AN INTRODUCTION TO GANGS

By

George W. Knox, Ph.D.

Revised and Expanded 5th Edition

An Introduction to Gangs, 5th Edition, 2000, New Chicago School Press, Inc, Peotone, IL.

ISBN 0-9665155-4-4

Library of Congress Catalog Card Number: 00-133631

This book is dedicated to my wife and my sons who are my sources of inspiration. I thank them for their patience with me during the labor of creating this expanded and revised 5th edition.

PREFACE TO THE FIFTH EDITION

This book has been written primarily to serve as a college or university level text on gangs or as a primary training book for those whose work is directly affected by gang members. It has the aim of being used as more than a simple "review of the literature" because of the discussion of theory, research, and policy. Also, because an effort is made here to avoid ideological bias and a defense of any particular doctrine or theory (by being interdisciplinary, and eclectic) this can also be of value to all who may be concerned about gang crime and violence in America today --- scholars, researchers, community groups, correctional institutions, law enforcement officials, social service agencies, educators, parents, and policy makers.

My own training has been quite interdisciplinary, even though my university degrees are in the discipline of sociology, and even though my current teaching is in the field of corrections and criminal justice. My commitment is to criminology, I am a life member of the American Society of Criminology and the Academy of Criminal Justice Sciences and have been so for quite some time. Criminology involves the social scientific study of crime.

This fifth edition is most timely given the continuing interest in the gang problem today. It incorporates much significant new research and information that has been generated since the first edition appeared in 1991, and since the second edition appeared in 1993, and since the third edition appeared in 1994, and since the fourth edition appeared in 1998. The first edition was widely adopted as a college textbook on gangs and I benefited from the feedback provided by a large number of persons both here and abroad. True to the prediction of Dr. Malcolm Klein, many such new college courses on "gangs" did in fact appear for the first time at colleges and universities throughout the United States and in other countries.

This fifth edition is much stronger and even more comprehensive because of the variety of new and ongoing gang research projects I have been involved in as the director of the National Gang Crime Research Center. I have obviously benefited as well in terms of being attuned to the best scholarship on gang issues by serving as the editor-in-chief of the Journal of Gang Research. This fifth edition therefore includes over 80 tables of relevant research data and over 50 different figures. Additionally, more internal documents from some of the larger and more sophisticated American gangs are also included in this new edition, along with new developments in the gang problem and the response to the gang problem.

A lot of new materials have been added to this fifth edition dealing with specialized subjects in the area of gang research and gang profiling. We have added actual "Gang Profiles" in the this book, which are organized in the appendices. We have added a lot of new and recent research findings on gangs and gang members. Many new developments regarding gangs are also included to provide students with the most "up-to-date" account as possible.

So the goal of this 5th edition is to make it a "one stop" reading and reference book for gang training in an institution of higher learning or applied setting. Finally, what is unique about the fifth edition as a major gang book? Unlike the various editions of the Thrasher classic (1927), which got smaller and smaller over the years with no updated information; this book has gotten larger and larger and steadily updated over the years. This was possible because of the continued dedication of the author to this are of research specialization in the social sciences.

TABLE OF CONTENTS

Pages

Chapter 1: An Overview: The Social Science Approach
    to Understanding Gangs... 1 - 15
Chapter 2: Classification Factors for Gang Analysis................. 17 - 36
Chapter 3: Major Milestones in Gang Studies........................ 39 - 60
Chapter 4: The Racism-Oppression Thesis for Gang Analysis........ 63 - 77
Chapter 5: Gangs: Underclass, Surplus Population, and Human
    Capital.. 79 - 89
Chapter 6: Politics and Gang Crime: Another Continuity in
    Thinking about Gangs.. 91 - 107
Chapter 7: The Oral History and Qualitative Gang Research Styles... 109 - 121
Chapter 8: The True Story About The Shaw & Mc Kay Tradition....... 123 - 132
Chapter 9: Shaw and Mc Kay on Gangs: With Commentary and
    Historical Analysis.. 135 - 145
Chapter 10: The Thrasher Criminological Riddle: What Was
    His Actual Research Methodology?............................. 147 - 159
Chapter 11: Gangs As An Urban Way of Life......................... 161 - 174
Chapter 12: An Organizational Approach to Gang Analysis.......... 177 - 188
Chapter 13: Gangs, Guerrilla Warfare, and Social Conflict......... 191 - 211
Chapter 14: Towards the Understanding of Gangs: The Group Factor... 213 - 225
Chapter 15: A Comparison of Cults and Gangs: Dimensions of
    Coercive Power and Malevolent Authority.................... 227 - 251
Chapter 16: Gangs and Drugs....................................... 253 - 264
Chapter 17: Gang Crime and Organized Crime....................... 267 - 277
Chapter 18: Female Gang Members and Rights of Children........... 279 - 295
Chapter 19: Asian Gangs... 297 - 311
Chapter 20: The Family and the Gang............................... 313 - 332
Chapter 21: The Promulgation of Gangbanging Through the Mass Media... 335 - 349
Chapter 22: The Community's Role in Dealing With Gangs........... 351 - 369
Chapter 23: Law Enforcement and Gangs............................. 371 - 391
Chapter 24: The Impact of the Federal Prosecution of the
    Gangster Disciples... 393 - 428
Chapter 25: Gangs and Adult Correctional Institutions............. 431 - 479
Chapter 26: Gangs and Juvenile Correctional Institutions.......... 481 - 494
Chapter 27: Gang Prevention and Intervention...................... 497 - 511
Chapter 28: Gang Programs: An Overview, Analysis and Critique..... 513 - 527
Chapter 29: Gang Theory.. 529 - 541
Chapter 30: Gangs and the Future: Towards Theoretical Integration
    and Policy Options For Reducing the Gang Problem.......... 543 - 560

Selected Bibliography on Gangs...................................... 561 - 596

Appendix A: Written Constitution and By-Laws of the Almighty
    Latin King Nation... 597 - 605
Appendix B: Written Constitution and By-Laws of the
    Spanish Gangster Disciple Nation............................... 606 - 611
Appendix C: Internal Documents of the Brothers of the Struggle.... 612 - 616
Appendix D: Written Constitution of the Vice Lords............... 617 - 630
Appendix E: The Illinois Streetgang Terrorism Prevention Act...... 631 - 633
Appendix F: The Gangster Disciples: A Gang Profile.............. 634 - 644
Appendix G: Gang Profile: The Black Gangsters, AKA "New Breed"... 645 - 652
Appendix H: Gang Profile: The Black Disciples.................... 653 - 662
Appendix I: Gang Profile: The Latin Kings....................... 663 - 680
Appendix J: Gang Profile: The Black P. Stone Nation............. 681 - 692
Appendix K: Crips - A Gang Profile Analysis..................... 693 - 698

Author Index... 699 - 702
Subject Index .... 703 - 708

FOREWORD TO THE FIRST EDITION (1991)
by
Malcolm W. Klein

Having studied street gangs off and on since 1962, and having written, thought, and lectured about them all these years, I have been asked on many occasions why I don't teach a course about gangs. My answer has always been that there is not enough at issue to justify a full semester course on gangs. Several lectures in a criminology or delinquency course, yes, but not a whole course on gangs.

The advent of this text by Professor Knox raises the question again, but in a different and far more effective way. He offers a very comprehensive coverage of pertinent issues. And if there is a legitimate text, is there not also a legitimate course to be offered? Is there enough knowledge to disseminate? Are there a sufficient number of intriguing intellectual questions (of theory, definition, method, and generalizability) to engage students in conceptually directed discussions? Upon considering these questions, and upon reviewing the materials offered us by Professor Knox, I am compelled to alter my position. Yes, there is now a course to be offered --- a good, worthwhile course. Why this should be true now, but not before, reflects at least the following points.

1. There has been a new explosion in gang knowledge. It was in the late 1950s and 1960s that much of our knowledge about gangs was developed. This happened in large part because of the research projects attached to intensive gang intervention programs in New York, Boston, Chicago, and Los Angeles. Professor Knox summarizes much of this material. In the period from the mid-1960s to the early 1980s, very little was added to that earlier knowledge base, as both private and public funders of research turned their interests to new directions. But from the mid-1980s on, there has been a renewed interest in gangs as their prevalence spread from the few major gang cities of the earlier era to well over 100 cities currently.

The earlier research told us much about the structure and dynamic processes within gangs. The current expansion places more emphasis on gang context -- the urban underclass setting of street gangs, their connection to drug markets, and the relationship of gang violence to institutions of social control (police, courts, prisons). And as we learn more about these contexts in an increasingly wider variety of cities, we learn more as well about variations in gang structure: street gangs have changed in age distribution and violence; Asian gangs have become far more prevalent, revealing less territoriality and more sophisticated racketeering; prison gangs have become commonplace; white gang forms, such as "stoners" and "skinheads", have appeared in suburban areas and posed different control and ethical issues; drug gangs have reportedly emerged in more pure forms, complicating our understanding of gang functions. Many of these developments, too, find space in the chapters to follow.

2. This proliferation of gangs and gang forms has forced scholars to turn to definitional issues to an extent not required earlier. I can recall vividly a "gang city tour" I took in 1963, sharing my initial impressions of Los Angeles gangs with established gang researchers in Chicago, New York, and Boston, and later in San Francisco, Seattle, and Philadelphia. Regardless of city, our gangs looked alike and our gang members acted alike. There was, thus, little pressure to attend carefully to issues of definition --- what is a gang, when is a group not a gang, what constitutes gang membership, or different levels of gang membership?

The luxury of such definitional innocence and ignorance is no longer affordable, for gangs in too many forms have now been described. A scientist who cannot define the phenomena being studied with sufficient clarity to allow comparison and replication by other scientists in the field is not in a position to contribute to the knowledge base of the discipline. And so Professor Knox gives considerable attention to the issue of gang definitions, and the student must come to understand that, far from being an arcane matter, this definitional problem is critical to our continuing capacity to understand, control, and prevent the negative components of the gang phenomenon.

3. Old gang theories need correcting; new ones need development. The gang scholars of earlier decades contributed theories that went far beyond gangs to become dominant themes of

delinquency causation generally. Theories of "Differential Association", "Strain", "Delinquent Sub-culture" and "Opportunity Structure" owed much or most of their form to gang research. While they were important first steps, they were also misleading in their parochialism. For purposes of understanding gang etiology, each usually covered only one portion of the problem; an amalgam was badly needed, but never achieved. Worse, each became a mechanism for explaining delinquency or crime generally, and failed to meet the challenges of such an expansion. Criminological scholars overlooked the very special nature of gangs as (a) lower class, (b) male, (c) young and (d) group structures whose character could not easily be translated into middle class or female or adult or individual crime patterns.

Theoretical developments throughout the past two decades have been all but non-existent, except as critiques of prior attempts. But the application to the gang world of William Julius Wilson's notion of the urban underclass is becoming widespread. A fair prediction for the 1990s would be that the urban underclass and other contextual approaches will replace the strictly etiological theories of the '60s. The spread of street gangs across the nation would seem to require theories of political and economic sorts more than those stressing developmental and family processes, or sub-cultural pressures. Thus the intellectual surroundings of gang theory must broaden. The college course on gangs must include discourse on economic and industrial changes in American cities, the politics of federalism and local control, racism and racial segregation, class structures, and -- perhaps above all -- some appreciation for the way social values affect where we do and do not expend our national resources.

4. Approaches to gang intervention have changed. Street gangs in prior times seemed relatively innocuous. They were only episodically violent; the damage they wrought was more to themselves and the life-chances of their own members than to those around them. A gang member's life was dull, rather than the stuff of West Side Story or Colors. In such circumstances, gang inter-vention programs were principally concerned with helping gang members prepare for their adult futures. Programs emphasized education, work skills, social skills, and connecting with the values of an adult world. Delinquency prevention was seen as the outcome of social development as much as a legitimate, direct target of intervention.

This story has been told elsewhere, and in part retold by Professor Knox, but these programs largely failed. Indeed, some of them contributed to increased delinquency. They underestimated the intractability of gangs, and overestimated their own capacities to affect the gang community. They completely failed to understand that they might have unintended consequences of a negative sort.

Now a new, diametrically opposed intervention philosophy has emerged, in part in response to the increased criminal involvement of street gangs and their spread to new cities. This philosophy -- retributive, punishment-oriented, suppressive -- is roughly based on deterrence theory but even more solidly grounded in political conservatism. It stresses arrests and convictions, police sweeps and crackdowns, new laws and policies to target street gangs as one might target the Cosa Nostra.

And, as with the socially oriented programs of earlier times, these gang deterrence interven-tions underestimate the intractability of gangs, overestimate their own capacities,, and completely fail to understand their unintended, negative consequences. It is my guess (if programs don't permit research evaluations, they yield guesses only) that the old and new approaches yield the same prod-uct -- greater gang cohesiveness and greater gang crime, including violent crime. A college course on the gang should prove a marvelous setting in which to explore these assertions.

5. The street gang is basically an American product. As a final element in my listing of issues deserving class coverage, this is in some ways the most important. The United States is not alone in being an industrialized nation, nor in having major urban areas with denotable inner cities, nor in having sizeable minority populations, nor in having failed social policies for the urban poor, nor in relinquishing much responsibility for social control to the criminal justice system. Yet, with very few exceptions, the United states is alone in its development of the urban street gang. Our gangs are like no others in the world - ours are far more prevalent, more permanent in their communities, larger and more complex, and more criminally involved by far. The American street gang is no temporary aberration; it is a permanent by-product of our inner city enclaves and many of their suburban sur-roundings. Its members are ruining their own lives, and endangering some others. Our societal response is to rant and rave about this, but not to undertake serious efforts to understand and change

the situation.

What does all this tell us about our nation, about its structure, its values, its place in the society of nations? Were I an instructor about to launch a course on gangs with the aid of Professor Knox' text, I believe I would introduce the course with this question, and end it by asking the question again in hopes of having achieved some clarity in its answer. America is known for its entrepreneurial success, its stress on individualism, its emphasis on civil liberties and rights, its success in implementing democracy, its political and charitable contributions to other nations -- and its violence. Street gangs have lately become synonymous with violence, however unfairly.

In my own city and county of Los Angeles, we have produced over 2,400 gang-related homicides over the past five years, at a current rate of almost 40 percent of all homicides in the area. Los Angeles is the leader, but there are over 100 less Los Angeles' out there, and more are added each year. To understand street gangs, we must come to grips with what there is to a society that -- however inadvertently -- permits, fosters, and fails to remedy this situation.

If Professor Knox has offered us the first full text on gangs, the developments and issues outlined above would seem to guarantee that it will not be the last. In preparing this first, massive effort, Professor Knox has done us a considerable service. Now, I fear, I shall have to return to the office to prepare my lectures; I have a gang course in my future.

ACKNOWLEDGEMENTS

Never before has so much been owed to so many by one person, me. Much credit is owed to many professionals, nationwide, who helped in one way or another. A book like this depends on a huge network of sources of good information. I want to thank the hundreds of law enforcement officials who responded to our national surveys on gangs. I am also indebted to similar hundreds of superintendents of juvenile correctional institutions, and wardens of adult prisons, jail administrators, and others for their cooperation in various phases of similar research on gangs reported in this book. I am also thankful for the similar cooperation from a sample of probation and parole officers nationwide. Many criminal justice professionals nationwide had some input into this work, through their generous sharing of time and information in cooperation with my gang research.

I also want to thank --- again far too numerous to list here --- my students and colleagues and a variety of other persons including program service staff, members of the clergy, school teachers, offenders and ex-offenders, and others --- many of whom shared their story, their files, their information, etc, with me at some point during the production of this book and in making improvements for this third edition. I am especially grateful for the information provided to me by those directly involved in the American gang scene: particularly persons who were at some point in their career "gang leaders", and active gang members, and their loved ones who shared information about their gangs. Most helpful, and most inspiringing, were those who had left the gang to lead highly productive and useful lifestyles, playing a positive and responsible role in society, and I thank them for confiding in me and for sharing their "story". These persons, whose stories of redemption or rehabilitation, would not want me to acknowledge them; but they know who they are, and I again express my gratitude to them.

I am sincerely appreciative of comments and suggestions from editors of the Journal of Gang Research whose advise in many areas helped to dramatically improve this fifth edition. I am, of course, forever indebted to my colleagues from the National Gang Crime Research Center for their ongoing support and assistance in a myriad of ways. Also, there have been a couple thousand gang specialists from all walks of life who have attended training conferences I have organized through the National Gang Crime Research Center that have read earlier editions of the book and have provided useful feedback to me, and I am eternally grateful for their useful input.

Mostly I owe the students who end up reading this kind of book for invaluabale feedback in various forms over the years. This has certainly included students from my own Department of Criminal Justice at Chicago State University for their keen insights, where I teach criminal justice courses on gangs and related topics. I am grateful as well to students from other colleges and universities (University of Minnesota at Duluth, Lewis University, College of Du Page, Loyola University, and many others) whose instructors used the early editions of the textbook and sometimes invited me to speak to the class --- as I am always eager to do. The feedback of students has been invaluable in preparing this third edition. I am also grateful for the help from the staff of the National Gang Crime Research Center, and especially fellow researchers in various gang research Task Force projects organized by the Center over the years.

I have been blessed to be the executive director of the National Gang Crime Research Center since 1990. In this capacity I have had the opportunity to work with a large number of other gang researchers throughout the U.S.A. and abroad, and to work with a large number of "real" gang experts who provide the best training on and about gangs and gang members. One of the most direct and positive types of impact I have felt as a human being in terms of influences on my work has been from a "new breed" of scholar: the cop scholar, someone who works in the criminal justice system but who also holds an advanced professional degree and who does conduct and carry out professional research. One of the most challenging duties in my position with the National Gang Crime Research Center has been that of serving as editor-in-chief of the Journal of Gang Research, now with a decade of service as a quarterly professional publication and the official publication of the National Gang Crime Research Center. What makes being a publisher challenging is that there is so much information available about gangs that a good deal of misinformation also exists. Fortunately, the keen observer of the gang scene and crime problem in America is quick to probably discover that there are "frauds" and "hustlers" who move into the gang arena not by a sincere motivation to study it with a "let the chips fall where they may" scientific attitude, but who rather enter this arena with a "chip on their shoulder" or an "axe to grind" or who are just "hustling the problem" (i.e., consultant pimps who follow the smell of government funding, and when the government money dries up so does their interest in gang problems). In this capacity of directing the activities of the National Gang Crime Research Center it has been literally possible to learn something new about gangs everyday. So if I had to list everyone who has helped to shape my view of the world of gangs, I am afraid that list would be almost as long as this book.

If there is one lesson I have learned in all my studies about crime it is this: when it comes to "crime", things are rarely what they seem; I advise my students to be as skeptical as the true social scientist and to not believe anything they hear and only half of what they see. When it comes to gangs this cautionary advice is of even greater import: gangs today have their own spokespersons who have academic credentials, gangs today have their own publications, gangs today have their own Internet websites, gangs today have their own counterparts in government who act in a "denial" or "cover-up" syndrome who benefit from downplaying the role of "gang crime" generally in the United States, gang today have their own political activists and "front groups" to give the appearance that they are "do-gooder groups", gangs today have an enormous ability to corrupt everyone from university professors to judges and sworn police officers and those working in the criminal justice system, especially corrections. Sadly, a lot of the misinformation about gangs comes from federal agencies that have sponsored "gang research", and while it is disseminated "free" and therefore is "most available" and most widely quoted, I think the axiom still applies "you get what you pay for".

Today an entire industry has been developed around gangs. This includes specialized criminal justice training and associations for networking on gang investigation, etc. This includes new roles in the areas of corrections, public schools, social service programs, youth development and recreation programs, and a variety of counseling and health care functions as well. These positions are not likely to disappear, as they have become new employment opportunities as well. There are a wide number of public and private programs that employ gang specialists in a service capacity.

One of the things that we can expect in the future is the international role played by some gangs. This is already occurring in the case of motorcycle gangs where there is aggressive and almost imperialistic development efforts to reach into new countries and territories abroad to spread the influence of American gangs. There has been an import-export function going on for years now with regard to some street gangs in America that have high numbers of illegal aliens within their membership. Their U.S. gang involvement gets exported back to their country of origin when U.S. immigration officials successfully return them to their homeland; and vice versa, gang styles in other countries are imported into the U.S. as well, to wit: the case of Jamaican Posses.

In some underdeveloped countries today there exist groups that are both "gangs" and "terrorist groups". This too is a something we can expect as a future development. This includes "narco-terrorism".

The future may also show new forms, or innovations, such as a blend between what we have traditionally thought of as "cults" and "gangs". Open societies are particularly vulunerable to this kind of development; as well as societies that are bitterly divided along the lines of religious doctrines.

There exists, in open societies such as America, an institutional vulnerability to gangs. Thus, it is reasonable to predict the future will show the capability of gangs to exploit these institutional vulnerabilities. For example, in places like Cook County, Illinois it is common for about 85 percent of the adults charged with felonies to "plead guilty" under plea bargaining arrangements: our criminal justice system now depends on this efficient way of disposing of court cases. But what if a gang leader ordered all of his jailed gang members to demand a jury trial? Would our judicial system have the capability to handle a 200 or 300 percent increase in jury trials? Probably not, and unless we can get them tried in 180 days, then they walk away free: that is the law, they have a right to a speedy trial. What is to stop a gang from taking over various fraternal and special interest associations by adding a new influx of paid members, voting out the established leaders, voting in new leaders, and giving a "new direction" to such groups? Attempts alone these lines for "gang take-overs" of legitimate groups have already occurred in the USA. And therefore we may reasonably expect more such initiatives in the future.

Finally on the matter of taking credit and sharing the blame, I share anything positive with the many others who helped me, but hold alone, as my own, full responsibility for any failures, oversights, inaccuracy, etc --- in short, any blame is all mine.

If I had to name my main influences, then it would be a short list: those who are my friends and colleagues --- Curtis Robinson, Dorothy Papachristos, Andrew Papachristos, Thomas McAninch, Shirley Holmes, Sandra Stone --- some of my primary influences, I owe them more than I can ever possibly repay for their generosity, their kindness, their ideas, and their leadership in "doing something" about the gang problem.

Lastly, if I had to name one main source of motivation that keeps me "at it", which has given me the stamina and "stick to it" attitude, I must give credit to the victims of gang violence in America. Children, toddlers, pregnant women, grandmothers, innocent bystanders --- all those who have died and have been maimed by gang gunfire. There are a lot of "gang books" that give credit to the gangs, and which "glorify" gangs to the point of being "gang apologists". If there is anything that distinguishes this gang book from all others, it is that I have remembered a lot of the gang violence victims, I have spoken to many, and seen some as well close-up. And it is my hope and prayer that eventually our society will "wake up" by achieving some level of "values clarification" and set priorities accordingly regarding the problem of gang crime and violence.

G.W.K., August, 2000.

Left: female members of
Simon City Royals.
Right: Infant being
raised to be member of
Simon City Royals.
Bottom left: Simon City
Royal "war sweater".
Bottom right: Another
folks gang.

Chapter 1

AN OVERVIEW:
THE SOCIAL SCIENTIFIC
APPROACH
TO UNDERSTANDING GANGS

INTRODUCTION

By today's definition a gang is a group, informal or formal in nature, whose members recurrently commit crimes and where these crimes are known openly to the members, often conferring status or profit upon those members who commit the crime. The crime must be openly known to the members of the group or organization and tolerated or approved of in order to qualify as a gang. The only exception to this definition is where the persons do not attempt to evade an arrest, but in fact want to be arrested, such as in protest groups, who seek to draw further attention to their cause through the mass media coverage of the arrests.

This new 5th edition of the book demonstrates that there has been a veritable explosion of new knowledge development about gangs during the last decade. So many new books and new groups exist today, and so many new specialized jobs have created a demand for gang experts (in corrections, in law enforcement, in schools, in community organizations, in social services, etc), that it is possible to say that "gangology" may exist today as a recognizable social scientific area of study. Many colleges and universities today offer courses on or about "gangs" and gang problems. About a fourth of all cities have some local municipal ordinances that deal with gangs or gang members. Millions of dollars are spent by government every year dealing with gang problems. And gangs remain the number one fear among young children in America today.

SOME OF THE PRIOR VIEWPOINTS IN THE LITERATURE ON GANGS

Chapter 3 of this book will review, in detail, a number of the major milestones in the field of gangology. Here we simply want to make note of the fact that a wide variety of viewpoints have been reflected in the gang literature during the last century. Some of these preliminary comments are necessary because there have been contributions to the literature on gangs that basically provide misinformation. It is also true that in the last twenty years, the gang problem in America has become much different; thus, contributions to the gang literature in the early 1900's and well up through the 1950's, need to be viewed in their own historical time frame.

Good students of gangology try to get the best information they can get on gangs - they do so by using a social scientific approach. The first and most fundamental requirement of a social scientific approach is not to ignore major contributions to this important area of research and scholarship. There are degreed experts in the area of gangs, and there are many practitioners in this field as well who may not have advanced graduate degrees, but who have contributed to the literature. Someone who ignores major contributions to the area of gang study is someone who lacks a sufficiently rigorous social scientific perspective: i.e., they have not really done their homework.

As the founder and editor-in-chief of the Journal of Gang Research, the present author has necessarily been required to become familiar with all well-known gang authors or their works. There certainly are a number of gang experts, and probably others, who may not yet be known to the present author. As already mentioned, it is an ever-expanding field of study. But if they exist, they have not published anything known to the present author. If you are such a person, you are urged to get in contact with the author, so that you are given your due respect and consideration in future editions of this book.

Some of our literature on gangs has described "social gangs[1]" which are similar to unsupervised play groups. Social gangs, according to this author, are not really gangs at all. While they could become real gangs they are little more than the kind of precocious youths represented in movie characters like Spanky and Alfalfa in "The Little Rascals"[2]. We should be less worried about the mischief caused by play groups. They do not represent a national crime problem.

Some of our literature on gangs tends to describe "wannabe" gang members, but discounts these "wannabe gangs" and their members as not posing a threat to society. Actually, we should be concerned about "wannabe" gang members. The reason is this: when one "wannabe" shoots another "wannabe" gang member, we do not have a "wannabe homicide", we have a real gang homicide on our hands. But we should be wary of anyone who discounts their gang problem as consisting only of "wannabe's", because in far too many cases the "wannabe" is really a "gonnabe". And "wannabe's" do eventually meet the "real thing" when they get processed into the criminal justice system.

Some of our literature on the "gang world" today is subdued political dogma where the primary conclusion is the insatiable need to criticize the establishment itself. This is commonly known as the gang-apology doctrine: giving gang members an excuse for their behavior. The excuse can be poverty, racism, etc. More often than not the excuse is that gang members get a bad label from their society. This gang-apology doctrine fails to recognize one fundamental fact: no one demonizes gang members more than gang members themselves. Gang members seek out the labels they acquire and collect. Gang members seek out the "reputation" of a "demon" or "bad person", it is not a gang researcher who puts this label on the gang member.

This book provides a study of the criminal gang. The most essential feature of the criminal gang is that its members routinely engage in law violation behavior. This is done individually, in small groups, and often in an organized continuing fashion. The nature of this involvement with crime will be seen to provide the basis for examining gangs from a social organizational perspective.

Thus, without crime, we would not have a gang: it would be a deviant group or deviant organization at best. Thrasher's (1927) early American approach to gangs probably included some such groups that today would probably not qualify as true delinquent or criminal gangs. Thrasher's original research included a large number of Social Athletic Clubs (SAC's) that today might be viewed at most as a nuisance, but not gangs.

When the first edition of this textbook was published in 1991 this was almost a taboo to define gangs in terms of their criminal behavior. But this definition has proved true to be held now almost universally by most esteemed gang researchers. A gang that does not commit crime is therefore really not a gang. This is not to say, however, that it is in anyway possible to basically "rehabilitate an entire gang". All this means is that gang behavior is intrinsically tied to crime, delinquency, and deviance.

Prior to the first edition of this book in 1991, a gang could be any threatening, or posturing, or deviant, or youthful group or clique that was not wearing Boy Scout uniforms. Without criminal conduct, over time, a group or organization would not be capable of being defined as a gang today.

This book studies the kind of gang that is found in both juvenile and adult correctional institutions. Correctional officers do not see "social gangs", those who never come to the attention of the criminal justice system.[3] They see, rather, the hardcore law-offending gangs[4]. It is mostly the criminal gang member we find in our jails and prisons.

Law enforcement faces little problem from small cliques of unsupervised kids who periodically engage in deviance or who test the norms of propriety. Thus, police do not face a very high threat from so-called social gangs. Law enforcement officers are, however, sometimes shot and killed by members of criminal gangs. It is the criminal gang that is the focus of this book. Later it will be shown how these gangs are classified in terms of the level of organizational sophistication.

You, and the public, are not worried about being killed by a random shooting where the shooter was Spanky or Alfalfa. You are probably concerned more about the hardcore criminal gang. Some of these well known criminal gangs are examined in detail in this book. Some gangs are highly structured and have written constitutions, some examples of these internal gang writings are provided in the appendices of this book. Some gangs are little more than small units of persons often no more complicated in their hierarchy than a burglary or armed robbery "ring".

Regarding the study of gangs there are many questions that must be answered if we are to truly attain a social scientific perspective. This book seeks to provide a social scientific view of gangs. That means being interdisciplinary.[5] That also means relying, where possible, on good criminological research about gangs. This means being "critical" where necessary of "research": to suggest to you, the student of gangs, in no uncertain terms, what kind of mistakes can be made in "misinterpreting" information about gangs, and helping you to defend yourself against "misinformation" about gangs. The propaganda is out there.

The ambiguity of defining characteristics of and about "gangs" in the literature can often mean more confusion the more we read. But there are two empirical questions about gangs in America that command our attention. (1) When does a loosely formed street corner group become a gang? And (2) if gangs are involved in crime, then how much of crime in America is explained by gang involvement? These two questions, so essential to the social scientific study of gangs, are not fully answered in the prior literature. Much new data is provided in this book to shed light on these and other important issues.

IMPROVEMENTS OF THIS BOOK OVER TIME

Obviously, a lot has changed since 1991 when this book first came out in its first edition. A second edition expanded the coverage of gangs and was updated in 1993. In 1995 a third expanded and revised edition was published. In 1998, a fourth edition expanded even more and revised and updated information on gangs. This new 5th edition includes even more information and updates on the gang problem in the world today.

SOME PRELIMINARY CONSIDERATIONS ABOUT GANGS

Some may say that gangs can be socially engineered (i.e., artificially created) and even experimentally manipulated (e.g., gang social service intervention, gang deprogramming services, or capable of being manipulated by political parties). The bottom line here is: can anything be done about the gang crime problem? Some may say that it is possible to exert much impact on gangs, perhaps even destroy them (e.g., gang busting). Others may say that through social services we can work directly with gangs and gang members; and perhaps show them a better way of life. The most extreme form of this therapeutic intervention would be that we can "deprogram" gang members. Before addressing the significance of such an assumption about social engineering and gangs, it is necessary to review some of the issues concerning gangs generally. Still others may say that as a crime problem no one has ever come up with the magic bullet of rehabilitation or prevention. Therefore it may be impossible to turn around the gang crime problem if we were to listen to some viewpoints. The truth is probably some-

where in between the two extremes that we can do a lot or we cannot do anything about the gang crime problem.

In this chapter we will only examine some of the general characteristics of gangs. In later portions of this text, however, the definitional overlap and variation in what constitutes a gang will be examined in much greater detail. This will involve the analysis of the gang in terms of what we know about social group formations generally.

The approach of this book is therefore incremental. It will address the major issues and at appropriate points in the book provide elements of a more integrated view of gangs, including a gang typology. The final chapter will review in detail the competing definitions of gangs and suggest an integrated definition of gang levels of "threat severity" and membership stages.

Gangs apparently need not have a publicly known label or name for their group[6], although most American gangs do.[7] Indeed in the early stage of gang formation the name itself emerges as a function of identity and crystallization. Gangs often do not consider themselves "gangs", but rather as types of "organizations". Gangs like the Gangster Disciples in Chicago deserve their preference for being called an organization, because they have been able to stage protests with several thousand members marching in unison in front of City Hall.

A historical review of American gangs would suggest that they emerged along racial and ethnic lines. Bonn (1984: 333), discussing gangs in the context of organized crime, reported criminal gangs existing in America as early as 1760. In the urban context, Bonn described gangs as clearly having ethnic homogeneity in terms of their organization. "Irish gangs were the first to emerge.." followed by German, Jewish and Italian gangs (Bonn, 1984: 333-334). This factor will be examined in much greater detail later in the book.

To some extent gangs gain legitimacy through the tendency of American culture to romanticize, and often idolize, gang exploits[8]. Al Capone as a gang leader has been significantly represented in fiction, myth, and through the Hollywood movie industry. As a byproduct of this element of culture, Chicago as a city must still today labor under the image of a "rat...tat...tat...tat" town associated with hoods carrying Thompson submachine guns. The cognitive map of many Americans places Chicago as "gangster land", which is not exactly a tourist attraction![9] And how does America compete as a tourist attraction, as a "peaceful place" in a democratic milieu, when gangs dominate the public imagination both here and abroad? The image of gang killings communicates "when travelling to America, bring your bullet proof vest".

There is also an important ideological factor involved in both the study of gangs and policy responses to the gang problem. Hagan (1987: 231-232) characterized the study of gangs as a fetish of criminologists during the 1950s and 1960s. While the gang problem did not disappear, the attention to gang research apparently did in the 1970s according to some sources. Hagan cited the literature review by Bookin-Weiner and Horowitz (1983) to the effect that ideological polarization in the 1970s was associated with a shift in analytical interests. Here the emphasis on macroanalytic problems such as social structure, SES (social economic status), and the community as the unit of analysis are characterized as being perhaps liberal while the emphasis on individual traits as explanations of criminal activity hold more weight for a conservative ideological orientation. The legitimacy of this claim is open to discussion[10], but perhaps rests with the common hypothesis that in some regard academic research follows the budgetary process. That is, in academia, the tail of funding for research can wag the dog of knowledge development.

This ideological factor cannot be overemphasized and we must be alert to its influence at all stages in the knowledge production process. By ideology we mean those values and assumptions about the world which have implications for the control and allocation of limited resources. In the study of sociology, for example, one of the concepts that students quickly learn is "value free". That is, one should not bring one's own values into play in research; for otherwise we are advancing not social science, nor policy for the improvement of corrections and criminal justice, but rather we are advancing ideology. The problem however is that society cannot be easily placed in an aseptic vacuum free from normative influences. That is, how we view the world may often influence how we portray the origin, structure, function, composition and policy recommendations for problems such as gang crime.

There has always existed a linguistic problem in the study of gang crime. The term "gang banger" itself is perhaps more fitting for use by sensational journalism than by a social scientist. It is a label containing stigma and implications that should engender fear and loathing. Indeed our language has much to do with the problem. When discussing "gangs" in America, one of the first things a student of criminology will learn is that in reviewing the literature what some conceive of as "gangs" are little more than conspicuously obnoxious youths running head strong against societal norms, as well as, of course, highly organized and armed groups with syndicated functions and hierarchical roles who are prone to violence.

The loose and pejorative use of the label "gang" is a source of confusion. We shall have to clarify our language to be able to objectively assess the gang problem in America today. The most common variation involves labelling all gang members in a tradition of much enmity (e.g., gang banger). Another variation, espoused by those in combat with gangs, is that some authors have apparently experienced the "Stockholm syndrome", or an over-identification with the rhetoric of gang members; almost in a tradition of Chicago's Rev. John Fry (Fry, 1969, 1973), that all that is important is that we "offer them something" (e.g., give them a bone), and we should therefore provide services and programs to serve them.[11] Both views suffer from a lack of clarity of what levels of gang sophistication we are talking about and the degree of individual integration into the gang subculture.

Vagueness and imprecision can get us into a lot of trouble. Mostly, it backfires in terms of social policy and legislation. Kamisar (1971: 52) described how the zeal of Detroit prosecutors to fight crime created a "public enemy act", as well as New Jersey which passed a law making "it a felony, punishable by 20 years' imprisonment, to be a gangster", were found to be unconstitutional, in New Jersey's case because of vagueness and uncertainty.[12] It also confuses us in the arena of social service intervention: some gangs at some stages of membership integration are clearly more "reachable" than others, and not paying attention to the details of such distinctions can mean exacerbating the very problem being used as a platform for social service intervention. Generally, what the study of gangs implies in criminology is some difference from loner or individual crime, chiefly in terms of a difference in organizational terms. A single gunman acting alone in a robbery, simply put, differs from a crime resulting from a gang. The gang implies something that the lone criminal offender does not have: some sense of organizational capability. The gang also implies a continuing or persisting threat over time that can increase. It is this emphasis on organizational characteristics that is common to the study of gangs, but which is at the same time most underdeveloped in the sense of linking what we know about social organization generally to the more specific problem of the study of gangs.

The study of gang crime has always implied some element of organizational life, although this aspect of gang analysis has not always emerged in the literature to the extent that we may desire. Indeed, there is radical disagreement on this issue. But this book develops such an organizational viewpoint, because it is also one that allows for more effective law enforcement, greater choices in managing the problem in the field of corrections, and much more latitude in addressing the gang problem from all levels of prevention --- primary, secondary, and tertiary (e.g., aftercare services).

Clearly, gangs do exist and their members do commit crimes. It is, then, a proper area of study for the social sciences. And yet some may say that gang research and analysis has barely risen above the level of an esoteric craft. These same cynics condemn not only intellectuals but applied knowledge as well, to the effect we really do not know much about crime, when in fact we do know some things. This book simply seeks to fill the gap in limited choices available for someone who has the responsibility for educating and training on the topic of gangs. The book therefore addresses many issues and includes many sources of data.

WHEN IS A GROUP A GANG?

Does calling a group a gang make it a gang? It probably depends on who uses the language. The voice of a community resident differs in definitive power from the voice of a United States Attorney or a local prosecutor.[13] The difference is power.

Legally, there are many definitionss of gang-related activities (e.g., gang loitering, etc), but for the most part, specific laws addressing gangs have only in recent decades come into being.[14] There is the federal RICO statute and its many mini-RICO versions at the state level of criminal law. These define organizations engaged in violation of the law and can be used for both criminal and civil prosecution. Again, however, language is no friend of social science here. For example, Illinois as does many other states, has a "mob action" criminal statute which covers crimes committed in a group including civil protest demonstrations. Literally thousands of persons have been arrested under this statute for protests associated with the "right to life" movement and in protesting abortion. Does arrest for mob action make one a "mobster"?

The answer is most probably, NO. That is, most of those arrested for protesting the operation of an abortion clinic would probably reveal a pro-social motivation of a higher social purpose and an intent to be arrested, not to avoid arrest, in their behavior as a matter of civil disobedience. Indeed, they may be very religious persons who know that mass media attention to their cause is most likely under conditions of the arrest of their members. But does that make them "mobsters"? No! It is a matter of intention to avoid arrest as well. Groups like those with internalized higher moral imperatives such as those who may engage in civil disobedience --- for example to protect the environment --- knowing they will be arrested for their behavior, and willfully continuing such behavior as a moral protest, cannot be considered "gangs" in any sense used in this book.

The reasoning here rests with the fact that their intent is not to do harm through violence or to benefit economically through criminal code violation, and further that in such civil disobedience they do not seek to evade arrest.

Another well known federal criminal law deals with Continuing Criminal Enterprises. These are the kind of federal statutes used to prosecute a number of gangs and others involved in organized criminal conduct, especially drug trafficking.

Thus, many persons being arrested for protesting abortion in the traditional civil disobedience style of political and moral protest cannot be considered gang members. However, in recent years violent attacks have been undertaken against individual physicians. Also, the medical buildings themselves have been burglarized, vandalized, and attacked in a different style where the perpetrators definitely do seek to cause harm and do seek to evade arrest. Such persons operating as a group would, therefore today, come under the umbrella of gang analysis if and only if the intent was to evade detection. Those who bomb abortion clinics are different than those who voluntarily seek to be arrested.

A new law did recently criminalize some abortion protest behavior, it is called the FACE Act: Freedom of Access to Clinic Entrances Act. It is a federal criminal misdemeanor where the first offense can result in six months in prison and a fine of up to $10,000 for blocking the access to healthcare services of patients trying to use an abortion clinic. The first federal charges against violators of this Act were made in June of 1994.[15]

So what we have here is a change from the time the first edition of this book appeared: a new criminal code defining that behavior as a crime. So the fact is the benefit structure here is ideological in nature, just as in political crime and in terrorism, and while we can expect this "gang" behavior to profile differently, it must still be treated analytically as gang crime if the abortion protestors violate the FACE Act. The fact that most do not try to evade arrest do however make them a unique exception to what we mean by gang crime.

This shows the "volatility" of "gang policy" in America. When the first edition of this textbook came out in 1991 we had to conclude by legal definition that abortion "right to life" protestors were not "gang related". By the time the 3rd edition came out, a new federal law "criminalized" such abortion protest behavior, making it ipso facto a "gang crime" of a sort. Still, during this same period (8 years), in spite of much effort to achieve the change, the FBI's Uniform Crime Report has still not been changed to include "gang member arrestee" information; thus, we continue as a Nation to "live in the dark" about "gang crime" regarding what information the Uniform Crime Report provides American citizens about the "gang problem in America".

A similar linguistic problem arises in considering gangs. And in this regard we choose at this point to forcibly eliminate the phrase "gangster" from any subsequent discussion, because it confuses more than it contributes to the scientific understanding of the problem. It carries a value connotation and a culturally prescribed image of evil. One fact that will emerge in the study of gangs is that not all of the 24 hour day spent by gang members is spent in a relentless search for evil as if it were the only goal gang members had. Gang members are not alien invaders from another planet, they are from and live in our communities.

The term "gang banger" is similarly not to be found in the ensuing discussion unless in the context of views from persons interviewed who do not represent a social scientific view of the world. It is a label of derision just like gangster and mobster. It connotes more in terms of values of derogation and the psychology of enmity (Keen, 1986) than it does in terms of scientific classification.

Anyone who grew up in the 1950s or who watches such re-runs may recall a "gang" that was portrayed every Saturday morning at cartoon time on television. It was the series about "The Little Rascals". Is that what we mean by a gang? It too is a misrepresentation, albeit one that gives a favorable image to "gang". But that is Hollywood, and the reader of this book must be willing to break free of those kind of stereotypes created by culture. Alfalfa and Spanky and their associates typified much of urban adolescents, but they hardly typified what is meant today by an American gang-affiliated youth.

Do gangs necessarily have to have illicit goals, functions, or engage in law violation collectively or as individuals? Or can a gang have pro-social purposes? The answer is historical. That is, historically the phrase gang has encompassed both sets of group affiliation. In doing so the study of gangs has suffered from more than a small amount of measurement error. There must be both a qualitative and quantitative difference between a voluntary association composed primarily of youths which simply seeks to have a good time as compared to one that has a high degree of criminality in its everyday life. In other words, if any clique or group of three or more youths together, unsupervised constitutes a gang, then all of America has at one time or another been gang affiliated.

How much deviance or crime must a group be responsible for before it is considered a gang? Are the Boy Scouts a gang if one of the ranking members is in fact secretly a cat burglar or a semi-professional car thief? No doubt about it, some legitimate social organizations and groups do routinely experience what is called a succession of goals. That is, these groups may be formed initially for a certain specific purpose, but may later in time change and come to take on a new and entirely different goal and purpose. So it is analytically possible for even a legitimate group to transform itself into a gang.

If the road to hell is paved with good intentions, then how do we account for the type of organizational climate change that took place when the Rev. Jim Jones began having his religious followers carry out the practice of drinking poisoned Kool-aid?[16] The tragedy that occurred in Jonestown, where 900 people died in 1978 bears much significance to the study of gangs in that it was collective behavior and it ultimately had what must be regarded as a criminal outcome --- mass suicide. How do gangs differ from cults? A cult engaged in crime, over time, is a gang.

Many "skinhead" groups and white racist groups must be considered gangs, because they often engage in what are called bias crimes.[17] But it means having more than the "skinhead", it means the actual commission of such acts of racial/ethnic/sexual preference bigotry in a manner that tends to violate another persons civil rights; or more commonly, for such "hate groups" it means groups that routinely engage in crimes of various sorts, including violence, with the fact that the same group may also hold extreme political views. Early scholars like Puffer, Furfey, and Thrasher did not include adult gangs such as the Ku Klux Klan, or vigilante groups. Rather, early scholars focused on youth groups who tended to go against the grain of mainstream society, its culture, its values, and its norms. That is, some sense of youthful deviance. The present analysis will show why we must also consider such groups like the Aryan Brotherhood, the Aryan Nation, the KKK, Neo-nazis, etc, also qualify as "gangs" for purposes of both criminological research and prosecution[18].

It is inadequate criminological analysis to not include a group or organization under the definition of gang just because they do not claim a turf in a ghetto or they do not put up graffiti. Mostly, it is biased as a gang analysis not to include groups like Skinheads and motorcycle gangs in a gang analysis; because what it would leave us with is a lot of minorities as gang members and exclude from gang definition a lot of caucasians. Thus, the KKK must be regarded as a gang. It is not necessary, in the criminological analysis advanced in this book, for a gang to hold down "turf" or identifiable territory or put up graffiti before it comes under the analysis of being a "gang". It is sufficient that any type of crime is conducted over time by the members of the group, formal or informal in nature, and where these crimes are openly known and approved of as such within the group or organization. It is not necessary for the group or organization to "vote" on whether to commit the crimes. Tacit approval or acceptance works just as well to define the group or organization as a gang.

Recent research by the National Gang Crime Research Center shows that white racist extremist gang members basically engage in literally all types of crimes that other gang members engage it: for profit crimes, drug sales, etc (Mc Currie, 1998). But if the federal government agencies "divide the turf" on dealing with these white racist extremist gangs in an internal political fashion, then a serious flaw exists that may help these type of gangs to flourish.

To be more specific, in this book the definition of gangs will be restricted to not simply involvement with or committing acts of deviance, but rather to crime. Crime is a special subset of deviance. In this sense, members of the Jonestown religious community could not be considered a gang even though they engaged in deviant practices and their behavior was deviant from our perspective[19]. The problem with using deviance as the key ingredient to define gang behavior is that it is far too encompassing.[20]

A group is a gang when it exists for or benefits substantially from the continuing criminal activity of its members. Some element of crime must exist as a definitive feature of the organization for it to be classified as a gang[21]. That need not be income-producing crime, because it could also be crimes of violence.[22] Examples would include such extremist groups like the Ku Klux Klan, the Aryan Brotherhood, young white racist group equivalents, and others who engage not necessarily in well known income-producing crimes, but who still commit crimes along a dimension of "bias". Often these crimes involve violence to property or persons, as "hate crimes" or "bias crimes".[23] This is a legitimate aspect of the gang problem because it is criminal behavior that is approved of, and often planned, as such by a group[24].

Crime involvement of a group must not therefore be a sub rosa function about which few of the members have knowledge if we are to consider the group a gang. Members of many legitimate voluntary associations and civic groups are sometimes arrested for a variety of offenses. But these are not offenses committed on behalf of their group, these are not offenses even necessarily known to their full social network, these are not offenses condoned and approved of in advance by their organization, or which enjoy their acceptance or blessing. To be considered a gang, the criminal involvement of members must be openly known and approved of as such.

Conspiracy laws have some application here. To prove a conspiracy it is generally necessary to prove one or more overt acts in furtherance of the conspiracy. The key word is "overt". It must be open and clearly regarded as law violation behavior. That is, they know it is wrong, they know it is against the law, and they do it anyway. Some element of criminal conspiracy to avoid detection for law violation must therefore be present, whether the actual/objective/material skill/knowledge/ability to avoid or limit the probability of arrest actually exists.

Thus, from the perspective of the analysis advanced in this book, a group is not a gang simply because it is labelled as being in some sense deviant. A group is a gang if and only if it meets the higher requirement of having a known involvement with crime. It can therefore include the Crips, Bloods, Folks, Peoples, Posse, Vice Lords, Latin Kings, motorcycle gangs (Pagans, Hells Angels, etc), and a host of others whose primary occupation is income-producing crime or who benefit substantially from it, and as well it can include those engaged in a mixture of traditional crime and political crime involving rightwing and leftwing extremism (e.g., Aryan Brotherhood, Supreme White Power, KKK, and others versus leftwing groups like the Symbionese Liberation Army, and others). Such crime patterns, particularly of more organized gangs who have been able to accumulate economic assets, can also include a mixture of legitimate income (small businesses, hustling, etc) and criminal pursuits.

A semantic problem that needs to be clarified here is that we cannot effectively use the phrase "youth gangs" in a logical and rigorous criminological analysis of the gang problem. If there are youth gangs, then logically there are "adult gangs" as well; and any student of human development will recognize that there are many possible gradations along the life span in terms of age-categories. First, the term "youth" is not easily operationalized in social policy. Secondly, there is no level one or higher "gang" known to this author which in its code of conduct or its charter or its written constitution or in its informal norms restricts membership to simply "youths"[25]. Groups like the Crips and the Bloods, the Vice Lords and the Disciples, etc, cannot simply be regarded as "youth gangs": it is more accurate to say these level three gangs have many youthful members. Youths are the easiest to exploit, particularly in drug-trafficking. As a general tendency, most street gangs have about half "juveniles" and half "adults" in terms of age of the members, so we cannot call these "youth gangs".

Some "gang researchers" think that there must be a certain "flavor" or "style" before classifying a group as a gang. Such an intellectual would disregard "white racist extremist groups" as gangs, because they do not "hang out on the street corner". Your present author would suggest that such intellectuals have inappropriately focused on "street corner" definitions to the point of over-concreteness. A gang could be a "street gang" operating from a street corner without a clubhouse, just as a gang could also be a "suite gang" that operates out of an office building somewhere in white collar America. Where the gang operates should not be part of the definition of a gang given the ease of mobility and communications.

Analysts who continue to use the phrase "youth gangs" find their results hard to apply to the real world of criminal justice: there are no "youth laws", there are juvenile laws, and adult criminal codes. Anyone 17 or older in Illinois, for example, is an adult under law; and their behavior in violating the law is not regarded as "juvenile delinquency", it is "adult criminality". It is also a data problem: we do not have any census of all gang members in the United States, so we cannot accurately say that the majority are "juveniles", or even "youths" --- whatever we interpret "youths" to mean operationally. Stephens, in quoting a police chief on gangs, says it is a myth that the majority of street gang members are juveniles, that is, in Los Angeles juveniles may constitute only about a fifth of the gang membership (Goldstein and Huff, 1993: p. 224)!

The problem, then, with using the term "youth gang" is that it inaccurately describes the social reality of American gangs. Further it implies that such gangs have no adult leaders whom they are accountable to. It mistakenly implies that just because they are "youths" they are therefore not culpable nor responsible for their acts: as if by compulsion to join a gang this would be any defense in committing violence against another citizen. No matter what their age, gang members young or old must be held accountable for their actions.

A "level zero" gang is really a "non gang": it is a group of persons who could become a gang. Thrasher's (1927) analysis of the etiology of gangs showed that a number of "precursor" group combinations could conceivably become a gang. But just because a group of youngsters dance and play music adults disapprove of is not a crime: it is not definitive enough to define such a group as a gang. Even if this group goes in public and in military precision "picks their nose" or engages in some violation of mores or folkways, it is still not a gang until it becomes dependent on its identity for criminal violations.

A level one gang is the most elementary form of a real "gang". At level four in the classification system advanced in this book, such a group is really "organized crime". A level zero gang is not really a gang at all, it is a play group, a peer group, call it anything you want: we have all been members of such groups who engage in many behaviors, but essentially not that of violating criminal laws over time in a context where the group knows and approves of such law violation behavior and in fact benefits from

it.

Finally, many students of criminology today ask "what is the difference between prison gangs and street gangs?", and here some answers are now known. Previously it was thought that many prison gangs like the Aryan Brotherhood existed only in prisons and were not reported to be a problem for local law enforcement, or for other criminal justice personnel (probation or parole officers, etc). Clearly, we now know that gangs like the Aryan Brotherhood and their youth counterparts DO EXIST outside of the context of correctional institutions. And prison gang membership will be in most cases equivalent to gang membership on the outside of the correctional environment as well. Although, obviously, there are situations such as in our county jails and other institutions where confined persons "ride with" or temporarily show an allegiance to a gang simply while in custody and somehow reduce --- perhaps to its absolute minimum --- any such post-release gang affiliation. There are few if any "prison gangs" that do not represent if not by the same name then by proxy a similar gang problem on the "street".[26]

The language of this book is not limited to what some authors call "street gangs". We cannot define gangs simply in terms of those who "hang out on the streets", or "use the streets", or "claim the streets as their turf". The kind of gangs studied in this book are those who commit crime. Too often the casual reader about crime comes to think of "street crime" as a code word for crimes by minority persons. This book demonstrates that all ethnic groups, all races have gangs today; or had them in the past. If our social science vocabulary is so limited that we have to use the layman language of "street gang", then minimally and logically there must also exist "suite gangs" as well: those groups and organizations who commit their crimes from offices.

Finally, some analysts have failed to analyze the reality of gang life by concluding that "prison gangs" are totally independent of or totally different than their identical counterparts in the streets or the "free world". Gangs get imported into prison for the most part when their members are effectively prosecuted for crimes. The larger gangs on the streets of America are also found in the prisons of America. This book provides an enormous amount of information about gangs in the correctional context: jails, prisons, juvenile facilities, etc. This book also takes to task some previous researchers who have, by the nature of their flawed research methodologies, systematically underestimated the scope and extent of the Nation's gang problem behind bars. What we know today is that about one out of four inmates in American adult prisons are in fact gang members. Previous federal research concluded this "density" was only six percent, and by drastically underestimating the problem, this disinformation has had negative effects during the 1990's for correctional institutions; this is true because it basically denied the scope and extent of the problem, and made it hard for Security Threat Group (STG) analysts to get the resources they needed to counter-act the gang problem behind bars. Today, much has changed, and gangs behind bars are often just called "Security Threat Groups" or "Security Risk Groups": because the correctional institution has one primary mission, to maintain security for the inmates and the public.

In sum, it is not where the gang operates, it is how it operates and functions that distinguishes it in terms of its sophistication and its objective crime threat. We will, later in this book, learn that "threat analysis" can be applied to gangs. We will learn that we can distinguish between gangs in terms of their organizational capabilities and this can be used to rate gangs in terms of what threat they pose to society.

THE BURNING QUESTION: How Much Crime in America is Gang-Related?

The study of gangs is justified as a portion of all curricula in every criminal justice, delinquency, criminology, sociology, psychology, etc program: if and only if gangs and their members constitute a significant portion of the overall American crime problem. This gets directly to the issue of what is a "gang-related crime". Or, alternatively, when can we count the value of "gang-impact" in assessing the overall threat that a gang or several gangs may pose in terms of their contribution to crime statistics in the United States? Some would have us believe that just because little Johnny robs someone, even though he was a member of a gang, as long as the gang did not order him to rob or as long as the robbery did not occur along with several other confederates who were members of the same gang, that this individual crime by a gang member should not be counted as "gang crime". The position advanced here is comparable to the Los Angeles law enforcement definition discussed later: if the crime was committed by a known gang member, it was a gang-related crime.

The reason is good logic: the offender in this instance has a larger more encompassing influence, the gang. Bad behavior while alone as a gang member may bring a violent punishment to the gang member from his/her own gang. Good behavior (i.e., defending the nation) would similarly --- as a lone person --- be behavior honored and perhaps even rewarded by the gang. Either way, there is little escaping the implications of behavior from the viewpoint of a larger social entity the offender belongs to: the gang. One is a gang member in some gangs 24 hours a day. Gang life in more organized or violent gangs is not a part-time commitment. It is more comparable to being a member of a cult or a total institu-

tion. One acts as a "gang member", and one may feel as a gang member he or she has greater protection for any individual acts. Thus, it is comparable to a police officer on duty taking a bribe: it is a police-based crime, whether the officer did it alone or as a member of a corrupt group. It should not be necessary to say that in the case of gang crime that the gang had to know and approve of the crime in advance before we consider it gang-related crime; for that could be considered gang legislated crime. We are far from having the nationwide facts about gang crime. Until we do it is best to have the widest possible definition until we know what that yields. When we are at the stage of adequately coming to grips with the scope and extent of this national problem, then we might be able to partial out those crimes which were known and approved of in advance by the gang itself, or authorized, or directed by gang leaders. It is a moot point at this time in history, because no one has the data. In this situation, your author elects to accept the definition of gang-related crime as any crime committed by a gang member.

So, back to the issue: do the facts currently justify the study of gangs in the sense that gangs and gang members tend to account for a sizable portion of the American crime problem? Yes, is the answer argued here. But sadly, all parameters of the answer are not completely known. Some attempts to estimate youth crime portions of national crime statistics suggested that about half of all such crimes were gang-related. The problem here is very complex and needs some explanation.

First, it is widely known that there are generally three sources of data for crime statistics. There is the FBI's Uniform Crime Report (UCR), but it does not ask local law enforcement agencies to "double-tag" offense reports so that we could even know nationally what the scope and extent of gang crime in America is. There is also the victimization survey, but it does not ask respondents if they believe the crimes that they were the victims of were gang-related. Finally, there are self-report surveys and these come closest, at present, to giving an indication, at this stage of social science, of what role gangs play in criminal law violation in America. None of these three sources are as of yet adequate to provide all of the answers needed regarding the problem of gang crime. By way of comparison, "hate crime" is something that became officially tracked only in relative recent history. This is not to say that America only had "hate crime" in its recent history only. This means that our official policy was to simply recognize it, like child abuse, as a new social problem worthy of systematically tracking and reporting. No state and no federal government agency is required by law to monitor and report all known gang-related crimes, or crimes committed by gang members at this writing. This can be expected to change in the future, because like "hate crime" or bias crime, or like child abuse crimes, crimes committed by gang members appears to be taking on the role of the new national bogeyman in America.

There is reason to believe, however, that gang-related crime constitutes a significant portion of all crime in America. It is for that reason that this study represents both a challenge and a knowledge development need for the future. Many of the gangs studied by Thrasher would probably not be considered gangs at all in this analysis. Indeed, the gangs which exist in America today represent a much more formidable challenge to law enforcement, corrections, and public safety. The "gangs" that Thrasher studied were lucky to have pocket knifes and baseball bats. Some gangs today have at their disposal fully automatic weapons and even military ordnance.[27]

Gangs are a national problem and are now reported to be a problem to some extent in nearly all states. The Camp and Camp (1985: p. 11) study showed only a few states not reporting a gang problem in their prison system (Alabama, Alaska, Delaware, Kansas, New Hampshire, North Dakota, Oregon, Rhode Island, South Carolina, South Dakota, Vermont, Wyoming and missing data on New Jersey and Tennessee).

Recent data on correctional institutions, described in later chapters, shows that there are no states in the USA that do not have a gang problem. Law enforcement data, described in later chapters, shows the same thing. While the "gang problem" in large urban areas is certainly different than the gang problem in a rural area or suburb, we are still faced with the situation that few jurisdictions in America today are "free" from any gang problem or gang presence in their community.

One of the most fascinating criminological research needs regarding gang crime is how much crime and violence committed by gangs is simply never recorded in our national crime statistics. Routine "drive-by" shootings and rival-gang shoot-outs in many inner city areas, while being well known to the residents, are simply never recorded as "real crimes" by the police. Kotlowitz (1992: p. 18) reports the case of a large-scale shoot-out between rival gangs at the Henry Horner Homes public housing complex on Chicago's near west side that when a reporter called the next day for a copy of a police report, the reporter was told no such police report existed! Many such crimes in Chicago are routinely "unfounded", that is: not listed as real crimes, and therefore never reported to the FBI for its national crime statistics: rather the police radio messages tell us what happens, because no "complainant" exists to sign a complaint, the police officer responding to the call (if a call is ever made) simply radios back it is a "nineteen

Paul", the code for "no problem", "no complainant", "no arrest", "no report". Anyone with a police scanner can listen to these police radio frequencies to hear of anonymous calls from "citizens" and actual complainants throughout the City of Chicago about such daily gang shootings, most of which get handled the same way "19 Paul".

What we have now as valid and reliable information is not sufficient to answer several basic national questions: how much crime committed in the United States is gang related, or committed by gang members? We don't know, all we have are estimates. How many gangs exist in the United States and how many gang members exist in the United States --- again all we have are estimates. The FBI's criminal division did recently estimate that there may be 400,000 gang members in the United States.[28]

HOW EASY IT IS TO OVER-GENERALIZE ABOUT GANGS

Some authors have sought to systematically root out the "myths" about gangs in America today (Sanchez-Jankowski, 1991). This generates far too much attention, because the problem is really empirical, not theoretical. Theoretically, gangs can vary in terms of a wide number of characteristics, functions, structures, and behaviors. Some gangs sell drugs, some may not. But generally, if it is a real gang (one that engages in crime), given the opportunity it is certainly capable of any type of crime. The reason this is an issue is that some studies may have focused on the strong linkage to either drug use or drug sales and such studies may seek to generalize their findings to the entire American gang problem.

The term "myth" is not used here (e.g., It is a myth that all gangs sell/use drugs). It is rather and more accurately called a logical fallacy that overgeneralizes from a specific instance to the larger scene. The phrase "All gangs or all gang members use/sell drugs" is therefore just that: an over-generalization. Just finding an exception does not mean we do not have strong evidence of the role of gangs in selling drugs, nor does it diminish the general behavioral profile showing that gang members abuse drugs more than other offenders, or than non-offenders.

Some of these types of definitional analyses are "straw-man" techniques to raise other social or ideological issues. While they are not unimportant issues, there is no limit to the logical number of such issues: the family's role, the role of single-parent families, the role of educational failure, the role of being stigmatized/labelled, etc. What we need are statistics: numbers that will help to clarify the parameters of such issues. Variation in illegal groups is to be expected in the same way that such variation is to be found in lawful groups. The global factors that vary with gangs are clearly: who, what, when, where, why and how. The variations in factors which help us to classify gangs are potentially endless.

Another common error made frequently by some newcomers to the gang issue in criminology is to assume that anything that applies to juvenile delinquents (e.g., treatment) automatically applies to "gangs". As stated earlier, we lack information over time on what percent of all American juvenile delinquents are in fact gang members, or even what proportion of all crimes committed by juveniles arrested represent such gang members. Thus, it is criminologically naive to think that simply because a "therapy" program that had some application to juvenile delinquency years ago may be of value for intervention with gang members today. All juvenile delinquents are not gang members, and not all gang members are juvenile delinquents. It is possible for a gang member to technically never be arrested for a crime and grow up as an adult with no "rap sheet" at all; perhaps even get hired as a police officer.

In the search for a honest view of gangs, the goal of this book has been to provide a holistic, interdisciplinary, and historical analysis covering the main issues. It is not easy to provide an overall theme that integrates material that has never before been provided in such a format. Indeed, some experts in the field when they heard of this plan for a textbook on gangs said that "it could not be done". They believed that viewpoints in the gang literature are so different and the research methods are so diverse, that it is "premature" to have the basis for a textbook on gangs. Actually, there are a number of commonalities in the literature as will be shown.

It is no easy task to organize into a coherent whole all of the extensive gang literature. The reader is strongly encouraged to closely follow the footnotes provided. Other reading in areas of interest from the recommended readings and bibliography provided is also suggested.

Where the author digresses at various points in the book to discuss historical issues, or matters of research ethics, etc, these discussions are provided because the author felt the issues were important to raise. Please pardon some cliches to be found in the book as a deviation from a professional writing style. While the author has endeavored to provide a comprehensive analysis of gangs in America, this book by no means "covers everything". No single book could ever claim to "know it all".

In no sense does the amount of space or attention provided to specific gang authors imply any relationship to their overall contributions in the field. This means some prior authors who may have been only marginally connected to the field of gang studies could be discussed much more than prolific gang authors. This book does not try to establish such a

"pecking order" of gang wisdom. New data is now emerging that will have much bearing on the analysis of gangs in America. It is, in short, a volatile field; partly because gangs are emerging as such a national problem.

Finally, not each and every "gang action program" in America is discussed here. Many are not known outside of their immediate area. There is no central "GANG CRIME INFORMATION AND REFERRAL SERVICE"[29]. The author therefore apologizes to the many local efforts not mentioned here, commends them, and hopes to hear from them[30]. Finally, "tone" in this book may vary at times. Some would say it could have been more dispassionate, perhaps softened, and much less sarcastic/argumentative/cynical in certain respects.

A QUICK OVERVIEW OF WHAT THIS TEXT WILL COVER

Chapter 2 will examine some of those factors that should probably be used in the classification of gangs. This is most important, since some current approaches to gang analysis see only three types of gangs: social gangs, delinquent gangs, and conflict gangs. Others add "drug" or hedonistic to the gang classification. That is not a precise scientific approach, it is rather a convenient such classification, based at the highest level of theoretical competence on attribution theory. We need a better classification system, because that is the first step of science. The author will at strategic points in the book provide the basic typology, and later add elements of the classification, and discuss its potential application. Towards the end of this book the reader will then be able to compare previous definitions of gangs and arrive at an integrated definition.

Chapter 3 provides an overview of the major milestones in the gang literature. The purpose here is to acquaint the reader with "major contributions". Hopefully the reader shall find that this book is not restrictive about the admission of evidence. In fact, quite the obverse, as will be seen in subsequent chapters, where many such additional contributions are summarized where they are most appropriately brought into discussion. But some major figures in the field of gang studies such as Malcolm Klein, Walter Miller and Irving Spergel have added so much to our knowledge about gangs that books could be written about them individually.

In chapter 4, a current view among some gang authors (Moore, 1978; Hagedorn and Macon, 1988) regarding the societal conditions or the social context under which gangs emerge, more specifically, the racism and oppression hypothesis, is examined in greater detail. Is this a political platform, not a theory? Is this based on social fact? Are there conceptual continuities in the literature and historical grounds for this view? These questions are answered in reviewing this gang thesis about racism and oppression.

In chapter 5, a related thesis about gangs is examined. It involves the underclass. As will be seen, it is a provocative, enduring issue, and one that suggests a changing research agenda for gang analysis.

In chapter 6, another historical continuity and organizational aspect is examined: the relationship of gangs to politics in America. This, too is an issue still significant in the modern era-- one that is multiplied in varied ways in many political jurisdictions. It is an issue over the control over and allocation of scarce resources, and the political-economy.

In chapter 7, one of the primary qualitative research techniques for understanding gangs is described. This is the oral history method. Sometimes called "conversation analysis", conducting "case studies", and "field research interviews". It too has been used with considerable variation over the years.

In chapter 8, we clarify the truth about two major early contributors to the understanding of gangs: Shaw and Mc Kay. And because current literature reveals a confusion about these authors, Chapter 9 as well examines Shaw and Mc Kay on the matter of gangs, along with some related historical context. Chapter 10 provides another interesting bit of history: a detailed examination regarding what, specifically, might have been involved in the research methodology used by Thrasher in his famous study of 1,313 gangs in Chicago.

In chapter 11, the gang is described not as a sign that America is "falling apart", or as a sign of its imminent collapse as a democracy, such as in a negativistic view of the future as might be implied in some of our Hollywood movies along the same lines (e.g., Escape from New York City, etc). In fact, we should view gangs (as group formations) as natural and normal. Their members may indeed engage in behavior that some of us may regard as unnatural and abnormal. But as a whole, gangs are normal under some conditions. Further, gangs are not new to America. And America is not the only society with gang problems. But America is alone, according to the current literature, in having such a conspicuous and violent gang presence in everyday life.

Chapter 12 provides a viewpoint on gangs from what we know about organizational life generally. It is an organizational approach to gangs that may help to clarify what types of gangs actually exist. They are, after all, more than groups. They have continuity and internal social organization.

Chapter 13 examines a historically legitimate issue: gangs, guerrilla warfare, and conflict. Here we find the interesting case of robber gangs from India and how the British military was able to suppress them. It is valuable because it shows that gangs have

another possible level of violence other than drive-by shootings. Can gangs be a proxy force for terrorism in the decades ahead? Was Jeff Fort's Chicago gang, the El Rukn's, the only gang in America to seek out funding from foreign governments hostile to America? These and related issues are also examined in this book.

Chapter 14 seeks to clarify, from what we know about social group formations, the group characteristics of gangs. Here we see as well some evidence that perhaps gangs can arise naturally under certain conditions (e.g., economic deprivation, social disorganization, ethnic antagonism, racial segregation, the underclass context, etc) but might in fact be capable of being artificially created. That is, creating a gang by social engineering. The author's previous research on Neo-nazi youth gangs is described here as well.

Chapter 15 takes the group analysis approach a step further by comparing the features of both cults and gangs. The analysis of the conditions of the group and organization found in comparing cults and gangs is quite revealing: there are more similarities than differences.

Chapter 16 addresses the controversial matter of legalizing or decriminalizing heroin and hard drugs as a strategy recommended (Moore, 1978) for gang neutralization. Would taking the economic incentive out of drugs truly reduce gang problems? Or are there at least two other scenarios: one where there was "no effect", and one where there was an unintended "compounding" effect. It also examines drug use and drug sales by gangs.

Chapter 17 examines the question, of concern to many, regarding the differences between gangs and organized crime. Here again we see the importance of examining gangs in the framework of a social organizational approach. Clearly, many criminal justice officials believe that there are some gangs that should be considered forms of organized crime.

Chapter 18 examines recent research on female gang membership and how they differ from non-gang members when matched by race, age, and education. It also examines aspects related to female members of gangs, and the issue about the rights of children as this pertains to the gang problem in America. Chapter 19 focuses on another unique aspect of gangs: Asian gang members.

Chapter 20 looks at family life and aspects about the family in relationship to gangs. Chapter 21 examines the thesis about the role of the mass media, particularly the movie industry, in portraying the gang problem in America. Similarly, Chapter 22 examines the community's role in dealing with gangs.

Chapter 23 involves a review of those issues, problems, and new directions in law enforcement relevant to gangs. It also examines adjudication and statutory problems regarding the handling of gang crimes. Data from recent research is also summarized here.

Chapter 24 provides a case study of an effective federal gang prosecution: the case of the notorious "Gangster Disciples" in Chicago.

Chapter 25 focuses entirely on the gang problem as it is experienced in adult correctional institutions. It shows some of the unique problems faced by correctional facilities and their limited choices in dealing with the gang problem. It also discusses the need for standards governing the control of gangs in custody. Data from recent research on this issue is also provided and discussed.

Chapter 26 examines the parallel problem of gangs and juvenile correctional institutions. This is based on recent national research and shows that gangs are truly a national problem. Again, much new information from national research on aspects of this problem are provided.

Chapter 27 discusses the importance of gang intervention and gang prevention initiatives. It describes some of the strategies and policies relevant for communities, educational institutions, and correctional institutions. It provides an analysis of those service components and program initiatives used in the past, and some new suggestions, for efforts involving gang intervention.

Chapter 28 provides a review and analysis of some of the gang programs around the country. It describes some of the best and some of the worst of such service programs. It critically addresses the issue of gang leaders being the administrators of government funded gang programs. Chapter 29 discusses gang theory and what exactly a gang theory should be able to explain about gang life today.

Chapter 30, in conclusion, seeks to integrate our knowledge about gangs and discusses the gang problem in terms of what the future holds. This closing chapter examines our options as a society for dealing with the gang problem.

SUMMARY

In criminological research, as in any research, the term gang must ultimately be put to test. It must be a concept that can be measured to be a meaningful concept. Clearly, there have been many loose definitions of what constitutes a gang in the literature. More precision is needed. Thus, the definitive criteria of what constitutes a gang is a central focus of this book in order to clarify more than confuse.

There is reason to be concerned about the gang crime problem in America. Minimally we need to know if gang-related crimes make up a large or small share of our national crime statistics. Unfortunately, little such hard, factual information exists. This too will be the focus on ongoing discussion in this book.

Additionally, a large number of persons who work in the criminal justice system --- in law enforcement, corrections, probation, parole, judges, private security, and others, as well as program/service/intervention staff, teachers and many others dealing with the problems of gang crime on a daily basis --- need as part of their training a comprehensive analysis of gangs in America today. This book may not answer all their questions. But it attempts to address all the major issues.

This book involves many sources of information and a variety of different research methods and research projects dealing with gangs. It uses official sources, it uses survey methods, it uses the oral history method or case studies, it uses secondary analysis; in short all known sources of information. Where the author has been selective about sources is in not including much from our newspaper accounts about gangs[31]. There is much good journalism being focused on gangs and dealing with topics that are worthy of investigation, and where ever possible some of these better media sources have been cited in the book as well.

Finally, we have not at this stage addressed the matter of what really makes a "gang" a gang. Or an effective gang, or a "threatening" versus a "non-threatening" gang for that matter. That is the focus of chapter two, and beyond. Chapter two begins to address this matter. The issue of gang classification, gang characteristics, factors on which gangs do or may be expected to vary.

Discussion Questions

(1) Assume Bobby J. and Billy K. are both members of an organized criminal gang. Acting on their own to increase their joint income they rob a store. Does that robbery count as a "gang-related crime"? Or is "gang-related crime" limited to those offenses that are officially sanctioned and approved in advance in a conspiratorial manner by the official full gang? If they had to share some of the loot from the robbery with their gang leader, would it be a gang crime then?

(2) If a significant portion of crime in America becomes known to involve "gang-related crimes", then would our traditional response to crime (e.g., imprisonment) be the best solution when our correctional system has historically been based on the lone offender, or could gangs become more organized in the correctional setting and operate more efficiently than correctional staff, or even function to become the de facto administrators of their correctional facility?

(3) Why would gangs emerge or organize along ethnic lines? And would the most effective gang be one that is racially/ethnically integrated or one that is homogeneous?

END NOTES:

[1] A "social gang" is what the author calls in later portions of this book a level zero gang. It is, at best, a "pre-gang" group. It commits few serious crimes. It is equivalent to a streetcorner play group such as Spanky and Alfalfa, et al, in the popular TV series "The Little Rascals".

[2] "The Little Rascals" was a TV series produced by Hal Roach in the 1930s. The series involves neighborhood kids, with a clubhouse at times, who are not adult supervised. Because they are not adult supervised some authors today would still consider them a gang. The present author does not consider them a real gang. Only a group involved in crime or benefiting from crime, over time, is a gang in the authors definition.

[3] We cannot oversimplify the definition of gang by taking the viewpoint that any organized group containing offenders must necessarily constitute a gang. Were that kind of ambiguous definition used in gang analysis, then correctional officials would have to conclude that any "pro-social" club or organization behind the walls of correctional institutions constitutes a "social gang". That is not the perspective advanced in this book. Even though some wardens may use this definition of gangs, particularly in reference to Muslims.

[4] A criminologist should be a social scientist --- someone who does not simply take an "official" definition as the gospel. In prisons today, some religious groups are classified by correctional administrators as "threat groups", essentially treated the same way gangs are.

[5] Gangs represent a group, collective behavior, organizational patterns, and other features that have historically been the turf of sociology. However, other disciplines have much to add to this area of study --- and these include the perspectives from law, psychology, social service administration/social work, human development, urban studies, anthropology, corrections and criminal justice, and other areas of specialization in the social sciences.

[6] Vigil and Yun (in Huff, 1990: p. 159) describe the uniqueness of Vietnamese youth gangs in not having a name even within their group "for fear that it would invite police recognition". Thus, a secret society with criminal functions would also be a gang in this sense.

[7] Malcolm Klein's definition of gang is that the members "recognize themselves as a denotable group (almost invariably with a group name)". This is generally accurate and covers most of the gang problem.

[8] Gorn (1987) reports the case of massive public attendance at a gang leader's funeral, involving 250,000 people back in 1855. What all gangs and those in the funeral procession seemed to have in common was their social class.

[9] The informed reader will note that the tourist industry in Chicago has adapted itself to this problem. Bus tours now routinely take tourists through the city to show them where Al Capone conducted business, where mobsters were slain, etc. An "Al Capone" museum was recently opened as a tourist attraction in Chicago as well. A bar in Peotone, Illinois is locally referred to as "Capone's place" and features a large picture of Al Capone and a sign reading "Gangsters Hall"; again a kind of reverence shown to figures like Al Capone.

[10] The bibliography for this book shows over 50 such contributions during the 1970s to the study of gangs or gang members. There was in no sense, then, a "black out" on gang studies.

[11] Perhaps contrary to many of such author intentions, they have also communicated by their provincial analyses that the only gang threat in America is that by "persons of color". Or that, there is no problem with Ku Klux Klan members, right wing extremists, hate groups that commit bias crimes and engage in anti-semitism, etc. In fact, our data shows groups like the Ku Klux Klan and the Aryan Brotherhood, and others prone to engage in bias crimes and illegal acts of anti-Semitism are very much a current problem facing America today.

[12] It is important to note, historically, that in spite of this problem there have been significant efforts that have induced much effect in terms of using criminal justice resources to target organizations as the focus of investigation. We need only recall how in the 1950s the American Communist Party was the target of an enormous investigation.

[13] The research in Hyde Park by Shireman, et al showed adolescent versions of the street corner group (Liebow, 1967; Anderson, 1978), but which were faced with fearful adults in the area who were most prone to define them as a gang or "up to no good".

[14] The State of California, in its penal code, sections 186.20 through 186.27 has the "Street Terrorism Enforcement and Prevention Act" which is addressed towards gang suppression. It has become an important tool for intelligence and prosecution.

[15] See: "6 Abortion Foes Are 1st Charged Under New Law", Chicago Tribune, June 7, 1994, Section 1, p. 3. These were the six arrested in Milwaukee.

[16] According to some sources, we might add to this list the case of Synanon. A drug treatment organization that for years was recognized as the best in the business. Then the press and mass media uncovered how the organization had controlled vast economic enterprises, operated with the use of firearms, and was less than a organization with a "wholesome" appearance.

[17] Some states do not consider groups like the Aryan Brotherhood or Ku Klux Klan "gangs"; rather they are considered "hate groups". Presumably hate groups prone to crime.

[18] It would appear to be somewhat discriminatory to con-

sider group criminal behavior as "gang crime" when it is committed by groups who consist predominantly of racial minority group members, and not applying the same standard to white groups who also engage in such continuing criminal behavior patterns. This is particularly important in terms of the legal validity of enforcing gang abatement or gang crime statutes. Allowing groups like the Aryan Brotherhood to escape the investigative and prosecutorial thrust of anti-gang legislation may make such statutes unconstitutional (see Destro, 1993: p. 235).

[19] The issue is: is it illegal to prepare for suicide or simulate it under the laws of the country in which this particular tragedy occurred? If they knew it was illegal to self-destruct, or encourage others to do so, then it is a criminal code violation behavior over time, a crime of violence, not income-producing crime.

[20] Obviously, social scientists are always free to use some literary license here in defining what they think should be considered to be gang behavior, just as criminologists rejecting the legalist definition of crime are free to declare what they think should be a crime. Such a list is potentially endless, particularly for youths given the tendency of adults to view with alarm any non-conformity among youths; and the historical tendency of each new adult generation to declare its youth population "gone to the dogs". The analytical focus here, to repeat, is on crime; not deviance; not "ill", "malo", or "immoral" behavior; and not even on what should be legislated as crime.

[21] When this definition was first advanced in 1991, it was almost heretical because of the liberal idea that gangs could be considered "gangs" also because they were inimical in someway, or threatening in someway to society or their community, without regard to the legal issue of ordinance or statutory violation. Subsequent works by Klein and others acknowledged this basis "definitive ingredient".

[22] The Ku Klux Klan and related political extremist groups are clearly included in the definition of criminal gang. Obviously, like some of our more organized gangs to be discussed in later chapters, some may believe they are really emergent varieties of organized crime.

[23] Typical examples of actual crimes committed involve: bombing business establishments and painting graffiti, such as anti-Semitic threats on synagogues. See: "Supremacist Guilty in Bombing, Vandalism", Chicago Sun-Times, Sept. 14, 1994, p. 19.

[24] Some gang analysts see only three possibilities: youth gangs, hate groups, and organized crime. The problem is, this is not a classification system where logic is on our side. Youths can be members of hate groups, and of organized crime. Some groups loosely considered "youth gangs" may simply mean "youth members" of various types of gangs, indeed: gangs whose top leadership structure is not in any sense "youth controlled", but is rather driven by adults with long criminal records.

[25] The notable exception are engineered gangs: those created by adult hate groups (e.g., neo-nazis) such as were created by the NSPA nazi movement in southwest Chicago in the mid-1970's. These were specifically age-graded "sects" of the larger adult neo-nazi organization. These are discussed in more detail in Chapter 13.

[26] The chapter on gangs in the adult correctional institutions also addresses this issue: for example, two such gangs were felt to exist only inside prisons in Illinois (e.g., Northsiders, and the S.I.A.). However, recent additional research has now shown "Northsiders" to be an identification used at the jail inmate level as well.

[27] Let us keep a historical perspective here on the armed offender in the gang context. Prior to 1968 anyone in America could readily acquire firearms over the counter, through the mail, etc. If Thrasher's gangs wanted them, at that time in history they could also purchase as much dynamite as they wanted in local hardware stores. Both explosives and weapons laws changed dramatically in 1968, making it somewhat more difficult for offenders to acquire these instruments of destruction.

[28] See: "Feds Can Help Cities Fight Gangs, FBI Says", by Jerry Moskal, Chicago Sun-Times, Feb. 10, 1994, p. 8.

[29] Shortly after the first edition of this book appeared in 1991, the National Youth Gang Information Center appeared as an information service on gangs similar to what the National Criminal Justice Reference Service does. But all it did was collect information on gang research, particularly federally funded projects on gangs. At the time of the second edition (1993), the NYGIC was under threat of closing and being absorbed by the NCJRS. It is now gone completely. A separate national clearinghouse on gangs and gang intelligence was still sorely needed. The fact that federal leadership on this has been lacking has resulted recently in correctional gang intelligence coordinators forming their own clearinghouse. When a major leader in OJJDP retired, a group in Florida suddenly became the National Youth Gang Center, receiving millions in federal funding, with the same retired OJJDP official at the helm of the group. We would hypothesize that as soon as the federal money ceases to go to this Florida group, it will cease as a "National Youth Gang Center".

[30] Actually, at this writing, such a national analysis of actual gang programs is underway; tracking all federal and foundation support to programs involving "gangs" or "gang members". The full and complete book on recent and contemporary gang programs has not yet been written. I am working on it now.

[31] This is not in any sense to denigrate journalism, in fact while some authors condemn the mass media for being "alarmists" the role of the media is also very positive when it documents the role of racial conflict in the study of gangs. Much information of that nature has emerged in the printed media. We should also recall that being a newspaper reporter was one of the background skills before training in sociology that Thrasher brought to bear on the analysis of gangs (see Geis, 1965: p. 17).

Simon City Royals: A Chicago White Gang

Chapter 2

CLASSIFICATION FACTORS FOR
GANG ANALYSIS

INTRODUCTION

Science begins with classification. The best form of classification would be that of the typology. A typology must meet two fundamental rules: (1) The categories must be exhaustive --- that is to say, the classification covers the entire gamut and the full spectrum of possibilities, there can be no exceptions to its categories, and (2) The categories must be mutually exclusive --- that is to say, something can fit into only one category, not two or more. This chapter describes those factors that may be useful for gang classification, threat analysis, and typology development. Classification, for example in the field of corrections, is also fundamental to effective processing and management.[1] We must examine factual data and background factors. In the correctional setting, we must also take into account adjustment factors. These are important and allow for public agencies like correctional institutions to more effectively carry out their mission. The same, it will be found, is true in the study of gangs.

Threat analysis, or applying screening for risk and profiling to gangs, must also be research based: using those factors known from research on gangs to predict and correctly assess their objective crime threat. That is, to be useful, and to hold up in court, it must be empirically demonstrated that such factors can significantly differentiate high risks of crime or violence from low risks. The rise of gang intelligence positions throughout the American criminal justice system in recent years is a response to the gang threat

problem. The direction of such developments seems to be headed towards something similar to Targeted Offender Programs, where strategic purposes of intelligence prove invaluable, particularly in gang member database development, and gang member tracking systems.

This chapter will not provide a full classification system, it will only identify some of the major factors that should probably be included in it. In a later chapter this classification approach will yield four such gang classification categories in terms of their level of organizational development and crime threat. How these factors might be figured into a scheme for examining the differences in gangs along organizational dimensions will be illustrated later in the book. We will alert the reader now, however, what the author means by Level Zero, Level One, Level Two, and Level Three gangs.

A Level Zero gang, in the typology developed by author, is not a true gang at all, it is at worst a "pre-gang". It is in the language of sociology an informal group. It is the kind of clique or "Spanky and Alfalfa" group that most human beings have belonged to. Some call a youth group unsupervised by adults a gang, unfortunately if we accepted this definition of "gang", then we could easily estimate how many gang members there are in the United States: over two hundred million, because everyone at one point or another during their childhood has done this. But this would confuse more than it elucidates in the

17

field of criminology. That is why the present author would not include such groups or Level One gangs and members in any estimate of criminal gangs and their members: because they are not a part of the national crime picture.

A Level One gang, in the typology developed by the author and discussed in greater detail elsewhere in this book, is an emergent gang, typically consisting of only one unit of operation. It may be less structured as an entity of human organization. All members belong and clearly function as a small organization, but a type of informal organization, without written rules typically. It typically consists of only one unit of operation. An example: A group of youths in a suburban community adopt the name for the gang as the Southside Crips because they live on the southside of the suburban community, they have no idea what "Crip culture" is really all about, they only have a small inkling of the "Crip lingo" from rap music videos, and they no absolutely no one in Los Angeles (the epicenter for Crip gangs) or California for that matter.

A Level Two gang, in the typology developed by the author, is a crystallized gang and has a definite structure. It is comparable to what could be called the formal group. It typically consists of several units of operation that are not geographically contiguous. An example could be any gang that has two or more "sets" that operate in cooperation with each other on a regular basis.

A Level Three gang, in the typology developed by the author, is sometimes called the "supergang" or the "corporate" gang. It is a highly structured gang. It can be regarded in classical sociological language as a formal organization. It may include numerous "chapters", "sets", or franchises throughout an entire society. A number of such gangs are found in almost all states (i.e., Aryan Brotherhood, Bloods, Crips, Gangster Disciples, Latin Kings, Vice Lords, etc). This type of gang typically has formalized its "code", and may have a written constitution and by-laws. Several examples of these types of written constitutions and by-laws, and other internal written memoranda are provided in the appendices of this book.

In theory, a gang can become Level Four: which would meet the traditional definition of being an organized crime group if it secures the advantage of political corruption for its operations and accumulates sufficient capital to penetrate legitimate business.

Thus, in the authors typology the levels Zero through Four in classifying gangs simply reflects the level of organizational development in these gangs. As will be seen, this enables a more objective way of looking at gangs. This is also a necessary foundation to provide a threat analysis on gangs.

In order not to overwhelm the student, however, the full typology advanced by the author will be presented and discussed at points further in this book where it is appropriate. Because the student must first understand the classification factors that might be used, the history of gangs, and a number of other empirical trends about gang members. In doing so, an incremental approach will be made. This will be based on the literature and on previous research. The objective is to provide a comprehensive set of factors that can be used for gang classification. These factors are also important in quantifying any gang threat assessment.

In specifying the various organizational features of gangs, it is possible to therefore expect as many different variations and permutations as there are such factors on which to classify them. This would not, however, offer a manageable approach to developing a gang typology. In practice we can expect hundreds, perhaps thousands, of such unique variations when a large number of such factors exist.

The following discussion therefore encompasses those factors which are relevant to gang classification.

One of the questions that is frequently asked of gang experts in America is "which is the most dangerous gang in America today?". That question can only be answered with reference to those factors which spell out the differential ability of gangs to exist and function in society. Thus, the factors discussed below can be used to classify gangs along dimensions of risk. These factors also help understand the myriad of ways in which a gang, as a form of social organization, develops and strives for greater sophistication.

LEVEL OF ORGANIZATION

Obviously, gangs vary by this factor, we do have criminal gangs that are not well organized and we have some that are very organized. This is the basis of the authors typology. This helps to make sense out of the literature on gangs, because some authors will simply deny that gangs have any organization, that is they are simply "near groups", not even real groups! Recently Spergel wrote "despite some police and media reports, especially reports by national law enforcement agencies, street gang organization and crime patterns are not highly organized" (1994: p. 3).[2] This may be an example of over-generalizing, because we do not have a complete national picture nor a very good empirical basis to say much about the national picture when we do not know how much crime gang members commit or even how many gang members actually exist. It is safer to assume that natural variation exists in the level of organizational sophistication of gangs. The fact is there are highly organized gangs, some do exist, and we cannot simply define them out of our analysis by saying "oh, those are organized crime groups" without at least documenting when and how the "street gang" transformed itself into a higher category of threat. Organized crime groups are, as will be illustrated in a later chapter, the epitome of gang crime. Why? Because they are criminal organizations.

LEADERSHIP

A gang crime specialist in Chicago once remarked that "gang leaders have been short in physical stature". They need not be intellectual giants either. But some level of charisma and an ability to use wits and cunning is presumably necessary. Being a trained military veteran might help. Krisberg (1975, Chapter VI) sees the most conspicuous feature of gang leadership as being "their superior verbal ability...a capacity to deliver emotional speeches" (Krisberg, 1975: p. 74); that is, "verbal talent...excellent language control...verbal abilities" (ibid, p. 75).

No doubt about it, there are different classifications of leadership. Our social sciences can help here. Thrasher's (1927) analysis suggests it is simply a matter of "natural leaders", or being older than followers. But today, does gang leadership fit the "crude democracy" pattern described by Thrasher? Or, as will be explained later in this book, is this leadership attribution mostly applicable to the lower end of the gang development spectrum. That is to say, we might assume some variation in leadership style along with differences in the level of organizational development among gangs[3].

It is probably too late to study this feature in its natural formative stages, but prisons would have been great opportunities to study the natural history of offender leaders.[4] Today, most prisons are highly impregnated with gangs. It is too late to be able to go in and set up an opportunity for leadership emergence and to study the characteristics of those who can dominate relatively innocuous prison organizations (Jaycees, A.A./N.A., Toastmasters, etc, etc). The problem with seeking to do this kind of study today would be that gangs already exist in these prisons and would naturally want to have some influence over these groups. Or these groups do not control the kind of resources that other sub rosa groups can control within the prison population, making them of little interest to the continuing offender.

Gang leaders in larger more structured gangs may be regarded as God-like figures to younger members of the gang. Most gang leaders at the upper end of the gang income flow are older adults. Often in their 40's and 50's. Some of these gang leaders are able to effectively run their gang operations from behind prison bars[5].

A typical description of a gang leader of a level three gang, like the El Rukns, was that description of Jeff Fort as follows:

"It was Fort's charisma, and his amazing recruiting skills, that made him special. He traveled with an entourage, wearing snappy clothes that dictated neighborhood fashion, and when he walked by Woodlawn's elementary schools, kids on the playground would pile up on the fence just to get a look at him."[6]

TERRITORIALITY

Presumably a gang must lay some claim to control of a specific turf, if we are referring to the classical "street gang". However, there are some known exceptions and it is worth further discussion (see Hardman, 1969: p. 176).[7] Basically, most street gangs do arise and have a local network with a specific geographical pattern of activity. They even recognize the specific boundaries of gang domination. But some gangs do not. The Aryan Brotherhood would seem to be a gang group, found in many prisons nationally, that on the outside of the prison has no specific territorial control at least that has yet been reported in the literature.[8] Also, there do exist "hybrids" as gang formations:

Turf defense is most conspicuous as a gang feature in the early stages of gang formation; and at the higher end of organizational development when turf also equates to market share or marketing area (e.g., drug distribution). Inside the correctional institution, turf can have its symbolic equivalent: an exercise area, etc, where turf translates to a "controlled resource" rather than "home".

Some believe the gang problem in America is easy to explain: it is nothing more than a "territorial imperative". That is, of course, an over-generalization and fails to consider the more important factors also discussed in this chapter on gang organizational features. Turf today for many criminal gangs in America means drug distribution territory.

Turf is often, but need not be present, to define a gang. Turf is sometimes economic or political territory as well. When most people think of "gang turf" they think of an area of the city where a specific gang has conspicuously marked up the area with its own unique identifying graffiti.

Often, in large urban areas such as Los Angeles and Chicago, what separates "turf" are natural geographic boundaries such railroad tracks, highways, and main traffic corridors.[9]

INTERNAL ORGANIZATION

There must be a certain level of sophistication regarding internal organization. This means a hierarchy of authority, a chain of command, and the division of labor. It is difficult to imagine anything being classified as a gang without some level of internal organization. On the other hand, gangs do differ on the factor of internal organization. We shall learn more about this in subsequent chapters.

Some of these internal functions include recruitment, discipline, inculcating the gang code of values, and other functions such as preventing defection.[10] How a gang spends its "treasury" tells us a lot about internal functions. If it is spending its money on guns and drugs, for example, its function is predisposed towards crime. Internal organization also means having at least a second layer of leadership: those who have sufficient experience or education to be on a "council", or to serve in a function of mid-management (e.g., "one star Maliks" in the Vice Lords, etc). For example, in the Brothers of the Struggle (B.O.S., aka Gangster Disciples), there is a "Board of Directors" composed of the Chairman (the top gang leader, "King" Larry Hoover) at the top of a rather complex organizational structure.

To have any level of internal organization, a gang is required, by definition to consist of three or more persons. Two persons would only consist of a dyad or duo and could not be capable of the most elementary function that a group or organization has: the ability to delegate a duty.

EXTERNAL ORGANIZATION

To function effectively, a gang must have alliances and outside connections, often with other gangs or subcultures. The highest level of functioning would be to have an apparatus that is capable of paying off local politicians and local law enforcement, as well as facilitating rewards for staff who work in the correctional facilities where gang members are incarcerated. External organization includes other resources such as political alliances and resources mobilization generally. In other words, a gang that has a lawyer on call 24-hours a day has a higher level of external organization than one that does not.

The important aspect about external organization is the public relations function a modern gang needs today. When a South Central Los Angeles member of the Crips uses the expression "we have only love for South Central", they use like many gangs a code word or subcultural argot. To a South Central Crip, "love" has the meaning: let our vision educate. Gang literature often provides some aspect of this propaganda function by presenting the gang image as something "positive" (e.g., fighting oppression, helping the community, etc). This dual image is very functional for a gang and some gangs go to enormous expense and effort to be able to present a positive public image. This includes providing fully catered large scale picnics such as that held at Starved Rock in 1992 to celebrate the gang leader Larry Hoover's birthday[11]. Existing community groups find gangs more than eager to cooperate with them, par-

ticularly when such groups are willing to hire their gang members as "liaison"/street workers, etc, because some gangs clamor for positive publicity. What young children hear about during gang recruitment are the external organizational features: the myth of the gang, its "front", its claim to be a protector of the community, its claim to be a defender of traditional values such as peace, loyalty, justice, you name it.

Many experts on cults offer us some additional insight into the way gangs gain new members. Cults like gangs have always existed in America.[12] In Chicago during the 1994 political season, a gang political activist defended the Gangster Disciples by saying the gang does not have to recruit members, rather than members want to join the gang. Cult experts remind us that in cults, the typical cult member is not necessarily recruited as a member; rather the person is deceptively seduced and enticed to join the cult. The gang has a similar variation to this cultural universal cult recruitment mechanism. And it works quite effectively on young children.

The reason a criminal gang adopts the "public relations" gimmick of claiming it has prosocial aspects, or may even want to venture into politics or community action, is real simple to understand. A gang that claims it is a political or religious group can hide from law enforcement investigation behind constitutional grounds. A gang that can claim it does something for the community allows it to deflect law enforcement attention. A child whose parent discovers he is in a gang, say the Gangster Disciples, can immediately claim to the parent that "we are not gangbangers, we are about growth and development for the community".

RELIGIOUS OR POLITICAL TRAPPINGS

This issue is examined elsewhere in the book, but it basically means the gang uses a religious or political front for its public image. It also means providing a basis for organizing and attracting members. This helps in prison and on the streets where the gang can hide behind constitutional safeguards. Willie Lloyd, leader of Chicago's Unknown Vice Lords, developed an extensive written guide to what was called "The Amalgamated Order of Lordism", a religious identity that was superimposed on the gang's business: drug dealing.[13] Willie Lloyd could use his "public relations function", his identity as a "do gooder", to claim he was a contributor to a "gang peace treaty" or truce in Chicago, in fact he was granted an award in an official ceremony held by school officials at Chicago's Englewood Public High School. Lloyd just did not come and accept the award, because at the time members of his own gang were trying to assassinate him and the federal government was also investigating him.

Jeff Fort was the master of this charade and

provided the blueprint for other gangs to follow. Fort used religion as a springboard for his first major foray in gang organization --- conning a minister to help him get money for the gang (i.e., Rev. Fry), and later establishing his empire as a legal religious identity, owning real estate under the same identity. The religious identity --- Moorish Science Temple of America and Islamic influences --- was just a front.

Gang members in prison know this routine: they go to chapel to act like they are a prayer group, but it is just a meeting place for the gang members to transact business. African-American gang members seem clearly represented in the religious front, just like neo-nazis who use the Identity Church variations for their front group activities. It is an interesting twist, that according to one source a member can effectively leave one gang, the Latin Kings, if the member makes a genuine conversion to religious life; that is, the individual must be sincere for it to be effective, because if it was just a ploy and the individual is caught subsequently in a compromised situation he will be violated the same way he would as if he tried to simply quit the organization --- a three minute "head to toe", which involves the exiting member standing in front of two of the largest members of the chapters who will beat the member for three minutes, and the member cannot fight back, if he fights back he may die. The three minute "head to toes" are in some cases replaced with a bullet to the knee.

WRITTEN RULES, CONSTITUTIONS AND INTERNAL GANG LITERATURE

Surprisingly, for the level of literacy and educational under-attainment that is so often typical of many individual gang members --- at least that is an "image" we get from much of the literature, some contemporary gangs have written codes and written rules (i.e., constitution and bylaws). Some examples of these gang constitutions are provided in the appendices. Some gang researchers point to the fact that this may have arisen because once a gang leader is imprisoned he has much time to spend applying his interests to gang development. No doubt about it, many of the written codes that are widely circulating throughout the criminological community regarding gangs have been confiscated while in some form of correctional custody (prisons, jails, etc).

Not all of this type of evidence surfaces within the walls of corrections. Gang crimes officers routinely come across this material. Over ten years ago, in carrying out oral history studies of gang members, and in evaluating programs designed to rehabilitate gang offenders, I routinely had individuals willing to turn over their written gang codes to me. Later in this text, it will be shown how in the early 1800s a group existed (similar to the Aryan Brotherhood)

which also had such an elaborate written constitution and by-laws. Also, some contemporary examples of written constitutions from major contemporary gangs will be analyzed. Parents sometimes discover the "homework" that new young gang recruits are studying: it is not school books, it is more often than not the gang "prayers" and constitution. These kind of documents are readily available from a variety of sources including the gang members themselves[14].

The internal gang literature also includes poems and prayers of various sorts. Figure 1 provides an example of one such poem from the Aryan Brotherhood. Some larger gangs have been around so long and are large enough (e.g., Crips, Black Gangsters) that some of their members have formed musical bands that have produced their own musical tapes and records (e.g., rap music). Such songs as much as they exemplify an art form and offer a way to perpetuate the symbols and values of the gang are also important aspects of organizational capability.

Figure 2 provides an example of such a poem for the Brothers of the Struggle (BOS), that is, their "Prayer". Inside the Illinois prisons the Black Disciples (the Freeman faction of the Disciples) and the Gangster Disciples (the Hoover faction of the Disciples) basically "ride together".[15]

Figure 1

A Poem of the Aryan Brotherhood

An Aryan Brother is without a care,
He walks where the weak and heartless won't dare.
And if by chance he should stumble and lose control,
His brothers will be there, to help him reach his goal.
For a worthy brother, no need is too great,
He need not but ask, fulfillment's his fate.

For an Aryan Brother, death holds no fear,
Vengeance will be his, through his brothers still here.
For the Brotherhood means just what it implies,
A brother's a brother, till that brother dies.
And if he is loyal, and never lost faith,
In each brother's heart, will always be a place.

So a brother am I and always will be,
Even after my life is taken from me.
I'll lie down content, knowing I stood,
Head held high, walking proud in Brotherhood.

FIGURE 2

B.O.S. PRAYER

Looking out the window as far as I can see,
All my BOS Brothers standing around me,
GD's and BD's has combined,
As we both unite our star will shine,
King David he recruited, gave the (G)
Strength on the street,
He recruited the (D) on the history of our G
We will last forever,
As the Brothers of the Struggle,
Struggle together.

ETHNIC HOMOGENEITY

Ethnicity should encompass culture, skin color, country of origin, and language[16]. Generally, gangs are ethnically homogeneous; that is, their membership constitutes a majority of a certain ethnic group. There are no known Jewish members of the Tongs. Gangs tend to be ethnocentric. This need not be, from a strict theoretical viewpoint. In fact, perhaps the most powerful gang conceivable would be one that was thoroughly integrated. The reasoning here is obvious: domination and control relies on ability to as smoothly as possible have as much penetration of the illicit market place as possible, and the more diverse the ethnic and linguistic content of the gang membership then the higher its capability for national and even international operations.[17]

One recent development in areas outside of larger urban gang scenes, has been the situation where gangs using larger well-known names often associated with a specific race, are in fact very integrated along racial lines. That is, it is not to find white youths not only active but holding leadership roles in gangs often thought to include only African-Americans. It is not difficult to find American Indian youths in gangs traditionally thought to be representing Hispanic/Latino members (i.e., the Latin Kings). The possibility of a rainbow gang could prove to be a formidable challenge. For as will be seen in the chapter on organized crime, there is a real limiting effect when the gang is homogeneous with respect to race or ethnicity.

A NEW TENDENCY TOWARDS HETEROGENEITY

While it is true that historically gangs have tended to be homogeneous with respect to race and ethnicity, there has been an interesting recent trend in some gangs to basically include the full "Rainbow" of race and ethnicity. In theory, the "Rainbow"-style of gang which includes members from all races and ethnic groups could be more formidable over the long run in terms of its potential to become a true organized crime group.

SHIFTING MEMBERSHIP

While it is a common practice for gang members to have their own business cards printed up with their gang logo imprinted on it, it is not the case in gang organization that all gangs are the equivalent regarding membership patterns. In the Aryan Brotherhood, for example, one of their favorite slogans is "kill to get in, die to get out", implying specifically, that you can never "drop your flag", that if you become a member then you become a member for life.

Our gang literature is not in agreement on this matter of whether it is easy or difficult to voluntarily terminate gang membership. The reason for this lack of consensus is not theoretical or analytical. It reflects simply the fact that our literature is quite diverse on the levels of gang sophistication data being analyzed. Certainly, at the lower end of the gang organizational development spectrum, it is probably easy to say "I quit". But at the higher end of organizational sophistication that same intent could mean "termination with prejudice". Most gangs found in the prison system are of the "no quit" variety. Camp and Camp (1985: p. ix) showed that "in nearly two-thirds of the gangs, membership is perceived as a lifetime commitment, "blood in, blood out".

The issue is paying dues and showing allegiance to the gang organization. A gang where a member can "float in" and "float out" as he or she chooses is less effective than one with strict guidelines regarding membership obligations.

We shall later analyze in greater detail this factor of group commitment, particularly in relationship to policy choices regarding gang dismemberment.

ROLE DEFINITIONS

One of the most interesting areas of research on prisoners has been those roles that they are allowed to take on within the correctional institution. There are many such roles that are legitimated for inmates. There are other roles that are regarded as being taboo (snitch, informant, etc). That gangs should provide the same kind of role differentiation is to be expected.

Clearly, it is known that one of the essential roles that must be filled in any gang organization is that of the disciplinarian. Someone who metes out punishment for violating gang mandates. Someone who is the "chief of violations".

Role definition is a matter of the bureaucratization of a gangs infrastructure. Ideally, the more status-enhancing roles that exist, the higher the rewardive capability of the gang; and the more it can integrate those who themselves experience a competitive social existence. America is a status-seeking society. Gangs can provide such status. The organizational infrastructure of the typical gang delineates various roles and functions which can be assigned to gang members.

LEVEL OF COHESION

Much of the literature on gangs is in agreement on the simple issue that gangs generally show some level of cohesion. However, gangs do vary on this factor, as do all types of social organizations. Clearly, anyone who studies organizational life will find that in addition to the existence of an actual formal organization, all such organizations also have an informal social organization. We would therefore expect the same for gang organizations. There is competition and there can be strife and there can be leadership battles within a gang.

Cohesion shows in mobilization and in attaining group goals and in accomplishing group objectives.

LEVEL OF MORALE

Generally, as in the military analogy, the higher the morale the higher the effectiveness of organizational performance. However, we can also expect morale to vary over time because of the periodic imprisonment or interruptions in gang functioning that are brought about, often randomly, by law enforcement initiatives. In the case of Chicago's El Rukns, the high number of ranking gang members who were willing to testify in federal court tends to bring with it an unrecognized measure of fighting the gangs from a law enforcement perspective: the fact that group morale deteriorates rapidly when multiple members are found to be in complicity with government prosecutors. Also, from the viewpoint of psychological warfare, it is generally known that there are measures that can be taken to erode morale. The point here is that morale, like self-esteem, is a factor subject to much variation over time and by experience.

For example, there is some evidence that after the successful federal prosecution of 39 of the top leaders of the Gangster Disciples, that this had quite a demoralizing effect on the members of the GD gang. This demoralizing effect included a reluctance on the part of some members to take on leadership positions that were offered to them, the reasoning was clear: they did not want to become a target of a federal prosecution. This new and expanded edition of this book includes a new chapter on gang prosecution, specifically dealing with the Gangster Disciples.

NORMATIVE CONSENSUS

Simply stated, do the members of a particular gang agree on what is expected of them in terms of conduct and behavior? There is a significant organizational climate difference between a gang which has explicit norms and mores in comparison with one that manifests a high degree of normlessness or anomie. This is a way of distinguishing between what some call the highly organized gang and the "loose knit" gang. Like any organization, the higher the normative consensus, the more effective it can be expected to perform. Conversely, a gang that has few such internalized guidelines for personal conduct can be expected to experience varying degrees of internal conflict between members --- simply because they do not agree on what is or is not expected of them. In some gangs "tree jumping" (a gang phrase for rape) might be approved of on a conditional basis if it is a target of opportunity or if it involves a rival gang or its turf; while in other gangs this particular type of personal conduct might be considered taboo and sanctionable. In the Black Gangster Disciple's literature, for example, forcible rape of an another prison/jail inmate is expressly forbidden; but consensual favors in terms of homosexual sex would apparently be allowed.

Gangs today enforce their internal norms by the use of rigid discipline involving fines and physical punishment. To break the gang rules as a member may often bring about more punishment than would occur from the existing law enforcement structure. More importantly, some things that are "crimes" as defined inside the gang ideology are not really "illegal" per se. A common version is "dropping the flag", or not upholding the honor of the gang organization; there is no law that compels someone to be a hero or to be a loyal member of any civilian organization, but in the gang this kind of "violation" brings about a most violent punishment. Gangs use such internal codes and behavioral expectations to increase the compliance structure of members. The more such internal gang rules and gang "laws" are enforced, the more the gang exerts its own formal social control over members by the use of force and punitive sanctions.

MEMBERSHIP EXPECTATIONS

What the command structure of a gang can consistently rely on from its members in terms of level of effort, resources, and time allocation has much to do with its organizational effectiveness. A gang requiring regular dues, that has meetings at which attendance is expected or a fine is levied, that charges special "franchise taxes" for drug operations/chop shop operations/extortion gambits, etc, is different from one that has a laissez faire philosophy. It is a matter of organizational centralization of the focus of personal identity as well. We would hypothesize that the higher or the clearer the membership expectations, the greater the organizational performance of the gang. Thus, the higher its potential threat as well.

Even former members of large gangs like the Black Gangster Disciples can be counted on for "aid and support" when confronted by current members of the gang. One female member of this same gang (an "intellectual sister", or S.O.S., Sister of the Struggle, the female counterpart of the B.O.S.) who is now attending college described how she was essentially forced to sign a petition demanding the parole of the B.O.S. gang leader during the summer of 1993. The gang members came to her house and asked her to sign. Could she have really said "no"? Not at some significant personal and imminent risk of harm!

LEVEL OF STABILITY

Stability has to do with both control over existing operations and the organizational membership and its hierarchy. A gang that changes chiefs frequently is one that has a low level of stability. A gang that cannot maintain its share of the illicit market is one with a low level of stability. Stability also has to do with the matter of aging membership. In other words, a gang that loses members to a rival gang because of the more lucrative or higher rewardive capability of the rival gang has a lower level of organizational stability in terms of its ability to keep and promote its recruits. A highly stable gang is one that will have its own investment portfolio, with a capability to provide a gang members family with its own form of subsidized housing in a residential building owned by the gang, or provide legitimate employment in a business owned by the gang to a "straight" family member.

LEADERSHIP QUALITY

The quality of leadership is perhaps the most vital ingredient in terms of any perspective that seeks to undermine or erode gang influence. Many gang researchers have commented on the emotional or psychological instability of gang leaders. As if it communicated to the rank and file, "hell, what will he do next?" Generally we must be willing to assume that someone that is more emotionally stable, who is fair, who is impartial, who weighs the facts, who provides the kind of image that most Americans would prefer in a boss, would generally have an organization more effective than one with the obverse characteristics.

To my knowledge, few discussions of management style have been provided about gang organizations in America. And yet from an organizational perspective this is most essential! We can generally assume that many, such as Al Capone, have been authoritative types. But not always, because things are not always as they seem or appear to be. In fact sometimes this means in the study of crime don't believe anything you hear, and half of what you see and you will probably have an adequately scientific level of skepticism about the difficult problem of measuring and understanding crime in America. It may be that some gang leaders have a cult-like hold over their members and that the introduction of religious and ideological content into their constitutions will make some gang leaders appear to have charisma.

RECURRENT ILLEGAL ACTS

Even college and fraternity organizations periodically engage, either collectively or through individual members, in acts of deviance and/or crime. But to be considered a gang we must be willing to add the additional requirement that it be a recurring type of action. Not a one-time act of vandalism or outrage. Not a singular, spontaneous, event. Indeed, to be considered a gang characteristic the emphasis on illegal acts must have the quality of being recurrent, indeed ongoing.

Some legitimate groups and organizations have their own equivalent of the Mardi Gras. The Mardi Gras in our culture is a way of once a year, or in a "planned release", to let the steam valve open and "let down your hair", to "get funky". A seasonal involvement in deviance differs clearly from a year-round capability to commit crime.

The point of this discussion is that an organizational environment that has a once a year "escape" is not generally an organization classifiable as deviant. Most voluntary associations, even professional associations, and trade groups, have what is commonly known as an annual meeting. A chance to party? Conventions!

To consider a group a gang, one of the required defining characteristics must be this factor of recurrent criminal activity. Activity committed as subgroups of the wider organization, activity committed as members of the organization in an approved fashion, or activity committed by leaders in cooperation with lower ranking gang members, all of this would qualify as a defining characteristic of a gang if and only if it was recurrent in nature. That is, if it was not an isolated incident. It must continue as a crime pattern over time.

AGE-GRADED PARTICIPATION

Gangs tend to be age-graded, like many other forms of group affiliation and social organizations in society. This is normal social behavior. But gangs may not necessarily be homogeneous with respect to age. That is to say, we have yet to see a gang in America that has its own retirement home for aging gang members[18]. Then perhaps we would see the true organizational epitome in the development of gangs in America. As extensions of a community or orientation, many gangs are intergenerational in nature. Typically, however, the leaders of the more serious gangs (the ones we have to worry about) are not youths, but are adults. The term "youth gang" is therefore only a heuristic device.

Age-graded participation does not mean necessarily having the complete life span accounted for, it means having specific roles available for special age categories, it means status variation by age. A gang can be a young gang, a teenage group. A gang can also be an adult-teen gang. A gang can be an adult-only group. And, theoretically, a gang can be a complete age-span organization having the capability to integrate members regardless of age status.[19]

One characteristic of most gang research and gang literature is that it specifies the attraction that gangs have for youths in America.[20] Particularly because of the special problems associated with the transition from youth to adulthood in America. We need only recall that the transition from youth to adulthood in America can be a turbulent period. A period of maladjustment. A period of chaos, of confusion.

These are conditions ripe for the recruitment of youthful members. Like a cult group carrying out a marketing analysis, looking for ways to recruit new members, a gang would probably rely heavily on the works of social scientists like Erik Erickson, because the identity crisis of American youth is almost universal. A major critique of American society today is in fact that youth has lost its innocence. There is no longer a genuine childhood free from stigma. Kids at all ages can get in trouble today.

Kids do kill. Kids do drugs. Kids do carry and use firearms. But these are things they must learn to do. The socialization process itself may have been significantly altered in recent years. And yet it seems that every adult generation in America condemns its youth as the most rebellious and most devil-worshiping generation that has yet hit the pages of American history.

A gang composed primarily of elementary school children does not represent as formidable a threat to public safety as does a group that also has adult gang leaders. The modern gang has adult leaders, who usually have extensive criminal histories as well. Most serious gangs have "pee wee" members: those being brought up into the gang. But while youths may constitute the most visible age-graded aspect of the gang problem, the term "youth gang" is used only sparingly in this book because it is a phrase that may obscure more than enlighten us about "gangs".

Because of the age differences among members of the same gang, a gang like any other group or organization in society is subject to the same social processes; thus, it is not uncommon to find gang members reporting a problem of a "generation gap"; essentially, older members complaining about the lack of respect and tradition among younger members.

GENDER-GRADED PARTICIPATION

Similar to age-graded participation is the issue of gender-graded participation. That is, separate functions and roles implied for female members of the gang. The "intellectual sisters" memorandum from the Brothers of the Struggle (B.O.S.) gang illustrates this. This document was apparently written in prison and rapidly found its way into the hands of gang members on the outside. Local Chicago gang research has revealed that some female gang members do now in fact regard themselves as "intellectual sisters" or as "Sisters of the Struggle". These adolescent gang girls are basically getting their marching orders from imprisoned male adult gang leaders. This memo is provided in Figure 3 below.

FIGURE 3[21]
Creed for the Intellectual Sisters

We the Intellectual sisters of the struggle believe in the teaching of our honorable chairman and executive staff. You and I will become as one and aid an assist each other and reach our fullest potential.

I feel strongly upon the six point star utilizing, Education, Economics, Political, Social Development, Unity, and Love. I will learn to look and listen to anything that may be conductive to the acceleration of our organization.

I will strive everyday to remain an outstanding member and never abandon the struggle; Therefore with no struggle there is no progress. We are special group of sisters with love and respect for ourselves and others.

We are endowed with a great leader, together we shall see and share in his vision, as we grow to be a powerful group of intellectual sisters.

7.4

ADVANCEMENT OPPORTUNITY

Ask yourself, would you rather work for a local fast food "burger joint" or a local gang? Part of the answer would probably lie in the matter of opportunity for advancement. That is, how can you personally achieve your own culturally prescribed goals through involvement and participation in the gang organization?

Clothing, getting a car, jewelry, items of conspicuous consumption, these are the things that a gang involved in the criminal subculture can most readily offer. At least they can offer them at a more competitive basis than can working at a fast food establishment. Because there is no wait, it is a "go for the gold" situation. It is an application of the crudest form of America's spirit of capitalism --- "go for it....grab what you want".

Here, as in all organizations, think of it as the "benefit package" of employment. Most persons want an opportunity for advancement, few want a dead-end position as a foot soldier for the duration of their life span. There must at least be the hope of achieving some important material goals through such an association.

The bottom line, in gang studies, is that there is a qualitative organizational difference between one that is "growth oriented" just as an employer would offer similar opportunities. There must be opportunities to achieve personal goals within the framework of the organizational goals. There is a significant recruitment and motivational advantage for a gang that offers opportunities for advancement. Unfortunately for American citizens, as will be discovered elsewhere in this book, our traditional criminal justice response to gangs has often meant inadvertently inducing leadership training opportunities for gangs.

In modern American gangs, one of the quickest ways to get a promotion is to go to jail. Someone who carries out a "hit" behind bars may spend a couple weeks in the "hole" and come out with an automatic promotion in rank that carries over once released from jail.

PRESTIGE

Along about payday at the university some academicians may have had occasion to find themselves in the position of saying what is often remarked about professors, "we work for the status, not necessarily the bucks". A university professor scores very high in what is called the occupational prestige scale. Gangs can also confer prestige. It is a rewardive function of the organization.

How a gang confers prestige can occur along several different dimensions. It is communicated through status and role within the gang organization. It is conferred by recognition for accomplishments. The military confers medals for almost everything, the Boy Scouts confer badges for a variety of competencies, and similarly the gang organization at least has the social capability to confer similar levels of status for social recognition to its members. Some gang analysts remark, in this respect, that going to prison is no long a fear for gang members: because

they might be able to meet their top gang leader, and in this way, in a social process not dissimilar from the cult member who would do anything to personally meet or be in the presence of the cult leader, the modern gang member may see prison not as a "punishment", but may rather see our modern expensive penal sanction as an "opportunity" to hook up with the top gang leadership structure.

Status and prestige go hand in hand. However, the capability to impart these conditions varies between gangs. Obviously, the gang capable of providing for these social-psychological satisfactions is the gang that is going to be more capable of keeping its rank and file members at an optimal level of morale. And the higher the morale, the higher the organizational performance.

A first lesson about Chicago politics probably goes something like this "reward your friends and punish your enemies". Clearly, the more powerful gang will be capable of rewarding its members, particularly along the dimensions of status attainment. Youths live for status, it is something they are deprived of structurally by society. A sense of "honor" is similarly important to gang members.

GANG MIGRATION VERSUS SOCIAL IMITATION AND EMULATION

Some gangs clearly do migrate, for example Vietnamese gangs that specialize in home invasion migrate from one city to the next looking for opportunities in their specialty area: robbing other Vietnamese who may keep substantial amounts of cash in their homes rather than using a bank account for their savings. This does not mean that the same Vietnamese gang specializing in home invasion is also seeking to develop a new franchise or cultivate new members in the same target areas of its criminal operations. It is important to note as well that individual gang members routinely travel domestically and abroad, so does that constitute "gang migration"? The answer has to do with intent and behavior: if the member is on a mission, it is gang migration; if the member seeks to develop his/her own chapter, it is gang migration.

Some gangs such as those that are formal organizations have roles equivalent to an "ambassador" for members who definitely seek out new areas for cultivating additional factions of the gang. This comes close to capturing what is meant by "gang imperialism", that is the intentional conquering or "taking over" of a new geographical area. It also captures what is meant by "gang franchising", that is the intentional cultivation of new chapters or sets in other jurisdictions or geographical areas, the intent of which often centers around basically developing new drug income markets.

Several other common methods by which

"gang migration" occurs are basically unintended consequences. Two examples can be provided here. One of the most common is transferring gang member inmates from one state to another, or from one location to another; in their new confines, they organize a local chapter of the gang. Another unfortunately all too common way in which gangs spread is when a parent/guardian either voluntarily (after realizing the youth is a gang member and thus wants to "protect" the best interests of the child: get them out of the "hood", send them to live with the parents in the south, or in Mexico, move to the suburbs, etc) moves the child to a new residential location, or is forced to do so because the youth has come to the attention of the criminal justice system. What happens, it appears, all too often is that once the youth is moved to a new location; the values the youth has picked up in the gang also move with the youth. That is, it is common to find the youth starting his/her own chapter of the gang of orientation in the new location to which he/she has been relocated. Such may constitute what are called "transplanted gangs".

The National Gang Crime Research Center recognized this problem and controversy several years ago and has continued to develop and monitor gang proliferation and migration. The problem, however, is attributing causality. It is relatively easy to identify the gang names that exist nationwide and where they are located. It is not easy to ascertain if in fact any national network actually exists. Nor is it easy to ascertain which gangs engage in intentional imperialism and the cultivation of new chapters or sets. This is a most important aspect of gang classification, screening for risk, and threat assessment. Some obviously do engage in this behavior. Some do, once they have established their "chapters", maintain routine contact with their "homebase" or gang of orientation. It is, after all, an efficient way to gain "rank" in the gang: simply declare yourself the local chief, and get as many members as you can to join.

Some of these gangs carrying the same names are regarded as "renegade" gangs. Sometimes, however, they are integrated into the established gang, and do function in an interstate and international capacity.

The truth is, however, we do not know how much of the gang proliferation that the United States has witnessed in recent years is due to genuine migration, or whether it is due to "emulation", transplantation, or social imitation via the "copycat" phenomenon. For example, the "Warriors" was a gang movie. It is not surprising, therefore, to find gangs existing by that name in cities such as Chicago and Boston, but they may not know each other if they actually met, they may not even know (unless they study criminological research) that another gang by the same name exists somewhere else in the United

States! The word "Warriors" is simply a threatening symbol produced by Hollywood that the gang has adopted as its own name. One of the truly most needed research projects on gangs is to ascertain how much of the gang proliferation can be attributed to mass communications[22]. The fact is that little such empirical evidence currently exists, in spite of the fact that many believe it to be possible that gangs might spread or proliferate (via emulation, social imitation, etc) because of the social space created for our youths in the negative images created by Hollywood movies and the mass media coverage given to gangs. Some gangs are clearly that: copycat gangs.

PUBLIC RELATIONS FUNCTION: "We are not just Gangster Disciples, we are about Growth and Development for the Black community."

Over a period of time, a more organized gang learns the value of having a public relations function. Not unlike the appeals used by members of the Rev. Sun Yen Moon cult ("Moonies") in their long history of effectively hustling donations by claiming they are a "patriotic group...we are trying to fight communism", etc, gangs today and for many years have made similar claims. In the early history of the Chicago's El Rukn empire, the El Rukn gang formed the Grassroots Independent Voters of Illinois and had it incorporated as a not-for-profit corporation.

The idea is to maintain some "positive public image" as a "do gooder" group or association. Gangs in Chicago today still provide large scale summer picnics (all you can eat, free transportation, etc) for such a public relations function. Some gang leaders that operate drug sale rings in and around public housing complexes have organized conspicuous "litter clean-up campaigns". The novice gang researcher is quick to believe in this "other side", or they want to believe in it perhaps; but the fact remains that such public relations functions are just that: a front, a cover, a smoke screen. Anyone who really knows the gangs, like the residents that have to put up with them daily, knows the truth: it is all a scam, not unlike the soup kitchens to serve the homeless that Chicago's Al Capone maintained. One prosocial act does not neutralize a crime spree; one good deed does not translate as a "pro-social" organization. Gangs have historically, however, been able to use such "put on's" as a social-political platform to provide a counter image to that which develops when the police and others want to "crack down" on them.

Hispanic gangs in southern California (Surenos) basically have a multi-colored glossy magazine that has catered to them since 1980. White extremists like the White Aryan Resistance (WAR) have produced a cable television show about "Race and Reason" which has been viewed in 50 American cities[23]. WAR, like other white racist gangs, also publishes its own newspaper.

INTERNATIONAL INVOLVEMENT

Some U.S. gangs have, apparently, show signs of international movement. This is true in several different ways. One is there the gang member flees the U.S. to another country, for example a Latin King or Mexican Mafia member avoiding a criminal warrant for their arrest and fleeing to Mexico. This is true also where gang members are sent back to their country of origin, for a variety of reasons, such as in the case of the TAP boys (Aka: The Arab Posse) in the Chicago area, who have been seen in middle eastern countries.

Another way this international movement occurs is when the U.S. Immigration and Naturalization Service (I.N.S.) does its work effectively in facilitating the deportation of illegal alien offenders. The I.N.S. in 1992 formed the Violent Gang Task Force to address gang problems among illegal aliens. In the United States such an illegal alien might be a member of a well known gang, and when deported to another country like El Salvador, they bring their gang orientation with them. It is the issue of the internationalization of gangs. They get their feet and operations established in several different countries. The I.N.S. deported 70 Salvadoran gang members back to El Salvador in 1993.[24]

And, of course, there are those cases where gangs that exist in other countries try to come into the United States and stage operations here.

The present author therefore clearly recognizes there is an international connection with some American gangs. This was illustrated in the killing of a Catholic church official mistaken for a "hit" target inside Mexico carried out by American gang members from San Diego under contract with a Mexican drug cartel. America certainly has no monopoly on "social gangs", as this must be regarded as a cultural universal, it is just an area not of concern to the present author because it does not involve crime. Finally, there is the known connection that American gangs have to drug cartels in other countries. Just as Latino and Hispanic gangs have their connections for drug sources in Mexico, Latin American and South American countries, African-American gangs have connections for such drugs in African countries like Nigeria[25], and Asian gang members have their counterpart connections as well.

OFFENSE PATTERNS

Knowing that a gang derives some or a substantial amount of profit from certain types of offense patterns is important to gang classification. A gang is what a gang does. Some offense patterns will therefore tend to suggest a gang is closer to organized crime.[26] These offense patterns can include levying "street taxes" (extortion), narcotics trafficking, and others discussed below.

NARCOTICS TRAFFICKING

There was a period in the study of organized crime when the concept was advanced in criminology that some major figures in organized crime considered it a taboo to traffick in narcotics or illegal drugs (e.g., heroin), because of the negative attention it brought to the organization. Thus, the willingness of a gang to engage in practices with the highest level of risk necessarily sets it apart from those who prefer to limit risk.

Most of the more organized gangs today have an unmistakable involvement in the narcotics trafficking area. Still, it would seem important to know those gangs that will not touch certain kinds of drugs in the distribution and sales function. Will all gangs sell all drugs? Probably not. Profit, risk, clientele, all enter into the equation. It is an equation that must also be taken into consideration in evaluating the nature of the gang organization. Gangs and gang members as drug users is nothing new (Dumpson, et al, 1952).

Collecting "street taxes" is a gang function as well. The gang may shake down other independent drug distributors, forcing them to pay a commission (e.g., 5 percent). If they do not pay up, such independent drug dealers may receive what gangs call a "money bag" (a hit is put out on them).

GAMBLING

Gambling has been the traditional mainstay and staple of organized crime in America. To the extent that a gang involves itself with this particular aspect of vice crime means something unique about it as a corrupt organization. There are many variations and scenarios for entering into this business. Obviously, there are also differing levels of penetration of this most lucrative field. The difference tells us much about the complexity and capabilities of the gang organization.

Because it is such a uniquely income producing offense, gambling also offers a major organizational incentive to its members with little risk. Many criminologists still discuss gambling as a "victimless crime", as if it is illegal but not really bad, because so many "so-called respectable people" do it.

That is not a position that will be advanced here. Both gambling and prostitution have definite victims and our laws reflect this moral consensus.

In Chicago and elsewhere, some gangs sponsor "Dog Fights", where the betting is on what dog wins and what dog dies. During the start-up, the "Ring Master" will often throw a cat into the fenced off ring where the dogs fight, when a champion "fighter dog" is first brought into the "ring", and the audience consisting of gang members and others shout and cheer as the dog rips apart the flesh and bones of the "sacrificed" cat.

LOAN SHARKING

Slums, ghetto, inner city, barrio, and other areas of economic under-development have traditionally been a prime environment for the operation of the juice business, or loan sharking. This crime pattern is a mainstay and prime characteristic of the income generating capability of organized crime. Thus, the extent to which a gang has generated a surplus revenue sufficient to allow the operation of loan sharking activities says much about its organizational capability.

Having this kind of crime pattern capability also speaks to the ability of a gang to replace traditional organized crime operations that may have been displaced by aggressive prosecution efforts of local and federal law enforcement authorities. We must at least consider the potential that the displacement effect in crime is also considered a benefit for indigenous organizations like street gangs, when higher visibility groups like the Mafia get prosecuted and put on ice, leaving much of their market open to penetration by independents and groups like existing street gangs.

Theoretically, we should also expect some of these functions of organized crime to come to be filled by the more local and more visible street gang.

The extent to which this does occur means a gang organization with a unique income-generating capability. The higher the income in low-risk enterprise, the higher the gangs ability to reward and increase gang effectiveness.

CHOP SHOP OPERATIONS

This is simply a very lucrative field and its operations are typically interstate in nature. The extent to which a gang involves itself in this type of criminal enterprise makes it especially troublesome to a community.[27] The scope and extent of these kinds of operations vary considerably from custom-order car theft procedures, and custom-order parts theft[28]. This can also involve the theft, transportation, and sale of farm machinery, aviation, and heavy construction equipment --- much of which also has an international market. But the routine local car theft ring enjoys the largest crime violation impact from gangs in America[29]. The theft of Harley-Davidson motorcycles, for example, is an organized activity typically carried out by motorcycle gang members.[30]

COUNTERFEITING AND CREDIT CARD FRAUD

In what seemed like a routine gang arrest in Chicago during early October, 1993, the police officers discovered that a faction of the local Disciples (Brothers of the Struggle) gang had something more than the typical assortment of illegal drugs in their "spot" (i.e., their operations center). They had video equipment used by the shorties (younger gang members) to videotape the police officers working in the district. They had police scanners. The police also found sheets of recently printed five, ten, and twenty dollar counterfeit United States currency.

In a recent article published in the Journal of Gang Research[31], Jackson (1993) describes a quasi-gang group that specialized in large scale credit card fraud. With the ease of using credit cards for a variety of purchases of goods and services, gangs and gang members can be expected to increase their involvement in this area in the future.

"Getting Birth Certificates and Drivers Licenses From the Latin Kings"

In 1999 an investigation into the Latin Kings street gang in Chicago revealed this group was heavily involved in the lucrative trade of selling fake, but high-quality, identity papers to illegal aliens. The gang sold birth certificates and driver's licenses, even green cards. A typical set of such illegal documents would sell for about $100. It appears the Latin Kings got involved first by simply extorting protection fees or "street taxes" from other vendors who would sell these kind of documents, but at some point got involved directly in selling them as well.

Source: "Latin Kings Prey on Need for Illegal Documents", by Gary Marx and Teresa Puente, Chicago Tribune, pp. 1,14, Section 1, Sept. 19, 1999.

PROSTITUTION/VICE

Many gangs have some level of involvement in commercialized vice operations. These can serve as additional opportunity crimes particularly in the area of extortion and robbery. Again, it is a crime capability factor that is important in the classification of gangs. It is also one that can be used in connection with extortion and attempts to compromise those who work in the field of law enforcement and corrections. One Illinois gang ran a prostitution ring for prisoners inside an Illinois state prison, inmates were allowed to have sex with female correctional officers who had been corrupted and compromised by drugs.

VIOLENT TAKE-OVER STYLE ROBBERIES

Gangs have also been known to specialize in, or be involved in, violent take-over style armed robberies of armored cars, banks, credit unions, and casinos. This scenario features gang members heavily armed who do use the weapons if they have to. The Aladin casino was one of seven recent such armed robberies of casinos in Las Vegas by gang members from Los Angeles during the first half of 1994. In the Aladin robbery the members came in violently with shoulder weapons, some holding citizens and security at bay while others jumped over cash counters to rapidly collect the money, and two minutes later they were out of the casino with $47,000. In some cases, as in the San Remo casino robbery, shots were fired to terrify the citizens. The robbery at Harrah's netted the gang members over $100,000 in cash. The Flamingo Hilton casino robbery netted the gang members over $125,000. The money from Harrah's and the Flamingo was not recovered in spite of arrests.[32]

FREIGHT AND WAREHOUSE THEFT

There are several variations of this type of offense pattern, but the target is any source of valuables: a freight shipment, by train or truck etc, a warehouse, or any place where such shipments or storage pass through. Sometimes this involves using the gang members to quickly unload such items, for example from a railroad car or container. Sometimes this involves gang members who work at the site and use their inside information to arrange thefts with the help of confederates from their gang who basically have a very limited risk: all they have to do is pick up the goodies. Axelson (1984: p. 3) documents where a gang will try to "rip off" trucks.[33] This type of pattern certainly extends far back in American history.

FEMALE GANG MEMBER INVOLVEMENT

The issue here is both equality and force strength. The equality issue has to do with two competing concepts in criminology regarding gender and crime. These are the chivalry hypothesis and the convergence hypothesis. The former implies that female gang members will be relegated to subservient positions, reflective of the sexist orientation of predominantly male members, such that female gang members will constitute almost an auxiliary group and will take second seat to male members[34], with no genuine hope of full advancement within the gang organization (as would be potentially the case if the member was a male). The latter (the convergence hypothesis) implies that just as wider society has now given much more power and responsibility to females in the legitimate opportunity structure, therefore gangs will follow suit and reflect these same wider normative influences by granting female members more complete rights within the gang organization. Mostly it is a matter of force strength: that is, what proportion of the gang membership is made up of females? This is simply an important parameter to measure and compare in terms of its relationship with other indicators of female representation in the criminal

justice system such as that of the imprisonment function in America (where females make up only about five percent of those incarcerated).

TATTOOS

For some time in Chicago, some gangs are so completely represented within the family structure, that gang involvement is very much an intergenerational experience. This includes gang members who report their father being a member of the same gang, and who now have children who are being brought up as gang members.[35] Indeed, this can mean having the baby tattooed with the gang insignia as soon as it was out of the hospital after birth.

There have been a variety of studies of inmates and tattoos, much of this couched within the framework of self-mutilation analysis from a psychological perspective. Many authors in the study of gangs quote examples of gang members being proud of their "red badge of courage" by having visible scars, self-induced or otherwise.

Clearly, it is a level of commitment that is measured by this factor of gang differentiation. Gangs that tend to require tattoos which identify the gang affiliation are going to be able to command more from their members. Sadly, we know little about this function within the gang organization: in what gangs is it required, or is it optional, does it convey any special capability for advancement in the gang organization, etc. These are questions that have simply not been answered in the literature.

Clearly, though, there is an important difference between those gangs that have many members that have taken this severe step as opposed to those that have not. As will be seen in a later chapter, simply having a permanent tattoo is a factor that significantly differentiates the variable of ever joining a gang.

ALIASES

Most genuine gangs routinely assign aliases to their members, these become "gang names". It is a basis for a new identity. An identity reinforced by gang life itself. It is obviously most useful within the law violation context as well. It is a factor of differential identity: gang members with aliases come to live up to that identity because it can be one of the few social networks that affords them what all human beings need --- praise and a sense of being a part of something larger than oneself.

Having a "monicker" or gang name (e.g., "Trigger", "Yummy", "Gator", etc) is therefore functional for the gang in several ways. It is a mechanism to socialize members of the gang to live up to their "gang identity". It establishes, most importantly, a deviant identity apart from the "self" that previously existed.

TOTEMS

Totems are symbols which carry much significance for those who hold them in importance, and these are associated with various taboos. Gangs routinely have symbols for their nation or their organization. These are considered sacred symbols and are treated uniformly with much reverence. Their origins are not as mystical as Sigmund Freud would have us believe, however, because for the most part they come into existence at the onset of the emergence of the gang organization. Sometimes it is little more than a set of numbers. Sometimes it is a variation on other legitimate symbols used in society. And any functional street gang has its own hand signs for signifying gang affiliation. This is complemented with color patterns, the typical variation of which is at least one color is black.

Customized cars with unique color patterns and symbols, any potential item of clothing with special symbols or color patterns, robes, jewelry, hats, shoes, pins and buttons, window decals, and a number of objects are designed and used by gangs to carry their symbols. The sale of this gang paraphernalia is big business[36].

Gangs and gang members use a wide assortment of cultural objects and artifacts as totems. Generally, the higher the sophistication of a gang and the longer its tenure, the more it uses and accumulates such totems. Businesses (tattoo parlors, sports clothing outlets, "airbrush" design your own t-shirt shops, jewelry stores, etc) respond to this market demand by gang members and therefore tend to encourage the gang problem.

INITIATION RITES

A large amount of social imitation is endemic to gang organization today. While there is some high level of organizational functioning in the contemporary gang problem no gang has yet been reported that uses Robert's rules of order for their gang meetings[37], but most gangs have some variation of initiation rites. Often this involves an element of violence. That is to say, for the male gang member it may involve enduring some physical punishment such as having every gang member present authorized to give a full force closed-fist punch to the chest of the gang initiate. For the female member it may involve the equivalent of a "gang rape", that is, allowing every gang member present to engage in any sexual act of his or her choice with the new female gang initiate[38].

Such initiation rituals vary widely from gang to gang. Sometimes this can be little more than learning to memorize a gang prayer, and sometimes this can involve both a symbolic humiliation and then some act of violence against the opposition. When gangs seek to develop new members in more affluent suburban areas, for example, such "blood in" ceremonies are purposefully de-emphasized. It is only after joining the gang that the member may have to shed blood or endure some other form of physical violence or humiliation.

"Bizarre East-Coast Crips Initiation Ceremony"

Do some gangs kill other people as a part of their initiation ceremony? Of course. In gangs like the Aryan Brotherhood their basic motto is "kill to get in, die to get out". Killing becomes the ultimate "blackmail" the gang can use against a member who might have second thoughts about their commitment to the gang.

This is not to say that all gangs do this, naturally. But some gangs do. This is a story of one of those such gangs.

This off-shoot of the Crips gang was based in North Carolina. Actually, there are a wide number of different Crip and Blood factions on the east coast, even though Crips and Bloods have their gang epicenter, or source of origin, in Los Angeles. Some gangs can get formed by just calling themselves a Crip or Blood gang. They do not need to have written authorization from Los Angeles gang headquarters to use a common name and get their own "thing" up and running. This is apparently what happened to this Crip gang in North Carolina: it was autonomous from the L.A. chapters, it just used all the same "dressings" (colors, language, codes, symbols, etc).

To make a long story short, this Crip gang felt it had to be "tougher" than traditional Crip gangs, this is called the "accentuation effect". So to accentuate their gang reputation, two new recruits into the gang, Francisco "Paco" Tirado and Eric Queen, were told to randomly kidnap and murder their victims to get into the gang. What the two new Crip members did was paint the tips of their bullets "Blue" (the Crip color of choice) and then go out hunting for victims. They did it: they actually kidnapped and killed Tracy Lambert, age 19, and Susan Moore, age 25; and pumped seven bullets into Debra Cheeseborough as well. But Debra lived to testify against the new Crip recruits.

Both of the Crips were sentenced in April, 2000 to the death penalty for doing this.

SOURCE: "Two Sentenced in Gang Slayings", Associated Press, 4-11-2000.

SUBCULTURAL DIFFUSION

An interesting organizational question must be raised regarding gangs from an organizational perspective: to what extent do they tolerate other forms of deviance within their own ranks? In other words, can an openly homosexual person operate effectively as a gang member of any level of authority?[39] It is a matter of the degree to which the gang organization is an open-system in terms of its subcultural diffusion. And by no means is this discussion meant to derogate sexual preference. Rather, the point is obvious here: some organizations that have a deviant function and purpose, such as gangs, may or may not allow such an open approach to wider societal influences. The level of variation here is between broad and narrow tolerance levels for subcultural integration outside of the gang context.

FORCE STRENGTH

Whether we conceive of only two levels of gang affiliation (periphery vs. core members) or as "regulars" versus "wannabees", or casual associates, ultimately after considering the specific crime pattern of any gang, we must come to the matter of risk assessment in terms of the actual force strength represented by any particular gang. That is simply: how many members can be mobilized for purposes of gang crime? We shall see later that because of the "franchising" of gangs, that outside of the correctional environment, gang leaders are themselves not really sure of exactly how many members they may or may not have at any given time. And at what level of involvement? This most critical aspect of an organizational approach to gang studies has only rough estimates in our literature as to what might constitute the actual parameters of the scope and extent of this problem facing America today.

ARSENAL

Some gangs, whether they are conspicuously engaged in income-producing crimes or not, tend to want to accumulate more weapons and firepower than others. Right wing extremist gangs like the Aryan Brotherhood, Ku Klux Klan, and others have historically sought to develop their own military-style arsenals. The differences in the scope and extent of the firearms acquired and used is a most important factor for assessing threat.

Any technological device that can be used in support of organizational operations should probably be included in this classification factor relating to the gang arsenal. Gangs today use "police scanners" that they can buy at their local Radio Shack and pick up a copy of the local police frequencies free of charge from the same place.

THE FUNCTIONAL AND PRO-SOCIAL ASPECTS OF GANGS

Some ethnographic researchers studying gangs have said that there is a good side to gangs[40]. Criminologists do not study the good side, they study the criminal side; a criminological researcher compares persons who violate the law with those who

conform to test and develop knowledge that helps us to better understand and predict crime and criminal behavior. Much of the nature of the status-seeking behavior, the role playing, learning the language of the gang --- is not criminal in nature. In fact, gangs and gang members do engage in a host of pro-social behaviors; some of these intentional in nature, such as the public relations function where the gang that controls the drug trade in a public housing complex will enforce anti-littering norms of its own, and actually clean up the litter, most conspicuously.

At another level, quite accidental, but creating a kind of symbiotic relationship between the gang and the community of which it is a part are the functional aspects that the gang plays for the neighborhood. While living in a Chicago neighborhood with a large gang population this can be understood, but not to the casual observer. When the cop on the beat is expected to write a quota of parking tickets, the non-gang member resident of the area may be less likely to get a "citation", particularly when the members of the gang routinely leave several beat-up cars, often stolen, often inoperable, where they accumulate large numbers of tickets. The police officer on the beat has a safe "hole" to write the tickets on, satisfying the expectations of the police administration, and giving a break to the rest of the citizens parking cars in the area. Eventually the "trap car" is towed away, often with twenty or more tickets. Having lived in such neighborhoods and on occasions not having always fed the parking meters, I am grateful to this function provided to the community by gang members. They take all the heat!

But on the other hand, most of what passes for prosocial behavior of the modern criminal gang is a smoke-screen and public relations function. Simply because the members of the same gang are friendly to one another, party and enjoy each other, is not to be taken as a finding that the gang is prosocial. Rather this means there are many social aspects to a gang.

WHAT COULD FOSTER GANG DEVELOPMENT?

It is interesting to ask what policies or conditions might inadvertently foster gang development, assuming naturally that gangs are viewed as a problem that citizens do not want to see expanded. There are some organizational features of gangs that are important to consider. Gang leadership should not be cultivated nor enhanced. Any community member who thinks gangs are good because they "help defend the neighborhood" legitimizes gang turf and accentuates the gang problem. Community based social services that work with gangs should not be in the business of improving gang morale. In the absence of competitive methods of recognizing and positively reinforcing prosocial behavior among law-abiding youths, youth gangs will dominate the market on prestige.

An inverted kind of "Horatio Alger" myth, which basically says "you can be filthy rich even as a child, and perhaps have your own new Mercedes, if you join the gang and sell drugs", also contributes to the problem. Because as long as it is believed or believable, it is then always a potential motivational force for new gang recruits. In this book we shall discover many such "lessons" on what could exacerbate or erode the gang crime problem.

We shall also discover many myths about gangs, aspects of misinformation that have systematically accumulated in the public imagination and perception of gangs today.

SUMMARY

Discussed here have been some of those factors that can be considered as important for the classification and assessment of gangs. Threat analysis assumes that gangs can and will vary in terms of the kind of impact they are capable of. Not all gangs are equal in crime threat. This form of inquiry is a question important to the gangs themselves. The question is: Who is the biggest? Who is the toughest? Who is the strongest? More specifically, how do we rank and evaluate gangs regarding their threat to the public in terms of crime or violence?

Gangs represent a national problem,[41] and many believe, a potentially increasing problem of violence. This discussion has advanced a basis on which to systematically evaluate gangs in terms of control and interdiction. As we know, prosecutorial resources and correctional resources are limited. The more we can focus in on the gang target for prosecution in terms of its objective threat rather than treating all gangs and gang members alike, the safer a community will be. But it is going to be difficult to translate much of our gang literature into such an applied manner, because of its tendency to focus on the personality and psychology of the individual gang member rather than the gang as an organizational unit.

Using a threat assessment or some type of objective procedure to classify gangs along a dimension of "risk" or "threat" is similar to the problem of dealing with terrorist groups. A risk assessment must be made in order to allocate investigatory resources and to expend resources in plans for intervention. The problem is there has not been agreement on what constitutes a high risk gang as opposed to a gang that represents a low level of threat to the community. Such a classification system will be advanced in later chapters.

What this chapter has hoped to accomplish is to establish the fact that theoretically gangs can vary along any variety of the types of factors used in their classification. As real or incipient organizations, like any social organization, they can go in a variety of different directions. Gangs today can take on a variety of shapes and functions, just like many of our legitimate groups and organizations function.

This chapter has pointed to a variety of factors that will emerge later as most important in the study of gang organization in America today. More is necessary to achieve a classification system, and we are not even close to having a typology yet. We have simply summarized some of these organizational features in a descriptive way.

Discussion Questions

(1) Could much of gang behavior be simply a matter of "emulation", that is "social imitation", a kind of "trying out" of organizational forms and social roles to which they have been socialized along a power/authority dimension as "the controlled" or subordinates seeking a super-ordinate position in a kind of role-reversal? Would the gang organization therefore attract members who have a combative personality or does the gang produce members with such a combative personality?

(2) Could the role structure, that is the specifically identified layers of authority and role positions that can be filled in a gang, be predicted from socialization? That is, among gang members with an experience of being incarcerated in correctional institutions, could we anticipate that they would evolve along paramilitary lines in the same fashion as American law enforcement agencies have a paramilitary structure?

(3) The student who closely reads the gang literature will find an interesting example where in Philadelphia, to reduce gang homicides, a private group arranged for a citywide gang meeting, bringing all gang leaders together, and the claim that this actually reduced gang-related killings "from 43 in 1973 to...one in 1977" (see Stephens, 1988: p. 41).[42] Is it a good idea, theoretically, to negotiate with gang members as "organizations"? Would "leadership training" for youths involved in gangs be a good service to provide through a local social work program?

What Lengths Gang Members Will Go To In Reaction to a "Status Threat"

A status threat is easy to understand. It is a "put down". Like "playing the dozens" or talking about someone's mother. The concept of the status threat, as originally advanced by Short and Strodtbeck (1965), is that it is a "challenge" perhaps even to the masculinity of the gang member. They must "defend" their image.   In 1998 Chicago gang leader Henry Brown, age 43, was sentenced to life imprisonment stemming from his role in the kidnapping and torture of Gaddis Johnson[43]. Brown believed that Johnson's brother had stolen money and a car from him. Brown wanted revenge and with Timothy Belin, age 20, they went looking for a Johnson, any member of the Johnson family would do. They first kidnapped Johnson and stripped him of all of his clothes. They then set Johnson on fire. When the fire burned out, then they poured bleach upon his wounds and watched the skin foam-up as Johnson screamed in mortal agony. When they ran out of bleach, then they sicced a dog on him.

SOME CULTS CAN ALSO BE CONSIDERED GANGS

Rod Ferrell was a teenager who was the leader of a small vampire cult in Florida.[44] Vampirism involves the drinking of blood. When it is done consensually it is deviance, and probably risky behavior given what we know about AIDS/HIV, but not necessarily a crime. Ferrell's group, though, arranged for sex between adults and underage minors. Ferrell's group included his own mentally ill mother, other teens, and young adults.

Ferrell's cult believed that through ritualistic murder they could open the "gates to hell". So they used a crowbar to beat to death two victims (Richard Wendorf and Naoma Queen) from Eustis, Florida. They also carved and burned their cult marks into the bodies of the two victims. Ferrell pleaded guilty to the two killings. Three other members of the cult are also charged in the murders.

This was not a street gang. This was a Level One cult-type gang. It did not have large numbers, it did not have more than one "unit" of operation, it did not claim turf per se. One of the newly added chapters to this 5th edition of An Introduction to Gangs includes much new and important information from comparing gangs and cults: are they really different? Decide for yourself if the commonalities outweigh the differences in the analysis of gang and cult organization factors.

END NOTES:

[1] It should also be part of any "gang awareness/gang training" curriculum. But it usually is not. Rather this type of training usually focuses on identification of gangs/gang members, and less on the social/historical context.

[2] Testimony of Irving A. Spergel, Feb. 9, 1994, Subcommittee on Juvenile Justice, Committee on the Judiciary, United States Senate.

[3] It is an issue, also, of "gang tenure": how long has the gang existed as a group entity?

[4] For example, prison riots prior to the 1970s tended to show a general consistency among the pattern of inmate leaders that emerged under such conditions. This ideal-typical profile was not dissimilar from Thrasher's "natural leader" and a pattern of "crude democracy". The pre-1970 riot leader was likely to be a "right guy", "tough" or having physical prowess. The problem is, with the advent of prison gangs, the inmate culture has changed. The 1950s inmate culture is a thing of the past.

[5] It should be noted that the lack of any scientifically based national assessment of prison gangs has helped to foster confusion and denial of the gang problem in state correctional facilities. In some state prison systems, the gangs basically run the show. This is less true in the federal prison system which has adopted more of a zero-tolerance approach.

[6] Tom Brune and James Ylisela, Jr, "The Making of Jeff Fort", Chicago, November, 1988, p. 202.

[7] A skinhead bias crime and drug specialty street gang known as the "Bomber Boys" were active in Chicago during the 1980s on Chicago's northside and were known to be nomadic; originating in San Diego, coming to Chicago for the warmer months.

[8] In our research on law enforcement, using data from a national survey sample of police chiefs, we can now report, however, that a number of sources have identified the A.B.'s (Aryan Brotherhood) as a community gang problem as well. That does not, however, mean A.B.'s are territorial, it just means we now see them operating outside of the prison context for which they have been previously known.

[9] For what could be the best ever analysis of territoriality among street gangs, see the study by Alejandro A. Alonso (1999).

[10] See Shukla (1981) for a discussion of these as-

pects of internal organizational.

[11]This event sponsored by the gang was very professionally done involving lots of rented buses, their own "picnic police", special T-Shirts, and obviously represented a major cost in food alone for about 1,000 or more persons. The event was also professionally videotaped (12 hours) by law enforcement.

[12]See: "Cult Leaders' Roots Deep in U.S. History", Chicago Tribune, April 8, 1994; section 2, p. 9.

[13]See: Anne Keegan, "Death of the Vice Lords", Chicago Tribune, May 15, 1994; Section 5, pp. 1,4.

[14]This fact that such constitutions do exist and that they have not previously been given any attention or discussion by some authors who have studied some of these gangs (whose constitutions are provided in the Appendices), may render their findings suspect. That is, if such authors were really studying "gang leaders" or had any level of serious penetration into the gang, they would have come across these documents. Even to an anthropologist such documents are a goldmine of information on the codified values and beliefs of a gang.

[15]The GD's (Gangster Disciples) are headed by Larry Hoover; and clearly outnumber the BD's (Black Disciples). On Chicago's southside alone (Gang Crimes South, CPD, 8-29-91), the BD's in police districts 2, 3, 5, 6, 7, 8, 21, and 22 were estimated at no more than 464 such members; compared to 5,755 for the GD's in the same police districts. Thus, the GD's basically constitute the B.O.S. as well. Any of the literature of the B.O.S. referring to the Chairman of the Board is therefore referring to Larry Hoover.

[16] On the matter of language and gangs, language communicates social values. Our social-anthropology analyses of gangs have not taken to heart the social-linguistic analysis by Barker (1950, 1979) which analyzed how the unique language pattern or subcultural argot was used by the gang. It is obviously an important factor to analyze. But we have not seen the level of analysis conducted on this matter since the time of Barker's study of the Pachuco's in Arizona.

[17] Similarly, when we address the issue of what differentiates the highest level of gang organizational development from traditional patterns of organized crime, we will see that the extent to which such a deviant organization can integrate into larger society shall certainly limit the degree to which it can dominate and control legitimate business enterprises in any society.

[18]Although, Kaplan and Dubro (1986: p. 137) document how a Yakuza gang conglomerate provides "retirement pay" for its members. See also Skolnick, Blumenthal, and Correl (1993: p. 200) who report regarding drug-dealing among California gangs that "if a gang member is sent to prison, largess is expected both to keep him well-equipped there and to ease his transition back into the drug business upon his release".

[19] Klein (1990) reports a major change in America's history of gang crime, the fact that modal age is now higher for gang members; while it "used to be around 16" it is currently "at 19 or 20" (p. 6).

[20] In a case study of a college-educated Latin King member, case LK-29, this showed, among other things, how a three-year-old infant had already been taught by gang family members to "throw up" the Latin King gang sign and "throw down" the rival gang signs; or the case, perhaps, of a very young "wannabe" gang member, but more likely a "gonnabe" gang member, because such a child faces an almost historical imperative to follow the tutelage and older sibling gang affiliation pattern.

[21]Transcribed exactly as it appeared in its original typed version.

[22]I am grateful for some ideas from Jeffery T. Walker, Ph.D., Department of Criminal Justice, University of Arkansas at Little Rock, who mentioned to me in a conversation how "mass communications" may be an important factor to examine regarding gangs.

[23]See "Hate Groups in America: Part One - White Supremacists", Jeff Mc Caddon, P.B.S.P., 1993, March, p. 30.

[24]Some 230 gangs are said to exist in El Salvador. These can be just as violent, use the same hip-hop dress pattern as in the U.S., but they have access to a lot of the military hardware from El Salvador's civil war. The violence of that civil was a socialization experience for children that would facilitate the combative personality syndrome and predispose youths towards violent gang behavior. See: "U.S. Gangs Hit Streets of El Salvador", by Tracy Wilkinson, Chicago Sun-Times, June 26, 1994, p. 37; "Deportees Find Willing Pupils for Violence", by Tracy Wilkinson, ibid.

[25]For how an African-American gang like Chicago's Gangster Black Souls (a folks gang) use Nigerian drug connections, see: "19 Are Charged With Operating Gang Drug Ring", by Lee Bey, Chicago Sun-Times, Jan. 7, 1994, p.23.

[26] Particularly if the crime pattern analysis reveals any capability of more sophisticated crimes such as might be regarded as traditional 'white collar' crimes (e.g., insurance fraud, etc) (see Johnson, 1981).

[27] See: "Motor Vehicle Theft in Chicago: An Examination of the Last Twenty Years", by Robert E. Smith, April 15, 1998, Chicago Police Department.

[28] Some motorcycle gangs specialize in the theft of Harley-Davidson motorcycles and are said to be involved in shipping quantities of these to Europe where their value is vastly increased.

[29] According to the Illinois Motor Vehicle Theft Prevention Council, "Organized street gangs have been and continue to be significantly involved in the motor vehicle theft problem". (p. 64, April, 1993, Statewide Motor Vehicle Theft Prevention Strategy, Chicago, IL).

[30] There is a law enforcement organization composed of investigators who specialize in "outlaw motorcycle gangs".

[31] The Gang Journal was published initially by Vande Vere Publishing, Ltd. (Buchanan, Michigan) as the official journal of the National Gang Crime Research Center. That publisher was fired for excessive delays and fiscal irresponsibility. The journal was reorganized during the summer of 1994 to become totally independent. It is now known as the Journal of Gang Research. Subscription information can be obtained by contacting the National Gang Crime Research Center, P.O. Box 990, Peotone, IL 60468.

[32] See: "7 Heists Jeopardize Resort's Family-Fun Image", Chicago Tribune, May 19, 1994, Section 1, p. 10.

[33] Roland G. Axelson, "The Psychological Influence of Street Gangs on School-Aged Youth: A Case Study in Hartford, CT", 1984, the I.N. Thut World Education Center.

[34] The written constitution of the Vice Lords, for example, contains various clauses on "queen power" and "queen ladies", but essentially establishes female gang members as subservient. Up to and including their role in housework, hygiene, and child rearing. Some of these written constitutions of gangs (from level three gang formations) are discussed in Chapter 15.

[35] Such an "intergenerational" feature of gang involvement, or its transmission from older siblings or relatives to young family members, must certainly be regarded as a problem worthy of social service intervention and prevention efforts.

[36] Shortly after the National Gang Crime Research Center aired its one hour cable television program "Gangs in the Schools" and detailed the sale of imported socks containing gang logos (people and folks symbols), and other items that are routinely sold in stores around and near schools, local media was quick to document and validate this issue. See particularly Robert Blau and David Jackson, 1993, "Jewelry to Die For: Teens Drop Big Bucks on Gang Totems", Chicago Tribune, June 22, Section 1, pp. 1,16.

[37] That is, outside of the context of prison and jail where gang members may "take over" such a legitimate group and use its structure and methods for gang purposes.

[38] A number of varieties of this kind of "sexual violence" initiation for female members occurs in gangs. Some gangs may use an element of chance, such as "rolling the dice" to see how many members the new member must have sex with. More typically, it means complete sexual bondage for a time period where any member of the gang can take sexual advantage of the new gang member in any way they want.

[39] Other authors have described "homosexual tendencies" of gang members (e.g., their preference for male contacts), but it was Leissner (1969: p. 13) who actually showed such homosexual relations among gang members in terms of a sociogram or social network form of analysis.

[40] See Joan Moore, 1993, "Gangs, Drugs, and Violence", pp. 27-46, in Scott Cummings and Daniel J. Monti (Eds.), Gangs: The Origins and Impact of Contemporary Youth Gangs in the United States, Albany, NY: State University of New York Press.

[41] I recall attending a so-called "gang crimes planning group" involving government agencies, private groups, and criminologists in Chicago over ten years ago. I was very frustrated because the law enforcement representation was strictly city in nature. I earned no level of positive attention when I remarked before the group "gangs travel interstate in their operations, so why do we not have the U.S. Attorney's office or the FBI represented here today?" It is not a local problem anymore. It has been a national problem for a long time. It might be an international problem.

[42] This and other recent claims are often made by the gang alliance spokes persons. However, as in the Philadelphia case there were so many extraneous variables involved (including the reduction in gang effectiveness through prosecution, mortality, etc), that it is not possible to attribute any reduction in gang deaths to such a variable. In some cities, with an increased political value attached to the "law and order" issue and "quality of life" issue surrounding gang homicides, the political response is sometimes to simply "unfound" or reclassify the incidents: they become to be called "drug related killings" not "gang related killings".

[43] See: "Life for Gang Leader", Chicago Sun-Times, Feb. 20, 1998.

[44] See: Mike Schneider, "Teenage Vampire Enter Guilty Plea in Cult Slayings Trial", Chicago Sun-Times, Feb. 6, 1998, p. 33.

A Look At Some Major Chicago Gangs: A Guide to Some of the Appendices

Some of the appendices to this book include what are called "Gang Profiles". You can examine these documents to get a better idea of how the classification factors work in gang analysis.

For example, Appendix F provides a Gang Profile of the Gangster Disciple Gang. Here you will see aspects of the gangs internal organization, its processes, how it interacts with larger society, how it accumulates resources from its environment, how there are special roles and tasks within the organization, etc. You could read Appendix F and then examine Appendix C for additional information on the internal operations of this gang. Then you could skip ahead to Chapter 24 and see a chronological analysis of the same gang in terms of how it functioned over the years, that is until it became a target of federal prosecution.

You could also examine Appendix I, the Gang Profile of the Latin Kings. This is the Chicago-based, original Latin Kings, not the New York spinoff faction. In Appendix I you will get a good idea of how a gang operates as an organization. You can then examine Appendix A to examine the internal rules and regulations for this same gang.

In Appendix G you will find the Gang Profile for the Black Gangster's gang, which is also known as the "New Breed". This is actually a local spin-off sect of the original Devil's Disciples gang. Gangs can "split away" from their origins, and take on an entirely separate identity is what this gang profile shows. All it seems to require is a charasmatic leader to pull it off.

In Appendix H you will find the Gang Profile for the Black Disciples gang; this is the gang that remained true to its traditions originating in the Devil's Disciples gang led by its original leader David Barksdale. When Barksdale died, that event left a leadership vacuum allowing for the emergence of Larry Hoover as a force to be reckoned with; and thus, the birth of the "Gangster Disciple" gang.

One of the most fascinating historical issues regarding gangs is found in Appendix J: the Gang Profile for the Black P. Stone Nation (BPSN) gang. This is Jeff Fort's gang. Jeff Fort is a legendary figure in American gangs. There have been a number of books written about the BPSN. This is the gang that successfully obtained millions in federal money and foundation grants through the help of Rev. John Fry. This gang remains an active and violent gang today.

Finally, you may want to look at Appendix D, the written rules and regulations for the Vice Lords to get an idea of how this gang operates. The Vice Lords are believed to be the oldest of such gangs in Chicago, originating in 1959 when disgruntled juvenile offenders locked up in St. Charles State Training School formed the gang inside the correctional institution. It was then "exported" to the community. There are several books about the Vice Lords as well.

Photo: Shot of the Gangster Disciple Picnic held in Kankakee, Illinois; held on a private farm; an estimated 10,000 attended.

CHAPTER 3

Some Major Milestones in Gang Studies

INTRODUCTION

In the field of corrections and criminal justice, as in any area of high responsibility, it is important to have as broad an understanding as possible about any given subject. In the study of gangs, we need to know much more about the actual nature of previous gang studies. To read all of these studies, as can be seen from the large bibliography on gangs which appears at the end of this book, could be a very formidable task indeed. One solution is to provide an executive summary of some of the more "formative" contributions to this literature.

The purpose of this chapter, therefore, is to provide a brief historical overview of major gang authors, their basic concepts, methods, and views regarding the study of gangs. The approach here will be chronological and a review of authors and their contributions by order of their appearance in the literature. This is not intended to be an "exhaustive" coverage. Other authors, books, articles, papers, etc, will be covered in this text. But examined here are the "major" milestones in the gang literature. There are a number of works that appeared prior to Thrasher, but these are not professional criminological contributions. These are, however, analyzed in some detail in later chapters of this book. Our real social scientific understanding of gangs begins with Thrasher.

Was There Anything Before Thrasher?

Yes, but for an introduction to gangs, Thrasher will do. If you want to go back a few years before Thrasher, you can find examples of the analysis of gangs easily enough, you just may not find the analysis sufficiently social scientific to be acceptable. You can go back a hundred years before Thrasher and find some useful works on gang conflict: these books are covered elsewhere in this book. You can go back to the 13th Century and examine the works of Islamic scholar Ibn Khaldun and find a great deal of material on "migrating gangs" (i.e., nomadic tribes). But this chapter is about "formative" influences on the emerging discipline of "gangology": the social scientific study of gangs.

Frederic M. Thrasher (1927)

The Gang, A Study of 1,313 Gangs in Chicago is worth discussing at some length not simply because it was an early study of gangs, but because of the enduring influence of Thrasher's approach to gang research. Thrasher's approach can be called the natural history approach which has been heavily associated with the "Chicago school" of sociology. But the gangs analyzed by Thrasher were at best periodically delinquent, and certainly did not reach the level of violence associated with gangs in the 1990s.

A most interesting etiological sequence is suggested by Thrasher for gang development. It is provided in graphical depiction by Thrasher - the Natural History of the Gang (Thrasher, 1968: p. 56). This developmental sequence recognizes five sources of gang input: (1) a spontaneous play group, (2) a casual crowd, (3) the family itself, (4) intimacy groups (adolescent dyads), and (5) the formal group. Importantly, Thrasher sees eight developmental outputs of the gang: (1) a mob (not implying organized crime), (2) a secret society, (3) public, (4) ring, (5) criminal gang, (6) orgiastic group, (7) political machine, and (8) a psychological crowd (both action type and orgiastic type). The three stages of gang development proposed by Thrasher were (1) diffuse (amorphous), (2) solidified (well-knit), and (3) conventionalized (formalized).

While we do not obtain a very high level of quantitative assessment in the profiles of the 1,313 gangs studied by Thrasher, what does emerge is the recognition of the variation in organization sophistication. This natural history of the gang gives a graphic illustration of gang etiology. It is this etiological sequence that makes it still of value as a primary reading today.

Thrasher's work is not statistically oriented. We never learn much about the overall picture of the 1,313 gangs, or their estimated membership, their estimated income enhancements from gang activities, etc. It is, plainly, an important historical work. The many photographs it contains are also valuable documentation of the urban context of the gang.[1]

Thrasher's gang etiology sequence recognizes a difference between the pseudo-gang, the gang itself, and separately the criminal gang (1968: 56). The gang itself can develop, incrementally, into three stages of development: (1) diffuse or amorphous, (2) solidified or well-knit, and (3) conventional or formalized. The gang in its embryonic state can first emerge from a variety of sources such as the spontaneous play group, a casual crowd, the family, a small intimate dyad, or even a formal group.

As we shall see later, the kind of gangs studied by Thrasher were mostly at the lower end of the organizational sophistication spectrum. Many criminologists simply do not know the full story about Thrasher. Thrasher's first research dealing with gangs was actually reported in his 1918 Master's thesis. Many criminologists simply assume from a casual reading of Thrasher that the 1927 study represented seven years of ethnographic field research, when apparently it was some level of effort less than this. The 1927 classic was really, word for word, Thrasher's 1926 Ph.D. dissertation in the Department of Sociology at the University of Chicago. The work of Thrasher is so important that a new chapter has been added for this third edition, which seeks to solve

a historical mystery about what exactly was the research methodology that Thrasher used.

William Foote Whyte (1943)

Street Corner Society is a study of one Italian community called Cornerville, circa 1937. Using the case study/oral history method, interviews with a gang member named Doc showed that gang fights were common and Whyte (1968: 5) describes one where the rival gang was armed with banana stalks and milk bottles. To fight with another gang was to "rally" on them. Doc's gang the "Nortons" was also highly capable of engaging in legitimate behavior including organized bowling tournaments. Doc matures and when he is 30, most of his fellow gang members have married and moved out of Cornerville.

But Doc wanted to run for political office. Lacking formal education, Doc received a short tenured job placement from a local community center. Doc left the gang, and withdrew from the election, even though he had mobilized some level of support. The Norton's disintegrated. The new "corner" gang was the Angelo's Boys. The latter was also highly integrated into legitimate activities such as the Cornerville Dramatic Club (Whyte, 1943: 49).

Chapter 2 in Whyte (1943) covers the etiology of an Italian social club that has all the characteristics of a traditional legitimate voluntary association. Chapter 4 is a summary of more traditional Mafia-style organized crime, and its involvement in gambling and pay-offs to law enforcement officials. Chapter 5 provides an analysis of the changing informal social organization of a voluntary association called the Cornerville Social and Athletic Club. Chapter 6 is a detailed discussion of the role of this in traditional electoral politics. The conclusion chapter discusses aspects of leadership traits and correlates of this lifestyle. Social structure here meant social economic status as well and the obvious difference in life chances between a "college boy" like Whyte and the "corner boys" who hang out in the slum. A very detailed appendix describes how Whyte came to choose this particular slum area for study.

In short, little of what Whyte (1943) analyzed is comparable to the nature of the typical urban street problem which characterizes American society today. The image of the gang that emerges in Whyte is that of the famous West Side Story. It is, however, a very important piece of research. Indeed, there are some important parallels between Whyte's (1943) work and some of those conditions which may exist today.

For example, Whyte sees the streetcorner gang arising from "the habitual association of members over a long period of time" (1981, p. 255).[2] When some gang members left the community, a group would disintegrate, and its members merge with another group. Family life and spending time with the family at home was absent for most of these corner boys. They did acquire and use aliases through the gang. Whyte pointed out the distinction in obligations between members who were single and those who were married, and the latter were allowed extra social space for meeting this social contract. The gang is a system of mutual obligations.

We shall see in a later chapter there are ethical problems in both studying gangs and in dealing with gangs. It is not a problem that should be addressed without advance knowledge of what we are doing.

Albert K. Cohen (1955)

Cohen's (1955) Delinquent Boys: The Culture of the Gang is a theoretical discussion of delinquent subcultures. The general theory of subcultures advanced by Cohen is termed the psychogenic model. It is not a research-based analysis, but it was clearly rooted in the scholarship of its time. Cohen alternately praised or criticized the Chicago school approach, favorably recognizing the works by Thrasher and Whyte, while often criticizing cultural transmission theory (Shaw and McKay, 1942).

Cohen's focus on social class has been a matter of much discussion even though it is secondary to the more pivotal argument he advanced that psychogenic factors such as status seeking behavior, age-graded norms, group loyalty, and other aspects of a social-psychological nature account for the onset and persistence of youth gangs. Cohen devoted much attention in this early 1950's publication about "growing up in a class system" when it was probably somewhat risky to give a candid analysis. It is a comparison between working class and middle class differences.

Cohen explicitly addressed the anticipated popular question of how do gangs originate, how do they arise? He assumed all behavior including gang behavior is problem-solving behavior (Cohen, 1955: P. 50). Gangs, therefore, to quote from a much earlier contribution (Merton, 1938) "innovate", that is, they solve problems uniquely in their particular adaptation to society.[3]

To the extent that Cohen was evasive about providing all explicit details of his theory for fear of criticism, many contemporary writers on the gang problem in America are quick to criticize Cohen on a variety of reasons.

Yet Cohen's (1955) work has had enduring impact on criminology today and still has much to add to the understanding of gangs. The entire subcultural theory of crime owes much to Cohen who brought to fore the elements of hedonism, negativism, and fate as differentiating persons prone to either delinquency or non-delinquency. Cohen's discussion and frame of reference may not be current, but it included aspects of enduring significance and represents like those others here an important contribution to the literature.

Basically, Cohen sees youth gangs emerging as a reaction formation to status frustration among working-class youths who are less likely to have been socialized into middle-class values. Cohen's influence on subsequent research is evident where Miller (1958) similarly considered the lower-class social status factor as a primary determinant of gang delinquency.

Cohen's value for criminal justice, then, lies in understanding the "larger picture" of societal forces at work in producing those situations favorable to gangs.

Bloch and Niederhoffer (1958): The Generation Gap

Herbert Bloch and Arthur Niederhoffer in their work entitled The Gang: A Study in Adolescent Behavior (1958) advanced the hypothesis that there is variation in all societies in terms of the mechanisms of status, rituals, roles, etc, made available to adolescents and that these also vary across cultures in terms of how difficult a transition it is from youth to adulthood. Basically, their position is that there is a large generation gap in American society, and that the more difficult the transition or the greater the identity-crisis, then the greater the likelihood of gangs.[4]

Bloch and Niederhoffer (1958) were quick to point out that gangs seem to provide the adolescent with those things not provided by traditional social institutions. Therefore the gang becomes a surrogate family and provides other necessary functions as well which may not be satisfied through the existing social structure. They were later roundly criticized by Cloward and Ohlin (1960: pp. 56-57) for their lack of definitional clarity in specifying what is or is not a gang. That is, Bloch and Niederhoffer (1958) tended to equate adolescent gangs with delinquent gangs.

This study is important because of the comparable problem faced everyday by offenders behind bars. They may be adults chronologically, but maturationally, and educationally, and in terms of moral development and personality they may still function at a less than optimal level of adult responsibility. The gang reinforces this commitment to deviance.

Cloward and Ohlin (1960): Differential Opportunity Theory

The seminal work by Richard A. Cloward and Lloyd E. Ohlin (1960) entitled Delinquency and Opportunity: A Theory of Delinquent Gangs is often cited as just a general theory of delinquency, but in fact like Cohen's is oriented to gang delinquency. That a great deal of research has been generated in support of the main propositions from differential opportunity certainly lends some credence to this theory. Basically, the theory assumes that in every community there are both legitimate and illegitimate opportunities, however when a youth experiences or perceives closure in the legitimate opportunity and simultaneously has chances to make a living in the illicit or illegal opportunity structure --- then delinquency occurs.

A factor cited by Cloward and Ohlin as well as many other contributors to the gang literature is the difficulty of being a youth in America. Social participation is age-graded, there is an identity-crisis factor, there is the gap between being young and dependent and being an adult and responsible. There is not a smooth transition from youth to adulthood.

Cloward and Ohlin were able to anticipate some developments in gang crime, particularly the hypothesis of ethnic succession. They discussed how domination of the lucrative rackets (e.g., gambling, drugs, etc) by the Italian and Jewish syndicates (1960, pp. 199-201) would eventually dissipate by control from local ethnic residents. They also correctly predicted "as a result of the disintegration of slum organization" that gang crime would become increasingly aggressive and violent in the future (1960, p. 203).

Cloward and Ohlin are especially important for correctional personnel because they suggest a solution: good training, and job placement. Develop good work habits, portable skills, and be prepared to enter the world of work. Aftercare services structured in such a manner to provide continuity with correctional industries can clearly make a significant difference in reducing recidivism.

Scholars and researchers interested in further insights into this major gang book are urged to read the recently published interview of Richard Cloward published in the Gang Journal (Rush, 1993: 51-53). After publishing the book in 1960, Cloward basically abandoned criminology.

Lewis Yablonsky (1962)

Yablonsky's work entitled The Violent Gang (1962) is often criticized under the global concern that early youth gang analysts did not consider anything other than the large cities (New York, Chicago, Los Angeles, etc). In point of fact, however, Yablonsky explicitly recognized the emergence of the same problem in smaller communities regarding the "kill for kicks" phenomenon (Yablonsky, 1962: p. 3). In point of fact, while Hagedorn (1988) would probably not legitimate the analogy, there is even a continuity in terms of how Yablonsky felt gang infrastructure was less formal than often conceived and how Hagedorn suggests gangs are truly less formalized

than they are sometimes portrayed to be. Yablonsky's work deserves a significant amount of discussion here.

Yablonsky's classification of gangs included three types: (1) delinquent gangs, (2) violent gangs, and (3) social gangs (1962: p. 149). These are discussed not as a pure typology meeting the requirements of exhaustive and mutually exclusive categories. Rather, Yablonsky describes them in the "ideal-typical" construct. In this fashion, what dominates the gang ethos explains its gang function (e.g., delinquency, violence, social, etc). Thus, what kind of gang it is depends on the type of norms, behavior patterns, and personalities of the gang membership.

It is the violent gang organization that Yablonsky analyzes in detail. The picture that emerges of the violent gang according to Yablonsky (1962) is as follows: the gang emerges spontaneously, it provides a sense of power, joining is easy, initiation rites are pretty much a myth, it is easy to quit the gang, but leaders and core members seldom leave the gang (p. 155), the leaders are self-appointed manipulators who "manifest paranoid delusions of persecution and grandeur" (p. 156), they use the myth of vast alliances with other gang nations and affiliates, gang warfare is like a group contagion and often has no clear purpose other than trivial things that trigger conflict. The sociopathic members live in slums in urban communities facing negative forces of decay and erosion. Prejudice and discrimination aggravate the gang problem (p. 184).

From Yablonsky comes the differentiation between "core" versus "marginal" members. Also provided is a discussion of the gang infrastructure in terms of a continuum of organized-unorganized. In this scheme a mob fits the pattern of unorganized, the violent gang fits the pattern of being a near group, and social/delinquent gangs fit the pattern of being most organized. Basically, the differences in personalities mediate all causal factors and the personality types determine what kind of gang a youth joins.

Yablonsky's final chapter was on gang intervention programs and services. It provided, perhaps prematurely, a blanket and glowing endorsement of Synanon as a vehicle for rehabilitating core gang members. Still, it is important for criminal justice staff because it provides some interesting insights into the psyche of gang members.

In 1998, Yablonsky came out with a new gang book: Gangsters: Fifty Years of Madness, Drugs, and Death on the Streets of America (New York University Press). This new gang book by Yablonsky provides a foundation for group counseling methods with gang members who are sincere in their desire to "give up" gang life. "Lou", as Dr. Yablonsky likes to be called, remains active in research and professional work in the area of gangs.

The Many Works of Malcolm W. Klein

A quick inspection of the gang bibliography for this book shows another important trend. Some authors are obviously not new to the study of gangs. For some gang researchers, like Malcolm Klein, the study of gangs has been a continual lifelong research interest. The many works of Klein date back over 25 years ago.

If there was a single summary statement from the works of Klein it is his 1990 Edwin H. Sutherland Award address to the American Society of Criminology (Klein, 1990). It says that some of what is contained in the gang literature is myth, particularly mass media accounts. It says we should realize that there are different varieties of street gangs and so all who study gangs, particularly criminologists, must be careful not to create an artificial image of the gang crime problem.

Klein's ties to Chicago involved interacting with a number of different researchers: "Short, Suttles, Spergel, Kobrin, Feinstein, McKay, Gordon, Miller, Ohlin, Simon, and Lerman" (Klein, 1990: p. 5) as well as Hans Mattick.

What has changed in American gangs according to Klein is modal age and propensity for violence (Klein, 1990: p. 6) as well as additional ethnic group representation in the gang scene, more specifically Asians (p. 7). Modal age appears to have changed from around 16 to about 20 (p. 6). More homicides are today associated with gangs and account for nearly 40 percent "of all Los Angeles County homicides -- a truly astounding figure" (p. 6).

Klein joins other contemporary authors, this author included, in noting that the tendency to blame and stigmatize among criminal justice agencies and other "labelling" institutions is itself a problem to be overcome. The gang problem is not a simple problem, it is a complex problem. And we still do not know why some cities have gangs and others do not, or why some persons in the same area join gangs and others do not (p. 12).

Law enforcement agencies and the mass media are quick to assume "street gangs are well-structured, cohesive collectives with strong individual leaders", but Klein says this is clearly in most instances incorrect (pp. 13-14). Also, gang members do not spend their 24-hour day enmeshed and engulfed in a full schedule of violence, they also have normal lives (p. 14).[5] The evidence does not exist that gangs truly control all or even a significant share of drug sales in America (p. 15). Finally, no evidence exists that L.A. gangs like the Crips and Bloods have franchised and exported crack distribution rings to the rest of the United States (p. 15).

But these are four misconceptions widely held by criminal justice officials and reinforced by the mass media.

Because he has devoted his career to the study of gangs, Klein will be referred to throughout this book. His contributions reflect an entire era, and are ongoing, like "Lou" Yablonsky's.

The Many Works of Irving Spergel

Two major works appeared in the mid-sixties, and ongoing contributions have come from the same author, Irving Spergel of the University of Chicago's School of Social Service Administration. The first monograph was Racketville, Slumtown, Haulburg: An Exploratory Study of Delinquent Subcultures (1964). The second was Street Gang Work: Theory and Practice (1966). Both works have had extensive and enduring positive impact on the study of gangs in America.

Spergel's (1964) Racketville, Slumtown, Haulburg is important for several reasons. First it describes three different community areas: (1) Racketville, (2) Slumtown, and (3) Haulburg. Each such community generates a unique type of delinquent subculture or gang. The organized crime syndicate or crime cartel emerges from the Racketville type of community. The conflict subculture emerges from the Slumtown type of community. And the theft subculture emerges from the Haulburg type of community.

What is exceptionally important about Spergel's work (1964) is that it anticipated perhaps the devastating impact of drugs and youth gang involvement such as is currently evident in American society. Spergel explicitly indicated that the drug-using or drug-addiction adaptation could arise in any of these three types of communities. Another important fact that distinguishes Spergel from previous researchers on gang studies is that hard data was collected on gang members. This information came from his work as a gang outreach worker in an eastern city. While the sample size was not exceptionally large (N = 125) it was given more analysis that was the case in any previous studies, such that we get a much stronger picture, quantitatively, of the differences between various gang and non-gang types of affiliation. Spergel clearly demonstrated that self-report data could be effectively collected from gang affiliated youths (1964) and used effectively to explain variations in their life chances and outlooks on life.[6]

Spergel's (1966) Street Gang Work: Theory and Practice is itself a milestone in developing a comprehensive strategy for working with the gang problem at the community level. Heavily influenced by the "Chicago school" of sociology and serving as a faculty member[7] there for a long time, he must also be regarded as an important contributor and shaping force in the Chicago criminological tradition.

Generally, it seems Spergel's work is under

appreciated, even though from an overall analysis it (1964) represented the most social scientific treatment yet offered of American gangs. It recognized problems still cited today as primary causal factors: high unemployment (p. 3), low income (p. 4), the "struggle for security and decency" (p. 14), age-role integration (p. 22), social and economic deprivation (p. 27), status aspirations/expectations (p. 29), criminal code norm internalization (p. 34), role-models (p. 36), and more. Further, Spergel was the first to empirically "test" major factors as hypotheses (p. 106) with hard data.[8]

Spergel's work shows continuity and growth and it is an enduring concern rather than a passing interest. There is little new being advocated for gang intervention that had not been proposed three decades ago by Spergel (1964, 1966).

Spergel's work is important because more and more corrections personnel are involved in family counseling and in aftercare services. A gang member often provides impetus for other family members to join the gang. Such works like those from Spergel suggest methods to "reorient" or work with gang members in the community. It may also provide, if structured properly, an alternative to working with gangs inside the correctional milieu itself. Thus, Spergel's contributions reflect an entire era, and are ongoing.

The Many Works of Walter B. Miller

Empirical research on gangs owes much to the pioneering and modern work of Walter Miller which covers half a century. Miller's 1982 report showed gang problem existing in slightly over one out of every ten of America's smaller cities (less than 10,000 population), and in two-fifths of medium size cities (populations 100,000 and above), and in five out of every six of our larger cities. It is from Miller that we find one of the only clues about the puzzle of how much crime in America is "gang related". Miller (1975, 1980) estimated that gangs may account for half of all juvenile crime in our largest cities. It was further hypothesized that gangs may account for as high as a third of all crimes of violence committed by juveniles (Miller, 1975: pp. 75-76).

In summary, as seen from the many contributions of Miller represented in the bibliography, Walter Miller --- like Malcolm Klein and Irving Spergel --- has had a career of gang research. Miller years ago established that gangs are a national problem and established national gang research as an essential knowledge development need. Miller's work also reflects an entire era.

Short and Strodtbeck (1965): Status Threats and Aleatory Risks

In <u>Group Process and Gang Delinquency</u> (1965) James F. Short, Jr. and Fred L. Strodtbeck extend the Chicago school tradition of gang studies to be the first major study with a large sample size using multivariate statistical analysis. It was a unique contribution set in the context of both field research and applying general social science skills to the social reality of urban life.

Generally, this represents an analysis that includes comparisons along white and African-American dimensions only, with no Latino nor Asian groups. Importantly, Short and Strodtbeck note that gangs in depressed inner city areas are not only normal they are also apparently universally expected because of their appearance in many other countries (1974, p. 1). It is the first major contribution to use multivariate probability statistics. It also recognized that since the time of Thrasher, "apparently the gang of today is not the gang of yesterday" (1974, p. 77). In providing the first comprehensive comparison along racial lines (1974, pp. 102-115) it also documents white racist bias crime through qualitative data.

The major concepts developed here involve status equilibrium in the group context. It involves the "status threat" as an immediate factor which may precipitate inter-gang violence. The authors are among the first to note the parallels between gang violence and guerilla warfare (1974, p. 200). They also note the problems of employment counseling and job placement services with the youthful offender (1974, p. 225) which was borne out in much additional research years later on the offender population generally.[9] The concept of aleatory risk is based on game theory and assumes a differing level of subjective evaluation of various decision outcomes.[10] It involves the utility-risk paradigm (1974, p. 254).

Thus, the basic position taken by Short and Strodtbeck (1964, 1974) is that status related to general society (employment aspirations, legitimate career potential, educational attainment, etc) is important but that status within the small group context is more immediately likely to have impact on outcomes like gang violence (e.g., status threats, and status enhancing functions of the gang). Both the social structure and the group process must be taken into account.

This book is important for a variety of reasons: its superior research method, its findings, and its implications that gangs cannot be dealt with as we deal with individuals. We are dealing with a group which takes on a higher level of significance, and requires "special handling".

Keiser (1969, 1979): Anthropology of the Vice Lords

This is a very short monograph and the 1979 reprinted edition with additional commentary follows the Whyte pattern and includes new personal insights from the author. The author sought to overcome racism and as a white researcher from Northwestern University "lived with" the predominantly African-American Vice Lords. The entre was telling the gang he wanted to write a book about them and share the royalties with them. It involved about four months of such fieldwork. It provides useful information on the gang infrastructure, its adaptation to the risk of arrest and loss of members to the criminal justice system, and the "franchising" of gang branches within the gang organization, including their operation of a restaurant, a recreation center, an employment service, their business office, and their status as a legally incorporated not-for-profit corporation as far back as 1968.

The importance of Keiser is in realizing that over twenty years ago we had highly organized (what we shall later call "level three") gang formations in our country. This is an important historical contribution documenting one gang in Chicago[11].

Poston (1971): Gangs as Grant Funding Hustlers.

Richard W. Poston's (1971) book, The Gang and the Establishment: A story of conflict rising out of the federal and private financing of urban street gangs, is a detailed historical chronology of an indigenous ex-gang member managed social program originally called the "Real Great Society" or RGS located in New York City. In short, it finds this particular type of indigenous community group to be 99 percent fluff and one percent substance. Its leaders use theatrics, myth, mass media manipulation and political grandstanding to generate contributions from government, corporate, and private foundation sources. The book epitomizes what might be imagined of the worst of the 1960s programs where the highest level of program accountability in reporting service impact was a year end statement to the effect "saw client, served same".

This is not a theoretical discussion of gang formation, nor a quantitative piece of research. Rather it is a policy case study with a substantial amount of inside information. It clearly cautions against knee jerk funding allocation decisions to programs with exoffenders or ex-gang leaders in administrative capacities.

To the extent that it documents an important historical phase of social policy reaction against providing funding to gangs, it was and remains a valuable contribution, however cynical. The reader is simply alerted to a more powerful manner in which this same kind of experience reported by Poston was analyzed quite differently in the work by Krisberg (1974). What Krisberg showed is that sure, gang leaders were hustling, but society hustled them too, programs themselves are "hustles" promising to fulfill broken dreams and never delivering.[12]

Haskins (1974, 1975): A Historical Perspective

Based largely on historical materials this work shows gangs have always existed in America. It includes many interesting photographs from historical archives, even some from Keiser's work. It focuses on the urban nature of gangs and the SES factors that foster gang activity. It sees the first organized gang in America as the "forty thieves" gang, circa 1826. It also traces the history of the Ku Klux Klan as a group that experienced a succession in goals towards bias crime. It makes very effective use of printed news media accounts of gangs in America. And also shows the political connection with gangs as well as the high levels of violence such that the National Guard was routinely called to quell gang disturbances.

Joan W. Moore (1978): Homeboys --- gangs, drugs, prisons, barrios

Moore's (1978) Homeboys: Gangs, Drugs, and Prison in the Barrios of Los Angeles brings the sensitivity and verstehen of the researcher to the deviant population not seen since the work of Sutherland. A potential criticism is that perhaps there was too much, in the sense that if "applied" persons or those working in the field of law enforcement or corrections would be required to read it, they might regard it as somewhat of an anomaly and that the writer appeared in some instances to be glamorizing the gang and accepting their definitions of the social reality, almost as a justification for gang violence. This is not a text that is easily adapted by law enforcement for the repression of gang organization.

Nevertheless, it is a remarkable and fresh contribution giving insights to the gangs having a Mexican-American ethnicity. It uses their language: pintos are convicts or ex-convicts, barrio refers to a named neighborhood and gang, tecato is a drug addict (1978, p. 4). The data comes from three "hardcore barrios of Mexican East Los Angeles" (p. 7).[13] The essence of the viewpoint presented tends to follow, to some extent, a racial oppression thesis.

Gang structure becomes defined as having the following components: territoriality based, age-graded "with a new klika, or cohort, forming every two years or so", and all Chicano gangs are fighting gangs, with high levels of drug use (35-36). The gang is regarded as a quasi-institution in the barrio and involves the adult world. The author is quick to defend gang intervention/service programs: "Chicano gang subculture is responsive to programs" (p. 41). Unlike other previous social workers that label and stigmatize the gangs, Moore assiduously avoids this and in fact allowed the gang members in her study to have much veto power and control over research functions such as instrumentation, data collection, etc.

Tremendous insights into drug trafficking and marketing in the barrio are presented which must be regarded as important contributions in their own right (pp. 78-87). A theme developed is that barrio men sent to prison made new connections and became more sophisticated in their criminal operations (p. 87). The policy implication is that prisons should do less experimenting with group therapy and start paying inmates work salaries commensurate with civilian life. Moore is an avid supporter of the prisoner and barrio self-help movement and writ writers[14] and also recommends the legalization of heroin.

Moore curiously limits the generalization of the research findings to the extent that such barrio "ethnic traditions in Los Angeles are quite different from those of blacks, and are even unlike those of Chicanos in other cities" (p. 169).

Anne Campbell (1984): <u>The Girls in the Gang.</u>

Campbell's study is a close-up look, using the oral history method and extensive dialogue with three female gang members. Two were from Brooklyn and one was from Manhattan. The estimate is that ten percent of gang members in New York City are female (p. 5). Gangs arise "from conditions of poverty and alienation common to those at the lowest levels of urban life" (p. 33). The researcher used the entre to the three gangs of a police officer from the local Gang Intelligence Unit. One photograph shows both the author and the policeman with a jovial relationship with several male gang members (p. 133).

This qualitative research is described as a form of participant observation. From the photographs of the author in the home and in other settings with the three female gang members highlighted in the book, much is conveyed. The gangs themselves were somewhat curious. Connie was one of the female gang members interviewed and belonged to a biker gang called the "Sandman Ladies", but it had only one operational motorcycle (a BSA 650) (p. 49). Sun Africa, one of the other two female gang members interviewed, belonged to the gang called the "Five Percent Nation" which turns out to be a quasi-religious organization emphasizing Islamic teachings.

There is no "theory testing" per se here, rather it is an elaborate descriptive account of the viewpoints of the three female gang members chosen for study.

The final chapter of the book (pp. 232-267), however, provides some interesting political commentary regarding gang life. Here we find that while these three women may have been unhappy with their economic plight, they had no aspirations to overthrow American capitalism; indeed they wanted to be in their highest aspirations members of the well-dressed, well-eating, high-consuming, happily married American middle-class.

Campbell notes that "72 percent of all juvenile homicides committed in 1974 were gang-related" (p. 232). Campbell takes the position that "youth gangs are not a universal phenomenon" (p. 233) and that it is pretty much an American social invention. Gangs become indirectly defined by their attributes of "membership initiation, demarcated roles, rules, names, "colors", territoriality, discipline, a specific philosophy, or feuds with other groups" (p. 233).

Gangs were nurtured and promoted by American politicians. The gang members have a geographical dependency that keeps them locked into a specific urban community area. They rarely venture out of these small areas, even when they are wanted by the police (p. 236). Those with the "least to gain from the status quo" are the ones who join gangs. Gang members are far from being potential revolutionaries, they often have conservative views (p. 237). Basically, "gangs do not represent a revolutionary vanguard rejecting the norms and values of a capitalist society that has exploited them" (p. 267).

Jackson and Mc Bride (1985 to present)

Jackson and Mc Bride have provided what many believe to be the single best law enforcement view of the gang problem in America. It was one of the first works to document that some highly organized gangs have written gang constitutions and truly do function as something comparable to a military organization. Much more than simply a law enforcement view, it provides a reasoned analysis of gangs that blends the practical problem of police work with the need to understand larger social issues that are associated with gangs in America.

The author Sgt. Wesley McBride is a leading figure in the California Gang Investigator's Association and was instrumental in organizing a national version. Sgt. McBride works for the L.A. County Sheriff's gang unit.

Hagedorn and Macon (1988): Gangs as part of the Underclass.

Hagedorn and Macon in their (1988) <u>People and Folks: Gangs, Crime and the Underclass in a Rustbelt City</u> focus on previously unexplored aspects of racial oppression in explaining predominantly minority group membership in Milwaukee's youth gangs. Joan Moore provides an insightful introduction to the book. Rather than a single theory developed per se, the authors present their tape recorded oral history data from 47 "top dogs" or gang founders, and then evaluate previous contributions in terms of what fits the Milwaukee context.

The authors denounce criminal justice research and law enforcement efforts, and certainly the use of the penal sanction against gang members, as being counterproductive. White sociologists are seen as part of the problem for "too much theory, too few facts" about gangs (pp. 26-27).[15] And criminology as a "white social science" is equally useless having "not produced any studies of note about modern gangs" (p. 28). For their own points of departure, the primary researcher (Hagedorn) describes a personal background of being a community activist and the other author (Macon) being a former Chicago street gang leader.

The introduction by Moore (pp. 3-17) provides a very cogent discussion of the definitive characteristics of gangs. Gangs are seen as: friends sharing common interests, from poor and marginal communities, in an age-graded system of gang participation, that are not hierarchical organizations (p. 5). Here underclass differs from previous uses of the phrase to mean "these are men and women permanently excluded from participation in mainstream occupations" (p. 7). That seems pessimistically tantamount to defining them as an American social caste rather than a part of the surplus population from which there might be some escape if adequate policies and service resources were available.

It seemed somewhat unbelievable, indeed contradictory, to see Moore declare "Gang members and their individual friends dealt in drugs, for example, but with very rare exceptions the gangs themselves did not become involved in crime" (p. 11).[16] It goes without saying that even the most hardened career criminal or organized crime member, if we were to conduct a time and motion study of their daily lives, would not be violating the law 100 percent of the time. Both Moore and Hagedorn seek to change the image of the gang and to challenge the stereotypical and alarmist portrayal of the gangs in the mass media.

Regarding any gang or offender research, as well as basic criminal investigation, it is a practical matter of social science to have a high level of skepticism when it comes to the matter of crime. What we need is facts. And there are many different research methodologies that have been used to acquire these facts about gangs. Perhaps the facts that Hagedorn seeks so vigorously.[17] The social reality of crime, especially gang crime, is sufficiently complex as to be least amenable to journalistic styles of investigation.[18] Unless of course we devalue the matters of validity and reliability.

The authors clearly sought to "change the public image of gangs" (p. 31), perhaps gangs had been getting some bad press behind the Cheddar Curtain. Employment data is cited to show a declining economic opportunity for inner city minority group members. Gang members are described as being uniformly school drop outs (p. 44). Gang formation occurred in Milwaukee in the context of a race relations crisis, thus racial oppression has some causal significance to gangs (p. 50). The authors reject the notion that gangs can be "exported" (p. 79), but clearly their data show that at least four gangs were imported (p. 58). The rest of the gangs arose out of dancing (N=3) and traditional street corner groups (N=10), or as female auxiliaries (N=2) (see p. 58).

Importantly, the authors document the interstate shipment of firearms (p. 74) between gang members. And that there are in fact high levels of continuing gang involvement from adolescence into adulthood for gang members (pp. 124-125). Most of the gang members they interviewed had at least one pistol, none of which had been acquired legally (p. 144). The authors describe the problem of police coverups and denial of a problem of gang crime as part of the public image for a city. The correctional sanction was not a deterrent to continued gang involvement (p. 162). They agree with Cohen that gangs have a rebellious aspect, but it is "cynical" and destructive of the communities in which they live (p. 164). The solution is jobs and education (p. 168).

Vigil (1988): The Multi-Marginality Concept

Focusing on the barrio gangs of East Los Angeles this ethnographic study sees the gang arising and persisting because of the marginality of gang members in terms of ecological, socioeconomic, cultural and psychological factors.[19] What Vigil argues is that it is not a simple matter of alienation, but rather gangs arise and persist because of an accentuated estrangement. The psychodynamic factors of gangs are discussed in terms of Erikson's identity and related ego and self-identity formations. Family conditions, when stressful, also are seen as important ingredients in gang affiliation; and why the gang itself becomes a kind of surrogate family.

Taylor (1990): A Close Look at Detroit Gang Data

Taylor's (1990) analysis of gangs is a modern one. It is social scientific, it lacks any obvious ideological bias, and it involves the multi-method approach. The hard data collected on gang members is of much value because it probes into areas of much concern to gang analysis. The qualitative data involves focused interviews on subjects of much relevance (industry, drugs, family, role models, etc).

Taylor (1990) advances the concept of the quisling effect in gang analysis. This is the notion that gangs are more than simply destructive to the community, they are "sell-outs", they are functionally --- in spite of their own rhetoric to the contrary (e.g., working for "oppressed peoples", etc) --- working to destroy their own country and community. The gang member as parasite and germ collaborating for destruction is the essence of this concept.

Huff (1990): Prior Gang Viewpoints in America

This is a reader containing fourteen papers on gangs in America. The forward by Albert K. Cohen is most interesting in its own right. These are selections written by persons who are well known gang authors.

There is much that is new, but not necessarily unanticipated. For example, Hagedorn's discussion is quick to point out the need for more "field work"[20]. Hagedorn also criticizes other authors in this reader (e.g., Spergel and Curry) as "courthouse criminologists", because they do not get their information directly from the mouths of gang members.

Knox (1991): The First Full Textbook on Gangs.

The first edition of this book appeared in 1991 and while several "readers" (collections of various papers by different authors) existed on gangs, the first edition of An Introduction to Gangs was the first serious effort by a single author to address all of the major issues is a textbook format since the time of Thrasher. It was the very first to provide actual full length written gang constitutions showing the formal structure of some of the more notorious criminal gangs. The 1991 first edition also included a geographical listing of gangs that was dropped in the 1993 second edition[21]. The publisher of the first two editions was also dropped with extreme prejudice. The third edition expanded somewhat in 1994. The 1998 4th edition was expanded even more. And, of course, this "expansion" continues and is reflected here in the newly revised and expanded 5th edition (2000).

Sanchez-Jankowski (1991): Ten Years Hanging Out With Gangs.

This work represented a major step forward in dispelling certain myths about gangs. It is based on ten years of qualitative research: hanging out with different gangs in several states. This is much more time than Thrasher (1927) ever spent with gangs. While the methodology of the author has been criticized, the quality of the results make this a book of enduring value. The criticism that the work may overgeneralize its research findings is a charge that can be put at the door of almost all gang researchers.

Goldstein (1991): Gangs as Hyperadolescents.

One of the biggest intellectual issues in the study of gangs today is the matter of "stigma" and "labelling". That is, there is a fear that some research and scholarship will add to the public fear of gangs. The work of Goldstein (1991) summarizes much of the sociological literature on gangs including a chapter on "Gangs as Communities", and also includes a unique psychological perspective as well by viewing gangs as hyperadolescents. What this concept implies is that younger gang members face more than the normal amount of tension and "trouble" in terms of identity formation and status seeking behavior problems. Thus, while gang leaders may in it for the money, young kids involved in gangs may be in it for the status itself.

Goldstein also believes in the "pro-social gang". Any public defender, any mother testifying at the sentencing hearing of her convicted killer son, will say something similar: gangs do not spend every second of every minute, every minute of every hour, and every hour of every day doing 100 percent evil. They do periodically have fun. They do periodically do things that are normal. But the idea that a gang is pro-social or can become pro-social is very ludicrous in light of the type of gangs discussed in this book. Maybe "Spanky and Alfalfa" can become less obnoxious and more "pro-social": but no psychologist and no "treatment" is going to "turn around" a serious criminal gang. It cannot be done.

Kotlowitz (1991): The Gang Stranglehold on African-American Public Housing Residents

This book details the everyday life events of several children growing up in the Henry Horner public housing projects over a two year period. Gangs and the violence and drug business the gangs control are examined from the viewpoints of youths like Pharaoh who are not gang members. This is one of the few such participant observation studies that takes the viewpoints of non-gang members into account. What we learn is that gangs like the Vice Lords who earned thousands of dollars a day in their drug business are a menace from the viewpoints of law abiding public housing residents.

Mc Lean (1991): The Evangelical Outreach to Gang Members

The author describes his early work at the Green Hill Training School in Chehalis, Washington to his present work with juvenile and adult offenders --- many of whom are gang members. While working in a juvenile cottage he was attacked and tied up in an escape effort. From 1982 to present, the Chicago gang scene is described; and covers many of the same aspects of the gang problem discussed elsewhere. It also describes ten years of experience in a "United Nations" component of the ministry to offenders where rival gang members were brought together for peaceful meetings[22]. This is the group that issued "Officially Retired Gang Member" photo I.D.'s. in the Chicago area.

The author has been effective in getting to know some of the more notorious gang members in "Audy Home" in Chicago. These are kids facing a life behind bars and who need someone to "speak up for them" at time of sentencing.

The 1992 Cervantes Gang Reader: Drugs and Gang Violence

This short work provides a lot of traditional discussion about drugs. The only new gang research presented is small sample (N = 81 cases). It provides a mental health focus by authors who are mostly from the L.A. area. It tells us nothing about gang drive-by shootings in relationship to gang drug disputes. The small sample of gang members incarcerated in L.A. focuses on the psychological issue of post traumatic stress disorder (PTSD); not the PTSD the gang members induce in the community, but rather their own PTSD.

Padilla (1992): The Gang as a Business Enterprise.

This study of former members of a Chicago gang focuses on an important aspect of gang life: drug selling as "work". Work that is not very rewarding, but provides a basically "hand to mouth" subsistence with the real profits going to the higher up gang leaders. Despite the rhetoric in their gang constitutions, the gangs basically mimic their capitalistic society and seek to exploit the "workforce" of gang members willing to push drugs or commit other crimes of economic profit.

Knox, Laske, and Tromanhauser (1992): Gangs and Schools.

This short monograph focuses exclusively on the gang problem among school children. It includes much new research showing the strong linkage between drugs and gangs. It provides a special look at Asian students and concludes the "gang profile" is similar across all ethnic groups. It specifically tests a variety of hypotheses from the gang literature using recent data (students, parents, teachers, police, etc). It is out of print. Good luck finding it.

The 1992 Covey, Menard, and Franzese Book on Gangs:

Some of the good features that this book contains make it a worthy contribution. It does consider skinheads gangs, along with other white supremacist gangs. It does provide a good penetration of the gang literature and a review of some of the major issues. It does appear to provide a balanced perspective on gangs. It does seek to develop some theoretical propositions about gangs. It is even appreciative of the early Chicago school of criminology.

The additional positive features of the book include the fact that it places the context of explaining gangs in terms of larger more well known criminological theories (strain, labelling, social control, etc). One chapter provides some interesting material on gang studies in western history and another

provides a review of the material on gangs in other countries. It even addresses the underclass issue and gangs in relationship to politics.

Having said this, the question here is whether or not the potential criticisms of this book outweigh its positive features.

The downside of this gang book includes the fact that it provides no empirical data on gangs or gang members compiled by the work of the authors. It continues to use the misnomer "juvenile" and "youth" gangs as if older members did not exist; and as if the kids really "ran" the gangs in America, not the much older adult members who are often incarcerated. It criticizes ethnographic accounts and other gang research for being too parochial, but the authors provide no research of their own, not even an effort to test their propositions as hypotheses.

The 1992 Gang Identification Guide by Dunston:

The author is primarily concerned with gang identifiers. He describes how gang graffiti is used to mark turf, list the gangs members, challenge rivals, and mourn deceased members. He gives special attention to the "Folks" and the "People" graffiti. But he also deals with the representations of skinheads, prison gangs, Cuban criminals, motorcycle gangs, and the occult.

A fifteen page glossary of terms is divided into Chicago-based gangs, west coast gangs, motorcycle gangs, and satanism/witchcraft terminology.

Also included are 34 representations of "runes" and "alphabets" felt to be potentially in use as secret writing codes.   The author is a captain in the Tupelo, MS police department. This book is not a historical endeavor, nor is it research-based, and for this reason does not target an academic audience. Rather it is a nuts and bolts type of essay that seems reasonable for its price.

The 1993 Books By Gang Members

One of the most popular, articulate and insightful books written by gang members was that by Luis Rodriguez (1993) Always Running: La Vida Loca - Gang Days in L.A. The Rodriguez (1993) book basically provides an anti-gang message and this redeeming quality distinguishes from two others that also appeared in 1993. The other two 1993 gang-authored books that deserve review here are:

Monster: The Autobiography of an L.A. Gang Member, by Sanyika Shakur, aka Monster Kody Scott, 1993, New York, NY: Penguin Books.

Shorty Four, by Albert Kinnard and Marlon Wilson. 1993, self-published, Chicago, IL, 100pp, stapled softcover.

Many have seen Monster, and this may be the first anyone has heard of Shorty Four, but both are also recent books written by gang members. Monster Kody is a L.A. Crip in custody, and the author of Shorty Four is a young leader in the Four Corner Hustlers --- a Chicago-based gang. The reviewer has no idea where the latter might be available, having had to pay cash ($10.00) to some unknown party for the copy reviewed here. Obviously, Monster is well-known, a glitzy product showing much editing polish by a Hollywood image producer, and available over the counter; while Shorty Four is a self-published street product, reflecting no such intensive external handling by the nature of its paper cover, stapled fold-over homemade format. Their physical appearance and availability is about all that makes them different analytically. Both books are about gangs. Both books are written by gang members. In both cases the gang leader is presently incarcerated. Monster Kody is the hero in Monster and at the time the book was first released he was in California's Pelican Bay Prison. Albert Kinnard is a Four Corner Hustler self-styled "chief" holding the last known rank of Prince going by the gang name "Magoo", serving time in the Illinois Department of Corrections.

Both books portray the main characters as gang members who were caught up in a screwed up society such that they had to become something equivalent to "freedom fighters" in a modern urban guerilla war fought on the streets of the USA. Both are African-American authors. Both books portray the main characters as products of oppression having no moral responsibility for their criminal behavior and violence.

There is little dwelling on guilt, remorse, or any of the attributes we might expect of someone who wanted to distance themselves from the gang. Indeed, both books are well-liked by gang members because of the authors do not denounce the gang. The authors do not denounce gang life, but rather denounce "social injustice". Both books apologize for gang life, gang violence, and gang crime by portraying gang life as not only an acceptable life style alternative, but by presenting gang life as an inevitable result of urban life today for many young children sucked into the gang scam. Not unlike the fact that the gang member who receives a beating from his own gang is not necessarily any less likely to try and quit the gang, these two gang authors lost many friends and experienced much personal pain in the process of pursuing their respective gang careers --- none of it resulting in a consequent denunciation of the gang as a way of life.

Both books are very prone towards presenting the author as a self-stylized gang hero, a legend in the urban community, a fierce warrior with a take-no-crap attitude, exposed to violence at an early age in life, using violence as the preferred solution to everything, hating larger society for its uncaring attitude towards the down-trodden, indeed --- puppets

popping, deadly wind-up toys propelled to produce mayhem. Kids who kill who grow up to be young adults in custody with a story they want to tell.

Both books achieve the same result with and without experimental inducements. Monster was the product of a related gang apologist, Hollywood writer on gangs, presenting the quality product of a large commercial investment; the proceeds of which in terms of royalties are not known to have been attached by civil actions by any of the victims of this particular gang member. Shorty Four was self-published in a cheap format of folded over pages stapled twice in the middle as a softcover binding, and sold on the streets of Chicago, carrying no copyright and no name of any publisher. Its only citation information for date of publication is that of a forward written to the book by Useni Eugene Perkins, dated July 9, 1993 who expresses his concern as to what will eventually happen to Albert. Thus, one of these books is professional produced and one is strictly low-tech, but both present an essentially identical perspective: gang life for them was a result of a social-economic-historical-political-racial predestined type of causal determinism --- they had no choice, therefore they do not have to feel guilty about their behavior.

Both books over-glorify gang life. Both books present the author as a gang expert caught up in a merciless criminal justice system run by corrupt officials. Both authors give the reader the best side of their story possible, with little discussion of their own culpability for various crimes against their own community. These are not "confessions", these are both examples of moral neutralization.

Anyone who works with gangs will quickly recognize the ethos or philosophy advanced in both of these books. It is a twisted rationalization bordering on nihilism (i.e., we need to "destroy it all, America is corrupt") and political extremism (much less so in Shorty Four where the political cause celebre is stressed to a significantly less extent, perhaps because of the lack of a good marketing promotions department).

Both books do not reveal upper echelon figures who may be responsible for their own crimes as manipulators of urban children today. Both books do want to make us believe they were swept up in this kind of powerful lure that the gang has today, just as a freedom fighter joins the underground in a nation invaded by foreign powers. In no case do the authors suggest the need for more police, both books denounce police and the "system" in general.

Both books do present the gang as a deadly source of violence today. For example, in Shorty Four a gang fight near the Henry Horner Homes is described in detail where at one point the author nearly has his gang use a rocket launcher against a building containing rival gang members in a shoot-out with gang rivals.   Can we believe the story of both authors is a real issue.   In <u>Shorty Four</u> in the rocket launcher scene, the Four Corner Hustlers dispersed because a police helicopter appeared on the scene.   The Chicago Police Department has not had helicopters for a very long time, too many of them were crashed, and the helicopter squad was eliminated many years ago.   So we have no idea who the lead character in <u>Shorty Four</u> might be talking about when he claims a police helicopter suddenly came on the scene to interrupt a gang gun battle.   Maybe another phenomenon occurs when gang authors write their own books, something similar to a mix of flashback and intermeshing this with, as gang members themselves might say, a little yeast.

On the other hand, these are issues that we must take seriously.   In the case of the Four Corner Hustlers, in October of 1994 several members of the same gang in <u>Shorty Four</u> did try to buy a rocket launcher to blow up a Chicago police station.   Are they trying to live up to the warrior scenario in their own book?   Will Crips follow the same pattern, or any other extremist group identifying along the same dimensions that includes such now politicized gang members?   Time will tell.

Obviously, these are not books written with criminal justice practitioners or criminologists in mind. These are books written by gang members who want to play on current interests on the topic, who want to exploit the "fear factor", and they diligently endeavor to develop sympathy for their cause in these books.

Cummings and Monti (1993):   Another Diverse Reader on Gangs

This reader --- a collection of various articles by different authors --- contains thirteen chapters, four of which were authored by the editors.   The viewpoints on gangs are very much grounded in the criminology and criminal justice literature.   It contains useful new contributions not previously published: particularly on gang graffiti as an art form in the study by Ray Hutchison.   Other useful contributions include new viewpoints on gang migration and on the civil rights of gang members.   It also provides an excellent summary of Thrasher's enduring value to gang analysis.

The Cummings and Monti (1993) reader contains more original gang research than most other "gang reader books".   The Cummings and Monti (1993) reader never deviates analytically from the more specific issue of "gangs" or "gang members". A much greater theoretical diversity of viewpoints on the causes of gangs and more realistic potential solutions to gang problems are to be found in the Cummings and Monti (1993) reader.

The theme of the Cummings and Monti (1993) reader is that the gang problem is very com-plex and no simple solutions like psychological therapy are going to suddenly "cure" a deep rooted and highly institutionalized problem like that represented by modern "gangs".

The 1993 Goldstein and Huff Gang Reader:

Containing eighteen chapters a third of which the editors contributed, this reader seeks to address the issue of gang intervention.   The assumption is that both the stick (criminal justice punishment) and the carrot (psychological and community services) are needed to intervene with gangs.   Much of the literature upon which gang intervention is based as discussed by a number of the contributors was not the more specific and unique form of deviance and criminology we call "gang literature", but was the wider "delinquency intervention" literature. Unstated assumptions for psychological intervention amount to little more than "attributions" and labels to gang members, by assuming that the literature on "conduct disorders" among youths has any proven effectiveness value in gang intervention.   It is a fairly large stretch of intervention logic to assume that any prior program intervention dealing with delinquency or psychological disorders can automatically be applied to gang intervention with the same results.   They are not the same phenomena!

Some mistakes in our previous gang literature such as that by Brooks (1952) were based on the same lack of logic.   The book on "Girl Gangs" by Brooks (1952) becomes on closer inspection not a documentary of a full gang composed ONLY of females who engage in serious crime.   Such a serious criminal gang composed only of females was not fully documented in the gang literature until the recent work of Lauderback, Hansen and Waldorf (1992). Thus, the title by Brooks like some others on gang issues, was really misleading; what the Brooks book did was simply discuss some of the more vicious accounts of female delinquency that had appeared in the mass media --- not gangs of girls, but the individual behavior of females mostly acting alone.   In other words, routine delinquency and criminology literature.   The fact is that the gang literature is a specialized subset of the crime and delinquency literature.

Calling it a handbook does not make it a single source reference book on gang programs.   The book describing the history of gang programs in America and their effectiveness has yet to be written.

Hamm (1993):   Skinheads as Gang Members

This is a major positive contribution to the study of white racist gangs.   It is a detailed and indepth scholarly monograph based on mainstream criminology and establishes that groups such as skinheads and neo-nazis who engage in bias crimes should be included in what we mean by "gangs". Such hate groups do accumulate military weapons and ordnance and should be regarded in the domain of domestic "home grown" terrorist threats. These are not just "kids", these are more often than not problems of crime and violence created by adult-led political extremist organizations. See also Jack B. Moore's work Skinheads Shaved For Battle: A Cultural History of American Skinheads (1993) for a view and analysis that complements the Hamm study.

Hamm believes white right extremists gangs drink too much beer. Some authors believe female gang members have behavior that is explained by this as well. Subsequent research on white racist extremist gangs by McCurrie (1998), Journal of Gang Research, showed these offenders are not really different in the crime patterns than other gangs: they extensive abuse and use and sell drugs, like most others, and beer would be a small matter to worry about in the larger picture of what gangs today have access to.

Sanders (1994): Gangbangs and Drive-Bys

Sanders provides the best sociologically-grounded approach to ethnographic research on gangs. Much analysis is presented within a wider social perspective that includes such well known theorists as Goffman. This particular study deals with gang violence in San Diego. It helps to explain why some social values like loyalty have different meanings to gangs than they do to others, or rather how in the gang context the value of loyalty is "grounded" in the specific gang culture. This may help to explain how some have regarded gang members as having twisted or upsidedown value systems. Gang members are gang-centric is what Sanders shows.

Goldstein and Glick (1994): The Prosocial Gang?

The idea of a prosocial gang seems to some to be a contradiction in terms and therefore an oxymoron. The authors of this book appear to have conducted a small program for juveniles, a psychological treatment program called aggression replacement therapy. They claim it works on gang members, although their own data (p. 95) shows the participants did not change in terms of anger control. They do claim a reduced recidivism rate that is significant. It is fair to say that the methodology for this evaluation was not the best. Calling a comparison group a control group implies an experimental design, when it is in fact not clear that random assignment was used. It is not clear what types of gangs may have been specifically represented in the treatment group, or their comparison group. The present author is highly skeptical that such a simple program could turn around anyone but the lowest level gang member of the lowest possible threat level. Why? Because the gang problem is not simply a psychological problem.

The gang problem is not something so simple that it could be chemically treated by an "anti-gangbanging" pill, or as some turn of the century writers believed that a "gang instinct" existed, that any biological or genetic manipulation will reduce the gang problem.

The 1995 Klein Gang Reader

The Klein et al (1995) reader is organized as follows: three papers on defining gangs; five papers on types of gangs; four papers on female gang involvement; six papers on understanding gangs, including an article from Ice T the famous rapper; three papers on group process; three papers on delinquent and criminal patterns; four papers on gangs and drugs; three papers on social intervention; five articles on law enforcement; and four articles on policy issues. It is broad and eclectic in coverage of a variety of authors and issues about the gang problem.

The 1995 Spergel Book

The Spergel (1995) book is organized into two major parts: I. description and analysis, and II. Policy and Program. The first part has chapters dealing with: historical perspectives, research and data sources, scope and seriousness of the gang problem, gangs drugs and violence, gang member demographics, the structure of the gang, gang member experience, the ecological context, and youth gangs and organized crime. The second part deals with theoretical perspectives, gang violence reduction, the police, prosecution, probation, corrections, social intervention, social opportunities, and local community mobilization. Throughout one will find rich new insights and views from Spergel on his research and field work.

The 1995 Anti-Gang Book by Mike Knox:

The book Gangsta in the House: Understanding Gang Culture, by Mike Knox, 1995, Momentum Books, Ltd., 6964 Crooks Road, Troy, Michigan 48098, has resulted in the author being a well-known national speaker to many diverse groups on the topic of gangs.

Another title could have been used for this book "Common Sense About Gangs and Gang Members". The author convincingly argues from experience the merits and disadvantages of various approaches to dealing with gangs. The book is not offered as a scholarly research book on gangs. The book does, however, provide true-to-form descriptive material about gangs and gang members, including a very useful chapter on female gang members.

The book is crafted quite logically into nine chapters: 1. Mind of a Gangster, 2. The Big Lies, 3. The families, 4. Girl Gangs, 5. The Look I Want to Know Better, 6. Graffiti, 7. Empowerment, 8. Denial, and 9. The Cure.

So, basically, the first six chapters are about the culture of gang life in America. The last three chapters deal with responses to gang problems. The chapter on "Denial" is worth the price of this book alone.

What is so refreshing about this book is that the author's language level is clearly designed to be read by any citizen who is seriously interested in doing something about the gang problem. The book is non-technical in nature. The book provides an enormous wealth of keen insight into the American gang problem. Parents of gang members should be required to read this book, it would possibly raise their level of understanding about what untapped powers they have to respond to the problem of having a gang member in the family. That makes this book perfectly suited for a common situation in the gang business: what to do when the parent contacts you, a sincere and caring parent, who wants to know what to do now that they have recently discovered, to their chagrin, that they have a kid who is a gangbanger. Give them the title and order information for this book, and you will be doing such a parent a valuable social service. The book is clearly designed to be used by parents and others as a "gang primer". And as such, it provides one of the best available in that genre.

This book is not "soft" on gang crime. The author's law enforcement background ensures that is not the case. It is a practical book that is abundantly filled with "common sense" about what to do and what not to do about gang members.

Any gang expert or anyone dealing with the gang problem should always have this book available: for when you get that visit from a parent who needs common sense advice about what to do. This book will help you deal with that situation more effectively.

The 1996 Cozic Book

The Cozic (1996) book contains materials carefully selected to try to represent diametrically opposing viewpoints on gangs. This can be illustrated by examining how the book seeks to achieve a "point counter point" type of effect about incarcerating gang members. For example, one can find a short selection by John J. Wilson and James C. Howell entitled "Convicted Gang Youths May Require Incarceration". The incredible insight implied by the title is exceeded only by the fact that the paper is after all a summary of some OJJDP materials. The article includes such original ideas like the notion that a small proportion of offenders may constitute a disproportionate amount of the crime or violence problem in America.

The 1996 Mitchell and Rush Gang Reader

This Mitchell and Rush (1996) book is a gang reader containing ten different articles that combines the best criminological science applied to the real life problem of gangs and gang members. The focused use of the book is therefore, obviously, in the criminal justice system. As Dean Champion points out in the Forward "several significant components of the 1994 Crime Bill were directed at street crimes perpetrated by youth gangs". The gang problem has become a national problem. Sadly, an examination of NIJ Awards in Fiscal Year 1995 (January, 1996, National Institute of Justice, Research in Brief, U.S. Department of Justice, Office of Justice Programs) shows literally no new basic research funding awards aimed specifically at gangs or gang members and what effect they may be having on the criminal justice system. There was only one gang program evaluation grant made by NIJ in 1995, in fact to one of the authors in this book being reviewed. So it is good to see the private sector, as exemplified by the ACJS/ Anderson monograph series, picking up the ball dropped by federal agencies like NIJ's Office of Justice Programs.

J. Mitchell Miller wrote the preface for this book about how different fields of thought in criminal justice are now responding to the gang problem. All of the authors of the ten articles, with one coauthor exception, are listed as being academics.

The 1997 State-Level Case Study by Oehme:

This is a book exclusively about the gang problem in the State of North Carolina. Why, then, would you want to read it if you do not live in North Carolina? That question is answered in this book review.

This book is both a case study of the gang problem in one state as well as being a statewide analysis. What is particularly valuable about this book is that it provides an in-depth and detailed analysis of the gang problem and the measures taken to deal with the gang problem in one state. As such, it provides an important historical "marker", and establishes some of the parameters of the gang problem in that state. Why is that valuable?

It is not the only state in the USA that has had the benefit of statewide gang analysis: some other states have undertaken this type of work, or the work has been undertaken on behalf of other states. This list of statewide analyses that the NGCRC has been involved in include: Wisconsin, Illinois, Georgia, South Carolina, and more. The customary methodology for such statewide assessments includes the kind of research strategy employed by Oehme in his study of North Carolina: it is a technique that basically involves direct surveys of law enforcement agencies using an attempt at saturation sampling (i.e., getting as many of the law enforcement agencies to participate as possible).

It is not easy to get full cooperation from all law enforcement agencies in any state. But Oehme has done a great job at getting a high response rate for the research that constitutes the basis for his book (i.e., 62.7%), as about the only way to get a better response rate than that is to have legislation in place requiring routine reporting for statewide analysis, something similar to the Uniform Crime Reporting system maintained by the FBI. Thus, in many ways the methodology of surveying law enforcement agencies on gang issues provides a "simulation" of what the FBI's Uniform Crime Report would say if it ever included information about gangs. Obviously, the FBI's Uniform Crime Report has never had anything to say about gangs since it was first started in 1930.

So lacking this local information from jurisdictions that have arrest authority, criminological researchers like Oehme must take the best shot they can at generating the best estimates of the scope and extent of the gang problem in their areas. Professor Oehme has, therefore, in carrying out this kind of analysis for North Carolina, provided an invaluable public and professional service by generating this local knowledge where it had not previously existed.

In generating this useful body of knowledge for the State of North Carolina, Professor Oehme has given that state the power of now having a statistical "bench mark" against which to measure subsequent efforts to deal with the gang problem. Will the gang problem increase or decrease over time? Only states that have had the benefit of such statewide analysis are going to be in position to be able to know exactly what direction their statewide gang problem is headed.

What is the best thing a State Governor could do for their respective state on the gang problem? Many establish various "commissions" to examine the gang problem. Some, such as in Illinois, have even held extensive public hearings on the issue of gangs. Often, therefore, the reports that get issued from these "gang commissions" are essentially worthless documents: they reflect the myopic opinions of those serving on the commissions or immediately jump into recommendations without the benefit of hard empirical research on the scope and extent of the problem. What is the best thing a governor could do for the citizens of any state? Find someone like Professor Oehme and carry out a similar study to provide the same kind of statewide gang statistical analysis.

If every state had the benefit of the kind of scholarship reflected in this book by Oehme, then truly it would be reasonable to assume that consensus on the gang problem would be within reach: something that is not necessarily true today, as there is extensive disagreement on the scope and extent of the gang problem, and of course, there are a number of variations of "gang denial" operating in many communities as well.

The 1997 "How To Fight Gangs" Book by Coghlan:

The book entitled How to Prevent Gangs and Drugs in Your Home, School and Community!!, by Michael Coghlan, a noted gang expert, is receiving a great deal of national acclaim by those who have seen it. It is available directly through the author, a former gang prosecutor in Illinois.

Whatever the cost of this book, you know you are getting a "big bang for the buck" because it is technically the largest book in the world on gangs in terms of page count. The NGCRC has for years held that honor until the appearance of this new book by Michael Coghlan, and now we are in the position of having to "catch up" with this new record of accomplishment.

A major accomplishment, this book certainly is. It is a major accomplishment not simply because of its length, but by the substance of what it offers: a new genre of gang book! This is truly a "how to do it" book to fight back against the gang problem in any community.

If we wanted to suddenly have a major positive impact on the gang problem nationally, then one thing that could be done is to get this "how to do it" book into the hands of as many proactive citizens and local policy makers and local leaders as possible. It would "arm" them in their battle to deal with their local gang problem.

This is finally a book that can be used by the ordinary American citizen to do something about their local gang or drug problem. There is no other book like it on the market. The book is an ingenious "mini-tactical office" of form letters, strategies, and methods to use existing law as a basis for waging war against otherwise intractable problems like those represented by how gangs and drugs become "entrenched" in some communities. Can anything be done? Absolutely yes, and this book is the only book of its type that provides some "sure fire" methods of putting the heat on these problems.

This is the kind of book that probably should have come from one of our Nation's better and more professionally staffed "Crime Commissions": i.e., those groups that claim to be looking out for citizens on crime issues. But it came not from the government, and not from organized entities, it came from one gang expert. In writing this book, the author has clearly done a major positive service to the American people on combatting crime. This is an award winning book.

The 1998 Evangelical Book by McLean, et al:

The book entitled <u>Too Young to Die: Bringing Hope to Gangs in the Hood</u>, by Gordon McLean, with Dave and Neta Jackson; 1998, Wheaton, Illinois: Tyndale House Publishers, is the second major book on gangs by Rev. Gordon McLean.

If you ever meet him, you won't forget him: that is Gordon McLean, and he is a historical figure in Chicago when it comes to unique ways to deal with gang members.   What he has to say in this new book is therefore valuable in several ways: for its own content and for its historical significance.

This is not intended as a "scholarly criminological" book about gangs. It does not provide any empirical research and analysis about gangs. But does it provide interesting insights? Absolutely yes.

This book chronicles some of the experiences over the years that the author has had in his ministry to gang members. McLean's program in the Chicago area is called "Juvenile Justice Ministry of Metro Chicago Youth for Christ" and dates back to 1982. There are a lot of individuals from the clergy over the years who have tried to "dabble" in gang problems. Some of these, like Rev. John Fry, came to Chicago and quickly started their programs to deal with gang members by handing out government and foundation grant money and other resources directly to gangs like the Black P. Stone Nation (then called the Black Stone Rangers when they were given such generous unconditional positive regard from Rev. Fry). Thanks to Rev. Fry, the same gang rapidly flourished, grew, expanded, and moved into other states as well and continues to plague many communities in an even more devastating way than before, almost like a "mad doctor" experiment gone awry: a kind of experiment that does not reduce gang crime, but rather expands it. This book is not of that genre, it is a different style of intervention that presumes individual change within individual gang members can be a useful service if it is available in a community infected with a serious gang problem.

If there was one member of the clergy nationwide who has generated an exemplary program, based on a dose of religion, then most independent analyses would probably all point to the author of this book. Why? Because of the long time span that the program has been in operation. With nearly two decades of experience, this program stands out for its "survivability" factor alone; as too many such initiatives get a strong start, but fail to survive the test of time, i.e., the ability to continue and persist over time.

Of course this book provides some worthwhile and useful insights into local Chicago gangs. The author is very "savvy" on gang issues, he is not operating as some have before him with "blinders on". Even before coming to Chicago, the author was in-volved with a ministry outreach to gangs in another state, so it is unlikely that a gang member could "con" the author.   And that is one of the things, unfortunately, that probably comes to mind when some skeptical gang experts hear of a person like Gordon McLean who tries to bring the message of Jesus Christ to gang members: they may say to themselves, "this is another Rev. Fry, out to self-aggrandize himself". It is not hard to find "gang apologists" within members of the clergy today. It would incorrect to say that this book is of that persuasion though. And even if you do not agree with the message, you may be impressed with some of the results reported in the book. Is there a vital role to be played by clergy in outreach to gang members? This book proves that case affirmatively.

The 1999 Reader on Female Gangs: Chesney-Lind and Hagedorn

This is an anthology of viewpoints on female gangs and female gang members. It includes some of the classical viewpoints (Thrasher, Quicker, Fishman, Giordano). It also includes some new and recent viewpoints as well. Fitting the typical "gang reader" profile, though, most of these are reprints of viewpoints and essays that have been in the literature for some time. Just two years earlier, there was a major milestone in actual new gang research on female gang members, it is the innovative work by Burris-Kitchen (1997), which examined the role of African-American women in the gang-drug economy.

The Grennan, et al, International Perspective on Gangs (2000):

The book entitled <u>Gangs: An International Approach</u>, by Sean Grennan, Marjie T. Britz, Jeffrey Rush, and Thomas Barker, 2000, Prentice Hall, Upper Saddle River, New Jersey, represents an important approach to gang studies. And it deserves analysis here in some detail.

Two factors made this, at first glance, a very appealing book: (1) the title of the book suggested something that was long overdue, a true international scope to the gang problem, and (2) the fact that the authors recommend a zero-tolerance approach to gangs and generally view gangs as a menace to society. While the book has a number of strengths, a closer analysis of the book reveals a number of flaws as well.

Some gang analysts who are familiar with cross-national gangs like the Mara Salvatrucha 13, will search this book to find it is a gang that is not even listed or acknowledged as even existing. It is a book that does, however, cover everything from traditional Italian organized crime to terrorist groups like the PLO all in one binding. However, it does so rather inconsistently. What distinguishes a terrorist group, or a classical form of organized crime, from street or prison gangs is simply missing in terms of organizational analysis.

The book does an excellent job of summarizing a large array of domestic and foreign newspaper stories about gangs. Most of the citations in the book's bibliography are newspaper accounts or documents from the federal government.

The book begins a look at what the authors were able to understand about gangs generally. Unfortunately, the effort appears to have been sophomoric at best. An example, is where the authors suggest that no knowledge exists about how people get into gangs (p. 18) with no differentiation provided about the important distinction in terms of modern modes of entry into the gang system: recruitment versus voluntary joining behavior. Obviously, the astute gang researcher would know that about half of all present living gang members join the gang voluntarily and about half are recruited into the gang. This important distinction has much import: as the volunteers are more hard core generally, and those who get recruited into the gang are somewhat more likely to try and leave the gang.

A full chapter (chapter 4) is provided on the Italian forms of organized crime. Much of this is dated information, the kind of material found in a variety of textbooks, giving a historical account of crime families. It lacks an up-to-date analysis of how the same strains of organized crime continue to function today. It is therefore somewhat stale in its treatment of traditional American OC.

Chapter 5 in the book addresses motorcycle gangs. This is a book that is declared to be intentionally pragmatic, and this chapter proves it is. Much of the material here is already well known to anyone who has ever attended a gang training session about outlaw motorcycle clubs. It includes some of the same kinds of material: a graphic depicting how a biker group will be organized in a convoy when on the road en masse. The book gives no attribution to the source of this and much other information though.

This problem of attribution surfaces again and again from the perspective of this author, as much information is presented as being authoritative information, but it is often not grounded with reference to the sources of the same information. It is somewhat troublesome and tends to raise critical concerns for this reviewer. Some of these issues will be addressed shortly.

Chapter 6 in the book is devoted to racist and racial supremacist gangs. How this chapter, and the one dealing with prison gangs, could ignore the Aryan Brotherhood is a complete mystery to this reviewer. Chapter 6 does not even acknowledge the existence of the Aryan Brotherhood; in fact, the ABs are mentioned only once in passing later in the book.

Chapter 7 devotes seven pages to "street gangs". It suggests, incorrectly, that there are only two gang epicenters in the United States: (1) Chicago, and (2) Los Angeles. This becomes, ultimately, a fatal analytical flaw in the book; particularly, when the authors finally address the "Latin Kings". Chapter 7 particularly is an example where the use of citations, references, and attribution to sources could have been useful as the authors try to give an account of Chicago gangs. The attempt fails due to historical inaccuracy and overlooking many significant events with regard to Chicago gangs. The discussion of Chicago gangs like the BPSN and GDs (pp. 122-125) acknowledges no source material.

Here is the major problem this reviewer had with Chapter 7: the authors try to explain the existence of current Chicago gangs and deal only with how when David Barksdale died, Larry Hoover and Shorty Freeman were in a power struggle, Hoover won out. Then, if we were ill-informed enough to believe the authors, Jeff Fort got jealous of the rising GD gang and the Black P. Stones were then up and running as the leading force in the "People's" gang alliance.

This is an inaccurate and misleading analysis for several reasons. First, Jeff Fort's group preceded the GDs, and there are a number of books about this history; unfortunately, they are not to be found in the bibliographic references of the book under review. Secondly, Hoover did not supplant Shorty Freeman, Hoover simply started his "own thing". Shorty Freeman continued to run the purest derivative of "King David Barksdale's" gang: and it continues today, the Black Disciples. The authors are simply not aware that Barksdale's original gang spun-off into three separate gangs: GDs, BDs, and BGs. Thirdly, and most seriously, this discussion of Chicago gangs totally ignores the Latin Kings and the Vice Lords, as well as white gangs like the Simon City Royals. The Vice Lords are the single oldest gang in Chicago, their origin dates back to 1959, and again, much literature exists on the Vice Lords, and their factions and derivatives, but this information is totally lacking in the book under review. Any discussion of Chicago gangs without reference to Vice Lords and Latin Kings is a discussion that cannot be taken seriously. Sadly, there is not one reference in the subject index of the book to one of the oldest and most prolific gangs in America that originated in Chicago: the Vice Lords, other than a casual mention that they are a "people" gang (p. 125).

Somewhat interesting is the discussion in Chapter 7 that attributes the alliance between the Crips and the GDs (Folks nation) to a 1992 gang summit meeting (p. 125). Again, the authors fail to give any reference to facts or citations: no city where the event occurred etc. The astute gang analyst may know what "gang summit meeting" the authors are referring to, as the authors claim the event was sponsored by funding from the federal government. But the NGCRC has always maintained that the alliance was an outgrowth of the 1993 Chicago gang summit meeting, which was dominated by GDs and a small spattering of cooperative Crips and their L.A.-based political-ideological activist groups. The NGCRC videotaped most of the 1993 Chicago events subject to the standard press-credentialed access.

Much later in the book we do find a limited discussion about the Latin Kings. The Latin Kings are analyzed as an "emerging high-profile gang" (p. 406). Emerging? They have been a high-profile gang for 40 years!

Another serious problem, and fatal flaw from this reviewers point of view, emerges with regard to the discussion about the Latin Kings. The authors quote from the east coast version of the Latin Kings only. The authors apparently have no idea that the version of the Latin Kings founded in New York may have the same colors as the Chicago-original, but the New York version is the renegade faction: the east coast version operates on a written constitution that is totally and completely different than the Chicago original. And now that some of those New York and east coast Latin Kings are in federal prison with some of the Chicago-OG's, they have faced the need to "pay the fiddler" so-to-speak for the song they have been dancing.

The NYC version of the Latin Kings is a renegade and independent spin-off of the original Chicago Latin Kings. The Chicago-based Latin Kings, by the way, are not pleased with the existence of the east coast renegade factions who are doing some serious perpetrating under the name of the Latin Kings. The authors of the book under review would have the reader believe that the only Latin Kings were the east coast variety!

The book does include Malcolm X and the contemporary Black Muslim movement as racial supremacist gangs. Oddly, however, whichever of the authors wrote this section about the Nation of Islam had only a superficial grasp of the nature of the organization. For we never learn about the Fruits of Islam (FOI). Conspicuously missing as well from the book is any discussion about Five Percenters.

The book does give a fair amount of discussion to some groups that are traditional terrorist groups like the PLO. But do not expect the authors to know about the Chicago and Chicago-suburb based TAP Boys gang; or other Palestinian gangs that do operate in the U.S.A. with extensive cross-national trafficking.

The book does a good job of codifying some of the Asian, African, and European gangs; although mostly on the basis of limited information available

in DEA and Justice Department reports; with some reference to Magloclen and the Asian gang investigators association materials. Some of the major contributors to the field of Asian gangs are ignored though.

This could have been one of the most interesting contributions to the study of gangs to appear in a long time. It had the dual goal of providing an international focus and being pragmatic. With regard to the international picture, the book failed on numerous accounts, and therefore must be regarded as a start in the right direction only. With regard to being pragmatic, the book also fails because of its errors and omissions.

We do, however, recommend that gang analysts get a copy of this book. It is the first gang book put out by a very large and well known publisher (Prentice Hall). It provides a model for what might be a very effective book of this genre in the future. That ideal book giving an authoritative international analysis has yet to appear. Thus, the persons who read this book might get motivated to be the future authors of what is needed in this regard.

SUMMARY

This chapter has provided a short overview of some of the major milestones in the study of gangs. We have not provided a simplistic summary of all criminological theories as they might pertain to, or could conceivably be interpreted as apply to, gangs.[23] Also, there are other books and monographs not cited here, which represent such distinct contributions (e.g., Klein) or such interesting accounts that these will be examined in detail in later chapters. We will also find the opportunity later in this book to examine the contributions of other authors, whose works are not always cited as gang contributions, and what they have provided for a more social scientific and historical analysis of gangs.

We have not reviewed here a number of books that serve as gang identification guides. The work by Olivero (1991) is based on newspaper accounts and includes a number of symbols and pictures[24]. One of the worst is by Fox and Amador (1993), which is little more than a local listing of some gangs, and their symbols. Probably the best privately published gang identification guide is that describing Peoples and Folks gangs, which provides a very detailed cross-reference manual for midwest gangs (Gang Prevention, Inc., 1994)[25]. A number of police departments throughout the U.S. have produced local gang identification guides. Chicago's has always been popular. Some statewide law enforcement groups have also recently began to design statewide gang identification manuals.

We have not reviewed a number of books that are basically fiction or apologia about gangs. The book by a Crip gang member, <u>Monster</u>, for example is not a professional contribution to knowledge, it is his autobiography portraying himself with the best of motives however stylized an account it is. Books by gang members are becoming a new genre and can be expected to increase in the future on the principle that we like to read about what generates much fear. Nor have we considered reviewing gang movies, as many of them that exist, just as we have not reviewed pure fiction works that while interesting, for example from a perspective on feminism (i.e., <u>Foxfire: Confessions of A Girl Gang</u>, by Joyce Carol Oates), are still more likely as non-professional contributions to reinforce stereotypes and give unfounded conclusions about the gang problem.

What this chapter demonstrates is a diversity of approaches to the understanding of gangs. And along with this comes a range of research approaches that have been used. The analysis of gangs has also represented a theoretical and social policy focus. All of these contributions must be taken into account to understand the history and evolution of gangs in society.

If it is solid and useful theory, if it is careful and replicable analysis, or if the concepts still apply, then just because their contributions are not recent ones is no reason to discount them as "dated" and therefore not of any value. Obviously, all of the gang members from Thrasher's analysis are now probably dead and buried. But we cannot at the same time reject out of hand the value of potentially useful concepts advanced in such prior analyses. It is not simply a matter of old theory and new gangs. As we shall see in later chapters there are some important historically grounded conceptual continuities in the gang literature.

Discussion Questions

(1) Could a plumber, carpenter, or bus driver carry out a study of gangs as equally scientific and valid in findings as a Ph.D. trained in criminology if the method of study was that of "hanging out" with the gang?

(2) Are ethics involved in the study of gangs? What should such ethical guidelines consist of?

(3) Why should a gang researcher be knowledgeable about the prior literature and theory, generally, before conducting research on gang members? Or do you think a chemist or a coroner having no exposure to the gang literature could do just as good a job as a sociologist or criminologist who was well-read in the gang literature?

"Us Versus Them: The War Mentality of Modern Gang Members"

So you are driving "past" Chicago at night. You know better than to get off the expressway and travel into an unknown neighborhood. So you keep driving, say on the Dan Ryan Expressway, and you think to yourself: I am safe here, I can always speed up! Wrong!!

Welcome to the Gang Expressway False-Flag Scenario Shooting. During early February, 1998 the following scenario happened several times on Chicago's expressways (Dan Ryan, Eisenhower, etc).[26]

It is late at night, about midnight. A car drives up right beside yours and travels at the same rate of speed, but pulls up on the driver's side of your car. That allows the passenger side of the approaching gang car to do this: get your attention and throw you a gang hand sign. What do you do?

You don't recognize the gang hand sign. Should you throw back a similar sign? Should you just wave? How about the international "peace sign"? You know, the "V" sign. (Don't actually throw the "V" sign, it could mean you are a Vice Lord in the hand sign language of gang members in the midwest).

Before we discuss what you should do, from a survivability point of view, let's describe what has happened, and why it happens.

What happens is that any sign returned to the approaching gang car or any failure to return a hand sign to the gang car, means they do not wait very long at all, under a minute, before they open fire on you with handguns. And you and anyone in your vehicle is subject to being killed by gunfire. That's what happens.

Why does it happen? This is a classic "false flag" routine that all gangs use in some fashion. They approach someone they do not know, and "throw up" or give the hand sign for their enemy. If the gang car has Gangster Disciples in it (they "ride" under the six pointed star), then the person in the passenger seat or rear seat will "throw up" a rival sign from perhaps a "Peoples" or "Brothers" gang. If you return the same sign, then you are a confirmed enemy. There is very little probability you could actually come up with the correct gang hand sign in a false flag operation. In a false flag operation, the gang members are just out cruising for an opportunity to "shoot up some rivals". In their "war mentality" it is simply "us" versus "them". "Them" is anyone who is not "us". In their mind the whole world is in a gang of some sort.

So, to survive Chicago's expressways: if someone pulls up along side your vehicle and some young men are trying to get your attention by throwing you what may appear to be "hand signs", what should you do? First, don't return any sign whatsoever unless you have a badge to flash on them; the probability of you returning the "correct" gang sign is very remote. Secondly, there really is no sure-fire safe way out of this mess. Here is what some students in my gang classes have said they would do in this scenario: Hit your brakes hard immediately, travel in reverse gear at a high rate of speed, make a power turn, use the shoulder of the road to travel in the opposite direction directly against the flow of traffic, if you have a cell phone, use it immediately. If you do not, keep going until you find a police officer. That's the best advice in a situation where you are damned if you do and damned if you don't, you are going to get shot either way by not returning a gang sign or by returning the wrong gang hand sign, welcome to the modern gang expressway false flag shootout. It would be totally improper to advise anyone to ram the gang car off the road before they could shoot if you were in a situation where you could not apply the brakes and turn around rapidly (i.e., flee for your life).

But out of curiosity, WHAT WOULD YOU DO?

END NOTES:

[1] For example, p. 11 (Thrasher, 1968) shows a picture of the "heart of Chicago's ghetto", the famous Maxwell street market. This area has been studied by a number of authors.

[2] While Whyte does not indicate any references to the literature in his book, it is fascinating to find the phrase "habitual association" also used by Sleeman (1849: p. 357). Sleeman's work will be described later in reference to guerilla warfare, terrorism, and gang conflict.

[3] Clearly, Cohen (1955, p. 59) seems knowledgeable of Merton's (1938) contribution of the typology of deviance by discussing "innovation" as something that should almost be avoided behaviorally. Cohen recognized the high value of Merton in accounting for adult crime, but criticized it for not being able to account for the non-utilitarian aspects of gang crime (see Cohen, 1955: 36).

[4] Unfortunately for this "age-role" integration theory of gang formation, suggesting that society does not allow enough status for youths therefore they become gang affiliated to acquire their equivalent status and role functions, is the position advanced by authors such as Denisoff and McCaghy (1973, p.153-154), quite au contraire, which sees no such version of the British rebellion against the status system, rather in fact, views the selection of gang targets as rarely representing the adult world which should, according to such a "youth rebellion" theory, be directed more towards those symbols of "unjust domination" by adults.

[5] Leissner (1969: p. 9-10) takes a similar position in avoiding the use of the term "gang" completely, because it implies "crime and violence" which overemphasizes the destructive factors of these groups. Thus, Leissner prefers the term 'street corner group', "because this term avoids the implications of exclusive preoccupation with violence and crime..." (1969, p. 10).

[6] The appendix in Spergel (1964) clearly indicated that only in the case of the Racketville (organized crime, crime cartel) type of community was there difficulty gathering data by qualitative and quantitative methods (p. 198).

[7] While many others of this era (Short, Miller, Klein, etc) have retired, Dr. Spergel still teaches in the Social Service Administration at the University of Chicago.

[8] Spergel (1964) typically analyzed three communities each having three groups for a nine-cell table, but usually reported only ten cases per cell, for a presumable sample size of only N = 90. That may not seem like an impressive sample size today by some standards, but for the time it was a major turning point in gang studies.

[9] The problem is job tenure, job retention, keeping the job, and conversely, quitting or getting fired from the job gotten through agency services. Current Chicago data shows that for one of the largest such offender job placement agencies in the country, that only about 1/3 get a job placement, and that after about 90 days only a fourth of them are still employed in the same job. This is not to deride job placement services: they are essential and based on good theory and they should be continued, indeed expanded and improved. Neither Short and Strodtbeck (1965, 1974) nor myself imply these types of services should be "cut back". Au contraire, they should be vastly refined qualitatively and quantitatively.

[10] As a rational-choice model, the aleatory risk schema must face the criticism discussed by Jackson and Mc Bride (1990, p. 15) in that gang murders "are committed by emotional, violent gang members who do not think of the consequences". Horowitz (pp. 37-54 in Huff, 1990) similarly brings out the issue of whether it is a matter of "instrumental" (rational, calculating) or "expressive" (integrative, spontaneity, etc) motivation. Actually, a third problem is that of the error of organizational aggregation: the social-psychological polarity of motivation involving integrative versus instrumental is one applied historically to individual actors, not GROUPS of persons or organizations.

[11] David Dawley wrote a similar book A Nation of Lords: The Autobiography of the Vice Lords (1973, 1992). This author includes a photography of himself showing the "gang sign" and claims to be "the only white Vice Lord". The author helped the gang get grants and loans to start business enterprises.

[12] For the other side of this Poston (1971) story, that is, an equally vigorous policy discussion but one that is pro-RGS (the Real Great Society) see the work of Mottel (1973) which includes an interesting assortment of gang views in terms of conversation analysis with gang members.

[13] Oddly, we never find out even in passing about their relationship to such other gangs as the Bloods and Crips, or the Aryan Brotherhood. These other gangs were perhaps less prominent at the time of the book's preparation. But there had to be other gangs

in outlying neighborhoods, and we never hear about this aspect of intergang relationships that extend beyond the Mexican-American community.

[14] That is, "jail house lawyers".

[15] Oddly, the authors have no problem quoting such contributions to their own use when it serves their purposes.

[16] To belabor the obvious: if they are selling illicit drugs, then they are committing crime; and depending on the type of drug, perhaps very serious crime. And with drug dealing go a host of other related crimes, including armed violence, retaliatory strikes, income producing crime to support drug purchases, etc.

[17] Where I can certainly stand in agreement with the authors is that what facts we seek shall certainly determine, limit, and constrain what can ultimately be said about gangs. Thus, the best mode of starting an investigation is not necessarily from an atheoretical point of departure. Indeed, while Hagedorn often quotes from the underclass, racial oppression, and economic urban infrastructure deterioration literature, these concepts do not appear to be operationalized in their own data collection instrument (Hagedorn and Macon, 1988: pp. 171-180).

[18] The case study by Olivero (1991) intentionally uses such a journalistic style and makes much reference for data to news media accounts.

[19] Appearing, simultaneously, was Harris (1988) who espoused a view of Los Angeles female gang members that was not dissimilar from Vigil's marginality thesis. At least Harris is quite compatible by seeing these gang members "caught in a socially non-existent place in terms of the dominant culture" (Harris, 1988: p. 189).

[20] Another lesson from the sociology of knowledge, to use an adage, is perhaps that sometimes we have to watch what we pray for, because it could come true. Which is to say, there is nothing new about getting "close up" to a crime problem to study it. Such was the essence of the early Chicago school. But getting "close up" is just as equally subject to be used from a conservative perspective (e.g., Slack and Schwitzgebel, 1959) as it might be from a leftist one. (see Slack, Charles W. and Ralph Switzgebel, 1959, "Interpersonal Research: A New Approach to Reducing Delinquency", Alabama Correctional Journal (6)(Oct): 32-40.)

[21] This reflected the "National Geographic Guide To Gangs", developed and maintained over the years by the National Gang Crime Research Center. This is now a very extensive listing of book length itself. It identifies the major gangs that are active in any capacity throughout the United States, using data from all sources: law enforcement, adult prisons, jails, juvenile correctional institutions, county sheriffs, etc.

[22] This was not meant as a serious academic book, it was meant as a serious religious view of the problem. The photographs in the center of the book are somewhat interesting, but appear to be contrived. For example, one page (following p. 96) shows a black youth holding a very small revolver with the caption "O.Z., a Chicago gang member, armed on a dangerous street" (he was actually posed, looking out a window), with the same young man in the same identical clothing, hat, same sunglasses, same shirt, on the bottom photo holding a Bible with the caption "and later, with his Bible", apparently not much later.

[23] Jackson's (1989) review of theories and findings about gangs is such a global assessment of the Chicago school, Miller and Cohen, plus other potentially applicable theories. It brings into discussion labelling theory and Matza's drift and bonding as potential such theories to apply to gang research.

[24] J. Michael Olivero, Honor, Violence, and Upward Mobility: A Case Study of Chicago Gangs During the 1970s and 1980s. Edinburg, TX: The University of Texas-Pan American.

[25] The Street Gang Identification Manual, is available from Gang Prevention, Inc, PO BOX 7400, Elgin, IL 60121.

[26] See: Stephanie Zimmermann, "Gunfire Rakes the Ryan: Second Gang-Linked Expressway Shooting", Chicago Sun-Times, Feb. 14, 1998, p. 1-2.

A New Gang Book in 2000:
The First Research-Based Gang Reader

There are a lot of "gang readers" on the market, and some are clearly better than others. Some have unique qualities, but all until this one were general collections, that typically included little new gang research. Most of the readers simply publish articles that have been previously published in journals, some of it very "dated" material.

What is unique about the book *Contemporary Gang Issues: An Inside View*, by Sandra S. Stone, is that its articles are all new and are all research based. What is also unique is that these various authors all worked on the same research project: thus, they had a research database in common to work from.

One of the most useful contributions in the new book by Stone is the article entitled "Bullying Behavior: An Invasion of Our Schools", by Shirley R. Holmes, Ph.D.. This article shows a consistent fact about the etiology of gang joining behavior: first a person in school is "bullied", and then, typically about a year later in grade school, himself makes the transition to being a "bully". Thus, the transition from bully-victim to bully-victimizer begins the behavioral roadmap that leads to gang membership.

How family dysfunction can account for the behavior of gang members is explored in the article by Jodet-Marie Harris, Ed.D., entitled "Family Dynamics: Gang Members Vs. Non-Gang Members". In this article Dr. Harris provides much new insight into how important family life is in the understanding of gang-joining behavior. Clearly, it provides much new evidence that the goal of gang prevention has a long way to go unless family conditions are addressed.

Clearly one of the most insightful pieces to emerge in years is the article by Alice P. Franklin Elder, Ph.D., entitled "Inside Gang Society: How Gang Memberss Imitate Legitimate Social Forms". In this article, Dr. Elder examines the gang in terms of an organizational analysis. The analysis reveals much in common between gangs and legitimate social forms with the obvious exception that gangs engage routinely in illegal activities.

Another article in this new book is entitled "Gang Activity in Juvenile Correctional Facilities: Security, Management and Treatment Challenges" and is one of the few pieces ever published on the subject of juvenile corrections from a research point of view. Further, it has the added value of offering advice to staff and administrators who work in the field of juvenile corrections on how to more effectively deal with the gang problem in juvenile correctional settings.

The book *Contemporary Gang Issues: An Inside View*, by Sandra S. Stone, Ph.D., 2000, ISBN 0-9665155-6-0, can be ordered from: New Chicago School Press, Inc, P.O. Box 929, Peotone, IL 60468.

BELOW: The Gangster Disciples at their peak level of organizational sophistication. Photo of the 1993 "Gangster Disciple" picnic held in Kankakee, Illinois. Elected politicians, some still in office, were present at this event which had a conspicuous "21st Century V.O.T.E." crowd - the political wing of the GDs.

Chapter 4

THE RACISM-OPPRESSION THESIS
FOR GANG ANALYSIS

INTRODUCTION

The serious reader of gang studies will sense that there is more than simple disagreement between some authors who have contributed to this line of inquiry. It is comparable in some sense to the more general question of does racism account for any variation in criminal justice outcomes, such as sentencing disparity, etc. This analysis, however, finds much historical continuity with regard to the linkages between factors related to racism and oppression and gangs in general.

The most complaints about this chapter come from white students, so a few words are in order here. First, this is a theoretical concept that is being explored and in the social scientific approach to finding solutions we must have an open mind about all logical possibilities. Secondly, this is not a line of argumentation that advances racial conflict or divisions, but rather brings the issue into the open light of public discussion; it is only how some react to this potential platform that might be a source of division, such as where the discussion prompts a person towards dogmatism by stating some over-generalization such as "all police are racists", etc. Thirdly, the evidence exists for this thesis and it deserves to be understood correctly, such as the fact that similar to

how the abused child without treatment reproduces this behavior by becoming a child abuser, the gang may arise and prosper during racial conflict but it also reproduces and exacerbates racial tensions.

Indeed there appears, at times, to be a striking, even ideological, difference between many authors in their basic orientations to the study of gangs. However, the astute observer will also find, upon much closer examination, that there are important conceptual continuities represented in the literature on gangs. One of these commonalities has to do with racial and ethnic conflict.[1] Racism can therefore be regarded as a factor causing the onset of gangs (Jackson and Mc Bride, 1990: pp. 8-9).

In short, there may be more consensus among gang researchers that we have previously been willing to recognize. This paper seeks to flush out one of these major commonalities in some detail. This cluster of related concepts will be called the racism-oppression thesis.

What it means for corrections personnel is that while no ACA[2] standards exist on programs for improving race relations within correctional facilities, we need to be keenly aware of the subtle nuances of race relations when gangs are organized along ethnic lines. What it means for modern law enforcement officers is that resolving racial and ethnic conflict must also be a goal within the context of community policing. Gang conflict often mirrors racial conflict, as is seen in violence that occurs in high schools. Also, contrary to some reports on gangs that see them as having predominantly conservative views, the view of the gang member may take on such a "world view" as to see larger society as a force that discriminates and oppresses along racial lines.[3] Some of the written gang constitutions typically contain such an "oppressed people" theme. Some recent research shows how racial beliefs are factors that vary significantly along the dimension of gang involvement.

OVERVIEW

The racism and oppression thesis basically holds that patterns of ethnic conflict and competition in America, the social structure and institutionalized patterns of race relations, the accommodation of poor and minority group members to an affluent society, and the individual experiences, patterns of enduring racial conflict, and perceptions of racism and oppression ---- all of these forms of social injustice, as objective and material conditions or as perceived by the individual, tend to be important causal determinants and reinforcing agents of gang delinquency and gang crime.

Indeed, there is some evidence, as shall be developed here, that the gang is a historically important and even contemporary apparatus through which racism is violently engendered, reinforced, and challenged at various levels (the community, prison, etc). The conservative reader will probably at this point conceive this to be a "no fault" conceptualization that relieves the individual gang member of social and moral responsibility. But that is not exactly correct. In fact, gang members may today be the leading cause of continuing racial violence in America; and certainly play a large role in "bias crimes".

Rather this is a more macro-analytic approach that focuses on larger issues and social forces beyond the level of the individual actor. These may not be things that can be easily or even ever controlled completely, but we need to be alert to these viewpoints.

ETHNIC HOMOGENEITY IN AMERICAN GANGS

A central axiom of the racism-oppression thesis is that institutionalized racism manifests itself in the context of deviance, delinquency, and criminality by the gang's tendency to be ethnically homogeneous. From a sociological viewpoint, gangs tend towards ethnocentrism --- the age-old concept of "ours is best, put down the rest".[4] However, there is an enduring and clear pattern of intellectual continuity in the identification of gangs as being ethnically homogeneous. This means that specific gangs more often than not consist of members who are predominantly of one racial or ethnic group.

That gangs are ethnically homogeneous has been cited by a number of authors over a long span of research and analysis (Thrasher, 1927; Thompson and Raymond, 1940; Bernard, 1949; MacIver, 1960; Gannon, 1967; Gordon, Short, Cartwright, and Strodtbeck, 1970; Hagedorn, 1988: p. 134; etc). As Suttles (1968) showed, African-Americans gangs had no members from other ethnic groups, while the other gangs tended to be predominantly of one or the other ethnic identification (1971, p. 164). This includes conflict along the dimensions of race, religion, ethnicity or nationality of origin (Asbury, 1927). It includes as Yablonsky points out, quoting from Thompson and Raymond (1940), certainly those gangs prior to the Prohibition Era being "classified by their national or racial antecedents" (1962, p. 116). It amounts to a kind of multiplicative relationship[5] between ethnicity and neighborhood ties: "The Irish controlled the West, and the East Side belonged to the Italians and the Jews" (Yablonsky, 1962: p. 116).

That gang crime involves conditions of competition and ethnic succession is also documented (Cloward and Ohlin, 1960: p. 200-202;) in the literature.

Earlier data from the Chicago Police Department on Chicago street gangs also shows this condition of ethnic homogeneity. Figure 4, below, shows this breakdown by gang and ethnicity. This excludes gangs listed as inactive. There are also various branches of the Disciples, Vice Lords, Latin Kings, and others in different areas of Chicago. Clearly, the vast majority of these major gangs operating in Chicago using official police statistics meet this criteria of being ethnically homogeneous.

Finally, we must take advantage of the rich detailed account provided by Thrasher (1927). Indeed, all of Chapter 10 in Thrasher's gang study involved this aspect of ethnic homogeneity and ethnic conflict via the gang. The historical change implied by this continuity of two such predominant factors that have appeared throughout the gang literature --- (1) the gang arising and persisting as a racially or ethnically homogeneous group, (2) in a depressed or inner city neighborhood: is social organization.

What has remained somewhat intact is that of social organization in the Chinese community, where their pattern of ethnic accommodation involves preserving traditions and local organization. It is the least changed in terms of ethnicity and inner city processes of ethnic succession and displacement. Thus, there has been a continuous gang problem dating back to the role of the Tongs over a hundred years ago.

Figure 4
Police Reports on Chicago Street Gang Membership

Gang Name	Racial Composition
**********	************************
Ambrose	98% Latin
Ashland Vikings	60% Puerto Rican, 35% Mexican, 5% white
Assyrian Eagles	100% Assyrian
Bishops	98% Latin
Black Eagles	100% Oriental
Black Gangster Disciples	99-100% Black
Black P Stone	100% Black
Black Souls	100% Black
Braizers	100% Mexican
C-Notes	90% white, 10% Latin
Cobra Stone	100% Black
Cullerton Boys/Duces	99% Latin, 1% white
Dragons	97% Puerto Rican, 2% Cuban, 1% white
Dueces (Insane)	70% Latin, 15% white, 15% Black
El Rukns	100% Black
Freaks	100% white
Gaylords	99% white
Ghetto Brothers Organ.	97% Latin, 2% Black, 1% white
Ghost Shadow	100% Oriental
Harrison Gents	70% Black, 30% Latin
Imperial Gangsters	90% Latin, 8% white, 2% Black
Kenmore Boys	90% white, 10% Latin
Kents/Stone Kents	100% Latin
Kool Gang	99% Black, 1% Latin & white
Latin Brothers	95% Latin, 5% white
Latin Counts	99% Mexican, 1% white
Latin Disciples	95% Latin, 3% Black, 2% white
Latin Eagles	80% Puerto Rican, 10% Mexican, 5% white, 5% Black
Latin Jivers	95% Puerto Rican, 5% Black
Latin Kings	90% Latin, 5% Black, 5% white
Latin Lovers	98% Latin, 5% Black, 5% white
Latin Saints	90% Latin, 10% white
Latin Souls	80% Latin, 15% white, 5% Black, 1% Arab
Orchestra Albany	95% Latin, 4% white, 1% Black
Paulina Barry Community	75% white, 22% Latin, 3% Black
Popes	95% White, 5% other
P.R. Stones	90% Latin, 5% white, 5% Black
Racine Boys	100% Latin
Reapers	50% white, 30% Latin, 20% Black
Uptown Rebels	100% white
Ridgeway Lords	White and Latin
Satan's Disciples	95% Latin, 5% white
Simon City Royals	97% White, 3% Black & Latin
Sin City Boys	97% Latin, 3% White & Black
Spanish Cobras	80% Latin, 18% white, 2% Black
Spanish Cobra Disciples	95% Latin, 5% white
Spanish Lords	90% Latin, 10% white
Tokers	100% Latin
Two-Six Nation	95% Latin, 5% white
Unknowns (Insane)	95% Latin, 5% Black & white
Vice Lords	100% Black
Villa Labos (Lone Wolves)	98% Latin, 2% white
Warlords	95% Latin, 5% Black & white

What changed in the 1960s was the civil rights movement and strengthened social organization among African-Americans. Latinos and Hispanics followed in this line of seeking ethnic parity. This backdrop provided an important historical opportunity for their representation among gang organizations as well. Along with equal opportunity to attend white schools came the equal opportunity to have your own gangs.[6] What was emancipated was social organization. Racial prejudice, discrimination, and oppression did not necessarily change drastically and certainly did not disappear.[7] When it does, however, and African-Americans and other persons of color are free to live wherever they want in America and have genuine educational opportunities, then perhaps we might see the emptying out of high rise ghetto buildings and inner city areas filled with the intergenerationally poor, and in so doing, removing one of the backbones that give rise to American street gangs.

HYBRID GANGS: BREAKING THE MOLD ON ETHNIC HOMOGENEITY

Hybrid gangs have arisen since the 1990's in many areas of the United States, particularly in smaller jurisdictions. What distinguishes these hybrid gangs is that they are multi-cultural, multi-racial, and often cut across all socio-economic classes. One expert on gangs in Florida, Det. Scott Lawson, sees these kind of gangs as a new model, something that can break all the stereotypes about gangs and race/ethnicity. The trend is certainly well documented, and to the extent that it is true, it could be viewed as a rival hypothesis to the racism-oppression thesis. This would be true because of the tendency towards heterogeneity in gang membership would erode any argument that gangs are forming because of perceived racism.

BIAS CRIMES IN THE GANG CONTEXT

From the most formative and early writers on American gangs comes the recognition of cases of bias crimes. While bias crimes were not formally recognized until the late 1980s[8], a bias crime involves simply bigotry towards race, ethnic, religious, or other (e.g., sexual preference) group attribute as the primary precipitating and motivational factor in the commission of a crime. That is to say, a person or group of persons are singled out because they have such an attribute (e.g., skin color, etc). This is most conspicuous when it involves acts of brutality involving white racism (Schwartz and Disch, 1970; Kovel, 1984). A neo-nazi skinhead spinoff gang group called the Bomber Boys, about ten years ago in Chicago, specialized in attacking homosexuals and African-

Americans on the near north side.

What has passed in our history as the recollection of "zoot suit" riots in California during W.W. II, was shown by Gonzalez (1981) to be little more than organized racist violence against any Mexican person. That is, a cultural difference of clothing or apparel (the "zoot suit" or "drapes") was a sufficient condition at the time to facilitate the social production of deviance; that is, whether they were or were not "gang" members, anyone wearing such apparel was automatically conceived to be a Mexican gang member.[9] And, often, whether they were or were not wearing such zoot suits when they met large angry mobs of military men on shore leave in California cities, they were still violently attacked if they were Mexican males.

There have been many variations on this theme, both here and abroad (Carey, 1985). Skinhead groups, neo-nazis, and other extremists (KKK) have figured prominently in this role. Suall and Lowe (1988) estimated only a couple hundred active skinheads in the USA, but that such "white power" groups may be growing.

RACIAL AND ETHNIC SLURS AS A CAUSAL VARIABLE IN GANG VIOLENCE

Racial tension as a provocation or precipitating factor in gang violence has been denied by Gannon's analysis involving a mail questionnaire approach with N = 80 gang outreach workers in New York City (see Gannon, 1970: p. 348). Yet the same research, curiously, showed that in 1964 among those factors cited by these gang outreach workers as "most often" being a factor related to group conflict, racial tension was the single largest factor most frequently reported as a precipitating factor of gang conflict (p. 347). This factor of racial tension was viewed as most often being a cause of, or being associated with, gang conflict by 45.3 percent of the detached workers responding to the survey. This was higher than for any other of the precipitating factors analyzed (drinking, girls, neighborhood group differences, individual reprisals, "sounding", price of liquor or drugs).

Yablonsky's (1962) ten hours of tape recordings with gang members was able to document the role of ethnic slurs and counter reaction as a prelude to gang conflict. This showed that "some boys used racial or ethnic discrimination as a reason" for intergang conflict (pp. 10-11).

RACE RELATIONS AND GANG PROBLEMS

Heavily influenced from the earlier research in Los Angeles showing similar conditions (Moore, 1978), the study by Hagedorn (1988) in Milwaukee was significant in contributing to the elements of analysis in the racism-oppression thesis. Denial and avoidance of the "race question" in gang research and analysis was ably demonstrated by Hagedorn (1988, p. 25). Some non-sociological or non-academic reports have simply taken the position of denying the significance of race and ethnicity.

Yet, if Hagedorn's thesis is correct regarding racial and ethnic subjugation, then confirmation comes from analyzing the differences in gang membership/structure during different periods of American history. Hagedorn's position regarding the etiology of Milwaukee's street gangs is that "gang formation took place in a context of continuing crisis in race relations" (1988, p. 50). The implication for the present would be, that those race and ethnic groups most subjected to racism and oppression (African-Americans, Latinos, American Indians[10], Asians,[11] etc) would be the most conspicuously represented in gang organization.[12] Similarly, those cities experiencing heightened levels of racial conflict would likewise be those more likely to show the stronger emergence of a gang problem.[13]

Racial and ethnic antagonisms were not born in the 1960s. Gangs have probably existed in America since the day America was first colonized. Thrasher's and Whyte's emphasis upon recent immigrants as a "feeder mechanism" for gangs can therefore be viewed not as the gang problem as originating among "aliens", but rather that these new immigrant groups represented the bottom of the social pyramid and faced harsh stigma --- because of their language, customs, cultural pattern/dress, etc.[14]

The Rodney King case provides another example of how a crisis in race relations can provide the ideal setting for the onset of serious gang violence and civil disorder. That gangs in Los Angeles were heavily involved in the rioting during 1992 is not to say they were the only ones involved. In conditions of civil disorder, the rule of law disappears and the only rule is that of force. Gangs and gang members obviously benefited after the rioting as well by the declarations, demands, and massive media coverage. Unfortunately no government agency has declared war on the race relations problem in America.

The continuing problems of race relations are to be found throughout the United States. In seeing the rise of the "cool pose" behavior typifying a crisis in manhood development which they go on to say provides the fertile ground for gang behavior as well, Majors and Mancini (1992) state:

"We are concerned with how some black males use coolness to counter the stresses of oppression...People of all racial...groups use cool behaviors to some extent. However, because of the legacy of slavery and because black males in the United States have been subjected to systematic discrimination...we suspect cool behaviors have emerged with more frequency and intensity among low income black males than in other groups (Majors and Mancini, 1992: p. xii)".

GANGS ON THE INDIAN RESERVATION

Native American Indians were the subject of intentional policies of genocide by the American government. Their lands have been taken from them, and they were placed on Indian reservations. In the 1980's and 1990's a new type of oppression had hit the "Res": gangs.

The modern "Res" is a place of continuing poverty where one can readily find the gamut of problems of social disorganization[15].

Gangs from large cities, Crips, Latin Kings, etc, found a brand new "ready made" type of youth for their membership: Native American Indian youths. It brought a new type of war to the "Res". It brought a new contagion as well. Today, it is unlikely that any "Res" does not have a gang problem at some level.

"A New Breed of Warriors: The Emergence of American Indian Youth Gangs", by Julie A. Hailer and Cynthia Baroody Hart, Journal of Gang Research, Volume 7, Number 1, Fall, 1999, pp. 23-33.

In their study of American Indian youth gangs, Hailer and Hart (1999) had hypothesized that they would find gangs on larger Indian reservations such as the Navajo Nation (N=190,000), the Puyallap Nation (N = 150,000), and the Cheyene/Arapaho Nation (N = 165,000). They did find such gangs in support of their hypothesis. But they also found gangs operating in much "smaller reservations such as Hannahville, MI (population 500); Bois Forte, MN (population 800); Nisqually, WA (population 400), and the Ak-Chin (population 573)" (Hailer and Baroody, 1999: p. 26).

ADULT PARTICIPATION AS AN INDICATOR OF MINORITY GROUP OPPRESSION

A second theme generated from Hagedorn is that adult participation in gang crime has as a fundamental cause "drastically changed economic conditions in poor minority urban neighborhoods" (1988, p. 111). Campbell (1984) came close to suggesting something compatible here, in the sense that the estrangement of the underclass, their detachment, their displacement, their disassociation, etc, ---- whatever we want to call it, has something to do with gang affiliation. In Campbell's view, those persons who join a gang are the same persons who have the least to gain from the status quo (p. 236). As will be seen in chapter 5, addressing the concepts of underclass,

surplus population, and human capital, this experience need not be an objective material condition --- it can also be a perception.[16] As Short and Strodtbeck note, gang members certainly express a feeling of deprivation (1974, p. 126).

RUMORS HEIGHTEN THE ANTAGONISM

Suttles (1968) showed that racial bias and racial fears were important ideological components of the content of rumors at the community level.[17] "Every spring for example, there were several rumors which preceded the closing of school: for instance, the Negroes are going to cause a riot in the Italian section, or vice versa" (Suttles, 1968: p. 197). If the Kerner commission, studying civil disturbances in the 1960s, was any indication; then rumors play an important role in the onset of conflict.

The Kerner report (Wicker, 1968) documented the historical role that rumor has played in racial strife in America. This included the 1917 race riot in East St. Louis: as several white men worried about the threat of African-Americans to their job security and status "were leaving City Hall, they heard that a Negro had accidentally shot a white man during a holdup. In a few minutes rumor had replaced fact: the shooting was intentional --- a white woman had been insulted --- two white girls were shot. By this time 3,000 people had congregated and were crying for vengeance. Mobs roamed the streets, beating Negroes. Policemen did little more than take the injured to hospitals and disarm Negroes" (pp. 217-218).

Rumors played such a large part in civil disturbances, that some law enforcement agencies such as in Chicago established rumor control centers "where individuals who hear rumors can call to find out what is actually happening. These centers have proved to be highly effective" (Revere, 1982: p. 301). Such rumor control "hotlines" were also used during the 1993 federal trial involving the Rodney King case.

In 1992 a "memorandum" became widely circulated throughout the African-American community of Chicago. To the casual observer it was real, or you wanted to believe it at least. It as a memorandum from the Ku Klux Klan, only it was spelled "Klu Klux Klan". It thanked gang members for their good work in killing Black people and encouraged them to "keep it up". It was later revealed that this was a moral joke played by an activist minister.

In early September, 1993, in Chicago another underground communication was quickly spread by fax machine --- the infamous "Lights Out" memorandum. It was believed by so many that it was often retyped by the recipient and spread rapidly throughout the city to all races, and all sectors. The present author received four versions, each produced by a different typewriter or printer. This memo panicked the city until a local television station revealed it to be a rumor gone astray. Here is the text of the memo:

"BEWARE!! There is a New "Gang Initiation". This new gang initiation of murder is brought about by Gang Members driving around at night with their car lights off. When you flash your car lights to signal them that their lights are out, the Gang Members take it literally as "LIGHTS OUT", so they are to follow you to your destination and kill you! That's their initiation. Two families have already fallen victim to this initiation ritual. Be aware and inform your families and friends. DO NOT FLASH YOUR CAR LIGHTS FOR ANYONE!!"

It was a hoax. But it showed how the public can panic and take these rumors as genuine truth: the element of fear takes over, the ordinary person wants to believe gangs are capable of such evil. The "Lights Out" memo was posted in colleges, in government offices, in businesses, and handed out in churches throughout Chicago until it was revealed about a week later as a hoax.

White racist groups are experts as trying to spread such rumors in their organizing efforts (see Ridgeway, 1990). It could have very well been such a source for the related "gang panic" rumor that spread rapidly through the sororities of the University of Illinois at Champaign in the fourth week of September, 1993. The gang rumor being spread was that a new gang initiation rite involved gangs sexually assaulting female students, and leaving a gang "brand" on the body of African-American co-eds. Computer bulletin boards are sometimes the source of such rumors.

THE RURAL-URBAN DIFFERENCE

William Kornblum's <u>Blue Collar Community</u> (1974) was a study of Chicago's southside steel mills. Kornblum lived in the area and worked in the steel mill during the period of study. While contributing much to the understanding of urban ethnicity, this study also documented conflict in the steel mills between African-Americans regarding gang affiliation. The basic difference was the that between the younger African-American male socialized in the urban setting, and often having a gang affiliation, and that of the rural older African-American (1974, p. 45). It was a "dimension of cleavage" (p. 45) and a source of "tension and disunity" (P. 48).

Importantly, in the "neutral turf" of the work place, "gang membership itself does not cause visible tension between members of rival gangs who work in the mill" (p. 48). Each gang would put its slogans and epithets on the bathroom walls.

Logically, however, while gangs in America have traditionally been studied as an urban phenomenon, it is equally possible to have gangs in rural areas and smaller cities.[18] That is, if the racism-op-

pression thesis is correct, such wider societal and social structural forces operate to impact equally strong outside of urban areas. These forces therefore could also play a part in the emergence of gangs outside of urban areas.

GANGS AS VEHICLES OF ETHNIC CONFLICT

Do white gangs function as surrogate defenders for the status quo of ensuring the continuity of racial segregation? Is the gang in American cities the contemporary vehicle through which ethnic rivalry is concentrated? Are white gangs the modern violent defenders of "ethnic purity"? These are research agenda items for future criminologists. For now we must speculate only towards their affirmation.

But first, it bears repeating that many skinhead and almost all neo-nazi and white racist groups can be classified logically as gangs using our definition of gang: it is a group that benefits from the continuing criminal activity of its members. The crimes in these instances may not be drug sales income, but are rather ideological crimes, that is bias crimes, offenses that reinforce their ideology. They benefit as well because such crimes occur in a group context, more often than not, and this is a mechanism for building greater solidarity among such group members.

Within the realm of "White Racist Extremist Gangs" (WREGs), there is much variation in organizational sophistication for these various groups. However, some of the Level One WREGs can in fact be suppressed almost completely by means of aggressive policing and prosecution. One example would be the group that earned its place in history by trying to "March on Skokie": the National Socialist Party of America (NSPA), led by nazi Frank Collin. Collin amassed a lot of followers in his one group based in Marquette Park on Chicago's southwest side. But when Collin was arrested and convicted of having sex with young underage boys not only was his image as a "tough nazi" tarnished, he went to state prison and was never heard of again acting out his "tough nazi" routine; this was coupled with some federal convictions for firearms violations for nazi's right under Collin, resulting in basically the complete effective suppression of this nazi gang. Suppression does work is the lesson of history: it works most effectively on lower level gangs who cannot "regain momentum" after a successful prosecution. Another example would be the Level One WREG called "White War Commission", basically consisting of a handful of hardcore neo-nazis, who caused more than their share of negative community impact in terms of their attacks on Jewish synagogues.[19]

That American race relations shifted from conflict to competition was demonstrated in the work of Wilson (1978[20]). But was some segment of the conflict modality then shifted to a less conspicuous form such as in the gang subculture is the question raised here? The continuing historical pattern of ethnic homogeneity among American gangs is of some import. As a struggle over power, privilege and resources, the gang is a natural combat force readily employed in this struggle to maintain or challenge the status quo. Any community has "plausible deniability": it was only the gang, it was not "us".

Terrorism was directed against African-Americans in the form of mob lynchings well up through the time of Thrasher's and Whyte's research. As Raper (1933: p. 1) documented, between the period of 1889 and 1930 at least 3,724 people were put to death by mob lynchings in the United States. We can correctly assume that much of this was directed at racial and ethnic minorities. According to Scwhartz and Disch (1970, p. 29), in fact, there were 3,811 African-Americans lynched between the period 1889 to 1940. When you can be lynched for attempting to vote, you do not develop a community infrastructure with social organizations allowing for political control and access to scarce resources. It is hard to develop a "tong" or protective society or gang that is conspicuous under such conditions of overtly targeted violence and repression.

Returning to the work of Thrasher (1927, Chapter 10), we find that only 7.16 percent of the 880 gangs about which ethnicity was known involved African-Americans. The rest were of a wide variety of white-ethnic groups, and they were all in this sense homogeneous with respect to skin color. Antagonistic relations between various white ethnic groups were "carried over into gangs and color many of their conflicts in Chicago" (Thrasher, 1968: p. 133). Indeed, "among the most bitter of these intercultural enmities transplanted from the old world is that between Jews and the Poles" (p. 133). Pogroms in Europe had their parallel forms with American gangs in cities like Chicago.

The infamous "march on Skokie" by a neo-nazi group in the 1970s had its equivalent form involving gang members in Thrasher's account of anti-semitism (pp. 134-135) in Chicago (Knox, 1976). Random violence, conflict at the mode of consumption and in recreational areas was common. And it was reciprocal ethnic antagonism, prejudice, discrimination and bias crime. Jewish gangs found their sport in the "Polock hunt" (p. 135). What Thrasher documented beyond gang activity was the important historical process of community change involving the "process of invasion and succession" (p. 137). Dating back over a hundred years ago, one ethnic gang would inevitably dissolve by its ethnic groups displacement to the arriving newcomers to the neighborhood, and the "new kids on the block" would

emulate the social organizational infrastructure they were exposed to, and develop their own ethnic gang.

Another important contribution from Thrasher that seems to have been missed throughout all subsequent discussions involving gang analysis, is that of race riots and the gangs (Thrasher, 1968: pp. 139-140). Clearly, Thrasher documents that white gangs were heavily involved throughout the 1919 race rioting in Chicago. "Gangs and their activities were an important factor throughout the riot. But for them it is doubtful if the riot would have gone beyond the first clash" (p. 140). These white gangs operated to perform bias crimes against African-Americans "without hindrance from the police" and quoting a judge Thrasher also noted "they (the gang members) seemed to think they had a sort of protection which entitled them to go out and assault anybody. When the race riots occurred it gave them something to satiate the desire to inflict their evil propensities on others" (p. 140).

Thrasher documents the rise of Chinese gangs, or "tongs" meaning protective society, in response to their victimization from white racism (pp. 144-149). Thrasher's (1927) chapter 10 should be required reading for everyone because of its richness of details about ethnic conflict, the culture complex (p. 149), the cultural frontier and oppression psychosis (pp. 152-153), and Thrasher's conclusion that the base "problem is one of reconciling these divergent heritages with each other and with America. If there has been any failure here, it can hardly be laid at the door of the immigrant" (p. 154).

IMPORTATION THEORY AND THE SPECIAL CASE OF THE ARYAN BROTHERHOOD

Importation theory relates to the correctional institution and how gangs came to have such a large and conspicuous presence in jails, correctional institutions, and prisons. It basically means the gang members were "imported" into the correctional milieu through aggressive "gang targeting" prosecution efforts. In other words, the more gang members were prosecuted, the more they were represented in the prison system.

Clearly, in the 1960s and 1970s those gangs most targeted for prosecution in American cities were not white gangs. They were minority member gangs. It came as no surprise that minority gangs were heavily represented in America's prison system. In fact, the racial composition of the American prison population has changed most dramatically since the time of Thrasher (1927). In 1927, only 21 percent of the inmates admitted to state and federal prisons were Black; this figure has steadily increased since 1927, to the point where by 1986 the proportion for Blacks had reached 44 percent[21]. Similar trends have been noted in the juvenile correctional population.

But did the Aryan Brotherhood fit the same pattern of being imported into the prison? Most suspect not. That is, AB's were not imported, at first, directly; even though, today, through transfers we find AB's in various correctional institutions. Some critical observers have taken the position that it was an invention fostered by correctional staff to "counter balance" the threat of disorder represented by minority gangs. The indigenous formation view is that the white inmates themselves entered into a gang formation that did not exist outside of the correctional institution because of the need to maintain parity in group power.[22] White inmates simply developed their own patterns of group cooperation to maintain such parity with other forces inside the correctional institution. This seems the most plausible explanation rather than believing the "conspiracy theory" that "white gangs" were artificially created. It is not easy to artificially create a gang. Even though, it can, technically, be done.

The existence of large numbers of juvenile correctional institutions reporting the existence of separate white gangs in their facilities, often skin heads, tends to suggest the possibility that such groups functioned outside of corrections and may have in fact been imported. Remember, if law enforcement is effective, or if correctional officials have to transfer gang members, then importation occurs.

What we do know about adult institutions is that "the phenomenon of racism is fierce inside prisons and gangs usually organize along racial lines" (Camp and Camp, 1985: p. viii). We also know that about half of all juvenile institutions in America report a problem with racial conflict; those who have problems of racial conflict in corrections generally are those same institutions more likely to report a gang problem as well.

An assessment of the research at this point must conclude that white extremist gangs are to be found throughout the United States. This includes skinheads and "A.B.'s" in many adult and juvenile correctional institutions. The recent work of Hamm (1993) views such bias crimes as racial terrorism and regards such groups as terrorist youth subcultures. The importance of preventing such domestic terrorism requires, according to Hamm, several recommendations: "Boycotting White Power Rock...Expanded Litigation Against Publishers of Racist Literature...Conservative Gun Control Legislation...Standards for Responsible Media Coverage" and research (Hamm, 1993: 219-220). The bottom line here is that skinheads who commit bias crimes are a gang, just as the KKK is a gang: they may not be on the street corner selling drugs, but they benefit from violating laws nevertheless. It is a mistake to simply regard them as "hate groups". Hating is not a crime. Putting hate into action in the

context of racial violence is a crime. The "benefit" may not be financial, it may be ideological. But it is a crime pattern all the same[23].

What will also emerge from national data is that wherever correctional institutions report a gang problem, they also tend to report a problem of racial conflict among inmates as well. This is a very consistent research finding in many contexts including schools.

VARIANCE IN CRIMINAL JUSTICE SYSTEM CONDITIONS AND OUTCOMES RELATED TO RACE AND ETHNICITY

Short and Strodtbeck (1965, pp. 224,258) estimated that for African-American gang boys their probability of an arrest for offenses related to violence are about .04 --- that is, in only 4 cases out of one hundred would the offense result in an arrest. Indeed, they argue for the more sophisticated or experienced offender this probability may be cut in half to 2%. However, does it make a difference if these are "Black on Black" crimes of violence, or if the victim is white? Such is an issue that must be resolved, empirically, regarding the racial oppression thesis.

Official data on homicides in Chicago for the year 1989 bears some relationship here. For the 480 African-American male offenders there were 353 victims, and only 21 of these victims were not cases of "Black on Black" crime (Chicago Police Department, 1989 Murder Analysis, p. 19). From the same report, among the 187 unsolved murders, there were 4 female whites and 18 male whites (p. 21), the other victims were persons of color.

MINORITY GROUP REPRESENTATION WITHIN THE RANKS OF CRIMINAL JUSTICE PERSONNEL

The 1964 Civil Rights Act gave minority group members a chance to begin working in law enforcement, corrections, probation and parole, and related criminal justice positions. This act required criminal justice agencies to have an affirmative action program to ensure that minority group members were adequately represented in these various governmental positions. It means recruiting from minority groups and having "policies and procedures protecting minorities from racial and sexual harassment" (Klofas, Stojkovic, and Kalinich, 1990: p. 20). Thus, simply hiring minority group members at the lowest echelon or entry level position is not enough. There must be a fair opportunity for advancement within the organization and there must be an atmosphere free of racism.

Regarding corrections alone, according to the 1987 Sourcebook of Criminal Justice Statistics published by the U.S. Department of Justice, Bureau of

Justice Statistics, 1,118 of the 7,076 employees of the State adult correctional institutions in Illinois were African-American (p. 37). Another 316 of the 854 employees of in community-based facilities were African-American (p. 37). Yet it is difficult to say that the institutional employee capability to relate to the inmate population along racial and ethnic lines holds when 15.7 percent of the prison personnel are African-American and over 60 percent of the inmates are African-American. This is a growing gap.

A report published by the American Correctional Association in 1988 showed that while African-Americans are 12 percent of the American census population, they constitute almost 50 percent of the prison population nationwide (Petersilia and Turner, 1988: p. 92).[24] Oddly, in Illinois, while whites constitute only about a third of the prison population, whites also receive over half (55%) of the placements in the community-based facilities in Illinois (see Table 6.62, p. 635, Sourcebook of Criminal Justice Statistics, 1988).[25]

In July of 1993 a class action lawsuit was brought against the U.S. Federal Bureau of Prisons by some 4,300 of its Black employees[26]. The law suit charges the federal prison system with discrimination in terms of promotions. About 18 percent of the federal prison system employees are Blacks, but few Blacks actually hold higher management positions.

That there exists evidence of institutional racism at various levels in the criminal justice system is felt apparently by some. Because of this, clearly our society must do more to encourage and cultivate minority representation within the corrections and criminal justice field. To conclude otherwise is to deny some important truths that must be faced. The point here is that this means not simply the treatment of those adjudicated and confined in custody, it also means hiring and promotion opportunities for minorities within this field. Clearly, much progress remains to be made in this area.

THE RELATED ISSUE OF THE DUAL LABOR MARKET

The dual labor market hypothesis basically argues that in American society our legitimate occupational opportunity system can be divided into two broad, but very different, categories: the competitive sector, and the monopoly sector. In the competitive sector, these are jobs with little potential for advancement, low pay, low job security, low benefits, and low prestige (e.g., burger flopper jobs at fast food restaurants). In the monopoly sector, these are jobs with high security, high pay, many benefits, and more prestige (banking industry, etc).

Crutchfield (1989) using Seattle, Washington census tract data and annual police reports showed some support for the dual labor market hypothesis where labor instability was found to be associated with violent crime rates. This is a critical issue in criminology. It is more directly related to the issue of the underclass, the surplus population, and human capital factors that are emerging as significant factors in gang research. This issue will be addressed in much greater detail in Chapter 5. But to the extent that it becomes the vehicle through which racial differences emerge in society, then it too must be taken into account for providing such an analysis of the racism-oppression thesis.

To test the racism-oppression thesis one cannot simply go to a correctional facility and ask the inmates if they believe that the reason they have a criminal record is because this is a racist society. That is not the best manner in which to test the racism-oppression thesis. Many so affected may not simply understand the larger societal processes. This is an area best suited for macrosociological analysis, not the individual level of analysis. Provided below is an effort that uses American juvenile correctional institutions as the unit of analysis.

CRIPS: ARISING IN A CONTEXT OF CONFLICT

If we believe the public relations imagery of more educated members of the Crip gangs, as in the story Monster, then we would believe that the gang was basically formed in response to institutionalized racism. Actually there are a number of rival explanations for how the Crips began, the five most common being: (1) They adopted their title from the TV movie series "Tales From The Crypt" starring Vincent Price to be "scary" in a tinsel town; (2) Some early members were suffered injuries to the legs, rendering them handicapped, the word "cripple" then being shortened to "crips"; (3) One phonetic explanation is that the Crips sprang from an actual group called the "Cribs" who were themselves the surviving influence of the Slauson street gang which dates to the earlier 1960s; (4) Another phonetic explanation is that "Crips" became the phonetic spelling of "krypts" the personified version of "kryptonite", which kills Superman, that is, the term simply was adopted to imply a powerful image; and (5) That youths were actually politically active in a protest orientation and that the very word Crip was an acronym that meant "Common Revolution In Progress".

About all anyone agrees in the facts about the origins of the Crips is the issue of when they were first brought to the attention of the criminal justice system. It was in 1969 that the Crips first got such attention. It was fighting behavior in Washington High School that got the Crips noticed.

RACIAL DIFFERENCES NOT RACIAL OPPRESSION

The issue is whether some gangs are simply different by the type of motivating force they have. One of the classic dichotomy's in any introduction to psychology course discussing motivation is the difference between expressive versus instrumental. In the expressive version of a gang, it is motivated by social and not economic concerns. In the instrumental version of a gang, it is motivated primarily by money making concerns.

Some authors have suggested this concept applies to modern gangs including the Crips and Bloods compared with Hispanic/Latino gangs. One in this line has interpreted differences in homicide rates among Chicago gangs to conclude that predominantly African-American gangs like the Vice Lords and Gangster Disciples were more likely to commit homicides because of money making concerns; while Hispanic/Latin gangs like the Latin Kings and the Latin Disciples were more likely to commit homicides because of expressive concerns like turf defense (Block and Block, 1993: p. 8).

This would appear to be reductionism or an over simplification of the gang reality. To extend it to its logical extreme, such a comparison between African-Americans and Hispanics would be arguing that one racial group has a monopoly on a human motivation. It would also, logically, be assuming equal variances in the extent to which gang members join a gang for chiefly economic reasons. It would also, logically, be assuming a lot more about racial differences than would appear to be justified by data.

But such overgeneralizations are easy to make about gangs as has been noted earlier in this book. We have not yet seen much empirical research on gang economic issues. What we do know from the literature is that such an expressive-instrumental classification is probably a fallacy even in Chicago. The work of Padilla shows Latin gangs are clearly concerned with making money too. But to future research, some of which is now underway, we can add these empirical questions to settle this issue: are there more ballers and high rollers in African-American gangs than in Latino/Hispanic gangs, that is those who are gang members because they are making money at it; are African-American gangs more dog city than Latino/Hispanic gangs, that is they are working for the money; are there differences by ethnic gangs in terms of making ends in the gang, that is making money in the gang; are African-Americans the only gang members trying to get their thirties on, that is making money selling drugs; are there differences by racial gangs in terms of living large, that is being able to make money and live a pseudo-wealthy lifestyle? These hypotheses have not been tested yet in the literature.

THE RACISM-GANG PROBLEM: A PRELIMINARY TEST

The gang problem appears to have some relationship to the problem in race relations as well. That adult prison disturbances have had racial overtones has been previously reported in the literature. Less is known about the juvenile context of this same problem. What is known is that in recent years the percentage of Black and Hispanic youths has increased over 30 percent among children in custody (Snyder, 1990).

Our question to juvenile correctional administrators was "are racial conflicts a problem among juveniles in your facility?". Some 155 institutions are included in this sample representing 49 states.[27] The findings show that nearly half (47.4%) indicated this was true. That some environments can foster a destructive demeanor appears to have some empirical support at least when examining this factor of racial conflict in relationship to reports of property damage, overcrowding, and recidivism.[28]

This factor of racial conflict is shown to significantly differentiate any extent of gang member damage to government property as seen in Table 1 below. This means that where a juvenile institution has a problem of racial conflict the chances are increased of having a problem of gangs damaging government property in the same institution.

TABLE 1
FREQUENCY DISTRIBUTION OF
RACIAL CONFLICT BY REPORT OF
GANG DAMAGE TO GOVERNMENT PROPERTY

		GANG DAMAGE TO GOVT. PROPERTY	
		NO	YES
RACIAL CONFLICT PROBLEM:	NO	51	26
	YES	20	52

Chi square = 22.05, p < .001

Also, overcrowding is shown to be significantly associated with racial conflict as seen in Table 2. This means those juvenile correctional institutions that are overcrowded are those more likely to report a problem of racial conflict.

TABLE 2
FREQUENCY DISTRIBUTION OF REPORTS
OF OVERCROWDING IN JUVENILE
INSTITUTIONS
BY REPORTS OF RACIAL CONFLICT

	Reported Racial Conflict	
	NO	YES
OVERCROWDING PROBLEM:		
NO	45	25
YES	31	48

Chi square = 9.4, p = .002

The reports of racial conflict in juvenile institutions appear to be associated with the problem of high recidivism rates as well. Table 3 shows the distribution for reported racial conflict by whether the same institutions also reported a recidivism rate higher than twenty percent. This means those juvenile institutions with racial conflicts are more likely to have higher recidivism rates.

TABLE 3

DISTRIBUTION OF RACIAL CONFLICT BY REPORTS OF HIGH RECIDIVISM RATES

		Recidivism Higher Than 20%	
		NO	YES
Reports of Racial Conflict	NO	47	26
	YES	34	39

Chi square = 4.6, p = .03

There is a need for standards to govern the handling of gangs within correctional settings and to address the matter of racial conflict. But these have not been forthcoming from the American Correctional Association in spite of its recognized ability to generate standards for just about every other aspect of care, treatment, process, and human behavior.

HOW PESSIMISTIC RACIAL BELIEFS VARY WITH HAVING EVER TRIED TO QUIT THE GANG AMONG A LARGE SAMPLE OF GANG MEMBERS

Gang members generally are more likely to have beliefs that exemplify a problem in relating to other races, particularly whites. Further, this appears to vary consistently along the dimensions of the gang risk continuum. The gang risk continuum represents the extent to which one is involved with gangs.

The data analyzed here come from a recent larger study of gangs and guns.[29] This data represents a large sample of criminal gang members surveyed in the midwest in the summer of 1994. The gang members are combined from four different social contexts: eight jails, a high school, a probation program, and an innercity social services program.

What this data shows is that the more hard core gang member has a significantly higher distrust of white persons. The survey question asked them to agree or disagree with the statement "It is usually a mistake to trust a white person". Among those who had tried to quit the gang, some 23.5 percent agreed. Among those who had never attempted to quit the gang, some 44.4 percent agreed. The significant difference here is shown in Table 4 below.

TABLE 4

FREQUENCY DISTRIBUTION OF BELIEFS ABOUT WHITE PEOPLE BY WHETHER THE PERSON HAS EVER ATTEMPTED TO QUIT THE GANG AMONG A SAMPLE OF MIDWEST GANG MEMBERS

		Ever Attempt to Quit The Gang?	
		NO	YES
It is usually a mistake to trust a white person.	AGREE	105	48
	DISAGREE	131	156

Chi-square = 21.1, p < .001

There are many white people who are not prejudiced.	AGREE	154	164
	DISAGREE	83	44

Chi-square = 10.4, p = .001

The findings about the more pessimistic views on race relations among the more hard core gang member (i.e., the ones who have never tried to quit the gang), shows that the stronger the commitment to the gang, the more the same person distrusts white people and views white people as prejudiced. This shows that among those who had never attempted to quit the gang some 64.9 percent agreed that there are many white people who are not prejudiced, compared to 78.8 percent among those who had tried to quit the gang. Clearly, it is the more committed the person is to the gang as measured by having never attempted to quit the gang, the more the same person has pessimistic racial beliefs about white people.

SUMMARY AND CONCLUSION

What has been so obvious, on a closer examination of the gang literature, is the undeniable fact that racism has played an important role in the onset and persistence of American gangs according to many authors.[30] This implies, also, that gangs will exist as long as ethnic or racial oppression exists. For poor whites in gangs this is less a matter of their ethnic or racial subjugation than it may be their competitive relationship with minorities in a context of mutually disagreeable economic conditions; particularly in social and human capital development terms.

In short, there is reason to believe historically that an important condition that fuels both the onset and persistence of gangs is that related to the racial-oppression hypothesis. It is remarkably predictive in the correctional setting, the educational setting, and the community setting. Research on juvenile correctional institutions shows where we have a gang problem in terms of damage to government property we also have high reports of the incidence of racial conflict.

Perhaps, then, from a larger point of view one method of dealing with gangs would be a strategy that involves improving race relations generally. Just as a sense of good will must be developed with inmates, such a network of interracial "good will" among correctional inmates could be an important factor in limiting the potentially destructive influences of gangs in our prisons today. That racial conflict among inmates in American correctional institutions is now becoming shown to be a very large problem. It simply reflects the enduring pattern of ethnic rivalry and ethnic antagonism and racial discrimination that is often at the base of much of the gang problem in America[31].

Unfortunately the strained race relations we have in our prisons and jails are only a reflection of the same problem in the outside surrounding communities. The escalation of racism and racial conflict will mean the escalation of the gang violence problem, because gangs step in to act as the power brokers in such conflict, and out of fear, others join the gangs of their particular ethnic and racial composition.

Discussion Questions:

(1) Can a peace treaty between gangs of only one ethnic group really be expected to solve the "gang violence problem"? Could such peace treaties, if they involved the entire "rainbow", eventually lead to the absence of a gang crime problem?

(2) Racial conflicts in high schools and other contexts can be the catalysts for deadly gang violence. What should be done to reduce racial tension?

(3) Can riots in the atmosphere of racial injustice be expected to be even more violent when a strong gang presence also exists in the same community?

RECOMMENDED READINGS

Breed, Allen F.
   1990 "America's Future: The Necessity of Investing in Children", <u>Corrections Today</u> (February): pp. 68-72.
Camp, George and Camille Graham Camp
   1985 <u>Prison Gangs: Their Extent, Nature, and Impact on Prisons</u>. Washington, D.C.: U.S. Dept. of Justice.
Crutchfield, Robert D.
   1989 "Labor Stratification and Violent Crime", <u>Social Forces</u> (68)(2): 489-512.
Fong, Robert S.

   1990 "The Organizational Structure of Prison Gangs: A Texas Case Study", <u>Federal Probation</u> (Mar): 36-43.
Knox, George W.; David Laske; and Edward D. Tromanhauser
   1992 <u>Schools Under Siege</u>. Dubuque, IA: Kendall-Hunt Publishing Company.
Kornblum, William
   1974 <u>Blue Collar Community</u>. Chicago: University of Chicago Press.
Kovel, Joel
   1984 <u>White Racism</u>. New York: Columbia University Press.
Linster, Richard L.; Pamela K. Lattimore; and Christy A. Visher
   1990 <u>Predicting the Recidivism of Serious Juvenile Offenders</u> National Institute of Justice Discussion Paper, Washington, D.C.
Perkins, Useni Eugene
   1987 <u>Explosion of Chicago's Black Street Gangs</u>. Chicago: Third World Press.
Petersilia, Joan and Susan Turner
   1988 "Minorities in Prison: Discrimination or Disparity?", <u>Corrections Today</u> (June).
Rader, Arthur F.
   1933 <u>The Tragedy of Lynching</u>. University of North Carolina Press.
Ridgeway, James
   1990 <u>Blood in the Face: The Ku Klux Klan, Aryan Nations, Nazi Skinheads, and the Rise of a New White Culture</u>. New York: Thunder's Mouth Press.
Schwartz, Barry N. and Robert Disch
   1970 <u>White Racism</u>. New York: Dell Publishing Co.
Smith, Melinda
   1990 "New Mexico Youths Use Mediation to Settle Their Problems Peacefully", <u>Corrections Today</u> (June): 112-114.
Snyder, Howard N.
   1990 <u>Growth in Minority Detentions Attributed to Drug Law Violaters</u>. OJJDP Update on Statistics. U.S. Department of Justice, Office of Justice Programs, Office of Juvenile Justice and Delinquency Prevention. Juvenile Justice Bulletin. Washington, D.C. (March).
Suttles, Gerald D.
   1968 <u>The Social Order of the Slum</u> Chicago: University of Chicago Press.
Vigil, James Diego and Steve Chong Yun
   1990 "Vietnamese Youth Gangs in Southern California", pp. 146-162, Chapter 7 in C. Ronald Huff (ed.), <u>Gangs in America</u>, Newbury Park: Sage Publications.
Wilson, William J.
   1987 <u>The Truly Disadvantaged</u>. Chicago: University of Chicago Press.

HOW MANY GANG MEMBERS ARE THERE IN THE UNITED STATES?

Our best estimate is that we can simply multiply the official federal government estimates by a factor of three to arrive at what the National Gang Crime Research Center believes is closer to the truth. The source of the information described here was: The 1996 National Law Enforcement Gang Analysis Survey.

The survey asked the responding agencies to estimate the total core and periphery gang membership in their jurisdiction. Data on this variable was available for N = 229 jurisdictions. The results ranged from a low of zero such local gang members to a high of 6,000 gang members. Overall, a grand total sum of N = 34,506 gang members were indicated in this sample.

The way to put the local gang member population into a more meaningful perspective is in comparison with two other variables: (1) the total number of sworn police officers in the same jurisdiction, and (2) the total civilian population in the same jurisdiction.

First, gang members outnumber municipal police officers by a factor of 2.3 to 1 is the finding of this research. This is very much consistent with previous research results along the same lines by the NGCRC.

Secondly, gang members in relationship as a component of the overall civilian population gives additional and interesting insight into the size of the gang member population in the USA today. Gang members in this sample constituted .005 percent of the overall civilian population. Thus, about 5 in every 1,000 civilians is a gang member is another way of expressing this finding. Given the extent to which large urban areas like Chicago, New York, and Los Angeles were not represented in the current sample, and rather the random sample does in fact contain many smaller towns and cities instead, it is reasonable to assume this figure of national gang density in the civilian at-large population (this excludes the number of gang members in prison, conservatively estimated to be 20% in the 1995 national survey of prison wardens, however the mean for juvenile facilities is closer to 50%) is also a conservative estimate.

If we extrapolate this parameter of .005 percent to the overall U.S. census population, we get an estimate of over a million gang members in the U.S. today that are on the streets. Add another 200,000 known to be in correctional custody, and we get the figure of about 1.5 million for the best estimate of the total American gang population in 2000[32]. This is far above FBI estimates and previous federally funded gang research.

End Notes:

[1] And, of course, with institutionalized racism (see Perkins, 1987).

[2] The American Correctional Association (ACA) is the professional membership society --- the largest of its type in the world --- which sets operating standards for jails, juvenile institutions, prisons, halfway houses, etc. To use an analogy, the ACA is to corrections in America what the AMA is to healthcare.

[3] Such a view of the world as controlled by white racists was typical of the gang members interviewed by Krisberg (1975: pp. 15-17).

[4] However, this is clearly implied in the work by Haskins (1975). Also, Vigil showed that prejudice and discrimination played an important role. That is, particularly in educational settings, ethnic derogation provided the impetus to the gang affiliation process; in defense of such threats to identity (Vigil, 1988).

[5] That there can be a multiplicative, rather than an additive relationship between two factors causing deviance, delinquency, or crime is traced to the statistical work of Blalock. In the work of Suttles (1968) this thesis is brought to the forefront as an analysis of the two factors of ethnicity and territory in the inner city.

[6] The interesting social scientific question is why did many northern cities see the proliferation of African-American street gangs, when similar inner-city conditions of racial oppression were also to be found in large southern cities (e.g., Dallas, etc)? Could this variation in gang emergence be explained to any degree by the differences in social organization?

[7] In fact, even qualitative researchers such as Keiser (1979) report the need to overcome racism even to carry out such a social-anthropological research method (Keiser, 1979: p. 85).

[8] It should be obvious to the reader that "bias crimes" have existed the entire history of American society, and well before that in other countries. The fact that these offenses have just recently been "discovered" is comparable to the discovery in the 1970s that there existed offenses called "child abuse". In either case, this is not to assume that these were non-existent before legislation made them sanctionable by imprisonment.

[9] The social-historical analysis by Gonzalez (1981) suggests that law enforcement still produces such gangs by the labelling process or by the social cre-

ation of such expectations of deviance. Again, however, Gonzalez points out that the role of institutional racism is a powerful force explaining the onset and persistence of gangs among Mexicans.

[10] While not widely known, American Indians or Native Americans either have their gangs too, or some believe it to be a substantial enough problem to warrant foundation grants. A grant from the Mc Knight Foundation (Minnesota) for $150,000 was made in 1988 for a "prevention program to reach gang prone Indian youth and their families" (source: Grants Index, DIALOG). Similarly, we have received field reports from an area in Oklahoma where a number of Cherokee youths clearly identify with the Crips, but would not tattoo Crip symbols on their body when a Crip leader approached them about the use of other Crip symbols in their embryonic stages of emulating the Crip gang.

[11] The research by Tromanhauser (1981: p. 188) based on a random sample of over 12,000 students in Chicago's public school system, is one of the few studies to compare American Indians, Asians, Hispanics, Blacks, and whites. In this data, American Indians reported the highest rate (18.2%) of any ethnic group for being solicited for gang membership when out of school, and (17.2%) for being attacked or threatened on or near the school by gangs, and (16.2%) for being solicited for gang membership while in school. This also showed that Asian students reported the highest level of fear from the presence of street gangs (14.7%).

[12] In fairness to Hagedorn, who postulates gang membership being a problem mostly facing African-Americans and Hispanics (p. 25), persons of Asian or American Indian background probably represent a special case. Certainly, there have been specialized gangs from East Asia (Vietnamese, Cambodian) operating in sections of Chicago and elsewhere as well as the Chinese dominated Tongs. American Indians, facing a policy of racial extirpation in America, however, have taken a different form of adjustment. In the urban area, this is markedly, to rely on previous terminology, a "retreatist" mode of adaptation --- alcoholism, governmental dependency, becoming institutionalized into the surplus population, or as Hagedorn calls it the "underclass", and on the reservation a pattern, recently, of parallelling traditional organized gambling operations. The point is that African-Americans and Hispanics are not the only targets of racism in America, and thus from a strict theoretical accounting, we can expect gang activities wherever racism rears its ugly head. On Chicago's far southside, a recent report shows the emergence of an Arab-American gang, emerging as a problem during the period when persons of Middle-Eastern heritage were subject to considerable stigma and discrimination in American society.

[13] For example, in explaining the development of Chinese gangs in New York, Chin (1988) describes how these were simply students living in fear and desiring to protect themselves in the context of ethnic antagonisms. That was in the 1960s. Later they experienced the organizational development cycle of greater sophistication and evolved into highly organized criminal groups, in relationship to organized crime (the tongs).

[14] The arrival of large numbers of Haitians in the recent years has in fact coincided with their representation in gang activities (Posses). Similarly, the Mariello boat lift operations, had subsequent Cuban gang activity. As did the Vietnamese. The point is that all three groups were racially mistreated by the media and by social stigma during and upon their arrival.

[15] There are a number of talented gang researchers and specialists who are studying and dealing with the gang problem in Indian country. Armstrong (1997) certainly provides excellent insight into this unique type of gang phenomena.

[16] I have found it useful to distinguish between these two forms in explaining the difference in measurement and equivalent impact. I often tell students that when it comes to oppressing someone, that is to destroy all hope of a decent future, there are actually two equivalent options: (1) let the person actually experience repeated discrimination and rejection, or (2) let the person believe that there is no hope. The latter amounts, in terms of impact, to the same thing.

[17] Cohen (1955) provides a fascinating and useful footnote on the matter of rumors (see footnote 2, pp. 186-187).

[18] Research shows this to be the case. Just because it is a rural or suburban area is no reason to automatically assume, also, that gangs in these types of communities cannot function at the higher end of the gang organizational spectrum.

[19] See: Suan Dodge, "Judge Declines to Move Man's Trial From Skokie", Chicago Sun-Times, Feb. 26, 1998, p. 23.

[20] The Declining Significance of Race: Blacks and Changing American Institutions, University of Chicago Press.

[21] See Race of Prisoners Admitted to State and Federal Institutions, 1926-1986, 1991, U.S. Department of Justice, Bureau of Justice Statistics, Washington, DC.

[22] The Aryan Brotherhood are said to have began as the "Blue Bird Gang...to protect white inmates from other racially-oriented non-white gangs" (Jackson and Mc Bride, 1990: p. 53).

[23] When the first edition of this book came out, it was not uncommon at national criminology and criminal justice conventions for other gang researchers to ask me "how can you include groups like the KKK and skinheads in a gang analysis?". The first edition included a preliminary version of the national gang tracking list and such groups like skinheads, the KKK, and other white-power gangs were even shown to be widely dispersed across the United States.

[24] Similarly, a federal survey in 1982 showed that 47.8 percent of all state inmates in America were African-American. (See p. 397, George F. Cole, The American System of Criminal Justice, Monterey, CA: Brooks/Cole Publishing Company.

[25] While few Americans will probably agree with me, let me go on record with a growing number of criminologists who take the position that there are in fact limits to the use of the penal sanction, and that America overuses this formal mode of social control. So much so, that it is anti-productive. We can recall the words of one spokesperson on this issue as follows: "It is not unfair to say", remarked Hans W. Mattick, "that if men had deliberately set themselves the task of designing an institution that would systematically maladjust men, they would have invented the large, walled, maximum security prison" (see Gordon Hawkins, 1976, The Prison: Policy and Practice, Studies in Crime and Justice, Chicago: University of Chicago Press, p. 45).

[26] See "Prison Workers' Complain", Nation Briefings, Chicago Sun-TImes, July 13, 1993, p. 8.

[27] This survey is described in more detail in Chapter 20.

[28] In Juveniles and Jail (National Coalition for Jail Reform, 1985, pp. 1-15) overcrowding is argued to be a condition that will contribute to violence and conflict.

[29] Gangs and Guns: A Task Force Report, National Gang Crime Research Center, November, 1994. Co-principal investigators included: George W. Knox, James G. Houston, John A. Laskey, David L. Laske, Thomas F. McCurrie, and Edward D. Tromanhauser.

[30] This includes even the law enforcement perspective of Jackson and Mc Bride (1986; 1990: p. 9).

[31] Apparently this is a universal phenomenon, as illustrated in the case of Japanese gangs. In Japan, the "burakumin" are like a "untouchable caste", and are subject to much discrimination. This minority group feeds many members into the various Yakuza gangs. See Kaplan and Dubro (1986: pp. 22, 145).

[32] This estimate would assume, based on research to that effect, that one out of every four inmates in the adult correctional population in the United States are gang members.

Scene at the 1993 Gangster Disciple Picnic in Kankakee, Illinois

Chapter 5

GANGS:
THE UNDERCLASS, THE SURPLUS POPU-
LATION, AND HUMAN CAPITAL

INTRODUCTION

We should perhaps begin this chapter with the admonition that it is really no new "criminological research finding" to find example of gang members who grew up in poverty or who faced problems of economic deprivation, or who "had a lot of bad breaks in life". However, one of the most popular views about gangs has to do with this same issue. We simply remind the reader that no society is lacking in poverty or problems of human capital development and the like. We simply remind the reader that there is no "cure" for this type of problem generally, even though national policy has much to do with the priorities for addressing the issue of human capital.

What students of criminology as well as corrections and criminal justice personnel of the 21st Century must realize, and we are shortly there, is that social scientists over the years have examined "mega trends" that may have something to do with gangs. In fact some recent gang authors take exactly the same view: that is, factors like the "underclass"[1] figure prominently in explaining the onset and persistence of gangs. This "human capital factor" is another truth that emerges from a meta-analysis of our gang literature.

In terms of theory in accounting for the onset and persistence of gang crime there are different levels of explanation possible. Cloward and Ohlin's (1960) approach can be regarded as a "middle range" theory because its level of generality and its unit of analysis involves the individual in relationship to their community's opportunity system. Psychological theories relying simply on individual traits or characteristics that can vary from one person to the next, such as Cohen's (1955) status-frustration/reaction-formation approach, can be regarded as being in the microanalytic range. At the societal-wide level of generality there are macroanalytic approaches which tend to look at the "bigger picture".

One such macroanalytic approach is represented in the attempts to apply underclass theory and surplus population theory to the problem under investigation --- gang crime. This chapter highlights this macro-demographic view regarding gang crime.

Gangs and the Underclass

A variety of contributions to the gang literature assume the important analytical role that the underclass concept has for explaining gang formation and persistence. The first such contribution in the gang literature that specifically saw the underclass status as a cause of gang forming and gang joining behavior --- and the crime and violence that gangs can be responsible for --- was the work of Moore, Livermore, and Galland (1973). The lead author had seen the process from several perspectives being the former superintendent of the Cook County Jail.

Hagedorn (1988) also argues the relevance of analyzing gang crime in terms of overall differences in "life chances" as represented through the application of underclass theory. Much more needs to be done to legitimize this approach if it is to also be linked with institutionalized racism. Hagedorn (1988) is careful not to call such persons in the underclass a "permanent underclass" and not to quote Karl Marx's closely related concept of the "dangerous underclass",[2] or the Neo-Marxist American version "the surplus population". In fact, the introduction written by Joan Moore alludes to such a fixed distinction as the permanent underclass[3], yet Hagedorn clearly sees it as something other than permanent by the optimistic potential for gang crime reduction represented by national policies emphasizing education/job training and job placement programs (Hagedorn, 1988: p. 168).

Vigil (1988) advances the concept of multiple marginality. It means persons of color who face prejudice and discrimination experience an accentuated estrangement or intense alienation and it involves a cluster of interrelated socioeconomic, cultural, psychological, and ecological factors. Thus, an examination of underclass life and how it affects gangs is essential for a macroanalytic analysis. To Vigil, "the underclass phenomenon entails the longitudinal effects of poverty" (1988, p. 11).

In linking the masculinity crisis --- the problems of manhood development experienced by Black males --- to gangs, Majors and Billson (1992) in their book Cool Pose: The Dilemmas of Black Manhood in America point to the extraordinary high unemployment rate among inner city Black teenagers (as high as 70 percent in some areas) and aspects of the underclass experience itself:

"Joining a gang is a way to organize and make sense of the marginal world of the inner city neighborhood....For black males who have been locked out of the social and economic mainstream, running with a gang can be a form of social achievement, as can engaging in fortuitous violence (Majors and Billson, 1992: p. 50)."

For the record, it is important to note that the concept of the underclass or its conceptual equivalent in relationship to crime has an important legacy predating Hagedorn, Moore, Vigil, etc. Indeed, the works of O'Connor (1973), Quinney (1977), and Young (1978) having direct bearing on this issue are not even cited by Hagedorn. As will be seen, however, there is much compatibility between these analytic approaches.

SURPLUS POPULATION THEORY vs. UNDERCLASS THEORY

Are they different? Not really. The concept of the surplus population has been brought up as a relevant theoretical concern by few scholars (O'Connor, 1973; Quinney, 1977; Young, 1978; Knox, 1980). The term "surplus population" is sometimes used in economics and demography, but some have clearly used it in the context of referring to crime (Quinney, 1977; Young, 1978; Knox, 1980).

According to O'Connor (1973, pp. 25-26) the surplus population, which is also a condition called technological unemployment, is further divided into the absolute and the relative. The relative surplus population (RSP) being the reserve army of the unemployed. Thus, the RSP includes those who have worked perhaps sporadically, seasonally, in the spot labor market, etc. So the RSP includes those with some work history who have some type of skill or labor potential, who are both willing to work and eager to work out of economic necessity. The absolute surplus population (ASP) being, apparently, a subset that traditionally has an even more difficult time entering the labor force. The ASP would therefore include youths, women, minorities, exoffenders, etc, and persons seeking employment for the first time.

The reader unfamiliar with the admittedly scant literature addressing itself to the surplus population may feel uneasy with this concept and its implications. Not being familiar with the overall concept, one might raise the humanist question of "how can there possibly be a surplus population --- are these people who are just not needed by America's legitimate opportunity structure?" This concept implies that some persons are simply "surplus" to the mode of production, while simultaneously, obviously, being highly oriented to the mode of consumption. A surplus population is that group which cannot be readily absorbed into a productive capacity in the economy through selling their labor and thereby attaining a legitimate source of economic livelihood.

In American society, the surplus population tends to be differentiated by ethnicity, language, and education.[4] Crime is expected to rise with the size of the surplus population as is the use of the criminal sanction and the number of persons placed in total control institutions. Crime and deviance are viewed as the natural outgrowth of a surplus population in a culture which constantly emphasizes material success.

The concept of the surplus population, for those persons whose educational training has instilled a repulsion towards "deterministic" philosophies such as Marxism, need not be viewed in such a mechanical fashion. This condition is felt to be somewhat amenable to policy intervention by social engineering schemes such as national level programs funded by the government. Some critics may claim this only tends to "cool out" the surplus population because it can be argued that no amount of welfare policy will truly restructure the economic system which might be viewed as the ultimate source of the problem.

Quinney (1973, pp. 131-140) cites a direct positive relationship between the use of the punitive sanction and the growth of the surplus population. The American criminal justice system is viewed in the Gramscian[5] sense as the state repressive apparatus which functions to control the unemployed --- and presumably dangerous --- surplus population. As will be seen, data on federal prison admissions and unemployment rates show a close association. This association cannot be automatically discounted as spurious and tends to be cause for much concern.

Being a part of the surplus population is an objective material condition which need not be a part of a conscious motivational force in order to produce criminality. The condition of deprivation which is implicit in this concept, as well, need not show that crime is rebellion --- although it may often be, or at least may have that appearance, ex post facto. Being a part of the surplus population is equivalent to being defined as having membership in the underclass.

Axial concepts of surplus population theory is an analysis of the nature of the opportunity (learning and performance) system itself and the role of work and occupations in society. We are not likely to find complete consensus on what the opportunity system really is (legitimate vs. illegitimate, monopoly vs. competitive sectors, etc) and how it actually works. The role of the state in all of this, however, is assumed to be prominent through social policy initiatives and governmental controls.

An understanding of the surplus population, like the concept of the underclass ala Hagedorn (1988), does lend itself to another way to interpret problems like crime and gangs. Here we shall consider the surplus population in the force it plays in both the process of initiation into crime and its systemic persistence and continuity in individual criminal careers. It will be argued that as a social condition, to be functionally defined as surplus to the legitimate opportunity system can be a necessary precondition in the chain of causal events that ultimately has as its deviant outcome criminality or gang membership.

Young (1978) advances the position that with the growth of the surplus population "we are driven to desperation to objectify and brutalize people who,

in other times, would be defined as kin, friend, or kind" (Young, 1978, p. 7). Authors who even have the appearance of being apologists for gang crime are themselves quick to point out the destructive impact that gang crime has on any given community in which it operates. We need only see the parallel between gang violence in the community, for example "Black on Black crime" etc, and observations such as those from Frantz Fanon's The Wretched of the Earth regarding colonialized persons and the way they internalize violence: they do not strike back at the cause of their frustration and oppression, they strike back at themselves more conveniently.[6]

The definitions of the surplus population certainly are congruent with most definitions of the underclass when it comes to operationalizing or measuring this concept. Young (1978, p. 7) suggests that the surplus population is composed of the following segments of society: the unemployed, those over 65, those on A.D.C., welfare, aid, etc, and those confined in correctional facilities. The historical analysis sketched by Young (1978) views the surplus population as a "deadly plan" of capitalism in the same sense that the growth of the capitalist middle class was for feudalism. An important distinction made by Young is whether the population is "surplus" to the mode of production or to the mode of consumption.

A concept similar, in definitional components, to that of the surplus population and underclass is that of structural unemployment in what might be called price theory in economics. Basically, some economists have argued that a certain level of unemployment is probably necessary in the sense that too high of an employment rate[7] will negatively impact on price stability. It is in this sense that Bergmann and Kaun (1966, p. 1) clearly assume the existence of the surplus population in their definition of structural unemployment as the "amount of employment (less minimal frictional and seasonal) which cannot be removed by monetary and fiscal policy without creating substantial continuing inflation deriving from shortages of labor". Other economists assume that there is a kind of "Phillips Curve" which accounts for the relationship between unemployment and prices in a fashion similar to the standard Phillips Curve relationship assumed between wage rates and unemployment rates (Phillips, 1958; Lipsey, 1965).

According to some liberal and conservative Keynesian economists there is a "trade-off" between unemployment and inflation as well. In other words, the government cannot take policy steps to reduce unemployment without also risking a rise in prices. It is also assumed that there is a "natural" rate of unemployment which is necessary for the economy. The accelerationist school of economics, sometimes called the Freidman advocates, happen to deny this trade-off; but they still assume a natural rate of un-employment --- almost in the Weberian tradition of the Protestant Ethic and the Spirit of Capitalism that "the underclass (and surplus population) shall always be with you" ---and feel that no policy intervention should be directed at the problem of unemployment. Indeed, they argue not for education, training, and job placement ala Hagedorn (1988) and others before him (Amandes, 1979), but rather for policy initiatives that should be directed chiefly towards the goal of price stability (Ginsburg, 1975, p. 23).

In the gang crime situation, the surplus population refers to those, who for a variety of reasons, do not have a functional relationship to the means of production. This includes those considered "unemployable" as well as the unemployed. This includes the "hidden unemployed", and those kept out of the work force by legal control. This includes those who could clearly function in the world of work, but who are dissuaded from doing so by pervasive forms of racial, ethnic, and other bias-oriented discrimination felt at the individual level, as a perceived "closure of the opportunity system" (Bailey, 1969). These persons are not involved in a productive capacity involving the competitive sale of their labor.

The role which the concept of the surplus population plays in a theoretical explanation of deviance, delinquency, criminality, and gang crime may best be conceived of as a structural or institutional social condition that amounts to an antecedent variable important to the initiation process itself, and for secondary deviation (repeated criminality, gang involvement, etc) or powering its continuity, rather than as a simple kind of direct cause and effect variable.[8]

While skin color, race, ethnicity, age, sex, and other important correlational variables cannot be experimentally manipulated, one set of factors that relates to the surplus population theory can be. This involves a cluster of human development traits often called "human resources" or "human capital".[9] While there are ample references to the so-called "K factor", the cognition and intelligence factor in which it is assumed there is natural variation among human beings (not ethnic groups or races), there are growing references to the human capital or what might be called "H-Factor" variables which are inextricably involved in any analysis of surplus population theory, the underclass, etc. This "H-factor" can be conceived of as either a factor at the individual level of analysis facilitating the onset of deviance, delinquency, crime, or gang activity or a factor that compounds the ability of society to reintegrate these persons into a legitimate career trajectory.[10]

What this suggests for corrections and criminal justice personnel as well as for our communities is HOPE. Something can be done about the problem. Job training. Educational upgrading. Skill en-hancement. Aftercare services involving job placement, etc, along with all of the counseling that is required in between these steps.

Throughout the criminology literature we will find consistent references to important variables that can be included in the "H-factor" (education, employment history, socialization, etc,).[11] This H-factor is not always explicitly identified, per se, in surplus population or underclass theories, but it is clearly present and important. More importantly, it is something we can do something about. The research by Berk, Lenihan and Rossi (1980) was not able to demonstrate the impact of these human capital attributes, however, their analysis did show that in looking at the number of arrests among exoffenders in Texas and Georgia (in the TARP program) that the single factor having the strongest inverse relationship from their regression analysis was that of "weeks employed" (1980, pp. 781-783).

At the level of the individual actor, these H-factor attributes tend to differentiate measures of crime, deviance, and gang affiliation. The corrections literature, dealing with the treatment of offenders and various program strategies, has focused extensively on experimentally manipulating these factors; ostensibly for purposes of rehabilitation. Some of this programmatic knowledge has been encouraging in the sense that from this body of evaluation research it can be concluded that genuine social policy alternatives do truly exist for reducing the crime problem.[12] Recall that these intervention strategies are valuable for consideration here because they occur at the most difficult level of impact: the tertiary level of prevention.

Whatever we call it --- human capital[13], human resource development, human potential optimization, etc, --- the "H" factor refers to the amount of investment in education, training, and skill development in human beings. This is relevant here for the understanding of gang crime because it includes consistent patterns of knowledge development about factors associated with deviance, delinquency, crime, and gang proliferation. Perhaps more important is the fact that the H-factor is amenable to experimental manipulation. It is a condition we can do something about.

Deviance, delinquency, criminality, and gang affiliation should not be viewed as an inevitable lifestyle for the underclass. It is probable, varying by historical conditions, and community structures. But not all persons with subordinated levels of human capital follow such a path of human development. Similarly, not all persons from an impoverished ghetto become offenders. There are other equally self-abusive or self-destructive options (alcoholism, suicide, mental illness, cults, etc). Moreover, the existential choice of the individual, to commit crimes or join a gang versus overcoming barriers to legitimate success, cannot be denied for some. Nor should we ignore the fact that if there is a net shrinkage in the sector of industrial and unskilled employment opportunity, then individual motivation reduces to little more than fierce rugged individualism in competition for these limited chances of productive affiliation. In such an economy one persons success in landing a job can often mean the displacement of another person.

The matter of what constitutes a radical political analysis in reference to these concepts centers around the attribution of intention and purpose. A radical with a hidden agenda in his or her criminological rhetoric would probably take the position that employers prefer such an industrial reserve army. That is, a vast pool of applicants for a job has always been used as a weapon against collective bargaining among workers.[14] Similarly, perhaps a large surplus population is a political benefit only to the ruling elite in that it artificially reduces wage rates and this itself generates more surplus value.

For the gang-affiliated person, who experiences a variety of rewardive power from the gang including its potential for income-producing opportunity however illegitimate, or any offender --- who may show the characteristics of the surplus population (through measured "H-Factors"), it may be difficult to convince them that entering an unskilled or semi-skilled occupation is a more rewarding alternative than a life of crime. Certainly the wages may not be satisfactory for someone used to issuing themselves an allowance or payroll advance, through drug sales or through illegally appropriating someone else's valuables. Further education and training, with some hope of advancement for a career ladder, would appear to offer the best inducement. The decision to enter the legitimate occupational opportunity structure is also a voluntaristic one; and this implies that manpower programs may have to rely entirely on motivational force alone to impact on this population.

The "H-factor" overlaps between concepts of the surplus population and the underclass. Underachievement in education and the dearth of skill training is clearly one of the most important features defining underclass status for most gang members. It is not uncommon at all to find among these youthful and adult offenders, that these are persons whom after their conviction and release from prison cannot correctly spell the crimes for which they were adjudicated. Persons who cannot spell the crimes they are committing may surely be expected to have problems integrating into the mainstream of society.

Occupational success in America is often a combination of marketable skills, perseverance, and ambition. At least in theory. At least if white skin

privilege has no effect. It is amazing sometimes to find the same tenacity of dedication among gang members to pursue delinquency and crime as might be found in the competitive business world. It may be a difficult task indeed to convince some of these gang members that they can "make it" in our society --- as if, via a positive mental attitude or the like, all they have to do is think and grow rich. That they lack marketable skills for America's labor force is obvious to most observers.[15] The problem is not lack of aspirations or motivation for having a better life, the problem is our society's institutional forces that would rather keep and maintain an expensive underclass that reproduces, ala Bell (1953), as much gang crime as we seek to manage through the repressive apparatus.

DATA SUPPORTING THE UNDERCLASS THESIS

Three themes using three different modes of analysis will be used to argue that there exists some amount of empirical support for the underclass thesis.[16] How institutionalized is the impact on the underclass law offender in America --- indeed, using the human capital aspect of educational attainment, can it be said that the gap or educational lag is of such magnitude as to constitute, along with legal restrictions on employment (for those convicted of a felony offense), a "caste"? Secondly, from a cross-sectional analysis can it be demonstrated that the effects of unemployment and welfare dependency are indeed factors that differentiate the likelihood of being arrested for a crime in America? Thirdly, using census data for three countries can it be demonstrated that there is any relationship between the size of the underclass and the use of the penal sanction? These three research questions are addressed here in an effort to shed some light on the issue.

The underclass thesis is important to address. If we must take the position that there is a "permanent underclass"[17] with no hope, then that leaves us few options. It suggests that nothing works. It provides few alternative recourses to the solution of the crisis.

THE EDUCATIONAL LAG IN THE AMERICAN OFFENDER POPULATION

From a research point of view there is little doubt that educational attainment is an important variable. It plays a significant role in explaining crime, especially recidivism. The level of educational attainment is also a very important variable affecting employability and earnings potential in America. That is to say, someone with at least a high school education has a greater likelihood of getting a job and staying "clean" than someone having less than a high school education. Educational attainment also tends to vary inversely with recidivism. As Spergel stated "it used to be that as gang members got older, out of their teens, they'd leave gangs to take decent-paying jobs, now there's no jobs for people like that".[18]

The historical trend in educational attainment in the United States has shown a continual decrease in the percentage of the adult population (those 25 years of age or older) who have not completed high school. Let us summarize this trend here by referring to the U.S. Census figures in Table 5.

TABLE 5

Yearly Distributions of U.S. Census Statistics For the Percentage of Adults Not Completing High School Since 1940

Year	% of U.S. >= 25 Years of Age with <= 11 years of Educational Attainment
******	********************
1940	74.6 percent
1950	63.8
1960	58.8
1970	44.9
1972	41.8
1973	40.2
1974	38.7
1975	37.5
1976	36.0
1977	35.1
1978	34.1
1979	32.3
1980	31.4
1981-2	30.4
1983	27.9
1984	26.8

SOURCE: Statistical Abstracts of the United States, U.S. Department of Commerce, Bureau of the Census, Social and Economic Statistics Administration. 1985, p. 134; 1982-83, p. 143; 1981, p. 142; 1980, p. 149; 1979, p. 145; 1978, p. 143; 1977, p. 136; 1976, p. 123; 1975, p. 119; 1974, p. 116; 1973, p. 115; 1971, p. 110.

Educational lag is defined here as not having a high school degree or GED or at least 12 years of education completed. Table 5 indicates that the distribution of this characteristic in mainstream America has steadily decreased from nearly three-fourths of the population in 1940 to less than one-third today. The question is, how does the offender population compare with the rest of America regarding this condition. To review this parameter for the offender

population we must necessarily make reference to a number of previous, independent, research projects that are summarized in Figure 5.

Figure 5

Research Literature Citations for Adult Offenders, Percentage Lacking a High School Education

Author	Sample	% <= 11 Years Educ.
**************	***********	**********
Clemmer (1940, p. 50)	N = 2,345 (adults circa 1931-1934)	97 percent
Rumney and Murphy (1952, p. 75)	N = 1,000 New Jersey probationers (1937)	92 percent
Simpson, et al (1976, p. 100)	N = 27,390 DARP Drug Addicts	63 percent
Diamond, et al (1977, p. 3)	N = 221 Chicago probationers	59.4 percent
Knox (1978d, p. 391)	N = 24,047 State of Illinois inmates	69 percent
Lenihan (1978, p. 55)	N = 431 Baltimore Parolees	88.3 percent

---

As seen in Figure 5, the research literature on offenders has consistently shown that the offender population lags behind their American peers in educational attainment. Current levels of educational attainment among America's offender population are characteristic of literacy levels of the general population only by comparison to this same human capital attribute before World War II. Some correctional researchers may also point out that the correctional process itself may be a co-determinant of this problem and that correctional facilities themselves may be responsible for some of the disruption in the educational process for both delinquents and adult offenders.

The finding of interest here is that the offender population is two to three times as likely to have a non-marketable level of educational attainment (e.g., not a high school graduate, or <= 11 years of education) when compared with America generally. The validity of this educational lag is mitigated only by the fact that the offender population itself tends to be increasing homogeneous with respect to SES (i.e., Social Economic Status) and ethnicity --- both of which correlate highly with educational attainment.

Ask yourself, how are these under-educated persons going to fit into the American economy in a productive, fulfilling, and integrative capacity?

THE UNDERCLASS AND CRIMINALITY

The notion that the underclass in America contributes disproportionately to arrest, conviction, and imprisonment rates is not a new one. Myrdal

(1969) has been interpreted to the effect that lower class delinquents can be viewed as part of the American underclass whose characteristics include poverty, substandard housing, limited opportunity, underemployment and under-education. Marxist authors have referred to the "dangerous underclass" in a similar vein. Some analysts have regarded the surplus population in terms of a subculture of poverty where, it is assumed incorrectly, there is little motivation for economic success and that poor people are the way they are because they have not internalized middle class success goals.

While contributions from liberal, radical, and conservative perspectives have tended to cite some relationship between crime and conditions of economic immiseration there is sharp disagreement on what the nature of this relationship really is.

Something pointed in the work of Glasgow (1981) is that to be defined as part of the African-American underclass is equivalent, functionally, to essentially lack any organized political interest or social organizational infrastructure to be recognized as an entity in the polity. It is often said that the reason prison reform movements persisted for decades, indeed longer, even as little more than a spark of an interest, with little more than technological progress in the effectiveness of physical security devices is that there is no substantive political base to support these kinds of major social policy changes and the public funding they require.

If there is anything pervasively common to the surplus population or the American underclass it is their lack of legitimate social organization. Where political clout is defined as the size of a financial contribution to an electoral campaign, and where poverty itself is stigmatized (as is unemployment), it is unrealistic to expect traditional forms of power seeking from a group that is functionally disenfranchised.

Johnson (1977) argues that the concept of the underclass may be more fruitful for testing delinquency theories than traditional measures of socioeconomic status (SES) such as father's occupational status. Johnson (1977) therefore focuses on the merits of alternative operational measures of social class such as: unemployment or marginal employment, poverty level income, recipient of welfare benefits, etc. According to Johnson (1977) these should show a stronger relationship with problems such as delinquency and crime.

The NORC (National Opinion Research Center) General Social Survey (Davis, 1980) data for 1980 was used to examine the effects of unemployment and welfare dependency on self-reported arrests. The unemployment measure is a dichotomous variable reflecting whether or not the person has been unemployed and looking for work for more than a month during the last ten years. Welfare dependency

is a general measure reflecting the receipt of any government welfare aid. The self-reported arrest variable reflects whether the person has been picked up, or charged, by the police for any reason other than traffic violations.

Table 6 below shows that within this nationally representative sample there is in fact support for the proposition that employment varies inversely with being arrested for crime. Those persons experiencing unemployment are shown in Table 6 to have an arrest rate of 20.8 percent. This is twice as high as the 9.3 percent arrest rate for those persons not experiencing unemployment. In summary, unemployment using this cross-sectional data significantly differentiates arrests.

TABLE 6

Unemployment and Arrests in the 1980 Sample
of the NORC General Social Surveys

		Were Americans Arrested?			
		NO		YES	
		N	%	N	%
Were Americans Unemployed?	NO	932	90.7	96	9.3
	YES	312	79.2	82	20.8

Chi square = 33.2, probability < .001

Similarly, government dependency (welfare recipient) is shown to significantly differentiate self-reported arrests among Americans. These findings are reported in Table 7. This shows that 17 percent of those receiving aid were arrested compared to 9.9 percent for those not receiving various forms of government aid.

TABLE 7
Government Dependency and Arrests in the 1980
Sample of the NORC General Social Survey

		ARRESTED BY THE POLICE?			
		NO		YES	
		N	%	N	%
Welfare/Aid Recipient?	NO	800	90.1	88	9.9
	YES	439	83.0	90	17.0

Chi square = 14.5, probability < .001

THE UNDERCLASS AND THE PRISON POPULATION

The relationship between the size of the surplus population or the underclass and the amount of crime or use of the prison sanction is also an important relationship to examine. Employment has been a variable examined that bears some relevancy to this question. While much research has been done in this area, much of it is also relegated to the "fugitive literature" and hard to find. For example, one of the most detailed analyses of unemployment and crime was that done by Kleeck, Winslow and Reid reported in 1931. It clearly showed a strong consistent relationship that the higher the unemployment the higher the property crime and this covered the period of 1893 to 1926 for the State of Massachusetts (p. 303, 312).

The research by Glaser and Rice (1959) uncovered a significant inverse relationship between employment and crime for the period 1932 - 1950 in the U.S. The ptolemic by Guttentag (1968, p. 110) sought to discount these findings without a secondary analysis or empirical approach to counter the evidence by Glaser and Rice, and others such as Fleisher (1966).

Here we examine related measures of the underclass thesis as an independent variable in determining the strength of the relationship with the volume of criminal justice processing. For the United Kingdom, covering England and Wales during the years 1859-1910 this involved the distribution of "able-bodied adult paupers" expressed as a rate per 1,000 of the population in census data. For lack of a better word we could call this the pauperization rate or simply the underclass ratio. When this is regressed against the rate per 1,000 criminals brought to trial in the same year a very strong positive correlation (r = .90, p < .001) emerges.

Data on Americans are taken from the U.S. census. Here the analysis focused on the unemployment rates and the volume of imprisonment for the years 1941 - 1978.[19] Here again we find what appears to be a moderately strong and significant correlation (r = .62, p < .001).

The Canadian experience with the Depression had a very similar skewed effect for imprisonment. The analysis reported here, therefore, dates from 1941 to 1968. The imprisonment variable reflects the total number of prisoners received during the year taken from the Annual Report to the Commissioner of Penitentiaries, and the unemployment variable taken from the Canada Year books. Again we find a significant (r = .73, p < .001) positive correlation between unemployment and imprisonment.

In summary, these aspects of the underclass experience of being defined as marginal to the economic mainstream of society, are shown to be significantly related to the rates at which the same three societies (America, Canada, England and Wales) adjudicate or imprison law offenders. The larger the underclass, the larger the prison population.

PERCEPTIONS OF HOPELESSNESS CAN HAVE THE SAME IMPACT

The perception of closure in the legitimate opportunity structure is itself significantly associated with delinquency, crime, recidivism, and gang affiliation. In other words, internalizing a defeatist belief that there is little hope for success via traditional means, regardless of objective material conditions regarding occupational opportunity, can itself be a tremendous social-psychological force operating to propel a person into deviance, delinquency, crime or gang membership.

This attitudinal measurement approach has dealt mostly with delinquency and is traced to opportunity system theory (Cloward and Ohlin, 1960). A number of independent efforts have shown basically the same finding: that perception of "blocked" legitimate opportunities is closely associated with delinquency (Elliott, 1962; Spergel, 1963; Palmore and Hammond, 1964; Blalock, 1965; Short, Rivera and Tennyson, 1965; Knox, 1978(b)). In short, the belief held by the individual that society offers little chance of legitimate success is shown to be a very significant variable differentiating delinquency.

COROLLARY RESEARCH FINDINGS

A good deal of research over the years has been undertaken on the relationship between employment and various measures of deviant outcomes (delinquency, criminality, recidivism, gang affiliation, etc). Suffice it to say, that in most of this literature, there is a significant volume of support for the proposition that employment varies inversely with crime. The more basic research by Zatz (1985) found that one of the most powerful variables differentiating gang members from non-gang members was that of their status of being currently employed.

In that much of this comes from program evaluation research, the interested reader should examine reviews such as those by Leiberg (1978) to examine aspects and details of these programs for adults, and Knox (1981) regarding delinquents.

The inverse relationship between employment and crime is documented in basic research (Glaser and Rice, 1959; Glaser, 1964; Fleisher, 1966; Holahan, 1970; Votey and Philips, 1974; Sedlak, 1975; Knox, 1978(a)) and in much evaluation research (Miller, 1972; Mills and Walter, 1974; Killinger and Archer, 1974; Easton, et al, 1974; Whitney, 1974; Bernardo, 1977; Bowker, 1977; Wadsworth, 1977; Greenberg, 1978; Knox, 1978 (d); Cook et al, 1978; Mills and Walter, 1979; Rulo and Zemel, 1979; Pirog-

Good, 1979).

We need not use conjecture here or rhetoric, we need only examine more completely the extant literature. The research like that by Fleisher (1966) clearly demonstrated "that change in economic position is a core element in the social control of delinquent behavior" (Janowitz, 1966).

THE GANG AS A NATURAL COMPETITIVE DEVELOPMENT IN A GROWING UNDERGROUND ECONOMY

Where we have one gang, another will shortly follow. The author calls this the law of natural group opposition formation. When the Crips arise, the Bloods shortly follow. When the Folks appear in an area, the People also appear. The vast amount of illegal income that could be made from the underground economy, particularly drug sales, may have provided a social environment that facilitated the formation and growth of gangs. This does not mean that the two warring or competing factions have to be necessarily equal in size or power or in terms of their market share. Because by some estimates, the Crips outnumber the Bloods three to one in actual numbers of members. Where they are equal is in the number of different locations they are found in throughout the entire United States. In all social contexts, where we find the Crips we will also find the Bloods.

The competition and rivalry therefore existed before and gives rise to such patterned varieties of organized conflict. It could be as simple as the Blues (Crips), extending a color from their high school symbols; and the Reds (Bloods) adopting their color from their high school[20]. Thus, the underground economy itself is advanced as an explanation for being the engine that powers the emergence of gangs, and that the competition in this market is normal behavior, such that while one group may tend to dominate, the competition will extend to all geographical areas.

HOW A STRAIGHT JOB IS LESS APPEALING TO THE MORE HARD CORE GANG MEMBER

Employment is no panacea, but most agree or assume it would have a positive effect. Rodriguez (1993) explains how he left gang life and would expect many others to quit the gang if they could get a job paying a livable wage. But there is some research that recently revealed that the more hard core gang member would not take a good paying job even if it were offered, one hypothesis being that perhaps the gang pays better. The data here come from the recent research on gangs and guns cited in an earlier chapter, and uses a sample of 476 gang members in the midwestern United States.

This data shows that among those gang mem-bers who have never attempted to quit the gang, some 16.9 percent would not take a job paying $9.00 per hour. This compares with only 6.2 percent who would not take a job paying $9.00 per hour among those gang members who have tried to quit the gang. This shows that even providing such jobs would appear to attract the less hard core gang member. The more hard core gang member, that is someone who has never tried to quit the gang, is less likely to want to take a job paying $9.00 per hour.

SUMMARY

The underclass thesis regarding gangs clearly involves a host of related concepts. Some of these are traditional Marxist (the dangerous underclass) concepts, others are related concepts without direct ideological classification (the permanent underclass, the truly disadvantaged, etc), but refer to comparable and historically similar such conditions. This set of concepts articulates a more societal wide "condition" favorable to the production of crime and gangs.

This thesis does enjoy both theoretical and empirical support dating back some time. It also poses some hard choices for America: what do to about the underclass? Some gang authors simply recommend legalizing heroin, and we shall see in a later chapter this might be equivalent to simply creating a true "caste" in America. That is, a group both functionally at the bottom of the social and economic pyramid, kept there by a variety of factors, and officially/legally recognized as such an entity.

One fundamental problem exists with this type of historical continuity in the literature about gangs. It is the issue of why some poor people never become criminals or gang members and do they therefore represent an ipso facto exception to the theory or does their very existence challenge the theory? Further, it is now well known that suburban gang members may be less likely to join a gang for chiefly economic reasons. It seems clear that a large percentage of members of more organized criminal gangs typically join "to make money", but this is not universal, and while characteristic of innercity gang members is not a profile factor for suburban or smaller town gang members who can float in and out of the gang, having a relatively comfortable home life and even middle class existence to return to.

Can we help them get out of this underclass? Can we instill the hope of a better life? These are the issues that must be faced and answered as America enters the 21st Century.

Discussion Questions

(1) Do you think there is any merit to the concept of the "underclass", "surplus population", etc, in describing societal wide groups of persons who are excluded from a productive relationship to their society? Is this the group most at risk of joining a gang?

(2) Can a society measure its strength by the size of its underclass or surplus population? What national policies do you feel should be adopted to reduce the size of such groups in America today? Is the human capital theory fatally flawed because gangs can be found in suburban affluent communities as well?

(3) If the federal government declared a war on gangs and appointed a Gang Czar that felt there was some merit to the underclass theory, or surplus population theory, or the multiple marginality concept, how would it be possible to implement such concepts in terms of doing something about the gang problem?

DO WE "MARGINALIZE" AND "DEMONIZE" GANG MEMBERS OR DO THEY SEEK OUT A MARGINAL LIFESTYLE AND SEEK OUT DEMONIZED LABELS?

Some writers in the gang literature really over-simplify the gang problem by claiming that the reason gang members are gang members is that they have been "marginalized" by their society. Some writers in the gang literature therefore feel we need to "help" gang members with special services rather than "demonize" them and give them "bad labels" that they will "live up to".

Such writers about how marginality causes gang involvement overlook an important alternative explanation that appears to have some merit. It is this: gang members want to be different, they want to project the "image" of living a life at odds with their society, and their "failings" at life typically begin early in their careers: being a bully in school, being suspended from school, threatening or assaulting teachers in school, running away from home, being expelled from school, being arrested, etc. From a perspective on the human development life span of gang members, therefore, it could be argued that something like "growing up poor" is a "cop out" and "apology" for crime: because not everyone who is poor makes the decision to become a criminal.

Such writers about how demonizing gangs is anti-productive to solving the gang problem also may be overlooking an important alternative explanation. Gang members do intentionally seek out "bad reputations", "tough images", and want to be feared. Society does not give them their "killer nicknames", they do this to themselves. Society does not give them their "criminal" gang names, they do this themselves.

Here is an important fact about gang members in the United States today: half join voluntarily, and half are recruited. Thus, for half of all gang members America today, the gang was like the "light bulb attracting moths": they sought out the gang life style, perhaps because it would offer them the opportunity to "be the best gangster you can be". By the way, those who seek out gang life by voluntarily joining it are harder to deal with than those who were "recruited" into the gang: the latter are somewhat more likely to give up gang life.

End Notes:

[1] Most authors of the underclass approach refer to the urban African-American underclass (Wilson, 1987; Duster, 1987), but it certainly transcends color.

[2] Again, for the record, let me point out that Joan Moore's use of the underclass was not the first applied to gangs. An earlier account which Moore (1978) and Hagedorn (1988) failed to acknowledge was that by Moore, Livermore and Galland (1973). In the Moore, Livermore, and Galland (1973) analysis the process of urban deterioration was analyzed and its accelerated destruction left behind "a dangerous underclass spawned by poverty, joblessness, misguided welfare policies, and ineffectual corrections and educational programs" (p. 43). Gangs in this process were described as having a terrorism function in the community.

[3] Moore says in referring to Wilson's use of the concept "underclass", "These are men and women permanently excluded from participation in mainstream occupations" (Hagedorn, 1988: p. 7).

[4] Short (1990) astutely applies the closely related concept of "social capital" to explain why one person may grow up in the same inner city area and go on to live a law-abiding life and be a good citizen and how another --- in the same environment --- might become a gang leader. Social capital, then, has to do with social skills; without which the more economic investments (e.g., a University of Chicago education, manpower training in business or the crafts, etc) as measures of human capital, will not be able to put to use effectively. See James F. Short, "New Wine in Old Bottles? Change and Continuity in American Gangs", pp. 223-239, Chapter 10 in C. Ronald Huff (ed.), Gangs in America, Newbury Park: Sage Publications.

[5] Gramsci is an Italian political economist who was at one time a political prisoner. See Antonio Gramsci, 1971, Selections from the Prison Notebooks, New York: International Publishers.

[6] This same tendency has it social equivalent in Douglas G. Glasow's The Black Underclass: Poverty, Unemployment, and Entrapment of Ghetto Youth.

[7] Note that Hagedorn (1988) rallies around the traditional call for "full employment".

[8] As has been amply demonstrated, however, and quite impressively, poverty has a strong relationship to crime, as measured by income and recidivism (see Berk, Lenihan and Rossi, 1980).

[9] I explain this concept to my students in a straight-forward fashion: Compare yourself, a university student, with someone in the penitentiary the same age, the same ethnicity, etc. Chances are you have a lot more "dollars" invested in the cultivation of your human talents. Your training, your formal education, your instruction, your documented skills, your health, your licenses and certifications, etc, etc. That amount of capital spent on refining and cultivating your talent as a human being is your "H factor", your human capital, your human resource development expenditure, your human development investment.

[10] Yablonsky is quick to point out that the goal of persons doing social work with gangs, outreach workers, detached workers, community organizations, etc, should have as their goal not simply making resources available to the gang members, but rather the "dismemberment", the disintegration of the gang itself, and thereby creating the opportunity to bring these persons back into the main stream. Clearly, such a proposition cannot be made in good conscience without first noting the discrepancy between their level of human capital development and what is expected in larger society. This includes language, social skills, even hygiene itself.

[11] I wish to anticipate some criticism and divert it now: this is not a "deficit" approach to stigmatize. Any deficit that is implied is not teleological by imparting purposive lack of motivation. Indeed, quite the obverse is true: these are human beings who have had their dreams of a good life crushed by the institutional forces at work in their way of life. They wanted good education, good training, skills and experience from a rewarding career opportunity --- but these doors were closed to them.

[12] At the time of interviewing for a university position, once, a high ranking member of the university administration posed the question to me "do you really think we can do something about crime, that is make society safer?" I answered, most definitely, but how much money are you willing to spend towards that goal, or if not that, how much of your civil and constitutional rights are you willing to part with.

[13] See James S. Coleman, (1988), "Social Capital in the Creation of Human Capital", _American Journal of Sociology_ (94)(S): 95-120.

[14] I speak to you, I hope calmly, and without wild-eyed fanaticism, in disclosing that while I teach at a University, the first thing I did after getting my Ph.D. was joining the American Association of University Professors. I am currently a union member, local 4100 of Illinois, AFL/CIO, University Professionals of Illinois. Yet I truly recall growing up in America, especially in high school, finding tremendous animosity and propaganda directed against anyone who was "pro union".

[15] Huff (1989: p. 527) notes, in support of the underclass thesis, gangs are clearly drawn from the urban underclass, and they are often "economically and socially marginal youth who has dropped out of or been expelled from school, and/or is without job skills" (Huff, 1989: p. 527).

[16] A note on meager resources with which to carry out the research reported here: This book was not written with funding of any sort. Obviously, with adequate funding a much more direct and more complete analysis of this kind of research problem could be undertaken. I am only alerting the reader that this analysis must be evaluated also in terms of the level of effort, which unfortunately in this case was a meager one.

[17] John Irwin's The Jail: Managing the Underclass in American Society sees the population feeding American correctional institutions as consisting of that social group loosely labelled "the rabble" who are a permanent underclass (1985: p. 103). This permanent underclass is therefore related to "persistent ("structural") unemployment among our least integrated citizens" (Irwin, 1985: p. 104).

[18] Irving Spergel quoted in: "The Gang's All Here", by Jennifer Halperin, 1994, _Illinois Issues_ (April): p. 16.

[19] The depression era (1930-1940) was problematic and masked any relationship because nearly a fourth of Americans were unemployed in 1933. Also, some crimes prosecuted vigorously under other historical periods (e.g., prostitution, gambling, drugs, etc) were less aggressively prosecuted during the early part of the 20th century because these offenses did not directly affect the affluent (see Gordon, 1972, p. 62; Clark, 1970, pp. 55-56). The depression era, also, tended to be a "good time Charlie" period of law enforcement, a more permissive period with regard to vice.

[20] The red color may have therefore represented Centenial High School in Compton, California where many of the OG's of this group are supposed to have lived. Blue was a clothing color from Washington High School in Los Angeles.

Latin Queens
(Female Faction of the Latin Kings)

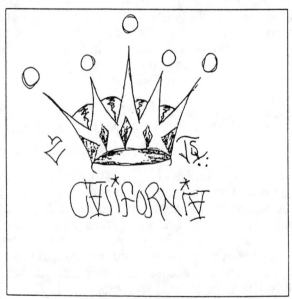

According to our top level informants in the Latin Kings, members treat Queens like they were their true sisters. The penalty for disrespecting a Queen is death. You can disrespect a male member, and depending on the rank of the person "dissed", the person doing the "dissing" may still walk away alive. However, a member can get killed for just calling a Queen a "bitch", especially if she is married to another Latin King. Says one informant in this gang: "we trained them to be just as ruthless as we were, we trained them to never back down from business, they realize they have to do what their gang asks them to do, they will fight any rival gang members over the flimsiest issue, they will shoot at rival gang members, they will go the whole nine yards, we trained them to do that."

Latin Queens are a subset of the Latin Kings. They are accountable to the male-driven Latin King gang. They are one of the most well-known female auxilliary gangs, and they develop a reputation for fighting other females. Such female Chapters of the Latin Kings are found in many suburbs of Chicago today. They always have the township or city name as a prefix to their chapter name. Their roles, duties, and rights are spelled out in writing in the written constitution of the Latin Kings

"There is one thing worse than a crook and that is a crooked man in a big political job. A man that pretends he is enforcing the law and is really taking 'dough' out of somebody breaking it, even a self-respecting hood hasn't any use for that kind of fellow. He buys them like he would any other article necessary for his trade, but he hates them in his heart".

Al Capone (See Landesco, 1929: p. 1049)

Chapter 6

POLITICS AND GANG CRIME:
Another Continuity
In Thinking about Gangs

INTRODUCTION

As demonstrated in Chapter 4 the historical continuity in the gang literature regarding ethnic homogeneity in American gang formations was supported by a number of authors. Similarly, there is another conceptual continuity when it comes to the matter of politics. How, exactly, such linkages and political ties or involvements develop and what form they take are examined here. Gang involvement in the modern American electoral process deserves closer attention.[1]

Correctional veterans of the 1970s will recall the political activism of prison inmates and the force they represented. Could gangs provide such a similar level of organizational challenge in the years ahead? Clearly, we need to understand the linkages between politics and gangs to be adequately informed in this area.

GANGS AND POLITICS: Another Historical Continuity in the Literature.

One of the other conceptual continuities in the gang literature is the matter of politics. As will be seen, since gangs were first described in America over a hundred years ago, a continuing study of American gangs has repeatedly found a relationship between the gang and political life (Short, 1975; Short and Molland, 1976). Yet many questions remain unanswered about this relationship.[2]

The strongest continuing theme that has emerged in the literature is that gang members have been cultivated and used as repressive or corruptive functionaires in the urban political scene.[3] A second related theme, regarding direct and indirect aid from political incumbents to gang organizations, is that in urban areas the gang is used to maintain hegemony on voting patterns. Thirdly, many authors cite the covert use of gang capability for extralegal functions. A fourth theme is illicit collaboration, a pattern of "quid pro quo", existing in one form or another between gangs and public officials.

The proof of the enduring relationship between politics and gangs can be found in many cities today. In Chicago, for example, during the summer of 1993 when gang leader "King" Larry Hoover was up for a parole hearing, some major Chicago elected political officials wrote letters to the parole board and even appeared before the hearing on his behalf. The gang itself had pledged to help bring in the votes. Many other studies are showing similar efforts by gangs to ingratiate themselves to liberal politicians. The longterm effects of collaborating with gangs is yet to be felt in such contemporary examples, but historically it dramatically backfires and has proven to be a major political blunder and liability.

Each of these four themes will be reviewed here. Part I simply provides a summary of this literature in relationship to gangs and politics. Part II provides a discussion of the voting rights of ex-offenders and gang members as well as an interview related to the gang-politics theme.

PART I:
What The Literature Shows on
Gangs and Politics

1. POLITICIANS CULTIVATING GANGS

Have some corrupt high ranking political figures in America intentionally rewarded, reinforced, and strengthened gang organizations through the sharing of their power, resources, and protection?[4] Absolutely yes, is the answer from the literature. But this should be viewed in the historical context.

Asbury's (1927) account devoted considerable length to the discussion of earlier American urban politics and gang life. In fact, both Thrasher and Whyte also gave separate chapters in their analysis to this matter of politics. Many other contributors to the gang literature have subsequently cited the interface between politics and gang.[5]

Asbury's contribution was in showing this continuity in the relationship between gangs and politics to a point before the American civil war. The intense competition for scarce resources between newly arrived ethnic groups in urban areas is quoted by Campbell (1984, pp. 234-235) as a precondition that allowed gangs to be "nurtured by politicians" (p. 235). Indeed, while the gangs that were cultivated by politicians as in a sense "political machine maintenance" staff for both Tammany Hall and for other corrupt regimes in Chicago and elsewhere have all but disappeared or have taken new forms, there continues some reference in the literature to the ongoing problem of politicians cultivating gangs. However, today it works both ways: gangs cultivate politicians, and vice versa.

Perhaps the most thorough account, however, is that presented by Landesco (1929). Here much painstaking documentation is provided of the role of both neighborhood gangs and "business gangs" in relationship to political corruption. Landesco gives many details, complete with addresses of bombings, indictments, etc. It concludes with a chapter from E.W. Burgess, suggesting the need to take politics out of law enforcement, and a host of other recommendations.

A more recent citation is that by Suttles quoted in Short and Strodtbeck (1974, pp. viii-ix) who indicated this problem had not disappeared well into the 1960s. That is, politicians still "cultivated" gangs. What is also important, however, is the contribution which Suttles made regarding the valence of political ideology among gang members. Clearly, Suttles indicated that any political sentiments shared by gang members in their ties to politicians were likely to be of the anti-leftist variety.[6] As if patriotism was the last refuge of the scoundrel, gang members clearly identified with conservative, even patriotic, political images. This was also to be subsequently reported by Campbell's study.[7]

Why did politicians cultivate gangs? According to Thrasher, politicians cultivated gangs because of their potential enduring use in the social organizational infrastructure of urban life. Gang members could be used to promote a politician's own interests, and it also meant that in having such an affiliation or tie with the politician, there was an indirect positive impact that could be mobilized in terms of the voting behavior of the parents and adult family members related to the gang (Thrasher, 1968: p. 313).

Let there be no mistake about the accuracy of Thrasher's observation as a continuing rule of thumb for politicians today. The larger the household or family network unit in the ward or precinct, the more a precinct captain, alderman, etc, can "overlook" in the deviance, gang affiliation, etc, of such a social unit. Such voting clusters represent persons related by birth and marriage.

Thrasher showed how politicians encouraged the increasing formal organization of the gang structure (p. 315), by encouraging it to become a "club". Why? Because many important politicians at that time had their start in such gangs. Such that at one point the Chicago city government was, in effect, in the business of promoting the growth of predominantly white gangs. This was indicated by Thrasher's account of how a park employee had a program involving the transitioning of these groups from recurring indigenous nomadic tribes into chartered organizations with a fixed base in a building or office (or clubhouse), with the rent either paid entirely by the politician or in some way subsidized (p. 316). An important detail about gang vitality and its ability as an organization to survive was also contributed by Thrasher in the context of the early American history regarding gangs and politics. There were two variations: "subsidized" and "self-supporting" gangs (pp. 316-317). The latter generally had a much higher rate of organizational failure and inability to continue. Without economic support --- direct aid or indirect subsidies --- these gangs simply "went under", that is they disappeared.

How were gangs used by politicians? Mostly in electoral politics. To some extent it was a seasonal function. That is, gangs were more likely to be actively mobilized by a politician during the campaign seasons (p. 317).

Thrasher quotes Robert E. Park on the feudalistic nature of gang cultivation by politicians (p. 322). In a sense, the politician was the "serf" or royalty in the feudal sense, and the gang member was a loyal "vassal" who comes to expect protection. A strong "us versus them" identification characterized this differentiation between those affiliated with the political machine and other citizens (pp. 322-323). Variations of this continue today in many areas, where political affiliation brings with it political patronage. Entire criminal justice agencies --- police departments, correctional systems, probation departments, etc --- experience the strangle hold that newly elected politicians place on their agencies, particularly in staffing and promotion. Political clout still matters a great deal today in the criminal justice system.

What were the "pay-offs", the incentives, and the reward structure for gangs affiliating with a politician and for engaging in what in their own minds must have certainly been regarded as rather pro-social activities? Jobs with the city government or in the private sector where the politician had significant influence are cited by Thrasher as part of this reward structure that could motivate gang members. It involved the traditional "spoils system" (p. 330).

Of course, political pressure on a criminal justice agency (e.g., police department, prison, etc) on behalf of a gang member, to give a sense of immunity, was also obvious (pp. 327-329). In this sense to demonstrate historical continuity, at least in the basic structural conditions that allow for this relationship between gangs and politicians, one should assess the basic problem of political encroachment upon criminal justice agencies such as the police department. If external political pressure can be applied to such agencies to impact on their own internal policies or in special individual cases, then the basic structural problem giving rise to illegitimate influence still exists.

The largest single chapter in Whyte's (1981) Street Corner Society was that entitled "Politics and the Social Structure" (pp. 194- 252). Here we see the exchange process function between the gang and the politician with favors, and quid pro quo. They have mutual influence and mutual interests in common (p. 205). Says Whyte "the politician must take the social organization of the neighborhood into account" (p. 213). Whyte documents the role of gangs in elections as "stooges" (p. 218), their "nuisance value" (p. 219), and in general campaign work and getting out the vote, or alternatively --- suppressing or redirecting it. For a more recent example, the study of children affected by gang violence in Chicago's Henry Horner public housing complex by Kotlowitz describes how a politician used gang members in the campaign after his life was threatened and his vehicle was shot up:

"At Henry Horner, a young local politician recruited gang members from playgrounds to pass out leaflets and accompany campaign workers in his successful 1987 bid for Democratic ward committeeman. He paid each gang member $20 a day (Kotlowitz, 1991: p. 39)".

2. AID FROM THE POLITICIAN TO THE GANG ORGANIZATION

As Whyte indicated, there is a system of reciprocal obligations or expectations in the relationship between the gang and the politician. What form that aid, direct or indirect, can take is of interest in the understanding of the etiology of a variety of contemporary problems such as political corruption, political violence, the integrity of the democratic process, and even racketeering.

Gang members tend to be predictably exploitive of any resource. Remember as well, that gang organizations and gang members are not from another planet: they are indigenous to our neighborhoods, they are someone's children. What seems incredulous is after nearly fifty years of different versions of the detached worker program, that little research has surfaced on the nature of the communications pattern between power brokers, opinion leaders, and influential community members in relationship to the gang.

White gangs seem to be able to take their cues from their respective communities along the lines of racist sentiments. White gangs have historically had a continuing function of fighting for their respective versions of "ethnic purity". It always means segregation. Further examples of this will be highlighted in a discussion of racism and gang crime in a later chapter.

Racism is political and in fact there is evidence that some gangs were able to be simply manufactured by adults, almost from blueprint specifications. Such was the case of the neo-nazi group called the National Socialist Party of America (NSPA) which operated in Marquette Park, on Chicago's southwest side, during the mid-1970s.[8] Two age-graded youth gang auxiliary groups were organized: (1) the White Youth Front, aka "The Young Wolves", ages 12 and under, and (2) the Young National Socialist Corps aka "The Exterminators", ages 13 to 17.[9] Anyone 18 or over was a regular storm trooper (see Knox, 1976). These were, by the way, neo-nazi's who were running for political office, and almost made it.

Preventing organized dissent or preventing organized attempts to undermine the political domination by a given elected official can be another circumstance in which gangs become useful to the politician. Beyond and including the American scene, there is ample historical evidence of using "thugs", or persons having predispositions similar to modern gang members, in a political context to maintain power, to reinforce power and dominance, and to have such political functions carried out, under some social contract. This process usually involves an expectation of reward from the politician. While there is likely to be much "buffering" of the communications between the politician and the gang member, making it difficult as Thrasher and Whyte showed to gather hard evidence that could be used in court, this relationship still constitutes a political reality of gang members as allies, hired hands, or in violent or criminal functions as mercenaries.

Some politicians, in areas such as Chicago, today make no effort to conceal their relationship to "street organizations" (i.e., gangs). Today politicians may in fact openly and conspicuously seek to work with gangs, for example seeking to influence the parole board to release an imprisoned gang leader. The political reality may in fact be that such politicians enter into such relationships by little choice of their own. Rather it may be simply be impossible not to recognize the power that such large gangs may represent in an urban area where a local alderman draws support from.

3. COVERT USE OF GANGS FOR EXTRALEGAL FUNCTIONS

It is in this instance that the linkage between a politician, or powerful individual who may not be a public official but who still seeks or exerts power and control, and a gang must be interpreted as something other than pro-social behavior. Here we are dealing with political crime and the gangs role in it.

Historically it has meant everything from cutting tires, breaking windows, violence to the individual or property, within election campaigns, and has extended most recently in the case of Chicago's Top El Rukn, Jeff Fort, to seeking contractual terrorist work with hostile foreign nations (see Useem and Kimball, 1989: p. 77) --- wanting to blow up American planes or installations for a price. As an organizational vehicle of conflict and violence, the gang deserves much comparative analysis and is also likely to have its parallels internationally. Campbell cites an example of a New York City police sergeant who is quoted to the effect that gangs have been actively recruited and paid for terrorist work (1984, p. 22). Tannenbaum also described the gang as a political instrument (1938, pp. 128-134) and noted their violent role played for management in labor disputes (p, 37). Cloward and Ohlin (1960, pp. 195-196) reference Asbury's account of gangs in politics, even before the civil war, and gang relationships with corrupt politicians in Tammany Hall.

Much of the gang violence that occurs in American cities today has many of the elements of urban guerilla warfare. This analogy and differentiation will be further developed later.

The literature shows gangs can provide a host of extralegal services and functions; from supplying sex and prostitutes, to providing drugs to campaign workers, etc.[10] Figure 6 below is only a suggestive list and certainly does not give an exhaustive list of these many and varied functions.

Another excellent example of the covert use of gangs for extralegal and even terrorist functions is found in recent research on Jamaican posse gangs (Mc Caddon, 1993). According to this source, two major Jamaican posse gangs now operating in the USA were used in the political infighting in Jamaica:

"The Spangler Posse was an enforcer for Michael Manley's People's National Party, while the powerful Shower Posse worked for Edward Seaga's Jamaican Labor Party" (Mc Caddon, 1993: p. 15). Some evidence of C.I.A. involvement with street level enforcement groups in Haiti's 1994 crisis did emerge, the goal being to control the groups to prevent anti-American leadership from emerging. In the United States, vote suppression emerged as an issue because of the remark of an aid involved in the campaign of New Jersey's republican Governor elect Christine Todd Whitman, the charge being that $500,000 was spent to suppress the African-American vote.[11] Theoretically, street gangs could be put to quite effective use in this regard.

4. GANGS AND POLITICIANS: Quid Pro Quo

"You scratch my back, I'll scratch your back", the essential meaning of quid pro quo, represents the application of the norm of reciprocity and the social exchange relationship between gangs and politicians. Another way of describing this relationship between a "gang" and a "government agency" is sometimes called the "client/patron" relationship. One uses the other for mutual benefit. Figure 6 below shows this enormous potential lure represented by "what" the gang has to offer to a politician.

FIGURE 6
WHAT A GANG CAN OFFER,
WHAT A GANG MAY WANT[12]

WHAT THE GANG OFFERS	WHAT THE GANG WANTS
********************	********************
Extra Legal Functions	Directed police discretion
Plausible Deniability	Freedom to Operate
Violence against detractors	Political Interference
Violence against property	Political Protection
Intimidation	De Facto Immunity
Help With Handbills	Tampered Court Cases
Help Tearing Down Signs	Resource priorities (e.g.,
Help Putting Up Signs	drug programs, etc)
Drugs for Campaign Workers	Laissez-Faire
Prostitution & Sexual Favors	Favors
Blackmail Capabilities	Privileges
Stolen Goods	Continuity

The gang clearly has a vast potential capability for operating outside of the legal system. When adequately "buffered" by various layers of contacts to the politician, then any of these essentially criminal acts where the objective material impact is to increase the power and control of the politician, the politician can also enjoy the covert nature of these operations. "I didn't do it", the gangs did; "I didn't run no prostitution ring", somebody else did; "I didn't take any illegal payoffs", the gang did.

Yet there is a norm of reciprocity that operates here and it has to do with an exchange relationship between the politician and the gang. A gang can build up a reservoir of such "good will" with a politician that can be "cashed in" at a later date. A gang can also contribute its unique resources for specialized favors negotiated in advance on a contingency basis: "if we prevent X from winning, then you will help get Y off on probation"; or "if we keep all X's political signs out of the neighborhood by constantly ripping them down and putting yours up, then you will transfer the current Police District Commander out of this ward"; etc, etc.

POLITICS IN THE GANG RIGHTS ACTIVIST MOVEMENT

Many level three gangs today represent themselves as political and civil rights groups, and they are successful in many instances. The Gang Summit held in Kansas City in 1993 was able to convince the Mayor of Kansas City to prevent police from interfering with the event; indeed, the Mayor welcomed the gang leaders at a special breakfast for those attending the Gang Summit. Some gang representatives make no apologies for their gang membership, and like Sharif Willis from Minneapolis indicate there is nothing "former" about their leadership: they are still the top ranking member of their gang --- the Vice Lords in this instance. A number of politicians in a number of cities have therefore met with such gang leaders, typically their public remarks imply that they can coopt the gang into doing prosocial work for the community. The gangs claim that too: that is, that they are the last hope to reverse the deterioration of our urban areas. Are we to believe them is the real question here.

The political "platforms" of gangs today are easily to predict. As a gang leader turned informant for the federal government told the author, "gangs are in favor of gun control...if there is a gun around, they want to be in control of it". Gangs would tend not to be attracted to a conservative political agenda. Gangs and gang members are more attracted to very liberal and even radical political ideals. There are some notable exceptions, however, as we have yet to see a gang really endorse gun control legislation and disarm themselves in the spirit of being politically consistent. It is useful to summarize some of the political issues that arise in what now exists as the "gang advocacy" press.

Gangs, then, often have a critical or even radical political slant. Often this includes some racial conflict analysis. An example that seeks parity in social policy is provided in the Teen Angels (Issue 122) magazine in its editorializing. Teen Angels is a gang magazine[13], particularly for Cholos, it includes glossy color photos of various Hispanic gangs (e.g., SUR 13, Surenos, 18th Street Gang, etc) mostly in California; but includes other western states as well (e.g., Texas, Colorado, Arizona, etc). It is the real thing. It has existed since 1980 and gives gangs and gang members what they want, in fact what they are willing to pay for: an outlet for their messages, and their art. Their art is predictable: guns and sex are the most common themes, followed by customized car scenes, always of course with the gang logo.

In the first issue of Teen Angels many young females had their photographs published; and it was in fact a "membership" type of association: one could join the Teen Angel Fan Club and buy Teen Angel T-shirts[14]. This magazine truly has the best gang art, being the first gang magazine in the world. Its first issue also included a full-page drawing of a gangster in a 1930s black car holding a Thompson submachine gun with the advertisement for the name and telephone number of a criminal defense attorney "He's On Your Side".

By its own description (Teen Angels, Issue 118: p. 2):

"Teen Angels Magazine is a "gang" Rights Activist News Agency Organization dedicated to informing the Barrio Youth of their Civil Rights and Liberties as defined in the U.S. Constitution, The Bill of

Rights and the Hildalgo Treaty between the U.S. & Mexico".

One will often find gang and gun photos in the magazine, but it does not include "drug stash" photos such as might be found in the centerfold of High Times magazine. One can find religious-based anti-gang ads from California groups seeking to get Cholos to quit the gang for Jesus. Since its first issue in 1980 and continuing to present, it has included specific gang contributions (e.g., SUR 13). Because it is exclusively focused on Hispanic gangs and gang members, and recognizing that such magazines are not known to exist for African-American gangs, the casual observer might be tempted to suggest some cultural difference in the need for expressive outlets. However, it is probably much more complex that this, and the present author would hypothesize that if a similar group such as that which tried to organize a National Truce in Kansas City in 1993 were to market a similar publication geared primarily to African-American gangs, it would be equally as successful as Teen Angels.

The magazine rarely includes editorials, but those that are included are of some political interest. One such editorial consisted of a comment or published reply to a letter/article by an inmate. The editorial (Issue # 106) was very pro-law enforcement and encouraged its readers to believe that most cops are good cops. What it also said was the real issue was how the network television news was controlled by the Japanese (called "Japs"), and that what readers needed to worry about was "the coming war with Japan!" Another editorial in the same issue raised the "double standard" problem of how some might complain about pictures of Chicano gang members with guns (who have the right to own guns, unless they are convicted of a felony), while pictures of white persons with guns and depicted in acts of violence can be found in many comic books.

Another editorial (Issue 122) was in the form of a one page poem entitled "Indian Drugs, War Drums are Beating!" and was accompanied by commentary that Americans have overly ignored Native American Indians. It goes on to raise a similar issue on overlooking the Latinos:

"The school system celebrates Black history week. Is there a Latino history week? HA! Latinos are now the official majority of the population of the state of California and don't even have their own week. Teen Angels Magazine demands that there be not only a Latino week, but also a Native American week!"

Articles from the ACLU are reprinted in the magazine, along with those written by prison reform/activist groups in California.

The July 15th 1993 Gang Summit held in St. Paul, Minnesota tends to epitomize what is meant by indigenous "gang politics". About 150 persons attended the meeting held at the Church, many of whom were not necessarily gang members but were long standing "community activists", and groups such as the American Indian Movement who can be counted on to attend and speak at such events that are critical of the status quo. The style and the rhetoric of the "march" held after the first day's Gang Summit meeting in St. Paul was remarkably similar to some of the 1960s and early 1970s radical political protests[15]. The main message was that of anti-racism and anti-law enforcement, particularly how cops had killed gang members. During the same time frame as the Gang Summit in the Twin Cities, sniper attacks continued on Minneapolis police (e.g., a police car was simply doing a traffic stop on the southside of Minneapolis when it was hit with five gun shots). Thus, in addition to the role of the gang in relationship to traditional politics and political corruption, there is the additional feature of gang rights and gang activist movements.

ON THE ISSUE OF ELITISM AND POLITICS

The law of the land is that you don't have to be a highly educated white home owner to vote. The voting franchise is certainly a right to be used by any gang member of age and so qualified to vote. Anyone who thinks that social status and stigmatizable qualities should restrict persons from voting in America necessarily operates under an elitist view of democracy. Modern gangs are definitely involving themselves in the electoral process. The issue is not whether they have the right to vote. The larger issue is that of responsible participation in the political process as opposed to something less prosocial.

On the other hand, we must recognize that as a typical scenario in the relationship of a gang to local politics, the gang volunteers to work for political candidates in handing out leaflets, house to house, etc. When the media hears about this, or rival candidates can use it, typically the candidate refuses such volunteered help. As a result, local newspaper editorials may attack the same candidate on the grounds that it was a chance for "steering the gangs into something pro-social". But we must simply recall from the limited data available on the subject (see Taylor, 1990) that most gang members are not normally in the habit of voting. One might ask, in light of this, is their interest in electoral politics, then, one of instrumental rather than integrative motivation? That is, does the gang want something, quid pro quo, for such volunteer work? Does the hidden agenda of the "21st Century Vote" initiative of midwestern gangs today include the release of high ranking imprisoned gang leaders or greater influence over local policing practices? In such a context, obviously, gang help could truly be a political liability and an astute candidate knowledgeable of the impact of the mass media might refuse such assistance in the same vein that constituents would expect an elected official to also refuse assistance and especially material support from organized crime.

My own position is, hopefully, clear: we cannot legally exclude gang-affiliated persons from the political process.[16] Nor can we automatically assume that if we see someone on televised videotape at a major "mass" event, open to the public, showing a gang sign, that this is in any sense "proof" that the official sponsoring or benefiting from the event is necessarily a cultivator of gangs, a benefactor of gangs, and a corrupt politician whose power is tied directly to gang crime. Finally, recall that differential access theory could predict more intense violence from gangs if they were excluded from the political process. This is true particularly where gang ideology takes on revolutionary or insurrectionist tones.

So here, guided by previous research, are the merits of doing focused oral histories with gang members. Such a case is shown below in the case of LK41. No names are used. And names of politicians, ward numbers, etc, have been edited out. Otherwise, it is an exact transcription of tape recorded interview material.[17]

CASE STUDY OF LK41:

I'm a Latin King. I figured getting involved in politics was an easier way to help other people that have created problems for themselves. For example, to help people pull a few strings here and there when it is possible. Being a Latin King member for 25 years and a former War Lord of the Boulevard, from the gang fights I have had, from the people I have destroyed in one way or another, the younger people look up to me. They respect me.

RELATIONSHIP WITH FORMER ALDERMAN E.V.: I was a part of the __nd ward, I was a part of the organizers. Ah, I was what they would call, in the field. My job was to try to recruit gang members into the __nd Ward to help build an army, not in the sense of against the police or anything, but for voters. My job was to get the gangs politically involved into the neighborhood.

I didn't receive anything, but I was promised Latino Youth Centers for the Latin Kings. I myself, I really didn't want anything, I felt that at that time being a part of the problem in the __nd ward, that I could put something back into it, such as Centers, educational programs, maybe even a boys club if possible, something to get the gangs off the street. That was my main objective.

E.V. didn't help, which was a promise that never given, because we lost to Ald. C_____ G_____. That was an issue, that if we won we would receive, if we lost we would receive nothing. I am currently involved with the __nd Ward with Mr. ____, and I expect the same thing I expected out of Mr. V_____ at the time. I expect at least youth centers. I expect to try to help the community. Yes, there is gangs, there is Latin Kings, there is gang members involved, as in all politics.

I believe that at if Mr. ____ is elected Alderman that he will keep his promise. Which is to try to curb the gangs by opening up a few centers. Maybe a few parks. Maybe even a possibility that to try and put some of these guys into jobs.
By keeping them on the streets all you are doing is creating a problem. Not solving it.

WHAT IS THE GANG SOLUTION? Education. I believe that low fixed income people would go with more than just a few dollars. Politicians have a habit of wanting to pay you two dollars for a hundred thousand dollars worth of work. I believe that if the politicians, aldermans, committeemen, congressmen, senators, that if they took a little more interest in their sons and daughters, who probably are gang members, would see another side of the coin.
I believe by creating jobs for them, by not just locking them up and creating problems, such as calling them animals, and dope fiends and drug dealers, these are the labels that people have put upon these people. And in return, they are reacting towards what society expects them to be. Not what they want to be.

I believe the politicians prey on the gangs, they use them to their advantage, they use them for their campaigns, they use em to bring an image into the neighborhood which they in return promise the public that they will curb once they are in office. I believe a lot of gangs are paid by politicians, to be used. I believe the police officers play the same role. The police have a job to perform but I think they only perform it due to the fact because the politicians want them to perform it. By arresting, twelve, thirteen, fourteen-year-old children for curfew doesn't resolve a problem, it creates a problem. The younger look upon the police and instead of respecting them look upon them with animosity. How can you expect a 12-year-old girl or boy to respect a police officer when he is slapping him or her upside the head with a club? Or using a term like bitches or punks in front of their friends, what if they are not a juvenile as the police makes them out to be, when they are 19 or 20 years old, how can you expect them to honestly trust and respect somebody that doesn't have no respect for them?

HOW MANY LATIN KINGS ARE THERE IN THIS __th District or __nd Ward?

I couldn't honestly say, possibly maybe a thousand. Active, maybe 5 to 6 hundred total. They range from probably 12 to, I'm 41 years old.

The Latin Kings, we started out originally, which may sound far fetched, ah, a social activity organization. Our main goal was to try to keep which all of em said, to keep the enemy out of the neighborhood. When we first formed, when I first became a gang member in 1965, my main objective was to try to clean up the neighborhood, there was drug addicts in the neighborhood, there was a lot of burglars, and a lot of killing. Our main thing was to join a coalition (pronounced "correlation") to try to keep and try to straighten out the neighborhood, not to create problems. As time went on, we were turning away from not only from the politicians but from the police officers, we were harassed because we went out on the corners and we fought against other gang members who were raping and robbing and stealing off of our own people. I don't think the Kings want to be known as the killers and rapers and drug dealers, child molesters, or whatever for the rest of their life. I would like to think they would like myself that they have done something constructive. By turning over a new leaf if given a chance. I mean how can you keep expecting somebody to try be a, try to be a citizen, when people keep putting them down. I mean even a dog has its own day. I think that the Kings, if given a chance, I think they would like to come into this neighborhood and clean it up. I think the Kings are just like anybody else. That given the right chance, I think what they are looking for actually is somebody to really sit down and talk to them. Not to disrespect them. I believe that if there was a program set up for some of the older guys to sit down with some of the younger guys I think we could at least eliminate some of the wrong doing that has been done in this neighborhood. Not total. But I believe that if we have helped one out of ten we are doing something.

WHO HAVE THE KINGS ELECTED TO POLITICAL OFFICE? Well, I know, C____ G_____ was one of them, as a matter of fact, the Kings had backed up Rudy Lozano. Rudy Lozano was one of our main image. He was somebody that was our savior for the neighborhood. He came into us, talking to us, relating what was expected of us, promising to help the neighborhood, but I am not saying that was wrong. I think he took an interest in us. But I do know that C___ G____ has used the Kings for his own benefit, by promising jobs, by working work with the kings that work with him, by knocking on doors, doing whatever is possible to get him

elected. By him being elected we had the neighborhood to ourselves, which was a false promise. C____ G____ used us and there is no doubt in my mind he has probably used other gang members, not only Kings, but probably the Two-Six also which is another gang in the neighborhood.

WHO DO YOU BELIEVE KNOCKED OFF RUDY LOZANO? I believe it was a political move. I don't believe that C___ G___, ah...I mean Rudy Lozano was killed because of drugs. I find that hard to, I knew Rudy Lozano, I sat down and talked to Rudy Lozano on several occasions. I believe because there was a struggle in the neighborhood for the, for politics. I don't think it was, so much that the, Rudy Lozano was not a drug user. And I would put my life on the line for that. Rudy was not, he didn't believe in drugs, that was not his image, he was for the people. I find it pretty hard to believe that people would even consider even thinking that he was a drug user. I mean, the man had everything to gain and a lot to lose, and he lost his life over it. And I believe it was over, what he was trying to do was form the unions in the neighborhoods, such as your tortillas, and your, ah, ah, and your restaurants, and I believe and this is to my heart that somebody put up somebody to kill him. He was much too strong for him to use drugs.

I believe it was true that what the newspapers reported, that the Two-Six gang member killed him, that he just got too strong, politically. They used it as, as, a drug issue. The individual was probably paid and probably his family got paid off also. Understand this, the man was becoming a political image in this neighborhood to a lot of people. Especially the poor people. Especially the Hispanic people. Now I am not saying it was a white or a black that killed him. We know that somebody killed him. And I had gone with Rudy Lozano on a few voyages through the neighborhood confront different store owners, and ah restaurants, and businesses. And they did not like Rudy Lozano. Due to the fact that because he was for the Hispanic people. He was trying to straighten the neighborhood out. He was trying to form a union here. A coalition for the Hispanic people, instead of the same thing, like I said for the Kings, instead of taking advantage of them, that he wanted to do something for them. And I believe that was the reason why they killed him.

Gangs and politics go hand in hand. I believe that an Alderman that has been an alderman for the last 20 years, and there aint no doubt in my mind, I would probably stake my life on it, he has probably taken a bribe along the way. Not all of them. But a good majority of them. But the record shows it for a fact. You have aldermen in the penitentiary. I believe the Kings are probably just waiting for something or somebody to come to relieve them. Of giving something. So they can start their life all over again. Put their life together. You know it is a funny part of this, the politicians ask for the Kings for the gangs help, but they refuse to help them when it is all over. And in every election you hear the same thing, you have to clean the gangs up, you have to take them off the streets, you have to build more penitentiaries, take the graffiti off, but in return it is the politicians who ask the gang members to go out and hang their signs, to destroy the other candidates as much as possible, to disgrace them if possible. And I am not going to sit here and say they would even go as far as to kill them. But I do know they will probably use them as much as possible to hurt another candidate if push comes to shove.

AN UPDATE ON THE RUDY LOZANO ASSASSINATION

In the summer of 1993 a high ranking member of the Latin King organization who had "flipped for the G" (i.e., being a confidential informant for federal law enforcement agencies) and who was now being held in a snitch farm was interviewed on the Rudy Lozano issue. Lozano was a very popular local political leader in the Chicago Hispanic community, as well as a labor organizer, who was assassinated on June 8, 1983. This was truly a "former member" or "ex" member of a gang, in this case the Latin Kings. He was really an "ex-member" of the Latin Kings because there was and still is a $250,000 "hit" out on him. Thus, he was being held in a very secure special protection unit. By special permission I was able to visit this secure facility and conduct in-depth private interviews with this person. This person had been a member of the Latin Kings for twenty years and had gained at his forced retirement the position of a Prince and carried the special tattoo that the position entailed!

Many of the details in the multiple in-depth interviews with this person proved to be corroborated. We were not paying for our information either. As the person in this instance, an inmate, explained the true story about Rudy Lozano:

"Rudy Lozano was going out with one of Baby King's sisters".

Baby King a/k/a "B.K." was then and is now the single highest top ranking member of the Latin Kings and may rise to the Sun God position in this burgeoning national organization. As our source further indicated:

"BK got with David Ayala, the chief of the Two-Sixers, because he was upset with Rudy Lozano and in the crime business, well the business part of it is you put your differences aside even if you are rival gang organizations. The dude who was arrested and

convicted for the Rudy Lozano killing he's in prison now, I've met him. He was Latin Folks, being a two-sixer, which I could not get along with being Latin Peoples. Well, his name is Gregory Escobar, he was the fall guy. He knows now that it was a King hit, it bothers him now. But he didn't know it was a Latin King hit when he did it."

Many including the present author had suspected the Rudy Lozano assassination of a major local grassroots political leader was at the time a crime that could be put at the doors of the Latin King organization. Obviously, the true facts of the crime had been effectively concealed a very long time officially[18]. But the true story was known apparently to many in these two gang organizations (Two Sixer's and the Latin Kings). Gangs continue today throughout America to seek to develop and cultivate ties to elected politicians. What those politicians need to know are stories like the Rudy Lozano case[19].

As some gangs approach the point of operating in the fashion of organized crime, this problem can be expected to escalate. For after all, being able to cultivate or use political corruption is one of the defining features of what we mean by organized crime. That some gangs are operating as groups that can mobilize thousands of votes (e.g., the Disciples Annual Picnics are an example: in their summer 1992 they attracted 5,000, in 1993 some 10,000 attended their picnic, all food and transportation free[20]), and that they engage in voter registration drives as well, and particularly to the extent the gangs use a public relations strategy where they manipulate the mass media into scenes showing their involvement in "Truces" and "helping the community" (e.g., anti-litter campaigns in public housing complexes, where they may themselves "fine" a litterer), then such grey areas of political "right and wrong" and outright ethical misconduct and worse can be expected in the political arena.

THE GANG ISSUE IN LOCAL AND NATIONAL POLITICAL CAMPAIGNS

During the 1992 presidential campaign, the incumbent President George Bush did not use the gang issue as part of his political campaign. Why? In a later chapter on gangs and law enforcement we will find part of the answer, as apparently a large portion of our Nation's gang problem basically exploded during President Bush's term of office. Presidential candidate William Clinton did refer to gangs in his nomination acceptance speech at the Democratic National Convention. In that speech, one of the "covenants" referred to addressing our Nation's gang problem by means of a new kind of "national service", involving college graduates who perform public services that might be useful in preventing some of the problems associated with gangs.

Another candidate running for the president's office in 1992 was James "Bo" Gritz, the famous Green Beret activist for P.O.W.'s. In a videotape used in his presidential campaign, entitled "The Healing of America" (1992), gangs are given much more prominent attention. The kind of discussion of gangs in the Gritz (1992) political platform basically sees major gangs profiting from drugs, and political corruption having a lot to do with the importation of drugs, and the rise of a secret-style military-police force who are ever present to hold back the rising threat of violence and riots from gang members and other groups driven to desperation.

In some local municipal elections, gangs are also a campaign issue. The most popular and effective political use of the gang issue is that of the get tough approach. In short, the gang problem has become an issue that is relevant to the campaign positions of candidates seeking office in all levels of government. Given the rising importance of the gang problem we can probably expect this trend to continue.

LEFTIST POLITICAL EXTREMIST GROUPS CULTIVATING GANGS

Some groups who regularly show up at Gang Summit Meetings, meetings of gang members and gang leaders held under the banner of working for peace sometimes directly or indirectly subsidized by the federal government held in recent years that this author monitored, are traditional and well known left wing extremist groups. They show up wearing radical T-shirts with their symbols of revolution, but stick out as some of the only white people present not representing the media. This happened in Kansas City, Minneapolis, and Chicago; three different gang summit meetings. In Minneapolis a variety of such groups appeared. In Chicago two white teenage members of the Revolutionary Communist Party, Chicago Branch distributed flyers calling for revolution. In the Chicago meeting another group using the black panther symbol superimposed over the globe called the New African-American Vanguard Movement (NAAVM) based in Los Angeles also distributed a flyer explaining its platform: peace and justice, better food and housing, reform of criminal justice, legalized drugs, sentence reductions, end of police brutality, end of military aggression, and religious tolerance. All of the political analysis was couched in traditional 1960s radical leftist language, but updated to specifically attract Crips and Bloods to their own way of thinking. There has also been a Latin and Hispanic version of this, where in Chicago some groups tending to be supportive of the terrorist group known as the F.A.L.N., have tried to cultivate gang members and have apparently succeeded in some regards as discussed elsewhere in this book. The

F.A.L.N. is a leftist group that seeks independence for Puerto Rico[21]. White gangs provide numerous examples of mostly rightwing cultivation.

"Government Gangs: Can They Exist?"

In the classical study of gangs by Frederick M. Thrasher (1927) one thing that was overlooked was the possibility that gangs could exist inside government. In Thrasher's original work, he developed a chart outlining the "natural history of a gang", it showed what groups could become gang, and what a gang could become (see p. 70, in Thrasher 1927). Thrasher did recognize that a gang could start as a gang, then become a "political machine" in a later etiological development sequence. But Thrasher did not conceive that where a group of individuals from a party existing and controlling government agencies could itself become a gang.

This appears to be the case in explaining how 28 people, as of early 2000 (the number will probably rise), were charged by federal prosecutors with taking bribes to sell "Commercial Driver's Licenses" (CDL's) to truckers who would probably not have passed the tests if they went through regular channels. While some of the bribe money got shared inside the group, by those working in the Illinois Secretary of State's office, at least $170,000 of the illegal bribe money found its way directly into the campaign fund for the candidate who was then running for governor and who would in fact win the Illinois race for governor (Republican Gov. Ryan). This group of individuals working in government had a specialized crime pattern. They had no "gang name", they had no "graffiti", they did not wear special colors. They were simply an informal social organization within a larger formal government organization that operated, collectively, and cooperatively, to carry out a large scale licensing scam. As a group involved in recurrent criminal acts, it must be defined as a gang using the social scientific definition of gang.

GANG POLITICAL INFLUENCE ON GOVERNMENT AGENCIES

In 1993 Gangster Disciple gang leader Larry Hoover engineered a public petition drive to influence the Illinois Prisoner Review Board to grant him a parole. The petition cover was endorsed by a number of African-American politicians and activists[22]. When it was submitted to the parole board it contained the names and addresses and signatures of nearly 5,000 persons.[23] By chance we had been interviewing female members of the gang at the time, and one who had "de-activated", basically trying to "socially slip away" from the gang, responded to a knock on her door one night and was basically told by the local gang members to sign the petition, and thus she expressed the view of being compelled to sign the petition. We did feel it was very curious to subsequently discover that such an important document was destroyed by the Illinois Prisoner Review Board.

This attempt by the gang to engineer the release of their gang leader included using well-known current and former elected officials to speak or write to the parole board on behalf of such a parole, in addition to a number of business and religious leaders. The parole was not granted[24], but another parole hearing was scheduled for December, 1994 which also corresponds to a time of a build up of political action by the gang. And it would appear from closer analysis that Hoover also has a back up plan for trying to get a parole from the Illinois Department of Corrections.

Hoover's back up plan surfaced in 1993, when Illinois State Representative Coy Pugh introduced House Bill 513 and House Bill 240 to the General Assembly.[25] The thrust of these bills, had they been passed, would have converted so-called "C-numbers" to a flattime sentence for inmates currently in the system. Hoover has a c-number, meaning it is an indeterminate sentence. The state law proposed by Pugh would have converted c-number sentences to fixed sentences, allowing many in prison to automatically be released. Pugh was one of several who wrote a letter on July 15,1993 to the prisoner review board in behalf of Hoover's attempt to get released.[26] Pugh is friendly to the "21st Century V.O.T.E." group and was featured in a press kit photo standing with their main leaders at the summer 1993 picnic held at a private farm in Kankakee, Illinois which drew nearly 10,000 persons --- mostly Gangster Disciples.

POLITICAL ACTION BY GANGS

When the Gangster Disciples in Chicago formed the Young Voters of Illinois in the mid-1980s, these folks were quickly followed by the same put-on among peoples. The Unknown Conservative Vice Lords (UCVL) in 1985 formed and obtained a state chartered not-for-profit group called the United Concerned Voters of Illinois (UCVL). This type of development is more of a public relations function for the gang than a serious attempt to enter politics and unseat incumbents. Jeff Fort's El Rukn gang formed the Young Grass Roots Independent Voters, similarly, but according to 1991 testimony apparently to suppress the African-American vote against Harold Washington by backing another candidate and then mayor Jane Byrne, that is a straight-forward contractual arrangement with the gang being paid for its power to intimidate.[27]

More recently, however, the Gangster Disciples have taken a more serious turn in political ac-

tion by forming "21st Century V.O.T.E."[28], and have developed a large war chest for the group to have some impact. This same group had very high access to political elites when one of its main gang activists, Wallace "Gator" Bradley, was able to meet with the President in the White House[29]. Some longtime gang analysts point to the fact that there is nothing new about gang leaders meeting with the President and cite the case of Jeff Fort and Richard Nixon in 1991. Actually, while Jeff Fort was invited to Nixon's inauguration, Jeff did not personally attend and in fact sent two of his lieutenants in his place to attend the inauguration.[30] However, some analysts of this development are less worried about the success of the GDs in electoral politics under the theory that in the light of day the group will be viewed as a deviant group and not be supported in spite of its efforts to hand out Thanksgiving and Christmas food baskets, even though they can be obviously effective in pressure politics by their simple ability to disrupt. The GDs did not need have to read up on Saul Alinsky to realize they can have an impact in Chicago just by showing up with 5,000 members in Chicago's loop with protest signs, chanting nasty slogans about Mayor Daley.

Current thinking seems to be that the recent more sophisticated approach to Chicago politics by the Gangster Disciples is no longer a put-on and that they are having a definite impact on elections. The first major battle was in the March 15th 1994 primary elections in which 21st Century V.O.T.E. supported Jerry Washington as a challenger to Rep. Daniel Burke[31]. While Burke won the election easily, gang involvement in the election was very obvious, and their preferred candidate Washington did do a lot better in terms of votes than in previous attempts in the same race.[32]

The spring 1994 election followed an earlier public relations event that drew harsh criticism when 21st Century V.O.T.E. had staged an awards ceremony at Chicago's Englewood Public High School. This ceremony and media event happened during the Chicago Gang Summit meeting held in October, 1993. Among the recipients of awards was of course Larry Hoover, but Willie Lloyd[33] the leader of the Unknown Vice Lords was also given an award like Hoover in absentia, along with other gang leaders active in the Gang Summit Meeting.[34] Students at the school had to attend this ceremony, and one teacher reported several non-gang members told her they now wanted to join the gang.[35] While it showed the ability of the gang to be able to use a public high school through sympathizers who worked there[36], the media generally gave it harsh reviews and it was roundly criticized as an inappropriate use of government property[37].

Still, late in 1994 it was the Gangster Disciple's front group "21st Century V.O.T.E." that was said to be responsible for an attempted takeover of the southside branch of Chicago's NAACP, when a group friendly to these same gang activists and which was also a co-sponsor of the 1993 Chicago Gang Summit (No Dope Express) walked into the NAACP office with 5,000 new and recently completed applications for membership in the NAACP --- along with nearly $50,000 in cash for the membership fees to go along with the applications, in an attempt to engineer a political takeover of this branch of the NAACP.[38] While erring on the side of flamboyance, the political education of gangs could improve over time, and with the ability to walk in with 5,000 new memberships there are few organizations, fraternities, not-for-profit groups, membership associations, etc, that could not easily find themselves held hostage in this fashion. This is a twist on the same type of "terrorist threat" style of shake-downs used by the Yakuza, where they would simply buy shares to a corporation, show up at the stock holders meeting and disrupt the activities therein, and literally shake down the corporation systematically in elections and stockholders meetings.

SUMMARY AND CONCLUSION

Politically, most gangs are opportunistic, conservatively oriented[39] in the sense that they have as their ideal type a function as a business organization, and their attachment to the legitimate social order through politicians tends to be characterized by lower-level field functions. Gang members are not, as a group, over-achievers in the field of higher education, particularly political science. They are not likely to be used as strategy or policy makers in a political campaign, rather their function is, like their life style, a "street function". The gangs attempt to form its own political organization can only further expose the same gang to systematic investigation and will thus backfire in the long run.

Chicago has a somewhat unique political context. Currently, an appointed Alderman sits on the City Council who is an "ex-member" of a large gang organization. Some like to loosely use the phrase that Chicago "has elected a U.S. Congressman who is a gang member" --- but they are referring to someone who had only a political association with the Black Panther Party[40]. In its time, certainly the Black Panther Party was treated as a gang[41]. Some in corrections still define Black Panthers in the same way, as they do the Fruits of Islam, as a threat group. And, of course, Chicago politics is somewhat unique in what can best be described as being an open-system capable of integrating most organized political factions, and accommodating the rest. Chicago is not any more or less corrupt than any other city in America it just has enjoyed more than its share of attention in that regard, so much so that Chicagoans themselves joke about it in the popular witticism "vote early and often".

The problem is that gangs are quick to learn the laws and the laws on financial disclosures for politicians are well known. Any cash donations below a certain threshold do not have to have a name or donor source associated with it for Ethical Disclosures in Financial Activity required by law. A gang is uniquely qualified to "wash" and "launder" very large hidden cash contributions, by having its many members hand-carry such smaller cash donations to the political function. This helps explain why in the fall of 1994 the Gangster Disciples political action committee known as "21st Century V.O.T.E." was able to file a financial disclosure report indicating over $100,000 in donations, but only $2,500 was accounted for by specifically named sources.

And yet, it is often remarked for gang leaders, like Jeff Fort that the extent of mind control over fellow gang members is extraordinary. Some also like to see the parallel qualities that some gang organizations have with cult groups in terms of the remarkable control of member behavior. This type of parallel of gangs to cults has the common elements of an authoritarian leader, a group that threatens harm to one who tries to leave it, and harsh discipline against its own members for violating internal rules. If the organizational efforts and energy of a typical modern organized gang were applied for pro-social activities, then it would be considered a heroic development from the underclass: just to get these persons on a trajectory out of a pattern of typically inner-city impoverishment. It is a political coup in its own right to be able to organize such persons to do anything positive. However, no evidence exists that anyone has ever been able to "treat" an entire gang, let alone rehabilitate it in terms of its individual members or its composite function and purpose as a group or organization. Thus, most of the conspicuously prosocial aspects of a gang are part of its public relations function designed to deflect law enforcement attention and just like in community policing where the police officer wants to have a friendlier relationship with the locals, the gang seeks more cordial relations with those locals who could potentially testify against them.[42]

The difference between the present position from that of implied prior positions in the literature is the matter of a gang member's right to vote and participate in the electoral process. Any offender has that right, if local laws allow it. Remember, over ten percent of all Americans have an arrest record according to NORC[43] data. Any view which implies exclusion of deviants or exoffenders is necessarily an elitist view of how democracy should work.

The reader who accepts, to any extent, the popular "reintegration" strategy for rehabilitation or preventing criminal relapse or recidivism, cannot have the cake and eat it too --- we cannot in policy claim to want to reintegrate offenders back into our communities and put them on a legitimate career trajectory and at the same time through elitist practice prevent them from exercising constitutionally guaranteed rights, such as the right to vote. Clearly both racism and the double standard operate here when it comes to how some ultra-conservative whites have characterized Jesse Jackson's or Operation PUSH's efforts to register Cook County Jail inmates to vote. That was not cultivating gang organization, it was a lawfully entitled effort to reach out to an important segment of America's "other half" ---- that half that never votes anyhow.

In the long run, the success of a gang in spurring an increase in voting behavior may be the penultimate solution to the historical question of "how do we increase voter turnout?". The reason this is answer is theoretically forthcoming is to be found in the work of Emile Durkheim. Durkheim informs us that norms are strengthened and social solidarity may increase because of crime in some instances by the application of sanctions and response to the crime problem. The American "lazy half" that never really votes might actually get off their bar stools, register to vote and actually vote if they knew the full extent of gang involvement in local American politics.

Finally, we cannot from a strict social scientific basis rule out the possibility that powerlessness and the search for power are codeterminants of gang organization. We shall see later that another contemporary theory says essentially the same thing: multiple marginality causes gangs, that is they are not simply alienated individuals, they are multiply labelled, some persons face "double", "triple" jeopardy, and beyond, in terms of their life chances for "making it in America". Or as Vigil (1988) says, they are multiply marginal. We should not alienate offenders from our mainstream political institutions, or else they have but one recourse: subcultural politics --- and political extremism.

Indeed, with advance knowledge of any gang's potential to abuse such political resources, it might be more effective to stimulate citizenship and voting behavior as a general thrust towards a more "pro social" orientation of the type of offenders we find in our correctional institutions today. The trouble comes when denying the political linkages and the tendency of gangs to gravitate towards sources of political legitimation.

Discussion Questions

(1) How do you think the evolution of the mass media has impacted on the relationship between the corrupt politician and use of gang members in the political arena? Is it as easy today as it was several decades ago, just to get away with it unnoticed?

(2) Campbell (1984) felt that gangs (at least the female gang members she studied) were not revolutionary. How then do we account for the existence within highly organized gangs (level 3 gangs) that have in their written constitutions, language that identifies "their struggle" with the Third World, and oppressed persons generally?

(3) Are neo-nazi, Aryan Nation-style, and skinhead gangs by most standards likely to be political by definition, and political extremists, if they organize along the dimensions of "white power"?

"I'm Not A Gang Leader, I'm an Organizer of a Street Organization Composed of Oppressed Minorities"

We all wish it were true, and there have been many versions of this "line". One of the best was from the New York City Latin Kings. The N.Y. Latin Kings and Queens Nation is spin-off of the original Chicago Latin Kings. The New York version wrote its own separate constitution. Word is the Chicago original is not happy with the New York "renegade" faction and a "hit" was put out of them, and a message was sent to them, and in fact as recently as of May, 1998 observers in New York were noticing a tendency for N.Y. Latin Kings to "flip" over to another gang (Neta's).

But this is a story about how gang's use the public relations function. Antonio Fernandez is "King Tone", the self-styled leader of the N.Y. Latin Kings[44]. In 1996 and 1997 and early 1998 he obtained a great deal of what must be regarded as "favorable media coverage" by insisting to the reporters that he was "turning the gang" into a force for good. The N.Y. Latin Kings had their own community newsletter they would distribute to "spread the word" of their good deeds for the community. He soon got help from lawyers and priests. He got his gang incorporated. He got on the payroll of a sympathetic church. Criminal justice professors in New York saw this as a "miracle": someone who could stop crime from within the gang. Cops, prosecutors, corrections officials, and anyone knowledgeable of the N.Y. Latin King gang, including the National Gang Crime Research Center which published the N.Y. Latin King gang profile in its Journal of Gang Research tended to be the only ones not sucked into this "con".

HONOLULU, Hawaii: An Editorial About Politicians Who Negotiate With Gang Members

(Republished from the Journal of Gang Research)

It is common knowledge that it is bad news to negotiate with terrorists or criminals. The message has yet to sink in among some politicians that it is bad news to negotiate with gangs, gang members, and gang leaders.

If it were an individual armed robber, a mentally stable human being would never suggest to the robber "could you just take my wallet and cash, and leave me with my money belt so I can enjoy the rest of my vacation?". You usually cannot negotiate with individual criminal offenders. And when you negotiate with "groups" or "organizations" of criminal offenders you are making an even larger mistake: you are giving them power. And the mistake is further compounded when a government official provides this power to the gang that enhances the status and solidarity of the gang.

In the summer of 1996, Honolulu's mayor Jeremy Harris joined a small but goofy number of politicians who have negotiated with gang members. On June 7th, a gang member was fatally wounded by a police officer and the decedent's gang, the Little Pinoy Bad Boys, threatened to wage armed retaliation against Honolulu's police officers.

What did the Mayor of Honolulu do? Well, he did what any good gang apologist would do, he asked the gang if they could do lunch with him. He invited ten of the gang members to his office and over lunch lectured to them that they should not declare war on Honolulu's police officers. The gang members left the complaining about police brutality, gaining an enormous amount of free and unwarranted publicity.

Sadly, the Mayor of Honolulu has not been the only politician to try and negotiate with gang members. In recent years we have seen other related cases:

• Mayor of Peoria, Illinois hires Wallace "Gator" Bradley to develop a gang peace treaty in his town.

• Mayor of Kansas City, MO treats gang members from across the United States to a breakfast and police protection for their National Gang Summit Meeting.

• Fort Worth, Texas: hiring gang members to walk the streets "to keep the peace".

• President Clinton himself meets with Wallace "Gator" Bradley in the White House in 1994.

These are bad examples for elected officials for one fundamental reason: they strengthen the gang by giving such recognition and status to gang members, as if the gangs were equal partners in the public safety mission! Gangs and gang members are a significant part of the crime, drug, and violence problem, they are not a part of any solution and politicians need to get this straight. We suspect those who do not get the message will get another message when re-election votes are tallied and the informed public can send its evaluation of the value of negotiating with gang leaders.

End Notes:

[1] Remember that in American politics, appeasement is always a factor. Is it is possible that some gangs sustain nourishment and legitimacy from such political appeasement? Through having "social programs" ostensibly created for gang prevention work, that may in actuality function au contraire in terms of actually providing the meeting grounds for gang organization development? And all with public monies or enjoying not-for-profit status? Poston (1971) described some of this problem.

[2] One of these is the interface with political forces. Not all gangs have such ties to larger political forces. Most can reasonably be assumed to want to exploit such relationships. If given the chance. The maxim "through understanding comes control" has more than some significance in this analysis of politics and gangs in the correctional environment.

[3] Bensinger (1984: p. 5) quotes the 1968 Senate Investigating Committee looking into the $927,341 OEO grant to the Blackstone Rangers where a gang leader named "Watusi" alleges "the federal monies were used to pay off gang members not to riot".

[4] Recently in Chicago when the City Council seat for the 22nd Ward became vacant, Mayor Daley appointed Ricardo Munoz to fill the open position. Much local media attention and editorials shortly appeared; because Mr. Munoz admits to prior gang affiliation and an arrest history for drugs and weapons charges. One letter to the editor by Hector Linares in the Chicago Tribune blasting the appointment said "The message his appointment makes to the gangbangers and drug dealers is clear --- the more you break the law, the better your qualifications for Chicago political office".

[5] Haskins (1975) provides a powerful historical analysis as well. That is, most local political leaders in New York City many years ago "had at least one gang working for" them, "thus the gangs of New York play no small part in the political struggles of mid-nineteenth century, starting under the approving eye of the politicians" (Haskins, 1975: p. 32).

[6] This is amply documented by Sale (1971, pp. 66-67) where Jeff Fort's gang, at that time in history known as the Black Stone Ranger's, was paid to keep the Black Panthers from operating effectively on Chicago's southside. Later Jeff Fort would also be paid for African-American vote suppression in the Harold Washington election.

[7] And, of course, in other studies as well, Jeff Fort's

early gang development formation, in the stage of the Blackstone Rangers, prior to the stage of "Moorish Americans" and prior to the "El Rukn's" was reported by Denisoff and McCaghy (1973, p. 155) quoting the work of Mc Pherson (1966) to be anything but "militant" and totally uncooperative with the Black Panther Party, they were in a nutshell, "out for themselves". Opportunists in every sense of the word. Ultimately, Jeff Fort's group (the El Rukns) would be vigorously targeted for federal prosecution when they made the decision to enter into the political arena and seek to carry out domestic terrorism functions for foreign countries.

[8]A current nationally known neo-nazi in Lincoln, Nebraska (Gerhard Lauck) began with this Chicago neo-nazi group that operated in Marquette Park. In fact, he was the chief propagandist for Chicago's NSPA headed by Frank Collin. Lauck has a history of exporting native American fascism to Germany. See: Rogers Worthington, "From A Distance, Nebraska Nazi Agitates At Will", Chicago Tribune, Section 1, pp. 21,24, Jan. 9, 1994.

[9]A neo-nazi with a similar profile to Frank Collin has established a similar operation, although less organized, in St. Paul, Minnesota. See: Conrad deFiebre, "Nazis Take Root: South St. Paul Keeps Watch on Neofascists' Activities", Star Tribune, June 2, 1993.

[10] Early American urban politicians quickly realized the potential extra-legal functions and roles that gangs could play and that such "arms-length" distance allowed these politicians plausible deniability for such extralegal acts. For example, "gang leaders were paid for taking care of jobs like blackjacking political opponents and voting many times over at the poles" (Haskins, 1975: p. 32).

[11]See: Editorial "Probe Vote-Suppression Charges", Chicago Sun-Times, Nov. 12, 1993, p. 35.

[12] This is a suggestive list only.

[13]Teen Angel, P.O. Box 338, Rialto, CA 92376.

[14]The gang art included in Issue #1 of the magazine includes a collage with young Hispanic men and teenage Hispanic females; one of the females holds a switchblade, another holds a pistol; the message written reads "Cliques all over Aztlan are uniting with the 'Teen Angels', de Aztlan, Together we are a powerful force! Join Today ese!" No page numbers are provided in Teen Angels. The notation and referencing system to be used henceforth in referring to such materials will count the front cover as page one. The above collage is therefore on page 19.

[15]See Tim Nelson, 1993, "Gang Members Launch Summit", St. Paul Pioneer Press METRO, July 16th, p. 1, 4C.

[16] The data from Taylor (1990: p. 133) would have us believe that this is probably not something to worry much about, as gang members don't vote, at least in Taylor's Detroit sample.

[17] This particular interview was conducted by a Hispanic leader and student of mine, Arturo Mota.

[18]The version presented here is consistent with another theory of the Rudy Lozano assassination, which is that the arrested and convicted killer Escobar was himself an accomplice during the early stages of the prosecution of the case, an accomplice in the cover-up of the murder. Escobar was prosecuted by then State's Attorney Richard Daley. See: Michael Rosenfeld, "Who Killed Rudy Lozano?", Grey City Journal, October 15, 1993 for an extensive review of the facts of the Lozano murder.

[19]How the Bamboo Gang was used by Taiwanese politicians to assassinate a Chinese-American journalist --- Henry Liu --- in San Francisco is described in Kaplan and Dubro (1986: p. 219). In fact, the "hit" was contracted with the Bamboo Gang through the Taiwanese Defense Ministry Intelligence Bureau.

[20]See George Papajohn, "Gang Shares Peace - and Potatoe Salad", (pp. 1,3), Chicago Tribune, September 12, 1993. In the 1993 version of the B.O.S. (includes BD's, GD's, BGD's) picnic, the front for the group was the 21st Century --- a voter registration campaign and political organization. Earlier in 1993 as the above story documents, the same "political" group staged a protest in downtown Chicago with 5,000 protesters.

[21] Another twist on this was reported by DiChiara (1997). DiChiara's study of the Los Solidos gang, showed members who had great admiration for the "Macheteros" (an FALN splinter group that carried out an armored car robbery). Perhaps this matter is really simple to understand: gangs are an "enemy within", the "quislings" as Taylor says, and it may not be abnormal psychologically for such gang members to identify with other "public enemies", such as Al Capone movies, and terrorist groups who also in some sense, like the gang itself, have "declared war" on American society.

[22]Among the politicians names that appeared printed and endorsing the front of the "Petition to Parole Larry Hoover" were: former Mayor Eugene Sawyer; Joe Gardner, Commissioner, Metropolitan Wa-

ter Reclamation District; Alderman Allan Streeter, 17th Ward; Alderman Shirley Coleman, 16th Ward; and Alderman Virgil Jones, 15th Ward. Under these pre-printed endorsements the petition included the paragraph "WE HEREBY, INDIVIDUALLY AND COLLECTIVELY, do believe, as evidence of his present actions, Larry Hoover, to be rehabilitated and of sound mind and judgement, and as such, an asset to the communities-at-large in the capacity of a prime component in the institution, maintenance and subsequent longevity of the existing United in Peace Coalition Nations' Truce that currently attributes to the continuous, dramatic drop in the percentage of violent crimes and homicides in the African-American communities from Chicago to Peoria and throughout the State of Illinois". Obviously, that "truce" was a farce, it never really did work.

[23]The National Gang Crime Research Center realizing the potential research value of this data, did make an official Freedom of Information Act request to the Illinois Prisoner Review Board, by registered mail to (Ill. Governor Edgar; chairman James K. Williams and Kent Stenkamp of the Prisoner Review Board) have access to this public information. However, the list "was disposed of...because it was not needed after the parole hearing" which denied inmate Hoover a parole. In his 1994 re-election campaign television ads, Gov. Edgar claimed to be the candidate to wage the best war against gang crime. As it was reconfirmed in October, 1994, the story was "we just did not need all the names, all we needed was an example of the front of the petition form used, which has been preserved in the file". Thus, one page of the overall petition was all that was kept for official files.

[24]One of the major opponents against the release of Larry Hoover was Cook County State's Attorney Jack O'Malley. Jack Hynes, supervisor of the gang prosecution unit under State's Attorney O'Malley, pointed out the following in a 1994 memorandum: "Larry Hoover is the leader of the Gangster Disciple street gang in Illinois. He was sentenced to 150-200 years in the Department of Corrections in 1973 for the murder of Joshua Shaw. Due to the sentencing law in effect in 1973, Hoover now comes up for parole every year. Last year supporters of Hoover organized a letter-writing and media campaign to gain his release. The tenure of this campaign was that Hoover is reformed and would be a positive role model for the community. It is the position of the State's Attorney's Office that this is not true. Information gathered from the Illinois Department of Corrections, police gang intelligence, and official court documents in criminal trials reveals that Hoover remains the undisputed "King" of the Gangster Dis-

ciples. His release would unify thousands of Gangster Disciples, enabling them to increase the efficiency in which they inflict injury and terror in our communities".

[25]See: "TO: C NUMBER PRISONERS, FRIENDS, FAMILIES AND SUPPORTERS OF C NUMBER LEGISLATION", by Shango, Inside Out, a publication of the Prison Action Committee, Dedicated to the memory of Fred Hampton and Mark Clark, Vol. 1, No. 5, December, 1993, p. 1.

[26]The letter read: "Please accept this communique as letter of support on behalf of Mr. Larry Hoover, who will be appearing before the parole board in August. I am personally endorsing his release at this time. From all indication concerning his personal reform and evident rehabilitation I strongly urge that the Board consider this case with due diligence and in a positive frame of reference. Mr. Hoover has more than demonstrated his willingness to take a responsible place in society. His work and efforts to bring about badly needed changes are quite known to myself as well as others in the community".

[27]See: Jim Merriner, "Gang Charges Set the Tone in 2nd Dist. Race", Chicago Sun-Times, Dec. 19, 1993, p. 5.

[28]A tape-recorded conversation between Larry Hoover, "King" of the Gangster Disciples from his prison cell and rival gang leader Willie Lloyd, showed Larry bragging "I got a political action committee, a 21st century vote". See: "Jailed Gang Chieftan Says He Started PAC", by Lee Bey, Chicago Sun-Times, Sept. 29, 1994, p. 20.

[29]Gator got his name from preferring alligator shoes when he was a Black Gangster Disciple (BGD). Of course he told President Clinton he represents a group called Better Growth and Development (BGD) for urban areas. See: "Gator Gets Say With Clinton", by Lee Bey, Chicago Sun-Times, Jan. 26, 1994, p. 3. This meeting between the president and Gator was widely criticized as an affront to countless victims of gang violence, see: "Outrage: Gator at White House", Editorial, Chicago Sun-Times, January 26, 1994, p. 31. Jesse Jackson defended the visit, noting that forgiveness is necessary, and we should not stigmatize such persons, see: "Personal View: Jackson Defends Gator Visit to White House", Chicago Sun-Times, Feb. 1, 1994, p. 24. At the time Gator met with President Clinton in the White House, Gator was out on bond for a charge of criminal trespass to a stolen vehicle and was not supposed to leave the jurisdiction without the permission of the judge, see: "Gang Activist's Trip Unlawful", by Lee Bey, Chicago Sun-

Times, Jan. 31, 1994, p. 3. Columnist Richard Roeper also criticized the President for this, see: "Gadflies Gator, Ziff Hang With Bubba", Chicago Sun-Times, April 17, 1994, p. 11. The motor vehicle theft charge resulted when Gator rented a Cadillac from Avis using the offer of credit card help from a news reporter, and later the bill for the car was reported in the computer as being unpaid, where in a routine terry stop Gator was arrested because Avis reported the car as stolen, see: Lee Bey, "Chance Meeting Steers 2 Into Trouble", Chicago Sun-Times, Nov. 27, 1993, p. 6.

[30]For an excellent history of Jeff Fort, see: Tom Brune and James Ylisela, Jr., "The Making of Jeff Fort", Chicago Sun-Times, November, 1988.

[31]See: "Group Tied To Gangs Facing Test of Voters", by George Papajohn and Steve Rhodes, Chicago Tribune, Section 2, p. 1-2, Jan. 23, 1994.

[32]See: "Losing Teaches VOTE Lessons for Next Time", by John Kass and George Papajohn, Chicago Tribune, Section 2, pp. 1-2, March 20, 1994.

[33]It was Willie Lloyd who captured much media attention during and after his release from prison, leaving prison in a fur coat and a limousine, and later in Chicago being the target of an assassination attempt from his own gang in the fashion of a roaring 20s style shoot-out on the Eisenhower expressway, which was followed by another failed attempt near the criminal court building at 26th and California. See: Jim Casey and Art Golab, "Gang Leader, 3 Others Shot on the S.W. Side", Chicago Sun-Times, Oct. 20, 1993, p. 76.

[34]See: Lee Bey and Fran Spielman, "Gang Awards Program Hit as Bad Message", Chicago Sun-Times, Oct. 27, 1993, p. 12.

[35]See: John Kass and George Papajohn, "High School Role in Gang Summit Hit", Chicago Tribune, Section 2, pp. 1,8. October 27, 1993.

[36]The assistant principal of the school had been one of those who wrote a letter on behalf of paroling Larry Hoover in 1993. The principal was seen in a press kit photo provided by 21st Century V.O.T.E. for their large picnic on a farm in rural Kankakee in 1993.

[37]See: "Gang Awards Send Appalling Message", Raymond R. Coffey, Chicago Sun-Times, Oct. 28, 1993, p. 3.

[38]See: Jerry Thomas, "NAACP Upstart Brings in 5,000 New Members", Chicago Tribune, Oct. 20, 1994, section 2, p. 2.

[39] This analysis does recognize the existence of language and written gang constitutions that indicate affinity with "third world" causes and "oppressed people" generally. But this is often little more than double talk.

[40]For a view of the Black Panther Party which could possibly define it as a gang in terms of its leaders and controlling figures having a pattern of criminal activity or corrupt practices, see Hugh Pearson, 1994, The Shadow of the Panther: Huey Newton and the Price of Black Power in America, Addison-Wesley Publishers.

[41]See also the book review by Sol Stern, "Charismatic Thugs: Exposing the Criminal Behavior of the Black Panthers", Chicago Sun-Times, Sunday Arts and Show Supplement, July 3, 1994, p. 12 (B).

[42] See the work of Brotherton (1997) for an example of where from a leftist point of view it is worthwhile to want to believe gangs, such as those in New York City, when they claim they are seeking to "improve the community". Gangs with critical views towards larger society are hard to find in New York City or anywhere else in America. But just because gangs have "politics" does not mean that they have given up on crime. It is more reasonable to believe that gangs know they live in a world subject to "impressions" and that any gang of size or magnitude will eventually have to implement a "public relations function" to help fight the law enforcement view about gangs. Simply put, some scholars who are leftist are therefore prone to swallow the theory of "reformed gangs" hook, line, and sinker.

[43] NORC (National Opinion Research Center) conducts the General Social Survey.

[44] See: Barry Bearak, "Gang Boss Seeks A Peaceful Image: Latin King Sincerity Doubted", New York Post, Nov. 20, 1997, A21.

Satan's Disciples
(AKA: "Satan's Gangster Disciples")

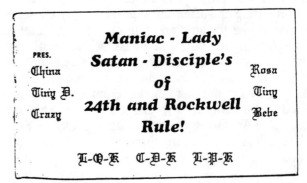

PRES.	Maniac - Lady	
China	Satan - Disciple's	Rosa
Tiny D.	of	Tiny
Crazy	24th and Rockwell	Bebe
	Rule!	

L-Q-K C-D-K L-P-K

Note the "put downs" or "status threats" printed on the bottom of the "business card" used by the female faction of the Satan's Disciples. Most gangs have this kind of "female wing" that functions as an auxilliary of what is mostly a male-dominated organization. Like loyal soldiers, note the female members in the example of the "business card" first challenge the Latin Queens by including the expression "LQK": meaning "Latin Queen Killer". While many university scholars studying gangs by means of ethnography try to capture the "meaning" and "significance" of gang life today, what gangs provide is an instant "clarification" of who is and who is not an "ENEMY". By joining a gang a person comes to know they do have a real and genuine enemy: it is an enemy-making human endeavor.

CHAPTER 7

THE ORAL HISTORY AND QUALITATIVE GANG RESEARCH STYLES

INTRODUCTION

Another continuity in gang studies has been in the application of qualitative research methods that approximate or aspire to the use of what will be described here as the oral history technique. This chapter focuses exclusively on the variations in the research methodology itself. This is of much practical importance in evaluating contributions to the gang literature that use some variation of this research method. What emerges here is that some approaches are better than others and while holding an advanced degree in the social sciences may not be required to effectively carry out this technique it may not be sufficient either, because from a human relations viewpoint this technique can be more complex than some would have us believe.

As will be seen, there are both similarities and differences between the classical oral history method and what has been done in sociology and criminology applications. There are also important ethical dilemmas of using recording technology in addition to the wealth of analytical complexities in the social encounter between the researcher and the law offender in the "oral history" interview situation. There are, simply, many strategy variations in use by researchers using this method. This needs to be clarified from a methodological viewpoint.

Field work as a research method for understanding gangs can encompass a variety of experiential factors. But ultimately it boils down to the differences in the strategy used to collect information from gangs and gang members using basically "talk therapy" or simply hanging out with them. This qualitative research strategy involves the use of narrative information and speech. It differs from quantitative approaches that may involve the use of surveys or questionnaires, where numbers become the primary data collected. As will be seen, there are different names for what may involve rather similar elements of the qualitative research method. Thus, the terms oral history, case study, field work, ethnomethodology, depth interviews, ethnography, participant observation, etc, all refer to "how to get it, and what to do with the verbal data" so acquired. In this sense we need to know much more about the oral history method and conducting oral interviews. The oral history technique deals with how to get "their story" for use in conversational analysis, case studies, depth studies, focused interviews, etc.

THE FIGHT FOR QUALITATIVE METHODS

The oral history or case study approach is clearly a type of qualitative methodology. In the last four decades the more quantitative research methods have been the preferred techniques for sociologists and criminologists, especially those studying the offender population. Two points must be made about this qualitative research approach: (1) it complements traditional quantitative methods and can be, and should be, used in conjunction with other research designs for the collection of data on the offender and gang population for the purpose of testing or developing theory, and (2) it makes for spicy reading in as much as it goes behind and beyond the mere numerical codification of human experiences and in this sense provides a more humanistic orientation to the study of deviants, delinquents, offenders, gang members, etc.

James Bennett, in Oral History and Delinquency, University of Chicago Press, 1981, presents a critical appraisal of the oral history tradition in the study of delinquency. It expresses skepticism about the quality of oral history studies conducted to date and discounts the worth of such a methodology for testing or illustrating theories.[1]

Bennett refers to the use of the oral history method as a humanistic tradition in criminology (1981, p. 6) and rightfully so; because most of the criminologists who have used this method have tended, it seems, to represent a liberal ideology as well. Logically, it does not necessarily follow that the oral history method is inherently humanistic. It has appeared to be this way in the American criminological literature. It is, of course, subject to abuse by scholars and intelligence agents who could very well have a conservative-reactionary ideology, although this has not surfaced in any significant fashion -- at least intentionally so -- as of this date. There is nothing to stop ultra conservative "law and order" researchers from using the same method to advance their particular analyses as well. Thus, it is a logical error to think that such a research strategy is inherently humanistic.

Scattered throughout Bennett's book are discussions of the variation in conducting oral history, but lacking is a systematic treatment of the components of the research method itself. One concludes from the book that the oral history method must be more art than science. In fact, Bennett reported trying to conduct such a method without success.

While there are fine gradients of methodological variation that will be explained later in this chapter, for now let us assume that the oral history method also encompasses much of what is also meant by the case study method in studying gang members.[2]

Importantly, this method itself is not unique to the Chicago school of sociology or criminology. Goffman (1961) used a variation of this method, focusing on the asylum as a total control institution. Thrasher and Whyte used it to observe street gangs. It has also been used to study college administration (Clark, 1960), political life (Dahl, 1961), and even casual sex contacts in cocktail bars (Roebuck and Spray, 1967). Using oral history, to record the story of the offender or gang member, is a technique that has been prominently identified with the Chicago tradition, particularly Shaw and McKay (1931) and Sutherland (1937). Obviously, however, no one has a patent on such a technique.

THE ORAL HISTORY INTERVIEW METHOD USED BY HISTORIANS

What we mean by the classical oral history method is that interview technique used by historians. It is an interview conducted under conditions of informality and in a relaxed atmosphere and it absolutely requires the use of tape recorders or high technology (e.g., video cameras). It focuses on the use of spoken words as data, transcribed fully, editing out only the "er's" and the "ah's", or pauses, and keeping intact any vulgarity.

Harris (1975, p. 3) favors tape recorders and the use of tapes as data because "the nuances, the inflections that human speech can convey have a subtlety that escapes the most accurate of transcriptions". Along with the use of the tape recorder, of course, comes the use of videotapes as well.[3]

The intellectual norms appear to differ in comparing the classical method with that used in sociology and criminology. In the former it is an accomplishment in its own right to document an important aspect of history for centralized use and secondary analysis by other researchers. In sociology, it often boils down to "what did you say from the data." And, of course, while there are quantitative data archives for criminologists, there exists no such "criminological or gang studies oral history archive" at this point in history, even though, obviously, it too could, from transcription, be stored on computer. There is not, as well, a "speech sample" data bank, for the investigation of offenders, yet.

The purpose of the classical oral history method is to collect tapes and transcripts that other scholars of history can use. That is, the method itself assumes the prominent role of secondary analysis; or the involvement of other scholars who will later use the same data. This forces a consideration of research and publishing policy. Our social science journals do not require the author to provide the dataset for each research article published, or insure its availability at a central repository, so that other social scientists can do a secondary analysis or even build upon previously published findings. The classical oral history method, then, differs from any such use ever made of this interview technique in criminology. As Bennett (1981) noted, even the hand written documents in the Shaw and McKay tradition were routinely disposed of after transcription thus making it impossible to confirm their authenticity.

ORAL HISTORY Vs. WRITTEN SELF-ACCOUNTS BY YOUNG OFFENDERS

In examining the writing samples of youthful and adult offenders one might easily conclude that their literacy level itself, their constricted vocabulary, their limited repertoire of communication symbols, prevents us from getting much in the way of systematic written "self-accounts."[4] The youthful gang member who can write lengthy, legible, detailed accounts of personal experiences is an exception to the rule. It requires a command of a language, a written language as well, but several such gang authored accounts have appeared since 1981.[5]

Having offenders write out such accounts about their life, and how they "got into trouble with the law, etc", has been used as part of the psychological diagnostic intake in some correctional facilities and programs. This type of data has not yielded much analysis that, to the author's knowledge, has been reported in the literature.

Many will probably want to cite the book Monster as an exception. The hollywood glitz and glamour is all over this book, romanticizing gang life as a cultural form and portraying the gang member/leader as a freedom fighter in an occupied land undergoing guerilla warfare. This book has had the benefit of much stylizing in the vein of Truman Capote's In Cold Blood, where the underdog never has to accept responsibility for anything. The book Monster was a commercial effort, not a social scientific effort. Still the book does tend to demonstrate what some recent authors have called the combative personality syndrome: someone who prefers violent solutions over all other alternatives to resolving a dispute. It is a person predisposed, by choice, toward violence; but where the person does not consider the moral implications of their behavior, and further refuses to accept any responsibility for their actions. Such a person is "fighting the system", a rebel with or without a cause but with little or no hope of success.

The skinhead neo-nazi who chose to tell his story in a way to denounce his gang in Germany, in the book The Reckoning: A Neo-Nazi Drops Out by Ingo Hasselbach, quickly sold 15,000 copies of this popular account.[6] There are other gang-authors who like the retrospective account by Rodriguez (1994) do not glorify gang life. Co-authoring with gang members dates back some time, Hagedorn's co-author describes himself as a Chicago gang member transplant to Milwaukee. The recent account by Padilla and Santiago (1993) takes this to the level of co-authoring with a wife of an imprisoned gang leader.

Oral history clearly differs from written self-accounts taken from gang members, either while in custody or in a community treatment/intervention program context. It means writing down notes and their comments during the course of a semi-structured interview. The use of the tape recorder, while a source of potential contamination with law offenders, has been reported by a number of gang researchers. The use of the tape recorder or higher technology could be problematic for several reasons.[7] It is reactive under some conditions and the subject may feel more inhibited, as if it were an interrogation. It could encourage "performing" for the interviewer, rather than generating natural speech patterns, because of the defensive posture induced by the presence of a tape recording device. Most importantly, for the gang member who is truly candid and discloses specific names, dates, and locations of serious crimes, this represents very sensitive information.[8]

TAPE RECORDERS AND THE PROTECTION OF HUMAN SUBJECTS

The use of the tape recorder in capturing oral history data on offenders raises some concerns and problems regarding the protection of human subjects. Criminologists who use the self-report method often come across many serious crimes that have not been officially detected or adjudicated; crimes for which the statute of limitation may not apply. While it has not been addressed in recommended policy by groups such as the American Society of Criminology, certainly the criminologist should not feel compelled under any circumstances to release this confidential information to law enforcement or any other authorities. Not using a tape recorder at least prevents the existence of any such material evidence that could be potentially subject to government interest. However, written notes have also been known to have been targeted, for example in the study of organized crime.

THE DYAD INTERVIEW AS A SOCIALLY DISTANCED ENCOUNTER

While Goffman would certainly say that interviewing the offender in a one-on-one situation consists of a social encounter, it is also one characterized by much social distance when carried out by a Ph.D, or someone who is obviously not indigenous to the community. We cannot dismiss the material differences in social class position, life chances, and other factors of social power in the context of interviewing gang members. These things do matter, and will impact on what ultimately is "heard." For many of these types of field interviews it comes to resemble, in some ways, the confessional relationship between a priest and the penitent.

The dyadic interview simply involves asking the offender or gang member to "share" experiences, amounting essentially to "giving up information." For researchers who have used this method with offenders effectively, and it may be argued that perhaps not everyone can from a personality requirement be expected to have the human capability to carry out this method, many have found the tendency in a number of these kinds of interviews for the relationship to be interpreted by the self-reporting offender as an opportunity to "snitch."[9] Hagedorn (1990) does not refer to gang members as "data sources" or "respondents", but frankly calls them "informants." We can probably be assured that Hagedorn did not approach these gang members and ask them "hey, would you be my informant for a study I am doing?"

To a certain extent we should probably expect that in an oral history interview session the offender is "performing" or "acting a role" that may be defined, by default, in terms of the status and authority of the interviewer. The oral interview is not equivalent to interrogation. And unlike the forced-choice item in the survey method the researcher must often be on a "fishing expedition" unless factors to be elicited or focused on are specified in advance, and the researcher is in fact skilled, clinically, at "probing."

STRATEGY VARIATIONS IN THE ORAL HISTORY METHOD WITH OFFENDERS

There appear to be a number of different strategy variations in the manner in which the oral history method is employed by criminologists. Described here are ten such component variations that may affect the overall interpretation of "how was this information generated?"

(1) Using Background Information Before The First Meet.

Reading the available reports, records, files, public information, etc, from official sources, and using related information readily collected on the individual's social milieu (neighbors, retail stores, bars, etc in the area where the person lives and is known) before the actual interview can play an important role in the oral history method. Can criminologists be conned? Certainly, and they are much more likely to be misled when they do not prepare for the interview by gathering as many facts as possible about the person before the first meeting. Not reading the prior offense data on an offender allows the interview session to unfold naturally without the interviewer focusing on specific offenses. From a related perspective, if the interviewer is not highly

trained, perhaps it could be argued that knowledge of this official criminal history and social background information could have the potential for interviewer prejudice. Generally, the author would recommend having as much information possible prior to the interview.

Such "advance information" allows at least the calibration of the interview data for genuineness and validity. Asking the obvious questions about which confirmed answers are already known in advance allows some judgement about the extent to which the person being interviewed is really cooperating. This validity factor is most important and is one of the most avoided points of discussion in many of the examples of field research involving such qualitative methods with gang members.

(2) Type of Entre or Introduction.

The type of introduction which assures access to the individual for being interviewed in the oral history fashion importantly shapes the ensuing interview. A preferred situation is one where a host agency or individual acts as a buffer or broker for the interview; ideally it is a host who is respected indigenously.[10] A common approach is that of the quality social service provider, a private agency known to provide jobs and education, etc, to the offender population. That is, one that is well known in the area. Lacking this, there is always the snowball method of using one offender to provide the entre to another offender.

This gets somewhat complicated in gang studies by the fact that different gangs are, naturally, known to compete and exist as bitter rivals. So the snowball method works best inside one gang group. To be seen with one gang may preclude obtaining valid data from a rival gang under conditions of intense distrust as may often exist in some of our urban communities today.

(3) Mode of Interviewer Dress/Appearance.

Casual and relaxed is the order of the day in oral history studies. It may be assumed that the variation in dress mode and appearance of the interviewer could have some relationship to the consistency and quality of the information gathered through the oral history method. Generally, what will be found is that social distance can be either minimized or maximized by dressing either casually or very formally. A suit and tie approach generates the least information on first interviews.

(4) Honorarium/Fee Offered for the Interview.

Offering to pay for the interview produces the highest rate of voluntary cooperation for the oral history method when dealing with offenders. Depending on the nature of the introduction with individuals, however, this is not necessarily required in all instances. The author has seen cases where the persons refused the "fee", and agreed to the interview for less instrumental types of motivation. Shaw and McKay (1931) report no use of stipends or fees paid to their sources[11], such as in the classic case study of "Nick".

Timing can be everything in offering even the smallest types of monetary incentives. Again, however, such tokens are not likely to be appealing to anyone who has a serious commitment to criminality. Someone who the previous night robbed a yuppie trying to buy $1,000 worth of cocaine is not likely to be very responsive to a small two figure cash honorarium. Similarly, we have yet to see anyone seriously entertain offering such petty "rewards" for interviews with more seriously involved criminal offenders (e.g., organized crime, and higher level gang organizations).

Such interview fees work best with the Alfalfa and Spanky type of gangs, and with the lowest possible level of involvement with criminal gangs. Why would a gang leader, presumably controlling a significant illicit income, want to "open his guts" for $25.00 and tell the world his secrets?

(5) Consumable Amenities.

Is it "breaking bread together" that establishes a mutual basis for interaction? Well, offering "goodies" at the time of the interview start-up is little more than a lure in some cases. But it does work. Offering refreshments without any advance notification of the availability of these consumable amenities (cans of cold soda pop, donuts, coffee, etc) establishes a "respect" for the respondent. It is a welcoming ritual.

Apparently there are more than some authors in our literature who have simply invited the gang members to their homes. In the "Streetcorner Research Lab" to be discussed in a subsequent chapter, the principal investigator (Schwitzgebel) always offered sandwiches, candy --- whatever they wanted to consume. Indeed, in some of our prior gang researchers reported experience, they offered alcohol. But at the point that a researcher is providing alcohol we are out of the realm of oral history method and into the realm of covert interviews and more.

(6) Interview Site Location.

The interview site location may figure prominently in the quality of the interview results. Interviewing an offender while still in custody is often difficult (distractions, noise, the security environment, etc). It would depend on the skill of the researcher in adjusting to this kind of situation to be capable of overcoming the environmental press that mitigates against good data. Interviewing the offender in a natural setting, in the field, is often difficult. Office

sites are convenient, along with universities, but also communicate an "officialdom" to the respondents.

While prisons and places of confinement have been criticized as "contaminated" zones; there is no theoretical reason to expect any difference in validity or reliability. Indeed, there is a higher motivation to want to talk. Certainly much more than exists in the field. Again, the issue may center around "what are we studying?" If we are principally focusing on the psychology of the individual gang member, then perhaps some conditions are better than others. But, again, there is no hard evidence that shows this to be true. And, of course, if we are not focusing on the self-reporting of the offender's deviance, but the deviance of "others" (e.g., the gang group/organization), it may not matter where we interview someone.

(7) Explanation of Purpose and Informed Consent.

The interviewer needs to explain the overall purpose of the interview and give some assurance of anonymity or protection of privacy, unless otherwise covered in written contract with the respondent. Informed consent is best accomplished by showing the person an example of a "case study" or "oral interview" or "oral history" and explaining in writing before the interview session and orally at the time of the first meeting, what type of content the interview may cover and what will become of the resulting "data".

A researcher whose entre to the respondent is through a community-based program who verbalizes an objective "to help out the program" may be eliciting a response shaped by the need of the respondent to present information in light of its most favorable interpretation to the program, not the research problem per se. A direct "honesty in interviewing" approach is probably best; telling the respondent "I am a sociologist/criminologist studying_____ and I want the truth about it" has a virtually neutral effect on interview response.

A gang researcher may potentially violate such a promise of anonymity to the gang member by subsequent publication. We should not assume that gang members cannot read our works. For example; assume one spent the summer interviewing gang members in Podunk, Arizona, promising them anonymity, and then published a book detailing their federal criminal law violations and providing probable cause to federal authorities to directly target such gangs in the city and state so explicitly identified in the book. Is that a violation of the promise of anonymity? It probably would be from the gang member's point of view, particularly when the feds started making arrests.

(8) Reliability.

In its most elementary sense, reliability in research means the degree to which the researcher can get the same story again and again. Would two trained Ph.D.'s conducting oral history studies of the same persons, simultaneously, get the same results? There could be much variation in results. But having the same respondent interviewed by two or more interviewers at least provides multiple observations on the same case and a basis for comparison whether the same story is coming through. That would be inter-rater reliability. Similarly, having the same person interviewed at two or more different points in time, with redundancy in the content of probes, provides more of what is meant by content reliability. The comparison of single cases by multiple interviewers, or the comparison of single interviewer responses at multiple points over time, allows for the assessment of the quality of the interview results.[12]

Again, this kind of "technical issue" has not been adequately addressed in our gang research literature.

(9) Validity Issues.

Is it really the truth or is it a crock of mumble jumble? It is a clear problem in determining whether "data" from oral history methods really measures what it purports to measure because of the obvious human tendency to misrepresent reality. However, some information is subject to verification. Also, if the researcher takes the time to use "test questions", or validity items, in the context of the interview, which correspond to items of known information relating to the respondent, known in advance, and there is not a consistent pattern of responses to these test questions, or if there is significant variation from these "base lines", then one would be well advised to assume some level of deceit emerging from the respondent.

A gang researcher may not know when a gang member is or is not under the influence of a controlled substance. Which, at least in the more controlled environment of the prison, jail, detention or treatment center, etc, we might assume at least has a somewhat lower probability; although, obviously, a matter not entirely to be dismissed. Do gang members in the community use drugs? Does the consumption of drugs or alcohol affect the validity of what might come from such field interviews? We might assume the affirmative. Again, we find no discussion of this matter in the recent qualitative research on gangs.

(10) Anonymity.

Anonymity should be assured to the respondent both verbally and in writing. Unfortunately when dealing with law violation behavior this means a slight alteration from the classical oral history approach. That is, names, addresses, etc, must often be blanked out or obscured so as to not give away, indirectly, the identity of the respondent. If we were in Podunk, Arizona for our gang "field interviews" and published the data showing that all of the gang members in that city have illegal, fully-automatic Uzi's, if government agents (ATF) used the publication as probable cause for targeting the group or as the basis for starting such an investigation, could we say that such anonymity has been violated?

It may not matter if the individual researcher is even willing to go to jail for "not disclosing" who exactly said they had an Uzi submachine gun. The issue is, from a policy and research utilization viewpoint, someone reads the report; sees a major federal law being violated, en masse, and targets the group in the city so identified in the book. When the gang members begin to go to jail for such a hypothetical case, would this be an ethical violation? Many may believe so.

Any promise made in good faith must be fulfilled to a respondent or data source. We live in an information age. And law enforcement agencies are obligated to act on information about wrong doing. The issue of anonymity is no small matter. If we do not promise it, then it is similar to the Miranda warning. But if we do promise it, it is something we should most certainly live up to. At least in the sense of limiting potential harm.

ORAL HISTORY Vs. INTERROGATION

In what respects does oral history differ from, or is it similar to, criminal interrogation? Surely the element of "confession" is common to both, but also common to both is that the interviewer be patient and consistent. Bennett's work (1981) touches on this to some extent.

Bennett critiques charity/service organizations dealing with offenders when they use the oral history method to "toot their horns", that is to proclaim their accomplishments and effectiveness, but mostly to seek financial support for their mission. Bennett (1981) amply shows oral history has been capable of being corrupted for such self-serving causes.

Bennett (1981) shows some interesting parallels between oral history and "confession". Regarding the introduction of solitary confinement in corrections, specifically the solitary cells of the Preston Jail in 1839, "W.L. Clay aptly dubs this oral history site the 'cell confessional' (Bennett, 1981: 73)". Clay's success in getting such oral history "stories" was his kindness to the inmates as a prison chaplain in a situation of stark contrast to the oppressive ethos of the jail environment after the introduction of solitary cells. Thus, Rev. Clay's "kindness" in that context was not functionally different than a traditional "Mutt and Jeff routine".[13]   Actually a current book on gangs from an evangelical point of view, while not knowing it was a legitimate research technique, actually produced very comparable results --- on the importance of the underclass, the role of violence, the role of the family, jobs, etc, as impacting on the growth and persistence of gangs --- suggesting any-one can "do" qualitative research (Mc Lean, 1991).

Many criminal interrogation textbooks point out the importance of the personality requirement to the effect that "you either have it, or you don't".[14] Similarly, in classical oral history methods "some people are simply incapable of properly conducting interviews" (Harris, et al, 1975: 10). Perhaps in this sense, the "art", as opposed to the "science", is reflected. Perhaps both interrogation and oral history are arts which should be approached scientifically.

As seen in Figure 7, there is more in common between interrogation and oral history than exists the differences between these two forms.

As seen in Figure 7, there are three differences and eight commonalities in looking at oral history methods and interrogation methods. The obvious difference, though, is that of purpose: the difference between documenting for social science and the law enforcement purpose of effective prosecution.

CRIMINAL JUSTICE TRAINING FOR INTERVIEWING GANG MEMBERS

The purpose of this kind of interviewing is the development of intelligence on gangs. A number of training manuals exist for gang training that address this issue of how to best interview the gang member. Most are largely consistent with the advice given in this chapter for the purpose of plain research. One of the best ideas is to ask the gang member not about his own deviance, or his own exploits and crimes, but rather to ask about the competition. The competition can be members or sets/factions of his own gang or other gangs.

While all gangs view "snitching" as the ultimate wrongful act of a fellow member, they do this regularly by "dry snitching" --- that is informally disclosing information about their associates. Some gangs tolerate this more than others. Some gangs go to great lengths to prohibit certain types of social interaction and disclosures to the "outsiders", such as the Latin Kings who in one incident shot a member in both knees for having an interview with a television station that came to the hood for a story.

FIGURE 7

COMPARISON OF ORAL HISTORY
AND INTERROGATION

Oral History	Rel.	Interrogation
1. Put your respondent "at ease"	D	Increase the psychological tension to confess.
2. An informal dress mode is preferred.	D	Conservative suit should elicit respect, not fear.
3. Make interview setting comfortable for having a conversation.	D	Use stiff back chairs; face to face, 27 inches apart in a bare room.
4. Show no emotion which may communicate that you are offended by what you hear.	C	Use emotional ploys; let "S" know that nothing they say will shock you, "we've heard it all before".
5. Don't be offended by what the offender might say.	C	Minimize the moral implications.
6. Show empathy: a genuine positive regard for the "R".	C	Sympathize with the "S" (e.g., "anyone might have done the same thing")
7. Be scholarly, but ask questions in plain words.	C	Speak in simple terms; use "their" language if necessary.
8. Interview cunning is always important.	C	Interrogation is a true battle of wits.
9. Personality is important.[15]	C	A flexible personality is required.
10. Even if you are nervous, don't show this to the "R" or they will "clam" up.	C	Don't show your nervous tension; don't smoke, and if you do, offer one first to the "S" as a gesture of kindness.
11. Review background info before the interview.	C	Interview victim and witnesses first; know all facts and the "S" records before the interview.

LEGEND OF SYMBOLS: "R" = respondent,
"S" = subject
Rel. = nature of the relationship
D = difference
C = Commonality

Some manuals are very specific and develop specific guidance for investigators about certain gangs like the Crips and the Bloods:

"If a particular Crip or Blood is not bragging about his very successful business, dealing, or womanizing; he will want to be known as a deadly, ruthless person. Insane-style tattoos and monikers will reflect their self-proclaimed reputation---examples being: Killer Kev, Crazy Ed, Psycho Mike, etc."

That is, gang members are egoistic, egotistic, and enjoy attention and performing their important roles. They will talk and provide information about others, but they do not consider this snitching when the others are competition. Still, some gangs train their members in how to resist interrogations by police and investigators, such as the training memo from the imprisoned Gangster Disciple leader to members on the streets, a copy of which is provided in the appendices of this book.

Some of the common tips for criminal justice personnel offered in gang training manuals today include these taken from a midwestern corrections training document on gang awareness: (1) work on their ego, (2) use their sense of individualism, (3) uses their self-proclaimed "playboy" image, (4) play on their entrepreneur self-image, (5) play on their hero/warrior/freedom fighter self-image, (6) have some background on them, (7) show interest in their politics and ideology, (8) show interest in how they able to lead an extravagant life style to get them to talk about how they make money, (9) show interest in how deadly they are and how fearsome their reputation is among their own gang members and to other rival gangs to get them to talk about weapons, monikers, violent incidents, etc., and (10) show interest in their leadership abilities to get them to talk about how the organization functions.

ORAL HISTORY AND THE "CASE STUDY"

In a classic paper on the sociological use of the case study approach, Burgess (1928) addressed the matter of rival interests between social workers and sociologists. Burgess explicitly detailed aspects of the "social case record" that should be focused on to make the data useful for research. Missing in the nearly 70 years after Burgess is a well developed approach for training in the methodology itself.

Yet there are interdisciplinary parallels in the use of this kind of qualitative method. In market research it can be called the case approach or a depth interview[16] and still bear much resemblance to what has been regarded as an oral history approach (Woodside and Fleck, 1979). The purpose is what is different, in market research the aim might be to find out why the person prefers one brand of beer over another. A similar comparison exists between oral history and "case analysis" in management or organizational change research.

Perhaps some of the current favor enjoyed by the case analysis methodology is its legitimacy established by the parallels in almost all of the behavioral and social sciences. The analytical potential of this research methodology is therefore best revealed when considering the diverse disciplines in which it has been applied. Different names for the variation in this methodology also are evident when the perspective is interdisciplinary.

In fact, case analysis is also called the case study method, the case history method, the depth interview, the case method, social casework, case research, the clinical interview, etc.

CASE ANALYSIS IN MANAGEMENT

Paine and Naumes (1982) place the matter of strategic management at the heart of using broad concepts and strategy to survive in a changing environment. Most of their book is devoted to actual cases (pp. 167-610). Here we find that:

"In the case study method, learning takes place as the students try to discover, refine, and answer critical questions using real-life situations. The end goal of case analysis is suggested management actions based on the analysis (Paine and Naumes, 1982: p. 167)."

Thus, case studies are used for a variety of purposes such as exploring values and their effect on decisions and to "demonstrate the methods, inputs, style, and environmental setting of such decisions" (p. 167).

Here are the basic analytical elements for a case study according to these authors. It means a current definition of the concern and the current objectives of the organizations and groups involved in it along with current strategic actions and policies (p. 168). It means taking into account the values and relative power of major constituency and policy-making groups. A "capability profile" must be developed to include: "a. key factors or mobility barriers, b. need for more information, c. competitive advantages, and d. strategic implications" (p. 168). The external environment must also be examined for such things as "competitive factors, economic factors, legal factors, regulation, and social issues" (p. 168). It should, in short, be a factual basis for decision-making based on a close relationship with reality.

Niehoff (1966) calls it not the case study method, but the case history method (p. 5). Its benefit is to be able to learn from study of past efforts. The many cases of change and development affecting peasant farmers in the Niehoff book are therefore "case histories" (p. 7) at the project level, not the planning level. Regarding the case history method itself, we are told not so much how to carry it out as to be able to recognize when we see it. The ideal case history method has these attributes according to Niehoff: "professional and complete...so the...reader can get a clear picture of what happened" (p. 7), "interestingly presented" material that is not dull, with the "most information presented in the most succinct manner" (p. 8).

The use of the case method, as White, Stamm, and Foster (1976: p. iii) call it, has been applied to health care facilities such as hospitals and other formal organizations. The case method is also used in teaching and the work by Sprague, Sheldon and McLaughlin (1973) explains its use in health care and provides more specifics on "how to" properly carry out the development of case materials (Sprague, et al, 1973: pp. 110-113). Burns and Stalker (1968) also explain in some detail this same method (pp. 12-

14).

SPECIFYING THE ELEMENTS OF THE CASE STUDY

The classic treatise by Neihoff (1966) identifies seventeen major elements, the first eight of which are innovator characteristics and the rest are recipient characteristics: (1) role characteristics, (2) communication by the innovator, (3) participation obtained, (4) utilization of local culture, (5) timing, (6) flexibility, (7) continuity, (8) maintenance, (9) communication among the recipients, (10) motivation of felt need, (11) motivation of practical benefit perceived, (12) other types of motivation, (13) leadership, (14) social structure, (15) economic pattern, (16) beliefs, and (17) practices (Niehoff, 1966: p. 12).

Whatever we call it, case study, case history, case method, etc, what is generally being dealt with are actual empirical examples described in an interesting way to depict important qualitative aspects at the individual, organizational/group, or societal level.

Observation is a key component of case analysis and in the methodology of Strauss, et al, (1985) observation means daily experiences and interviews over a long period, in their case five years (see Strauss, et al, 1985: pp. 291-296). This can produce significant details which are normally not documented and yet which give more meaning to understanding the project's success.

GOING UNDERCOVER: QUALITATIVE RESEARCH ON GANGS

There have been a large number of researchers who study the gang by in someway "going undercover". However, most of the time the researcher is never "concealing" their role as someone who is gathering information. The ethnography of a Moroccan gang in the Netherlands was based on the ability of the researcher to become "a barkeeper in a youth home, a youth worker and a social worker" (Werdmolder, 1997). One of the most widely read ethnographic studies of American gangs is that by Sanchez-Jankowski (1991), where the author claimed to have spent ten years with the gang and was even shot in a gun fight during the research.

HANGING OUT SAFELY: TO GET ACCESS FOR STRATEGIC INTERVIEWS

One of the classic variations in the qualitative research methods as it has been applied to gang members is for the researcher to use a "safe site" as the basis for making contact with the gang members. There are a number of ways in which this strategy has its benefits in terms of accountability and reducing risk for the researcher. An excellent example would be the book: The Hot House: Life Inside Leavenworth Penitentiary by Pete Earley (1992).

Earley provides some of the best insights that have ever surfaced in the gang literature on the gang known as the "Aryan Brotherhood". The "Aryan Brotherhood" (AB's) have the motto: "Kill to Get In, Die to Get Out". AB's are not easily studied as you might imagine.

What Earley (1992) did was get permission as a journalist from the Federal Bureau of Prisons to "hang out" inside the prison and eventually he was able to gain the confidence of some of the top ranking members of the Aryan Brotherhood. In fact, Earley's analysis provides the best insights into this particular gang. But Earley did not "join" the AB's, nor did Earley have to compromise his ethics to study these gang members, because he did so under relatively safe conditions.

PARTICIPANT OBSERVATION AS A SOURCE OF MISINFORMATION

Participant observation with real gangs, not wannabes, could put the researcher at more than some risk: is the researcher going to collaborate in terms of drug sales, consume drugs and get high with the gang informants, and become a party to their patterns of criminal law violation? Non-participant observation is probably the concept that more aptly describes what some researchers have done in "hanging out with gangs". No non-offender scholarly researcher has yet to report going undercover to join a gang and report on its activities.

Many such gang researchers who employ such a "field work" research technique are often viewed by the gang as "egg heads". Hanging out with gang members in a neutral setting where an observer has a legitimate right to essentially "be there", as in drop-in centers, Boys and Girls clubs, etc, offers one way to overcome this problem. Yet there are still substantial problems in terms of validity regarding the data obtained through such types of participant observation.

The fact is offenders are prone to lie. Talk to any gang member long enough and you will hear at some point a presentation of self as a "gang leader" of some sort; even if they were only the "leader" of one housing unit of one juvenile detention center for one time in the distant past. The astute and responsible researcher who engages in participant observation as a research method would use social network analysis to ascertain who is in fact a leader, rather than relying on self-report.

A close reading of the contemporary gang literature reveals that taking such statements from gang members as the "gospel truth" also may fatally flaw ones research conclusions and analysis. One such participant observation study of Milwaukee street gangs, for example, claimed that the El Rukn gang had never existed or penetrated the city. The fact is

Jeff Fort was paroled to Milwaukee and started his first El Rukn organization there, and with success returned to Chicago to expand[17].

The issue of validity here is a cognitive one: some gang members simply may not be knowledgeable about the history, facts, and functions of gangs (especially rival gangs) that they may be more than willing to comment on. An example of how and where this would be likely to occur could be in studying a gang that identifies itself as a Latin King chapter, say somewhere in Florida, but which was started by a transplanted lower level member; and few of its members know much of anything about the original Chicago group and its two main branches (the northside branch from Humboldt Park, and the southside branch from 26th Street). Asking such an emulation/social imitation gang about Latin King gang organization could not be generalized to the Chicago or national picture. It is simple: you cannot get the truth from someone who may not know the truth or the big picture.

Another related possibility that some critical analysts of the gang literature have recently surfaced is the problem of the "Stockholm syndrome". The profile here is of someone who discovers and becomes involved in criminology only after hanging out with a gang. One should be thoroughly familiar with criminological literature well prior to trying to interpret and understand gang phenomena. This is more than accepting what the gang member says as the gospel, thus publishing essentially a public relations document for the gang (e.g., the gang is not about crime and drugs, it is about growth and development for the community), it involves overidentifying with the gang to the point where the "gang research" if we are to call it that basically amounts to an apology for the gang. Thus, the researcher affected by the Stockholm syndrome somehow converts to being some kind of an academic/professional/intellectual member of the gang[18].

ETHNOGRAPHY AS A SOURCE OF INTELLECTUAL DISHONESTY

Ethnography basically means "hanging out" with the gang or the gang members. One issue here is simple: it takes a special kind of person interested in deviance to want to hang out with gang members anyhow. The main issue, however, is this: how do we keep this kind of investigator "honest"? A person can choose to see and hear what they want to hear, and they can see through an ideological "lens" and hear selectively what supports a preconceived idea about gang life. So most ethnographic studies of gang life basically ask you to swallow the "social construction" of gang life as perceived by that one investigator's experience. This kind of literature often makes for "interesting reading", but it can also

be a source of intellectual dishonesty by the very nature of the research method being used.

The issue of accountability is very large here and it may very well be that the only way we can monitor the qualitative researcher using ethnography or participant observation as a methodology for studying gangs is to "wire them up" like an undercover cop. No one has reported doing this for scholarly purposes, because this would pose its own problems. But there has been a recurrent historical trend where naive liberal-minded researchers "hang out with the gang" and end up being sucked into their way of life: defending the gang, apologizing for the gang, helping the gang, becoming a "public relations" spokesperson for the gang, and in this fashion basically becoming a part of the problem itself.

SUMMARY AND CONCLUSION

This chapter must be regarded, contra Bennett, as a clear defense of the oral history or "own story" approach. The primary evidence of its enduring utility is that it has comparable approaches in other disciplines. The oral history or case study method must be regarded as being slightly more complex than a simple open-ended item in survey research where there is no time limit. Methodologically, there are subtle differences and variations, but essentially much of what is called by various names --- field approach, ethnographic studies, case studies, depth studies, etc, and at the highest level of analysis, the oral history method --- much of it entails a direct face-to-face and personal approach. To get the story right from the gang member in a qualitative way.[19]

The other obvious criticism of this qualitative approach, from a strict methodological perspective, is that it has yielded little in the way of content analysis reported in the literature. Content analysis is a rigorous method of quantifying such qualitative data as might emerge in open-ended questions or even the oral history or case study approach. No one has yet to report an inter-rater reliability coefficient for assumed findings from the oral history approach; rather, the raw data has simply been presented as ipso facto "proof" for author assertions --- sometimes along ideological dimensions. Some of the best such accounts (e.g., Taylor, 1990) have simply sought to obtain data on specified topical areas of relevance to a descriptive analysis of gangs.

Secondly, just "hanging out" with a gang, or even moving in with them to study their lifestyle (ala Keiser), presents its own ethical dilemmas. Most importantly, the more organized gangs have strict rules in their constitutions against disclosure of such privileged information about their organization. A necessary implication of this tendency of higher level gang organizations to punish their members who disclose information to outsiders is that the so-called field study approach is not really going to be likely to generate much quality research on higher level gang organizations. That is, it is considerably easier to do field research on groups like Spanky and Alfalfa than it is to do so on groups like the El Rukns, Aryan Brotherhood, etc.

Hopefully what has been established here is that there are some interesting parallels across the social science disciplines for what essentially involves the same types of research strategy. This method is sufficiently complex that it can be regarded as irresponsible to basically send out someone untrained into the field, maybe because they are not skilled in quantitative methods, and expect them to automatically be good at qualitative research methods such as oral history interviews[20].

In this sense, perhaps it is incumbent upon researchers in this area to demonstrate their efficacy in some manner where through secondary analysis with the "raw materials", independent analysis can ascertain the quality of such interview results. A basic standard may be where multiple professionals interview the same gang member. Much gets edited out. And the problem of over-identification during close contacts with gang members represents another potential source of invalidity of this method. Getting "conned" into assuming the ideological accentuations preferred by the gang member, or "adding yeast" as the offender might say, would mean that some "case study methods" could potentially have the impact of disinformation as much as they could objectively inform us about the gang reality. It bears repeating here, as stated elsewhere, that the study of crime at the individual level is sufficiently complex to require a certain level of skepticism about verbal information gleaned from simply talking to gang members. So much hinges on what motivates the gang member to disclose information in the first place. Also, in some cases, a politically active scholar with a "leftist" slant, may have ears that want to hear "how gangs uplift the community" or are a new type of force of good seeking to "transform inner-city neighborhoods in a positive way": for gangs of all ethnic and racial persuasions are certainly capable of giving such a "slant" on their business.

DISCUSSION QUESTIONS

(1) In the absence of a full disclosure of all details of a field study, does what gets "edited out" in terms of information, come to function overall as a "black box" problem where we really do not know for sure what went on?

(2) If oral history, case studies, etc, can be abused, then what would be the most likely scenario for such intellectual dishonesty?

(3) When can "hanging out with the gang" become social science and when can it become an invasion of privacy to the extent of covert undercover operations? Similarly, when does "hanging out with the gang" become complicity in gang crime? Should higher standards of ethical behavior be established for such types of "hands on" research where the researcher intends to become intimately involved with the gang and its activities?

F.B.I's Sins of Omission A National Shame

Our nation's Federal Bureau of Investigation, arguably the most powerful law enforcement agency on earth, each year releases a voluminous document called the Uniform Crime Report (U.C.R.).

Within the hundreds of pages in this report, one can scan statistical data about arrests for offenses as minor as public intoxication right up to murder one. This document can tell you age, sex, race of the offenders and victims, the weapons used, the time of year, and circumstances surrounding the event.

But if you rely only upon the FBI's annual U.C.R. to learn about crime in modern day America, you will conclude gangsters and gang violence became extinct right along with Prohibition.

This could change in 1997 if Congress would authorize a modification of the FBI's Uniform Crime Report to include gang information on arrestees in the United States. This would be a prudent, practical response to the growing gang problem.

Some recent studies conducted by the National Gang Crime Research Center (NGCRC) and published in its journal reveal: (1) about two-thirds of all American cities, large or small, now have a gang problem; (2) about one-fourth of all inmates in adult correctional facilities are gang members; (3) about half of all persons confined in juvenile correctional facilities are gang members; (4) that the current estimate of the total U.S. gang member population is about 1.5 million; and (5) the gang problem shows no sign of abatement as we enter the 21st Century.

Congress and the executive branch need to realize that the most important tool to combat to the gang problem is information. But it literally takes an Act of Congress to modify or enhance the FBI's Uniform Crime Report (UCR).

The time is overdue to mandate that the FBI's Uniform Crime Report now include two new data elements: (1) was the arrestee a gang member? If yes (2) the name of the gang.

Without this factual data in the report, there can be no objective assessment of anti-gang initiatives.

Without this information, communities outraged into action by the latest driveby murder of a child, senior citizen or other innocent currently lack information about the true scope of the gang problem in their municipality.

By mandating that the FBI's Uniform Crime Report include gang membership data on arrestees, this would also put an end to the phenomenon of "gang denial."

Cities like New Orleans have only recently admitted they had a gang problem, with others (New York, Washington D.C., the list goes on) continue to deny it, despite the gang graffiti scrawled on their buildings and the bloodshed on their streets.

American citizens and police officers don't deny the truth-- that gangs exist and are conducting their deadly business within their borders.

Smaller cities and suburban areas have responded more swiftly-- about a fourth of all such municipalities have now passed laws or ordinances aimed at the gang problem.

If the FBI's UCR included detailed information about gang members and the harm they do, this political policy of amnesia and denial would end.

In a recent survey conducted by the NGCRC of several hundred police chiefs, we found that most assigned a "D" grade to work elected federal officials were doing to address the gang problem. Clearly the real "troops" fighting the war against gang crime --- the local and municipal police departments in the USA --- are not very impressed with the gang-fighting performance of the federal government.

Churches, civic associations, and other entities concerned about the gang problem will continue to labor in the darkness of an informational blackout.

This lack of reliable national statistics has contributed to a lack of consensus and coherent strategy on what direction our national social policy should take on the gang crime problem. Until Democrats and Republicans in Congress can "talk sense" about gangs, the deadly destruction directly attributable to gangs will spread like wild fire within our large cities and small towns.

The true cost of this informational blackout is felt in every town, large or small, where parents fear their children will be recruited to throw signs, sell drugs and carry guns.

It is felt each time decent citizens fear to cross a local intersection to go to church or work or school because that street corner is "owned" by a local gangster.

Further, where there is no real information, misinformation prevails. Gang propaganda efforts, an American tradition ever since Al Capone started his own soup lines, thrive when there is no official report on their criminal activity.

Citizens striving to live decently and raise their children in neighborhoods terrorized by local gangs have in some cases suffered the further indignity of watching gang members declare themselves "community leaders" and their gang a legitimate "community organization." In some cases, gangs have been successful in duping the local government and press into advancing their public relations efforts.

The time is now for the FBI to include data about gangs, gang members and gang crime in its annual Uniform Crime Report.

When that day comes, it will be possible to assess the threat gangs pose to this nation and to create real strategies to target gangs on a national, state and local level.

We might see creative legal strategies, such as seizing gang assets and awarding them to the families of the murdered and maimed. We might see community groups finally having sufficiently accurate data to effective plan a course of action to attack the local gang problem. We might see an end to "gang denial" by police departments because of the politi-

cal encroachment from local politicians "dabbling" in law enforcement policy.

The efforts of a gang to subvert the press and local government to gain legitimacy will then appear ridiculous when detailed information is suddenly available about the number of murders, arsons, thefts and rapes committed by its members.

End Notes:

[1] Remember this was directed at the abuse of methods in explaining delinquency. For example, Kramer and Karr (1953) would be one such example. In Kramer and Karr (1953) the authors call their method "dramatic narrative", which turns out really to be a kind of journalistic/impressionism from talking with detached workers and on this basis making fictionalized "composites" describing gang rumbles, the gang life, etc. Yet Kramer and Karr (1953) were certainly liberal reformers, advocating preventative measures rather than prison sentences, and being a social-political lobby for expanding detached worker programs.

[2] The qualitative method reported by Vigil (1988) is described as the "life history" using "case informants" or alternately, the "life history and self-reflexive history method" (Vigil, 1988: p. 174). It is clearly in the oral history tradition.

[3] Video products must generally have a "signed release form" from the subject. Also, to my knowledge no one has ever applied forensic psychology to this data in the same fashion that the polygraph has been used to determine the validity of traditional survey data. That is to say, could "voice stress analysis" uncover important variations in speech patterns, again using words as data.

[4]The notable exception to this is in using high ranking adult imprisoned gang members who have become confidential informers --- thereby denouncing the gang --- for the government. In visiting such persons, the present author has found that it is useful to have them call you (they will always have to call collect from the prison) and tell them what you intend to discuss in advance, they will often prepare "statements" from their recollection in their eagerness to assist.

[5] For a most excellent such exception, see Dino Malcolm, 1981, "D To the Knee! Stone To the Bone!", pp. 81-91, <u>Best of Hair Trigger: A Story Workshop Anthology</u>, Chicago: Columbia College Writing Department. Which provides an insightful experience of the Disciples and Black Stone Rangers gangs in Chicago.

[6]See: Thom Shanker, "A Skinhead Recants", <u>Chicago Tribune</u>, Section 5, May 11, 1994, p. 1,3.

[7] Keiser found that simply whipping out his notebook and pencil when in public with the gang induced panic among the gang members present (1979). Also, some authors report the complexity implied by transcribing tape recorded material.

[8] Hagedorn was able to secure a federal government agency "protection" against subpoenaed disclosure.

[9] Generally, known offenders tend to under-report their own extent of deviance and law violation and over-report their degree of legitimate integration. Which means, when interviewing a known gang member, such a person is more likely to report on the deviance of friends and associates than their own acts or behaviors at variance with society values, norms, and laws. Thus, it may be a more valid focus to raise questions about the gang as an organization and focus on other actors in such an enterprise.

[10] Sometimes it seems like the researcher in some previously published reports was trying to "go indigenous". That is, communicating at least an indigenous status to the offender being interviewed, perhaps with something that on its surface may seem innocuous such as "I've done things too, everyone has, I just wasn't caught like you", or something. But to what extent would such a strategy have the reverse intended effect in research? Could the respondent interpret such an admission as patronizing?

[11] I want to apologize for using the word "subjects" at this point, recalling once how Morris Janowitz lectured me similarly that in sociology "we don't have subjects, only kings and queens have <u>subjects</u> .... in sociology we have data sources and respondents". I fondly recall, in his spirit of egalitarianism, during this encounter adding "and don't call me Doctor Janowitz, I don't deliver babies" (circa, 1978).

[12] I will not address the matter of using unskilled, indigenous persons, or offenders belonging to the same network carrying out this kind of data collection as a hired hand. It is not the best idea if quality data is the goal. As will be seen, even in simple interviewing techniques, social skills and personality come into play. Training is important, but not everyone perhaps can be a good interviewer.

[13] A "Mutt and Jeff" routine involves two interrogators, each playing a separate function: one to play the good guy, one to play the bad guy; so as to elicit a confession. The "bad guy" there was the situation: the harsh reality of the prison; the "good guy" was the kind Reverend willing to show kindness, and get a story.

[14] The implication should be clear and is even more obvious from a critical review of former works involving "field work" with gangs (Whyte, Schwitzgebel, etc): to belittle the sophistication required for doing effective field work with groups as potentially violent as gangs is to take an equally serious ethical risk. Some authors might say it is "easy" to conduct field work. But that does not address the matter of quality of data gathered or the risk of deleterious impact through unintended negative consequences as a result of the "experimental/manipulator" overzealousness.

[15] To this point "some interviewers are born, some are made, and some never make it regardless how hard they try" (Harris, et al, 1975: p. 45).

[16] Arnold (1965) called his gang interviews "focused interviews" and used this subjective social encounter as the basis for collecting essentially quantitative data, for a remarkable analysis that is rarely cited in our gang literature.

[17]A number of sources verify Jeff Fort's formation of the El Rukn gang organization while in Milwaukee after his release from federal prison, and in a continuing fashion well into the 1980's. See, for example, p. 21 of the <u>Gang Awareness Module</u>, #17, Corrections Training Academy, Illinois Department of Corrections, 7/1/90.

[18]Paul Hoffman's (1993) review of the book by David Dawley states "This book contains many photographs including one of Dawley signifying, apparently, his gang allegiance: crossing his arms in the fashion of 'Peoples' (Dawley, 1992: p. 204)". Dawley claims to be the "only white member" of the Vice Lords, the group he hung out with in the late 1960s and early 1970s.

[19] This conversational analysis approach therefore crosses over many disciplines of the social sciences. Particularly sociology, psychology, and anthropology. But obviously, potentially others. Recently some authors have restated the argument by Hogrefe and Harding (1967) that gangs can be studied <u>only</u> through such methods as participant observation. Such quantaphobia and "anti-number crunching" is, of course, while reminiscent of a period of the 1970s referred to by Bookin-Weiner, etc, little more than intellectual posturing. (see Hogrefe and Harding, "Research Considerations in the Study of Street Gangs", 6 <u>Applied Anthropology</u> (21), 1967).

[20] Horowitz (1986) showed this complexity in the different types of researcher identities and how these can shape the efficacy of the data collection process.

Mafia Insane Vice Lords

MAFIA
☾ M·I·V·L·N 6·4
TILL THE WORLD BLOW UP
M.I.V.L.N

This is want MAFIA Means and other things.
Mother
And
Father
In
Africa
MAFIA

MIVL
4th Vice Lord CVL
TVL
MAFIA O SOlo
64 still
the WORld blow up
Chief APRIL
G.D Killer Nigga
MAFIA for LIFE

Mafia
Insane
Vice
Lords
64
Mafioso
Shabazz

M-I-V-L-N
AL-Shabazz
Mophia Insane
Vice Lord Nigga

Q. How hard is it to get a gang started?
A. It is easy. Take 4 or 5 guys who are working together in drug sales, they eventually see the benefits of continuity and formal structure. The moment they adopt a "name" for their group, they move from a "crew" to a "gang". The only downside: in most areas of the USA today, they will have to "pick a side" in the civil war of the underground economy: people/ bloods or folks/crips. The only other option is: white extremist groups/motorcycle gangs. But those are "tied up" and internally regulated too. A new gang today basically has to face this decision tree: what affiliation it will have.

CHAPTER 8

THE TRUE STORY ABOUT THE SHAW AND McKAY TRADITION

INTRODUCTION

Too often the novice to the study of gangs is quick to denounce all prior studies as "dated". Which is to say the neophyte entering the gang social science literature may take the viewpoint "they didn't know what they were talking about", or it is simply a case of "old theory and new gangs".[1] In criminal justice and corrections, as in all of society, that is not simply the case. We cannot denounce prior research in psychology or economics on such a similar basis or we would have to basically find ourselves in the odd situation of creating new "theories" every time a new gang problem emerged.[2]

This is not to deny that society itself has not changed since the 1920s. Indeed, many major changes have occurred since then in terms of technology, demography, values, and economics. These include changes in technology (mass communications, transportation, etc), changes in demography (i.e., a shift of population to urban areas, increased educational attainment, new groups entering American society, etc), changes in values (e.g., a new recognition of the rights of children and the creation of "child abuse" laws to protect the young), economic changes (i.e., the shift from an economy characterized primarily by industrial occupations to one that consists mostly of jobs in the service sector), and many other such structural change factors. These changes also include the fact that America has now surpassed the Soviet Union and South Africa in terms of penal incarceration.

The value of studying the past lies in understanding historical continuity and more generalizable concepts that can still be applied today. Such a historical focus also increases our understanding of continuing problems that have yet to be resolved. In corrections, we still have yet to conquer the "recidivism problem" and, curiously, this emerges in the gang literature; if we are astute enough to find it. In law enforcement, we have yet to eliminate political encroachment; and this too surfaces in the gang literature; if we look closely enough.

This chapter therefore seeks to place an important historical tradition in criminology, especially as it pertains to gang crime, in closer and more accurate focus. We need to know the truth. Too many students must rely on second-hand versions of what was represented in the Shaw and McKay tradition. It will be demonstrated that this tradition is often unfairly criticized and inadequately credited regarding concepts central to the understanding of gang crime. In fact, the truth is that many of the variables used by Shaw and McKay in their early research are the same variables being used in contemporary gang research.

Just what were the contributions of this tradition for the study of gang crime? Does the criminological literature really provide the true story?

Are many authors on gang issues today influenced, whether they know it or not, by Chicago's "Shaw and McKay" tradition?

Let's find out.

123

UNFAIR CRITICISM

Both Clifford R. Shaw and Henry D. McKay in fact were applied criminologists. But then, just as today, such applied competency does not mean they were any less scholarly or that what they had to say was of any less theoretical significance. Hagan (1987) implies it is "ironic" then that they are associated with the "Chicago school" of criminology, because "they never enjoyed faculty status at the University of Chicago" (p. 439).[3] Clearly, Shaw and Mc Kay attended the University of Chicago and both continued to interface with academics, many academics, not just at the University of Chicago. But as Hagan says (p. 439):[4]

"Snodgrass (1972) indicates that neither Shaw nor McKay received their doctorates due to foreign language requirements, but worked closely with many faculty and students from the university (Carey, 1975, pp. 84-92)."
Again, however, one gets the impression from this kind of introductory text that the only contribution was their basic thesis that social disorganization implies it is not abnormal persons as offenders, but abnormally disorganized social environments that produce crime. Hagan, like many contemporary writers, gives no credit to Shaw and McKay in a contribution to the understanding of gangs (pp. 231-232).

There appears to be a very unfortunate tendency among some writers to want to "pigeon hole" and give salient caption labels to other authors. However, when we are talking about an entire life tradition of criminological research ideally a more holistic examination would be the fairest way to go. Only a lazy scholar, someone without the energy to go back and actually read the originals, could make some of the untruthful and disparaging attributions that have been made to the Shaw and Mc Kay tradition. Shaw and Mc Kay used many research techniques to come to a better understanding about crime and delinquency and gangs. They basically helped to legitimatize and establish a research tradition used by those who could seem most prone to denounce Shaw and Mc Kay today. Shaw and Mc Kay, unlike some contemporary gang researchers, did not simply conduct one little research project on gangs or crime and then move on to some other sociological problem --- they carried out many, many different research projects, focusing on much of the same thing. One research project hardly makes anyone a gang expert.

Any contemporary gang researcher who thinks they have discovered the "best way" to get "close-up" to real criminals or real gang members, or that something they did they felt they did uniquely (e.g., collaborate with the persons being studied), is probably suffering from delusions of grandeur if not a total blindness to the history of the criminological

literature, particularly about the contributions from the Chicago school. But then again, intellectual politics being what it is, some are prone for whatever reason to take shots at the "Chicago school" of criminology. And there is nothing wrong with that, no one is perfect; and debate is healthy. But the fact remains, there is little that is new under the sun in terms of human relationships and human interaction --- and that is what we are talking about when we are talking about qualitative research methods, simply getting cooperation in a non-exploitive way.

Unlike most contemporary gang researchers, Shaw and Mc Kay used both qualitative and quantitative research methods.

Shaw and McKay are sometimes criticized for being naive about the use of obviously unreliable, under or misreported official statistics (see Siegal, 1983: p. 193). Siegal felt this reliance on official data "seriously damages the potential value of their work" (pp. 172-173). Hagedorn (1990) would later call this "courthouse criminology" in a criticism of modern Chicago school authors Spergel and Curry; the idea being that any information that comes from "official" sources like police or courts is unreliable and not the best source of information on gangs or gang members. First, Shaw and Mc Kay supplemented this "official data" with extensive qualitative data in the form of case studies and oral histories the quality and rigor of which have not yet been surpassed. Secondly, let's keep this in historical perspective. While the formative Shaw and Mc Kay monograph discussed and cited below is dated 1931, the Uniform Crime Report system maintained by the F.B.I. was not itself authorized for a go ahead until 11 June, 1930 (Inciardi, 1984: pp. 119-120).[5] Thirdly, as will be shown later in this chapter, it is just not true that Shaw and Mc Kay were unaware of the problems of official data, they were aware of the limitations and reported these qualifications. Fourthly, it is absurd to think that in criminology we can ignore official statistics and what happens in the criminal justice system as if any one research method (qualitative vs. quantitative) was scientifically superior.

Also it is worth noting that Shaw and Mc Kay used important data that is not analyzed in the FBI's U.C.R. statistics, or the BJS (Bureau of Justice Statistics), or even in most "self-report" surveys (because they must often be anonymous) ---- they used one thing: the home address.[6] It is doubtful that a cogent argument can be made to the effect that the courts, etc, didn't really know the correct address of the offender, which would provide some basis for a criticism of Shaw and Mc Kay on the basis of systematic measurement error.[7] Shaw and Mc Kay's ecological analysis involved marking the location of the address on a geographical map of the city of Chicago: an approach being revived today by researchers using computer mapping of crime complaints and incidents to support innovations in community policing.

At this point it is useful to specify what works by Shaw and McKay will be examined here. The issue may simply be that when we are talking about these two criminologists maybe we have not been talking about the same known works. Two works in particular never seem to be examined very closely in our recent literature when crediting or discrediting Shaw and McKay. One is the 1931 monograph that served as the blueprint for their most frequently cited 1942 text.[8]

COGNITIVE DATING OF SHAW & McKAY

Pardon the neologistic expression, but hopefully the astute reader has heard of cognitive maps.[9] Cognitive mapping is to associate a certain attribute with a certain geographic area on any city map. Cognitive dating is the only expression that seems to put this matter into perspective, but refers to the tendency for scholars to "time stamp" in history, a given authors contribution. So when should we chronologically date the major Shaw and Mc Kay contribution to American criminology?[10]

Many persons use the year 1942, but the well read criminologist will suspect this intellectual charting is due to an inadequate and superficial reading of Shaw and McKay. The 1942 publication, entitled Juvenile Delinquency and Urban Areas: A Study of Rates of Delinquents in Relation to Differential Characteristics of Local Communities in American Cities, should have probably earned Shaw and Mc Kay the contributory salutation in terms of theory classification as "differential social organization"[11] to append to the long list of other such "differential this and that" in the Chicago school of criminology.[12] Most such one liner definitional attributes for Shaw and Mc Kay give them the phrase "cultural transmission theory" or "social disorganization theory", or when referring incorrectly to only one of the analytical tools they used "concentric zone theory",[13] or ecological/ area analysis.

The 1942 text by Shaw and Mc Kay included separate contributions from six other authors.[14] The document that clarifies the problem about dating Shaw and McKay's theoretical contribution and their gang analysis was really published in 1931. This was volume II, National Commission on Law Observance and Enforcement, Report on the Causes of Crime, United States Government Printing Office, Washington, D.C. (price 50 cents). It is formally entitled Social Factors in Juvenile Delinquency: A Study of the Community, the Family, and the Gang in Relation to Delinquent Behavior, (416 pages).[15]

In truth, a sizable portion of what Shaw and Mc Kay reported in the 1942 text was taken paragraph by paragraph, and map by map, from the 1931 monograph. The 1942 text simply updated some of the data. Admittedly, the 1942 text dropped the title reference to gangs, just as their 1942 index contained no such reference to the gang.

It is possible to suspect that the 1931 monograph may have been the origin of the alternative moniker applied to the Shaw and McKay theory being called "cultural transmission theory". In the 1931 monograph, gangs are treated as evolved forms of play groups.[16] They spoke of the "transmission of delinquent tradition" (pp. 223-240) and its norms and values. More of Cohen's work than is probably acknowledged as Shaw and Mc Kay influenced may be found here when it comes to the matter of delinquent norms and values, also a topic examined in elaborate detail by use of case studies and oral history materials (pp. 240-250).

Technically, the introduction to the 1942 text, which was written by Ernest Burgess (pp. ix-xiii), should have been sufficient to unquestionably cement and legitimize Shaw and Mc Kay in the hall of criminological fame referred to, so loosely at times, as the "Chicago school".[17] Shaw and McKay worked closely with Burgess. But Shaw was unquestionably the senior of the Shaw and Mc Kay team. Shaw's title in 1931 was Head of the Department of Research Sociology, Institute for Juvenile Research and Behavioral Research Fund; while Mc Kay's title was Associate Research Sociologist. A later document, dated in 1949, carries the identifier of simply "Shaw and Associates".

Much of the material in the 1942 text clearly appeared in the 1931 monograph and this is a summary of that reprinting. The 1926 police series (N=9,243) appears in both (1931, p. 67; 1942, p. 80). The 1917-1923 court series (N=8,141) appears in both (1931, p. 41; 1942, p. 59). The 1900-1906 juvenile court series (N=8,056) appears in both (1931, pp.49-50; 1942, Maps 12 and 13).

What Shaw and Mc Kay did not continue in their 1942 text was a discussion regarding gangs. One can only speculate, but perhaps because of this, and the fact that their 1942 text is what they are identified with, they are lumped with generic delinquency theories rather than with those having direct implications for gang crime. But the fact is, the 1931 monograph did focus on gangs. Oddly, Shaw's 1951 natural history study of the delinquent career continued the reference to organized gangs and criminal groups (p. 15),[18] as did the 1931 version of Shaw's "The Natural History of a Delinquent Career" (Shaw and Morre, 1931).

Chapter 6 in Shaw and Mc Kay (1931) was an effort to show that most delinquency is group activity. What else is noteworthy about this chapter is that the authors were fully aware of the limitations of "official data", as will be seen. An earlier study by Shaw and Meyer (1920) is quoted showing that among some 6,000 cases of stealing in the juvenile court, only 9.6 percent of these involved lone offenders, the rest (90.4%) were group offenders (1931, p. 196). Additional data collection on another 4,663 youths with theft charges showed in chapter 6 that 89 percent were group offenders.

In chapter 6, Shaw and Mc Kay were clearly aware of the limitations of official data and perhaps this can dispel some of the criticism leveled at them for being criminologically naive regarding this. It is well to quote Shaw and Mc Kay in their entirety here:

"It should be borne in mind that these statistical tabulations have been restricted to offenders known to the juvenile court authorities. It is not assumed therefore that the relative frequency of lone and group offenders in the general delinquent population is identical with the percentages presented in this study. Obviously, not all of the boys engaged in delinquent activities are known to the court". (Shaw and Mc Kay, 1931: p. 198).

They actually anticipated such criticism and advanced the defense that their estimates for lone offenders were very conservative, and in fact overestimated their representation involving theft cases because of the natural tendency of gang boys to not "squeal" on each other when caught. Further, "it is obvious that not all such group delinquencies are committed by well-organized gangs" because while "many of the delinquents may be members of such gangs, they usually commit their offenses in the company of one or two other boys" (p. 199).

Chapters 7 and 8 in Shaw and Mc Kay (1931) involve the delinquent group and their traditions. Chapter 7 describes the case of Sidney Blotzman, who over the period from 1913 to 1928 was actually involved with three different gangs. The residential mobility of this youth meant that by moving from one neighborhood to another, within Chicago, he also found himself in a different gang (p. 201). Admittedly, at times the playgroup, the companionship group, and the gang tend to be concepts used interchangeably (p. 204). Sidney's first gang was not a highly organized gang (p. 214), but the 3rd gang was the lower age grade affiliate of an adult criminal group, the membership of which "included some of Chicago's most notorious criminals" (p. 218). In this third group, Sidney became involved in armed robbery and rape (p. 219).

Clearly, a most significant difference between the 1931 monograph and the 1942 text is the use of many case studies and oral histories. While many are provided in the former, few are given in the latter. The 1942 text contains mostly quantitative data. Many of the 1931 case studies referred directly to various aspects of gang activity.

Yet there are other analytic differences even in the focus on quantitative measures in comparing the 1931 monograph with the 1942 text. As seen in Figure 8 below, there were continuing analytical measures in common between both works. What is significant is the expansion in the 1942 text. The 1942 text included new measures of differential social organization giving rise to delinquency such as: rental values, truancy, infant mortality, tuberculosis rates, mental disorder rates, home ownership, and economic segregation. Clearly, in the 1942 text Shaw and Mc Kay see racial differences having the common origin of economic segregation. In the 1931 monograph broken homes were shown to have a negligible relationship with delinquency and perhaps because of this was excluded from analysis in the 1942 text.

Figure 8
Comparison of Community Measures in the Two Shaw and Mc Kay Contributions

The 1931 Monograph *****************(pp.)		The 1942 Text *************(pp.)	
Economic dependency (AID)	74-75	Families on relief	34
Condemned Buildings	69-70	Demolished Buildings	28
Changing Population Size	71-72	Changing population	31
Race/Ethnic segregation	79-80	Black Segregation	32,37-42
Neighborhood Succession	82-94	Ethnic succession	42
CJS Ethnic Intake Change	94-98	Same	152
White Racism	117-129	Similar	149
Presence of Adult offenders		Adult offenders	100
Broken Homes	265-268	Not analyzed	
Not Used		Rental Values	35
" "		Truancy	86
" "		Infant Mortality	94
" "		Tuberculosis Rates	96
" "		Mental Health Rates	99
" "		Home ownership rate	144
" "		Economic segregation	33

ANALYTICAL PARALLELS TO CURRENT APPROACHES

It is certainly the case, from the official record, of contemporary published materials about gang crime that some authors acknowledge more familiarity with the work of Shaw and Mc Kay than do others. This review pertains only to major works, not journal articles, or presented papers at professional societies. What this may demonstrate is an enduring influence from Shaw and Mc Kay, whether it is acknowledged, whether it is unconscious, or whether it is simultaneous independent discovery of the same factors examined by Shaw and Mc Kay within some of the current approaches to gang crime. This review shows, then, that basically the same variables used by Shaw and Mc Kay are still in use today by an array of authors on the topic of gangs.

Hagedorn (1988) likes to have the cake and

eat it too, but does not quote a single contribution from Shaw and Mc Kay and makes only one indirect reference to a quote of Shaw via Miller (1976, p. 120) (see Hagedorn, 1988, p, 20, fn p. 185). This is most curious considering that some of the factors examined by Hagedorn include those also previously analyzed by Shaw and Mc Kay. These factors in Hagedorn (1988) include: adult involvement (p, 110), the minority experience (p. 17), disorganization and deprivation via Bogardus (p. 43), racial economics (pp. 25-26), the gang as a launch pad for criminal careers via Tannenbaum (1938) (p. 9)[19], ethnic conflict (p. 44), gang loyalty (p. 184), the repudiation of middle class standards via Cohen, the role of AFDC and public assistance (p. 190), ethnic and nationality conflicts via Cloward and Ohlin (p. 194), not truancy but school dropouts (p. 199), the stage of immigration (p. 203), urban prejudice via Yablonsky (p. 183), social and economic discrimination via Yablonsky (p. 184). Now are we supposed to believe none of this was examined in the works of Shaw and Mc Kay?

Moore's (1978) emphasis on the relationship between the barrios and the prisons could have certainly been strengthened by reference to Shaw and Mc Kay's findings on gang affiliation and the correctional experience. How dissimilar is the structural condition between bootlegging under the prohibition described by Shaw and Mc Kay and the bootlegging in drugs described by Moore? Moore surely quotes the importance of government aid and welfare (p. 30), clique succession (p. 60), and the strong sense of nationalism (p. 107) in analyzing gangs in Los Angeles. And there are no parallels drawn by Moore with the prior work of Shaw and Mc Kay.

Campbell (1984) refers to Shaw (1929) only in terms of ecological pressures (see Campbell, 1984: fn, p. 268).[20] There are also references to issues of immigration and how New York neighborhoods are segregated along ethnic lines (p. 234). Does it seem more reasonable to conclude that many of the factors studied by Shaw and Mc Kay are more or less the same factors subsequently used by other criminological researchers?

Yablonsky (1962) seemed so heavily influenced by the work of Shaw and Mc Kay he used the phrase "differential socialization" (p. 232)[21]. Yablonsky was certainly aware of the 1931 monograph and quoted it (p. 124, 126). Also discussed in Yablonsky were themes related to the Shaw and Mc Kay work such as "the twisting threads of prejudice and discrimination" (pp. 184-185), the gang as an outlet for bias crimes (p. 186), ethnic conflict and rivalry (p. 187), and in fact five of Yablonsky's seven causal factors (p. 232) seem tied to the Shaw and Mc Kay tradition.

Suttles (1971) cites the 1942 Shaw and Mc

Kay text (p. 18), the problem of white vs. African-American school tensions (p. 58), and presents a fascinating ecological analysis involving the short distance between place of gang offense and gang members closest residence (pp. 208-209). It is certainly a theoretical refinement on differential social organization, by showing that communities such as those examined prior to Suttles (1968) were not monolithic conditions of equal forms of social disorganization. Indeed, they often have more "infrastructure" than casual observers credit them with; that is, they have ordered segmentation.[22] Ordered segmentation, we assume, is a function of ethnicity and territory, and allows for the management of social relations within and between neighborhoods, which is further refined by normative patterns paralleling differences in age, sex, kinship, and residential groupings, so as to facilitate regulated assembly, a localized provincialism and pattern of movement in face to face aggregates, having standardized role capacities.

Spergel (1964, 1973) must be considered part of the Chicago school of criminology, even though if a person seeks to take course work at the University of Chicago they will find no such division called "the School of Criminology", they will find only the existing Department of Sociology, and other social sciences that work closely with it. There is no "major" in criminology, although obviously a Ph.D. special field examination can probably be taken in this topical area. Spergel is currently an associated faculty member, teaching as he does from the Social Service Administration on the other side of the "Midway". In the Chicago school tradition, he also coined the phrase "differential life styles" (1973, pp. 63-92)[23].

What Spergel proves is that one can both build directly upon a prior acknowledged tradition and advance new theoretical structures that are largely consistent with the Chicago school tradition. Spergel (1971) gives no credit or mention to Shaw and Mc Kay in the East Coast community he studied, but by means of independent discovery or simple good research basically discovers and identifies many of the same variables. For example, Spergel does include indexes of social breakdown"ization"[24] that measure public assistance and aid, infant mortality, venereal disease, and psychiatric discharges in the three communities he studied (p. 5). Spergel also discusses relationships with adult offenders (pp. 145-146) which Shaw and Mc Kay dealt with as a problem for a community, it provides the opportunity for delinquents to acquire adult tutelage in gang crime.

Spergel (1971) seems to wrestle with two conceptual themes, not one as he has been unfairly criticized (ala Hagedorn). There is both the implied community social disorganizational structural backdrop and the social-psychological aspect relating to perceptions of the opportunity system. Figure 9, below, tries to place this in graphic form.

FIGURE 9
THE SPERGEL ANALYSIS OF TWO THEMES:
SOCIAL DISORGANIZATION   AND
OPPORTUNITY SYSTEM TYPOLOGY

The Nature of the Neighborhood Opportunity System
****

		Legitimate	Illegitimate
		**************	**************
Community		Nice, low crime,	Racketville and
Social	LOW	middle class,	Outfit, Inc
Disorganization		ideal neighborhood	type neighborhood
Levels			
	HIGH	Working class poor,	The slumtown
		pre-deindustrialized	extraordinaire,
		neighborhood	Moore's Gulag
		(Haulburg?)	neighborhood.

The only problem with such a scheme is the first quadrant, the "nice, low crime, middle class, ideal neighborhood": how do we promote and develop it? Sometimes students of criminology are told that in order to understand criminality we must first understand why persons conform to the law. Perhaps what this problem in criminology indicates is the more general problem in the search for the ideal community structure and environment.

Cohen (1955) directly quoted the 1931 monograph by Shaw and Mc Kay regarding the fusion of versatility and malice in one of their oral histories (p. 29). Once the reader of Cohen becomes acclimated to a "stream of consciousness" monologue writing style, and diction such as "niggardliness" (p. 52), Cohen could actually be quoted perhaps contra original intellectual intentions in support of a segmented labor force thesis (pp. 94-95). Cohen does call the 1931 Shaw and Mc Kay monograph "cultural transmission theory". But sees Shaw and Mc Kay's cultural transmission approach being rehashed in "criminal behavior" theory by Sutherland "couched in what are essentially cultural-transmission terms" (p. 180).

Cloward and Ohlin (1960), clearly a part of the Chicago school modern criminological tradition, call Shaw and Mc Kay "cultural transmission" theory as well (pp. 35-36). They refer to Shaw and Mc Kay's 1940 version of Delinquency Areas and Shaw's (1933) article on delinquency as a group tradition (Cloward and Ohlin, 1960: pp. 37,162). It has been pointed out that perhaps the best way to "label" Shaw and McKay is by their own intended terminology: differentiall social organization theory.

WHAT SHAW AND MC KAY SAID ABOUT "CORRECTIONAL INSTITUTIONS"

Getting personal, I am having the same problem explaining Shaw and Mc Kay as I did in the early 1980s explaining the social reality of "nothing works, oops, I'm sorry, maybe it does" Martinson. Martinson had been the chief ideologue for a long time that "nothing works in rehabilitating offenders". Then on November 20th, of 1978, at the Second National Workshop on Criminal Justice Evaluation, in Washington, D.C., in a panel where I was also presenting a paper[25], he stunned the standing room only audience when he announced to the effect "I know many of you may be expecting me to tell you more about how rehabilitation does not work; but I was premature in my conclusions; in fact I am here to tell you that perhaps some things do work, now that I have started using real data".

I would tell my students about this story and Martinson's self-inflicted death just shortly after the above presentation, and students in the class would make the strangest comments. Such as "I bet the CIA killed him and made it look like a suicide, didn't he get a lot of money from the feds?", etc, etc. Mostly the students began to distrust what they read. This is probably good, because the research monograph I am going to summarize here, from Shaw and Mc Kay (1949), also has incredible implications. But this is an authentic document, so I think we had better believe these previously unknown findings from Shaw and Mc Kay.

This is an unpublished study entitled Subsequent Criminal Careers of Juvenile Delinquents, School Truants, and Special School Pupils, dated 1949. On the yellowed by age copy that I inherited is marked boldly Confidential and has what may or may not be the signature of "C. Shaw" in the same ink. Penciled on the front of this sixty page monograph was the writing "Note: This study was financed by Wiebolt $49,000 and was never published because of the effect it would have on collections for work in juvenile delinquency". How I got it is a longer story that can be told somewhere else.

It is an extensive follow-up study of official efforts to rehabilitate children through sending them to institutions whose purpose had that stated goal of "the reconstruction of human lives" (Shaw and Mc Kay, 1949: p. 1). There are no case studies here. This is a straight forward quantitative study. It studied cohorts of four dispositions for these children: (1) boys who are repeatedly delinquent as children and are sent to the State Training School, (2) boys whose delinquency has brought them into the juvenile court as official delinquents, (3) boys who have been found to be repeatedly truant, and (4) boys who "are problems in the school system" (p. 3).

The data from the Illinois State Training

School for boys (St. Charles) includes: (1) "a series of 327 boys committed to the State Training School from Chicago during the year 1930", (2) "a series of 435 boys paroled from (St. Charles) to Chicago during the years 1942-44", and (3) "a summary of the findings of an earlier....follow-up of 263 boys paroled (from St. Charles) for the first time during the years 1923-25" (p. 13).

The data on delinquent boys brought before the Cook County Juvenile Court includes: (1) "a series of 1,336 boys brought before the Juvenile Court during the year 1930", and (2) "a series of 1,178 boys brought before the Juvenile Court during the year 1920" (p. 13).

The data on boys adjudicated as school truants by the Cook County Juvenile Court included: (1) "a series of 408 boys committed to the Chicago Parental School by the Juvenile Court during the year 1930", and (2) "a series of 543 boys brought before the Juvenile Court on truant petition in 1930" (p. 13).

The data on boys who are behavioral problems in the Chicago Public School system included: (1) a series of 382 boys admitted to the Montefiore Special School during the years 1932-33 (p. 13).

Table 7 below summarizes the findings from this Shaw and Mc Kay study (1949). These statistics are vulgar in the extent to which they demonstrate how juvenile institutions appear to be in the business of systematically producing adult criminals. These figures are beyond being alarming, they should be indictable. And such results from the City where juvenile processing was supposed to be the best in the United States? I fear for those other jurisdictions and their own rates of mass producing adult criminals. What shame there must be in needing to reproduce crime along the lifespan to feed adult prisons!

Or can we simply discount these powerful findings from Shaw and Mc Kay?

I suspect these findings are true. We cannot assume that any major societal impetus has given us reason to believe, also, that these same parameters have changed in the direction of reduced levels of recidivism. What it implies for gangs, and correctional staff, should be clear.

We are not doing the best job in preventing recidivism.

In fact, apparently, as a society we really do not care to address this matter of the hidden industry in our criminal justice system that systematically produces adult criminals from the raw materials of errant youths.

In fact, recidivism problems among juvenile institutions are as equally problematic today as they were in the time of Shaw and Mc Kay's study (1949). The problem has never been tackled. The problem

has been systematically ignored.

TABLE 7

Summary of the Shaw and Mc Kay (1949) Findings on the
Percentage of Juvenile Boys in Chicago Who
After Being "Cared For" By Institutions
Designed to Redirect Their Lives
Actually Became Adult Criminals

	FUP (yrs) ********	%SJ& AR *********	% ARA ********	% ARC ********	% ARI ********	MEANS ***************** ANA *******	ANC *******	ANI *******
ST. CHARLES:								
1930 Intake	17	82.9	76.1	68.5	60.5	5.1	3.0	2.2
1930 Intake	5	78.3	68.8	61.2	52.9	NR	NR	NR
1942-44 Parolees	5	71.0	63.9	52.2	42.1	3.0	1.9	1.7
1923-25 Parolees	5	80.2	75.7	69.6	58.2	2.9	1.8	1.6
JUVENILE COURT:								
1930 Intake	18	73.3	66.2	52.2	36.1	4.7	2.5	2.0
1920 Intake	28	67.8	59.6	42.7	22.5	5.5	2.8	2.3
TRUANCY SERIES:								
1930 CPS Intake	18	69.6	57.8	44.4	32.1	5.0	2.7	2.2
1920 Juv. Court	18	71.3	58.2	45.3	31.9	4.8	2.6	2.1
MONTEFIORE SERIES:								
1932-33 Intake	15	74.6	53.7	42.4	30.9	4.2	2.5	2.1
1932-33 Intake	9	71.2	47.9	36.6	28.5	NR	NR	NR

Legend of Symbols:

FUP = Follow-up Period
%SJ&AR = Percentage with Subsequent Juvenile & Adult Record
%ARA = Percentage with Adult Record of Arrests
%ARC = Percentage with Adult Record of Convictions
%ARI = Percentage with Adult Record of Imprisonment
ANA = Average Number of Arrests as in adult record
ANC = Average Number of Convictions in adult record
ANI = Average Number of Imprisonment commitments (adult)

COMBINING TWO SHAW AND MC KAY THEMES ON THE PRODUCTION OF CRIME

The theme for which Shaw and Mc Kay are known, or should be understood from their published literature, is that at the level of the community, above and beyond the control of those who are born there or who reside there, are structural forces in society having to do with what Shaw and Mc Kay called aspects of social disorganization and conditions of inequality, including racism, prejudice, discrimination, and segregation --- and these forces, while being discernible from communities without or with less delinquency, gang crime, etc, in terms of their variation or differences in social organization, basically bring about the onset of delinquency and gangs. What the 1949 study shows is that once the government becomes involved in the welfare of these youths brought to the attention of "authorities", through a series of repressive institutional life experiences, we as a society also take these young errant boys and make them into adult criminals.

That's how I read Shaw and Mc Kay. And I believe them.

SUMMARY AND CONCLUSION

The Hollywood caricature of the arch conservative-bigot in the persona of Archie Bunker tends to communicate "it's not what it is, it's what it appears to be, that's important". Along these lines, I do not consider myself a defender of Shaw and Mc Kay, although obviously it may appear that way. I have to "call em' as I seem em'". But I do feel some authors have either not known the whole story or else simply discount Shaw and Mc Kay for reasons we cannot readily surmise. The whole truth needs to be told.

The truth is that Shaw and Mc Kay indeed contributed much to the gang literature, as demonstrated in their 1931 monograph. Also, whether we acknowledge them or not, there appears to be a large influence from Shaw and Mc Kay or minimally, there are research parallels with many current approaches to gang research.

Finally, perhaps what could have been their most powerful contribution to criminology was never allowed to be released to the public and remained "confidential" (Shaw and Mc Kay, 1949).

So the truth is that Shaw and Mc Kay probably have been unfairly maligned in some of the literature, under-acknowledged often, and even misinterpreted in some of our literature. Perhaps this is somewhat related to what Martinson (1978) said "I was premature in my conclusions...", because it would appear that these same authors bent on criticizing Shaw and Mc Kay may not have had a grasp of the larger picture --- the other contributions from Shaw and Mc Kay.

We need a much fuller grasp of this literature before taking on any responsibility and authority to "do something about it". This should not discourage such attempts at rehabilitation, it should incite and further motivate them. But just as in tackling the gang problem, we should do so not based on intuition and "hunches" of what programs should be put in place, it should be a strategy based on social science and known research results of "what works".

DISCUSSION QUESTIONS:

(1)   In early radical intellectual circles during the 1960s and early 1970s, "empiricism" itself, that is, using numbers in research, was considered the supreme act of academic fascism: reducing the problem to numbers. This belief system did change when radicals found they could use computers too. So does the denunciation of gang research because it uses "official statistics" mean that only "first hand qualitative methods" are the answer to generating knowledge about gangs in America? Or can some official statistics be used effectively? Is this a problem of political rhetoric or science? Census data are "official statistics" too, so can the same radical criticism apply? Is the ultimate radical position that any data collected by any governmental agency or governmental representative necessarily means a "big lie"?

(2)   Do you feel that Shaw and Mc Kay have become "type cast" in our criminological literature?

(3)   What do the recidivism statistics reported by Shaw and Mc Kay (1949) imply about America as an advanced civilization?

End Notes:

[1] James Short (in Huff, 1990) sees much historical continuity in his analysis of "new wine, old bottles".

[2]   In fact, if we are truly to have a social scientific perspective, we must at least strive for a cumulative body of knowledge. Even if a student of criminology is to deny such a cumulative body of social science, then minimally we should at least be informed about the mistakes of the past or run the risk of repeating errors.

[3]   My data indicates that during the Fall Quarter of 1946, that Henry D. McKay was the instructor of record for Sociology 271, a course entitled "Crime & Juvenile Delinquency". My source of information for this is the personal files of the late Don T. Blackiston, Ph.D., who took this course, and others from Mc Kay. Shaw apparently taught "Criminology" and others (Soc 377) "Community Organization and Delinquency Prevention", (Soc 397) "Criminal Careers".

[4]   We have a boundary maintenance problem here in defining what is meant by membership in the "Chicago school of criminology". Hagan seems to imply one must teach in the sociology department of the University of Chicago, and have completed the Ph.D. requirements. Does this mean that many of the fine

and unique contributions from many, many Master's theses completed at the University of Chicago's Department of Sociology are not genuine contributions either? Does this mean that any of the many U of C Sociology Ph.D.'s that worked in the Illinois prison system as "sociology actuaries", because it was field work, not academia, were somehow less legitimate? We shall have to come up with some working definition of what is and is not "Chicago school" tradition. I suspect, however, because of the complete variation in both methods and ideology that there is no one-dimensional tradition, but rather many different traditions focused on much the same thing.

[5] Not to belabor the obvious, but at the time of Shaw and Mc Kay's early work there was not even a messed up national system of "official statistics" to worry or lament about!

[6] I often ask students undergoing criminal investigation training about how to solve crimes involving the residential propinquity factor when no centralized, routinely updated, arrest/event dated address file really exists in the U.S.A. Perhaps Shaw and McKay should be read more closely by law enforcement students.

[7] Shaw and Mc Kay were admittedly descriptive and bivariate in their (1931,1942) statistical analysis, using maps, bar charts, percentage distributions, rate calculations, and correlation coefficients rather than multiple regression. But they were dealing with large volumes of data as well, without the use of a computer other than that their Creator gave them!

[8] I am indebted to the wife of the late Don T. Blackiston, who graciously turned over his personal files to me. Blackiston had earned his Ph.D. in sociology from the University of Chicago. He never taught, he worked his entire life as an applied criminologist. The works I shall be quoting from in this chapter came from Blackiston's collection.

[9] This is similar to what Suttles (1971) refers to as a process by which any given location in a city may have a stigma associated with it, such as the housing projects being associated with persons of color (Suttles, 1971: p. 16).

[10] Many persons seem to place Sutherland's theory of differential association before the contribution of Shaw and Mc Kay. Differential association theory had its first version in 1939, in the 3rd edition of Sutherland's Principles of Criminology. As I shall argue here, whatever we call Shaw and Mc Kay's theory, its first version was in the 1931 monograph, not 1942.

[11] Indeed, Shaw and Mc Kay (1942) use this particular phrase, differential social organization (pp. 177-183). I have always presented the Shaw and Mc Kay tradition to my students in this terminology, only to have them find, quite to their confusion, that other criminologists do not use this phrase in reference to Shaw and Mc Kay.

[12] Sutherland (1939) differential association; Cloward and Ohlin (1960) differential opportunity structure; Daniel Glaser's differential identity, etc, etc. Actually, Cloward and Ohlin also made reference to "differential integration" (1960,pp. 189-192); but seeing that no one called their framework by that, I used the phrase myself (Knox, 1978).

[13] My point is this: we as human beings probably want to pigeonhole everything; and maybe one document can be so classified if it has a single thrust, but we cannot as readily pigeonhole a person's whole lifespan of productivity.

[14] So let's be fair here, the 1942 text was Shaw, et al.

[15] Not all gang authors were unaware of this important contribution. Morash (1983) was one who certainly cited this work.

[16] Shaw and Mc Kay clearly, however, distinguished between the play group and the gang (see 1931, p. 240).

[17] And, of course, Short and Strodtbeck's (1965, 1974) legitimation of Shaw and McKay as part of the old Chicago school that compiled natural histories (p. 77).

[18] Cultural enrichment is a service intervention style often held out for delinquents, gang members, etc, at a primary to secondary level of prevention. Depending on your view if this works to reduce crime or not, one can alternately blame or credit, perhaps, Shaw, at least to some extent, for the later emergence of many variations of the cultural enrichment programs for delinquency treatment and prevention. Because the 1951 study by Shaw emphasized the disjunction between a delinquent boys environment and the "little access to cultural heritages of conventional society" (p. 15).

[19] This cites the 1929 study by Shaw and Myers.

[20] Similarly, perhaps due to the historical "pigeon holing" of the intellectual contributions of criminological authors, Shaw and Mc Kay become "type cast", such that authors (e.g., Denisoff and Mc Caghy, 1973: p. 150) continue to refer to Shaw and Mc Kay's

contribution as little more than the "ecological theory".

[21] Please note, as part of the ongoing concern about boundary maintenance with WHO is really a part of the "Chicago school" of criminology, that simple use of the prefix "differential" is not necessarily an automatic means of inclusion within this intellectual tradition. Otherwise anyone could generate frameworks such as "differential assimilation", "differential competition", "differential whatever", and lay legitimate claim to such an intellectual gang/ingroup.

[22] Suttles notes that among African-Americans there may be less such spatial ordering because of lower amounts of mobilizable resources for local social organization in their community infrastructure (p. 226).

[23]Many of the criminological theories from the Chicago school have this "differential" prefix: differential association (Sutherland), differential social organization (Shaw and Mc Kay), differential identity (Glaser), differential opportunity (Cloward and Ohlin), differential integration, etc.

[24] Pardon my added suffix here.

[25] My paper was "A Comparative Cost-Benefit Analysis of Programs for Illinois Offenders", and was certainly a defense of and an argument for expanded resources targeting aftercare and prevention services for youths and adult offenders. I was a young turk who just got his Ph.D. two months ago and was there arguing "for rehabilitation" and I did not know until I got in the room and looked at the name plates on the speakers table that Dr. Martinson was also presenting. Needless to say, I felt at the time like I was "set up" for a clashing debate between the renowned and highly funded Dr. Nothing Works and me the Dr. Young Turk Who Thinks Something Works. It didn't happen. In fact, when Martinson took the podium, he recanted his whole "nothing works" doctrine, which generated much verbal stirring in the huge mostly governmental audience. I had the distinct impression that he almost wanted to be "let back into the fold" of such groups like the American Society of Criminology, where he was not too popular. I guess we will never know the full story.

The Scholarly Significance of Shaw & McKay:
An Aspect of Value Yet to be Discovered or Appreciated

Most people in America learn about Shaw and McKay in an introductory level course at a college or university. Such courses deal with criminology, juvenile delinquency, criminal justice, etc. Most people who provide information today about Shaw and McKay are criminologists and others who write the books for these courses.

What every single textbook today that addresses Shaw and McKay fails to point out is the value that Shaw and McKay had for larger society through some of their lesser-known research. In fact, the single largest research project that Shaw and McKay worked on was their follow-up study of what happens to youths who are sent to juvenile correctional facilities in Illinois. Few scholars today are even aware of the existence of this study. This study was describe in Chapter 8 here.

Here is what the study seems to say: in the name of having the government be the "parents" of errant children, and at great cost to taxpayers, and often in the name of the protection of the children themselves, we as a society for over a century now have been incarcerating juveniles and claiming that we are "rehabilitating" them. What we have actually been doing, it appears from Shaw and McKay, is producing adult criminals.

Few who work in adult correctional institutions today actually believe in any aspect of "rehabilitation". But there are a large number of persons who work in juvenile corrections today who still believe in rehabilitation and feel that they are genuinely engaged in rehabilitating juvenile offenders. But missing is any aspect of accountability to the tax paying public: routinely reported outcome studies of the juveniles being released from these facilities are rare. Often called "recidivism studies", these are rare because they are a source of criticism to the stated goals of such facilities.

So those who work in juvenile corrections harbor and internalize these beliefs about rehabilitation in a noble way: they have hope for turning the children around and producing better citizens. But often it is just that: hope alone. And more often than not their hope exists in spite of the overwhelming evidence of continued failure to achieve any measure of effectiveness in that regard.

Does your state publish or disseminate outcome studies or recidivism reports of the juveniles confined in your state? How can you find out? Contact the State Corrections Commission or Department in your state. Some states have separate departments for juveniles, in some states juveniles are simply are separate division in a larger corrections agency.

As a very expensive and very ineffective aspect of government, juvenile corrections has yet to be discovered as a topic of debate in the minds of the average American citizen. Perhaps it will someday become an issue.

Crips (Various Active Midwest Sets)
(SOURCE: Ohio)

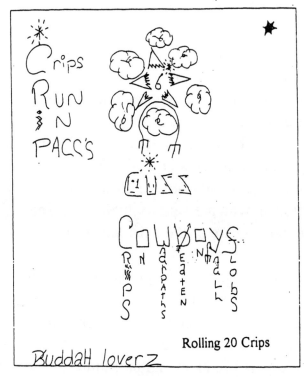

Rolling 20 Crips

Buddah loverz

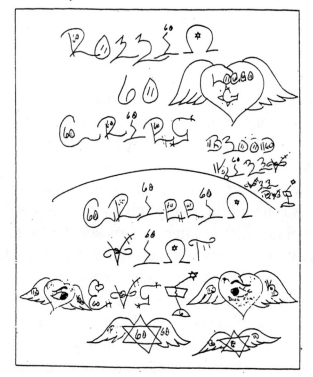

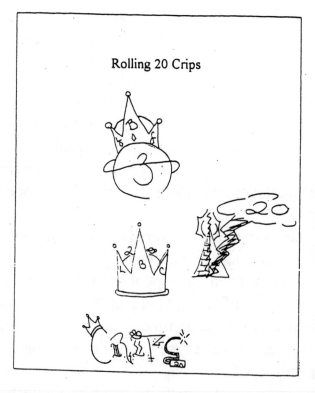

Rolling 20 Crips

CHAPTER 9

SHAW AND MC KAY ON GANGS:
With Commentary and Historical Analysis

INTRODUCTION

It remains somewhat of a sociological mystery why Shaw and Mc Kay gave so much emphasis to gangs in their 1931 monograph and seem to have mostly abandoned it thereafter. Clearly, few contemporary authors credit Shaw and McKay with any contribution to our understanding of gangs. That is a historical mistake. Recall that Thrasher's (1927) work was gaining acclaim as the definitive study of gangs, as was Asbury's analysis. Factually, we can only recount what Shaw and Mc Kay had to say about gangs and provide some background material. That is the purpose of this Chapter.

The implications for the field of criminology should be evident. We have missed an important segment of the knowledge development spectrum if we do not understand that Shaw and Mc Kay had more to say about gangs than contemporary authors give them credit for. This is particularly important for those readers concerned about the future of America's gang problems and what social policy initiatives or programs should be put in place. We need more than a casual understanding of the past, for otherwise we make a major risk of misinterpretation; indeed a risk that should not be taken when dealing with a problem as significant as gangs.

The same applies to the field of law enforcement. It is a mistake to ignore the past. Thus, any analysis of gangs must be able to offer an understanding of the past, present, and the future. Hopefully, the present analysis is such an account. Which is not to say that criminologists should write first of all for policy makers, but rather that social science findings bearing on such obviously important topics have an obligation, morally, to not ignore the possibility that such findings could be misinterpreted in the absence of any such policy suggestions or overall position statements.

By providing a summary of what Shaw and Mc Kay contributed to our understanding of gangs, this is more than simply giving historical documentation to their role in the study of gangs. What they have to offer is of continuing significance.

DISORGANIZED NEIGHBORHOODS, ORGANIZED GANGS

In comparing economically depressed inner city neighborhood life with a more prosperous neighborhood, what is of importance regarding the propensity for law violation are the sources of norms and values, "conceptions of right and wrong" (Shaw

135

and Mc Kay, 1931: p. 111). In the urban poor enclave a youth has restricted access to the established social order in the sense that it may be limited to "formal contacts with the police, the courts, the school, and the various social agencies" (p. 111). In a more prosperous community, perhaps a youth could have extensive formal relations with the established social order: through tutors, nannies, adult supervised travel and tours, and a host of other socialization functions. This might include those at the young adult collegiate level, like that of the anticipatory socialization/training grounds often found at prestigious or private universities like the University of Chicago, and their "student run" Society for Social Research.

This points to a fundamental aspect of youth socialization: a condition of normative ambiguity or normlessness, as a condition of anomie, is going to be a source of much alienation; therefore in the natural search for human meaning in a social or collective setting, when the formal mechanisms do not work, informal ones take over. It is truly a matter of the qualitative differences between having a positive and functional relationship to the adult run apparatus and being warmly welcomed into it; or conversely, of being in a "control mode" by major social institutions, where the most frequent contact with the legitimate adult authorities is in a combative relationship with the established social order. We can add, of course, to this the variations in power, privilege and racism ala Wilson to see that while everyone might in theory be "equal under the law", by the nature of their social attachment to the social order some are clearly going to be "more equal" than others.

According to Shaw and Mc Kay (1931) it is more than a material difference, it is a difference between being "excluded" or "included" from channels of normative learning (p. 111).[1] These are conditions of the social structure of society and how they impact locally at the neighborhood or community level.[2] What the social structure communicates to many of our nation's youths is therefore that "you are NOBODY". Today, in the 1990s we often have heard the call in educational policy discussions for "value added" education, that is to put values back into the curriculum. Today's students get "valued added" education anyway: they get it in the subcultures surrounding the school zone, they get it from gang members, they get it from our mass media --- but not necessarily adding the values conducive to pro-social behavior or good citizenship.

Shaw and Mc Kay were keenly aware of the societal forces that produce gangs. That is to say, if the major social institutions (family, school, church, economy, government) are not functioning for America's children, then informal or indigenous institutions will naturally arise:

"Very often the child's access to the traditions and standards of our conventional culture are restricted to his formal contacts with the police, the school, and the various social agencies. On the other hand his most vital and intimate social contacts are often limited to the spontaneous and undirected neighborhood playgroups and gangs whose activities and standards of conduct may vary widely from those of his parents and the larger social order" (p. 111, Shaw and Mc Kay, 1931).

The family sticks out as a social institution in that it is regarded as the last line of defense. The family is expected to be the primary agency of socialization.[3] The problem is, and was demonstrated by Shaw and Mc Kay, that the inner city or poor family differs in not having or controlling resources with which to carry out this mandate. It becomes a social institution in effect with high levels of social responsibility and low levels of functional authority (e.g., use of rewardive power, incentives, etc). Most observers of social organization would say that if such a family does prevent its children from deviance, delinquency, gang affiliation, etc, in a condition of having responsibility without authority, that we have witnessed a kind of socialization miracle.

What Shaw and Mc Kay seem to imply is that a parent today should not pray for a miracle, they should pray for social justice. That is, the hope that child development in America does not translate for them as criminal development. What Shaw and McKay would later (1949) find is that the their worst fears were true: our nation does in fact systematically produce, with alarming effectiveness, adult criminals from the raw materials of school behavior problems, truants, and delinquents.

Demographic transitions and demographic changes translate into social changes in the population. Population changes and the immigrant's adjustment to American society, were factors taken into consideration by Shaw and Mc Kay[4]. The importance of these factors, overall in terms of America's social structure, to use an illustration, is that between the period 1900 and 1910 immigrants accounted for about two-thirds (about 10 million) of the total population increase in the United States (about 16 million). Between 1930 to 1940 immigrants accounted for less than ten percent of the increase in the U.S. population. Thus, expressing total immigration in relationship to the total size of the U.S. population shows an important aspect impacting on American society. Table 9 below shows this data on the United States.

Table 9

Comparison of U.S. Total Population and Size of
Immigration Waves Over Time

Year	Total U.S. Population	Total U.S. Immigration Volume	Immigration Wave Date
*****	***********	*******	*********
1990	248,709,873	7,338,000	1981-1990
1980	221,700,000	4,493,000	1971-1980
1970	204,351,000	3,322,000	1961-1970
1960	179,245,000	2,515,000	1951-1960
1950	150,697,000	1,035,000	1941-1950
1940	131,669,000	528,000	1931-1940
1930	122,775,000	4,107,000	1921-1930
1920	105,711,000	5,736,000	1911-1920
1910	91,972,000	8,795,000	1901-1910
1900	75,995,000	3,688,000	1891-1900
1890	62,948,000	5,247,000	1881-1890
1880	50,156,000	2,812,000	1871-1880
1870	38,558,000	2,315,000	1861-1870
1860	31,443,000	2,598,000	1851-1860
1850	23,192,000	1,713,000	1841-1850
1840	17,069,000	599,000	1831-1840
1830	12,866,000	152,000	1820-1830
1820	9,638,000	38,689	1820-1824

Note: Near 1911-1912, about the time of Puffer's (1912) book on gangs, almost 1 out of every 10 Americans had immigrated to America in the last decade. This was the highest period for immigration rates.

The early works on gangs that came before Shaw and Mc Kay, like that by Puffer (1912) and Furfey (1926), reacted in response to some of these demographic changes impacting on American society in terms of its potential relationship to social conditions and gangs. Shaw and Mc Kay quote Puffer regarding, then, the ability of the family to function in capacities of normative socialization for children or for a recent immigrant parent, who may not speak English, to be able to truly exert control over a child --- because for one thing, the child will have more power: the power to buffer information and to function as the translator, when the child understands English as a second language (Shaw and Mc Kay, 1931: p. 112).

Actually, Shaw and Mc Kay (1931) had to battle intellectually against much prevailing social-Darwinist theory which was then so popular in American conceptions of how society works. Puffer (1912) was one such social Darwinist theory. Puffer like others before (Franklin Chase Hoyt, Quicksands of Youth; etc, see Thrasher, 1968, p. 34) argued from what was called "recapitulation theory" that the child is just a savage, and the gang is his tribe, such that ones ancient animal history means that all boys (girls don't have it) have a "gang forming instinct". Thrasher was quick to attack this "gang instinct" approach. Says Thrasher: "It is not instinct, but experience---the way he is conditioned---that fixes his social relations." (Thrasher, 1968: p. 35).

Recognizing that there has been a kind of resurgence of bio-sociology in recent years, perhaps we should digress shortly to comment further about Puffer's approach. Not to encourage it, but to demonstrate some of the mistakes of the past. The 1990s is a time of gene splicing and much genetic knowledge development. The 1960s saw the appearance of the XYY chromosomal anomaly as a controversial (but convenient and conservative) explanation for crime, the so-called "super man" deviant, who has an extra "Y" gene.[5] Perhaps the modern bio-sociologist should read Puffer closely and begin searching for the "gang instinct" genetic code marker.

PUFFER'S (1912) SOCIAL-DARWIN THEORY OF GANGS

We must preface this discussion with the statement now widely accepted that "genetics" does not cause "crime", it has a complex social, cultural, and economic inter-related cluster of causes. If you think boys are apes, or men are naturally savage, or if you believe in channeling and "getting in touch" with your primordial self, or if you believe in transcendental multi-generational ancient-ancestral or contemporary-New Age gobbledygook, then you are going to truly enjoy Puffer (1912) about American gangs.

First the "gang-forming instinct" is only felt by boys. Girls, then, must have, if we are to carry this to its logical extreme conclusion, a "follower or self-debasement" instinct when they are represented in the ranks of gang membership. Or maybe there is something called the "super woman" equivalent to the XYY "super male". We should doubt it all.

But the gang has a desire for "local habitation...its own special street corner, its club room, its shanty in the woods" and the gang instinct is therefore "set deep in the soul" and accounts for "their spontaneous organizations" (Puffer, 1912, p. 24).[6] Recall the imagery of Lord of the Flies as Puffer explains gang etiology:

"The typical boys' gang, then, is no mere haphazard association. Accidents of various sorts...age, propinquity, likeness of interests,..bring together a somewhat random group...One or more leaders come to fore. The gang organizes itself, finds or makes its meeting place, establishes its standards, begins to do things...in some sort, a collective mind...the gang is, in short, a little social organism...it is the earliest manifestation in man of that strange group-forming instinct, without which beehive and anthill and human society would alike be impossible" (Puffer, 1912: p. 38).

Certainly there are studies of social groups that point to the existence of the "group think" tendency (Janis, 1972), but this was analyzed in terms of how our nation's leaders made decisions. The "risky shift" phenomena is also routinely cited in social-psychology and group behavior (Stoner, 1961; Wallach, Hogan, and Bem, 1962) and can affect any age-grade of group. Risky shift means a person is more prone to commit a crime in a group than as a lone individual. The risky shift concept has much use in explaining gang behavior today. But these are social process theories, they are not concepts that argue for genetic determinism.

Puffer felt that the risk of gang formation was a problem endemic to a certain phase of the lifespan[7]. That is, the "gang age...is from ten to sixteen", a period of "organized group life" that can theoretically begin slightly earlier and therefore can probably last longer; mostly, however, it appears to be a period in which "boys prefer boys" and boys scorn girls, because we know they are exiting from this phase or stage, when the boy "cultivates individual friendships, or courts a girl" (Puffer, 1912, p. 26).   Did Puffer (1912) therefore influence, or manifest conceptual parallels with, subsequent gang authors such as Bloch and Niederhoffer (1958)[8] and Yablonsky (1962)? If we could believe Bloch and Niederhoffer (1958), then we must revise the human development life-span theories, including Erickson and identity, Kohlberg and moral development, to realize that:

"the adolescent period in all cultures...<is a>...striving for adult status...<such that when>...society does not make adequate preparation...for the induction of its adolescents to the adult status...equivalent forms arise...<therefore>...the gang structure....appears to...(satisfy)...deep-seated needs experienced by adolescents in all cultures. Such, very briefly, is our

hypothesis" (Bloch and Niederhoffer, 1958: p. 17). Reading Yablonsky, we find a neo-Freudian observation compatible with the "boys only" approach of Puffer, to the effect that Yablonsky sees gang boys as kind of closet homosexuals[9] or latent or manifest homosexuals[10]:

"Fear of responsibility and emotional isolation from females generates the gang as a kind of 'homosexual' community. Consider...the projections of felt internal homosexual problems. Most gang leaders, in particular, manifest homosexual attitudes in their ridicule, exploitation of females, and their closer feelings about members of their male peer group. Along these lines there is evidence of homosexual experimentation among gang boys" (Yablonsky, 1962: p. 200).

Apparently Puffer's analysis was that all boys were bad news, they were savages:

"The normal boy between ten and sixteen is really living thru the historic period, which for the races of northern Europe, began somewhere this side of the glacial period, and came to an end with, let us say, the early middle ages. He is, therefore, essentially a savage, with the interests of a savage, the body of a savage, and to no small extent, the soul of one. He thinks and feels like a savage; he has the savage virtues and the savage vices; and the gang is his tribe" (Puffer, 1912: p. 77).

In Puffer's less than social scientific viewpoint, then, gangbanging must be natural for the innate savage boy. The idea that the gang is a tribe has recently been getting an increased amount of analysis in the gang literature as well (Etter, 1998). Oddly, though, a Pufferistic viewpoint again recently surfaced in the gang literature that sounds remarkably similar:

"There are many similarities between the turf-marking behavior of gangs and the territory-marking behavior of certain animals...the stratification dynamics and competitive behavior of many gangs are quite similar to the dominance and deference rituals of wolves and other animals...Understanding Darwin also helps in understanding certain aspects of the gang's behavior, especially male dominance and deference rituals and the predatory victimization of 'the weak' on the streets (Huff, 1993: p. 18)."

This kind of syllogistic logical fallacy (it is similar to animals, therefore crime must have a biological/genetic cause) was certainly not to be taken seriously by the Chicago school. Thus for completeness, perhaps a few words should be added about the record of the "Chicago school" of sociology.

THE CHICAGO SCHOOL WASN'T PERFECT, BUT IT WASN'T RACIST

Shaw and Mc Kay cannot even remotely be accused of an "anti-Foreigner" or "anti-alien" ideological theme.[11] Indeed, the critical thinker will note that it was Shaw and Mc Kay who implied that American society constantly replenishes its groups that live under conditions of social disorganization, as if it were a perpetual need for a "group" at the bottom of the social pyramid; and it is from this group that comes the arrests, the convictions, and the swelling of the prisons (Eisenstadt, 1951). Indeed, as some ethnic groups have advanced up the ladder and out of the inner city "arrival zones", they were proportionately less represented as offenders in the criminal justice system and perhaps more integrated into its defense.

The Chicago school of sociology and criminology has never been accused of racist dogma or ideology. The early sociologists included those being arrested for protesting racism and social injustice in the 1920s onward. Many had left of center or liberal views. It is useful to briefly demonstrate the point, legitimately included as a methodological concern in gang analysis, that high quality oral history material can, like quantitative data, be used for secondary analysis. Here the oral histories were done on sociologists from the "Chicago school".

The data collected by Carey (1976) in the historical archives collection at the University of Chicago contains high quality oral histories (see Carey, 1975) on major figures of the Chicago school of sociology. Carey (1975) showed that the source of legitimacy for the Chicago school was the practical use of sociological knowledge and policy input. In some ways, this supported the conception by Schwendinger and Schwendinger (1974) arguing that corporate liberalism dominated the ideological precepts of American sociologists,[12] as did that data collected in the Luther L. Bernard survey (1927).[13]

These two data sources were used for the content analysis reported here. Only three of these sociologists were intensely religious (3); eight were mildly religious, and most (26) were non-religious. Along political lines, ten were socialist oriented, four were conservative or anti-socialist, and most (23) were not active or apolitical.[14] Data on party affiliation was not available for 16; but for those who did report this information, most indicated (13) they were democrats, or liberals (3), or independents (2), with only 3 republicans.[15]

This information shows the Chicago school sociologists were more likely to be fighting racism. For example, Herbert G. Blumer said "by and large the members of the department and faculty they were what we would speak of as genuine liberals in their perspective" (Carey Collection, Box I, Folder 2, p. 12). Leonard S. Cottrell recalled "we were for radical justice....and I remember that some of us got at least as far as joining the socialist party and contributing money for Normal Thomas" (Carey Collection, Box 1, Folder 6, p. 5). E.R. Mower recollected that

"there were marches at the Bug House square. Louis Wirth used to enter in these. He was arrested, I remember. He came to class, a Burgess class, after being absent for a couple of weeks, and he had been in jail or something" (Carey Collection, Box 1, Folder 16, p. 19).

In fact, some of the Chicago school was under physical attack from the ultraright. An antecedent to the political violence of May 5, 1969, when Professor Richard Flacks was attacked in his office and severely beaten by a rightwing extremist group[16] is found in the fact related by Edgar T. Thompson that once the home of professor Herbert Blumer was attacked and the Ku Klux Klan burned a cross in front of it (Carey Collection, Box 1, Folder 24, p. 8).

If the climate in the Chicago School was a politically liberal one, then it must have also been reflected in its relationship to interpersonal aspects of racism. The Bernard sample contains an autobiography of an early African-American sociologist from the University of Chicago, George F. David who states:

"Later I attended the University of Chicago and it was my first contact with whites on a basis of equality of any kind. At that time there was only about twenty Negroes in attendance here and we rarely came in contact with each other on the campus" (Bernard Collection, Box I, Folder 21).

Franc L. McCluer related the following anecdote about Robert Park:

"I remember the story they used to tell about Park. He was making a study of race relations in the South, which you probably heard. He lived with 'em, according to the story, for awhile - the Blacks in Kentucky or Tennessee. He blackened his face, and one of them said to him one day after they'd become friends with him, he said: Brother Park, you dress yourself up and go up North, you can pass yourself off as a white man." (Carey Collection, Box I, Folder 14, p. 17).

Mc Cluer also told how the Society for Social Research, the sociology student organization of the University of Chicago, would hold its meeting at the Hyde Park Hotel and when they would invite guests like Black poet Kelly Miller to their meetings that the hotel officials "wouldn't let him eat with us" (Carey Collection, Box I, Folder 14, p. 6).

Do not jump to conclusions too fast about the Chicago school, because my data also supported the contention by Schwendinger and Schwendinger (1974) on another point. While the Chicago school had many liberal types among the faculty-student body, the ideology officiated from at least one prominent member of the faculty, the Chairman Albion Small, appears to have been a fervently anti-Marxist one. Asked to characterize the political climate of the department of sociology, John Dollar said:

"It was firmly anti-Marxist that I knew, and I had already read to a certain degree in Marx before I became a student there. It was very clear that sociology was something distinct from Marxism and it was not revolutionary---it had no revolutionary thrust" (Carey Collection, Box I, Folder 7, p. 7). According to Dollard students were not reading Marx because it was officially dismissed as a monolithic error. This is more clearly explained by examining statements made about the Albion Small seminar on Marx. For example, E.R. Mowrer recalled:

"It's very strange, but I had a seminar with Small and I hadn't the slightest idea of what it was all about. He had taught before a seminar on Marx, Karl Marx. I guess his seminar had always been on Karl Marx for several years. And the year I took it he shifted to something else. I had hoped it would be Karl Marx. But it turned out not to be. I've seemed to have forgotten what it was about at all". (Carey Collection, Box I, Folder 16, p. 19). Similarly, the following statement from Martin H. Neumeyer is also quite revealing:

"I took only a few courses (from Small). He offered one on Marxism. He told us why there were some professors in another department who were too much inclined to accept Marxism and he wanted the students to know the fallacies of Marxism, so we had a seminar. Incidentally, we had a Marxist in the class, who was taking it and after we discovered it we went after him and argued nearly every week, and I guess Dr. Small thought that was a good teaching procedure, finally Dr. Small leaned forward and said "once a Marxist, always a Marxist, and no amount of objective evidence can convince him different". (Carey Collection, Box 1, Folder 18, p. 3).

TO RECAP, WHAT HAVE WE LEARNED ABOUT SHAW AND MC KAY?

The answer is, truthfully, not a hell of a lot. But it's been a slice of history that we need to understand. Therefore, onward and aggressively forward in a continuing discovery of what, if anything, Shaw and Mc Kay had to contribute to our understanding of gangs.

BACK TO SHAW AND MC KAY

Imagine Shaw as a detective, interviewing a young gang member, what would be Shaw's first question? Quite possibly it might be this "okay, what kind of values and norms do you have and where did you get them from, whose are they?" Because clearly Shaw and Mc Kay pointed to the socialization of youth under conditions of social disorganization such that two things occur:

"The child in this situation is not only isolated from the traditions of our conventional culture but is subjected to a great diversity of behavior norms, some of which come from the family, others from the schools and courts, and still others, perhaps the most stimulating and enticing, from the undirected play groups and neighborhood gangs." (Shaw and Mc Kay, 1931: p. 115).

Exposure to the pattern of social relations in the gang therefore can make it harder then for traditional outreach to the youth through the family.

That the family has a difficult time competing with the social lure provided by the gang was indicated in Case # 1 of the many case studies provided in Shaw and Mc Kay (1931). Says the youth "We did everything in the gang, anything for a thrill and excitement. I can honestly say that we never went home unless we had done some kind of excitement, summer or winter" (p. 118). Often that excitement had the thrust of being white racist violence. The content of that excitement therefore deserves some analysis here and the case studies by Shaw and Mc Kay (1931) provide that content. Many readers will find a remarkable similarity of the basic human elements of these cases with contemporary examples.

Is baseball exciting enough? It is when you can fix the game according to Case # 2:

"We didn't play baseball on the square, for we always had an umpire who could really cheat for us, so we would win all our games. If he would cheat for the other team he sure would get a licking...if he ever showed up again he sure would be caressing a sore jaw and head" (Shaw and Mc Kay, 1931: p. 121).

This excitement also took racist forms:

"All the kids hated a negro and if any made an attempt to touch us we sure would give them a fight. They use to bar us from swimming at the lake and would steal and burn our clothes up. So if they came in our neighborhood, we sure would mess up them tar babies. They sure would get slaughtered" (Shaw and Mc Kay, 1931: p. 122).

Another common scenario in the "thrill and excitement" content of gang life was when the group agreed that an income-producing crime had to be committed, and they would all agree that a designated offender to pull off the job would be chosen fairly, by chance, such as the following account in Case # 3:

"I remember...one afternoon where we needed something to smoke but didn't have any money to buy smoking tobacco with, so the oldest of the crowd suggested shaking dice. The loser had to grab the purse of the next woman who passed along the street. The loser happened to be the bully. Well, just then an old lady came by with one of those old-fashioned purses and the bully walked over and grabbed her purse" (Shaw and Mc Kay, 1931: p. 124).

Parental complicity in delinquency takes many

forms, from covertly endorsing delinquent stealing "oh, mom, look I found this new television in the alley...and I've got it working" and it continues to work and be enjoyed by the family, to obvious direction and overt manipulation and encouragement of law violation behavior.   Similarly, adults who are upstream beneficiaries[17] of ill gotten gains is a factor also demonstrated in Shaw and Mc Kay's case study # 4:

"You can just about judge for yourself how the adults in the naborhood thought about delinquency. The way they looked at it was 'let him steal if he wishes to, so long as its not from me, but for me'....It seemed to me that many of the people encouraged young boys to crime by buying stolen articles...They never asked any questions. They didn't care how, what, or when the goods were gotten, just so they were able to buy them. Some of the money would go for the mothers and fathers of these children, so nine times out of ten they will encourage the child's mind to work for easy money" (Shaw and Mc Kay, 1931: p. 125).

Case # 5 in Shaw and Mc Kay (1931: 128-132) provided much discussion, then, of adults in the "fence" role and how their existence in a neighborhood also contributes to the ongoing thefts by gang members. The existence of such adults willing to buy stolen property in a neighborhood gives it an illicit infrastructure and subeconomy that economically sustains gang organization. Just as "fences" would send out the word to gang members that a certain item was "needed" to facilitate crime on a custom order basis (e.g., "I'm in the market for new caddy tires with spoke rims"), so too apparently can this occur in the family. As case # 6 shows sometimes theft proceeds were directly profiting the parents and it became a family affair:

"After a year of breaking into box cars and stealing from stores my stepmother realized that she could send me to the market to steal vegetables for her. My stealing had proved to be very profitable for her...I knew it was for my own good to do what she wanted me to do...anyway, I didn't mind stealing, because William (stepbrother) always went with me, and that made me feel proud of myself, and it gave me a chance to get away from home" (Shaw and Mc Kay, 1931: p. 133).

Case # 7 in Shaw and Mc Kay shows the scenario where an unrelated adult cultivates a band of youths in a quid pro quo arrangement, where he provides them with adult legitimacy and resources, and they provide him with custom-ordered stolen property. It can involve a creative mix of what on the surface appears to be legitimate employment, but which is substantially supplemented through illicit activities of the young gang members. As a social formation, we must ask ourselves, does this still exist today in some variation:

"Across the alley was Mr. Smith's shanty, where he kept his coal and did his business...our gang, use to help Mr. Smith make his deliveries. He would sell coal by the bag at 35 cents a bag. Whenever another coal man was making his deliveries and left his wagon load of coal sit in the alley or street, a couple of us kids would steal the wagon load of coal and take it down to Smith's shanty and unload the wagon of coal...Smith had a junk yard, too, and he bought junk and sold it. He had a big bunch of us kids that stole all the kinds of junk for him in the neighborhood and in other neighborhoods....Smith let us have our clubhouse in his barn as pay for stealing for him" (Shaw and Mc Kay, 1931: pp. 134-135).

In a large family, sometimes the small gang formation took the variation of involving the boy siblings as the nucleus and with several other youths from the neighborhood. In Case # 8 Shaw and Mc Kay describe this kind of situation. It involves the older brothers being involved in more serious crimes (burglary, etc) and the younger brothers being involved in routine theft. Importantly, it means the tutelage down the birth order from one sibling to the next in law violation.

Part III of the Shaw and Mc Kay (1931, pp. 189-257) monograph addresses "The Companionship Factor in Juvenile Delinquency" and is the more direct contribution to understanding gangs. It includes chapters 6, 7 and 8, each of which will be examined here.

Chapter 6 in Shaw and Mc Kay (1931) addresses "Male Delinquency as Group Behavior" (pp. 191-199). While most youths form social groups, often spontaneously, and which "constitute a primary group relationship" they "differ widely in regard to cultural traditions, moral standards, and social activities" (p. 191.). That is, "in certain areas of the city the practices and social values of many of these groups are chiefly of a delinquent character" (p. 191). And clearly, at a higher stage of gang formation the group can become a kind of social institution "some of these groups are highly organized and become so powerful in their hold on members that the delinquent traditions and patterns of behavior persist and tend to dominate the social life throughout the area" (p. 192).

The primary concept developed in Chapter 6 is that much delinquency is, in fact, group behavior. Data on 1,886 juveniles was used to determine this, by going back and determining if other juveniles were involved in the offenses. For all such offenses, Shaw and Mc Kay found that 81.8 percent involved a group of offenders, mostly in groups of two (30.3%), three (27.7%), or four or more (23.8%) (Shaw and Mc Kay, 1931: pp. 194-195). However, when the offense pattern was limited to include only offenses of stealing, then 89 percent of the cases involved this element of group behavior (p. 196). And finally, that:

"It is obvious that not all such group delinquencies are committed by well-organized gangs. While many of the delinquents may be members of such gangs, they usually commit their offenses in the company of one or two other boys" (Shaw and Mc Kay, 1931: p. 199).

Many researchers have tried to emulate the life-span or developmental analysis presented by Shaw and Mc Kay in Chapter 7 of the 1931 monograph. It is time-series oriented to analyze one gang member, the case of Sidney Blotzman[18], and his involvement over the years 1913 to 1928, and an "active" offense pattern period within this time span including first offense at age 8 and last offense at age 20, and Sidney's complete known record of offenses, and the three different gangs he committed these offenses with over this period of time (pp. 200-201). Not unlike what can happen today, here the youth was a gang member, moved to another neighborhood, became a gang member there in a second gang, moved again and in that neighborhood became a member of a third, and different, gang (p. 201).

This delinquency career was punctuated with trips to jail and all the "child saving" agencies and institutions designed to redirect wayward youths. Sidney went through, successively, (1) a home for dependent children, (2) the police lock-up, (3) juvenile court and release to parent, (4) juvenile detention home, (5) the Chicago Parental School, (6) probation (supervision), (7) back to the Chicago Parental School, (8) escape from Chicago Parental School, (9) committed to the Chicago and Cook County School, escape from there, returned, and eventually paroled, (10) St. Charles, and then state prison for a twenty year stint.

Shaw and Mc Kay would discover in 1949 how serious this problem of recidivism and criminal relapse is. And there is no reason to believe that the pattern of "Montefiore...Audy Home...St. Charles...adult prison" has changed. Shaw and Mc Kay were keen to point out that the system changes little, what changes is the ethnic input to the criminal justice system. Such that today it probably reproduces mostly African-American and Latin adult offenders; or those groups, including poor whites, who are essentially, ala Gans, "trapped" in the inner city conditions of social disorganization.

Finally, chapter 8 addresses "The Activities and Traditions of Delinquent Groups" and includes 27 more case histories (pp. 222-257). It is here, perhaps, that some writers have felt that Sutherland's theory of differential association was influenced by Shaw and Mc Kay:

"It is clear from the study of case histories that very frequently the boy's contact with the play group or gang marks the beginning of his career in delinquency. These groups, with their fund of delinquent tradition and knowledge, often become the chief source from which the boy gains familiarity with delinquent practices and acquires the techniques that are essential in delinquency. Many forms of delinquency require special skill and knowledge which are usually acquired through contacts with older and more experienced delinquent companions" (Shaw and Mc Kay, 1931: pp. 222-223).

This chapter also demonstrates the formation of ties with other gang members inside correctional institutions and the continuity of their gang crimes after release (see Case 2, p. 227). In Chicago today, expensive gym shoes are frequent targets of gang strong-arm tactics. Consider, then, Shaw and Mc Kay's case # 4 that occurred back in the 1920's:

"We did the same with them fancy gym shoes. Me and Sheenie bummed from school one day and went downtown, and we were both basket-ball players, and some of the other fellows had a pair of good gym shoes that cost $4 or $5 dollars; so Jack and myself decided to get ourselves some (e.g., steal them)" (Shaw and Mc Kay, 1931: p. 233).

Shaw and Mc Kay noted the gang's tendency not to pass up "crimes of opportunity" (p. 234). Again, perhaps all that has changed is the price of gym shoes and who needs to steal them.

The gang, according to Shaw and Mc Kay (1931), transmits criminal behavior "through the intimate personal contacts" and in this medium "the boys gain familiarity with the attitudes, standards, and code of the criminal group" (p. 240). Theirs is an upsidedown value system, at odds with conventional society. Stigma from courts and jail strengthens their commitment and status within the gang hierarchy (p. 241). For the gang member his behavior is normal, so that he has low levels of respect for the law, and "efforts to suppress his delinquent tendencies by formal methods...often give rise to attitudes of rebellion and hostility" (p. 242). The reason is that "like conventional social groups, the delinquent and criminal group demands conformity to its code and ideals on the part of its members" (p. 243). Gang members detest "snitches" and traitors to their in-group.

The gang member is viewed by Shaw and Mc Kay as normal and motivated by normal human factors:

"Like the nondelinquent boy, he is apparently motivated by those common and universal desires for recognition, approbation and esteem of his fellows, for stimulation, thrill and excitement, for intimate companionship, and for security and protection" (Shaw and Mc Kay, 1931: p. 250).

It just so happens that in areas of conspicuous gang activity, these normal human desires are being fulfilled by the gang, not legitimate groups.

Finally, whatever their value in contributing to our understanding of gangs, we should point out also that Shaw and Mc Kay (1931) must take some of the blame (or credit, however you see such developments) for the fads in "group therapy", "guided group interaction", "confrontation group therapy", and the myriad of other such forceful invasions on the privacy of the confined involving mandatory group counseling techniques. Because it was Shaw and Mc Kay who felt there was a "great need for developing methods of group treatment in the field of delinquency, since it appears that delinquent behavior is in many cases a form of group activity" (p. 257).

SUMMARY AND CONCLUSION

Hopefully what this discussion has demonstrated is that Shaw and Mc Kay have probably not been adequately credited with contributing to the gang literature. Clearly, they had much to say about gang membership, gang crime patterns, motivational factors, the confinement-to-community gang linkage, and more. Apparently they said more than some have been willing to give credit for.

Gangs have always existed in America. It is important to understand previous research on gangs. Understanding the historical continuities about gangs also helps us to arrive at a more theoretically sound analysis of the gang problem. More importantly, a conceptual framework for "doing something about the gang problem" requires more than a casual grasp of the gang literature.

DISCUSSION QUESTIONS:

(1) To what extent is the work of Shaw and Mc Kay compatible with the "multiple marginality" gang theory advanced by Vigil (1988)? Can this be synthesized in the hypothesis that the greater the social disorganization, generally the higher the marginality?

(2) Can Puffer's approach be reformulated to imply that gang affiliation is not only normal behavior, it may even be prosocial behavior within distressed communities? Or is Puffer's work a pre-scientific contribution to the gang literature? Is any biological determinism model of crime causation likely to be frought with controversy?

(3) Can Shaw and Mc Kay's analysis of gangs, and factors involved in gang crime (e.g., parental complicity), be just as appropriate today? Or useful as hypotheses for gang research? Can you give some examples?

VIEWS FROM GANG SPECIALIST POLICE

"What parents should do to effectively keep their children out of the gang is...know where their children are and who they are with. 95% of the gang members I come into contact with come from single parent families or those families that are very dysfunctional.

What teachers should do to more effectively deal with the gang problem is...be able to recognize gang members and their activities and report this information to the proper authorities. I was a School Liaison Officer for 7 years and every year I would give a short seminar on what teachers should know about gangs. I received 100% cooperation from the faculty and staff which helped to curtail the gang problem immensely.

What police should do to more effectively deal with the gang problem is...provide training for parents and teachers. Parents are the first line of defense against gangs. Acknowledge the gang problem and work with the community, i.e., parents, government, and schools. Set up at least one officer to be technicallyl aware of gangs and develop intelligence. Finally, police should take a zero tolerance stance on gangs by arresting gang members whenever possible."

"What parents should do to effectively keep their children out of the gang is...provide them with as good a home life as possible (emotionally). Take time out to spend time with their children, show an interest in what they are doing in school and in home activities. Encourage their interests in other activities (Boy Scouts, sports, etc).

What teachers should do to more effectively deal with the gang problem is...no tolerance for gang activity or representation in the classroom or school. Emphasis on school work and not just passing students for the sake of getting them out of school. Constant interaction with students and parents. We should also educate our children about gangs in the same manner we now use for drug prevention.

What police should do to more effectively deal with the gang problem is...I think the police organization has to take more than just a law enforcement role. It must be willing to sponsor youth activities or groups and make a commitment to funding and providing manpower for these groups to make them effective. Parents should also be targeted for education programs (i.e., gang awareness programs)."

(Views From Gang Specialist Police Are Continued on Page 144)

VIEWS FROM GANG SPECIALIST POLICE

"What parents should do to effectively keep their children out of the gang is...parents should find things of interest for the children and themselves to be mutually involved in; parents should be more involved in their child's education.

What teachers should do to more effectively deal with the gang problem is...teachers shuld learn to recognize gang activities in the school. They should not allow a gang member to organize or recruit within the school. Teachers should also be willing to work with the local police if a gang problem exists.

What police should do to more effectively deal with the gang problem is...police should be aggressive with gang patrol and protective sweeps. I feel some police are intimidated by gangs which gives the gang the upper hand. Police should continue to arrest gang members for law violations to get them into the justice system. Police should try to push more family type programs for young children."

"What parents should do to effectively keep their children out of the gang is...be alert for the early signs of gang affiliation (i.e., bad grades, poor attitude, never at home) and be aware of the type of clothing worn on a day to day basis. Parents have to be more educated to the gang problem, at least enough for them to understand the problem and not be deceived by their children. They need some knowledge on the gang problem.

What teachers should do to more effectively deal with the gang problem is...the teachers role should not end at the end of of the school day. Maintain and enforce strict rules about dress (i.e., wearing colors, or symbols), grafitti, flashing of gang signs, and any violation should be reported to parents immediately.

What police should do to more effectively deal with the gang problem is...be able to place officers in the schools such as D.A.R.E. officers, etc. Especially with the smaller kids. Unfortunately by the time the kids are joing the gangs, they have a negative view of police officers."

"What parents should do to effectively keep their children out of the gang is...promote more family outings; wake up and notice if your child is in a gang; if you suspect gang involvement, become more involved in the childs whereabouts; try to steer the child into non-gang activities.

What teachers should do to more effectively deal with the gang problem is...recognize that gangs are well-organized, highly structured, and in every community. Try to be more familiar with the differ-ent gang factions in their respective schools. I'm not trying to be sarcastic, but they should be able to cold cock the punks.

What police should do to more effectively deal with the gang problem is...arrest the judges who let the punks out of jail or better yet, let the judges be more accountable for when those that they have released commit new crimes."

"What parents should do to effectively keep their children out of the gang is...provide their children with some moral code or religious ethic to help them understand their responsibility to society. Become more involved in educational exercises; help with homework, etc.

What teachers should do to more effectively deal with the gang problem is...not be intimidated; report all violations; identify those students who are on the verge of falling prey to the gangs, e.g., look for signs of low self-esteem, family instability, etc. Then through counseling and self-help programs attempt to turn these youths around.

What police should do to more effectively deal with the gang problem is...depends on the type of police department, but better education mostly. Suburban gangs are not like inner city gangs. Inner city gang members have to belong, suburban members want to belong. Develop community progrdams to steer juveniles in different directions than gangs. Involve the park district in these programs."

End Notes:

[1] This theme of "exclusion", in multiple ways, would later be amplified by Vigil (1988); as an entirely independent intellectual contribution; because Vigil gives us no clue to his understanding of the literature summarized here from Shaw and McKay. Vigil's theory of gangs, called "multiple marginality", is discussed later in this book.

[2] They must, we presume, operate at a more macro-analytical level as well; as for instance, in the differential patterns of human capital development nationally tending to correspond to ethnic and social class positions. If ever there was a need for strong policy statements from criminological research, then it is here: we need more educational investment. We need also to formally educate our prison populations.

[3] The family seems to be expected to be everything to everyone; and, simultaneously, not be equipped with the resources to accomplish it; it cannot be deducted from taxes for those who can earn a living, and it cannot be supported from supplemental aid for those below the poverty line. The family is much discussed, and much ma-

ligned.

[4] Vigil (1983) predicted that continuing Mexican immigration would feed barrio gangs.

[5] See Sarbin, Theodore R. and Jeffrey E. Miller, 1970, "Demonism Revisited: The XYY Chromosomal Anomaly", Issues in Criminology (5)(2)(Sum): 195-207.

[6] Redl (1945) would later suggest, well after Puffer, that such clique behavior may be due to a genetic factor, perhaps not unlike the XYY chromosomal anomaly (see Fritz Redl, 1965, "The Psychology of Gang Formation and the Treatment of Juvenile Delinquents", 1 Psychoan. Stud. Child. 367).

[7] Puffer can in this context be considered a close friend of more conservative views in criminology; that is, the popular conservative doctrine often identified with the "burn out" hypothesis holds that an offender is never really rehabilitated, they simply burn out, usually in their 30's. (see Knox, 1980).

[8] An interesting implication of the "status attainment" frustration approach has to do with the duration of the socialization period and when should youths take on adult responsibilities? My own research shows that many of our offenders behind bars had to take on, perhaps prematurely, such adult responsibilities as those pertaining to family roles and functions. The reader should be alerted then to not inferring that we should necessarily expedite transition to adult roles, but that this is an issue for further analysis. Should the socialization and nurturing period be shortened or lengthened? Should there be a mandatory "national service" for all youths as they approach adulthood? These are interesting questions.

[9] Perhaps this comes from the prior work of Blanchard (1959) who in explaining gang rape noted the homosexual implications of boys sharing sex, or of the gang leader having a kind of brutal "constant fear" homosexual hold on gang followers.

[10] In Jungian analysis, gang members can be seen as exemplifying a kind of "masculinity crisis" by the very nature of their over-compensation of trying to give off the constant appearance of "toughness". Some work has begun in applying a Jungian psychological analysis to gangs (Tripp, 1997).

[11] But the one contribution that can be is that by Davis (1982, pp. 5,8) who offers the same conception of gang history shown by Gonzalez (1981) to be a fraudulent and scurrilous misconception advanced by law enforcement officials. Davis sees the rise of gangs in southern California (pp, 5,8) as having been importantly shaped and affected by the arriving waves of Mexican "aliens". The dissertation by Gonzalez provides a thorough analysis of the early 20th century history of California, especially in relationship to the "Zoot suits" and the rioting and racial violence directed against Mexicans.

[12] See also Ort (1975, pp. 66,69). Or the notion that sociology "served primarily as a conduit through which European conservative social thought was introduced into the American academic milieu" (Nicholaus, 1973: p. 49). Or counter, that there was much ideological heterogeneity (Baker, Long, and Quensel, 1973; Baker, Ferrell, and Quensel, 1975). Mills (1943) contended that American sociology was rural, protestant, and pragmatic.

[13] Now held in the Historical Archives section, Special Collections, Regenstein Library, University of Chicago. These have been described elsewhere (Baker, Long, and Quensel, 1973; 1975).

[14] In an interview of Daniel Glaser (Carter, 1972), Glaser did say that when he arrived back at the University of Chicago in 1949 "there was an instructor in sociology at the University of Chicago named Joe Lohman, who was active in politics and close to Adlai Stevenson. When Stevenson became Governor he made Joe chairman of the Parole and Pardon Board. Lloyd Ohlin, then a Chicago graduate student while employed as a sociologist-actuary at Joliet, became Lohman's Research Sociologist...and in 1950 they hired me to work at Pontiac, the youth prison, to revise the prediction tables there" (Carter, 1972: p. 24).

[15] By the way, for the enthusiastic reader, Henry McKay is included in the Carey sample. When Mc Kay was asked about what persons had intellectually influenced him, he quoted: Park, Burgess, Farris, and Shaw.

[16] See the Chicago Tribune, December 19, 1975.

[17] Adults who knowingly benefit financially from acting such roles or functions as "fences", etc, for youthful gang members is itself another cross-national continuity in the study of gangs. See Patrick's (1973, pp. 28-29) discussion of the "punter" role, essentially an adult who collaborates with younger gang members, exploiting their risk-taking criminal behavior. Also Taylor (1990, p. 102) describes how some "businesses covertly cater to gang types".

[18] Who is given a complete case study in Shaw's 1931 "The Natural History of a Delinquent Career", University of Chicago Press.

BELOW: This is a "gang logo" drawn by a confined juvenile in California representing his gang, the East Side Bounty Hunter Watts Bloods. The "streets" where this gang is active are also represented in the logo, which are the "sets" of the gang this juvenile gang member is representing.

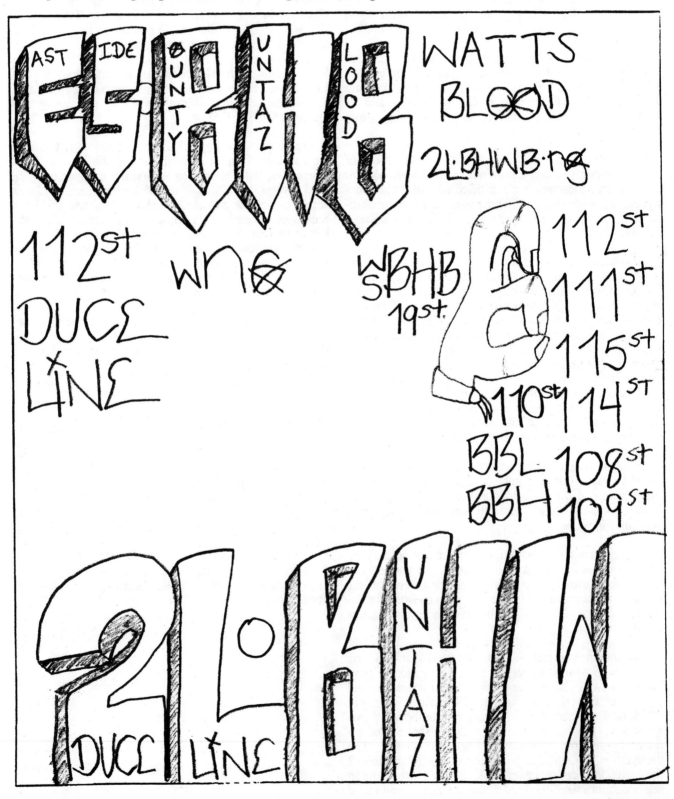

Chapter 10

"THE THRASHER CRIMINOLOGICAL RIDDLE: What Was His Actual Research Methodology?"

INTRODUCTION

Everyone doing serious research on gangs ends up quoting or referring to the work of Frederick Milton Thrasher. Unfortunately, few copies of his full and complete original and unabridged version of the book The Gang actually existed. What researchers did was quote from abridged versions that did not have all of the material from the original version of the book by Thrasher.

This changed in the summer of 2000 when the full and complete version of Thrasher's The Gang became available again. At least now the full version of Thrasher is in fact available to be read in its entirety.

But what no one has been able to resolve about Thrasher is a scholarly riddle dealing with the actual "research methodology" Thrasher used. No version of his book ever included a chapter on his methodology. Thrasher's original preface to the book indicated it was a seven year project. Yet the "data" used in Thrasher's gang map (something only a handful of people living today have ever seen until the reprinting of the full Thrasher original in the summer

of 2000), indicated a time frame of 1923-1926. What was Thrasher's methodology? This chapter seeks to provide some insights on this issue.

A close inspection of Thrasher's (1927) classic study of N = 1,313 gangs in Chicago shows almost complete ambiguity about what exactly the research methodology consisted of. Historical records are analyzed to reconstruct what is factually known about basic questions in the actual research methodology Thrasher used. These elementary inquiries consist of "who", "what", "how", "when", and "why". The answers from this historical research shed new light on the life and times of Thrasher and answer an important and, until now, continuing criminological riddle.

Why is this important to do? The "novice" at gang research makes important historical mistakes. It is important to know a lot more about gang history. One type of "novice" today is the gang author who is so scatologically appreciative of Thrasher's work that the "novice" assumes Thrasher was literally out in the field codifying and interviewing the leaders of all of the 1,313 gangs that were spread all over the Chicago area. Our analysis shows that is not likely. Thrasher may have been enjoying more credit than is due in that regard.

THE RIDDLE: HOW DID THRASHER REALLY CONDUCT HIS RESEARCH?

An important social science issue that enjoys some salience is the matter of defining gangs in empirical research. Thrasher's definition included any playgroup that did not have proper adult supervision and included, it appears, all social athletic clubs in the City of Chicago during 1923-1926. Social athletic clubs (SACs) to those who do not know what is going on inside, because they are after all "private", may arose suspicion; but it is extremely doubtful that all social athletic clubs fit today's modern definition of gangs, particularly with regard to the matter of "ongoing criminal activity".

As a criminological classic, Frederic M. Thrasher's 1927 book entitled The Gang: A Study of 1,313 Gangs in Chicago, is certainly well known today. Many contemporary contributors to the specialized area of gang research recognize its enduring value. Even the critical extreme view, which discounts its relevance under the historical analysis which asserts "gangs are different today", recognizes the importance of how Thrasher's research had a large impact on the field. Still, all would agree that a major criminological riddle exists here: what was Thrasher's actual research methodology and could it be replicated today? This paper seeks to clarify this one aspect of American criminological history.

Thrasher's 1927 book was actually his 1926 Ph.D. disssertation at the University of Chicago, Department of Sociology. Many who quote Thrasher in the gang literature today really misinterpret his work and really do not have a clue about what really constituted his "research methodology".

Few details have been previously reported about the methodology that Thrasher used[1]. This paper began out of an interest in replicating Thrasher, only to find that a much larger problem exists from a validity point of view (Knox, 1992). As the historical record is less than clear, some of the possible methods that Thrasher may have used are discussed in relationship to recently discovered historical materials. A large number of documents and sources of information on Thrasher were collected and examined and are discussed here. In a comparative sense it also vindicates Thrasher from the harshest contemporary criticism.

What seems, therefore, a simple question: How many gangs are there in Chicago; or the USA for that matter; is really much more complicated than it may appear and requires a much more complex social organizational analysis than has yet surfaced

in our literature. Examining this issue helps to shed light on one of the many historical puzzles about American gangs.

The riddle is answered as best as historical records allow in terms of how Thrasher actually collected his data. We begin this historical analysis by examining Thrasher's "data". Then simple historical questions are analyzed in relationship to documents from the period. These questions focus on why, when, what and how the data was collected. We begin first, however, with a brief and somewhat more complete biographical sketch of Thrasher.

THE LIFE AND TIMES OF FREDERIC MILTON THRASHER

Thrasher (1892-1962) was born in Shelbyville, Indiana, the son of Milton B. Thrasher and Eva Lacy Thrasher. He is most noted for writing The Gang: A Study of 1,313 Gangs in Chicago. In 1911 he worked as a newspaper reporter in Frankfort, Indiana where some of his family members still live today. He obtained his B.A. degree from DePauw University where he was also elected to Phi Beta Kappa. In 1917 he became an instructor in sociology at Ohio State University. He completed his M.A. degree from the Department of Sociology at the University of Chicago in 1918. It was his 1918 Master's thesis which represented his first known research involving gangs. The 1918 thesis dealt with the history of the Boy Scout movement. The Boy Scouts were viewed as offering the kind of socialization that could prevent young men from joining gangs. It was this early formative research on youths that would set the stage for his entire life specialty in sociology. He would later work extensively with a variety of organizations like the YMCA. This concentration on keeping kids out of trouble and especially out of gangs became a life long quest for Thrasher. Much of his theory and wisdom on gangs is still of value today even though America has a more violent gang problem and a problem that today is not necessarily limited to large urban areas.

In 1923 he became an assistant professor in sociology at Illinois Wesleyan University. His Ph.D. degree was awarded from the Department of Sociology at the University of Chicago in 1926. This period of 1923-1926 was also the period of time listed on what is known as the Thrasher gang map, a document that appeared in the first edition of his book only. It is an important historical document because it dates in print when the gang data was collected.

In 1923 Thrasher was the mover and shaker who established the Department of Sociology as a separate department at Illinois Wesleyan University. Prior to 1923, which was when Thrasher arrived, there existed only the Department of Economics and Sociology. Under Thrasher a separate department of sociology was established of which he was chair, which today is called the Department of Sociology and Anthropology.

By 1926 he was the chairman (Head) of the Department of Sociology at Illinois Wesleyan University. He had earlier in his career additional experience in teaching sociology courses at DePauw University, the University of Chicago, and Indiana University. Records at the university reveal that Dr. Thrasher taught what would be considered very heavy course schedules, teaching numerous courses on a variety of topics. In other respects this period of his life also prompts some to say he is a real enigma because important details are not readily accounted for with regard to social facts about Thrasher himself. An analysis of articles about Professor Thrasher in the Argus, the student newspaper at Illinois Wesleyan University, suggested to one source that perhaps Thrasher commuted to and from Chicago to the university located in Bloomington, IL. Regular train schedules during that time period could have allowed rather efficient travel to and from Chicago on a daily basis.

With a heavy teaching schedule, possibly travelling to and from Bloomington during the week, and doing his Ph.D. dissertation research on The Gang: A Study of 1,313 Gangs in Chicago how much time and when was he able to gather much information and geographically plot out the 1,313 gangs in the Chicagoland area[2]? Newspaper clips and book order advertisements during the period provide some of the only clues. Consider these early comments in a flyer describing "How Professor Thrasher Gathered His Data" written by Henry Justin Smith in Collier's Weekly:

"Thrasher is a lively and ingenious fellow. A man who wore a solemn face or asked questions carelessly could never have "got in" with the wary Black Hands and Tomahawks, not to speak of the Night Riders or the Skeiks and Wailing Shebas. He would have been forced to run for his life in the North Side Jungles, the West Side Wilderness, and the South Side Bad Lands - the three empires of gangdom in Chicago.

But Thrasher could sing songs; he could tell stories; he could even do 'magic tricks.' He was such an amusing and likeable fellow altogether that he was simply adopted into this tribe and that. Now he knows the rank and sobriquets of more than 1,300 gang leaders in Chicago alone, and has gathered not only data -- as they call it sociologically -- on the 50,000 or more gangsters in Chicago, but also facts of interest to other cities."

In 1927 he took the position of Assistant Professor at New York University in the field of Educational Sociology. He was involved in a number of different research projects dealing with delinquency prevention and other issues. He was the organizer of the American Friends of Turkey in 1930 and a past president of that organization. In 1931 he was promoted to Associate Professor of Education at New York University. In 1933 he was appointed the Chairman of the Council of Lower West Side Social Agencies in New York City.

Some of his other interests and activities during this time frame included being the director of the American White Cross Association on Drug Addiction, chairman of New York City's Action Committee for Delinquency Prevention, and president of the Metropolitan Motion Picture Council.[3]

In 1937 he was appointed to full professor at New York University. His contributions to the field of sociology after the Ph.D. were centered primarily in the specialty area of educational sociology. He was in fact one of the founding fathers of this special field of sociology today. By 1945 he served as an associate editor of the Journal of Educational Sociology published by the Payne Educational Sociology Foundation in New York, NY.

Until the mid-1950's his classic enjoyed almost complete domination of the field of gang studies. His gang book went through several editions including one posthumous edition in 1960 and then the abridged version in 1963 edited by James F. Short, Jr. all by the University of Chicago Press. All the editions after the first in 1927 dropped the use of the "gang map" however. The gang map plotted the 1,313 gangs by dots on a street grid of the City of Chicago. It was historically important because the gang map contained the only data on geographical dispersion of two types of gangs (those with and without "club houses"). Most of those with club houses were actually known as "Social Athletic Clubs". Perhaps because of their autonomy we find that Thrasher and the project he worked on were more inclined to view "SAC's" as unwholesome or "gang-like" influences. The actual gang map itself is indicated as being compiled by Thrasher during the time frame of 1923 to 1926.

On March 9, 1955 he submitted a plan for a new book on gangs to the University of Chicago Press. All copies of his classic had sold out by then and it appears the publisher wanted something fresh that would reflect the gang problem after World War II. His plan of attack for the new gang book, entitled "The Delinquent Gang in the American Community: Cause and Cure" was never to be realized however.

In 1956 he began teaching half-time in preparation for retirement. He had just achieved Professor Emeritus status in 1959 and began his retirement, when on February 5, 1959 he was in a accident as a passenger on a bus that was in a collision with a truck. He sustained a major head injury requiring hospitalization, from which he would never recuperate. On June 12, 1959 he was transferred to Bellevue Hospital for treatment and observation. On September 24, 1959 he was certified incompetent and transferred to the Central Islip State Hospital in Long Island. He died in March, 1962 at the age of 70. He is buried in the family cemetery in Frankfort, Indiana.

His estate was inherited by a 20-year-old adopted son, adopted in 1963. He had previously married and divorced after completing his Ph.D. degree.

Shortly after his death, the University of Chicago Press hired noted gang researcher and author James F. Short, Jr. to publish an abridged edition of his famous study of 1,313 gangs in Chicago. The abridged edition eliminated two chapters that were not important at the time, but which later emerged as being of enduring value: a chapter on "Wanderlust" (travel, migration), of potential value today with regard to gang migration issues, and a chapter on "Dime Novels, Crime Movies and Cinema", of enormous value from the viewpoint of how the mass media contributes to gang emulation behavior, the "copycat" phenomena, or as some call it the contagion effect as seen in the many gang movies that exist today. The full Thrasher book is finallly available today in 2000, complete with the original "gang map".

Many of the social conditions which Thrasher analyzed in relationship to gangs remain salient today. These include the variation in the organizational sophistication of gangs, their involvement with politics or political corruption, their ethnic homogeneity, the role of racism or racial prejudice, gang warfare, gangs and organized crime --- these and other historical continuities were first analyzed in a detailed way by Thrasher. It is in this sense that while today there are important differences reflecting historical changes as well in the composition of gangs, their level of penetration into the criminal justice system, and the intensity of violence itself, some basic social phenomenon have remained the same even though the type and behavior of the social actors may have changed.

His other written works include numerous articles on delinquency published in the Journal of Educational Sociology from 1927 to 1949.

But Thrasher's foremost legacy is contributing to our understanding of gangs. Unfortunately, if the Thrasher research cannot be replicated it is not research at all. How could be replicated? Well, first we must understand a lot more about what remains an enigma in our criminological history. It is the question of exactly how did Thrasher carry out and implement a research methodology, and what was it? We can begin to unravel this historical riddle by first examining Thrasher's data.

THE THRASHER DATA

Some current gang analysts assume that Thrasher was an autonomous actor whose definition of gang in his research was not defined by social control agencies, but rather reflected his own definition in close interpersonal contact with the gang:

"Researchers from Thrasher to Keiser to Jankowski have done excellent studies with virtually no reliance on the police for defining their topic of inquiry --- gangs." (Sanders, 1994: pp. 178-179). This is a historical interpretation of Thrasher's methodology, but it appears to be based on insufficient information. More specifically it might be an inference based on the ambiguity of Thrasher's methodology, because Thrasher did not provide many such details, thus one might assume --- perhaps incorrectly --- that because Thrasher did not say he relied very much on social control agencies like the police, that perhaps one could conclude to that same negative effect. We shall see in a later section on "how" Thrasher collected his data that recently discovered historical materials do in fact show Thrasher relied heavily on reports from police and social control groups (e.g., Chicago Crime Commission). Thus, to prevent future incorrect conclusions about the historical record of Thrasher's data, it useful here to briefly review what Thrasher's data consisted of.

Statistically, the original Thrasher (1927) work is less than complete[4]. The N = 1,313 gangs are never listed by name. In fact, there were only four data elements quantified by Thrasher: age range (1968: p. 60), race and nationality (p. 130), whether from a foreign nationality (p. 131), and number of members (p. 222) as seen in Table 8.

TABLE 8
THRASHER'S DATA REPORTED IN RELATION
TO THE N = 1,313 SAMPLE

Variable	N of Cases Reported	N of Cases Missing
Age range	1,213	100 (7.6%)
Race/nationality	880	443 (33.7%)
Foreign nationality	396	n/a[5] (n/a)
Number of members[6]	895	418 (31.8%)

Clearly, as seen in Table 8 the Thrasher gangs were not very well documented. Thrasher's strongest data is for the age range variable with only 7.6 percent of the cases missing. The race and nationality of a third of the gangs was not known and for 31.8 percent of the gangs the number of members was not known. This was the basis for the earlier questioning of the validity of Thrasher's information (Fletcher, 1964).

Actually, a fifth variable was available to Thrasher about these 1,313 gangs but it is never analyzed in relationship to other factors in either the dissertation (1926) or the book (1927). The fifth variable comes from the plotting of the 1,313 gangs on a grid map of the City of Chicago; with two types of gang markers: one symbol for gangs with clubrooms, and another symbol for gangs without clubrooms. A fourth of the 1,313 gangs had such clubrooms. Thrasher called these gang with clubrooms the conventionalized type of groups (Thrasher, 1968: p. 52). These were typically social athletic clubs. Thrasher's original "Table VIII" was dropped from the book edited by Short, and it was crucial to gang research issues as it detailed the deviance and criminal activit ty of the N=1,313 gangs. It is reasonable to assume that most gang experts living today have never read the full original "Thrasher".

WHY DID THRASHER WRITE A GANG BOOK FOR HIS DISSERTATION

The answer here seems simple enough, Thrasher's interests in youth socialization became his area of lifetime specialization in sociology. The fact is, the 1927 first edition of the gang book was actually Thrasher's 1926 Ph.D. dissertation in sociology[7]. Another less known fact is that this was not Thrasher's first professional writing on the subject of gangs.

Thrasher's first formal writing on gangs was not the 1927 book based on the 1926 dissertation, but was rather his Master's thesis entitled "The Boy Scout Movement As a Socializing Agency" (1918)[8]. It is here that Thrasher first wrote about "wanderlust", which was again to appear in the gang book (1926, 1927) but which was dropped from the most recent abridged edition (1965). Thrasher also examined the "gang spirit" in his master's thesis.

This early coverage of the "gang" included such topics as the following:

"The boy demands activity and excitement. If there is no chance to get it in a constructive way, he will take advantage of every opportunity the city offers, and there are many, to get it in ways that lead to disorganization. If he has no club, he will find a "gang" (Thrasher, 1918: 8-9).

"*A critical examination of original human nature....reveals certain tendencies...like gregariousness (the "gang spirit")....which may easily be socially useful or the contrary depending upon whether or not they are carefully directed*" (Thrasher, 1918: 37).

In fact, a long section was devoted to "Scouting and the Gang Spirit" (Thrasher, 1918: 53-58). These and other materials have been analyzed here. While the 1918 master's thesis gives no clue as to his research methodology for <u>The Gang</u>, it does give the same conceptual blue print: the idea is that the gang is a corrupting influence on youths, and that adult supervised recreation such as that provided by pro-

fessional socialization groups like the YMCA and Boy Scouts are to be preferred over allowing youths to entertain themselves.

Thus, in many ways the cognitive foundation for his famous book on gangs was actually established some time earlier in his 1918 master's thesis. There is continuity in the ideas presented in both works.

WHEN DID THRASHER COLLECT HIS DATA?

Many criminologists have suffered from only a casual reading of the classic by Thrasher (1927) and have assumed typically that Thrasher conducted seven years of fieldwork. This is apparently a false assumption.

The social base map of gangs lists the location of nearly all 1,313 gangs[9]. It was a fold-out map provided in the dissertation, and an enlarged version was sold with the 1927 book by Thrasher. The dissertation itself gives few specific details on methodology. In fact, the original dissertation plan submitted by Thrasher and included in the Burgess files at the University of Chicago described this work as "The Gang: A Study of Collective Behavior". It had thirty chapters and five appendices. Other documents authored by Thrasher included a "Plan of the Investigation", "Sources of Data and Their Use" and "Specimen Questionnaires". But none of these documents which might have enlightened us as to the specific nature of Thrasher's research methodology have yet to surface in the literature[10]. The gang map created by Thrasher suggests the data was collected during the period 1923-1926.

A 1927 University of Chicago Press flyer promoting Thrasher's book stated "Professor Thrasher spent six years in his study of gangland -- the poverty belt which surrounds Chicago's loop district".

The gang map by Thrasher suggested three years of data collection (1923-1926).

A fund raising flyer used by the Y.M.C.A. of Chicago in seeking to raise money for the year 1925 quoted Thrasher as an endorsement: "The only way to overcome the present situation is to establish institutions like the Y.M.C.A. which will prevent their gang formation in many instances and in others, change them into clubs with the right leadership, having their sports and fun in a wholesome way". It also indicated Thrasher "spent two years investigating these gangs".

In a book endorsement by Smith (1927) included in the book order form (the book cost then was $3.10 postpaid), we get a different figure:

"*I take these facts - for facts they are - from the notebooks of my friend Frederic M. Thrasher....For a year he went out among groups, big and little, formed because boys flock together, hunting -- or being hunted -- in packs. A man who wore a solemn face or asked questions carelessly could never have "got in" with the wary Black Hands and Tomahawks, not to speak of the Night Riders or the Sheiks and the Wailing Shebas....But Thrasher could sing songs; he could tell stories; he could even do 'magic tricks.' He was such an amusing and likeable fellow altogether that he was simply adopted into this tribe and that. Now he knows the rank and sobriquets of more than 1,300 gang leaders in Chicago alone, and has gathered not only data --- as they call it sociologically --- on the 50,000 or more gangsters in Chicago, but also facts of interest to other cities"* (Smith, 1927).

Was it six years, three years, two years, or one year? Fortunately, additional evidence exists having implications for answering this question. Clearly, the 1,313 gangs were identified on or before 1926 as indicated in the Gang Map (1923-1926), so factually at best it was three years. In as much as the entire Ph.D. dissertation was printed in 1926, it is more reasonable to assume that the field work or codification of the gang data occurred sometime prior to this. The best estimate is therefore in the range of one to two years.

In the fall of 1924, when Thrasher was teaching sociology at Illinois Wesleyan University[11], the student newspaper carried a story (Argus Nov. 19, 1924, #3, p. 2) explaining how Thrasher just completed his "survey" of Chicago gangs. If the gang research began in 1923, then it was about one year until all 1,313 gangs were identified, because the news story specifically used that figure and others. The 1,313 gangs had an estimated population of 50,000 members. Some 579 of the gangs met in streets and alleys, 147 in vacant lots, 368 in club rooms or donated spaced, and 194 in pool rooms or shacks. Gangs in Illinois, Thrasher states in this newspaper story, date back to 1810 "when a gang of murderous thieves operated throughout the state, victimizing travellers...they had taverns and inns as their hang out and were recognized murderers".

The first indication of the start of the gang study for data collection was 1923. By November, 1924 a front page story in the Chicago Daily Tribune carried the feature headline "Finds 1,313 'Gangs' In City: Crime Cradle, Says U. of C. Professor". Thus, along with the detailed comments provided in the 1924 November issue of his own school newspaper, two such extant sources show the data was in by 1924.

The use of magic would help in identifying 1,313 gangs through fieldwork alone --- hanging out, participant observation, etc ---in that limited time frame. If someone today said they worked with N = 1,313 gangs "in the field" during that short of a time period, they would probably be accused of "fudging" their data or at least be regarded with some critical attention with regard to validity.

WHAT WERE THE DATA SOURCES FOR THRASHER?

Here the historical record has helped us, although the book by Thrasher is certainly less than complete on this issue. In a student newspaper interview where he taught sociology (Illinois Wesleyan University) during the time of the gang research, Thrasher did reveal some of details of what, specifically, were the data sources for his famous gang study[12].

According to the story (Argus, Nov. 19, 1924), "Mr. Thrasher obtained much of his information from the police and crime commissions...some was obtained from politicians, but in this instance, the men did not know for what use the information divulged was to be put." So, clearly it can be said that some systematic approach to data collection was evident in the Thrasher's methodology. But it also appears to have been a research methodology that used multiple sources, including actual gang members interviewed in juvenile correctional settings.

The same story goes on to state that Thrasher did some observation of youths 17 to 19 years old in their play and recreational settings. But he also apparently got much information from gang members who were interviewed in the context of juvenile corrections. The part of data collection Thrasher enjoyed most was that part involving the interviewing "of the boys in the Chicago and Cook County School....some of those lads whose goodwill the researcher worker gained by entertaining them with mind reading and sleight of hand stunts, came to visit the college instructor when they had been released from the school...in many instances, the young professor was invited to parties, and played tennis with his young gang protegees...he stated that he became interested in this work after following the Boys Scouts movement for some years" (Argus, student newspaper of Illinois Wesleyan University, Nov. 19, 1924, #3, p. 2).

It seems reasonable to believe based on this historical information, therefore, that Thrasher began his research using a methodology that was designed in one sense to be the first guide to gang identification in Chicago. A kind of systematic cataloging using official sources like the police, agency reports, information obtained from political groups, and young offenders themselves. If Thrasher used a "worksheet" or note cards for each gang he ran across this way, and tried to collect as much information as he could on each gang, and included each and every gang anyone ever reported to him as ever having existed, then a simple alphabetical listing could easily account for the large "sample" (N = 1,313). The unit of analysis is, after all, the gang itself in this research methodology.

There is a potential for over-estimation of the

number of such groups based on age-grading and multiple faction names. This is discussed in greater detail shortly, but basically it could mean double or triple counting what might amount to one gang. There is no evidence uncovered from this study, however, which indicates this potential criticism actually applies to Thrasher. It is an operational issue: would the "Sheiks" and the "Pee Wee Sheiks" be counted as two gangs or one? If the polish members were, as a clique within the "Sheiks", sometime referred to as the "Sheikowskis" would that be included as a third gang? Would the female auxiliary, perhaps the "Sheikettes", be a fourth gang? This is a potential problem, however, if anyone actually replicated Thrasher's today. Perhaps one important reason no one has yet to actually replicate Thrasher's study is that much remains a mystery about how, exactly, Thrasher actually collected his data.

HOW DID THRASHER COLLECT HIS DATA?

Thrasher was clearly prone to quote statistics and numbers provided by the Chicago Crime Commission and local groups such as the YMCA. The promised appendix on methodology by Thrasher never actually surfaced in print. We can only speculate, then, on how Thrasher collected his data.

HYPOTHESIS #1: THRASHER USED A CARD INDEX FILE TO IDENTIFY GANGS. Many documents cited by Thrasher are never specifically identified other than examples such as "see document 231, p. 231". It is fair to assume many of these came from the 26 different organizations or government agencies that Thrasher acknowledged as a source of reports, bulletins, and records (Thrasher, 1926: p. 544). We must be willing to assume that Thrasher took these reports and supplemented this data with some degree of actual field work. It is therefore reasonable to assume that Thrasher simply went on a quest to find as many gangs as he could from all sources and treated each source with equal validity.

In other words, Thrasher may have had 1,313 index cards about what he assumed were different gangs in Chicago. Some cards had ethnic identification, some did not; some had age estimates, some did not; some had membership estimates, some did not; some had age-ranges, some did not. This would explain the missing data situation faced by Thrasher's quantitative presentation. One thing he also had: the geographical location of the gang. He used either an address or a geographical coordinate in order to prepare the gang map.

HYPOTHESIS #2: THRASHER USED A QUESTIONNAIRE/CENSUS FORM. Another possibility based more directly on the specific language of documents not widely known[13] is that Thrasher's methodology involved the approximation of a census. This could have involved a questionnaire form seeking basic data elements and eventually Thrasher ended up with N=1,313 of these, with previously mentioned amounts of missing data.

If we are willing to accept a certain historical reporting format as continuous prior to the time of Thrasher among Chicago agencies working with gangs, then this method becomes even more plausible as the manner in which Thrasher identified his 1,313 gangs. Other information of import here was obtained from the Chicago Historical Society. For example, a reporting form used by the YMCA as recently as 1963[14] contained the same kind of statistical information used by Thrasher: age range, sex, ethnicity, location; and often included other information --- opposing gangs, agency/worker information dealing with the gang, when the gang was formed, its hang-out and area of operation.

The issue, then, is whether this 1963 YMCA format for gang data was based on Thrasher's 1927 work or Chicago school researchers working with these agencies at the time (Short and Strodtbeck, 1965), and thus the YMCA simply sought to emulate the gang tracking system of Thrasher or as recommended by Chicago school researchers; or whether the YMCA data format was in existence in substantially the same manner prior to and during the period 1923-1926 when Thrasher codified these 1,313 gangs. One thing is not disputed by the historical record: Thrasher worked very closely with the Chicago YMCA and in fact endorsed their work in their fund raising initiatives; and generally saw them, like the Scouts, as a positive force for adolescent socialization.

Another agency reporting format would be ideally suited to such a secondary analysis using a kind of census questionnaire coding form and would provide additional gang names and identifiers because its program services targeted different groups in different areas of the city than the YMCA efforts. Another agency reporting form used by the Welfare Council of Metropolitan Chicago in its Youth Services Division[15] shows, similarly, the name of the gang, age range, sex, ethnicity, hang-out location, area of operation, allied gangs, name or worker/agency contact.

If similar forms were in use by agencies during the 1923-1926 period, then all Thrasher would have had to do is take these regular reports, complete his own tracking/census form with their information, and perhaps on the basis of unique names or variations in the names --- and with some unknown amount of field work during a period of less than two years supplemented this agency and official information (e.g., from interviews with criminal justice officials) to generate the sample of N=1,313 gangs.

The issue of how Thrasher documented his 1,313 gangs is relevant to contemporary research and especially to the important historical issue of validity. Our best evidence is that Thrasher spent some unknown about of time in the field "face to face" with gang members, maintained some type of data collection form on each gang, the "data" being collected in about a year from a variety of sources: but a secondary analysis of agency reports and interviews with officials appear to dominate as such sources; and finally, any "club" that was not a part of the YMCA or other "approved" social service/social control apparatus was considered a "conventionalized gang" --- constituting one-fourth of the Thrasher sample. And further, that all 1,313 gangs had been recognized as early as 1924.

Any subcultural group of three or more members might be mistaken for a gang if there are no rules of evidence in data collection. Some would regard the Black Panther Party as a "gang" of the 60's and early 70's[16]. Some would improperly regard the American Indian Movement (AIM) as a gang today[17]. These are both minority groups with essentially political purposes; and it is not surprising that some of their members have had contact with the criminal justice system subsequent to their politicization. However, these two groups are not themselves "criminal", nor even "deviant", but are only labelled as gangs by the criminal justice system which views any potentially disruptive group as a "gang".

Criminologists as social scientists cannot allow journalists or social worker files to define "gang" if we are to ultimately have a valid and reliable national or even local analysis of gangs. A social service agency like the YMCA during the time of Thrasher (1923-1926) had a political-economic investment in labelling some groups as "gangs": in as much as these represented a growth market for the expansion of the legitimacy and service apparatus of the YMCA. Criminologists or serious researchers cannot afford to have their research methodology compromised by allowing someone else to "define the situation". The issue is a large one for the sociology of knowledge and research ethics.

How then are criminologists to ultimately answer the simple question that many have assumed was adequately answered by Thrasher --- the estimation issue of "how many gangs and gang members are there" in a given city or jurisdiction? Collecting and codifying agency reports from government, news media reports, and social service agency reports (presumably a dominant source of Thrasher's data) represents only the first step. Collecting primary data on youths and young adults is the main and logically necessary step.

It may be necessary to collect multiple self-report samples (school population, out of school population, probation, parole, detention, jail, drug abuse treatment, etc) to adequately tap into the full subculture of any city or jurisdiction. Again, this is only a beginning step. It will then be necessary to codify the gang identifiers and actually go back to the population and determine how these groups are or are not related to each other. Ultimately, a social network analysis is going to be required to answer the question; and it would require an enormous research undertaking to provide a longitudinal assessment of some of the types of real gangs that exist in America today. While gangs are dynamic groups our research methods have to date been very static in nature.

Anyone who today thinks they can study a serious gang like the Aryan Brotherhood solely through the use of social worker files is truly delusional. Nor are most such groups readily accessed by qualitative researchers eager to "get into the field"; as their reports often reflect they made most of their contact with those most prone to respond to an educated adult (often of another racial/ethnic group): kids. Yet it is clear that the preferred analysis is one that includes all sources of information, very strong quantitative methodologies supplemented with qualitative data.

The alliances between gangs must also be taken into account. Within an institutional social control setting --- such as the public high school --- gangs with slight different names may actually function as one allied group. This gang aggregation phenomenon appears to function similarly in correctional settings where "folks" and "peoples" differentiate most of the gang population in Illinois corrections.

Some harder and more replicable research basis is needed to answer the question of "how many gangs and gang members" there are in any social context or geographical area (e.g., City of Chicago). It is certainly not sufficient to rely on reports from agencies of socialization (schools, churches, etc) nor from agencies of social control (e.g., police). For gangs, this may come only from social network analysis. It would be important to establish that a gang exists and functions as an autonomous group rather than just in name within a community. Several different variations of the "Vice Lord" gang can be obtained by simple semantic shifts in prefixes (Insane Vice Lords, Undertaker Vice Lords, Cicero Vice Lords, Conservative Vice Lords, etc[18]). If its members exist only in name --- say, hypothetically, the Cicero Insane Undertaker Vice Lords --- and function only as "Vice Lords", then gangs of similar variation cannot be counted as separate gangs. They may be instead conceived of as cliques, units, or factions of a larger gang organization.

On the other hand, if the gang functions both as an autonomous group in the community and in the institutional setting (e.g., high school) it may very well be possible to call it a separate gang; albeit a variant, chapter, or unit of a larger gang identification. But if it exists in the institutional setting by its proclamation or admitted membership, but does not exist as a group which functions specifically by that name in the larger outside community, then what we have is a gang chapter; not a separate gang.

The issue then is clear: if we include "gang chapter" as a distinct gang even if it does not function as an autonomous group by that specific identity outside of an institutional setting, then we may be in the situation of grossly overestimating the number of different gangs existing in time and space[19]. Without documenting any form of systematic communication and cooperation between the Aryan Brotherhood that exists in California and that which exists in Texas, are we to then assume that these are two separate gangs?

The logical tension confronts us: those who believe gangs are "loose knit" groups that do not function in interstate relationships must then be willing to grossly overestimate the number of gangs in any census of gang groups. The Aryan Brotherhood reported by one California prison would be counted as a separate gang from the AB's from one Texas prison. The same or roughly similar gang name in different settings or different jurisdictions would be assumed to be different distinct gang groups. In cities like Chicago where the official police estimate is that there are 42 different gangs[20], it may very well be easy to generate a listing well in excess of that by Thrasher if the same group name is found in separate jurisdictions or geographical areas. The potential multipliers would only be limited by the number of different analytical settings (schools, program service sites, police beats, community areas, neighborhoods, parks, prisons, jails, service caseloads, etc).

THE THRASHER MYSTIQUE

Beyond the simple mystery of how Thrasher collected his "data" there is a certain mystique to The Gang classic. A large part of this is the projected persona of one who dangerously enters the close-up intrigue of real gang life. Thrasher was not bounced from a bar like Whyte (1942), nor ripped off for his booze like Schweitzgebel (1965), nor shot like Jankowski (1991). At least nothing has surfaced in the official records to effect that Thrasher faced the threat of personal harm in his work, even though clearly the promotion of his book did claim such a related mystique about dealing with the underworld.

During the course of investigating Thrasher, tracing all names and figures and events, a surviving close friend of Thrasher was located. This was some-one who moved to New York City about the time Thrasher did and also some who literally was his boyhood friend of several years younger. They grew up in the same home town. In a series of open-ended oral history interviews with this survivor, he revealed what I had probably wanted to relegate to unwritten history, because at the time I thought it to be totally unbelievable. But it, too, now that corroborating evidence exists, shall now become part and parcel of the Thrasher mystique. Because apparently Thrasher really did face some danger.

Thrasher's boyhood friend told me "he was run out of Chicago, that's why he went to New York". That is, basically Thrasher had made some kind of serious enemies in Chicago and that he was forced to leave town. The chronological life-event record for Thrasher does reflect that he was the chairman of the Department of Sociology that he himself founded at Illinois Wesleyan University when in 1927 he took a lower position (i.e., assistant professor) at New York University. One published story (Argus, Nov. 19, 1924, #3, p.2) quotes Thrasher in a kind of moral panic as follows:

"The real significance of the survey is the baring of the alliance of gangs and politicians. The politicians protect them in their practices and in return, receive the support of the gangs. We have obtained enough stuff on politicians, which if published, would turn the whole government of Chicago upside down. We also have much discreditable information on state and national politicians. The whole city political situation is unspeakably corrupt --- it is impossible to exaggerate it."

It is easy to see how in the nationally covered newspaper coverage about Thrasher during the time frame of 1924-1927 that he may very well have earned the ire of some individuals.

SUMMARY AND CONCLUSION

It was not Thrasher's (1927) assertion that the N = 1,313 gangs he studied represented all existing gangs in Chicago. Using the more restrictive definition of gang from Knox (1991) which does not include simple deviance or acting out behavior among streetcorner groups[21], it is not possible to ascertain how many of Thrasher's gangs were active in crime[22]. The issue is whether Thrasher can be replicated and in doing so how would it be possible to measure how many gangs exist in any city.

There are certain validity problems with self-reported deviance data from officials, students, and other such respondents. The Thrasher temptation would be to consider all sources equal in validity. The problem with this assumption is that it may be prone to overestimate the scope and extent of the gang problem as illustrated in the case of the single high school closely examined in the present research.

It is simply a matter requiring much more definitional clarity. Students who are members of a gang but are not active while in the school setting can be counted as a separate gang that is represented in the school population. But this may not translate as equivalent to gangs presenting a problem in the school environment.

Are we to count "midget vice lords" and senior "vice lords" as two distinct gangs? Are we to count the same gang name with a unique prefix typically representing different geographical areas as separate gang (e.g., Cicero Vice Lords vs. Undertaker Vice Lords)? If we are willing to assume that a gang by the same name reported as active in any jurisdiction or facility is a separate gang because it may reflect a "unique chapter" or faction, then we must be willing to assume that literally thousands of gangs exist in the United States today[23]. And compound this by a rule of evidence clause that allows any reported gang from any social control agency as admissable into the sample.

There is a need to examine the relationship among and between gangs in any estimation of the gang problem. There is also a need for establishing whether such gang factions are in fact autonomous groups and organizations existing substantially apart from their gang "nation".

How Can You Get A Copy of the Full and Complete Original The Gang by Thrasher?

The full and complete book by Thrasher is available from: New Chicago School Press, P.O. Box 929, Peotone, IL 60468.

REFERENCES

Fletcher, Colin
    1964 "Value or Validity", A Review of
        Thrasher, New Society (21 May).
Jensen, Eric L.
    1994 "An Interview With James F. Short,
        Jr.", The Gang Journal: An Interdisciplinary
        Research Quarterly,.
Knox, George W.
    1991 An Introduction to Gangs. Berrien Springs,
        MI: Vande Vere Publishing.
    1992 "The Thrasher Temptation: Over Estimating the High School Gang Problem", paper
        presented at the Annual Meeting of the
        American Society of Criminology, Nov. 7,
        1992, New Orleans, LA.
    1993 An Introduction to Gangs. 2nd Edition.
        Buchanan, MI: Vande Vere Publishing.
Knox, George W.; David Laske; and Edward D.

Tromanhauser
    1992 Schools Under Siege. Dubuque, IA:
        Kendall-Hunt.
Landesco, John
    1932 "Crime and the Failure of Institutions in
        Chicago's Immigrant Areas", Journal of
        Criminal Law and Criminology (23): 238-
        248.
Rosenbaum, Dennis P. and Jane A. Grant
    1983 Gangs and Youth Problems in Evanston:
        Research Findings and Policy Options. Center for Urban Affairs and Policy Research,
        Northwestern University (July 22).
Sanders, William B.
    1994 Gangbangs and Drive-bys: Grounded Culture and Juvenile Gang Violence. New York:
        Aldine De Gruyter.
Smith, Henry Justin
    1927 "How Professor Thrasher Gathered His
        Data", book endorsement, University of Chicago Press book order form. Quotations from
        Collier's Weekly.
Thrasher, Frederick Milton
    1918 The Boy Scout Movement As A Socializing Agency. M.A. Thesis, University of Chicago, Department of Sociology.
    1926 "The Gang as a Symptom of Community
        Disorganization", Journal of Applied Sociology (XI): 3-21.
    1926 The Gang: A Study of 1,313 Gangs in Chicago.
        Ph.D. Dissertation, University of Chicago,
        Department of Sociology.
    1926 "The Gang", Survey LVII: 71-75.
    1927 The Gang: A Study of 1,313 Gangs in Chicago. Chicago: University of Chicago Press.
    1928 "How to Study the Boys' Gang in the
        Open", Journal of Educational Sociology
        (I)(Jan): 244-254.
    1968 The Gang: A Study of 1,313 Gangs in
        Chicago. Abridged with a new Introduction
        by James F. Short, Jr. Chicago: University of
        Chicago Press.

Discussion Questions

(1) Why is the "data" so important to understanding Thrasher's research methodology?

(2) Why should Thrasher probably be credited with being the father of the field of "gangology"?

(3) Why does the legacy of Thrashser still exist today in ongoing concerns about basic gang issues? Do you think that today some of the gangs studied by Thrasher would not even be classified as "gangs"?

THRASHER'S F.B.I. FILE: WAS HE REALLY "RUN OUT OF CHICAGO"?

Frederick Milton Thrasher's FBI file is # 62-32551. There is a lot of stuff in the file. None of it shows anything bad or criminal about Thrasher. There is absolutely zero evidence of any sort that Thrasher was "run out of Chicago" because his gang book was embarrassing to "corrupt politicians in Chicago".

J. Edgar Hoover had files on everyone, that was his job, and he did a good job of keeping track of important people and less important people. In the times that Thrasher lived, Thrasher played a "big role" in his society, so it was not surprising that a lot of material was in his FBI file.

One thing is clear, however, from the Thrasher file: J. Edgar Hoover personally knew Thrasher, and they were friends.

For example, in August of 1934 when Thrasher's mother died, the Special Agent in Charge of the FBI office in New York City wrote a memo to J. Edgar Hoover as follows: "Believing that you may desire to convey expressions of sympathy to Dr. Frederick M. Thrasher, Associate Professor of Education, New York University, a present conducting a series of lectures on crime which are being attended by a Special Agent of this office, I desire to advise of the death of Professor Thrasher's mother during the past week".

On August 11, 1934 J. Edgar Hoover wrote to Thrasher: "My dear Professor Thrasher: I have just learned with sorrow of the death of your Mother and I am writing this note to extend my profound sympathy upon your great loss. Sincerely yours, J. Edgar Hoover."

What else was in his FBI file? Nothing really exciting.

Someone sent Thrasher an anonymous letter once "informing" him of a "fence for stolen goods", Thrasher turned it over to the FBI, the FBI investigated thoroughly, the person was a "nobody" and not a "fence".

In the fall of 1933, a young man tried to extort $2,000 from Thrasher's father. Thrasher's father owned a dry goods store in Frankfort, Indiana (where Thrasher grew up). Thrasher asked for and received enormous FBI help on the case. The offender was quickly caught and ended up with a prison sentence.

The FBI had high regard for Thrasher's work on exposing gangsters in Chicago. But there was no evidence whatsoever that Thrasher was "run out of Chicago" which surfaced in Thrasher's FBI file.

The Wanderlust Gang: The Freight Train Riders of America (FTRA)

Many who read intensively on the "gang issue" will notice that in Thrasher's original version of his book (1927), he had a full chapter on "Wanderlust" as it related to gangs. In the subsequent editions of the book, this chapter was dropped. So few people have actually read it. Today, however, the full original version is available; having been reprinted in the summer of 2000. Thus, many students of gang life may "rediscover" this issue of wanderlust as having a lot to do with the issue of "gang migration".

How, we ask, can "wanderlust" be applicable in the type of gang we have in today's modern society, when gang members cannot go one or two blocks in either direction from their "home" because of the existence of "rival" or "opposition" gangs? Well, there is one gang today that fits the "wanderlust" profile: the FTRA[24].

By most accounts, it is a predominantly white gang, older members, typical profile includes a military vet who has become a societal drop-out, who uses drugs, and who is "constantly on the move": by means of hopping freight trains. The FTRA member wears a special decorative item for his handkerchief, which is worn around the neck. Their membership is estimated to be anywhere from 2,500 to 5,000 all of whom are older adult "transients": constantly on the move. They leave a lot of graffiti. They are suspected of a number of homicides along the national railroad lines and rail yards. They are particularly active on the west coast.

END NOTES:

[1]James F. Short, Jr., who wrote the introduction for the latest edition, was also not aware of what exactly this Thrasher methodology entailed (personal letter).

[2]Thrasher's 1927 book was the only one to include this gang map. The map specifically indicates the 1923-1926 period for data collection and plots out all 1,313 gangs on the Chicago street grid. No subsequent edition of the book included this map.

[3]Anticipating some contemporaries, Thrasher felt the mass media needed more regulation because of its possible effect on juvenile behavior. See the recent interview of James F. Short, Jr. (Jensen, 1994) for a similar view that takes the mass media to task as a possible cause for gang emulation behavior.

[4]The book by the University of Chicago Press released in 1927 is based on the Ph.D. sociology dissertation by Thrasher (1926).

[5]This was a dummy variable: whether the gangs represented a single foreign nationality group.

[6]Actually, some work prior to the 1927 publication was more specific that the book itself. Thrasher claimed in 1926 that these 1,313 gangs contained a total of 25,000 members (boys and men). See "Chicago's Gangs", Religion and Social Service, The Literary Digest for November 6, 1926 (pp. 28-29). A YMCA fund raising flyer for 1925 highlighting the 1,313 gangs identified by Thrasher indicated "1,313 different gangs enrolling 50,000 boys in the city have been studied".

[7]No copy of the original dissertation exists in the Department of Sociology at the University of Chicago, or at least that is what I was told when I tried to examine it. I was told one such copy did exist up until around the mid to late sixties, a student borrowed it and it was never returned.

[8]Department of Sociology, University of Chicago (August, 1918).

[9]The actual map itself appears from a Nov. 19, 1926 letter by the University of Chicago Press to be the work of the Local Community Area Research Committee: "Mr. Thrasher has confirmed my opinion that the Base Map which he has for his study of Chicago gangs was prepared by the Research Committee, and he has released us from royalty for any use of the Map without the gang material." Thus, Thrasher took this map (containing industrial, parks, railroad, and language group information and simply marked in symbols for the distribution of the 1,313 gangs.

[10]The present author in 1994 had been working on a project to bring back the availability of the full Thrasher book. It was tentatively, in 1994, to be called The Unabridged Thrasher, and the plan then was to have it published by Vande Vere Publishing Company, Buchanan, MI. That publisher deteriorated in reliability, attorneys were brought in, etc. And the project sat limbo for awhile, but regained momentum in 1999, and came to fruition in 2000, such that the full original Thrasher is now available once again.

[11]I am grateful to David L. Laske, Ph.D., for assistance in collecting historical records from this university. Officially, however, the most important records there (e.g., his personnel file) are missing, or so we were told.

[12]I am grateful to Dr. Jim Sikora, chairman of the Department of Sociology, Illinois Wesleyan University for sharing transcribed copies of early news items in Argus, the school newspaper, pertaining to Thrasher.

[13]One document examined here was what appeared to be a 1927 letter from Thrasher to Burgess along with a detailed program/research proposal for further research and intervention/experimentation on Chicago gangs. Never subsequently published or referenced in our literature, these materials make use of the methodological descriptors of both "census" and "survey" of gangs.

[14]Source, Chicago Historical Society; a report by Fred D. Hubbard, Director; Program for Detached Workers; March, 1963; funded by NIMH Grant 5R11 MH541-3 (1959-1963).

[15]Available: Chicago Historical Society, March 10, 1959 document from the Hard-to-Reach Youth Project.

[16]The typical law enforcement definition of gangs as any group that is threatening to the community allows a white-dominated police department to label the Black Panther Party as threatening, ergo, a "gang"; threatening not necessarily to the African-American community, but to the status quo.

[17]To the extent that stigma and collective national guilt are also factors mediating the labelling process, we can anticipate that some may want to define groups like ACT UP as a gang.

[18]A more recent gang identification guide by the Chicago Police Department (1991, p. 125) recognizes ten factions of Vice Lords: (1) Conservative V.L., (2) Cicero Insane V.L., (3) Traveling V.L., (4) Unknown V.L., (5) Rockwell Garden V.L., (6) Renegade V.L., (7) Horner Home V.L., (8) Four Corner Hustlers, (9) Insane V.L., and (10) Undertaker Vice Lords.

[19]During the 1923-1926 period it is unknown, because Thrasher did not report the list of gang names, how many of the 1,313 gangs in Chicago were really "unique and autonomous" functional groups; or how many were variations of a smaller such number. For example, Pee Wee Vice Lords and Anciano Vice Lords might simply count as two gangs the younger Vice Lord identification and the older Vice Lord identification.

[20]The author makes no evaluation here of the validity of Chicago police estimates of either how many gangs exist or how many gang members exist.

[21]Indigenous organizations like Social Athletic Clubs, included as gangs in Thrasher's work, are therefore

not considered genuine gangs in the Knox (1991) definition. Rather, such "conventionalized groups" as Thrasher called them, would be regarded as Level Zero groups whose social organizational formation and development pattern took them away from an ongoing involvement in or benefit from crime.

[22]Major sources of information and established ties in the historical record between Thrasher and the Chicago YMCA help explain why about a fourth of the 1,313 gangs probably were not gangs in the Knox (1991) definition; they were SAC's. These SAC's were in competition with the YMCA for leisure time legitimacy. Simply labelling these SAC's as "unwholesome influences" was not then nor is now a justification to be defined as a gang: it is patently ideological.

[23]The Geographical Guide to U.S. Gangs data file maintained by the author consists of 100 single-spaced pages of gang names reported from criminal justice officials in all states.

[24] For one of the few types of coverage on this gang, see: Mark Matthews, "Train Tramps Ride Rails of Crime Across United States", Police magazine, November, 1997, pp. 14-18.

Latin Kings
(AKA: "Almighty Latin King Nation")

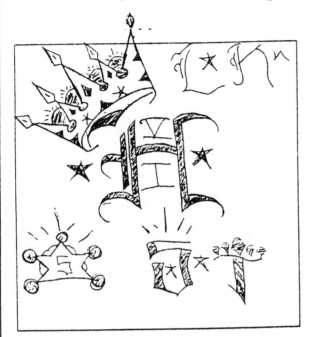

The Latin Kings are one of the most stable gangs in the USA today . It is one of the few gangs to have never changed its ideology: its internal written belief system still prevails. Its command structure has remained intact since the 1960's. The gang has a rigid authoritarian centralized authority structure. The gang spends a lot of time disciplining (i.e., administering "violations", or ritualized torture beatings) its members. The gang keeps elaborate written records of dues and membership. All chapters are frequently visited by an upper management representative of the gang.

CHAPTER 11

GANGS AS AN URBAN WAY OF LIFE

INTRODUCTION

If a correctional officer, or a law enforcement officer, or a probation/parole officer, or a school teacher --- someone who must deal with gangs and gang members in everyday life --- had to read some of our prior books about gangs and try to relate these concepts to their work, they would probably experience more than a little confusion or dismay in being able to do so. The scene of a police officer facing a march of 5,000 gang members protesting in Chicago's loop, or the scene of a correctional officer watching as a gang leader controls the entire inmate body, or the scene of 10,000 gang members and associates holding their own "Woodstock" style gang picnic on a farm just south of Chicago (these are all real scenes) --- one would be tempted to remark "Near-groups nothing, these are real groups alright, in fact too damn organized for my good". Those gang researchers who study less formidable gangs may find it easier to interview Spanky and Alfalfa types of kids, but they will not be able to understand more complex gang organizations such as those found in Chicago and elsewhere.

Part of this problem is "over simplifying". Some of our literature describes gangs as a cultural form that are wrongly labelled by an over-reacting public and the government both caught up in a moral panic. Some of our literature sees the urban gang member as the new urban guerilla or political messiah. Some of our literature sees the urban gang member as a quisling, that is an enemy within, someone whose very presence deteriorates the neighborhood. The biggest problem in understanding the truth about gangs is that it is not a subject that can be simplified, because it is a complex problem with equally complex explanations.

Clearly, the problem of gangs is not new[1]. Not to the United States. Not to other countries[2]. What we need to understand is the context and environment in which gangs do arise and persist.

It is a misconception to view gangs as being anything other than social organizations with varying degrees of formalization and complexity. They are more than simple social groups and they are less than bureaucracies. They can be much more destructive than they are now, and their association with killing, the use of firearms, and explosives or military weapons is not new. Every major newcoming ethnic group in America has had its role to play in gangs. The gang is an expected outgrowth of social institutional arrangements and grows as a new fabric to community infrastructure when these social institutions are inadequate to meet human needs.

While any society can theoretically generate gang formations, those with social orders of recurring inequality such as slavery and racism in the U.S., must take account of the historical character of social relations in any theory of gangs. Such societies have as much crime as they can manufacture and process through the criminal justice system, and the same applies to gang crime. Not much is truly new in gang life in America. Every ethnic group in America has had its gangs. The current gang crime crisis is one that reflects only the continuing lag between hope for a better life and its fulfillment for persons of color.

ORGANIZED GROUP AFFILIATION PATTERNS

The fact is that American society is a nation known for its multi-graded clubs, special interest groups, voluntary associations, membership associations, professional associations, and even secret societies. Gangs are but one variation on this natural tendency of organized group affiliation. America has always had gangs in one form or another and probably always will. It is also true that the failure to appreciate the organizational characteristics of gangs has to some extent been associated with reinforcing the strength of gang organization through ill conceived policies of the past.

Rival football teams from local high schools provide another historical context for competition and moderated conflict. But we must recall the Crips and Bloods arising in two separate high schools in Los Angeles and adopting their school colors as their gang colors to recall that group conflict is part and parcel of American society. One finding in this regard has the overwhelming statistical evidence to be regarded as a social law: the law of natural group opposition formation --- when one threatening group arises and makes a presence, another opposing group will shortly follow and exist in the same social context.

THE AMERICAN NIGHTMARE

American society has not yet necessarily seen the worst case scenario in terms of gang organization. We must gauge potential by the history of such related organizational forms. What the 1920's showed is that gangs can be involved in the assassination of political leaders, state's attorney's, they put out "hits" on police officers who obstruct their operations[3], etc; gangs can be the forces that both foment urban race riots as well as actors that escalate such violence. As organized forms of deviance, theoretically all such historical variations could appear.

If Rev. Jim Jones could sway several hundred followers to mass suicide, if cults can use drugs, hypnotism, sleep deprivation, "love bombs", and an ever increasing social grip on the individual to achieve nearly total compliance among its members, then could an educated, highly skilled, or very charismatic individual organize or assume leadership of a vast gang umbrella organization ---- citywide, statewide, nationwide, or even international? Organizationally, anything is possible.

The "bad news" of continuing patterns of inter-gang homicides throughout the United States is really the good news in terms of indicating that no such syndication or higher level gang organizational functioning yet exists; even though some gangs operate throughout many different states in America today. The fierce competition among and between gangs in fact has shown, in the past, that a next potential stage is that of monopoly formation. Clearly, the potential exists for such hybrid variations of the gang structure and function to emerge.

GANGS, GUNS AND KILLINGS ARE NOT NEW

Students of gang crime must be careful to avoid the direct comparison of contemporary gang organizational patterns with "play groups" and "street corner groups" described by Thrasher and Whyte. Most certainly, even during the period of Thrasher, America had an enormous problem with armed offenders --- including, of course, the use of fully automatic weapons and explosives in routine daily business. The reader should simply be cautioned that the first instinct in reading works like Thrasher and Whyte is that one is also cognizant of higher levels of gang organizational functioning and the natural tendency is therefore to assume that this is a problem of "old theory, and new gangs". One needs to examine the early historical periods, such as the 1920's, to discover that the best analogy is that between contemporary gangs and organized crime groups of an earlier era.

The analogy breaks down, of course, in terms of the factor of ongoing, conspicuous political corruption. Today that corruption pattern is likely to be much more concealed; in fact, it is likely to at least have the "plausible deniability" feature. We are, after all, dealing with other changes in society here as well; including the role of the mass media.

Regarding gang-related homicides and shootouts when comparing the 1920's period of Thrasher to present day conditions, this shows one thing that Shaw and Mc Kay predicted: the ethnic composition of gangs in America has changed.

FROM GANGS TO ORGANIZED CRIME

The prison of language is such that many who write about and carry out research on gangs, never use the adverb "gangster" in referring to one who is a functionally active gang member.[4] Clearly a "street corner play group" whose most serious impact on crime statistics involves a few burglaries over a period of several years is hard to equate as "organized crime". It therefore seems that the inadequacy of prior gang studies have been in terms of their inability to account for that circumstance in which the gang is effective and successful over time, such that it truly becomes an equivalent form of an organized crime group or cartel.

It is a matter of organizational development and maturation, and the gang must be at least conceived of as a point of origin for organized crime.[5] The gang is a manifestation of all social institutional fabrics of any given community in which it is found. In any community the social institutions include the family, employers and business (the economy), religion, schools (education), and the government, and some would have us add healthcare as a sixth social institution. But the inferior quality of life in many of America's communities means that in terms of power and being functionally viable, the gang is more dominant than all such social institutions and takes on, by neglect from without and by lack of developmental resources from within the community, its own localized status as a social institution in its own right.

Racism is the missing link between gangs and a transition to organized crime. White skin privilege allows organized crime to use illicit gains to enter traditionally legitimate business, and once inside the mainstream economy, to milk it and defraud it for everything it is worth. That is less of an option, regardless of how effective the gang is in developing a war chest (capitalization money for gang use or investment), among persons of color.

Many contributions to the gang literature are explicitly directed at whites, others have trouble analyzing the minority communities. Most certainly there is a notable exception to most gang theories and that is the matter of the historical patterns of racism in America. All things are not treated equal when it comes to race and gangs. Two variations exist: (1) Persons of color, notably African-Americans and Latinos, have experienced continued intergenerational disadvantages[6], and secondly (2) white gangs have historically tended to be more explicitly racist[7] in their function and purpose.

GANGS ARE VERY NORMAL, GROWING UP IN THE INNER CITY WITHOUT AN ARREST RECORD IS NOT

By most accounts in the gang literature, another empirical continuity has to do with the norms of the gang. Such social values internalized by the gang members as: loyalty, "follow the rules", personal sacrifice, etc, these are attributes actually in high demand by American employers and they are to be found in most active gang members. The gang

ethic and the spirit of capitalism have much in common. Particularly, the aspect of rugged individualism.

But one aspect of crime tends to put the community-gang relationship in better context. It is the fact that members of minority groups face a disproportionate chance of being arrested in the first place when they live in a high crime inner city area. Gangs are normal in the sense that they rationally seek to attain power and respect. It is not "abnormal" to want a better life. The problem of gangs cannot be reduced to any simple psychological generalization, as gangs are fundamentally social in character. For complex reasons, members of minority groups simply do face a higher chance of being arrested. The gang is the one place where an arrest or even a prison record is a "positive" resume item. When there are more African-American young adults under the correctional sanction than there are enrolled in higher education, we can see how larger processes within the American social structure also operate to limit the power of any community to "do something" about the gang problem.

THE STUDY OF THE BARRIO

A gang rights magazine called <u>Teen Angels</u> released its first issue in 1980. Few whites, and literally no Blacks, are included in the many, many photographs that the gangs send in (for a small fee) to have their group or individual message published in the magazine. It is clearly focused on the Hispanic market. As with all other gangs, a favorite type of photograph the gangs send to the magazine to be published is a small group holding guns or displaying gang hand signs. "Placas", are also common: drawings of gang symbols and a listing of the gang names.

Like the work by Moore (1978), a strong emphasis is placed on the role of the prison. Most the magazines include pictures sent in by prison inmates; and many names and addresses of inmates seeking pen pals. Another common type of material in the magazine are memorial "R.I.P." statements on recently killed members of the gang. A wealth of barrio "gang art" in these magazines could be analyzed in the fashion of Hutchison (1993).

The magazine reprints articles by the American Civil Liberties Union and strongly encourages its readers to join the ACLU. Erotic sketches of attractive partially clothed Latinas are to be found in most of the magazines. It is a magazine for Hispanic gangs, not anyone else. Of course, through the mail rival Black and white gangs could readily purchase a complete set of these magazines (some of the older back issues cost as much as $35.00 at this writing); as could, and presumably have, law enforcement agencies. A published photograph in this magazine where they are signifying the gang dress and signs could easily be used to establish gang membership for purposes of prosecution using recent laws that provide for stiffer sentences if the prosecutor can prove gang membership. Knowing this, will gang members continue to send in photographs of themselves in gang poses? A recent trend appears to be sending in just a photograph of the "arsenals": a long display of AK-47's, machine guns, sawed-off shotguns, etc, on display with no human faces, just the gang logo. Which, of course, may provide probable cause for such a gang facing an investigation by the ATF.

Clearly, the American economic market has found the gang to be a large consumer group; we may expect such magazines for other gangs as well. In many cities "air brush" clothing logo "SLANG WEAR" shops have sprung up: putting the gang logos and symbols on T-Shirts, pants, and other clothing items. Some gang paraphernalia is professionally produced abroad (e.g., Brothers[8] and Folks socks embroidered with their respective symbols), imported and sold in inner city sports stores. An enormous market exists in the sale of gang jewelry items. Gangs in Los Angeles and Chicago and perhaps elsewhere also have their own musical bands thus some of the organized gangs (e.g., Crips, Disciples) also sell their own gang records and tapes of music --- typically rap --- that portrays their own gang in a positive light.

THE PRISON SYSTEM AT THE MACRO-ANALYTIC LEVEL

Does the prison system or the use of the criminal sanction have a natural "limit", or can a society have the capacity to truly punish everyone? And what are the trade-offs for such an over dependence on the use of such methods of formal social control? How do we as a society firmly instruct new groups and successive generations left behind in urban squalor residing in our inner cities that we "are about business"? Step out of line and they'll come and take you away. To prison. But the American prison was designed for the individual recalcitrant. Can it really function equally effectively with larger organized groups as its primary class of prisoners? The evidence suggests the gangs are winning in the prison system; that is, the gangs are becoming in some jurisdictions the de facto administrators of our nations prisons (see Lane, 1989).

GANGWEAR: BUSINESS ENTERPRISES ADAPT TO THE GANG MARKET

It is common today to find a variety of specialized "sports shops" which sell what amounts to gang clothing and gang attire. Some examples from the midwest include custom-designed socks with the gang symbol and initials of the gang. Jewelry stores have tapped into the enormous profitability of sell-ing gold medallions and symbols used by gangs on necklaces, rings, and pendants. Custom "air brush" shops are now common to create uniquely designed slogans and multi-color symbols for gang T-shirts.

FRAME OF REFERENCE AND UNIT OF ANALYSIS IN GANG THEORY

The gang literature is quite fragmented in terms of the frame of reference and the unit of analysis. This problem for theory development deserves our attention here. Despite the existence of rich and highly detailed qualitative data collected on gangs since and including the time of Asbury and Thrasher, the more disciplined reader will search unproductively for an integrated and systematic analysis of gangs.

Figure 10 below gives a graphic depiction and overview of this problem for gang theory. Few contributions have been offered in the higher end (sectors 3,1 and 3,2) of the analytic spectrum encompassing causal forces or channels (micro vs. macro) and units of analysis (individual, community, society). Yet such an approach can help to clarify our thinking considerably and allows, hopefully, transcending the personal bias that appears to be present in reading the gang literature, over and over again.

This should not be construed as an attempt to reduce approaches to a specific area of relevance, but should rather force a consideration of what roles particular contributions have played in extending the social scientific analysis of gangs.

FIGURE 10

GANG STUDIES IN TERMS OF BOTH THEIR LEVELS OF EXPLANATION AND UNITS OF ANALYSIS

Unit of Analysis	Levels of Explanation in Gang Theories	
	1. Microanalytic	2. Macroanalytic
1. Individual	(1,1) Almost all psychological theories, e.g., Yablonsky	(1,2) Social process and social exchange theories; e.g., Short and Strodtbeck
2. Community	(2,1) Social control theory, e.g., Thrasher	(2,2) Social disorganization theory, e.g., Shaw and Mc Kay
3. Society	(3,1) Differential opportunity theory	(3,2) Underclass and surplus population theory.

As seen in Figure 10, virtually all psychological approaches would have as their level of analysis, the microanalytic level, and their unit of analysis as that of the individual. Such is Freudian psychology and behaviorism, and Yablonsky is appropriately classified here. Similarly, social process and social exchange theories derived from social-psychology may have a more macroanalytic level of analysis in terms of being generalizable beyond specific aspects of human behavior but are still focusing on individuals as the actors in this transaction and are therefore appropriately using the individual as the unit of analysis (that is, does the individual invoke a norm of reciprocity, is it quid pro quo for the individual, etc).

A somewhat larger unit of analysis than that of the individual actor is that of the community. As seen in Figure 10, Thrasher's emphasis on the breakdown of social control at the individual level, manifested in communities with gangs, puts Thrasher at an intermediate unit of analysis but at a microanalytic level of explanation. Compare this with Shaw and Mc Kay, whose work was macroanalytic in implying more universal processes that apply to all cities in America, albeit at the community level of analysis.

Finally, where society itself is the unit of analysis we find a much higher level of measurement. Such works as Cloward and Ohlin qualify here for the microanalytic level of analysis in terms of differential opportunity structure. Similarly, surplus population and underclass theory apply to a more macroanalytic explanation, also using society as the unit of analysis. We should probably be sufficiently convinced that because of the problem of inter-rater reliability in such global content analyzing, we are probably not going to generate much consensus with classifying all such previous gang research authors, and the present book has therefore made no attempt at such a classification.

This observation is offered only as a prelude to what is possible in theory and research on gangs. Obviously, there is a "middle range" between microanalytic and macroanalytic because these two terms are little more than heuristic devices. Already perhaps this position has confused more than it has enlightened, but the point bears repeating: we need to consider what the causal forces are in their explanation of human behavior (levels of explanation) and we need to then consider what impact these explanatory concepts have as they are measured (i.e., the unit of analysis: individual, community, organization, society, etc).

The reader who compares and closely follows various contributions to the gang literature will, it is believed, discover that our greatest gaps in the literature are not at the individual or community unit of analysis, but at the societal level for both micro and macroanalytic explanations.

WHYTE: A CRITICAL VIEW

William Whyte's Street Corner Society has been critically analyzed by Geis (1965). By his own account, Whyte was not highly experienced in dealing with lower class communities, he was rather a middle-class, ivy league graduate student who studied a community in Boston's north end via a Harvard University fellowship.[9] Louis Wirth at the University of Chicago would later criticize the merits of Street Corner Society as a Ph.D. dissertation. Whyte appears to be the Chicago school's version of Poston (1971).[10] On much closer reading Whyte is not simply atheoretical as was Poston, but worse may be anti-theoretical![11] And yet no one criticizes Whyte[12]? Why?

Whyte never quoted one piece of literature or social science in his book. Whyte smugly rejected all previous knowledge on the subject as "irrelevant". He obviously rejected even Chapter nine in Shaw and Mc Kay which described in detail where Whyte could have found delinquency subcultures. Chapter nine in Shaw and Mc Kay's 1942 version included an analysis of Boston. Whyte admits he was not sure for a long time what, exactly, he was studying or what he was doing in Boston other than collecting fellowship support from Harvard.

If a social scientist or applied criminologist is truly committed to developing knowledge in the field, then there is a moral obligation to not be deceitful, to not conceal, to test theory, even theories we may not personally favor.

If Louis Wirth, from whose famous essay comes the spirit of this present analysis, knew that Whyte had intentionally engaged in voting fraud in Boston's elections in order to "study gangs", then would he have been as gracious and accommodating as he was in agreeing to a compromise in allowing Whyte to obtain the Ph.D. from the University of Chicago? It's an interesting question. The informed reader cannot tell what Whyte's approach really was: was it as an economist, as a fiction writer, as a street psychologist? Or some of all three with the cloak of sociology?

The point at which a researcher must commit crime to study crime is a point of ethical no return.[13] Had Whyte committed this type of election crime in Illinois he might be subject to prosecution even today; because forgery has no statute of limitations in Illinois, prosecution can commence at any time --- the clock never "runs out". And for Whyte to sign ballots using names and signatures other than his own, just to have a window of opportunity to study the politics in relationship to the gang, amounts to just that ---- forgery. Moreover Whyte, by his own account of this self-reported deviance, would have no legitimate legal defense such as "compulsion" or acting under duress. He was simply naive, gullible, low on internal locus of control, and apparently as well unwilling to read works like that by Landesco (1929) documenting in elaborate detail the manner in which such political crimes could be researched. Stated alternatively, Whyte could have read Landesco (1929) and would have had a variety of ways to study the linkages between politics and gangs rather than being a political stooge himself. By reading Landesco he could have been alerted to the etiology of political crime in America.

This is not an indictment of all participant observation research, field research, or ethnographic accounts in the study of gangs. Obviously, many such accounts exist which do not involve joining in the deviance, but rather involve joining in activities such as football, board games, and social conversation (Santamaria, et al, 1989; see also, Sanchez-Jankowski, 1991[14]).

This is not a repudiation of Whyte, nor is it an assertion that nothing he had to say was worthwhile. This has been a straightforward criticism along other dimensions. It is equally notable that one of the youths that Whyte worked with recently shared his story in the Journal of Gang Research in a regular feature called "Interview and Focus on History". In this story Angelo R. Orlandella credits Whyte with showing him how to deal with organizations in a prosocial way, because he went on to lead a productive life including a military and government career.[15] This new information was developed through the recent interview of William F. Whyte by Joe (1993).[16]

GANG STUDIES AS AN IDEOLOGICAL BATTLEGROUND: A Personal View

It shouldn't be, but life is not always fair; even to the social sciences. Is there so much riding on the answer to "why we have gangs in the USA?" that author ideology triumphs over scientific method itself? The present analysis has entered this fray cognizant of the undercurrents of such ideological conflict. Let this analysis go on record as being non-aligned to any such ideological camp.

Bookin-Weiner and Horowitz (1983) advanced the notion that seemed to say we found less gang research because leftist scholars in a rightwing national political climate did not want to study gangs. Recent contributions to our gang literature should dispel that analysis. In fact, Bookin-Weiner and Horowitz should have noted that the comparable problem of research on the Mafia gangs did not increase during the period of fascism (see Hobsbawm, 1965: p. 44). It significantly decreased. So one can technically argue, from a social-political rhetoric standpoint, either direction of blame: the left wing, or the right wing.[17]

This, however, takes us no where analytically. Like anything else, the gang crime problem certainly has its political and ideological issues. But just because a gang, as we will see in Chapter 15, has a written constitution dedicated to working for "oppressed peoples" should not, ipso facto, be any simi-

lar basis for assuming a new urban insurrectionist mass movement is developing in America[18].

On the other hand, if there is one thing the present author has learned about gangs it is this: never say gangs lack certain capabilities just because they have not yet been documented in the literature. What is historically unique about gangs in America today is that by taking advantage of technological advances in communications and the ease of travel, some gangs in the United States today are in communication with each other from shore to shore. Gang "summits" and national meetings sponsored for the gangs under the guise of reducing their own violence have facilitated this new national networking among and between gangs. We shall now face the future of gangs in America with the certainty that more is being done to facilitate organizational development in gangs than is being done to prevent their growth and expansion. If there was any place in the world to form a gang and enjoy a host of civil and constitutional rights, then it is in the United States. Unless we are willing to allow our constitutional rights to be systematically eroded, then without a substantial shift in federal policy there may be little that can be done about the gang problem in many communities.

GANGS AND THE QUEST FOR HUMAN SIGNIFICANCE

Between the two extreme conditions of absolute powerlessness and having an inordinate amount of social power are the many gradations of human existence that most of us probably call our own. As a way of affirmation of self it is normal to seek out something larger and more significant than ones own self. For many this may be accomplished through religious institutions, for others perhaps the corporate world or politics, or even academia. Gang life is a natural mechanism for the fulfillment of this human need, particularly when avenues to more legitimate sources of fulfillment are either blocked or found wanting.

To belong, to be accepted, to be recognized and esteemed by like-minded persons, to have a sense however fragile that you are in some way important or needed --- you fit in --- this is what the gang offers. It is an offer that is apparently taken and accepted by those American youth who are subjected to intense forces of alienation. The result is their marginal connection to the established social order and its highly routinized manner of "getting ahead" in the world. Because whatever the tenuous tie the youth may have had to the legitimate social order prior to joining a gang, this subcultural integration tends to further erode legitimate ties.

GANGS AND SOCIAL INSTITUTIONS

Social institutions are relatively permanent forms of group affiliation that do not just persist over time, but which have legitimacy; and serve crucial functions of socialization and social control. That which externally erodes the effectiveness of a society's social institutions at the neighborhood level is, in no necessarily ranked order of negative impact, basically: poverty, prejudice, discrimination[19], political neglect, economic exploitation, and double standards. This includes the lack of needed national policies and the existence of those that are less needed or which may counterproductive at the macroanalytic level.

As an invisible societal wide process, then, the social institutional erosion becomes added to conditions of deprivation and human capital lag to present America with a sad twist on the Turner slave rebellion thesis --- because when gangs become predominantly persons of color, particularly African-Americans who are not new to America, but who have been subjected to the repeated onslaughts of prejudice and discrimination (something most youths do not need a university education to understand), with the effect of intergenerational poverty, then we truly have a new variation on gang crime in the United States. And a new variation in race relations as well.

For the law abiding and well adjusted reader it must simply be asked: conduct a self-inventory of your own social institutional experience. Did educational agencies or institutions at any time "work" for you? Did the Church, Synagogue, Mosque or place of religious worship at any time work for you? Did the economic structure in terms of the transmission of wealth or the world of legitimate employment ever work for you --- do you have a work history or did you derive indirect benefits from it? Was your relationship to the government a generally positive one, Laissez faire, or a negative one? Was your family structure a viable and functional one, useful in learning mainstream social values or was it such that you hit the streets to feed yourself when you would wake up about noon and sought out nurturance elsewhere? Both the nature and quality of such institutional ties have much to say about the human condition.

If even a single social institution "worked" for you at a formative period in your life, then that may be much more than what we can expect from a great many members of our society for whom these institutional structures have never worked properly, or who have given up on them once they became gang affiliated. And when they do break down as viable and functional sources of social control and socialization, what you have is someone that no one can "reach" but the gang. Gang affiliation must be regarded not only as normal, but as expected under some of these conditions. It is normal because gang affiliation is but one possible result for those who do

not "fit in" to their society. There has always been the options of self-destruction, the asylum ala Goffman, alcohol and drug dependence, and of course crime and the gang life. What should be of most concern to social scientists curious about what is "possible", is that the gang can become itself such an institution competing quite effectively with malfunctioning mainstream social institutions.

THE GANG AS A SOCIAL INSTITUTION

In a 1949 journal article, Henry Mc Kay showed that the gang was different than a play group and different from organized crime. The gang, because of its higher level of organizational formalization and persistence as a group formation, is actually an indigenous social institution (Mc Kay, 1949: p. 36).[20] Recent discussions by some authors of gangs being "institutionalized" in American society, are therefore, whether or not they read Mc Kay (1949) or acknowledged him, simply repeating what has already been specifically described in the gang literature.

Not all indigenous social institutions (as alternatives to the big five: family, education, economy, government, religion) are deviant or criminally inclined. Saul Alinksy proved such indigenous social institutions could take a political and self-help form. Mc Kay calls these "conventional" forms of indigenous social institutions because the thrust of the group activity is related to mainstream society and these could include: social athletic clubs, ethnic group organizations, and perhaps neighborhood block/watch clubs/committees. Visibility and continuity are the life blood of such indigenous social institutions.[21] The nonconventional or unconventional or deviant such indigenous social institutions include the gang, organized crime, perhaps even political extremist groups, or even cults.

What is more fragile about these indigenous social institutions is that they often disappear upon the two conditions of loss of leadership and loss of resources. The second, loss of resources, makes leadership succession or the emergence of new leadership unattractive if there is no worthwhile instrumental goal worth shooting for. Loss of leadership alone is not sufficient to neutralize an indigenous social institution, or dismember it. Hopefully we have realized at this point in history that simply sending a gang leader to prison is also not accomplishing true "loss of leadership".

In summary, that gangs are often "institutionalized" is not a new observation.[22] Mc Kay (1949) noted this long ago. The real question is one of social organization. More specifically, in what sense do gang organizations function to attract and promote gang membership? That is, by what organizational mechanisms is the gang able to persist over time and compete with the big five social institutions and even other indigenous social institutions? These are questions that must be answered by gang theory.

THE RELIGIOUS TRAPPINGS OF SOME GANGS: A LOOK AT THE BLACK P. STONES

Called "Brothers", the African-Americans who compose the Black P. Stone Nation, ride under the five point star (which they have now attached the letters A, L, L, A, H clockwise along the five points, as a symbol. As they operate today in Chicago, a new recruit truly does his "homework" and must literally completely and correctly memorize a number of different "prayers" and aspects of the gang constitution. The recruits are given materials to study, and are frequently quizzed on their rote memorization of the materials. The following materials come from someone who did not enjoy the rigid indoctrination methods and volunteered to cooperate with police. The "Stones" still exist, and are also called the Cold Soldier Army.

The Stones, riding under the five point star, are categorized as "People"; but over the last few years, the African-American gangs riding under the five point star call themselves "Brothers". So the major two factions are Brothers and Folks. Oddly, the largest "Folk" gang (BGD's) are to themselves known as the Brothers of the Struggle (B.O.S.). The language of gangs sometimes becomes confusing. The "Ye" language in the following document is socio-linguistically reminiscent of something out of the Bible, but is used in a context that actually denounces Christianity in favor of Islamic teachings:

"BLACKSTONE FOUNDATION

The Foundation of our Nation must not perish within the ignorance of self. For the love we have bonded has connected and linked, one to the other, with the greatest of strength. As knowledge be ye cup and wisdom be like that of water, ye shall walk those miles together. If ye fall lame ye shall be broken. If ye forsake our Bound ye shall be formed into dust. Peace and blessings are for the righteous who shall carry the message to the four corners of the world for all nations to see. Behold, Blackstone Foundation.

Allah is most great, there is no God but Allah, and Mohammed is his prophet, come to prayer, come to salvation, Allah is most great, there is no God but Allah."

Consider the following gang written document to see how the gang identity "Stones" is intermeshed with a mystical Black Stone[23]:

"BLACK STONE CREED

Out of the darkness into the light, Black Stone gave me courage. Black Stone give me sight, Black Stone give me something no man should be deprived of, a true and Divine Happiness called Stone love.

For many are called, but few are chosen, a head sees but only a few know that 9,000 miles due east across the waters likes a Black Stone which was placed there by the Holy Kaba. Many have tried to remove the Stone, but failed. For it is written that whom so ever falls upon the Stone will be broken. Whom so ever the stone falls upon shall be ground to dust. We hold to the bone, Almighty Black Stone.
ALL WELL
(Prayer for Feasting)

As Allah is my creator and I his image, I bless the fruits of the earth that I'm about to eat in knowledge and growth and of good health. Amen"

The "Cold Soldiers" army or nation appears in another highly secret oath of the Black P. Stones, as in the other internal documents above, the exact transcription is provided here and the present author suspects that some words were not correctly recalled by the informant:

"COLD SOLDIER'S OATH

My right hand to my father, God Allah and mister Emir, I hereby do declare to preserve the sacred doctrine of all Cold Soldiers silent brotherhood and keep the secret covenant of Cold Soldiers hidden from the non-believers. This I will do even to death. While I live the man and the Mecca remains safe, I will build upon and assure foundation stone and enforce law seven times both in and out. Those in relation in the sweet and honorable name of the Emmand the most high Allah, with my own hand will IL create, save, and destroy and woe unto the unbelievers. Allah speaks to man through man in a still small voice and those who hear will act as the soul dictates and the end shall always be right. But if ever I fail to perform my duties thus being a Cold Soldier or violating the universal laws of Allah and the Cold Soldiers Nation, thus at the risk of anothers life let my name be there after Judas peace and book of the dead. Let the finder of Dersvia point mental strength. Let the wrath of Allah's avenging angels strike 7 times upon the diaplate of heaven and my life span by the right hand of my brother man shortened."

The enormous social control of such religious and military language spells an enormous challenge to any urban area that contains such gang formations. In traditional "neutralization theory" in criminology, the offender minimizes the moral implications of the criminal behavior, or is able to rationalize the crime. Here we see such matters taken to a higher extreme, where the gang claims religious authority for its mission. Such ideologies are truly believed similar to the indoctrination of those who join or are recruited into cults. This has become more apparent to the present author over the years, and as a result, this edition has a new chapter to that effect.

A CRITIQUE OF GANG THEORY

What it is that constitutes the foundation for gang life in America seems to fundamentally revolve around three separate functions all of which must be present to some extent. First is the condition of social institutional erosion, either materially or functionally experienced as such, so that conventional social institutions are not effective sources of social control or socialization. Secondly, there is the function of either relative or absolute deprivation, either symbolic, or perceived; real or imagined; which is more specifically a test of what "hope" exists in traditional routes to success (e.g., through mainstream conventional social institutions). Thirdly, there is the more psychologically oriented state which functions as a human development or human capital lag or breakdown --- essentially a condition of underdeveloped or abused human capital, where society communicates loudly and clearly "there is no room for you in a productive capacity in America".

To the extent, therefore, that gang theory either fails to address these major and necessary components, such theory does not enjoy a firm foundation in the existing social science literature. It is very much a binary process whereby such incrementally adverse conditions virtually assure deviance or societal displacement. Those who are normal under these conditions probably gravitate towards gangs. One condition added to another compounds the problem of social adjustment. To restore even one of these conditions in conventional function, therefore, offers some hope of re-directing the lives of those who constitute the American gang population. Placing these youths in juvenile detention and state training schools serves no purpose other than to accelerate the binary process of dehumanization.

It is much as some may perceive it to be, a problem in the "value of human life" itself.

The initiation sequence to create and propel gang membership seems, from the existing literature, to require one or more of these three conditions. The higher the instability represented in these conditions, the higher the probability of gang crime. The existence of all three seems to assure a gang problem.

THE MILLER MISTAKE

Miller (1958) followed the psychological tradition of a microanalytic level of explanation for individual differences in "focal concerns of the lower class".[24] The logic offered was that Miller assumed a relationship between two macroanalytic concepts (e.g., culture and class) but used data from detached worker reports on gangs --- and some of his own participant observation and tape recordings (i.e., micro level data).[25] Miller (1958) assumed that if a household was "female-based", then it was lower class and associated with delinquency. In this fash-

ion he estimated that about half of all the USA is "directly influenced by lower class culture" with about 15 percent being a hard core lower class group.

This is fascinating social commentary but what does it really say about the origin and persistence of gangs in America? What is the causal nexus for Miller (1958)? Is this really anything more than academic stereotyping using gang motivational components?

Was Miller blowing smoke or did he have something to say based on good research? His primary data consisted of "over eight thousand pages of direct observational data". Social worker files is more like it. And unless it was data specifically collected with the purpose of measuring the concepts Miller was researching, it is little more than an ex post facto content analysis without the methodological rigor implied by content analysis. Eight million pages of nothing will not lead to something. It was a research mistake. A mistake that is often pointed out to students in the manner "calling a person something does not make them that".

If we are to believe Miller (1958), then cultural values or as Miller dubs them "focal concerns", are also by way of the causal chain in some sense "cultural imperatives". Overall what really was Miller's "motivational theory" of gangs?

First, it implied no structural problem for American society other than that of the lower class' own making. It was a convenient way to both label and stigmatize those who were poor and who were represented in gangs. The blame, if any, was the offenders. It had an aseptic analytical quality to the extent that it implied "you wouldn't be a gang member if you hadn't internalized those lower class values which have kept you out of the mainstream".

Secondly, it diverted attention from social policy initiatives. That is, little could be done to change "hillbilly cultural beliefs" of trouble, toughness, smartness, excitement, fate and autonomy. This thinking became a convenient way to avoid discussion of more systematic bases of the problem, e.g., at the macroanalytic level and the societal level which might call for some measure of social change. By which it is implied that the only blame is that on the individual hillbilly or Eurobilly for having such "lower class" motivations. It is a an individual "deficit" analysis.

If we were to extend Miller's (1958) analogy to the present, then our explanation of gangs would be little more than a variation of the "deficit" or "culturally deprived" thesis.[26] That is, the explanation of contemporary gangs ala Miller would be that the large numbers of African-Americans and Latinos represented in contemporary American gangs is explained by their version of being culturally disoriented or deprived. That is, they are hedonists, with an instinct for kicks, incapable of deferred gratification, who believe in luck rather than individual initiative. Or expressed somewhat differently, they "are not interested in what white people are interested in" or "they don't want to make it in America", which may be a convenient analysis for not doing anything about the problem other than locking them up.

The real danger here is twofold: (1) the Miller mistake deflects analysis from more critical aspects of our society wherein the option to change and reallocate resources might imply a corresponding change in the gang problem,[27] and (2) it is a cultural or motivational variation of the demonism theme --- i.e., the tautology that "they are gang members because they are lower class persons motivated by lowerclass focal concerns".

Let us examine this mistake by Miller by using a slightly higher level of disciplined thinking. Let us analyze this in terms of an axiomatic theoretical model. Here would be such a version:

A ---+----> B   lower class people have lower class values

B----+----> C   lower class values are found in gangs

Therefore, by transitivity, the proposition that:

A---+---> C   that lower class people constitute the gang threat. An equally vicious logical fallacy could be constructed along more patently racist lines. It casts blame, it does not explain. It exploits elitist preconceptions, it does not offer genuine solutions. It is a mistake. A mistake social scientists should assiduously avoid to truly understand the gang problem in America.

"WE ARE NOT A GANG, WE ARE...."

Another universal phenomenon in the urban context about gangs is that eventually when they become the target of close criminal justice scrutiny, like the Moonie who denies he is a cult member, the gang denies it is a gang and claims to be something else entirely --- indeed, it makes a claim of being a positive force in society, a prosocial organization. In some cities, the gang name itself is used for the duality: Gangster Disciples say they are not a gang, they are a community organization about "Growth" and "Development". In some cities in the northeast and southeast, spokespersons come forward to tell the mass media that gangs like the Latin Kings are not really gangs at all --- they are cultural groups. Thus, raising a charge of racism against the police and others who may want to investigate them.

This is not a new situation in the field of criminology. Cults usually deny they are cults, they profess instead to be firm believers in their religious doctrines. Very firm, apparently. Similarly, when major organized crime figures face the mass media, they deny that a "mob" even exists. It is common for

such major organized crime figures to say, typically on their way to being sentenced or in responding to an indictment, that "this garbage about a Cosa Nostra or a Mafia is all a hoax...we are only legitimate businessmen...we are being persecuted because we have Italian last names and belong to the same social athletic club".

Gangs must be expected to want to exploit any propaganda and misinformation they can put to effective use. Much of their propaganda centers around their recruitment myths: they are progressive even revolutionary organizations seeking some higher form of justice and greatness for all of humanity, then the kids join the gang to find out it was a crock! Similarly, gangs in prisons throughout the United States have used religious and ethnic group organizations as "covers" and "fronts" for their gang organizations. Jeff Fort's El Rukn gang organization claimed to be an Islamic sect of the Moorish American variety. It also happened to engage in murder and heroin trafficking, and eventually terrorism.

Gangs in places like Chicago make effective use of propaganda stunts like "litter clean up" campaigns. Maybe once in a lifetime they conspicuously do something genuinely positive, like help an elderly person across the street, and in their own minds this vastly outweighs the myriad of crimes and negative effects they have had on the community. Another common scenario is where they claim to be some contribution to law enforcement itself: they help identify or help to turn in some serial rapist, etc. Gang peace initiatives, commonly called "Gang Truces", represent another scam that gangs are prone to promote in order to claim bargaining power in restoring public order. Gang truces are discussed in greater detail later in this book. The idea is that they want to be included and recognized as a power broker in reducing gang violence. It is an issue not unrelated to that of negotiating with terrorists.

SUMMARY AND CONCLUSION

The above discussion has broken tradition somewhat by a criticism of two earlier examples of gang research (Whyte, 1943; and Miller, 1958). Only the historical record can show whether this was correct or incorrect. And the historical record is something we should be keenly concerned about. Indeed, this author believes it has been overly ignored or perhaps even misrepresented in some contemporary gang analyses. This is especially true regarding the tendency where Shaw and Mc Kay appear to have been some of the most influential and the least recognized contributors to this literature.

Any systematic and integrated theory of gangs must, as pointed out here, contain the elements for being tested by all three units of analysis: (1) the individual, (2) the community, and (3) the society. It should also speak to both the micro and macroanalytic concerns raised by social scientists.

A frequent first impression in reading the gang literature is that almost every author seems to begin with an expression of frustration to the effect that "unfortunately, we know nothing about gangs". Truly our literature is fragmented and does not answer all of our questions. But it does contain some historical truths as well.

The other problem is that some authors find it convenient to engage in a denunciation of all past scholarship, as if gangs had just landed in a space-ship. Such writers follow the mold of an Evangelical preacher who is the only one with the "true story", with the "word". Serious students of criminology should beware of such pretensions, because that is not social science, that is intuition and revelation.

Gangs today are so strong in some communities around the United States that they are the "power" to be reckoned with. Some level three gangs are intergenerational in nature: the children and the parents are members of the same gang. The homogenizing process that generates new potential gang recruits is the criminal justice system itself, by the propensity to use the criminal and penal sanction against minority group members and poor persons. The gang is the one place such "records" and deviant labels take on a reverse effect. Perhaps we should, in our communities, seek to resolve human conflicts by methods proven at the international level: dispute resolution, mediation, conflict management, etc. The alternative to peaceful means to resolve the underlying issues of the gang problem is a military style solution, and one of suppression. Do you want surveillance video cameras permanently installed on light and telephone poles on every street corner in your community, where the police monitor everything you do? Do you want --- as has been seriously discussed[28] --- sophisticated listening devices (applications of defense and munitions industry technology) also monitoring your entire community --- such technology exists that can identify the precise location of the sound of shots from firearms, and could help catch those persons shooting guns in gang dominated communities. Do you want police agencies to handle the gang threat the same way the federal government handled the David Koresh religious cult in Waco, Texas?

DISCUSSION QUESTIONS:

(1) In a 1956 article entitled "Is Gang-Busting Wise?" by Shaw and Sorrentino[29], it is suggested that what this book calls level zero gang formations can be redirected into prosocial community activities. Every community probably has level zero gang types. Do you believe these groups can be prevented, through local adult involvement, from patterns of serious crime or delinquency?

(2) What limitations does the qualitative research method (oral history, field studies, etc) have in terms of unit of analysis in relationship to "levels of explanation" in terms of theory?

(3) What basic human needs would have to be satisfied in order to counteract the attractiveness of gang affiliation?

HOW MANY CHILDREN MUST DIE BEFORE WE GET SERIOUS ABOUT GANGS?

In early November of 1996 six-year-old Nichols "Nico" Contreras was asleep in bed at his grandmother's house in Aurora, Illinois. The gang nightmare caught this child sleeping: gang gunfire in the neighborhood. A bullet from the gang gunfire outside entered the house and hit the six-year-old "Nico" who died immediately. When a child is literally not safe in bed at his grandmother's house anymore, it really is time to "wake up" the citizens on the gang issue.

Hundreds of citizens were galvanized to "do something" about the gang problem because of this tragedy. A year after the killing of "Nico", 250 people marched in the town of Aurora to get their message out: "Stop the Violence".

But what legal powers can we use to get "smarter" as society in dealing with violent gangs and gang members?

LIKE SEX OFFENDERS, REGISTER GANG MEMBERS: AN EXAMPLE OF A NEGATIVE TOLERANCE POLICY ON GANGS

Under the concept of "negative tolerance", the idea is to increase the cost of doing "gang business". One benefit gang members currently enjoy without cost is a "master status" of being a gang member, witnesses are afraid to testify against them, thus many criminal cases are "dropped" (Miethe and McCorkle, 1997: p. 425). Maybe it is time to take away this "hidden benefit" for gang members.

Sexual predators are feared by the public. Sex offenders throughout the United States are now required to register with their local police department: if they go "AWOL", they can be re-arrested for the crime of not registering. Sex offenders contested this in court, all the way up to the Supreme Court, they argued that this was "cruel and unusual" punishment and they argued that it was also unconstitutional because they already "served their time" and that the registration process was therefore like being punished twice for the same crime. The United States Supreme Court responded: sorry, but it is in fact constitutional for a society to protect itself from a perceived threat to public safety.

Gang members are also feared by the public and wreak much havoc on any community they live in and travel to. It is a realistic possibility that one of the future "smart laws" would therefore be to create a special category of offender in the criminal code, similar to the "sex offender", which would be called the "gang offender". Making the "gang offender" register with police and publishing their names and addresses would do much to take away the gang member's sense of "anonymity": they would be known to the public.

Do you think this is a good idea? Or is this taking things to extreme measures and "over-reacting" to the gang problem?

End Notes:

[1] Geis quotes the rather vicious account of a London gang circa 1712 known as the Mohocks who would today be regarded as a middle-upper class organized, continuing variation of "wilding" and far more brutally violent than anything surfacing in the contemporary media about such events (Geis, 1965: p. 6).

[2] See Tompkins (1966) for citations by state in America, as well as citations of gang literature from localities such as Japan, Canada, Britain, Australia, Ceylon, Taiwan, and France (pp. 71-77).

[3] This, too, appears to be a historical continuity in terms of gang crime threats. As recently as the Fall of 1993, a Disciples gang leader let it be known that he was putting out a hit on one or more police officers working on the southside. Other police officers did not immediately swell to their defense, because the officers so targeted or threatened with a "hit" had been accepting pay-offs from the same gang to facilitate the gang crime pattern (typically, drug sales operations). Once compromised, it is difficult for a police officer to enforce a "crack down" order; the gangs expect their protection regardless seems to be the historical trend.

[4] Whyte, for example, uses extensively the verb form "ganging; not "gangbanging" as is popularized in layman's terminology today.

[5] Chapter 15 addresses this issue in much greater detail.

[6] So much so for women Latinos, in fact, that a recent census report showed their earnings declining; that is, while historically women in America have tended to make about 70 cents on each dollar that the American male makes, this figure had dropped considerably for Latino women.

[7] And, of course, anti-semitic.

[8] Today, in Chicago, members of what have been called "Peoples" gangs (Black P. Stones, Vice Lords, etc) now refer to themselves --- among African-Americans at least --- as "Brothers", not "peoples".

[9] See appendix A of the 1981, third edition of Whyte (pp. 279-360).

[10] The reader should note, for the record, that what you see is not always what you get. Hagedorn (p. 26) takes the position that apparently its not how you study gangs, but "when" that's important. Ergo, Whyte's study was the best book since Thrasher till

Hagedorn, because its data dealt with the period of the depression. The serious reader should examine Rundquist and Sletto.

[11] Hagedorn's criticism of Spergel, we recall, was that Spergel was a good example of theory misguiding research. A social scientist without a theory is like a soldier shooting blanks. Hypothesis testing cannot be done until there is a theory operationalized to guide data collection. The problem for many social scientists, those reviewed here included, is their dogmatic and male authoritarian bias puts them in the situation of denouncing all other theories than their own. That, at least, is their justification for testing only their own theories.

[12] Geis (1965, p. 22) is one of the few to take notice of Whyte's admission of vote fraud. Geis also takes Whyte to task over the bar scene where Whyte, intent on meeting a girl as a data source over drinks, which if we are to extend Hagedorn's criticism of "courthouse criminologists" in this case means adding "cocktail criminologists", because when Whyte approached a threesome at a bar table a man promptly threatened to throw Whyte down the stairs, and needless to say Whyte immediately abandoned this particular research methodology.

[13] Keiser (1979) reports some emotional distancing trouble in doing participant observation with Chicago's Vice Lords. "As a participant observer I was involved in the first stages of one actual gang fight, and was part of the preparations for another that never materialized" (Keiser, 1979: p. 88). Remember Patty Hearst? When she passively participated did that mean she was no longer a hostage, but a confederate in the crime? That's why she was convicted.

[14] Some scholars obviously are more motivated than others to get the truth: Professor Martin Sanchez-Jankowski was shot in his efforts over ten years to study gangs in three states. The Sanchez-Jankowski (1991) study shows it is not always easy to carry out true participant observation research on serious gangs. Obviously, prior to Sanchez-Jankowski (1991) a variety of authors have shown us it is easy to collect data on playgroups or level zero gangs (e.g., Alfalfa and Spanky groups).

[15] See Angelo R. Orlandella, "A More Effective Strategy for Dealing With Inner City Street Corner Gangs", Journal of Gang Research (in press).

[16] See Karen A. Joe, 1993, "The Legacy of Street Corner Society and Gang Research in the 1990s: An Interview with William F. Whyte", The Gang Journal (now the Journal of Gang Research), Volume 1, Number 4, pp. 45-51.

[17] Also, not to belabor the obvious, but to the extent that gangs were a problem in the 1970's (some say there was a "lull" in gang crime in the seventies), there were a number of gang studies --- and some current authors should be delighted to see many of these were qualitative affairs. And some of the authors published their results in critical criminology journals.

[18] A gang crime unit officer in Chicago during September 1993 disclosed that he had heard rumors of gangs getting together nationally for the purpose of staging large scale "rioting" three years from now to influence national elections. I remarked, disbelievingly, "that is impressive that they could plan anything that far in advance".

[19] Poor whites in Appalachia, etc, as well as those clustered on the fringe of or inside our nation's urban areas may not admit it as readily, but they too feel such prejudice and discrimination; not along the lines of race, but along the lines of social status and social worth. Indeed it is a social complexity all its own to find such persons derogated as "white trash" who themselves become the often frequent basis for actual conflict with African-Americans.

[20] On the continuing theme of the importance of theory, this article by Mc Kay tends to clarify some of the problems now being rehashed in our literature regarding "what can be done" to help solve or prevent gang crimes. Mc Kay argued that even treatment must be based on a theory of crime causation (1949, p. 40).

[21] The research findings on Chicago's Safe School Study reported by Tromanhauser (1981: p. 183) showed that at least half of all public school students reported some street gangs in their neighborhoods (56%) or some street gang members in their school (52.3%).

[22] Hagedorn and Moore's discussion of such institutionalization (1988) uses language remarkably similar to Mc Kay's (1949), but this contribution by Mc Kay (1949) is never apparently acknowledged whether or not these authors were aware of its existence.

[23] Another source provides this typed version reproduced exactly: "CORNER STONE. Man is the corner stone of all creations. Many are called but few are chosen. We are those chosen few symbolically proclaiming our national birth rights of all creation [29]

to do so. We must measure within the bonds of moderation reason. We must practice to free our selves from one bondage matters. Man is god allah within himself. Allah is mind and mind made all creations. The corner stone represents all four branches of stone belief for the uplifting of peace and unity among all stones. In the east sites of the holy city of meca, in the holy city of mecca sites the holy kabba, in the upper left hand corner of the holy kabba sites the eternal black stone which we all represent for his everlighting our sunrise for it's the last giving love light to all peace 360 of knowledge and wisdom. (amen)."

[24] Note, however, that the many continuing, lifetime, contributions well after and beyond this 1958 contribution by Miller make Miller a major and ongoing contributor, like Malcolm W. Klein, to the gang literature.

[25] It is, at a minimum, a large problem of what researchers call the "rules of correspondence" between concepts and what is actually measured.

[26] For an excellent critique of these "deficit-deficiency" stereotyped concepts, see Joseph L. White, 1984, The Psychology of Blacks: An Afro-American Perspective, Englewood Cliffs, New Jersey: Prentice-Hall, Inc.

[27] I have always assumed that a social problem, like gangs in America, is a problem about which something can be done. That does not emerge from Miller (1958). What would Miller have us do to fight gang crime? Perhaps instill conservative values, I don't know.

[28] See John Mintz, "Agencies Listen to New Crime-Fighting Idea: System Would Hear Gunfire and Inform Police", Chicago Sun-Times, p. 38, Oct. 1, 1993. The little known research by Johnson (1949) showed some merit to such an approach. It is an approach that is also well-grounded in the literature: that not every waking moment of a gang member's life is spent in a ruthless pursuit of crime and wrong-doing. See also: Jereczek, 1962.

"Gang Members Who Get On The Police Force in Large Cities Like Chicago"

There have been a number of such cases over the years, and it involves the situation where a gang member is also a police officer. How can this be? Students are encouraged to read books like the *Blue Collar Community* to get a foundation for how this happens. In the book *Blue Collar Community*, 1974, by William Kornblum, you will see examples of how gang members import their gang conflicts into the work setting when they take jobs at a local steel mill in southeast Chicago.

Kornblum helps us to understand how the broad culture impacts on the work environment; and part of that culture is gang life. One of the least researched aspects of gang activity in the United States is its impact on the work and business environment.

For a disturbing story about gang members who become police officers and the inevitable problems that emerge from this kind of "bad guy with a badge", see the case of former Chicago Police Officer Edward Lee Jackson. Jackson was a member of the Conservative Vice Lords and also a Chicago cop. This story is described at the CNN website: http://cnn.com/CNN/bureaus/chicago/stories/9702/gangcop/details/index.html

This story describes what are called "rogue cops": those who, like "Pacman" the gang member cop, used their badge and authority as a basis to shakedown, extort, and criminally victimize others.

Apparently, "Pacman" did not operate alone: he was a tactical police officer who worked out of a police station in the Austin district of Chicago, on Chicago's westside. There the rogue cops would routinely engage in shakedowns of drug pushers, or help drug dealers by providing them an "security escort" to transport drugs, and in other cases simply rob persons suspected of being drug dealers. Actual undercover photographs of these kind of events are shown on the CNN website. It is the story labelled "Gang-Member Cop" dated 2-18-97.

Insane Gangster Disciples
(AKA: "White Gangster Disciples")

Somewhat autonomous gangs that may have few Black members, and where the typical member is white, when using a gang name traditionally associated with Blacks or African-Americans, will often arise in areas away from the gang's epicenter and will use the prefix "Insane". Often "Insane Gangster Disciples" is equivalent to "White Gangster Disciples". Often called "wannabes" because of their overidentification with Hip Hop culture and gangster rap, they become the "real thing" when they easily meet the real opposition or when they enter the criminal justice system.

Chapter 12

AN ORGANIZATIONAL APPROACH TO GANG ANALYSIS

INTRODUCTION

A common fact about modern higher threat level gangs is that they mimic, imitate, or emulate sophisticated organizations by the very nature of their titles of authority and their authoritarian chain of command structure. Gangs like the Gangster Disciples (i.e., the Gangster Disciples, aka the Brothers of the Struggle, B.O.S.) use a corporate structure that includes the very top gang leader as the Chairman of the Board (also known affectionately as their "King"), and includes a large network of gang management staff, as depicted earlier in this book. Within the Latin or Hispanic "folks" gang conglomerates like the Spanish Gangster Disciples (SGD's), they have an Executive Committee, the top leader of which holds the business style title of "C.E.O."[1]. The SGD "Latin Folks" conglomerate currently includes a number of gangs such as the Two Sixers, the Imperial Gangsters, the Maniac Latin Disciples (M.L.D.'s), Ambrose, Latin Eagles, and others[2]. Gangs like the Insane Spanish Cobras include positions of national rank as well[3] and represent organizational interactions of gang leaders across state lines. In some gangs like the Imperial Gangsters the various chiefs of the "sets" or "factions" of the same gang act as major shareholders in the corporate crime decision making structure of the gang[4]. Gangs like the Maniac Latin Disciples (M.L.D.'s) include positions of authority that imitate government organizations[5]. Gangs have their own organizational language to define anyone as outsiders or non-members or as members of the opposition (e.g., "flakes"). Some early internal literature from the Crips emphasized their money making purpose in life, such as "power in this society is money, so the sword we must possess is money...we must adopt a business organization mentality". It is important, therefore, to examine the organizational factors about gangs.

The best evidence is that which comes from social science research. Anyone can hypothesize, or guess, at what causes a gang to form and what causes someone to join a gang. Anyone can conjecture about it and anyone can form an opinion. Opinions are like noses, everyone has one. But hard information, quantifiable information, data and findings from empirical research is probably going to enjoy greater merit. Particularly when the data collection has been guided by theory or the prior social science literature.

One such body of theory that needs to be applied to gang analysis is that of organizational theory and our knowledge of group affiliation and group dynamics. The value of such an approach will be developed here along with suggestions for research methodology and the application to present problems.

177

WHAT KNOWLEDGE DO WE WANT TO DEVELOP ABOUT GANGS?

What knowledge we want to develop will be importantly shaped by what our framework of analysis is and what data is collected. Clearly, there are different knowledge development needs regarding gang crime in America. Here are just a few of these different types of knowledge needs.

1. Law enforcement. From a law enforcement point of view a gang analysis is useful if it helps to triage in terms planning and response to gang problems. There is also the need for an analysis that can guide the use of criminal investigation strategies. More importantly, there is a need to prevent serious gang crimes like drive-by shootings.

2. Parent's and Child Development. From the point of view of the parent who learns that gangs exist in the community, the parent wants to know how to avoid having their child end up as a gang member. The parent wants to be able to know the "warning signs" of gang affiliation, so it can be confronted at an early point a child's development. Such would be gang prevention at the primary level.

3. Primary and Secondary Level Educator's. From the point of view of our primary and secondary level educational institutions, both public and private, it is a matter of "keeping the peace" --- at least during school hours and throughout the school term. Their mission to educate the youths of our society is threatened when gang violence or intimidation has a significant impact on the social climate of the educational institution. What the educator wants is better control strategies. Educators cannot revitalize the community infrastructure in which they work. Their only option is to employ better management techniques to deal with the gang problem. Perhaps much more could and should be done to also address, by prevention efforts, one of the most consistently significant background factors found among gang members --- the fact that the typical gang member has a significantly higher likelihood of having an experience where he or she assaulted a school teacher. Patterns of suspension and being expelled from school also are highly correlated with the gang member profile. Thus, a working agenda for schools would be to being to provide more prevention of events likely to label a student as violent and propel someone further into the criminal justice system, and also improve school safety by simply reducing assaults on teachers. This would in turn reduce suspensions and expulsions.

4. Community Organizations. From the viewpoint of local community organizations, they need to know what can be done to pacify and prevent the escalation of the gang problem. It is a damage control operation, the gangs may already be present, the problem is how to limit new recruits, encourage periphery members to attach themselves to more legitimate pursuits, while targeting core members and leaders for something else --- prosecution, reintegration, rehabilitation, etc. Taking the bang out of the gang would mean removing its economic incentives and preventing new recruits. Combined with pro-active law enforcement efforts this might give the community back to its citizens by taking power away from the gang. Where there exists a modest gang problem already, efforts to deal with it will be those at the secondary level of prevention and intervention. It is easier to prevent the problem than to rehabilitate those who manifest the problem.

5. Correctional Service/Treatment Programs. Whether it is in the public or private sector, as a not-for-profit organization that is citywide in its catchment area, or whether it is a service modality that becomes a part of regular "probation" or "post-release" aftercare services within a correctional agency, there is a different kind of knowledge need here. What is needed here is: how to prevent secondary deviation, how to prevent relapse and recidivism in light of the more obvious threat posed by a return to gang crime, and the powerful resources that the gang can offer in both rewardive and coercive ways. This would constitute prevention and intervention at the tertiary level.

Add to this a host of basic questions from all avenues of life. From the business world, from academia, from architectural and community planners, etc. The point should be clear: depending on how the gang problem impacts on someone, such will tend to shape their specific knowledge needs. The homicide investigator is not going to want to know very much about the potential for rehabilitating gang offenders. Similarly, the public official charged with the responsibility to "do something about" the gang problem is not going to be particularly interested in social-anthropology dimensions of the rites, customs, and special language in the gang. That kind of material from participant observation may make interesting reading, but it is not likely to help an elected official develop a solution to the gang problem. We will need hard data for policy analysis and program development.

In fact, this is really an issue having to do with "solutions". Perhaps some scholars will take the position that there are no solutions to gang crime, just as it can be argued it is a problem about which something can clearly be done. For the gang crime victim, the solution desired more often than not is the use of the penal sanction: imprisonment. The issue is: "what is to be done" about the gang crime problem in America.

How we conceive of the gang problem is therefore going to determine what we can say about what should be done, if anything. Good research is a way to impact on or change social policy. One fear is that even if there was an unlimited research budget and the principal investigator was able to completely replicate all prior research, we would still be in the situation of having a great many unanswered questions.[6] It is a matter of being able to generalize findings beyond a specific sample or specific time period or situation. It is here that organizational theory has as much a role as research methodology to play in future knowledge development regarding the gang problem.

WHAT DO WE MEAN BY ORGANIZATIONAL THEORY?

In the social sciences organizational theory is the study of a variety of organizational forms and processes. In business management, in sociology, in political science --- depending on what the discipline of orientation is, there are different aspects of organizational life that are examined. The advantage of organizational theory is that it has this interdisciplinary aspect: it is relevant to psychology, sociology, business administration, political science, and others.[7]

Organizational theory, no doubt about it, is often associated with the study of formal and complex organizations, and bureaucracy. The critic might say that trying to apply a social organizational theory to the gang problem is tantamount to overkill. Some might say, as well, that we need to study the gang in the social-psychological laboratory which has been the primary knowledge development approach for small group behavior. The problem is that gangs are more than small groups and less than bureaucracies.[8] But is a mistake to believe gangs do not have some things in common with formal organizations and we should recognize from our organizational literature the gradients of formality and organizational development in groups.

Some of the larger gangs do have elaborate written codes as will be discussed later. They do issue written "memos" and "updates". Some have complex mechanisms, including the creation and operation of for-profit and not-for-profit corporations. White racist gangs even make use of computers.

So, here an effort will be made to demonstrate the value of such an organizational approach to the study of gangs. It shall set the basis for a method of gang analysis in terms of level of organizational development that is provided in Chapter 14.

THE VALUE OF RETIRED OR INACTIVE GANG MEMBERS AS DATA SOURCES

The value from an organizational approach is this: one of the best ways to study any organization is to interview its former members or employees. Indeed, from what we know about data contamination and measurement error from self-report methods with offenders, there is another justification

as well. It is this: most law offenders under report their bad qualities, and over report their good qualities. Mostly, offenders are less likely to report their own deviance, and more likely to report on the deviance/crime of their confederates/associates/friends.

What we are recommending to be studied here is not the individual gang member, but the gang as a group, the gang as a social organizational unit.

OVERCOMING METHODOLOGICAL PITFALLS IN ETHNOMETHODOLOGY

The problem with Whyte, discussed in a previous chapter, is but one of the problems of ethnomethodology involving gangs and crime. Remember, that with some white gangs it can also be essentially the study of an extremist hate-group not dissimilar to the KKK or Nazi party. Any scholar who "hangs out" with a gang must at some time report, if the gang is really doing anything illicit or illegal, that the researcher is regarded with distrust. Not just as an outsider, but as someone who could be a government agent.

The marginality of the ethnomethodology research, the participant observer, is that if it truly involves a Ph.D. or graduate level researcher studying a deviant group, then the researcher is basically in the position of trying to get information as a "hanger on", not as truly a confederate in crime. Even Saul Alinsky's participant observation of the Chicago mob meant simply being a "groupee", not being privy to authority.

What must be challenged is the notion often made from an ethnomethodology viewpoint that the only way we can understand the gang problem is from such an "inside" story. For to understand the social organization in question one truly need not "join". The difference between Whyte's "joining" behavior, and that of traditional law enforcement infiltration techniques, is that the latter definitely can take on leadership roles and make use of experimental conditions to assess organizational functioning. Whyte did caution against such "controlling" influence. What we have here is also an enormous ethical problem for researchers.

One of the pitfalls is obviously ethical. A real sociologist is bound by the ethics of the American Sociological Association which explicitly forbids conduct such as Whyte's involvement in vote fraud. To "join" a gang or an extremist organization is to essentially be a part of the very problem which is being researched. To what extent would the confused, well-meaning, liberal researcher, by simply "hanging out" with the gang also become an important resource for them to exploit and manipulate? If gangs thrive on attention, then they will certainly prosper with the kind of sympathetic treatment they get from some authors.

While some may be reluctant to do it, it should not be viewed as objectionable for some authors to routinely invite what they portray to be "heavy hitting criminals" into their homes. But let's be honest here: there is an immense social distance between the social status of most Ph.D.'s and typical gang members or offenders. They are in different social worlds.

Indeed, while such risk-taking is often essential, and it was this willingness of the researcher to get away from the office and prison cell type of interview situation that led to some of our most important contributions to criminology (e.g., Sutherland's research).[9] Rather, the issue has to do with the quality and the nature of the data being gathered specifically on gangs as social groups and organizations, not individual offenders.

The problem is this, even for a researcher to become a "non-crime involved hanger-on", it must be recognized that the moment a researcher declares an affinity to group goals and values with the target organization/group, then the researcher necessarily accepts the definition of the situation offered by such respondents/cases/informants, etc. What gives us the assumption that gang members have such high levels of personal insight that they can explain "their own story" satisfactorily and objectively to be able to test theory? A sociologist today cannot ethically conceal his/her identity, disguise self to under represent educational attainment, or through a regression in vocabulary try to impart that deceit. Human subjects have rights. So do gang organizations.[10]

The other problem is that of group or inter-gang conflict. One cannot become identified with a particular gang and as easily make a transition to a rival gang group. To collaborate with one group may very well preclude the possibility of getting any cooperation from other groups. Here again the tendency in prior research to focus on the "individual" as a way to understand an essentially group and organizational problem does not lead to a logical accumulation of social science knowledge --- it gives us only a larger puzzle.

For example, Horowitz (1983, 1987) describes the importance of a sense of honor in the etiological sequence leading to gang violence. In some sense, personal autonomy, independence, or self-management equates as a cultural basis for honor. As Reid (1990: p. 84) correctly notes along this basis, then:

"For a parent to supervise the gang member's behavior too closely would compromise his honor and development as a man. It also might alienate him from the approved family and community activities in which he takes part" (Reid, 1990: p. 84).

What remains unclear is how does either the ethnomethodological researcher or a detached worker impact on or threaten this same variable? Is such a close involvement with individual gang members or their "top dogs" viewed as honor enhancing or honor threatening? On the basis of the gang classification system that will be presented in full later in this book, it would appear to me that at the lower level of gang formalization, such intrusion is status enhancing because it involves highly educated adults recognizing youths as a group power; but at the higher end of the gang development spectrum, such "hangers on" must clearly be regarded as a threat to honor, in the sense that to divulge too much information to such "hangers on" is to certainly place gang crime operations in potential jeopardy.

There is a problem when gang research that depends for its "evidence" as that of simple routine field reports from detached workers and social workers "hanging out" with gangs, such as that research methodology used by Miller (1958) and others. The difficulty is that even though such persons presumably remained on the "periphery", did not join in the deviance or crime, did not do drugs with the gang members they were studying, etc, there is still the complication of the interpersonal involvement arising from such a reporting source. Whether it is a university student doing an internship, being paid for the research/service, or as a hired hand using indigenous aids or ex-offenders, these persons are important new actors and if they are at all effective in making a surreptitious or open entry into the confidence of the gang members, then they still must face the criticism that the role structure they entered into will importantly color and shape whatever information they garnish or collect.

The research dilemma with participant observation and gangs is that you are damned if you do join in and you are damned if you don't. If you do join in their illicit activities like Whyte did, then you are producing the very deviance you are studying. If you don't join in, then you are not "privy" to the real "inside story".

Interviewing offenders is not the easiest task. In fact if someone does carry out a quality "oral history" interview, they are going to hear some shocking details of crime. And like the interrogator they cannot afford to provide editorial comment to the offender, or go off into a treatment modality providing "counseling". As much as you might like to or want to do so, particularly when an offender is describing in bloody detail his accomplishments at "tree jumping" (i.e., rape) or victimizing senior citizens, to do so is to cut off further disclosures. So in light of this, we must evaluate data sources from such detached workers and similarly employed data collection persons to the effect that if they were in the business of informal counseling and covert therapy, then what they heard is probably not the real story.

The moment you attack or question the morality of a gang member, that is the moment the relationship changes and what gets disclosed to the "observer" is probably self-fulfilling ---- they hear what the gang member thinks they want to hear.

In summary, it may be less problematic for solid research to focus not on the individual offender, but on the group; and this can be accomplished, as indicated above, by alternatives to traditional "participant observation" or related ethnomethodology approaches. Indeed, perhaps these approaches if they are to prove their worth should be applied in the analytic context suggested here: for the group or gang organization as the unit of analysis, not the individual member. As an example, the case study approach used by Shaw and McKay did not simply mean a "depth interview" with the offender in question, it also meant using all other outside information --- interviews with family, neighbors, significant others, and of course, official information from secondary data sources (police records, school records, public records, etc).

ELEMENTS OF AN ORGANIZATIONAL ANALYSIS

The value of specifying the elements of an organizational analysis is to provide the agenda for future research in terms of measurable variables; factors that can be used for gang analysis and classification. One of these primary factors that distinguishes a formalized gang from that of an informal group is the existence of a formalized written or oral code. But, as we shall see later, there are many other such social organizational factors to consider. A fuller accounting of the elements of an organizational analysis will be provided in chapter 14. For now it is important to simply introduce some of these elements such as the formalized "code".

The value of specifying these measurable elements of organizational analysis was previously demonstrated by the research of Arnold (1965). Arnold was one of the few gang researchers to take earlier definitions of the gang such as those by Thrasher and to quantify these factors in order to generate a rating system for gangs. Indeed, Arnold's research is one of the few to actually measure gang membership size and to recognize some of the commonalities and differences between gangs and other forms of group affiliation.[11]

THE FORMALIZED WRITTEN OR ORAL CODE

With the publication in 1847 by J.H. Green of The Secret Band of Brothers or, The American Outlaws[12] comes the first reference to gang formations in America having a written Constitution and by-laws dating back to 1798 (Green, 1847: p. 90).

It reads like a precursor to a mixture between the Aryan Brotherhood and the Ku Klux Klan. It specifies the authority differentiation between members and officers, the latter known as Grand Masters. It explicitly allowed for male or females (pp. 90-91). It had religious undercurrents, but was clearly against organized religion, speaking often of the "God of Nature". In so doing, it represented an early form of the "quasi-religious" or "religious front" gang formation such as Jeff Fort's El Rukns.

Like many contemporary urban variations it had a Robin Hood clause as well:

"Article 13.   We pledge ourselves to take from the rich and give to the poor....we agree to take from the one, and give to the other; and that the wealthy, or the enemies of this society, shall be the ones we will strive to harass, by disapprobation of their tyrannical course." (Green, 1847: p. 94).

The official name of this gang was the Holy Brotherhood also known as the Secret Band of Brothers. Its constitution and by-laws explicitly paralleled the contemporary Aryan Brotherhood gang norm of "kill to get in, die to get out" in its Article 22. And, as will be discussed in a later chapter it had in common with more sophisticated gangs and organized crime the capability of "enforcement":

"Article 22.   Having now informed you of some of the benefits and duties falling upon you, as a Brother, I now come to an article of penalty, which you will find requires your close attention, as follows: If you betray a Brother, this Constitution allots to you but one punishment, which is ---DEATH BY VIOLENT MEANS!---and this sentence will surely be carried into effect---as sure as that there is a sun at noonday, or stars at night; and the Brother, so terminating your career, shall receive, in compensation, the sum of THREE HUNDRED DOLLARS, which shall be paid to him by a Grand Master, for this society" (Green, 1847: p. 100).

Like many contemporary gangs, language itself had explicit double meanings in terms of a cipher code.[13]   The gang described by Green used a numbering code as well, with values between zero and nine. For example, the word "naugh" associated with the digit "9" meant an African-American:

"Third: Naugh --- a flash word, signifies Size and Complexion --- and, therefore, each number has a double meaning. No. 1 signifies the person to be large and tall, 2 low and heavy, 3 tall and slender, 4 medium, 5 small, 6 sandy complexion, 7 light complexion, 8 dark complexion, 9 Coloured" (Green, 1847: p. 109).

For the record, these white gang offenders predated contemporary forms by using the word "crib" as slang or subcultural argot to refer to ones "house" (Green, 1847: p. 113).

If we can believe Green, then this group was either the first known gang with its own formalized constitution and by-laws or it was clearly an antecedent of organized crime in America. Either way it deserves our interest and tends to support the proposition that gangs are not only normal, they have always existed in one organizational form or another in America. It also shows the enduring historical commonality among gangs that they adopt special symbols and use a linguistic code that allows them --- like the 19th century Budhuk gangs in India --- to maintain the duplicity of gang affiliation when interacting with or in the presence of non-gang members: they can literally carry on a conversation using gang argot (e.g., slang) that a non-gang member would not normally be able to truly understand.

As the study of African-American psychology, and other cultures as well, has shown, this can also consist of an oral tradition. If it formalizes roles or language or sanctions for the violation of group norms, then whether it is a written or oral code it still qualifies as a formalization of gang structure. Its existence means the difference between a gang organization and that of simple recurrent aggregative social encounters (e.g., meeting persons you know by face on an ongoing basis, but with little normative consensus, for example at a bus stop on the way to work in the morning, etc).

CONSOLIDATION, ALLIANCES AND GANG MERGERS

While many social scientists discount the work by Sale (1971) because it was clearly the work of a journalist, not a trained social scientist, such accounts are useful to the extent that we can assume they are factual. A gang as an organization if it is to survive over time must face the possibility of consolidation, alliances, and mergers. Sale's description of the etiology of Jeff Fort's gang career prior to the emergence of the El Rukns is illustrative. In describing the emergence of the Blackstone Rangers, Sale narrates that:

"He told me then how, back in 1959, there had been a small street clique on 66th St. that had a modest ten members. Jeff Fort was the man at its head and it controlled a turf known as Jackson Park. But there had been a rival gang, small one as well...on 70th Street...the gangs clashed...They fought together many times. When they found that neither one could inflict a final, decisive defeat, they came together and talked. A short time later they combined" (Sale, 1971: pp. 63-64).

It is curious, in light of this general trend in the literature showing such varieties of conflict/alliance/new formations, that conflict theory itself has not been applied to the gang problem.

Clearly, the existence of gangs that have undergone organizational development processes such as consolidation, the creation of alliances, and even mergers sets this type of gang apart from one that is in its incubational stage or its embryonic level of development. It is the role of the criminal justice system that plays an important part in the creation of such alliances, mergers, and even consolidation. Consolidation by sheer minority number strength may be a possible hypothesis for the emergence of the Aryan Nation white racist gangs in prison. Such a natural consolidation hypothesis must compete with the rival explanation of fostered development and informal cultivation from prison staff themselves, where the existence of such a white gang counterbalances the domination of minority group gangs in the correctional setting.

The bottom line here is that we do not know how exactly the Aryan Brotherhood emerged to be represented in so many different prisons throughout the United States and in many different communities outside of prison and no such news report like R.T. Sale has been able to "get the story". Nor has any sociologist, ethnographer, or activist reported such knowledge. The only explanation offered to date is that prison transfers of such gang members meant the reproduction of such gangs to all new environments to which the inmate gang members were shipped. From an organizational viewpoint, that might mean the need for a central national unit to which to ship such inmates rather than to other institutions that are not experiencing a gang problem.

In fact, we know really little about the "franchising" of gangs outside of limited data (Waldorf, 1993), some estimates on the problem of gang migration from police, and the one case reported in the present study of the franchising of the Latin Kings to the State of Indiana through Chicago's southside "bush" chapter of the Kings. It is the issue of whether gangs can be "exported" from one state to another. Klein takes the DEA and others to task for simply assuming such a direct exportation or "national conspiracy" kind of explanation, for example, of the existence of Crips and Bloods in many different states (1990). It is an issue needing more research and less conjecture. Like other controversies in the gang arena, the truth is probably somewhere in between the extreme polar views (i.e., no gang migration occurs versus much gang migration occurs).

COMMUNITY AND SOCIAL STIGMA

Without stigma as a deviant group, the gang would not be a gang it would be a legitimate voluntary association in the pre-incorporation stage. The stigma arises, mostly, from fear of criminal victimization. Shireman, et al (1958)[14] described one such gang at its most embryonic level of organizational development called the "Clovers" who came to be regarded as a gang by the community and by the process of the self-fulfilling prophecy were, ipso facto, a gang in spite of their lack of formalization in other organizational qualities:

"The group of Negro boys, who later became known as the "Clovers", range in age from 14 to 18. Most of them are new to the community, are of Southern background, and have lived elsewhere in Chicago before moving to Hyde Park. Although most of them live within a five block radius of the HPNC, ninety-five percent of them were not members of the agency and had no previous experience in the HPNC program. They attended the local elementary and high schools. Most of the youths would be classified as being from upper-lower class families, if we take into account the realistic and preferred values and economic status of the Hyde Park community. The boys did not identify themselves as being a group or gang, although they were identified in this manner by the adults of the community because they gathered frequently in front of the home of one of the youths, and often traveled together within the community. They were also accused, by the neighborhood people, of thefts, purse snatching, intimidations, assaults, unnecessary noise, insults and crowding sidewalks" (Shireman et al, 1958: p. iv).

Clearly, a hostile adult community towards youths appearing organized gave rise to an escalation of stigma. A group committing acts of deviance, public disorder, and crime is more severe than single individuals in such capacities. Shireman et al, who helped pioneer the detached worker approach to gang work in Chicago, demonstrated early this factor of community and social stigma associated with a particular group of such young persons.

That the media play a role in this is demonstrated by the account from Zatz (1987). It is an image, akin to the psychology of enmity (Keen, 1986), which portrays youths --- especially minority youths --- when in a group as being a priori evil. That is, "they are up to no good".

The analytical variation exists, of course, to operate outside of ones community of orientation in an illicit fashion or to function without a territorial boundary. In such cases, the gang assumes a higher level of organizational functioning by avoiding the stigma and potential recrimination from those in the most advantageous position to informally monitor their life style and thereby be sources of information for law enforcement efforts against them. Clearly, some of the robber gangs of India reported by Sleeman (1849), to be discussed later, fit this profile.

A number of authors have cited this factor of the gang arising from an informal group given formality through their treatment from the social order. Parents and community members, the media, crimi-

nal justice officials --- responding to an informal group as if it were more formalized may tend to add more cohesiveness and organizational capability to the gang through the expectations such images communicate. It is here that we are truly lacking in our gang literature an adequate classification system that can help guide both research and policy initiatives. We should not be in the situation of treating all groups as an equal threat to society, because we know there are some important differences. The classification system that will be developed in Chapter 14 therefore includes an analytical spectrum ranging from the informal group (pre-gang formation) to the formal organization (a formalized criminal gang).

FAMILY AS A VEHICLE OF GANG INSTITUTIONALIZATION

Just as the family as a social unit can be a powerful source of socialization and training for legitimate pursuits, it can also be one that takes on the more deviant function of solidifying gang organization. To the extent that a gang organization has membership of siblings and successive generations --- parent/child --- it also has a higher level of institutionalization. What the history of India's gangs --- to be discussed in more detail in the next chapter --- seems to imply is that in the absence of social control efforts to the contrary, when the family reinforces gang values and purposes by directly benefiting financially, these gangs continue to exist from one generation to the next.

Adults, particularly family members or those with some legitimate status in society, therefore function as gang sponsors when they lend legitimacy to the gang as a group entity. Within any particular gang the existence of members from the same family of orientation must constitute, at a minimum, a collective identity heightened and accentuated by these internal bonds. There is an important qualitative difference between a gang that has no such family-related infrastructure and one that does. By implication, then, any social institution probably carries this capability of, through its gang membership, reinforcing the gang's organizational strength: members of the same school, members of the same religion, members of the same political party, etc.

THE ORGANIZATIONAL FEATURES OF GANGS

Useful for analysis if nothing more than the classification of gangs are a host of organizational features. Does the gang have satellite units, is there interstate involvement, is the leadership a "cult of personality" or democratic, the internal organization -- is it age-graded, does it have a female auxiliary, is there a territorial control claim, is the level of adult participation high or low, what level of institutional permanency exists in terms of the number of years of operation for the gang, is its membership local in character, citywide, or not bound by geographical limits, are the weapons in use by the gang of low threat (clubs, rocks, knives, zip guns, etc) or high threat (automatic and shoulder weapons, ordnance, etc), what is the force strength in terms of mobilizable numbers, is there a formal initiation mechanism, how complex is the role structure, and what special language (argot) exists, is there a uniform, is there a written code, what alliances or networking exist, is there a headquarters or does the gang own its own property, is decision-making regulated by gang hierarchy or is it spontaneous, what sanctioning mechanisms exist to enforce the gang code, the process and extent of mind control over gang members, what are the rewardive powers of the gang, what is the nature of delegating responsibility and authority in the gang --- these are but some of the organizational questions that have yet to be answered systematically regarding gangs in America.

Further, these are questions for which answers are needed through a national level research initiative. Our gang research literature is too fragmented to be able to piece together an overall picture of the current state of gang organization in America. The need is great for such a research initiative.

THE NEED FOR A NATIONAL CONSORTIUM RESEARCH APPROACH

We need as a society to conduct a version of what Short and Strodtbeck (1974) were involved in, but at a national level. This should include freedom for individual researchers, if they are not comfortable with the collective research design, to control a portion of the resources for individual initiatives. All quantitative and qualitative data collected should a priori, that is by agreement prior to data collection, be available for secondary analysis and future researchers. This ideal national approach would have to be interdisciplinary in nature[15].

TYPES OF SOCIAL GROUP FORMATION AND GANG THEORY

The basic distinguishing features of present, and probably former, gang formations have to do simply with formality and the difference between groups and organizations. Figure 11 shows this basic typology for gangs, based not on individual attributes which may change over time, or on behavior which may not be culturally universal, but rather on the factors of formality and group formation.

Figure 11

A Gang Typology Based on
Type of Social Group Formation

	Level of Social Formality *****************	
Type of Group Formation	Informal *******	Formal ******
Group	Level 0	Level 2
Organization	Level 1	Level 3

Perhaps many of what prior authors have focused their attention on have been these level zero informal groups. Every community, rural or urban, can be assumed to have these. A level 1 or emergent gang means having at least the implied goal of psychic or economic benefits from crime and typically means simply the emulation of an organization, not a true formal organization, it is striving to be such a social formation, and is often little more than an emerging, ad hoc gang[16]. A level 2 or crystallized gang has attained, in pursuing crime, a certain level of formality by its hierarchy and division of labor but functions like a single pseudo-family in a single-tiered but often multi-level group structure. A level 3 or formalized gang has satellite units, organizational goals, is diversified in its criminal income sources, has highly stable leadership and is comparable analytically to what law enforcement officers call the "super gang" or some authors call the corporate gang. This typology would suggest that level zero gangs can readily be given adult supervision and perhaps redirected into prosocial functions for a community or neighborhood as Shaw and Sorrentino (1956) claimed; because it is not, truly speaking, a gang --- it lacks the pattern of law violation. A level one gang might be that most readily reached through such initiatives as detached worker or street outreach programs; again, because the level of commitment, the level of threat, the level of group cohesiveness, and illicit income sources are low or limited.

This typology, based on organizational and group theory, would also suggest that a level two gang might be the easiest to target using conventional law enforcement strategies. But, conversely, a level three gang is not going to be readily put out of business, and might even gain further strength through conventional law enforcement strategies including the traditional use of the penal sanction. All a level three gang has to do to become what many regard as an organized crime cartel is to shield itself from prosecution more effectively via political corruption and to penetrate the legitimate opportunity structure. This will be discussed later in this book.

SUMMARY AND CONCLUSION

The serious student of criminology must recognize that some gangs are easier to study than others through qualitative methods (ethnomethodology, participant observation, etc). From an organizational perspective we must also recognize that gangs do not necessarily have to originate from an urban tradition, although that has been the predominant pattern in America. In fact, later in this book we shall learn that the gang problem has certainly penetrated many smaller towns in America.

Gang organization, to parallel what we know from organizational theory generally, can therefore have different levels of organizational development: incipient, mature, formalized, and institutionalized. Thus, attempts to control gang crime must recognize this basic distinction. How prior attempts to "help society" in the name of such social control initiatives have actually functioned, objectively and materially, to strengthen gang organization also deserves our critical attention.

To the extent that interviewing itself can constitute "therapy" by its dramatic personal thrust and a re-awakening of charged emotions, then to what extent, we must ask from an organizational perspective, does inviting the gang to the university for "study purposes" also give it more legitimacy and organizational strength than it deserves if our interest for society is a reduction in gang crime? This discussion has attempted to point out some of the pitfalls of ethnomethodology regarding the production of knowledge about gang crime. It has also argued the merits of shifting attention from the individual to that of the group or organization itself.

That those who do not understand history are condemned to repeat it is a claim made throughout the ages. That our gang research literature contains some mistakes that should not be repeated should be evident. Clearly, the work by Asbury (1927) differed from Thrasher (1927) in that the former included a more historical analysis which showed gangs operating in America prior to the civil war. The work cited here by Green (1847) also reinforces the claim that America has probably always had gangs. Indeed, the important work by Sleeman (1849) appeared about the same time frame to demonstrate gangs operating in British colonized India. It is a mistake to assume that these works are not of value in understanding group forms of criminal conduct[17].

This chapter must, therefore, be interpreted as an argument for an organizational analysis or a focus on the gang organization itself. All answers, all questions, all issues have yet to be raised in this regard. It is a continuing concern for us all.

Finally, returning to the issue of "what knowledge do we want developed?", it is useful to conclude with some remarks concerning scholarship and the political-economy arena. If we really are not concerned about the future of gang crime in America or its escalation to heights as yet unseen in terms of devastation and societal cost, then we should probably continue a national policy that provides little incentive for social science research, we should probably continue to associate "sociology research entrepreneurs" with the infamous Senator Proxmire "golden fleece awards" describing the absurd use of public funds. Gangs in America will thrive under such an atmosphere of anti-intellectualism. If the Senators want to do something about the quality of research they should insist that agencies like the National Institute of Justice and the Department of Health and Human Services establish true competitive bidding and eliminate political influence in "who gets what".

Implied here, in regards to the political economy, is that some scholars may be importantly influenced by what side their bread is buttered on. Therefore, what is studied can be that which is rewarded. For criminological interpretation, we need only recall how some such cases of intellectual prostitution regarding "nothing works in terms of rehabilitating offenders" meant millions of dollars in "do nothing, say what we say" research money in the 1960's which justified a more punitive national policy. This resulted in the official philosophical ethos being remarkedly repressive in America during the 1970's. So if we don't want to be really serious, we can continue to focus on the "how do you feel?" kind of individual gang member as the unit of analysis as a preferred research agenda. Unfortunately, those who have been the heaviest advocates of setting as a national research priority the conducting of "field work" with gangs tend also to contribute to the national image that the only gang problem in America is a problem of "color". Hopefully the national findings reported in this book will establish that whites can also constitute a gang problem.

It is, after all, a matter of what knowledge do we really want developed. Someone, for example, in a rendition of misquoting Durkheim could say "gangs are good for America....look how they keep our prison systems expanding, and providing jobs for corrections and law enforcement.". Or, alternatively, gangs are the "bogeyman" we all fear in our sleep and the repressive apparatus must therefore be expanded.

A true social scientist must probably be strictly eclectic in showing no allegiance to theory per se, but rather a comparable enthusiasm to "test theory". It should not be a mission of establishing support for one's own individualistic view of the world, it should rather be a mission of gang research to be more responsible to gang members and gang victims and the gang's society by a willingness to consider all views -

-- especially an organizational view --- as they might improve our ability to account for these developments.

Let us hope that, in the process, no one seriously entertains the function of reinforcing these gang developments. Because it is possible to argue, from an organizational analysis, that just as gangs can be manipulated[18] gangs can in fact be artificially generated, created, propelled, given direction and resources, and yielding predictable functions. A national policy of America as the ostrich with its head in the sand surrounded by gangs having varying levels of sophistication, avoiding general research, avoiding facts, avoiding the truth ---- that is the nightmare.

DISCUSSION QUESTIONS:

(1) Do you think a focus on organizational characteristics can help classify or "triage" a response to the gang crime problem?
At what level of the gang threat continuum would you classify the "Clovers" studied by Shireman?

(2) Should all gangs be treated alike, or is it possible that some strategies and programs may be differentially effective depending on the type of gang? Is it ethical for a researcher who studies or treats lower level gang members in low threat gangs to try and generalize findings to all gangs?

(3) In correctional settings, non-gang affiliated inmates are called "neutrals" or "neutrons" but experience an enormous pressure to affiliate with a gang. Do you think the correctional environment is a good opportunity to study what may or may not work to prevent gang affiliation or to evaluate gang deprogramming or gang dismemberment strategies?

DO GANGS EXPLOIT ORGANIZATIONAL WEAKNESSES IN YOUR JURISDICTION?

Gang members are masters at exploiting organizations for their personal benefit. Gang members continue to do this, in part, because we as a society have thought it over sufficiently to formulate specific-enough policies to prevent it.

Let's take a real case from the real world. Donte Redding is a teenager who in the summer of 1996 did what a lot of gang members do: shoot guns. In his case, a 9-year-old girl having nothing to do with gangs was gunned down in cold blood and died as a result of stray bullets from Redding. At his sentencing in late 1997[19], Redding received a sentence of 38 years, a co-defendant, Joseph Taylor, age 21, got off completely when a jury agreed with his defense attorney that in a gang war a citizen has the right to defend himself, and this twist on "self-defense" worked for the jury, and Taylor walked away a free man.

One reason Redding, however, got such a comparatively light sentence was that two staff members working in the Audy Home (Cook County Temporary Juvenile Detention Center) showed up to testify, in mitigation for Redding, that Redding was "a model student" while at the Center and "stayed out of trouble". This free help in mitigation testimony has its ongoing equivalent in the Cook County Jail as well, where particularly cunning gang members can con the school and social service staff at the jail to testify on their behalf as "mitigating circumstances". When Chicago's Mayor Daley is urging citizens to get more involved in "court watch" programs to monitor such gang cases, it seems a fundamental contradiction that personnel who work in a corrections capacity can be allowed to manipulated and volunteer themselves to come to the aid of gang members.

Are you in favor of having a written policy for those who work in juvenile and adult correctional facilities (detention centers, and jails) that civilian staff (teachers, social workers, etc) cannot voluntarily offer their services in mitigation testimony to help out convicted offenders, unless of course the offender had "flipped" and was an intelligence asset to law enforcement or the prosecution, in which case the services of any civilian would be unnecessary anyway in as much as prosecutors and police do routinely speak up at sentencing for "deserving" offenders who helped make the "case"?

Today, staff at both the Cook County Jail and the Audy Home still continue to routinely get "sucked in" to providing such mitigation testimony on behalf of gang members. Does this go on in your jurisdiction? Could you change it by writing to the county board in your jurisdiction? Do you think involved citizens volunteering for "court watch" services would be less demoralized if a "zero tolerance" policy existed in terms of not allowing civilian staff at correctional centers to be able to testify for gang offenders?

End Notes:

[1] His gang name is "Shakey"; he was also chief of the Milwaukee, Wisconsin chapter of the Latin Kings; but he broke off from the Latin Kings; changed colors from Black and Gold (King colors) to Orange and Black.

[2] Other members of their executive committee according to our sources include: "Maddog" (Ronnie Carrasquilo), a cop killer now imprisoned in Dixon, Illinois, who is Chief of the Imperial Gangsters; "Tuffy" (Anibel Santiago), president of the SGD's, and Chief of the Spanish Cobras; David Ayala, Vice President of the SGD's and Chief of the Two Six boys; Fernie, vice president of the SGD's and Chief of the Maniac Latin Disciples; Paul Villa Gomez, Vice President, and Chief of the Ambrose; and "Drac" AKA Dracula, vice president and Chief of the Latin Eagles.

[3] The Spanish Cobras headquarters are said to be located near Maplewood and Potomac in Chicago. The key figures in the Spanish Cobras, according to our very reliable source, include: Anabel Santiago "Tuffy", the King Cobra (i.e., chief of the Cobras); Edwin Losario (a rappy or crime partner of Tuffy's, AKA "Rabbit"), who is chief of all Spanish Cobra's inside the prisons; Slim, the National President; "Burner", the executive National Vice President (a name that in gang slang means Killer); Lil Man (Tuffy's brother), and an Advisor to Tuffy; Bradley C., an advisor; Fro (a derivative of Afro haircut), an Enforcer; Mr. Mike, a treasurer; Horse, a Lt. Governor; Polaco (means Pollock in Spanish), a Lt. Gov.; Blancito (means White Boy in Spanish), a Lt. Gov.; Alex and Pico (brothers), Lt. Gov.'s.; "Drac", a Lt. Gov.; Lurch (killed Hector Sanchez, a major gang figure), a Lt. Gov.; Rubin Santiago (Tuffy's cousin and now in a wheelchair, but still said to be active), a personal hitman who shot our informant; and Charlie C. (chief of the Milwaukee, Wisconsin chapter of the Cobras), a Lt. Governor as well.

[4] According to our source the key players in the Imperial Gangsters include: Ronnie Carrasquilo, chairman of the SGD's, and Chief of all Imperial Gangsters, now imprisoned in Dixon, Illinois; Paulie Carrasquilo (brother of Ronnie), chief of the Imperial Gangsters on the streets; David Ramirez, AKA "T-Bags", treasurer and Maddog's personal enforcer (someone said to have killed twelve rivals but never caught for it, who also owned a $6 million dollar a year cash business called Dirt Busters, a car wash business, that was confiscated by the feds); Hector G., an enforcer for all chapters of the Imperial Gangsters; Jose Martir AKA "Casper G.", chief of the

Grand and Division chapter of the Imperial Gangsters (the Imperial Gangsters are said to have originated at the Cammeron School nearby); "Mems", chief of the North Avenue and Central Park chapter of the I.G.'s; and "Chico", chief of the Armitage and Drake chapter of the I.G.'s in Chicago where they own several buildings.

[5] The key players and roles in the Latin Disciples, according to our sources, include: Fernando Zayas, AKA "Fernie", chief of all the Maniac Latin Disciples (M.L.D.'s); Pachaco, Minister of Finance; Victor Matas, Minister of Defense (an enforcer role or title); "King Vic" (who used to be chief of the MLD's and who wrote the literature for them), Minister of Literature; "Mousie", a chapter treasurer; "Ricky D." (Ricky Garcia actually), an assistant minister of defense; Victor Nieves, a chapter treasurer; Miguel, a chapter treasurer; and Pete "The Burner", semi-retired, but still considered to be the Latin Disciple of all Latin Disciples as he helped start the gang with co-founder "Hitler" (Hitler is now deceased, killed by the C-Notes).

[6] This would be particularly true if gang research continued to focus explicitly along psychological-deficit dimensions of the individual gang member, as if, in a continuing quest to find a personal trait causing gang affiliation we can in the same sense "cure" them of their gang affiliation patterns.

[7] Such as "educationists" (Parsons, 1969: p. 32).

[8] The view of organizations by Parsons seems to be comparable to many gang authors who deny hierarchy or complexity in gangs. According to Parsons "cliques of friends, and so on, are not in this technical sense organizations" (Parsons, 1969: p. 33). For Parsons "organization" was almost equivalent to "bureaucracy" and was a highly restricted definition (Parsons, 1969: p. 32).

[9] Professor Martin Sanchez-Jankowski (1991) is such a highly trained, sociological version of this "close up" research approach. But it is anything but easy. In fact, Professor Sanchez-Jankowski was at one point shot and wounded during his research.

[10] Here we see a potential liability associated with field research, participant observation, and ethnographic "get in there" kind of approaches. Hagedorn (1990: pp. 255-256) in describing his relationship with one of his "informants", (Howard) related the experience where rumors began circulating about Hagedorn being a cop and that the informant (Howard) was "informing". Howard was threatened. Hagedorn went out into the community with Howard

to defuse the situation. But what if Howard had been killed? Or any of the other data sources? A prison warden that uses an "informant" to snitch or penetrate a target group faces legal liability if anything happens to the snitch. Is there not a comparable problem in such "field work" situations? I fear that should Milwaukee gang members get a copy of Hagedorn's book, and gang members do read, they would see the word "informant" and perhaps renew their threats on Howard. Police have informants, researchers have data sources and respondents.

[11] See also Muehlbauer and Dodder (1983: pp. x-xi) for another view of gangs as deviant organizations, "something more tangible than a subculture" (p. x).

[12] Published in Philadelphia by G.B. Zeiber and Co, No. 3 Ledger Buildings.

[13] The use of codes reported by Green were far more complex than those more recently reported among prison gang members by Fong (1990, pp. 41-42).

[14] The document referenced within the selected bibliography was prepared by Willie C. Watson, Street Club Worker of the Hyde Park Neighborhood Club (HPNC) of which Charles H. Shireman was the director through the Hyde Park Youth Project (HPYP), and John M. Gandy, Director of Research (HPYP), and John Ramey, director of the HPNC. Watson and Gandy are indicated as the senior authors. See also Gandy, 1959.

[15] See "Preliminary Findings from the 1992 Law Enforcement Mail Questionnaire Project", Gang Journal: An Interdisciplinary Research Quarterly (1)(3), 1993 for an example of how such projects can work.

[16] The report by Dunston (1990, p. 6) on New York gangs gives an excellent example of a level one gang. New York is not seeing the highly organized "super gangs" found in Chicago and elsewhere. Rather "the typical New York State gang is a loose association of irregularly anti-social youth, often anonymous, more nomadic than territorial, and of shifting or changeable leadership" (Dunston, 1990: p. 6). In fact, "these groups are like pick-up basketball teams. They live all over the city and come together at school. They meet on a subway platform, a leader steps forward and they're off and running" (Dunston, 1990: p. 6).

[17] The recent viewpoints expressed by Covey, Menard and Franzese (1992) illustrate this kind of blatant disregard for historical works as if gangs suddenly landed in a spaceship in the 1980's; that, at least, is the implication when they say that criminologists know little about gangs and what is known in criminology is out of date with regard to gangs. Of course, the very title of their book is a misnomer: Juvenile Gangs; for as discussed elsewhere in the present analysis, no gang is known to expel members when they reach adulthood, thus no pure 100 percent "juvenile" gang exists at the higher level of the gang organizational spectrum (i.e., the more notorious gangs that present communities with the largest threats).

[18] Ko-Lin Chin (Huff, 1990: p. 135) describes in Chinese gangs how gang mentors induce conflict intentionally.

[19] See: Lorraine Forte, "Teen Gets 38 Years in Slaying of Girl, 9", Chicago Sun-Times, Dec. 13, 1997, p. 12.

Want to Find Out If A Youth is a Gang Member, Give Them A Test!

INSTRUCTIONS: These are serious questions. Please do not talk or share your answers or feelings about these questions during the time period that you complete this survey. Your information will be kept confidential by school staff.

(1) How many physical fights have you been in during the last 12 month period? (CHECK ONE)
____0 ____1 ____2 ____3 ____4 ____5 or more

(2) How many of your close friends and associates are gang members? (CHECK ONE)
____0 ____1 ____2 ____3 ____4 ____5 or more

(3) How many of your close friends and associates use illegal drugs? (CHECK ONE)
____0 ____1 ____2 ____3 ____4 ____5 or more

(4) How many members in your family are gang members? (CHECK ONE)
____0 ____1 ____2 ____3 ____4 ____5 or more

(5) How many times have you carried a weapon (knife, gun, etc) to school during the last 12 month period? (CHECK ONE)
____0 ____1 ____2 ____3 ____4 ____5 or more

(6) How many times have you been suspended from school in your entire lifetime? (CHECK ONE)
____0 ____1 ____2 ____3 ____4 ____5 or more

(7) How many times have you been picked up by the police for suspicion of having done something wrong? (CHECK ONE)
____0 ____1 ____2 ____3 ____4 ____5 or more

(8) How many times have you threatened a school teacher? (CHECK ONE)
____0 ____1 ____2 ____3 ____4 ____5 or more

(9) How many times have you wanted to run away from home during the last twelve months? (CHECK ONE)
____0 ____1 ____2 ____3 ____4 ____5 or more

(10) How many times have you been asked to join a gang during the last twelve months (CHECK ONE)
____0 ____1 ____2 ____3 ____4 ____5 or more

INSTRUCTIONS FOR SCORING THE GRIP SCREENING DEVICE:

The overall score for any student will range from an absolute low of ZERO to a maximum score of 50.
The lower the score, the lower the "risk" the student is facing.
The higher the score, the higher the "risk" the student is facing.
To derive the individual student's score: simply add up the values for each of the ten questions.
EXAMPLE: student checks "zero" for all ten questions, the overall total score would be "zero".
EXAMPLE: student checks "one" for all ten questions, the overall total score would be "ten".
EXAMPLE: the student checks "5 or more" for all ten questions, the overall total score would be "50".

ABOVE: Three "security staff" for the 1993 Gang Summit Meeting
in Chicago.

BELOW: Members of the Guardian Angels protest the GD-led gang
summit meeting as a "joke".

"Gang conflicts have become a form of ur-ban-guerilla warfare over drug trafficking. Informers, welchers and competitors are ruthlessly punished; many have been assassinated."

Newsweek (Jan. 28, 1988: p. 23)

CHAPTER 13

GANGS, GUERILLA WARFARE, AND SOCIAL CONFLICT[1]

INTRODUCTION

Gang violence and conflict has been previously described as guerilla warfare (Short and Strodtbeck, 1974: p. 200). The Crip gang member who gave his glamorized story of gang life in the book Monster similarly describes himself as a trained combat veteran and freedom fighter in an undeclared urban guerilla war. The rebellion theme has similarly been common in the gang literature (Hagedorn, p. 164;) as is the relationship of gangs to various forms of social conflict (Tannenbaum, 1938). The gang member as warrior (Pound, 1930: 178-179) is a similar theme corresponding to the book title of Keiser (1971).[2] Is it only that, a simple analogy?[3] Or do gangs represent the highest threat yet seen in terms of maintaining the security of our nation's communities and public institutions and, comparably, do gangs represent a continuing threat[4] or menace in terms of the essence of what is implied by "terrorism" (Davis, 1978)? Similarly, calling gangs "urban terrorists" as an official criminal justice council in California did (California Council on Criminal Justice, 1989: p. viii) is strong language, but again does labelling gangs terrorists make them terrorists?

This issue exemplifies one of the intellectual debates about gangs today. Some authors had concluded earlier that gangs --- whatever their rhetoric --- were simply not well organized and in no sense constituted a revolutionary group. Some contemporary gang analysts in direct contradiction of such assertions may point to groups like the Black Guerrilla Family as a clearcut example of such a revolutionary gang. As in some of the other debates about gangs, what we must realize is that there are sufficient variations in group function and organizational capability that all dimensions (apolitical to that of revolutionary, rightwing to that of leftwing, etc) can probably be found in the modern reality of American gangs. The "debate" in this and other instances is more often than not simply a problem of authors overgeneralizing from inadequate previous research. It is an error to consider all "gangs" equal --- either in terms of the threat they may represent, or in terms of the potential for intervention.

For those who have studied guerilla warfare and unconventional combat forces there is a striking commonality between the basic affinity group repre-

191

sented by the typical urban street gang, of whatever stage of organizational development, and guerilla combat operations. Further, the nature of the conflict --- its direction, its intensity, the means by which it is moderated and controlled --- is also of some comparable interest. At least this provides the rationale for introducing to the reader the gang "study/research/experimentation" by Lieut.-Col. W.H. Sleeman from Calcutta in 1849 and other authors and views in the analysis of social conflict.

JEFF FORT'S MISTAKE ABOUT IDEOLOGY

Jeff Fort, the leader of Chicago's El Rukn gang, seemed to follow a historical pattern in organizational emulation. When Louis Farakhan was able to get a five million dollar no interest loan from Libya's Moammar Gadhafi, Jeff felt he could get some too, and proceeded to seek $2.5 million to engage in domestic terrorism inside the United States on behalf of Gadhafi:

"In five years, Federal agents taped some 3,500 hours of conversations. Eventually they heard what sounded like an extraordinary transaction: Fort was trying to cut a deal with Moammar Gadhafi. For $2.5 million ("two dinners and half a lunch" in El Rukn code), the El Rukns would bomb government buildings and commit other terrorist acts in the United States, the Feds believed.

But they needed proof. It came when an El Rukn bought a rocket launcher from an undercover agent. And the icing came when Trammel Davis, an El Rukn amir, agreed to turn state's evidence in return for $10,000 for his family."[5]

Had Jeff Fort's Chicago gang, the El Rukn's, not contemplated seriously the ideological exploitation value of being a terrorist for hire organization for a foreign nation hostile to America (Useem and Kimball, 1989: p. 77), do you think Jeff Fort would still be operating on the streets of Chicago, indeed perhaps throughout America today? In the late 1960s, during a time of intense ideological strife in America, much of it having to do with civil rights and the antiwar movement in reaction against the war in Viet Nam, was it not the Black Panther's who were attacked rather than Jeff Fort's gang of thugs and robbers?

That gangs in America, whatever their skin color, have previously had the overall characteristic of being rightwing, and reactionary, supportive of the status quo, tends to be supported from most of the extant literature.[6] But that may have changed today with the advent of greater sophistication in the organizational structure of gangs.

Some early gang authors (e.g, Campbell) have said that gangs are anything BUT revolutionary organizations --- they are rather thugs and exploiters, mostly opportunist, often reactionary. Unthinking.

Unreflective. Functionary operatives. Grand scheme of things followers. Defenders of the social order. They seek not to overthrow and revise, rather they seek their fair share. They seek the equal opportunity to exploit.[7] But let me remind you, that has been the preceding historical variation. There are, obviously, some alternative social-political variations. What we see now may not be what we get in the long term. Gangs, as armed peasants, could become a larger problem than they are now. Some of the level three gangs in America today have well articulated political beliefs, some formalized, and they are well armed as well.

Also, many of the recent researchers who have contributed to our prior literature on this issue have focused almost exclusively on African-American gangs. White gangs may be different as implied earlier. Groups like the KKK, Aryan Brotherhood, and many others can be assumed to have a clear and unmistakable rightwing ideology or philosophy. And yet even among African-American gangs there do exist at least some contemporary forms that take on what amount to essentially leftwing beliefs.

The early 1970's Krisberg (1975) study provided an excellent analysis of gang views on racism and revolution. Interviews with gang members showed, as might be expected, a projection that most white prison guards are racist (Krisberg, 1975: p. 16). That is, there was little more than enmity towards white people with the noted exception that "if some rich white man will buy guns for Black revolutionaries, then he would be spared" (Krisberg, 1975: p. 16).

Apparently, the group studied by Krisberg saw themselves ready for revolution, where revolution meant "a large rumble (gang fight)" (ibid). Said one of the gang members "we're the experts in revolution...I know how to stab, he knows about dynamite, and none of us is afraid to use a gun" (Krisberg, 1975: p. 16).

MONSTER'S MEDIA SUCCESS VIA IDEOLOGY

The author of Monster in a "60 Minutes" interview (July 31, 1994) outlined a chronology of how he gave up the life of "Crips" as "Monster Cody" and converted to a revolutionary ideology supportive of the New African Republic. Prison, he said, was just a place for studying revolutionary science. He denied he was a sociopath, "I am just an ordinary guy" he said, in response to a sound bite from the prosecuting attorney who put Monster in prison. "He is extremely intelligent" and uses his cunning and personal power to manipulate others is what the prosecuting attorney implied.

Since writing the book he has gained much attention in the mass media. He renounced any loyalty to the United States in the interview, but vowed support for revolutionary ideals. With tears dripping from his eyes during a period of questioning about his football star legend father, whom Monster said he hated for essentially "not being there", he was quick to point out how he can be regarded as a political prisoner because he was a "political organizer" in the California prison system prior to being transferred to Pelican Bay.

The book Monster is highly stylized and superbly edited to defend this Crip gang member and present him in the most embellished positive light in a way that he avoids taking any responsibility for his behavior because he was a freedom fighter in an urban war. To the extent that apologists for gangs are themselves fair in terms of a policy of equal time coverage, we should therefore expect a Blood version of the same book. And in order to give fair play to midwestern gangs this could, naturally, rest on the bookshelf next to "The Historic Rehabilitation of a Criminal Gang Into A Prosocial Gang: Changing the Gangster Disciples into The Growth Developers".

GANG INVOLVEMENT IN THE LOS ANGELES RIOTS

No one disputes the fact that gang members and gangs were actively involved in the Los Angeles riots after the "not-guilty" verdict regarding Rodney King. Gang rights activist and advocacy views tend to downplay the role of gangs in the riots and point to the widely viewed television news footage showing entire families and many diverse individuals who were looting stores. The record shows that during the riot over 800 buildings were torched resulting in property losses exceeding $750 million dollars. Among the subsequent arrests made for arson related to the riot, about a third were gang members or gang-affiliated[8].

In a riot situation, a condition of civil disorder and the breakdown of legal regulations, it is the individual "one-time" rioter or the novice (e.g., a homeless person, a mother, etc) who is most likely to be arrested. A gang member could be expected to operate with members of his/her own gang; and thus, acting as a group they are much more formidable, and therefore less likely to actually be caught. Gangs are predisposed to criminal activity, and therefore are more likely to systematically benefit from looting in a riot or civil disturbance. Gang members were not stealing Pampers or canned food goods, they were targeting businesses like the 29 gun shops that were looted of about 5,000 firearms. Gangs in L.A. were believed to have taken most of those guns including two hundred police uniforms that were also stolen[9].

POLICE POLICY AND AMERICAN GANGS

In Chicago, an ancient tradition of dealing with gangs involved simply picking up a gang member, asking for information and when not getting co-operation, driving the gang member to another part of the city, indeed an area known to be thoroughly controlled by a rival gang, and dropping the gang member off, out of the police car, right then and there. "Fend for yourself". It was a control policy reflecting the cultivation of internecine violence between rival gang members. This policy was not much more sophisticated than a "divide and conquer" approach. Without the "conquer", because these gangs were never "conquered".

Most gangs in urban America, through ill-designed social and law enforcement strategies, have been unintentionally cultivated and organizationally reinforced, if not through their imprisonment, then through their official recognition, and the legimation accorded them. Or through the conflict that is increased which gangs thrive on. Or through ill-conceived gang programs and policies that increase rather than decrease the problem.

Chicago is instructive in this instance regarding law enforcement policy. For a period in Chicago, the gang abatement/control policy hinged on using the "disorderly conduct" statute to simply arrest and detain, for whatever short period of time, any conspicuous accumulation of persons on a "street corner" who looked like a gang formation --- most characteristically, persons of color from inner-city neighborhoods. When the federal court later ruled this unconstitutional, and ordered the Chicago Police Department to: (1) go back to their files and notify each such person so unlawfully arrested that they had the right to bring suit against the City of Chicago for false arrest, and (2) to erase 800,000 such records of unconstitutional arrests for disorderly conduct, this approach of "street gang control" was modified.[10]

VOLD: THEORETICAL CRIMINOLOGY AND GANGS

Vold (1958) reviewed the shortcomings of anomie theory and gang formations via Cloward and Ohlin as well as the work of Cohen. More importantly, however, Vold advanced the discussion of crime as minority group behavior (see Vold, 1981: pp. 288-292) as well as discussing the political nature of crime (pp. 292-296). It is here that Vold argues that the gang as a collective enterprise is by its very nature a minority group, not necessarily a racial minority group, but one that is clearly at odds with the larger society.

The nature of this structural conflict is one where the gang is the outgroup and legitimate society is the ingroup. Similar to underclass theory, the gang member becomes defined as being marginally important to his/her society, and with different values come different goals and methods to attain those goals. As Vold indicated:

From a more general point of view, however, this prevalence of collective action in crime may reasonably be interpreted as an indication of the banding together for protection and strength of those who are in some way at odds with organized society and with the police forces maintained by that society (Vold, 1981: p. 289).

In essence, the gang is normal in wanting to exert power over resources for the benefit of its individual members. In seeking to expropriate the wealth of others, by the use of illegitimate or coercive power, the gang therefore is in a natural state of combat with the criminal justice system. States Vold further:

The delinquent boys' gang is clearly a minority group in the sense that it cannot achieve its objectives through regular channels, making use of, and relying for protection on, the police powers of the state (Vold, 1981: p. 289).

Vold was clearly aware of how for white gang members in America the gang maturation process often meant a springboard for entering the legitimate opportunity structure, of escaping from the competitive sector of the economy, such as Chicago's famous Mayor Richard J. Daley, the "Boss" who was a member of the Hamburg street gang in Chicago's Bridgeport neighborhood which later became a powerful political organization.[11]

Thus, at the individual level this conflict with larger society can be accommodated under conditions of white skin privilege. For the individual who is a person of color, however, who faces racism in daily life as well as institutional racism, the social structure is less accommodating in the transition to adulthood legitimacy. Says Vold:

The juvenile gang, in this sense, is nearly always a minority group, out of sympathy with and in more or less direct opposition to the rules and regulations of the dominant majority, that is, the established world of adult values and power (Vold, 1981: p. 290).

Further, the use of coercive force such as imprisonment or any such label as "treatment/intervention" by the majority group is not likely to succeed with a minority group. It is similar to the typical resistance that any prisoner-of-war experiences who holds loyalty to ones own group (see Vold, 1981: p. 291).

Gang members, then, do not accept the definition of the situation offered by the criminal justice system of their behavior, however illegal or violent, as being anything other than honorable and acceptable to their own group code. As Vold says, the gang as a microcosm of larger society manifests a larger and more general problem of conflict:

The more basic problem, therefore, is the conflict of group interests and the struggle for the control of power that is always present in the political organization of any society (Vold, 1981: p. 202). Herein is the problem that gangs appear to seek control of the streets, of a street corner, of an area of "turf", of exerting influence over a particular institution such as a public school, or a recreational area they seek to dominate and control for their own. According to Frantz Fanon[12], violence is power as well.

To the extent that a gang entity is highly predictable in its behavior in terms of its propensity to want to exploit any valuable resource, then the gang functions normally in a quest for such power and control. It is equally of interest to note that for those persons of color who may be objectively and materially powerless in terms of economic and social power, this is an even more escalated function. It accounts for the relative importance of something as simple as a "status threat" as the precipitating factor in serious acts of violence.[13]

Vold clearly speaks to the racism-oppression hypothesis as one of the four variations of the political nature of crime. Basically, much crime arises from attempts to induce social change in the context of institutional racism. For example, both South Africa and the United States are cases in point where the person of color is historically expected to assume a subordinate role and position in society. Attempts to rock the boat of the "caste system of racial segregation" (Vold, 1981: p. 295) therefore often result in various crime charges.

As we will see, social caste subjugation in ethnic status was also highly associated with the robber gangs of India as well.

THE EARLY GANGS OF INDIA

Here we shall rely on the wealth of information on robber gangs operating in India reported by Sleeman (1849). This is an oversized, 433+ page military government document describing the nature of the "Budhuk" gangs of India and their suppression by the military[14]. Here we find, among other things, an assortment of "confessions" or depositions taken from gang members and gang leaders about their exploits. The clear difference between these and later American "oral history" methods is not in the content, because they have been meticulously transcribed and translated into English; what differs is that these were taken by force.

The basic structural elements of these gangs had some factors in common with American gangs today and some very important differences. The commonality is that these gangs reflected a constituency of those at the very bottom of the social ladder with little hope of legitimate advancement in society. Gang membership was very much intergenerational through the family. Additionally, in and outside of the periodic episodes with prison life the gang members generally considered themselves more adept at crime than their non-gang counterparts. The commonality, to reiterate, between these early 19th century gangs in India and those in America today had much to do with the surplus population theory of crime: both were marginally tied to their society, both were surplus to having a productive role to play in the overall economy.

The major difference is that these gangs were, like guerrilla forces, based in very "wild" or dense jungle type of rural areas[15]. In fact, they located their entire families in these swamp/wood regions where it was difficult for government troops to effectively pursue them. When government military troops did pursue them into these jungles, they often had high casualties (mortality losses) from fever.

Their specialty, to give it a historical update, was that of what might be comparable today to robbing "big scores", either treasuries, or Brink's trucks, and secondly, home invasion of the rich. Theft, kidnapping, murder were commonplace to these gangs. Their notoriety was for being "robbers" or "decoits". Like gangs today, they had their own subcultural argot, and could communicate in the presence of a potential victim without alerting the latter of their intent.

These were very professional and dedicated criminals: they would often travel hundreds of miles, in disguise, to "pull a job" based on their intelligence gathering capabilities, and would take over an entire section of town while the "score went down", doing so typically at night under cover of darkness, with swift and unexpected violence against all who might resist. Often, in these frays, they would never lose a single fellow gang member. They carried out highly organized attacks on specific pre-identified targets of crime opportunity.

The life style of these gang members, was therefore, one of the ideal-typical contemporary income-oriented criminal: they would make a score, and live the rest of the year in their version of luxury --- drinking, feasting, having fun with as many wives as they could support.[16] What this revealed about the effectiveness of the gang organization, and its high level of morale on such criminal expropriation "quasi-military/insurgency" maneuvers, was that the wealth from such "scores" was shared with all in the gang. The wives got a share, all children got a share, if a member was killed or in jail, he still got a share. It was the primary source of economic support for a large number of persons and their families. None of them worked legally, they condemned "hard work" with great ferocity.

That these gangs continued from one generation, in a family, to the next was clearly evident. The gang was an organization with a clear leader, no necessary written code, but an extensive oral code including subcultural language/argot that allowed them to communicate with others. The gang was rarely in conflict with other gangs. Their targets were not the street corner, their targets were often chosen within the city for example, home invasion of an important "banker", but would equally focus on the informal calculation of risk/benefit ratios designed to maximize their ability to get away with the crime --- to be able to move as rapidly as possible out of the area of the crime undetected and with the loot intact.

If there is a primer on how to be an effective gang, this military report by Sleeman (1849) is it. When your gang membership numbers fall to prison, sickness, death in action, etc --- take new children into the "family fold". These gangs were often accused of kidnapping babies and youths. The economic incentive was clearly there: the women in the clan would receive an extra portion of the share of booty if they had more children, it did not matter if they were their own children. The children would, if they survived, be raised to serve the gang. The haunting question for America is, then, have any of our Nation's many missing children "disappeared into the gang"?

Like the modern gang member counterpart, these Indian gang members were prone to engage in conspicuous consumption with the spoils of their successful income-producing crimes. They did not mind paying higher rents, when the landlord knew they were gang members, because the landlord became that way a confederate and supporter, someone whose best interest was in having the gang member stay "as long as you like". Paying in cash, such merchants then as now are upstream economic beneficiaries of gang crime.

Like similar accounts of American gangs on their way, en masse, to a foray, conflict, or event --- they never travelled so as to draw police attention, they travelled "separately, by two or three and four" (Sleeman, 1849: p. 33). These gangs also provided quasi-political control functions of a repressive nature for local property owners or officials of significance. They provided "protection" to the status quo and the local ruling elite from depredations by outsiders by their conspicuous presence.

These gangs had small arms comparable to those in use by the military and police, but lacked the artillery which the military was able to employ frequently to successfully attack their forts and demand their surrender. With the spoils of their "war on society" they simply outfitted themselves with rifles and pistols in the open market.[17] If they needed a boat to pull off a job, they would buy it and sink it later to cover their tracks.

These gangs were not about theatrics, and "representing" their colors. They were about business. The business of income-producing crime. They were unlike many contemporary gangs that conspicuously allow their identification, such as the El Rukn's who during Jeff Fort's reign were easily identified even on a name search by computer because they would in addition to wearing their colors daily add the "-el" to their last name such that "Jackson-el" was readily identified to anyone cognizant of this "put on". These Indian gangs would more frequently adopt a variety of disguises that allowed them to more effectively travel and commit their crimes. A common variation was the "religious/holy person" journey ---- to bury a persons remaining ashes, to attend a wedding, to a pilgrimage, etc., all the time enacting a role of religion to avoid critical scrutiny. They would frequently "hire" genuine such "holy men" for frontline effect in these deceptions.

To those interested in the nature of social conflict and its relationship to exchange theory, the "pay off" matrix was such that many officials would not hazard an attack on the gangs, because of the direct costs associated with it and the obvious risk to life and limb, while the same officials in taking a Laissez-Faire attitude or "hands-off" position, had benefits without risks. To attack the gangs is to risk much loss ---- personal and political, to acquiesce to the gangs (that is, to permit them relative freedom of operation or a zone of comfort for their staging area) means benefiting indirectly with no risk at all. It is here that Sleeman (1849) makes the assertion that many of "the first nations in Europe, countenanced and supported the Algerine pirates, from the same feelings and views" (Sleeman, 1849: p. 79). Gang members can spend their money too, seems to be the general drift. And today, of course, gang members and their families also represent a political vote sector as well.

"Pirates: Gangs in Boats"

Gangs who do their business on motorcycles are called "motorcycle gangs", so what do we call criminal gangs who operate out of speed boats or ships? Answer: pirates, and yes, they would have to be classified as a gang.

In the year 1999, there were 258 raids or attempted raids by pirates on the high seas according to the International Maritime Bureau. This was an increase from 202 such incidents, world wide, in the year 1998. Knives and guns are the primary weapons used by pirates in these raids. These raids resulted in 78 deaths in 1998.

Source: David Rennie, "Raids on Yachts and Ships on the Rise", Chicago Sun-Times, Jan. 25, 2000, p. 21.

The value of Sleeman is showing the continuity with gangs of modern America. Sleeman (1849) showed that in some instances the gang leader "assumed the character of the high priest, and all the rest that of his followers and disciples" (pp. 80-81). This is not dissimilar from some variations of American gang formation reported in the literature, including Jeff Fort and the El Rukns. And, of course, just as the "gang-breaking" philosophy has characterized much of the American law enforcement response to gangs (see Needle and Stapleton, 1983: p. 30) which involves targeting gang leaders, this was also essentially the mission of Sleeman.[18]

Gangs then were nomadic when they had to be, that is they would leave their encampment and establish a new one if cause necessitated it. What we know about urban gang members, urban felony offenders generally, is that they too have a high level of residential mobility. They are the counterpart in being urban nomads. Probation and parole officers often remark that they seem to move as frequently as they have to submit monthly reports. From my experience in interviewing gang members, many shared something in common with these Indian gang members: their behavior being influenced significantly by superstition. They also had in common the societal-wide social stigma: not of color, but of being "eaters of anything", e.g., pork, meat, even snake in a culture that was rather reverent towards the cow.

What the British military did was of some significance in law enforcement policy for gang control[19]. One law passed in 1836 made it an imprisonable offense to be a member of such a gang:

ACT No. XXX of 1836. It is hereby enacted, that whoever be proved to have belonged, either before or after the passing of this Act, to any gang of Thugs, either within or without the Territories of the East India Company, shall be punished with imprisonment for life, with hard labor (Sleeman, 1849: p. 353).

The military also recognized the value of separating these gang members from their territory of operation and legislation was passed in 1843 (Act No. XVIII) to allow a more federalist approach, because local jurisdictions lacked the capability for secure detention, and this 1843 legislation allowed for the confinement of gang members in other parts of India. Another law, Act No. XXIV made it illegal for any person to receive economic benefit from the gang, in the language of "the offense of unlawfully and knowingly receiving or buying property stolen or plundered" by the gang (Sleeman, 1849: p. 354-355).

"Habitual association" with like-minded individuals was the key definitive ingredient in defining who was or was not a gang member in the 1848 law instituted for the suppression of Indian gangs (Sleeman, 1849: p. 357).[20] Here again, child steal-

ing, was a major emphasis or concern of the established social order; there was at least the widespread fear that these gangs routinely engaged in "child stealing", using murder if necessary, in order to replenish their members lost in combat or to the criminal justice system.

Of vital significance is the effort reported by Sleeman (1849) to experiment with these organized gangs. One proved effective: it meant, offering conditional pardons to those who would become informants, called "approvers", and rather than seeking to suppress them all, asking them once in custody to submit to what was an elaborate oral history method to identify all other names of gang members operating in India, and in this way develop a very large gang data base.[21] This was effective for the military in repressing the gangs and in carrying out even assassination against key gang leaders, and mostly, of effecting their eventual capture. It amounted to a kind of informal social network analysis, where the interrogators had means to cross-check the validity of such self-reports. Again, as recommended earlier in this book, the focus was not on the individual, but rather on what the individual knew about the gang organization and their previous exploits. It proved to be a powerful mechanism of law enforcement.

Secondly, another experiment was somewhat less successful, but appeared to have some positive effect, and that involved what to do with all the gang members in custody. The military established a "school of industry" where the gang leaders' children and the "approvers" (snitches) were held in a somewhat more comfortable facility and the hard core gang members and leaders were housed in a more secure facility. The idea was to have the inmates produce goods for sale. Mostly they produced textiles; rugs, tents, clothing, etc. Like many modern prison industries in America, they made little profit, but it looked good.[22] Evaluation research and "recidivism" had not yet come into the terminology of such corrections personnel, so we have little knowledge of whether this really "worked". The idea of separating confidential informants, snitches, "approvers", from the gang they have turned on has apparently come back into vogue recently. California now uses the Pelican Bay Security Unit involving a no-human contact status to encourage gang members to "debrief". Other states have created "snitch farms", physically separate facilities for informants.

Clearly, during the "interrogation"/"plea bargaining" version of the oral history data collection phase of military intelligence gathering on gang force strength and social network analysis, another frequent question that appeared in the "depositions" was to the effect "how much money, per diem, do you think it would take to get these gang members to be happy with their life style and stop their gang crimes?". This

was used to formulate the school of industry approach, and to provide a rough approximation of what was needed to contain and control the gang members once they were in custody. Curiously, there is no mention of whether these gang members, including the snitches (approvers) were allowed conjugal rights.

What must be emphasized here is that this was a national problem for India, it meant during the time frame from 1803 to 1848 some 516 persons killed, and 1,270 wounded in gang attacks (Sleeman, 1849: p. 429). And this was official data: it was clearly recognized that many such gang crimes never got recorded. What constituted "gang related crime", then, has as much relevancy in the 19th century in India as it does today in America. No one really knows. Or if they do, they are not talking.

"12-Year-Old Boys Lead Armed Rebellion in Burma"

In early 2000, the ongoing battle against the military dictatorship in the country of Burma got renewed attention when "God's Army" commanded international headlines.

"God's Army" is a band of Karen freedom fights, heavily armed insurgents or guerrillas, who fight against the Burmese military dictatorship. What is unique about this particular army? They are led by two twins who are only twelve years old.

The two young twins, Johnny and Luther, actually began leading "God's Army" when they were about nine years old. The two twins have developed a mystique to the effect that they have mystical powers, i.e., bullets cannot "hit them".

Sources: Terry McCarthy, "Leading God's Army: The Bizarre Tale of Boy Twins With Mystical Powers Who Command a Rebellion", Time, Feb. 2, 2000, pp. 60-61. Patrick McDowell, "Myanmar's Twin Rebel Leaders on Run After Loss", Chicago Tribune, Jan. 28, 2000, section 1, p. 13.

ON GANGS, VIOLENCE, AND REVOLUTIONARY THEORY

Not to confuse those who thought up to this point they had a complete grasp of the "Chicago school of criminology" through the recognition of the recurrent prefix of "differential" this and that, let me add at this point, with some obvious risk of confusion, the introduction of a non-Chicago school use of the "differential" logo, another such "differential" theory. This use of the term comes from the political science area dealing with guerilla warfare, terrorism[23], and violent conflict. It is called "differential access", a derivative of deprivation theory. As Nieburg (1970) describes it:

Differential access focuses on the disparities in political influence and power as the most salient and influential factors. The less access to a remedy for its grievances a group has, the more violent it tends to become in demanding such access (Nieburg, 1970: p. 40).

It is an issue of dispute resolution as well. Where can the gang member go to resolve a conflict? To the police? To the court system?

In light of this "differential access" is it not possible that much of what might appear on its surface to be utterly senseless violence, devoid of value for human life, might such, unfortunately, ongoing incidents in America actually represent another possible view of reality? Before interpreting this in best light of those who are gang members please note that this may also imply that routine offenses, from drive by shootings, adjudicated as "manslaughter" may more forcefully be conceived of as being, more seriously, premeditated "murder one" offenses.

That gangs are more prone to internecine violence rather than random violence against civilians seems to be the evidence to date on the American scene. Most accounts of gang victimization show that there are innocent victims, but other gang and former gang members seem to be the target (see Rothman, 1974: p. 10). These victims, too, are typically of the same social status of the gang member pulling the trigger. These drive-by shootings are not occurring in our most lavish and wealthy areas. They occur, indeed recur, one feeding on the other in an endless succession of retaliatory feuding, in our more impoverished inner city areas. Areas where the quality of life has and continues to be a problem for us all.

THE URBAN GUERILLA ANALOGY

A gang may use "guerilla tactics" but most gangs in America today certainly could not, in their present form, be regarded as a guerrilla army. As Janowitz said "guerrillas are a part of an organization, proceed with a plan, prepare paths of withdrawal, and develop sanctuaries (Janowitz, 1970: p. 182)." To other authors, they also seek to control a given area or territory at a successful stage of development. Oppenheimer (1969) was one of the few authors on urban guerilla warfare to at least address the unique nature of gangs and social conflict.

The early Indian gangs would seem to fit the definition of guerilla offered by Janowitz. Are gang members a part of an organization[24], even if it is an organization with varying degrees of formalization, sophistication, and permanence? Do some gangs direct planned activities including drug sales and retaliatory violence?[25] Do gang members prepare paths of withdrawal --- in their own turf and in other jurisdictions? Do gangs develop sanctuaries, areas where they feel protected? Most certainly is the answer to

all of these analogous factors that might fit the definition by Janowitz (1970).

What the reader must ask is this: is it just an analogy[26], perhaps a false one at that, or is it a potential scenario for American gang development? Sibley recently observed that "the police and the public are facing an enemy army with its own uniforms, weapons and rules" (1989, p. 403). Some conspiracy buffs feel gangs are being fostered by home-grown communists and the domestic violence is being allowed to develop in order to implement the National Security Act and thus suspend the Constitution. There is a lot of misinformation being published by and about gangs[27]. And, of course, there are many views seeing the gang-drug connection nationwide to represent a very formidable and apparently growing problem[28].

Oppenheimer discussed gangs in several contexts, including a mention of Jeff Fort's Blackstone Rangers involved in political activities (1969: p. 38), but sees them generally, like Hobsbawm, as "bandits", with the caveat that one scenario could allow for the blurring of distinctions between criminal bandits and guerrillas, allowing for an escalation of conflict. From Oppenheimer's view:

People with guns but without ideology are bandits; people with ideology but without guns are liberals....the analogous social formation in the urban area is the gangster, or on a less organized level, the juvenile fighting gang (1969: p. 34).

Presumably gangs need only an ideology of pro-social systematic self-help to become, then, guerrillas by most definitions. The author's appraisal would suggest that this exists already.[29]

Moore's (1978) work tends to suggest similarly a "self-help" internalized ideology in the context of a visibly obvious in-group/out-group relationship between the gang member and larger society. Oppenheimer had recognized that:

From time to time urban gangs (mainly juveniles, not racketeers) go "social", that is, abandon fighting and adopt tasks of a "social welfare" character, such as recreation, clean-up campaigns, and so forth (1969, p. 35).

Perhaps what made the Symbionese Liberation Army different than the Crips or Bloods was their epitomizing this "social welfare" character in their role in food give-aways to the poor.

The haunting question, knowing that Jeff Fort's gang could be eager to carry out, for a price, terrorist activities in America, is this: How have other gangs have fared in this developmental direction[30]? Do gangs carry out political assassination?[31] Are gang members terrorists by definition?[32] Some new research on this issue is now emerging, in terms of access to military weapons by gang members, and their firearms usage patterns. This new research does show the gang member to have greater access to better firepower including fully automatic weapons, explosives, and military weapons, and a higher likelihood of wearing body armor during the commission of a crime.[33] A recent development in Chicago's gang community exemplifies this trend, several leaders of the Four Corner Hustlers gang were so angry about the effectiveness of a recent community policing initiative that was cutting into their drug operations income, that the gang members tried to acquire missiles and machineguns to blow up the local police station and wage a total war against the local police. They had turned over a large amount of cash and cocaine as their deposit on the purchase of an M72A2 LAWS anti-tank rocket. They were very serious about wanting to blow up the police station.[34]

The issues here are many. Could today's street gang be tomorrow's terrorist/urban guerilla group in armed warfare or low intensity conflict? Organizationally, the early India gangs were able to effectively function much like guerilla groups.[35] That they kept their apolitical and ethnocentric views of the world, as professional bandits, may have kept them from seizing political power. What qualitative aspects of ideology must be present before we can consider the gang as a guerilla group? In the absence of such a formalized ideology is their opposition to be interpreted as little more than mercenary behavior? Or as Taylor (1990) would call it, "quisling" behavior? Or is the typical military terminology used by higher level gang formations just a social "put on"?

For the record, several scenarios are obviously possible. The research by Hans Mattick was the basis for what we know about the "Dirty Dozen".[36] What Mattick showed was that offenders paroled to the U.S. Army fared well, and in fact, such military socialization was useful in reducing their recidivism. Again, the question seems to hinge on this: "is there a productive role for these persons to play in America?" If not, get ready for the worst case scenario.[37]

Finally, some readers may find the analogy to guerilla warfare in terms of solutions, in terms of the battle against gangs. For example, the Chicago Area Project sees the struggle for community control as a "neighborhood by neighborhood" approach to provide greater community empowerment.[38] Some readers may find that not dissimilar to "house by house" military fighting often associated with urban warfare.

"The Heavily Armed Gangs in Jamaica Today"

When gang problems erupt in Jamaica, the problems are of sufficient threat-level to require calling out the military and imposing curfews. In 1999 gang violence resulted in 71 killed in a three-week period, such that Jamaica's Prime Minister P.J. Patterson called it "a spate of criminal madness".

What happens when gang wars erupt in Jamaica is that local residents flee the area like refugees, often taking up temporary residence at the nearest police station.

In Jamaica the gang leaders are called "Don's" in their respective gangland kingdoms. Jamaican gangs have a long history of being used in the traditional patron/client state sponsored crime pattern; that is, they are often used for political purposes by various factions in the political arena. These "posses", as they are known, have certainly made their mark in American cities as well, bringing high levels of violence with their involvement in illegal drug trafficking.

POLITICAL EXTREMIST GANGS: The Case of the Black Guerrilla Family

The Black Guerrilla Family (BGF) is typically found in adult prisons, but has also been reported as active by local law enforcement, in adult jails, and in juvenile correctional institutions. While it is found throughout California, the BGF has been reported in a number of other states (Arizona, Georgia, Indiana, Minnesota, Missouri, Nevada, New Jersey, Texas, Washington, and Wisconsin). The written constitution of the BGF consists of 16 pages of single spaced typed text. This is one of the few gang constitutions that clearly indicates an intent to engage in armed conflict.

The BGF in its written constitution clearly regards other gangs like the Aryan Brotherhood and the Mexican Mafia (EME) as enemies; in fact, as "tools" of the penal administration. Of all the written gang constitutions, that of the BGF is clearly the most politically sophisticated. Yet much of it seems as if it could have been copied --- in terms of phrases, "pat expressions", etc --- straight out of radical leftist newspapers or periodicals. The BGF also recognizes its beginnings in the "guiding example and teachings of George Jackson". George Jackson was a famous African-American militant who died of gunfire while imprisoned. He helped ignite the "prisoner rights/reform/protest" movement of the 1970's (Jackson, 1970).

The BGF oath like that of their arch enemy (the Aryan Brotherhood) rhymes in the form of a poem[39]:

OATH OF THE BLACK GUERRILLA FAMILY
> If I should ever break my stride,
> And falter at my comrades side,
>> This oath will kill me.
> If ever my world should prove untrue,
> Should I betray this chosen few,
>> This oath will kill me.
> Should I be slow to take a stand,
> Should I show fear to any man,
>> This oath will kill me.
> Should I grow lax in discipline,
> In time of strife refuse my hand.
>> This oath will kill me.

Under its section on Exemplary Punishment, the BGF constitution specifies a death sentence to any member who basically doesn't go along with the program. Several gang laws are listed, such as "use of heroin", "selling or giving weapons to the enemy", etc. Many gangs have the rights of trial for members, but not the BGF which includes this very efficient clause: "Time not permitting a chance of review, the Generals, for security reasons, may order and have a sentence of death carried out against a member for violation of one of the above laws".

In addition to its "do's" and "don'ts" in terms of expected behavior (basically political indoctrination), the BGF constitution includes a very elaborate "Party Platform". It specifically identifies the "Party" as the overall reference group, apparently the Communist Party from this paragraph in Part III of the BGF constitution:

"We use Marxism, which is positive in spirit, to overcome liberalism, which is negative. A communist should have largeness of mind, and he/she should be staunch and active, looking upon the interest of the revolution as his/her very life and subordinating his/her personal interests to those of the revolution. Always and everywhere he/she should adhere to principles and wage a tireless struggle against all incorrect ideas and actions, as to consolidate the collective life of the Party, and strengthen the ties between the Party and the masses. He/she should be more concerned about others than about himself/herself. Only thus can we be considered a Communist."

In its ideal and self-described form, then, this particular gang does in fact see itself by name and intention as a group that is "about revolution". Guerilla warfare and political terrorism are definitely potential interests of this gang.

It is of some interest, as well, that gangs behind bars in states like Illinois such as the Brothers of the Struggle (B.O.S.) refer in their internal literature to their development goals as a "movement". A number of such internal written documents of the B.O.S. gang (basically another name for the Gangster Disciples) are provided in this book. As reported else-where[40], this same gang that operates inside jails and adult prisons (and juvenile correctional institutions as well) has evolved to the point where it now has it own written "Disciplinary Report Forms" that it completes on its own members when they violate one of the internal rules and regulations of the gang.

A PRELIMINARY TEST ABOUT POLITICAL EXTREMISM USING CONFINED JUVENILE OFFENDERS

While some authors may claim gangs have no ideology, emerging data shows some gangs are truly formalized. Obviously, if we are to consider groups like the Ku Klux Klan and Aryan Brotherhood "gangs", as is done in the present analysis, then we must admit that some gangs do have such fairly developed ideology (Helmreich, 1973). Some gangs even have written constitutions which express this ideology. Many observers in the study of guerilla warfare and terrorism also observe that the element of ideology must be present as well. Described here are results from the survey of juvenile institutions reported more completely in a later chapter of this book.

In the Fall of 1990 all juvenile correctional institutions (training schools and camps) were sampled using a four page survey instrument designed to be completed by the Superintendent. Some 155 institutions responded representing 49 states. Below are some of the findings relevant to the present analysis.

When asked "to what extent are gang members involved in extremist political beliefs" on a scale from zero (not at all) to a high of ten (a great deal), 61 percent indicated zero. The ideology variable was then recoded to reflect a dummy variable of the presence or absence of any such reported extremist beliefs. In this fashion, its effects on other gang problems is most significant as seen in Table 9.

TABLE 9
Significant Relationships Between Gang Political Extremism And Indicators of Gang Population Size, Reports of Gang Damage to Government Property, and Racial Conflict

		Any Level of Political Extremism Reported Among Gang Members?	
		NO	YES
Institutions Reporting 10% or More of their Population Are Gang Members	NO	66	16
	YES	35	39
		Chi square = 19.1, p < .001	
Institutions Reporting a Problem of Gang Damage to Government Property	NO	67	8
	YES	32	47
		Chi square = 43.1, p < .001	
Institutions Reporting a Problem of Racial Conflict	NO	58	20
	YES	39	34
		Chi square = 7.2, p = .01	

What these findings suggest is that the extent to which gangs do have such an element of ideology as measured by the presence or absence of political extremism is itself significantly related to problems such as gang force strength, the damage they do to government property, and reported problems of racial conflict. Ongoing research dealing the same problems in adult institutions and other criminal justice settings is now underway by the author.

GANG MEMBERS SEEKING FIREARMS AND ORDNANCE FROM FRIENDS IN THE AMERICAN MILITARY

The findings reported here are based on a exploratory study of N = 91 members of a unit of the Illinois National Guard. On the morning of October 13th, 1992 a 7-year-old child named Dantrell Davis was killed by sniper fire from an AR-15 rifle in the Cabrini Green public housing complex on Chicago's near north side. The shooter who had served in the Army, was determined to be a gang member. It was a gang-related killing that occurred as the child was being walked with his mother on the way to school.

Enormous attention was given to this incident in the mass media and a public outcry ensued that gained national attention. During this aftermath several city officials were quoted as giving was serious consideration to bringing in the National Guard to help suppress the gang problem in Cabrini Green.

Outside of the official report by Sleeman (1849) documenting the role of the military in the suppression of the Budhuk gangs of India there is little in the literature that provides any linkage between the two separate issues of "gangs" and the "military"[41]. One notable exception is the analysis of the Yakuza by Kaplan and Dubro (1986, p. 200) who mention how the Yakuza operating in South Korea in their production and sales of illegal drugs, more specifically methamphetamines (i.e., "speed", a drug of choice in Japan) had spread in terms of illicit use to U.S. soldiers stationed in South Korea[42]. But little documentation and no indepth analysis of the possible impact that a gang can have on military personnel is provided anywhere in the public literature.

Most of the literature on gangs that provides any citation to the military is therefore cursory at best. The "Zoot suit" riots, which could have equally been called "military riots against Pachucos", are an example of this cursory treatment. Most analysts have had to rely on what was printed in the newspapers and on oral history recollections from the viewpoints of the Pachucos, with no known follow-up on the members of the military who were obviously very important actors in the fray. Similarly, the early role of the National Guard (19th century, New York City) in the suppression of gang street battles is mentioned in the literature only in passing, that is they were effective in dispersing the gangs fighting in the streets (Haskins, 1975: p. 29)[43].

A magazine called Teen Angels published since 1980 in California, describing itself as a gang rights activist news organization, routinely includes pictures and names of Hispanic members within the military and encourages military enlistment[44]. It is not implied that these are "gang members"; but everyone else in the magazine indicates they are...complete with the photos the gangs send in of themselves, their arms caches, and their "placas". It is a magazine for west coast Hispanic gangs.

The book about gangs from an evangelical view of a minister providing outreach to gang members describes the case of "Trigger", a gang member who wanted to do well in school and join the Marine Corps for the benefit of subsequent college education benefits, and the gang leader encouraged this goal (Mc Lean, 1991: p. 78)[45].

Some very limited newspaper coverage has been given to the problem of gangs near large military bases. One of the best of these journalistic efforts deserves some recognition here[46]. First, military kids were considered potential risks to gang membership because they are very transient, moving from one place to the next. A local police officer near a military base in Oceanside, California stated that he knows of military children who were heavily influence by gangs, some of whom still live on the military base. Staff running youth programs for the Defense Department acknowledge such problems, although military spokespersons are quick to say they are just "wannabe" gang members. One military base commander was quoted as saying "The general has a strong policy....if you're caught in gang-related activities, you're [moved] off base" (Jowers, 1993).

An anonymous survey questionnaire was designed to measure various aspects of the gang problem. The instrument used is a one page, double-sided questionnaire. The front page contained forced-choice items and the back page contained open-ended items[47]. Many of these items replicate previous research on groups that deal with gang problems (e.g., law enforcement, etc).

In mid-November 1992 the data collection began using a student who is a member of the same military unit who sought informal cooperation from other members of the National Guard unit where he was stationed. The unit sampled is located on Chicago's southside and is predominantly African-American.

Because of the sensitive nature of the questions about gangs and crime no identifying variables were included in the survey. Only one background variable was used: length of service.

The sampling technique used here qualifies only as a purposive or exploratory study and is not generalizable.

Only about one third (32.2%) of the respondents expressed the belief that the National Guard should be sent to Cabrini Green (or any other gang environment) to stop gang warfare. Half (50%) rejected this utilization of National Guard troops. Some 17.8 percent indicated they were not sure.

These National Guardsmen were asked if the armed forces should try to recruit gang members just in case the military has to be used in response to a riot situation where many gang members could be involved. About a third (34.4%) accepted the validity of this notion. The majority (65.6%) rejected the idea of recruiting gang members for use by the military.

The overwhelming majority (95.6%) of the respondents expressed the belief that the federal and state government has not done enough to try to prevent the gang problem.

These members of the National Guard were presented with the scenario where they should not be used to deal with gang problems and were asked "who should" be used instead. The single largest group (41.4%) indicated the local police should be used. Some 10.3 percent indicated the state police. Some 24.1 percent indicated federal troops. And 24.1 percent indicated "other".

These members of the National Guard were also asked to estimate based on their knowledge what percent of all U.S. armed forces personnel they believe are probably gang members themselves. Only 2.8 percent indicated "zero percent of the U.S. armed forces are probably gang members". In fact, the percent of estimated gang membership within the U.S. military ranged from a low of zero to a high of 75 percent. The mean, or arithmetic average, was 21.5 percent.

Table 10 presents the findings for a somewhat more general inquiry of "what would be your estimates for the percentage that are current or former gang members by branch of military service". As seen in Table 10, the Coast Guard is shown to have the lowest estimated current or former gang member population, followed by the Air Force. The Coast Guard are shown to have a mean estimated former or current gang membership of 6.3 percent compared with 7.8 percent for the Air Force. It is of some interest that these National Guard respondents gave their own outfit the highest mean average of former/current gang membership (mean = 25.6%).

Table 10

ESTIMATES OF THE % WHO
ARE CURRENT OR FORMER
GANG MEMBERS BY BRANCH

	Low ****	High *****	Mean *****
Army	0%	90%	16.3%
Navy	0%	80%	10.9%
Marines	0%	70%	14.8%
Air Force	0%	60%	7.8%
Nat'l. Guard	2%	80%	25.6%
Coast Guard	0%	50%	6.3%
Army Reserve	1%	90%	19.8%

Asked if the National Guard can truly stop the problem of gangs in places like Cabrini Green, over half (58.2%) indicated in the negative. Only 12.1 percent expressed the belief that the National Guard could truly stop the problem of gangs in places like Cabrini Green. Some 29.7 percent indicated they were "not sure".

Just over a fourth (26.7%) expressed the belief that the National Guard are adequately trained to go into a place like Cabrini Green to stop gang violence. Most (73.3%) felt the National Guard lacked adequate training for such a mission.

These members of the National Guard were also asked if they have ever, as individuals, been approached by a gang member who wanted to acquire military weapons or ordnance (e.g., grenades, etc). Most (90.8%) said no. However, some 9.2 percent indicated they had in fact been approached by such gang members seeking military weapons. It is not known, because of the brevity of this particular survey, whether any of these events were ever reported to authorities. Nor is it clear what specific reporting guidelines or policies are in place with regard to this matter.

These members of the National Guard were also asked their opinion on whether the U.S. armed forces should discharge a soldier who is determined to be a current gang member. The respondents were almost evenly divided on this issue. Some 59.1 percent felt that the military should not discharge gang members. Some 40.9 percent felt that gang members should be discharged.

These members of the National Guard were asked if they believe that gang members are depicted as an overblown "threat" by the news media, politicians, and others. Over half (59.5%) expressed the belief that gang members are not depicted as an overblown threat. However, some 40.2 percent affirmed the belief that gang members are depicted as an overblown threat.

These personnel of the National Guard in Chicago were also asked "how many of your close friends and associates are gang members". The distribution of results for this item was as follows:

How many of your close friends
or associates are gang members?

	0	1	2	3	4	5 or more
N	62	1	7	3	2	11
Percent	72.1	1.2	8.1	3.5	2.3	12.8

Thus, over a fourth (27.9%) of these members of the National Guard had one or more close friends or associates who are gang members. It is unlikely that those social forces calling for the utilization of the National Guard in Cabrini Green were aware of the fact that the same military personnel might be in the situation of confronting gang members who could --- at some unknown level of probability --- be friends or associates of the soldiers assigned to such duty.

It is of some interest that 12.8 percent of this sample of National Guardsmen reported having five or more such close friends or associates who are gang members. This type of question is often a measure of subcultural integration and a predictor of gang membership itself. It is also of interest that one respondent chose to mark a large "Star of David" six-pointed star symbol on the back of his survey instrument; which is the insignia/logo used by the Disciples (BDs, GDs, BGDs, B.O.S.) in the Folks gang nation.

The survey also included the question used with other populations (e.g., police, etc) to the effect "do you believe that if many of today's gang leaders had entered the military instead of joining a gang they could put their leadership skills to better use as good soldiers"? Three-fourths (77.8%) of the respondents expressed this belief that such gang leaders could have made good soldiers. Just over a fifth (22.2%) rejected the idea that gang leaders would make good soldiers.

Almost two-thirds (65.2%) of the sample felt that they knew how --- with relative certainty --- to identify a gang member by their colors, behavior, or language. Just over a third (34.8%) did not know how to identify a gang member in this fashion.

When asked how long they themselves had served in the National Guard, the distribution showed a low of one year to a high of 21 years. The mean, or average, was 6.3 years.

About one in ten (10.2%) reported that in the last year they had been a victim of a gang crime.

A bivariate analysis was made of a number of variables in the survey. This was accomplished by recoding some of these variables the details of which are explained below. Described here are some of the significant findings from this inquiry.

Table 11 shows that, among this sample of National Guardsmen, by recoding the "gang friends" variable (none versus having one or more) and the "belief pattern about what percentage of all U.S. Armed Forces personnel are probably gang members" yields a statistically significant relationship. In other words, the profile that emerges here is that the gang friendship variable is significantly differentiated by the level of perceived gang membership throughout the armed forces. Specifically, those National Guardsmen who have one or more close friends and associates who are gang members are those more likely to perceive a higher representation of gang members in the U.S. Armed Forces.

Recall that overall some 27.9 percent of this group had one or more such friends who are gang members. Table 11 shows that among the low belief pattern only 19.4 percent have one or more such gang friends; but among the high belief pattern some 44.1 percent have one or more such gang friends. There is clearly a relationship between these two variables.

TABLE 11

BELIEF ABOUT GANG REPRESENTATION IN THE
U.S. ARMED FORCES IN RELATIONSHIP
TO HAVING ONE OR MORE GANG FRIENDS
AMONG A SAMPLE OF NATIONAL GUARDSMEN
(FREQUENCY DISTRIBUTION)

	Have One or More Close Friends Or Associates as Gang Members	
Belief Pattern of What % Gang Members Are in all U.S. Armed Forces:	NO	YES
Low (<=15%)	29	7 (19.4%)
High (>=20%)	19	15 (44.1%)

Chi-square = 4.93, p = .02

This finding is similar to that uncovered in gang studies in high schools where the gang member is more likely to project a higher estimate of the percentage of the student population who are gang members. In fact, this tendency for perceived gang representation levels becomes even more pronounced in relationship to having one or more gang friends when the more specific variable of gang members in the National Guard is examined as seen in Table 12.

Table 12 shows the same pattern profile where the gang-friend variable is significantly differentiated by low-high perceptions of the extent to which gang members are represented in their own ranks (e.g., the National Guard). Those who have the low perception of gang members in their own ranks show only 16.6 have one or more gang friends themselves. But among those with a high perception of gang members in their own ranks some fifty percent have one or more such close friends who are gang members.

Finally, these perceptions are clearly directly related to one another. That is, those who perceive low levels of gang representation among the ranks of the U.S. Armed Forces generally are pretty much those who also perceive low representation of gang members among their own ranks of National Guardsmen. This finding in shown in Table 12.

TABLE 12
BELIEF ABOUT GANG REPRESENTATION IN THE RANKS OF THE NATIONAL GUARD
IN RELATIONSHIP
TO HAVING ONE OR MORE GANG FRIENDS
AMONG A SAMPLE OF NATIONAL GUARDSMEN
(FREQUENCY DISTRIBUTION)

	Have One or More Close Friends Or Associates as Gang Members	
	NO	YES
Belief Pattern of What % Gang Members Are in the National Guard:		
Low (<=15%)	25	5 (16.6%)
High (>=20%)	16	16 (50.0%)

Chi-square = 7.68, p = .006

As seen in Table 12, not only are the perceptions of gang penetration into the military related to having gang friends, but the perceptions overall are related to the perceptions in their own ranks. This is highly significant (p < .001).

Table 13 also shows that among those who have a low level perception of the extent to which gangs are represented in the overall U.S. armed forces most of these (22 out of 28) also perceive low levels of gang representation among their own ranks. Vice versa, those with high perceptions of the gang presence within the overall U.S. armed forces mostly see their own ranks as also penetrated by gang members.

TABLE 13
FREQUENCY DISTRIBUTION OF PERCEIVED LEVELS OF GANG MEMBERSHIP IN THE OVERALL US ARMED FORCES IN RELATIONSHIP TO PERCEIVED LEVELS OF GANG MEMBERSHIP WITHIN THE NATIONAL GUARD AMONG A SAMPLE OF NATIONAL GUARDSMEN

	Belief Pattern of What % Gang Members are in the National Guard	
	LOW (<=15%)	HIGH (>=20%)
Belief pattern of what % gang members are in the overall U.S. Military.		
LOW (<=15%)	22	6 (21.4%)
HIGH (>=20%)	5	26 (83.8%)

Chi-square = 23.11, p < .001

Another factor that significantly differentiates the perception of gang members within their own ranks is their belief about what the military should or should not do if a soldier is discovered to be a gang member. Table 14 provides this test.

TABLE 14
FREQUENCY DISTRIBUTION OF BELIEFS ABOUT WHETHER GANG MEMBERS SHOULD BE DISCHARGED FROM THE MILITARY IN RELATIONSHIP TO PERCEIVED LEVELS OF GANG MEMBERSHIP WITH THE NATIONAL GUARD AMONG A SAMPLE OF NATIONAL GUARDSMEN

	Belief Pattern of What % Gang Members are in the National Guard	
	LOW (<=15%)	HIGH (>=20%)
Should the U.S. Armed Forces Discharge Anyone Determined to Be a Current Gang Member?		
NO	13	23 (63.8%)
YES	16	10 (38.4%)

Chi-square = 3.92, p = .04

As seen in Table 14, those with the more tolerant position about gangs in the military who believe current gang members should not be discharged show some 63.8 percent with a high perception level of gang representation among their own ranks. Conversely, those with a less tolerant view and who do believe a soldier discovered to be a current gang member should be discharged show only 38.4 percent with a high perception level of gang representation among their own ranks. This factor of gang policy in the military significantly differentiates this perception of the extent to which gang members are present among their own ranks (p = .04).

The only genuine "background" factor within the data environment of this survey is years of service within the National Guard. Recoding this variable to reflect recent versus long term soldiers reveals a significant finding in relationship to perception levels of the gang presence among U.S. armed forces. This is shown in Table 15. Also, Table 15 shows that this factor of tenure in the national guard also significantly differentiates those who have one or more close friends who are gang members.

This background factor of years of continuous service in the National Guard was recoded to create roughly two groups: the young guard, and the old guard. The young guard are those with less than or equal to four years of service. The old guard are those with between five to twenty-one years of service. Therefore this difference between young and old guard does not reflect actual age, but is rather a surrogate measure of age, experience, and military socialization by measuring specifically the years of service within the National Guard.

TABLE 15
FREQUENCY DISTRIBUTION OF PERCEIVED LEVELS OF GANG MEMBERSHIP IN THE OVERALL U.S. ARMED FORCES IN RELATIONSHIP TO SERVICE TENURE LEVELS AMONG A SAMPLE OF NATIONAL GUARDSMEN

| | Years of Service Within The National Guard ************************** | |
	Young Guard (<=4 yrs) *********	Old Guard (>=5 yrs) *********
Perceived Levels of Gang Membership Overall in the U.S. Armed Forces		
LOW (<= 15%)	10	25
HIGH (>=20%)	20	15

Chi-square = 5.83, p = .01

Table 16 shows that the old guard are more likely to report a low perceived representation of gangs in the overall ranks of the U.S. armed forces.

Duration of service appears to be inversely related to the perception of gang membership levels in the overall U.S. Armed Forces.

Similarly, Table 16 shows that it is the younger guard who have a statistically significant higher likelihood of having one or more close friends and associates who are gang members. In other words, the actual condition of these National Guardsmen having such gang friends itself is a factor that profiles quite differently by years of service.

TABLE 16
FREQUENCY DISTRIBUTION OF THE PROFILE OF HAVING ONE OR MORE CLOSE FRIENDS OR ASSOCIATES WHO ARE GANG MEMBERS IN RELATIONSHIP TO SERVICE TENURE LEVELS AMONG A SAMPLE OF NATIONAL GUARDSMEN

| | Years of Service Within The National Guard ************************ | |
	Young Guard (<=4 yrs) *********	Old Guard (>=5 yrs) *********
Have one or more close friends or associates who are gang members?		
NO	23	38
YES	16	7

Chi-square = 6.81, p = .009

It seems reasonable to believe that some gang members are present within the ranks of the U.S. armed forces. However, very little is actually known about this aspect of gangs. It would reflect what is called an adaptation of marginality: high integration into legitimate organization (e.g., the military) and high integration into an illegitimate or subcultural organization (e.g., the gang). What side is such a person really on? No one knows, this has been the first effort reported in the literature to examine the issue. So, hopefully, this study has begun to shed some light on the issue of gangs and the military.

The one respondent who did intentionally affect a gang posture by inscribing a large gang symbol on his survey may reasonably be assumed to be a gang member. However, the situation under which this data was collected did not lend itself to such self-reported gang membership research. At the time of this study these same members of the military were under consideration for being sent into a housing complex (e.g., Cabrini Green) to quell gang violence.

Indeed, there is another reason this standard self-report question was not included here: if discovered, it could be cause for serious difficulty.

Therefore the present study focused only on surrogate measures of the self-report research method by asking the respondent to report on the deviance of their friends and associates not their own. This meant asking these national guardsmen how many of their close friends and associates were gang members rather than asking if the respondent was currently in a gang. Self-report research among deviants shows that they are more likely to report on the deviance of their friends and associates than their own.

A gang member in the military must be regarded as a unique condition of deviance: someone who literally marches under two sets of colors and to two different drummers, one legitimate (the military) and one illegitimate (the gang). How pervasive this situation is cannot be objectively estimated from simple perceptions or beliefs as are measured in this survey. What orders of the day would the gang member in the military actually follow if they were on a domestic mission to suppress a gang-related civil disturbance: those from the military, or if they were facing their own gang those from the gang?

While exploratory in nature, several findings from this research deserve serious attention[48].

What should be the position on gang membership among military personnel? Not all gang members have criminal records. It is real simple to understand: not all gang members who commit crimes are always caught and even if caught always convicted. There are well known cases where a gang member committed a possible homicide (he still to this day does not know if the person died from the gunshot wounds) as part of an initiation ceremony and later "chilled out", went to college, and is now working in the criminal justice system. He has no police record. He was never caught.

It is very similar to the situation for dealing with the marginality of some police officers. A police department cannot terminate the employment of someone who simply associates with "undesirables". It is a freedom of association and constitutional issue that has not been given much legal analysis.

No military code of conduct is known to the present author that specifically prohibits members of the U.S. armed forces from having close friends and associates who are gang members. It is an issue having enormous implications.

THE POWER OF GANGS IN SOCIAL CONFLICT

Could a criminal gang literally take over a legitimate organization? Yes, it is theoretically possible. The reasons why a gang might want to engage in this type of social conflict would have several potentially diverse explanations. One would be the monetary resources such a legitimate not-for-profit or membership or fraternal organization might own, resources that under the right leadership could be rapidly liquidated or exploited. Another reason might be the political platform base that such a group might represent as a target for a take over.

Some discussion on this issue has focused on the case of the Gangster Disciples, through their political arm the "21st Century V.O.T.E." group, in late 1994 tried to wrench control of a branch of the N.A.A.C.P. in Chicago. A surrogate force was said to be used here, a group that had for a couple years established itself as an anti-drug program or drug rehabilitation/counseling program, which while very popular in some circles (No Dope Express), was actually a co-sponsor and heavily involved in the October 1993 Gang Summit meeting held in Chicago. Some have indicated that the gang in this instance is being used to divide and fractionate the political infrastructure of the African-American community, almost to a blueprint plan.

The tension that had existed in Chicago's southside branch of the NAACP reflected an induced conflict between the older vanguard of the civil rights struggle, including noted figures like Vernon Jarrett, and the new and much younger sector. Earl King, from No Dope Express, apparently had only about a year or so membership in the chapter and ran for president. By doing so, the "split" or social conflict began. When Vernon Jarrett joined in with the opposition, within a short time later, Earl King walked into the NAACP office in Chicago and handed in 5,000 newly completed applications for membership along with the $50,000 in cash. Some read this development as an effort by the gang to take over this chapter of the NAACP.[49]

The potential exists, of a gang which can rapidly generate large numbers for a turnout, for a gang to take over a legitimate organization. The disruptive legal impact of this type of tactic carries enormous implications for social conflict. The astute observer of this scene will also be able to recall examples of some political extremist groups sympathetic to and/or existing as an above ground propaganda vehicle for a terrorist group like ALF, where such activists were able to take over legitimate groups in the animal rights arena, converting their funds and assets to a different use. While in the terrorism example of ALF and its front groups was successful, the Chicago gang strategy to take over a chapter of the NAACP was much more directly combative and designed to backfire because it was not done in a quiet, subtle, fashion --- but rather in a Rambo-style display of conspicuously threatening force. Any group that can rapidly generate 5,000 to 10,000 members or associates for a picnic, like the Gangster Disciples were able to do in recent years, is obviously a group also capable of having such persons fill out membership applications to join any association legally, and literally take it over by overwhelming numbers of voters in any election of officers.

SUMMARY AND CONCLUSION

Stinchecombe's (1964) analysis of youth rebellion is useful here in coming to a summation on the matter of gangs, guerilla warfare, and social conflict. It advances the "articulation hypothesis" which amounts to this element of hope: to those who can articulate little relationship between their current socialization and relationship to dominant social institutions (e.g., the schools, etc, which are designed to train persons for such future productive roles in American society) and their subsequent life chances in the hope for a better existence --- it is among these for whom rebellion is strongest. Whether it is perceived or objective, the net effect is equally the same: alienation. In a high school context it became, ala Stinchecombe (1964), "expressive alienation". In a subsequent gang maybe it can become "active alienation" to the extent that these same persons carry on a war against their own society.

Perhaps this is all too conjectural. The cynic could say whatever the potential for gangs becoming guerilla's, undereducated drug abusers do not make good soldiers[50]. So perhaps another variation would be a toned down variety of social protest, without the use of arms. There are certainly a lot of different scenarios for what could happen to America's gangs.[51] One thing we can probably rule out, however, was an option used by the military suppression effort against gangs in India: exiling the gang member for life "across the seas".

Clearly, there is a need for further and more indepth research on the potential for gang involvement in terrorism, civil disorder, and low-intensity conflict. We have much to do in the analysis of the gang crime problem in America.

The serious student of criminology knows that a wide variety of "wilderness" and "survival" programs have been used with delinquents throughout the years. If "boot camp" training is all we as a post-industrial society (where theoretical knowledge is supposed to be the principal basis for social change)[52] can come up with, then we are certainly headed for disaster. Not dissimilar from the well-intending social service program that makes its resources available to a gang for manipulating/abusing in the interest of "reaching out" to them and then finding out too late (e.g. Chicago's Fry) that something has truly "gone awry"; the correctional fad of "boot camps" when it comes to gang members should be viewed with some caution as a "solution".

Some hard historical facts remain undisputed about the role of gangs and higher levels of violence. Some of these facts remind us of how pitifully little we have done about the gang problem; and of how scant the answers are to major gang questions like "how many gang members are there in America?". The two top Catholic leaders of Mexico were gunned down in 1993 in Guadalajara, Mexico near the airport because their car resembled that of a rival drug lord targeted for assassination. The shooters that killed Mexico's Cardinal on May 24th, 1993 were American street gang members hired by a Mexican drug lord to hit a rival[53]. The facts show that important linkages have been made between foreign groups and American gangs: Islamic terrorist groups and the El Rukns, the Yakuza and the Latin Kings, and the above instance of a Mexican drug lord and the 30th Street Gang in San Diego. It would seem gangs may be expected to figure prominently in such future scenarios unless our society confronts this problem most forthrightly.

It was not until February of 1998 that arrests were made in the mistaken-identity/assassination-style killing of Roman Catholic Cardinal Juan Jesus Posada Ocampo. It turned out that the Arrelano Felix drug trafficking gang based in Tijuana, Mexico recruited ten (10) gang members from San Diego, California for this "hit". The gang members were from the Logan Heights neighborhood in San Diego. They were supposed to kill Joaquin "Chapo" Guzman Loera. "Chapo" is a rival gang/drug kingpin competing with the Arelano Felix drug gang.

What happened at the Guadalajara Airport parking lot in 1993 was that seven people were killed, including Cardinal Ocampo. Guzman was there, but he escaped injury. Guzman was in an armored car. Several of the shooters are, like the Felix brothers, fugitives living somewhere today in Mexico.

The Arellano Felix drug gang is led by Ramon Arrelano Felix and his brother, Benjamin Arrelano Felix. A two million dollar reward was offered by the FBI for information leading to the arrest of these two fugitives from justice.

DISCUSSION QUESTIONS:

(1) Up until the present, patterns of gang violence at the highest level (e.g., those involving homicide as a routine outcome) tended to involve a pattern characterized by retaliatory shootings (vengeance for the death of a fellow gang member) against rival gang members, drive-by shootings in areas where the cognitive maps tend to identify the area or residential location as a gang member site, arson against residential buildings known to be occupied by gang members, street stops (attacking persons who wear colors or look like rival gang members in streets controlled by a rival gang), assassination within the correctional setting by any of a variety of violent means including planned or opportunistic attacks upon rival gang members as well as correctional staff, and "false flag" random shooting (driving through a neighborhood, displaying a false gang hand sign and shooting the person who responds with the same gang hand sign). Can you envision any other future patterns of violence based on human history?

(2) Is it possible to have true nationwide gangs, functioning in virtually every state and major city in America? Do you feel that Philadelphia's MOVE group was a gang? Was the Symbionese Liberation Army a gang?[54] What problems can arise in using a definition of the gang as not simply that it is involved in crime over time, but that it or its members come to the attention of the community which views it as in some sense "threatening"? That is, could any political group be then defined as a gang if the local power structure felt "threatened by it"?

(3) If gang members are so hostile to legitimate authority, as is often presumed in the gang literature, then why are many rank and file gang members so highly compliant with the directives of the gang leaders, up to and including the order of carrying out a homicide or other serious assault involving great personal risk?

GANG MEMBERS WITH BOMBS

It is a growing trend: gang members with bombs. In early April, 1998, Rahshan Hodge, age 22, was wanted by police, having been indicted along with 43 others on drug and related charges, all those indicted were associated with the GI (Gary Indiana) Boys gang, also known as "Young Boys, Inc". While Young Boys, Inc was first established in Detroit, it eventually became active in Gary and Columbus, Ohio.

Police received a tip that Hodge might be coming into Columbus, Ohio on a Greyhound bus. Staking out the bus terminal, police spotted Hodge and arrested him. He had ten (10) pipe bombs in his possession at the time.

What do you think a gang member would do with ten bombs?

"It's Like Bosnia Around Here Sometimes",Former Chicago Police Department's Gang Crime Commander Donald Hilbring, 1998.

A place as large like Chicago with its own gang epicenter always has some kind of gang war going on. In late 1997 and early 1998, however, the gang violence became so terrifying near the Robert Taylor Homes, which are Chicago public housing buildings on Chicago's southside, that children were not attending school[55]. Their parents kept the kids home: there was too much "gun fire" during school hours.

Chicago's public schools receive funding based on what is called "ADA": Average Daily Attendance. So if attendance by the vast majority of enrolled students suddenly slips, the school is going to be hurting in a big way financially. The Robert Taylor Homes are located on Chicago's southside, with the most intense gang violence appearing at about 51st Street South along State Street (which runs north and south through Chicago).

With the onset of gang gunfire, attendance at one school dropped from 90 percent to 60 percent over night.

Extra police and new emergency initiatives were put into place, including "human shields" called "walking school buses" to protect children from the gang gunfire, in an attempt to restore confidence in being able to safely walk to and from the local school which is only blocks away.

Some of this conflict was tied to the displacement of a gang called the "Mickey Cobras", who lived at "the Hole", a building in the Robert Taylor Homes that was scheduled for de-commission and demolition. The Mickey Cobras are "People" and are literally surrounded in the adjoining high rise "projects" by "folks" gangs which are rivals. During this same time frame, the trained and armed security guards working for CHA had been "cut back". Clearly, there is a need for much enhancement of the gang sophistication in terms of training and preparedness among public housing officials in the United States who work, ultimately, for the U.S. Department of Housing and Urban Development.

THE DIFFERENCE BETWEEN LIVING IN NORTHERN IRELAND AND CHICAGO

In Northern Ireland, the terrorism and the battles between groups like the Irish Republican Army and Protestant Military Groups has rightfully given everyone an image of this piece of real estate as being "one very violent place". But just how different is Northern Ireland and the City of Chicago with regard to such lethal violence by combatants?

In Northern Ireland, there have been more than 3,000 deaths since 1969 because of the fighting there.

But Chicago is not too far behind in terms of gang deaths alone: from 1969 to present there have been 2,334 gang-related killings in Chicago.

The combatants in Northern Ireland usually have some training in the use of weapons and the shooters there usually hit their mark. A sizeable portion of the shooting in Chicago's gang wars are "stray shots" that end up hitting innocent bystanders.

So it is true that technically Chicago is safer than Northern Ireland in regard to number of killings by "combatants". But not by much.

End Notes:

[1] I am indebted to Professor Thomas F. Mc Currie for help on establishing the interface between the gang literature and the terrorism literature and who helped co-author a closely related paper on the same subject.

[2] And, of course, the gang member as "quisling" in Taylor (1990).

[3] Chapter 15 discusses some of the written gang constitutions and by-laws and shows the important element of "oppressed peoples" ideology. In fact, in the Spanish Gangster Disciple Nation the language of greeting to fellow gang members is "comrade", indeed these higher level gang formations come to view their fellow members as comrades in arms.

[4] As Sibley says "the police and the public are facing an enemy army with its own uniforms, weapons and rules" (1989: p. 403).

[5] See: Tom Brune and James Ylisela, Jr., "The Making of Jeff Fort", Chicago, November, 1988.

[6] Clearly, the strongest evidence yet to emerge that gangs have a left-wing ideological base is from the present study of gangs. In later chapters, in examining actual written gang constitutions, it will be noted how some major Chicago gangs have a common ideological component regarding their official declaration as being the avant guard for "oppressed peoples" generally, or at a minimum identifying with struggles of the oppressed groups.

[7] See Campbell and Muncer (1989) for how American gangs have historically lack a revolutionary ideology, in fact, their values have tended to be those of the "mainstream" society, albeit somewhat distorted.

[8] "Probers Hint Gangs Used L.A. Riots To Get Guns, But Not All Agree", Chicago Tribune, June 18, 1992: Section 1A, p. 41.

[9] Chicago Tribune, ibid.

[10] Hagedorn (1988: p. 203) was knowledgeable of this "street sweeping" tactic of gang repression.

[11] See Royko's (1971) Boss.

[12] See his The Wretched of the Earth.

[13] It also accounts, across race, for the ability of sting operations to net large numbers of such offenders using a "double con" method. See also, the related honor threats resulting in gang homicides in Quebec (Cusson, 1989).

[14] See Srivastava (1981) for a recent discussion of these "robbery gangs", which also links the conflict to caste and social class factors.

[15] See Cole and Momen (1986) for a similar example of how urban gangs functioned in political violence and did control entire towns, involving a coalition of gangs (circa 1843, Iraq).

[16] The contemporary, updated, drug-related version would therefore include drug consumption, and perhaps thereby, a shorter "crime free" time span of rest and relaxation.

[17] Patrick (1973, p. 47) reports the case of a Glasgow gang routinely acquiring its firearms in the local "black market" (e.g., criminal subculture), and one case of the gang burglarizing a military installation to steal fully automatic shoulder weapons, hand grenades, and other military equipment.

[18] Keiser (1969, 1979) should have been sufficient for law enforcement analysts to realize that this "gang-breaking" approach, while often "used by insurgent groups to weaken the effectiveness of organized governments, societies, and competing organizations" (Needle and Stapleton, 1983: p. 30), may not be effective with gangs at the higher end of the organizational development spectrum --- particularly the Vice Lords, which were studied by Keiser, which as a gang basically planned for their leaders to face such targeted prosecution programs and therefore to provide gang organizational continuity, the Vice Lords "institutionalized" leadership within roles. That allows for leadership succession in much the same way that the military command "passes" down the ranks to those eager to fill these positions.

[19] For a contemporary version, see Sibley (1989, pp. 420-421) who describes California's 1988 Street Terrorism Enforcement and Prevention Act, a piece of anti-gang legislation passed making it a felony to "participate in a street-gang" or if convicted of a gang-related crime (p. 421), which carries another three years imprisonment.

[20] William Whyte (1981: p. 255) used the same phrase "habitual association".

21 This allowed for an early form of a Targeted Offender Program; identifying those gang members most active, in leadership roles, and at large for law enforcement initiatives.

22 What we know did fail, as a third such experiment, was integrating the gangs into the military en masse into one unit. This did not work at all.

23 Most training materials would have us believe that terrorism usually implies the use of violence for political, religious, or ideological goals, with the noted exception of criminal terrorism which means the opportunistic use of violence for instrumental purposes (e.g., income motivated), planned or unplanned.

24 Some contemporary gang experts when talking about the goals of many action programs since the 1950's to present (e.g., New York City Youth Board, Chicago Youth Development Project, Community Youth Gang Services) use the term "to destabilize gang structures", as if they were small foreign countries, and such youth workers were CIA SOC/INT social engineering agents.

25 "Planning" was a necessary ingredient in Thrasher's definition of the gang and its behavior.

26 Most of such contemporary gangs would fail to even meet Cuba's revolutionary hero/theorist, Che Guevara's, three tenets of guerrilla warfare: constant vigilance, ok; constant distrust, ok; but constant mobility --- probably not, because to the extent they are "homies", bound to a specific turf or street corner or geographic "base", they are then vulnerable. Che's three guidelines (constant vigilance, constant distrust, constant mobility) were either not enough to be an effective guerrilla or he simply did not himself live up to them, having met a violent death at the hands of counter-insurgency forces.

27 In describing how large gangs get their guns and bombs, one recent book aimed at the layman audience (not a social scientific analysis or study of gangs) claimed "they buy these weapons from international arms dealers" (Webb, 1991: p. 75). Some gangs would probably like to have such a connection, but it is substantially less than factual to claim major American gangs have and use such connections now.

28 See for example the article quoting everyone from Malcolm Klein, Sgt. Wes Mc Bride, to the FBI on the nationwide expansion of the gang-drug-violence problem by Robert Mc Garvey, 1991, "Gangland: L.A. Super Gangs Target America", The American Legion (130)(2)(Feb): 25-27,60-61.

29 Recall that the California prison gang, the Black Guerilla Family (BGF), is very political and "is an adjunct of the Black Liberation Army (BLA) which operates as a Marxist-Leninist terrorist organization on the streets of America" (Jackson and Mc Bride, 1990: p. 53). But outside of the prison context, Jackson and Mc Bride see the BGF as apolitical, due to the waning of the political movement, such that this

gang is "now almost totally a criminal group trafficking in narcotics" (ibid).

30 According to a gang informant a relationship does exist between a known terrorist organization (the F.A.L.N.) and a street gang (Spanish Lords). This is a cultural tie, both being oriented towards and composed of members descending from Puerto Rico. This has a prison connection as well. Luis Rosa, the informant indicated, was tied to the FALN; and is like a brother with Carlos Vega, who was said to be a leader in the Spanish Lords. Further ties become established in the prison setting when, for example, in 1988 in Stateville Penitentiary a Latin Exchange Cultural Committee (an inmate organization with outside ties) was established to increase political awareness among inmates.

31 The murder of Chicago's Rudy Lozano is one such case known and documented. But, apparently, still not completely "solved".

32 The work of Davis (1982) is worth some attention here. It is a short book filled with pictures and horror stories; everything from a prison gang rape to "how to" approaches to making explosives. It does provide much discussion about terrorism generally (Davis, 1982: p. 50) and does tend to equate gang members with terrorists (Davis, 1982: p. 52).

33 See: "Gangs and Guns: A Task Force Report of the National Gang Crime Research Center", Nov. 11, 1994. For release at the Annual Meeting of the American Society of Criminology, Miami, FL. Co-principal investigators on this Task Force included: George Knox, John Laske, Jim Houston, Tom McCurrie, and Edward Tromanhauser.

34 See: "Plot To Blow Up Police Alleged Gang Sought Rocket Launcher, Feds Say", by Tom Seibel and Art Golab, Chicago Sun-Times, Oct. 21, 1994, p. 1, 12. See also: "Five in Gang Accused of Plan to Blow Up Police Station", Chicago Tribune, Oct. 21, 1994, section 2, p. 10.

35 Program literature from the BUILD, Inc program in Chicago described in Chapter 17 for example states "Youth gangs are like street armies, marching to a different drummer".

36 The "dirty dozen" were more like the dirty thousands. Mattick only analyzed several hundred from the Chicago area. These felony offenders were integrated into regular units during W.W. II and did well. See his Master's thesis, Department of Sociology, University of Chicago.

37 Cynicism here would mean this: for some white gangs like the Aryan Brotherhood, Ku Klux Klan, SWP, and others, these are not persons facing racial discrimination. They are often simply right-wing extremists, and not because of any condition of their own poverty.

38 Based on personal interviews with current staff and training materials used by the Chicago Area

Project.

[39]I am grateful to correctional gang investigator and researcher Jeff McCaddon for internal documents and indepth analysis materials on the BGF and other major gangs.

[40]George W. Knox, Ph.D., "Gang Organization in a Large Urban Jail", American Jails (January/February), 1993: pp. 45-48.

[41]Lt.-Col. W.H. Sleeman, 1849, Report on Budhuk alia Bagree Decoits and other Gang Robbers by Hereditary Profession and on the measures adopted by the Government of India for their Suppression. Calcutta: J.C. Sherriff, Bengal Military Orphan Press.

[42]David E. Kaplan and Elec Dubro, 1986, Yakuza: The Explosive Account of Japan's Criminal Underworld. Reading, MA: Addison-Wesley Publishing Company, Inc.

[43]James Haskins, 1975, Street Gangs Yesterday and Today. New York: Hastings House Publishers.

[44]Such as in Issue #107, two pages were devoted to the military men and women (including full names, rank, and photos); usually the Teen Angels magazine lists this type of material as "Green Angels", and gives the P.O. Box 338, Rialto, CA 92376 - the same address as Teen Angels magazine.

[45]Gordon McLean, 1991, Cities of Lonesome Fear: God Among the Gangs, Chicago: Moody Press.

[46]Karen Jowers, "Kids at Risk: The Spread of Gangs Has Some Military Communities Antsy, and Getting Involve", Life In the Times, 1992.

[47]A literal and exact transcription of the responses to the open-ended items is provided in Appendix B.

[48]I am grateful for the help in data collection from a member of the same military unit; who would prefer not to be explicitly mentioned in print.

[49]See: "NAACP Upstart Brings in 5,000 New Members", Chicago Tribune, October 20, 1994, section 2, p. 2.

[50]But they may make good surrogate terrorists. See Rachel Ehrenfeld, Narco Terrorism: How Governments Around the WOrld Have Used the Drug Trade to Finance and Further Terrorist Activities, 1990, Basic Books.

[51] Another variation is intense violent partisan conflict an example in Jamaica of which is described by Harrison (1988).

[52] Or so says Daniel Bell, in The Post Industrial Society.

[53]Hugh Dellios, 1993, "Mexican Drug Lords Recruit U.S. Street Gangs", Chicago Tribune, July 11, Section 1, p. 3.

[54] Remember it is convenient, for example, to exclude some groups like the Posse from gang analysis by saying "they are not gangs, they are organized crime" even though they have significant numbers of juvenile members. Does that mean we are simply being convenient by expanding our "inclusionary definition" of organized crime?

[55]See: Rosalind Rossi, "Taylor Homes Gunfire Cuts School Attendance", Chicago Sun Times, Jan. 7, 1998, p. 20.

TOP: Picture of Larry Hoover,
"The Chairman" of the GDs.
RIGHT: The Gang Never Forgets
Your Birthday Party.
BOTTOM: Speaking Out At The
1993 Gang Summit Meeting in
Chicago, Illinois (held at
the Congress Hotel).

Chapter 14

TOWARDS THE UNDERSTANDING
OF GANGS:
The Group Factor

INTRODUCTION

It is the "group" aspect of the gang that challenges our modern criminal justice system. It is the unique context of the group as a crime committing apparatus that also constitutes the definitive feature of a gang. The nature of the gang as a cohesive group behind bars also poses a new and formidable management problem for adult and juvenile correctional institutions. The study of group behavior is the legitimate domain of sociology, as the field of criminology is rightfully grounded in sociology as well. In this chapter we will examine aspects of gang group behavior much more closely.

Much of the variation in definitions of what constitutes a gang seems to be explained by the conceptual differences within a variety of theoretical orientations among gang authors. Here we review in as precise detail as possible some of the previous definitions of gangs in terms of their group components. Regarding group behavior our gang literature is surprisingly aloof from our social science knowledge of groups and what can or cannot be accomplished in doing something about gangs. So by addressing some of these issues and questions regarding the "group" factor and gangs, our analysis is at least one that is more explicitly grounded in our knowledge of social group formations from the social sciences.

In sociology a group is defined as two or more persons, and thus "threat group" can then be an umbrella from which to also examine political extremist groups and gang groups. But in much of the gang literature, it is generally agreed a gang must be a group of three or more persons. The reasoning is organizational: only in a group of three is it possible to achieve the primordial act of organizational life, the delegation of duty, the delegation of tasks. The Three Stooges could therefore constitute a level zero gang of mischievous adults, because it is possible for Moe to tell Curly to have the third stooge do something. Sending orders down through the command structure, that is delegation of responsibility or duty or even authority, is the primordial function of any organization. So the other truth that emerges here is that some gangs can become real organizations, and some function much more informally. Numbers of members and resources available to the gang are the determinants of whether the gang evolves into a greater level of organizational complexity and sophistication. And generally, the higher the organizational sophistication of the gang, the higher its crime threat.

This focus is important because when, for example in corrections, when we think we are dealing with individual inmates we may be actually dealing with groups of individuals related by gang affiliation.

Therefore, to understand these group dynamics is an important leap forward in being better prepared to deal with the gang problem in any situation.

ALL DEFINITIONS AGREE GANGS ARE A GROUP

While not all contributions to the gang literature provide an operational definition of the "gang", among those who at least provide us with the elements of what they consider a "gang", all definitions of gangs agree that gangs are a group of persons.[1] What remains rather ambiguous and uncertain is the logical question: what kind of social groups are gangs? And finally, what group characteristics do they have? Are gangs primary or secondary groups, membership or reference groups[2]? Formal or informal groups? And can a group become something more sophisticated?

It does not intellectually advance our understanding of gangs to simply categorize gangs as being outside of the extensive literature on social groups such as: conflict groups, deviant groups, subcultural groups, etc. That becomes little more than a definitional tautology: they are gangs, because they are deviant groups; ergo, because they are deviant, they are gangs. It is tautological because they become defined in terms of themselves.[3]

The one contribution to the gang literature which was clearly grounded in this "group" literature was that by Short and Strodtbeck (1974).[4] Strodtbeck is, of course, represented within the social-psychology literature on groups (Bales and Strodtbeck, 1951). The study of groups has been an area studied primarily by sociology, and by social-psychology. It is not an area of analysis carved out traditionally by the field of psychology which is more oriented towards the analysis of the individual mind, although obviously some such authors have advanced their analyses of gangs apparently aimed at a social-psychology or psycho-social explanation.[5]

Returning to our question: what kind of group is the gang, the analysis advanced here will take the position that the gang can be at its earliest formative stage a secondary[6] group, and at its higher stage of development is certainly somewhat more than a primary group. Most important to the linkage of this discussion of gangs to the wider social group formation and affiliation literature is the assertion that social organization is necessarily implicit to any gang analysis. Therefore, to the extent that we simply "label" the gang as having no formal organizational aspects or denying such paramilitary or "pyramidal" types of infrastructure as police are allegedly prone to believe, we are avoiding a closer analysis of this most important aspect relating to the social organization of gangs.

A social group, as differentiated from temporary collectives of human beings (as in aggregate recurrent interaction at a bus stop, etc), must by its definition have social organization. It must not only be a recurrent collectivity, it must have social organization and it must have an identity and objectives in common. Size is only one of the factors that will complicate all group analysis.[7]

Inside the gang, as a social group, is such affiliation principally integrative or is it instrumental? That is, is gang membership enjoyed and valued for its own sake as an end in itself, or is it instrumental: as a means to an end, to earn money, boost one's reputation, get protection, etc. Clearly, Thrasher had some grasp of this literature, by showing such a powerful influence from the work of Tarde.

From the gang literature, most conceptions of the gang see it as more than a social group, they generally see it as a primary group. But in addition to this, there are other characteristics of the group formation as a gang unit that have been cited in the literature. Figure 12, below, summarizes some of these group characteristics defining the gang. Clearly, these factors differentiate the gang from simple "Bowery Boy" or "drinking buddy" street corner groups that may be considerably more pro-social indigenous organizations.

Perhaps this lack of clarification on what type of social group formation being analyzed as a gang has accounted for some of the reader's sense from reviewing the American gang literature that "these authors are not talking about the same thing".[8] How many of Thrasher's 1,313 gangs were "gangs" and how many were "loose knit", "recurrent street corner adolescent gatherings", with little group behavior function qualifying as "criminal"? By the same adult tendency to view with alarm youth culture generally, in all generations as being rebellious, is its racist equivalent that of defining any group of two or more males of color gathered together as a gang?

Can there be a gang of two persons?[9] This is the question of group characteristics and group functions that has been assiduously avoided in most prior discussions of American gang formations. Let us examine Figures 12 and 13 below to answer this Socratic inquiry.

FIGURE 12

GROUP CHARACTERISTICS
IN DEFINING THE GANG

GROUP CHARACTERISTICS[10]:	AUTHOR(s)
Interstitial group	Thrasher
Recurrently associating	Klein
Gathered together on continuing basis	Wrobleski & Hess
Forming allegiance for common purpose	Jackson & McBride
Having an identifiable leadership	Miller
Having internal organization	Miller
Territorial oriented	Miller; Bobrowski
Attached to local territory	Thrasher
Adolescents	Klein
Perceived as a gang by others	Klein
Self-recognized as a distinct group	Klein; Rothman; + more
Integrated/strengthened thru conflict	Thrasher
Meeting face-to-face	Thrasher
milling, movement thru space as a unit	Thrasher
Conflict and planning: resulting in:	Thrasher
Tradition	Thrasher
Unreflective Internal structure	Thrasher
Esprit de corps	Thrasher
solidarity, morale, group awareness	Thrasher
Prone to possess and use weapons	Most authors
A system of mutual obligations	Whyte
Relatively stable composition	Whyte

Figure 13

FUNCTION AND BEHAVIOR OF THE GANG
AS A GROUP

FUNCTION AND BEHAVIOR:	AUTHOR(s)
Organized to protect turf by violence	Rothman, p. 2
Engage in anti-social behavior	Wrobleski & Hess
Unlawful and Criminal Activity	Jackson & McBride
Involved in conflict with police	Arnold (1965)
Individual or collective violence or illegal behavior	Miller
Violent or illegal activities defined as collective actions	Horowitz
Involved in enough delinquency to get a negative response from their community or law enforcement	Klein
Today have M-16's, grenades, and C-4	Vetter & Territo (1984)
Training and propelling others into a criminal career	Early Chicago School[11]
Create an atmosphere of fear and intimidation in the community	Dunston (1990: p. 6)

CAN A DYAD GROUP BE A GANG?

A group of two persons could certainly have all of the following characteristics generally attributed to gang organizations: it could be homogeneous with respect to race or ethnicity, recurrently associating, gathered together on a continuing basis, forming an allegiance for a common purpose (legitimate or illegitimate), having an identifiable leadership, having internal organization (with two persons obviously the minimal levels of vertical and horizontal dimensions), being territorially oriented, or attached to a local territory or turf, they could be persons of any age including adolescents, could be perceived as a gang (whether they are or are not) or recognized as a distinct group, and could recognize themselves as a gang (regardless of their objectively minimal size and force), their bonds could be strengthened further by being labelled or through conflict with others (including adult authority), they meet face-to-face, mill around and have mutual movement through space as a unit, they experience or engage in conflict and planning, they develop a tradition, have an esprit de corps, a sense of solidarity, morale, group awareness, have boundary maintenance functions defining "in group" and "out group"/friend and foe, it can be an open system with mutual obligations and a relatively stable composition. That could describe any dyad, triad or larger group in America.

What differentiates gangs from conventional forms of group affiliation is "what the group does, how the group functions". That is, its group behavior. When it serves a protective or any other illicit function through violence, engages in anti-social conduct that is also unlawful and criminal activity, in either individual or collective violence or illegal behavior, when it is involved in sufficient amounts of delinquency to get a negative response from either the community or law enforcement officials, or when it trains and propels others into a criminal career ---- then we are talking about a gang.

To borrow from the psychology of Yablonsky (1962) perhaps two sociopaths together meeting the above qualifications, but otherwise functioning perhaps in governmental service, would technically meet, sans the definition of violent or law violating deviance, etc, the qualification of being defined as a gang (Yablonsky, 1962: p. 196). We really do not want to be in the intellectually limited situation of having to agree, by an insufficient definition, that two persons engaging in anal sex in Georgia --- where such behavior is illegal, even felonious --- therefore constitutes a "sex gang".[12]

The consensus of gang researchers and criminal justice practitioners alike is that there must be three or more members to be considered a "gang". A dyad simply constitutes a "team" at best. With three persons, it is possible to engage in the primordial act of any organization: delegation, actor X can instruct actor Y to have actor Z commit a crime.

CAN GANG MEMBERS BE DEPROGRAMED?

The most extreme extension of this logical inquiry must be this: can gangs be artificially created, in either a laboratory situation or in real life in their natural habitat? The answer on both accounts appears to be yes. But before elaborating further, let us add to Figure 12 some of the other definitional continuities found in the literature, one previously discussed as ethnic homogeneity. Let us consider a variation on this, that being social homogeneity.

In the "Robbers Cave" experiments by Muzafer Sherif, et al (1961) the basic pattern of adolescent group conflict was artificially created. This involved using young boys (11 and 12 year olds) in the situation of a summer camp who were randomly separated after a short period of time. In a few days, both groups of boys developed their own group names "the eagles" and "the rattlers" along with a corresponding level of group loyalty. The groups were experimentally manipulated to induce group rivalry and inter-group conflict. The enmity induced became real to the point where bringing the two groups together under any pretext of "making peace" actually accentuated and increased the level of potential violence between them. It increased aggression towards the "out-group" and increased cohesion and solidarity for the "in-group".[13] When Sherif and his experimenters created the artificial situation of a common "external" enemy, a superordinate goal, they had to act together and in so doing all inter-group conflict was eliminated.[14]

A somewhat related piece of evidence is found in the work of Schwitzgebel, who started a kind of "gang drop-in center" that sought to create a laboratory "subculture" (Schwitzgebel, 1965: p. 21). Few quote this research even though a close reading of it suggested that the author claimed some success in using professional psychological services to help youths leave the gang. Obviously, the "gang" in this instance, however, was probably a level zero or level one type of gang formation. That is, not a more highly organized gang organization.

In our correctional gang research we included "gang deprogramming" as a service in a list of such services for incarcerated juveniles as a validity item. We expected no one to say they provided such "gang deprogramming" services. We were more than somewhat surprised to find more than a few claimed to provide this service that we thought at the time was only a figment of our gang researcher imaginations.

THE INTERESTING AND CURIOUS WORK OF SCHWITZGEBEL (1965)

The research by Schwitzgebel at Harvard offers a similar affirmation of the thesis that gangs can be artificially created, albeit from a somewhat different angle. Schwitzgebel as a graduate student in psychology, set up an elaborate off-campus laboratory. They rented a store front and made it appear like a scientific laboratory, with electrical equipment, and even a rat until they had to get rid of it. When Schwitzgebel went out cruising on his "hunt" for street-corner/gang-affiliated delinquents telling them he would "pay them in cash" to come near the university to his laboratory and "talk into his tape recorder", most of them thought he was a homosexual, not a cop.[15] Few contemporary scholars seem to acknowledge the self-professed contribution to gang analysis and research by Schwitzgebel (1965) entitled Street-Corner Research: An Experimental Approach to the Juvenile Delinquent so it bears some attention here.

It is unclear from reading Schwitzgebel (1965) what if anything was his guiding theory prior to engaging in such "street" research. He quotes everyone from Nietche to Freud, to the Nuremburg trials and sado-masochism in France.[16] But he was very sophisticated and effectively outfitted with resources desired by youths. His described statistical project involved 30 white males with an average age of 17.8,[17] but other cases were also described from this Research Laboratory Street Center known as the Streetcorner Research Lab (SRL).

It was a remarkable improvement on Whyte's research project, which Schwitzgebel was aware of and positively disposed towards.[18] First, according to Schwitzgebel this project "did not begin with a logical design later given to others to complete" (p, 12).[19] Rather it was --- like Whyte --- a very risk-taking and personal, psychological, approach; almost "interviewing as therapy" as Schwitzgebel coined the term (p. 26).

The language here is very clear. Schwitzgebel was always the "experimenter", and the gang member (50% were gang members) or delinquent was the "subject". He was clearly an affectively inspired experimenter:

The participants in the therapeutic experiment, whether called doctors and patients or experimenters and subjects, may thus proceed "inspired by love and guided by knowledge" toward that excellent life so fervently advocated by Spinoza long ago (Schwitzgebel, 1965: p. 93).

His approach to obtaining research cooperation from delinquents was quite unique. It meant in one case hanging out playing pin ball for a long period and doing this so effectively at "winning free games" that he naturally attracted the attention of a nearby young male who eventually confessed to him a pattern of delinquency and agreed to come at once to the lab with him to be a "subject". In another case it meant pulling up to a street corner in a car in front of a group of boys and saying he wants to meet "Bongo" a delinquent, to make movies:

The experimenter stopped his car...several boys were standing there...the experimenter explained that he was looking for Bongo to give him a job. The job would be taking movies. "I'm on the level, and here's the camera." The gang was noticeably impressed by the new, streamlined camera. (Schwitzgebel, 1965: p. 95).

Schwitzgebel was not only in vogue, knowledgeable of research, but also anticipated "electronic monitoring" for offenders. He was aware of the difficulty of gaining public understanding:

Certainly a part of the difficulty lies in the great difference between the standards of "proper" behavior established by law and custom and the actual, covert behavior of many "proper" people (Schwitzgebel, 1965: p. 107).

The Streetcorner Research lab was so successful in penetrating the subculture that it attracted others not included in the statistical analysis of delinquents. One was a sailor with a drinking problem who was treated with syrup of ipecac (an emetic) for aversive conditioning in stopping his crime of writing bad checks (ISF, insufficient funds). Another was a homosexual college student who:

referred himself to the laboratory for treatment of "homosexual tendencies". He agreed to participate as an assistant in the designing of an experimental treatment procedure (Schwitzgebel, 1965: p. 127).

For baseline data collection, the homosexual recorded his sexual impulses in a log over a thirteen month period before the "treatment with syrup of ipecac was begun" (P. 128).

Schwitzgebel reports the convenience or appearance of success in aversively conditioning this homosexual away from "gay bars". The subject eventually got married and was "very content". Although, the man still had such impulses, but just didn't consider them a problem (Schwitzgebel, 1965: p. 128).

Schwitzgebel did not claim to have totally rehabilitated all these delinquents, perhaps because after all he and his Streetcorner Research Lab was an elaborate "black box". Who knows what, if anything, did work? Was it the priest, the philosopher, or the experimenter that brought about the desired change towards law abiding behavior? We wouldn't know.

What is interesting is the apparent eagerness of these youths to engage in deviance under the direction of the "experimenter". One situation was described where several boys came in to the lab, got a couple dollars, and:

On the way back to the amusement center, the boys asked me when the <u>real</u> job started --- meaning when do we roll the drunks or do the actual work (Schwitzgebel, 1965: p. 16).

That is, apparently these youths wanted to perform delinquency under experimental conditions for Schwitzgebel. Once the "lab" was underway, the written instructions asked the youths to defer to the seasoned veterans of the laboratory for any questions they might have. This method set up a natural group

formation by introducing one delinquent to the next, thereby creating groups that would have never possibly formed in the absence of the Streetcorner Research Lab (SRL).

If it took an attractive young blond female with a convertible car to impress the kids, then it was used; and in so doing, imprinting significantly on their tendency to be more attracted to the SRL. Cash, bonuses, tickets to ball games, beverages, sweets, sandwiches ---- whatever lured them.

Before rushing to get a copy of Schwitzgebel (1965), please note that no theory of gangs was ever offered or developed. It is certainly made more reference to the scholarly literature and it was more quantitative than Whyte, but is not a direct contribution to gang theory. It has an indirect value through possibly being linked to the conception that gangs can be artificially created or socially engineered, as shown by the offering of resources to be exploited, or pooling together delinquents who would not have otherwise engaged in group delinquency together. So in a "prisoner's dilemma" of owning two books and being told by prison officials you would have to dispose of one of them, a good hypothesis would see Whyte's book staying, and Schwitzgebel's going to the trash --- if it was an astute prisoner. We did not need Schwitzgebel to know that desired resources can be used to attract offenders. For as much discussion as he gave to the ethics of research and getting "informed consent", he would have probably also advised these youths: "you will be meeting other delinquents and statistically you could perhaps find yourself engaged in new crime patterns with these other offenders should you develop close ties to them".

For the record, Schwitzgebel did provide in an appendix some information on client "outcomes" (after association with the laboratory). Here it gets confusing. In the first table of data (N = 30), 22 of the subjects are indicated to have been gang members before lab association, and only 3 afterwards. Were it not for the fact that at best this might have entailed a level zero to level one gang formation, such results based on psychological intervention would constitute a miracle from a gang dismemberment or gang deprogramming point of view. And accomplished apparently without syrup of ipecac. But we are not given any indication of the nature of the time lapse for the follow-up period. As experiments go, this one was more than sloppy.

CAN AN ADULT OR AUTHORITY CREATE A YOUTH GANG?

The position advanced here is: affirmative[20]. But as an artificially produced social group formation, not arising naturally from conditions of conflict, deprivation, etc, this should be qualified by saying as well: with varying degrees of effectiveness and continuity.[21]   Basically, it is much easier to manipulate than to create. The question is not dissimilar to this: can a powerful country like the USA help create, foster, cultivate, support and give direction to an insurgent force in a foreign hostile nation? Can it succeed is the real question, and the answer again in some situations is a historical yes. Such groups can obviously be created, even in the laboratory. This raises, analytically, the again unanswered and unaddressed question in our gang literature: how long must a gang operate to be considered a quasi-institution? Is a one-night escapade sufficient to define a group with extra-legal goals, objectives, and illegal functions as a gang?

A similar analytical difference exists between that which is legally defined as a "gang" or "mob" in terms of law violation behavior, which can be punished as such, and the need for the criminologist to have a more social scientific definition. For example, mob action statutes, such as those in Illinois:

Chapter 38, Section 25-1 **Mob Action.** (a) Mob action consists of any of the following: (1) The use of force or violence disturbing the public peace by 2 or more persons acting together and without authority of law; or (2) The assembly of 2 or more persons to do an unlawful act; or (3) The assembly of 2 or more persons, without authority of law, for the purpose of doing violence to the person or property of any one supposed to have been guilty of a violation of the law, or for the purpose of exercising correctional powers or regulative powers over any person by violence. (b) Mob action is a Class C misdemeanor. (c) Any participant in mob action which shall by violence inflict injury to the person or property of another commits a Class 4 felony. (d) Any participant in a mob action who does not withdraw on being commanded to do so by any peace officer commits a Class A misdemeanor.

In such mob action statutes, which addresses as seen above cases involving rioting or vigilante groups, do not require the group to have previously existed as a group entity for purposes of prosecution. It is rather sufficient that they existed as a group at the time they collectively engaged in what amounted to a violation of the criminal code. Thus, analysis of "mob action" convictions will not be a good source of data for the explanation of gangs.

On the other hand, if aggression is a measure of violence or its potential, then a low threshold of frustration can apparently be induced in groups of children from laboratory experiments relating to this aspect of artificial gang formation. Such was the nature of the lab experiment by Davitz (1952). Twenty children (7 to 9 year olds) were used to create 5 groups of 4 each. These children were trained to be aggressive through physical games similar to "king of the hill", etc (Spot). Another 20 children were

given constructive training on how to deal with frustration. This was a comparison of "aggressives" versus "constructives" by inducing both qualities in the child groups. Aggressives were trained to damage property and their aggressive interpersonal behavior was both praised and positively reinforced. Later comparisons of both groups (aggressives vs. constructives) showed that such training significantly differentiates reaction to frustration. Did the Davitz lab provide adult legitimacy for this aggressiveness without which it may not have surfaced? We don't know, it is a plausible rival hypothesis. Just as it is plausible to believe that natural experiments in the field occur along the same lines, such as when one high school originates a gang like the Crips and another nearby high school follows with the Bloods, as happened in Los Angeles in 1969. Two gangs rising to play their version of "king of the hill" in the underground economy of illegal drug sales income, and then spreading nationally in the late early 1990s to the point where today sets of Crips and Bloods can be found in all states, in all social contexts, in many cities large and small. Crips and Bloods gangs do not persist because they are unsupervised kids, they are supervised by adult leaders of the same gang, their "OGs" (original gangsters).

A prototype of the Davitz social training model for engineering gang violence would have to: (1) segregate by sex to allow the macho hypermasculine factor to operate as happened in the movie classic Lord of the Flies, (2) allow them to self-segregate on the basis of ethnicity to artificially create the ethnic homogeneity factor so historically associated with gang life, and (3) induce hostility towards wider society and an increase their levels of aggression[22]. Obviously, the efficiency of manufacturing gang violence/aggression could be increased or accentuated by screening out those youths who had high levels of internal locus of control, and conversely, screening in those most likely to be influenced by their group setting: those with strong scores for having an external locus of control. Such would be the social engineering model for producing gang violence based on prior research involving essentially the manufacturing process of youthful aggression. Further, this tells us much about how we might go about preventing gang violence as well by reversing or neutralizing these principles.

The question of artificially creating a gang is comparable, in group control terms, to the issue: can someone start, develop and expand, and continue over a relatively long period of time with high tenure among members and low turnover, and function as a total control "cult"? Some knowledge of cults, as groups, can perhaps help us to understand the internal group dynamics of gangs. Cults, like gangs, "exist outside of the mainstream of society" and often have "strong, flamboyant leaders" (Popenoe, 1983: p. 443). Cults, like gangs, have been described as arising in reaction to feelings of deprivation (Glock, 1964).

What social-psychological fulfillment, then, does the cult and gang provide is the question from a control or dismemberment point of view, because that will have to be known to create equivalent such "counter functions" to be able to effectively, through propaganda or other means, "weed out" gang members by attracting them to something equally fulfilling but more pro-social in nature. Such a question must be answered prior to any responsible effort to "intervene" with gang members, for otherwise we are, by the lack of social scientific guidance, unwittingly taking the risk of strengthening or reinforcing gang organization or increasing its members level of commitment to the gang through our otherwise good intention to target gangs and gang members for social services.

We shall, in a later section, address more directly the matter of social service intervention, outreach, detached worker programs, etc, for social policy purposes. Just as the lack of theory before engaging in research or experimentation is an intellectual danger, we know from the past (e.g., Fry) that program initiatives not based on social science are similarly inclined to failure --- indeed, worse, can even help foster gang development. It bears repeating here that if a program has no analytically sound direction it will have no logical basis for what to expect in terms of impact or results. The difference in probability terms of achieving desired results is one between a crap shoot and playing a million-to-one lotto. Even with good theory, it can still be a crap shoot: there is still the problem of correctly implementing the theory. But with the atheoretical program, anything could happen, there could be as many possible outcomes as there are definitions of the situation. We would be best advised to take the crap shoot any day over the atheoretical program, it is a simple matter of the probability gain in doing some good.

The other evidence that a gang can be artificially created is found in what we know about native American fascism movements (Knox, 1976). One such group, which gained national attention for its "march on Skokie" was the NSPA (National Socialist Party of America) based in Chicago's southwest side neighborhood known as Marquette Park in the mid to late 1970's. The group thrived on the ethnic antagonism in the area; Marquette Park was virtually all white, and the neighboring community to the east was predominantly African-American. It developed and "outfitted" two such neo-nazi gangs.

The NSPA created the "Young Wolves" for children ages 12 and under, and it created "the Ex-terminators" for youths between the ages of 13 and 17. Anyone 18 or above could be a regular storm trooper. Both of these youth groups were organized as violence-oriented gangs and were given much reinforcement by adults in the NSPA. Both youth groups were given their own "publications" to extol their commitment to the nazi cause. In so doing the youths would put their "by line" on articles and increase their commitment to the nazi group. Through this kind of publication the NSPA youths would distribute the publications at schools, etc, to attract more delinquency-prone youths and encourage racial violence. Youths were offered free "white power" t-shirts, nazi arm bands, and were offered training from the adult nazis in "how to shoot all kinds of rifles and pistols at a real range with live ammo" to draw youths into the nazi organization.

In keeping with the overall anti-intellectual tendency of NSPA ideology the nazi youths were encouraged to drop out of schools where they had to "sit behind a desk all day". The public schools were portrayed as Jewish-communist dominated institutions which forced the youths to take liberal "social studies" and which "tease your mind with algebra formulas you'll never use after you graduate".

To support the contention that youth gangs can be artificially created, at least in the context of white racist gangs, it is helpful to quote directly from some of the publications from these two youth auxiliary units of the NSPA. One such newsletter, for the "exterminators", had several photographs of youths participating with the NSPA "white power" marches and notes that:

The Youth were the most active marchers of all. They bombed the windshields of passing Cadillacs with rocks and bottles. They even clashed with the police and went to jail for their race.

The Youth are always in the forefront for the struggle for White Power. In 1966, it was mainly the Youth who burned the cars of Martin Luther King and his invading Black hordes. They lit the night skies of Marquette Park with the fires of total resistance. That same spirit of White resistance in the Youth will someday strike a nation-wide up-rising against Black terror and White betrayal!

Similarly, the "young wolves" in their publication noted that:

At the first march, on August 23rd, White Youth members bombed cars with rocks and bottles along 71st street. Even a bus-load of coons was attacked by the "Young Wolves" of the White Youth Front! After the second march, on October 12th, the Youth stormed the house of a nigger who just moved into the white neighborhood east of Western avenue. The White Youth Front is at the head of the fight for White power.

It was clear that the NSPA adults offered these youths a good deal of serious recognition and provided for social interaction with adult NSPA members. The youths were given a sense of identity and purpose which enabled them to be manipulated for performing illegal acts of violence consistent with the racist goals of the NSPA leaders.

Of more than some interest to the gang student, this Chicago neo-nazi group was effectively put out of business through coordinated and effective criminal prosecution of the core members. The top leader went to state prison for deviate sexual assault on a minor, and other high ranking nazis caught federal beefs for firearms violations, etc. Had their leader gone to prison for anything other than being a homosexual pedophile he might have effectively used this to continue gang operations. But he was not, to the present author's knowledge, able to come back to Chicago from prison and effectively continue such large scale operations.

CAN A GANG BE DISMEMBERED?

If we are to view gangs with some degree of concern if not simply a recognition that they are destructive to the community, then how could a community-based program be structured to achieve the specific objective of gang dismemberment? This assumes we should not repeat the gang suppression criminal justice policy of the past, to simply "lock up" all such gang members, because at a late 1980's average cost of $75 per day for juveniles, that is an average cost of $27,375 per year and is likely to be a very expensive proposition not to mention its obvious potential for being counterproductive. America's prisons today are overcrowded to an all time high. We do not have the capacity to lock them all up. The only answer is that which is to be found in the communities of our nation. So in light of this, can the value of gang membership be undermined or used to triage in an effort to instill new values or dislocate periphery members to a more pro-social type of group affiliation? The answer, on the basis of social science research, is yes. But it could also mean inadvertently inducing a variation of "Gresham's law of conflict".[23] The research by Kelley and Volkart (1952) is instructive here.

Kelley and Volkart (1952) tested a Boy Scout troop on their valuation of group membership in the scouts. Then they gave the scouts an experimental propaganda speech by an adult outsider to the effect "camping and woodcraft are evil --- camping destroys nature and threatens our ecosystem, and its dumb too, the city is more fun, and scouts don't need a knowledge of the forrest, they need a knowledge of city life to survive". They found a definite inverse relationship between prior value placed on group membership and the strength of induced new values

via propaganda. That is, those scouts who least valued their membership or group affiliation were those with the highest induced value change from the propaganda; and vice versa. Remember, this is only inducing attitudinal (values and beliefs) change, not behavioral change. Kelley and Volkart did not after their psy-war phase create another organization that could be used to float off scout members alienated from their troop. It is one thing to change attitudes, and it is an altogether different and more difficult task to change behavior; especially group affiliation.

It has not been the custom to directly refer to gangs or offenders generally and in the same context of social services to make reference to the use of psy-war or propaganda techniques. At least most of the literature seems to avoid such mentioning of psy-war or propaganda. But to be intellectually honest many programs explicitly have this function or intent. Secondly, propaganda and psy-war can work under some conditions. This is not to recommend or endorse, but rather a recognition of a larger body of social science that can inform us more precisely about our expectations for gang intervention strategies having to do with dismemberment. Mostly, it is an honest and open recognition from an interdisciplinary perspective which is taken here to best understand group dynamics relevant to gangs.

Viewing the gang as a group in which their members make public commitments sheds some light on the difficulty of swaying their hearts and minds. A gang member has much that is expected in terms of behavior and values from the group. The research by Hovland, et al (1957) showed that propaganda is only minimally effective among a group with a public commitment. That is, their research showed only 14% vulnerable to propaganda in such a "public commitment" group (students who were told their views would be published in the student paper) as compared with a much higher vulnerability (41%) to propaganda among students who were allowed to be anonymous, or for whom there was no induced "public commitment". Such rituals of public declaration, oaths, etc, become, apparently, strong reinforcing mechanisms and the higher the commitment to the gang, the less likely any propaganda initiative is going to be effective at achieving voluntary dismemberment.

Clearly, the difference is one of having to defend and "stand up" to such a groups public views and beliefs. When a person feels no such external expectation or environmental press, then propaganda is likely to be much more effective. Finally, to achieve gang dismemberment, more than value change will be required. There will have to be alternative such organizations, perhaps something like the WPA, or relocation programs providing for income-generating opportunities and residency, genuine alternatives, perhaps a national service program, who knows, but it will have to represent a genuine alternative to the gang organization before we can expect the gang members to defect.

If we want them to defect then we will have to offer something to defect to. What that might consist of entails the much larger issue of how our society decides what are or are not appropriate government expenditures. That is a political science question beyond the scope of the present analysis.

IS INDIVIDUAL CRIME COMMITTED BY GANG MEMBERS "GANG CRIME"?

Assume a motorcycle gangs rides into town for a good time. You are in the wrong place at the right time and one of the members of the motorcycle gang has a verbal altercation with you. The next thing you know, you are mortally wounded. Would you consider this a "gang crime" even though it was not approved of in advance by the entire membership of the gang on a voting referendum on whether to kick your ass or not? Or take a more typical example: you are in the park with your children, gangs are selling drugs nearby unbeknownst to you, and a rival gang approaches the area in a slow moving car and opens fire with an AK-47, spraying the area with gun shots, and your child is accidentally killed from stray gun shots meant perhaps for the gang members nearby. Would the death of your child be considered an urban accident, or would you consider it a gang-related homicide?

This is a most profound issue because it has many implications for the suppression of gang crime in America. Perhaps the way to begin this analysis is to note that group dynamics that a gang provides are different from the kind of lone-ranger criminal who acts alone as a sole actor. A crime committed by a gang member may bring status to the member. There is an incentive to commit crimes of violence that the lone-ranger or individual non-gang member criminal lacks. Further, the "risky shift" effect operates in a gang context all the time: persons commit crimes, sometimes excessively brutal, that they may not have had the guts to commit as lone individual non-gang member criminals. The group gives them some sense of a larger reference group, a strength and support group.

The gang may have the good sense not to declare in its written constitution that "we are official enemies of the USA and we commit our lives to the commission of any and all crimes that will facilitate the erosion of the American way of life; and thus, all members are encouraged to commit crimes daily with our blessings and protection." In other words, the gang need not officially approve of the crime, nor need the entire gang be involved in the crime, before the crime by a gang member can be consid-

ered "gang-related" crime. Why this is so deserves some criminological background that some commentators have failed to acknowledge in their efforts to minimize the criminal impact or threat of gangs today by claiming that most such crimes are not "gang crimes" at all, they are simply the errant behavior of individual gang members.

An ethnographer who wants to study the social linguistic behavior of gangs rather than their criminal behavior patterns would be on solid ground in speaking to such unique aspects about gangs --- further it would be a worthwhile contribution that has not yet surfaced from such "hang out with the gang" researchers. But it would not be appropriate to jump disciplines and begin asserting that "gang crime" does not exist....only individual crime exists by individuals who may or may not be members of gangs. The reason this is faulty is that to deal with crime issues one must be linked into the much larger body of cumulative knowledge called criminology. Then and only then do such assertions become defensible in relationship to the previous literature on crime and gangs. Any analysis of gang behavior or its impact on crime that is not grounded in the wider social science of criminology runs the risk of being little more than wild-eyed rhetoric or pseudo-intellectual demagoguery. Why? Because it ignores what we already know!

What we already know about juvenile delinquency, for example, is that by far the largest amount of it in America is group related. It is committed in small groups. This was one of the many contributions documented by the early work of Shaw and Mc Kay in their Chicago research on crime and delinquency. Delinquents and criminals seek out "partners", they feel safer somehow having a "rappy". Morally, the very presence of a partner in crime helps to neutralize the moral implications of normative violation: whether it is robbing an elderly person, or a run of the mill burglary. The presence of a "partner" means socially "I am not doing wrong....I am doing my necessary business".

Many crimes of gangs simply are never reported, particularly the crimes of violence against their own members. In fact, in the typical violent initiation ritual, few prosecutors are successful in prosecuting a "beating" that someone agrees to accept as part of a gang initiation ritual. But how voluntary was it? Taken to its extreme, citizens do not have the right to go to the gang and say "please end my life...I am suffering from a terribly painful disease". Gangs --- for a fee --- would probably accommodate anyone who could not be served by physicians who have become prominent in the media for their "right to die" practice of supervised suicide.

The real issue here in resolving whether any given crime committed by a gang member is or is not a "gang-related" crime is legal and social: it is the issue of accountability and motivation. In short, would the crime have been committed if the offender had not been a gang member? Using this standard, most such crimes committed by gang members would be considered "gang-related". Let us take a real case to examine this more closely.

In Chicago's Cabrini-Green public housing complex, gang shootings did decrease for a time after the public outcry over the killing of Dantrell Davis in October 1992 and the "gang truce" that followed. But in 1993 gunfire claimed another victim: two rival gang members vying for the affection of a young lady quarrelled, the result --- one of them pulled out a gun, and killed the rival. Was this simply a "crime of passion"? Or could it be considered a gang-related homicide? If they were not gang members, would they still have such easy access to firearms or actually be in the normal routine of carrying concealed firearms? It is use of the firearm, after all, that caused the death. If the gang facilitated possession of the firearm, or if the offender carried the gun in performing gang duties or "defending his nation", then it was clearly a gang-related crime: the offender used the power the gang gave him to commit the crime. Did the fact that both men were members of rival gangs accentuate the conflict and thus increase the likelihood of using lethal violence to settle a dispute? If so, then it could be considered a gang-related homicide because the enmity predisposed the two suitors in the love triangle toward a higher level of violence, the loser in any non-violent resolution to who will win the affection of the lady in question would lose much face with his own gang --- particularly knowing a rival gang member persevered. Gang members are required to attack if their gang is "put down", or else it is "dropping the flag" and can be severely punished if discovered by fellow gang members. If both combatants exchanged verbal gang put-downs as well, then the crime is clearly "gang-related" no matter what the crime was: it is not a matter of whether both gangs gave each of these two men authority in advance to use lethal violence to win a romance war, rather they acted not just as "individuals", but as members of a larger reference group to which they are accountable.

The gang exerts enormous social control over its members. It also psychologically empowers the individual gang member into possibly committing crimes that he or she would not do alone or if they were not a gang member. As gang members are prone to claim, once a gang member they have "back up". Thus, under the theory of plain accountability most crimes of violence as well as income-producing crimes committed by gang members can still be considered "gang-related". Without crime as an ongoing pattern of activity by its members it would not be a gang

at all. The gang facilitates crime by its individual members by providing the group approval and support for such deviance.

Would the millions of dollars in damage to American property every year by gang graffiti in the endless series of "throw ups" (putting up the gang logo) and "throw downs" (putting down the rival gang logo) occur if the individuals who are responsible for these acts were not gang members? Not likely. Thus, gang graffiti in terms of criminal damage to property is almost always a gang-related crime. Similarly, most violence by individual gang members can be considered gang-related; the reason, similarly, is that while it may have been committed as an "individual", it was not just an individual lone actor that committed the violent crime: it was someone who is uniquely under the web of influence from a larger group that is supportive of such crime.

Beyond this issue lies the legitimate criminological inquiry into how much crime in America can be attributed to gangs and gang members. Without the sense of personal power that a gang provides to a gang member it would be possible to argue that much such "individual crime" is not gang-related. But the fact remains: the gang exists and persists because of this social-psychological empowerment and reinforcement of criminal behavior.

If we listened to and believed the gangs, then the "gangs" per se commit no crime. That is an apology for gang crime, not a social scientific analysis of gang crime. The gang provides the psychological reinforcement for crime, the motivation for crime, and the social environment that morally neutralizes the stigma of crime and violence. The gang is a group structure that therefore facilitates the crime of its members. If it is not possible to isolate the definition of the situation any gang member experiences in his or her larger society away from the gang and other gang members, then it is not possible to say that the gang has no effect on the crime the person commits as an individual. Ergo, the lone gang member in a forest who sets it afire thinking he is getting back at the "system" is acting out his own interpretation of the gang manifesto, and this would be a gang crime. Similarly, the gang member who has a "reputation" to uphold for his gang, who commits an act of domestic violence is still committing a gang crime, because it is a part of the motivational sequence and the predisposition of the offender.

SUMMARY AND CONCLUSION

We have, in opening up the discussion of the gang as a social group, only touched the surface of a wealth of social science research and literature that can help inform us more about both understanding the gang in modern society and in devising policy for "what" if anything to do about the gang problem.

The inquiries made here raise questions that the astute student of criminology would want to raise: can a gang consist of two persons, how long must they so associate to have the "gang" label, etc. This focus has the goal of leading to a clarification of some of the critical issues surrounding gangs today.

Finally, this chapter has offered an initial basis for the assertion that gangs can be artificially created,[24] in the laboratory and elsewhere. Which is to say that adults can create youth gangs. The evidence is scant at this point, but is still quite suggestive.[25] On the same basis, little direct evidence exists regarding dismemberment and therefore this chapter has tried to bring into discussion what are considered to be related conceptual difficulties.

Clearly, we have only begun to understand the gang as a group.

DISCUSSION QUESTIONS:

(1) Do you think that experiments without an Institutional Review Board (giving input on issues of ethics and the rights of human subjects in research) involving gang members could "go astray" or potentially have a reverse-intended effect? How might this happen?

(2) Given sufficient resources, do you think an adult could create a youth gang? If so, what would it take for that gang to become institutionalized over time?

(3) Raising a child to hate is no accomplishment. How could raising a child to be a gang member or inculcating beliefs and values of racial or ethnic hatred be construed as "child abuse"?
Why do you think it is still not a crime for adults to recruit or lure children to be gang members?

"Five Year Old Boy Refuses To Steal Candy For Gang Members: He is Then Thrown Out The Window of the 14th Floor".

The concept of the "risky shift phenomena" is easy to understand: just watch the movie Lord of the Flies. In the absence of social control from responsible adults, children in a group context are capable of anything under the sun.

On October 13, 1994 two young gang members were extorting and shaking down a five year old named Eric Morse. Eric Morse lived at the Ida B. Wells project. Eric refused to go out and steal candy for the two gang members. So what did the two gang members do? They dropped him from the 14th story out the window. Eric died immediately.

The fact is: human beings will do things in a group context that they would just never do as single, lone individuals. In theory, there is no logical limit to the level of brutal violence that someone is capable of engaging in if the "risky shift phenomena" kicks in.

Did you ever do things on Halloween night as a child in a small group context that you probably never would have done if you were alone?

LIBERAL AND CONSERVATIVE DEFINITIONS OF "GANG CRIME"

To have a liberal definition of gang crime, one applies liberal standards: if a gang member did it, it is a gang crime. To have a conservative definition of gang crime, more "conditions" must be satisfied: in fact the ultra orthodox conservative version if one gang member kills another, it cannot involve drugs, because then it gets categorized as a "drug homicide", and the killer must shout out "gang slogans" that someone hears, or must leave a "gang card" at the crime scene, and must have been planned out and approved as such by the gang in advance.

What is your tendency now: to take a liberal or conservative definition of gang crime?

Often our instinct here depends on the gang. And the type of gang crime. So let's give an example, and ask you to categorize it as a "gang crime" or "non-gang crime": a member of the KKK has a run-in with a co-worker (who is a racial/ethnic/religious minority), and spray paints racial/ethnic slurs on the car owned by the minority co-worker (including swastika's, KKK signs, etc). Now the KKK offender did this alone and without getting permission from the KKK itself to engage in this behavior. No one hears or sees the offender commit the offense. Is this "hate crime" a "Gang Crime" as well?

End Notes:

[1] Yablonsky's "near group" may imply it is not a genuine group, and certainly not an institutionalized group. Again, Yablonsky's concept probably applies at the lower end of the analytical spectrum: to level zero gangs, the "Spanky and Alfalfa" playgroups. A more updated version of Yablonsky is found in Oetting and Beauvais (1987) who use the phrase "peer clusters". Takata and Zevitz (1990) also resurrect "near-group" analysis in the case of Racine's apparent lack of a gang problem. That is, apparently gangs exist in Racine only in the minds of individuals.

[2] Harris (1988) provides an interesting account of female gang members using a larger sample than Campbell and found that the gang functioned as a reference group for these females in stronger fashion than did families or other social institutions.

[3] The need for more analytical rigor here is evident in several gang authors who describe their three or four "social types" of gangs, and call them, if there are three, "the following three typologies", etc, abusing the very essence of what is meant, linguistically, by the word typology. What these authors probably wanted to do was advance "a typology". This will be addressed in more detail later.

[4] Leissner (1969, p. 9) takes Yablonsky to task for denying that gangs are truly "groups" at all, that is that gangs are simply "near groups". Leissner (1969: pp. 8-9) terms them "dynamic groups" ala Hubert Bonner (1959). But Leissner rejects the usage of the term "gang" or "gang clusters" and prefers to use the term "street corner groups" because the term gang connotes wrong doing. We might simply remind Leissner that ignoring their wrong doing will not make go away, no matter how sensitive our language gets.

[5] From an educational perspective (of course, showing a heavy influence from mainstream sociology) Harris (1988) provides an analysis of the gang in terms of reference group theory, "the group as an important factor in the motivation of human behavior" (Harris, 1988: p. 189).

[6] Sheu's (1990) presentation describing nonsyndicated organized crime groups in Taipei, Taiwan characterized gangs as secondary groups.

[7] The significance of group size is this: using the formula $R = n(n-1)/2$; where R = number of potential relationships, and n = size of the group; a gang size of 35 would have 590 possible different combinations of relationships for the gang infrastructure, points of possible internal alliances, and possible internal conflicts. As Wilson (1971) showed, the arithmetic increase in number of group members has a geometrical increase in the number of possible relationships. This means the need for more "chiefs" in the internal social organization of the gang the higher the group number size is (see DiRenzo, 1984: pp 246-247).

[8] Vetter and Territo (1984, p. 517), also seem to agree that today's gangs are not those of the day of Thrasher, but in fact "have a tighter, more cohesive, and more durable structure" (p. 517), with a wide variety of hierarchical roles in an almost paramilitary style of organization.

[9] Arnold (1965) says no, a gang cannot consist of simply two persons. To be a gang it must be integrated (identify with itself), have a leader, have a place to meet, and engage in conflict; further gangs must have at least six members (Arnold, 1965: p. 73). Arnold's was one of the first such efforts towards an empirically-based classification system of gangs. Arnold argued the merits of examining these "structural" characteristics (group integration, leadership, mode of conflict, size, meeting place, etc) to supplement the traditional emphasis on cultural factors.

[10] We can add to this list: boundary maintenance functions, the fact that the gang as a group is always an "open system", and that as an organization it will have both an informal social organization (e.g., cliques inside it) as well as its declared formal social organization.

[11] This is Yablonsky's (p. 127) attribution.

[12] Bobrowski (1988, p. 8) reports the interesting case that came to the attention of the Chicago Police Department --- a gang of one called the Latin Devils. That is one leader who created the illusion of a gang and proceeded to compel three members to "join", all three of which testified against him. Miller apparently believes a gang must have at least three members (ibid).

[13] Recall, similarly, the famous experiment by Zimbardo (1972) in the creation of the "Stanford Jail", where students were randomly assigned to be either "hacks" or "cons". The gang of hacks became overtly authoritarian, the gang of cons became disruptive. Both groups were so highly charged emotionally, in fact, that the experiment had to be prematurely cancelled.

[14] The implication for gang violence here is clear. But is may amount, perhaps, to only a choice of victims of violence. Any charitable group, social worker, political activist, etc, type of person, could probably with some degree of difficulty, get feuding gangs to come together for a meeting, to "call a truce", and establish a hot line of communications between rival gang leaders. But would this then mean the guns are fired at other citizens rather than rival gang members? It is hard to envision such a superordinate goal other than one of natural disaster or world war that could provide the means to draft gang members into national service. On the other hand, it is a fascinating theoretical issue as to what would be required to re-focus, even temporarily, inter-gang conflict to-

wards a larger and mutual external enemy, wherein society as a whole would ultimately benefit.

[15] "The experimenter was nearly always seen in the role of a homosexual, cop, bigtime operator in the underworld, or a psychiatrist looking for interesting cases...The most frequent and immediate perception of the experimenter was that of a homosexual. This was not entirely unrealistic since delinquent and homosexual populations are often involved in activities of mutual exploitation" (Schwitzgebel, 1965: p. 16).

[16] Including lengthy, flowery quotes from Aldous Huxley, e.g. "how can we increase the amount of love in the world?", etc, (1965, p. 103).

[17] This age is apparently only for those two-thrds of the sample who had served time. The overall mean, one must calculate from the raw data (Schwitzgebel, 1965: pp. 136-137), age for the full group (N = 30) was 18.

[18] Like Whyte, Schwitzgebel found on his first outing to "find a delinquent", he had to offer the delinquents a half-pint of vodka, which they promptly took from him and exited from his car.

[19] Am I wrong then by inference in concluding on the basis of this assertion that Schwitzgebel's SRL was an illogical design never intended to be taken seriously?

[20] For the record, on the "hot dispute" in the area of gang ideas regarding can gangs be "exported" or franchised, I must to be consistent from such a social organizational perspective say "yes they can and are". But this is not to say that the national picture is so singularly explained by only this. Obviously there is some combination of both local conditions and indigenous formation as well as intentional imperialism.

[21] Throughout the United States there are "Fagin" cases involving older adults who were able to manage a "team" or group of youths or young adults, often gang members, in various criminal activities (burglary rings, auto thefts, etc). But these are level one gangs, operating as a single unit usually in a single jurisdiction.

[22] This should sound familiar to the criminology student. It is, after all, what we do in corrections (prisons, jails, juvenile detention, etc).

[23] Gresham's law of conflict is this: if the harmful and dangerous elements drive out those who would keep the conflict within bounds, what results is an even more menacing level of conflict. The distinct organizational possibility exists, at least, that siphoning off all periphery members and leaving "hard core" members could result in an even higher magnitude of violence proneness.

[24] The fact that such neo-nazi youth gangs could be produced by an adult has much significance when looking at the extent to which groups like the Ku Klux Klan exist throughout America.

[25] This is where the issue of "franchising" and gang imperialism come into play. Can gangs be franchised like a fast food operation in any community in America? Any literature showing that some individuals can exert influence over, or manipulate gangs, would then tend to support the notion of gang social engineering. And would, of course, also have to recognize the potential for gang dismemberment or something roughly equivalent to gang deprogramming.

Satanic Cult Gangs

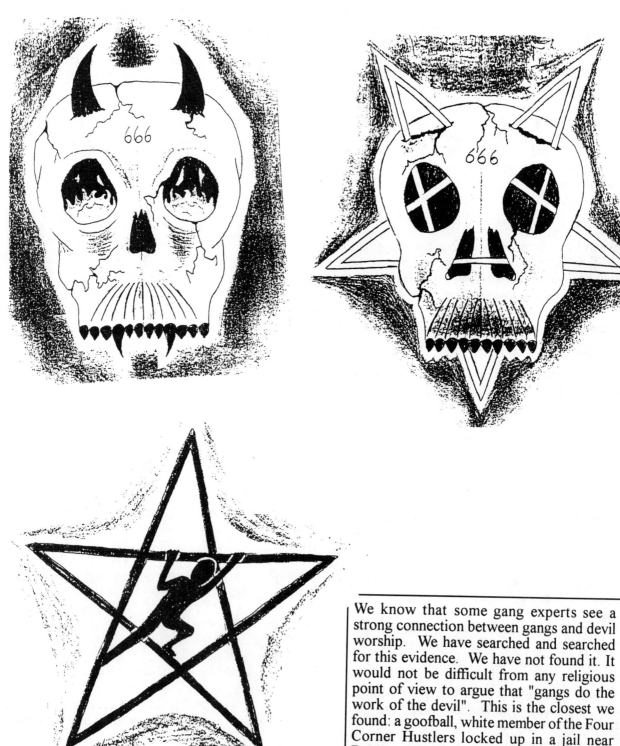

We know that some gang experts see a strong connection between gangs and devil worship. We have searched and searched for this evidence. We have not found it. It would not be difficult from any religious point of view to argue that "gangs do the work of the devil". This is the closest we found: a goofball, white member of the Four Corner Hustlers locked up in a jail near Davenport, who adorned his "cell" with these drawings. We bought his drawings while surveying the jail inmate population (cost: a couple extra small bags of Famous Amos cookies we used for rewards or honorariums given to incarcerated respondents).

Chapter 15:

A COMPARISON OF CULTS AND GANGS: DIMENSIONS OF COERCIVE POWER AND MALEVOLENT AUTHORITY

INTRODUCTION

This chapter explores the similarity and differences between gangs and cults. It examines several concepts such as: the risky-shift phenomenon, the group-think effect, the concept of collective moral neutralization, and the dependency-critical thinking effect. Recent data is analyzed to examine the effect that violence from within the gang (i.e., intragang violence) has on its members. Other concepts examined include the coerced-motivation phenomenon and the how the conversion process is almost identical when we compare cults and gangs. Finally we address the matter of reconciling free will and mind control in the gang.

Are gang members sometimes drawn into acts of violence that are basically outside of their own control? Is much of the behavior of the ordinary gang member classifiable as "compulsive behavior"? Is there any merit to the proposition that for many involved in gangs, their behavior is fundamentally beyond their own control? Is gang life in many ways "addictive"? These questions and more are addressed here in an analysis of the kind of coercive socialization that is experienced by gang members in modern American society.

MIND CONTROL

We believe there is sufficient proof to establish that some gang members in some situations operate under a certain type of mind control. The proof for those who reject this type of strong social and psychological impact on gang members in the modern American gang is easy to establish. We would propose that the skeptic do as follows: walk into an existing gang neighborhood; having identified the local gang's symbols and colors, carry a sign with the totems and symbols upside down, and wear clothing with the colors of a rival gang. Any gang expert knows what would happen anytime of the day in such a case. The person would quickly be identified by the neighborhood gang and subjected to great violence and quite possibly die as a result of the ensuing gang violence.

Why would the person die for expressing their opinion and color preferences and therefore really only exercising their constitutionally guaranteed right of expression? Because gang members will rarely consider constitutional rights about the freedom of speech. Because gang members would regard this as an attack on their way of life itself. Because gang members would not think first, they would shoot first;

they are extremely impulsive with regard to such issues. Indeed, a closer analysis will reveal that much of the behavior of gang members reflects a lack of critical thinking, they do not operate as independent or autonomous actors, but rather they operate more often than not in a pattern of social compulsion that is part and parcel of modern gang life.

Below we examine some of the elements of mind control, beginning with the issue of the similarity between gangs and cults. We then examine how, to some extent, the differences between cults and gangs are declining with the recent historical developments in American gangs. We also look at some differences between cults and gangs that still persist today.

To understand the dynamics of the comparison between cults and gangs we also need to look at a number of other conceptual issues. These include the risky-shift phenomenon, the group-think effect, the concept of collective moral neutralization, and the dependency-critical thinking effect.

Using research findings from the largest studies ever done on gangs, we also demonstrate below the mediating effect that violence from within the gang (i.e., intragang violence) has on its members. This helps to establish the coerced-motivation phenomenon. We then look at another conceptual parallel between cults and gangs: the conversion process over time, to uncover almost identical developmental events.

Finally we address the matter of reconciling free will and mind control in the gang. Some note is made of how "gang deprogramming" services are claimed to exist. We examine the implications of this analysis and provide relevant conclusions.

THE SIMILARITY BETWEEN GANGS AND CULTS

We can provide a number of elaborate similarities between gangs and cults. It is useful to simply delineate these areas of similarity. It will be seen that there is much in common between what we regard as "cults" and what we regard as "gangs" in modern American society today.

(1.) Members of cults lack the freedom to think and believe what they want to (Berger, 1985: pp. 9-10). In most gangs, a gang member similarly lacks the freedom to have such an individual level of freedom and autonomy. The reason is that there are many restrictions imposed on gang behavior. These restrictions include: colors that can be worn, colors that are taboo; words and expressions that can be used, and certain words and phrases that are taboo; certain symbolic representations, such as hand-signs and non-verbal methods of greetings and salutations. Some of these become "musts" and "requirements" for life in a gang. Simply put, a gang member lacks the freedom to do a lot of things, such as associate with rival gang members, or even persons who are not in their own gang.

(2.) Cults demand unquestioning obedience from their members (Berger, 1985: p. 11). Gangs are similar in this respect of demanding compliance from their members, and this is enforced by means of violence within the gang itself: members who "violate" gang rules are "violated". A gang often has a "chief of violations", someone who imposes such discipline. The discipline can be anything from a monetary fine to a ritualized beating of the gang member in the presence of other members of the same gang. One of the most common areas of "unquestioning obedience" is in the area of beliefs and values that a gang transmits in its written constitution and bylaws and in its "prayers". Some of these gang constitutions are so irrational and contradictory that one wonders how the gang would attract anyone with a questioning mind in the first place. But the fact remains: when a gang member does question the authority structure of his gang, or questions the validity of a gang's constitution or belief system --- these are serious threats to the gang. Today's gang requires unquestioning obedience from members just like a cult does.

(3.) Cults usually have self-appointed authoritarian leaders. Gangs today do not "elect" their leaders, there is no democratic procedure for becoming a gang leader today, one cannot "run for office" in the gang organization: top gang leaders are the gang leaders because they are basically self-appointed authoritarian leaders. They are self-appointed because they often formed the gang, or were "ancianos" (i.e., members for a very long time, survived, and were ruthless enough to "take over"). Gang leaders are clearly the types of persons who fit the "authoritarian personality" profile as well. A modern gang leader is like a despot, a "junta ruler", a "dictator" and the ideal-form of this method of "rule" is the lifestyle represented by someone like Al Capone: a ruthless killer who will impose his own "order" with the use of a baseball bat if necessary against errant members.

(4.) Once persons join a cult, they are said to undergo or manifest certain predictable personality changes. One of the most common assumptions in the gang prevention and gang intervention literature today is that there are such "warning signs" of personality and behavior changes that appear once a youngster is becoming involved with gangs or actually joins a gang. The assumption is that this involves things like: sudden downturn in grade performance at school, sudden onset of a combative personality syndrome, possible increase in drug/substance abuse, the onset of tattoo's and body markings, etc. One of the most obvious such changes in personality is the "us versus them" mentality: the new gang member by joining a specific gang automatically inherits a clearly defined "enemy" and has become a kind of "street soldier".

(5.) Cults routinely engage in the use of lies and deceptive practices especially against non-members. Gangs clearly and indisputably practice deception against non-members: it is the issue of maintaining a "front", or a "public image". Some gangs like the Gangster Disciples go to enormous lengths to try and carry out a public relations campaign, including the publishing of their own books for such use, to counter-act the public perception of their group or organization as a "gang". Gangs like the Gangster Disciples therefore will adopt phrases like "Growth and Development" as a "put on", and when they encounter non-members they try to give the impression they are a community group dedicated to the "growth and development" of the community. Some gangs intentionally practice the use of lies and deception particularly when it comes to attracting or luring new members: this is called the "courting process" in the gang. The gang will sponsor "parties" and try to convey the impression that the gang is predominantly a "fun thing", the gang recruiters will downplay any issue of violence or crime or drug dealing until the youth actually joins the gang. Once a youth has joined the gang, only then do they actually learn the awful truth and at that point it has become an irreversible decision: they may have to forfeit their life to actually get out of the gang.

(6) Cults systematically recruit certain types of persons with lures designed for young people. Gangs use "bait" that is designed for "catching" kids. If the gang leader were a fisherman, then the type of fish he is trolling for is clearly a young kid, the ideal age of about 12 years of age. Gangs offer such children the myth of protection: they will be protected against other harms they face in life. Gangs offer such children the myth of a concerned and loving "family". The gang leader becomes in this fashion the new "father" figure. The gang may also use the lure of "all for one, and one for all", "share and share alike", and similar doctrines that sound attractive to an underage child. Add to this the type of "excitement" and "kicks" that the gang can offer, and the gang becomes a formidable organization that can probably attract any type of child. Our best data on gang membership in the United States today shows that about "half" of all gang members alive have "voluntarily sought out the gang", wanting to join it, in fact eager to join it; while the other half have in fact been recruited into the gang.

(7.) Cults, like gangs, fall clearly in the realm of deviance; and there is a lot of overlap with crime or criminal behavior. Gangs are in fact the most powerful force in the underground economy of any society, the gang is the type of group or organization that dominates over all other deviant subcultures: because of its use of violence. Gangs are more dangerous than cults in this respect because gangs would not be "gangs" if they were not systematically involved in the commission of crimes.

(8.) In both cults and gangs, what is conceived of in social psychology as consisting of the "self" becomes unreflective, uncritical, and becomes situationally dependent on the "group identity". In this sense, then, another commonality in comparing gangs and cults is to be found in the realm of abnormal psychology where once inside such a powerful and controlling influence like the gang or cult, the individual members undergo a kind of brainwashing that ends in the fact that their "self" has changed. Their "self" no longer questions authority if the authority is that of the cult or gang leader; their "self" no longer questions the logical merits of "beliefs" in their organization; their "self" becomes primarily modelled after other like-minded persons who collectively accept a certain unspoken deception that they are in some way leading the "good life". They come to "worship" and "idolize" their cult or gang leaders, attaching "king-like" or "god-like" qualities to their leaders, even when such leaders are functional illiterates.

(9.) Both cults and gangs exploit the natural and normal human desire for group affiliation: the need to be a part of something larger and bigger than one's own "self", the search for an affirming community, the quest for a sense of community and affirmation from like-minded persons. Many normal people find this affirmation in religious institutions. Some people find it in a cult or a gang. For youths, in particular, this becomes a powerful attraction: because gangs "rule" the streets and the subcultures of a society. Gangs deftly blend youth culture into their lifestyle and seek to offer youths something that legitimate society has a hard time generating: the "thrill-seeking" adventures of outlaw life.

(10.) Finally, both cults and gangs are organizations typically administered by older adults which abuse younger and more susceptible persons like children or youths. Almost all gangs today that pose any problem to law enforcement are not "youth gangs" in the sense that at the top of the gang hierarchy we will find an underage minor in charge of the gang, rather and more typically the gang membership may include about "half juveniles", but as a general rule of thumb the gang leader is an older adult. The older adult gang leader simply exploits the younger and more gullible members of the gang.

Other similarities and parallels exist in comparing cults and gangs and these will be addressed elsewhere in the present study. But these ten similarities are sufficient as a beginning effort to demonstrate the need for a rigorous examination of what exists in common between cults and gangs, and what might possibly be the genuine differences between cults and gangs. Obviously, both cults and gangs are "deviant" groups or organizations, but there are important conceptual issues that must also be examined here.

"The Many Books and Authors Who Tell Us Satanism Is Not Nothing to Worry About"

There are a great many books of this genre that basically use a strawman method of argumentation to the effect that "satanic cults" either do not really exist, or that any concern about "satanism" and those who dabble in it is misplaced and over-rated. One of the most popular styles of this type of book is to argue that society has "over-reacted" to a kind of moral panic that is really not real and genuine.

In fact, some one could use the "moral panic" thesis to equal effect to say that police brutality is not really a problem in America at all, given the statistical rarity of its documentation; or someone could juggle philosophy a little bit and using the argument that the media "socially constructs" excessive force by police officers, and that given that overall it is a small issue affecting a small number of people by a small number of police in a larger system, it is not important. That is basically what a lot of the scholarly books about satanism end up saying about the issue of satanism and the occult: something we really should not worry about.

Hicks, Robert
　　1991　In Pursuit of Satan: The Police and the Occult. Buffalo, NY: Prometheus Books.
Jenkins, Phillip; and Daniel Meier-Katlin
　　1992, "Satanism: Myth and Reality in a Contemporary Moral Panic", Crime, Law and Social Change (17)(1): 53-71
Peterson, Alan H.
　　1988　The American Focus on Satanic Crime. South Orange, NJ: American Focus Publishing Company.
Victor, Jeffrey S.
　　1993　Satanic Panic: The Creation of a Contemporary Legend. Chicago: Open Court.

THE DECLINING DIFFERENCES BETWEEN CULTS AND GANGS

Among all of the cult and satanic experts and source materials consulted with, most are quick to point out what most commonly is felt to be the primary difference between cults and gangs: the former have as their axial principle of organization some spiritual/religious/ideological belief system, while gangs are commonly perceived to have no such advanced belief system. In other words, the common perception is that cults have as their primary basis for existence a spiritual need, while gangs might be primarily organized along crime, violence, or other functions (drugs, race, etc).

The issue here is real and genuine and needs to be examined in some depth. A major difference is commonly felt to exist in comparing cults and gangs: cults are seen as having some kind of "higher consciousness", while the common image of gangs is that they attract a non-thinking criminaloid. This examination should begin, therefore, with how gangs have been characterized from a historical perspective. We will examine two major factors: (1) political ideology, and (2) spiritual/religious beliefs.

1. The Factor of Political Ideology.

In terms of shaping perceptions about gangs and gang life, the early work by Campbell (1984) describing the activities of three female "gang" members, certainly demonstrates that having a sound research methodology is not the prerequisite tool for having a powerful impact in the field of criminology. Many today continue to point to this early work of Campbell (1984) as evidence to the effect that "street gangs do not have ideologies", thus "street gangs are not primitive rebels" (ala Hobsbawm, 1959). Specifically Campbell concluded "gangs do not represent a revolutionary vanguard rejecting the norms and values of a capitalist society that has exploited them" (Campbell, 1984: p. 267). For the record, though, Campbell did acknowledge that gangs have been manipulated by politicians, and that gangs often have conservative views.

Some other misconceptions about gangs are traced to the early "fathers" of gangology: scholars like Frederick Thrasher. Thrasher's research is still not totally understood by many contemporary gang experts, particularly what his "methodology" really entailed, as many have the misconception that Thrasher spent a great deal of time in "field research". That misconception has been laid to rest with the historical analysis reported elsewhere on the life and times of Thrasher (Knox, 1998). But this early and formative study of gangs only tended to show, like many studies that followed, that "politicians use and manipulate gangs". Thus, the idea continues today that gangs are not and never have been involved with electoral politics in any substantive capacity. Those astute readers of the Journal of Gang Research now different, particularly from gang profiles like that of the "Gangster Disciples", and the "Black P. Stone Nation", that some gangs clearly have made their own mark in politics.

Cults clearly have been characterized by extreme political ideological beliefs. We need only to recognize that whether it is the case of the Branch Davidian compound in Waco, Texas, or the case of "suicide cults", some "political beliefs" are part and parcel to their central way of life: as a way to define their existence as different from the rest of a misguided society perhaps. The political doctrines or belief patterns found in cults are commonly politics of conflict with the government or some perceived powerful entity. In many respects the gang adopts similar political baggage in its ongoing battle with the society in which it operates as well.

Some cult experts in fact define cults along a dimension of conflict with their larger society: those without conflict with their larger society come to be more like what Thrasher called "conventionalized gangs". Thrasher (1927) claimed to study 1,313 gangs in Chicago during 1923-1926, a fourth of which were "conventionalized gangs": i.e., they had their own clubhouses, which meant that a lot of "Social Athletic Clubs" were probably automatically classified as gangs according to Thrasher. A "conventionalized cult" would be one that styles over and tries to become more "acceptable" to a society, one that defies the label of "cult" and often succeeds in court in doing so, and thus operates freely and openly in a society, careful all the time to not make too many waves.

An organization that for years studied and researched cults was based in the Chicago area, it was called the "CULT AWARENESS NETWORK". It was sued by one of the groups it labelled as a cult. It lost the court case. The group that sued today answers the phone at the same organization which still has a listing in Chicago's phone directory. The group basically came to "own" the organization that it sued. Unsuspecting people who might call the Cult Awareness Network will today, therefore, find a different message when they call and inquire about whether certain groups are or are not "cults".

Some gangs like the "Black Guerilla Family" are extreme leftists. Most white racist extremist gangs are predictably extreme rightists. American society can be said to be blessed by the fact that hostile foreign national involvement in manipulation and influence over American gangs is negligible to non-existent at the present. We need to remember that at one point the gang leader of the Black P. Stone Nation (aka "El Rukns") was willing to do contract terrorism work for one such hostile foreign nation: Libya. There is hard data on the extent to which modern American gangs get involved in politics. This comes from the Project GANGECON (1995) research, a study of over 1,000 gang members in 5 states carried out by the National Gang Crime Research Center. Below we provide some of the details of this research.

The Project GANGECON survey asked the gang members "have you ever worked for a politician in any way" and just under a fourth of the sample (23.1%, N = 228) indicated they had worked for politicians. Three follow-up questions along the same lines sought to clarify the nature of this political involvement. Nationally some 13.8 percent (N = 136) had worked in voter registration, where half had been asked to do so by their gang leader, and half had been asked by a local politician. For the voter registration work, half were paid, and half were doing it in an unpaid capacity.

There is much variation, however, in comparing type of gang alliance system with regard to this factor of being involved in politics. Table 17 shows how "Folks" gangs tend to have a significantly higher degree of political involvement.

Table 17

**Percentage Distribution of Having Ever Worked For
A Politician By Type of Gang Alliance System
For A Large Sample (>1,000) of Gang Members
From Project GANGECON (1995)**

Have you ever worked for a politician in any way?	Type of Gang National Alliance System				
	People	Folks	Crips	Bloods	Other
% Yes	22.9%	29.7%	21.1%	13.6%	18.4%

Chi-square = 13.1, p = .01

As seem in Table 17, some 22.9 percent of the members of the "People" gangs report having worked for a politician. This is comparable to the 21.1 percent figure for members of "Crip" gangs. Only 13.6 percent of the members of "Blood" gangs reported working for politicians. The "other" category includes non-aligned gangs, motorcycle gangs, and white racist extremist gangs, and some 18.4 percent of the members of this type of gang that is outside of the Crip/Blood or People/Folks alliance system reported working for politicians. Clearly, however, the type of gang with the highest rate of working for politicians appears in Table 17 to be "Folks" gangs. Some 29.7 percent of the members of "Folks" gangs reported working for politicians.

Obviously, from Table 17 we cannot ascertain if any of this "work" for politicians was lawful or unlawful in nature. The fact is: politicians have been prone to try and enlist the aid of gang members in local elections. What we can say, definitively, about this political involvement of gang members will be illustrated in Table 18: it is the more experienced and highly committed gang members who are more likely to report working for politicians.

Project GANGECON, among other types of analysis, examined this political involvement issue from the standpoint of a threat/risk analysis of the type of gang member involved. The threat analysis scale used, in this instance, is a very simplistic design where the risk classification system varies from a low of zero to a high of three. The higher the numerical score, the higher the gang risk. All gang members begin by having a score of zero. Then three questions are used to give their risk rating:

(1) Are you still active in the gang, if yes, add one point.

(2) Have you ever held rank or a leadership position in the gang, if yes, add one point.

(3) Have you been in the gang for 6 or more years, if yes, add one point.

Let us summarize the profiles of these four gang risk/threat types.

Type 0: constituted N = 143, or 14.1% of the sample, all had joined a gang, none were current members, none had ever held rank, and all had gang tenure levels of less than or equal to five years.

Type 1: constituted N = 350, or 34.5% of the sample, all had joined a gang, a third (30%) were current members of the gang, 25.8 percent had held rank in the gang, and gang tenure varied.

Type 2: constituted N = 365, or 36% of the sample, all had joined a gang, 70% were current members of the gang, 78% had held rank in the gang, and gang tenure varied.

Type 3: constituted N = 157, or 15.5% of the sample, all had joined a gang and all were currently members, all had held rank in the gang, and all had gang tenure of equal to or greater than 6 years.

Thus, Type 0 is the lowest level of gang involvement, while Type 3 would tend to be the more "hard core" type of gang member. Table 18 shows that there is a significant difference in analyzing this threat/risk scale measuring the type of gang member in relationship to whether the same gang members have worked for politicians.

Table 18

Percentage Distribution of Having Ever Worked a Politician by the Gang Risk/Threat Classification in a Large (>1,000) Sample of Gang Members From Project GANGECON

Percent who have	Gang Risk/Threat Classification System			
ever worked for	Type 0	Type 1	Type 2	Type 3
a politician.	17.5%	20.1%	22.2%	36.3%
	Chi-square = 19.5, p < .001			

As seen in Table 18, this factor of working for politicians increases as the "seriousness" of gang involvement increases. The more committed and longterm ranking member of the gang is the type of person who is more likely to get involved in politics. Only 17.5 percent of Type 0 gang members reported having worked for politicians. This rises to 20.1 percent for Type 2 gang members, and 22.2 percent for Type 2 gang members. Then it jumps to the high of 36.3 percent for the Type 3 gang member.

So we would like to put to rest the misconception that gangs are not involved in politics, because certainly gang members are. Some gangs like the Gangster Disciples and Black P. Stone Nation have elaborated their political involvement to the point of having special political actions. Some gangs do in fact have "ideology" would seem to be the most accurate conclusion in describing contemporary American gangs.

2. The Factor of Religious/Spiritual Beliefs.

Cults have always been studied in the context of how they are unique as spiritual movements, they are not branches of established traditional religions, nor have they broken off from established religions to become a sect. Rather, cults are seen as unique religious or spiritual entities lacking the tradition and connection to larger society. Some social scientists would consider it possible for a group to break away from an established religious institution to become something other than a sect (i.e., still functioning in society without major conflict with its society), and perhaps become a cult. Under law today, almost anything, including witchcraft, could be protected as an established system of beliefs (i.e., having the protections afforded to mainstream religions). Prison inmates in America have certainly discovered this loophole.

Thus, in comparing gangs and cults, many uninformed readers of the literature on gangs might make the mistake of assuming that gangs have no religious or spiritual contexts. Actually, there is much that we can point to in gang life in America today that tends to suggest there are strong components of religious or spiritual beliefs tied into the very fabric of gang identity --- in some gangs.

Look at the lengthy constitution of the Vice Lords, and here we find the entire "Code" as one that is embellished with language from Islamic beliefs (see Knox, 1991, 1993).

Look at the Chicago Latin Kings constitution (Knox, 1998) and here we see how the Sun God is the mythical highest ranking member of the Latin Kings. The Latin King constitution, like many others, is loaded with its own versions of "Prayers" that all members must memorize and be able to recite.

In a recent gang profile of the "Brotherwood Gang" by Bonner (1999) published in the NGCRC journal, we see how one white racist extremist gang formulated its odd internal beliefs around the "religion" of Odinism.   In developments within other white racist extremist gangs, there is a clear affinity with the "Identity church" movement and its many variations; where white racism is justified by a twisted conception of in someway being "holy" or followers of God.

Other gangs have developed unusual types of written internal literature to their gangs to reflect their belief system, and these are typically documents that portray the top gang leader as a Godlike figure, just as most cults have self-appointed leaders who try to portray themselves in this same fashion.

The truth of the matter seems to be, in reference to some of the larger and some of the more dangerous gangs in America today, that they do in fact embellish their codified set of beliefs and values with various sect-like interpretations, or off-brand and cult-like, spiritual beliefs, including "gang prayers". Gang meetings themselves are often called "Prayer Meetings" by the gang members. But this is little more than embellishment and a propagandistic effort to make the gang sound like something other than a group or organization in pursuit of illicit income and deeply involved in criminal activities. It is also functional by bestowing more implied symbolic power to the leaders of the gang.

What is our best data about gangs and spiritual beliefs? It comes from some of the Task Force projects of the National Gang Crime Research Center. It suggests gang members are indeed more prone than non-gang members to claim have bizarre spiritual beliefs; in fact, we see variations even within the gang member population that are important in this respect. The data we will be presenting comes from Project GANGFACT, a study of N = 4,140 gang members from 17 states, which also included about another N = 6,000 non-gang member offenders in youth and adult correctional settings.

The Project GANGFACT survey included a variable to measure those who believed in God and those who were self-declared atheists. The survey therefore asked the question "Which best describes you: ___ I believe in God ___ I do not believe in God". In the total national sample of the ten thousand offenders in the study, the vast majority (93.1%, N = 8,998) indicated they do in fact believe in God. Only a small minority (6.9%, N = 665) reported they do not believe in God. However, there was a small but important difference in comparing gang members and non-gang members. Some 94% of the non-gang members indicated they believed in God compared to 91.8% of the gang members (Chi-square = 17.9, p < .001).

As a follow-up on some earlier research from the NGCRC, Project GANGFACT included a way to identify those who were basically self-declared "followers of Satan". This is not equivalent in our appraisal to "devil worshipers" as a collective identity, but it does indicate an aberrant belief system whenever someone would indicate they are a "follower of Satan". The survey asked "Which best describes you: ___ I'm on God's side ___ I'm on Satan's side". There was a significant difference on this variable comparing gang members and non-gang members (Chi-square = 84.9, p < .001). Some 4.0 percent of the non-gang members indicated they were on "Satan's side", compared to 8.7 percent of the gang members.

Additional analysis of these two religious factors was undertaken by looking at the gang member population alone, and comparing male gang members with female gang members. Some 7.7% of the male gang members, compared to 11.7 percent of the female gang members, claimed they do not believe in God (Chi-square = 6.41, p = .01). Further, some 8.2 percent of the male gang members, compared to 12.7 percent of the female gang members, indicated they were on "Satan's side" (Chi-square = 7.22, p = .007). Thus, the female gang member would appear to be more attracted to aberrant spiritual systems.

Efforts to explain the variation in such aberrant spiritual beliefs were undertaken in Project GANGFACT. One factor that seemed to account for a significant difference within the gang member population was the matter of coming from a dysfunctional family. A family dysfunction scale measured low and high levels of family dysfunction in the Project GANGFACT research. Some 5.9% of the gang members from better families indicated they do not believe in God, compared to 10.3% for gang members from dysfunctional families (Chi-square = 26.3, p < .001). Similarly, some 6.0% of the gang members from better families indicated they are on "Satan's side", compared to 11.4% for gang members from more dysfunctional families (Chi-square = 34.8, p < .001).

As an aside, one of the commonalities between gangs and cults is also about family: how the group or organization functions to gradually cut-off relationships with the family, that is eroding the positive strength of traditional family ties and such social bonds and the social control they represent, in exchange for greater social and emotional and/or spiritual dependence on the cult or organization. Someone from a dysfunctional family would therefore have an easier transition into cults and gangs would be a necessary corollary of this general finding.

Another measure of the "hardcore" gang member was used in Project GANGFACT. The "hardcore" gang member was defined in this particular analysis as: (1) someone who had joined a gang typically at an early age in life, (2) who remains until the time of the study an active gang member, (3) who comes from a dysfunctional family, and (4) who has ever fired a gun at a police officer. This group of "hard-core" gang members represented only 6.2 percent of the national sample of N = 10,166 offenders from 17 states. So when we compare this "hard-core" gang member with all other offenders, some interesting results emerged.

Among those who were not hard-core gang members, 6.3% indicated they did not believe in God, compared to 14.9% among the hard-core gang members. Also, among those who were not hard-core gang members, only 5.1% indicated they were on "Satan's side", compared to 19.6% for the "hard-core" gang members. Thus, among the "hard-core" gang members, it appears about a fifth (19.6%) are indicating an aberrant spiritual belief system if they claim they are on "Satan's side".

The best evidence, to conclude this component of analysis, is that gangs and gang members also have important dimensions of spiritual and religious beliefs and practices, making them not unlike cults.

SOME REMAINING DIFFERENCES BETWEEN GANGS AND CULTS

There are a couple areas of differences between gangs and cults that should be addressed here. These types of differences remain factors that tend to differentiate what we know about gangs and what we know about cults.

(1.) Mass suicide. Cults have clearly established themselves as the leaders in this phenomenon known as "mass suicide". We have not yet seen such a phenomenon as exemplified in Jonestown or Heaven's Gate yet appear in gangs. Recall some 900 members of the Jonestown cult committed suicide or murder in Guyana under the direction of their cult leader, Rev. Jim Jones. Some might point to small scale examples of "homicide/suicide" patterns within some gangs, a good example being what happened with the "Trench Coat Mafia": gang members go on a shooting spree in the local school, and after their planned violent attack, they take their own lives. Or examples such as white racist extremist gang members who go on a shooting spree, trying to kill as many of the "enemy" (racial minorities, etc) as they can, and when they are near capture they take their own life. However, we have not seen en masse suicide in the gang as of this date. Is it a logical possibility? Certainly, there is no known reason why a gang could not or would not do the same thing that a cult could do.

(2.) Total control institutions. A genuine cult is typically a total control institution: the individual lives with the cult 24 hours a day, seven days a week --- there is no "life" outside of the cult. Gangs are not typically of that nature: members float in and out of the web of gang influence, they "gangbang" at

night, go home take off their gang clothes, and perhaps appear normal in all other respects to unsuspecting parents or school authorities. Some motorcycle gangs have this kind of arrangement where members are gang members 24-7: they will "congregate" by living together in homes, perhaps because of the issue of "safety in numbers". Some white racist extremist groups have their own "compounds". But generally, gangs do not have this constant around the clock control over members. One exception to this rule is the correctional setting: in juvenile correctional facilities, in jails, and in prisons, the gang becomes a "security threat group" or a "disruptive group", and in this type of controlled setting, the gang actually has more control over its members once the gang is imported into or created in such a facility.

In cults, like the ones that claim they are not cults and have the tendency to be quite litigious, it is common for them to take a single family house, fill almost all rooms with "bunk beds" that go four-up on three sides, so that a single room could easily hold 12 members; and at night the shoes of the members are "locked" down in a shoe cabinet, thus during the winter, in a place like Chicago, one would not be tempted to simply "run away" or "step outside" for any reason. The members eat, work, socialize, and congregate together around the clock: they have no other social network other than their "in-group". They generally sever ties to former friends, colleagues, and family members in favor of the cult. That is they renounce their former community for their new cult community. Admittedly, gang members do this to some extent, but not anywhere near the 24-7 capability that a typical cult is capable of.

Is there anything to stop a gang from developing such a level of influence? No. In theory, any modern gang can make a transition to the next logical step of "control over members" by creating its own residential program: requiring gang members to live with other gang members. We need to remember the historical precedent for criminal groups using this "residential congregation" effect to its advantage: groups like the Symbionese Liberation Army (SLA), groups like M.O.V.E., and others have historically been the source of a number of critical incidents. The "residential congregation" effect clearly accentuates any level of risk factor the gang or criminal group might represent. Perhaps the gangs of the future will take greater advantage of this kind of organizational enhancement device.

(3.) Type of Socialization Process: Voluntary Versus Coercive Socialization. A person enters a cult in many of the same ways a person enters a gang, but in most ways, except for perhaps the matter of diet control and sleep deprivation, cults tend to show a voluntary socialization process. In the cult, the socialization process is one where the individual gives up more individualization gradually in exchange for the group identity, but it is primarily a voluntary process. In the gang, the type of socialization process is primarily coercive in nature. In the gang, the gang itself will "discipline" its members by means of ritualized violence. This is often called the "violation process": a gang member who fails to perform a chore, who "drops his flag" (i.e., does not defend his gang's identity when encountering rivals), who fails to pay required dues, etc --- all of these and a long list of potential behaviors can be sanctioned by the gang itself. The gang uses coercive socialization because it can use violence against its own members to maintain discipline and control over its members. Thus, in the re-analysis of the etiological sequence for how a gang becomes a gang and what a gang can become later in time, in the original formulation offered by Thrasher (1927), perhaps one clear sign that a "gang" is becoming something other than a "gang" (i.e., going legitimate, becoming a political entity, or in theory at least becoming a legitimate organization), would be where it drops the coercive socialization components of the organization. But clearly, and indisputably, a gang distinguishes itself as a group or organization by its ability to enforce internal rules and regulations by the use of violence and other punitive sanctions against their own members.

In an early study by the National Gang Crime Research Center, in examining coercive socialization, we had hypothesized that normal human beings would possibly feel more alienated from a group or organization that ritually and violently abused them: i.e., going through a "violation ceremony", which typically means being beaten by one's fellow gang members in a group context. The theory was that no normal human being would want to be so humiliated in the presence of their peers and experience pain in the same process. We hypothesized, therefore, that gang members who had been "violated" would be more likely to want to "quit the gang". We were sorely wrong! What we found was that gang members who had been through such a ritualized violence ceremony were actually more "hardened" and "hardcore" members of the gang: they became even more committed to the goals of the gang organization, they became less likely to want to quit the gang. We learned in that research project a fundamental fact about coercive socialization in gangs today: it is very much a matter of "brain washing" in one sense, because the individual gang member "invests" more in the gang, the "identity" of the gang member becomes such that it is almost like getting a "whooping" from a parent early in life, this perhaps unconscious need for discipline tends to reshape the identity to make it even more strongly committed to gang life. There are, perhaps, some parallels with the use of low-intensity torture and brainwashing, or what has been called

"re-education" efforts, by the communist Chinese military dating back to the Korean War and continuing up to the Vietnam era, in which prisoners-of-war (POWs) were subjected to such brutality along with specific messages designed to weaken the "will" of U.S. and allied forces who were taken into captivity.

Some possible disagreement exists, for the record, on cults and what type of socialization process they exemplify. The present author has examined such a cult that operated in Chicago until its leader went to jail, to find that it can as a cult be regarded as one that uses coercive socialization in a more subtle way. There is a need for basic research on this issue would be recommendation here.

THE RISKY-SHIFT EFFECT

Like the classic situation of a Halloween trick-or-treat outing, a child out alone would just never throw eggs or commit small scale offenses like criminal damage to property that we find typically when a group of children are together as a group and the risk taking activity is accentuated by simply being in a group. It is universally true that people do things in a group that they would probably never have the audacity to do when alone. In a group context a "critical mass" exists in terms of having to achieve group approval and this is particularly evident in risk-taking behavior.

The risky-shift effect is a classical social-psychological concept explaining risk-taking behavior in groups (Stoner, 1961; Wallach, Hogan, and Bem, 1962). Applied to the situation of crime, the risky-shift effect is simple to understand: some people will be more aggressive, more violent, and simply more prone to commit some types of crime in a group context that is supportive of such criminal offenses. The risky-shift effect affects all human beings, but is particularly strong in a gang situation.

For the reader with a research interest in studying the risky-shift phenomenon in relationship to gang behavior, note that an entire issue of the Journal of Personality and Social Psychology was devoted to this concept in 1971. What it means for gang behavior is basically "throwing caution" to the wind: embracing risk often for the sake of risk itself, or risk as an "end in itself". In the context of a gang, the small group process operates such that the decision made is often a decision that individuals alone would not make themselves. Risky-shift is an effect that occurs in a group context.

The gang offers one of the most fascinating examples of the risky-shift phenomena. Those interested in working with gangs should have probably focused on this matter years ago for intervention purposes: it is the matter of possibly "de-escalating" conflict with rival gangs. Gang outreach workers, or "detached workers", or a host of related terms (curbstone counseling, streetcorner therapy, etc), describe how basically paraprofessionals or indigenous workers (sometimes former gang members themselves) try to moderate the intensity of gang violence. In theory, insulating gang members against the "risky shift" effect would appear to be a promising intervention strategy, but unfortunately most such "interventions" are atheoretical in nature; which perhaps accounts for their general lack of success as well.

THE GROUP-THINK EFFECT

The group-think effect is a classical concept in the social-psychological study of groups and organizations. It will be shown that gangs certainly exhibit a high level of the group-think effect.

Like the cult, there is an "us versus them" antagonism that permeates the value system of the modern gang. The gang has its own language, special symbols, and ways of communicating that the gang thinks are secrets known only by its gang members. The gang emphasizes unity in a world view. The gang does have an ideology. An ideology is a system of beliefs and values. Some of the more organizationally sophisticated gangs also have written codes as well as elements of political and religious ideology.

The group-think effect, as a theoretical concept, owes its origin to the work of Janis (1971). In its original formulation, it was applied to legitimate groups as a way to explain how bad outcomes can arise when there is an enormous pressure to have complete consensus on a decision-making issue, such that with the pressure to "agree", no one would dare to disagree with a proposed decision that could a very poor decision indeed.

For example, in its original formulation, the group-think effect was used to account for the Bay of Pigs fiasco in poor planning by the Kennedy administration. In the Bay of Pigs invasion planning meeting, President Kennedy was so intent on carrying out the mission based on poor intelligence information, that only one dissenting voice was heard and no one was allowed to comment on that one critical voice which predicted the failure of the operation to topple Fidel Castro.

Gangs are not democratic organizations, they are violent authoritarian organizations. It is useful, however, to examine the some of the classical elements of the group-think effect in relationship to what we find today in the gang situation.

In its original formulation, the group-think effect described the situation where group norms "bolster morale at the expense of critical thinking" (Janis, 1989: p. 223). While the group-think effect definitely increases cohesiveness, it results in "a deterioration in mental efficiency, reality testing and moral judgments as a result of group pressures"

(Janis, 1989: p. 224).

Group members begin to operate with an "illusion of invulnerability" and are prone to "take extraordinary risks" (Janis, 1989: p. 225). Group members "ignore warnings", "believe unquestionably in the inherent morality of their in-group", hold stereotypical images of enemy groups as being innately evil, pressure other members to not question the group's mission or goals and to "keep silent about their misgivings", so that an illusion of unanimity exists in the group, and is maintained by "mindguards" who protect "fellow members from adverse information that might break the complacency they shared about the effectiveness and morality of past decisions" (Janis, 1989: pp. 226-229).

Whether he knew it or not, Janis (1971) was clearly on target in describing some of the social-psychological functions inside modern gang life. There is nothing in the original formulation that does not apply to modern gang life. What we actually find in gangs is probably something a lot stronger than "group think". In the original formulation as applied to legitimate groups someone who questioned the leader's visionary effectiveness might face at worse case scenario simply being fired from a job. In gang life, questioning such matters could result in the member being murdered by his/her own gang.

So a stronger version of the group-think effect actually operates in gang life today.

COLLECTIVE MORAL NEUTRALIZATION

In its original formulation, moral neutralization (Sykes and Matza, 1957), was a theory that was useful in explaining deviant behavior, juvenile delinquency, and crime generally. It was particularly useful as a theoretical explanation for certain types of crimes like violence, rape, etc. Here is the moral neutralization theory in a nutshell: the offender uses an upside down value system, or a moral code that denigrates the victim, such that even if violence is being used against a victim the victim somehow "deserves it", thus the offender is able to do the evil deed and in his/her own mind still justify or rationalize the event away by an alternative moral code. The alternative moral code can include a "dog eat dog world", "they steal from me, I should steal from them", "they will not miss it, so I might as well steal it, they can afford to lose it, they are insured", etc. These types of rationalizations are the "inner message", the kind of "movie script" for bizarre behavior, the kind of "taped message" that repeats itself in the mind of an offender.

Sykes and Matza (1957) delineated five principles to explain the process of moral neutralization as a theory of juvenile delinquency: (1) denial of responsibility (i.e., "I had to shoot back, they were probably going to shoot at us."), (2) Denial of injury (i.e.,

"It's a war, some people will die in a war."), (3) Denial of victim ("The guy that got shot had it coming to him"), (4) Condemnation of the condemners ("I'm being arrested for what police do all the time: protecting the community"), (5) Appeal to higher loyalty. In the last principle, the original language of the Sykes and Matza theory was this: "Sometimes adolescents may justify illegal behavior by claiming that they committed the act for someone else, such as the gang, the peer group, or an ethnic group" (see Regoli and Hewitt, 1991: p. 117).

Historically, the "moral neutralization" concept has been applied only at the level of the individual actor. It has not been applied at a group, organization, or collective entity level.

So, the way to provide a new look at gang life in the context of comparison with cults, would be this: if there is any merit to the concept of moral neutralization for explaining individual behavior of individual criminal or delinquent offenders, and the present author does accept that notion, then we must necessarily recognize that a group version of the same phenomenon can exist.
In the group version of moral neutralization, gang members will do things far beyond their individual violence potential. In the collective context of a group or organization, a different kind of social-psychological environment exists, particularly when we are talking about a coercive organization like a gang.

In the group version of moral neutralization, we would need to add a couple more principles to the original theory: (6) Denial of normative constraints - where the compulsion to violate norms gets momentum in the group context, such that the individual experiences the risky-shift phenomenon and becomes literally a person capable of violating any normative code or law in a process where the group may tend to reward such risk-taking behavior; and (7) Fear of disapproval or group sanctioning - where the person feels the group's goals are such that failure to do what was done could result in disapproval from the group or even a sanction (i.e., "violation") from the group for failure to do what was done (i.e., some element of duress).

By adding these two additional features to the original formulation of the moral neutralization theory, we can certainly view the behavior of gang members as they themselves view it.

THE DEPENDENCY-CRITICAL THINKING EFFECT

Gang life is as addictive as drugs in some respects. It is socially addictive. We see this phenomenon when an agency, or a professional therapist, after much work is able to work with a family to get a child away from gang life, going to the extreme of physically moving out of the old neighborhood, and

the hope was that the child would terminate his/her gang association, and suddenly the child simply uses public transportation or other means to return to his/her old haunts. And tragic results often occur for the gang member upon return to the old neighborhood.

Gang life is similar to the context of a person who invests a great deal of his/her lifestyle in a bar, saloon, pub, or nightclub "role". They compulsively carry out a routinized script of social life, they are always at the same bar stool, at the same time, most of the week, and particularly when the "action" is going on. Often mixed with alcoholism, and other forms of substance abuse, this type of person becomes a "fixture": more than just what the bar itself calls a "regular", the person may define and shape their entire life around that identity they have at a "bar scene". In other words, it is possible that some social thrills are so powerful as motivational forces that they come to shape one's everyday lifestyle and overpower the ability to "withdraw" from the situation. American culture has romanticized this situation in classical television series, where all of the actors have their common denominator and central axial principle in life as that of their identity at the counter of a bar where they are swilling down booze. Gang life is similar in some respects, particularly because of the intensity of its "risk taking" adventures that are routinized into daily gang life.

But similar to the cult, the gang has a strong "hold" on its members and it is fundamentally social in nature. Gang members often describe their gang as a "family", they describe their fellow members as their "brothers" and "sisters". Oddly, they do not describe their gang leader, though, as their "father", however they tend to act in this manner, with a hero worship style of dedication and uncritical orientation (i.e., their gang leader can literally "do no wrong"). This is called the "dependency effect" and it occurs with equal strength in cults and is therefore another conceptual parallel in our continuing analysis of gangs and cults.

What happens in both cults and gangs is a systematic deterioration of critical thinking skills for the individual member and a systematic increase in the level of dependency on the group and organization for one's personal affirmation and identify as a human being. Is it theoretically possible to "intervene" in this process? Yes, perhaps just as it would be possible to intervene in the life of a person who is entering into the drug subculture and exhibiting early or intermediate stages of substance abuse; but with very mixed and not necessarily high effective results using contemporary traditional methods of intervention.

Some have pointed to examples of "highly effective" drug abuse treatment programs, like Synanon, as strategies that can work better to facilitate someone to become a "recovering addict", but a closer inspection of the basic methodology of Synanon shows it is a total control institution and perhaps in some ways coercive. Other programs have replicated the total control and coercive socialization aspects of this "treatment", particularly through methods such as "confrontation therapy" which enjoyed decades of popularity in correctional circles. Perhaps this is analogous to the axiom "it takes a thief to catch a thief", or alternatively "it takes coercion to counteract a coercive hold on an individual", which would explain some of the more dramatic methods of so-called 'Cult Deprogramming' interventions that in some cases involved kidnapping the cult member and keeping them in bondage until they "realized the errors of their ways" (only to find that such persons typically immediately returned to their cults when they were released from restraints and high security confinement or control).

Similarly, while the quantitative evaluation research on Scared Straight suggests it is not necessarily the "Silver Bullet" of rehabilitation many of its advocates seem to believe it really is, it is, like Synanon, a program of intervention that is based on using fear and the threat of violence, i.e., coercion, in an explicitly vulgar and demeaning format to the "clients". Television versions of the "aftermath" of the Scared Straight program, 20 years later, suggest that a number of the participants were in fact "scared" straight. No such known "counter-gang" based on coercion and a total control format has emerged yet to the knowledge of this author in terms of private or publicly funded gang deprogramming services. But is it a likely future possibility? Yes, of course.

Viewed from the continuum of "dependency" versus "critical thinking", what happens in both cults and gangs is that the individual enters with some level of critical thinking, but this is systematically extinguished through the socialization process, and what emerges in both cult and gang organizations is a high dependency effect. The cult or gang member "depends" on their group or organization for their basic definition of their "self" and their mission in life. Nothing, absolutely nothing, else matters other than their self-selected group or organization, be it the gang or the cult: that is their moral compass, their sense of "right" and "wrong" is all dependent on the norms and values of their cult or gang.

THE MEDIATING EFFECT OF VIOLENCE FROM WITHIN THE SAME GANG

According to some experts on the topic of mind control, "brain washing" cannot be easily accomplished without the use of violence, particularly torture. What most people do not realize is that torture is a common aspect of gang life in America today: it is called the "violation" process. Gang members violate gang rules and face a "violation" from their own gang. The violation almost universally consists of the use of ritualized violence against the errant member in a group context where other members watch and take part in the ceremony.

We have described this in the context of coercive socialization. But perhaps we need to reiterate its important role in gang life today. The reason is many are simply not acquainted with this type of phenomenon. In fact, many persons subscribe to the fallacy that "gangs provide protection" to their individual members and therefore would be the last source of injury or violence. When in actuality, a gang member is probably, from an actuarial point of view, if we were an agency providing insurance against "gang violence", more likely to be a victim of violence from their own gang than from rival gang members who they assiduously avoid.

In this regard, the gang is more formidable and more dangerous than the cult. The gang does routinely "torture" its own members. Here is how it would work in a gang like the Latin Kings: say Johnny, a young gang member, losses his "stash" of drugs that he was selling for the gang; Johnny will have to report back to the gang that he was robbed, typically by a rival gang; Johnny will go to a brief summary trial at the next scheduled weekly gang meeting; he will then receive something like a 30 or 60 second violation. A 30 second violation means that Johnny would have to stand up and let three or four, or more, fellow gang members present, including the "Chief of Violations", pummel him, with closed fists, in punches to the chest and other areas, without resisting whatsoever (i.e., "taking his punishment"), for a period of 30 seconds. Not surprisingly, a number of such gang members develop conditions such as angina (i.e., heart problems). In a gang like the Gangster Disciples, if a member such as David did not fire back when his "crew" was attacked by a rival drive-by, he would go to summary trial at the next "prayer meeting" (i.e., weekly gang meeting), and he might receive the punishment of a "pumpkin head". A "Pumpkin Head" would mean that the Chief of Violations and other members could "beat on" David, hitting him with closed fists and kicking him, upon the head, resulting in profuse swelling of the head and facial tissues. And the gang member who "resists" or "fights back" would, of course, be subject to a "Death V": a sentence of death itself.

Gangs often gain their "reputation" by how "rough and tough" they treat their own members. For example, in a gang like the Aryan Brotherhood a member must "kill to get in, die to get out". It is more than an exclusive fraternity, it involves the element of coercive socialization which in contemporary legal circles is not at this date covered by statutory law. What this means is that when, using the case of Johnny from the Latin Kings, and David from the Gangster Disciples above, if both suffered paralyzing and life-threatening results from this kind of aggravated assault, this kind of mob action, this kind of forcible battery: a prosecutor could still not prosecute these cases as "crimes of violence", the reason is that the victim, in this instance, volunteered to sustain the effects of the violence or "treatment". Like a sexual liaison involving accentuated effects of sadism/masochism, the persons in the eyes of justice voluntarily entered into these relationships by their own consent, and there is no existing criminal sanction remedy to bring such cases into the criminal justice system. Recent collective moral developments in the United States concerning persons who engineer suicide have shown, however, that society is somewhat concerned as we enter the 21st Century, about the situation of "suicide doctors", or those who facilitate the event of suicide by assisting in the process and contributing physically and by other acts to the process of taking the life of another person. This may signal a moral awakening and future developments in state statutes with regard to the same phenomenon as it applies to gang life and ritualized violence that occurs inside gangs, often against juvenile underage members who are presumed, generally, to lack the ability to give such "consent"! The perspective of the present author is that such laws protecting underage children from ritualized violence received at the hands of groups or organizations administered by adult career criminals, such as "violations" received from a gang, would be long overdue. And the such future laws should include both criminal and civil penalties against the gang and the adult gang leaders responsible.

It is useful to examine some large scale gang research to address this issue of the effect of intragang violence: violence within the gang against its own members from other members in the same gang. Below we describe some of the findings from Project GANGECON.

Project GANGECON was the Task Force put together by the National Gang Crime Research Center to study The Economics of Gang Life. Among other things, it did look at what effect "violations" had upon gang members. The original hypothesis was that, perhaps like in a work situation, a "bad boss" would be a motivating force to "look elsewhere" (i.e., perhaps a greater tendency to quit the gang). The report was first released on March 11, 1995 at the Annual Meeting of the Academy of Criminal Justice Sciences in Boston, Mass. The citation used here will be Project GANGECON (1995).

The methodology of Project GANGECON involved ten researchers who interviewed over 1,000 gang members in five states. Among other findings in the book length report was this: a frequent activity

of the modern American gang is order maintenance, this means sanctioning its own members for infractions and "breaking the rules" of the gang itself, including violations that involved physical violence for such behaviors like not paying regular dues to the gang. Such sanctions are typically violations involving ritualized violence at a gang meeting. The violations are beatings from typically about 3 or 4 members of the same gang, and the beatings last varying amounts of time: such as 30 seconds, 60 seconds, etc.

A full one-third of all gang members in the United States appear to have experienced violent beatings from their own gang (i.e., getting a violation). The Project GANGECON survey instrument asked the gang members "have you ever been violated (received a beating) by your own gang for a violation?". Some 35.3 percent of the national gang sample indicated that they had in fact been beaten by their own gang for misconduct within their gang.

While the national norm was about 35 percent, the actual "rates" for violations differed between the type of gang alliance system as indicated in Table 19.

Table 19

Distribution of Violation Rates By Type of Gang Alliance System

Have you ever been violated (received a beating) by your own gang for a "violation"?	Type of Gang National Alliance System				
	People	Folks	Crips	Bloods	Other
% Yes	44.2%	40.9%	40.0%	25.7%	22.0%

Chi-square = 25.6, p < .001

Table 19 shows that actually there is some significant differentiation in the rates of violations by type of gang alliance system. But this really indicates that "Bloods" and the "other" category (unaligned, local, homegrown, white extremist, motorcycle etc) basically had the lower rates of such violations. When we look at "People" versus "Folks" gangs: there is no difference here, about two-fifths of all gang members who are People or Folks are reporting that they have been violated by their own gang. Actually, Folks and Crips are also identical in this respect: about 40 percent are reporting they have been violated by their own gang. This rate of being violated by ones own gang drops to 25 percent for "Blood" gang members, and to 22 percent for the "Other" gang category. A gang like the Trenchcoat Mafia would have necessarily been classified in the "Other" category: as it was not aligned with the

People/Folks or the Crips/Bloods national alliance systems.

So what we have learned so far is this: being physically beaten by ones own gang is not a rarity, it is a very common event in the modern American gang. The best estimate is therefore that from about a fourth to two-fifths of all American gang members have had this experience of being beaten by their own gang.

It is useful to explain how "violations" function as a method of coercive compliance inside the gang organization before taking a more detailed look at this matter. The administration of "violations" in a gang is an aspect of gang organization sophistication, because "violations" mean the members of the gang are subject to being physically punished for breaking the internal rules of the gang. Gangs that are less sophisticated, along organizational development lines, are less likely to have this function of coercive compliance. Gang members know this coercive function of the gang organization as the matter of "receiving a violation". A "violation" means getting a beating from one's own gang for breaking an internal rule, often written rules, such as not paying dues on time, dropping their flag, and even more typically disrespecting fellow gang members, etc.

A gang that does engage in coercive compliance using violations (i.e., the administration of corporal punishment for breaking rules) is therefore more authoritarian than a gang that lacks this capability of keeping its gang members "in check". The more sophisticated gang organization would be one that has this control capability for its members, because it is a ritualized activity: the member is often given a "hearing", goes to "trial", fellow gang members "vote" guilt or innocence, or in case of not paying dues or losing a gun or other gang resources (i.e., drugs that they may be selling), it could mean an instant violation without any trial (i.e., automatic punishment and summary judgement). The errant gang member must voluntarily submit to this punishment process.

When we look at specific gang organizations, we can find interesting variations that give us additional insight into the gang. Table 20, for example, shows the difference between the Vice Lord gang and the Gangster Disciples gang with regard to this matter of the percentage of members who are reporting that they have been "violated" by their own gang. It shows that 37.7 percent of the Gangster Disciples are reporting that they have been violated by their own gang, while this rises to 54.2 percent for members of the Vice Lord gang. In conclusion, when we look at the typical Vice Lord gang member, we can expect that about half of them have been beaten up by their own gang.

Table 20

Distribution of Violation Rates by Comparing Two Gangs: Gangster Disciples and Vice Lords

Have you ever been violated (received a beating) by your own gang for a "violation"?	Gangster Disciples	Vicelords
% Yes	37.7%	54.2%

Chi-square = 4.70, p = .03

Additional data suggests an important mediating effect of intragang violence and it is this: undergoing a "violation" by ones own gang does not, over time, necessarily lead to a greater motivation to attempt to leave the gang. Our data for this test comes from Project GANGGUNS, a 1994 Task Force Report on Gangs and Guns, by the National Gang Crime Research Center. Project GANGGUNS (1994) involved an analysis of N = 505 gang members in the midwest. It included the same language of "violation" in the survey instrument (i.e., have you ever been violated (physically beaten) by your own gang?).

In Project GANGGUNS we had hypothesized that perhaps the gang member who has been beaten by his own gang, that is he has been "violated" for a "violation" of gang rules, that such a person might be more prone to want to attempt to leave the gang. Our data from this study showed we were wrong. Two tests were done on two different variables of impact from being "violated". First we look at the move towards "inactive" status, a behavioral effort to get out of the gang. Second, we look at attempts to actually leave the gang.

First, the test about moving from active to inactive gang membership status. What we found here was that a significant difference does exist in comparing inactive and active gang members in terms of whether they have received a beating from their own gang for a violation of gang rules (Chi-square = 8.94, p = .003). However, it is not a finding that suggests the more one is beaten by the gang the more one is likely to move to an inactive status. In fact, quite the obverse is actually true. The inactive gang members had the lower percentage of being beaten up by their own gang (32.5%). It was the active gang member who reported the higher rate (48.4%) of being beaten up by his own gang. So, from the standpoint of the tendency to move from active to inactive status in the gang, it would almost appear as if this factor of ritualized intragang violence (i.e., corporal punishment against members for violating their own gang rules) is a variable that actually increases commitment to the gang in terms of continuity of gang membership. It is the closest evidence yet to suggest that this type of "torture" works to induce greater compliance among members of the gang.

Secondly, we now proceed to the test about efforts or attempts to formally quit the gang and leave the gang. Table 21 presents these results. We felt that this issue of commitment to the gang needed this separate additional test. But it too reinforces the previous conclusion: being beaten by one's own gang is not a factor associated with a lower commitment to the gang. The additional test made here was to examine whether having been beaten up by one's own gang was a factor that significantly differentiated the variable of having ever attempted to leave the gang.

Table 21

Frequency Distribution of N = 427 Gang Members Comparing Those Who Have Been "Violated" By Their Own Gang With Those Who Have Ever Attempted to Leave The Gang

Ever Been "Violated" (physically beaten) By Your Own Gang?	Ever Attempt to Leave the Gang?	
	No	Yes
NO	116	120
YES	106	85

Let us examine the findings in Table 21 which were not significant. There is no significant difference in comparing those who have and have not been violated in terms of attempts to leave the gang. Among those (N = 236) who reported "NO" they had not previously been "violated" by their gang, some 51% reported having attempted to leave their gang. Among those (N = 191) who reported "YES", they had been beaten by their own gang, some 45% reported having attempted to leave their gang. So the magnitude of the difference, in attempting to leave the gang, is not significant at all in comparing those who had and had not been "violated". The tendency, however slight, is for those who had been violated to be less likely to attempt to leave the gang.

Project GANGPINT was another large scale Task Force report of the National Gang Crime Research Center. Sixteen researchers collected data from N = 1,994 gang members in 8 states in 1994-95. This study offered the best evidence that the more gangs use "violations" against their members, the more the gang members are "hardcore". So the tendency is towards coercive compliance in the developmental sequence of gangs in America. The language of the variable was again identical (have you ever been violated, received a beating, by your own gang for a violation?). In this study, some 44.3 percent of the gang members nationwide reported that they had in fact experienced this violent internal disciplinary procedure commonly used by American gangs today.

What Project GANGPINT did was look at "violations" from the perspective of "level of gang involvement". Three levels of gang involvement were identified: Level 1, Level 2, and Level 3. The higher the level, the higher the level of gang involvement and/or commitment and investment in the gang as a lifestyle. Using a number of separate variables in the study, fifteen different factors of how "hard core" the gang member was were used to create an index called the "level of gang commitment". We will briefly explain this "scale" or index of gang commitment.

Fifteen factors were used in creating an additive index score of level of gang commitment.

Does the person have one or more close friends and associates who are gang members, if yes, add one point.

Does the person have family members who are in the gang, if yes, add one point.

Does the person consider himself a current "associate" of any gang, if yes, add one point.

Does the person have a gang tattoo, if yes, add one point.

Has the person ever joined a gang, if yes, add one point.

Is the person still active in a gang, if yes, add one point.

Has the person been in a gang for 5 or more years, if yes, add one point.

Has the person ever held rank or a leadership position in the gang, if yes, add one point.

Has the person ever helped recruit new members into the gang, if yes, add one point.

Has the person ever fired a gun at someone because they were threatening the drug business of their gang, if yes, add one point.

Has the person has never attempted to quit the gang, if no, then add one point.

Has the person ever been a shooter in a drive-by shooting, if yes, add one point.

Has the person ever fired a gun at someone in defense of their gang turf, if yes, add one point.

Does the person expect to continue to be a gang member for the next five years, if yes, add one point.

Is the person willing to die for their gang friends, if yes, add one point.

These fifteen factors were used to create three separate levels of commitment to the gang. Thus, a Level 1 would be a low level of commitment to the gang: this is someone who is not really doing much, and has a low level of gang involvement. A Level 2 would be an intermediate level of gang involvement.

And a Level 3 would be clearly what most people call the "hard core" gang member: someone who does violence and claims they are willing to die for their gang.

Table 22 presents the results of analyzing "violations" by the level of gang commitment or involvement.

Table 22

Percentage Distribution of Having Ever Been Violated By Level of Gang Involvement

Have you ever been "violated" (received a beating) by your own gang for a "violation"?	Level of Gang Involvement/Commitment		
	Level 1	Level 2	Level 3
Percent YES	25.1%	42.9%	51.8%

Chi-square = 83.7, p < .001

What we see in Table 22 is a very significant trend that is consistent and clear: those who do get "violated" tend to become the more hard core members of the gang. At a Level 1 level of gang involvement we find that only a fourth (25.1%) had been violated by their gang. This rises to 42.9 percent for the intermediate level of gang involvement (Level 2). At the highest level of gang involvement, what we probably regard as the "hard core" gang member in America, we see that half of these (51.8%) have been violated by their own gang. So the more the gang "violates" its members, the more it produces a more "hard core" member: more thoroughly committed to the gang organization.

Most certainly this represents strong and compelling evidence that "torture" works in the modern American gang to create a type of individual that becomes more highly committed to the gang enterprise. The gang member that is "violated" appears to be more eager to serve his/her gang, not less likely.

So, to summarize this issue, the mediating effect of violence inflicted upon members from within their own gang is a clear and predictable pattern: we see these persons as being shaped by coercive compliance to become more committed to their gang. There is almost an accentuation effect going on here: being beaten by the gang a person belongs to actually increases their involvement in the same gang.

THE COERCED-MOTIVATION PHENOMENON

It is a very common situation to find gang members who have been coerced to commit various crimes including murder. The basic chain of events in the coercion process always involves the threat of violence from the gang the person is in fact a member of. One of the most common ways this happens is at the time the person initially enters the gang. This coerced-motivation effect shows how gang members commit crimes they would otherwise not normally commit.

Gang members, for example, as part of an initiation ritual to get into the gang, are often told "do XYZ, or else". They are told to do this by their gang as the method of "testing" their faith and level of commitment to the gang. It is not uncommon to find cases in all types of gangs in all areas of the United States where the gang member has been basically coerced into committing a crime as part of an initiation process or other function in modern gang life. Someone who refused to carry out the directive of "do XYZ" would clearly face a violent mob: their own gang members.

Another common scenario for the coerced-motivation effect is found where the gang member is directed or compelled to commit a crime, often involving violence, as a way to achieve higher status inside the gang. Universally, gang members experience this kind of "respect maintenance" function. The norms of the gang basically require the gang member to defend the images and values of the gang. Some gangs describe this in terms of "don't drop your flag", which translated roughly means: "defend your gang nation at all cost". Translated, this means the gang member is compelled to respond with violence in certain situations where the gang's turf, its symbols, its image, etc, are "challenged" by either a rival gang or a "no body" (no body = non-gang member, as in "he's nobody", i.e., "he is not a gang member").

Because of the incredibly strong effect the gang has upon an individual, very similar to the cult situation, what often prevails as a norm of expressive conduct in venting personal opinions to others in the group or organization is not dissimilar to the proverbial "school yard" rule of elementary forms of social bonding: do not say anything to others unless you are absolutely certainly that they agree with you about what it is you are going to say to them. There is little room for dissension, and there is no room for challenging the primary edicts of the written gang constitution or the cult manifesto, and in this sense the world the gang and cult member lives in is a false world, however symbolic, and however serious, it is still a product of an illogical past and enjoys no democratic tradition. The cult, like the gang, is inimical to the democratic concept of freedom of speech.

CONVERSION INTO CULTS AND GANGS: ANOTHER CONCEPTUAL PARALLEL

In some respects we know more about how people get into gangs than we do how people get into cults. In gangs, recent data suggests that about half "join" voluntarily, that is they seek out the gang as a lifestyle they want to lead; while the other half are basically "recruited" into gang life with the "lures" and "attractions" that the gang offers. But we do not know, generally, the same statistical parameters with regard to cults. What we know about cults is that some are very aggressive recruiting organizations.

But in one important respect we can recognize another basic similarity between cults and gangs and this is to be found in the fact that whether one enters a cult or a gang, a definite process of "conversion" occurs for the individual. In the cult, the conversion is social, psychological, spiritual, and more. A new "lifestyle" must be adapted to, and the conversion process in cults has been seen by cult researchers (Lofland and Stark, 1965) to be predictable in one respect: often a disruptive life event occurs just prior to the decision point when the person enters a cult. In fact, data reported by Richardson, et al, (1979) shows that about half of those who entered a cult had been through a "disruptive life event" immediately preceding the point at which they entered into a cult group. There has been no specific research directed at gang members to examine this same possible phenomenon, but it would appear to be a worthwhile area of future investigation; particularly because the results could have much import for prevention.

In the cult situation, a "disruptive life event" could entail the situation where a promising college student whom many thought had lots of talent suddenly experiences a "failure", and the college student had never dealt with "failure" before, and lacking the coping skills to deal with a "failure", the student has a kind of breakdown. A physician explained to this researcher that a similar process exists in how some students have a nervous breakdown when they fail in the rigorous process of medical school and that it is common for some teaching physicians in medical school to try and "predict" informally who will typically have such a nervous breakdown and be forced out of medical school: typically, it is the same type of person: someone who throughout their life has been an gifted student, but who has never been socially experienced in dealing with the situation of "failure", and thus when a "failure" occurs it has devastating results. Obviously, in the context of cults a "disruptive life event" could entail a lot of other situations: financial hardship, unemployment, being fired from a job, marital disruption, etc, etc.

It is indeed possible that gang members could have a similar pattern involving the process of first experiencing a disruptive life event and then gravitating to the gang lifestyle. We do not have hard data on this situation, but there is some anecdotal information from case studies, etc. Here would be the typical profile for this situation: a person gets

killed by gang gunfire, that person has a brother or sister who during the grieving process develops a need to "get revenge", and as a way of coping with the loss of a loved one, what they do is join any gang that is "opposed" to, or which is "fighting with", the gang that killed their loved one. If a "Crip" killed the loved one, then the person joins any "Blood" gang; and vice versa. The idea is to join a gang that affords the opportunity to get revenge against an imaginary enemy force.

Both cults and gangs instill phobias and somewhat strange fears in their members. In cults this can often consist of the fear of going insane if the member leaves the cult. In gangs, it can mean other types of fears and phobias such as the following example from a typical "Crip" gang member. The word "clock" would always be intentionally misspelled as "clocc" by a Crip gang member, because Crip gang members have become conditioned to the fear of using the two letters "CK" in any word or phrase. Rival gangs, like the Bloods, use the initials "CK" to mean "Crip Killer".

Another conceptual parallel in examining cults and gangs is to be found in the type of vulnerable person who ends up in such groups or organizations. Certainly, the subtle nuances of the types of organizations are different, most cults are simply deviant groups. But gangs are not only deviant groups, they distinguish themselves additionally as being criminal in nature. But the seriousness or impact of the social decision to enter a cult or gang can probably be equal in its impact. We might hypothesize as well that there exist, plain and simple as a social truth, certain types of vulnerable individuals in any society and that such persons become the potential new "joiners" and "recruits" to cults and gangs. Both cults and gangs tend to take in persons who are pliable and willing to undergo a certain kind of transformation for the perceived benefit of enjoying membership in an exclusive type of alienated community of like-minded individuals.

Another conceptual parallel between cults and gangs can be found in what is called the internal/external locus of control concept of personality measurement. This is more than a concept, it is a personality measurement test as well: its results tell us a great deal about how "susceptible" a person would be to either march to their own drummer, or to march in lock-step formation with the crowd they are in. The basic question here is whether the person is predominantly controlled from within, or from without? A person with high internal locus of control would be a person with high critical thinking skills, who "marches to their own drummer", who is not easily swayed by group thinking or mass hysteria, and who would therefore in theory be much less likely to be a kind of person to join either a cult or a gang.

Cults and gangs do not tend to recruit individuals who have high levels of what is called <u>internal locus of control</u>. Cults and gangs, do however, tend to recruit individuals who have high levels of what is called <u>external locus of control</u>. To illustrate this concept, a police officer or a genuinely good leader must be able to have an exceptionally high level of internal locus of control: they are driven from within, a crowd or mob scene would not be able to influence them in terms of their decisions, they must carry out their mission and uphold the law or do what is best in any situation or calamity. But a person who tends to have a high level of external locus of control is a person who is easily "swayed" by the group or surrounding social milieu: the decisions they make are often not their own, they are little more than "parrots" of the group ethos, they tend to lack a mind of their own and are therefore prone towards extreme risk taking behavior. In the "Simon Says" child play game scenario, the person with a high level of external locus of control will do anything "Simon Says".

Those skeptics who doubt the possibility that a gang has the ability to exert extraordinary control over its members, and do not accept the possibility that in some cases gang members "know not what they do" (i.e., are acting under duress and a strong element of compulsion to carry out an act of violence for example), need to refresh their reading of the early experiments by Stanley Milgram. Milgram (1965) used large samples of mainstream American adults for his research on obedience and disobedience to authority. He was the implied authority, in a research lab where subjects where duped into believing they would be administering "electronic shocks" to subjects who were undergoing a "memory experiment". What he found was that most people are susceptible to this implied "authority/power" dimension of following orders, directives, admonitions, etc, even when it involved administering violence to another human being. Obviously, the "violence" in this case was not real, but the experimental subjects did not know that: in fact elaborate measures, including screaming, banging on walls, hollering in pain, etc, were "effects" created for the benefit of the experiment. But most people were willing to administer "shocks", up and including those that would be dangerous or harmful voltage levels.

One of the main conclusions of Milgram was that "one must always question the relationship of obedience to a person's sense of the context in which he is operating" (Milgram, 1965; see Steffensmeier and Terry, 1975: p. 192). Applying this axiom to the gang situation, how much possibility of disobedience exists when a gang orders or compels a member to carry out a violent act, such as in an "initiation ceremony" where the new gang recruit is asked to go out on a "drive-by" to shoot an opposition gang mem-

ber? The same problem emerges in a cult: how can a cult member seriously not comply with a request or directive from a leader of the same cult, even if it means doing something they did not want to do?

We can shed some light on this issue from data reported in Project GANGFACT (1997). Project GANGFACT included data on over 4,000 gang members. In that research, the largest study yet of gang members in the United States, over one-third of all gang members studied, some 36.6 percent, reported that they had in fact experienced this kind of compulsion in their gang: they had been asked by their gang to perform an act they knew was wrong. The survey from Project GANGFACT asked "has anyone in your gang (i.e., leaders, etc) ever told you to perform an act that you felt was wrong". Some 63.4 percent (N = 2,367) of the gang members surveyed said "no": they have not experienced this compulsion to do anything for their gang that they felt was wrong. Still, some 36.6 percent (N = 1,366) of the gang members indicated "yes", that they have in fact been told by gang leaders to perform an act that they felt was wrong.

So, not unlike the Milgram experiments, gangs today seem to be able to obtain a great deal of "compliance" and "obedience" from their members through directives from the leaders of the gangs. The data from Project GANGFACT would suggest that about a third of all gang members in the USA probably have experienced this compulsion phenomenon of anti-social obedience to illegitimate authority.

One of the other prominent conceptual parallels between cults and gangs has to do with the issue of alienation and/or conflict or tension with the larger societal environment. It is common to find one of the possible "symptoms" of potential future gang membership as that of alienation, unhappiness, disillusionment, conflict with the social order, etc. What it describes is a failure to adequately adapt to society, experiencing some level of social disorganization in community life. We know from some prior research on cult members that "the person frequently feels alienated from conventional society and those who are a part of it" (Light and Keller, 1985: p. 401; Downton, 1980). It is sufficient to characterize this condition leading to cult and gang membership as one of either alienation or anomie (e.g., a situation of normlessness). Perhaps an even better term to describe this condition would be "social estrangement".

What happens if an individual experiences a "disruptive life event" and then experiences a condition of alienation from society or disillusionment and social estrangement? Two possibilities exist: one is where they meet persons in a gang or cult, and through this intimate process of social interaction with significant others, the person learns of a new social alternative or a new social lifestyle. In the field of criminology, we call this differential association: it is the theory first advanced by Sutherland (1947), which states that persons become criminals or delinquents through symbolic interaction with other criminals or delinquents, and they learn the tricks of their trade in the same way (i.e., the notion that prisons are "schools of crime"). In the field of cult studies, this is simply a condition of "exposure" and one of the sequences a person goes through before becoming a cult member. But they are identical social processes! So in theory, if we had a youth who had recently experience a disruptive life event and it deteriorated to a condition of normlessness, alienation, and social estrangement, and the youth never could "hook up" with gang members, it is likely that the process would be "severed" at this point in the chain of events. Put alternatively, the gang joining behavior would be "naturally prevented" by the very lack of opportunity to associate with significant others who are involved in a gang.

This issue of differential association presents a fascinating research issue for the field of gang studies. One of the basic issues is this: how many youths in America are potentially at risk of gang membership due to their diagnosis as having recently experienced "disruptive life events" and the condition of "social estrangement"? Is it possible that a tremendous potential reservoir of potential new gang recruits exist in American communities and that the gangs are on the prowl while the parents and responsible adults are blind to the potential hazards of the children they are responsible for?

Indoctrination is the final outcome for both cult and gang members. Once they "join" or are "recruited", and we point out that these are different methods of entering the organization, they must take on the color and values and language and beliefs and practices of the group or organization they have entered. They must "style over", they must learn to "talk the talk" and "walk the walk". They must show their obedience to the group or organization and its leaders. They must often "prove" themselves. They must support and sacrifice for their new "cause". They ultimately come to have few if any friends and associates, or significant others, outside of their cult or gang. Their cult or gang becomes the central matter of their lifestyle: it shapes the way they dress, the way they think, the way they talk, the way they behave, and the beliefs and social values they have. Whatever their former life was like, it changes dramatically when they enter a cult or gang. But they must all go through a kind of indoctrination process to become like the others in the cult or gang.

What we see in the larger societal picture, to recap from the preceding analysis, is an etiological sequence of events and conditions that lead predict-ably to the same outcome: gang or cult membership (Lofland and Stark, 1965; Light and Keller, 1985: p. 401). It begins with the "disruptive life event". This is followed by a condition of disillusionment or what we have called "estrangement" or alienation from legitimate or larger society. Then differential association kicks in: by association with significant others who are themselves involved in a cult or a gang, the individual gets exposed to the new potential lifestyle represented by the cult or gang. The end result is indoctrination into the life of the cult or the gang.

This etiological sequence is graphically depicted in Figure 14. The same process seems to apply to both cult and gang members. It is a significant conceptual parallel in analyzing the chain of events that propel an individual into cult or gang membership. In theory, cutting off this chain of events at any point before "final indoctrination" is something that would prevent cult or gang membership.

Figure 14: Chain of Events Leading to Cult/Gang Indoctrination

DLE ==> A/SE ===> DA ===> Indoctrination

Legend:
    DLE = Disruptive Life Event
    A/SE = Alienation/Social Estrangement
    DA   = Differential Association

RECONCILING FREE WILL AND MIND CONTROL

Astute gang observers know that the gang attracts criminal offenders: persons who are predisposed to do what gangs do. Older adult gang members and leaders are simply career criminals whose gang functions like a kind of union guild, giving the opportunity structure for further criminal behavior. Do gang members operate with a genuine type of "free will" in the decisions they make or are they under the influence of an unshakable type of group control?

The absolute issues of free will versus mind control can be reconciled by viewing these conditions as relative or variable conditions which have differential impact at different points in time or in different circumstances or situations. The best argument appears to be, therefore, that gang members experience differential levels of mind control in their gang experience.

1. The Honeymoon Factor: Initial Adverse Influence Followed By Realization of Exploitation and Desire to Eventually Leave the Gang.

There are several ways of reconciling the matter of the free will versus mind control issue regarding gang life. One would be to assert that free will operates for the most part just as it does for any ordinary criminal offender, with the caveat that gang membership is a factor accentuating the negative. Therefore the decision to join a gang may be little different than the type of decision made when a person joins a cult or authoritarian extremist group: they are voluntarily surrendering to a collective force. It is what happens later on in the developmental lifespan of a gang member that may be important to examine: when they realize, as most presumably do, that the gang simply exploits them, and that the real "spoils of gang war" are shared primarily among gang leaders, not ordinary members.

At the time the gang member comes to the realization that he/she is being exploited, it is often too late to simply quit: they are loaded with tatoos and a rap sheet and a long list of enemies they have made over the years; so while many may have contemplated quitting the gang, there really is no "safe zone" for them to land in. This way of reconciling the free will versus mind control issue therefore views the early part of gang life as the "honeymoon", and yes at that point they are under an incredibly intensive adverse influence from their group, but that at some point in their later gang career the "romance" wears off, and they realize their gang involvement was a life course decision that is for the most part irreversible.

In the honeymoon scenario of freewill versus group control, we see a kind of upside down "J-curve" over time where we could plot the level of group influence on the gang member: it rises constantly until the honeymoon is over, and then the level of group influence or mind control takes a sudden downturn as the gang member comes to the realization that this type of adverse influence is not adaptive for his/her survival. It could be an event of betrayal, an event of wrongfully accused of something by his/her gang, an arrest for a major crime, or any event that is likely to have a sobering effect on the gang member. The point at which group influence takes a sudden down turn would be the point at which we could predict defection from the gang, or a willingness to testify against other gang members, or a willingness to sever ties to the gang once and for all. This theory may have great applicability to institutional environments where data could be monitored to assess this condition on a regular and ongoing basis.

2. The Upsidedown U-Shaped Hypothesis: Initial Autonomy, Followed by Absence of Autonomy and Group Control, Ending in Regretful Autonomy.

In this formulation, it may be possible that free will exists intact initially at the point of joining a gang, and gradually declines in direct proportion to the level of group influence, until a dramatic event, such as in the "J-Curve hypothesis", at which point group influence then begins to dissipate over time, leading eventually to abandoning gang life. Viewed in terms of the level of loyalty and commitment to the gang, if we plotted this over time it would look like an upsidedown "U": low level of group influence at first, followed by continuing escalation in group influence, until a dramatic event occurs, at which point the level of commitment and loyalty to the gang begins to decline over time.

Under the upsidedown u-shaped hypothesis, a gang member is most likely to kill a rival gang member or anyone for that matter if it is connected with gang life, when the person is at the midpoint or the top of the upsidedown "U" in terms of the level of group influence over time. Once the group influence starts to take a downturn, that is when a gang member can be "flipped": converted to a 'snitch' or 'informant', that is when the gang member is looking for a way out of the gang. But typically few take that option of collaboration with law enforcement. Most simply accept their fate and try to live out their life with the added weight of gang involvement and the fact that they "owe" something to the gang, that they can always be subject to gang influence, that they will always have to show their loyalty in some way to the gang the rest of their lives...unless they go "underground". What the gang member does under this scenario is gradually withdraw from the gang over a long period of time.

3. The Scaling of Expected Variation: The Comparison to DUI Testing.

In this formulation, the extent of adverse group influence or mind control varies naturally, between persons, and over time, and can be viewed similar to how "Driving Under the Influence" (D.U.I.) testing is conducted. Some may have the gang influence, but not become impaired because of low levels of impact from the adverse nature of the group influence. Just as some others may indeed become intoxicated with gang life so much that they mindlessly follow gang directives like a lemming marching over the proverbial cliff of doom.

Perhaps, therefore, one of the most practical ways to view and analyze the extent of mind control exerted upon gang members is through this analogy to the way our society measures D.U.I. levels: we expect, above a certain arbitrary point, that the level of adverse influence is indicated. What that level would be is a subject of recommended future research. We cannot with confidence currently determine when a gang member is an "automaton" of his/her gang leadership. No "gangalyzer" test of this nature currently exists.

Clearly, we know or should assume that youthful age would interact in a multiplicative way with susceptibility to gang influence, such that it may be possible to go back and analyze a number of youthful gang violence cases as cases involving gang compulsion. The issue here is that "they know not what they do". It is possible to conceive of some younger gang offenders as being "wind up robots" of gang violence, given direction and momentum from older adult gang leaders.

The "Greenhorn Irish Travelers": Cult, Gang, Neither or Both?"

By most definitions, a "clan" is a group of persons related by birth or marriage who often live collectively to preserve unique traditions of their ethnicity and culture. In theory, such a group overlaps with the definition of cult when it has a unique or deviant belief system in which all members are expected to be socialized.

An Associated Press story entitled "Texas Fatalities Fuel Doubts About Clan" (see: Chicago Sun-Times, Jan. 17, 2000, p. 19) described a unique group called the Greenhorn Irish Travelers. The size of the group is impressive. Estimates suggest 7,000 members live in the United States, mostly in Texas and South Carolina; but that world wide there may be many more as 40,000 members may live in other countries like Ireland and England.

So little is actually known about the Greenhorn Irish Travelers that it is not possible to label this group as a cult. No one seems to know what if any belief system they may possess, or what their traditions really entail. It may be nothing more than a harmless ethnic subculture.

Then, again, if we are to believe some sources it may be a group that facilitates or is often associated with certain unique crime patterns. A variety of police reports have drawn attention to this clan. The AP story noted several arrests for members involved in fraudulent activities, con games, etc.

The group occupies two trailer parks in the Fort Worth, Texas suburb of White Settlement. The AP story described how many of these members spent their winter months in Texas, and spent their summer months working in northern states doing manual labor. It is, then, simply a group like "carnies" (e.g., people who work at carnivals) who do seasonal and migratory labor?

Is it a tight ethnic group, where in any large such collective one might expect some members to be arrested? Thus, if the group itself does not approve or endorse the criminal activity, it could not collectively be viewed as a gang? It is not clear if criminal activities are committed in group contexts, but where the individual members operating in a criminal fashion, if there were three or more involved in the enterprise, it certainly could be defined as a gang unit. It is a fascinating issue, but one that begs for empirical research.

DEPROGRAMMING GANG MEMBERS

There certainly exists an unusually high level of belief in some circles that gang members can be "deprogramed" from gang life. Perhaps those who are most likely to be working in a setting that presumes the effectiveness of rehabilitation or intervention are also the ones most likely to want to believe that gang members can in fact be deprogramed. I offer an interesting story about this with regard to some of the early gang research on American juvenile correctional institutions.

In 1990, and again in 1991, two yearly surveys of all juvenile correctional institutions in the United States, carried out by the NGCRC, we wanted to include a "validity item". We have always used validity items in surveys of gang offenders, because everyone knows offenders tend to over-report their good qualities and underreport their deviance. We were interested in having some type of deception detection capability in the survey of juvenile institutions because typically the surveys were completed by the administrators of these juvenile correctional facilities.

The research team considered a number of possibilities for developing a validity item for the 1990 and 1991 juvenile correctional institution research, where the unit of analysis was the institution itself (i.e., size of population, staff, number of gang members in the population, types of gang incidents during the last year, etc) and the survey instrument was typically completed by an institutional administrator. What we did was design a "service program" that we knew, or reasonably believed, did not really exist anywhere, and in a standard "check off" list of existing service programs, slipped this validity item into the list. The idea was to have a better idea about the extent to which administrators were being truthful in the representation of the facts disclosed about their respective institutions.

The type of "program" we listed was something we just invented in 1990: "gang deprogramming". It sounded good, but from our perspective at the time it was so ludicrous as to be a perfect validity item. It sounded even feasible and worthwhile, but we knew from our collective mastery of the literature that really no such program existed. We basically invented the idea, feeling at the time it was so preposterous that it was equivalent to asking juvenile institutions if they had a "sex change program" for boys and girls who wanted to change their gender identity.

What we found was that 16.6 percent of the institutions in 1990 claimed they had a gang deprogramming program, and that even though we pointed out in our report that this was a validity item and we were therefore skeptical about such responding agencies and made sure all respondents received a copy of the 1990 report, in the 1991 survey some 23.8 percent claimed they had a gang deprogramming program or service component in their institution (Knox, 1998: pp. 338-339).

Subsequent investigation into those who reported having programs that we thought were non-existed revealed the term "program" can include informal initiatives in governmental settings. That is, any efforts undertaken to erode "gang ties", to "dismember" gangs, to "coopt" those who are not hard core gang members, and to basically "siphon off" gang members whose commitment level was not very high to begin with, were considered "gang deprogramming services" by juvenile correctional administrators. We felt that the same administrators may have wanted, to some extent, to claim they were a modern treatment facility and may have been fooled into believing that "gang deprogramming" was a type of proven and accepted program on the cutting edge of child saving.

Most scholars who study cults know that "cult deprogramming" is just not a recommended strategy for a number of reasons. Mostly, it just does not work. To synthesize what many scholars have had to say on the topic, it appears the best strategy is not deprogramming, but rather a cautious use of "exit counseling" (Tucker, 1989: p. 27). The best idea appears to be this: when someone is ready to leave, determine if it is authentic and then intervene. The cautionary screening, however, is still vital: someone who just before they face sentencing by a judge who suddenly says "I want to quit my gang" could be considered less than genuine in some regards.

SUMMARY

We now summarize the basic findings of this analysis involving a comparison of cults and gangs. Our analysis has led to one fundamental conclusion: gangs have almost all of the features that cults are attributed to have, but gangs are more sinister in terms of the use of violence against their own members and others. Disobedience in a cult might mean having to get "K.P." (i.e., scrubbing dirty dishes, cleaning toilets, etc), but the same disobedience in a gang could result in the death of the member.

Figure 15 provides a summary table of the basic commonalities between cults and gangs. As seen in Figure 15, we can delineate about forty (40) various factors from the present study that seem to be common elements of both cults and gangs. In a great many ways, then, cults and gangs are similar. In fact, it may be possible to argue that one of the developmental paths that present gangs may take for the future is to improve their operational control over members by adding two factors from Figure 16 and that gangs generally lack today (i.e., functioning more like a total control institution and arranging marriages

for members).

Other possible differences could include factors such as a restricted diet. However, in some Islamic-influenced gangs like the Black P. Stone Nation, and to some extent in Vice Lords as well, there is a specific prohibition against eating pork.

Figure 15

Summary Table of Some Basic Similarities in the Comparison of Cults and Gangs

	Cults	Gangs
Self-appointed leaders	Yes	Yes
Top leader acts as a "father" figure	Yes	Yes
Have special "prayers"	Yes	Yes
Have secret signs, code words, and rituals	Yes	Yes
Have specialized language code	Yes	Yes
Have an ideology or codified belief system	Yes	Yes
Members basically lack freedom/autonomy	Yes	Yes
Demand unquestioning obedience	Yes	Yes
Undergo personality changes after joining	Yes	Yes
Use lies/deceit against non-members	Yes	Yes
Target certain types for recruitment	Yes	Yes
Basically a deviant group	Yes	Yes
Group-dependent definition of self	Yes	Yes
Exploit normal desire for group affirmation	Yes	Yes
Top leaders typically older adults	Yes	Yes
Sometimes involved in politics	Yes	Yes
Literature defines leader as God-like figure	Yes	Yes
Members show high external locus of control	Yes	Yes
Members show low critical thinking ability	Yes	Yes
Use coercive compliance to maintain order	Yes	Yes
Use special totems and symbols	Yes	Yes
Have strong "in-group"/"out-group" norms	Yes	Yes
Throw "parties" to recruit new members	Yes	Yes
Members show alienation/tension with society	Yes	Yes
Disruptive life events occur before joining	Yes	Yes
Members get "new" names (e.g., aliases)	Yes	Yes
Members develop a "new" identity	Yes	Yes
Go through indoctrination after joining	Yes	Yes
Members experience risky-shift effect	Yes	Yes
Members experience group-think effect	Yes	Yes
Members develop tight bonds to the group	Yes	Yes
Experience collective moral neutralization	Yes	Yes
Expected to financially support the group	Yes	Yes
Leaders financially exploit the members	Yes	Yes
Membership group becomes new "family"	Yes	Yes
Deprogramming generally not effective	Yes	Yes
Group will punish its disobedient members	Yes	Yes
Not easy to leave the group after joining	Yes	Yes
Members prosyletize to recruit others	Yes	Yes
Membership is considered a life-long matter	Yes	Yes
Have special "commemorative" dates	Yes	Yes
Instill phobias/fears in members	Yes	Yes

Figure 16 provides a list of the major differences that still appear to exist in comparing gangs and cults.

Figure 16

Summary of Major Differences in the Comparison of Cults and Gangs

	Cults	Gangs
Functions as a total control institution	Yes	No
Historically involved in mass suicides	Yes	No
Corporal punishment often used on members	No	Yes
Kill members who try to leave the group	No	Yes
Kill members who are disloyal to the group	No	Yes
Engaged in conspicuous illegal activity	No	Yes
Membership base includes mostly offenders	No	Yes
Arranges marriages between members	Yes	No

IMPLICATIONS

It may be worthwhile to dwell, momentarily, on the matter of some of the implications that could be reached from an analysis of coercive socialization in gang life today.

Some might take the issue to the logical extreme conclusion that if there was a form of mental illness that lead to or culminated in "gang banging", that therefore certain necessary corollaries must also be assumed to be true. One would be that there would exist a "treatment", perhaps something equivalent to "Ganganon", as a recovery program. One would also be tempted to conclude that defense lawyers could have a field day with the affirmative defense of compulsion for many crimes other than murder. Another would be convenient for gang apologists and those who have as of yet failed to condemn gang behavior for what it is, because to the extent that one could argue gang behavior is compulsive behavior, then to the same extent it could be argued to be a diseased human condition requiring service intervention like other addictions, not penal sanctions. Taken to its logical, or perhaps illogical, extreme: If we could redefine much of gang behavior within the context of contemporary definitions of mental illness such as those promulgated by the American Psychological Association, that is provide a powerful excuse for gang behavior, then perhaps gang status itself could

be protected under laws such as the Americans with Disabilities Act.

Clearly, there are many important and far reaching implications of the present analysis. What remains to be done however is a great deal of new large scale research on this issue. Some of the things we need to know about have simply been neglected in the prior literature: what kind of "disruptive life events" do we find in the life cycle of gang members prior to their decision to join the gang, and what level of "social estrangement" is necessary before a youth begins to consider entering into a gang? There is anecdotal data along these lines: a youth loses a close friend or family member to gang violence from the "X" gang, and then seeks to join the "Y" gang in order to carry out a retaliatory mission of violence against a perceived enemy in the long American tradition of extralegal solutions to personal problems (i.e., vigilantism). But it would be useful to know the full range of possible disruptive life events that could trigger the motivation to join a cult or gang.

Researching the gang as a "malevolent authority" that uses its prestige-granting mechanisms and status-enhancing capabilities for vulnerable youths to command these same pliable youths to carry out acts of great violence and brutality against other human beings, would appear to be a worthwhile line of future investigation.

Some of the other research needs have been addressed inside the body of this article. Unfortunately, most of this is the kind of recommended research that would probably never be funded by public agencies that pay for gang research (NIJ, OJJDP, DHHS, etc). We must assume, then, that some of these issues will remain clouded by lack of hard data for years to come.

CONCLUSION

A close colleague of mine, who is an expert on satanic cults and related deviant cult-like groups, is fond of telling the following "war" story of his extensive experience in the field of gang training. He has done a lot of gang training to diverse groups all over the USA: parents, teachers, police, etc. He tells the story of going into some communities and trying to warn parents about the "threat of gangs" to their children, and often finds his audience "yawning", that is, in effect having a low level of such fear. But when he would mention how some gangs operate as cults, the sheer thought of a "cult" getting one of their children was enough to suddenly get riveted attention from an audience that listened attentively to each and every word the trainer spoke.

The trainer, my colleague and friend, discovered an important aspect about gang life in America today: many parents have already been de-sensitized to the issue of gang life, they know gangs are part and parcel of everyday life in many communities, and the same parents think they know enough to deal with a situation where their child would become contaminated by gang association. But the same parents were terrified of the idea their kids would become involved with cults. This lesson shared with me from this colleague was enough motivation to begin studying the similarities between cults and gangs and eventually led to the writing of this article.

What we can now definitively say about the relationship between cults and gangs is this: there is, in fact, a lot that gangs and cults have in common. They have more in common than many casual observers would suspect. Most certainly one thing is true: the similarities outweigh the differences in comparing cults and gangs. And there is a great need to begin conducting large scale research on some of these issues in greater depth.

Discussion Questions:

1. What do you think is the most important single difference between cults and gangs, justify your answer.

2. Describe a "cult" and a "gang" from the real world, compare them as a case study.

3. How should a free and open society fairly deal with cults and gangs?

Selected Bibliography

Appel, Willa
    1983 Cults in America: Programmed for Paradise. Holt, Rinehart & Winston: New York, NY.
Berger, Melvin
    1985 Mind Control. Thomas Y. Crowell: New York.
Bonner, Roger
    1999 "Gang Profile: The Brotherwoods - The Rise and Fall of a White-Supremacist Gang Inside a Kansas Prison", Journal of Gang Research, Spring, Volume 6, Number 3, pp. 61-76.
Breese, Dave
    1975 Know the Marks of Cults. Victor Books, Wheaton, IL.
Bromley, David G. and Anson D. Shupe
    1981 Strange Gods: The Great American Cult Scare. Beacon: Boston, Mass.
Campbell, Anne
    1984 The Girls in the Gang: A Report from New York City. New York: Basil Blackwell Ltd.
Chambers, W.; M. Langone; A. Dole; and J. Grice
    1994 "The Group Psychological Abuse Scale: A Measure of the Varieties of Cultic Abuse", Cultic Studies Journal, (11)(1): 88-117.

Cinnamon, Kenneth and Dave Farson
    1979 Cults and Cons. Nelson-Hall Publishers: Chicago, IL.
Downton, James V., Jr.
    1980 "An Evolutionary Theory of Spiritual Conversion and Commitment: The Case of Divine Light Mission", Journal for the Scientific Study of Religion (19)(4): 381-396.
Enroth, Ronald
    1977 Youth, Brainwashing and the Extremist Cults. Zondervan: Grand Rapids, Michigan.
    1979 The Lure of the Cults. Christian Herald Books: Chappaqua, New York.
Forrest, Alistair and Peter Sanderson
    1982 Cults and the Occult Today. Marshalls Press: London, England.
Fraser, George A.
    1997 The Dilemma of Ritual Abuse: Cautions and Guides for Therapists. American Psychiatric Press, Inc: Washington, D.C.
Gruss, Edmond C.
    1982 Cults and the Occult. Eerdmans: Grand Rapids, Michigan.
Hanna, David
    1979 Cults in America Tower: New York.
Hobsbawm, E.J.
    1959 Primitive Rebels: Studies in Archaic Forms of Social Movements in the 19th and 20th Centuries. New York: W.W. Norton & Company, Inc.
Hunt, Dave
    1978 The Cult Explosion: An Expose of Today's Cults and Why They Prosper. Harvest House: Irvine, California.
Hunter, Edward
    1956 Brainwashing. Farrar, Straus & Cudahy: New York.
Janis, Irving L.
    1971 "Groupthink", Psychology Today Magazine, American Psychological Association.
    1989 "Groupthink: The Desperate Drive for Consensus at Any Cost", chapter 15 (pp. 223-232) in J. Steven Ott (Ed.), Classic Readings in Organizational Behavior, Brooks/Cole Publishing Company: Pacific Grove, California.
Jenkins, Phillip
    1992 "Investigating Occult and Ritual Crime: A Case for Caution", Police Forum, Academy of Criminal Justice Sciences Police Section, Vol. 2, No. 1, Jan.: 1-7.
Kahaner, Larry
    1988 Cults that Kill. New York: Warner.
Knox, George W.
    1991 An Introduction to Gangs. 1st Edition. Berrien Springs, Mich.: Vande Vere Publishing, Ltd.
    1998 An Introduction to Gangs. 4th Edition. New Chicago School Press: Peotone, Illinois.

Larson, Bob
    1982 Larson's Book of Cults. Tyndale House: Wheaton, Illinois.
    1989 Satanism: The Seduction of America's Youth. Nashville: Thomas Nelson Press.
Lewis, Gordon R.
    1966 Confronting the Cults. Baker: Grand Rapids, Michigan.
Lifton, Robert Jay
    1969 Thought Reform and the Psychology of Totalism. W.W. Norton: New York.
Light, Donald, Jr.; and Suzanne Keller
    1985 Sociology, 4th edition. New York: Alfred A. Knopf.
Lofland, John; and Rodney Stark
    1965 "Becoming a World-Saver: A Theory of Conversion to a Deviant Perspective", American Sociological Review (30): 865-875.
Lucksted, Orlin D.; and D.F. Martell
    1982 "Cults: A Conflict Between Religious Liberty and Involuntary Servitude?", FBI Law Enforcement Bulletin, April, May, and June.
Martin, Walter
    1985 The Kingdom of the Cults. Bethany: Minneapolis, Minnesota.
Milgram, Stanley
    1965 "Some Conditions of Obedience and Disobedience to Authority", Human Relations (18): 57-75.
Petersen, William J.
    1982 Those Curious New Cults in the 80s. Keats: New Canaan, Connecticut.
Project GANGFACT
    1997 The Facts About Gang Life in America Today: A National Study of Over 4,000 Gang Members. Chicago, IL: National Gang Crime Research Center.
Project GANGGUNS
    1994 Gangs and Guns: A Task Force Report. Chicago, IL: National Gang Crime Research Center.
Project GANGECON
    1995 The Economics of Gang Life: A Task Force Report. Chicago, IL: National Gang Crime Research Center.
Project GANGPINT
    1996 Gang Prevention and Gang Intervention: Results from the 1995 Project GANGPINT National Needs Assessment Gang Research Task Force. Chicago, IL: National Gang Crime Research Center.
Regoli, Robert M. and John D. Hewitt
    1991 Delinquency in Society: A Child-Centered Approach. New York: McGraw-Hill, Ic.
Richardson, James T.; Mary White Stewart; and Robert B. Simmonds
    19779 Organized Miracles: A Study of Contemporary, Youth, Communal Fundamentalist Organization. New Brunswick, NJ: Transaction Books.

Robbins, T.
    1988 Cults, Coverts and Charisma. London: Sage.
Schein, Edgar
    1961 Coercive Persuasion. W.W. Norton: New York.
Schrag, Peter
    1978 Mind Control. Pantheon Books: New York.
Singer, M.T.; and R. Ofshe
    1990 "Thought Reform Programs and the Production of Psychiatric Casualties", Psychiatric Annals (20): 188-193.
Sparks, Jack
    1979 The Mindbenders: A Look at Current Cults. Thomas Nelson: Nashville, Tennessee.
Stark, R. and W. Bainbridge
    1985 The Future of Religion: Secularization, Revival and Cult Formation. University of California Press: Berkeley, CA.
Steffensmeier, Darrell J.; and Robert M. Terry
    1975 Examining Deviance Experimentally: Selected Readings. Port Washington, NY: Alfred Publishing Co., Inc.
Stoner, J.A.F.
    1961 "A Comparison of Individual and Group Decisions Including Risk", c.f. Stephen Wilson, 1978 Informal Groups: An Introduction, Englewood Cliffs, NJ: Prentice-Hall.
Stoner, Carroll and Jo Anne Parke
    1977 All Gods Children: The Cult Experience - Salvation or Slavery? Chilton Book Co.: Radnor, Pennsylvania.
Streiker, Lowell D.
    1983 Cults: The Continuing Threat. Abingdon: Nashville, Tenn.
Sutherland, Edwin H.
    1947 Principles of Criminology. (4th Edition). Philadelphia: J.B. Lippincott Company.
Sykes, Gresham M. and David Matza
    1957 "Techniques of Neutralization: A Theory of Delinquency", American Sociological Review (22)(Dec): 664-670.
Tucker, Ruth A.
    1989 Another Gospel: Cults, Alternative Religions and the New Age Movement. Academic Books: Grand Rapids, Michigan.
Wallach, Michael A.; N. Hogan; and D.J. Bem
    1962 "Diffusion of Responsibility and Level of Risk Taking in Groups", Journal of Abnormal and Social Psychology 68: 263-274.

Party Photos of the
Satan's Disciples in
Chicago, Illinois

CHAPTER 16

GANGS AND DRUGS

INTRODUCTION

As gangs and crime are inextricably related it comes as no surprise that gangs and drugs are also tied together in a complex way. There are several issues that must be examined to understand the relationship between gangs and drugs. One is the matter of drug use among and by gang members. Another is the involvement of the gang and its members in profitable illegal drug sales activity. Gangs like the Crips and Bloods and many Folks gangs and many Peoples gangs derive most of their income from the enormous underground economy in terms of illegal drug sales. Gangs will change their internal values if the money is right, as in the case of the El Rukns who for a long time would not sell heroin because in their written constitution they felt it was too destructive to the community, but decided to go ahead and provide this commodity for the African-American community when the income margin was profitable and when there was too much competition in other drug user products (i.e., cocaine, marijuana, etc).

Drug abuse and drug sale income are two aspects along which gangs can and do vary. Thus, from a social organizational perspective it is possible that a gang may exist that prohibits any involvement with drugs, just as it is possible to find a gang that sells drugs as its primary income source. "Stoner" gangs are portrayed as consisting of members who use and abuse drugs as an ongoing and regular activity in their recreational lifestyle[1].

Some gangs like the Latin Kings have mixed policies on drugs and drug abuse: making money from drug sales of any kind is fine, using soft drugs is acceptable, but using hard drugs by means of I.V. injection is prohibited and can be severely punished as a violation of written gang laws and rules in their constitution.

It is fair to say that a great deal of crime and drug abuse goes on in America. Neither of which is always detected, and only a portion of which ever comes to the attention of the criminal justice system. It is not true that we know everything we need to know about the linkages between the two topics of "gangs" and "drugs". In this chapter we examine drug abuse among gang members, as well as the more interesting aspect of drug sales by gangs and gang members. Finally, the issue of hard drug legalization is examined in relationship to gangs.

DRUG ABUSE AMONG GANG MEMBERS

Using the individual gang member as the unit of analysis shows that gang members are more prone to drug abuse than non-gang members. This is true inside the offender population itself, this is true in the student population in public high schools, and this is also true for special groups such as Asian students. What this trend suggests is support for the hypothesis that, generally, gang members are more prone to deviant behavior including substance abuse than their non-gang member counterparts. This is little more than common sense because gangs are, after all, important aspects of the deviant subculture due to their involvement in crime.

Three different studies of this issue will be summarized here examining the relationship between drugs and gang membership among: (1) high school students, (2) juveniles in short and long term correctional facilities, and (3) Asian students.

(1) Drugs and Gang Membership Among High School Students.

A sample of 552 Chicago high school students in an anonymous survey administered in the Fall of 1991 showed that overall, some 10.3 percent of the students reported that they had ever joined a gang. For male high school students, this was significantly higher, 17.2% compared to only 4.7 percent among females. The effect of gender on self-reported gang membership is therefore statistically significant (Chi-square = 23.05, p < .001). This particular one high school was chosen as a case study because it was uniquely integrated in terms of race: almost equal proportions of the student body were African-American, Hispanic, and white.

Self-reported gang membership is also a factor that significantly differentiates whether the same high school students have seen drug sales occur in or near the school. This finding is provided in Table 23.

Table 23

The Frequency Distribution of Self-Reported Gang Membership by Having Seen Drug Sales in or Near the School Among a Fall 1991 Sample of Chicago High School Students

	Seen Drug Sales in/near the School?	
	No	Yes
Gang Member:		
No	323	122
Yes	26	24

Chi-square = 9.15, p = .002

As seen in Table 23 above, among gang members some 48 percent have seen drug sales occur in or near the school compared to 27.4 percent among the non-gang member high school students. Gang members are significantly more likely to have seen such drug sales, in part of course because they could have been selling the drugs themselves.

A variable that taps into the drug use dimension is actually a surrogate measure of self-usage. It asks the student how many of their close friends and associates use illicit drugs. This is considered by some to be the best true measure of deviance: as the natural tendency is to over-report good qualities, and underreport deviance. By focusing on the deviance

of "friends", this measures both association with and integration into the deviance represented by the drug abuse subculture. The essential finding among this sample of high school students is that among gang members 57.1 percent reported having one or more such close friends and associates who use illicit drugs, compared to 29.9 percent among students who were not gang members. This is a very significant difference, suggesting clearly that the gang member is more deeply tied into the drug abuse subculture than the non-gang member in the same student population.

(2) Drugs and Gang Membership Among Confined Juveniles.

The data used here was collected in the summer of 1991 and reflects a very large sample (N = 1,801) of juveniles confined in short and long term correctional institutions in five states (New York, Massachusetts, Tennessee, Wisconsin, and Texas). The survey instrument provided for anonymity of the juvenile: no names were used. The thrust of this study was that of the health risks of confined juveniles, such as drug and substance abuse, suicide, etc. But gang membership is a factor that significantly contributes to the morbidity and mortality rates among our Nations juveniles. Thus, this factor of gang membership allows us to examine a large sample of juvenile delinquents who have had to be incarcerated. Examined here is how gang membership among the confined juvenile population is related to drug and substance abuse at the individual level of analysis.

Just under half of all the confined juveniles (46.1%) reported having ever joined a gang. Unlike the public high school population, in this confined juvenile population no significant difference by gender existed in terms of self-reported gang membership. Thus, the gender difference in gang joining behavior while significant in the general population seems to disappear at the point the juvenile is incarcerated.

The strong evidence from this large study is that gang members are significantly more likely as individuals to report more substance abuse than non-gang members using eleven different drug and substance abuse variables. These factors can be summarized as follows.

1. Gang members were significantly more likely (p < .001) to report smoking cigarettes.

2. Gang members were significantly more likely (p < .001) to report first drinking alcohol at an early age.

3. Gang members were significantly more likely (p < .001) to report more drinking episodes (days when they had at least one drink of alcohol during their lifetime) than non-gang members.

4. Gang members were significantly more likely (p < .001) to report more incidents of heavy

drinking (during the 30 days prior to being incarcerated, how many days they had five or more rinks of alcohol in a row, that is, within a couple of hours) than their non-gang member counterparts.

5.   Gang members were significantly more likely (p = .02) to report first using pot (i.e., marijuana) at an early age.

6.   Gang members were significantly more likely (p < .001) to report more pot use episodes (number of different times using marijuana during their life) than non-gang members.

7.   Gang members were significantly more likely (p < .001) to report first using cocaine at an early age than when compared to their non-gang member counterparts.

8.   Gang members were significantly more likely (p < .001) to report a higher frequency of the number of different times using any form of cocaine (powder, crack, freebase) than compared to their non-gang member counterparts.

9.   Gang members were significantly more likely (p < .001) to report a higher frequency of the number of different times using crack[2] or freebase forms of cocaine than compared to their non-gang member counterparts.

10.   Gang members were significantly more likely (p = .03) to report a higher frequency of using sundry other illegal drugs (e.g., LSD, PCP, mushrooms, speed, ice, heroin, pills) than compared to their non-gang member counterparts.

11.   Gang members were significantly more likely (p = .004) to report that they had ever injected (i.e., shot up) any illegal drug (including skin popping or injecting steroids) than compared to IV drug abuse among their non-gang member counterparts. This most serious drug abuse behavior in relationship to ever joining a gang is analyzed in Table 24 below[3]. This "riskier" behavior among those who have been gang members is also examined in chapter 16 where along with sexual behavior, this type of health risk behavior may lead to higher risks of contracting sexually transmitted diseases, particularly AIDS/HIV infection.

TABLE 24
Frequency Distribution of Having Ever Joined a Gang by Having Ever Injected (Shot Up) Any Illegal Drug Including Skin Popping or Injecting Steroids Among Confined Juvenile Delinquents

	Ever an I.V. Drug User?	
	Yes	No
Ever Join a Gang?		
Yes	112	722
No	91	896

Chi-square = 8.08, p = .004

The strong consistent evidence here among 1,801 youths surveyed from juvenile correctional institutions and facilities in five states suggests clearly that gang members profile differently than non-gang members in terms of greater drug and substance abuse. The gang member is significantly more likely to report such drug and substance abuse than the non-gang member among confined juveniles. Additional information from this study of confined juveniles as the unit of analysis is discussed in chapter 20.

(3) Drugs and Gang Membership Among Asian Students.

In the Spring of 1992 a national Asian educational association facilitated data collection for the present author. This meant using an anonymous questionnaire, administered by Asian teachers to Asian students in eight states (Washington, Hawaii, Colorado, Minnesota, Louisiana, Maryland, New York, and California). The sample size used here consists of over three hundred Asian students[4].

The same relationship described previously from a sample of Chicago high school students was tested for this sample of Asian students. Thus, Table 25 shows that similar to the Chicago high school sample consisting of almost equal proportions of Black, Hispanic, and white students, that among Asian students the gang member is more likely to have one or more close friends and associates who use illicit drugs than non-gang members.

TABLE 25
Frequency Distribution of Ever Joining a Gang by Having One or More Drug Abusing Friends Among a 1992 Sample of Asian Students

	Have 1 or More Close Friends and Associates who Use Illicit Drugs?	
	No	Yes
Ever join a gang?		
No	233	72
Yes	6	20

(Chi-square p < .001)

As seen here among Asian students who report never joining a gang, just under a fourth (23.6%) report having one or more close friends and associates who use illicit drugs. Over three times that proportion is shown among Asian gang members! Among the Asian students who report having ever joined a gang, some 76.9 percent had one or more such close friends and associates who use illicit drugs. In short, it appears that across the board, a universal aspect of the relationship between gangs and drugs regardless of ethnic group differences, is that gang members have a higher integration into or association with the illegal drug subculture. Again, this is only logical inasmuch as being a gang member is itself a form of subcultural integration and association. The drug subculture appears to substantially overlap with the gang subculture is what this finding suggests.

Similarly, Table 26 below shows that identical to the Chicago student sample, these Asian students show another common profile. That is, gang members are significantly more likely to report having seen drug sales in or near the school than compared to their non-gang member counterparts. In fact, as shown in Knox, Laske, and Tromanhauser (1992) the factors predicting gang membership among a school sample where the white, Black, and Hispanic racial groups were almost equal are factors that are also significant predictors of gang membership among Asian students.

Table 26

The Frequency Distribution of Self-Reported Gang Membership by Having Seen Drug Sales in or Near the School Among a 19921 Sample of Asian Students

	Seen Drug Sales in/near the School?	
	No	Yes
Gang Member:		
No	241	67
Yes	8	18

Chi-square = 28.4, p < .001

GANGS AND DRUG SALES

The senseless killing of Mexican Cardinal Juan Jesus Posadas Ocampo on May 24th in 1993 illustrated one shocking truth --- that at least one foreign drug lord did have a connection with at least one American street gang. A Mexican drug lord recruited an American street gang for "hits" abroad in the fierce competition of the international illegal drug trade. The gunfire that killed the Cardinal at the airport in Guadalajara, Mexico came from the Calle Treinta (30th Street) gang in San Diego, who while recruited for the hit, actually shot the wrong person --- the top Catholic cleric in all of Mexico, the Cardinal[5]. Apparently the San Diego gang members fired at the Cardinal's car because it "looked like" that which they were supposed to target, a common phenomenon of the "mistaken identity" shooting trend found throughout the United States where gangs engage in such violence.

The fact is the kind of gangs analyzed in this book as level three gangs have been shown to have international connections for their illegal drug

supplies. It is not uncommon to find large drug seizures for gangs with connections in Nigeria and Columbia[6].

The issue of gangs being involved in the profitable and illegal venture of drug sales is a more common trend than gangs being cultivated as labor pools for hitmen. Drug sales are only one of a number of crimes that gangs are involved in. To illustrate this some important recent data from American law enforcement executives will be summarized here.

The 1992 Survey of Law Enforcement was a joint project between gang researchers at four universities[7]. The data was collected in late 1992 and early 1993 by means of a mail questionnaire. A total of 398 law enforcement agencies responded: 248 police chiefs, 137 sheriffs, and 13 "other" or missing this particular variable for the type of jurisdiction[8]. Also discussed in Chapter 18 of this book, it is important to note that 89.5 percent of the police chiefs nationally and 79.4 percent of the county sheriffs reported that youth gangs were a problem in their jurisdiction. Thus, for cities of 25,000 or more and the component counties of metropolitan areas which constituted the sampling frame for this survey, the city or county without any gang problem is truly becoming the exception to the rule.

Table 27 below provides the results from a series of questions to these police chiefs and county sheriffs about what kinds of problems youth gangs cause in their jurisdiction. One of these crimes that gangs are involved in is that of drug sales. But as will be seen, drug sales are not the most common nor the least common type of crime that gangs are involved in according to the reports from these law enforcement administrators.

Table 27
Percentage Distribution of the Types of Crimes That Gangs Are Involved in Among Jurisdictions Reporting A Gang Problem by a National Sample of Law Enforcement Administrators

TYPES OF CRIMES:	Police Chiefs	County Sheriffs
Violence	87.8%	81.5
Drug Sales	73.8	80.6
Graffiti	82.4	73.1
Burglary	67.9	71.3
Robbery	52.5	43.5
Drive-by shootings	61.1	50.9
Arson	12.2	11.1
Prostitution	2.7	7.4
Car Theft	63.8	62.0
Other	18.1	18.5

Table 27 shows that among those police chiefs reporting that gangs are a problem in their jurisdiction, some 73.8 percent of these police administrators also report that gangs in their area are involved in drug sales. Similarly, among county sheriffs reporting that gangs are a problem in their jurisdiction, some 80.6 percent of these law enforcement administrators also report that gangs are involved in drug sales. Violence, however, tops the list as the most frequent type of crime that gangs are involved in according to both police chiefs and county sheriffs. Similarly, gangs are least involved in prostitution at this stage of their development nationally.

GANGS AND GANG-CONTROLLED DRUG IMPORTATION INTO PRISONS

The 1992 National Survey of Prison Wardens is described in greater detail in chapter 19. It includes the viewpoints of 325 prison wardens from all 50 states. Reported here is evidence of another unique aspect of the gang-drug connection: the extent to which gangs control the importation of drugs into state correctional institutions. Summarized here are some of the findings from a much larger research project. The specific findings here show how gang drug trafficking inside American prisons is significantly related to two other problems: threats of violence by gang members against correctional officers and racial conflict among inmates.

This problem of gang members threatening staff is shown to be significant in relationship to the extent to which gangs are felt to control the importation of illicit drugs into the correctional facility and to the extent which gangs are felt to dominate the illicit drug trade behind bars. These findings are shown in Table 28.

TABLE 28
DISTRIBUTION OF DRUG IMPORTATION AND DRUG DISTRIBUTION GANG-CONTROLLED ACTIVITIES INSIDE PRISONS BY REPORTS OF THREATS BY GANGS ON STAFF

		Problem: Gang Threats Against Prison Staff?	
		NO	YES
GANG CONTROL OF ILLICIT DRUG IMPORTATION INTO THE CORRECTIONAL FACILITY	Low[9]	94	11
	High[10]	60	43
		Chi-square = 26.45, p < .001	
GANG CONTROL OF ILLICIT DRUG DISTRIBUTION INSIDE THE CORRECTIONAL FACILITY	Low[11]	98	10
	High[12]	61	48
		Chi-square = 33.50, p < .001	

As seen in Table 28, where gangs have high control over the importation and distribution of drugs in these adult state correctional institutions there is a statistically higher probability of an associated report of threats by gangs members against correctional staff in the same facilities. This finding regarding gang control over drug importation and distribution and its statistically significant relationship with a factor of violence faced by staff (e.g., threats) is very consistent with the emerging national research literature on gangs showing that the higher the gang-drug problem the higher the individual risk of violence.[13] Similarly, Table 29 shows that gang involvement in drug importation and distribution inside adult corrections is also significant in relationship to racial conflict. That is, the more gangs are involved in drug importation and distribution, the more racial conflict is reported from the same prisons.

TABLE 29
DISTRIBUTION OF DRUG IMPORTATION AND DRUG DISTRIBUTION GANG-CONTROLLED ACTIVITIES INSIDE PRISONS BY REPORTS OF RACIAL CONFLICT AMONG INMATES

		Racial Conflict?	
		NO	YES
% of illicit drug importation into the facility controlled by prison gang members	LOW[14]	60	52
	HIGH[15]	37	77
		Chi-square = 10.28, p = .001	
% of the illicit drug trade in the facility that is controlled by prison gang members	LOW[16]	61	55
	HIGH[17]	35	83
		Chi-square = 12.70, p < .001	

THE HARD DRUG LEGALIZATION ARGUMENT

Many different recommendations on decriminalizing drugs or legalizing drugs have been made. There is only one issue here and it has to do not with the moral or the financial implications of such arguments, but rather has to do with the relationship between drug legalization and crime --- in fact, more specifically, gang crime. The book about barrio gang members in Los Angeles by Moore (1978) specifically concludes that we need to legalize heroin and suggested that gangs would cease to be a problem in America if only we, as a society, were not so hypocritical about our drug policies. Decriminalization is a less extreme version, it simply would recommend reducing the penalties associated with such drug problems. But legalization implies openly tolerating, even controlling by government supervision, such hard drug distribution and use.

Moore (1978) basically argues that if we could take away the profits from hard drugs like heroin, then the resources for American gangs would "dry up". Thus, the legalization argument as presented by Moore (1978) specifically predicts a "gang-fading scenario". As will be seen, it is not the only possible scenario for what would happen if American society took this extreme measure by legalizing heroin or other hard drugs.

Some may regard this argument as an example of the economic-determinism model of gang theory: that is, that gangs exist and persist only because of the income they can generate for their leaders and members. It is not possible to simply reduce the world of gangs to either "cultural" gangs (those who function for essentially cultural reasons and motivations) and "entrepreneurial" gangs (those who function to seek profits and wealth). It is not "gang theory" we are creating when we make up images of such pure types of gangs, such as the recent conclusion by Skolnick, Blumenthal and Correl (1993) that gangs in southern California are "cultural" and those in northern California are "entrepreneurial" gangs. Such over generalizations are also overly identified concepts[18] that truly stretch the imagination and distort the reality by being so oversimplistic[19]. Illegal income is one of the many factors along which gangs can be classified in terms of the array of social organizational features.

In summary, the argument favoring drug decriminalization or legalization in the gang context basically assumes that without penalties, or when anyone could buy their drugs at the local store legally, monetary resources would no longer be so plentiful for gangs. It further assumes that gang violence would be reduced, because the fight over drug territories would be eliminated if citizens could buy their drug of choice over the counter. The logic concerns the immediate effects in terms of how street gangs would cease to shoot each other over issues of "holding down" local drug turfs, not the long term effects on society or gangs.

There is, of course, another side of this argument regarding the legalization of highly addictive drugs like heroin. Perhaps our analysis should begin with the potential of any group to dissolve, shrink into impotence, or to swell in ranks in more solidified terms. Instead of gang dismemberment it is theoretically possible that we could see gang consolidation as well under conditions of hard drug decriminalization. In any event, it is an issue that deserves to be informed by what we know about the mechanics of group structure, group goal formation, and succession of goals. We begin this analysis, therefore, with an open mind towards both potentials: while decriminalization and legalization advocates emphasize the obvious immediate direct effects (e.g., economic disincentives for gangs involved in drugs), we must of course, in an objective spirit, recognize that often policies as drastic as this can have other unintended consequences. Which is another way of saying that the gang literature demonstrates that sometimes the most liberal imaginations have had the most deleterious effects (e.g., Fry, 1969) in terms of solidifying gang organization[20].

THREE DIFFERENT HARD DRUG DECRIMINALIZATION SCENARIOS

If we are to believe Moore (1978) and other advocates of drug decriminalization, then gangs will cease to be a major problem in American society after market forces no longer provide the economic momentum to gang organizations. This is the "gang fading" scenario and will be discussed at some length. But there are at least two other scenarios if we are willing to look at more than the simple immediate effect of such a social policy on gangs.

Another scenario of the same policy could be an unintended nightmare: gangs previously in conflict, whose members are now free to have drug habits without facing criminal sanctions, will unite along new lines of differentiation. Perhaps even ethnic lines. Ethnicity has always been a factor of gang conflict and there is little in the drug decriminalization argument that promises better race and ethnic relations in America. Unless, of course, such decriminalization advocates are willing to assume that all bigots will turn to legalized drug dependency. Such a precarious assumption should force a consideration of alternative scenarios such as the reverse intended effect that will be called the "gangs merging/consolidating" scenario, perhaps even at a national level.

Finally, there is a midway effect or impact view which could conceivably be this: that such drug decriminalization has no real effect on gang dismemberment, in fact, because of the intractable nature of gangs as an organized subculture, legal drugs would simply mean a different mode of association. Remember, unless the government is going to give away heroin and cocaine, then these addicts are still going to have to pay for it. And how? So the third scenario is a "null effect" version, with no substantial change in the size of the gang force strength in America or its involvement with income producing crimes.

1. THE GANG-FADING CRIME-FADING SCENARIO

"UPI - Today, the President reached an all time high in popular support by signing dramatic new legislation authorizing all physicians in America to dispense heroin, cocaine, and other previously illegal narcotics."

Such might be the newspaper headline signaling the decriminalization and/or legalization of hard drugs. But what would be the parameters of such a policy? Do we truly envision legislation allowing minors to consume in this legal drug market as well? It would probably, like alcohol, be 21 years of age, or at least the age of 18 or consent. Thus, an large lucrative juvenile market would still exist for gangs to exploit.

Adding to the social control function of the health care system in America as is reasonably assumed in the drug legalization argument there is still the issue of who pays for the drugs and the drug dispensing service? The most pragmatic projection would be that like America's current and fragmented health care system which allows for health to the degree that you can pay for it: if you can't pay for it, you don't get it. So where are the addicts going to get the income for their habits? Thus, a large population of drug dependent persons desperate for cash could create a new income-producing crime wave that gangs will certainly want to get their share of.

The other possibility would require convincing the rest of American tay-payers that in terms of a cost-benefit analysis, that rather than allowing addicts to commit street crimes and force the criminal justice system into additional high costs, it might be cheaper to provide a ready supply of hard drugs and some form of group shelter for American drug addicts. It could involve a national registration system for addicts. But with free drugs and a home, just how large would the addict population grow to? As institutionalized addicts they could be defined out of the work force, reducing unemployment in a most revolutionary way. Would some lawyers, politicians, and Wall Street businessmen drop out of the rat race to join this addict population (i.e., the "cross over" effect)? What proportion of the American society would become addicts under this scenario, and at what point would society basically collapse because of the magnitude of drug addicts?

Who would want to work when you can get "high" and have the government take care of your basic needs? Most decriminalization advocates assume a minimal or no "cross over" effect: those who have been casual users of soft drugs turning to harder drugs because of the lack of penalties attached to this kind of deviance. That would appear to be an assumption that carries significant risk.

Because drug legalization sounds almost too good to be true it is well to remember that laws change. Remember the Prohibition Amendment to the U.S. Constitution, it was repealed allowing Americans to drink legally. So assume a national program of registering addicts began, and the gang members came forward en masse leaving their homies for the good life of government grade dope. Needing their fix, the physician would be their new gang leader. It would be a great opportunity to identify all the addicts almost over night. They would be registered, fingerprinted, photographed, DNA analyzed, and HIV tested.

The one war on drugs that no one seems to quote from, one that was quite successful at its time, was that by China's Mao Tse Tung. After Mao's communist forces seized power, they discovered a large population of Chinese addicts existed among their comrades who were not in any sense eager to participate in the restructuring of Chinese society according to Marxist-Leninism or anything else that did not get them high. But Mao had a sure fire solution: firing squads and labor camps. Thousands of addicts disappeared quite literally over night.

The point here should be clear: what if such drug legalization legislation was overturned or reversed after a period of time that allowed for the identification of America's addict population? Clearly, then, law enforcement agencies would have the intelligence base for monitoring what might be expected to be a crime prone population. What is not realistic is in thinking that America has the resources to prosecute or incarcerate all or even a major part of the criminal and/or gang population.

Let us return now with more analytical rigor in looking at the after effects of drug decriminalization. Suppose our decriminalization legislation had this clause: free drugs, but no other help. And then systematically, throughout America, we find these persons leaving the "happy houses" of approved physician drug dispensing facilities, and following their own propensity toward polydrug use, taking other substances, and routinely dying of chemical reaction and overdoses, or dying of other drug-related diseases. Knowing that drug addicts will not rank high in the triage system for health care, perhaps the highest point of gang impact of such decriminalization would be the latent extirpation policy implied in the evaluation of the social worth of the drug addict. The drug addict will not score high on social worth and thus they would not receive health care treatment, and would die off. This could truly impact on the gang problem but perhaps not in the way envisioned initially by Moore (1978).

That is the most cynical scenario. A more optimistic version would be as follows. Gangs previously in conflict over turf, racial and ethnic differences, or market share of criminal enterprises, suddenly become dissuaded from conflict because of the more powerful lure of personal psychic and pleasure gratification through legalized drug abuse. Gang members from all gangs like the Crips, Bloods, Vice Lords, Latin Kings, Aryan Brotherhood, etc, all become intoxicated with the pursuit of personal gratification and hedonism --- getting high. Gang drive-by shootings in our neighborhoods come to be replaced by drug-line riots: the fighting is no longer over color or turf or gang colors, but over who is going to be first in line to get their fix. And the non-drug abusing gang members suddenly find themselves impoverished because they no longer have a steady source of drug-sale income; so they quit the gang too and take jobs somewhere, straighten up and fly right. Legalized drugs could be a great leveler indeed.

Some don't buy it. But according to Moore (1978: p. 177) heroin should be legalized, because even as a drastic measure, it would take away the economic incentives for gang strength. However, for the record, Moore was aware that such a policy change "would have a major impact, although the precise effect is still a matter of speculation" (ibid).

2. THE GANGS MERGING-CONSOLIDATING SCENARIO

It is important to consider what effect the legalization of heroin and other hard drugs would have outside of the obvious economic destabilizing effect that it is assumed to impact on gangs. One such post-drug legalization scenario that must be considered a logical possibility is therefore an unintended nourishing of the gang problem. This negative scenario would mean that gangs could merge, consolidate, and expand rather than shrinking into impotence. How might this happen?

One variation would be the possibility that gangs with a local character --- from Los Angeles, to Chicago, to New York, etc --- might be brought together in closer non-combative association with the potential that they could form a nationwide gang structure. Hardcore criminal gangs don't like junkies anyway, they do not make reliable gang members, perhaps because it is too easy for them to compromise their gang organization: if arrested, police can "sweat" them, going "cold turkey" in lockup they might provide any information a police officer asked if they knew they could be released and thus get a chance to get their fix. Gangs like the Latin Kings deal with these issues in their written constitutions:

"Those who are known to have previously used heroin for the purpose of addiction cannot obtain a position of rank without the approval of Las Coronas." (Source: Latin King Constitution).

The "gangs merging-consolidating" scenario could therefore involve a much larger national network created out of such recent efforts as "gang summit" talks. Drug crime profits are not the only income-producing offense patterns that gangs engage in. The possibility exists, therefore, that gangs could simply continue in tact and simply adapt to the lack of drug income by specializing in other and new crimes. Perhaps they would follow the lead of the Yakuza and in the context of an open and democratic society become sophisticated "shake down" artists against American corporate business enterprises. The Yakuza have refined this to an art: buying one share of stock, allowing them to attend the stockholders annual meeting, and then threatening to disrupt the entire proceedings through skullduggery; or like the Yakuza, move into lucrative sex crime, or gambling (see Kaplan and Dubro, 1986).

Recall that legalizing the consumption of alcohol did not automatically put the Mafia, La Cosa Nostra, the Outfit, the Mob, out of business! If some of today's American street gangs were actually able to collaborate on a national level, then they could truly provide a formidable form of competition to traditional organized crime. What is known about gangs is that they do of course aspire to such an ultimate level of control and power. The heroes of the ordinary gang member are not scientists, progressive American Presidents or civil rights leaders, rather their hero worship types are major organized crime figures like Al Capone. The fact that under drug legalization they would lose some income is a given, and the fact that gangs might lose some of their "weaker" members to the legalized drugs is also a given --- but this could strengthen the gang by removing those who are not zealots of the gang organization. What would remain is a more fit and more dedicated gang core structure. One would have to be using some powerful drugs to want to assume that suddenly such gangs would simply cease to exist or would make a "succession in goals" to become a prosocial and legitimate group in American society.

3. THE "NULL EFFECT" SCENARIO

Logically, a final scenario for the effects that legalizing hard drugs like heroin would have on gangs in America would be the "null effect" scenario. As alluded to above, under this potential development existing gangs could simply experience a succession in goals or a restructuring. Drugs are not the only source of illegal income. So, like many entrepreneurial organizations with a diversified income base, or like many of our social service organizations, the gangs might simply "chase the buck"[21]. If its gambling, commercial sex, pornography, chop shop operations, counterfeiting, extortion, loan sharking, etc, then these become natural alternative recourses to the solution of the gang income crisis. Further, such traditional organized crime specialties are the natural and expected progression for an effective gang. The logical fallacy in Moore's (1978) recommendation about legalizing heroin as a way to curtail the gang problem has to do with advancing an essentially economic solution to what amounts to a socially caused problem: the social and cultural imperative for gangs. If gangs organize, spawn, and persist to any extent because of the nature of the culture represented by its members, and develop over time into the social institutional fabric of any segment of the American population, then no simple economic quick fix is going to work. If gangs arose and persisted chiefly out of the quest for drug profits, then the drug legalization argument would at least be on more consistent grounds; as pointed out above, however, it would still be untenable, for there would still exist an underage drug market. The problem is Moore (1978) provides much keen insight into the cultural and social institutional basis for Hispanic gangs in the barrios which she studied very close up in Los Angeles over a decade ago. One cannot have it both ways and recommend legalizing heroin as a solution to the gang problem. Eliminating heroin profits from the gang would not simultaneously eliminate the cultural imperative giving impetus to gang joining behavior or the persistence of the gang as a collective or group entity.

DRUG POLICY: ASSESSING THE SCENARIOS ON LEGALIZING HARD DRUGS

This moral and ethical quagmire about legalizing heroin as a way to curtail the gang problem provides an interesting basis for discussing a variety of developmental scenarios and issues about gangs in America and elsewhere. Looking at more than the obvious and immediate effect of such a drug policy helps us to understand the underlying issues about any policy that seeks to "dismember", ameliorate, neutralize, suppress, or redirect gangs in America. Depending on the type of the gang, such a drug policy could be expected to have different effects as well.

The gang classification system used in this book recognizes Level 1, Level 2, and Level 3 gangs as "real" gangs --- they are involved in and benefit from crime over time. A Level 0 gang is not involved in crime and is therefore outside the area of discussion here. A more organized gang (e.g., Level 3) is more likely to have a written and declared policy on drug use by members of its gang; usually restricting such use, if any restriction exists, to "soft" drugs. Yet all real gangs (levels 1, 2, and 3) can be involved in both drug use and drug sales; just as it is possible to conceive of some exceptions to this rule. It is the income potential from illegal drug sales that is of most

attraction to the modern American gang. Thus, a level three gang might be expected to be more capable of exploiting the illegal drug sale market. The reason this is true is that it exists in several jurisdictions. A level one gang involved in drug sales might simply constitute a local "drug ring", it controls only one small area of the much larger drug trade.

WINNING GANGS AND LOSING THE WAR ON DRUGS

No American drug czar has yet won the war on drugs. The term itself is ludicrous, as drug "czar" implies not a combat role such as that of "Generalismo" might, but rather implies --- like the culture of authoritarian aristocracy from which it is social linguistically derived --- control and benefiting from the drug market. But it raises an important concern: could the war on drugs, or similarly a war on gang crime, ever be basically "won"?

The answer is --- at what cost of liberty are we willing to sacrifice rights, including basic civil liberties Americans all claim and often assume such as that of the right to privacy. All retail theft and basic street crime in a controlled area of any density can theoretically be prevented: it would require the equivalent, however, of a "state of siege" mentality in law enforcement, and could very well involve some finely tuned version of martial law itself! In the summer of 1993, a released prisoner who had formerly been the governor of a large midwestern state, declared an intent to run again as governor; some of his first words uttered in political campaigning amounted to the following: If he were elected to be the Governor, he would look at areas with high crime and high violence and if necessary declare martial law in these areas and have the National Guard stop the crime if the local police cannot!

So, without knowing it, the above recycled politician was recommending exactly what Taylor (1992)[22] was fearful about in criticizing the federal governments "Weed and Seed" approach to the war on drugs. Weeding means specifically targeting "gang activity in high-crime neighborhoods" (Gurele, 1991: 1)[23]. A recent effort to implement this in Seattle drew harsh criticisms from the local American Civil Liberties Union (Taylor, 1992). The weed and seed operation was described as "one more overblown weapon in the federal government's discriminatory and ineffective war on drugs - a war largely directed at minority Americans" (Taylor, 1992: 1). The operations involved "street sweeps" and were felt to be functionally equivalent to transforming parts of Seattle into "virtual martial law zones". That is, the Weed and Seed approach "seeks to establish a federal paramilitary operation in our inner city" (Taylor, 1992: 2).

Modern technology in electronic surveillance could itself crush the drug dealers in America and the users. National pen registry systems are but modest computer and minor storage problems. Assume that 100 million residential and cellular phones were used on any given day in the U.S.A., assume further that nationally each of these separate 100 million lines made five calls each. Recording the 10 bytes of the caller and the 10 bytes of the other party (their area codes and seven digit phone numbers) would require only 10,000 megabytes of computer storage --- more than 80 typical Personal Computer hard drives (i.e., 120 Meg. each), but not much in comparison with large main frame computers. Having such a phone line registry data base over time would allow a retrospective identification and analysis of the social networks of drug pushers. Having such data local law enforcement would know everyone a captured drug pusher dealt with and like a real war, the rest could be "rounded up" rather easily over time using the same "on-line" data. Are you personally willing to allow such a data system to be used for anything other than national security interests of which local drug dealing is not a qualified issue? Does simple association with someone who may later be determined to have sold drugs make you a "drug pusher" suspect if you had even accidentally dialed their number?

The role of electronic surveillance in combatting other crime in America has risen dramatically in the last decade, because of its effectiveness in prosecuting more complex and sometimes organized types of criminal behavior. Gangs are ideal crime problems for using modern surveillance equipment. Public gatherings of gang members can be monitored with pole cameras and aerial surveillance, versions of which are often shown in gang training. If they are at a park, and you are there too strolling by, are you someone who should have a police file even though you have never been arrested or convicted of anything? If yes, you may be saying that everyone should have a police file; and if police have the right to investigate everyone simply by association or like the typical victim of a gang drive-by shooting --- being merely an innocent bystander --- then you are actually advocating that many features of the Bill of Rights in the United States Constitution be systematically violated in a fashion that ultimately would come to be a police state.

The moral lesson here is that if you are not the kind of person who would like living in a police state, then you should be happy that as a society we have over the years of the ongoing "war on drugs" witnessed a series of competent individuals in ineffectual roles called drug "Czars", rather than having incompetent or especially competent individuals in effective roles such as may be implied --- to use a social linguistic source other than that from which "Czar" is derived --- in the stronger title of "Drug Fuehr" who might be operating under conditions where basic freedoms could be temporarily suspended.

This is the ethical dilemma of any suppression effort directed towards drugs or gangs: to do it most efficiently may mean some impact on civil liberties to the extent that effectiveness is also an issue.

SUMMARY AND DISCUSSION

We have tried to examine a variety of issues in terms of how the topic of "drugs" overlaps with and interfaces with "gangs". The policy recommendation by a contemporary gang researcher that to do something about the gang problem in America we should legalize heroin was critically examined. The three scenarios reviewed therefore included not just the most positive scenario ("gangs fading"), but also include a "gangs merging-consolidating" and a "null effect" scenario. What this issue highlights is actually the paucity of income data on gangs: we need more research on this underground economy. What we need most are not "vignettes" reflecting how one researcher hangs out with one gang, what we really need is national data giving us hard numbers on this problem. We currently lack such information in the gang literature. We have only rough estimates of how much money is involved in American illegal drug sales and it would be even harder to ascertain with any validity and reliability how much of this economic activity is controlled by gangs or gang members.

DISCUSSION QUESTIONS:

(1) Marijuana is said to be the largest cash crop in America today. Would legalizing it mean an extension of the material temptation of "free will"? Or would it imply a societal acceptance of varying degrees of drug or substance abuse resistance and the concomitant belief that "some people will always try it if it is available"? What do you think?

(2) Do you think it would be better, because it might be cheaper, to maintain a large population of addicts under a government heroin-assistance program rather than sending these same types of persons to prison for felony offenses associated with their addiction?

(3) Should police have the right to investigate a group just because it is perceived as deviant? Or should such intrusions on privacy be limited strictly to known and substantial patterns of law violation? Could a college "clique" or three or more persons who recurrently acquire and use illegal drugs in a small group be considered a gang?

"Gang Ties to Domestic Terrorist Group: Or Just Anti-Drug Vigilante's?"

The gang is called "Straight Edge". It created much attention in Salt Lake City, Utah in 1997. Their typical activity? They go out, dressed in "punk rock" clothing, and try to find other youths using drugs. One night in 1995, they found Rich Webb, he was smoking a joint, a group of Straight Edgers caught him, pummeled him and carved an "X" in his back with a knife. Straight Edgers don't like junkies or people who abuse drugs, they have heard the message "say no to drugs" and they are doing something about it apparently.

But police have reason to believe the "Straight Edgers" have made a connection to a domestic terrorist group: A.L.F., the Animal Liberation Front. ALF has a clear "signature" in its terrorism: it attacks companies that sell "fur clothing", hospitals that experiment on animals, and "fur farms". Firebombings of several businesses near Salt Lake City (1. mink feed cooperative, 2. McDonald's restaurant, 3. Tandy Leather Craft and Supply Store, and 4. an animal trap business) apparently has some connection to the "Straight Edge" gang.

END NOTES:

[1] The gang literature typically portrays "Stoner" gangs as white groups whose worst crime threat is they routinely engage in "getting high". In communities and college campuses across America, regardless of race, a social organizational approach to gangs as advanced in this book would consider such groups "level one" gangs if there was a continuing pattern of law violation behavior by essentially the same core group. Such gangs are very horizontal: the "leader" is the one most esteemed, the one with the drug supply connections! Thus, a gang need not have a name and identity as such to function as a gang.

[2] "Crack" drug laws are more severe than the "powder form" cocaine drug laws. In 1994 federal Judge Clyde S. Cahill of St. Louis struck down the federal anti-drug laws giving harsher penalties for crack cocaine possession. The harsher "crack" penalties were seen as an unconscious form of racism against African-American offenders.

[3] This analysis of the effects of joining a gang on I.V. drug abuse uses a slightly larger sample than first reported in Knox and Tromanhauser (1991). The early report included 1,801 cases; but more data came in and was used in a slightly larger sample that was used for this test.

[4] For additional information on the Asian student survey, see Knox, Laske, and Tromanhauser (1992) Schools Under Siege.

[5] See Hugh Dellios, 1993, "Mexican Drug Lords Recruit U.S. Street Gangs", Chicago Tribune, July 11, Section 1, P. 3.

[6] For an example, see: Fran Spielman, "City Seizes Drugs; Daley Blasts Feds", Chicago Sun-Times.

[7] Issued in May of 1993 to all respondents in the survey, the monograph entitled "Preliminary Findings from the 1992 Law Enforcement Mail Questionnaire Project" involved the following universities and respective researchers: Chicago State University, George W. Knox, Ph.D., and Edward D. Tromanhauser, Ph.D.; Rhode Island College, Pamela Irving Jackson, Ph.D. and Darek Niklas, Ph.D.; St. Ambrose University, James G. Houston, Ph.D., and Paul Koch, Ph.D.; and James R. Sutton, then at the University of Illinois at Chicago. A copy of the report was printed in Volume One, Number Three of the Gang Journal: An Interdisciplinary Research Quarterly, 1993.

[8] The data used for this analysis reflects all data collected, including a police chief who responded after the May 1993 report was issued.

[9] Low gang control of the illicit drugs brought into the correctional facility by prison gang members was measured by those respondents that indicated less than or equal to four percent of all illicit drugs brought into their facilities were attributable to gang members.

[10] High gang control of illicit drug importation (smuggling) into the correctional facility was measured by whether the respondent indicated that five percent or higher of all illicit drugs brought into the prison were the result of gang members.

[11] Low gang control of the illicit drug trade behind bars was measured by less than or equal to four percent of the illicit drug trade in their facility being dominated by prison gang members.

[12] High gang drug distribution control was measured by five percent or higher of the illicit drug trade behind bars being dominated by prison gang members.

[13] See Schools Under Siege: A Study of Gangs, Drugs, Crime and Violence in the Modern American School, George W. Knox, Ph.D., David Laske, Ph.D., and Edward Tromanhauser, Ph.D., Kendall-Hunt Publishing, Chicago, IL, 1992 (to be released in August, 1992: for information write: Kendall/Hunt Publishing Company, 2460 Kerper Blvd, P.O. Box 539, Dubuque, Iowa 52004-0539. TEL (319) 588-1451.

[14] Low = less than or equal to four percent ($< = 4\%$).

[15] High = greater than or equal to five percent ($>= 5\%$).

[16] Low = less than or equal to four percent ($< = 4\%$).

[17] High = greater than or equal to five percent ($>= 5\%$).

[18] It appears that Skolnick, Blumenthal, and Correl (1993) were limiting this over-generalization to Black gangs.

[19] The real problem with Skolnick, Blumenthal, and Correl (1993) is their rather cavalier attitude towards minority groups. Which is to say, their language is less than sensitive. For example, in describing how most of the gangs studied by Thrasher (1927) were white-ethnic gangs, they generalize "Their moral posture seems scarcely different from today's black youth" (Skolnick, Blumental, and Correl, 1993: p. 193). Not "Black gangs", but the more general and inclusive "black youth". Thus, whether they meant it or not, implying that all Black youths were gang members. Similarly, in claiming their theory of gang migration applies outside of California, they state "This theory may also be applicable to Eastern U.S. gangs, such as the Jamaicans" (Skolnick, Blumenthal, and Correl, 1993: p. 195). They probably meant Jamaican Posse groups or Jakes as some call them. Not everyone who emigrates from Jamaica is in a gang. The point is our language must be much more clear when dealing with a problem as complex as gangs.

[20] It was not Rev. Fry who was indicted for defrauding the U.S. government for his gang program, it was his indigenous worker, one Jeff Fort. The history of gangs in America shows numerous examples of this kind of gang intervention initiative where a local activist is provided with funding to do "his thing" with the gang. No theory, no guidelines, no standards, no evaluation --- it sounds good or it uses the right buzz words that bureaucrats in Washington want to hear, and thus it is funded. Was Fry duped? Or was this social experimentation with gangs (providing money to the gang that would eventu-

ally become the notorious El Rukn organization) irresponsible on its face?

[21]To "chase the buck" is a phrase used in American social service organizations where the social work agency tends to specialize in whatever the government is willing to pay for it to perform. To wit: an agency founded initially with legislative funds that run out, or which were provided by a government agency that may be dismantled by Congress, may not simply just cease to exist and disappear. Social service organizations simply adapt by having a succession or modification in their service delivery goals. This is normal organizational behavior, and thus we should not rule out the possibility that gangs can evolve in a similar fashion.

[22]Taylor, Kathleen, 1992, Letter by Kathleen Taylor (Executive director of the American Civil Liberties Union of Washington) to Mayor Norman Rice), RE: Operation "Weed and Seed".

[23]Gurule, Jimmy, 1991, Operation "Weed and Seed". Reclaiming America's Neighborhoods. U.S. Department of Justice, Office of Justice Programs, National Institute of Justice, Washington, D.C.

**Facts About Gangs and Drugs: Project GANGFACT
A Study of Over 10,000 Offenders by the NGCRC**

Involvement in Organized Drug Dealing

The survey asked "have you ever been involved in organized drug dealing". Some 55.0 percent (N = 5343) reported that they had in fact been involved in organized drug dealing. Some 45.0 percent (N = 4372) indicated they had no such prior involvement in organized drug dealing.

A very significant difference emerged here in comparing gang members and non-gang members (Chi-square = 1162.0, p < .001). Some 40.2 percent of the non-gang members reported having been involved in organized drug dealing, compared to 75.3 percent of the gang members.

Organized Drug Dealing: Individual Versus Gang Reasons

A follow-up question for those who indicated they had ever been involved in organized drug dealing was included in the survey: "if yes, which best describes the drug dealing: ___I did it for myself, ___I did it for my gang". There is little room for doubt here any "why". Some 91.0 percent of those who had ever been involved in drug dealing reported they had done so "for myself". Thus, only 9.0 percent "did it for my gang".

One further necessary statistical distinction must be made here: controlling for those who were in fact gang members. So, among those who had ever been involved in organized drug dealing and who had ever joined a gang, some 87.9 percent reported having done so "for myself", while only 12.1 percent reported having done so "for the gang". The explanation that seems to emerge here is that argued previously in the NGCRC national study called Project GANGECON, where the gang seemed to function as a kind of "trade union guild" for criminal offenders: if they wanted the illegal income opportunity from selling drugs, the gang was perfectly able to provide them with that opportunity, and here we see that it is in most cases a voluntary activity for individual gain. The profile is consistent with the longstanding "income oriented crime" pattern: the person is seeking personal benefit.

Attempting to Smuggle Drugs into the Correctional Facility

The survey asked "have you tried to smuggle in any illegal drugs while in this facility". Most of the incarcerated respondents (85.0%, N = 7287) reported that they had not attempted to smuggle in illegal drugs while incarcerated. But some 15.0 percent (N = 1282) did report attempting to smuggle in illegal drugs while incarcerated.

This factor was significant in the comparison of gang members and non-gang members (Chi-square = 384.6, p < .001). While 8.0 percent of the non-gang members had tried to smuggle in illegal drugs, some 23.4 percent of the gang members had tried to do so.

Do Gangs Try to Corrupt Correctional Staff to Bring in Drugs?

The survey asked "do gangs seek to influence staff members to bring in drugs/contraband in this facility". About two-thirds (68.8%, N = 4795) reported that gangs do not seek to corrupt correctional staff for this purpose. However, some 31.2 percent (N = 2170) did report that gangs seek to influence correctional staff to bring in drugs/contraband.

There was a small difference in comparing gang members and non-gang members on this factor (Chi-square = 30.0, p < .001). While 27.8 percent of the non-gang members indicated that gangs seek to adversely influence staff for the purpose of smuggling in drugs/contraband, some 34.0 percent of the gang members reported this.

The Real Chicago "Outfit": A Rare Photo of Chicago's Mob.
Seated far left rear and working to the right towards the front:
Joey Aiuppa, Dominque Dabela, Vince Celano, Al Pillatto; standing:
Jack Cerrone; Joey Lombardo. Seated far left front and working to
the right: Tony Accardo, Joe Amato, Joe Cesare DeMarco, and Jimmy
"the Turk" Turrello.

Chapter 17

GANG CRIME AND
ORGANIZED CRIME

INTRODUCTION

It is common for descriptions of the gang crime problem to make the analogy with organized crime when gangs appear to function in a sophisticated manner.[1] Many see "supergangs", or corporate gangs, or what the present author calls level three gangs as simply being a new form of organized crime. But lacking in our literature is any discussion that helps to distinguish what exactly these factors of sophistication are.

Also, those previous gang authors who base most of their conclusions about the gang crime in America on the sole data of their ability to penetrate the confidence of Spanky and Alfalfa type of gangs through ethnographic studies, are not in the position of being knowledgeable about higher level gang formations --- those that exist with written gang constitutions. Some of these national gang constitutions will be discussed here. For some authors gangs in America constitute little more than hostile playgroups. That is not the full truth, but does reflect the continuing problem of gang researchers who tend to overgeneralize their findings. Clearly, there do exist some very formidable and highly organized gangs in America today[2].

While many working in the field of corrections and criminal justice may take the view that some of today's gangs should be considered new forms of

"organized crime", we truly need to think such a prosecution process through. Targeting them as "Mafia" groups may give them the identity they have long sought and will seek to live up to. In a "lock em' up" atmosphere, it may be convenient to label such gang members as "organized crime". But clearly there are social organizational differences. And there may be unintended risks for society associated with targeting all gangs and gang members in such a blanket manner, to "get the terrorists off the streets". The danger is that how we officially define them may constitute what they become.

If gangs can be roughly defined along a social organization continuum of complexity, where at the lowest level we find our spontaneous "play group" formations, and at the highest level we find our more complex gang nation or "super gang" having the characteristics of advanced social organization, then at this higher end of the gang spectrum the observant student of criminology must ask: what then is the difference between a highly organized criminal gang and organized crime? To answer this question is to provide a wider method of viewing gang and group crime.

The approach here will be to begin with a summary of what we know about the structure and function of organized crime. Then we shall return to the gang classification system discussed earlier to see what differences, if any, exist between a level three gang and "organized crime" as discussed in the criminological literature. Within this context we shall also discuss in some detail the written constitutions and by-laws of several Chicago gangs.

The value of this approach is that it helps to identify, as well, those aspects of contemporary gangs that we are clearly not informed about and yet should be so obvious to even the most casual observer. It helps, therefore, to set a research agenda for the future that will help advance our social scientific understanding of gangs. It will be seen that having enough capital to penetrate legitimate business and having political corruption that can be put to use are about the only two things stopping some major gang organizations from making a transition to forms of organized crime.

DEFINITIONS OF ORGANIZED CRIME

What are we talking about when we focus on "organized crime"? Is this the "Mafia", the "Camorra", the "Cosa Nostra", the "Syndicate", Chicago's "Outfit", international illegal drug cartels, the "Black Hand Society", the "Dixieland Mafia", or what? We must seek greater clarity and precision in our review of "organized crime". Some gangs use the word "mafia" in their name (e.g, Mexican Mafia, etc). Gangs like to use "strong, virile" names. What gangs do strive for in their most idyllic goal is to emulate if not surpass their cultural hero of Al Capone.

If we wanted to induce confusion here, our definitional clarity could suffer immensely by references to areas outside of the social sciences, such as the printed mass media. Newsweek, for example, offered one of the best tautologies of defining it in terms of itself, almost to the point of comic relief in making the assertion "I feel the Mafia is controlled by organized crime":

"The Mafia is a loose confederation of gangs spread around the country" (Newsweek, 1981: p. 35).

Here apparently, organized crime "families" are "gangs". And that certainly seems to simplify everything we wanted to know about the difference between gangs and organized crime. Not really, as we shall see. Indeed, perhaps our problems with both gangs and organized crime is our tendency, in dealing with the government and the wider lay public, to do exactly that: over simplify, to the point perhaps of adding nothing to our understanding and analytical framework. So to begin with we see that there are some enormous definitional contradictions in both the "gang" and "organized crime" literatures. If organized crime is so "loose knit" organizationally and pulls in billions in profits, then how come ordinary criminals do not enter this field in competition or even

unethical business persons for that matter; clearly, these are some remarkable human beings who can accomplish so much economically with such little social organization. And finally, if these organized crime "families" are so "loose knit" why is it so difficult to successfully prosecute their members? Or finally, are many of our criminological analysts so worried about making the error of reification --- treating as real or as a concrete material form something that is really just an abstraction? Another impression from reviewing the gang literature is that our abstractions have not been such very powerful theoretical generalizations that we have to worry too much about it.

Vetter and Territo (1984, p. 36) define organized crime as *"a business that provides illegal, but desired, goods and services for the noncriminal public. Also known as syndicated crime"*.

Cole's (1983: p. 45) definition is that organized crime is *"a social framework for the perpetration of criminal acts, usually in such fields as gambling, narcotics, and prostitution, where a service the public desires is illegal"*.

The definition by Thio surfaces the same conflicting problem found in the gang literature about whether gangs are, or are not, organized. Thio (1988) recognized that:

"organized crime has been viewed in two conflicting ways --- as a tight and as a loose organization. The reality seems to lie somewhere in between. As a highly lucrative enterprise, organized crime involves selling illegal goods and services, racketeering, large-scale thievery, infiltrating legitimate businesses, and corrupting public officials" (Thio, 1988: p. 417).

The definition of organized crime by the President's Commission on Law Enforcement and Administration of Justice tends to focus on size of both organization and profit potential. It is a definition implying "massive scale as a business enterprise" (Di Renzo: 1984, p. 409).[3] Here was the President's Commission (1968) definition of organized crime, which was not too dissimilar from President Reagan's attribution of organized crime as being "an invisible, lawless empire" (see Thio, 1988: p. 403):

"Organized crime is a society that seeks to operate outside the control of the American people and their governments. It involves thousands of criminals, working within structures as complex as those of any large corporation, subject to laws more rigidly enforced than those of legitimate governments. Its actions are not impulsive but rather the result of intricate conspiracies, carried on over many years and aimed at gaining control over whole fields of activity in order to amass huge profits" (President's Commission, 1968: p. 437).

A slightly less "alarmist" and somewhat more analytical definition of organized crime was provided by the 1986 President's Commission on Organized Crime:

> *"Organized crime is the collective result of commitment, knowledge and actions of three components: the criminal groups, each of which has at its core persons tied by racial, linguistic, ethnic or other bonds; the protectors, persons who protect the group's interests; and specialist support, persons who knowingly render services on an ad hoc basis to enhance the group's interests* (President's Commission, 1986: p. 25)."

Some definitions of organized crime simply include gang crime as one of the possible variations. That is, gang crime is a subset and included in a wider definition of organized crime. Wrobleski and Hess (1987: p. 104) quote the lengthy definition that views organized crime in terms of these five categories of criminal activity:

> *"1. Racketeering. 2. Vice Operations (narcotics, prostitution, loansharking, gambling). 3. Theft/fence rings (fraud, bunco schemes, fraudulent document passers, burglary rings, car thieves, truck hijackers). 4. Gangs (youth gangs, outlaw motorcycle gangs, prison gangs). 5. Terrorists."* (Ibid, p. 104).

COMPONENTS OF ORGANIZED CRIME

Does a successful criminal venture mean that only when the group becomes national in scope that it is considered "organized crime"? No. But the federal government's Organized Crime and Racketeering Unit, which was formerly decentralized and operated under the direction of local U.S. Attorneys, is now centralized for a more coordinated effort. Clearly, organized crime implies a multi-jurisdictional boundary problem by the potential such a group has for expansion. Nor should it imply the need to be an "interstate" operation, even though obviously that is helpful for federal prosecution, and even though as Cole notes organized crime operations can indeed often cut "across state and national boundaries" (1983, p. 45).

A hierarchical structure is definitely a component of organized crime according to leading sources like Cressey. The collective or organizational groupings carrying out "organized crime" are often called "families". This does not mean that all such members of any given "family" are related by blood, come from the same family of orientation, or are related by name or by "family of procreation", although obviously, there is considerable "bonding" and potential for strengthening organized crime ties through such marriages. What "families" implies is that the "chief executive officer", if his name is Tony Acardo, well, then his organized crime family becomes known as the "Acardo family". The astute student will sense,

perhaps at this point, some common problem in definitional clarity also to be found in our gang studies literature. Clearly, then, the value of a social organizational approach to gang studies is that it provides for the analytical linkage to a wider analysis of other forms of collective or organized crime. This, at least, is the hope of the present analysis.

ELEMENTS IN COMMON BETWEEN HIGHER LEVEL GANG FORMATIONS AND ORGANIZED CRIME

Clearly, there are a number of characteristics that the gang and organized crime have in common.[4] At least this is true of the higher level of organizationally sophisticated gangs.[5] They both have a code of conduct. At the higher end of the gang organizational spectrum this code of conduct is in fact more than an oral tradition and can take on the form of a written constitution and bylaws.[6] Both formalized gangs and organized crime also make use of "buffers".[7] These are often "middle management" roles, lieutenants, trusted henchmen, etc, who hold status and power above the rank of regular members.

Both organized crime and gang crime involves conspiracy. Both gangs and organized crime also have "enforcement power". In the more sophisticated gang, this means having a gang role equivalent to the "chief of violations", someone who dispenses punishment for errant members, someone who "puts a hit out" on a former member turned snitch, etc. In terms of conspiracy and enforcement, both gangs and organized crime are much alike.

Violence in both organized crime and gangs has an important element of honor. In organized crime, while most violence is instrumental, not expressive, it still has the element of defending honor; particularly among those who threaten the honor of the organization. Honor is associated with gang violence in several ways (Horowitz, 1983, 1987), but mostly in relationship to defense of the "hood" being controlled, or symbolic honor as in the correctional institution where there is little "turf" to defend, or even to fellow gang members who violate one of their internal laws.

THE ETHNIC SUCCESSION HYPOTHESIS

Most useful to understanding the potential of even a highly sophisticated gang making a transition to what is ordinarily implied by "organized crime" is our comprehension of the ethnic succession hypothesis. Ianni (1974) takes essentially the definition of organized crime discussed above, which differentiates gangs from organized crime in terms of expansion into legitimate income areas. That is "organized crime activities illustrate the mixture of legal, semilegal and illegal activities that make up that segment of the American economy we call organized crime"

(Ianni, 1974: pp. 246-247).

In appreciation of Ianni (1974) the one feature that distinguishes organized crime is its systematic fulfillment of demands from the culture and society which cannot be fulfilled through legitimate channels. Indeed, chapter 5 of Ianni (1974) "The Gypsy Cabs: Organized Crime or Minority Business Enterprise" is a striking example of the large "spot market" in such illicit areas. Gypsy cabs functioned illegally, had bitter competition with legitimate cab companies, often struck up creative arrangements with prostitutes and drug pushers, but fulfilled an essential need desired by a specific public. Bribery was a feature of this kind of enterprise, as was the cultivation of political influence. Ianni sees this "gypsy cab" industry being eventually legitimized.

Ethnic succession here meant that for African-Americans and for Puerto Ricans this method of "making it in America" is not dissimilar from other patterns of how ambitious, "rugged individualists" who got their piece of the American pie (e.g., economic success) also had less than saintly beginnings. We shall avoid, for the moment, analysis of the idea that many of our nations gangs could likewise make such a transition, and if they did make such a transition towards a more legitimate business enterprise, what implications that might have for our communities.

The value of Ianni should be clear and will emerge even more strongly below in the analysis of gang constitutions. As demonstrated much earlier in this text, gangs tend to be ethnically homogeneous. The hypothesis by Ianni (1974) is therefore of much potential value to gang analysis, because it provides a means of analyzing the transition from "street gang" to "organized crime".[8]

Sale (1971) describes how during the 1960's, Chicago's Mayor Daley was upset because the money flow from Washington did not go through city agencies before being distributed to programs such as the one in which the Black Stone Rangers through Rev. John Fry were able to acquire such funding. Sale also suggests that Senator McClellan's committee investigating funding abuses was spurred by Daley's animosity towards not being able to get an administrative share of these federal funds by processing them through City Departments:

Pressure from Mayor Daley helped to explain why McClellan was making such bitter charges, claiming, for instance, that federal money was financing the formation of a new "Black Mafia" (the Stones) which was supposed to be taking criminal control of the South Side (Sale, 1971: p. 87).

THE INDIVIDUAL TRANSITION AND ORGANIZATIONAL CHANGE HYPOTHESIS

A number of authors have shown cases of youth to adult transition in crime careers. It involves both the individual and organizational forms. At the individual level, it means essentially graduating in terms of membership from a street gang to the ranks of organized crime.[9] At the organizational level, the entire gang functions with stronger leadership and a greater division of labor. As Taylor states, the gang can evolve as in the case of Chicago's "Forty Two Gang" in the 1930's from a "scavenger/territorial to corporate/organized" gang (Taylor, 1990: p. 7).[10]

The organizational change hypothesis is described mostly in current literature as showing organizational evolution. That is, the evolving higher level of organizational sophistication in gangs. The term organizational change is used here to cover the other direction of development. That is, there can also be disintegration, dismemberment, and dissolution if we are to accept the notion that gangs as social groups can either be put out of business or can sometimes put themselves out of business.

DIFFERENCES BETWEEN ORGANIZED CRIME AND GANGS

The two major differences between organized crime and gangs are: corruption and capitalization represented in the extent of penetrating legitimate business. That gangs have their own small business enterprises has apparently been the case for some time in Chicago. They are said to have video stores, game rooms, and smaller such cash business enterprises. Gangs have not been too successful in corrupting public officials or law enforcement.

The Herrera Family is an interesting case here. Is it a gang or is it organized crime? Clearly, to carry out such an ongoing high level of control of the heroin importation and distribution market it must be able to bribe --- certainly, we would assume, in Mexico. But perhaps not as effectively in the U.S.A. Yet it is also well known that many business enterprises are controlled by the Herrera family through the accumulation of wealth in the heroin trade.

Similarly, Taylor (1990) argues that many such corporate style gangs have already become forms of organized crime. This would probably include as a good candidate list: Aryan Brotherhood, Bloods, Crips, Vice Lords, Disciples, El Rukns, Latin Kings, Mexican Mafia, Black Guerrilla Family, Nuestra Familia, Ku Klux Klan, various motorcycle gangs (Pagans, Hells Angels, etc) and probably more. But we cannot simply say that we do not have a gang problem by defining the gang into a different category of analysis: organized crime. Organized crime is a gang phenomenon, indeed it is the highest level of gang development, a goal aspired to by most gang members in all gangs in America. Crips and Bloods, Peoples and Folks, all admire major organized crime figures as legends of ruthlessness and conquest, as models for achieving instant wealth and fame.

We can now add some more analytically based criticism to the policy recommendation of legalizing heroin as a primary method of gang dismemberment in America. Organized crime has found pornography to be a very profitable area. It is an area, obviously, where gangs could clearly compete. Taking away drug income could simply force gangs to diversify their income base, and enter into such fields traditionally associated with organized crime (e.g., pornography, gambling, loan sharking, protection, etc).

The real key to further understanding these differences is the extent to which American gangs have associated, directly or indirectly, with organized crime figures[11]. Do organized crime figures look at gangs and gang leaders as "dope fiend renegades" or as potentially serious competitors? We don't know for sure, because most researchers know that once we reach the top of the gang organizational continuum ladder (i.e., organized crime), obviously no one talks to skilled or naive researchers. What we do know is that when Crips gang members robbed a series of Las Vegas casinos in 1994, we can probably assume they got the attention of organized crime. There is simply limited data on this key question about the extent to which gangs interact with or cooperate with or simply compete with organized crime.[12] Ko-lin Chin (1988) did, however, indicate that the Chinese gangs in New York City worked as "protectors" for the tongs who are regarded as organized crime.[13] There was some evidence that Jeff Fort, at a point in his career when he was in the transition from the Moorish Americans operating in a political context as the Martin Luther King Movement march against neo-nazis on Chicago's southwest side during 1976-77, and before he organized the El Rukns formally, he had some contact with organized crime figures. But apparently Jeff could not work very effectively with them. But he is today imprisoned in the same place with some important organized crime figures (i.e., the federal facility in Marion, Illinois). Such federal correctional staff are the best at assessing the nature of any such relationship between gangs and organized crime. This is an important intelligence aspect that should be used in any threat assessment of gangs.

AN ORGANIZATIONAL CONTINUUM

For the purposes of noting how modern gangs can make the transition to organized crime, a brief version of the gang typology offered by this author is provided here. In chapter 23, more details of this gang typology are provided. Basically four levels of

gang sophistication are developed in terms of their differences in organizational development. It is helpful here to simply discuss this classification system to focus specifically on how a higher level gang formation differs from organized crime. Figure 17 presents this gang to organized crime organizational continuum.

Figure 17

A Group/Organization Crime Continuum

Operational Characteristics:	Organizational Continuum Gang Threat Levels[14]				
	Level 0	Level 1	Level 2	Level 3	Level 4
CRIME IMPACT	None	Low	Medium	High	High
BUFFERED LEADERSHIP	None	Little	Some	Much	High
MULTI-JURISDICTIONAL	No	No	Maybe	Yes	Yes
LEGIT. Bus. Control	No	No	Rarely	Often	Always
Own Property	No	No	Sometimes	Yes	Yes
BRIBERY/CORRUPTION	No	No	Sometimes	Often	Yes
CARE OF INMATES	No	Rarely	Sometimes	Often	Always
ASSETS ACCUMULATION	No	No	Low	Medium	High
KILL SNITCHES	No	No	Sometimes	Often	Always

LEGEND:
Level 0 = Not a true gang, not involved in ongoing crime.
Level 1 = A formative gang, not highly organized.
Level 2 = An intermediate gang formation.
Level 3 = A formalized gang, often with written constitution.
Level 4 = Syndicated, Organized Crime cartels or families.

As seen in Figure 17 above, where a level three gang (the most organizationally developed and the most sophisticated) differs from organized crime (a level 4 group crime phenomenon) is chiefly in the ability to permeate throughout the society.[15] To carry out bribes and to corrupt public officials. To have a widened source of income including legitimate income from business enterprises under control, and to penetrate other legitimate business enterprises, and to in this way keep the accumulation of capital "moving" in an investment strategy rather than a milking "hand to mouth existence".

The true difference, then, between organized crime and higher level gang formations is simply a matter of degree.[16] Both level three gangs and organized crime must be regarded as formal organizations. But a highly organized gang with thousands of members and different chapters in many areas must still achieve two things that distinguish most gangs from organized crime: the ability to use political corruption and the ability to penetrate legitimate business. More specifically then the difference between more organized gangs and organized crime is the degree to which the group can operate in wider society: bribing officials, getting protection, investing and diversifying its capital, and maintaining connections with many others who are obviously not in their group. In this sense, traditional organized crime groups are more "pro social" than gangs; they have the ability to maintain cooperative ventures and alliances with a wide variety of persons, in chiefly economic relationships, outside of their own limited subcultural integration. Organized crime, therefore, requires a higher level of legitimate integration. Some gangs today try to achieve political power as a step in that direction.

Where some gangs parallel this matter of legitimate ties to larger society is in the political arena. Formalized gangs in Illinois have established their own not-for-profit corporations chartered often as "voting leagues".[17] Their ability to "get out the vote" translates into quid pro quo for whatever politician that is willing to accept their assistance.

Mafia Snitch Gets Involved With White Power Gang

A strange thing happened to Sal "Sammy the Bull" Gravano when he went underground after testifying against John Gotti: he got involved with a small white power gang to make a little extra money from the gang's ability to sell ecstasy pills.

In February, 2000, Gravano was arrested in Phoenix, Arizona along with 35 other members of the gang. Gravano is suspected in 19 murders.

Getting involved with a small white racist extremist gang to make money selling ecstacy at youth concerts and rave parties turned out to be a big mistake. Obviously, someone in this small gang did not believe in the "omerta" concept (i.e., keeping silent).

Source: Patrick Graham, Feb. 24, 2000, "Ex-Mafia Hitman Gravano Arrested", Associated Press.

THE FEDERAL ROLE IN GANG PROSECUTION: RICO STATUTES

No correctional administrator wants gang offenders in a facility that structurally lags behind the social change in the offender population itself represented by inmate gangs. They are most problematic. Our society has few examples that are equivalent to the infamous Alcatraz. One might be the U.S. Penitentiary at Marion, Illinois; inmates there are out of their cells only one hour a day. Another more recent example might be the Pelican Bay prison in California where violent gang members are sent; inmates there are kept under the "no human contact" security status.

The literature on India's robber gangs (Sleeman, 1849) showed that local law enforcement was not able to effectively deal with this crime problem. A national approach was required to make progress on a national problem. Then again, just because the gang is armed and organized comparable

to a military unit, is that sufficient justification for bringing our own military forces into this fray? We shall examine this possibility of a stronger federal role to play in addressing the gang problem in Chapter 18. But in the absence of a stronger federal role, state's must probably rely on the "mini-RICO" statutes, which can be effective prosecution tools.[18]

GANG CONSTITUTIONS AND BY-LAWS

Another area of commonality between higher level gang formations and traditional forms of organized crime is in this area of declarations of official purpose.[19] It has been a recurrent pattern for some organized crime families to have their "social athletic clubs", basically "fronts" for crime. Here we shall see that level 3 gangs, or more sophisticated gangs in terms of organizational development, also have this aspect in common with organized crime. Because according to these written gang constitutions and by-laws, the cloak of "do gooderism" is common to all.

The documents discussed here consist of the following: (1) the constitution of the Almighty Latin King Nation, (2) the constitution of the Spanish Gangster Disciple Nation, (3) the constitution of the Vice Lords, and (4) Black Disciple's Nation internal memoranda. Three major commonalities, worth discussion here, are to be found in all of these lengthy gang written documents.[20] First, they declare a "pro-social" intent. Secondly, they have some element of spiritual or religious legitimation.[21] Thirdly, they all claim to be "oppressed" and part of a larger struggle for freedom and justice.[22] All quotations of these documents made here are direct and reflect any original errors in spelling, etc.[23]

(1) A Pro-Social Intent. The most fascinating, but perhaps not unexpected, aspect that these all have in common is their written and official declaration of being essentially "pro-social" organizations. The Black Gangster Disciples, for example, in a memo describing progress with getting a not-for-profit corporation started up, declaring themselves intent on stopping the commission of crimes within their communities. It is like the skeptical professor says to students in criminology, don't believe anything you hear and only half of what you see and chances are you'll have a scientific footing in the area of crime. It is absurd to conceive of the Black Gangster Disciples as a community-development organization intent on eliminating crime[24]. It is comparable only to the Ku Klux Klan suddenly claiming an official intent and purpose of improving ethnic and race relations in America. It is a very big lie, but an interesting one none the less.[25]

It is interesting because of the potential of such a definition of the situation being promulgated in the group context. It serves an important social-psychological function to have such a "cloak" of social acceptability, even moral superiority. It is more than moral neutralization. It is moral stabilization. One can commit serious crimes and acts of violence with little of shame in this kind of group ethos. In written form, any such declaration of intent as a kind of Masonic organization or association (ala Hobsbawm, 1965: p. 50) as a "mutual aid" society, is only that --- a declaration. Indeed, it is a declaration without regard to goals, functions, or overall societal impact.

(2) The Spiritual/Religious Emphasis. Another commonality between gang constitutions is their claim to a spiritual approval for their existence. Or the use of religion as a source of legitimation, cohesion, and internal social control for the gang[26]. Clearly, one megalomaniac tendency in some gangs is to portray a particular gang leader as such a "holy person".[27] For the Black Gangster Disciples, this means "the religious faith of this organization, tribe and nation, is founded in the very nature of all things; one religious doctrine, teachings and philosophy is that of truth...the doctrine of truth embraces and reflects every religion known to man, from the beginning of recorded time, and history reveals that all religious doctrines claim their god to be the father of all creation; but none yet have given an image to their god which can be manifested from one age to another." Here, obviously, the gang leader is the Chosen One.[28] Recall, for the historical record, the same religious backdrop for legitimation represented in the elaborate written gang constitution described by Green (1847).

For the Spanish Gangster Disciple Nation we find significantly less emphasis on religion, but a potential mysticism nevertheless[29]. Referring to their insignia, "the Spanish Cross derives from our heretic ways, the first word in our Nations name, in which we find our race, our creed, our essential beliefs and our faith". There is but a glimmer of religiosity: "we as a Nation have to have morals, to teach our young in every subject, to abide by our set of laws, to carry our Nations oath in our heart, to accept our prayer for our deceased...". In fact, there is no mention of God whatsoever in the "prayer" for "our Brother's & Sister's who have lost their lives in being part of our Nation's struggle".

In the Latin Kings written constitution and by-laws we find again the difficulty that any type of ethnographic research approach is going to encounter in trying to study this type of gang. Revealing internal affairs of the gang organization to outsiders is explicitly forbidden, and takes on much significance as a potential violation. Most interesting, therefore, is the "holy prayer" of the Latin Kings which appears to be a prayer not to God, for there is no reference to God or Jesus or Allah, but rather might be interpreted as a prayer either to gang ancestry or some visionary "sun god" who rules the gang nation. It, along with the "Kings and Queens Prayer", portrays God as a fellow gang member, where God is the Almighty King; again, however, the original author fearing some moral abomination never uses the descriptor "God" or "Jesus". We do find, however, an explicit declaration that "The Almighty Latin King Nation is a religion which gives us faith in ourselves, a national self-respect, power to educate the poor and relieve the misery around us".[30]

In the Conservative Vice Lord Nation, their oath, which all members are required to know, more specifically reflects an Islamic influence. Recall that the Chicago Vice Lords and the Chicago El Rukns are allied gangs (i.e., "peoples"). The Vice Lord oath within the Illinois State Prison setting is as follows[31]:

"In the name of almighty Allah, I lord cocaine as a representative of a C.V.L.N. will not dishonor our most sacred weapon Lord Unity nor under the threat of death will I deny those who stand beside and as a representative of the a.C.V.L.N. I will listen to the truthful teaching of our elites so that upon my release I may be useful to myself and my community as a whole. Let the black god Allah bear witness to this oath. Behold Vice Lord".

Similarly, the "star" in Vice Lord totems symbolizes "the eye of Allah watching over his people". This Islamic influence is also to be found in the Almighty Black P. Stone Nation.[32]

(3) The "oppressed peoples" belief system. Here we find the strongest evidence yet that many of our nation's prison inmates may in fact be "political prisoners", in the limited sense that if they were gang members, they might have subscribed to an official code that had clear elements of a revolutionary or resistance ideology. We can loosely call this the "oppressed peoples" belief system.[33] Oddly, an analysis of these organizational belief systems from written constitutions of higher level gangs, shows they actually have much in common; such that it does present some interesting possibilities in terms of scenarios for the future.[34] Let us consider some of these different "oppressed peoples" themes.

In the Black Disciple's Nation, their logo, the Star of David, is described as follows: "*THE DEVIL'S PITCH FORKS REPRESENTS OUR NATION'S POWER IN OUR STRUGGLE TO OVER COME THE OPPRESSION WE ARE UNDER....THE DEVIL'S TAIL REPRESENTS THE OPPRESSION BLACK'S, LATINO, AND THIRD WORLD PEOPLES LIVE UNDER AND IS NOT A WHITE ISSUE*". We shall find this same explicit identification with a "third world struggle" in other gang, including rival gang, constitutions.[35]

In the Spanish Gangsters Disciple Nation, fellow gang members are greeted as "comrades in arms". Their work is the "struggle". In this written constitution we find a fascinating hodge-podge of pseudo-political ideology:

"Through our nations decades we've enjoyed providing security, a sure safety and domestic tranquility among the lives of our people...We, brother's of the S.G.D.N. must ordain and abide by the nations constitution, to eliminate poverty and inequality among our people, to provide a structure of potential developments for the individual of our nation, to maintain a liberty for our children and a more gratifying style of social living."

From gang leader Vic, however, we find this element of ideology to be more honestly a patent and clearcut form of individual opportunism. That is to say, at least in this gang's internal written material we find the declared purpose to be "the social elevation of it's members". Presumably the social-economic elevation of its members as well. It is essentially the same doctrine found in the India robber gangs (Sleeman, 1849). These guerilla fighters want their share, but they obviously have no plans on restructuring society and its political institutions. They are decoits, brigands, and opportunists; and only by a stretch of the imagination "political prisoners", because they are by their own account "out for themselves". What this particular constitution also shows is the important tendency of social imitation; that is, gang organization mimicking legitimate organizational forms.

In the Almighty Latin King Nation, we find a constitution that is more specifically identified with the "third world struggle against oppression". Here we find the strongest written evidence of such an official dogma, but the reader should obviously view this kind of declaration with some skepticism in terms of its sincerity not its authenticity:

"The name of this association shall be the AL-MIGHTY LATIN KING NATION. An organization of international brotherhood with[36] exists for the purpose of: 1. Promoting prosperity and freedom through love and understanding to all oppressed people of the world, 2. To train our People to become aware of our social and political problems and of the conditions we are subjected to live under as a Third World People, 3. To provide the aid and way in our search for peace and unity, 4. To promote and encourage education and vocational learning in order to train our People in the art of survival".

It is most interesting to compare this kind of global statement of purpose to the actual written chapter meeting notes for a long time frame.

The fact is some gangs do have regular meetings, and while Hagedorn (1990: p. 245) tells us gangs do not keep membership rosters, we should be careful in studying gangs what we say they cannot do. It is a problem of over generalizing, as many prior gang authors have been very prone to do; often on the basis of lower level gang formations (e.g., level zero gangs). Because some gangs do keep rosters, obviously for paying dues. What one such chapter meeting minutes, made available to the author, showed is this: numerous "violations" against fellow gang members, where violation implies more often than not physical punishment and ridicule, the gang chapter apparently spent much of its time disciplining its own members. Secondly, the gang chapter's monetary proceeds (from dues chiefly) were certainly not spent on community improvement; they were spent on firearms, gang paraphernalia, and spray paint "to fix the hood".

What is interesting about the Latin Kings is that they specifically deny membership to rapists, at least in their constitution. Again, however, one should view this with some skepticism; which is to say, there can be a large difference between official dogma and reality. The present author recalls interviewing a gang member from the Disciples in the 1970's and seeing one of the best examples of moral neutralization, where the youth described a common practice of "tree jumping". It was rape, but in the language of this gang member is was not violent rape but simply "tree jumping".

Generally, the totems and written codes for higher level gang formations serve the purpose of allowing allied gangs, or satellite gang units separated geographically, to share in a common system of symbols and beliefs. Thus, as true Masonic organizations have their various "lodges" separated geographically, so do level three gangs have their franchises[37].

SUMMARY

What we have tried to accomplish in this chapter is two fold. First, to those gang authors whose conception of modern gangs is that they lack any sophisticated internal organization particularly those who deny "centralized, hierarchical organizations" in the spirit of disagreeing with strawman law enforcement definitions, the position taken here, based on a classification system that reflects an organizational capability/sophistication continuum, is that essentially all such views may be correct but only in the limited context to those levels of sophistication that exist in gang formations. Level 0 groups are our typical "clicks" or "cliques", or "street corner" groups, a natural and normal and essentially non-criminal operation. Levels 1 thru 3 represent the true gang organizational development patterns, with level 4 being essentially what is meant by organized crime.

For those who continue to deny the existence of highly organized, pyramidal hierarchies, or any equivalent form of organizational sophistication and development, we have offered for analysis here several such written constitutions and by-laws for several Level 3 gangs.[38] These are fairly lengthy typed documents. Your author did not, nor did law enforcement officials intent on psy-war, manufacture these written codes. They are genuine. Indeed, as anyone who comes to understand the magnitude of the problem and discovering privileged information, here it has not been possible to present all such information because of its sensitivity, which is to imply one of many sources of data, and an appraisal that to disclose this information is to place some persons in jeopardy and perhaps to obstruct justice.

Secondly, in this chapter we have sought to compare and contrast gangs with organized crime. Higher level gang formations assuredly have much in common with organized crime. Where they differ is also important.

DISCUSSION QUESTIONS:

(1) All crime is organized to some degree or another. White collar crime begins and exists only because of organization. Can gang crime begin because of social disorganization and thrive thereafter as a natural social organizational form? Does defining level two and level three gangs as "organized crime" allow law enforcement to say they no longer have a "gang problem"?

(2) What in social policy should be changed to discourage gangs from evolving into organized crime? Or, what should the federal role be in combatting gang crime?

(3) Logically, do you think we should find organized crime patterns to be as equally differentiated as gang formations?

"What's Worse Than Accidentally Driving Through Beirut, Lebanon During An Israeli Air Attack?"

This happens more frequently than many probably suspect, and it happens anywhere you can find gangs.

In Cypress Park, California, one Sunday evening, on Sept. 17, 1995, the Kuhen family was driving home from a picnic with some of their friends. The car's driver was a family friend, but he made the wrong turn, and turned into a dead-end street. A gang called the Avenues was there and thought the Kuhen family car loaded with children was a threat. The gang opened fire on the Kuhen family car. Inside the Kuhen family car, three-year-old Stephanie Kuhen was shot in the head and died instantly; a younger brother was shot in the foot, and the driver was shot in the back.

GANGS AS FORMS OF ORGANIZED CRIME: RECENT RESEARCH FINDINGS

The 1996 National Law Enforcement Gang Analysis Survey carried out by the National Gang Crime Research Center included a strict random sample of N = 283 municipal police departments from 48 states.

A Fourth Consider Some of the Gangs in Their Area An Organized Crime Problem

The survey asked "do you consider any of the gangs in your jurisdiction to be an organized crime problem". Some 28.3 percent indicated they did in fact consider some of the gangs in their area an organized crime problem.

Gangs Considered Forms of Organized Crime

The survey asked "do you feel any of the following gangs could be considered forms of organized crime" and the respondents were instructed to "check all that apply". The results for six specific gang categories showed the following results:

Percentage Who Considered These Gangs Forms of Organized Crime

Type of Gang	% Feel it is a Form of O.C.
Crips	64.0%
Bloods	60.7%
Gangster Disciples	53.9%
Vice Lords	43.9%
Latin Kings	51.7%
Aryan Brotherhood	58.8%

Gang Owned Business Enterprises

The large national study of the economic function and structure of American gangs by the National Gang Crime Research Center (Project GANGECON, 1995) showed that some of the more organized gangs, and even those with regular sources of large illegal income from drugs, are able to buy and operate what may seem to be legitimate business enterprises. This is a very common and expected gang development in larger urban areas where gangs have enjoyed the tenure of existing over a long period of time.

The survey therefore asked "has you agency uncovered any gang involvement in local legitimate businesses". Some 9.2 percent of the respondents in 19 states indicated that "yes" in fact gangs had been detected as being involved in business enterprises in their areas. A follow-up question asked "if yes, what kinds of businesses (CHECK all that apply'" for a list of commonly used gang fronts for laundering their illegal money in what are mostly cash-based businesses. Of the 25 respondents who indicated that gangs had some involvement in local businesses here are the results for type of business establishments gangs were actually involved in: restaurants and fast food businesses (N = 8), pool halls (N = 6), gang rooms and video arcades (N = 7), car washes (N = 6), taverns (N = 5), car repair businesses (N = 8), dance clubs (N = 8), beeper and cellular phone stores (N = 6), jewelry stores (N = 1), and auto paint and body stores (N = 9). Obviously, some of these types of businesses work well in mixing legitimate business with crime as well.

End Notes:

[1] See, for example, Dean Murphy "L.A. Black Gangs Likened to Organized Crime Groups", Los Angeles Times (Front Page), January 11, 1987.

[2] Apparently the "community denial" syndrome has many variations, including academic denial of some highly organized gangs.

[3] Di Renzo like many authors also tends to define "organized crime" in terms of its monopolistic tendency, its use of legitimate businesses as "front groups", and its high profit volume, that is, "it was estimated in 1967 that organized crime "earns" approximately $9 billion annually, a figure that could safely be doubled or tripled" today (DiRenzo, 1984: p. 410).

[4] Whether it is a "put on" ala the research on deviance by Robert Stebbins, or if it is some process of linguistic emulation, one gang member interviewed in 1991 (LK27) used the phrase common to the Chicago "outfit" or organized crime of being "made" as a member. Where "made" translates in meaning as to being accepted into the gang organization.

[5] Hoenig (1975, p. 159) was one of the first to discuss the gang transplant/diffusion/franchising issue in noting that there was "some official speculation that there are links between Brooklyn gangs and the Blackstone Rangers, a Chicago gang of the early sixties that eventually grew so large that it swallowed up much of Chicago's organized crime business...". Hoenig may be referring to what is now known as Jeff Fort's El Rukn gang; or to the current derivative of the "stones", the Black P. Stone Nation.

[6] Jackson and Mc Bride (1990: p. 52) report that the Nuestra Familia, a California prison gang, "has a written constitution and an identified rank structure from warrior to general".

[7] From the law enforcement view, when leaders are insulated against arrest, this is a feature considered typical of organized crime (Sibley, 1989: p. 406).

[8] As early as 1974 one sociologist observed about gang leaders inside prison that "certain leaders speculate about the development of a grand alliance and the rise of a Black Mafia to challenge the syndicate for control of Chicago vice (Jacobs, 1974: p. 407)".

[9] One might also call this the "continuity" hypothesis. That is, it is an alternative to the maturation hypothesis. The maturation hypothesis suggests persons leave the gang when they become adults, marry, or just settle down. The continuity/ individual transition hypothesis would be more compatible with contexts such as the underclass, etc, because it implies no such disavowal of gang ties. It may only imply the person has been in prison before and now knows how to limit risk.

[10] Taylor cites the work of Sifakis (1987) regarding how "in 1931, two University of Chicago sociologists did an in-depth study of this gang of forty-two tough juveniles who were aggressive, reckless scavengers" (Taylor, 1990: p. 7).

[11] Here we mean outside of the prison context. In the prison context, organized crime figures and gang leaders might be assumed to have a "truce", or a mutual respect for their power base. But outside of the prison context is the real test of any

ties between traditional organized crime and American gangs.

[12] As Bensinger (1984, p. 2) reports, at least the appearance of organizational sophistication by close observers of the crime scene, led the Chicago Crime Commission to hold a conference to discuss the link between gangs and organized crime in July, 1983 (see Chicago Tribune, July 7, 1983).

[13] And further, that these Chinese gangs followed the organizational development pattern suggested in this text; first arising out of ethnic conflict, then solidifying for illicit gains, and becoming professional criminal organizations. Indeed, Kolin (1988) predicts that with their overseas connections these same gangs will likely play a larger role in the international drug trade in the future.

[14] See legend below.

[15] It is a matter, perhaps due to human capital, social skills, language, culture, and racism, to be able to "integrate" into the wider society: its businesses, its organizations, and its groups. A good cross-national example of ability to integrate into such a larger social network including businesses, would be the Jakuza gang in Japan - it is organized crime.

[16] Of some relevance here is the recent testimony of a Chicago gang crimes police commander who, in referring to the El Rukns, said "I don't even consider the El Rukns or the Blackstone Rangers a gang. I'll tell you why they have gotten outside the thing we are talking about. I think a lot of emphasis or the complaints that we receive based on gangs are no more than disturbances, ordinance violations. When you are talking about the El Rukns, you can't equate El Rukns with Gypsies. El Rukns are organized crime. They have buildings, they have lawyers, they have doctors, they have banks. It's completely out of the realm of what we consider street gangs" (see Nash, 1984: p. 70).

[17] Chicago's Vicelords incorporated (not-for-profit, Illinois corporation) formally as the United Concerned Voters League; for the Black Gangster Disciples, they were also known as the Young Voters of Illinois. The entity "Young Voters of Illinois" traces far back into the 1980s, while the contemporary entity "21st Century V.O.T.E." is very recent (1993), just enlarged in scope. Most theorists believe this recent development is simply a gambit fostered to get their gang leader out of prison.

[18] This same hope for "stronger teeth" in the criminal code was expressed by Alderman Ivan Rittenberg who testified before the Illinois Gang Crimes Study Commission: "There's no reason why the State of Illinois and this Commission could not write a state law and make this thing for member that we can show is part of an organized gang and their attorneys, if you could show that the attorney knows in fact he's working for an organization, that is, everybody is entitled to a defense, but nobody's entitled to have their attorney participate in the crime. I believe that this Commission, and I am a member of it, I'm going to urge some serious consideration of a statewide anti-racketeering statute which will be able to reach any person who seeks to profit by professional criminal activity similar to this federal one with the same requirements of the minimum 10 years on a conviction, and I think that could be a beginning of the end of gangs, these vicious street gangs organizing and becoming organized criminal entities" (see Nash, 1984: p. 70).

[19] A number of authors have shown some gangs in America to have such written constitutions (Arnold, 1969: p. 177; Fong, 1990).

[20] Obviously, there are other commonalities as well, such as a special cryptic language, or its own subcultural argot; and there are differences as well. We have only a limited space here for such analysis of these and other documents that cannot be shared in this text. These are single spaced typed documents typically of about 20 - 25 pages long each.

[21] The Marielitos, Cuban offenders, are also said to have their own "jailhouse religion". Their impact on America was a result of the Mariel Freedom Flotilla of 1980 in which 130,000 Cuban refugees came to the United States, of which 25,000 were believed to be hardened criminals.

[22] Note, for the record, this was a common theme reported by Camp and Camp (1985) particularly for prison gangs like the Black Guerilla Family.

[23] Note, for the record, that Camp and Camp (1985) reported no such major themes for white prison gangs like the Aryan Brotherhood.

[24] Or similarly, from the written constitution of the Black Guerrilla Family (BGF), if a reader were to simply believe the BGF Code of Conduct one might believe these are inmates truly seeking to rehabilitate themselves.

[25] The CRIPs, which stands for Common Revolution in Progress, is similar in having such a cloak of a "cause celebre". But as Camp and Camp (1985: p. 110) report, such fragmented gangs operating under the same "CRIP" banner may come together under a consolidated or confederation of CCO (Consolidated Crips Organization) and could be a dominant force in and outside of correctional institutions in a more nationwide gang problem. Current juvenile corrections research shows the Crips and Bloods in a number of different states throughout America.

[26] The Vice Lords are similarly based on the front of Islamic religion. Mostly, the M.S.T. --- the Moorish Science Temple of America. And commit crimes hoping that a verbal acknowledgement and written constitution that places trust in the Almighty Allah will spare them of any actual guilt for the harm they cause. The M.S.T. was apparently founded in Newark, New Jersey in 1886 according to the Vice Lord constitution.

[27] See for example, Campbell's (1984, p. 189) description of "Sun-Africa" whose involvement with a quasi-Islamic group in which leaders were regarded as "gods" (e.g., Shamar and Barsun). Similarly, in Chicago's Mickey Cobra gang (allied with El Rukn's, and other "peoples"), in the Cobra totems of symbolism "The Red represent the blood that was shed by all stones/Cobras of our family tree, and the Holy Prophet Mickey Cogwell".

[28] There is, then, more than some elements in common between cults and gangs. The Vice Lords, for example, in their constitution (which shows a heavy influence from the El Rukn's) in explaining what "Vice Lord" means: "The meaning behind the name? Vice means having faults (the human being) and second in importance (Man being second only to god). God being Rule of all worlds and universe. Man was elected by him to be his Vice Lord or (Vice Ruler) of the physical world. Lord means one having dominion over others, a ruler. We see ourselves (man) as god's highest creation, his custodians of this physical world. His Vice Lords. We believe whether you address yourself as Muslim, a Christian, a Jehovah's Witness, or etc. By the definition of that which just been defined you are still Vice Lord, the only difference is one interpretation and acceptance". Which gobblygook is typical of cults.

[29] A gang constitution conspicuously lacking any reference to "God" or religion is that of the Black Guerrilla Family which is specifies in writing an allegiance to revolutionary Marxism. Still, however, there is some comparable idealism as is evident from the following BGF passage "I fully understand, without any reservations whatever, that our revolutionary mission is never done until our will has been complete, and the light of freedom, justice, and equality sine down on all mankind like a star in the night."

[30] Latin Kings are also "peoples", that is allied with the Nation of Gangs which includes Islamic-influenced El Rukns and Vice Lords. But as case LK27 illustrated, some Latin King gang members routinely attended their local Catholic church and had every outside appearance of being staunch Sunday Christians. Indeed, they would say "thanks God" for not being caught after various escapades.

[31] The gang constitution at the community level shows an almost identical "oath".

[32] Keiser (1969) describes the case of a Black gang retaliating against a white neighborhood where the gang member quotes Malcolm X to the effect that "violence sometimes serves its purpose" (Keiser, 1969: p. 8). That is, the gang member apparently believed in deterrence theory by also saying, after such a planned foray, "they'll think twice before they do it" again (ibid).

[33] Such political leanings are much more clearly articulated in gangs such as the Black Guerilla Family (see Camp and Camp, 1985: p. ix).

[34] Hobsbawm (1965) in his chapter on the Mafia found similarly such tendencies in the criminal associations, gilds, or fraternities, to believe in a kind of ruthless justice against an unjust political situation.

[35] In the Chicago Vice Lords, this ideology appears in their totems and use of symbols. The circle means "360 degrees of knowledge that black people rule the world and will again rule the world". Fire "represents the Black Nation's true knowledge of being suppressed and their inability to reach knowledge because of the heat created by the fire". See also the Vice Lord prayer which makes reference to "all poor and oppressed people of color nationwide" (Nash, 1984: p. 55).

[36] Presumably, the gang author meant "which" rather than "with".

[37] The constitution of the Vice Lords, for example, creates a special ranking membership category for "ambassadors". They act as missionaries, to "propagate and promote Lordism", to intentionally proselytize and spread the gang influence.

[38] Fong's (1990) analysis of Texas prison gangs also acknowledges the existence of such constitutions for internal member regulation (Fong, 1990: p. 40) as well as the military style of gang role structure/organization.

When Do Gangs Become "Organized Crime?"

I tell my students: when gangs can effectively buffer and shield themselves from investigation and prosecution through bribery of criminal justice personnel, and in addition to their illegal income sources, also get involved in legitimate businesses as well, THEN they have probably made the transition to organized crime.

Getting a lot of illegal income is not enough; size is not enough; ferocity is not enough. The gang must be able to "corrupt" the legal system and also impact on the legitimate economy. Then it would fit almost all classical or mainstream definitions of "organized crime".

BELOW: Cobrette's, female members of the Spanish Cobra's (a
Folk's gang), "throw down" their opposition (i.e., the Latin
Kings).

CHAPTER 18

FEMALE GANG MEMBERS AND
THE RIGHTS OF CHILDREN

INTRODUCTION

The female gang member and especially the female gang leader is often neglected in our gang literature. This chapter has the goal of increasing practical and social scientific knowledge about female gang members. In Part I of this chapter the reader will find important new research findings about the female gang member. In Part II of this chapter, larger issues about the role of females in gangs today are discussed and analyzed. Additional discussion is made in Part III regarding the rights of young children in the larger societal context of clarifying our moral values and legal codes.

THE CHIVALRY VERSUS CONVERGENCE HYPOTHESES

The chivalry hypothesis is advanced as a way of explaining female crime generally. It assumes that there is a bias against locking up females. It may assume that at the gates to the criminal justice system, females are treated differently than males. An example would be if it could be shown that females are more likely to receive "discretion" and therefore screened out of the criminal justice system at the point of arrest.

Touted as the major rival explanatory hypothesis to the chivalry idea is the convergence hypothesis. The convergence hypothesis suggests that females may in some ways be "catching up" to their male counterparts in the criminal justice system as offenders. The convergence hypothesis rears its head every time anyone suggests there is a rise in any aspect of female crime, delinquency, or punishment.

If the chivalry hypothesis is that females receive special treatment in the criminal justice system, then actually, and more logically, the reverse of the chivalry hypothesis would not be convergence, but would rather be something akin to rudeness towards females (e.g., female harassment). Finally, and perhaps more likely, exists possibility that males are simply more prone to crime than females cross-culturally.

How then do we explain, in criminological terms, the female gang situation today? First, enormous evidence suggests that in the overwhelming number of cases involving the larger and more formidable gangs that exist in America today, that these are male-dominated activities: females play a role in these gangs, but not in the top leadership positions. Why would this be true? Criminal offenders are not generally known for being activists against sexism and for the women's rights movement. Criminals abuse women, plain and simple, would be the better bet.

By most actual empirical research conducted, the percentage of female gang members existing in America tends to roughly parallel the percentage of females in the American prison system. About 5 to 6 percent.

Many gangs have female auxiliary units, this is a common phenomenon. Many gangs allow females to associate with them, in a supportive capacity. Some gangs allow females to hold rank and even direct male members. But few major gangs exist that are genuine criminal gangs that are in fact 100 percent female. If we wanted to use Thrasher's definition of gang (any group unsupervised by responsible adults that may engage in deviance), the obviously, such "gangs" would exist everywhere. But few all-girl gangs exist as autonomous gang organizations. How could they exist very long? What would they do? It would have to involve something other than claiming geographical turf, because they would attract every gang that ever heard of them. It would have to involve something other than drug sales, because eventually they would end up in competition with any of a number of male dominated gangs.

There is only one place this author knows where we can easily find all female gangs operating: behind bars, in juvenile detention centers, in juvenile correctional institutions, in adult jails, and in adult correctional institutions that, by definition, allow only females as inmates. Inside some of these facilities there are conflicts and rivalries between the members representing their various gang groups and organizations.

A FACTUAL BASED APPROACH TO UNDERSTANDING FEMALE GANG MEMBERS

It is possible to theorize about female gang members in terms of how the processes work for females entering gangs, how female gang members compare to their male counterparts, what differentiates female gang members from females in the same social milieu who never join gangs, and whether aspects of abuse and discrimination are significant developmental milestones in female gang careers. However, a "theory" is just that: an argument or opinion that may have nothing to do with the "facts" or the social reality of the issue.

It may be more fruitful to the student of female gang members to begin with some reliable facts about female gang members. In this way, we can begin with the "reality" of female gang members. These, then, would be some of the facts that a good theory would have to account for. There have been a number of different gang research projects reported

in recent years that have advanced our knowledge about female gang members.

Let us now turn to some of these "facts" about female gang members in America today.

PART I. FINDINGS FROM THE MATCHED PAIR DESIGN

The research reported here seeks to add to our understanding of female gang members and how they may differ in some respects from their peers who are not gang members. The findings discussed here relate specifically to African-American female high school students[1]. The analysis compares a sample (N = 100 Folks) of those who self-report gang membership with a sample (N = 100 Neutrons) who have never joined a gang[2]. Thus, the fundamental hypothesis explored here is whether or not among African-American females gang members are really different from those who have never joined a gang. Very little systematic research on female gang members has been reported in the social science literature. What literature does exist on the topic of female gang members shows research efforts where the "sample" size was as small as N = 3. This project was undertaken to specifically add to our knowledge about female gang members.

THE MATCHED-PAIR SURVEY RESEARCH DESIGN

As reported previously (Knox, Laske, and Tromanhauser, 1992), gender is a factor that significantly differentiates self-reported gang membership among high school students. Females have a lower base rate for gang membership than do males. The research problem, then, was to over-sample female students to such an extent that a sufficient group size could be obtained for female gang members. To accomplish this research goal, two versions of the same survey were created: one for males, and one for females.

Several public high schools on Chicago's southside were used for data collection. The male version of the survey is not analyzed here and was not the primary research objective, and thus served a placebo function to basically keep the boys busy in the coed classrooms. Both versions of the survey instrument were five pages long and contained 99 different questions, some of which had multiple parts, and thus well over 99 different variables. Data collection began in early 1993 and continued until May, 1993 when a sufficient number of self-reported female gang members had been reached[3].

All survey instruments were stored by the school and classroom in which they were collected. Manual checks were made to identify self-reported gang members and then the gang member was matched by race, age, and grade level often from the same classroom with a non-gang member respondent. The analysis reported here therefore reflects a matched-pair design of African-American female high school students, half (N=100) of whom self-reported that they had previously joined a gang, and half (N=100) of whom reported that they had never joined a gang.

MATCHED SAMPLE DESCRIPTION

All of the female gang members (N = 100) are members of the Folks gang nation. More specifically, they self-identify as Sisters of the Struggle (S.O.S.), Intellectual Sisters, Intellectual Sisters of the Struggle (I.S.O.S.), or simply members of the Gangster Disciples gang. The "Intellectual Sisters" identity comes from the written internal literature of the Brothers of the Struggle (B.O.S.), which is essentially the conglomerate group of the Disciples Nation. While other "Folks" gangs exist which have female members, our data allowed the identification of specific gangs to which the respondents self-reported their membership in. For all practical purposes, then, the female gang members analyzed here can be regarded as "Intellectual Sisters" or S.O.S. -- the female constituency of the clearly male dominated B.O.S. organization.

All of the African-American females (N = 100) who have never joined a gang are typically regarded as "Neutrons" in the context of the high school and community environment. A "Neutron" is a person who is not gang-affiliated, having never joined any gang and not being aligned with any gang nation (e.g., People or Folks, Brothers or Folks, Crips or Bloods, etc).

The school grade level among folks and neutrons was almost identical as seen here:

	Neutrons	Folks
9th grade	29	30
10th grade	28	27
11th grade	22	24
12th grade	21	19
TOTAL	100	100
Mean	10.3	10.3

Similarly, the age distribution among folks and neutrons is very similar as seen here:

		Neutrons	Folks
AGE:	<=14	12	9
	15	22	23
	16	33	28
	17	22	26
	18	10	10
	>=19	1	4
	TOTAL	100	100
	Mean	15.9	16.1

The family structure in terms of number of siblings (brothers and sisters) and total number of persons living in the household also show the two groups are similar, but with tendency being for somewhat larger sizes among those who self-report gang membership as seen below:

		Neutrons	Folks
Number of Brothers	Mean	1.75	2.36
Number of Sisters	Mean	1.77	1.83
Total Household Members	Mean	4.66	4.91

Family function in terms of "openness" also appeared to vary little between these two groups. Two separate questions addressed this issue, asking "how easy or hard is it for you to speak with your mother" and father, using a response mode of zero (very hard) to ten (very easy). Openness for communication with mother showed a mean of 6.60 for neutrons compared to 7.17 for folks; and with fathers a mean of 5.34 for neutrons, and 5.16 for folks.

FINDINGS COMPARING FOLKS AND NEUTRONS

It is helpful to begin this discussion with a summary of those factors for which no significant difference emerged in comparing those African-American females who had, or who had not ever, joined a gang. Figure 18 lists those factors from the survey for which no significant difference emerged using the Chi-square test (p > .05). As seen in Figure 18, some factors reported recently in the literature to be important with regard to gang membership (e.g., suicide ideation) are shown here to be factors not significantly differentiated by gang membership within this sample.

FIGURE 18
FACTORS NOT SIGNIFICANTLY DIFFERENTIATED BY HAVING EVER JOINED A GANG AMONG AFRICAN-AMERICAN FEMALE HIGH SCHOOL STUDENTS IN A MATCHED-PAIR DESIGN

Description of Survey Instrument Question or Variable:

Do you think some types of rap music encourages crime or violence?
Are you mother and father either divorced or separated?
Have you ever given birth to a child?
Do you plan on graduating from high school?
Have you ever joined Girl Scouts?
During the past 12 months did you ever seriously consider suicide?
Have you ever tried cocaine?
Do both of your parents live in the same household with you?
Are girls more likely to get a break from police?
I often think people are talking about me.

Figure 18:   Continued

I am not as emotional as other people.
Do you have any regular part-time or full-time job?
What is your official Grade Point Average for high school?
Do you have a lot of resentment about the way some racial groups   are treated differently than others?
Nobody tells me what to do.
I want to eventually marry and have children.
This is a sexist society that discriminates against women.
Have your parents verbally abused you one or more times in the last   two months?
Has your boyfriend verbally abused you one or more times in the   last two months?
Have you defied your parents' authority to their face one or more   times?
Have one or more close friends and associates who have been wounded   by gunfire in a gang shooting?

Table 30 provides the frequency crosstabulation of those variables that were significantly differentiated by gang membership among this sample of African-American female high school students in Chicago. These results can be summarized in terms of six profile patterns: family life, substance abuse, school discipline, dating, violence socialization, and aggressive personality characteristics.

(1) The Family Life Profile. Female gang members are significantly more likely to report that they have siblings (brothers or sisters) who are also gang members. Female gang members are significantly more likely to report prior pregnancies. Female gang members are significantly more likely to report that their family receives Public Aid. Female gang members are significantly less likely to report that they regularly attend church. Female gang members are significantly more likely to report having struck (hit) a parent one or more times. Female gang members are significantly more likely to report ever having run away from home. Female gang members are significantly less likely to report receiving an allowance from their family.

(2) The Substance Abuse Profile. Female gang members are significantly more likely to report that a lot of kids in their neighborhood use illicit drugs. Female gang members are significantly more likely to report using marijuana at least once a week. Female gang members are significantly more likely to report drinking alcohol at least once a week. Female gang members are significantly more likely to report having close friends who have shot up/injected drugs (e.g. IV drug use) and who use illicit drugs[4].

(3) The School Discipline Profile. The female gang member is significantly more likely to report knowing the police officers who work at the school. The female gang member is significantly more likely to report having been (a) suspended from school, (b) having an 'in school' suspension, and (c) having an 'in-school' detention. The female gang member has a lower educational aspiration by being significantly less likely to expect to graduate from a 4-year college. The female gang member is significantly more likely to report also having been previously arrested.

(4) The Dating Profile. The female gang member is significantly more likely to report having a boyfriend who has an arrest record. The female gang member is significantly more likely to report having ever been beaten or assaulted by a boyfriend. The female gang member is significantly more likely to report that she could marry someone who is an active gang member; and, reminiscent of the classic Westside Story, apparently more willing to date a rival gang member if he showed respect. The female gang member is significantly less willing to marry someone of another race.

(5) The Violence Socialization Profile. The female gang member is significantly more likely to report having been previously threatened with gang violence. The female gang member is significantly more likely to report having ever carried a weapon to school for protection. The female gang member is significantly more likely to report having been in one or more fights during the last year. The female gang member is significantly more likely to report having ever had to pull a knife on someone. The female gang member is significantly more likely to report having had experience in shooting a handgun. The female gang member is significantly more likely to report having a permanent tattoo.

(6) The Aggressive Personality Profile. The female gang member is significantly more likely to believe she can take a beating just like a man. The female gang member is significantly more likely to report that she would never back out of a fight. The female gang member is significantly more likely to report that she sometimes feels like smashing things for no apparent reason. The female gang member is significantly more likely to think of herself as someone who fights first and asks questions later. The female gang member is significantly more likely to report that other persons consider her a very defiant individual and to distrust other people.

TABLE 30

SUMMARY TABLE: FREQUENCY DISTRIBUTION OF VARIOUS FACTORS IN RELATIONSHIP TO GANG MEMBERSHIP AMONG AFRICAN-AMERICAN FEMALE HIGH SCHOOL STUDENTS

EVER JOIN A GANG?

	NO	YES
In your neighborhood, do a lot of kids use illicit drugs?		
NO	23	12
YES	24 (24%)	40 (40.4%)
DON'T KNOW	53	47
Chi-square = 7.81, p = .02		
Has your boyfriend ever been arrested for any crime?		
NO	71	39
YES	27 (27.5%)	60 (60.6%)
Chi-square = 21.82, p < .001		
Have any of your brothers or sisters been in a gang?		
NO	74	44
YES	25 (25.2%)	56 (56%)
Chi-square = 19.48, p < .001		
Do you know the police officers who work at your school?		
NO	40	15
YES	60 (60%)	85 (85%)
Chi-square = 15.67, p < .001		
Have you ever been beaten or assaulted by a boyfriend?		
NO	88	75
YES	12 (12%)	23 (23.4%)
Chi-square = 4.47, p = .03		
Do you plan on graduating from a 4-year college?		
NO	15	29
YES	84 (84.8)	68 (70.1%)
Chi-square = 6.11, p = .01		
Do you have a permanent tattoo? NO	90	43
YES	10 (10%)	53 (55.2%)
Chi-square = 45.89, p < .001		
How many times have you been pregnant? 0 times	75 (75%)	59 (60.8%)
1 time	21	23
2 or more times	4	15
Chi-square = 8.32, p = .01		
Do you use marijuana at least once a week? NO	96	60
YES	4 (4%)	40 (40%)
Chi-square = 37.76, p < .001		

	NO	YES
Do you drink alcohol at least once a week? NO	92	62
YES	8 (8%)	37 (37.3%)
Chi-square = 24.52, p < .001		
Have any of your close friends ever injected (shot up) drugs? NO	95	87
YES	4 (4%)	13 (13%)
Chi-square = 5.11, p = .02		
Have you ever been arrested for anything? NO	88	37
YES	12 (12%)	60 (61.8%)
Chi-square = 52.77, p < .001		
Is it hard to get out of a gang? NO	5	48
YES	24	36
% Yes	(24.4%)	(37.5%)
DON'T KNOW	69	12
Chi-square = 77.38, p < .001		
Have you been helped by a police officer before?		
NO	66	44
YES	33 (33.3%)	53 (54.6%)
Chi-square = 9.03, p = .003		
Would you go out with a rival gang member if he showed respect for you? NO	46	21
YES	50 (52%)	74 (77.8%)
Chi-square = 13.96, p < .001		
Do you think you could marry someone who is an active gang member? NO	79	32
YES	20 (20.2%)	64 (66.6%)
Chi-square = 42.91, p < .001		
Do you receive an allowance from your family? NO	29	47
YES	69 (70.4%)	53 (53%)
Chi-square = 6.34, p = .01		
Have you ever been suspended from school? NO	61	25
YES	38 (38.3%)	73 (74.4%)
Chi-square = 26.10, p < .001		
Have you ever had an 'In School' Suspension? NO	67	49
YES	31 (31.6%)	50 (50.5%)
Chi-square = 7.24, p = .007		
Have you ever had an 'In School' (hit) detention?		
NO	57	37
YES	42 (42.4%)	62 (62.6%)
Chi-square = 7.68, p = .006		
Do other persons consider you a very defiant individual?		
NO	60	39
YES	34 (36.1%)	51 (51%)
Chi-square = 7.77, p = .005		

Table 30: Continued
EVER JOIN A GANG?

		NO	YES
Does your family currently receive Public Aid?	NO	69	49
	YES	29 (29.9%)	46 (48.4%)
		Chi-square = 7.19, p = .007	

		NO	YES
Have you ever helped to recruit other females into a gang?	NO	95	50
	YES	3 (3%)	47 (48.4%)
		Chi-square = 52.68, p < .001	

		NO	YES
Do you regularly attend church or religious worship?	NO	49	61
	YES	50 (50.5%)	30 (32.9%)
		Chi-square = 5.98, p = .01	

		NO	YES
Do you think you could marry someone of another race?	NO	38	55
	YES	59 (60.8%)	37 (40.2%)
		Chi-square = 8.02, p = .005	

		NO	YES
Have you ever run away from home?	NO	76	56
	YES	23 (23.2%)	37 (39.7%)
		Chi-square = 6.11, p = .01	

		NO	YES
In the last year, have you ever been threatened with violence by a gang member?	NO	82	68
	YES	17 (17.1%)	28 (29.1%)
		Chi-square = 3.95, p = .04	

		NO	YES
Have you ever carried a weapon to school for protection?	NO	78	42
	YES	21 (21.2%)	53 (55.7%)
		Chi-square = 24.56, p < .001	

		NO	YES
I can take a beating just like a man.	FALSE	83	45
	TRUE	17 (17%)	51 (53.1%)
		Chi-square = 28.21, p < .001	

		NO	YES
I would never back out of a fight.	FALSE	43	28
	TRUE	56 (56.5%)	68 (70.8%)
		Chi-square = 4.28, p = .03	

		NO	YES
I sometimes feel like smashing things for no apparent reason.	FALSE	70	48
	TRUE	27 (27.8%)	49 (50.5%)
		Chi-square = 10.47, p = .001	

		NO	YES
A person like me fights first and asks questions later.	FALSE	82	46
	TRUE	17 (17.1%)	51 (52.5%)
		Chi-square = 27.10, p < .001	

		NO	YES
I have had experience in shooting a real handgun.	FALSE	84	46
	TRUE	15 (15.1%)	50 (52%)
		Chi-square = 29.91, p < .001	

Table 30: Continued
EVER JOIN A GANG?

		NO	YES
At least once, I've had to pull a knife on someone.	FALSE	78	41
	TRUE	19 (19.8%)	56 (57.7%)
		Chi-square = 29.75, p < .001	

		NO	YES
A person is better off by not trusting anyone.	FALSE	64	44
	TRUE	35 (35.3%)	53 (54.6%)
		Chi-square = 7.36, p = .007	

		NO	YES
Have one or more close friends and associates who use illicit drugs?	NO	72	47
	YES	28 (28%)	51 (52%)
		Chi-square = 11.92, p = .001	

		NO	YES
Been in one or more fights in the last year?	NO	56	22
	YES	42 (42.8%)	74 (77%)
		Chi-square = 23.63, p < .001	

		NO	YES
Ever struck your mother or father (hit them) one or more times?	NO	81	61
	YES	19 (19%)	35 (36.4%)
		Chi-square = 7.47, p = .006	

HAS FEMINISM AFFECTED GANG LIFE?

What do these female gang members report in terms of convergence and chivalry hypotheses? Are the females in this particular gang on equal status and enjoy equal opportunity for advancement as found in the male gang member counterparts (the convergence hypothesis)? Or are females given special duties because of their gender and are still basically relegated to a subservient position in a male dominated organization (the chivalry hypothesis)? Here we can test these issues by taking a closer look at the viewpoints of our sample of female gang members.

About half of the female gang members (52.1%) report that their boyfriend is also a member of the same gang.

When asked "within the gang, are female members treated the same as males (i.e., do they have the same status and privileges as males)", some 60 percent said "yes". About a fourth (26.3%) said "no". And the rest (13.7%) were not sure.

When asked if the females in the gang are used for specific jobs or tasks because they are females, about half (53.7%) said "no". About a fourth (28.4%) said "yes". And the rest (17.9%) were not sure.

When asked if females in the gang have special duties which males do not have, some 37.8 percent said "yes". About an equal proportion (40.8%) said "no". And about a fifth (21.4%) were not sure.

When asked if female members are permitted

to date males who are not members of the same gang, about two-thirds (65.6%) said "yes". Some 17.7 percent said "no", and the rest (16.7%) were not sure.

When asked if female members are allowed to be leaders within the gang nearly three-fourths (74.2%) said "yes". Some 9.7 percent said "no", and the rest (16.1%) were not sure.

When asked if female members are allowed to lead or control male gang members this story of equal opportunity tends to unravel. About half (51.6%) of the respondents said that they were not allowed to lead or control gang members in their gang. Still, some 29.5 percent said it would be possible for females to exert this power over males. And some 18.9 percent were not sure.

One of the classical ways in which male gang members exploit female gang members and female gang associates is to use them to limit their risk of apprehension and arrest. Numerous examples exist in the literature, for example, showing that female gang members are often asked to carry guns for their male members as Dawley described in his tenure with the Vice Lords that the females were used for "whatever was needed" including sex:

"A Vice Lady was also used for carrying guns. The police couldn't search females so she could carry a shotgun up under her dress and the fellas could walk alongside" (Dawley, 1992: p. 31).

When asked if female gang members are expected to carry guns for the male gang members, some 32.3 percent said "yes". About half (50.5%) said "no". The rest (17.2%) were not sure.

Theoretically some gang organizations can be expected to display more of the chivalry pattern than others. This is true, as documented elsewhere, because some gang organizations like the Black P. Stones and the Vice Lords have a strong Islamic ideological influence in their internal beliefs and in their written gang internal literature and belief system. Historically, women have not gained the same power and status as men in Islamic groups or societies. The group studied here is not one that has a pronounced Islamic influence. The "Brothers" gang nation has the more pronounced Islamic identity. Thus, theoretically it is possible to hypothesize that greater convergence would be found in this group (S.O.S.) than among gangs composed primarily of the same racial group representing a rival or opposition gang nation (e.g., Stones, Vice Lords, etc).

No clear cut answer, thus, is forthcoming on this issue. The data suggest a mixed set of findings in a gang that held the best possibility for convergence. To a large extent, however, it would appear that females have not exactly liberated this particular gang organization. While this particular gang organization is very adept at sponsoring regular educational meetings for its members called "Awareness Ses-

sions", not one of them in the list of subjects known to the present authors has dealt with "Feminism Today".

What is very clear from this research is that female gang members differ in significant ways from their non-gang member counterparts matched by the same race, age, and school grade level. This still does not answer the more fundamental question of whether female gang members differ significantly from the social, psychological, and behavioral or background profile found among male gang members.

PART II: THE MANY OTHER ISSUES ABOUT FEMALE GANG MEMBERS

We know so very little about the role of females involved in gangs consider the scope of the problem. In the recent research on 232 police chiefs an 25 county sheriffs in Illinois, when these law enforcement administrators were asked whether females were also involved in the gangs in their areas, some 74.2 percent of the police chiefs and 68.2 percent of the county sheriffs indicated this was true.[5] Thus, it is a problem much larger than its knowledge base.

There are many other interesting issues about female gang members that need further research. Some of these larger issues are described here, and where possible new and other additional hard data is provided. Finally, the rights of children are examined in the context of the gang problem today.

Are Female Gang Members More Violent In Some Situations Than Their Male Gang Member Counterparts?

I recall witnessing my first female gang member violence. It happened in Bridgeport, a community area in Chicago, one of the many Chicago communities I have lived in. This particular incident occurred in the mid-1980s, and it involved about ten female members of the Satans Disciples. The female gang members had lured another female into an ambush on the corner of Racine and 31st Street. I ended up taking the victim to the hospital, so both witnessing the event and debriefing the victim afterwards as a resident of the community, this gang experience is treated as nothing more than anyone who lives in an urban area may have also had in terms of life experience. It is direct observation and focused interviewing with the victim.

First this particular gang violence was exceptionally brutal. The victim was 18 years old and in a late stage of pregnancy at the time she was attacked. What I saw caused me to holler from a second floor window to down below on the street and rush to take the victim to the hospital. The female gang members felt slighted by this neutron at the high school. The victim had said something that was taken as verbal insult to one of the female members of the Satans Disciples. No chance for an apology was to ever come.

What happened was a classic physical assault ambush. A confederate of the female gang members had lured the victim out to meet at the corner "store" (a small lean-to mom-and-pop style grocery that catered mostly to kids for snacks, but also sold drug paraphernalia). Once the victim was out of her house and got to the corner where the store was located, the other female members of the Satans Disciples "swooped" from three directions, waiting in hiding nearby.

There were about ten female gang members, ranging from 15 to 19 years of age, including Mexican-American and white members. The first few punches to the face and head of the victim from the first several female gang members that ran up on the victim were sufficient to knock the victim to the ground. Subsequent kicks by the female gang members that surrounded her body, on and about the head, rendered the victim helpless as she laid on the sidewalk with the gang girls pummelling her. This all happened in a quick instant and lasted only a minute and then the female gang members had dispersed in different directions leaving behind a bloodied victim. Actually two victims. Because the victim in this instance was in a late stage of pregnancy.

The female gang members eagerly tried to get close to the victim on the ground and kick the victim in the stomach. It was obvious the victim was pregnant. But the female gang members focused their attention on kicking the fetus. As the attack happened I hollered to the gang members to stop, and then ran from the building to the scene. Just as I got to the scene the female gang members had retreated.

With a neighbor I took the victim directly to the hospital and notified the police.

The issue here is whether female gang members are, as some have alleged, more violent or more vicious than their male gang member counterparts? Much informal information developed by numerous interviews with gang members and others has often led to the final appraisal of this issue by responses to the scenario: if you were in alley and at one end you faced the male members of the gang, and at the other end of the alley you faced the female members of the gang, and there was no way out, which end of the alley would you prefer to taking your beating from? I have never seen someone prefer the female end of the alley. Many seem to point to a kind of overcompensation phenomenon where the female gang member will be predictably more violent.

No systematic research has yet answered this question. There is other evidence that speaks to this issue. But for the most part, the gang member problem in America is a male problem; the vast majority of the leaders of serious criminal gangs are older adult males. The traditional exploitive arrangement seems to be the norm: where the female gang members act almost as the "Womens Auxiliary" of the male dominated gang culture.

"The Study of Confined Juvenile Gang Girls by Rosenbaum (1996)"

The study by Jill Leslie Rosenbaum ("A Violent Few: Gang Girls in the California Youth Authority", Journal of Gang Research, Vol. 3, No. 3, Spring, 1996: 17-23) pointed out that a lot of misconceptions about "female gang members" have been previously published in the criminological literature. Among these misconceptions was the generalization from Cohen (1955: p. 45) that female delinquency generally consists primarily of sexual delinquency.

Rosenbaum studied $N = 70$ female gang members confined in the California state juvenile correctional system. The profile that emerged was this: 94% had been arrested for a violent crime; most joined the gang at age 12; about half "had other family members who had served time in jail or state prison" (p. 19); about half of these female gang members reported being the early victims of sexual or physical abuse in their generally dysfunctional families.

Rosenbaum takes Chesney-Lind (1993) to task for the claim that violent girl gang behavior is a social-construction of the mass media. Says Rosenbaum, "she obviously has not looked closely at the female gang members who have found their way to the California Youth Authority" (p. 21).

ARE THERE ALL FEMALE GANGS?

Yes, is the clear answer here. There do exist, just as among males, gangs of varying levels of sophistication in terms of their organization and in terms of their level of crime threat, which are gangs composed almost entirely if not exclusively of female members. Most examples of this type of all female gang are those at the lower level of the gang crime threat continuum. However, some recent research does show that the all female criminal gang does in fact exist.

Perhaps the strongest evidence documenting the all female criminal gang is the work entitled "Sisters Are Doin' It For Themselves: A Black Female Gang in San Francisco" by Lauderback, Hansen, and Waldorf (1992) published in what is now the Journal of Gang Research. In their work they documented the group called the Potrero Hill Posse, or PHP. Their study basically showed this all female gang to be primarily involved in drug sales operations. It also seemed to attract less attention from the police, in fact their study showed that only a half of the members had an arrest record. Is it possible that the Chivalry hypothesis operates here: that is citizens are more likely to call the police when a group of boys hang on the corner, and be less likely to call the police about a complaint of suspicious girls on the corner? This would make for a fascinating actual field experiment for those interested in future research on gangs.

What happens to male dominated gangs also happens to female gangs is another finding of the Lauderback, Hansen, and Waldorf study. When one group forms, another will form to oppose it. This has been called the law of natural group opposition formation; where a blue gang starts, a red gang will shortly follow; where a folks gang starts, a peoples gang will shortly organize to counteract it. The Potrero Hill Posse had their opposing local gang in a group called the Valencia Gardens Mob, also composed primarily of African-American females.

THE CORRECTIONAL ENVIRONMENT FOR FEMALE GANG MEMBERS

Nationwide a lower gang density is always reported for females than for males. This consistently appears in research on the different types of correctional environments as well: juvenile short term detention facilities, juvenile long term correctional institutions, local jails, and adult state correctional institutions. However, this lower gang density is that reported as the official estimate only. There is reason to be somewhat skeptical about the official estimates from those who are the chief administrators of the same facilities.

The fact remains, however, that in the female component of the correctional system what we have are groups of females that interact along gang lines. One thing appears to be true and deserving of much more research: that females are in this context much less violent than their male counterparts. One can readily find numerous examples of male gang members behind bars who kill other inmates and who even assassinate correctional officers, and who routinely "riot". In a recent gang riot at Cook County Jail, a male gang member situation, the Vice Lords fought the Disciples over who would have first use of the shower. Seven inmates were stabbed, and two were killed in this frivolous fight over who showers first.

We do not seem to hear as much such gang violence in the female correctional context. Is this a problem of statistical proportions that is masked and biased by the very nature of the use of the penal sanction in America? Possibly so. For please recall that historically in America about only five percent of the prison inmates have been female, and this trend is largely consistent over a very long period of the history of American criminal justice. One possibility we can rule out for those that would claim that female gang members are less violent in custody than

their male counterparts, is the idea that female inmates are treated better. The fact is most correctional programs are geared towards males, especially the rehabilitation and vocational training programs. Much fewer resources are allocated to the womens division of most state correctional systems. So one cannot effectively argue that women gang members are less violent because they are treated better than male inmates.

What we do know about inmate roles is that female inmates take on more of a quasi-family function, and do appear to have social skills to be able to avoid and mediate conflicts. What we do know about male inmates is that many, particularly gang members, have a kind of combative personality syndrome that prefers conflict over all other options for problem solving. Still the issue is a gnawing one that deserves greater research. Our correctional institutions provide a natural arena in which to ascertain the nature of the differences in gang violence and much more research needs to be done in this area.

"Queens of Armed Robbery: Short-lived All Female Gang"

An example of a small all-female gang that specialized in armed robbery demonstrates that all-female gangs can exist and can be involved in violent crime. This particular example, though, is rare.

Four girls made up the gang called the "Queens of Armed Robbery". They came from an affluent suburb of Houston, Texas. Their gang behavior: armed robbery, no graffiti, just armed robberies, typically convenience stores. The girls were linked to at least five different robberies during the summer of 1999.

Two of the girls (both 17 years old), Lisa Warzeka and Katie Dunn, were sentenced to 7 year prison terms for their role in the armed robberies.

SOURCE: "Texas: Girl Gang Members Get 7-Year Terms for Store Robberies", Chicago Tribune, Jan. 29, 2000, Section 1, p. 10.

BURNING OUT: Slowing Disengaging From Gang Life As Some Approach Adulthood.

A number qualitative interviews with female gang members have shown this type of scenario. The basic situation was that of where the female gang member of a larger male dominated gang, usually a very structured criminal gang, slowly disengages from the gangs routine activities. The end result is the ex-gang member or what could also be called the inactive gang member. Some simply "grow out of it", their affiliation with the gang was contextually centered, that is typically in a high school situation, so when they reach their early 20s, their social network changes, and they find themselves progressively avoiding the trouble that gang life provides.

Case #1: White Female Member of White Gang.

A white female gang member of the Simon City Royals, a predominantly white gang in Chicago, simply found herself hanging out with the gang less and less over time as she had to find a job, and pay her own bills. Quitting shortly after high school, re-locating to a new neighborhood, and not renewing high school contacts, she established an entirely new social network of friends and associates. She still has the gang tattoo, but it is on an area of the body not normally exposed in public. And so it is easy to simply act like she knows nothing about gangs and live a law abiding existence. Which is what she does. Gang life for her was a temporary adolescent fad, it had its value in high school, but it lost its value as she faced the need to seriously address how she was go-ing to fit into her society --- and pay the bills and the rent. She is today a highly responsible citizen, who works like anyone else for a living at ordinary jobs.

Case #2: African-American female member of the Gangster Disciples.

An African-American female member of the Gangster Disciples provides another example of this disengagement theory about severing ties to the gang. This person began to sever the ties to the gang at the time she enrolled as a student in university. By the time she had graduated she still lived in the area where she grew up, but she no longer was active in gang life on the streets. In fact, she had thought that she was completely out of the gang until one night in 1993 some Gangster Disciples came to her house. While she still lived on the southside, she had moved and did not think her gang knew where she lived. But they appeared at her door one night and handed her a petition and basically ordered her to sign the petition. The petition was that being circulated in the Chicago area, which ultimately had over 5,000 names on it, demanding that the Illinois Prisoner Review Board (i.e., the parole board) grant Larry Hoover (their gang leader) a parole because he was now rehabilitated.

The Gangster Disciples are and always have been male dominated. We can demonstrate this by examining the infrastructure of the Gangster Disciples below. This particular chain of command was ana-lyzed and created by someone in law enforcement. The author has not been able to verify how accurate the list is currently, as this gang as all others are open-systems, and do change, gang members particularly gang leaders are killed routinely. So it has not been completely updated. But using it as a basis for rou-tine interviews with gang members including high ranking members, does suggest it is accurate.

Gangster Disciples Chain of Command[6]

Larry Hoover
"King Larry"
IR # 190647
CHAIRMAN OF THE BOARD

ASSISTANT CHAIRMAN: Melvin Haywood, "Head".

BOARD MEMBERS: Leon Bolton, "Bo Diddley", IR # 2692948; Duffy Clark, "Guy", IR # 257920; Ernest Wilson, "Smokey", IR # 255775; Robert Dordles, "Coal Black", IR # 385784; Vincent Gallo-way, "Legs Diamond", IR # 342983; Robert Lowe, "Big Lowe", IR # 181344; Michael Scott, "Speedy", IR # 362031; Henry Griffin, "Money", IR # 10010; Charles Harris, "Sundown", IR # 472523; Gregory Sharpe, "G Sharpe", IR # 289496; Jeffery Hatcher, IR # 295827; Ernest Hope, "Junior", IR # 141819; Michael Smith, "Michael G.", IR # 369474; Kirk Williams, IR # 510708; Andrew Howard, "Dee Dee", IR # 69789; Michael Johnson, "Pair a Dice", IR # 269463; Gregory Shell, "Shorty G", IR # 704666; Carey Smith Jr., "Lucky G", IR # 112018.

FINANCE AND COMMUNICATIONS: Lucy Kemper, IR # 29623; Bertha Mosby, IR # 393682; Stephanie Powe, #IR # 827544; Johnny Jackson, IR # 899836; Miranda Goodloe, IR # 132030.

GOVERNORS AND AREA COORDINATORS: Dontay Banks, "Dirk", IR # 786407; Michael Baptiste, "Bap / White Mike", IR # 343836; Dave Smith, "Heavy D", IR # 640147; William Baptiste, IR # 624366; Victor Thompson, IR # 582181; Darryl Brent, "Pee Wee", IR # 350360; Willis Richardson, "Dollar Bill", IR # 605286; Samuel Bryant, "Big Wayne", IR # 509590; William Edwards, "Too Short", IR # 887190; Antoine Stewart, "Magellan", IR # 597036; Alexander Faulloner, "Champagne Black", IR # 562872; Delano E. Finch, "Trouble", IR # 901570; Ricky Harris, "Slick Rick", IR # 668316; Dan Wesson, "Dan Tanna", IR # 431704; Darryl Johnson, "Pops", IR # 672416; Tommy Lon-don, IR # 739111; Lamont O. Mattick, "G Money", IR # 865244; Terry McClinton, IR #752581.

REGENTS/STREET ENFORCERS: Robert Berry, "Renegade", IR # 633222; Eddie Clark, IR # 930027; Johnny Walker, IR # 680305; Kevin Reed, IR # 952171; Arthur Jones, IR # 821482; Darnell Thames, IR # 872922; Kyle Dunqy, IR # 558602; Vincent Martin, "Peanut", IR # 404140; Michael Mason, "Midnight", IR #834077; John Williams, IR # 376872.

Clearly, there are few females in this command structure. Where the female gang members are concentrated are in the finance and communications area. The leaders, then, are primarily males. Returning now to the case study, this particular former female member reported that she basically had to sign to petition. She had no choice, the gang members knew who she was and simply told her to sign the petition. When she explained this situation to me, she was obviously somewhat frightened and now alarmed that the gang had discovered her again. She had effectively avoided the gang for several years and was on the verge of graduating from the university and going on the establish a normal American career.

She did decide at this point, however, to move far from the community she grew up in. She did not want to be surprised again by a knock on the door and find herself facing the same gang associates she had grown up with. As a postscript to this case study, I had realized that the petition would represent a legitimate source for gang research, therefore on May 9th, 1994 I did make a Freedom of Information Act request for the full petition containing all names and pages. A month later, no results, so I made the same request again by registered mail to several officials. Then I was told that because the petition was not needed any longer, now that the parole hearing was over, that the petition and all its contents had been destroyed, that is discarded. The full truth here may never be known. Was it really destroyed? And if so why? We could not afford an attorney to challenge the agency in court to comply with the Freedom of Information Act, so it must remain a mystery until someone else examines the issue. We did view it as a goldmine for gang research because it might be one case where gang members actually gave their true and correct names and addresses --- for if they did not, and they belonged to the gang, they could certainly count on stiff sanctions from their own gang, that is a "violation". But the fact remains, the agency through its staff reported to us verbally that they had disposed of the petition and thus could not comply the FOIA.

Case #3: Female Associate of Latin Gang.
This case shows the classic situation of being dually integrated at a high level into conventional society and into the subculture, a kind of marginal adaptation. She prefers the Barrio life even now as she is capable of moving out and starting a professional career. Why? Because that is where she grew up and has many friends there. She was able to basically leave the gang alone, and to this day remains friendly with them, because they are part of the very fabric of the Hispanic Chicago community she lives in. She still knows the gang members, and the gang leaders, and has family members in the gang. She is

not, however, likely to be active in any gang criminal operation nor involved in its street life. She is, however, cordial to the homies. And has simply been able to disengage over a period of years while working and attending college, a period of time that corresponded to her own maturation and entry into young adulthood. Not uncommon, she has no arrest record and plans to work in the criminal justice system. She would like to work, in fact, for the FBI now that she is a college graduate and considering going to law school.

She was not sure what she would do when I posed the moral dilemma to her as follows: she graduates from law school, still lives in the same area, and because of her language and cultural skills she is assigned as a new FBI agent to investigate and develop indictments on her own brother who is a local leader of this particular chapter of the Latin Kings. It was not possible for her to tell me precisely what she would do. She was in a quandary over this moral dilemma situation. Being a part of both worlds, the non-gang and the gang life, this situation describes a number of persons who are able to do a fine balancing act: having close ties with the gang world, and the "straight" world. But not unlike the undercover vice detective immersed in a deep cover investigation, they take on language and habits that expose them systematically to personal risks. It is the marginal adaptation: and the lure of the subculture is addictive, and sometimes deadly.

In the Hispanic and Latino gang structure, the culture is one of male domination. Female "members", or associates, are basically a supportive function, with some noted exceptions. The notable exceptions do capture front page newspaper headlines: such as the case in Chicago where two female gang members lured members of an opposing gang into a park late at night, under the pretense of romance, and then summarily executed the two rival male gang members with shots to the back of the head.

Female gang members do take the initiative in some situations. Female gang members are able to hold positions of rank in traditionally male-dominated gangs. Female gang members are able to at least feel as if they are treated equally, and "part of the family" by gangs that have mostly male leaders. Female gang members are able to get in a gang through means other than offering themselves as sexual objects, and to be "blessed" into the gang by having family members or others in high position who give them special status, or who simply decide to take their licks like the male counterparts in a "jumping in" type of ceremony. That is, the violence can be physical punishment or sexual in nature as a part of the initiation. Being the sexual object as a part of the initiation process can mean total humiliation by a variety of measures: including shaking the dice to see how many members they will have to have sex with, or more usually having to submit to any and all sexual acts desired by anyone present at the initiation ceremony. It is less status-enhancing to a career in gang life for a female member to opt for the sexual object version of gang initiation. It is more status-enhancing to a career in gang life for a female member to want to be jumped in or who is willing to make her bones in a retaliatory attack on an opposition gang (i.e., a gang drive-by shooting, etc).

Female gang members do congregate and create a critical mass in public conflicts just as do their male gang member counterparts. Still there is something very unique about the female gang member that deserves further analysis --- motherhood.

> **"The Tabula Rasa Treatment Program for Female Gang Members"**
> The study by Ernest M. De Zolt, Linda M. Schmidt, and Donna C. Gilcher ("The 'Tabula Rasa' Intervention Project for Delinquent Gang-Involved Females", Journal of Gang Research, Vol. 3, No. 3, Spring, 1996: 37-43) described a promising program for female gang members in Cleveland that grew out of a reported 22 percent increase in female delinquency. The project involved a "rites of passage" approach that included: an educational component, a "wellness" component, and a job skills or vocational component. Thus, tutoring and mentoring were part of this holistic approach. It included bi-weekly group counseling by a licensed psychologist as well.

A GANG MOTHER RAISING HER CHILDREN AS GANG MEMBERS

It happens more often than many would suspect. Young mothers active in the gang and having children, raising them from infancy on how to properly show their gang signs and the like. The fact is our current laws do not define raising a child to be a gang member as a crime or even as constituting child abuse. The fact is that white extremist gangs routinely raise their children in the same doctrine of hate and this is also not defined anywhere in America as a crime or as a prima facie case of child abuse. The sadder fact remains that in spite of the many agencies designed to protect the rights of children and the public of children throughout our federal and state government bureaucracies, we have no idea of how pervasive this problem may be, nor what it may portend for the future.

The astute reader must recall the history of this issue of the moral awakening of American society. Up until the 1970s in some parts of America child abuse as a crime was limited to unique situations where the child was admitted to the emergency room with multiple bone fractures. Today, obviously,

a lower standard of "proof" of child abuse exists. It was not until the 1980s that we saw actual criminal laws appear defining "hate crimes" or "bias crimes" in America. Obviously, this does not mean that it America only had criminal child abuse until after the 1970s, or that we only had bias crimes until after the 1980s; what this means is that it took us this long to get laws passed reflecting the moral consensus of Americans. We still have a very long way to go to get our policy makers and our law makers serving the best interests of the American child today.

Should mothers who raise their kids to be gang members lose their rights of being responsible parents? That is, should there be a law enabling the public guardian of any community to take custody of such a child and put the child up for adoption or in foster or group homes until it an adult? Or is it an inalienable right of any parent to raise their child to be a racist or klansman? And what of the rights of the children involved here? Do they have any rights? And how do we weigh these against the rights of the parents and the public?

ABUSE OF FEMALE GANG MEMBERS BY MALE MEMBERS

This scenario has many variations, and is well documented, painting the picture of the traditional exploitative relationships that male gang leaders have over female members. Many were shocked to hear the case in Texas where two adolescent females were required to have sex with what they were told was an HIV positive gang member as a mandatory part of their initiation ceremony into the gang, for which they did comply. Other cases of violence against female members emerge when the female member is suspected of "knowing too much" about the gang, particularly its criminal operations, at which point the female member becomes a liability to the male gang leaders and she is executed. The case of Yummy is similar to this scenario, he knew too much too, and was executed by his own gang before he could talk.

One particularly brutal case of violence was in the case of 20-year-old Kristin Ponquinette, a high school graduate, and the daughter of the school superintendent in Aurora, Illinois. In this case, Ponquinette had simply been a wannabe, hanging out with lower level gang members. She witnessed the gang business operations, became sexually involved with some of the male gang members, and after a confrontation with jealous female members of the gang, she was targeted for execution[7]. This execution was described thusly:

"On April 17, 1992, according to testimony in the trials, Mobley's gang tied and gagged Kristin Ponquinette in a basement garage, threatened her with a chain saw, chopped off her hair, beat her and locked her in a closet.

Then they led her to a railroad bridge at 127th Street and Eggleston Avenue, where they smashed her over the head with a chunk of cement, wired a manhole cover to her feet and threw her into the Cal-Sag Channel.

The body eventually broke loose from the manhole cover and was found floating miles downstream in Alsip nine days later by a Coast Guard boat".[8]

"Females Represent About Six Percent of the Gang Problem"

The study by George T. Felkenes and Harold K. Becker ("Female Gang Members: A Growing Issue for Policy Makers", <u>Journal of Gang Research</u>, Vol. 2, No. 4, Summer, 1995: 1-10) noted that "gang membership is predominantly male-oriented, 94 percent male and 6 percent female" (p. 5). Their study provided insight into Hispanic female gang members in the Los Angeles area.

Among other findings, the research noted: (1) female were more likely to want to be successful in life, (2) over half (61.1%) were from a two-parent family, (3) two-fifths (41.2%) had dropped out of school, and (4) while most believed in God (91%), only 18.4 percent attended church regularly.

VIOLENCE AGAINST THE FAMILIES OF GANG MEMBERS

This is another common scenario, particularly with level three gangs that recruit children. The youths find out that once in the gang, it is very hard to get out, in fact they simply try to slip away. But the gang knows where they live, and shows up looking for the kid. In one recent case, the kid was not at home, so when the gang members broke in, they simply shot his parents instead.

For female gang members who like in the case above, try to avoid taking their "outing" or violation for leaving the gang, that is a physical beating in a ritual ceremony, the same result happens to them as happens to male members. They will be targeted for worse violence. This happened in the case of 15-year-old Connie Ayala in Elgin, Illinois, where the gang put out an S.O.S. (Slaughter On Sight) order on her for not taking her beating to get out of the gang. Then one day on the street with her aunt, Connie was again attacked by female members of the gang, who ended up stabbing the aunt.[9]

Gang members present a collateral risk to anyone who associates with them; this includes everyone, police officers simply standing by gang members on the street, kids who just hang with gang members, and in cases involving dating with gang members. In June, 1992 Victor Garcia, age 17, was convinced that he could join the gang if the gang could have sex with his girlfriend. Garcia agreed with this unique arrangement for his gang initiation ceremony in Chicago. The girl was subsequently lured to a party where the gang members lay in wait. She was then physically assaulted and repeatedly raped by four gang members until the following day when she was let go.[10]

PART III: THE RIGHTS OF AMERICAN CHILDREN AND GANGS WHO WANT THEM

The incontrovertible and historically documented argument that exists across all cultures and is that a society is civilized to the extent to which it protects and provides for the nurturing of its young. Even wild animals protect and safeguard their young. But in America today, a parent has a right to be a bad parent, and parents generally want to deny responsibility for the acts of their underage children.

How then do we reconcile this cultural universal with the fact that no where in American society today will we find that it is against the law for adult gang leaders to systematically corrupt innocent children by attracting them and allowing them to join the gang? Our lack of any such laws stand in stark contrast to many other criminal codes that provide stiff sanctions for crimes against children --- harsher penalties for violence against, and the sexual exploitation of, children are now common place in all fifty states and the federal criminal code as well. Simple possession of child pornography can result in an automatic prison sentence. This type of law reflects the moral awakening of a society and its attempts to overcome the sexual exploitation of children.

But what laws do we have to prevent, even monitor, the gang exploitation of children? We have none. We have had laws dating back over twenty years making it a crime to "conscript" a person into the gang. This is also known as compelling gang membership. It means the person must join because they were intimidated to do so. But we do not have a single law, to the knowledge of the present author, which holds any adult gang leader accountable for systematically corrupting the values of the underage members, the children not of legal age, who become the new cannon fodder of almost every criminal gang in America today.

The highly trained gang expert knows that there is only one way to effectively suppress gangs in a society like our own: viewing the gang as an open-system, and counteracting on its ability to attract new members. The new members are always children. Underage teens and pre-teens. Adolescents. Even infants. A gang that cannot attract new members is a gang that will not survive, because as an open-system it will lose members by defection, death, and imprisonment.

American society makes it easy for a gang to flourish today. How? By enabling the gang to freely recruit new gang members from the ranks of American children at no legal risk --- civil or criminal. Some of the only statutes on the books in many jurisdictions are traditional "contributing to the delinquency of a child" laws. These are not easy to prove, and often have weak punishments (i.e., misdemeanor offenses typically). In this regard American gangs are proliferating and evil is triumphing because good citizens did nothing: nothing to protect the rights of children.

A child like "Yummy" is a case in point. This Chicago case gained instant international attention in 1994, when "Yummy" a member of the Black Disciples, only eleven years old, was executed by his own gang for fear that he may testify against others in a gang-related killing. Yummy typifies how American society really looks after the rights of children. Those government agencies that are chartered "in the best interests of the child" allowed this eleven year old, and many more just like him of all ethnic groups in many places in America today, to basically fall through the cracks of public interests.

YUMMY: Executed At Age 11 By His Own Gang.

Robert Sandifer's gang name was "Yummy", because he loved to eat cookies. As a member of the Black Disciples gang, the BDs', he was "folks". But the BD's often fight with the GD's on the streets. In jail and behind bars they will routinely "group up" in a mutual assistance pact, to discourage attacks from their mutual enemies the "peoples" or "brothers" among African-American members of the Peoples gangs (Black P. Stones, Vice Lords, etc). Yummy hand a long criminal record at the time of his death, even though he died violently at the age of 11. A lot of newspapers and television news programs in the USA and abroad described the story of Yummy. A lot of versions of this story exist. It was the cover story in Time magazine for September 19, 1994. It was front page news in many areas of the country, and it was also international news.

Yummy had his own extensive record of arrests and convictions, including robbery and arson, but he was also a victim of child neglect and child abuse. Yummy got his name from the gang he joined, the Black Disciples, for his love of cookies and other sweets. On August 28, 1994, perhaps seeking an elevation in rank or other rewards from his gang, Yummy opened fire with a weapon supplied by the gang to shoot at a gang rival, he wounded his target but not fatally, but a stray bullet fired by Yummy killed an innocent bystander, and a child named Shavon Dean became added to the mounting toll of innocent bystanders killed by gang warfare in Chicago. The police manhunt ensued, the heat was on the gang,

and the gang did what was expedient: they executed Yummy in a dark underpass.[11] This is not uncommon for a gang to protect itself, for if Yummy talked, older adult leaders would be implicated. The gang had been hiding Yummy during the manhunt, so when it came time to execute him, they simply conned him into thinking that a car was waiting at the other end of the tunnel to take him out of state. Yummy entered the tunnel and was carried out by the coroner. Another expendable child used as cannon fodder by American gangs is the statistic Yummy represents, lured into the gang with candy money from gang business, manipulated as a young gang member, and then simply eliminated when by accidentally shooting an innocent victim he changed from an asset to a liability.

SUMMARY AND CONCLUSION

The gang attracts female gang members who have a history of abuse and abuses them further is what our data suggests. There are exceptions, but generally gang life for female members continues to pattern itself after an exploitive pattern of male chauvinism rather than providing genuine equal opportunity across gender lines. There are few female members in high command in level three gangs today, this remains a male business, open for female customers. At the high school level it is easy to find a significant difference by gender in the general population in terms of who has or who has not joined a gang: males predominate. However, our evidence from juvenile correctional populations using the confined juvenile as the unit of analysis, that is surveying these confined children themselves, revealed in a 1991 study of nearly two thousand detained juveniles that no significant difference existed in terms of the proportion who were gang members by gender. That is, inside juvenile institutions, when we ask the youths confined there if they have ever joined a gang, we will not find the difference we find in high schools out in larger society. What we will find in juvenile institutions when we ask the children themselves if they have ever joined a gang is convergence: about half of all males and females admit to such gang membership.

There are a number of factors that significantly differentiate the non-gang member from the gang member among female students surveyed in Chicago is also a major finding from this chapter. The female gang member profile is consistent with the hardening effect found among gang members generally: having been exposed to trauma, the person produces more trauma, and the cycle continues to play itself out. It is rare to have a happy ending to such a cycle, it is more likely one preprogrammed for a casualty in the making. So it is not uncommon that the cycle ends in the death of the player, or a long prison sentence.

Much more research is needed on female gang members and on very young gang members as what we have here appears to be the crime within a crime: the systematic exploitation of persons by criminal gangs. Crimes that never get reported because there is no one to report them too without great immediate danger. Your author has used some rather harsh language in this chapter, particularly calling the body of laws we call our own legal statutes as a fallacy when it comes to the protection of the rights of children. I shall not apologize for this slight against our policy makers until there are no more Yummy's and no more incentives for the adult gang leaders to use our Nation's children to do their bidding. We cannot continue with our head in the sand like an ostrich in this matter. Gangs are using children. We need to wise up.

Imagine, for a moment, that you were in the following scenario. You are a young student in a public school. Your principal and teachers routinely escort you and all the other students to the auditorium for another lecture on good citizenship. This time you hear a group of well dressed men addressing you in the audience of other school children and all the teachers, these men are surrounded by cameras and therefore obviously very important persons as well. The men tell you they represent a group called Truth Heals Urban Groups, they make speeches, everyone applauds. They hand out awards, and everyone is attentive. They do not hand out membership applications for their group, but would you consider joining too given that these men were so important that they commanded the respect and admiration of the principal and all other school staff, plus government elected officials, and others who appeared to be dignitaries? You might, just as some kids might be swayed and influenced by such messages.

How then to we interpret what happened in a Chicago Public High school? Gangs grandstanding, showing they control school infrastructures, they have contacts in high places, and that they are an acceptable lifestyle for children? Or do we take the most logically extreme redemptive explanation: these were not gang members at all, sure some awards were given out to what the government calls gang members (King Larry Hoover, leader of the Gangster Disciples, and Willie Lloyd, leader of the Unknown Vice Lords), but you cannot believe the media and certainly not what the government says about them, for these leaders claim to be doing something good for the community, and if they say they have had a change of heart, well then we should have an open heart and listen to them, right? Wrong. You forgot about the children.

You might have that right to extend any amount of forgiveness you want to a gang leader, you might have that right to forgive by the book, the Great Book, 70 times 7, and then realize that the gang leader only has committed and been convicted of 489 crimes....so he should still be forgiven even if you were the victim of all of these offenses; you have that individual right to act upon whatever moral beliefs you want to believe in. But you do not have the right to communicate to children that gang members run the school, and that gang activists are such important people that the children begin to believe that what their parents may have said about gangs is all a lie, that joining a gang could be a good thing, they are not thugs, they are a group committed to the idea that Truth Heals Urban Groups or any other such non-sense that a cult or a gang might come up with.

The awards ceremony held in a Chicago public high school in October of 1993 was exactly as given in the scenario above. The students heard about a group called Growth and Development, and teachers reported that afterwards some students who had not been gang members now wanted to join that gang[12]. Some 2,500 persons were in the assembly at the school auditorium, a lot of gang activists and all the school children, when two well known top gang leaders each received an award.[13] If you were attending that school and shortly after joined the honored gang, then would your parents have a right to school the Chicago Public School system for facilitating not your educational growth and development but your membership in the Gangster Disciple gang?

Some gangs still continue today to conscript young children with the simple message: "join or die".[14] The more common pattern is covert recruitment: the child is systematically cultivated, or "courted" as the gangs say, allowing the youth to come with on trips, and to parties, eventually growing closer and closer to a new group of "friends", until one day sometime early after gaining complete membership by an often violent ritual ceremony, the youth learns these are not friends at all, and it is very hard to actually quit. The enormous fear that gangs have instilled in children across our country has children now thinking about and planning their own funerals, kids fantasizing about what color patterns they want on their caskets.[15] And few if any legal penalties await the adult gang leaders who benefit from the young new recruits who systematically replenish the membership base of gangs throughout the United States today. How many kids do we have bury, killed from gang violence, until we consider the rights of these children? What will it take to wake up complacent adults and have them recognize that their children have the right to live free from gang recruitment, indeed gang recruitment so systematic in some cases that it can include proselytizing the entire school assembly? The rights of children to live free from the fear of gang violence remains one of the most important and most neglected issues in the current debate about the gang problem in America today.

DISCUSSION QUESTIONS:

(1) In English literature, the older cunning criminal Fagin who used young hungry street children to steal and pickpocket on his behalf is actually a cultural universal. With the ability of adult gang members to manipulate children, should much stiffer legal provisions be enacted, "Fagin laws" or "Yummy protection" laws, whatever we want to call them? What language would you use in such a proposed amendment to your state criminal code? Write it and send it to your elected officials.

(2) Do you think that gangs attract alienated female members who may have a history of neglect and high risk behaviors, or do you think that the gang reinforces these traits?

(3) Is the violence that female gang members experience symptomatic of how women in general in our society are the targets of male violence? Does the gang simply provide a new vehicle by which to accomplish the exploitation of and violence against women?

FEMALE GANGS NATIONWIDE: RECENT RESEARCH FINDINGS

The 1996 National Law Enforcement Gang Analysis Survey carried out by the National Gang Crime Research Center included a strict random sample of N = 283 municipal police departments from 48 states.

Three-Fourths Report Female Involvement in Local Gangs

The survey asked "are females also involved in the gangs in your area". Some three-fourths (74.7%) of the respondents indicated that females were in fact also involved in the gangs in their local gangs. So, three out of four cities in America, regardless of size are reporting the presence of at least some female gang members in their jurisdiction.

A separate follow-up question asked "if yes, estimate what percentage of the total gang member population in your jurisdiction are females". The results ranged from as low as zero percent to 50 percent. But the mean, or average, was that 11.4 percent of the gang members nationally were females.

So if we assume that females, nationwide, constitute about 10 percent of the total American gang population, that gives 150,000 female gang members under the best assumption that the total existing American gang population in 1998 is 1.5 million.

END NOTES:

[1] The findings presented here are a part of a larger study of female gang membership. Currently, data collection on Hispanic, Caucasian, and Asian females has not been of appreciable size to warrant serious analysis. Such research will continue to examine the same issues with other ethnic groups. The present analysis, however, is limited to African-American females.

[2] The analysis reported here, again, is restricted to one "folks" gangs. The Black Gangster Disciples, B.O.S., is the largest such gang in Chicago in terms of actual gang membership. In the summer of 1993, some 10,000 persons attended a "picnic" sponsored by the political arm of this group (21st Century Vote). Other and similar data on various other factions of "folks" and "Brothers" gangs (Black P. Stone Nation, Vice Lords, etc), or what has traditionally been regarded as "Peoples" gangs (Peoples and Brothers are used interchangeably, with the latter being the current and politically correct referent for African-American gangs), like the Latin Kings. The sample sizes for "Brothers" or "Peoples" gangs were not large enough at the time of this writing to warrant in-depth analysis; nor of comparisons between such gang nation affiliations.

[3] I am grateful to a large number of research assistants who helped at various stages of this project. Usually, this meant having at least one university student assist by being trained in the administration of the anonymous survey, and standing by in each of the classrooms to maintain the conditions of the research (no talking or sharing of responses, collecting the completed surveys, etc).

[4] The recent qualitative research by Laidler and Hunt (1997) showed that shoplifting, drug sales, and theft were the most common "hustles" or crime income sources of female gang members.

[5] See: Results of the 1994 Illinois Law Enforcement Survey: A Preliminary Report on Gang Migration and Other Gang Problems in Illinois Today. A Task Force Report of the National Gang Crime Research Center. Co-Principle Investigators: George W. Knox; Thomas F. McCurrie; James G. Houston; Edward D. Tromanhauser; John A. Laskey. March 31, 1994.

[6] Note: When first published, somewhat before the federal indictment and trial of Larry Hoover and 38 of his top gang leaders, this list was accurate. Since the time of the prosecution and conviction of the 39 GDs, including Larry Hoover, the "organizational chart" has changed somewhat as one might expect.

[7] See: Cameron McWhirter, "Gang Member Convicted of Drowning Aurora Woman", Chicago Tribune, Jan. 11, 1994, section 2, p. 2.

[8] See: Tom Pelton, "Gang Leader Guilty in Woman's Murder", Chicago Tribune, June 17, 1994, Section

2, p. 6.

[9]See: "For Ex-Gang Members, Violence Hasn't Stopped", Chicago Sun-Times, Aug. 22, 1994, p. 17.

[10]See the commentary on how this overlaps with the gang true issue by: Richard Roeper, "Here's Your Chance, Gang Peacemakers", Chicago Sun-Times, Nov. 10, 1993, p. 11.

[11]The underpass was marked with gang graffiti and the lights in the tunnel did not work. After the killing of Yummy there, the lights were immediately fixed and the walls were immediately painted.

[12]See: John Kass and George Papajohn, "High School Role in Gang Summit Hit", Chicago Tribune, Section 2, pp.1-2, Oct. 27, 1993.

[13]See: Lee Bey, "Principal: I Don't Favor Gang Honors", Chicago Sun-Times, Oct. 28, 1993, p. 3.

[14]See: Tamara Kerrill, "Pilsen Teenagers March to Reclaim Turf From Gangs", Chicago Sun-Times, May 2, 1994, p. 16.

[15]See: "Black Youths Tell How Gangs And Guns Have Them Planning Their Own Funerals", Jet, Jan. 31, 1994, pp. 26-28.

Aryan Nation

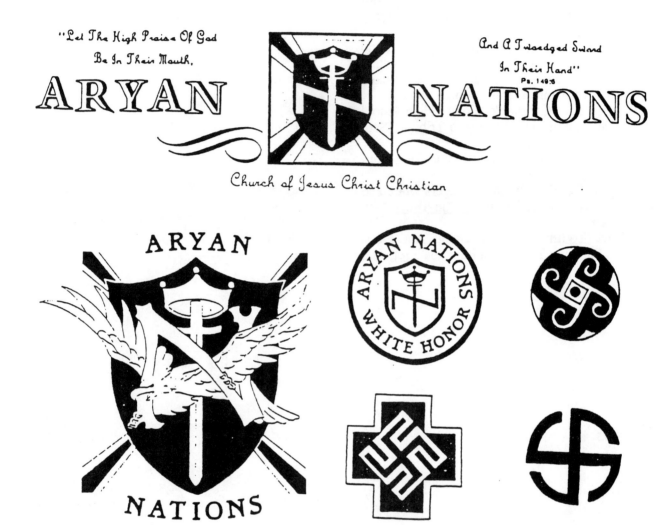

Operating behind the cloak of "Christian Identity", some white extremist groups gain greater protection (i.e., constitutional protections) by operating as a "religion". Not surprisingly, the Aryan Nation is very aggressive at "proselytizing", i.e., attempting to gain new members. This is a national organization with many "chapters" or "factions", official and unofficial. It is a group that is particularly supportive of any SKINHEAD who is also a white racist. The "Church of Jesus Christ Christian" has its national HQ in Hayden Lake, Idaho (PO Box 362, 83835). What are their beliefs: anything that neo-nazis believe, they probably believe: (1) the USA is "run" by Jews in an international conspiracy, (2) Blacks and other minorities get preferential treatment at the cost of whites , (3) race mixing is a bad idea, (4) the WW II "Holocaust" was a "myth", etc. So they do not like Jews and most racial and ethnic minorities. Like the KKK they sell a lot of "paraphernalia" to anyone who will buy it.

CHAPTER 19

ASIAN GANGS

INTRODUCTION

This chapter is divided into two parts. Part I explores some general issues about Asian gangs. Part II provides an actual test of some of these issues.

Part I: General Issues About Asian Gangs.

The purpose of this section is to briefly cover some recent research findings on Asian gang activity in the United States. The research projects described here were those organized and carried out by the National Gang Crime Research Center (NGCRC). The NGCRC has sought to improve the knowledge base about gangs since 1990, publishes the Journal of Gang Research now in its eighth volume, and is currently based in Chicago.

Specifically, the thesis will be argued that: (1) the Asian gang problem is small in comparison with the overall gang problem, (2) much of our research suggests there is little that is unique about Asian gangs or Asian gang members, (3) a strong homogenizing influence exists today so it is not uncommon to find Asian gangs allied with Crip/Folk or Blood/People gangs, and (4) most Asian gang members apparently do not belong to "Asian" gangs.

THE ASIAN GANG PROBLEM PALES IN COMPARISON WITH THE OVERALL NATIONAL GANG PROBLEM

This is a comparative declaration. Overall, in the United States today about two-thirds of all cities, large or small, currently report a gang problem of some level. However, only about a fourth of all American cities report any Asian gangs or Asian gang members have been active in their jurisdiction. Let us explain the importance of this basic trend.

All ethnic groups in America at one time or another have had gang involvement. Ethnicity is related to gangs in several important ways: (1) racism provides both a "fuel" for gang conflict and for gang formation, (2) newly arrived immigrant groups in the Shaw and McKay tradition have often faced some level of social disorganization that contributes toward youth gang involvement, and (3) ethnicity and race can be an organizing principle for a gang's collective identity. Please refer to the issue of the historical continuity of racial conflict earlier in this book, for additional information.

Those who work in law enforcement must study the gang, learn to read or learn to bleed, and be able to "decipher" the meaning of gang slang, its subcultural argot, and unique verbal expressions used by the gang in its extensive and very symbolic language system.

Gangs learn from each other, they mimic and replicate "what works" for each other, and they do this most effectively once they have been inside the criminal justice system of the United States where they are afforded a great many statutory and constitutional rights. They copy each other's "organizational structure": if one gang develops a written constitution and by-laws, the other gang quickly follows. If one gang develops a written code of conduct, or written rules for its members to ensure greater discipline and cohesiveness among the membership, other gangs follow and replicate this trend. If one gang develops an icon, the other gangs quickly follow. They learn from each other in much the same way that Sutherland first advanced in his theory of differential association. The lay or non-professional public have simply called this same phenomenon: "monkey see, monkey do". Others who have tried to raise the issue to greater abstraction have called it the contagion effect: the copycat phenomenon.

MOST ASIAN GANG MEMBERS DO NOT BELONG TO "ASIAN" GANGS

The 1995 study of nearly 2,000 self-reported gang members in eight states (see Project GANGPINT, 1995) contained N = 160 Asian or Chinese respondents. Some N = 99 (61.9%) were gang members. The high density comes from the fact that the research intentionally sought to survey "high density" social contexts (jails, boot camps, juvenile detention centers, juvenile correctional institutions, alternative high schools, etc).

There were Asian gang members who did belong to well known Asian gangs. These Asian gangs included: Wah Ching, the Tiny Rascal Gang, Pinoy Real, Black Dragons, Red Door, Oriental Boys, Asian Boys, and the Asian Dragons. These gangs clearly identified as "Asian" gangs accounted for only 20.8 percent of the gangs to which these Asian gang members belonged. A long list of Crip and Blood sets, as well as People (Vice Lord, Latin King, etc) and Folks (Gangster Disciples, Two-Sixers, etc) gangs, constituted the bulk of the gangs to which the Asian gang members belonged to.

We interpret this finding as another "fact" any researcher can test empirically, but one that supports the thesis of homogenizing influences on Asian gang members. We argue, further, that it is a normal process for Asian members to exist as members in gangs not thought of as "Asian gangs". There is a strong and growing tendency for gangs to exhibit ethnic diversity.

We will test this hypothesis again in the new and larger 1996 gang research (Project GANGFACT, 1996). However, if what we have found here so far is in fact true, then this has much import for the validity of some methodological approaches to the study of Asian gangs. Those studying Asian gangs by qualitative or other techniques will have limited generalizability by being relevant only to Asian gangs, and not to most Asian gang members. It appears that most Asian gang members do not really belong to what most would regard as "Asian gangs".

SUMMARY AND DISCUSSION OF FINDINGS

Asked to address Asian gang issues, we went back to some of our recent research to perform additional analysis that was perhaps not included in previous reports. Our research strategy has always been the larger gang problem, and not one limited to Asian gangs or even Asian gang members. However, we did learn some important lessons from examining Asian gang issues. It is important to summarize these here.

(1) While two-thirds of all cities in the U.S. today report some degree of a gang problem, clearly the problem posed by Asian gangs or Asian gang members is less substantial. Only a fourth of American cities are reporting a problem of Asian gangs or Asian gang members being active in their jurisdiction.

(2) Most Asian gang members simply do not belong to "Asian gangs". While additional research is now underway to provide another test of this concept, it appears that only about a fifth of Asian or Chinese gang members actually belong to what might be regarded as "Asian" gangs. The vast majority belong to more integrated gangs.

(3) It seems untenable to claim much that is "unique" about Asian gangs. While it is not hard to find differences in the general population analysis comparing Asian citizens with non-Asian citizens (Song, Dombrink, Geis, 1992), a strong homogenizing influence exists that impacts on gang life in the United States today. The result is remarkable similarity between gangs and gang members for a large number of variables. We continue to hear experts express the opinion that certain crimes (home invasion, kidnapping, extortion, etc) are peculiar to Asian gangs. This is simply not true. A number of works report on the activities of organized crime figures (Irish, Jewish, Italian, etc) and their involvement in these and whatever other crimes it takes to make money (Mustain and Capeci, 1988; Lacey, 1991; Touhy, 1959; Roemer, 1995).

Part II: ASIAN GANG MEMBERS: A Risk Profile Common to Student of Other Ethnic and Racial Groups

INTRODUCTION

A number of previous gang studies have involved surveys of school students (Tromanhauser, 1981; Morash, 1983; Rosenbaum and Grant, 1983; Spergel and Curry, 1990; Fagan, 1990; Thompson and Jason, 1988; Schwartz, 1989; Sherer, 1990; Takata and Zevitz, 1990; Bastian and Taylor, 1991). Missing from this prior literature, however, is research that specifically focuses on the Asian student population. The research reported here seeks to examine some contemporary gang concepts using data from a national sample of Asian students.

DERIVING HYPOTHESES FROM THE LITERATURE

While Asian gangs are portrayed in the mass media as a major threat and new menace to American society[2], Ko-Lin Chin (1990: p. 130) estimates no more than 2,000 Chinese members nationwide; further, that Chinese gangs recruit "vulnerable youths...those who are not doing well in school or who have already dropped out (p. 134)." Most importantly, Chin describes how Chinese gangs are portrayed as significantly different than other ethnic gangs (p. 136) and portrays unique aspects of the Chinese gang organization, its income, investment in legitimate business, and extortion. All the present research can do is speak to whether Asian students as gang members show a different trend than that of their white, Black, and Hispanic counterparts.

Both the works of Chin (1990) and that by Vigil and Yun (1990) assert that students with high academic achievement have a lower risk of gang affiliation. The proposition that Asian youths who experience low achievement in terms of grades in school and who come to be labelled through the school disciplinary system are those who are more likely to join and be involved with gangs has, however, not been empirically tested. The present research addresses this and other issues.

Much of the research literature about gangs can be reduced to three dependent variables for which explanations are sought: (1) why gangs arise, (2) why persons join gangs, and (3) why gang members behave the way they do. Why gangs arise, or the etiology of gangs, is exemplified in the early work of Thrasher (1927), the social disorganization theory of Shaw and McKay (1942), and perhaps even the racism-oppression thesis (Knox, 1991). Other theories are best at explaining why persons join gangs as in the subcultural approach of Cohen (1955), Yablonsky's (1962) sociopathy approach, Stinchcombe's (1964) articulation hypothesis and the

Cloward and Ohlin (1960) opportunity approach. Finally, some theories specifically focus on explaining specific gang behavior such as violence, fighting, and drug abuse (Short and Strodtbeck, 1965; Sanchez-Jankowski, 1991; Fagan, 1990).

The research reported here sought to test the hypotheses in Figure 19. The issue is whether these hypotheses, most of which are based on traditional gang concepts, still hold value for explaining aspects of the gang problem among Asian students.

FIGURE 19
AUTHOR(S), CONCEPTS, AND HYPOTHESES ABOUT GANGS

Author(s)	Concept	Hypothesis
Cohen (1955)	Subculture: Belief in "good luck".	The higher the belief in good luck, the more likely the gang affiliation.
Stinchecomb (1964)	Articulation Hypothesis	The higher the articulation of present education for future value, the less likely the gang affiliation.
Vigil and Yun (1990)	Asian Pragmatism	Asian gangs (e.g., Vietnamese) are less likely to engage in "persistent fighting that characterizes African-American and Chicano gangs" (Huff, 1990: p. 158).
Chin (1990)	Vulnerability Factor	The higher the academic failure, the higher the gang affiliation.
Sanchez-Jankowski (1991)	Defiant-Individualist Character	As gang members have this defiant individualist character, they are more likely than their non-gang member counterparts to report a higher level of fighting and involvement in violence.
Cloward and Ohlin (1960)	Legitimate Opportunity	The higher the legitimate employment and income, the lower the gang affiliation.
Knox (1991)	Self-esteem[3]	The higher the self-esteem, the lower the gang affiliation.
	Internal-locus of control	The higher the internal locus of control, the lower the gang affiliation.
Yablonsky (1962)	Paranoia	The higher the paranoia, the higher the gang affiliation.

METHODOLOGY

The Asian student survey used here was the result of a probono research project conducted by the National Gang Crime Research Center for the National Association for Asian and Pacific American Education (NAAPAE). Asian teachers were identified who were teaching classes to predominantly Asian students. The selection of geographical sites was designed to stratify by size of the Asian population cluster and therefore the eight cities used reflect both large and small Asian communities. An officer in NAAPAE then called the selected Asian teachers (also members of the association) to secure their co-operation for data collection in the following sites: Aurora, Colorado; Minneapolis, Minnesota; Harvey, Louisiana; Tacoma, Washington; Kahului, Hawaii; New York City; Alhambra, California; and Rockville, Maryland[4].

In March of 1992 each of the target sites was sent several letters explaining the Asian student study and giving explicit written directions on how to collect the data. The sample size generated from this survey was 361 Asian students. The instrument used was an anonymous five page survey that was pre-tested earlier on Chicago students. For further analysis based on this national assessment of Asian gang members see Knox, Laske, and Tromanhauser's (1992) Schools Under Siege.

DEFINITION OF GANG

As described elsewhere (Knox, 1991) gangs vary by the nature of their social organization and the level of affiliation. The present author defines a gang as a group of persons who individually or collectively commit crime, or who as a group knowingly benefit from the crimes committed by its members, and where law violations persist over time. The present analysis does not use the gang as a social organization as its unit of analysis. It uses self-reported gang membership. Figure 20 shows a listing of the types of gangs that these Asian students self-reported joining. This is traditional self-report survey research. Some 15.7 percent of the Asian sample reported that they knew the names of the gangs active in their school[5]. It was not possible to control for the level of organizational sophistication or the level of membership involvement with the various gangs identified in this research.

INDEPENDENT VARIABLES: MEASURES USED FOR THE HYPOTHESIS TESTING

Three demographic measures were used to determine if variations existed with regard to the gang problem among Asian students: grade level, age, and sex.

To test implications from the work of Chin (1990) three dichotomous variables were used: (1) ever suspended from school, (2) ever had an in-school suspension, and (3) ever had an in-school detention. In addition to these measures of academic failure and labelling, another measure is also used: (4) high grades. High grades is recoded from the self-reported grade point average (GPA) to reflect a dichotomous variable: those with "A" or "B" grade point averages, versus those with lower GPA's.

The Stinchecombe (1964) articulation factor was operationalized here in terms of its career or em-ployment prospects. The articulation hypothesis argues that if students do not know what they will be doing after completing educational requirements they will be more likely to be gang active or at risk of joining a gang[6]. This work articulation factor is a dichotomous variable reflecting whether the students know what career or profession they will enter after completing their education.

The Cloward and Ohlin (1960) hypothesis includes two measures of legitimate opportunity. These are dichotomous variables reflecting: (1) whether the student has any full or part-time job, and (2) whether the student receives a regular allowance from the family.

The self-esteem measure is based on the full ten item scale by Rosenberg (1965). The internal-locus of control scale consists of five items taken from James (1957). The median score on these scales was used to group the sample into a dichotomous measure reflecting high or low values.

The Cohen (1955) subculture variable of "belief in good luck" is an item taken the internal-locus of control scale (James, 1957). The item asks the student to agree or disagree with the statement "when things are going well for me I consider it due only to a run of good luck."

Fighting behavior was used to test an implication of the Sanchez-Jankowski (1991) concept of the defiant character. This is a dichotomous variable reflecting whether the student has been in one or more physical fights during the last calendar year[7].

DEPENDENT VARIABLES: MEASURES USED FOR THE HYPOTHESIS TESTING

In some concept frameworks, due to temporal ordering differences, what some treat as an independent variable, others treat as a dependent variable. Some of these independent variables that can also be examined as dependent variables include: high grades (academic success), fighting behavior, knowledge of drug sales, having gang friends, and having drug abusing friends.

Ever joining a gang is a dichotomous variable (yes/no) and simply measures prior gang membership[8].

Ever being asked to join a gang (yes/no) is a related dichotomous measure of gang recruitment attempts.

Knowing the names of the gangs active at the school is a dichotomous variable (yes/no) that measures cognition of gang activity in the school.

DEMOGRAPHIC CHARACTERISTICS OF THE SAMPLE

The student sample included grades six through twelve and ages eleven through twenty-one. About a fifth (21.6%) were in grades six, seven and eight, with the rest distributed as follows: 15.2 percent in grade nine, 24.7 percent in grade ten, 18 percent in grade eleven, and 20.5 percent in grade twelve. Just under half (45.2%) were 15 years of age or less. The students are equivalent with regard to gender: 50 percent males, and 50 percent females.

Ethnicity and national origin showed the following distribution: 19.9 percent Chinese, 8 percent Japanese, 9.1 percent Pacific Islander, 0.3 percent Native Alaskan, 11.1 percent Vietnamese, 8.6 percent Cambodian, 0.6 percent Laotian, 6 percent Hmong, 19.9 percent Filipino, 0.9 percent Thai, 6.5 percent Korean, 0.3 percent India, 0.3 percent Indonesia, 0.6 percent Asian/Hispanic, 0.9 percent Tongan, 6.8 percent Hawaiian, 0.3 percent Marshalese, and 0.3 percent Micronesia.

The distribution by state was as follows: 50.3 percent of the Asians student in the present analysis were surveyed in Hawaii[9]; 11.5 percent from Washington; 5.1 percent from Colorado; 4.2 percent from Maryland; 8.1 percent from Minnesota; 2.5 percent from Louisiana; 12.6 percent from California; and 5.6 percent from New York.

OVERALL FINDINGS AND THE EFFECTS OF AGE AND GENDER

Age significantly differentiates fighting behavior, observing drug sales in or near the school, joining a gang, being asked to join a gang, and number of close friends who abuse drugs. Here the age variable has been recoded to compare two age groups: <=15 versus >= 16. Table 31 provides the frequency distributions for those variables significantly differentiated by age.

As seen in Table 31, it is the younger age group that appears to report a larger gang problem. The younger Asian student group was significantly more likely to report one or more fights during the recent year (36.2%), to have seen drug sales in or near the school (31.5%), to have ever joined a gang (11.3%), having ever been asked to join a gang (19.4%), and having one or more close friends who use illicit drugs (34.2%).

Gender significantly differentiates the following variables: fighting behavior, ever joining a gang, ever being asked to join a gang, number of drug using friends, and knowledge of gang names. Table 32 provides the frequency distributions for these variables. As seen in Table 32, as in other high school studies, males predominate in the area of gang activity. Female Asian students are were less likely to report one or more fights during the last year (22%), to have ever joined a gang (4.5%), to have been asked to join a gang (9.2%), to have one or more friends who are gang members (19%), to have one or more friends who abuse illicit drugs (20.7%), and were less cognizant of the names of the gangs at their school

(9.4%).

THE EFFECTS OF SCHOOL DISCIPLINE AND HIGH GRADES

The measures of academic failure and labelling are shown to be among the strongest variables from this analysis. For example, ever being suspended from school is shown to significantly differentiate all the dependent variables except for the knowledge of gangs variable. The measure for ever having an in-school suspension significantly differentiates all of the dependent variables. The variable for in-school detention significantly differentiates all but joining a gang and knowledge of gang names. The high grades measure significantly differentiates fighting behavior, joining a gang, being asked to join a gang, number of gang and drug abusing friends.

It would appear from these findings that schools are either good at picking out 'gang prone youths' among Asian students and meting out deserved discipline to them for their deviance in the school environment, or that these social ceremonies of stigma and labelling become clearly associated with higher gang problems (Peiar, 1985).

TABLE 31

FREQUENCY DISTRIBUTIONS OF VARIABLES SIGNIFICANTLY DIFFERENTIATED BY AGE AMONG ASIAN STUDENTS

		>= 1 Fights in Last Year	
		NO	YES
AGE GROUPS:	<= 15	95	54 (36.2%)
	>= 16	125	31 (19.8%)
		Chi-square = 10.1, p = .001	

		Seen Drug Sales At School	
		NO	YES
	<= 15	102	47 (31.5%)
	>= 16	150	37 (19.7%)
		Chi-square = 6.11, p = .01	

		Ever Join a Gang	
		NO	YES
	<= 15	141	18 (11.3%)
	>= 16	182	8 (4.2%)
		Chi-square = 6.34, p = .01	

		Ever Asked to Join a Gang	
		NO	YES
	<= 15	120	29 (19.4%)
	>= 16	167	20 (10.6%)
		Chi-square = 5.11, p = .02	

		>= 1 Friends Who Use Drugs	
		NO	YES
	<= 15	100	52 (34.2%)
	>= 16	140	41 (22.6%)
		Chi-square = 5.48, p = .01	

TABLE 32

FREQUENCY DISTRIBUTION OF VARIABLES SIGNIFICANTLY DIFFERENTIATED BY GENDER AMONG ASIAN STUDENTS

>=1 Fights in Last Year

		NO	YES
GENDER:	Male	101	53 (34.4%)
	Female	120	34 (22.0%)

Chi-square = 5.78, p = .01

Ever Join a Gang

	NO	YES
Male	159	18 (10.1%)
Female	166	8 (4.5%)

Chi-square = 3.97, p = .04

Ever Asked to Join a Gang

	NO	YES
Male	131	33 (20.1%)
Female	157	16 (9.2%)

Chi-square = 8.01, p = .005

>= 1 Gang Member Friends

	NO	YES
Male	119	47 (28.3%)
Female	140	33 (19.0%)

Chi-square = 4.01, p = .04

>= 1 Drug Abusing Friends

	NO	YES
Male	108	58 (34.9%)
Female	134	35 (20.7%)

Chi-square = 8.45, p = .004

Know Names of the Gangs

	NO	YES
Male	131	36 (21.5%)
Female	153	16 (9.4%)

Chi-square = 9.38, p = .002

Increased marginality via such labelling is clearly associated with higher deviance (Graham, 1986). While this profile is not unique to Asians, it clearly supports the academic vulnerability hypothesis derived from Chin (1990): the higher the school adjustment problems, the higher the gang involvement; and, vice versa, the higher the academic achievement, the lower the gang involvement.

Table 33 provides the frequency distribution for variables significantly differentiated by whether these Asian students report ever having been suspended from school. Clearly, this condition of ever having been suspended from school shows: significantly lower grades, higher fighting, higher observation of drug sales in or near the school, and a greater likelihood of joining a gang, being asked to join a gang, and having one or more friends who are gang members and drug abusers.

Having an in-school suspension, as seen in Table 34, significantly differentiates all of the dependent variables examined here. Again, as in the research on white, Black, and Hispanic students in Chicago, this factor of problematic school adjustment is highly associated with the gang problem among Asians. Similarly, having a "hit" or an in-school suspension, as seen in Table 35, is a factor that significantly differentiates all but two variables: gang joining and knowledge of gang names variables.

TABLE 33

FREQUENCY DISTRIBUTION OF VARIABLES SIGNIFICANTLY DIFFERENTIATED BY BEING SUSPENDED FROM SCHOOL AMONG ASIAN STUDENTS

High Grades (Overall GPA)

		C or Less	A or B
EVER SUSPENDED			
FROM SCHOOL:	No	78	199 (71.8%)
	Yes	24	18 (42.8%)

Chi-square = 14.08, p < .001

>= 1 Fights During Last Year

	NO	YES
No	200	56 (21.8%)
Yes	14	26 (65%)

Chi-square = 32.12, p < .001

Seen Drug Sales Near School

	NO	YES
No	222	62 (21.8%)
Yes	20	22 (52.3%)

Chi-square = 17.85, p < .001

Ever Join a Gang

	NO	YES
No	275	17 (5.8%)
Yes	37	8 (17.7%)

Chi-square = 8.11, p = .004

Ever Asked to Join a Gang

	NO	YES
No	255	27 (9.5%)
Yes	24	21 (46.6%)

Chi-square = 42.63, p < .001

Have >= 1 Gang Friends

	NO	YES
No	228	56 (19.7%)
Yes	20	23 (53.4%)

Chi-square = 23.24, p < .001

Have >= 1 Drug Friends

	NO	YES
No	220	65 (22.8%)
Yes	17	25 (59.5%)

Chi-square = 24.73, p < .001

THE ARTICULATION FACTOR, SELF-ESTEEM AND LOCUS OF CONTROL

The work articulation factor is shown to significantly differentiate observation of drug sales in or near the school and ever joining a gang. Table 36 shows the frequency distributions for these two variables. Prior theory predicts that the higher the articulation, the lower the rebellion (Stinchecombe, 1964). Unfortunately, while significant in relationship to two variables, the direction of the effect is in reverse of that expected. As seen in Table 36, those Asian students who do articulate future benefit from present schooling (as reflected in they know what occupation or profession they will enter after completing their education) are more likely to have seen drug sales near the school, and they are more (not less) likely to have ever joined a gang.

The self-esteem variable appears less predictive than the literature suggests regarding gangs, at least among the Asian students studied here. Table 37 shows the frequency distributions for the three variables that high self-esteem should impact on. The first two are not unexpected: the higher the self-esteem, the higher the grades; and the higher the self-esteem, the lower the fighting. Those with higher self-esteem were also more likely to know the names of the gangs in their school.

The internal locus of control scale scores yield no significant effects on any of the gang variables, and are only able to differentiate the high grades variable. This shows that those with higher internal locus of control scale scores are more likely (76.4%) to report high grades than those who do not (60.9%).

TABLE 34

FREQUENCY DISTRIBUTION OF VARIABLES SIGNIFICANTLY DIFFERENTIATED BY HAVING AN IN-SCHOOL SUSPENSION AMONG ASIAN STUDENTS

High Grades (Overall GPA)

EVER HAVE AN IN SCHOOLSUSPENSION:	C or Less	A or B
No	76	189 (71.3%)
Yes	27	25 (48%)

Chi-square = 10.7, p = .001

>= 1 Fights in Last Year

	NO	YES
No	186	57 (23.4%)
Yes	25	26 (50.9%)

Chi-square = 15.76, p < .001

Seen Drug Sales Near School

	NO	YES
No	214	57 (21%)
Yes	25	28 (52.8%)

Chi-square = 23.16, p < .001

Ever Join A Gang

	NO	YES
No	264	17 (6%)
Yes	45	9 (16.6%)

Chi-square = 7.13, p = .008

Ever Asked to Join a Gang

	NO	YES
No	242	29 (10.7%)
Yes	34	20 (37%)

Chi-square = 24.39, p < .001

>= 1 Gang Member Friends

	NO	YES
No	217	54 (19.9%)
Yes	28	26 (48.1%)

Chi-square = 19.32, p < .001

>= 1 Drug Abuser Friends

	NO	YES
No	212	60 (22%)
Yes	22	31 (58.4%)

Chi-square = 29.2, p < .001

Know Names of Gangs at School

	NO	YES
No	230	35 (13.2%)
Yes	38	15 (28.3%)

Chi-square = 7.59, p = .006

TABLE 35

FREQUENCY DISTRIBUTION OF VARIABLES SIGNIFICANTLY DIFFERENTIATED BY HAVING HAD AN IN-SCHOOL SUSPENSION AMONG ASIAN STUDENTS

	High Grades (Overall GPA)	
	C or Less	A or B
EVER HAD AN IN-SCHOOL DETENTION: No	76	187 (71.1%)
Yes	26	28 (51.8%)

Chi-square = 7.6, p = .006

	>= 1 Fights in the Last Year	
	NO	YES
No	186	53 (22.1%)
Yes	29	28 (49.1%)

Chi-square = 16.81, p < .001

	Seen Drug Sales Near School	
	NO	YES
No	214	56 (20.7%)
Yes	28	29 (50.8%)

Chi-square = 22.2, p < .001

	Ever Asked to Join A Gang	
	NO	YES
No	245	26 (9.5%)
Yes	35	22 (38..5%)

Chi-square = 31.7, p < .001

	>= 1 Gang Member Friends	
	NO	YES
No	216	56 (20.5%)
Yes	34	23 (40.3%)

Chi-square = 10.08, p = .001

	>= 1 Drug Abusing Friends	
	NO	YES
No	207	62 (23%)
Yes	30	29 (49.1%)

Chi-square = 16.44, p < .001

TABLE 36

FREQUENCY DISTRIBUTION OF VARIABLES SIGNIFICANTLY DIFFERENTIATED BY THE WORK ARTICULATION FACTOR AMONG ASIAN STUDENTS

	Seen Drug Sales Near School	
	NO	YES
Know what occupation or profession will enter when finished with education: No	82	20 (19.6%)
Yes	147	64 (30.3%)

Chi-square = 4.01, p = .04

	Ever Join A Gang	
	NO	YES
No	105	3 (2.7%)
Yes	194	22 (10.1%)

Chi-square = 5.54, p = .01

TABLE 37

FREQUENCY DISTRIBUTION OF VARIABLES SIGNIFICANTLY DIFFERENTIATED BY HIGH SELF-ESTEEM SCORES AMONG ASIAN STUDENTS

	High Grades (Overall GPA)	
	C or less	A or B
High Self-Esteem Score: No	66	83 (55.7%)
Yes	27	106 (79.6%)

Chi-square = 18.3, p < .001

	>= 1 Fights in Last Year	
	NO	YES
No	91	43 (32%)
Yes	105	27 (20.4%)

Chi-square = 4.64, p = .03

	Know Names of the Gangs	
	NO	YES
No	138	15 (9.8%)
Yes	102	32 (23.8%)

Chi-square = 10.33, p = .001

BELIEF IN GOOD LUCK AND PARANOIA

It is fair to say that most gang concepts in the literature have not been vigorously tested. A subcultural belief in good luck could be expected to be associated with higher gang affiliation according to Cohen (1955). A higher level of paranoia would be expected to be associated with gang affiliation according to Yablonsky (1962).

Table 38 provides the frequency distributions for those three variables significantly differentiated by belief in good luck. Consistent with the hypothesis, those who agree with the good luck question from the internal-external locus of control scale: are less likely to have high grades[10], more likely to have had one or more fights in the last year, and more likely to have one or more close friends and associates who are gang members.

Table 39 provides the results for the paranoia question. Consistent with the hypothesis, those who express this measure of paranoia: have lower grades, more fights, are more likely to see drug sales near school, more likely to be asked to join a gang, and are more likely to have one or more gang friends.

TABLE 38

FREQUENCY DISTRIBUTION OF VARIABLES SIGNIFICANTLY DIFFERENTIATED BY BELIEF IN GOOD LUCK AMONG ASIAN STUDENTS

	High Grades (Overall GPA)	
	C or Less	A or B

"When things are going well for me I consider it due only to a run of good luck."

	C or Less	A or B
Disagree	32	114 (78%)
Agree	64	85 (57%)

Chi-square = 14.86, p < .001

	>= 1 Fights in Last Year	
	NO	YES
Disagree	110	29 (20.8%)
Agree	97	45 (31.6%)

Chi-square = 4.24, p = .03

	>= 1 Gang Member Friends	
	NO	YES
Disagree	122	27 (18.1%)
Agree	113	47 (29.3%)

Chi-square = 5.36, p = .02

TABLE 39

FREQUENCY DISTRIBUTION OF VARIABLES SIGNIFICANTLY DIFFERENTIATED BY THE PARANOIA QUESTION AMONG ASIAN STUDENTS

	High Grades (Overall GPA)	
	C or Less	A or B

"I often think people are talking about me."

	C or Less	A or B
False	50	131 (72.3%)
True	52	75 (59%)

Chi-square = 5.97, p = .01

	>= 1 Fights in the Last Year	
	NO	YES
False	129	36 (21.8%)
True	79	42 (34.7%)

Chi-square = 5.85, p = .01

	Seen Drug Sales Near School	
	NO	YES
False	147	37 (20.1%)
True	88	45 (33.8%)

Chi-square = 7.58, p = .006

	Ever Asked to Join a Gang	
	NO	YES
False	163	21 (11.4%)
True	109	26 (19.2%)

Chi-square = 3.81, p = .051

	> = 1 Gang Member Friends	
	NO	YES
False	153	31 (16.8%)
True	89	47 (34.5)

Chi-square = 13.3, p < .001

EMPLOYMENT AND INCOME

Some recent research has challenged long-held views about the value of employment for youths with regard to its ability to prevent deviance. The present findings must be added to this exception to opportunity theory. In this analysis knowing whether a youth has a full or part-time job has no effect on any of the gang variables. In fact, those respondents with full or part-time jobs appear more likely to have one or more drug abusing friends, and to know the names of the gangs. Thus, the nature of the relationship is obverse to that which might be expected from Cloward and Ohlin (1960). This is shown in Table 40 and is consistent with similar findings among non-Asians (Knox, Laske, Tromanhauser, 1992).

TABLE 40

FREQUENCY DISTRIBUTION OF VARIABLES SIGNIFICANTLY DIFFERENTIATED BY HAVING FULL OR PART-TIME EMPLOYMENT AMONG ASIAN STUDENTS

	>= 1 Drug Abusing Friends	
	NO	YES

Have any regular part-time or full-time job?

	NO	YES
No	180	55 (23.4)
Yes	54	38 (41.3)

Chi-square = 10.4, p = .001

	Know the Names of the Gangs	
	NO	YES
No	206	31 (13%)
Yes	72	20 (21.7%)

Chi-square = 3.79, p = .051

The Chicago high school research found that youths with jobs were in fact more likely to be asked to join a gang, not less likely. Perhaps because of the disposable income which such employment provides, it may provide a youth with greater access to the drug subculture.

Finally, the income variable (whether the student receives a regular allowance from the family) is significant in relationship to all variables except that of high grades as seen in Table 41.

TABLE 41

**FREQUENCY DISTRIBUTION OF VARI-
ABLES SIGNIFICANTLY DIFFERENTI-
ATED BY HAVING AN
INCOME ALLOWANCE
AMONG ASIAN STUDENTS**

>= 1 Fights in Last Year

		NO	YES
Receive an allowance			
from your family:	No	114	29 (20.2%)
	Yes	99	51 (34%)

Chi-square = 6.94, p = .008

Seen Drug Sales Near School

	NO	YES
No	135	28 (17.1%)
Yes	102	54 (34.6%)

Chi-square = 12.69, p < .001

Ever Join A Gang

	NO	YES
No	160	8 (4.7%)
Yes	145	18 (11%)

Chi-square = 4.50, p = .03

Ever Asked to Join a Gang

	NO	YES
No	147	13 (8.1%)
Yes	122	35 (22.2%)

Chi-square = 12.37, p < .001

>= 1 Gang Member Friends

	NO	YES
No	130	29 (18.2%)
Yes	115	45 (28.1%)

Chi-square = 4.37, p = .03

>= 1 Drug Abuser Friends

	NO	YES
No	125	35 (21.8%)
Yes	103	54 (34.3%)

Chi-square = 6.15, p = .01

Know Names of the Gangs

	NO	YES
No	149	16 (9.6%)
Yes	123	34 (21.6%)

Chi-square = 8.77, p = .003

The problem, however, is that the nature of the observed relationship is not that which might be predicted from opportunity theory. The youths with family allowances appear to have higher gang problems than those youths who do not receive an allowance.

Apparently not receiving an allowance from the family may be a blessing in disguise according to the findings in Table 41. Students who receive a family allowance are more likely to have been in one or more fights during the last year (34%) than students who do not receive an allowance (20.2%), they are more likely to have seen drug sales occur in or near the school (34.6%) than those who do not receive an allowance (17.1%), they are more likely to report having joined a gang (11%) than those who do not receive an allowance (4.7%), they are more likely to have been asked to join a gang (22.2%) than those who do not receive an allowance (8.1%), they are more likely to have one or more close friends and associates who are gang members (28.1%) than those who do not receive an allowance (18.2%), they are more likely to have one or more close friends and associates who use illicit drugs (34.3%) than those who do not receive an allowance (21.8%), and they are more likely to know the names of the gangs in their school (21.6%) than those who do not receive an allowance (9.6%).

These findings run directly against the grain of conventional thinking and opportunity theory. It may be that gangs find youths with allowances more attractive to recruit because they can pay their regular dues. It may be that youths with allowances and disposable income are more likely to be exposed to the drug subculture. It may also reflect some aspect of change in traditional family function among Asians[11].

FIGHTING BEHAVIOR

Prior research shows that gang members report a higher level of fighting behavior than non-gang member youths. It may be tied to some aspect of the defiant individualist character described by Sanchez-Jankowski (1991). But does this same finding documented for whites, Blacks, and Hispanics also apply to Asian students?

The frequency distribution for the effects of fighting behavior are shown in Table 42. This shows that fighting behavior is clearly associated with lower grades and with a higher likelihood of observing drug sales, joining a gang, being asked to join a gang, having one or more gang member friends, having one or more drug abusing friends, and knowing the names of the gangs.

Fighting shows a consistent significant effect for all gang variables and is consistent with the finding by Knox, Laske and Tromanhauser (1992) that gang members face a higher likelihood of fighting and assault than their non-gang member student counterparts.

TABLE 42

FREQUENCY DISTRIBUTION OF VARIABLES SIGNIFICANTLY DIFFERENTIATED BY THE FIGHTING VARIABLE AMONG ASIAN STUDENTS

		High Grades (Overall GPA)	
		C or Less	A or B
One or more fights in the last 12 months:	No	51	150 (74.6%)
	Yes	35	44 (55.6%)

Chi-square = 9.55, p = .002

		Seen Drug Sales Near School	
		NO	YES
	No	171	45 (20.8%)
	Yes	43	37 (46.2%)

Chi-square = 18.83, p < .001

		Ever Join a Gang	
		NO	YES
	No	215	7 (3.1%)
	Yes	70	16 (18.6%)

Chi-square = 21.41, p < .001

		Ever Asked to Join a Gang	
		NO	YES
	No	190	20 (9.5%)
	Yes	56	27 (32.5%)

Chi-square = 23.37, p < .001

		>= 1 Gang Member Friends	
		NO	YES
	No	181	31 (14.6%)
	Yes	48	37 (43.5%)

Chi-square = 28.71, p < .001

		>= 1 Drug Abuser Friends	
		NO	YES
	No	170	41 (19.4%)
	Yes	39	44 (53%)

Chi-square = 32.68, p < .001

		Know the Names of the Gangs	
		NO	YES
	No	185	30 (13.9%)
	Yes	63	19 (23.1%)

Chi-square = 3.66, p = .056

PREDICTING GANG MEMBERSHIP

Prior efforts to predict aspects of the gang problem involved variables similar to those examined in the present research and in one case was able to correctly classify 74 percent of the cases (Truckenmiller, 1983).   More recently another research project was able to correctly classify 8 in 10 youths (Winfree, Vigil, and Mays, 1991: 14). Taking some of the factors shown to strongly be associated with gang membership it is possible to compute a discriminant function using these predictor variables. This linear model is basically a "one-way multivariate analysis of variance" (SYSTAT, 1986: 107). The F-values for the predictor variables used are shown in Table 43.

TABLE 43

UNIVARIATE F STATISTICS IN PREDICTING GANG MEMBERSHIP

Variable	F-Value	Prob.
>= 1 Gang Member Friends	37.99	< .001
>= 1 Drug Abuser Friends	22.16	< .001
>= 1 Fights in Last Year	20.08	< .001
Age: (0=LE15; 1=GE16)	7.38	.007
High Grades (1=A,B;0=LE C)	6.61	.01

The actual group membership (gang/nongang) compared to the predicted group membership (gang/nongang) is provided in Table 44.   This shows that 83 percent of the cases were correctly classified as either gang or nongang members.   The largest error in predicting gang membership here is among those who are not gang members who are predicted to be gang members (N = 42).

TABLE 44

ACTUAL VERSUS PREDICTED GANG MEMBERSHIP

		Prediction	
		Gang	Nongang
ACTUAL	Gang	19	3
	Nongang	42	201

SUMMARY AND CONCLUSION

The basic finding of interest from this research is that in many respects Asian students face the identical "gang problem" or "gang risk" that is documented among white, Black, and Hispanic school students (Knox, Laske, and Tromanhauser, 1992). The sample of Asian students used is a purposive rather than true national random sample and the findings reported here are at this point only suggestive.

High self-esteem while clearly related to high grades, fighting, and the cognitive variable (know gang names), but was not significant in relation to joining a gang, being asked to join a gang, or having gang friends.   Similarly, the measure for high internal locus of control was significant only in differentiating high grades; and not any of the gang involvement variables.

Whether the student had a full or part-time

job was shown to be significant only in relationship to having drug abusing friends and knowledge of gang names. Yet the allowance variable showed significance in relationship to all variables other than having high grades. Unfortunately both of these legitimate opportunity variables were shown to have the reverse effect than that which would have been logically expected. They are not associated with a lower, but rather a higher gang problem.

The belief in good luck variable is shown to be significantly related to high grades, fights, and having gang friends. Similarly, the paranoia variable was shown to be significant in relation to high grades, fights, seeing drug sales, being asked to join a gang, and having gang friends. The fighting variable was shown to be significant in relation to all variables. The academic vulnerability hypothesis tested from Chin (1990) yielded the strongest consistent support in the analysis undertaken here. Fighting behavior, examined in terms of Jankowski's (1991) defiance hypothesis also yielded consistent results.

The variables most predictive of gang membership were: having one or more close friends who were gang members, having one or more close friends who use illicit drugs, and having one or more fights in the last year. Age and grades were also significant in predicting gang membership.

In summary, this survey research sought to test various hypotheses from the literature on gangs using an Asian student sample. In fairness to the opportunity model, future research should examine perceived closure in educational and occupational structures, as well as illicit income sources. An urgent need exists for more comparative national research using ethnicity as a control variable.

DISCUSSION QUESTIONS:

(1) Among some Vietnamese gang members in America it is not uncommon to find them using the phrase "Toi o gica", meaning "my crazy life", or "I do not care about anything". Is this commonality with other ethnic groups, for example in the barrio, a possible cultural universal or do you think this is simply a part of the personality syndrome adopted or shaped among gang members?

(2) Some Vietnamese gang members have a rather violent way of targeting Vietnamese businessmen, where it typically involves a home invasion, and the use of violence even torture, to force the victim to turn over their money. Is this another possible cultural universal about gangs, that is that they do their most damage to their own ethnic and racial groups, or is this a function of opportunity itself?

(3) How do we explain the rather common "profile" that emerges for Asian gang members that is also found for the most part among gang members of most other racial and ethnic groups? Is this the homogenizing influence of gang life, the common desensitization about violence?

REFERENCES

Bastian, Lisa D. and Bruce M. Taylor
1991 School Crime: A National Crime Victimization Survey Report. U.S. Department of Justice, Office of Justice Programs, Bureau of Justice Statistics (Sept).

Bergman, Brian
1991 "Terror in the Streets: Young Asian Gangs Are Spreading Fear, Violence, and Death in Canadian Cities", MACLEAN'S, Canada's Weekly Newsmagazine, March 25, pp. 18-26.

Berland, David I; et al
1989 "Adolescent Gangs in the Hospital", Bulletin of the Menniger Clinic (53)(1): 31-43.

Chin, Ko-lin
1990 "Chinese Gangs and Extortion", pp. 129-145 in C. Ronald Huff (Ed.), Gangs in America, Newbury Park, CA: Sage Publications.

Chin, Ko-lin; Robert J. Kelly; and Jeffrey A. Fagan
1993 "Methodological Issues in Studying Chinese Gang Extortion", Journal of Gang Research, Volume 1, Number 2: pp. 25-36.

Cloward, Richard A. and Lloyd E. Ohlin
1960 Delinquency and Opportunity. New York: Free Press.

Cohen, Albert K.
1955 Delinquent Boys: The Culture of the Gang. Glencoe, IL: The Free Press.

English, T.J.
1995 Born to Kill. New York: William Morrow and Company.

Eyres, John
1997 "On the Rise of Vietnamese Gangs in Southern California: An Analysis of Los Angeles Times News Reports", paper presented at the Annual Meeting of the American Society of Criminology.

Fagan, Jeffrey
1990 "Social Processes of Delinquency and Drug Use Among Urban Gangs", pp. 183-222 in C. Ronald Huff (Ed.), Gangs in America, Newbury Park, CA: Sage Publications.

Gardner, Robert W., et al
1989 "Asian Americans: Growth, Change, and Diversity", Population Bulletin (40)(4)(Feb).

Goldstein, H.S.
1986 "Conduct Problems, Parental Supervision, and Cognitive Development of 12- to 17-year Olds", Psychological Reports (59)(2-I): 651-658.

Graham, J.
1986 "Schools and Delinquency", Home Office Research and Planning Unit Research Bulletin (21): 21-25.

Hochhaus, Craig and Frank Sousa
1987 "Why Children Belong to Gangs: A Comparison of Expectations and Reality", High School Journal (71)(2)(Dec): 74-77.

Huang, Hua-lun
1996 "Chinese Secret Societies/Gangs and Transnational Organized Crime: The Triads and Chinese Gangs in the Global Enterprise of Human Smuggling", paper presented at the Annual Meeting of the American

Society of Criminology, Chicago, IL.

IAACI News
1992   Newsletter for Law Enforcement on Asian Gangs, International Association of Asian Crime Investigators, P.O. Box 7221, Falls Church, VA 22046.

James, W.H.
1957   Internal Versus External Control of Reinforcement as a Basic Variable in Learning Theory. Ohio State University, Ph.D. dissertation.

Jan, Lee-jan
1993   "Asian Gang Problems and Social Policy Solutions: A Discussion and Review", Journal of Gang Research, Volume 1, Number 2: pp. 37-44.

Knox, George W.; David Laske; and Edward Tromanhauser
1992   Schools Under Siege: An Interdisciplinary Study of Drugs, Crime, and Violence in the Modern American School. Dubuque, IA: Kendall-Hunt.

Knox, George W.; Thomas F. McCurrie; John A. Laskey; and Edward D. Tromanhauser
1996   "The 1996 National Law Enforcement Gang Analysis Survey: A Research Report from the National Gang Crime Research Center", Journal of Gang Research, Vol. 3, Number 4, pp. 41-55.

Lacey, Robert
1991   Little Man: Meyer Lansky and the Gangster Life. New York: Little, Brown and Company.

Liang, Bin
1997   Chinese Tongs and Gangs in America, Master's Thesis, Arizona State University.

Loeber, R., et al
1989   "Continuity and Desistance in Disruptive Boys' Early Fighting at School", Development and Psychopathology (1)(1): 39-50.

Long, Patrick Du Phuoc; with Laura Ricard
1996   The Dream Shattered: Vietnamese Gangs in America. Boston: Northeastern University Press.

Mok, Bong Ho
1990   "Community Care for Delinquent Youth: The Chinese Approach of Rehabilitating the Young Offenders", Journal of Offender Counseling, Services & Rehabilitation (15)(2): 5-20.

Morash, Merry
1983   "Gangs, Groups and Delinquency", British Journal of Criminology (23)(4)(Oct): 309-335.

Mustain, Gene and Jerry Capeci
1988   Mob Star: The Story of John Gotti. New York: Bantam.

Peiar, J.
1985   "School as a Mechanism of Social Control", Revija za Kriminalistiko in Kriminologijo (36)(4): 318-329.

Project GANGECON
1994   The Economics of Gang Life: A National Investigation. National Gang Crime Research Center, Chicago, Illinois.

Project GANGFACT
1996   Facts About Gang Life Today: A Study of 3,000 Gang Members in 20 States: With a Large Offender Comparison Sample. National Gang Crime Research Center, Chicago, Illinois.

Project GANGPINT
1995   Gang Prevention and Gang Intervention: The First National Needs Assessment - A Large Scale Gang Analysis. National Gang Crime Research Center, Chicago, Illinois.

Roemer, William F., Jr.
1995   Accardo: The Genuine Godfather. Donald I. Fine, Inc.

Rosenbaum, Dennis P. and Jane A. Grant
1983   Gangs and Youth Problems in Evanston: Research Findings and Policy Options. Center for Urban Affairs and Policy Research, Northwestern University (July 22).

Rosenberg, M.
1965   Society and the Adolescent Self-Image. Princeton, N.J.: Princeton University Press.

Sanchez-Jankowski, Martin
1991   Islands in the Street. Berkeley, CA: University of California Press.

Schwartz, Audrey J.
1989   "Middle-Class Educational Values Among Latino Gang Members in East Los Angeles County High Schools", Urban Education (24)(3)(Oct): 323-342.

Shaw, Clifford R. and Henry D. Mc Kay
1942   Juvenile Delinquency and Urban Areas. Chicago: University of Chicago Press.

Sherer, Moshe
1990   "Criminal Activity Among Jewish and Arab Youth in Israel", International Journal of Intercultural Relations (14)(4): 529-548.

Short, James F. and Fred L. Strodtbeck
1965   Group Process and Gang Delinquency. Chicago: University of Chicago Press.

Song, John Huey-Long; John Dombrink; and Gilbert Geis
1992   "Lost in the Melting Pot: Asian Youth Gangs in the United States", Journal of Gang Research, Volume 1, Number 1: pp. 1-12.

Song, John Huey-Long; and Lynn M. Hurysz
1995   "Victimization Patterns of Asian Gangs in the United States", Journal of Gang Research, Volume 3, Number 1: pp. 41-49.

Spergel, Irving A. and G. David Curry
1990   Differential Patterns of Gang Involvement Among Hispanic and Black Adolescent Males: Promise For Prevention. School of Social Service Administration, University of Chicago.

Stinchecombe, Arthur L.
1964   Rebellion in a High School. Chicago: Quadrangle Books.

Takata, Susan R. and Richard G. Zevitz
1990   "Divergent Perceptions of Group Delinquency in a Midwestern Community: Racine's Gang Problem", Youth and Society (21)(3)(Mar): 282-305/

Thompson, David W. and Leonard A. Jason
1988   "Street Gangs and Preventive Interventions", Criminal Justice and Behavior (15)(3)(Sept): 323-333.

Thrasher, Frederick M.
1927   The Gang. Chicago: University of Chicago Press.

Touhy, Roger
1959   The Stolen Years. Cleveland, OH: Pennington Press, Inc.

Toy, Calvin
1992   "Coming Out to Play: Reasons to Join and Participate in Asian Gangs", Journal of Gang Research, Volume 1, Number 1: pp. 13-29.

Vigil, James Diego and Steve Chong Yun
1990   "Vietnamese Youth Gangs in Southern California", pp. 146-162 in C. Ronald Huff (Ed.), Gangs in America, Newbury Park, CA: Sage Publications.

Winfree, L. Thomas; Teresa Vigil; and G. Larry Mays
1991   "Social Learning Theory and Youth Gangs: A Comparison of High School Students and Adjudicated Delinquents", paper presented at the Annual Meeting of the American Society of Criminology, San Francisco, CA.

Yablonsky, Lewis
  1962 The Violent Gang. New York: MacMillan.
Yan, Wenfan and Eugene L. Gaier
  1991 "Causal Attributions for College Success and
         Failure: An American-Asian Comparison", paper
         presented at the Annual Meeting of the American
         Educational Research Association, Chicago, IL (Apr).

FIGURE 20

**RANK ORDERED LISTING OF MOST FRE-
QUENTLY LISTED GANG NAMES ACTIVE IN
SCHOOLS ATTENDED BY ASIAN STUDENTS**

Hawaii Gang Names:
Bloods
Crips
Tongan Crip Gang (T.C.G.)[12]
No Guts, No Glory
H.H.B.
Delta
Tao-Gama
Gamol
Baung Gang
Akuat (Akyat) Bahau (Bahay) Gang
Scorpios; Scorpians
Central Bloods
Upcountry Boys
Cross Sons
P.S.I.
Crazy Samoan Warriors (AKA Warriors)
Sons of Samoans
Peace Makers
Hawaiian Boys
Baja Gang
F.O.B. (Fresh Off the Boat)
C.I.A. (Criminals in Action)
Lahaina Mob Squad
Hydros
Homeboys
Boys from the Darkside
Jkalihi Valley Home Girls
The Posse
B.G.C.
Lahaina Boys
H.W.A.
The S.I.
L.M.S.

Washington Gang Names:
Crips
H.T.C.G. (Hill Top Crip Gang)
O.L.B. (Original Local Boys)
O.L.G. (Original Local Gang)

Colorado Gang Names:
Born To Kill
K.P.
L.L.K.
Dojoyby
Hojing
White Dragon
Korean Dragon
Blue Dragon
C.P.
J.K.P.
C.C.K.
Maryland Gang Names:
Flying Dragons
Pythons
Wolfpack

Figure 20:   Continued

Minnesota Gang Names:
White Tigers (W.T.'s)
Cobras
Lost Boys
Laos Boys
R.C.B.
O.C.S.

Louisiana Gang Names:
Dragons

GANG CRIME PROBLEMS IN CHINA
        Mainland China, or communist China, is an oppres-
sive country to live in. Example, you do not have "rights" or
enjoy many constitutional protections there. If a mother has
two children and becomes pregnant again, the village sends a
"state counselor" to convince you to get an abortion, if you
refuse, you are punished; which is the Communist Chinese
method of population control.
        Chairman Mao Tse Tung, who started the "commu-
nist revolution" in China, used techniques of crime control
that are just not available in countries like the United States.
When Chairman Mao wanted to reduce the problem represented by heroin and opium addicts, he sent his military troops
into every village and rounded up all drug addicts: they were
told "say no to drugs, or we will be back and say no to your
life". Sure enough, follow-up visits resulted in thousands of
drug addicts being lined up and summarily executed.
        One recent piece of research on the gang problem in
China (Zhang, Messner, Lu, and Deng, 1997) reminds us of
the problem of "getting a handle" on what kind of crime problem communist countries have. In the Soviet Union, for example, when the "Iron Curtain" was still up, Russian Communists routinely reported to the outside world that they had
no crime problem; when in fact, the rest of the world knew
better. Communists, after all, lived in a "workers paradise":
and there is little crime under such socialist conditions.
        The research by Zhang, et al, (1997) reported from
one survey that there was a relatively small, low level of orga-
nizational-development, gang problem in China. Yet they also
gave clues from quoting official sources to what may be a much
larger problem: "officials reported hat 200,000 criminal gangs
were cracked down upon nationwide in the 1983 campaign
against crime and gang related crime decreased as a result"
(p. 300). If China had 200,000 gangs in 1983, they have a lot
more today: and the statistical likelihood is that some of these
are probably very well organized, knowing that they face a
formidably oppressive "enemy": the Chinese communist government.
        China has over 1 billion citizens. Do you think they
might have a gang problem? If a "trade deal" could be worked
out with China for "correctional services", would you be in
favor of funding a program where American gang members
could serve their sentences or their probation/parole terms
under Chinese authority, assuming the offender "volunteered"
to this arrangement?

END NOTES:

[1]For an excellent analysis of "state sponsored" gangs in Mexico, see: Mark Stevenson, "Shadowy World of Death Squads: Mexican Gangs Spread Terror at Night", Chicago Sun-Times, Dec. 31, 1997, p. 22.

[2]See "Asian Street Gangs Emerging as New Underworld," The New York Times Metro, Wednesday, April 1, 1992, by James Dao.

[3]A variety of authors have cited the importance of self-esteem in relationship to gang involvement (Berland, et al, 1989; Mok, 1990).

[4]I am indebted to Dr. Kay Tokanaga (Chicago Board of Education) for this assistance.

[5]The survey by Takata and Zevitz (1990) showed students perceived the gang as less formalized than did adults.

[6]This is true, according to Stinchcombe Rebellion in a High School, because from this poor articulation of the present status in relationship to the future the student will be more prone to rebellion.

[7]See Loeber, et al (1989) for a related psychiatric concept called "high oppositional behavior" shown to be highly related to fighting in school.

[8]Current gang membership was also measured in the survey. About half of those who admitted joining a gang were willing to admit that they were still considered a gang member. Current gang membership (self-reported) therefore has a very small base rate (3.8%).

[9]Gardner, et al (1989) showed that by the 1980 Census about half of Asian Americans resided in California or Hawaii. Thus, the sampling here does tend to roughly mirror the geographical cluster desired.

[10]This finding is consistent with that by Yan (1991) who found that academic success among Asians was attributed more to effort than to good luck.

[11]Betty Lee Sung, in The Adjustment Experience of Chinese Immigrant Children in New York City, suggests such major family changes combined with the increased role played by the school, create the context where peer groups such as gangs play a more prominent role. The present research did have one variable about family function: Whether parents helped or encouraged the student with homework, but it was not significant in relation to gang membership, being asked to join a gang, or having one or more gang member friends.

[12]The Tongan Crips were documented in 1990, 1991 in Utah's juvenile correctional system (see Knox, 1991 An Introduction to Gangs). The Kingdom of Tonga population is estimated to be approximately 8 percent Morman which may be related to the migration pattern to Utah.

Mickey Cobra's

(Excerpts From the printed program of a 1992 Annual Meeting of the MC's in Chicago)

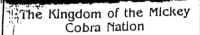

The Kingdom of the Mickey Cobra Nation

This is your Great Nation, Chief, speaking to you Chief, and from the heart Chief, and Chief with each and every one of our lives we will uphold your Great Nation to the highest, even if it means going to jail or even losing our lives. But this great Nation will never, never die. We love you and miss you and your dream will be fulfilled.
That's Law.

Chief Mickey Cogwell

Cobra Love

THE KINGDOM OF MICKEY'S C.O.B.R.A F.O.R.C.E.S.

Committed to organizing believers against racism and apartheid. Fraternal order to revitalize community environmental services.

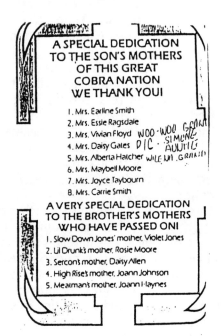

A SPECIAL DEDICATION TO THE SON'S MOTHERS OF THIS GREAT COBRA NATION WE THANK YOU!

1. Mrs. Earline Smith
2. Mrs. Essie Ragsdale
3. Mrs. Vivian Floyd
4. Mrs. Daisy Gates
5. Mrs. Alberta Hatcher
6. Mrs. Maybell Moore
7. Mrs. Joyce Taybourn
8. Mrs. Carrie Smith

A VERY SPECIAL DEDICATION TO THE BROTHER'S MOTHERS WHO HAVE PASSED ON!

1. Slow Down Jones' mother, Violet Jones
2. Lil Drunk's mother, Rosie Moore
3. Sercon's mother, Daisy Allen
4. High Rise's mother, Joann Johnson
5. Meatman's mother, Joann Haynes

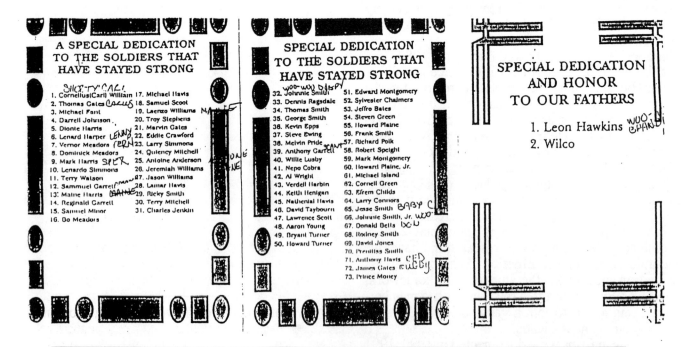

A SPECIAL DEDICATION TO THE SOLDIERS THAT HAVE STAYED STRONG

1. Cornelius(Carl) William
2. Thomas Gates
3. Michael Fant
4. Darrell Johnson
5. Dionte Harris
6. Lenard Harper
7. Vernor Meadors
8. Dominick Meadors
9. Mark Harris
10. Lenardo Simmons
11. Terry Watson
12. Sammuel Garrett
13. Maine Harris
14. Reginald Garrett
15. Samuel Minor
16. Bo Meadors
17. Michael Havis
18. Samuel Scoot
19. Laenzo Williams
20. Troy Stephens
21. Marvin Gates
22. Eddie Crawford
23. Larry Simmons
24. Quiency Mitchell
25. Antoine Anderson
26. Jeremiah Williams
27. Jason Williams
28. Lamar Havis
29. Ricky Smith
30. Terry Mitchell
31. Charles Jenkin

SPECIAL DEDICATION TO THE SOLDIERS THAT HAVE STAYED STRONG

32. Johnnie Smith
33. Dennis Ragsdale
34. Thomas Smith
35. George Smith
36. Kevin Epps
37. Steve Ewing
38. Melvin Pride
39. Anthony Garrett
40. Willie Lusby
41. Nepo Cobra
42. Al Wright
43. Verdell Harbin
44. Keith Henigan
45. Nathenial Havis
46. David Taybourn
47. Lawrence Scott
48. Aaron Young
49. Bryant Turner
50. Howard Turner
51. Edward Montgomery
52. Sylvester Chalmers
53. Jeffro Bates
54. Steven Green
55. Howard Plaine
56. Frank Smith
57. Richard Polk
58. Robert Speight
59. Mark Montgomery
60. Howard Plaine, Jr.
61. Michael Island
62. Cornell Green
63. Efrem Childs
64. Larry Connors
65. Jesse Smith
66. Johnnie Smith, Jr.
67. Donald Bells
68. Rodney Smith
69. David Jones
70. Prentiss Smith
71. Anthony Havis
72. James Gates
73. Prince Money

SPECIAL DEDICATION AND HONOR TO OUR FATHERS

1. Leon Hawkins
2. Wilco

What many "gang experts" have missed over the years in postulating and pontificating about gangs and gang members, is how some gangs operate today like "criminal cults": where the gang leader, living or dead, is the God to be worshipped and sacrificed for. Here is another example. As adult-driven enterprises, these groups hold no less appeal than someone like Rev. Jim Jones, regardless of how "crazy" they may behave. Will American society ever seek to "tighten" the loopholes that allow such groups to systematically exploit American children? Will it be too late before such progress occurs ?

Chapter 20

THE FAMILY AND THE GANG

INTRODUCTION

When a member of a Crip gang greets a fellow member he calls him "Cuz", meaning cousin. Just as Blood gang members call each other Blood, as in family blood. Is it just a put-on, a thin veneer of friendly language that disguises a pattern of ruthless competition among and between gangs and gang members, or do some gangs actually function like a surrogate family? As a primary agency of socialization, the family as a social institution has a crucial role to play in understanding gangs. Reid (1990: p. 84) suggests that males and females join gangs for essentially the same reason, that is "to find a sense of belonging that they have not otherwise found". This would suggest that the family and other institutions are not functioning at such an optimal level to provide an attractive form of belonging for America's young gang members. Therefore, it is important to focus on the family in relationship to the gang for this and other reasons.

Emerging national data, to quote from preliminary results of the author's law enforcement survey discussed in a later chapter, shows that among police chiefs nationwide 73.2 percent agree that parents are to blame for the gang membership of their children. Nearly all agree that the family is an important agency that can be used to prevent gang affiliation. And when asked to choose who has the pri-

mary responsibility for dealing with gangs among five options (family, religious institutions, businesses, schools, local law enforcement), about half of the police chiefs designate the family. We clearly need to know more about the family factor.

As gang affiliation is high among prison and jail inmates, and as felons in state and local custody tend to reflect the same socio-economic and community background as gang members, our knowledge of this inmate population has some bearing on gang members as well. Interviewing family members is also a way to better understand the social world of the individual gang member[1].

It is relevant to consider any family factors that are related to crime. This also represents a knowledge development need in terms of gang research. Some findings like Jeffrey Fagan's (in Huff, 1990) show measures of family integration having less impact than the role played by substance abuse. But the effect is as theoretically expected: the higher the family integration, the lower the gang problem. But not everyone agrees that the family matters regarding gangs, for example Sanchez-Jankowski[2] (1991) observed in his fieldwork with gang members that their family situations were like anyone else's: they did not all come from bad or dysfunctional families. Obviously a great need exists for more hard data on the relationship if any of family factors to gang problems. Some new research findings are therefore presented in this chapter.

FAMILY AS THE FIRST LINE OF DEFENSE

When the family provides for all the basic human needs of American youths, then we can safely say that the influence on youthful behavior from other sources such as the community will be negligible. But when the family does not provide for all of the needs of its children, as Wrobleski and Hess (1987: p. 75) point out, this weight of responsibility will have to be carried elsewhere to produce good citizenship, and if this burden of citizenship training is not taken up, then what we can look forward to is a greater probability of gang problems.

GANG DISATTACHMENT THROUGH MARRIAGE

Several authors in the gang literature have referred to the transition from youth to adulthood represented by entering into marriage as a common means by which a gang member severs his ties to the gang organization (Denisoff and McCaghy, 1973: p. 153). According to this argument marriage can be looked upon as a legitimate social commitment and as a means of avoiding gang life. But again, there is little hard data on this topic.[3] Secondly, this would seem to apply mostly to those gangs at the lower end of the organizational development spectrum. Thirdly, if a gang member marries someone from within the gang social network, then we are not at all necessarily in the context of disjoining the gang, but could, like the data from India's gangs (Sleeman, 1849), be in the position of producing gang members from the family institution itself.

Marriage, then, is seen as the epitome of the transition from youth to adulthood; and somehow signals the end of gang affiliation. This has been, admittedly, a common theme of earlier works on gangs; but may not adequately represent contemporary standards of gang affiliation. But if it did, then we have at least the element of a viable gang intervention strategy: help these offenders "settle down" and raise a family, to drop their flag and give up gang life.

But again, before anyone interprets this as advocating a marriage matchmaking program for gang members, let it be pointed out that absolutely no experimental data has been yet reported on this matter supportive of such a position.

One thing is known: the more a gang member marries into the same social network that constitutes the gang social organization, the stronger the commitment is to be expected to the gang; and it can often mean raising offspring as gang members (see Sleeman, 1849). In the more sophisticated gang organizations it is not possible to simply say "I quit", or "hey homes, I'm married now...I don't have time to gangbang". Only in lower level gang organizations is marrying out of the gang ever going to be a feasible option.

PARENTAL HELP WITH HOMEWORK

Knowing whether or not parents or extended family adults (grandmother, etc) help a student at home or encourage a student to do their school homework appears to be an important factor that significantly differentiates gang membership. The dimension of family life this measures is one of family function and family structure. It is an aspect of family structure in as much as we are presuming such parental figures are present. It is an aspect of family function because helping a child with homework is a common element of socialization and support provided by the family unit.

A sample of 552 Chicago high school students in an anonymous survey administered in the Fall of 1991 provided a way to directly test whether this family variable had any effect on gang membership. Table 45 shows the results of this test.

TABLE 45

Frequency Distribution of Whether Parents/ Grandparents Help or Encourage With School Homework by Having Ever Joined a Gang Among A Fall 1991 Sample of Chicago High School Students

	Ever Join A Gang?	
	No	Yes
Does your mother, father, grandmother, etc, help you or encourage you with		
homework? NO	59	13
YES	411	41

Chi-square = 5.42, p = .02

Table 45 shows that the chances of ever joining a gang appear to double where the family does not provide such help or encouragement with school homework. Thus, among those students reporting that their family does provide such help with homework only 9 percent reported they had joined a gang. Yet among those students who report that their family does not provide such help with homework some 18 percent report having joined a gang. This factor of family function therefore significantly differentiates gang membership among this sample of high school students.

DO ALLOWANCES KEEP KIDS OUT OF THE GANG?

One aspect of family function for youths, particularly high school age youths, is whether or not the family provides any regular financial "allowance". In the spring of 1992 a national Asian educational association collaborated with the present author to conduct an anonymous survey of Asian students in eight states. Some of these findings about gangs are also discussed in chapter 14. Greater details on the findings from this study are described in Knox, Laske, and Tromanhauser (1992).

There are as many possible hypotheses to test in the relationship between "family" and "gang" joining behavior as there are different aspects and functions of the family. Normally, the higher the functional level of family life it is presumed that the lower will be the probability of a youth from such a family joining a gang. Thus, a family that provides an allowance for its school age children is generally assumed to be more structured or perhaps more economically advantaged. The curious finding here, at least among this sample of Asian students, is that gang membership as measured by ever joining a gang was actually higher among those students who were provided with a regular allowance from their family. This somewhat counterintuitive finding is provided in Table 46.

TABLE 46

FREQUENCY DISTRIBUTION OF WHETHER FAMILY PROVIDES A REGULAR ALLOWANCE BY EVER JOINING A GANG AMONG A 1992 SAMPLE OF ASIAN STUDENTS

		Ever Join a Gang?	
		No	Yes
Do you receive an allowance from your family?	No	160	8
	Yes	145	18

Chi-square = 4.50 p = .03

Table 46 shows that among those Asian students who did not receive a family allowance, some 4.7 percent also reported ever joining a gang. Yet among those receiving an allowance, some 11 percent report joining a gang. Thus, a student with an allowance appears to have a higher risk of joining a gang.

One possible explanation for this curious finding is that gangs may seek out members who can pay dues, who have expendable income on a regular basis. Because no "causality" can be proven with snapshot survey research like this, another possibility is that the "allowances" began after the youth became a gang member: as if the family could "buy back" the loyalty of their family member from the gang. Either way, this finding suggests the need for greater national quantitative research on this important issue.

WERE GANG MEMBERS EVER SEXUALLY ABUSED?

Sexual abuse is an important variable to examine in relationship to gang membership. This is not to say that in all or even most instances the perpetrator of sexual abuse of a minor is a family member, although that is a common scenario of such sex crimes. The issue here is examining sex crime victimization among juveniles to ascertain if differences exist by comparing gang members with their non-gang member counterparts.

The data source used here is described in greater detail in Chapter 20. It represents an anonymous survey of confined juveniles in five states during 1991[4]. The survey did measure whether the juvenile had ever joined a gang; further males and females did not differ significantly on this variable as they often do in research on high school samples. These juveniles were confined in both short term and long term correctional institutions.

The variable measuring sexual abuse among these juveniles asked if they had ever been forced to have sex through abuse or assault. Here we can directly answer an important question not previously addressed in the literature: are gang members more likely to be sexually abused during their childhood?

Table 47 shows the effects of gang membership on having ever been sexually abused among a large sample of confined juveniles. As seen here, gang membership is not a factor that differentiates self-reports of sex abuse among confined male juveniles. That is, among confined male juvenile delinquents gang members and non-gang members report about the same levels of sexual abuse. However, among female juvenile delinquents a much different pattern emerges.

TABLE 47

Frequency Distribution of Having Ever Joined a Gang by Having Ever Been Sexually Abused Among Male and Female Confined Juveniles

		EVER BEEN SEXUALLY ABUSED?			
		Males		Females	
		Yes	No	Yes	No
Ever Join a Gang?	Yes	86	632	48	41
	No	87	751	46	72

Chi-square=.99   Chi-square = 4.57
(p = .31, n.s.)   (p = .03)

The sad story that begins to emerge here is the high rate of sexual abuse among those juveniles who are found in our nation's juvenile correctional system. As seen in Table 47, overall some 11.1 percent of the confined boys and an amazing 45.4 percent of the confined females report that at some time in their past they have been forced to have sex through abuse or assault! Obviously, females are significantly more likely to be sexual abuse victims.

Among the males in Table 47, no significant difference emerges in sexual abuse victimization by the factor of prior gang membership. As seen in Table 47, 11.9 percent of the confined juveniles who had ever joined a gang report such sexual abuse. This differs little from the rate of 10.3 percent among confined juveniles who never joined a gang.

The significant relationship in Table 47 is not among males, but it is among females where the sexual abuse history is shown to be significantly differentiated by gang membership. As seen in Table 47, among the confined females who have joined a gang some 53.9 percent report being previously sexually abused. Similarly, among confined females who had never joined a gang, they show a significantly lower rate of such sexual abuse (38.9%). It is the female gang member who appears in this instance to be significantly more likely to also report being sexually abused.

An important matter that cannot be solved in Table 47 is causality: which came first, the sexual abuse, or the gang membership? While age at joining a gang is a variable available in the survey data, and age at time of completing the survey is available in the survey data, the age at time of first sexual victimization would be needed to test the two rival hypotheses about sexual abuse and gang membership among females. Unfortunately this question about age at time of first sexual abuse is not a question that was included in the survey. The two rival hypotheses about sexual abuse and gang membership are as follows:

(1) Females who have been sexually abused are more likely to subsequently join a gang out of a social-psychological breakdown. The logic being that the trauma, personal outrage and anger that can be expected in the aftermath of the life of a young child abuse victim may propel or predispose such a juvenile to join a gang subculture.

(2) Females who join gangs are more likely to subsequently be sexually abused --- as is often the case in the initiation ritual that among females may involve sexual violence and sexual humiliation. The logic here is that gangs are basically composed of males in control whose sexist views of the world and other interpersonal qualities tend to ensure that females are invited and even enticed into joining a gang --- the payoff being the right to sexually conquer the female juvenile. We need only recall the infamous case from San Antonio in 1993 where female juveniles were required as a part of their gang initiation ceremony to have sex with an AIDS/HIV infected gang member.

Analytically, however, with the two variables that are available (age at time of the survey, age at time of first joining a gang) it is possible to investigate this phenomenon of sexual abuse among confined juveniles more closely in a way that has implications for the two rival hypotheses. But to begin this analysis we will need to first test whether there is any difference between males and females in terms of the age at which they joined a gang. Table 48 below provides this test.

TABLE 48

Frequency Distribution of Gender by the Age at Time of First Joining a Gang Among Confined Juveniles

Gender:	Age at time of first joining a gang					
	<=8	9-10	11-12	13-14	15-16	>= 17
Males	40	107	215	254	125	15
Females	6	12	24	36	13	1

As seen above, 47.8 percent of the males joined a gang when they were twelve years of age or less. This differs very little from the females, where 45.6 percent joined the gang at the age of twelve or under. In other words, there is no significant difference among confined juveniles in terms of the effect of gender on age at joining a gang. This is useful to know in further investigating gang membership among the unique subpopulation of sexually abused confined juveniles.

Table 49 shows the effect of ever joining a gang on current age at time of the survey among the select population of confined female delinquents who also are sexual abuse victims. This shows an important finding: among confined juvenile sexual abuse victims, the younger the age the more likely the female is to also report having joined a gang. Among those confined juvenile sexual abuse victims who have joined a gang, 54.1 percent were less than or equal to fifteen years of age at the time of the survey. This compares to 34.7 percent among those who had never joined a gang. This is a substantial difference suggesting that gang membership among females does carry an added risk of earlier sexual abuse.

TABLE 49

**Frequency Distribution of Ever Joining a Gang
By Current Age Group
Among Confined Female Sexual Abuse Victims**

	Current Age	
	<= 15	>= 16
Ever Join a Gang?		
Yes	26	22
No	16	30

The above findings show that the younger confined juvenile sexual abuse victim is more likely to be have joined a gang. While this does shed some light on the issue, a complete testing of the rival hypotheses is not directly possible here.

FERTILITY IN RELATIONSHIP TO GANG MEMBERSHIP AMONG CONFINED JUVENILES

There is nothing that more directly gets at an important aspect of whether the complex factor we call "family" has any effect on gang membership than that of fertility itself. The fertility variable used here from the same study described above measures how many times the females have previously been pregnant and among the males how many times they have gotten someone pregnant. The important finding that emerges here is that both male and female gang members are apparently more likely to engage in sexual behavior that results in pregnancy than their non-gang member counterparts.

The other issue of fertility in relationship to gang membership as in all underage pregnancies, is the matter of children having children, and thus by physiological capability alone being prematurely catapulted into the adult role of a parent. This gets at one of the most fascinating aspects of gangs and family: how gang members raise their own children. Our data on confined juveniles, however, allows us only to test the null hypothesis that there are no differences in fertility by whether or not a juvenile has ever joined a gang.

Table 50 below shows the results of this test for confined juvenile males.

TABLE 50

**Frequency Distribution of Ever Joining a Gang
by Number of Times the Male Has Gotten
Someone Pregnant
Among Confined Juveniles**

	How many times have you gotten Someone Pregnant?		
	None	Once	Twice or more
Ever Join a Gang?			
Yes	276	221	128
No	455	203	91

Chi-square = 39.9, p < .001

As seen in Table 50 above we can reject the null hypothesis that no significant difference exists with regard to this aspect of fertility in comparing male juveniles who have and who have not joined a gang. In fact, as seen in Table 50, among the non-gang joining youths, 60.7 percent have never gotten someone pregnant. For youths who have joined gangs, however, some 44.7 percent have never gotten someone pregnant. Youths reporting prior gang membership clearly have a higher likelihood of reporting that they have gotten someone pregnant.

Finally, we can examine the same issue of fertility among female confined juveniles and this test is provided in Table 51 below.

TABLE 51

**Frequency Distribution of Ever Joining a Gang
by Number of Times Ever Being Pregnant
Among Confined Female Juveniles**

	How many times have you Been Pregnant?		
	None	Once	Twice or More
Ever Join a Gang?			
Yes	48	17	23
No	72	34	14

Chi-square = 7.92, p = .01

Table 51 above shows the interesting finding that among confined females juveniles who have joined a gang, some 26.1 percent of them have been pregnant twice or more, compared to only 11.6 percent among their non-gang joining counterparts. The factor of ever joining a gang is shown to significantly differentiate the number of times these female juvenile delinquents have ever been pregnant. The trend in the data shows higher pregnancy rates among the females who have joined a gang.

SEXUAL BEHAVIOR AND GANG MEMBER-SHIP AMONG CONFINED JUVENILES

The simple question about whether gang members are more promiscuous has never been quantitatively researched in the previous literature. Yet the sexual behavior of gang members represents an important domain of human behavior itself and as shown above, at least the sexual experiences of some gang members, particularly females as discussed previously, may play a prominent role in explaining some aspects of their behavior. Here we provide the first known national data on this crucial topic of sexual behavior in relationship to having ever joined a gang among confined juvenile delinquents.

The variable used here to measure sexual behavior in the 1991 survey of confined juvenile delinquents actually measures age at the time of first consensual sex. It asks how old were you the first time you willingly had sex. Let us begin this inquiry by examining Table 52 below. This shows the separate distributions for males and females on age at time of first consensual sex.

TABLE 52

Frequency and Percentage Distribution of Age At Time of First Willingly Having Sex Among Male and Female Confined Juveniles

How old were you the first time you willingly had sex?	Males N	Males %	Females N	Females %
I Never willingly had sex	65	4.1	24	11.1
Less than 12 years old	647	40.5	37	17.1
12 years old	396	24.8	50	23.1
13 years old	252	15.8	45	20.8
14 years old	145	9.1	40	18.5
15 years old	60	3.8	12	5.6
16 years old	27	1.7	6	2.8
17 or more years old	6	.4	2	.9

As seen in Table 52 above, there are some juveniles in this sample who report that they have never in their life willingly had sex with anyone. Some 4.1 percent of the males and some 11.1 percent of the females indicated that they have never willingly had sex. Thus, in order to truly evaluate the issue of consensual sex among these confined juveniles, it is useful to eliminate these persons who have never had sex or who have never willingly had sex. Table 53 below shows the adjusted distribution among males and females for age at time of first consensual sex where we have eliminated from the sample those who claim to never willingly have had sex.

TABLE 53

Frequency and Percentage Distribution of Age At Time of First Willingly Having Sex Among Male and Female Confined Juveniles (Minus Those Who Claim to Never Willingly Have Had Sex)

How old were you the first time you willingly had sex?	Males N	Males %	Females N	Females %
Less than 12 years old	647	42.2	37	19.3
12 years old	396	25.8	50	26.0
13 years old	252	16.4	45	23.4
14 years old	145	9.5	40	20.8
15 years old	60	3.9	12	6.3
16 years old	27	1.8	6	3.1
17 or more years old	6	.4	2	1.0

As seen in Table 53 above, males are twice as likely as their confined juvenile female counterparts to report that they first willingly had sex before the age of twelve. Some 42.2 percent of the males and some 19.3 percent of the confined females report that they first willingly had sex before the age of twelve. What this shows is a substantial gender difference in human sexual behavior in terms of those first reporting consensual sex before the age of twelve among confined juvenile delinquents. Thus, we enter the gang membership question in relation to sexual behavior knowing this important difference does exist.

Whether gang members have sex at an earlier age than their non-gang counterparts among confined juveniles can now be directly tested. Table 54 below provides the breakdown of ever joining a gang by age at time of first willingly having sex among males, Table 51 provides the same results for females.

TABLE 54

Frequency Distribution of Ever Joining a Gang By Age of First Willingly Having Sex (Eliminating Those who Never Willingly Had Sex) Among Confined Male Juveniles

Ever Join a Gang?	<12	12	13	14	15	16	>=17
Yes	343	178	107	60	24	9	5
No	302	216	144	85	36	18	1

Chi-square = 20.3, p = .002

As seen in Table 54 above for males, the significant difference here is the factor of first having consensual sex before the age of twelve. Among males who have joined a gang some 47.2 percent report first willingly having sex before the age of twelve, compared to 37.6 percent among confined males who have not ever joined a gang. If we are willing to arbitrarily use the age of twelve as the point distinguishing when someone enters the period of adolescence, then gang members clearly seem to engage in more pre-adolescent consensual sexual behavior than their non-gang member counterparts in this sample of confined juvenile delinquents.

Table 55 below provides the same test what effect the variable of ever joining a gang has on the factor of human sexuality involving the age of first consensually having sex among confined female delinquents. Again, a substantial difference emerges here, but to see it we have to go one year in advance of the males and examine the percentage of females who first had sex not before the age of twelve, but on or before the age of 12.

TABLE 55

**Frequency Distribution of Ever Joining a Gang
By Age of First Willingly Having Sex
(Eliminating Those who Never
Willingly Had Sex)
Among Confined Female Juveniles**

	< 12	12	13	14	15	16	>=17
Ever Join a Gang?							
Yes	21	28	12	14	6	1	1
No	16	22	33	26	6	4	1

As seen in Table 55 above, among females who have joined a gang some 59 percent report first having consensual sex on or before the age of twelve; compared to 35.1 percent for their counterparts who have never joined a gang. This says that female gang members are more likely than those who never joined a gang to have consensual sex at an earlier age (i.e., twelve or under). It is fair to assume that the gang as a subculture of deviance appears to accelerate deviance and risky behavior at an earlier age; it is the gang socialization and the effects this has on the individual that can be expected to propel such a person into greater difficulty and trouble.

PARENT AND OTHER ADULT GUIDANCE ABOUT AIDS AND HIV INFECTION

Generally, most would be willing to assume that the more functional family structure is one that has the capability where the parents or other adults can and do talk to the child about the risks of AIDS or HIV infection. It is not just a sex education issue. Minimally, the lines of communication as a family function, would be higher in the family that is able to have such a dialogue with a child on the dangers of AIDS and HIV infection. Here we can directly test one very limited aspect of whether kids who join gangs come from less functional or dysfunctional families than those who do not join gangs. For here we will examine the effects of ever joining a gang on the variable of whether youths from the confined juvenile sample have ever talked about AIDS or HIV infection with a parent or other adult outside of school[5].

Table 56 below shows the effects of joining a gang on this factor of family/other adult guidance about AIDS/HIV infection. The null hypothesis that there is no difference in this factor that relates to parent and other adults providing such guidance between youths who join gangs and youths who do not join gangs cannot be rejected. No significant difference emerges here for confined juvenile males.

TABLE 56

**Frequency Distribution of Ever Joining a Gang
By Whether Parent or Other Adult
(Outside of School)
Has Ever Talked to the Confined Male Juvenile
About AIDS or HIV Infection**

	Parent/Adult Talk About AIDS?		
	Yes	No	Not Sure
Ever Join a Gang?			
Yes	448	257	38
No	542	288	31

Chi-square = 2.73, p = .25 (n.s.)

Similarly, no significant difference in this factor emerged among confined female juveniles as shown in Table 57 below.

TABLE 57

**Frequency Distribution of Ever Joining a Gang
By Whether Parent or Other Adult
(Outside of School)
Has Ever Talked to the Confined
Female Juvenile
About AIDS or HIV Infection**

	Parent/Adult Talk About AIDS?		
	Yes	No	Not Sure
Ever Join a Gang?			
Yes	68	20	3
No	83	33	7

Chi-square = 1.52, p = .46 (n.s.)

In summary, virtually no difference exists among confined males with regard to this possible family function of parents or other adults talking to the youth about AIDS or HIV infection. Males who had joined a gang (60.2%) were almost identical to those who had never joined a gang (62.9%) in terms of reporting that they had in fact talked to a parent or other adult outside of school about AIDS/HIV infection. Among females a slightly higher percentage (74.7%) of the females who had joined a gang had received such talks from parents or other adults outside of school, than had their non-gang joining counterparts (67.4%); but again this is not a significant difference.

In summary, the fact that this factor of ever joining a gang fails to significantly differentiate this aspect related to family life would tend to support the contention by Sanchez-Jankowski (1991) that gang members like non-gang members are equally likely to come from good or bad, functional or dysfunctional families. This is not, however, the strongest empirical evidence for such a claim, as has been pointed out, because the other findings in this chapter would tend to vastly outweigh such an overgeneralization. The fact seems to be, yes, the family does matter. It simply depends on what we are looking at, where we are looking, and how we are looking (i.e., doing research)[6].

Another way of looking at this finding of no significant difference regarding gang joining behavior and reports of parents/adults talking about AIDS/HIV infection to them emerges when we examine more specifically the rates of sexually transmitted diseases (STD's) among juveniles who join gangs and those who do not. If those who join gangs are significantly more likely to report having been diagnosed with an STD, which would be logically consistent with the fact that early sexual activity and I.V. drug use being more prevalent among youths who join gangs, then perhaps what we have here regarding "talking about AIDS" is a greater failure among parents of gang members to monitor their behavior and to therefore adequately protect them through such counseling and guidance.

GANG MEMBERSHIP IN RELATIONSHIP TO SEXUALLY TRANSMITTED DISEASES

Do juveniles who join gangs differ from their non-gang joining counterparts in terms of whether they have ever been diagnosed as having a sexually transmitted disease? Here we can directly test this relationship using the confined juvenile sample. The variable about STD's asked the youth whether they have ever been told by a doctor or nurse that they had a sexually transmitted disease such as genital herpes, genital warts, chlamydia, syphilis, gonorrhea, AIDs or HIV infection, including common slang terms such as "clap" and "drip".

Table 58 below provides the results of this test. As can be seen here, joining a gang significantly differentiates contracting an STD only among males. And it is the male juvenile who reports ever joining a gang who is more likely to report acquiring an STD than the juvenile who does not join a gang. However, among females no such significant difference exists with regard to gang joining behavior.

TABLE 58

Frequency Distribution of Ever Joining a Gang By Being Diagnosed with a Sexually Transmitted Disease Among Male and Female Confined Juveniles

	Ever Diagnoses With an S.T.D.?			
	Males		Females	
	Yes	No	Yes	No
Ever Join a Gang?				
Yes	123	597	32	58
No	99	739	34	86
	Chi-square=8.80		Chi-square=1.24	
	(p = .002)		(p = .26, n.s.)	

A closer inspection of Table 58 above shows what appears to be a much higher prevalence of sexually transmitted diseases among confined females. It is worthwhile, therefore, to examine without regard to gang membership, but more generally, whether gender is a factor that significantly differentiates STD's among these confined juveniles. For if it is, the much higher rate among females may obscure any effects of gang membership.

Table 59 below provides this test of gender by contracting STD's among confined juveniles.

TABLE 59

Frequency Distribution of Gender by Ever Being Diagnosed With a Sexually Transmitted Disease Among Confined Juveniles

	Ever Told You Had an STD?	
	Yes	No
GENDER:		
Male	222 (14.1%)	1342
Female	66 (31.2%)	145
	Chi-square = 39.9, p < .001	

As seen in Table 59 above, gender is very significant in differentiating the health factor of ever being diagnosed with an STD among this sample of confined juveniles. In fact, confined female juveniles are twice as likely to report having been diagnosed with an STD than their male counterparts (14.1% male vs. 31.2% female). We can probably assume --- given the gynopeia[7] of male dominated social policy making bodies like those who make the recommendations and who control the budgets --- that our national social policy on STD awareness is not proportionately balanced in terms of prevention efforts in line with the vastly higher objective health care risks that apparently serious female juvenile delinquents face in comparison to their male counterparts.

It is useful, in light of this issue, to examine another variable about individual behavior and responsibility regarding sex: the use of condoms. Table 60 below shows the effects of ever joining a gang on use of condoms during the last sexual encounter among male and female confined juveniles. No significant difference emerges here[8].

TABLE 60
Frequency Distribution of Ever Joining a Gang By Condom Use the Last Time They Willingly Had Sex Among Male and Female Confined Juveniles (Eliminating Those Who Never Willingly Had Sex)

	The last time you willingly had sex, did you or your partner use a condom?			
	MALES		FEMALES	
	Yes	No	Yes	No
EVER JOIN A GANG?				
Yes	226	497	29	54
No	273	530	28	80

Chi-square = 1.29   Chi-square = 1.82
(p = .25, n.s.)   (p = .17, n.s.)

A test was made of the gender difference, if any, on this variable of using a condom during the last time having sex; but no significant difference emerged in comparing male and female confined juveniles. Some 32.6 percent of the males and 29.6 percent of the females indicated they made use of a condom during the last time they had sex.

DO CHILDREN OF ADULT INCARCERATED TODAY BECOME TOMORROWS GANG MEMBERS?

It is a tragic possibility that the large numbers of children left behind by our American prison inmates may themselves be the most likely candidates to feed gang membership.[9] All we can hope to do here is develop such a hypothesis based on the magnitude of the problem represented by incarcerating mothers and fathers and leaving behind, in our cities,

large numbers of children.[10] These are children in unknown conditions of care and supervision, and presumably from the same environment as that which placed their parents in prison.[11]

The "baby boom" that fed our prisons in the 1960's and 1970's might be artificially created in terms of large numbers of children without adequate care and supervision if in fact our nation's inmates are leaving behind children whose career trajectory places them directly in line for deviance, crime, and gang affiliation. Just how serious is this problem?

The 1991 first edition of this book described statistics on the offspring of adults incarcerated in Illinois state prisons. More than half of these Illinois prison inmates had one or more children regardless of their marital status.   Now comes the interesting work of estimating how many children in our nation have parents in prison. Any way we go, we are talking about substantial numbers of children who have parents in correctional custody.

Estimate # 1: Using as a parameter the 55 percent of IDOC inmates who report having children, under the assumption that Illinois inmates are not significantly different than others in the USA, then for the prison population alone which at this writing is approaching two million in state and federal prisons[12], we are talking about at least one million inmates with children left behind in our communities.

Estimate # 2: When we adjust for the mean number of children left behind, and the additional numbers of persons in local jails, and for those incarcerated in juvenile correctional institutions, our estimate of children left behind rises to somewhere between two and three million.[13]

FAMILY "MORAL PANIC" IN RELATIONSHIP TO GANG IDENTIFIERS

Just because the public is not in panic does not mean there is nothing to be panicky about. But all too often some element of hysteria regarding gang affiliation is to be found among parents in relationship to their perceptions of their own and other youths. What it also boils down to, usually, is a moral panic. The fear that our best children in the best of families have fallen into the clutches of gang organization.

The "evidence" to some parents is anything unusual, certainly earrings, different color shoe laces, language, hand signs of greetings or solidarity made to other youths, etc. Parents will know when their child is a gang member by a variety of factors other than so-called "tell tale" signs of clothing and demeanor. Arrest, carrying a weapon, tattoos, ongoing illegal income --- these are the real signs of gang involvement for youths.

In a school environment an effective gang/delinquency management specialist assigned to the school will certainly know through the grape vine who is and who is not gang affiliated. A parent need only consult their school officials and local law enforcement to ascertain the truth if they are too socially blind to determine it themselves. Along these same lines, it may be useful to present some findings on behavioral correlates of gang affiliation.

THE GANG IS SOMETHING THE FAMILY CANNOT MOVE AWAY FROM

The idea of the contagion effect in the study of how the mass media may encourage some crimes is an idea that has also been extended to the situation of where a parent discovers a child to be a gang member and tries to relocate thinking just moving will squash the gang problem. They move, and nothing changes, but the child starts a new chapter of the gang in the new area. As explained by Laskey (1994)[14], one of the ways in which the gang problem spreads or proliferates may be unintentional in nature, resulting from the otherwise good intentions of parents. It means the parent relocates to a new area knowing their child was involved in a gang, and basically the gang gets "transplanted" to the new area. This would account for one of the many sources of what now constitutes the proliferation of gangs throughout all areas of the United States. Laskey's (1994) survey of 232 police chiefs and 25 county sheriffs in Illinois showed that 62.4 percent of the police chiefs and 60 percent of the county sheriffs reporting having seen cases of this familial transplanting of the gang problem. Thus, the old witticism may apply here having some moral implications: you can take the boy out of the country, but you can't take the country out of the boy; that is, simply moving without any change in values or orientation will not likely stop a child's gang involvement unless the child really and seriously wants "out" of the gang. When the child does not want out of the gang, moving will not change things is what this research would suggest. On the other hand, most observers would suggest that if a child does want "out", that moving would be very appropriate.

FAMILY, SELF-ESTEEM AND OTHER THEORETICAL FACTORS: Findings From A Study of a Gang Program.

Apparently there are some important attitudinal and behavioral differences when we compare gang offenders versus their non-gang affiliated offender counterparts. A common attribution to gang members is that they have low self-esteem or that self-esteem is a factor that may impact on gang behavior. Prior to adulthood, it is the family that is most responsible in terms of socialization to instill self-esteem. But among those collecting lists of "gang myths", another might be asserting that it is a myth

that the self-esteem of gang members differs from that of their non-gang member counterparts[15]. If self-esteem is only important after the criminal justice process sets in, then self-esteem like other factors (e.g., family) may have sufficient variability and conditions and contexts under which it sets in, particularly in relationship to recognizing differences in the level of social organizational functioning in modern gangs, that the lower self-esteem may have no impact in some areas but much impact in others. Summarized here are some such relevant findings that were reported previously (Knox, Mc Clendon, and Garcia, 1983).

"Suing the Parents for the Behavior of Gang-Involved Underage Children"

Can the parents of gang members be sued just because they have kids who are bad kids and who do bad things? Yes would be the general response. Most parents cringe at the idea. They cringe at the idea because they want to be off the hook in terms of responsibility for the behavior of their underage children.

Actually, there are many routine cases in civil procedure where parents are in fact held financially liable for the behavior of their underage children. This typically shows up in automobile accident cases, rather than gang cases. Two of the most popular theories of parental liability are: (1) negligent entrustment, and (2) agency. Under negligent entrustment the parent knowingly entrusts a child with the use of a car, knowing the child is irresponsible (e.g., bad driver, drinker, etc), and should something adverse happen, then the parent can in fact be sued under this theory of liability. Under the agency concept, the parent may act as an agent in some cases, for example asking the child to deliver a package using a car, and if the car gets in an accident, the parent is the agent responsible here, because the parent directed the activity to take place, and is therefore liable.

Can the theories of negligent entrustment and agency be applied to gang cases? It would seem so.

Using "civil sanctions", particularly involving lawsuits for financial damages, represents the trend that can be expected in the future against gangs and gang members of any age.

When it comes to juveniles, some states set "limits" on how much a parent can be sued for in terms of actual damages. In Illinois, the ceiling is $2,500 plus court and attorney fees.

SOURCE: "Here Comes Trouble: How Much Will It Cost if Your Child Runs Afoul of the Law?", by Ross Werland, Chicago Tribune, Section 13, p. 1, 5; Feb. 6, 2000.

Using a community-based program for ex-offenders that provided educational services to youthful offenders below the age of 21 located in a predominantly Latino area on Chicago's westside, in a project of collaborative empiricism involving the program staff and clients, anonymous surveys were completed by N = 97 youthful offenders (16 - 21 years of age). These youths were adjudicated offenders, whose mean age of first arrest was 14.8 years of age. Two-thirds of this group are Latino and it is predominantly male.

More than half (52.6%) of these youths reported that someone in their immediate family was economically dependent on welfare benefits. Some 38 percent indicated that at least one of their siblings had also been in trouble with the law.[16] Mostly, for purposes of analysis here, it is important that 53.6 percent of these ex-offenders reported being a gang member at some time in the past. These were youths who were clearly on their way to more trouble unless they could turn their lives around. The mean number of self-reported prior arrests for this group is 14.3!

Relying on previous research which has shown the value of trying to overcome the natural reporting bias introduced when a researcher tries to obtain data on deviance from a known offender population --- that is their tendency to over report their "good" qualities and to underreport their deviance --- a number of the questions focused on not their own deviance, but the deviance of their friends. Offenders are much more likely to report the deviance of their associates than their own. Therefore, following the findings of Hardt and Peterson (1968), "friends" deviance may be a better indicator of true deviance than that which these offenders report for their "self".

Table 61 below provides some of these findings about the deviance of their associates. These four items all asked "how many of your current friends" had previously been in prison, belonged to a gang, were hustling and stealing to make a living, and who had been in trouble with the law. What all of these questions tend to measure is the extent of subcultural integration among these youths. That is, the extent to which their own social and friendship networks consist of those persons who have either an ongoing deviant lifestyle or have been labelled as deviant.

TABLE 61

PERCENTAGE DISTRIBUTION FOR SUBCULTURAL INTEGRATION FACTORS

Type of Friend	Number of Current Friends					
	None	One	Two	Three	Four	Five or more
Previously been in prison	19.6%	4.1%	9.3%	9.3%	4.1%	53.7%
Who belong to a gang	46.4%	1.0%	6.2%	2.1%	4.1%	40.2%
Who are hustling or stealing to make a living	31.9%	10.6%	10.6%	3.2%	2.1%	41.5%
Been in trouble with the law	11.5%	1.0%	11.5%	9.4%	4.2%	62.5%

An interesting picture emerges here from focusing on the social relationships these offenders have as seen above in Table 61. By asking these youthful offenders about their friends, not themselves, we do get a better picture of just how subculturally integrated they are. Over eighty percent reported having one or more current friends who have served time in prison. Over half (53.6%) report having one or more current friends who are gang members. Over two-thirds report having one or more current friends who are hustling or stealing to make a living. And only 11.5 percent indicated their current friends had not previously been in trouble with the law.

The severity level is the more serious finding in Table 61 above. By examining the percentage distribution for type of friend where the youthful offender responding to this survey reports having five or more such friends, gives us a higher level of subcultural integration in terms of severity. Over fifty percent report having five or more such friends who are ex-cons. About forty percent report having five or more friends who belong to a gang, as is also the case for friends who are currently hustling or stealing to make a living.

We did ask them about their own deviance, but as stated above that is not the most reliable approach given the tendency of known offenders to under report their own deviance. Some 14.7 percent said they smoke marijuana every day, 11.6 percent "a couple times a week", 29.5 percent "now and then", and 44.2 percent "little or none". Only 12.4 percent reported getting high off of any drugs other than marijuana. We also asked them about what crimes they either "committed or were involved with" during the last two month period. Obviously, these respondents generally expressed an unfavorable reaction to this item, but it still uncovered some levels of self-reported crime: armed robber - 3.2 percent; burglary - 5.3 percent; assault - 6.3 percent; theft valued over $50 - 11.6 percent; drug sales - 11.6 percent; car theft - 3.1 percent.

These youths had already completed the educational program at the time they were invited back to participate in this survey research, and 32.3 percent reported having been arrested for some offense since completing the program (less than a year). Generally, when youths such as these who have had such a history of academic and school failure are able to complete their GED's, this is known to give them a better prognosis in terms of the risk of recidivism (see Knox, 1980).

What is valuable about this research is not the recidivism, for which we have only self-report information, but rather the fact other theoretically relevant data was collected on these same youthful offenders. This data actually replicates previous research and involves attitudinal scales that can be used to analyze the strength of association with the known pattern of gang affiliation. Let me briefly describe the scales and their value.

The perceived closure in the legitimate opportunity structure scale (Short, Rivera, and Tennyson, 1965; Knox, 1978) measures the extent to which a person perceives the legitimate world (education and occupation) closed to them. That is, someone with high levels of perceived closure sees no hope for a legitimate life; they see obstacles, not opportunities. It is an attitudinal approach to the testing of differential opportunity theory (Cloward and Ohlin, 1960). Generally, previous research shows that the higher the perceived closure in legitimate opportunity the greater the likelihood of being an offender. Here we are concerned about whether this is also related to gang affiliation.

Self-concept and self-esteem are two widely known social-psychological factors that have been researched extensively among offenders. Here two such self-esteem attitudinal scales were used. This included the Rosenberg (1965) self-esteem scale and the Tennessee Self-Concept Scale. Generally, from prior research a youth with higher levels of self-esteem and a better self-concept is less likely to become an offender. Again, however, here we are not using a dependent variable of initial criminality or recidivism; instead we are examining gang affiliation patterns.

Finally, another scale called the Rundquist-Sletto Respect for the Law Scale (1936) was also used. This measure can be loosely conceived of as capturing some element of the legitimation crisis; that is, the extent to which anyone has respect for our legal institutions, police, etc.; or conversely, the extent to which they feel our legal system is corrupt

and unfair at all levels. That is, under the racism-oppression thesis we would expect persons to have a very low level of respect for constituted authority, or "the system" as it were. It measures a social-political dimension; that is, one's attitude toward the status quo.

Figure 21 below summarizes the statistical results from examining these attitudinal scales in relationship to measures of gang affiliation. The statistic used here is the Pearson zero-order correlation coefficient. Its meaning can be summarized readily. The correlation value ranges from a complete low (no association whatsoever) of zero to a complete high (perfect correlation, e.g., between life and death the Pearson correlation coefficient is 1.0) of one. The higher the value, the stronger the association.

FIGURE 21

SIGNIFICANT CORRELATIONS[17] BETWEEN SELECTED ATTITUDINAL SCALES AND MEASURES OF GANG AFFILIATION

SCALES: *******	Pearson Correlation ***********	Measure of Gang Affiliation ***********
Perceived Closure in the legitimate opportunity structure	.19	Ever been a gang member
Rosenberg Self-esteem scale	-.12	
Tennessee Self-Concept Scale	-.19	
Tennessee Self-Concept Scale	-.19	Currently a Gang member
Perceived Closure in the legitimate opportunity structure	.41	
Rundquist and Sletto's Respect for the Law scale	-.15	Number of Current friends who are gang members
Tennessee Self-Concept Scale	-.19	
Rosenberg Self-Esteem Scale	-.21	

What the findings in Figure 21 above show is largely consistent. This data shows a decidedly inverse relationship between self-esteem and gang affiliation. That is, the higher the self-esteem level, the lower the likelihood of gang affiliation. Or conversely, the lower one's self-esteem or self-concept, the higher the association with gang life. Also, respect for the law varies inversely with the number of current friends who are gang members.

The magnitude of the correlation coefficient is what is also important here. While all of these relationships in Figure 21 were significant (p < .05), that is we expect them in terms probability to occur by chance in less than five times out of 100, we also see some large differences emerging here in what kind of gang affiliation measure we are analyzing.

When examining the gang affiliation variables of (1) have you ever been a gang member previously, and (2) are you currently a gang member, there is virtually no difference in the magnitude of the strength of the association between the three scales --- perceived closure, self-esteem, and self-concept. Only the valence or the direction of the relationship varies. Perceived closure has a positive relationship, the higher it is then the higher the gang affiliation. Both self-esteem and self-concept have consistent inverse relationships with gang affiliation.

Indeed the Rundquist and Sletto (1936) respect for the law scale is only significant in terms of its correlation with the third measure of gang affiliation --- number of current friends who are gang members. And it too, like self-esteem and self-concept shows an inverse relationship. That is, it has a negative correlation coefficient value.

Therefore, in using as our measure of gang affiliation the simple direct question to known offenders --- have you ever been or are you currently a gang member --- we see that virtually no difference emerges in terms of a higher explanatory power between the theories thought to have some relationship to gangs (opportunity theory, self-concept/self-esteem, and legitimation). In fact, it is only when we examine the more indirect measure of asking the offender about friends who are gang members, where we probably get a more accurate measure of gang affiliation as discussed earlier, that we see some important differences emerge.

In fact, looking at the last measure of gang affiliation in Figure 21 (number of current friends who are gang members) we see that the sociological theory (differential opportunity) yields a relationship that is twice as strong as any of the others. In fact, all such correlations in Figure 21 are low except for the moderately strong relationship between perceived closure and number of friends who are gang members (r = .41).

While the Cloward and Ohlin (1960) theory has been found to be useful for explaining generalized delinquency, just as the measure of perceived closure has been able to significantly differentiate delinquents and non-delinquents in past research, recall that their theory was explicitly directed at gang delinquency.

THE EFFECTS OF PRIOR GANG MEMBERSHIP

Recall that nearly half of these offenders self-reported that they were at some time in the past a gang member. Therefore this one variable of prior gang membership is useful in examining some other dependent variables. What this shows, with alarming consistency, is that prior gang membership for this Chicago sample of youthful offenders significantly differentiates a variety of adjustment outcomes. These results are presented in Table 62 below.

The statistic used here is the Chi-square which is a measure of independence. If it is significant, then it suggests there is some relationship between the variables. Generally, such a chi-square value is considered significant if the probability is less than .05. Meaning it would occur, by chance, in less than one time out of twenty.

TABLE 62

THE EFFECTS OF PRIOR GANG MEMBERSHIP ON DEVIANCE MEASURES

Arrested After the Program

		No		Yes	
		N	%	N	%
Prior Gang Member:	NO	35	77.8	10	22.2
	YES	30	58.8	21	41.2

Chi square = 3.92, p = .04

Use of Drugs Other than Marijuana or Alcohol

		No		Yes	
		N	%	N	%
Prior Gang Member:	NO	41	95.3	2	4.7
	YES	37	80.4	9	19.6

Chi square = 4.56 p = .03

Currently "Tied in" To a Gang

		No		Yes	
		N	%	N	%
Prior Gang Member:	NO	44	97.8	1	2.2
	YES	39	75.0	13	25.0

Chi square = 10.13 p = .001

One or More Friends Who Are Hustling/Stealing for a Living

		No		Yes	
		N	%	N	%
Prior Gang Member:	NO	21	47.7	23	52.3
	YES	9	18.0	41	82.0

Chi square = 9.51 p = .002

As seen in Table 62 above, this single factor of prior gang membership significantly differentiates four different measures of deviance among youthful offenders. This includes whether they report being arrested after completing a community-based literacy program, whether they report getting high off of drugs other than marijuana or alcohol, whether they have a current "tie in" with any gang, and whether they report one or more friends who are currently hustling or stealing to make a living.

As also revealed in Table 62, there appears to be a minimum risk of bringing such gang and nongang offenders together in a collective treatment setting. Only one person is shown to have reported no prior gang membership but has some current "tie in" to a gang.

In the interest of ethically disclosing all known findings some other results should also be summarized here. Data was also collected on the number of program hours each such offender spent in the program. Apparently, the program was reimbursed on such an hourly treatment basis as is customary in aftercare performance contracts for such counseling and assistance. This yielded the intriguing result that those who were prior gang members had an average of 20 more hours enrolled in the program than non-gang members. This amounted to a mean of 138 hours for prior gang members compared to 118 for those without prior gang membership.

There was also a significant difference found for age of first arrest. Prior gang members showed a mean age at first arrest of 13.9 years compared to 15.9 for those who were not prior gang members. Clearly, two full years difference!

SUMMARY

In the best of all worlds, the family as an agency of socialization and informal social control would be the best "first line of defense" against the gang problem. But dysfunctional families do exist, even more families experience enormous economic stress or feel the effects of residential segregation and failing relationships to other mainstream social institutions --- and these families might theoretically be expected to be less effectively instill in their youths an internal "buffer" against joining a gang. Fatalism is not an attitude we can simply change and expect the problem to go away. But fatalistic outlooks on life could reasonable be expected among families of some gang members, particularly those who lost loved ones to gang violence.

There is a need for more hard and quantifiable data on gangs in relationship to the family and the many factors involved with what we regard as "family". More often than not it is the family of the gang member that comes to suffer the effects of gang violence.[18] The family of orientation is usually what

most of the gang literature issues have dealt with to date: the issue being that maybe some family conditions may be associated with a higher likelihood of ever joining a gang. But the family of procreation for anyone who has joined a gang is also a highly relevant area of much needed research, as basically very little is currently known based on any systematic national objective approach. It is a matter of civil rights: children have rights to live free from ongoing physical or mental abuse from their parents or the risks to personal harm that they may pose; and thus some civil libertarian could theoretically argue that raising a child to be a gang member by parents who are members of the same gang could be construed legally as child abuse: thus, such parents could forfeit their parental rights, and the state could take custody of their children as wards of the court, or put them up for adoption. No one knows how many children have ever been raised to be gang members. That and many other "unknowns" tends to describe the rather elementary stage of development yet attained by gang research in criminology today.

What we do know is that it would be comparable to dogmatism to say that the family does not matter in terms of gangs, gang members, or gang problems, because the family means so much: all its relationships, its functions, its structure and the variations in between. So this chapter has shown that some family variables do matter in relation to gang membership. It is therefore useful to enlist parents in the goal of gang prevention initiatives[19].

One of the haunting questions in the gang literature is whether we, as a society, tend to systematically reproduce new gang members when their parents are placed in prison.[20] Very large numbers of children are simply left behind.

We have examined several different research projects dealing with gangs that involved family issues and factors. Most of the research shows that having ever joined a gang was a significant variable in relationship to a variety of family variables. However, from a social science point of view, the causality issue is one that is not likely to be resolved easily.

DISCUSSION QUESTIONS:

(1) From a position of economic comfort it is easy to say the family should be primarily responsible for preventing gang affiliation. But what of those families living in poverty? And under economic distress? Can such families really be expected to exercise social control over members whose activities or behavior results in economic benefit to other family members and parents?

(2) Should there be a modernized "Fagan" law, to make it a felony to encourage or cultivate law violation among ones own children or for whom one is a legal guardian, where benefiting economically from their known or assumed illicit activity would be sufficient grounds for conviction?

(3) Why would marriage be more likely to be a route out of the gang for lower level gang formations (level zero and level one) as opposed to higher level gang formations (level two and level three)? Should teacher and parent "gang awareness" training be provided by the federal government nationally?

(4) Should a parent who knowingly allows their child, or who encourages their child, to become a gang member be subject to state intervention for "child abuse"?

(5) Should parents of juvenile gang members be sued for the damage done by their children?

RECOMMENDED READINGS:
On Family and Crime.

Adams, Paul L. and Jeffrey H. Horovitz
1980 "Psychopathology and Fatherlessness in Poor Boys", Child Psychiatry and Human Development (Spr)(10)(3):135-143.
Allen, Walter R.
1979 "Class, Culture and Family Organization: The Effects of Class and Race on Family Structure in Urban America", Journal of Comparative Family Studies (10)(3): 301-313.
Alston, Doris N. and Nannette Williams
1982 "Relationship Between Father Absence and Self-Concept of Black Adolescent Boys", Journal of Negro Education (Spr)(51)(2): 134-138.

Ansari, Anwar and Bharati Ghose
1957 "A Study of Family Attitudes of Children withContrasting Socio-Economic Back ground", Educ. Psychol. Delhi. (4)(2): 90-102.
Aronus, Sidney
1970 The Black Middle Class. Columbus, OH: Charles E. Merrill Co.
Ball, Richard E.
1983 "Family and Friends: A Supportive Network for Low-IncomeAmerican Black Families", Journal of Comparative Family Studies (Spr)(14)(1): 51-65.
Billingsley, Andrew
1974 Black Families and the Struggle for Survival. New York: Friendship Press.
Brodsky, S.L.
1975 Families and Friends of Men in Prison: The Uncertain Relationship. Toronto: Lexington Books.
Brodsky, Stanley L. and H. O'Neal Smitherman
1983 Handbook of Scales for Research in Crime and Delinquency. New York: Plenum Press.
Brown, Waln K.
1978 "Black Gangs as Family Extensions", International Journal of Offender Therapy and Comparative Criminology (22)(1): 39-48.
Brooks, William Allan
1952 Girl Gangs. New York: Padell Book Company.
Bullard, Robert D.
1984 "The Black Family Housing Alternatives in the 1980's", Journal of Black Studies (14)(3)(Mar): 341-351.
Burgess, Ernest
1928 The Prediction of Marriage. University of Chicago Press.
Campbell, Anne C.
1980 "Friendship as a Factor in Male and Female Delinquency", in Hugh C. Foot, Anthony J. Chapman, and Jean R. Smith (Eds.), Friendship and Social Relations in Children, New York: Wiley.
Chapman, J.R.
1980 Economic Realities and Female Crime. Lexington Books.
Cherlin, Andrew and Shiro Horiuchi
1980 "Retrospective Reports of Family Structure: A Methodological Assessment", Sociological Methods and Research (May)(8)(4): 454-469.
Coleman, Marilyn, et al
1985 "Family Structure and Dating Behavior of Adolescents", Adolescence (Fall)(20)(79): 537-543.
Cosby, Bill
1986 Fatherhood. Garden City, NY: Doubleday.

Curtis, R., W.J. Crow, L.A. Zurcher, and A.V. Connett
    1973 <u>Paroled But Not Free: Ex-Offenders Look at What They Need to Make it Outside</u>. New York: Human Sciences Press.
Daly, Martin and Margo Wilson
    1985 "Child Abuse and Other Risks of Not Living With Both Parents", <u>Ethology and Sociobiology</u> (6)(4): 197-210.
Daniel, Jessica H., et al
    1983 "Child Abuse and Accidents in Black Families: A Controlled Comparative Study", <u>Journal of Orthopsychiatry</u> (Oct)(53)(4): 645-653.
de Anda, Diane
    1984 "Bicultural Socialization: Factors Affecting the Minority Experience", <u>Social Work</u> (Mar)(29)(2): 101-107.
Dobash, Russell P.; R. Emerson Dobash, and Sue Gutteridge
    1986 <u>The Imprisonment of Women</u>. New York: Basil Blackwell, Inc.
Dornbusch, Sanford M., et al
    1985 "Single Parents, Extended Households, and the Control of Adolescents", <u>Child Development</u> (Apr)(56)(2): 326-41.
Drake, St. Claire and Horace R. Cayton
    1945 <u>Black Metropolis: A Study of Negro Life in a Northern City</u>. New York: Harcourt, Brace, Inc.
Dressler, William W.
    1985 "Extended Family Relationships, Social Support, and Mental Health in a Southern Black Community", <u>Journal of Health and Social Behavior</u> (Mar)(26)(1): 39-48.
Duguid, S.
    1981 "Prison Education and Criminal Choice: The Context of Decision-Making", <u>Canadian Journal of Criminology</u> (23)(4): 421-438.
Dunbar, Ellen A.
    1963 "How to Help the Gang Member Through His Family", Special Service For Groups, Los Angeles: Unpublished.
Duncan, Otis Dudley and Beverly Duncan
    1957 <u>The Negro Population of Chicago: A Study of Residential Succession</u>. Chicago: University of Chicago Press.
Edelman, Marian Wright
    1987 <u>Families in Peril</u>. An Agenda for Social Change. Harvard University Press.
Edwards, Ozzie L.
    1982 "Family Formation Among Black Youth", <u>Journal of Negro Education</u> (Spr)(51)(2): 111-122.
Ekland-Olson, Sheldon, et al
    1983 "Postrelease Depression and the Importance of Familial Support", <u>Criminology</u> (May)(21)(2): 253-275.

Fishman, S. and A.S. Alissi
    1979 "Strengthening Families as Natural Support Systems for Offenders", <u>Federal Probation</u> (43): 16-21.
Fogel, Robert William and Stanley L. Engerman
    1974 <u>Time on the Cross: The Economics of American Negro Slavery</u>. Boston: Little, Brown and Co.
Gibbs, C.
    1971 "The Effect of the Imprisonment of Women Upon Their Children", <u>British Journal of Criminology</u> (11).
Gray, Susan W. and Kristi Ruttle
    1980 "The Family-Oriented Home Visiting Program: A Longitudinal Study", <u>Genetic Psychology Monographs</u> (Nov)(102)(2): 299-316.
Griffith, Ezra, et al
    1984 "An Analysis of the Therapeutic Elements in a Black Church Service", <u>Hospital and Community Psychiatry</u> (May)(35)(5): 464-469.
Harrison-Ross, Phillis and Barbara Wyden
    1973 <u>The Black Child -- A Parent's Guide</u>. New York: Peter H. Wyden, Inc. Publisher.
Heiss, Jerold
    1975 <u>The Case of the Black Family: A Sociological Inquiry</u>. New York: Columbia University Press.
Hill, Robert B.
    1972 <u>The Strengths of Black Families</u>. New York: Emerson Hall Publishers, Inc.
    1975 <u>Black Families in the 1974-75 Depression: Special Policy Report</u>. New York: National Urban League.
Hindelang, Michael J.
    1973 "Causes of Delinquency: A Partial Replication and Extension", <u>Social Problems</u> (Spr)(20): 471-487.
Hirschi, Travis
    1969 <u>Causes of Delinquency</u>. Berkeley: University of California Press.
Holt, N. and D. Miller
    1972 "Explorations in Inmate-Family Relationships", <u>California Department of Corrections</u>, Report No. 46.
Homer, E.L.
    1969 "Inmate-Family Ties: Desirable But Difficult", <u>Federal Probation</u> (43): 47-52.
Jensen, Gary F. and David Brownfield
    1983 "Parents and Drugs", <u>Criminology</u> (Nov)(21)(4): 543-54.
Klaus, Patsy A. and Michael R. Rand
    1984 <u>Family Violence</u>. Bureau of Justice Statistics. Special Report.

Kriesberg, Louis
   1970 Mothers in Poverty. Chicago: Aldine
         Publishing Co.
Lee, Laura J.
   1983 "Reducing Black Adolescent's Drug Use:
         Family Revisited", Child and Youth Services
         (Spr)(6)(1-2): 57-69.
Leslie, Gerald R.
   1973 The Family in Social Context. New York:
         Oxford University Press.
Liebow, Elliot
   1970 "Attitudes Toward Marriage and Family
         Among Black Males in Tally's Corner",
         Milbank Memorial Fund Quarterly
         (Apr)(48)(2): 151-167.
Liker, J.K.
   1980 "Nobody Knows the Troubles I've Seen:
         Post-Release Burdens on the Families of the
         Transitional Aid Research Project", pp. 299-
         317 in P.H. Rossi, et al (eds.), Money, Work
         and Crime. New York: Academic Press.
Lindblad-Goldberg, Marion and Joyce Lynn Dukes
   1985 "Social Support in Black, Low-Income,
         Single-Parent, Families: Normative and Dys
         functional Patterns", American
         OrthoPsychiatric Association: 42-56.
Linden, Eric and James C. Hackler
   1973 "Affective Ties and Delinquency", Pacific
         Sociological Review (16): 27-46.
Linden, R.; L. Perry; D. Ayers; and T.A. Parlett
   1984 "An Evaluation of a Prison Education
         Program", Canadian Journal of Criminology
         (26)(1): 65-73.
Lyman, Stanford M.
   1972 The Black American in Sociological
         Thought. New York: G.P. Putnam and Sons.
Malson, Michelene Ridley
   1983 "Black Families and Childrearing Support
         Networks", Research in the Interweave of
         Social Roles (Jan)(44): 76-85.
Mannino, F.V. and M.F. Shore
   1974 "Family Structure, Aftercare and Post-
         Hospital adjustment", American Journal of
         Orthopsychiatry (Jan)(44): 76-85.
McAdoo, Harriette
   1977 "A Review of the Literature Related to
         Family Therapy in the Black Community",
         Journal of Contemporary Psychotherapy
         (Sum)(9)(1): 15-19.
McCullum, S.G.
   1977 "What Works. A Look at Effective
         Correctional Education and Training Experi-
         ences", Federal Probation (41)92): 32-35.
McCord, J.; W. McCord; and P. Verden
   1962 "Familial and Behavioral Correlates of
         Dependency in Male Children", Child Devel-
         opment (33): 313-326.

McCord, J.; W. McCord; and E. Thurber
   1962 "Some Effects of Parental Absence on Male
         Children", Journal of Abnormal and Social
         Psychology (64): 361-69.
McCord, J.
   1979 "Consideration of the Impact of Parental
         Behavior on Subsequent Criminality", paper
         presented at the American Sociological
         Association, annual meeting.
McCord, W. and J. McCord
   1959 Origins of Crime: A New Evaluation of the
         Cambridge-Somerville Study. New York:
         Columbia University Press.
McCord, William, et al
   1969 Life Styles in the Black Ghetto. New York:
         W.W. Norton and Company, Inc.
McCubbin, H.I.; B.D. Dahl; G.R. Lester; and B.D.
Ross
   1975 "The Returned Prisoner of War: Factors in
         Family Reintegration", Journal of Marriage
         and the Family (Aug)(37): 471-478.
McLanahan, Sara S.
   1983 "Family Structure and Stress: A Longitudi-
         nal Comparison of Two-Parent and Female-
         Headed Families", Journal of Marriage and
         the Family (May)(45)(2): 347-357.
Minor, W.W. and M. Courlander
   1969 "The Post-Release Trauma Thesis: A Re
         consideration of the Rise of Early Parole
         Failure", Journal of Research in Crime and
         Delinquency (16)(July): 273-293.
Moore, Helen B.
   1982 "Motivating Black Learners to Excel", Jour-
         nal of Negro Education (Spr)(51)(2): 139-
         146.
Morris, P.
   1965 Prisoners and Their Families. London: Allen
         and Unwin.
Mullin, James B.
   1973 "Birth Order as a Variable of Probation
         Performance", Journal of Research in Crime
         and Delinquency (Jan)(10)(1): 29-34.
Norman-Jackson, Jacquelyn
   1982 "Family Interactions, Language Develop-
         ment, and Primary Reading Achievement of
         Black Children in Families of Low Income",
         Child Development (Apr)(53)(2): 349-58.
Patalano, Frank
   1977 "Height on the Draw-A-Person: Compari-
         son of Figure Drawings of Black and White
         Male Drug Abusers", Perceptual and Motor
         Skills (Jun)(44)(3,2): 1187-1190.
Pederson, Frank A., et al
   1979 "Infant Development in Father-Absent Fami-
         lies", Journal of Genetic Psychology
         (Sept)(135)(1): 51-61.

Petty, Douglas and George A. Robinson
  1982 "Common Philosophical Themes in the Oral History and TCB Content of Four Black Octogenarians", Journal of Non-White Concerns in Personnel and Guidance (Jan)(10)(2): 57-63.
Poussaint, Alvin F.
  1972 Why Blacks Kill Blacks. New York: Emerson Hall Publishers, Inc.
Queen, Stuart A. and Robert W. Haberstein
  1974 The Family in Various Cultures. New York: J.B. Lippincott Co.
Rainwater, Lee
  1970 Behind the Ghetto Walls: Black Families in a Federal Slum. Chicago: Aldine Publishing Co.
Robins, Lee; Patricia A. West; and Barbara L. Herjanic
  1975 "Arrests and Delinquency in Two Generations: A Study of Black Urban Families and Their Children", Journal of Child Psychology and Psychiatry (16): 125-140.
Robinson, Ira E., et al
  1985 "Self-Perception of the Husband/Father in the Lower Class Black Family", Phylon (Jun)(46)(2): 136-147.
Ross, Arthur M. and Herbert Hill (eds.)
  1967 Employment, Race, and Poverty. New York: Harcourt, Brace and World, Inc.
Sager, Clifford J., et al
  1970 Black Ghetto Family in Therapy: A Laboratory Experience. New York: Grove Press, Inc.
Scanzoni, John H.
  1971 The Black Family in Modern Society. Boston: Allyn and Bacon, Inc.
Schaefer, Earl S.
  1965 "Childrens Reports of Parental Behaviors: An Inventory", Child Development (36): 413-424.
Schneller, D.P.
  1975 "Prisoner's Families: A Study of Some Social and Psychological Effects of Incarceration on the Families of Negro Prisoners", Criminology (12)(Nov): 402-412.
  1975 "Some Social and Psychological Effects of Incarceration on Families of Negro Inmates", American Journal of Corrections 29-33.
Silvers, Steven B., et al
  1984 "The Role of Racial Identity Constancy on Children's Perceptions", Journal of Social Psychology (Apr)(122)(2): 223-226.
Schultz, David A.
  1969 Coming Up Black: Patterns of Ghetto Socialization. Englewood Cliffs, NJ: Prentice-Hall, Inc.

Spain, Johnny
  1972 "The Black Family and the Prisons", The Black Scholar (4)(Oct): 2-
Staples, Robert
  1971 The Black Family: Essays and Studies. Belmont, CA: Wadsworth Publishing Co.
  1971 "Towards a Sociology of the Black Family: A Theoretical and Methodological Assessment", Journal of Marriage and the Family (Feb)(33)(1): 119-138.
  1973 The Black Woman in America: Sex, Marriage, and the Family. Chicago: Nelson-Hall Publishers.
Stack, Carol B.
  1974 All Our Kin: Strategies for Survival in a Black Community. New York: Harper and Row.
Steelman, Lala C. and John T. Doby
  1983 "Family Size and Birth Order as Factors on the IQ Performance of Black and White Children", Sociology of Education (Apr)(56)(2): 101-109.
Studt, E.
  1967 The Re-Entry of the Offender Into the Community. Washington, D.C.: Government Printing Office.
TenHouten, Warren
  1970 "The Black Family: Myth and Reality", Psychiatry (33)(2)(May): 145-173.
Willie, Charles V. and Susan L. Greenblatt
  1978 "Four 'Classic' Studies of Power Relationships in Black Families: A Review and Look to the Future", Journal of Marriage and the Family (Nov)(40)(4): 691-694.
Wilson, James Q. and Richard J. Herrnstein
  1985 Crime and Human Nature. Chapter on the Family. New York: Simon and Schuster.
West, Donald J.
  1982 Delinquency: Its Roots, Careers and Prospects. Cambridge: Harvard University Press.
Wilson, Melvin N.
  1986 "The Black Extended Family: An Analytical Consideration", Developmental Psychology (Mar)(22)(2): 246-258.

SPANISH COBRA GANG MEMBER KILLS 3-YEAR-OLD BOY

The Spanish Cobra gang in Chicago, like most others, runs large scale drug sale operations. One "spot" used for "drive up" drug sales can easily bring in $5,000 a day to the gang. Gangs protect their drug "spots".

Two days after Christmas, in 1997, 3-year-old German Morales was outside playing with a toy near the 2600 block of West Potomac. Spanish Cobra gang member Edwin Orta was there at the same time. Orta fired a gun at what he thought was a rival gang member, but the 3-year-old German Morales was the one hit by the bullet. The child died immediately of the gun shot wound.

Chicago Police were quick to send his gang a message. Operation Mongoose resulted in 31 arrest warrants for members of the Spanish Cobras, for drug sales, in late January of 1998[21].

Gang member Edwin Orta, age 25, was charged in connection with the shooting of the 3-year-old infant.[22] Orta had fired six shots from a .45 caliber pistol, trying to hit rival gang members, but hit the infant German Morales instead.

Gang members lack good "shooting skills", we think a lot of the astute observers of the gang scene know this. We do pray that just because gang members lack good target practice opportunities --- a legitimate type of opportunity of the highest order --- that no gang apologist has the audacity to urge that gang members should be provided with compensatory marksmanship training to make them "better shooters". Gang members lack a lot of skills, social skills particularly, and generally are not good "shots" with guns, getting their "training" from television shows and alleys.

End Notes:

[1] One exception to this is the brief, but directly focused, oral history data reported by Taylor (1990: pp. 62-65). This data by Taylor involved an approach similar to the original work by Shaw and Mc Kay's case study method involving interviews with family members and what they had to say about a family member who was involved with the gang.

[2] Sanchez-Jankowski runs the risk of overgeneralizing from very limited data, but the iconoclastic viewpoint expressed is sure to have an overall positive effect by stimulating further research. Basically, Sanchez-Jankowski says it is a myth that gang members come from "bad families", because he found numerous cases where the family was a very functional and very nur-

turing one. For the record, it is not hard to find such cases.

[3] In the written constitution and by-laws of the Latin Kings we find the fascinating application of what appears to be a human development life span "stage theory" authored by a well placed gang member. Here we find in the second stage, the Latin King constitution explicitly recognizing and warning against the maturation hypothesis, that is the tendency to "marry and settle down" avoiding fellow gang boys and a lowering of commitment to the gang.

[4] The analysis reported here was beyond the scope of the initial project undertaken by Knox and Tromanhauser (1991) and which is reported elsewhere (Knox, Laske, and Tromanhauser, 1992). Thus, the analysis of sexual abuse and fertility in relationship to gang membership by gender is new and additional analysis. Because this occurred well after the project completion, which had a data submission deadline, and because additional data did in fact "come in", the sample size used here reflects N = 1,844 confined juveniles.

[5] The important methodological limitation that must be pointed out here is that many juvenile correctional institutions now routinely provide AIDS and HIV "awareness" information to the youths entering these facilities. Thus, in the analysis that follows, the validity of the findings must take account of this potential confounding influence from "other adults outside of school" who could potentially include correctional staff!

[6] The technique used by Sanchez-Jankowski (1991) relied apparently only on the reports of gang members themselves, and did not involve a validity check by actually assessing the family situation of said gang members. The more recent research by Scott Decker and his colleagues in St. Louis, Missouri provides a more rigorous research method: where both the gang member and his/her family members and parents are interviewed.

[7] Gynopeia in sociology means the "BLINDNESS TO FEMALE ISSUES" among males.

[8] The results may have been different if the question specifically ruled out all sexual activity that might occur inside the juvenile correctional institution (i.e., homosexuality). The fact is, we cannot rule this out. The question did not specifically say: prior to coming to this institution, the last time you willingly had sex did you or your partner use a condom. The last time, for some unknown number of them, may have been inside the institution in which they resided at the time of the survey.

[9] Spergel states that "male offspring may also follow in their father's or uncle's footsteps as gang fighters" (Spergel, 1984: p. 220).

[10] Jackson and McBride (1990: p. 11) discussed families with gang lineage and stated that "in these cases

the parents are usually graduates from gangs themselves and see little wrong with their children belonging to gangs. In fact, such parents often encourage their children to belong".

[11] Johnstone (1981) in describing suburban gangs points to this factor of absent parents or single-parent families as being important.

[12] See Jackson, et al, (1989, p. 120). Ronald W. Jackson, Edward E. Rhine, And William R. Smith, 1989 "Prison Overcrowding: A Police Challenge for Parole", Corrections Today (Aug.): 118,120, 122-123. Going to press, the figure approached 2 million in the year 2000.

[13] In a recent nationwide sample of inmates in American prisons Wright and Rossi (1985) reported that 62 percent of the male inmates had fathered a child.

[14] "The Familial Gang Transplant Phenomenon", paper presented by John A. Laskey, Morton College, at the Annual Meeting of the Academy of Criminal Justice Sciences, Chicago, IL, 1994. See also: The 1994 Survey of Illinois Police Chiefs and County Sheriffs by the National Gang Crime Research Center.

[15] See Knox, Laske, and Tromanhauser (1992) for where self-esteem as a variable was not really different in comparing gang members with non-gang members among high school students.

[16] Percent of siblings with juvenile court records was also a very significant variable that differentiated gang and non-gang members in the research reported by Zatz (1985).

[17] Pearson zero-order correlation coefficients.

[18] The case of the young Korean student, Jeanin Earl Ghim (age 17), is a case in point. He joins a Chicago-area gang, tries to quit without his violation, and the gang busted into his parents' house one night looking for him, and not finding him, they killed his mother and shot his father and sister. See: Philip J. O'Connor and Lee Bey, "Gang Member's Family Shot In Suburban Home Invasion", Chicago Sun-Times, Apr. 7, 1994, p. 1, 26.

[19] The McGruff headquarters has recently offered a kit for $24.95 on "Tools To Involve Parents in Gang Prevention". This is not a product endorsement, but simply an acknowledgement that such materials are now being produced under the assumption --- a good assumption from the present review --- that the family CAN do something about the gang problem.

[20] Campbell (1990: p. 182) quoting Hagedorn and Moore states that among gang girls "94% will go on to have children, and 84% will raise them without spouses"

[21] See: Fran Spielman, "Cops Smash N.W. Side Gang", Chicago Sun-Times, Jan. 28, 1998, p. 24.

[22] See: Dave Newbart, "Neighborhood Weeps for Tot: 250 People Mourn Child, Protest Gang Violence", p. 1, Chicago Tribune, Dec. 29, 1997.

How to "Gang Proof" Your Child:
Ten Rules to Help Parents

Can you do anything to prevent the anguish and misery that comes from having a child who is a gang member? Yes you can. You can be a pro-active parent to prevent this most serious form of delinquency.

As a rule of thumb, the more dysfunctional the family, the more likely the child is to become a gang member. However, we have seen exceptions where children from very stable, affluent, intact families with highly educated parents find out the hard way their child is a gang member. We have had police officers come to us as parents asking what to do after they discovering their own child was a gang member. So do not assume just because you are a good "role model" and you have a "good family" that it could not happen to you. Here are the "ten rules":

Rule #1 If your child is ever bullied is to make sure a retaliation or revenge syndrome does not set in: that could transform your bullied child into a bully. Once a child is a bully, he is on the road to gang life.

Rule #2: Make sure you really know who your child's friends are. You need to know not only all of the friends and associates of your child, but their parents as well.

Rule #3 is emphasize conflict avoidance and conflict resolution skills, keep your child out of fights. Tell your child "your mind is your primary weapon".

Rule #4 is avoid drug using friends who would facilitate or approve of drug abuse by your child.

Rule #5 is to make sure that your household communicates a zero-tolerance policy on gangs and gang members.

Rule #6 is to emphasize school success above all else, including self-esteem.

Rule #7 is simple: do not have gang members as friends or associates. Those who hang out with gang members are often regarded legally as "gang associates" and may show up on police intelligence files even though they have never been arrested.

Rule #8 is to remember it is your house, and you have the right and the duty to periodically assess what your child has in his/her possession.

Rule #9: do not fall victim to the "we just have wannabe's" fallacy.

Rule # 10: alert your child to the "false flag" routine that gangs use. This could save your child's life. The way the "false flag" routine works is easy to understand. A car drives up to a street corner or area on the street (store, arcade, etc) where your child may be standing. Someone in the car, typically a young man, smiles and waves a gang salute. The gang salute is simply a hand-sign. There are as many hand-signs as there are gangs (hundreds). But in the typical "false flag" routine, the gang member in the car is acting friendly, but is actually putting up a false flag: he is giving the hand-sign for a rival gang. For example, a Blood gang member in the car may give the "C" gang hand-sign. Bloods hate Crips. The "C" sign is the hand-sign of the Crips. The person in the car may be undergoing an initiation ceremony, and he is out to kill a Crip or a Crip-associate, or anyone who sympathizes with Crips. When your child tries to act friendly and returns the same sign or acknowledges it in a friendly way, your child gets shot. Tell your child to scream, run, take cover, and call the police immediately if they are ever exposed to a "false flag" routine.

Photos of the Media Frenzy That Occurred
When The Guardian Angels Showed Up to
Protest Against the Oct., 1993 "Gang
Peace Treaty Summit Meeting" Held in
Chicago, Illinois at the Congress Hotel.

Chapter 21

THE PROMULGATION OF GANG-
BANGING THROUGH THE
MASS MEDIA

INTRODUCTION

In an analysis of the mass media in relationship to gang issues, we must necessarily address the following fundamental concern: does the mass media have a significant negative effect on society in the extent to which it promotes or facilitates an increase in, or dependency on or unhealthy fascination with, violence as a problem-solving technique? Beyond this, it is important to identify and provide some assessment of what specific components of the mass media may be contributing to the "gang problem". And, of course, there are many fascinating issues that surface in analyzing the mass media in relationships to problems such as gang crime and gang violence. We will now examine some of these issues in greater detail as the necessary groundwork for understanding the thesis that the mass media does in fact, in certain ways, promote or exacerbate the "gang problem" in the United States today.

THE EXPLOITATION OF MASS COMMUNI-CATIONS BY GANGS TODAY

A subsidiary issue of the thesis that the mass media contributes to the gang problem is the assertion that gangs themselves systematically use and exploit forms of mass communication.

Gang graffiti itself is a threatening form of mass communications, it is a kind public advertising,

it communicates the symbols of a gang, who its leaders are, who its enemies are, and it often commemorates the gang's fallen or deceased members, or the members of rival gangs that the same gang is intent on killing in the future. Some may want to argue the semantics of how much "mass" there is in this form of low-tech communication. As a medium of communication it mixes symbols, art, and messages typically to mark its own territory, to threaten other gangs, and to disrespect any opposition gangs. The best estimate is that 9 out of 10 cities in America, regardless of size or location, probably have gang graffiti in their jurisdiction whether they know it or not.

There are in fact today printed and published gang publications that take on a sophisticated form of the print media. These include books, magazines, and newsletters.

Several American gangs have produced their books, having these published by vanity presses and being their distributor. One of the most well known is the book produced about the Gangster Disciples by the Gangster Disciples. It is useful to explain the GD book in some detail.

The GD book is formally entitled From Gangster Disciple to (The Blueprint) Growth & Development. The indicated author is Rod Emery with a preface by Dr. Nehemiah Russell. The latter "doctor" was the assistant principal at Chicago's

Englewood High School where the "gang leader awards ceremony" was held in 1993, coinciding with the GD-led "gang peace" summit meeting. The book is a short (110 pages) paperback. The format is unique: the ink color on all of the inside page printing is "blue ink", coinciding with the gang's color pattern (blue/black). So the double-entendre is noted (i.e., "blueprint" for growth & development). The book was formally released on Sept. 17, 1996 during the time that 39 of the top leaders of the GDs were being tried in federal court in Chicago, all of whom were subsequently convicted, most getting federal life prison sentences as a result. The pre-printed price of the book on the back page is $14.99, and includes order forms for getting additional copies of the book on the last page (indicating the book is available for $15 plus $2 shipping and handling, 7% tax for Illinois residents, through: African-American Institute for Urban Youth Studies, 3333 W. Arthington - Suite 105, Chicago, IL 60624).

The "book release" ceremony was held at Northeastern Illinois University's Center for Inner City Studies located near the old "Fort" (i.e., Jeff Fort's headquarters for the El Rukn's on Chicago's near south side).

The book and the press release information designed to promote the book describe the GD leader "Larry Hoover" as someone who rose from being a "dysfunctional illiterate with a speech impediment" to being a great community leader with a "post-Newtonian mind". The book's message coincided with the defense strategy that Larry Hoover used, albeit unsuccessfully, in federal court: that he was a political prisoner.

The GD book was clearly a book about the gang produced by the gang and distributed by the gang, and it was very sophisticated, and included a number of the gang's beliefs and public relations gimmicks so that others could start their own version of the GD's in their own town anywhere in the world by just reading this book.

Prior to the GD book there was another Chicago gang book that was "self-published". It was entitled Shorty Four, published in 1993, authored by Albert Kinnard & Marion Wilson, and must be considered authentic because it included an introduction by Useni Eugene Perkins, a gang book author who works at Chicago State University. It was a cheaper production. It did not have the professional "gloss" and pseudo-political hyperbole that the GD book had. It was in fact stapled together in the spine as the binding method. It was a story extolling the virtues and romanticized urban warfare experiences of one member of the Four Corner Hustler gang. It was a story of sex, drugs, and violence; and the main character's experiences in the juvenile correctional system.

On pages 70-73 of Shorty Four the main character is locked up in Chicago's Audy Home (formally known at the Cook County Temporary Juvenile Detention Center), he intimidates what the book calls a "bitch" (anyone male or female who caves into his subtle threats and demands, an adult male correctional officer in this instance who works in the Audy Home) into giving him the use of the officer's cellular phone, which is used to order drugs (an ounce of cocaine, cash, several bags of marijuana, and several cartons of cigarettes) that the officer smuggles back into Audy Home for the gang member. In subsequent sections, when the main character is sent to the state facility (St. Charles), the drugs continue as well as allowing hookers from the outside have conjugal relations with the juvenile gang member. Is it all fiction? Who knows, it was never investigated, few people even know the book exists.

In 1993 we also saw the publication of the book Monster: The Autobiography of an L.A. Gang Member, by Sanyika Shakur, aka Monster Kody Scott (Penguin Books). This was certainly not self-published, it is a commercially published book by a mainstream publisher. It is a highly polished and stylized revisionist account of how a gang member is really a "new urban freedom fighter".

In our "gang book review" above we have not included the book about the Vice Lords written by David Dawley. David Dawley claims he was the first white member of the Vice Lords, and clearly wrote one of the books that has been published about the Chicago Vice Lords. While the book clearly provides an apology for the crime and violence by the Vice Lord gang, the point here is not to try to be exhaustive in covering all such books, but to simply illustrate a point, which has been done. Due to limited space available here it is sufficient to establish through the above examples that gangs themselves have found ways to exploit the print media in book form.

There does exist a "gang rights activist press" as the slick California magazine called Teen Angels describes itself; as well as to examples of gangs like the New York Latin Kings operated their own community newsletter in the effort to maintain the charade of respectability in a standard "public relations" scam where the gang robbed, killed, and dealt drugs while simultaneously trying to maintain the image of being a leftwing revolutionary or avant guard Puerto Rican Liberation-style community organizing group.

What does it all boil down to: gangs using the print media as propaganda and as a means to promote their own causes directly and specifically gang-related in nature.

THE MASS MEDIA AND VIOLENCE CONTROVERSY

In analyzing the mass media in relationship to gang issues, we necessarily enter into the longstanding debate about media and violence generally. The primary issue is the extent to which the mass media is responsible for the spread, onset, replication, and/or persistence of acts of violence, or simply increasing the human tendency towards violence through a myriad of ways. Some of the specific questions that need to be addressed include the following questions.

(1) Does the mass media teach people how to be violent or how to commit crimes? Does the mass media, as in the MacGwyver series, informally train people in ways to improvise and develop field expedient devices and techniques necessary to carry out violent acts or as ways to fulfill pre-existing violent tendencies? We have no national data system in effect to be able to assess these intertwined questions. Much debate on the issue remains at the finger-pointing stage. Certainly, we can find examples of this, but it may be more worthwhile to ask a research question that can be answered by analyzing existing data (i.e., the collection of gang movies available in the American market today): do these gang movies provide informal training on the continuity of violence, more specifically the individual or group level vigilante response to gang violence? This is something that we can address in the present paper.

(2) Does the mass media desensitize people by the constant barrage of violence, so that people are more likely to commit, tolerate, or expect violence as reasonable behavior? Alternatively, and perhaps something more researchable, do the gang movies portray the gang as being in some sense "omnipotent", that is that gangs are so powerful that literally nothing can be done about them, so that the overall message sent to the viewing public is that gang violence is a necessary evil that we must all tolerate? We do believe that a number of gang movies develop and promote a theme that gangs are omnipotent.

(3) Does the mass media instill or promote negative or destructive social values which, once internalized or acted upon, result in acts or patterns of criminal or violent conduct? There are many possible ways to test this issue empirically, but perhaps one of the most direct ways would be in traditional criminological terms: that is, are some gang movies presented in a fashion that erodes a basic respect for the law itself? We do believe that it is easy to demonstrate that a number of gang movies qualify in terms of such a thematic or overall thrust.

(4) Does the mass media distribute and disseminate misinformation on and about gangs in a fashion that results in a further problem with regard to properly educating citizens about the public safety threat from gangs? In otherwords, does patently false and fabricated and clearly fictional information get communicated in gang movies that later becomes "believed as real and genuine" by the general public? Perhaps the best example we analyze here would be the myth about "gang truces" or "gang peace treaties".

We will keep these questions in mind as we explore the world of gang movies in the present research and report conclusions in regard as well later in this paper.

MASS MEDIA EXPERTISE

In a court of law one becomes recognized as an expert on any subject matter generally by showing legitimate training, education, and experience in the subject matter at a level that significantly exceeds that of the average citizen who might sit on a jury.

I think is reasonable to characterize my knowledge of the mass media as being above that of any average citizen. This comes from both formal study and experience. In terms of formal study, when we are dealing with the "mass media", this is covered under the study of mass communications in the field of sociology as well as that of journalism. But by far, I would rate my personal experience as the best learning source in regard to the mass media.

My personal experience with the mass media includes being a producer of televised educational programs about gangs and being a publisher of research information about gangs.

My personal experience with the mass media is therefore certainly far above that of the average citizen. It includes being interviewed by newspaper writers, radio talk show hosts, television reporters, etc, over the years on hundreds of occasions. Over the years I have retained the belief that a free and active press serves a vital and useful purpose. Thus, I have found newspaper and magazine reporters (i.e., credentialed "newspaper reporters"), generally, to be more sincere in their coverage of gang issues. With some notable exceptions.

EXAMPLE OF ONE NOTABLE PERSONAL EXCEPTION ON NEWSPAPER COVERAGE

Being inaccurate in gang coverage in a newspaper story can be a problem. I would like to illustrate this through the following true story involving my own personal experience.

A couple years ago, a small town newspaper in Illinois called our Center to get information on the Disciples. I freely volunteered information to the reporter. The information I gave was correctly reported in the newspaper account that the reporter wrote. The error that the reporter made was in my name: the reporter gave me the name attribution of

Dr. Charles Knox.

At the time of the story, "Charles Knox" was being sought by the Federal Bureau of Investigation or was already in custody having been indicted for using false information in trying to visit an inmate in a federal prison. The real "Charles Knox" had been visiting the notorious Chicago El Rukn gang leader Jeff Fort, posing as a "member of the clergy". The real "Charles Knox" was connected to a university but not mine, he was teaching "social justice" at Northeastern Illinois University in Chicago. But the bottom like is: the FBI wanted Charles Knox. Perhaps all the FBI knew was that Charles Knox was clever enough to have someone else "stand in" for him to do his time, because as I understand it he was already in custody at the time.

I have learned long ago, when giving an interview, to ask "are these questions for background information or for attribution to me?". And where my response is going to attributed to me, I always ask the reporter to fax me or mail me a copy of the story as soon as it is published. This particular reporter did comply and faxed me the story, and I knew immediately I would have troubles, because "Charles Knox" was now supposed to be running the National Gang Crime Research Center at Chicago State University. Anyone in the gang business knew who Charles Knox was.

About the time I slammed the phone down after expressing my intense dissatisfaction to the editor of the newspaper that gave me the name "Charles Knox", there was a knock on my door. Two FBI agents, showing identification in one hand, and keeping their gun hand near their pieces, announced themselves and said: "Are you Charles Knox?"

Now I am sure that there are probably some good investigative leads that can periodically come out of newspapers, but I was not in the proper frame of mind to respect that type of investigative strategy at the time the two FBI agents showed up at my office door.

Charles Knox is black, I am white. I discovered later that Charles Knox was in fact in federal custody in Chicago at the time they appeared at my door.

So my response to the FBI at the time was not gracious, I believe I retorted something to the effect, "do I look like Charles Knox?"

One of the FBI agents quickly responded, "a newspaper story indicates that Charles Knox is the Director of the NGCRC and he is here at Chicago State University".

I am going to skip over my further responses to these two agents and note that my level of civility reached its lowest point after the two FBI agents left, and an older gang banger arrived wanting to see me because he also thought Charles Knox was in my office. The gang banger looked at me with eyes of amazement when I said "yeah, I am Knox, they call me Knox Man Doggy Dog". But at least he left swiftly when he looked at me and he saw that there was no way in hell I could be Charles Knox. As he sauntered away he just said "yeah, well I was looking for Charles Knox".

A story like that would be hard to make up. The record is clear. It really did happen.

THE BASIC COMPONENTS OF THE MASS MEDIA

It is clearly a complicated and controversial issue to assert that the mass media in any shape or fashion tends to promote gangbanging. We must first isolate what aspect or component of the mass media we are talking about. Generally, as I have said, newspaper reporters are more responsible. So the print media in terms of major daily newspapers are a general exception. We note elsewhere in the present study that in American gang history, Thrasher (1927) devoted much attention to another aspect of the print media: "dime novels" that glorified gangsters and "the life of crime" generally. We will have much more to say about this shortly.

This leaves the following components of the mass media up for scrutiny: the movie industry, television news and television programs, radio, and the internet. Let us briefly examine these components of the mass media.

THE INTERNET

Some gangs already have their Internet Web pages. The Gangster Disciples were among the first to take advantage of the Internet to sell their new line of "gangster" clothing, and promote the image of "Larry Hoover" as a political prisoner. Prior to this, a large number of white racist extremist groups had made their presence known on the Internet and remain a large problem. Cult groups, satanists, witchcraft, etc, also exist on the Internet.

We have yet to see a full scale analysis of the trouble associated with the Internet with regard to gangs and threat groups. But one unmistakable conclusion can be reached: there are some evil people out there who have computer expertise and they want your children! They can legally spread their hate messages and/or their deviant cult group beliefs.

There are a host of gang sites on the Internet today. Some of these clearly are sites designed by someone claiming to be a peacemaker to gangs, but allows the symbols of various gangs and their messages to be distributed via the Internet, including chat rooms.

THE RADIO

Some radio stations deserve an audience that is educated about the power of complaints about the station license renewal process that should be made to the Federal Communications Commission. Some radio stations routinely allow "shout outs" to various gangs and gang members. Often couched in subcultural argot, these are difficult to decipher by the "non-gangwise" person. But most who are aware of this situation recognize the negative effect it has by giving positive recognition to destructive and criminal groups and their members (i.e., gangs).

"Shout outs" on the radio often relay messages to a gang, but more commonly are simply ways of allowing the gang to get positive recognition on a radio station playing their kind of music.

There have been numerous examples of groups like the KKK trying to get "equal air time" on the radio, particularly college or university radio stations. Recently, at the University of Missouri at St. Louis, this took the variation where the Ku Klux Klan wanted to be a "sponsor" of college radio programs. In late 1998, a federal court rejected the Klan's law suit that their First Amendment rights were being violated by not being allowed to be a sponsor of college radio programs on WKMU-FM, the U of MO at St. Louis radio station.

This paper, however, is not designed to analyze the situation with regard to radio stations per se.

TELEVISION AND NEWS PROGRAMS

It is sufficient to say that because what drives the engine of television programming is the almighty dollar, that clearly we have seen some terrible mistakes in terms of gang coverage on television and news programs. Some of the biggest violators consist of the "usual suspects" when it comes to television "confrontation talk" programs that exploit the seedier side of society. And we all know about these programs. Any goof can get on a program, the goofier the better usually. Usually we can place the blame on nationally syndicated programs in the larger networks. However, local cable television access programs also have been known to be exploited by "gang activists".

Due to limited space available here, however, we will not analyze the situation with regard to television coverage in the mass media.

THE ANALYSIS OF MOVIES AND MOTION PICTURES

The advantage of analyzing movies and motion pictures with regard to the gang issue is that many of these can today be obtained in video format. Thus, the analysis reported and undertaken here on movies and motion pictures rises to the level of so-cial scientific inquiry by being able to be analyzed by anyone else who may disagree with the conclusions reached here. In otherwords, the "data" is publicly available for purposes of secondary analysis: unlike the situation with regard to other forms of the mass media.

Many local newspapers are not widely available for secondary analysis. Radio station tapes are not available for purposes of content analysis. Television stations are not in the habit of releasing their broadcast tapes for purposes of any research that could possibly bring them undue attention and therefore threaten their profit motivation.

So from a strictly research point of view, when trying to analyze the mass media with regard to gangs, the best avenue appears to be that of examining movies and major motion pictures.
This, therefore, is the subject of analysis in the present study.

THRASHER'S 1927 ANALYSIS OF MOVIES AND GANGS

Most gang experts are simply not aware of Thrasher's analysis of how movies and other forms of the mass media contribute to, and can exacerbate, the "gang problem". The explanation for this lack of appreciation of Thrasher's original work on gangs is easy to understand: after the original 1927 release of the book The Gang: 1,313 Gangs in Chicago, some chapters were deleted. In fact, most people today that think they know what Thrasher had to say about gangs have probably only read the 1967 abridged version of the Thrasher book which was edited by James F. Short, Jr. The edited version means that a number of "chapters" in the original Thrasher book were simply "left out" and intentionally excluded.

In the original 1927 version of the Thrasher's book, The Gang: 1,313 Gangs in Chicago, chapter 6 (pp. 102-115) was entitled "The Movies and the Dime Novel". In this original chapter by Thrasher, he criticized Hollywood movies, radio, newspapers and print media. Some of Thrasher's sharpest criticisms and remarks seem to have been directed at movies because the strongest evidence suggested this was the medium gang boys are most attracted to. Thrasher concluded that gang boys prefer violent imagery in their movies and they prefer hypermasculine heroes.

Thrasher's basic position was that the mass media "awakens the spirit of imitation...making vice and crime attractive...many of the exploits of the gang undoubtedly involve imitating the movies" (Thrasher, 1927: p. 107). Thus, the basic mechanism by which movies become a demoralizing influence is through the natural human process of social imitation. Thrasher also provided numerous examples of what we today call the contagion-effect or the copycat phenomenon: of how various types of crime (e.g., kidnapping) or violence (e.g., suicides) become repeated in an almost epidemiological fashion.

Additionally, Thrasher noted that the very techniques of crime and violence communicated through the mass media are the means by which a number of criminal offenders and gang members gain their "skills". This includes everything from robbery, extortion, kidnapping, safe-cracking, burglary, etc.

Some of what Thrasher had to say back in the 1920's is still very relevant today. Thrasher takes a classical sociological position in this regard, one that examines the effect of communications as a function of social change itself and its effect on society, as illustrated in the following quotation:

"Every new invention which facilitates human mobility both as to rapidity and range of locomotion -- every new device which increases the vividness, the quickness, and the spread of ideas through communication -- has in it the germs of disorganization. This is because such innovations as the newspapers and the movies, as well as the automobile and the radio, tend to disturb social routine and break up the old habits upon which the superstructure of social organization rests" (Thrasher, 1927: p. 114).

METHODOLOGY

For approximately ten years, the author has assiduously sought after and identified and obtained access for analysis to a large number of movies and motion pictures that deal with gangs. Hundreds of hours of analytical viewing were spent watching and re-watching these movies for purpose of taking notes on major events and themes with regard to gangs. Some of these field notes are provided here in this research report.

While some effort was spent in analyzing foreign language films (Chinese and Mexican), having discovered a wealth of such gang materials, these will not be included in the present analysis. The present analysis includes only English language movies.

VALIDITY

In some qualitative gang research, where the researcher "hangs out" with the gang, we are basically asked to believe everything happened exactly the way it was reported. We are asked to believe that the researcher was honest, we are asked to believe that the researcher has no political "axe" to grind, we are asked to believe that the researcher is skilled enough to understand the situation he/she faced, and we are asked to believe the conclusions even though it is entirely "impossible" to go back and verify anything. In most qualitative research, it is impossible to verify anything. This is why some of the greatest examples of misinformation about gangs today have surfaced from qualitative research.

In qualitative research the validity is what the reader of the report attaches to the value of the message being heard. It is impossible for another researcher to come and say "let me go back and interview your subjects to make sure you reported everything completely and accurately". It is impossible to go back and find "mistakes" a qualitative researcher would make. Thus, it is attractive as a research style for gang researchers to use qualitative research methodologies as a way to spread their version of the "gospel". In research language, anything they say cannot be "falsified". In good research, the conclusions or hypotheses should be falsifiable: they should be able to withstand the rigors of evidence that anyone can obtain and, like a jury, decide for themselves.

In this regard, the present analysis focuses exclusively on data that is readily available and we will in fact identify a number of such movies and provide a short summary of what these were all about. Thus, clearly from a validity point of view, the present analysis is able to claim a level of validity far above that of any qualitative research which cannot allow other researchers to "go back and analyze the data" so-to-speak. In the present analysis, anyone can go back and analyze the movies that will be discussed and analyzed here.

HYPOTHESES

The hypotheses that will be examined here with reference to gang movies include the following:

(1) Do gang movies do a disservice by promoting the vigilante option as an effective response against gangs?

(2) Do gang movies promote the false view that gangs are omnipotent?

(3) Do gang movies promote a reduction in or decrease in respect for the law?

(4) Do gang movies promote myths and therefore have the net effect of spreading misinformation about gangs, as in the case of "gang truces"?

Having stated these basic hypotheses to be explored and tested, we will now turn to the findings of this research.

FINDINGS: MOVIES PROMOTING THE VIGILANTE OPTION AS AN EFFECTIVE RESPONSE AGAINST GANGS

A gang movie communicates false and demoralizing information to the public when it either implies or suggests that <u>more violence</u> is the solution to the onset of gang violence. That is, that citizens should "take the law into their own hands", perhaps "fight fire with fire".

Let us examine the movie <u>Tuff Turf</u>. This is a white gang in a high school context. It implies, by example, that someone with a B B gun can overcome a gang that has real guns. Violent confrontation with the gang is what works is the message from this movie.

Movie Title: "Tuff Turf" (1984)
Producer: New World Pictures

Fantasy love story involving a level one gang in a California high school. Begins with girl gang associates helping to rob a businessman. White male gang members are foiled in the robbery by a bicycle riding main character named Morgan. Morgan sprays the gang members with paint. Morgan begins school the next day, gang members also attend this school, and they proceed to run over his bike with a car. Gang leader, Nick, goes to jail briefly because of Morgan. Nick returns quickly. Nicks girlfriend, Frankie, becomes the target of Morgans affection. Morgan gets beaten by the Nicks gang in a shower room. Morgan's father gets shot by Nick. Frankie, now engaged to Nick, is present at the shooting. Nick returns and beats up Frankie's father because of her disloyalty. Final scene of a fight: Nick is shooting bullets, and Morgan is shooting B B's; but Morgan wins, because his friend shows up with two doberman's. All white cast except for one gang member who hangs with Nick and who affects a Hispanic persona.

A similar theme emerges in the gang movie Defiance. Here the victims are white, the gang is Hispanic. The lead character establishes the policy of confronting the gang. It culminates in one huge battle: the image of the good citizens in the community against the gang members. The gang members are beaten and taken away to jail. Anyone watching this movie would clearly get a vigilantism message as a solution to the gang problem.

MOVIE TITLE: Defiance (1980)
PRODUCER: America International

Tom Campbell the main character later known popularly as "Mac Gyver" is the unemployed merchant seaman (wannabe artist) who moves into a new apartment in a working class area of New York City, as he does, he notices a group of Latino youths in the hood who check him out closely. Tom calls one of them a punk the next day, and the gang catches him in the subway restroom and assaults him. Tom is called an "ambassador" by the neighborhood residents who like his hutzpa. The gang robs a Catholic bingo event in take-down style and terrorizes all, including the priest. The older men in the neighborhood have a SAC called the "Sportsmen" where they drink and talk. Tom has a brief affair with Marsha Bernstein a woman living in the same tenement. The gang is called the Souls, apparently a Puerto Rican gang, and is led by Angel Cruz. As Tom is about to "ship out", all hell breaks loose; a local man dies, a

big rumble scene ensues; what looks like Custer's last stand among the good guys fighting the gang members, is saved when the entire neighborhood joins in to give the gang members a beating and have them all arrested.

In the gang movie The Class of 1984 is another gang in the high school context script. A music teacher becomes taunted and provoked by the white gang. The music teacher fights back, kills a bunch of the gang members. It is a clearcut "vigilante" formula movie.

Movie Title: The Class of 1984
Producer: Guerilla High Productions Ltd.

Andy Norris, a young music teacher replacement, is the main character in this racially mixed high school which uses a walk-through metal detector and C.C. surveillance cameras in the hallways. The gang is a white group, emulating a corporate style, has an "office", involved in drug income chiefly. A while female wants "toot" and agrees to hook for the gang, a gang member is ordered by the leader to "test the merchandise". The gang assaults Andy and another teacher off campus, then firebombs Andy's car. A young white student Arthur (Michael Fox) is stabbed by the gang for being suspected of cooperating with cops, in the hospital he does finally cooperate. The white gang breaks into Andy's house, kidnaps his wife, takes her to the school at night (where Andy is having a music performance). Andy kills three of the white gang members in hand-to-hand combat, 1 other member of the gang a female is killed trying to escape, and 1 more is severely injured. Andy was, of course, provoked into the violence against this gang of white students.

In the gang movie Showdown in Little Tokyo we seek a white cop fight the Japanese Yakuza gang. It is a kung-fu fighting movie, where the white cop and his Japanese-American cop partner single-handedly end up killing virtually every one of the gang members, including blowing up their gang headquarters. For another type of "formula" Yakuza gang movie the reader is referred to Black Rain.

Movie Title: "Showdown in Little Tokyo"
Producer: Warner Bros. Inc, 1991

The Japanese Yakuza gang is portrayed here as capable of street level shakedowns against Japanese business proprietors as well as bringing the drug "ice" to Los Angeles. The entire movie is a changing battle scene between a white cop who was born in Japan where his parents were killed by the Yakuza (and therefore his childhood memory is of a particular gang tattoo), and thus, his kung-fu style vendetta against the Yakuza. The white cop is aided only by a

Japanese-American cop who also in the Hollywood tradition is an ernest kung fu fighter. Together they both kill virtually every Yakuza gang member and blow up their headquarters. This is pure hollywood hype.

The gang movie <u>Original Gangstas</u> provides another variation on the theme: where the older members of the community fight the young thugs in their same community. By engaging in battle with the local gang, the community wins by claiming to be the "toughest gang", i.e., "the original gang". Again, sending the message that what works is vigilantism.

MOVIE TITLE: Original Gangstas
PRODUCER: Orion Pictures Corporation (1996)

Filmed mostly in Gary, Indiana. Black youths battle black adults in an urban setting. Black adults arm themselves against black youths trying to burn down their stores, etc. Black youths claim the gang title of "Rebels". Black adults conquer the black youths and tell them "We are the Original Gangsters, the original Rebels".

People who are wondering why our society saw such a rapid development in paramilitary groups in the late 1980's and early 1990's need only examine a few of these gang movies as a possible explanation for some of the "fantasy acting-out behavior" of these various militia groups. In the gang movie <u>Annihilators</u> we find the basic formula: violent white gang terrorizes the community, four Vietnam vets come to the rescue, armed to the teeth, the vets kill off the gang threat to the community. Basic message of the gang movie: respond to force with greater force, i.e., a vigilante justice message.

Movie Title: Annihilators
Producer: New World Pictures (1986)

Four Vietnam vets come to Atlanta to revenge the death of a friend who was killed by gangs. They form a vigilante group. Eager community residents assist them and learn self-defense, tapping three times to make a sound of a general alarm. One of the four dies in an ensuing "gang war". The remaining vets attack the gang's heroin shipment with help of "inside" cop. The climax is the battle with the gang. The mostly white gang dies at the hands of the mostly white vigilante group. The cops take credit for the heroin seizure.

A school-age version of the idea of waging war against the local gang is exemplified in the gang movie <u>Street Soldiers</u>. Here a local adult helps gang victimized youths form a karate school where they learn how to defend themselves. The basic message

of the movie: fight back with violence against the gang, elementary vigilantism.

Movie Title: Street Soldiers
Producer: Action Brothers Productions (1990)

Two gangs --- the J.P.'s (a level one gang) and the Tigers (initially a level zero gang, then provoked into conflict) --- fight each other for "turf" and "representation" near a high school. Spider and Priest are the two J.P. leaders; with the latter exerting more control as he was just released from prison. The JP's attack the Tigers ("schoolies"). Some girls get involved. A non-aligned Asian youth (Charlie) helps in a fight; his uncle helps train the Tigers in a karate school, who eventually gets drawn into the conflict. At great cost, the Tigers triumph in a campaign of vigilante justice.

In the gang movie <u>Chains of Gold</u> we find a similar theme of individual level "take up the sword" solution against the gang: where someone is trying to get a youth out of a gang is basically forced to fight the top powerful gang leader to the death. Again, part and parcel of the "vigilante" theme is that police are no where around to help: that there is no system of law enforcement that a citizen can turn to when he/she has a problem with a criminal group like that of a gang. This blindness to the role of law enforcement and investigative agencies in society is an intentional affectation of the movie plot: designed to create the basic logical tension necessary to give someone the goofy idea that alone, as a kind of individual terrorist, they could conquer the local gang problem through violent conflict.

Movie Title: "Chains of Gold" (1990)
Producer: M.C.E.G. Productions, Inc

John Travolta plays one Scott Barnes, a social worker who no longer abuses alcohol. Scott is very friendly with a poor-white family consisting of Tommy (the boy), Rachel (the sister), and Martha (the mother). Martha has been accepting expensive gifts from the young boy Tommy (new television, new dress, money). Tommy did not "find a wallet", he joined a gang called "YIP" (Youth Incentive Program) that sells crack, corporate style.

Tommy wants to quit the gang. Scott begins to help. Scott meets an old flame (Jackie) who is now a lawyer representing the YIP gang. She gets Tommy a meeting with Carlos, the gang leader. The gang shows him the full operation, gives him the red carpet treatment as if he were a Harvard Ph.D. organizational consultant. The gang owns its own huge, private night club/casino where Carlos ceremoniously gives away 18K gold chains to his hard workers (sales recognition).

Scott is discovered going into a police station to

snitch. Jackie is killed. At the gang's warehouse where Tommy is waiting to be executed, Scott comes to the rescue. Scott triumphs over Carlos in hand-to-hand combat, Carlos gets fed to alligators, while police siege the building. Scott gets the young boy and leaves.

These gang movies that send the message that the solution to the gang problem lies in arming yourself and in developing a local militia, or in a campaign of vigilante justice waged against the gang, all do an incredible disservice to the American public. There is nothing more threatening to law and order than that of vigilante justice. Movies that even suggest the viability of vigilantism as a solution to the gang problem are movies that might as well have been produced in some distant hostile foreign country that wanted to systematically erode respect for the law in our country.

The idea of solving a crime/violence problem by encouraging a local citizen to commit his/her own campaign of crime/violence against errant citizens is inimical to our contemporary system of justice that is predicated on the rule of law. Thus, a movie that tends to advocate vigilantism, such as those gang movies reviewed here, is a movie that must be regarded as one that exacerbates the gang problem for one fundamental reason such film makers clearly overlooked: gangs thrive on conflict. Without conflict, without someone to "hate", gangs would probably not exist.

FINDINGS: MOVIES PROMOTING THE FALSE VIEW THAT GANGS ARE OMNIPOTENT

While gang movies, as illustrated above, do a substantial disservice to the public when they imply that the only solution to gang violence is to bring a higher level of violence against the gang itself, there is also the other extreme: where gang movies imply that gangs are so very powerful, perhaps omnipotent, that absolutely nothing at all can be done about the gang problem.

Let us consider a gang movie where we have both elements: the frustrated vigilante syndrome and the situation where the gang appears omnipotent. Such an example is provided in the gang movie Massacre at Central High. As seen in this gang movie, the violence by the gang in the school context is portrayed in a world view where literally no responsible adults can be found anywhere doing anything. Responsible adults in this gang movie are completely invisible in the casting of the movie. What message does it send to school-age youths: that they are "all alone", that there are no responsible adults, that adults simply just do not care or cannot be trusted.

Movie Title: "Massacre at Central High"
Producer: Evan Company, 1976
David the main character is a transfer student to this rural middle class high school in California. The movie opens with a student marking a swastika on a school locker and he is caught doing it by the level one gang of bullies (a little league gestapo group). David knows one of the bullies (Mark) from another school where they were friends. David originally helps the other kids, but then after losing his leg to the group of bullies, he systematically plots their death and ends up killing them one by one --- all of which appear to be accidents. In the absence of the former bullies, previous bully victims now seek to fill that power vacuum and to become bullies themselves. After killing about nine students throughout the movie, where we never see a single teacher or adult in the high school until the end when David was going to blow up an alumni dance, but changes his mind and gets blown up himself.

The gang movie New Jack City is one that must regarded as staging the overall image of the gang as being both omnipotent and invincible: i.e., literally nothing can be done about the gang, the gang will commit atrocities, the gang will even kill off the older local mafia population, the gang will get off in court if someone from the gang is arrested, and the frustrated citizen has no other choice than to lay in ambush at the door to the courtroom and execute the gang leader as the gang leader tries to leave the building. It sends the message: there are no ways to empower a community, there is no way to fight the gang without sacrificing perhaps your own life. It sends a very demoralizing overall message to society.

Movie Title: New Jack City (1991)
Producer: Warner Bros. Pictures
The preview commentary states the film has two levels: yes, its a gangster movie, but also its a "say no to drugs" movie. The violence and killing begins early as a white drug dealer is thrown off the bridge into the East River of NYC by the gang called the Cash Money Brothers (CMB). A foot chase ensues in a separate incident where a Black youth tries to steal the money from a Black officer (Scotty) in an undercover drug buy. The cop shoots the kid (Pookie) in the leg. The CMB leader "Nino Brown" refers to his members as "the Crew" suggestive of the Posse style gang language. Nino makes an elaborate plan to take over a large city housing development to use it as a large crack house, complete with computers to keep track of all the money. He succeeds. Pookie gets off drugs and agrees to be an informant; he is killed when his cover is blown.

Meanwhile the Italian Mafia wants their share from Nino; Nino says get lost. Scotty reveals his mother was killed by a junkie which later turns out to be Nino. Nino's gang kills 11 Italian Mafia members. Nino is eventually caught, but gets off with a trick in the courtroom. As he leaves the courtroom with a short sentence, a Black man from the housing project kills Nino by shooting him as he leaves the courtroom.

That gangs are omnipotent is a message clearly sent in the gang movie <u>Assault on Precinct 13</u>. In a most preposterous and unthinkable script, the local gang literally attacks the local police station. Ultimately a cop, an inmate, and a secretary fight back to kill off scores of gang members assaulting the police station. The message: that cops themselves are afraid of gangs, that gangs are so powerful they can attack and kill significant numbers of police right in the police station itself.

**MOVIE TITLE: Assault on Precinct 13
PRODUCER: A C K K Corporation (1976)**
The scene is an L.A. ghetto. Six members of the "street thunder" gang are gunned down, it is an interracial gang. The media reports the gang problem out of control. A Lt. Ethan Bishop gets assigned to close out the precinct thirteen police station. A father watches as his infant daughter is killed by the gang, retaliates and kills one gang member, but is chased into the police station. Three inmates on their way to prison were dropped off at the station. The phone lines are cut, the electricity is cut. Then the gang attacks the precinct station. Five police officers are killed, along with two inmates, and one secretary. The Lt., secretary and inmate team kill about 20 attackers in the first wave, another 10 or so in the final wave.

So very many of citizens receive their knowledge about gangs through the mass media. As many gang experts provide gang training services to the public, we frequently run across persons with outrageous assumptions about the gang problem and we wonder how such persons could become so very miseducated and misinformed about the gang problem. We need only remember that a lot of those citizens get what knowledge or information they have about gangs from gang movies such as those reviewed here.

FINDINGS: MOVIES PROMOTING A DE-CREASE IN RESPECT FOR THE LAW
Gang movies are notorious for promoting stereotypical images of police officers which seriously erode and therefore have the net effect of decreasing "respect for the law". Even if it is a Hollywood arti-

fact, the image of a white racist maniac violent cop is one that clearly can be found in a number of gang movies. It exploits the predisposition of some to want to believe that such attributes are common characteristics of white police officers. It therefore promotes racism as well by generalizing the phenomenon as if it were common practice.

We have previously examined the gang movie <u>Showdown in Little Tokyo</u>. It provided a case of race-revenge killing, where a white cop aided by a Japanese-American cop, literally kill the entire local chapter of the Yakuza gang. It presented the image of the vindictive, hateful, revengeful cop who goes unchecked and who can use any and all methods, regardless of legality, to fight the gang. In doing so, of course, it feeds the "killer cop" suspicion and the false notion that police can do almost anything they want to do against gangs.

Let us look at the gang movie "Gang in Blue", a case which is explicitly "anti-cop". This is the ultimate in disservice to the American public by creating a totally fabricated script, embellishing it with the image of a white racist cop and a black cop hero, and then making the larger police force look like a gang of nazis. It exploits a predisposition to hate white cops. It feeds a frenzy to be paranoid of law enforcement generally. It clearly erodes and reduces respect for the law in an intentional format.

**MOVIE TITLE: Gang in Blue
Producer: Showtime Network,Inc (1996)**
Black cop discovers white cops are acting as a vigilante force responsible for 25 murders. Disciples gang member kills officer in shoot out. The rogue officers are called the Phantoms. One Phantom kills a retiring police officer who planned to talk to the grand jury, and at the crime scene puts up "Disciples" graffiti. Actual Disciple leader arrested and killed by police at the jail. ----
What did the movie <u>Gang in Blue</u> communicate? It communicated the belief that gang murders are really carried out as a genocidal strategy of local white police and are just blamed on local black gangs. It even uses the "Disciple" identifier specifically, thus helping to explain the magnitude of the rapid proliferation of "Disciple" gangs throughout the United States. Anyone could simply adopt the title "Disciples" gang and be assumed to be "doing good work" by fighting against bad cops.
Let us analyze the formula for <u>Gang in Blue</u>: portray white cops as corrupt racists who seek to systematically kill black people. How could this formula not result in a reduction of "respect for the law" among impressionable viewers?
Other variations exist on this theme. The movie <u>Crack House</u> uses a similar formula, where the evil genius is not a white cop but a white high

school principal. The idea being: another white authority figure that should be challenged, with the net effect that again an impressionable viewer would come away with a reduced "respect" for the "system". Let's look at the basic elements of the movie called the Crack House.

Movie Title: "Crack House"

Key actor: Rick Morales. Ricky is a Hispanic teen, on leave of absence from gang ("dropped out" for benefit of his girl friend Melissa). He was not "jumped out" of the gang because his relative is the gang leader (Jesus). Rival gang member, Black Jammer, kills his relative. Rick puts back on his gang colors and assumes gang leadership. After a fire assault on Black gang house, Ricky is arrested. In jail, Rick's girl is assaulted by the Pauncho's, a rival Hispanic gang. Black drug dealer connection arrives (B.T. = Big Time) to save Melissa from assault. Rick's brother confined to wheel chair because of a drive by shooting in the distant past. In a group context Rick's girlfriend Melissa smokes rock cocaine and B.T. seduces her. Rick's brother visits him in jail. Rival Hispanic gang attacks B.T. and robs him of crack. Melissa becomes a crack addict. Mr. Stedman, a big time Black drug dealer, becomes police target with help of rollover Rick released from jail. Rick burns up B.T.'s van and beats him up. Police raid the crack house. The white high school official turns out to be the head crack supplier.

How far was this movie formula from the invented misinformation that the Central Intelligence Agency was responsible for introducing crack cocaine into the inner city drug market? People believe the worst and most far-fetched fears or suspicions that they can conceive of, and when any shred of secondary support emerges, such as can be found in a Hollywood movie, then that latent suspicion becomes an actual "belief" and the basis for continuing disrespect for the law generally, and an unhealthy disrespect for law enforcement agencies in particular.

Many who read of the accounts from the California newspaper reporter who mistakenly claimed the CIA was responsible for crack cocaine distribution, still continue to believe it. All they needed was some shred of "evidence". Irreparable damage was done when that newspaper story was published. Because it exploited a pre-existing condition of fear and distrust.

Sometimes the erosion of respect for the law occurs in a more subtle way. In otherwords, the movie may caste characters in a discriminatory fashion to achieve the same net effect of casting a net of suspicion towards a specific group. In some ways this is evident from the gang movie South Central (1992)

where the only white people in the movie were social control characters.

Let's take a look briefly at South Central.

Movie Title: "South Central"
Producer: Central Productions, Inc (1992)

Bobby exemplifies three generations of gang behavior in the same family in this all Black cast. The only white actors are the cops and corrections staff. When young Bobby is released from juvenile detention he hooks up with his homies --- a gang called the Deuces. Bobby's father is in prison for something back during the Watts riot.

Ray Ray DeWitt is the main leader of the Deuces. The early portion of the movie is about Bobby and his newly born son, who he brings with everywhere and calls "Deuce".

The Dueces decide to kill Snake, a heroin dealer. Bobby is eventually caught and sent to a California prison. In prison Bobby hooks up with some Muslim inmates and wins a parole. Bobby is released and finds his own boy is now as a Deuce locked up in a juvenile care facility. This leads Bobby to confront the Deuce leader Ray Ray. Love conquers all, and Bobby exits the final scene with his son, presumably to lead a happy life ever after as a non-gang member.

As seen in the gang movie South Central, the only white actors were those wearing a uniform and a badge: figures of governmental control in the criminal justice system.

Movie Title: STREET KNIGHT
Produced: 1993

White kung-fu fighting ex-cop named Barrett working as an auto mechanic is the hero. The movie portrays two Los Angeles gangs as having achieved a lasting peace, until a group of largely white older men in a well financed and highly organized FBI-style task force foment a war by actually killing members of each of the rival gangs. The two gangs (Latin Lords and the Black Blades) prepare to fight. Hero Barrett brings gang peace back to L.A. and is invited to rejoin the LAPD.

Similar "kung fu" fighting solutions to the gang problem can be found in two series of Vanishing Son. It is helpful to review these briefly.

Movie Title: Vanishing Son
Producer: series

Two brothers escape mainland China as key players in the Tienamen Square protest. Arriving in America, granted ____, both try to "make it in America". The older brother is a violinist and becomes the good guy. The younger brother joins a gang. Frequent violence flares where both brothers are able to use their martial arts skills. Violinist brother leaves town after saving brother in gang hit scene.

Movie Title: Vanishing Son II
Producer: (1994)

Younger brother continues with his gang which is now fighting the Triads. Older brother settles in with Vietnamese fishing community in Louisiana which is then attacked by the KKK. Younger brother reads the news of the KKK attack and returns to help his brother fight off a KKK attack. Older brother leaves for a violin competition, younger brother returns to his gang in California.

FINDINGS: MOVIES PROMOTING THE MYTH ABOUT "GANG TRUCES"

One of the first and most easily found examples of misinformation that is generated in gang movies is that surrounding the myth about "gang truces". Most gang investigators and true empirical gang researchers know that "gang truces" are social constructions: they are false, they are fabrications, they are social myths, they are simply not true statements of fact.

A newswire story that was printed in newspapers throughout the USA in late December, 1998 provided a similar misleading analysis about "gangs". The primary focus of the story was the "decrease in violent crime" in the USA as reflected in the FBI's Uniform Crime Report data. A professor was asked to explain the decrease in violent crime and speculated that, among other things (i.e., the Brady Bill, etc), that perhaps one reason for the decrease in violent crime recently in America was the "local gang truces" organized by local community groups.

We have previously examined the case of the gang movie Street Knight. It communicated one thing: that the local gangs had achieved a local "peace treaty", but that cops wanted to undermine it. Los Angeles, the scene of the movie, has never had any success with a "gang truce". Los Angeles, like other cities, has had pseudo-political leaders from gangs and activist organizations step forward claiming to be able to facilitate such "gang truces", but there have been no successful examples in American history of such "gang truces". They are a hoax. People want to believe that such "gang truces" work, because of the simplistic conceptions the same miseducated persons have about how gangs operate.

Here is the rule of thumb about "gang truces": the talk about these "gang truces" typically emerges after gangs have killed some very young or very innocent non-gang bystanders, and the "heat is on". To avoid further scrutiny and to deflect continued escalation in law enforcement investigation, gang activists will suddenly step forward with their own "plan" to solve the problem: a "peace treaty" between gangs. Gangs have manipulated the mass media throughout the United States on this issue for years.

Let us examine some of the Hollywood movie sources of the general population's misguided belief that "gang truces" work.

Within the Mac Gyver Series there was a segment that aired in 191 entitled Gunz N Boyz. This is summarized below. Only in Hollywood imagery could we find it possible for local mothers to arrive at a large gang fight to find the gang members laying down their weapons and being towed away by their ears. The misguided message: that everything would work out fine and the gangs would lay down their weapons if the mothers and grandmothers would just talk to their gang-involved kids.

Movie Title: "Gunz N Boyz"
Producer: Mac Gyver Series, 16 December,
1991

Black gang and crack selling young adult male seeks to corrupt younger male youths. Police roll up as gang member draws gun on MacGyver and Brian "cold blood" Jeffries who belongs to the Ice Boys gang attending a service center located in a rival gang territory (the Challenger's Club, a gang drop in center). The local Oliver Street Gang gives them trouble. Brians older brother died of gang violence. Gang driveby shoots up Brians house, whose mother runs the Challenger's Club. Mom is shot, MacGyver is ok. Baby boy of the family is at risk of joining gang. White gun dealer shoots Oliver Street gang leader, it is blamed on Brian. MacGyver catches gun dealer. Mothers all arrive suddenly on the battle scene, led by the bartender. Both rival gangs lay down their guns with their mothers and grandmothers behind them.

A kind of science-fiction spin on the gang problem that uses a classic plot for "gang truces" is found in the gang movie Class of 1999. Here two warring gangs "get together" to fight a common third party enemy: a government funded "killer robot" teacher. Together the gangs work together to fight a common third party enemy. The message that viewers receive: warring gangs can work together towards peaceful goals. The message really is social science fiction.

Movie Title: "Class of 1999" (1989)
Producer: Vestron Pictures, Inc (Lightning
Pictures, Original Pictures, Inc)

Actor Stacey Keach stars as Dr. Bob Forest representing the Megatech company seeking to gain a multimillion dollar grant from the Department of Educational Defense by providing android/robots refashioned from military surplus to work in a gang infested school. The Kennedy High School in Seattle is the scene where the three robot teachers called Tactical Educational Units (TEU's) are put to work. It is located in a "free fire zone" where police will not enter and where the gangs have taken control of the surrounding community. When the school is again opened, the students must check their machine guns in when they arrive at school. The main character is released from a juvenile prison for the experiment. This young white male is attract to a female student who is the principals daughter. The TEU's first kill two students in the school who were "disciplinary problems", and the main character discovers this. The TEU's encourage a fight between the two rival gangs, in which the TEU's kill about 20 of the gang members. The principal discovers the experiment has gone awry and wants it stopped. The TEU's kill the principal. The two gangs (Blackhearts and the Razorheads) join to attack the school to get the three TEU's. Finally, Dr. Forest is killed by one of the last remaining TEU's. Sci-fi futurism at its most pessimistic level regarding gangs, drugs, crime, violence, and schools.

MOVIE TITLE: First-Time Felon

Fictional story about the Impact Incarceration Program (Boot Camp) of the Illinois Department of Corrections. After initial conflict, shows a Vice Lord and a Disciple can work together. One quits boot camp goes to prison. Other remains in boot camp, helps with flood in small town.

THE DEARTH OF RESPONSIBLE GANG MOVIES AND DOCUMENTARIES

Some of the gang documentaries that have been produced in the United States are clearly sophomoric efforts that were subject to local manipulation and while making for "good ratings" tend to be exploitational like all of the other gang movies reviewed in this research.

Are there some good gang documentaries that have been produced? Yes. The gang documentary China - Beyond the Clouds is one such example. We should examine it briefly.

MOVIE TITLE: China - Beyond the Clouds
PRODUCER: National Geographic

Documentary 1991 on China; provides a time series look at gang crime (hooliganism) in a rural province; gang involvement with drugs; at a pool hall; fighting; a death by a gang fight; the arrest scenes; interrogation scenes; public sentiments about the death of ASAN (the boy killed). Some of the gang members attend a stern lecture from a Party Official; kind of like a fiery Baptist preacher, but a political official lecturing them on how immature they

are and what he thinks they need to do to improve; the parents of ASAN see a lawyer who will then SUE the persons family who killed their son ASAN.

GANG MOVIES: FURTHER ANALYSIS

Are there realistic movies about gangs? Yes there are. We can certainly recommend the gang movie American Me as being very realistic. But the level of violence is such that it is not likely to be of benefit to younger viewers: it is too obscene to show to children as a strategy of "gang prevention", it is obscene violent because gangs like those depicted in this movie are clearly of that genre. A similar prison gang movie would be that of Bound by Honor.

Movie Title: "American Me" (1992)

Story of Mexican-American youth through adulthood staring Almos from "Stand Up and Deliver" describes the gang called the "Mexican Mafia". Said to be based on a 1974 script much of the footage is based on gang activities in the prison context. The Mexican Mafia is a level three gang reflecting a formal organization that is represented in a number of different states. It is not just a prison gang.

To summarize the way a lot of gang movies have been written and casted is simple: urban violence exploitation, no overall redeeming message, just a message of hopelessness. As if nothing can be done except "move away from the hood". We get this message, certainly, in the classic gang movie Boyz N The Hood.

Movie Title: "Boyz N The Hood" (1992)
Producer: Columbia Pictures

Story of one youth named "Tre" (pronounced "tray") as he grows up in L.A. in the midst of gang violence and drugs. Tre first gets kicked out of school and his mother sends him to live with his father (a Vietnam vet). Living with his dad, he lives in an area of ongoing conflict. Scene shifts suddenly from 1984 to 1991 when Tre is college age. Tre's closest friend Rick is smoked (killed) in a status threat context. And the post-script indicates Rick's brother (Doughboy) is killed two weeks later perhaps as a result of killing the three who shot his brother. The message is "they don't care what's going on in the hood". Tre, however, is indicated as having successfully enrolled in college out of state along with his girlfriend.

The overall message of despair and hopelessness is typically just punctuated with rapid-fire scenes of "shoot outs" and violence is a typical gang movie formula. Sometimes a newer gang movie will take a previous formula component (i.e., gang member from

X gang develops love relationship with girl from rival Y gang) such as the doomed love story from <u>Westside Story</u>. *The gang movie* <u>Colors</u> *simply induces this love conflict in a larger drama of constant gang violence.*

Movie Title: Colors (1988)
Producer: Orion Pictures

Main stars are Sean Penn (Pac-Man, Danny) and his partner Robert Duvall who are both gang crime cops in L.A. Entire movie is one gang shoot out, drug pushing, drug using scene after another. Begins with CRIP gang member Rocky shooting Blood gang member in drive-by shooting. Crip members dressed conspicuously in blue colors, Bloods dressed in red clothing items. Pac-Man is attracted to Luisa a young female Latina; later love scene with her and Pac-Man, and even later with her and gang members. Community speech scene by cop and a gang outreach worker yields an angry crowd: frustration and outburst at the cops. At a Blood funeral scene, gang members flash signs over the casket, minister preaches against the gangs just as Crips spray the church with automatic weapons. Gang members snitch on each other, everyone gets arrested, then back on the streets. Pac-Mans partner Duvall is killed in a raid on a drug party. Pac-Man gets a new partner. End of story.

"In India, Movie Makers are Real Victims of Gangs"

Bombay, India is the context. Movie makers are routinely preyed upon by gangs, usually involving extortion attempts. When the movie makers do not pay, they get hurt. According to a recent report, about 50 movie producers in India are under 24-hour protection from local police because of the seriousness of the threat. Young gang members are often used as the trigger-men in cases where a movie producer is targeted for violence. Typical price to shoot a movie producer: $120 will do it (5,000 rupees in Indian currency).

Source: "Gangs Prey on Bombay's Filmmakers: The Sequel to a Movie Hit - All-Too-Real Hit Men Came Calling", by Celia W. Dugger, <u>New York Times</u>, International Section, p. 8, Feb. 27, 2000.

SUMMARY AND CONCLUSION

We need to put gang movies in perspective, they are not new and date back to 1911, when the first "gang movie" was produced. The first gang movie produced was <u>The Gangsters Feudal War</u> by D.W. Griffiths (1911): the same person who produced the movie <u>Birth of A Nation</u> several years later. The 1911 gang movie by Griffiths featured classic shots

that would be equally applicable today: gangland fights, alley scenes, violence in a big city (New York City), and all of the imagery of the "power" that exists below the surface of law-abiding American society: the "underworld", the criminal subculture.

We can find almost every type of gang movie on the market today, in otherwords there is little that has not been done on the subject matter. We can find the classic <u>Bad Boys</u> describing the gang problem in a juvenile correctional institution. Everyone has probably seen the classic <u>Warriors</u>, an attempt of one gang to escape the power of other gangs. Some of the classics also include those like <u>Cooley High</u> as typical "gang scenes" in the high school context. A number of gang movies have used white racist themes, such as <u>Prayer of the Roller Boys</u>. We can find illogical foundations for gang movies such as having a white leader for a black gang (i.e., <u>King of New York</u>). There are a number of gang movies not reviewed here that have the standard fatalistic theme as well (gang bang and you go to prison), such as <u>Menace to Society</u>. But few citizens understand that gangs behind bars can operate just as effectively as if they were still on the streets, and simply putting them in custody is no "end" to the gang itself.

What, then, from a review of gang movies in America can we say that is redeeming about these messages with regard to the gang problem. At present, very little, unfortunately. It is probably a problem of poor writers: persons who have no clue as to what the gang problem is really all about in America today. For fear of inadvertently steering future film makers in the right or wrong direction, we will not summarize what clearly could consist of prosocial themes of genuine success in dealing with local gang problems. But those of you in our area of expertise know these stories of what works.

It seems clear from an analysis of a number of gang movies that the vast majority of these are pure Hollywood hype; many of which in an objective and material way can actually be construed as increasing the gang problem itself.

As we have explained in this paper, the ways in which gang movies can actually promulgate gangbanging behavior include: 1, 2, 3, and 4.

Any analysis of American motion pictures, such as "gang movies", is also really an analysis of the culture of entertainment per se. It tells us something about ourselves as a society: it tells us "what sells to the imagination". It is an issue of "lower culture", not "higher culture". It is an issue of the gravitation towards the lowest possible threshold of being "legal" and at the same time providing the highest volume of drug abuse, sexual scenes, and graphic violence that can possibly be put on a screen in what today appears to be an escalating pattern.

There are no forces at work inside the mass media, internal to that profession and economic sector itself, that can work to moderate the intensity of the moral degeneracy that seems to drive this particular class of motion picture. There is one thing, however, that has had an effect: liability insurance and law suits against the individual movie theaters that have played these movies during their initial first runs --- a number of these have been violent escapades resulting in shootings or violence in or around the theater complex itself. These developments have provided a new market factor that can affect the feasibility of marketing and producing such movies.

A "wannabe" gang member can go to a local video store, and perhaps through ordering from other video chains, watch the movies reviewed here and get about a hundred hours of informal training in how to be a gang member. These movies provide the new gang member with the lingo, the techniques, the technology, the style, the strategies, and the "how to do it" information that a new gangbanger needs in order to gangbang in modern America.

So, in conclusion, we need to recognize that one of the forces at work in producing and promulgating the continuity of the gang problem in America today has been visible all along: it is in our culture, it is found in the mass media, most clearly in the English language "gang movies" produced and disseminated throughout the United States. The overwhelming vast majority of these gang movies send the absolutely wrong message to those foolish enough to pay to watch them.

DISCUSSION QUESTIONS:

1. Review some gang movies from your local video store, what "themes" emerge? Are these realistic or designed for pure entertainment purposes?

2. To what extent could the "copycat syndrome", also known as the contagion effect, impact on young impressionable children through available gang movies?

3. Does the masss media "demonize" gangs, or do gangs seek demonized labels as part of the package of being at odds with their society?

Chapter 22

THE COMMUNITY'S ROLE IN DEALING WITH GANGS

INTRODUCTION

The last defense against gang crime is the community itself if we cannot rely on the family as an effective agency of socialization. It may also be the best defense. This chapter will examine those practical measures such as program initiatives that can be undertaken by community groups as well as community-development strategies. Further and more detailed issues about gang programs --- particularly what not to do --- are also reviewed in a later chapter.

The experience with gangs and the community has often led to a recurring and common situation found in many of our communities. It is the complaint about gang crime as if it were a problem of "outsiders". More often than not it is not outsiders. They are not monsters from another galaxy. We do not intentionally import gang members into the United States from abroad. These gang members are our neighbors, perhaps our relatives. They are members of our own community or local neighborhood.[1] In fact, from at least one empirical study on the issue the younger the gang member the more likely the same gang member is to live in the immediate neighborhood (Suttles, 1968: p. 168).

Since the time gangs have first been recorded they have been described as having a territorial function. Most urban gangs still do have a sense of territoriality. Or at least a cognitive map of where they are or are not "safe". This has explicit meaning for a community that wants to do something about the gang problem.[2]

THE TERRITORIAL FUNCTION OF GANGS

Since Thrasher's early work on gangs, and including gangs today at all levels, the territorial function continues in one way or another. A major difference between the gang territorial claim of today and that during the time of Thrasher is probably that today's territorial claim also has the hallmark of being a market territory (e.g., drug sales) as well in many instances. What this means is that the base of operations for gangs will continue to be in our own American communities.

A typical gang meeting in Chicago today can be of two varieties: a regularly scheduled weekly meeting, or a special emergency meeting. In either case, the meeting is usually held in someone's home and in the same community area of its territorial claim.

It will include the use of at least one fellow gang member who will be posted in a "security or sentry" role function to alert gang members inside of any potential outside threat (other gangs, police, etc).

Sadly, in some of our American neighborhoods the gang seems to function much more effectively and meet more regularly than do the local community organizations. To the extent that information is power, the gang meetings which facilitate the dissemination of local information to other gang members, means that from a social structural point of view we as community members are basically giving the gang more power than they deserve. Comparatively, that is. The local community organization at the neighborhood or block level that meets only infrequently if at all, and on a unpredictable basis, is one that functions as a group at a very low level of effectiveness.

Finally, there is another problem here in dealing with gangs at the very local level. Even if the neighborhood "crime watch" or related "improvement association" does meet regularly, and if it is open to all who live in the area; then what do you do when the identity of local gang members are known, along with their errant behavior patterns, and their "families" are so integrated into the same neighborhood that among many persons, any suggestion that "Johnny XXX" is a gang member engaged in crime or other destructive influences in the community brings the critical reaction "I have known the XXX family for twenty years or more, and they are good people".

Someone who has even a tenuous social tie to the XXX family will find themselves sharing in the guilt of any accusation that a member of the XXX family is a gang member. That "someone" may be the first to stand up and deny any such gang involvement with the XXX family. They may use their voice to further suggest "it is an outside problem", that is "it is not the XXX family". Which shows another variation of the "denial syndrome": it is not "our people", it is a problem of "outsiders".

In fact, often at the early stages of such antigang crime groups, many of the local members who join in the initiative are of the impression that these gang crimes "must have been committed by persons from outside our neighborhood",[3] when in fact, the obverse is true. That is, these offense patterns are explained often by the existence of local gang members who sense that to commit these offenses in their own "turf" gives them a higher level of protection and a reduced level of detection from law enforcement. Or, the very existence of such a gang means a rival gang may intentionally chose such an area for more serious property crimes (car theft, burglary, etc).[4]

VIDEOTAPED GANG AFFILIATION PREVENTION/AWARENESS EDUCATION

Videos such as that produced by the Ontario Police Department ("Gangs, Move 'Em Out of Your Life", 1989) can be useful educational tools for heightening community awareness of the signs of gang activity. Most community members know if they have a gang problem through the existence of pockets of "gang graffiti", and periodic gang-related crimes, most typically criminal damage to property, and thefts associated with motor vehicles (stolen radios, tires, batteries, parts, etc) or damage to vehicles in a systematic fashion (serial puncturing of tires, breaking car windows, etc).

Perhaps the best such videos are those that are locally produced. Because just as gangs are each unique as social organizational forms varying in terms of a number of such factors previously described, every neighborhood in this sense has unique gang problems. That is, some gangs are a greater threat than others. Those gangs that are represented in various jurisdictions, that cross state lines and in some instances traverse the entire country, (e.g.,Bloods, Crips, Disciples, Latin Kings, Posse, Aryan Brotherhood, some Asian gangs, etc), and those gangs which are represented in many state correctional system, are also higher level gang formations (e.g., level three) and naturally have the capacity to be a larger crime threat. But, truly, much less is known of this more national picture. Clearly we need comparative research on gangs in America and this is one of the practical reasons for such a knowledge development strategy.

BLOCK/NEIGHBORHOOD WATCH PROGRAMS WITH AN EMPHASIS ON GANGS

There is a axiom that takes on the status of a social law regarding the role of community members and effective law enforcement and it is this: snitches alone, paid informants, and thorough detective work are not sufficient to adequately lay the basis for effective criminal prosecution --- it rests, ultimately, with the willingness of citizens to come forward, to share information, and to testify if necessary. That is, producing more eyes and ears for gang abatement.[5] Today, it is routine for correctional officers, law enforcement officers, and school teachers to have, as part of their required pre-service and in-service training, some degree of exposure to the gang problem; typically, "gang recognition/gang awareness" training. Citizens involved in cooperative alliances with local law enforcement also need this training, as do larger segments of our society (media, business, education, religious institutions, health care, etc). Gang awareness training most commonly involves a summary of local gang names, colors, hand signs, etc. It rarely involves more in-depth training on what is known from the literature about gangs that might help in making decisions or implementing policy correctly.

Here, again, is a prominent role that the federal government can play. In providing more generalized training materials that can be adapted to local conditions and variations in the gang crime problem. No one argues that the basic social-psychology of gang members in New York City differs from that of their gang equivalents in any other jurisdiction in the United States. While there are obvious differences in community areas and neighborhood composition, there is a remarkable similarity in some of the patterns of gang behavior nationwide. This is, therefore, an area of emphasis that federal initiatives should come to grips with in research, knowledge development, and training materials designed for state and local impact.

Some initiatives that a community group can start are low or no cost options. One good first step would be a simple photographic inventory of what gang graffiti exists in the neighborhood. How it changes, what keeps getting "put back up", and what is "crossed out" by rival gangs, is of more than some interest in determining which gangs are active in the area.

PROTECTING THE NEIGHBORHOOD

One of the profound contradictions of a community organizing against the threat of gang crime is to be found in this motivation to want to "protect the neighborhood".[6] From what we know about neighborhood watch groups, those most likely to get involved are those with the most invested: typically an employed middle-class male homeowner. It is less easy to get unemployed, lower-income, renters involved in such an initiative.

But oddly, at least one piece of research (Fagan, 1989: p. 658) suggests that gang members themselves, when asked "why did you join the gang", answer "to protect the neighborhood". That almost sounds prosocial, until we analyze it more closely. Protect it from what? From all "outsiders"? From persons of different ethnic, racial, or cultural groups? From what, indeed! Apparently, as a dominant theme, gangs as vigilantes defending ethnic homogeneity or the provincialism[7] of their neighborhood.

And to what extent is this mission informally communicated to our youths from the social structure of their community? This appears to be another unfortunate by-product of racism and discrimination. One cannot buy into racist conceptions and simultaneously desire to eliminate the gang problem. They are one and the same. And this may explain differential effectiveness of community efforts "to do something about the gang problem".[8]

The irony of all of this is or should be clear: indeed, we need to "protect the neighborhood", but

like Pogo said "I have met the enemy and the enemy is us". We also need to protect the neighborhood from the destructive forces within. Psychologically we need to take away any such self-conception of the gang member as "protecting the neighborhood". Because any conception they have of their behavior as being prosocial shall certainly serve to reinforce their commitment to gang organization, not community organization.

USING THE GEVEVA CONVENTION TO TARGET GANGS

One of the most unique perspectives on "gangs in the community" is the notion put forward by Robert A. Destro, constitutional law expert, Catholic University of America, in Washington, D.C. Here is an excerpt from an August, 1994 news release.

"As gangs spread from metropolitan areas to small communities, officials should think twice before allowing gang summits or hiring members as street counselors."

"It's dangerous for leaders to view gang activity as related to the civil rights struggles of law-abiding citizens", Destro says.

"Gangs are really organized criminal syndicates, not the legitimate representatives of a political cause. When civic leaders condone a summit, they're conceding they've lost control of their own communities", Destro says.

The news release describes community residents as "hostages in the hood", living in "war zones", if they live with gangs.

"The Fourth Geneva Convention provides for neutralized zones to protect medical services, children and expectant mothers. Geneva IV also imposes penalties for terrorism, looting and reprisals against persons and property. Perhaps we should look to Geneva IV's articles for inspiration in protecting citizens caught in the crossfire", said Destro.

"It's time we take the rights of the innocents in our own country as seriously as we do the rights of those caught in the crossfire in places like Beirut, Sarajevo, and Belfast", said Destro.

Source: Office of Public Affairs, The Catholic University of America, Washington, D.C., "Residents of Gang-Controlled Areas Often Hostages in the Hood", August, 1994.

I CAN'T BECOME INVOLVED, I'M A BUSINESS PERSON

Small business operators and proprietors need to be approached and involved in a community's response to the problem. Often, it is my experience, they will tell you "I can't become involved, I'm a business person". They need to be reminded of how they will have to pay now or later on the gang problem. It will cost them more if they let the problem get out of control, as some Englewood neighborhood stores and businesses can attest today in Chicago. The Gangster Disciples used their political wing, 21st Century V.O.T.E., as the vehicle to seek hefty donations from store owners; those who did not donate were picketed by the GDs. The Black Disciples in the same area did not honor the GD picket line however. Extortion and "protection payments" are what some business persons can look forward to in a neighborhood where the gang is allowed to thrive.[9]

CHURCH INITIATIVES

Asserting moral superiority is the essence of effective guerilla warfare and is also closely tied to the effectiveness of organized religion's role in combating local crime. Where to begin may not be with the obvious direct target of local gang members, it may rest with conditions, structures, or policies that symbolize such an internal moral decay. In Chicago, one Catholic priest has been, many believe, wrongfully accused and arrested for being the sole agent of an "anti-billboard campaign" involving painting over local billboards advertising alcohol and tobacco to inner city residents. The fact is, historically, this one member of the clergy started a campaign of civil disobedience and protest against stores that sold drug paraphernalia; a movement that was successful by its impact --- state laws were eventually passed making the sale of such drug pipes, and paraphernalia illegal.

The symbol in the billboard painting incidents are more important than the real or alleged act of criminal damage to property. The symbol of the local billboard glamorizing alcohol and tobacco dependency to the youth of an inner city neighborhood is the manifestation of a larger economic structure dependent upon consumer patterns and bold enough to make such propaganda lures in economically depressed neighborhoods which are the least able to cope in larger society. Attacking such billboards, with paint rollers or paint-filled balloons has in the years 1989-1990 in Chicago generated much mass media coverage.

Some feel that the Chicago priest had been wrongfully accused of being the "ring leader" of this moral campaign[10]. It is equivalent in one sense to any citizen wanting to paint over gang graffiti such as in the case of an abandoned building or an absentee landlord who does not take care of the building. What must be evaluated here, from a perspective of what the church can do to combat gang crime, is the larger issue of asserting effective moral leadership. It may simply not be possible to begin with an anti-gang member crusade. It may be necessary to begin with a more generalized "crime prevention" agenda.

It is not easy to advocate the arrest or detention of one's fellow community members. Although, ultimately a more developed moral consensus may demand that.

Using a more conspicuous external enemy is going to be more effective in generating moral support than simply pointing the finger at errant members of one's own community. If we were to apply Kohlberg's moral development stage theory to a community level of analysis we should conclude almost equally the same thing. That is, we cannot begin at a higher stage of moral analysis, we must begin at the basic level of moral evaluation. We cannot skip to higher levels of moral functioning through a simple, single sermon or pronouncement. It is a matter of religious and moral education. We must walk before we run.

So, to the extent that some religious leaders at least acknowledge this problem of the necessity of their communities to take moral charge of their environments, they are most certainly exerting a powerful and positive influence. An influence that should undoubtedly be duplicated in many other areas of our country if the commitment to moral development is to be taken seriously. It is a strategy that can work in the long run.

It is a strategy of taking moral responsibility for one's own individual environment, one's neighborhood, one's block, one's home. It is a strategy of peace. And of overcoming racism and discrimination.

Direct confrontation with symbols of moral threats are equally effective. In Harlem, an Islamic group that takes upon itself the responsibility to confront those persons generally regarded as selling narcotics, is a force of direct pressure to inform gang members that they are not existing in the area without moral opposition. Indeed, it is not as a vigilante action, but as a moral confrontation action, that brings to bear community awareness and greater solidarity in opposition to such collective enterprises as drug dealing. It can be an exceptionally effective tool in re-asserting the community's legitimacy, and its control.

But like the Chicago Area Project today, which has a fundamental goal of community empowerment, more specifically neighborhood empowerment, does our political apparatus really want to replicate such a project that trains local leaders to take civic responsibility, to assume responsibility, to "take charge"?

A number of churches and religious groups are now becoming involved in outreach to the gangs. Some of these are very new, others have as a part of their outreach to the confined adults and juveniles dealt with gang members for a very long time. One of these evangelical groups is described in the book

Cities of Lonesome Fear: God Among the Gangs[11]. It is called the Juvenile Justice Ministry, which has had a long history of bringing rival gang members together in a "peace making" session that is called the "United Nations"[12]. This same group issued photo i.d. cards with the logo "Officially Retired Gang Member" to the youths[13].

"Rising Role of Clergy In Dealing With Gangs"
        A truly unique but small number of clergy, nationwide, are getting involved in responding to gang and crime problems. This is not something normally taught at a seminary. But some clergy, today, are getting more involved in this issue.
        Students interested in this concept need to read the "cover story" of Newsweek magazine, June 1, 1998: "God vs. Gangs: What's The Hottest Idea in Crime Fighting? The Power of Religion.". This story represents the best summary of developments todate. It describes, in detail, the work of Rev. Eugene Rivers in Dorchester, Mass.; as well as the work of a number of other clergy throughout the U.S.A. It is not necessarily the most accurate or comprehensive story about the clergy in dealing with gangs, because obviously it has ignored a number of persons in the clergy who have written books on gangs as well.

USING WHAT GANGS UNDERSTAND
        One of the more aggressive methods used by some community groups to combat the gang problem is that of direct confrontation. Some members of Chicago's Northwest Neighborhood Federation took advantage of the national statistic that non-gang members do outnumber gang members. They sought the goal of residential displacement for gang members living in their community. They wanted the gang members and their family to move out. So they would hand the gang members a brick with a kind of Hallmark card attached to it saying "We Heard You Were Moving".[14]

THE DISPLACEMENT EFFECT IN COMMUNITY POLICING
        Prior to the rising interest in what is now known as community policing we called the displacement effect "dumping your problem on someone else". Presenting a paper on how one gang program was able to claim success by relocating some more hard core gang members to the suburbs brought one suburbanite to the point of intellectual combat, claiming this is criminal to have someone push or relocate gang members out of their community to someone else's community, and that it certainly should not be claimed as a success, it should be claimed as a damage.[15]

But today, when a community can displace its gang members out of its area, or its operations out of its area, then it is definitely considered a successful milestone in community policing. We need to understand that the problem has become so pervasive that this new technique for gang abatement is now a legitimate option.
        Some, obviously, have strong views on this issue[16].

SCREENING TENANTS FOR GANG CRIME PROFILES
        The issue here hinges on the rights of a landlord to screen potential tenants in a process that would systematically discourage gang members from living in any given area, community, or city. There are actually a number of ways this can actually be done. But it boils down to identifying potential problem makers before then can move into a building as tenants. Rental and lease agreements can theoretically contain a number of restrictive clauses, and require security deposits for a wide variety of risk factors (i.e., water beds, pets, etc), and born out of necessity has been some new innovations in this regard that have the net effect of screening out gang members as tenants. And it appears to be completely legal, where discrimination against gang members is treated as an objective risk factor, much in the same way that a bad driving record is legitimated considered in automobile insurance rates.
        What landlords in Aurora, Illinois are doing is doing criminal background checks on applicants for leasing or renting apartments and properties. With the cooperation of local police, the tenant simply completes an "Authority for Release of Information Form", and pay the police department $5.00 for a record check. Clauses in the rental or lease agreement may also include a provision for eviction for a subsequent offenses (i.e., drug sales, etc).[17] This type of policy would tend to discourage hard core active gang members from moving into the area.

THE NEW BLACK PANTHERS
        Recently the group called the New Black Panthers, tracing its beliefs to the original Black Panther Party of a previous era, has emerged in a number of cities nationally. In the present book we have not regarded the original Black Panthers as a gang, primarily because a close study of their internal structure reveals numerous "internal rules" about crime; it was a group that realized it could be jeopardized by the crime of its members. This is not to say that some of its members did not commit well known crimes. But still others who were members went on to become well known elected officials. Supreme Court Judge Clarence Thomas is said to have admired the Black Panthers when he was a college stu-

dent. Recently, the New Black Panthers have taken to patrolling Dallas neighborhoods, outfitted for combat, apparently to send a message to the gangs and drug dealers.[18]

Perhaps the best story about the Black Panther Party in relationship to gangs is found in Chicago oral history about how some gangs, like Jeff Fort's Black P. Stone Nation (then called the Blackstone Rangers) were used, in a patron/client format of state-sponsored gang activity, to have Jeff Fort's gang intimidate the Black Panther Party members on the streets. There seems to be a great deal of evidence supportive of this claim.

CITIZEN PATROLS AROUND SCHOOLS

This type of community program initiative goes by a number of names, but it basically means enlisting parents and community adults to form a "citizen security patrol" to protect students on the way to and from schools in the area. Such a program at Austin High School on Chicago's west side was formed when residents felt that police could not effectively protect students from violence and gangs. Such a program can be easily established by working with area churches and other community activists.[19]

GANGS ON THE UNIVERSITY CAMPUS

Some communities have college or university campuses and in fact some communities are "college towns". Unfortunately, the university or college campus can also have a gang problem. If drugs can be sold at the campus, then gangs can make an in-road to the campus.

Historically crime on college campuses has been systematically "downplayed". The problem is "image". The college or university is often unwilling to make arrests for crimes that can be prosecuted because of this "image maintenance" problem. Thus, some colleges "look the other way" regarding gang activity. Where is gang activity likely to show up in records other than the campus police? The answer is the "student disciplinary board" for a campus, but their "data" is not usually available to public scrutiny.

Is there a gang presence at any given college campus? One of the easiest ways to check is by inventorying the graffiti on campus.

THE SOCIAL POWER OF A CONSPICUOUS ANTI-GANG PRESENCE

While the program names differ nationally, a number of different cities give the obvious example of one such effective use of a social power against on-going flagrant organized threats to community life. It is the role of indigenous leaders. Men and women who take to the streets in a moral crusade to communicate "they are not going to tolerate drug deal-

ers" or gang activity.[20] Recall that Thrasher's formulation of gang development scenarios implied that a gang could become a secret society. So push the gang toward even greater levels of subcultural buffering from larger society. Make the gang drug dealers take the utmost steps to hide from our streets, from our corners, from our areas of legitimate social activity. Force them deeper underground.

Such can be an effective strategic ploy in showing that the gang has no legitimacy in the areas in which they operate. Forcing them underground takes away the related element of social power of hegemony over the streets after sunset. It can emasculate the gang structure. And in so doing, undermine one of the primary social-psychological ingredients of gang affiliation: the sense of power and identity with an organized enterprise. There is no "hyper masculinity" associated with living underground, with a fear of showing your colors under penalty of neighborhood and law enforcement sanctions.

THE CHICAGO AREA PROJECT

According to a recent Annual Report of the Chicago Area Project (CAP), "unlike other agencies, CAP has always worked with Chicago's gangs - identifying and meeting with gang leaders, discussing community and individual needs, and turning negative behavior into a positive force to create change for all members of a neighborhood"[21]. Also, CAP is unlike the Saul Alinksy or overt political approach to community organizing. In fact, training materials show local neighborhood committees are supposed to be non-partisan in ideology. The Saul Alinksy approach was "issue" oriented. CAP is development oriented.

The issues change, and when other political organizers leave the community behind, CAP is still there. CAP has been in many Chicago neighborhoods for decades. A fifty-year evaluation of CAP by the Rand Corporation concluded CAP was a promising program (Schlossman, et al, 1984). But CAP was not selected as an exemplary program during the LEAA years, and has not been replicated in its present form in any other city in America. In spite of this, according to CAP staff, representatives from other countries have come to examine the CAP process of developing neighborhood solidarity and local leadership.[22]

CAP literature quotes Irving Spergel and staff explain that a possible reason why CAP has not been replicated in other American cities is that Chicago is unique in having ethnic neighborhoods and enclaves. But if it truly works to build local neighborhood organization, then theoretically it can work in any city, in any part of the world. No federally supported or privately supported national project has yet been established to test whether CAP can work in other cities in America in spite of the strong support for CAP initiatives and the obviously strong theoretical underpinnings from the Shaw and McKay tradition which gave birth to CAP.

CAP literature can be interpreted as being compatible with the "multiple marginality" hypothesis of Vigil (1988). This program literature can also be interpreted as being compatible with much of the underclass theory:

"It's a simple fact. If young people can get out of the ghetto..get a job...and get some schooling...they leave the gang. But while individual gang members or ethnic groups may move beyond the gang experience, for others, gangs remain a way of life".[23]

It employs techniques similar to the detached worker program or street worker method, but it is called "curbstone counseling". This curbstone counseling is described as being most effective for what might best be described as level zero gang problems: "petty larceny, vandalism, and lewdness".[24] Curbstone counseling is most effective when it is carried out by adults or leaders indigenous to the neighborhood, rather than by outside university trained social workers who do not live in the neighborhood. It is doubtful that curbstone counseling would work very well with a deeply entrenched highly organized gang. For such a curbstone counselor would find the gang members saying "get out of my video" --- that is, stop interfering with gang business on the curbstone.

A PROGRAM THAT CLEARLY DIDN'T WORK

The Midcity Project described by Miller (1962) involved targeting seven gangs in disadvantaged Boston Communities. This "total community" method differed from the Chicago Area Project in several ways. It meant using not paraprofessionals or indigenous leaders for detached workers to provide outreach to the gang, rather it meant employing degreed social workers. For whatever reason, perhaps hoping to "integrate" the gangs into the mainstream of American life, these detached workers sought to serve the gang members almost as "organizational consultants":

"The detached gang workers changed the gangs from loosely organized near-groups to formal clubs, served as intermediaries between gang members and adult institutions, such as employers, schools, police, and other professional agencies...(Lundman, 1984: p. 69)."

Was it possible that the individual gang members viewed this "special positive attention" from the straight adult world as "manna from heaven"? There appeared to be no behavioral contracts with the individual gang members to the effect "you do this, and we'll do X for you"; thus, it was an unconditional

offering of special services. That included a heightened level of organizational capability: the transformation from informal to formal organization. Did organizing the gangs, along with trying to improve local citizen groups, even providing psychiatric family counseling to gang families, work? That is, work in the sense of reducing delinquency among those known to be involved in this Midcity Project? Absolutely not was Miller's answer.

It illustrates an important problem for the community's role in gang prevention, intervention, and crime reduction efforts. It is this: if the "theory" behind the program or project, in terms of answering "why we should expect good results" is not sound, then we should not be too alarmed to find less than good results. Worse still is the situation of having "no theory" to guide the design of efforts "to do something about it". Lacking as we are in hard evidence of what works in gang abatement (Miller, 1990), then perhaps our only option is to take a theory with some degree of more generalized support in the field of criminology and apply these to the more specific area of gang crime abatement.

What was found in the Midcity Project is the same problem of affording gangs a sense of "legitimation" through recognition that has plagued correctional institutions as well. A social worker's or psychologist's training is, normally, in working with the individual unit of analysis. We are in a different ball game when working with the gang as an organized group in an unorganized community. Just how "detached" are detached workers like these? Are they detached from the goals of larger society? Does "detached" imply they will serve the gang in any capacity but not as a member?

Our knowledge about gang formation and intervention strategies is beginning to become codified. It suggests we should definitely have a plan of action, one based on a more specific theory of "what to expect" from such initiatives. In chapter 19, for example, we will see how "well intentioned" efforts to "experiment" in the prison environment with gangs meant recognizing such gang leaders and allowing them some privileges. That backfired dramatically. It contributed to the eventual rise of "supergangs" in the late 1970's.

It is frankly beyond being irresponsible to take such risks without good process and product evaluation research in addition to having a theory of what to expect.

Why should detached workers assume it is their job to help gang members by intervening as an ombudsman when they have trouble with the police? Recall Vold's theory of gangs: the gang members are a "minority power group in the sense that they are out of sympathy with and in more or less direct opposition to the rules and regulations of the dominant majority, that is, the established world of adult values....police ordinarily represent the power and values of the adult world" (Vold and Bernard, 1986: p. 274). Thus, for a detached worker to ask the police for leniency on behalf of the gang is to reinforce this conflict between the gang and law enforcement agencies. Psychological theories stressing the need for individual responsibility for one's behavior also apply here (Glasser's reality therapy, etc). Don't be a chump, get a good theory of human behavior before offering any resources to a gang that can be exploited, unless the offering is intended to simply identify the gang infrastructure and then withdrawing the resource after accomplishing the identification mission.

SHORT AND STRODTBECK (1974) AND THE YMCA's DETACHED WORKERS

Oddly, the research described by Short and Strodtbeck (1974) was based on the Chicago YMCA's Detached Workers Program. Which we shall see below, in describing the Chicago's BUILD Program apparently basically "went out of business" by the time Short and Strodtbeck's (1974) book came off the press.

But the concept of working with youths at risk of becoming gang members is an enduring one that is still supported and recommended policy today and the community is the preferred place in which to carry out such programing (see Dunston, 1990: p. 43).

B.U.I.L.D.: A CHICAGO PROGRAM

The Broader Urban Involvement and Leadership Development (BUILD) not-for-profit corporation began in 1969. It works with "gang prone" and "gang involved" youths. Its 1983 level of service involved 3,500 youths in six contiguous areas of Chicago through a $400,000 yearly budget. Its fiscal 1989 report shows it served 2,378 young people. Currently, it has three components: (1) the prevention program, (2) the remediation program, and (3) the community resource program.

According to Hank Bach, the founder, BUILD filled the void when the YMCA Detached Workers program stopped in 1969.[25] The YMCA was moving out of the gang field. Several left the YMCA project and started the BUILD program. When it was first started it focused on remediation, similar to the detached or street worker approach. The prevention component was added later. Then the community resource component was added.

BUILD is explicitly based on a theory about human behavior. Its program literature calls it social development theory and is the basis for implementing program services. It appears, actually, to be what is more commonly known in criminology as social control theory. BUILD literature describes social development theory as follows:

This theory suggests that delinquency results from weak or absent social control, and that it happens because it has not been prevented. Social development suggests that there are factors which help provide social controls for youth. They are the family, the school, and the law. The greater the degree of bonding between each youth and these social institutions, the less is the probability of delinquent behavior.[26]

Obviously, all social institutions can provide for social control, and we can add the church and the employment/business community to the above list on this basis, even if the BUILD program does not explicitly identify these other agencies of social control. Also, there are both formal and informal social controls. And informal social control is probably going to have greater merit in preventing gang crime. The "law", or the government, comes to represent the agency of last resort and involves the application of formal social control.

An evaluation of the prevention component of BUILD is reported by Thompson and Jason (1988). The prevention service involves going to local schools and providing youths a specialized "classroom training" essentially in how to resist joining a gang, and can also involve an after-school services. What Thompson and Jason did was to compare a sample of those receiving the prevention services (N = 74) with those not receiving the prevention services (N = 43). Towards the end of the school year, the dependent variable for evaluation was "determined by comparing targeted youths' names with gang rosters provided by gang members involved with BUILD's remediation program" (Thompson and Jason, 1988: p. 329). This showed four of the nonserviced youths joined a gang compared to only one of the serviced group. The authors were aware of the problems of such an analysis, but the results approached statistical significance and tended to support the notion that something can be done about curtailing or preventing gang joining behavior.

BUILD's third and newest program service component parallels the leadership development strategy used by CAP. It is, at least, compatible with the CAP model, or complements it. Both CAP and BUILD are based on a theory of crime/delinquency. In fact, both programs made presentations in a well attended session at the 1993 Annual Meeting of the Academy of Criminal Justice Sciences.

THE YOUTH SERVICE PROJECT: A CHICAGO PROGRAM

Also called the "Second Chance" program, the Youth Service Project in Humboldt Park, a westside Chicago neighborhood, was founded by

Nancy Abbate[27] in 1975, and it works with gang involved or gang prone youths who come to the attention of the criminal justice system. It is a secondary-prevention program with a rehabilitation thrust. It works with mostly juveniles; males and females. It has been very successful at working with these youths, with education and job placement services, etc,[28] and involving the youths in graffiti removal projects. In-house statistics compiled on these juvenile clients are very promising: showing the youths do sever ties to the gang, and do not get re-arrested or committed to corrections at a very high rate.

GETTING THE <u>EDGE</u> ON EARLY GANG PREVENTION

This program initiative was designed in the field by a gang crime specialist police officer assigned to work in schools, Tom Fleming of the Park Forest Police Department in Illinois. EDGE was the acronym for Education for Gang Evasion. It is designed to reach students in the sixth grade, and like some other similar models, is stretched out over a six to seven week period for the full curriculum. It has been particularly effective in the suburban context of gang prevention.[29]

PARENTS AGAINST GANGS (PAG)

PAG was formed by gang crime victims James and Betty Major-Rose after their daughter died as a result of being a gang crime victim.[30] Goals of PAG include establishing on-site programs in housing developments, drug and substance rehabilitation programs, witness/victim assistance, individual and family counseling, community outreach and referral, promoting educational opportunities, providing supportive services, gang and drug awareness programs in schools and communities, a legislative clearinghouse for information and public education, and a Ginneria Major Scholarship Program. Program services already in place include: grief support groups to families who are crime victims, victim/witness crisis intervention, court advocacy, sibling support groups, youth at risk placement in alternative school and job programs, substance abuse counseling, parents and youth support groups, and Students Against Gangs and Drugs. The Parents Against Gangs staff also made a presentation at a well attended session of the 1993 Annual Meeting of the Academy of Criminal Justice Sciences.

COMMUNITIES DARE TO CARE

This group grew out of an enlarged application of the Parents Against Gangs mission statement. Some of the key figures in the Parents Against Gangs group while still supporting that mission, went on to start their own larger inter-community mission of building the ability of community groups to respond

to the gang problem. This is accomplished by training community leaders, educating parents and children, and general gang awareness. It is a model that was particularly designed to be adaptable to areas where "community policing" initiatives are undertaken. For it provides structure and direction to citizen initiatives which involves strengthening ties not only to law enforcement, but to other social institutions and influences in the community.

This organization, Communities Dare to Care, established the first Illinois statewide "Gang Awareness Week". It was also effective in bringing together representatives from across all ethnic and racial groups, and all political dimensions, into a common forum for attacking the gang crime problem. It goes beyond simply working with victims, even though staff are obviously still very much concerned about this, but rather it extends the model for public education to include potential new victims such as school children and their parents in a stronger prevention orientation.[31]

MOTHERS AGAINST GANGS IN COMMUNITIES (MAGIC)

MAGIC works with the Urban League of San Diego. It did receive some meager support from the Gannett Foundation for its program to get youth off the streets and away from drugs, gangs, crime and violence. This amounted to a $5,000 grant from the Gannett Foundation in 1989. But as will be addressed later in this book, clearly our foundations have not provided much in the way of funding to gang services or gang research. That will have to dramatically change if we are to provide any national climate that encourages individual initiative in dealing with the gang problem in our American communities.

MOTHERS AGAINST GANGS: Chicago and Suburbs

Founded in 1986 by Frances Sandoval after her son was killed by gang members, this group has earned much positive media attention, but equally --- at least in Cicero --- has earned the retaliatory attacks from gang members against the homes and residences of MAG members. It serves a public education function and advocates for family support, prevention, and lobbying for anti-gang policy reform, as well as neighborhood organizing. It also provides an important "court watch" service, monitoring judges who handle gang crime cases.

CHILDREN OF WAR

This program was founded by Judith Thompson and works with the modern version of "shell shock", gang violence trauma for innercity kids, and it also works with those children exposed to wartime brutality from Third World countries. They conduct workshops for junior high school students.[32] Such program services should probably be established in larger cities where the loss of life is routine for children, because this type of service may help to ease the shock to children when one of their school mates is killed.

THE CHICAGO INITIATIVE

This was a privately funded strategy to make sure Chicago did not have the kind of riots that plagued Los Angeles. It apparently worked. It was based on good theoretical ground: attacking racism, poverty, and gangs. Providing jobs, extending services, increasing recreation and teen programs, and creating a very large "safety net" seems to be a strategy that can work.[33]

LOCAL MEDIA

In the Soviet Union under its previous years of more totalitarian tendencies (i.e., before the period of openness), what got reported in the media (print and electronic) was what the government wanted reported. The author is aware of no opinion poll conducted in America regarding news media coverage for the printed press regarding the item: "Generally, do you favor knowing the names of persons arrested and/or convicted in your area and their charges?"

Chicago not too long ago used to at least publish sentencing outcomes. Perhaps with the influx of large numbers of such persons routinely processed through the criminal courts it is as difficult as preparing the accuracy of the classified section of any newspaper. Most smaller towns still routinely publish detailed "police blotter" sections to at least give the reader an idea of who was arrested and for what charge.

Clearly, in a city as large as Chicago, the nightly arrest report would take up a lot of space; and a weekly report, perhaps an entire page or more. But would citizens at least have more information on how law enforcement operates? Many believe so.[34]

Indeed, if gangs are not going to be abated, perhaps someone will recognize that this arrest and conviction information can be put to income-producing use; by publishing such "crime caper" materials where the larger newspapers simply avoid such coverage. One thing anyone who deals with offenders will tell you: the first thing they do when they read newspapers is look for the crime news, then they tend to also read the horoscope section, because many are said to be superstitious as well.

A true sign of the times in gang institutionalization in America within our inner cities will be when such a "crime newspaper" emerges and publishes specific sections pertinent to all existing rival gangs[35]. Who knows, perhaps a gang will fill this void.[36]

Gangs have in the correctional setting tested the limits of the freedom of religion, what remains in the community is the freedom of the press.

In the years ahead, we will see what progress can be made in gang abatement/prevention or whether the federal governments role will continue to be a doctrine of laissez-fair and handing all this responsibility back to the state and local governments. Without substantial national level efforts, expect to see a gang with its own newsletters or publications.

What many authors agree, regarding the media's role, is to at all costs avoid sensationalism (Kramer and Karr, 1953: p, 194; Bell and Sullivan, 1987). Also, giving attention to any one particular gang, and its specific identity being given such coverage, may not be the most responsible way to cover gang crime stories, if it can be construed as a "recognition" for a gang.[37] Sometimes publishing the address of a gang member does result in providing a rival gang the opportunity for retaliation. The fact is we have both sensationalism[38] and responsible journalism. And it is a market issue: what the public wants is what the public pays for.

The study by Kramer and Karr (1953) took a definite position on this matter of providing recognition to gang members in much the same way that it can be assumed recognizing gang leaders in the correctional setting tends to be counter-productive by legitimizing them. That is, Kramer and Karr (1953) purposely avoided use of any gang member names because:

Gang members are apt to be proud of seeing their names in print, and further inflation of sick egos is hardly desirable. In many cases the individuals mentioned are trying to reform, and more notoriety might interfere with their rehabilitation (Kramer and Karr, 1953: p. 194).

The impact of mass communications is a macro-analytic question regarding gangs; and it is not easily answered. Often the mass media is "damned if they do, and damned if they don't". But another historical continuity in the gang literature, indeed a cross-national one, is that in spite of the attribution of widespread illiteracy among gang members, they do read the papers and the first thing they look for is the recent crime news. As Patrick (1973: p. 66) stated "the papers were...scrutinized every morning for the slightest reference to gangs or gang warfare". Patrick also documents the effect of mass media and movies in terms of the emulation or "copy cat" phenomenon (p. 85).

OVERCOMING COMMUNITY DENIAL

"We don't have a gang problem" is the response of many adults and community residents, when in fact the graffiti, the local crime patterns, and repeated gang incidents point to nothing other than a gang problem. It is the classic reaction by the casting of blame externally which relieves the person of any sense of responsibility: "it must be outsiders." One of the conclusions from the national conference reported by Bryant (1989) was this very need to overcome community denial.

As in a treatment situation, help is not possible until there is an admission of a problem. Law enforcement cannot be effective on the basis of good detective work alone. Indeed, without the help of citizens, the civilian counterpart to sworn police officers, we would have few such criminal convictions. We need witnesses, we need testimony, we need leads and information. Community's must come to recognize they have a gang problem. It cannot be "outsiders" for everyone.[39] Some, many of us in fact, live in such neighborhoods with a gang crime problem.

Evidence suggests the way we learn about it may have something to do with such an appraisal. Adults may learn about gangs primarily through the mass media, while school age youths may learn about gangs through educational institutions and their peers.[40]

REBUILDING COMMUNITY FABRIC

Gang crime does not occur in a cultural-social-political-economic vacuum. It occurs in the community. If social disorganization can be said to have some positive role to play in the onset of gang crime, then we can assume as an equally strong force that gang crime also has a most deleterious impact on the very institutional fabric of any given community. The damage to these institutional linkages shall have to be repaired if a community is to successfully overcome the gang crime problem or even play its expected role in larger policies regarding gang abatement.

Here again is where federal resources are needed. Because when gang crime flourishes, those first to leave the community are those most likely to be the more upwardly mobile portion of the tax base. What gets left behind are those least able to contribute in an economic sense. Cities like Chicago are experiencing "crime flight", citizens leave because they do not feel safe; they fear having their children in public schools where only half the incoming freshmen ever finish high school, they fear the spread of drugs and the gangs with which they are associated. It will not be easy to reverse this process but it can be done.

One of the most under researched aspects about gang crime in our literature is the social impact of gang crime and how it shatters and tears asunder relationships within the community and between the community and other social institutions. Durkheim was right in the limited historical context with which he said crime can have a positive impact,

but if any only if the perpetrator is caught and punished and in so doing this tends to reinforce and strengthen the norms of the group. But in the context of gang crime this may be less sound; because even if a gang offender is incarcerated, the gang structure remains intact within the community and the criminal justice system simply plays a latent role by facilitating leadership training. That is, the pattern has been to target gang leaders for prosecution, inducing status promotional opportunities for other gang members who are not on their way to the penitentiary.

Citizens of our inner city community's become polarized and progressively isolated from mainstream America. We need to reverse that process. We need to allow the "system" to work for them. That means taking seriously some of the recommendations by Bell and Sullivan (1987), such as establishing conflict/dispute resolution centers perhaps in the structure of a multiservice community program that enhances the institutional linkages of these citizens to their larger society --- through healthcare, through education, through employment opportunities, family counseling, community-based corrections, through a more positive relationship with their government and the services it offers. The local religious institutions would have a prominent role to play here, if they wanted to.

In essence, the best way to arm the citizens who face our nation's gangs on a daily basis is to rebuild and strengthen this community infrastructure; its institutional linkages, its very fabric and identity as a "community". This is, after all, the essence of what Shaw and Mc Kay intended through the Chicago Area Project as a general delinquency prevention strategy. Summaries of the overall effectiveness of the Chicago Area Project such as those by Kobrin (1959) are not able to point to direct conclusive evidence that the initiatives produced significant reductions in delinquency, but then again no one to your authors knowledge has ever taken the position that this was a counterproductive effort as a variety of other intervention/control projects have tended to be.

THE ROLE OF LOCAL COLLEGES AND UNIVERSITIES

Here is where we can get some good advice, and a theory or two. Professors in the social sciences, in criminal justice, etc, are often expected to provide some level of "community service". It is good for them to have this contact with the community on behalf of their university. And they are not supposed to charge for it. It should be pro bono. Otherwise it is not community service, it is proprietary hustling. A community organization should take definite steps, in writing, to contact local colleges and universities: the various departments of Sociology, Psychology,

Criminal Justice, etc., and express an interest in working with any faculty members who are willing to help. Or agree to accept student interns.

Many faculty members would be pleased to assist local community organizations. But like anything, you don't the get the help unless you ask for it. This can be a "win/win" situation. Greater involvement by university faculty in the real world means research opportunities for them, it means they get credit for community service, and the community gets knowledge and hopefully good advice. It can be a creative partnership and it should definitely be expanded throughout American society. It too could help "rebuild the fabric" of our communities.

The recent work by Takata and Tyler (1994)[41] illustrates how nicely the skills and capabilities of individuals from a local university can dovetail with the pragmatic needs of a local community in terms of "doing something constructive" about the gang problem. Creating a Task Force as in their case is usually a good first step. Using university experts in criminological research is then a next good step to determine how serious the problem is and what if anything might be feasible in terms of "doing something about the problem".

Colleges and universities need to be concerned about the gang problem because more and more they are now feeling the effects of gang violence. Numerous instances of gang violence targeting campus areas and university students have appeared recently. Gang graffiti and drive-bys on campus appear on the rise.[42]

THE FEDERAL GOVERNMENT's (OJJDP) "I.D.E.N.T.I.F.Y" STRATEGY

The early federal government included many different agencies so it is not really accurate to say that any single coherent and coordinated federal response to the national problem of gangs really even exists. Almost all federal agencies have someone who interfaces in someway with gang issues. But as mentioned earlier, no "Gang Czar" exists. But a variety of "concepts" have been offered by federal agencies, one deserving mention here, the IDENTIFY strategy.

Bryant (1989) reports a recommended strategy for dealing with gangs at the community level based on what the Office of Juvenile Justice and Delinquency Prevention was able to compile. It recommends prevention, intervention, and supervision. IDENTIFY is the acronym for:

Identify the problem. Define the system components. Enumerate polices, procedures, etc. Needs clarification. Target strategies. Implementation plan. Focus agency responsibilities. Yell.

It suggests what criminologists have been saying for centuries: "schools, law enforcement, recre-

ation, mental health, housing, community agencies and churches --- all part of the prevention component --- must work together" (Bryant, 1989: p. 4). The trick is: how to do it. It is good advice. But for many of our nation's neighborhoods where this strategy is needed, these same neighborhoods are also going to need some federal resources to really carry it out.

The educated reader who examines gang issues will eventually find that if any blame is to be cast on anyone regarding the proliferation of the gang problem, then it is not the family, it is not the local police, and it is not the local community that should be blamed. Rather, the federal leadership in Washington deserves much more blame for seeing the gang problem begin to rise and fester all across the United States and virtually adopting an ostrich with its head in the sand type of response. It seemed like throughout the Reagan and Bush administrations about all they did regarding the gang problem was develop acronyms for what could be done about the problem. It is interesting, of course, to note that even the IDENTIFY acronym ends with "yell": perhaps "yelling" at our elected officials might help. Because not much has changed as we enter 1995.

This early effort by OJJDP was followed up by a number of other initiatives. Students will find a host of free materials on the topic of gangs available through OJJDP.

THE CLINTON COVENANT TO COMBAT GANGS: AN UNFULFILLED PROMISE

President Bill Clinton advanced a novel idea in his nomination acceptance speech at the 1992 Democratic National Convention. But is it a good idea? His concept for combatting gangs was couched within a larger social policy idea of allowing recent college graduates to repay their college loans by community service. A kind of highly educated Urban Community Corps perhaps. A closer examination of this idea shows some historical mistakes that deserve special consideration.

Efforts to combat gangs are not new just as gangs are not new. Our social science literature contains numerous examples of gang service programs and projects at the street level. Some worked. Some worked significantly in the reverse intended direction. We need only recall how in Chicago during the 1970's when Reverend Fry helped the El Rukn gang leader Jeff Fort gain federal grants. Some volunteers of the past have helped gangs become stronger.

Not every volunteer, whether possessing a college degree or not, is capable of combatting gangs in our communities. They would need direction, supervision and training before entering the field. Two well-known programs that use volunteers and do have a positive impact on combatting gangs are

Chicago's BUILD program and Parents Against Gangs. There are still costs associated with using volunteers and especially training them properly.

There are genuine anti-gang programs, and there are anti-gang programs. The genuine ones, like BUILD and Parents Against Gangs, have experts with considerable experience in the area and they operate with both a theory of achieving a positive effect and a well defined plan of action.

Other programs sound good, but are upon closer scrutiny bad ideas. One genuine bad idea is providing gang members with leadership training skills. Another bad idea is providing gangs with organizational development skills. Both of these bad ideas are still being promoted today in less educated circles. Helping gang members to be better organized under some guise of coopting them is not a well founded concept. Hopefully Bill Clinton did not have either of these two ideas in mind in recommending the use of volunteers to combat gangs in our urban areas.

There does exist considerable expert opinion that youths can be prevented from joining gangs. What it would take, however, to prevent this gang joining behavior would be providing something equal to or greater in attraction than the lure of the gang itself. Excitement, kicks, status, a sense of protection, a tight-knit group that provides a sense of identity, and more often than not income itself --- these are the things that the gang offers. The Clinton covenant would not work unless it could effectively compete with the current attractions that the gang affords. To prevent youths from joining gangs is slightly more complicated than simply providing a bunch of English major volunteers with recent bachelor's degrees.

To combat the gang problem through the use of college graduate volunteers will require specialized training in our social sciences, particularly sociology and criminal justice. These are the disciplines where full gang courses are taught in our nations universities. If we expect any volunteer to do good, then they must be trained. We cannot assume all college graduates have completed courses dealing with urban gangs. Institutions such as Chicago State University, Loyola University of Chicago, Lewis University, and many others throughout the U.S. --- they regularly teach courses on gangs. To use most of our recent college graduates to combat the gang problem the Clinton covenant would require additional college work in this specific area of expertise.

There is growing support among gang researchers for the value of a WPA-style, depression-era mass public employment or public service program to be able to offer poor and minority youths an alternative to drugs and the gang. Perhaps it is here, in the context of providing adult supervision for recreation, educational upgrading, vocational training, etc, that recent college graduates could best be put to use in working with the several million underclass youths who could benefit from such a program. Still the potential for major mistakes in dealing with gangs must be taken into account in any implementation of the Clinton covenant to combat gangs. Such a program initiative would require a national advisory commission staffed by professional gang researchers. Gangs have benefited in the past from political corruption and attempts to pay them to "chill out". If the Clinton covenant seeks to provide recognition to the gang as an organization and basically give it legitimacy, it would be equivalent to negotiating with terrorists.

To effectively combat gangs in America will truly require enormous new federal resources. It will take more than a bunch of volunteers. It will cost a great deal. But it will be worth it. It could save many lives, it could prevent the burgeoning costs associated with imprisonment, and it could truly help to restore a sense of community in some of our nation's troubled urban areas. The Clinton covenant, then, is not a bad idea. However, it will require considerably more thinking and planning and therefore must be regarded as a pie in the sky plan at this point.

Years of neglect by the Federal government with regard to the gang problem began to change only recently in 1991-92 when federal agencies received the command to get concerned about gangs. Research funding and prevention programs are still extremely meager in relationship to the scope of the gang problem. Agencies like the National Institute of Justice that have recently gotten interested in funding gang research are not required to have true competitive bidding. So the 'good ole boy' network of political favoritism in providing such funding still exists in our federal agencies. No one has promised to clean up this problem.

What the federal government should be doing is not experimenting with gang problems, rather it should use what current knowledge exists and apply this in a single, standardized, national model of gang prevention and suppression. As discussed in a subsequent chapter in this book, some very recent federally funded "gang programs" may have resulted in situations remarkably similar and equivalent in impact to the notorious mistakes of providing federal funding to gang leaders like Jeff Fort via Rev. Fry in Chicago, where the money was not really spent on trying to put the gang out of business, it was spent in a fashion to increase the strength of the gang. That kind of federal government blunder has not entirely disappeared is what a subsequent chapter will reveal.

BUILDING CONSENSUS TO COMBAT CRIME

Most of the ethnomethodological, participant observation, "hang out in the hood" qualitative studies about gangs do not take into account the viewpoints of the vast majority of the citizens. The viewpoints of adults and juveniles alike who are not tied into gangs have not been heard from systematically. Yet many appear to be willing to speak on their behalf, usually without any objective assessment of citizen views. A way to build consensus to combat the gang crime problem is to start with a systematic social survey of the viewpoints of those who live in the community: particularly those who are registered voters, and of course those who invest in and work in the community.

CREATING A CITYWIDE GANG-FREE TASK FORCE

Using official agencies, churches, political groups, citizen volunteers, schools, business people --- the entire gamut of social institutions, one of the best things a city can do is create a citywide Gang-Free Task Force or a Violence Free Task Force[43]. Such a committee needs to be as broad-based as the gang problem is itself, and include all segments and levels of society.[44] Examples of such initiatives exist in many parts of the country.[45] It can help target aspects of the gang problem that can be easily remedied: such as removing gang graffiti. Having the Governor or Mayor declare a certain week as "Gang Awareness Week" can then allow some groups like this to hold numerous functions across the city working with all segments of the problem: recreation, school, etc.

WHERE TO BEGIN?

A community anti-gang organization can begin with one interested citizen. We can even assume that such a person knew absolutely nothing about criminology or how to fight crime. But what they should do is immediately contact the National Crime Prevention Council.[46] This is the "Mc Gruff" headquarters. They have an assortment of helpful materials that can be put to use at the community level for "taking a bite out of crime". Or they could be adapted in the spirit of "taking the bang out of the gang". These are the type of very elementary materials for persons who have no knowledge about crime or gangs. It is recommended, however, that any local effort invite local police and criminal justice personnel to their Task Force for the most effective way to apply concepts to local problems.

"The Legacy of Arnold Mirales: Community Activist Against Gangs"

The story of Arnold Mirales is an experience that has probably been felt in numerous cities across the United States by a large number of persons who take action in their communities against gangs. What makes the story of Arnold Mirales different is the fact that he was killed by the gangs in his neighborhood because he was becoming too effective in his work.

As a community organizer, Arnold Mirales worked to rid his Chicago neighborhood of "problems" like drug sellers, gangs, dilapidated buildings, etc. He worked, in fact, in cooperation with the Chicago Alternative Policing Strategy (CAPS).

One particular slumlord in the neighborhood did not like the fact that he had to make a number of appearances in "housing court" because of the efforts by community organizer Arnold Mirales. The slumlord then contracted with local gang leaders, who resided in his buildings, to assassinate Arnold Mirales. When Arnold Mirales was killed, the investigation quickly revealed the slumlord and the gang members were involved, they were arrested and convicted. But at that time the maximum sentence for first-degree murder was 60 years.

After the assassination of Arnold Mirales a new state law was passed in Illinois. This new law went into effect January 1, 2000. The new law provides that if anyone kills a community policing volunteer they now face a mandatory life imprisonment or the death penalty.

SUMMARY AND CONCLUSION

A high ranking police official who grew up on Chicago's southside once remarked to the present author, about his own adolescence, that one of the things that has changed through the years in Chicago that may have some bearing on the gang problem is the role of parks and public recreation. "There were a lot of adult supervised park programs that kept us busy", he remarked. Today in Chicago these socialization resources are unevenly distributed and probably at a premium. But such park programs as a community resource probably have been under represented in our gang literature in terms of their capability to "do something" (positive) about the gang problem.

It is unrealistic to expect the gang problem to be solved independently throughout America at the city and state levels. Federal assistance is going to be necessary (Huff, 1989). While much can be done at the local and state levels, it cannot be done effectively alone. First, local initiatives that are successful must be able to be replicated in other jurisdictions, and such a clearinghouse function can only be effective at the national level. Secondly, coordination is also vital at the state or regional level, because gangs are not simply a problem to our communities, they are also a problem for state correctional institutions and their boundaries of influence extend to different and often non-contiguous geographical areas.

Local schools are going to be required to play a much more prominent role than they have historically played in dealing with the gang problem (Ackley, 1984). Stephens (1988) shows a variety of ways in which this can be done.[47]

By most accounts the community itself can play a formidable role in both prevention and in gang suppression. It is a question only of organization, effort, support, and resources. If our nation's gangs are so "loosely organized"[48], then why are we so ineffective at all levels of society in gang dismemberment? The answer appears to be this: we have been doing the wrong thing. And typically these failed efforts have also been those with no theory as to what to expect from any given experiment, program or initiative.

Two Chicago programs that are based on good theory were described here (CAP and BUILD). They appear to work, or have great merit in terms of design. And, of course, there is much more to be done. Neither of these programs have been replicated elsewhere in America. They truly deserve to be.

DISCUSSION QUESTIONS:

(1) Should local community groups and programs try to work with level zero and level one gangs and their members, seeking to reintegrate these youths and young adults in more prosocial activities, and leave more sophisticated gangs (level two and three gangs) to law enforcement?

(2) Could a program be designed for a community other than Chicago that reflects the best of both the BUILD and CAP programs? What would it involve as a solution to the gang problem? Could it be established as part of a strategic plan for community gang-violence reduction using a local Gang Violence Reduction Advisory Task Force? What would your ideal program for gang abatement be like?

(3) Poston (1971) was highly critical of direct funding to gangs and gang members because of their propensity to exploit the "establishment" as Jeff Fort did with Rev. Fry's assistance in Chicago. But if the government knew it was going to get ripped off, could this also function as a Trojan Horse strategy (recall Jeff Fort received a felony conviction out of such funds misappropriation) to make gangs more amenable to intervention?

THINGS THAT WORK: FOLLOW THE MONEY TRAIL FOR OWNERS OF BUILDINGS THAT ARE GANG CONTROLLED OR A NUISANCE BECAUSE OF DRUGS OR RELATED PROBLEMS.

While somewhat rare and requiring a community, and local community leaders (i.e., "block mayor's", and "indigenous leaders", and "moral leaders": the real thing in informal community leaders), with the "guts" to fight back; there have been some "success stories". This is one of them.

In Chicago's northside Edgewater and Rogers Park community, one landlord owned four different buildings that were all "run down" and which where sites of frequent criminal activity[49]. The landlord used a variety of names and aliases, complicating normal communication. Two community groups where the buildings were located formed a coalition and took the landlord to court in conjunction with community policing initiatives. They convinced the U.S. Department of Housing and Urban Development to terminate the "section 8" rent subsidy program eligibility for this particular landlord. Most of the rent money was federal "subsidized housing" money. This hit the landlord's "pocket book".

In addition, they worked with the Cook County State's Attorney's Office in seeking "nuisance abatement" laws to be enforced against the landlord. Successful at this initiative as well, the landlord ended up paying $10,000 in fines for each of the four buildings. Eventually the landlord had to sell the buildings.

The "Nuisance Abatement Statute" is an Illinois state law that can be used in any community in Illinois. It is specifically geared to gang and drug houses. If your state does not have a similar law, then maybe you should go to the law library, look up the Illinois criminal code, and lobby to get a similar version passed in your State.

WHAT PERCENTAGE OF GANG MEMBERS ARE JUVENILES VERSUS ADULTS?

If most gang members were underage minors, then it would be proper and fitting to refer to gangs today as "youth gangs". Perhaps some communities could be less concerned about "youth gangs", but would be troubled by having "adult gangs". Here is an important lesson that communities need to learn fast.

The best available data and information on gangs and gang members shows that when we analyze the age range of gang members, clearly we can find a lot of young gang members. The typical American gang member first joins the gang at age 12. Some can be born into the gang. But guess what? These are still not gangs run by kids, these are gangs having adult leaders: older adults who are typically hardened career criminals.

The best information is that when we analyze the "age range" of the American gang member population, that we get almost an equal 1/2 split between "underage juveniles" and those old enough to be tried as adults.

So, while it is true that as many as half of America's gang members are underage juveniles, the language of referring to gangs as "youth gangs" becomes another way in which a community can "discount" the threat and "over look the problem": those are just kids. Those are not just kids. The kids you see, especially the ones coming to our attention for their brutal and shocking violence, are typically kids under the influence of adult gang leaders.

The Case of Chicago's Arnold Mireles: Assassinated Because of His Fight Against Gangs and Related Community Problems

This is not the first case, and it probably is not going to be the last case, where one brave person has such an extraordinary impact in fighting against gangs in the community - that the person is killed because of this good work.

Arnold Mireles fit a common "good guy profile": he had a lot of friends in his community, he worked hard for his community, he tried to "clean up" his community, he was a dedicated type of person, and while he was non-confrontational he probably made enemies because as a community activist he had no "protection".[50]
What Arnold Mireles distinguished himself doing most was "fighting gangs".[51] And he got the gang's attention.

Arnold Mireles worked in a southeast Chicago neighborhood fighting gangs, drugs, and slum landlords[52]. He worked in the community policing program as a citizen volunteer. One day, one of the landlords he had problems with, Roel Salinas, decided to hook up with the local gangs that lived in his properties. The plot was hatched: for a few dollars the gang members would simply kill Arnold Mireles. Sadly, in 1997 this is what happened.

The aftermath brought a loud hue and cry from communities everywhere. Swiftly a new state law was passed in Illinois: citizens like Arnold Mireles who work with police departments in "community policing" and "neighborhood watch" type programs would now be given additional protection under law. Killing a citizen in Illinois, now, in connection with their work in community policing and the like will now carry an automatic death penalty. And, for the first time in over twenty years, the Cook County State's Attorney himself, Richard Devine, walked into court to personally try the case against slum landlord Roel Salinas.

END NOTES:

[1] Suttles (1968, p. 168) showed a direct inverse relationship between age of gang members and local residence patterns. That is, the younger the gang member the more likely such a youth is to live in the same neighborhood. In age categories and residence, Suttles found those in the 11-14 age group showed 100% lived in the same neighborhood area, in the 14-16 age group some 88% lived in the same area, and in the 16-18 age group 80 percent lived in the same neighborhood area (Suttles, 1968: p. 168).

[2] Some legislative efforts directed against youth gangs have sought to declare "safe zones" where the commission of a gang related crime in these areas constitutes grounds for more severe criminal penalties (e.g., schools, etc). Including section 8 housing and "projects" extends this institutional protection to the law abiding poor and is a worthwhile protection.

[3] The research by Suttles (1964: p. 207) showed that 94% of the malicious mischief or property damage was committed inside the same neighborhood area, as well as 55 percent of all theft cases (Suttles, 1964: p. 208). However, Suttles also hypothesized that gang offenders would be reluctant to victimize those persons who live in close proximity to them. What matters is the type of offense. Some offenses are more likely to occur in the local area than others.

[4] If local gang members are not the source of local property crimes, which I am reluctant to accept as a hypothesis even with some of the empirical support advanced by Suttles; then obviously, from the same hypothesis, gang rivalry can be extended to include intentional choice of a neighborhood for serious offenses because of this potential for "insulting" the local gang. Here, most obviously, is an area of much needed research that has significant practical impli-

cations. Such findings do emerge from more recent studies such as Moore, Hagedorn, etc.

[5] Sometimes all it takes is a "tip" from a citizen. A routine tip on Chicago's southside led to the arrest of 61 gang members. Tips do pay off for law enforcement. See: Phillip J. O'Connor, "Tip Leads to 61 Gang Arrests", Chicago Sun-Times, Oct. 20, 1993, p. 22.

[6] That is, one of the other historical continuities in the gang literature is the tendency of the gang members to express the view that they are "just defending the hood", and in some fashion therefore performing a valuable function, sanctioned by their social structure, or at least such a desired role function is communicated to such gang members, often along the lines of ethnic and racial conflict.

[7] Is provincialism a good thing or a bad thing? Or is it everything, but in moderation? In an increasingly inseparable world community, and even within nations and cities with an increasingly more mobile population, is provincialism the denunciation of a more cosmopolitan view of the world? Provincialism implies territoriality. It can also be the refuge of residential segregation patterns (e.g., ethnic purity, etc).

[8] The excellent summary about the lack of previous program effectiveness in gang crime intervention programs described by Walter Miller (1990) points to the problems of lack of theory, lack of hard evaluation research, and service organizations that continue "business as usual" even when they know their services don't work or may in fact be counterproductive.

[9] See: George Papajohn, "Korean Store Boycott Splits South Siders; ties to gangs, politics seen", Chicago Tribune, Dec. 28, 1993, section 2, p. 1,4.

[10] See Tom Siebel, "Surprise Defense Delays Priest's Vandalism Trial", Chicago Sun-Times Thursday, March 21, 1991, p. 22.

[11] See Gordon McLean, 1991, Cities of Lonesome Fear: God Among the Gangs, Chicago: Moody Press.

[12] According to Mc Lean (1991: p. 92) "More than forty representatives from twentysome Chicago street gangs and organizations have attended the sessions, currently being held at Calvary Memorial Church in Oak Park".

[13] As McLean (1991: p. 94) indicates "It often causes a stir when used as identification on the street".

[14] See: Art Golab, "Group Gangs Up on Crime", Chicago Sun-Times, Mar. 21, 1994, p. 1,14.

[15] This was a presentation at the Annual Meeting of the American Society of Criminology.

[16] Should the government do this? Actually, some in government are the least supportive of it, for a very selfish reason: for example, one of the larger obstacles to emptying out highrise public housing projects and dispersing the tenants to suburban areas where they

might prefer to live, and where they could be assured of much greater job opportunities resulting in a substantial decrease in public expenditures on welfare, is that the politicians who get elected from such high rises are the least supportive of any such dispersal plan --- and for good reason, they might lose their voting base.

[17] See: Philip Franchine, "Arrest Records Weed Out Bad Aurora Tenants", Chicago Sun-Times, July 11, 1994, p. 15.

[18] See: Pamela Burdman, "Black Panther Philosophy Coming Back in Vogue", San Francisco Chronicle, Aug. 29, 1994, pp. 1,6.

[19] See: The Austin Voice, March 1-8, 1994, Vol. 9, No. 12, pp. 1,4.

[20] Often this is sexually divided, as a men only group, or as a group that emphasizes predominantly mothers (MAG and MAGIC), but also parents (PAG) together.

[21] Chicago Area Project, The Nation's First Community-Based Delinquency Prevention Program, Chicago Area Project, 407 S. Dearborn Street, Suite 1300, Chicago, IL 60605 (312) 663-3574, p. 12.

[22] Personal interview with CAP staff on 12-7-90.

[23] Page 12, Chicago Area Project, The Nation's First Community-Based Delinquency Prevention Program, no date, late 1980s. Chicago Area Project, 407 S. Dearborn St., Suite 1300, Chicago, IL 60605.

[24] Material quoted from staff training documents supplied by CAP.

[25] Personal interview, October 26, 1990.

[26] Page 3 of BUILD, Inc document entitled "Program Profile".

[27] Nancy Abate, the founder, left the program she founded after the staff working in the program voted to become "unionized".

[28] Counseling (individual and group), sports/cultural/recreational outings, home visits, teen parenting skills, and the like.

[29] See: Barbara Dargis, "Park Forest Police Officer Trying To Help Area Youth", The Star, Feb. 13, 1994, A-4 CUP.

[30] PAG is located at: Lower North Center, 1000 N. Sedgwick, Chicago, IL 60610 (tel. 312 - 787 - 2490).

[31] Contact information: Communities Dare To Care, Dorothy Papachristos, Co-Founder, 7059 N. Greenview, Chicago, IL 60626. Telephone: (312) 338-CARE.

[32] See: Chicago Sun-Times, May 4, 1994, p. 12.

[33] See: Leslie Baldacci, "Show More Initiative For City, Daley Urges", Chicago Sun-Times, May 4, 1993, p.4.

[34] The issue here is adequate information. If gangs do engage in drive-by shootings based on their knowledge of where rival gang members live, then do you think that the families that may also live in such a building or next door have the right to know whether

such a building contains known gang members?

[35]Teen Angels magazine first published issue #1 in 1980 and is now in issue #124. The target audience for this magazine are "those who live and grew up in those areas where gangs have evolved for many years" (personal communication, May, 1993). It services the California area primarily. TEEN ANGELS, P.O. Box 338, Rialto, CA 92376.

[36] Recall the fondness of gang members keeping scrapbooks "describing their gang exploits" discussed by Jackson and Mc Bride (1990: p. 24).

[37] At a public hearing, before the Illinois Gang Crimes Study Commission someone in the audience asked for more detailed "hand outs" from the police department, in responding to this a police commander said "That's a danger because what happens, the competition --- did you read the article in the Chicago Tribune about a month ago about gangs? The Tribune Magazine had about a nine-page article where they interviewed me and two of my people rode with them. It covered all gangs. We had some shootings as a result of that article because they involved one gang symbol and the other then in competition started up" (see Nash, 1984: p. 72).

[38]See: Ken Parish Perkins, "60 Minutes in Little Rock's War Zone", Chicago Tribune, Section 5, pp. 1,3, August 1, 1994.

[39] Horowitz's (1987) article "Community Tolerance of Gang Violence" is most useful here. Horowitz says "Parents often can maintain the fiction of their son's conventional conduct outside the home if he behaves properly when at home (Horowitz, 1987: p. 443)". We want to believe little Johnny is a good boy. But are we willing to join a recent Chicago campaign reported extensively in the mass media to "turn in a family member" who sells or uses drugs?

[40] The biggest sample of hard data relating to this question so far was reported by Tromanhauser (1981). Regarding youths in school it showed: males know more about gangs than females, the older the student the more they are likely to report gang members in their school, the younger the age the greater the fear of gangs and percentage of youths reporting they are solicited for gang membership in school varies inversely with age (p. 187).

[41]Susan R. Takata and Charles Tyler, "A Community-University Based Approach to Gang Intervention and Delinquency Prevention: Racine's Innovative Model for Small Cities", Journal of Gang Research (in press, 1994).

[42]See: Roger Flaherty, "Security Beefed Up at NIU As Crime Shakes Campus", Chicago Sun-Times, Sept. 17, 1994, p. 12.

[43]Several examples of these exist, one with some apparent success is that in Duluth, Minnesota "Violence Free Duluth", founded in response to a growing number of homicides in that northern Minnesota town.

It does much direct outreach to teens.

[44]For example, prosecuting gang leaders can often mean discovering everyone around the gang member was liable. The gang leader has an enormous "web of influence" that may also be tainted. This was the case in the leader of the Four Corner Hustlers, Rufus "Weasel" Sims featured on "AMERICAS MOST WANTED" television series. Pretty much everyone who worked with Sims was a co-conspirator. Convictions in the Sims case included: "his lawyer, Richard Goldstein, his 63-year-old mother, his wife, and a girlfriend". See: Tim Gerber, "Fugitive Sims Caught by L.A. Cops", Chicago Sun-Times, July 8, 1994, p. 20.

[45]See the story for the one in Springfield, Illinois: Stephen Beaven, "Gang Presence Paints Hazy Picture", The State Journal-Register, July 10, 1994, pp. 1, 4.

[46] National Crime Prevention Council, 733 15th Street, N.W., Suite 540, Washington, D.C 20005, telephone (202) 393-7141.

[47] This document by the National School Safety Center also includes a listing of projects, and programs, nationally involved with gang intervention. One problem, however, appears that it advocates a program component of what amounts to the same mistake made by correctional institutions in terms of acknowledging and even negotiating with gang leaders (Stephens, 1988: p. 28). By suggesting that any strategy should be discussed "with student gang leaders and solicit their support", this is not too different than what correctional administrators did in earlier years.

[48] Spergel (1989) summarizes some of the gang literature and concludes, generally, that gangs are "loosely organized". That is, consisting of core, regular, peripheral and recruit members. But apparently not as organized as we would think. Which were sentiments expressed similarly by Short to wit: that "gangs are characteristically unstable as a form of association and organization" (Short, 1974: p. 16). We must keep in mind, that when authors like Horowitz and Schwartz (1974) involving only one gang in one area of one large city is hardly enough data to be able to quote, as a generalization, when they say "the gang's organization is rudimentary (Horowitz and Schwartz, 1974: p. 239". It was rudimentary to their gang studied in a park in Chicago's lower west side because it was a level zero to level one gang formation. But we cannot generalize to all gangs from such limited findings.

[49] This "success story" is taken from: Brenda Warner Rotzoll, "Neighbors Triumph Over Building Owner", Chicago Sun-Times, Feb. 11, 1998, p. 20.

[50] See: Teresa Puente, "Gunning Down of Activist Stirs New State Legislation", Chicago Tribune, Jan. 1, 1998, Section 2, P. 4.

[51] See: Bryan Smith and Jim Casey, "Activist Shot

Dead: Tried To Rid Community of Gangs", Chicago
Sun-Times, p. 1,2, Dec. 31, 1997.
[52]See: Lorraine Forte, "Devine Will Try Murder Case
Himself", Chicago Sun-Times, Jan. 21, 1998, p. 19.

Gangster Disciples

Twists on the Gang Identity

The Gangster Disciple (GD) (also known as the Black Gangster Disciple (BGD) or by its original name, the Black Gangster Disciple Nation (BGDN). It is also referred to as the "Brothers of the Struggle", and thus females are also called "Sisters of the Struggle" (AKA "intellectual sisters"). The GD's have also effectively used modern "public relations" gimmicks, including efforts to convince some politicians they have made a transition from "Gangster Disciples" or gangbanging to a new prosocial gang called "Growth and Development". That was how Wallace "Gator" Bradley presented himself when he had a personal meeting with President Clinton in the White House in 1994.

Chapter 23

LAW ENFORCEMENT AND GANGS

INTRODUCTION

Normally, a police officer cannot arrest someone for simply belonging to a gang, as much as citizens might want to give them that power. Recalling the military-based legislation from India (Sleeman, 1849) there is no law that makes it a punishable offense to simply belong to such a group or to be associated with such a group. Further, not everyone who is a gang member is necessarily criminally active.

What then can police do? That is the focus of this chapter. As will be seen, there are a variety of policies, programs, and initiatives that can be undertaken. Many of which could be beneficial in reducing gang crime. It requires planning, coordination, strategy, good information, and the necessary resources and support. This assumes that the fundamental responsibility for gang abatement and suppression is in the hands of law enforcement alone.[1]

GANGS ARE INTERESTED IN LAW ENFORCEMENT TOO!

Shortly after the L.A. riots when a "truce" existed between the Crips and the Bloods, these two gangs are credited with devising a plan for reconstructing their city[2]. They demanded $3.7 billion dollars for their budget to rebuilt L.A. with the threat *"Meet these demands and the targeting of police officers will stop: you have 72 hours for a response*

and commitment, in writing, to support these demands. Additionally you have 30 days to begin implementation" (p. 66).

Was it real or was it a fraud? No one knows, as no names of the authors appeared. But in addition to other ideas, they had a full law enforcement proposal which was as follows:

"The Los Angeles communities are demanding that they are policed and patrolled by individuals who live in the community and the commanding officers be ten-year residents of the community in which they serve. Former gang members shall be given a chance to be patrol buddies in assisting in the protection of the neighborhoods. These former gang members will be required to go through police training and must comply with all of the laws instituted by our established authorities. Uniforms will be issued to each and every member of the "buddy system", however, no weapons will be issued. All patrol units must have a buddy patrol notified and present in the event of a police matter. Each buddy patrol will be supplied with a video camera and will tape each event and the officers handling the police matter. The buddy patrol will not interfere with any police matter unless instructed by a commanding officer. Each buddy patrol will also be supplied with a vehicle. $6 million shall be appropriated for this

program over and above existing appropriations" (p. 66).

Whoever wrote this surely does not understand modern American law enforcement. Whoever wrote it does not know that most "police matters" do not involve subduing resistant arrestees, they involve order control: responding to domestic situations, etc --- where the last thing you need is a civilian "buddy" with a video camera. Gang members clearly are interested in law enforcement. Some without arrest records, or only minor juvenile records, actually become police officers. They are certainly eligible!

The close examination of the gang literature will show numerous examples of persons who report to being such "former gang members" as juveniles who later became responsible police officers. But were they "killers" and "drug dealers" in their youth? No. They were more typically level zero gangs, involved in local turf and periodic or seasonal very low intensity fights with rivals. Should police applicants be screened about prior gang membership? It is an interesting issue.

RICO PROSECUTIONS

As discussed elsewhere in this book, the federal RICO and state "mini-RICO" statutes are very effective tools against gangs. This 1970 federal law called the Racketeer Influenced and Corrupt Organizations Act was originally designed for use against traditional organized crime. It includes both provisions for criminal and civil prosecution. Anyone may initiate a civil prosecution under RICO, even against an employer. But the criminal sanctions and provisions in this law are effective against gangs because of the stiffer penalties against those charged, indicted, or convicted under the RICO act.

A number of effective prosecutions of gang members where almost total gang suppression, of that particular gang, occurred has been reported. This does not mean that a new gang will not come along and try to fill the void. But it does take out the gang in an effective way.[3]

CHICAGO'S EDGE AND SNAG INITIATIVES

Two recent police programs in Chicago include EDGE and SNAG. EDGE stands for Enhanced Drug and Gang Enforcement and is a proactive unit of "six sergeants and 60 officers in a unit to harass gang members and drug dealers in crime-ridden areas".[4] SNAG stands for Stop Narcotics And Gangs and involves using surveillance and sting operations against the gang, for example identifying a large scale drive-up drug retail operation, arresting the operators, and quickly setting up shop using undercover officers to arrest all the suburbanites who drive into the area asking to buy narcotics, selling them the

drugs, arresting them, and impounding their vehicles. The Chicago public seemed happy to have these new programs. Unfortunately, some programs have to basically stay one step ahead of the American Civil Liberties Union which has taken upon itself to challenge a number of new laws and efforts directed against gangs.

WITNESS PROTECTION

At a cost of $19 million per year the federal government's witness protection program has provided "new identities, houses in different locations, and new jobs to over 4,889 informers since 1970" (Thio, 1988: p. 403). This has been primarily to support federal prosecution of traditional organized crime figures or racketeers. Any successful prosecution of gang leaders, using other gang members, is going to necessarily entail the same kind of witness protection program. What it means is having law enforcement agencies and prosecutors working together to offer genuine protection to gang informants.

Simply creating the propaganda illusion that those who are high-ranking gang members and who defect for purposes of prosecution to law enforcement are provided with "great comfort" can itself be a powerful mechanism for inducing defection. Sometimes it is useful to simply allow such a gang member to accept conditions of controlled witness protection and relocation, not because the offender may in fact be useful for prosecution, but rather because it may instill the legitimacy of such a choice among other gang offenders. And, of course, it has a demoralizing influence on the gang organization itself. No one is certain exactly what such an offender can or cannot testify to.

Such defection creates a powerful negotiating ploy for inducing other gang members to accept such immunity and protection. Witness protection is a key ingredient to spurring key gang informants to "roll over" and should be made available for strategic use by law enforcement personnel responsible for gang crime investigation[5]. It is an expensive proposition. But used effectively and strategically it can have optimal effects on successful gang prosecution.

Some research by the National Gang Crime Research Center tends to suggest that this kind of service might result in more effective prosecution of gang crime. It is not uncommon to find well placed gang members who area willing to testify against their gang leaders, and basically cripple the gang, for a small price; such as $10,000 for their family to relocate when the testimony is needed. Illinois in 1999 created the "Gang Crime Witness Protection Act", as a pilot program, it allows for payments for temporary living costs, moving expenses, rent, security deposits and other expenses involved in relocation for witnesses involved in gang prosecutions.

VICTIM ASSISTANCE

Generally, only twenty percent of all reported crimes in American society result in an arrest (Senna and Siegal, 1984: p. 24). For even serious felony crimes among those actually arrested only a fourth of these offenders do time (Senna and Siegal, 1984: p. 102). Here the math means only five percent of those offenders arrested among reported crimes, for serious offenses, actually serve a correctional sentence. Recall, that not all such serious crimes are even reported to the police. Thus, the actual probability of doing time in America for serious crime is most likely less than this five percent figure.

This is not to recommend more prison sentences. But rather to suggest in dramatic terms the fact that perhaps something could be done, through victim assistance programs, to at least increase the effective adjudication of many of the serious offenses that occur in our society. The fact is: victims of crime need more help, and their immediate sense or perception that they are alone or "left hanging" translates into their non-appearance at court and that means offenders go free.

Experienced police officers know how to handle victims to ensure their appearance at court. They make sure the victim has a number they can call for any problem that arises regarding the case. They make sure they call the victim the night before court and arrange, if necessary, for transportation to and from the location of the court appearance. They also try to give some sense of reassurance and confidence in the psychologically vulnerable period during the first stages of trial. They make sure victims are not intimidated by the offender in or out of the courtroom.

In too many our of cities, when victims appear at criminal court, they are left to their own devices to manage somehow to appear as state's evidence. What happens is all too common. In spite of the existence of such "victim assistance programs" within the State's Attorney's offices, victims still must find their own place to park, must still go through metal detectors in the same fashion as offenders out on bail, must wait in the hallways often side-by-side with the offender they must testify against when they have the eagerness to arrive for a court appearance early, and are often placed in the less than friendly environment of a cold and hard atmosphere that communicates little support from wider society for the victim or witness who must appear in court: that is, they often must sit side-by-side on the same bench, often ending up sitting next to the person they must testify against. Clearly, even minor accommodations could be made to have a more dramatic improvement of the environment that facilitates a stronger and more effective judicial handling of criminal cases for the purpose of reinforcing pro-social behavior on the part of victims and witnesses. This is even more important in the context of gang crimes.

To the victim and crime witness, such a "bureaucratic" treatment, forcing a levelling effect, where they are treated just like the offender, means ultimately they may never come back after such a first appearance. We lose testimony and witnesses systematically, because of the callous disregard for the social-psychological state of such potential witnesses for the prosecution.

Which brings up the organizational effectiveness hypothesis that perhaps we need not necessarily increase law enforcement strength in the gang crime specialty area, rather we need to ensure that we do not lose our witnesses "through the cracks" of bureaucratic justice! Higher conviction rates would occur if more could be done to reinforce cooperation with the judicial level of the criminal justice system. This should not be left to simply the law enforcement officials, nor to local community organizations, indeed it ultimately has its responsibility with the local state's attorney or U.S. Attorney. When a gang crime victim has never met the prosecutor before the time of court appearance, we are dealing with an environment that communicates only one thing to the potential witness "you are not important" or "we don't really care about you".

Gang crime victims and witnesses are those who especially need such assistance. Many of these crimes occur in their own neighborhoods and the offenders are also likely to be on the same streets. Victims and witnesses need "orders of protection" to ensure that as a matter of official record, such offenders, once convicted, cannot if let loose on probation, harass by their presence such citizens who have the courage to come forward and make the judicial system work.

SCREENING FOR RISK (SFR)

Gangs can be classified in terms of their level of organizational sophistication. Similarly, in an earlier chapter dealing with organized crime, it was seen that the scope and extent of criminal violations and the magnitude of illegal income or numbers of persons involved in such crime, are also important. Here both should be tied together in a screening for risk (SFR) application. This is the type of quantitative research methodology that is also called threat analysis when it focuses on the measurable danger represented by a gang.

The primary justification for SFR rests with the limited resources any society has for "control". We do not have an unlimited supply of criminal investigators. We do not have a unlimited supply of prison cells. By targeting offenders who are "high risk", "high volume", or "high impact" an SFR application applied to gangs would mean focusing law enforcement efforts on those gangs representing the largest threat to law and order. That is, those gangs involved in the highest levels of crime and violence.

Here, for the sake of simplicity, we shall revise the classification system from a range of "level zero thru level three" to that of including level "four" where level four corresponds to organized crime groups. Then we shall be able to add a numerical "crime potential severity code rating" to each such gang formation. This numerical assessment of a gang's real or potential capability to represent a threat of crime or violence to the public shall vary between zero (the lowest) and nine (the highest) in terms of threat analysis.[6] In this configuration, the lowest gang threat problem in America is the "Spanky and our gang" variation of Level zero-zero (0-0), corresponding to the pre-gang (streetcorner, playgroup, neighborhood clique) with no major potential for crime and violence; to the worst case gang scenario of a Level 3-9, corresponding to the "super gang" armed with fully automatic shoulder weapons and controlling a vast empire of illicit income-producing crimes. This leaves level 4 crime threats for organized crime groups. Figure 22 below summarizes this screening for risk (SFR) application to law enforcement.

Figure 22

A Screening For Risk (SFR) System for Gangs In Relation To Their Organizational Sophistication and Crime/Violence Potential in Law Enforcement Applications

GROUP LEVEL OF
ORGANIZATIONAL
SOPHISTICATION:

		CRIME AND VIOLENCE[7] LEVEL OF THREAT FROM
		0 1 2 3 4 5 6 7 8 9
LEVEL 0	(not a true gang, a pre-gang)	
LEVEL 1	(emergent gang)	
LEVEL 2	(crystallized gang)	
LEVEL 3	(the supergang, the corporate gang)	
LEVEL 4	(organized crime groups)	

In Figure 22, a Level 0 group at level 0 of crime and violence threat is the least possible threat. A Level 4 group at a level 9 of crime/violence threat would be the worst possible threat.

"Chasing Monsters: When The Gang Unit Itself Gets Corrupted"

Most people have heard of the abuses that took place inside the Los Angeles police department's gang unit. Obviously, similar incidents can be found elsewhere as well.

In February of 2000, the FBI itself began investigating L.A.'s gang unit, because 20 officers had been suspended and 40 criminal convictions had to be reversed, when one gang cop testified about the corruption in the "CRASH" unit. As many as 3,000 criminal convictions could eventually be overturned because of the alleged abuses by the L.A. gang unit.

One of the aspects of the CRASH unit was that it used the INS to deport over 150 Hispanic immigrants who may have witnessed abuse by the gang police. Apparently, in 1997 and 1998 some of the LAPD gang unit officers in the Rampart division CRASH unit (CRASH = Community Resources Against Street Hoodlums) violated a longstanding policy prohibiting municipal police involvement in deportations.

This "heater case" emerged after Rafael Perez, an officer with the LAPD CRASH unit, was caught stealing eight pounds of cocaine from a police evidence room. He cooperated with federal investigators, and return got a reduced sentence (5 years). He has alleged that gang officers routinely framed innocent people and lied in court, even shot innocent people, in the Rampart area of Los Angeles. At his sentencing, Perez said in court: "whoever chases monsters should see to it that in the process he does not become a monster himself".

Targeted Offender Programs (TOPS) operate under similar guidelines. Intelligence gathering is conducted to show which offenders are "highly active", typically as repeat offenders. A case file is prepared and a review process is conducted to make a decision as to whether a police department should, through its targeted offender program, "accept" such a case. Once accepted, the offender is targeted for prosecution.

It can involve the use of all techniques of criminal investigation, covert operations, and undercover techniques. The purpose is to "get that offender" off the streets, because the offender is highly active in local crime functions.

The same successful strategy can be adopted for gang crimes. But it will mean more than a subjective appraisal of any such gang offender's individual "threat". A more quantitative appraisal is needed to supplement the investigative strategy suggested for gang prosecutions by Burns and Deakin (1989). As they admit, the major problem is finding those gang members willing to roll over.[8] Otherwise, their method is not too dissimilar from the ancient "vice ladder"; that is, giving up small fish to catch bigger fish.

Obviously, such SFR values may change and fluctuate over time and would need constant updating. As an example, assume a local Posse group is used in this SFR rating system. It would minimally be a level three gang, being interstate in character. Assume that prior arrests in the area are high, that it is believed from intelligence sources to be highly armed, and that it has many fiscal resources to draw upon from its ongoing criminal activity. It might rate an SFR score value of 3.75 compared to 3.25 for a local group of the Miami Boys who met only one of the same three factors. It is never as simple as this and screening for risk methods require much more statistical analysis than is implied here. But basically, it would mean wanting to allocate investigatory resources in a manner that focuses on the higher risk gangs. And then, of course, adjusting the strategy to the results of prior efforts; through a continuous appraisal of the problem.

"The Ultimate Gang Leader: Hooking Up With Corrupt Cops"

Chicago provides a model for the ultimate in gang leadership. It would require the gang leader to hook-up with a corrupt cop, ideally a gang cop. That is what happened in the case of Nelson Padilla, leader of the Latin Lovers street gang in Chicago.

Padilla established an alliance with a cop in the gang unit. When Padilla's gang members did get arrested, the cop was often able to get them released immediately. Now this was a gang that had something going on! Federal court records would show that even when Padilla was in jail on serious charges, that the cop would come and get him out so Padilla could go home to be with his wife. When Padilla was facing a long prison sentence, the cop actually testified on behalf of Padilla allowing him to get a reduced sentence in state prison in Illinois.

When Padilla was released, he started up the cozy operation again. Padilla would identify large-scale drug dealers, order large quantities of cocaine, then alert the cop: the cop would break in and arrest the drug dealer, seize the drugs, etc. The drugs would then be given to Padilla to sell on the street.

This story came to light when Padilla was under federal charges and faced life in federal prison. Padilla realized he had a "bargaining chip": the story about dirty cops in Chicago. It worked.

Source: "Gang Boss Says He, Cops Were Hand in Glove: Confessed Killer Claims Dealings With Police Spanned 2 Decades", by Todd Lighty, Chicago Tribune, Mar. 17, 2000, pp. 1, 22, section 1.

THE CHALLENGE OF GROUP DISRESPECT FOR THE LAW

The "risky shift" phenomena means basically that persons will act more severely in a group than they would perhaps behave as individuals. The challenge for law enforcement, then, is dealing with gangs as a group phenomenon and one flavored with more than a little disrespect for the law. According to some authors, gangs simply do not fear law enforcement:

"Gang members are getting so bold that not only do they show total disregard for their fellow man, but they have no fear of police or any formal consequences for their actions" (Trojanowicz, 1978: p. 402).

It is a serious crisis of legitimation for law enforcement that is represented by the contemporary criminal gang. If not dealt with effectively, then it shall surely manifest erosion of confidence in law enforcement among other civilians.

MULTI-JURISDICTIONAL EFFORTS

A simple truism is that gangs, while often having a territorial claim or a historical beginning that may be dependent on a specific "turf", do not limit all their crime activities to any specific political jurisdiction.[9] The problem in any given state is going to be, depending on the level of gang formation, multijurisdictional in nature. Task Forces and programs designed to address the gang problem must also, therefore, be able to cross traditional lines of political jurisdiction.[10]

This must include information sharing and subpoena power. Here both the state and federal courts have an important role to play. The one genuine organizational feature reflecting a change from earlier gang formations in the criminological literature is this matter of operational mobility. And the creation of satellite gang crime operations, often involving drug distribution, in other geographic areas. The California Council on Criminal Justice and its State Task Force on Gangs (1989) recently concluded, similarly, that gang drug trafficking is no local matter --- it is a statewide problem.[11]

State's today need enabling legislation to both create Metropolitan Enforcement Groups, or MEG units, and to allow these units to purse gangs and gun crimes just as they are traditionally enabled to investigate drug crimes. The simple fact is drugs, gangs, and violence are very inextricably related. More federal Gang Task Force groups that can work with local law enforcement can achieve the same effective results.

LOCAL AND STATEWIDE GANG INTELLIGENCE FILES

Most gang members, as part of the social-psychology of individual identity that reinforces gang affiliation, have gang names or monikers. The San Diego Police Department reported the value of maintaining a moniker file. It cross-indexes such nicknames, monikers, and aliases with true names and other identifying information (e.g., date of birth, gang of affiliation, etc) (see Kolender, 1982: p. 20). Alpha files are used for making name checks, and vehicle files are used to keep track of what vehicles and license numbers are known to be used by gang members.

The state-of-the-art in this area, however, is having a statewide gang and gang membership database maintained for intelligence purposes. The Illinois "SWORD" is one such example.

The Statewide Organized Gang Database (SWORD) Act became effective in Illinois on January 1, 1993. It provides model legislation for other states in seeking to coordinate and monitor the scope and extent of the gang problem. The SWORD computer system is maintained by the State Police. The details of this model legislation are provided in their entirety here:

"Illinois Criminal Code and Procedure. (1993). Chapter 20. Executive Branch. Act 2640. STATEWIDE ORGANIZED GANG DATABASE ACT.
Section
2640/1. Short title.
2640/5. Definitions.
2640/10. Duties of the Department.
2640/15. Duties of local law enforcement agencies.

2640/1. Short title. This Article may be cited as the Statewide Organized Gang Database Act.

Title of Act: An Act to create the Statewide Organized Gang Database Act and the Illinois Streetgang Terrorism Omnibus Prevention Act.

2640/5. Definitions. "Department" means the Department of State Police. "Director" means the Director of State Police. A "SWORD terminal" is an interactive computerized communication and processing unit that permits a direct on-line communication with the Department of State Police's central data depository, the Statewide Organized Gang Database (SWORD).

2640/10. Duties of the Department. The department may:
(a) provide a uniform reporting format for the entry of pertinent information regarding the report of an arrested organized gang member or organized gang affiliate into SWORD;
(b) notify all law enforcement agencies that reports of arrested organized gang members or organized gang affiliates shall be entered into the database as soon as the minimum level of data specified by the Department is available to the reporting agency, and that no waiting period for the entry of that data exists;
(c) develop and implement a policy for notifying law enforcement agencies of the emergence of new organized gangs, or the change of a name or other identifying sign by an existing organized gang;
(d) compile and retain a historic data repository relating to organized gangs and their members and affiliates, in a manner that allows the information to be used by law enforcement and other agencies, deemed appropriate by the Director, for investigative purposes;
(e) compile and maintain a historic data repository relating to organized gangs and their members and affiliates in order to develop and improve techniques utilized by law enforcement agencies and prosecutors in the investigation, apprehension, and prosecution of members and affiliates of organized gangs;
(f) create a quality control program regarding confirmation of organized gang membership and organized gang affiliation data, timeliness and accuracy of information entered into SWORD, and performance audits of all entering agencies;
(g) locate all law enforcement agencies that could, in the opinion of the Director, benefit from access to SWORD, and notify them of its existence; and
(h) cooperate with all law enforcement agencies wishing to gain access to the SWORD system, and facilitate their entry into the system and their continued maintenance of access to it.

2640.15. Duties of local law enforcement agencies. Local law enforcement agencies who are members of the SWORD system may:
(a) after carrying out any arrest of any individual whom they believe to be a member or affiliate of an organized gang, create or update that individual's electronic file within the SWORD system; and
(b) notify the prosecutor of the accused of the accused individual's gang membership or gang affiliate status.

There is only one good feature missing from this Act, and that is the provision for logging in known gang members previously arrested in a given period, for example within the last five years; and all of those currently in confinement at the local and state level. It will take awhile to "feed in" the data, but eventually it will be a very powerful tool. It would be even more powerful if it had a provision for "priming the pump", and thus requiring local law enforcement agencies to report all such gang members or gang affiliates arrested in the last five years. Then, once the data was processed into the system, it would be operational in a very short period of time.

Citizens who live in states where this kind of law does not exist, and who want to do something to help empower their law enforcement agencies to "win the war" against gangs, should endeavor to have such legislation passed in their own states. Gang researchers will someday discover this kind of systematic data is the real way to answer many of the questions in our literature about gangs in America.

CHANGING POLICE PATROL STRATEGIES

Wilson and Kelling (1989) describe the value of changing police patrol functions from the traditional "incident oriented response" to a "problem oriented response". The incident oriented or traditional patrol technique is to simply respond to radio dispatches from citizen complainants. The problem oriented response means allowing the police officer more flexibility and having the police work more closely with the "good guys" rather than seeing their fundamental mission as being only to "lock up the bad guys". It also means, essentially, being more proactive with regard to the gang problem.

It is, by the way, a recommended solution that can be very compatible with gang neighborhood programs such as CAP and BUILD described earlier. The idea is to put police into guarding and maintaining the local social infrastructure through their conspicuous presence. It is an idea whose time has truly come, and seems to genuinely offer a way to reduce fear of crime as well.

But it would mean, according to James F. Short, also changing what police are trained in and capable of doing. It would mean giving our police more skills in mediation, in conflict resolution, in consensus building, true "peace making", such that "police might become community advocates...rather than community adversaries".[12]

CHANGING THE CRIMINAL LAWS

Gang crime cannot be effectively prosecuted or investigated unless state criminal codes are consistent with regard to such organized threats against law and order. State criminal codes should not have "holes" or "prosecutorial gaps" such as those in Illinois. For example, Illinois criminal law technically allows an adult gang offender between the ages of 17 to 20 to direct a younger gang member in facilitating a felony crime by a juvenile, and cannot, if detected, be prosecuted under the more serious statutes for contributing to the delinquency of a minor. Let us review this Illinois "Fagin" law in some greater detail, for the large "hole" it contains favorable to gang crime operations:

"Chapter 38. Illinois Criminal Code. Section 33D.1. Contributing to the Criminal Delinquency of a Juvenile. 33D-1. (a) Contributing to the criminal delinquency of a juvenile. Any person of the age 21

years and upwards, who with the intent to promote or facilitate the commission of a felony, solicits, compels or directs any person under the age of 17 years in the commission of such felony commits the offense of contributing to the criminal delinquency of a juvenile. (b) Sentence. Contributing to the criminal delinquency of a juvenile is a felony one grade higher than the offense committed, except when the offense committed is first degree murder or a Class X felony. When the offense committed is first degree murder or a Class X felony, the penalty for contributing to the criminal delinquency of a juvenile is the same as the penalty for first degree murder or a Class X felony, respectively (see Illinois Criminal Code, St. Paul: West Publishing, 1989 edition, p. 168).

Certainly, anyone 17 years of age or older charged with a felony is going to be prosecuted as an adult; but, oddly, this particular statute leaves a "gap" between the ages of 17 through 20, and can allow for such stiffer prosecution only at ages 21 and above. This kind of gap must be eliminated. The first segment of any society to come to understand the criminal code is the offender portion. They should not be able to "slip through the cracks" so easily. It is a good law, but one that was poorly constructed in terms of its scope. It allowed for a gap. Thus, technically, a fellow gang member 17 to 20 years of age can direct a juvenile to commit a serious crime and escape the prosecutorial impact of this criminal code.

State laws should also bolster local enforcement powers through the ability to confiscate vehicles and real estate property used in the commission of gang crimes, and explicitly authorize intelligence gathering activities related to crime to overcome restrictions such as those faced by Chicago police.

In the urgency to "do something" about the gang problem at the local city level, some municipal governments like Chicago have passed ordinances that were aimed at the gang problem. One law made it illegal to sell spray paint to persons under 18 years of age. The idea was to reduce access to the spray paint and maybe reduce gang graffiti. Passed in 1992, it was challenged, and in the fall of 1993 a federal judge ruled that the ordinance was unconstitutional under due process grounds. Similarly, a Chicago ordinance making it unlawful for known gang members to conspicuously loiter on street corners was ruled unconstitutional by a Cook County judge --- it was too vague, and thus subject to abuse[13].

DO POLICE HAVE THEIR "HANDS TIED" IN GANG CRIME INVESTIGATION?

"Our hands are tied", rang the sentiments of many police officers after the famous Miranda decision. But the Miranda decision did not, in the long run, have any deleterious impact on criminal investigation. In fact, it might have induced an element of professionalism that may have otherwise never been adopted in policy.

It is, however, a legitimate issue for discussion. But not about the Miranda warning. Rather it involves intelligence gathering activities, data processing capabilities, use of fingerprints and photographs of juveniles, and related issues that can be critical to solving any crime, including gang crime which often involves underage youths.

To illustrate these limitations of power and authority that law enforcement must work with, let us use a scenario. Assume someone, while you are away, breaks into your home and takes everything of value. A neighbor sees the youths leave your home with the "goods" and could identify them. So you insist that the neighbor be able to look at "mug shot files". You are also knowledgeable about forensics and insist on an evidence technician, one in facts arrives on the scene and collects some good fingerprint sets on the crime suspects. Now you must feel your case is solved, right? Wrong.

In Illinois the Juvenile Court Act does not allow police officers to show photographic "mug shots" of known gang members previously arrested to victims of crimes. These youths have the right of privacy under the law. So there goes the neighbor as witness, unless you can somehow catch the offender yourself.

In many jurisdictions, the Automated Fingerprint Identification System (AFIS) involves only a database for adult offenders. Juveniles, again for the protection of their privacy, are excluded from such computerized data sources. If you were really smart you might want to check about two and a half years later (that is, in Illinois most felony offenses including residential burglary have a three year statute of limitations, so you hope maybe that the offender is arrested again later as an adult and gets into the AFIS system), but then you may find that few police departments with the AFIS technology keep separate "unsolved crime" physical evidence files for "aging/follow-up" purposes.

In fact, let's assume you get really lucky. You and your neighbor spot one of the burglars and you are able to effect an arrest. Theoretically, in Illinois anyway, the offender could be taken into custody and could conceivably have four or five other outstanding felony warrants, but the fact that no centralized computer index exists for juveniles for purposes of a "name check" means the offender could be let free even with a series of outstanding felony warrants. And if the arresting police officer wants to do a "station adjustment" (a verbal reprimand, "don't do it again", and lets the offender go) you really have little recourse other than to grin and bear it..

But let's assume you were indeed very lucky, the offender was arrested and placed in custody and now it is court time. In Illinois, you do not have the right to be privy to all the matters before the juvenile court. In fact, you as the actual victim may be the only one allowed into the juvenile courtroom. In Illinois juveniles have more rights than adult offenders; what juveniles cannot have that adult offenders themselves do not take much advantage of anyhow is the jury trial.

In late 1993 an appeals court took away an effective tool for law enforcement: the use of mug shot books for gang suspects was ruled to intrude on individual liberties (Police, 1994: p. 15).[14]

Police in many smaller jurisdictions have new recent ordinances about curfew and graffiti, some of these efforts are more effective than others. In some towns there have been backlashes against such efforts. But most seem to believe there is some value in hardening the target of smaller jurisdictions to make it harder for gangs to move in.

CHICAGO's "GANG LOITERING" LAW: A New Version for 2000

The original Chicago "Gang Loitering" ordinance went into effect in 1992 and made it possible for police to arrest gang members massing on public property (streetcorners, etc) in a menacing way. The law was challenged in various lower level courts and the City of Chicago was forced to suspend enforcing the ordinance in December of 1995. During the period of 1992 through 1995, however, some 42,000 persons had been arrested under this municipal law.

In the summer of 1999, the ACLU was victorious in having the U.S. Supreme Court declare the Chicago ordinance unconstitutional. What is interesting about the Supreme Court decision, however, is that Justice Sandra O'Connor gave an opinion that basically advised the City of Chicago on how to make the law be able to pass constitutional testing. Taking this as encouragement, Chicago Mayor Richard Daley began developing a new "Anti-Loitering" law that would be aimed at both gangs and drug pushers. In February of 2000, the new anti-loitering law was passed through a City Council committee vote after two days of testimony. So the City of Chicago plans on continuing to have such a law on the books.

And, in March of 2000, Chicago passed its revised ordinance on gang and drug loitering. This ordinance was passed about a week after the Chicago Police Department also made a big change: dismantling the gang unit itself in the wake of local examples of what was happening in Los Angeles.

USE OF THE GRAND JURY

During the 1960s and early 1970s the grand jury was often used as a device to investigate groups. Largely those groups, often student leftist groups, who opposed the war in Vietnam or who espoused a radical philosophy (SDS, Black Panthers, etc). Fishing expeditions were common. It is curious, then, to see that the same relentless use of the grand jury has not been as prominently used in the prosecution of genuine law violation behavior on the part of organized criminal gangs.[15]

The value of the grand jury is that it can develop much more information than lone investigators. In fact, the fundamental investigative advantage of the grand jury, over individual efforts of local law enforcement investigators is that the grand jury is more suited to "unravel a complex criminal structure" (see Kasimar, La Fave, and Israel, 1990: p. 636). It can grant immunity from prosecution, apply psychological pressure, and operate in secrecy to essentially force a known gang member to testify.

Simply issuing large numbers of such subpoenas to members of the same gang can induce an enormous amount of infrastructure damage to morale and cohesiveness. It is a legal way to make an effective arrest as well among those who are most prone to resist legitimate authority. Arresting such offenders routinely for "disorderly conduct" charges has been shown to be less than effective. But not responding to a grand jury subpoena means contempt of court and an opportunity for strategic arrests.

States that in their criminal code of procedure authorize the investigative subpoena power function through mechanisms other than the grand jury, the so-called "one-man grand juries", typically a judge and a special prosecutor (see Kasimar, La Fave, and Israel, 1990: p. 641), can eliminate the high cost and complexity of grand jury criminal investigations of gangs. Thus, the "special prosecutor" approach represents a genuine low-cost alternative to a grand jury investigation. The advantage of the "special prosecutor" approach is its county wide jurisdiction, and through the intelligence gathering function, to be able to share information with other jurisdictions in the same state. Because few states have "state-wide grand jury" mechanisms. Even though, these will come to be more politically attractive as the gang problem posed for states increases beyond city and county jurisdictional lines.

Police Author of Two Gang Books

Loren W. Christenson is a police officer with the Portland Police Department. He has authored two books on gangs, making him unique in this way. He first wrote Skinhead Street Gangs, a critical look and how these white racist extremist gangs are literally all over America. Most recently he completed the book Gangbangers: Understanding the Deadly Minds of America's Street Gangs. Both books can be ordered through: LWC Books, PO Box 20311, Portland, OR 97294-0311. These books are particularly useful for law enforcement viewpoints on the gang problem. The books are also available through Paladin Press, 1-800-392-2400. Check his website to order these and other books:

http://www.aracnet.com/~lwc123

THE CONTRADICTION OF COMMUNITY RELATIONS

What is the best policy for dealing with a community that is experiencing high rates of gang-related crime? To disclose the full severity of the problem to such residents and induce a panic that has obvious political implications to the effect that the status quo is not geared up to provide for adequate police protection and thereby possibly eroding respect for law enforcement? Or is it best to "triage" and through such law enforcement functions as Chicago's "beat representative" program to alert those more responsible and pro-law enforcement citizens to the "bigger picture"? That is, a balanced approach to disclosing the severity of the local crime threat.

In 1990, opinion polls showed that large numbers of persons living in New York City would move elsewhere if they could. Because of street violence. Presumably much of it owing to a gang origin. Cities like Chicago continue to experience a declining population; a "flight to the suburbs", a flight to greater security, a flight away from gang crime.

The contradiction, then, is that to be brutally honest with all citizens of the extent to which they face gang crime in the urban area is to risk both political and economic impact of a deleterious nature. Those most capable of moving out are those who have the higher incomes, leaving behind those who are more economically dependent.

Ultimately, it is a political issue. And local law enforcement agencies should be free from outside political pressure or influence regarding their decisions about responding to citizen pressures to brief them on the scope and extent of the problem. They have just as much right to know exactly how serious the gang crime threat is as they do to know whether their home is constructed on top of a toxic or radioactive waste site.

Universities and their police departments are by now totally familiar with the so-called "third party law suits". If they do not provide adequate protection, and a serious crime occurs, or if they are knowledgeable of such a clear and present crime threat and do not alert students and staff to its existence, and such a crime subsequently occurs, the "third party" law suit means not suing the actual offender, but suing the university or the facility in which the crime occurred, including employers. The issue is negligence. Failure to inform of real dangers, and thereby exposing innocent persons to undue risk of life or limb.

Finally, there are absolute limits on the scope and extent of social service functions that a police department can provide to its community. If they wanted social workers, then why train them to be crime fighters? Is it really that easy to wear both hats? Also, remember that the gang problem is not simply a law enforcement problem. In fact, as Muehlbauer and Dodder have stated "a community has failed its youth when its police force becomes the principal vehicle for the expression of community interest in young people outside the school" (1983: p. 129).

TRACKING, MONITORING, AND REPORTING "GANG-RELATED CRIME"

The police study by Needle and Stapleton (1983, p. 35) showed that "only four of the 27 departments reporting youth gang problems have written policies and procedures" dealing with gangs. That means chaos for police organization and management. Without adequate on-going training, without standards, without even a common definition of what is or is not a "gang-related crime", a law enforcement agency cannot ever hope to get a handle on the problem.

The definition of "gang-related crime" cannot be left up to the discretion of each and every police officer on the force. There must be clear guidelines for this, for otherwise any information reporting system faces the "garbage-in, garbage-out" (GIGO) problem of having no reliability.

JACKSON AND MC BRIDE: A LAW ENFORCEMENT VIEW OF GANGS

Jackson and Mc Bride provide a detailed, nontechnical discussion of the gang crime problem in the Los Angeles area. All of Part II of their book (1989, pp. 87-136) is devoted to law enforcement. Chapter 5 describes the difficulty of measuring gang violence and how some police departments have very conservative definitions of gang crime such that if there are not at least five more gang members who attack five or more rival gang members, it is not gang crime (p. 91). Which is, of course, a very convenient way to

"define out" any local gang crime problem.

Chapter 6 in Jackson and Mc Bride describes the gang unit of police organization and management. It provides one of the most complete discussions to date on management information systems applied to the gang problem, and what information needs to be collected. Chapter 7 in Jackson and Mc Bride discusses police patrol issues. This advises a positive, fair relationship with street gang members, because the police officer "whether he realizes it or not, is a de facto role model" (Jackson and McBride, 1990: p. 110).

Chapter 8 in Jackson and Mc Bride covers techniques of gang investigations. It suggests that the gang related crime scene should be considered a more expanded one than non-gang crime scenes. It provides helpful suggestions for investigating gang crime, including the cultivation of informants[16]. It also advocates witness protection not just for "violent cases, but in many others as well" (1990: p. 134).

These authors have also played a very positive role in setting law enforcement policy regarding gangs in America. Their book remains the single best law enforcement perspective on gangs today. The second author, Mc Bride, remains probably the most well known gang cop in America today.

CHRISTENSEN: A MORE RECENT LAW ENFORCEMENT VIEW ON GANGS

Christensen's (1999) book on gangs is written by a law enforcement officer. It extensively quotes other law enforcement officers on the issue of gangs. It also covers skinheads, white gangs, and Southeast Asian gangs; in addition, of course, to Black and Hispanic gangs. It also includes a small glossary of gang terms. The author had worked in a gang unit in Portland, Oregon.

Christensen (1999) enjoys the distinction of having written a number of books, including a separate book about Skinhead Street Gangs.

BURNS AND DEAKIN (1989): CHANGING INVESTIGATIVE APPROACHES

Traditional investigation techniques may not work as effectively with gangs is what Burns and Deakin (1989) argue. The gang crime problem reflects a pattern of such crimes and the traditional police response has been to look at these crimes in isolation, not as a recurrent pattern. Many of these individual crimes, alone, may therefore appear on the surface "senseless"; however in terms of a crime pattern may tell a different story.

These authors argue that there are varying levels of loyalty to the leaders among gang members and this can be exploited. One such method is the use of the grand jury investigation to heighten the psychological tension among gang members to provide information. The assumed prosecution policy here being to target leadership alone. Allowing some discretion for cooperative lower level gang members. Two other methods included: controlled arrest situations, and routine interviews of any arrestee who is a gang member. Again, the goal being that of getting greater amounts of information.

No difference is implied here between strategic or tactical intelligence on gangs. The authors express the belief that it is next to impossible to find out the exact force strength of any particular gang, only the top gang leader would know that if anyone.

SUCCESSFUL PROSECUTION METHODS: Sibley (1989)

The discussion by Sibley (1989) ties together successful criminal prosecution methods against gang offenders. It notes the difficulty of prosecuting gang leaders and takes the position that standard criminal prosecution techniques are ineffective (Sibley, 1989: p. 406). Importantly, it shows a growing body of criminal case law that allows as admissible evidence the factor of gang membership itself (p. 407). Gang membership or affiliation has probative value and can often establish a key element of motive (p. 408), and, of course, as a factor relating to witness credibility (p. 410).[17]

Bringing gang membership into play will mean using expert witness testimony on gang crime.[18] Typically police gang specialists (p. 412). Going up the gang organizational ladder to prosecute mid-management and leaders will mean the use of conspiracy charges (pp. 413-416). New criminal statutes are also emerging such as California's Street Terrorism Enforcement and Prevention (STEP) Act regarding violent gang activities.

In Illinois, the "Streetgang Terrorism Omnibus Prevention Act" was put into law at the same time as the SWORD gang computer information system discussed earlier. The Streetgang Terrorism act is a mini-rico statute that allows for additional criminal and civil penalties for crimes committed by gangs or gang members. States that do not have such statutes need to adopt them. Citizens and policy makers who want to do something to strengthen the laws, to be able to more effectively confront the gang problem, should ask their state legislature to pass a similar Act. The concerns about the constitutionality of new laws aimed against gangs --- typically raised by the gangs or gang apologists themselves --- are moot issues when considering the right of any legislative body to seek to protect its citizens against known crime threats. Such laws are not directed against Spanky and Alfalfa, they are directed against groups whose members routinely commit crimes on behalf of or with the aid of the group, organization, or other members. That is, they commit crime, over time.

That is what makes a gang. Put more simply: a gang is a more formidable crime threat than any sole, single, individual acting criminal offender.

THE G.R.E.A.T. PROGRAM

First known for its popularity in Phoenix, this has become a program nationwide through the Bureau of Alcohol Tobacco and Firearms (ATF). However, only in the fall of 1994 was a systematic effort unleashed to provide for program evaluation, so we shall have to wait for results on this federal research. It is a program similar to the DARE training for students, but applied to gangs it is Gang Resistance Education And Training (GREAT). An early evaluation of GREAT and two other gang prevention programs did not yield enthusiastic results (Palumbo, Eskay, and Hallet, 1993)[19] however.

NEW RESEARCH ON GANGS AND GUNS SHOWS POLICE ARE TARGETS OF GANGS

A Task Force Report on Gangs and Guns released at the Annual Meeting of the American Society of Criminology in 1994 by the National Gang Crime Research Center showed new important findings about how gangs get their guns and how they use them. This was a study of over 500 gang members in the midwest. Gang members have many sources in the underground economy for firearms and explosives. It is not uncommon for gang members to wear body armor during a crime. Another alarming trend is the tendency for gang members to be more likely to be involved in a police shoot out. Some gangs like the Insane Popes of Chicago make it a game in their initiation ritual to have the new member break into the home of a police officer and steal the firearms.

THE FBI SPY CHASERS ENTER THE HOOD

With the collapse of the Cold War, the FBI in 1992 reassigned 300 agents from its counterintelligence division to the violent crime divisions. These FBI agents work very closely with local law enforcement, and are having a stunning effect in the short time they have been on this mission. Federal convictions against gang leaders have soared in recent years, and much more work remains to be done in this regard.[20]

AN EXPERIMENTAL APPROACH: THE WESTMINISTER POLICE DEPARTMENT's PROGRAM

One of the most professional law enforcement programs implemented and a successful one is the TARGET program in the City of Westminister, California: Tri Agency Resource Gang Enforcement Team (TARGET). This program was necessary in order to adapt police work to new laws such as the STEP

Act. The STEP Act provides for increased prison sentences, where gang membership is viewed as a factor in aggravation, and carries an increase in penalty. In order to obtain a conviction under the STEP Act, however, certain intelligence needs must be met. Proving the gang membership of the offender, that the gang has three or more members, etc.

A very useful feature of the TARGET program is that it interfaces with other criminal justice personnel. An interface is established, for example, between probation officers and the police, and of course the district attorney. Probation and parole officers have an important role to play in gang crime suppression. The TARGET program has been viewed as a successful effort because of the increased arrests, gun seizures, and incarceration of gang leaders (Cook, 1993).

GANG MAPPING AND GANG TRACKING SOFTWARE

A number of different studies have shown the value of gang mapping for crime analysis (Kennedy, Braga, Piehl, 1996). The basic idea is to provide a new empirical foundation for "problem solving" and "community policing" law enforcement program initiatives. The City of Houston, Texas has found this technique of mapping gang crime to be particularly useful in their Mayor's office of anti-gang initiatives.

Clearly, there are a lot of "software" vendors today selling or marketing "gang analysis" and "gang tracking" software to police departments and correctional agencies. But one of the best and one of the first ever implemented is the SWORD or STAGIS model used in the State of Illinois. This is operated by the Illinois State Police. It can "track hits" on gang members in other jurisdictions, showing the "travel patterns" of gang members, and thus where they are likely distributing drugs or conducting related types of gang business and recruitment, etc.

ESTABLISHING A LIAISON/PARTNERSHIP PROGRAM WITH LOCAL SCHOOLS

In the midwest many gang analysts know of the program started by one concerned juvenile police officer specializing in gangs. The Police-School Liaison Program was basically started in 1985 and continues today under the impetus of police officer Thomas Flemming from the Park Forest Police Department in Illinois. As the program literature describes it, this kind of interactive program is beneficial to both police departments and students: "Positive personal contacts with young people by police officers is therapeutic for both parties...students and police officers need to see each other as real people."[21] It certainly fits nicely into any community policing initiative, because it essentially means establishing linkages and rapport where it did not previously ex-

ist. Such an initiative is low-capital intensive, it requires very little "start up" funding.

THE 1990 NATIONAL POLICE CHIEF SURVEY

Based on the prior literature and relevant issues, survey items were designed and used in a national survey of police chiefs. This mail questionnaire approach was based on the 1990 Directory of Law Enforcement Agencies. This involved a ten percent random sample of all municipal police departments in the United States. The sample size of N = 236 used here therefore reflects those police chiefs responding to the survey.[22]

Of the police chiefs responding to this survey some 160 indicated that gangs have existed as a law enforcement problem in their jurisdiction for some period of time. Among this group (N = 160) when asked how long have gangs existed as a law enforcement problem in their jurisdiction, most (81.3%) indicated for under five years; 11.3 percent stated gangs have been a problem for between five and ten years, and another 7.5 percent indicated the gang problem had existed for over a decade.

Nationwide, among all responding to the survey, only 36.8 percent of these police departments receive pre-service training in handling gangs or "gang awareness". However, about half (50.7%) receive such in-service training.

When asked to estimate the total core and periphery gang membership in their jurisdictions, about a third indicated "zero" such members. The remaining police departments reported numbers ranging from 2 (small rural town) to 45,000 members (L.A.). Overall, among the police chiefs responding to the survey reported a total of 17,786 sworn law enforcement personnel on their force at the present time, compared to a total of 72,657 core and periphery gang members in their jurisdictions. It would appear worse than assumed: that gang members not only outnumber municipal police officers in America, it may be a situation of being substantially outnumbered by a factor of 4 to 1 or higher.

Here we sought to get directly to the issue of how much crime in America can be attributed to being "gang-related". When all police chiefs regardless if they reported they had a gang problem responded in percentage terms to the question "what is your estimate of gang involvement (gang as a group <u>and</u> as individual gang members) in all reported crimes" in their city, 46.5 percent indicated "zero", .4 percent indicated "one percent", .4 percent "two percent", 2.2 percent indicated "five percent", 30.4 percent indicated "ten percent", and 7.8 percent indicated 20 percent, 6.1 percent indicated "thirty percent", and the remainder indicated levels of up to 70 percent. This indicates an overall mean or average of 9.6 percent of all crimes among all police chiefs in America, regardless if they report a gang problem, being viewed as "gang related crimes".

When asked the same question, framed "how about gang involvement as a percentage of all crimes committed by youths in your city", 44.7 percent indicated "zero", .9 percent indicated "one percent", 1.8 percent indicated "five percent", 25.4 percent indicated "10 percent", and the remainder indicated levels of up to 80 percent of the youth crime problem being explained as a function of the gang. For an overall average, 13.5 percent of the crimes committed by youths in their city were considered to be gang related; whether or not the same police chiefs reported that they had a gang problem.

Here then are the most conservative estimates of what gangs contribute to the overall crime problem in the United States. It would range from 9.6 percent for all crimes, to 13.5 percent for all crimes committed by youths. But obviously, some cities contribute to more of the overall national crime picture than others. So it is useful to select as a subsample those police chiefs who report a definite gang problem, and within this set of cities to report the same "GRC" (Gang Related Crime) statistics.

Among those police chiefs responding who indicated that gangs have existed as a law enforcement problem in their jurisdiction for at least some period of time we find somewhat higher estimates of what gangs contribute to the overall crime problem and the youth crime problem. This "partials out" those police chiefs who report that gangs have not yet existed in their jurisdiction as a crime problem. Among this group (N = 160) who do acknowledge a gang problem existing for some period of time we find these police chiefs reporting a mean or average of 13.6 percent of all crimes in their city were gang related and 19.1 percent of all crimes committed by youths were gang related. At a higher level of gang crime problem seriousness, in terms of whether gangs are reported to currently be a crime problem in their district, which is a smaller sub-sample (N=74), we find figures of 21.6% and 29.4% respectively for gang percentage of all crimes and all youth crimes.

Most (64.2%) believe that federal agencies should play a greater role in the investigation and prosecution of gang crimes. Also, only 26.1 percent felt that the mass media and newspapers tend to over estimate the extent of the gang problem. And, most (73.2%) felt that parents are to blame for the gang membership of their children.

Nearly all (93.5%) believed gangs in their city were loose knit groups as opposed to (6.5%) highly organized groups. This actual belief reported by police obviously varies significantly from the belief in "military pyramid" style gangs attributed to them by Hagedorn (1988: p. 86). Klein (1990: pp. 13-14)

stated that law enforcement agencies are quick to assume "street gangs are well-structured, cohesive collectives with strong individual leaders". Even when we examine the same data among only those police chiefs reporting a gang problem has existed for "any period of time" we find that 91.7 percent say the gangs are loose knit groups rather than higher organized groups (8.3%).

Seeking to compare the implications of the Short and Strodtbeck (1974) probability estimation with police chief estimates, they were asked "if a gang member committed a crime of violence in your city (other than homicide), what do you estimate the chances are that the gang member would be arrested?". Table 63 below shows this perceived probability of arrest distribution for gang assaults. Obviously, police chiefs see themselves as much more efficient than Short and Strodtbeck do in terms of making an arrest for a gang-related assault.

TABLE 63

DISTRIBUTION OF POLICE CHIEF ESTIMATES OF THEIR PROBABILITY OF MAKING AN ARREST FOR A GANG RELATED ASSAULT

Probability of an Arrest	Percentage
0%	7.4
10%	6.4
20%	4.9
30%	2.0
40%	4.4
50%	14.8
60%	5.4
70%	11.8
80%	15.3
90%	13.8
100%	13.8

Most police chiefs responding (66.8%) rejected the idea that male police officers are better able than female police officers to handle the gang crime problem.

Regarding the efficacy of federal research dissemination we find police chiefs are equally likely to report a knowledge of the actual research of Needle and Stapleton (1983) as they are to report a knowledge of a non-existent study. Most (90.2%) were not familiar with the Needle and Stapleton (1983) report. And an almost identical percentage (90.3%) were not familiar with a totally non-existing report included as a separate question in the survey as a validity factor.[23]

Nationally, about half of the police chiefs (54.9) felt that gang members were not at all involved in extremist political beliefs. But then, again, only 32.7 percent (N = 74) felt there was a current problem with gangs in their district. But 57.7 (N=123) percent felt it is a growing problem.

Most (84.5%) believed that there are some street gangs that should be considered forms of organized crime. Nearly all (96.4%) believed that the family is an important agency that can be used to prevent gang affiliation. About a third (30.9%) indicated that correctional institutions cooperated to address the gang problem. And nearly all (99.5%) would like to see more systematic interfacing between corrections and law enforcement in terms of information sharing.

Similar data will be reported in a subsequent chapter regarding the survey results from juvenile corrections superintendents, but among these police chiefs 43.3 percent felt we could more effectively deal with the gang problem if convicted gang members could be transferred to a central-national federal unit.

Most police chiefs (77.6%) believed that the "occult" or "satanism" (worshipers or dabblers) are also involved with gangs, although obviously no major research has surfaced on this issue yet in the literature. But increasingly, such material is also included in law enforcement and corrections "gang awareness" training.

When asked "do you feel that motorcycle gangs are a crime problem", 81.7 percent indicated yes.

When asked, do you feel that "detached workers" (social workers assigned to work with gang members on the streets) is an effective way to reduce gang violence, some 47.6 percent indicated "yes", and 52.4 percent "no".

It is interesting to note, in comparison however, that 46.5 percent believed that the military should be permitted to play a role in addressing the gang crime problem.[24] And 81.1 percent believed that expanding witness protection services would be helpful in addressing the gang crime problem.

Overall, when asked if they believed the gang crime problem is primarily a local problem or a multi-jurisdictional one, nearly all (91.5%) indicated it was a multi-jurisdictional problem, not a local problem (8.5). And most (88.9%) felt that we need tougher laws specifically dealing with the gang problem.

When asked, do you feel that local law enforcement should have the same options regarding juvenile offenders as adult offenders in terms of computer name checks on both, AFIS file checks on both, and authority to release names on both, nearly all (97.8%) indicated they wanted the option for computer name checks, 89.7 percent indicated they wanted AFIS for both juveniles and adults, and 68 percent indicated they wanted the authority to release names on both juveniles and adults.

About two-thirds (71%) felt that the grand jury should be used more to deal with the gang problem.

When asked, who has the primary responsibility for dealing with gangs (family, churches, business, school, police), a majority indicated (53.8%) the family, .5 percent the local churches, zero percent for business, 1.0 percent for the school system, and 44.8 percent indicated local law enforcement.[25]

All believed that the formation of regional gang intelligence meetings to brief each other and share information between different criminal justice agencies would be useful in addressing the gang crime problem.

A significant finding that warrants attention here is that while only about half (53.7%) of the police chiefs responding to the survey stated "yes" that the gangs in their jurisdiction were primarily of one ethnic or racial group, that the factor of in-service training significantly differentiates this belief. That is, among those police chiefs reporting that their departments provide in-service training on gangs, they were much more likely to report that in fact the gangs in their areas were of course primarily ethnically and racially homogeneous. Similarly, those police chiefs reporting that gangs were a problem in their district were also significantly more likely to report that gangs are ethnically homogeneous. What this cognitive factor means is that among those who are most truly likely to know about the gang crime problem, they are indeed more likely than not to affirm the historical continuity of gangs being ethnically and/or racially homogeneous.

THE 1992 LAW ENFORCEMENT SURVEY

This survey project was a collaborative effort among editors of The Gang Journal[26] representing researchers from four universities[27]. The analysis here simply summarizes some of the major descriptive findings about gangs from this large national sample of police chiefs and county sheriffs[28]. This study includes 248 police chiefs and 137 county sheriffs, and their assessments and views of the gang problem. The data was collected in late 1992 and early 1993.

Asked if youth gangs are a problem in their jurisdiction, 89.5 percent of the police chiefs and 79.4 percent of the sheriffs answered affirmatively. The percentage ratings of how serious a problem gangs represented were as follows:

	Police Chiefs	County Sheriffs
Major problem	18.4%	11.9%
Moderate problem	53.8	46.8
Minor problem	27.8	41.3

The higher percentage among police chiefs rating the gang problem as a major problem may reflect the urban-rural difference between these two types of law enforcement agencies.

The survey also asked the law enforcement administrators to provide two estimates: one for the percentage of the total crime in their jurisdiction that is caused by gang activity, and one for the percentage of total juvenile crime caused by gang activity. The results are as follows:

	Police Chiefs	County Sheriffs
% of Total crime caused by gangs:		
Range	0-67%	0-60%
Mean value	14.4%	11.1%
% of Juvenile Crime caused by gangs:		
Range	0-90%	0-100%
Mean value	26.7%	19.2%

This suggests, again, a somewhat larger overall average of what proportion of the total crime statistics can be attributed to gangs among police chiefs. Police chiefs on the average attribute just over a fourth of all juvenile crime (26.7%) to gangs. To date, these are the best estimates for what percentage of the overall crime problem in the U.S. is "gang related". Obviously, as well, it varies immensely from one jurisdiction to another.

It is further interesting to compare these figures with the degree to which these law enforcement agency budgets are specifically focused on the gang problem. Only 1.8 percent of the police chief budget and .5 percent of the county sheriff budget was directed toward the youth gang problem. In that gangs represent for many of these departments a relatively new phenomenon, perhaps these organizations have not yet adapted to accelerated social changes represented by gangs. Only 35.2 percent of the police chiefs and only 22.1 percent of the county sheriffs indicated that their department has a strategic plan for dealing with youth gangs.

Has gang activity become more violent in recent years? Most definitely, is the answer from this survey. Some 80.4 percent of the police chiefs and 66.7 percent of the sheriffs felt that gang activity has become more violent in recent years. Few felt it had become less violent (3% for Chiefs, .8 percent for Sheriffs), suggesting gang political activists have a long way to go before they can convince these respondents of any success in reducing gang violence through "gang truces".

These law enforcement professionals were also asked to rate the extent to which social programs are available in their jurisdiction that are designed to reduce/prevent the gang problem. On a scale of 0 (few programs) to 10 (many programs), the mean rating for police chiefs was 3.36 compared to 2.68 among county sheriffs. In their view, then, little is being done about the gang problem in America in terms of social programs. About half of the respondents (54.8% police chiefs, 45% county sheriffs) agreed that "detached workers," defined as social workers assigned to work with gang members on the streets, represent an effective way to reduce gang violence. Some 41.6 percent of the police chiefs and 21.3 percent of the county sheriffs reported that their departments have programs or services specifically aimed at youth gangs or youth gang members.

One of the most interesting findings has to do with the specific year the gang problem first came to be recognized in the communities represented in this survey. While cities like Chicago, Los Angeles, and some others have always had gangs, the present data suggests recent proliferation of the problem. The mean for police chiefs was 1985.2, compared to 1987.2 for county sheriffs; thus, on the average nationwide police chiefs first recognized the gang problem in 1987, county sheriffs in 1987. In fact, 95.6 percent of all gang problems by county sheriffs were first recognized in their jurisdictions on or after 1980! Further, some 85.6 percent of police chiefs first recognized the gang problem in their jurisdiction in the time frame of 1980 to present.

It is useful to examine this regarding in what year did gangs first become recognized as a problem in the jurisdictions of the respondents to this survey. In terms of recent presidential time periods, the findings are as follows:

	Police Chiefs	County Sheriffs
In what year did gangs first become recognized as a problem in your jurisdiction?		
On or before 1980	14.9%	6.1%
1981 - 1984	10.0	7.1
1985 - 1988	35.6	36.8
1989 - 1992	39.5	50.0

As seen here, about three-fourths of the city and county jurisdictions in America first recognized their gang problem during the time period between 1985 and 1992. During this eight year period --- the last term of President Ronald Reagan and the one term of President George Bush --- the gang problem quietly exploded in American cities and counties. Whatever the claims of these two presidents to being "crime fighters" the historical record reflected here shows that the gang problem vastly proliferated and expanded across America on their watch.

When asked, specifically, to rate the degree to which sworn police officers in their departments are provided with adequate ongoing training to successfully confront the modern gang problem, on a scale of zero (poor) to ten (excellent), both police chiefs and county sheriffs offered somewhat less an average answers. The mean or average value for police chiefs was 4.3 compared to 3.3 for county sheriffs on a scale from 0 to 10. Among police chiefs, about half (49.6%) report that their officers receive pre-service training in gang awareness or handling gang problems; compared to 43.8 percent among county sheriffs. Similarly, 70.2 percent of the police chiefs and 64.7 percent of the county sheriffs indicated that their officers receive such in-service training.

These law enforcement administrators were also asked to rate the extent to which the lack of a coordinated national policy has increased the youth gang problem in American cities. Again, a scale from a low of zero (no effect) to a high of ten (large effect) was used. The mean value for police chiefs was 5.7, and 5.4 for county sheriffs for the sample overall.

About four-fifths of police chiefs (83.3%) and county sheriffs (82.2%) agreed that tougher juvenile laws would aid the law enforcement response to the youth-oriented gang culture. Most similarly felt that the increased use of computer systems which store information on gangs will be an effective device in aiding investigative action against gangs (98.8% for police chiefs, 96.3% for county sheriffs).

The respondents were also asked to rate the extent to which language and cultural barriers may be a problem affecting their own law enforcement efforts at curbing the increase of Asian gang activity. On a scale of 0 (not a problem) to 10 (a large problem), the average value for police chiefs and county sheriffs was identical - a mean of 5.1 on the scale.

Overwhelmingly the respondents expressed the belief that the observed expansion of city gangs to suburban areas will continue through the mid-1990s (99.2% police chiefs, 99.3% county sheriffs).

The survey also asked the respondents whether their department can identify the leaders of the gangs within their jurisdiction. Some 82.1 percent of the police chiefs and 65.9 percent of the county sheriffs said they could identify the gang leaders in their area.

About three-fourths of the respondents believed that parents are to blame for the gang membership of their children (77.5% police chiefs, 74.4% county sheriffs).

When asked if the gangs in their area are loose knit or highly organized, most of these police administrators also do not believe the gangs in their areas are highly organized. In fact, 89.4% of the police chiefs and 91.6 percent of the county sheriffs thought the gangs in their areas were loose knit groups. Thus,

only 10.6 percent of the police chiefs and 8.4 percent of the county sheriffs felt their gangs were highly organized.

The respondents were also asked to estimate the total gang membership in their jurisdiction. For police chiefs providing this data (N=214), this ranged from a low of zero to a high of 58,300; an overall sum for all police chiefs of 231,574 and a mean of 1,083. For county sheriffs providing this data (N=103), this ranged from a low of zero to a high of 13,000; an overall sum for all sheriffs of 75,151 and a mean of 749.

Most of the respondents (73.5% police chiefs, 66.4% county sheriffs) expressed the belief that federal agencies should play a greater role in the investigation and prosecution of gang crimes.

This is easier to understand in light of figures on how many sworn officers are assigned full-time to work on the gang problem: an average of 5.3 officers among police chiefs, and an average of 1.3 among police chiefs. Almost half (47.7%) of all police chiefs and nearly a fourth (24.8%) of all county sheriffs indicated that their department does have a special unit to handle gang problems. Most of these law enforcement professionals also felt that the gang unit should be centralized rather than decentralized (65.4% police chiefs, 75.6% county sheriffs) where centralized was defined as city/county wide gang unit. Those supporting a decentralized gang unit, meaning each area commander responsible for a specific community area has his/her own gang crime officers for deploying locally, were in the minority (34.6% police chiefs, 24.4% county sheriffs).

Motorcycle gangs were felt to be more of a crime problem among county sheriffs (34.1%) than among police chiefs (22.7%). Further, some 29.7 percent of the police chiefs and a larger 43.7 percent of the county sheriffs felt that "hate groups" (KKK, neo-nazis, skinheads, etc) are a crime problem in their area.

The vast majority of the respondents (93% police chiefs, 94.7% county sheriffs) felt that the gang problem was multi-jurisdictional problem rather than simply a local crime problem. Nearly all of these law enforcement officials (98.4% police chiefs, 98.5% county sheriffs) expressed the belief that some gangs can migrate to jurisdictions like their own[29]. In fact, nearly four-fifths (80% police chiefs, 78.8% county sheriffs) expressed the more specific belief that at least some of the gang problem that existed in their jurisdictions was due to gang migration.

As a cross-check on this migration issue, the respondents were also asked additionally to rate the extent to which the gang problem in their area arose because of gang migration defined as outside gangs coming into their area to develop their own local franchises or local chapters; a scale of zero (not a factor) to ten (major factor) was used. For police chiefs the mean was 4.97 compared to 4.61 for county sheriffs.

Another question asked the respondents to estimate to what extent the gang problem in their area arose because of the "copy cat" phenomenon defined as youths who use the names of national groups without really having ties to the same groups in other areas; the scale varied from a low of zero (not a factor) to a high of ten (major factor). For police chiefs the mean was 5.4 compared to a mean of 5.2 among county sheriffs. Clearly, when put in this comparative context, the officials in this sample give greater credence to the "copy cat" syndrome than they do to intentional gang imperialism (i.e., developing franchises) in terms of the higher mean scores.

Over two-thirds of the respondents (71.2% police chiefs, 72.1% county sheriffs) also agreed that the grand jury should be used more to deal with the gang problem.

It is interesting to note that when asked if they believe the public recognizes that there is a problem with gangs in their area, 30.3 percent of the police chiefs and 55 percent of the county sheriffs said "no". What this means, clearly, is that more law enforcement agencies recognize the problem than the public does.

Only 27.5 percent of the police chiefs and 24.2 percent of the county sheriffs felt that elected officials have worked to sufficiently educate the public about youth gangs. About a fourth of the police chiefs (25.2%) and about an eighth (12.8%) of the county sheriffs believed that their local governmental bodies (city councils, county boards, etc) have allocated sufficient resources to combat the gangs in their area.

PUBLIC EDUCATION "BROCHURES" ABOUT GANGS

Many police departments that have gotten over the "Gang Denial" problem, or who never faced this political matter, now distribute "public education brochures" about gangs. These are often aimed at "parents" and interested citizens. There are some commonalities in these brochures, they typically list some of the local gangs, colors, signs, etc. There is enormous variation in the quality and accuracy of these "brochures".

Consider the version from the Oklahoma Gang Investigator's Association, P.O. Box 1439, Norman, OK 73070-1439 entitled "Gangs: A Guide for the Community". It contains this section about rap music:

"GANGSTER RAP MUSIC

The American entertainment industry has helped to spread the gang lifestyle. Unfortunately, the rush to make money has overshadowed the risks associated with providing this type of ma-
terial. Gangster rap, for instance, is available at most music stores in the country. Have you ever listened to the lyrics of these songs? This is music about the violent gang lifestyle, and it's often sung by former and present gang members. The music is very popular with gang members, has helped to spread the gang culture across the country. Children often listen to this violent and profanity-filled music, then attempt to imitate the criminal activity detailed in the songs" (p. 6, "Gangs: A Guide for the Community", 1997).

Someone in the 1950's could have said the same about rock music. We could analyze "country western music" to find enormous examples of violence, crime, and unethical behavior: but does the cultural values implied in the music form produce the market for the music, or does the musical form produce the culture itself? Does the behavior of listening to country music necessarily make someone a "hillbilly" or "red neck"? What do we find in country western music themes: Cheating, guns, violence, fighting, crime, etc. If we assume rap music produces gang members, then we must also be willing to assume the same applies to other musical forms.

A study of over 1,000 gang members known as Project GANGECON by the National Gang Crime Research Center (The Economics of Gang Life: A Task Force Report, 1995) was actually the first to shed any real light on the matter of "rap music" and "gangs". The survey asked two questions on this issue, first it asked "do you listen to gangster rap", and most (87.2%, N = 856) indicated they do. The survey then asked "does it influence you", and here only 21.3 percent indicated it actually influenced them (N = 197). So while most of the gang members in this national sample listen to gangster rap music, a much smaller percentage report that they are really influenced by it.

THE CASE OF C-BO's "TIL MY CASKET DROPS"

Certainly this case illustrates how some police officers have a justifiable concern about rap music and gangs. Shawn Thomas or "C-BO" as he is called is a rapper from Sacramento, California[30]. Convicted of a 1993 crime for firing a gun that killed a man, "C-BO" received a four year prison term. He served 15 months of the 4-year sentence and was paroled under the condition that he sever his ties to gang culture, engage in more violence including threats to police officers in his song lyrics. In early 1998, however, he produced a new gangster rap album with a song called "Til My Casket Drops" which included the following commentary about the "3 strikes you're out law" in California:

"You better swing, batter, batter swing,
'Cause once you get your third felony, yeah 50 years

you gotta bring,
It's a deadly game of baseball
So when they try to pull you over, shoot 'em in the face, ya'll'.
The lyrics were seen as specifically threatening a specific police officer, Sacramento Sheriff's Department employee Sgt. Jim. Cooper who had arrested a lot of gang members.

When "C-Bo" was taken into custody for a parole violation as a result of the release of the song, he remarked that he could not change into something like Vanilla Ice and still be a popular rap artist.

SUMMARY AND CONCLUSION

There are many issues in law enforcement related to gang crime. These are issues of policy, of structure and organization, and of resource allocation. Obviously, as well, there are many other issues in the overlap between law enforcement and gangs that have not been discussed here[31].

What this shows is that some things can and do work and deserve being expanded significantly, such as witness protection and victim assistance. Changing police patrol methods and using more innovative investigation techniques have also been recommended ways of addressing the gang problem.

Greater use of the grand jury and the increased belief that gang crime represents a multi-jurisdictional problem also have major implications for change in law enforcement. While the data collected and reported here represent some of the largest studies of their kind since the earlier work of Needle and Stapleton (1983), clearly more research is needed. Most smaller police departments do not have their officers trained on gang issues, and do not have a strategic plan for dealing with gangs.

Finally, there is one thing that can be done at little cost to help American law enforcement address the crime threat represented by gangs. Many smaller police departments are isolated and do not routinely interface with other law enforcement agencies to receive updated information on the gang problem. In some areas of the USA, "Gang Investigator" associations have formed. The two largest being the California Gang Investigators Association and the Midwestern Gang Investigators Association. Some other states like Arkansas have started their own statewide Gang Investigators Association. What is needed is a National Gang Investigators Association! Many criminal justice personnel other than police have vital roles to play in these types of training and education associations, including those who work in prisons, in juvenile institutions, in probation and parole, etc. Here again, the federal government has not been a leader in stimulating what could really pay off immediately for those who are responsible for protecting citizens from the threat of gang crime.

DISCUSSION QUESTIONS:

(1) Why would a decision support system be useful to law enforcement in managing the investigation of gang crime? Indeed, what planning issues should be dealt with in a "strategic plan" to deal with local criminal gangs?

(2) What special problems might arise in a gang crime unit where different policies and laws apply to the handling of juvenile versus adult offenders? How should a gang unit operate under the terms of what is known as "community policing"?

(3) How would you explain the discrepancy reflected in the data reported in this chapter in terms of the proportion that gangs contribute to the overall crime pattern and the much smaller organizational readiness of these law enforcement agencies to "tackle the problem"?

RECOMMENDED READINGS:

California Attorney General's Youth Gang Task Force
1981 Report on Youth Gang Violence in California. California: Department of Justice.
California Council on Criminal Justice
1986 Final Report: State Task Force on Youth Gang Violence. Sacramento, CA.
1989 State Task Force on Gangs and Drugs. Sacramento, CA.
Collins, H. Craig
1977 "Street Gangs of New York: A Prototype of Organized Youth Gangs", Law and Order (25)(1)(Jan): 6-16.
Dahmann, J.
1981 "Operation Hardcore: A Prosecutorial Response to Violent Gang Criminality", interim report, MITRE Corporation, McLean, VA.
David, J.J. and M.H. Shaffer
1988 Intelligence Gathering in the Investigation of Motorcycle Gangs, National Institute of Justice, NCJRS, Rockville, MD.
Day, D.
1987 "Outlaw Motorcycle Gangs", Royal Canadian Mounted Police Gazette (49)(5): 1-42.
De Leon, Aleister
1977 "Averting Violence in the Gang Community", The Police Chief (44)(7)(July): 52-53.
Duran, M.
1975 "What Makes a Difference in Working with Youth Gangs?", Crime Prevention Review

(2): 25-30.

Florida House of Representatives
1987 Issue Paper: Youth Gangs in Florida. Committee on Youth. Tallahassee, FL.

Gott, Raymond
1991 (Audio training tape) "Juvenile Gangs and Drug Trafficking", available through the National Juvenile Detention Association, 217 Perkins Bldg, Richmond, KY 40475-3127.

Haire, Thomas D.
1979 "Street Gangs: Some Suggested Remedies for Violence and Vandalism", The Police Chief (46)(7)(July): 54-55.

International Association of Chiefs of Police
1986 Organized Motorcycle Gangs. Gaithersburg, MO 20878.

Jameson, S.H.
1956 "Policeman's Non-Official Role in Combatting Gangs and Vandalism", Association for Professional Law Enforcement, Quarterly Journal (3)(June): 1-3.

Johnson, W.C.
1981 "Motorcycle Gangs and White Collar Crime", The Police Chief (47)(6)(June): 32-33.

Juvenile Justice Digest
1980 "Police Community Relations: Crime Prevention of Gangs", (Feb. 22): 7-8.

Kasimer, Yale
1971 "When the Cops Were Not 'Handcuffed'", pp. 46-57 in Donald R. Cressey (ed.), Crime & Criminal Justice, Chicago: Quadrangle Books.

Kennedy, David M.; Anthony A. Braga; and Anne M. Piehl
1996 "The (UN) Known Universe: Mapping Gangs and Gang Violence in Boston", forth coming article in Crime Mapping and Crime Prevention (Eds.), D. Weisburd and J. Thomas McEwen, New York: Criminal Justice Press.

Klein, Malcolm W.
1965 "Juvenile Gangs, Police, and Detached Workers: Controversies About Intervention", Social Service Review (39): 183-190.

Klein, Malcolm W.; Cheryl Maxson; and Margaret A. Gordon
1986 "The Impact of Police Investigations on Police-Reported Rates of Gang and Nongang Homicides", Criminology (24): 489-512.

Kobrin, Solomon
1964 "Legal and Ethical Problems of Street Gang Work", Crime and Delinquency (10)(2): 152-156.

Lyman, M.D.
1989 "Street Youth Gangs", (From Gangland: Drug Trafficking by Organized Criminals, pp.

95-111), Newbury Park, CA: Sage Publications.

Mc Guire, P.
1986 "Outlaw Motorcycle Gangs - Organized Crime on Wheels", National Sheriff (37)(2)(Apr-May): 68-75.

Mc Kinney, K.C.
1988 Juvenile Gangs: Crime and Drug Trafficking. U.S. Dept. of Justice, Office of Juvenile Justice and Delinquency Prevention, Washington, D.C.

Miller, Walter B.
1982 Crime by Youth Gangs and Youth Groups in the United States, report prepared for the National Youth Gang Survey, Washington, D.C.: Office of Juvenile Justice and Delinquency Prevention.
1989 "Recommendations for Terms to Be Used for Designating Law Violating Youth Groups", paper presented at the Conference of the National Youth Gang Suppression and Intervention Project, Chicago.

Moore, Mark and Mark A.R. Kleiman
1989 The Police and Drugs. Washington, D.C.: National Institute of Justice.

Morash, Merry
1990 "Gangs and Violence", in A.J. Reiss, Jr., N. Weiner, and J. Roth (eds.), Violent Criminal Behavior, Report of the Panel on the Understanding and Control of Violent Behavior, National Academy of Sciences, Washington, D.C.: National Academy Press.

Ontario Police Department
1989 "Gangs, Move 'Em Out of Your Life", (video), Ontario, CA 91761.

Pennell, Susan and Christine Curtis
1982 Juvenile Violence and Gang-Related Crime. San Diego: San Diego Association of Governments.

Philobosian, R.H.
1986 State Task Force on Youth Gang Violence. Sacramento, CA: California Council in Criminal Justice.

Reuter, P.
1989 Youth Gangs and Drug Distribution: A Preliminary Enquiry. RAND Corporation, Washington, D.C.

Sipchen, Bob
1993 Baby Insane and the Buddha. New York: Doubleday.

Spergel, Irving
1989 Report of the Law Enforcement Youth Symposium. National Youth Gang Suppression and Intervention Program. University of Chicago, School of Social Service Administration.
1990 Law Enforcement Definitional Conference

- Transcript.
Stapleton, W. Vaughn and Jerome Needle
    1982 Police Handling of Youth Gangs. Washington, D.C.: Office of Juvenile Justice and Delinquency Prevention.
Weiner, Arthur K.
    1965 "C-R-A-C-K-I-N-G The Hard Core Area", Police Chief (32)(Jan): 27-31.
Werthman, Carl and Irving Piliavin
    1967 "Gang Members and the Police", in David Bordua (ed), The Police: Six Sociological Essays, New York: Wiley.

A GOOD IDEA FOR A RESEARCH PAPER: Comparing and Analyzing the Messages and Accuracy of "Public Education Brochures" About Gangs Distributed by Police Departments.

A national survey of local municipal police departments in 1996 by the National Gang Crime Research Center showed that 16.8 percent had produced such "public education brochures about gangs". Typically, the larger the city, the more likely they are to produce these brochures; or the longer the gang problem has existed in the city, the more likely such brochures have been produced. What this means is that about one out of every six police departments, regardless of size, probably has such local versions of these "Gang Brochures". You could call or write to some agencies, collect some, and analyze them.

END NOTES:

[1] Huff (1989, p. 525) reports research that most school principals view police as having the primary responsibility for dealing with gangs. Presumably, we are talking about criminal gangs. A level zero gang formation, a "pre-gang", is not within the legitimate purview of law enforcement until it comes to the attention of local police through law violation.

[2] The Bloods and the Crips, 1992, "L.A. Vision: Program to Rebuild Los Angeles", Z Magazine (5)(7/8)(July/Aug): 63-66.

[3] See: "U.S. Drives Out Bronx Drug Gang", by Matthew Purdy, Chicago Tribune, Oct. 20, 1994, Section 1A, p. 33.

[4] P. 9, Chicago Tribune, June 9, 1994, Section 2, p. 9.

[5] Lacking any federal support in terms of facilitating the linkages and information sharing across law enforcement jurisdictions, in recent years "gang investigator associations" have formed. California has one. There is also the Midwest Gang Investigators Association covering Minnesota, Wisconsin, Iowa, Illinois, Michigan, Indiana, Ohio and other states. What is needed is a national version. Many southern states (Florida, Texas, etc) lack this information sharing network.

[6] Daniels (1987, p. 126) recommends in addition to regional gang intelligence sharing the same opportunity to conduct, among gang crime investigators and those charged with dealing with the gang offender in the correctional areas (prison, parole, probation, etc) the use of such regional meetings to update "threat analysis" of various gangs.

[7] There are numerous ways to derive "threat level". One of the simplest is a percentile of all known gang members who have a history of serious felony convictions. It could focus on the "violence proneness" in a similar format. Recognizing that such "force threats" would have to be re-calibrated and revised periodically.

[8] We might suggest that opportunity is everything. Gang infrastructure requires periodic internal discipline. It is invariably of the nature of a violent assault upon the gang member, with the ending admonition, "be a better gang member" and "all is well". Like a fatherly spanking. But psychologically, these routine internal "violation" events have not been adequately researched. We do not know if there are lasting effects of such "violations" from a social-psychological account. The idea, here, is that those "expecting" a "gang trial" soon, or expecting a serious violation, or who have recently suffered from such a beating, may be those more susceptible to law enforcement cooperation --- assuming that law enforcement could genuinely provide some alternatives (e.g., witness protection, relocation, etc, or rely on the myth of the effectiveness of such methods used strategically).

[9] Contemporary gang authors are not in agreement on the matter of whether gangs can be "franchised" or exported from one state to the next. But the evidence that emerged from the present study in the case of LK29 is that at least in the case of the Chicago Latin Kings, there was an intentional development effort to create such a franchise in Indiana. The gang member, in this case a former gang member, is in fact college educated (lacking 22 hours for a Bachelors degree) and currently works in the court system. He is considered very reliable and admits to his own violence for purposes of being "made" into the Latin Kings.

[10] This was also a recommendation by the Committee on Youth to the Florida House of Representatives (1987), where the recommendation for dealing with the increasingly severe gang problem involved a more comprehensive approach, one that was multicounty in nature.

[11] Vigil (1988: p. 175) reports that the California Gang Investigators Association meets to discuss and share information along the lines suggested here.

[12] See James F. Short, "New Wine in Old Bottle? Change and Continuity in American Gangs", p. 232,

in C. Ronald Huff, 1990, <u>Gangs in America</u>, Newbury Park: Sage Publications.

[13]See "Laws Struck Down on Gangs, Graffiti", p. 1,4, <u>Chicago Sun-Times</u>, Thursday, Sept. 30, 1993. However, Mayor Daley instructed the police department to continue to enforce the ordinance on gang members loitering, saying the people needed the law and that judges don't live in the real world. See Fran Spielman, "Police to Ignore Gang Law Ruling", p. 12, <u>Chicago Sun-Times</u>, Oct. 1, 1993.

[14]"Police 'Gang Book' Photos Ruled Illegal", <u>Police</u>, January, 1994, p. 15.

[15] Recently (Burns and Deakin, 1989) the grand jury has been used to induce psychological pressure and as part of a new strategy in gang prosecutions Baltimore.

[16]For an excellent case study in the development of a very useful gang informant see Sipchen (1993), which describes how a member of a San Diego Crip gang was cultivated and put to effective use.

[17] From the defense attorney viewpoint, however, there is another side of the story. Professor Pamela Hill, Department of Corrections and Criminal Justice, indicated "the first thing a prosecutor wants to bring out is that the defendant is a member of a gang...but from my perspective as a defense attorney, if it is an individual crime, then gang membership is irrelevant...some gang members get accused of crimes just because they are gang members" (1991, personal interview).

[18] Again, Professor Pamela Hill reminds us that in this process many "have failed to take into consideration why young people join gangs, it may not be initially for a purpose of crime; crime is secondary, crime was not in most instances the primary purpose for joining a gang...and all members do not necessarily partake in criminal activities....those are often individual acts more than group decisions (personal interview, 1991).

[19]Dennis J. Palumbo, Robert Eskay, and Michael Hallett, 1993 "Do Gang Prevention Strategies Actually Reduce Crime?", <u>The Gang Journal</u>, (1)(4): 1-10. The Gang Journal is now known as the <u>Journal of Gang Research</u>.

[20]For an excellent summary of this FBI initiative, see: Thomas Ferraro, "The FBI Takes Aim At Gangs", <u>Insight on the News</u>, October 5, 1992.

[21]From the Park Forest Safe School Consortium brochure.

[22] This is a preliminary analysis of this data, and the sample size will most surely increase, but has been analyzed here up to the point in time when this book had to go to press (March, 1991).

[23] There were two separate questions, "Are you familiar with the 1983 Needle and Stapleton report on the <u>Police Handling of Youth Gangs</u>?" and "Are you familiar with the 1985 Springer and Detwyler report

on <u>Police Response to Gang Problems</u>?" Springer and Detwyler were two students of mine involved in phases of this research, and they never wrote such a report, and the report simply does not exist.

[24] Recall from Haskins (1975, p. 29) that in early American history when local law enforcement was not sufficient to deal with gang urban disorders, the military was called in. The military generally "had no trouble dispersing the gangs" that were in group conflict (p. 29). So there is a historical context under which the military has been brought into play regarding gang violence.

[25] Obviously, to compare with the findings from Huff (1989, p. 525) what we seem to see here is a general tendency of "passing the blame". Educators say the police are primarily responsible, the police say it is mostly the family, etc.

[26]<u>The Gang Journal: An Interdisciplinary Research Quarterly</u> was formed in early 1992 and released its first issue in November, 1992, it is the official journal of the National Gang Crime Research Center at Chicago State University. The journal reorganized in 1994 as a totally independent journal, and is now known as the Journal of Gang Research.

[27]Chicago State University: George W. Knox and Edward D. Tromanhauser; Rhode Island College: Pamela Irving Jackson and Darek Niklas; St. Ambrose University: James G. Houston and Paul Koch; and the University of Illinois at Chicago: James R. Sutton.

[28]All data was used, which means the present analysis was able to use one or more additional "cases" that came in by mail after the release of the Preliminary Report on this research.

[29]The prior evidence on gang migration has been, prior to this survey, been primarily anecdotal. Bartollas (1993: p. 20) describes interviews with gang leaders and reported the gang intentionally sought to develop a national organization, more specifically the gang member made the claim "it won't be long before we are coast to coast", and accomplishing this goal by means of sending out gang ambassadors to develop "sets" or factions of the parent gang organization. As Bartollas notes, gang migration also occurs by means of shipping prisoners from one prison to the next, and when gang members are involved in interstate travel and are caught and prosecuted in another state, they often set up their own local chapters of the gang.

[30]See: Brigid O'Malley and J. Freedom Du Lac "Rapper's Words May Jail Him", Chicago Sun-Times, Friday, March 6, 1998, p. 48.

[31]One issue not discussed is the power of the gang to corrupt police officers. Knowing what history shows us as "possible" can help predict what is probable to occur. Kaplan and Dubro (1986: p. 159) describe the crisis in law enforcement in Japan when a closer investigation revealed hundreds of Japanese police officers were accepting bribes from Jakuza gangs.

BELOW: Some of the 39 Gangster Disciples who were convicted in "Operation Headache", the federal prosecution of Larry Hoover and 38 of his top associates.

TIMOTHY NETTLES-IR693439
11823 S. Yale
M/B, 11 Nov. 66, 6-0, 155
Warrant #886114078

TIRENZY WILSON-IR810615
414 W. 57th Place
M/B, 23 April 69, 5-8, 140
Warrant #885736424

KEVIN WILLIAMS-IR828303
10832 S. Edbrooke 2nd fl.
M/B, 8 Feb. 69, 5-7, 130
Warrant #886103887

DION LEWIS-IR868061
11931 S. Lafayette
M/B, 11 Aug. 66, 6-0, 180
Warrant #886104686

WILLIAM EDWARDS-IR881796
3833 S. Federal Apt. 309
M/B, 19 Feb. 71, 5-7, 150
Warrant #885732310

QUAN RAY-IR898870
12852 S. Lowe
M/B, 11 Nov. 72, 5-6, 300
Warrant #886107899

JOHNNY JACKSON-IR899836
9917 S. Union
M/B, 5 Aug. 72, 5-9, 160
Warrant # 839355498

DARRYL BRANCH-IR350360
2621 W. 83rd Street
M/B, 11 Sept. 57, 5-10, 155
Warrant #885740002

RUSSELL ELLIS-IR549066
7845 S. Emerald
M/B, 10 Aug. 59, 5-7, 170
Warrant #885730304

Chapter 24:

The Impact of the Federal Prosecution of the Gangster Disciples

INTRODUCTION

Examining the historical issues surrounding the effectiveness of the federal prosecution of the Gangster Disciple's gang means focusing on an interesting aspect of the criminal justice system (CJS) to examine this issue of prosecutorial impact or effectiveness. A lot of agencies in the CJS have special programs or initiatives that are routinely "assessed" or "evaluated". For example, in looking at initiatives such as D.A.R.E., it is expected that the program will have an evaluation of its outcome effectiveness. But when it comes to federal prosecution of gangs like the now famous prosecution of the Gangster Disciples in Chicago, in which 39 of the top leaders including Larry Hoover were convicted, we generally do not have a "follow-up study" that is built into the prosecutorial function.

The future of the prosecutorial function in the American CJS may actually include such an impact assessment or evaluation, but presently there is no such function. We will summarize some informal and anecdotal evidence about the impact of the GD prosecution in Chicago. This paper will also specify what should probably go into a formal impact assessment. It will also reveal a wealth of information not previously disclosed about the Gangster Disciple gang.

This therefore provides a comprehensive chronology and analysis of what many gang experts believe to have been the single largest and most notorious gang of the 20th Century.

ORAL INTERVIEWS

The oral interviews were conducted in correctional environments as well as at a university location. Thus, both confined gang members and gang members at large in the public were included in the oral interviews. The oral interviews were structured to examine the impact of the GD prosecution on the structure and function of the GD gang. Below we describe the advantages and disadvantages of oral interviews.

Oral interviews are a necessary ingredient of an impact assessment such as that being developed here. There are some advantages to oral interviews and these can be briefly described: (1) they allow for great flexibility in terms of capturing information directly from those affected, i.e., the gang members themselves, (2) they allow for interesting reading material in as much as this type of qualitative research technique generally produces useful insights into gang life, (3) they provide an excellent basis for more pinpointed analysis such as would be necessary in a more quantitative approach to impact assessment by the use of a questionnaire or survey technique designed to reach large numbers of such offenders, and (4) there is a long and rich tradition in gang studies where the oral interview is often the only research method employed to generate "data". The "data" in oral interviews consists of the information gathered during the interview process itself.

There are clear and definite limits and dangers represented in terms of validity when using oral interviews as the sole basis for an impact assessment. We will briefly list some of these issues: (1) there is always the issue of "validity", as offenders do "lie", (2) the oral interview requires a flexible personality and training that not everyone necessarily has, and thus some people are better "interviewers" than others, i.e., they know when to "probe" and when to "motivate" the gang member, etc, (3) ideally oral interviews are combined with secondary data of a quantitative nature to achieve some level of convergent validity so that one can have confidence in the overall conclusion from the impact assessment, and (4) there is always the issue of "judgement calls" when the researcher must reject certain "interviews" due to a belief that the gang member is in fact being deceptive or less than honest, and therefore there is a lot that often gets "edited out" in such interviews.

A SHORT HISTORY OF THE GANGSTER DISCIPLES

Larry Hoover was born on November 30, 1950. He grew up in a small rural town in Mississippi; migrating to Chicago in the late 1950's.

In 1960 Devil's Disciples were formed with David Barksdale, Shorty Freeman, and Don Derky being main "shot callers". Larry Hoover was involved with this low level emerging gang.

In 1966 the Black Disciples (BD) gang was formed by King David Barksdale; it began a new gang identity, one that persists even today. Larry Hoover was not known to be involved with the BD gang organization, it exists today as a rival to the GD gang. Larry Hoover remained involved with the Devil's Disciples however, up until the BD leader was neutralized by rival gunfire.

In 1969 Barksdale was wounded by rival gang gunfire, this effectively took Barksdale out of gang action. This would ultimately make the founder of the BD's a legendary cult figure in gang mythology. It would also position Larry Hoover for a major organizing opportunity to establish his own gang.

From approximately 1970 and continuing until 1973 Hoover forms spin-off group called "The family" includes "Supreme Gangsters". His group would include figures who would continue for the next 25 years to build up the gang organization known as the Gangster Disciples. This young kid from Mississippi with a serious speech defect (i.e., stuttering problem) would emerge shortly as a major player in Chicago gangs; ultimately, making him possibly the most serious gangster of the 20th Century. But his first effort to run an empire falls short due to his violence: he wanted to send a message to the rest of the gangs that he was someone to be "reckoned with". Thus, on February 26, 1973 Larry and his associate Andrew Howard killed a drug dealer who refused to pay them for a drug supply. The murder victim was William Young.

In 1974 David Barksdale died from kidney failure due to 1969 wound he received. This leadership void in Black gangland would provide Larry Hoover the ultimate window of opportunity to launch his new gang empire.

In 1974 Hoover's growing influence in "the family" and the "Supreme gangsters" culminates in a new identity: "Gangster Disciples". They were called variously "Black Gangster Disciples (BGD's)", "Black Gangster Disciple Nation (BGDN)", but always were GD's. What is significant? The gang was basically formed while Larry Hoover was in prison, serving a life sentence for a murder conviction.

In the next four years, Larry's influence would rapidly grow behind bars, making the GDs the most formidable gang inside the Illinois prison system. Thus, in 1978 a major prison riot in IDOC erupts at Pontiac prison: and, yes, the GD's were heavily involved; some say Larry Hoover even masterminded the entire prison riot.

Three correctional officers were killed in the 1978 riot. Larry Hoover was indicted, but charges had to be dropped against him, because no one would testify against Larry Hoover at that time.

In 1979 the one and only assassination attempt was made against Larry Hoover by gang member named "Nissan", he was a Black Gangster (the BG's are a third derivative gang from the original Devil's Disciples). The attempt to kill Larry Hoover involved using a homosexual to stab him, but it did not succeed, and the homosexual inmate died violently.

The 1980's would be owned by Larry Hoover, due to his enhanced ability to administer his gang by being eventually transferred to a minimum security facility where he would get constant access to visitors and phones, enabling his communications even with his underlings in other institutions, and on the streets. It was in the early 1980's that Larry Hoover's official title expanded: he was now "Chairman of the Board". While we doubt that he actually drafted the memo's, as our information indicates that these materials were crafted by the "Minister of Information" for the GDs, who is a highly educated GD member, and who was not prosecuted in the federal case against Larry Hoover and his top 38 associates, it is clear that Larry was eager to take the intellectual credit for these missives, orders, and memoranda issued routinely to the "troops".

Larry Hoover masterminded a detailed organizational plan to formalize the Gangster Disciples behind bars. Here is how the managerial flow chart worked, obviously, Larry was the "Chairman of the Board": (1) The Board of Directors, appointed only by the Chairman, establish policy and amend Nation laws, they approve programs and assist in the education of the Nation, and hear all complaints and grievances for the GD nation; (2) The Institutional Coordinators, appointed by the Chairman, there is one for each prison or institution; they appoint Unit Coordinators, the equivalent of a "cellhouse leader", they oversee the functions of the gang, communicate weekly with all their unit coordinators, they ensure that all laws and policies governing the GD nation are enforced, and report <u>daily</u> to the Chairman on the function and progress of the gang nation; (3) Institutional board secretary, appointed by the Chairman, oversees all correspondence and literature for the GD nation, re-screen all incoming and outgoing members, function as an emissary of the Board of Directors, and <u>communicate daily</u> with the Chairman; (4) Institutional legal coordinator, appointed by the Chairman, oversees legal affairs of the GD nation as well as complaints and grievances from members, and reports daily to the chairman on all complaints, grievances, reports and the functions of the organization; (5) Educational program director, appointed by the chairman, oversees teaching within the institution to GD members, oversees classes and quizzes on GD literature, and reports daily to the Chairman on the functions and progress of the teaching staff; (6) Institutional exercise coordinator, appointed by the chairman, coordinates sporting and social events within the institution for the GD members, ensures the exercise program is functioning properly, and reports weekly to the Chairman; and (7) Institutional Treasurer, oversees the operations of the Nation's finances, communicates weekly with all Unit Treasurers and the Institutional Coordinator.

Now obviously, prior to getting his federal prison sentence, Larry Hoover was literally "micromanaging" his gang. That is no longer possible for him to do.

Once Hoover approved, perhaps editing here and there to a limited extent, the memo's became LAW for his gang. The NGCRC maintains a large collection of these early type-written memo's from the GD gang. Some of these fit importantly into the chronology of events for the GD gang and will be mentioned where appropriate in time. Only a portion of these memo's are actually described or acknowledged here. The rule of thumb in deciding which one's to use was this: was there something unique about the memo? If so, we have provided an exact translation of the memo, complete with its original syntactic and spelling errors, and with its special "highlighting" (i.e., capitalizations, underlining, etc).

In 1981 Larry Hoover issues a memorandum to his troops: no one in the GD gang can ever assault, threaten, or even disrespect a correctional officer without his "blessing"; threatening or assaulting a correctional officer would mean a serious "violation" from the GD's. It becomes one of the 16 "laws" that all incarcerated GD's must follow: it was Law #7 "Guards: no member shall engage in any unnecessary confrontation with any officers or administrative personnel". It works, his troops obey him. This lands Larry Hoover, even though serving a life sentence for murder, the reward of eventually being transferred to a "college campus-like" minimum security facility in downstate Vienna, Illinois. Hoover would be transferred out of high security to minimum security status in 1987. Larry Hoover would use this additional "freedom" to great advantage in further building his gang empire. There are no walls or even fences around the Vienna correctional facility. Larry Hoover would live in relative luxury. When GD's would be transferred to the Vienna facility, Larry would arrange for them to come and meet him: Larry would give them marijuana, money, cigarettes, whatever they wanted, and cultivate potential new middle-management leaders of the GD gang in this way.

The year 1981 is when the GD's came up with the "New Concept" as well: some revisions and expansion of their internal written codes. If there is a "date" we can hang the time of when the GD's became a centralized, almost bureaucratic organization, run by meetings, by-laws, dues, lots of rules, reporting requirements, and a constant onslaught of "memo's from above" etc, it would be the year 1981. GD gang members would get these memos, after they had been xeroxed and xeroxed again and again, and read them and study them as their internal gang literature. Eventually, there would be "training sessions" for some members who might be in the "reluctant reader" category.

The prison-based GD's become called the "Brothers of the Struggle (B.O.S.)", it is an all-encompassing umbrella identifier for GD's in custody not only in prison, but in jails, and juvenile institutions. The identity of the B.O.S., as an umbrella identity, also covered the GDs who operated on the streets. Obviously, the "Chairman" of the "Board of Directors" for the Brothers of the Struggle is Larry Hoover. This becomes real clear in reading the memos. It is also real clear that the B.O.S. is simply the larger identity for the Black Gangster Disciple Nation (BGDN) or simply the "Gangster Disciples".

In a memo dated October 1, 1981 from Larry Hoover to his troops, the GD's are urged to study the written rules, regulations, and written codes and creeds developed by the GD organization. Obviously, every GD is expected to have a full copy. See Figure 23 for a copy of this memo. It is important, historically, for several reasons: (1) it instructs the membership that they will be getting more memos, and it therefore becomes a formal organization, centralized with Larry Hoover at the top; (2) a decade before the GDs would become visibly active in politics, here Larry Hoover alerts his troops to this long-term developmental strategy; and (3) he instructs GD's behind bars to "take jobs" in all possible areas of the prison where profits can be made for the gang (i.e., sensitive positions, etc, "unassigned" in prison means the inmate has no job, they are idle).

Figure 23
The Oct. 1, 1981 Typed Memo From Larry Hoover to His GD Troops

Date: October 1, 1981
From: The Chairman, Co-Chairman and the Board of Directors
To: All Brothers of the Struggle

The Chairman and the Board of Directors wish to extend our love, Life and loyalty to all Brothers of the Struggle! We are pleased with the support and the participation of many of you that has helped us in making a transition from the Old to the New.

Many of you have a copy of the Organization's <u>Preface</u>. The Preface explains the New Concept and the direction that the Organization has taken. As we stated in the Preface, "In the process of going from the Old to the New, we will have a few complications". As predicted, we have had our share of complications, but we refuse to allow anyone or anything to stagnate our progress or expansion. In spite of the few complications, we are happy to report that we are making progress. In order for us as an Organization to continue to progress and expand, we must become more <u>educated</u>, <u>politically motivated</u> and aware of the <u>economical realities</u> of Black America.

Laws and Sentences have become more stiffer and longer and more prisons are being built with us in mind. We as an Organization of young Black Men cannot allow ourselves to stay confined behind walls and locked in cages to slowly grow old and useless. Through <u>Business</u> and <u>Politics</u>, we can build an economical base that will insure us boundless power and wealth. But if we stay uneducated and without political power, prisons and death will continue to be a way of life for many of us.

<u>Now</u> is the time to put down the Donald Goins books. It is time for us to pick up the <u>business</u>, <u>law</u>, <u>political</u> and <u>economical books</u>. It is time for us to go to school, learn trades and develop all of our talents and skills, so that we will become stronger in society. We cannot wait for the system to teach us, we must take it upon ourselves to learn all that we can about this world. We must not be afraid to change

or grow. We, as an Organization will not stand still and die.

All Brothers are to have a copy of the Preface and the Laws of the Organization, these papers are to be kept at all times, they are for you to study and learn. These papers are important and should be treated as such. From time to time, you will be requested to attend and participate in meetings to read and discuss all documents that has been issued to the membership. It is important that you as a member of the Organization, know exactly what the Organization is about and where it is going.

Many of us are unassigned, it is important that all of us have assignments. We need to be everywhere, capitalizing on the learning experience and the profits that each assignment has to offer.

Everyone will be required to fill out an application. The reason for the application is for the Chairman and his Board of Directors to know more about you and help place you in a program or assignment that will best suit you as an individual and as a member of this Organization.

Some of our brothers have been indicted for murder. We are to give these Brothers all of our support. We encourage you to help in any way that you can. If they are found guilty, they will face the electric chair. We as an Organization will do all that we can to see that they are free.

Many of the Laws that govern our Organization are still being disregarded and disrespected. All Laws are to be adhered to and respected. Those that continue to disregard and disrespect the laws of this Organization will be violated and eradicated (removed) from this Organization.

Again, Thanks for your cooperation and participation.

SINCERELY,

CHAIRMAN AND BOARD OF DIRECTORS

The June 18, 1982 memorandum from Larry Hoover to his troops signaled another organizational development: how to constantly replenish the middle-management functions within the gang. By stressing the need for education to the rank and file members, this memorandum from Hoover is clear in outlining why their growing gang needs "a constant influx of competent replacements". See Figure 24 for a copy of this memo. It also documents how their gang (e.g., their Nation) is becoming more organizationally complex ("technical") as well.

Figure 24
The June 18, 1982 Memorandum from Larry Hoover to His Troops in Prison

Date: June 18, 1982
From: Chairman of the Board
To: The Brothers of the Struggle

Greetings Brothers:

In the name of the leadership (The Chairman and the Board of Directors), we bid you Love! Brothers, we say this in all sincerity. When you say the words, "Love To You!", you are really saying: "I am willing to accept responsibility for you; and I am willing to share responsibility with you." Many of us have used this phrase without really meaning it, or knowing the definition of it.

Our Nation is becoming highly technical (e.g., Written Reports, Bookkeeping, Program Proposals, Codes, etc). Some of our more qualified members who held positions of authority have been released. We need a constant influx of competent replacements. It is our responsibility to acquire the necessary skills to keep our Nation functioning at it's capacity. We must take the initiative to learn what we must, in order to preserve our heritage!

It is our duty to inform you that we, (The Leadership) have declared war! Our enemies are twofold: Complacency and Apathy! Before we can conquer our enemies, we must first identify them. Complacency, is the absence of initiative. Our membership is replete with guys who have no goals in life, other than enjoying their recreational periods; or just laying back watching television. These guys don't know anything of worth, and don't want to learn! When asked if they would participate in our school program, a program that would teach them the necessary skills to fill a position of authority, they have the audacity to be offended; as if someone were trying to belittle them. Our second, and greatest enemy, is Apathy. Apathy is the suppression of initiative. There are some of us who are highly qualified to take on roles of Leadership, but choose to shirk responsibility. Either they don't care what happens to this Nation, or they feel they won't get the proper acclaim for the effort they're required to give; or because of envy or hatred they're willing to let another fail, saying all the time to himself or others, "I could have done better". Brothers, we will stand for you, and with you! But the fight cannot be won by us alone, it will take your support and participation. Your Leadership doesn't want to force you to attend school, but due to our struggle to maintain

adequate personnel, it is our sincerest hope this cause will inspire you to rise to the occasion.
"Love To You".

The July 14, 1982 memo from the Chairman of the B.O.S. (Larry Hoover) announced what they called "Awareness Sessions" for the troops. These were mandatory. Think of it as "training" sessions. The idea was to get everyone on the same page. A copy of the July 14, 1982 memo is provided in Figure 25.

Figure 25
The July 14, 1982 Memo To the Troops on "Awareness Sessions".

Date: July 14, 1982
From: The Chairman and Board of Directors
To: All Brothers of the Struggle
Subj: Awareness Sessions

The Movement

It is a fact, without contradiction that the success of any movement depends largely upon the participation of the mass of people involved in that particular struggle. Leadership without active support, is as useless as spitting in the winds to aid in putting out a major fire. (The fire in this case is the burning effects of poverty, lost direction, and progressive states of self-destruction.) The same is true with the lack of Leadership for the people. The two must combine to coordinate the movement, and each part must do it's share in reaching the goals of the group. What is more important is that the directions of the Organization be set forth, and that each concerned member adhere to those directions, making the necessary sacrifices required to accomplish the objectives.

The Objectives

A group of people organized around the idea of reaching common objectives is called an Organization. Without that unit that comes from having a common purpose, that same group of people qualifies as a Mob, Gang, etc., Therefore, it is essential that each member realize the objectives of the group. Know what it is that inspire the need for unity, and what it is that binds them One to the Other. Otherwise, their membership becomes questionable.

One of the basic objectives of the Black Gangster Disciple Nation is: "To obtain the means to Self-Determination for our People." We can not possibly determine anything without being AWARE of our situation, as well as our alternatives.

This AWARENESS does not come from acting foolish, nor from being lax in your efforts to learn. Therefore the Leadership has opened up avenues for you to gain a perspective on life, our situation, and all aspects of progressive AWARENESS. One such avenue is the AWARENESS SESSIONS, conducted by the Legal Arm of the organization.

Awareness Session

The interest of our members are many, therefore the subjects of the Awareness Sessions are many. Listed below are the objectives of the Awareness Session.
1. Bring a vast range of Intelligence to the availability of the people.
2. Promote an environment of creativity among the people.
3. Practice the art of debate.
4. Inspire dignity in our people, by introducing them to a Black History, as well as a Black Heritage.
5. To in general, uplift the mental, emotional, and spiritual growth of our people.

All sessions shall be in accordance with the six points of the Star of David, signifying the six principles upon which our Organization is founded. These principles are: Love, Life, Loyalty, Knowledge, Wisdom & Understanding.

The goals we have set to reach in these AWARENESS SESSIONS are valid goals. We expect to range from politics to Stock Markets. We shall speak of wars and cultures, as well.

The August 27, 1982 memo from Chairman Larry Hoover specifically identifies the B.O.S. as actually being the Black Gangster Disciple Nation, in a routine "morale building" notice to his troops. A copy of this memo is provided in Figure 26.

Figure 26
The August 27, 1982 Memo From Chairman Larry Hoover

Date: August 27, 1982
From: The Chairman and Board of Directors
TO: All Brothers of the Struggle
Subj: Initiative

As the Chairman and Board of Directors strives for each of us, so should each of us strive for the movement (Struggle); and this is done through Initiative. We must understand that it is not initiative to shout "G.D.", nor to stand in a six-point stance, although each of these have their sentimental, as well as symbolic values.

Initiative cure ailments, builds and destroys governments, and have been the main factor of our survival. It takes initiative to achieve any intentional outcome. If you had not taken initiative to walk to the John, you would have left behind one hell of a mess...

Initiative is a self-reliant enterprise. It is impossible to be successful self-determinative without allying one's self with initiative. If your conscience is lowly, it is because you have not taken the initiative to heighten it. Your consciousness of the moral right and wrong of your own acts and motives. Initiative is the ardent wish that all goes well with the struggle; that every act exhibits one's own contribution to what he believes in, and what he stands against. It is assuring that all people gain spiritually from their association with you and your brethren, as you gain spiritual strength from the teachings of our Organizational Empire; called Black Gangster Disciple Nation....A noble sacrifice; a helpful hint to the wise; a constant striving under the inspirational leadership of our Chairman and Board of Directors.

"Love to you".

The September 4, 1982 memo from the Chairman reports to the troops inside Illinois prisons how their gang is succeeding in getting people registered to vote in Chicago. It contains the one and only piece of evidence yet to surface on how Hoover had tried to transform his gang into something a little more positive: it notes that GD members on the outside will no longer be able to rape females among their own membership at least. It is an example of the kind of "feel good" memo that counterbalances the constant onslaught of the kind of "crack the whip" type of memo's the GDs were famous for issuing to their troops. A copy of this memo is provided in Figure 27.

Figure 27
The September 4, 1982 "Feel Good" Memo Claiming Success in Chicago Voter Registration.

Date: September 4, 1982
From: The Chairman and Board of Directors
To: All Brothers of the Struggle

WHAT'S HAPPENING, INSIDE AND OUT!!!

Fellow Brother of the Struggle!

I don't know if you've recently heard the latest, but Our Organization stacked a Full House at the Voter's Registration Board (as the Chicago Suntimes de-

scribed). Yes, our fellow brothers on the street are moving out. Our new concept that we have adapted (Preface) of Organization is not only being enforced here, but outside of these walls also.

Our brothers have been involved in the cleaning of the 16th and 17th ward. And now they are involving themselves in a Voters-Registration-Drive. We also just recently informed our brothers that there will not be any drafting or raping out of our membership.

We have many goals and objectives toward our Organizational Growth. We shall be keeping you in touch, in the future about our goals and objectives through this bi-weekly information sheet (What's Happening - Inside and Out). We also encourage all of our brothers to step forward with your knowledge, Wisdom and Understanding of our Organization and it's direction. Get in touch with what's really happening, and forward your proposals, ideas, and Mind to us. Study and Read your literature. Check out the last few pages that you just recently received (Proclamation, Letter and Presentation). And watch for the Awareness Sessions coming soon!!! A lot of beneficial knowledge will be coming from these sessions to you, as a individual and member of this Organization.

We want you to give us your eyes and ears, so that you can begin to plug in. Because, We are for Real about what we propagate. Our Concept is to prepare us for the Political and Economical Realities of Black America, and We are going to live and flourish into something great.

SINCERELY,

Your Chairman and Board of Directors

The September 21, 1982 memo from the Chairman of the GD's has got to be a history-making piece of internal gang literature. What other gang in the USA do you know that has its own "Suggestion Boxes" for the members to give ideas or complaints to their gang leaders? If we made this up it would sound preposterous, but the document speaks for itself as a factual piece of American gang history. It is provided in Figure 28. Some of these typed memo's carried the top title of "What's Happening, Inside and Out", and this continued for years as a variation on the memo's, where they functioned as a kind of routine underground newsletter for the prison inmates in Illinois, as well as being distributed throughout Chicagoland and elsewhere for the GDs who were "on the streets".

Figure 28
The September 21, 1982 Memo From Larry Hoover Establishing "Suggestion Boxes" For Members of His Gang.

Date: September 21, 1982
From: The Chairman and Board of Directors
To: All Brothers of the Struggle

What's Happening, INSIDE AND OUT!!!

Fellow Brother of the Struggle!

Once again we come to you extending our Love, Life, and Loyalty to all the brothers of the struggle. We hope that some of the information that we are going to render here will benefit you as an individual member of this organization. Because TIME is essential, and as we stated in our Organizational "Preface", we have wasted enough TIME dwelling on insignificant matters. It is TIME to prepare ourselves for the world. And that is what this issue is all about! Some more enlightening factors about our objectives, goals and accomplishments reaching toward the world.

We would first like to congratulate all of our fellow brothers who have made our struggle a success up to this point. We are celebrating ONE YEAR, since taking on our new concept of Organization. Although there has been many difficulties through our struggle, many things have been accomplished. We also understand that after difficulty will come ease. Only saying, we are still reaching... During this SECOND YEAR, we aim to establish ourselves more firmly as an Organization to be reckon with by everyone doing their share, and contributing more to our cause (objective) which is toward the world!

On the streets, our brothers have been diligently involving themselves in Voters-Registration-Drives. They realize that POLITICS is the science of who gets what, where, when and most importantly, How! As we previously manifested to you, "Through Business and Politics, we can build an economical base that will insure us boundless power and wealth". THis is what direction we are moving in.

Many of you complain about this brother benefiting, and that brother benefiting. Also you complain about not receiving any benefits for yourself as a member of this organization.. Our brother, once again we will spell out our concept, which is Organization. (and this is defined as a unified and consolidated group of people with an executive structure that deals with the well-being of all it's people. It's an executive structure of business and enterprise for individual growth and collective excelleration of the body as a whole.) which means; once we have really established ourselves collectively as a Organization, our boundary of progression will be without measure. First, there must be dedication and sacrifice. We must give ourselves totally to the organization and begin to plug in to what's really happening, by molding ourselves around our organizational direction.

Recently, we had a meeting of Minds. It was recommended that we establish a Suggestion Box in each unit. We encourage all our members with any suggestions that you feel will aid us in our direction to forward these suggestions to your Unit Coordinator who will insure that they are properly delivered for review.

And again, we thank all our brothers for their cooperation and participation during this past year, as we venture into another year, may our progress be a success toward our objective, the World! as a ORGANIZATION...

Plenty Love

Your CHAIRMAN and Board of Directors

The September 27, 1982 memo from Chairman Larry Hoover instructs all gang members to mobilize their families to vote against republican incumbent Illinois governor Jim Thompson. It uses the cunning and guile and cult-like language of how to cultivate youths on the streets by "feeding them" the "New Concept" (i.e., they are not a gang). This memo is provided in Figure 29.

Figure 29
The Sept. 27, 1982 Memo From Chairman Larry Hoover

Date: September 27, 1982
From: The Chairman and Board of Directors
To: All Brothers of the Struggle!

What's Happening Inside and Out!!!! - Special Issue

Fellow brother of the struggle!

Due to the election being right around the corner (in November). Once again we are coming to you extending our Love, Life and Loyalty to all brothers of the struggle. We also hope that some of the information rendered in this Special Issue will benefit you,

as an individual and member of this organization.

We want you to be proud of this Organization that you represent. We encourage all our members to relate to their families and friends on the street about our direction and encourage them to VOTE - because, Your Life and their Life is on the line; we must utilize our POWER to VOTE. For us to be a success on the path that we're traveling, Politically, Economically, and Socially, we need our families to support our efforts/direction.

Being a member of this Organization is not being tough, but being intelligent....which will dictate respect. We want our message to reach our younger brothers & sisters on the streets about our direction and concept. We are NOT a GANG. Our Youth is our future. Through communicating with them, you will help us in many ways on the streets. Many of you incarcerated here, are looked up upon by the Youth on the streets. Begin to feed them our New Concept. Show them from your own experiences that cause to you fall into this pit, that this has become a gain in your wit. And show them the seriousness of the VOTE, which will determine their future, as well as yours. Tell them about how THOMPSON is trying to pass a law to convict the youth at the age of (14) as Adults, which will place them under the Class X.

And lastly, remember that COMMUNICATION is what bring forth Knowledge, Wisdom, Understanding, Love, Life and Loyalty. Your Chairman also wants you to know that he do not want anyone thinking that they cannot communicate with him. He wants you to feel free to communicate with him at any time. We are a not a Organization of Big I's or Little you's. Our strivings (struggle) are collective toward the WORLD.

Listed below are the various offices for which candidates will be elected on TUESDAY, NOVEMBER 2, 1982. We encourage you to inform all your family members and friends that are eligible to vote of this information. Ask them to take a friend to stop THOMPSON in this LIFE AND DEATH SITUATION...

Governor and Lieutenant Governor   Treasurer of Cook County
Attorney General
Assessor of Cook County
Secretary of State
Reg.Supt. of Schools -Cook
Comptroller
Commissioners Bd of Appeals
Treasurer
*   Pres., Cook Co. Board*

Trustees of the Univ. of Ill.
County Commissioners of
Representatives in Congress
 Cook County
State Senators
    (ten from Chicago and
Representatives in the
 seven outside of Chicago)
  General Assembly
Judicial Offices and
Commissioners of the Metropolitan
 Judges seeking retention
  Sanitary Dist. of Greater Chgo.
Sheriff of Cook County
County Clerk of Cook Co.

   Sincerely,

   Your Chairman and
   Board of Directors

A fascinating memo dated October 28, 1982 from Chairman Larry Hoover to his troops revealed how he saw gangs in Chicago such as Jeff Fort's Black P. Stone Nation (B.P.S.N.) as "experiments" on the Black community carried out by a government counter-intelligence program, presumably he was referring to the FBI's Operation CO-INTEL-PRO. Basically, the memo suggests that gangs disorganize the community. How could the GD members read this and not think that they were a part of another kind of grand experiment of some other sort? It is bizarre, but it is gang history. Figure 30 provides a copy of this memo.

   While this Oct. 28, 1982 memo tends to be a put-down on the B.P.S.N., Larry Hoover was not incapable of speaking favorably of the B.P.S.N. when interviewed by a <u>Chicago Sun-Times</u> reporter in 1995. In the 1995 interview Larry Hoover remarked "Black Stones, El Rukns, ex[gang-members], they formed an organization to make a change in the community" (see: Lee Bey, "Inmate Hoover Wields Power on the Outside", <u>Chicago Sun-Times</u>, April 11, 1995, p. 12).

Figure 30
The October 28, 1982 Memo From Chairman Larry Hoover to His Troops

October 28, 1982

To: All Brothers of the Struggle !!!
Fr: The Chairman and Board of Directors
Re: Introduction to Awareness Session Document

Due to Sessions beginning soon !!! All members having received this document. A brief elaboration is
being given here concerning this documentation to erase some of the mis-concepts that have been gain from many of our members. Hereby, we hope that you will be motivated to <u>read</u> and <u>study</u> this document in your possession, so that when the sessions begin; you will come in the right frame of mind...

This documentation (so-called experiment) is not merely about or on the B.P.S.N., but a well conceived plan of <u>manipulation</u> and <u>infiltration</u> inside <u>our</u> community. The main objective of this so-called experiment was to <u>create</u> Gangs, (as it stipulates on page 1) and keep us way from the concept of <u>organization</u>. Because as we <u>consolidated</u>, <u>unified</u>, and being a <u>power to reckon with</u>. Their main goal was to bring disorganization among the ranks of our people.

Through these <u>Aware</u>-ness Sessions on this document. We want our entire membership to become <u>aware</u>, <u>educated</u>, and <u>knowledgeable</u> of the effects/defects that plagued our community. This so-called experiment was no more and no less than another phase of the governments counter-intelligence program. It was a part of the same program that caused the suffering of Black People all across the country. This was the local manifestation dealing with Chicago area youths <u>in</u> <u>particular</u>.

Becoming <u>aware</u> of this document will enable us to be more knowledgeable and alert in this giant arena we're in. Awareness will help us to obtain an amount of understanding to cope with our adversary/adversaries as we courageously and wisely step into the oceans of where control, tricknology and power is at. Then if some of us should begin to <u>sink</u>, we can lend a helping hand to bring our fellow brother up. Because without everyone being aware of how our people can so easily be manipulated, our concept of organization can so easily be disrupted by opposing forces - Disorganizers/Organizers. This document is like a map showing us the many directions which can be used to attack us and our objectives.

Through these Awareness Sessions on this document. We hope that our brothers will be able to "SEE" (understand) "WHY" it is necessary for us to plug in upon the new concept of organization with "Discipline", "Unity", "Respect" and "Love" leading our path against these various types of Infiltrators and Manipulators surrounding us. Because AWARENESS is the main key to our SUCCESS here and in the FREE WORLD!!!

Sincerely,

Your Chairman
and Board of Directors

The March 15, 1983 memo from Chairman Hoover to his troops explains that some of the money from dues that flows upward in the organization actually gets used to help some of the less fortunate members. A copy of this memo is provided in Figure 31.

Figure 31
The March 15, 1983 Memo From Chairman Hoover to His Troops

March 15, 1983

To: ALL BROTHERS OF THE STRUGGLE
Fr: THE CHAIRMAN AND BOARD OF DIREC-
TORS
Re: WHAT'S HAPPENING INSIDE AND OUT!!!

Our fellow brother,

The Chairman and Board of Directors wish to extend our Love, Life and Loyalty to all the brothers of the struggle. Once again we are coming to you in all sincerity and dedication, hoping that you will be inspired to arise in helping us make this a ORGANI-ZATION to be reckon with; as we stated from the very beginning of formulating our New Concept.

In previous issues of What's Happening Inside and Out, we have asked our membership to re-read all of the literature that has been passed down to them. We have constantly re-elaborated upon this point, because we want our members to be sincere and proud of the Organization that they are a part of. And this Pride and Sincerity can only be accomplished by each individual member molding himself completely around the concept. This is called: PLUGGING IN! We are a growing Organization. Our objectives and Concerns are many. What you as a individual member of this Organization put in, this is what you get out.

The Leadership is very disenchanted with Lack of Participation of the Membership to the overall growth and development of the Organization. The map of Organization is layed out before you; but you as a member refuse to look up the road at the markings. At a recent Steering Committee Meeting, the number ne problem that each Unit Coordinator spoke upon existing in their particular unit was: "Lack of Participation by the Membership: Members not wanting to Plug In; Members not wanting to get involve in various functions of the unit."

Our brother, we refuse to force or coerce any individual to take a position. We highly encourage all

qualified members to step forward, as we stated in the past. But with you or without you, we are going to be successful.

A few of our brothers have been forced to do time in an unfortunate setting. We want our entire membership to know that we haven't and don't forget about these members. Your Leadership on a weekly base, send cigarettes, cosmetics and other commissary items to these members. We're constantly striving to make their time over in this unfortunate setting as easy as possible. There is also an established program for al new members that arrive to receive cigarettes and the necessary cosmetics when they enter their perspective units. The Treasuries are for the benefit of the entire membership. We want all our members to know that they are there for you. Get with your Unit Treasurer and Gallery Treasurers. Ask them about the various programs that are offered to you.

In upcoming issues, we are also going to present an "Honor Roll Sheet", honoring outstanding members in the Organization. Members who have achieved their G.E.D.s, Con-Artistes etc,. We also plan to sponsor many sporting competitive events in upcoming months. With your cooperation and participation, a successful flow of events and programs follow us up the road.

It is also suggested to you to begin to use the Suggestion Box in your unit by simply writing down any suggestions that you may have to help our Organization grow. This is done by merely submitting them to your Unit Coordinator who will ensure delivery to the proper authority.

Sincerely,

Your Chairman
and
Board of Directors

The July 1, 1983 memo from Chairman Larry Hoover fits the profile of another "crack the whip" message. Most of his memo's are either of the genre of "cracking the whip" to get members of the gang "in line", or "plugged in" as they like to say; or else the memo's are filled with "feel good" motivational messages. This July 1, 1983 memo is of the "crack the whip" variety. A copy of it is provided in Figure 32.

Figure 32
The July 1, 1983 Memo - Cracking the Whip Again on His Gang.

July 1, 1983
To: ALL BROTHERS OF THE STRUGGLE
Fr: THE CHAIRMAN AND THE BOARD OF DIRECTORS
Re: WHAT'S HAPPENING INSIDE AND OUT!!!

Fellow brothers of the Struggle,

In this issue of What's Happening Inside and Out, the subject matter which we will be speaking upon is two-fold. The first part will be upon some of the problem areas which many of our members continue to suffer upon, and We, the LEADERSHIP will not continue to tolerate these actions disrupting Organizational Unity. Therefore, by bringing them to the surface, we hope that they will enable you to see yourself. The second part will be upon solutions to these problems.

Problem #1 - LAZINESS - Many of you suffer with this problem, wanting somebody to cater to you, provide for you and give you their all. Our brothers, be it known that this is an enemy to our people and our community. We do not have time to carry you, and we will not cater to your laziness. Organization, which is our concept is a group of people <u>combined</u> together, <u>pushing all together</u> toward the same objective. This is with everybody pushing and pitching in to make things work. You have to stand up to be counted, to move. If you remain seated, that's where you're be; Sitting by the wayside looking... in your seat upon Problem #2.

Problem #2 - SELF HATRED - Hating your fellow brother for getting out of his seat to be somebody. Sitting back with animosity, speaking down upon him for having the initiative to try a task that you refuse to attempt. Feeling that he is conceited, when he doesn't have time to play crazy games with you, but he is trying to be Somebody in this world. Many of our brothers suffer from this mental disease. Be it known that we will not tolerate you down-rating a brother putting forth a effort in this organization, which you refuse to put forth. Our concept teaches you to aid and assist your brother in righteous endeavors. Instead of speaking down upon him, aid him by rendering your assistance to him if needed. This is Organization...

Problem #3 - Disrespect - Our concept teaches us to be respectful and dignified to all, but many of our brothers continue to disregard respect. They feel

that for them to be acknowledged by their peers, they must be loud and disrespectful with long Adjectives proceeding out of their mouth like running water. Be it known, that we will not tolerate disrespectful acts and dispositions in this Organization. Your disrespectful acts and dispositions has no place within this organization. It is a must that you respect your fellow brothers and others to avoid unnecessary confrontations. We are not a ignorant wild bunch of radicals, but a Organization upon <u>Intelligence</u> which demands our respect from others. Mold yourself accordingly...

Lastly, Problem #4 - LYING - Many of our brothers feel that by lying, they have gotten over on somebody. They fantasizes lies to cover up the real truth. You feel that once you get away with one lie, you can keep on and on. You feel that you can get away with anything. Our brother, whether you realize it or not, "all the darkness in the world cannot put out the light of <u>one</u> truth". The truth is bigger than a lie, and 99% of the time, it exposes a lie. Be it known that we will not tolerate you lying to us. Many of you lie on insignificant (small) things, and when you get away with it, you feel comfortable and continue to lie. Be yourself, and stand up upon the truth, which is yourself, because you are you, and Nobody else. Be that, so that you may be accepted as you are, and then learn what you can possibly become.

Our brother, we are for you, and not against you, as long as you're following the dictates of the Law. Only when you go outside of these dictates are we against you, because you are then disrupting Organizational Unity, becoming a Out-Law to the Law, and this will not be tolerated.

<u>*THERE ARE THREE KINDS OF PEOPLE*</u>
1. THOSE WHO MAKE THINGS HAPPEN
2. THOSE WHO WATCH THINGS HAPPEN
3. THOSE WHO WONDER WHAT HAPPENED

THIS IS WHAT'S HAPPENING!!!!

SINCERELY,

YOUR CHAIRMAN AND THE BOARD OF DIRECTORS

The July 1, 1983 memo to the GDs was one that was generated from middle-management, signalling the fact that the "memo's" had now proliferated to the point that these were becoming a burgeoning body of written and codified policy making materials for the gang. This particular memo deals with GD's teaching GD's, i.e., an educational program for the GD membership. But it is actually not about getting GD's GED's or something, it is really a continuing effort to indoctrinate the GD troops in the written code and written materials of the GD gang. It is another initiative to get the GD's all on the same page: internal gang training for the membership. Figure 33 provides a copy of this memo.

Figure 33
The July 1, 1983 Memo Establishing an Internal Education Program for the GD Membership.

JULY 1, 1983

TO: ALL BROTHERS OF THE STRUGGLE
FR: ALL UNIT HEAD INSTRUCTORS, ASS'T INSTRUCTORS AND STAFF
RE: SELF MOTIVATION AND SCHOOL STUDY EVALUATION

Fellow Brothers of the Struggle,

The Educational program consist of Teachers administering to the needs of the entire membership, in regards to members having problems; and those who would like to have a broader understanding of the OBJECTIVES of the Organization. This is done through members exchanging thoughts in group sessions, discussing the Organization's literature more indepth with other members, under the guidance of a Teacher. The general academic aspect of our Educational Program entails; reading, comprehending, spelling, math, science, political science, economics, social science, history, etc... Basically, we try to provide all of the basic areas of education essential to a society of people, such as ourselves, who understand the value of education in reference to progress and achievement of a Organization.

As you should be aware of by now, we're going to be dealing with the world on an intellectual level; and to make our NEW CONCEPT of Organization a reality within ourselves, it's going to be essential that we present ourselves intelligently to the world. This entails "Education"!!! It has been noted that some of our members have problems climbing up the Ladder of Knowledge and Understanding, because of us missing some of the basic tools that are needed in order to arrive at a level of intelligence sufficient to compete in the realities of this highly competitive society we live in.

We want you to know that the whole purpose of our School program is geared toward brothers helping each other in the different areas that we may have

problems; in education as well as other areas.

It is our sincerest hope that through your participation in these programs provided for you; with each of us working together. The rewards will be the kind to keep us moving in the right direction; inspiring our fellow members to get involved in the various programs and activities that our LEADERSHIP is offering us. Programs and Activities designed to be beneficial to us as INDIVIDUALS as well as within the framework of ORGANIZATIONAL united strength, if we take advantage of these positive programs.

Our aim is "Seeking True Strength and Solidification" as "A Strong People" organization that can be a Power to be Reckon With; that can be instrumental in helping achieve the strength and solidification of an over-all community of the brotherhood of Man. And to do this, we acknowledge that we must become truly Men (Minds).
SUPPORT YOUR EDUCATIONAL PROGRAM, AND IT MOST CERTAINLY WILL SUPPORT YOU....

Sincerely,

Your Units Head Instructors
Ass't Instructors and Staff

The July 23, 1983 memo from Larry Hoover to his troops signals training the rank and file in terms of resistance to gang intelligence gathering agencies such as the Illinois State Police, State's Attorney's, and others who may have cause to investigate their gang. This is the famous parable of "The Duck". Figure 34 provides copy of this memorandum.

Figure 34
The July 23, 1983 Memo From Larry Hoover to His Troops: The Famous Duck Parable

July 23, 1983

TO : ALL BROTHERS OF THE STRUGGLE
FROM : THE CHAIRMAN AND THE BOARD OF DIRECTORS
RE : MIRANDA WARNINGS

FELLOW BROTHERS OF THE STRUGGLE:

"Nothing hurts a duck, but its Bill (MOUTH)". The leadership is sure that you all are familiar with this old and truthful saying, because if any one of you have ever had the opportunity to go on a hunting trip (in the free world) before being locked up, then

you know full well that if the duck had kept his mouth shut, instead of quacking, he wouldn't have given his position away, and naturally, wouldn't have been our dinner.

This comparison with the duck, our Brothers, is used to stress home to everyone the value and importance of keeping your mouths shut, especially when you are confronted by investigators for the D.O.C., police, Counselors, med techs, even the ministers and others.

As you are all aware, situations occur where it may be necessary to take care off organizational business. Naturally it should be understood that there will be steps taken by D.O.C. messengers to find out who, and how the business was taken care of.

In cases where nation business has been taken care of the smooth way, without a large mass of people actually seeing what has taken place, but even then there are people around in the immediate area, and naturally you should know that there will be a general round up of everyone in the vicinity.

Let's recount these steps very briefly, because they are very important. First some business is taken care of. Second, some one saw what happened and gave your names, cellhouse, etc, or, no one saw what occurred, but due to the amount of people in the vicinity at the time of discovery, everyone is detained and checked out.

Third, Whether your name was given by a notorious messenger, or you are being checked out by a group of investigators, state police, state's attorney, etc, due to the fact the group you're in at the time (recreational period etc), is being questioned etc. The main question is "How do you handle yourself at this time?" What will be your reaction while you and maybe two, three, four, or more (B.O.S.) are being singled out as the persons who allegedly took care of the business, what would you say to these investigators who you know are trying to pin something on you with hopes of getting you the electric chair?

If, for whatever reason, you said you would talk to them in any way, (regardless of the exchange of words) you have just made the biggest mistake of your life, why? Because you are not, or were not to say anything at all to them. Let us explain further, here is the situation, the police, investigators, etc, don't have enough information to go on that would give them a better than average chance to obtain a conviction. The only hold they have is that they can make you convict yourself by breaking, thus implicating others, and making confessions, etc. Say for

instance that those of you being charged or investigated, were separated from one another and placed in different rooms, or different joints so you couldn't communicate with each other to find out what the other is saying or has said so far.

While you are in separate rooms, by yourselves or awhile, in comes two, three or more investigators with a pen, pad or tape recorder. One of them offers a cigarette, coffee, food, or whatever, you accept it, or you Don't, its up to you. If, however, you take their offerings, then you have implicated by your acceptance that the possibility of you breaking is very great, because not everyone has the strong will to reject their offerings and turn around and say, "Go to hell", or "I have nothing to say".

Before any questions have been asked, you were supposed to have been given or read your rights, formerly known as the Miranda Warnings.

These warnings comes from a 1966 case, (Miranda vs. Arizona), Under these warnings you must be informed of the following:

1. You have the right to remain silent under the due process of law, 5th and 14th Amendments, and that anything you say can and will be held against you in a Court of Law.

2. You have the right to have a lawyer present and to consult with a lawyer during questioning. If you cannot afford one, a lawyer will be supplied by the government.

3. You are entitled to make one free telephone call so don't waste it, contact a lawyer or somebody who can obtain one for you.

While this is going on and afterwards, it is extremely important that you don't sign anything, papers, etc., without the advise of your lawyer.

Our Brothers, all of the above must be remembered, as well as, al that you say, if you made a statement or statements to the investigators in the presence of others, but did not sign it, it may still be used against you, so it is best to just remain silent, its as simple as that.

The investigators, police, state's attorney, etc, use a number of techniques to get a person to tell on himself and implicate others.

That which seems natural our brothers, is often times unnatural, let us explain. Say for instance you were on your way to take care of some business and the cop stopped you, asking you for your pass but you don't have one and he tell you to return to your cellhouse, then somebody, member, non-member etc, came passing by you and the cop, but the cop said nothing to them as he had you, and you blurt out to the cop "you let them go by, why did you stop me", and he call them back and ask for a pass, but the don't have one. This may appear to be a natural question, but, what you have done is told on someone and kept them from taking care of their business because of your big MOUTH.

This is called dry snitching and will not be tolerated from anyone, what one do reflects on the whole which you all know. To say that you let so and so do this or that, or they are doing this why can't we do it, seems a natural question to ask the authorities. But it clearly is not and cannot be justified, and most certainly will not be tolerated.

SINCERELY,

YOUR CHAIRMAN AND BOARD OF DIRECTORS

The September 17, 1983 memo from a lower middle-management functionary in the GD gang shows that the infrastructure at the institutional level itself was predisposed to issuing "memo's" to the local troops. An "institutional coordinator" is a GD member in leadership who has responsibility for the affairs of the gang in one specific correctional institution. An "assistant institutional coordinator" works under this GD leader. In Figure 35, we see how one chapter of the GDs deal with internal strife.

Figure 35
The September 17, 1983 Memo From The Assistant Institutional Coordinator to the GD's In One Illinois Prison

Date: September 17, 1983
From: THE ASS'T INSTITUTIONAL COORDINATOR
TO: ALL BROTHERS OF THE STRUGGLE!!!
SUBJ: POSITIVE THINKING/MORALE

Fellow brothers of the struggle:

It has been two (2) years since the teaching of the new concept began. One of the issues that the new concept focus upon over this two year span was "NEGATIVE THINKING". In spite of those teachings, there seem to be a syndrome of negative thinking amongst the rank and file. Here this problem will be elaborated on, and from this point on; these slurs will no longer be tolerated.
THE PROBLEM

There are those of you who sit around constantly in your buddies cell; downrating everyone else. Saying things like: "that person is faking", "I don't associate with half the guys who profess to be a part of this organization", "If certain people weren't here, that guy might be this or that".

That way of thinking is bad for this organization as a whole; and if you sincerely believe that everyone is "Faking", except for you, then do yourself a big favor and remove yourself from the ranks and file of this organization. It is impossible for you to constantly downrate everything and everybody, and still profess to be a true brother of the struggle!

SOLUTIONS
Our brother, instead of always tripping on the few negative aspects of the organization, let's trip on the positive side. Let's talk about the tremendous progress that has been made over the last two (2) years. Let's talk about all the good (reliable) brothers that are working day and night to keep this organization moving.

The governing body realizes that there are those who have no business amongst our ranks; and eventually these few will be weeded out. You can help speed up this process. If you see a brother or know of a brother who's faking; don't sit around in your buddies cell talking about it; because you will give the impression that it is a rule rather than the exception for the organization to harbor brothers of this character. Instead, bring the matter along with your evidence/reasons (rumors not included) to the attention of the proper authority.

The brothers of the struggle! are like a team, and without confidence in ourselves we can't win. Let's stop concentrating on the few who's not, and start concentrating on the countless brothers who are!!! We must start congratulating each other and pepping each other up.

One of the main reasons that the U.S.A. lost the war in Viet Nam was that the morale of the soldiers was low. Morale is the issue (confidence). This point is stressing that, "We can't win unless we believe in each other". There are a lot of god brothers who believe in the organization and who give their all, just as you will. Let's start acknowledging that fact.

In closing, the next time you are somewhere and you hear a member talking about how much everybody is faking, and that he only associate with a chosen few; suggest t him thta if he truly believes what he's saying, "It would be appropriate for him to excommunicate himself from he organization, because in all reality, he's the one that's faking".

We must think more positive thoughts and believe in one another; and when it's necessary, we'll be able to rally and overcome whatever situation we are faced with......This is ORGANIZATION....

Perhaps the most important "milestone" in 1983 for the GDs was that this was the year that Larry Hoover would become eligible for parole. He would appear before the parole board 13 times, being rejected for parole each time, before he would eventually enter the federal prison system as a result of the federal prosecution against the GDs.

The August 23, 1984 memo from Chairman Larry Hoover established a "new annual dues system" for the GDs. The memo explains to the troops that the money will be used to catapult the gang into economic power, and to support their "righteous endeavorments (sic)". A copy of this memo is provided in Figure 36. It is also quite practical for a gang: many gangs like the Latin Kings beat their members when they cannot come up with their monthly "dues". The GDs had their equal share of free-riders claiming they did not have the money to pay dues on a monthly basis. But a "yearly" amount would avoid monthly beatings, and perhaps accumulate in the case of deadbeats so that the members would have to "work off" their dues debt to the gang.

Figure 36
The August 23, 1984 Memo From Chairman Hoover Establishing a New Annual Dues System for the GDs

DATE: August 23, 1984
To: ALL BROTHERS OF THE STRUGGLE
Fr: The CHAIRMAN
*   and BOARD OF DIRECTORS*
Re: NEW ANNUAL DUES SYSTEM

We, the Governing body have decided to establish a new annual, instead of monthly system of payment. This system is designed to show and mold us into that "POWER" to be reckon with, as stated in the Organizational Preface of the First Resurrection. Our purpose is to show the overall consolidation of everyone's responsibility toward helping each other in the righteous endeavorments toward the preservation of our unique concept under the leadership of our Honorable Chairman.

History has shown us that in every society, where a nation, an organization, or any collective group of people are united together for one common cause. Their integrity is measured on one hand; by the capacity of their physical strength of the battles and struggles they've won, which have proven to be of great significant toward their survival; however, on the other hand - there lies the REALITY of the world such as ours; whereupon integrity is foremost measured by the wealth that one has to put into effect their organizational goals, ideas, and purposes. For an Organization to grow and sustain itself; capital is of utmost importance. The Organization must be able to have purchasing power! This is the only way to attain: tools, raw materials, goods, services, properties and a long list of other resources that are essential for us to have; in order to pursue our organizational objectives and goals. For if we would just reflect back for a moment; and contrast our old concept with our NEW CONCEPT - Past experiences will be a motivating force/factor to keep our minds focus upon the REALITY that this is the only way. WE MUST RESURRECT AND RISE UP TOGETHER IN PREPARATION FOR THE POLITICAL AND ECONOMICAL REALITIES OF AMERICA.

Just as all armies, all businesses, and all other groups of people united together for whatever purposes; they must have purchasing power to be able to buy the equipment and supplies needed to aid them in their struggles for success. So it's an absolute must that our organization begin to establish an economic base. Churches, Businesses, Boy Scouts and even Social Groups have some form of a financial foundation. In order for our organization to elevate, expand and even exist; it's imperative that we too - NOW - start ours........

Establishing an economic base will enable us to purchase, build and perpetuate the financial power we need to start our objectives enroute to our organizational goals. These goals are integrated into the goals of every individual in our PROUD and GLORIOUS ORGANIZATION. We are a SPECIAL group of people and can be a SUCCESS with everyone contributing to our cause. The growth of our organization and unique design is a contribution; not only to the organization, but to individual's personal growth as well. PRODUCTIVE organizations produce PRODUCTIVE PEOPLE. It is thereby important that we represent and reflect each other righteously. The Governing body has decided to begin initiating the developmental stages of our economic base. The implementation of our "Annual Dues System" will be the catalyst (springboard). This system will help us to collectively acquire the necessary capital for economic growth.

We, the Governing body have the concerns of all our people at heart, and we want to see all of us progress and not regress. The NEW CONCEPT is the guiding light that should NOW be well lit in all our hearts and minds; FOR IT IS LIGHTEN TO KEEP US ON THE BRIGHT SKYWAYS TOWARD SUCCESS AND OFF THOSE DARK ROADS OF REGRESS!!! To become a POWER to be reckon with, it takes the wholehearted consolidation of all of us; PUSHING AND PLUGGING into the organization's causes, under the leadership and direction of our HONORABLE CHAIRMAN, whom all praise and honor is due......

SINCERELY,

Your Chairman
AND BOARD OF DIRECTORS

The "organizational preface" referred to in the memo in Figure 36 is a lengthy document, thus, for the sake of brevity, some of the basic and most important materials from this larger collection are provided in Appendix C of this textbook.

The September 5, 1984 memo from the Board of Directors specified that all GDs were to try and help get Larry Hoover, their esteemed Chairman, released from prison. It would be the basis for later efforts that nearly succeeded in gaining Larry Hoover a parole. We say "nearly succeeded" in a theoretical way, because if Larry Hoover had perhaps not tried to make himself out to be a political hero of some king, and had used a more subdued approach to appearing before the parole board, he might have gotten out given the kind of "letters" and endorsements he was capable of generating for himself. A copy of this memo is provided in Figure 37.

Figure 37
The September 5, 1984 Memo Demanding That All GDs Get Involved in Trying to Get Their Leader Larry Hoover Released.

Date: *September 5, 1984*
To: *ALL BROTHERS OF THE STRUGGLE!!!*
Re: *THE CALL ! ! !*
Fr: *THE BOARD OF DIRECTORS*

Our fellow brothers of the Struggle, this letter is by the Board of Directors on our Honorable Chairman, whom all praise and honor is due. As his Greatness is realized by us, this same realization must flow through the chambers of your Mind, Body and Soul as we move into this Reckoning Power under the dictates and guidance of this GREAT MAN.

History has shown us that Great Leaders inspire their followers, causing them to strive towards greatness. Our Chairman is a Great Man, a Great Leader; and like most men of greatness - He is fair, but firm; Wise, but tolerant of lesser men; He gives his all, but like most leaders, he does not ask for the many things that his most loyal want to give him. He does not ask for what in fact, he has coming. He is held accountable for our actions, but he never mentions it. If he was not; who he is - He would have long ago been free. Instead, he is held in Prison, because his FIRST loyalty is to us - THE B.O.S., and Everyone knows the Powers that behold him for fear that without his leadership, we would turn into a group of Gangbangers in every prison in this state. Without him, they fear that there would be a constant bloodbath, so in fact; Our beloved Chairman is being held here because he is the MAN; He is the number one #1 Brother of the Struggle.

The time has come that we work, fight, consolidate our efforts, pay and demand his release. The time has come for us to frankly get him out of here. The time has come for us to prove to him that our Loyalty, Faith and Love for him is, as great as his for us. He has proven his - He has been framed for us; He faced the Chair for us; An attempt was made on his life for us; He has gone to his pocket, his heart and his mind for us; and He has never weakened. He has suffered in strong silence, and we repeat - The TIME has come for us to prove we are, were and will remain worthy of what he has done for us.

We, the Board Members now demand that he must be freed at all cost, and we are assured that all B.O.S. feel the same - not out of fear, but out of Love, Respect and our Need to have him out on the streets to lead us further; to show the world what our Honorable Chairman is to us, to himself and to this world.

This letter is a call to all B.O.S. to plug in, so we can have our Leader out. The time has come for us all to show him that his hardships, his leadership, his teachings and his Love for us has not been in vain/ wasted. The line for Volunteers to aid the Chairman starts at the bottom of all true B.O.S. hearts and ends when we die. There is no need to say more, the time has come for us to open the door; let's all show "OUR" beloved Chairman how much we love him!

IN PRAISE AND HONOR
TO HIM FROM US TO YOU!!!

THE BOARD OF DIRECTORS

The Sept. 7, 1987 memo from Chairman Larry Hoover to his troops was a kind of lesson in gang etiquette, urging members to keep their word, i.e, "my word is my bond". A copy of this memo is provided in Figure 38. The most important event that occurred in 1987 was that Larry Hoover was transferred out of maximum security status to the minimum security status of the Vienna Correctional Facility, located far in downstate Vienna, Illinois.

Thus, the year 1987 figures prominently in the developmental lifespan of the GD gang for a number of reasons. Mostly, the relaxed security environment of the Vienna Correctional Institution, having no bars, no walls, etc, afforded Larry Hoover greater opportunities to "reach out" through visitors, through unlimited phone access, etc, to the outside world. This direct contact would include, it would be later alleged in the 1995 federal indictments against him and his gang, proselytizing underage juveniles to commit crimes in furtherance of the gang's continuing criminal enterprise.

Figure 38
The Sept. 7, 1987 Memo to the GD Troops:
A Message of Gang Etiquette
(My Word is My Bond)

DATE: SEPTEMBER 7, 1987
TO: THE BROTHERS OF THE STRUGGLE
FROM: THE CHAIRMAN AND BOARD OF DIRECTORS
SUBJECT: WORDS OF WISDOM
           MY WORD-MY BOND

When someone says, Yes I will, No I won't, I do, yes or no, this person is usually giving his/her word to a particular someone or something. When someone gives their word, they are giving up something of value, something personal or important to them. They are in essence saying, "you can hold me to that or I commit myself to that particular someone or something". A person lives their word to show that they can be trusted.

When a person commits themselves, for example, to a baseball team, job, school, a particular organization or group of people, you are saying you will not default on this. If a person defaults on his word they are usually ashamed, embarrassed or looked down upon.

No responsible individual with self respect will allow upon himself this type of degradation and humiliation. So a person of dignity will be aware, and take the initiative to guard himself and say, "Is my word my bond? Can I be relied upon and trusted?". Do you give you all (100%) to your commitments? If you do, then its because of your dignity and loyalty to yourself and your cause.

Always be sincere when giving your word, be a person to yourself and one that can be relied upon and trusted.

"Always be the type of individual whom people can look upon and say, there goes a person
you can count on.".
Make your word, your bond.
Sincerely,

The Chairman and the Board of Directors

In 1989, then Director of the Illinois Department of Corrections, Michael Lane, publishes a report about gangs in prison, suggesting quite critically that some Illinois prisons today are "defacto gang administered"; this story appears in <u>Corrections Today</u>, the official publication of the American Correctional Association. It would signal the change in the regime, and the end of Lane's involvement in state government; he would eventually retire to operate a restaurant in Springfield. His candor in trying to explain the growing gang menace behind bars basically cost him his job and his career, even though he was "eased" out of the management of the prison system, and into another high level state job before leaving state government completely.

Some of the negative press coverage of IDOC Director Lane involved his use of an IDOC or state-owned air plane; there were reports that the plan had landed at a runway or airstrip at the minimum security correctional institution in Vienna, Illinois.

One high ranking gang informant would later claim that Lane was seen walking with Larry Hoover in the grounds of the Vienna facility, perhaps consulting with him. This and other claims of being "coopted" by Larry have never been verified.

In 1989 a Latin King gang member named David Starks ambushes and assassinates IDOC correctional officer Lawrence Kush; Kush was on the gang's hit list. Gang tension heats up inside the Illinois Department of Corrections. It also generates a large reservoir of anger among correctional officers working the line about administrative policies that "allow" or "overlook" certain gang behaviors that are threatening to the work of a correctional officer.

The other very significant event that occurs in 1989, having great future impact, is that this was also the year that the U.S. Attorney's Office for the Northern District of Illinois started a long-term investigation of the GDs. This federal task force would eventually culminate on August 31, 1995 with the indictment of Larry Hoover and 38 other top GD gang leaders. This federal task force included state, local, county and federal investigators.

The July 20, 1991 memorandum from the Board of Directors gives 19 detailed suggestions to the GD membership on how they can help strengthen their gang organization. A copy of this memo is provided in Figure 39.

Figure 39
The July 20, 1991 memorandum from the GD Board of Directors to the GD Troops on How to Strengthen Their Gang Organization.

TO: ALL BROTHERS OF THE STRUGGLE
FR: BOARD OF DIRECTORS
DT: JULY 20, 1991
RE: PLAN OF ACTION

"HOW TO STRENGTHEN OUR ORGANIZATION"

What can I do to put new life into our organization? This is a question countless of thousands of us are asking. Groups or associations are in constant need for renewal from within. This applies whether they be civic, religious, educational, business, labor, political, fraternal or any other type of organization.

It is up to thousands of rank and file members to realize that the continued renewal of our organization is the business of each and everyone of us. These considerations may enable you to do your part:

1) *ATTEND MEETINGS REGULARLY.* Make it a matter of principle to attend meetings regularly. You can't participate unless you are physically present. Be more than just one of the folks. If you think an organization is worth joining, then it deserves your personal, intelligent, active and continuing support. Don't stay away from meetings because they are not ran the way you think they should be. Strive to improve them and encourage them, and encourage others to do the same. Remember you have no right to complain about the nations business, if you don't attend meetings.

2) *KEEP IN MIND THE PURPOSE OF OUR ORGANIZATION.* Any organization can lose sight of it's objectives and drift into side issues. So occasionally review the concept and laws, as well as the operating procedures for the nation, (i.e., policies, past/present decisions made by the leadership, etc.). Also, encourage others to do the same, as well as stick to the goals of the *"BLACK GANGSTER DISCIPLE NATION".* If the goals of the nation appear outdated, make steps to up-date them.

3) *LIVE UP TO THE DUTIES OF MEMBERSHIP.* These are the marks of a real G.D.:
    a. He/she willingly fulfills the responsibilities that goes with his/her rights.
    b. He/she knows that what he/she does or leaves undone helps or hurts everyone.
    c. He/she realize the limitations of a G.D., but does what is reasonably expected of him/her.

    d. He/she opens their ears to listen, as well as their mouths to speak.

4) *SHOW A PERSONAL INTEREST.* Nation business can become quite cold and impersonal unless all brothers of the struggle go out of their way to inject a personal note to everything they do. Try to be in harmony instead of being distant or hostile. Blend gentleness with firmness when you must take a stand. Respect the viewpoint and feelings of others no matter how much you may differ.

5) *THINK FOR YOURSELF.* It takes effort to be a thinker instead of a yes man. Unless you take some initiative you may be depriving yourself, as well as others of the benefits of the knowledge you secretly possess. Study the various aspects of issues so that you can make a judgement on your own. Base your views on reasons, principles, personalities and on the common good; not emotions or narrow partisanship.

6) *DEVELOP YOUR ABILITY TO COMMUNICATE.* More than one organization has been saved from an embarrassing decision by the voice of a lone individual who stood up and made his voice heard. Know what you are talking about in the first place. Unlock your own powers of leadership and everyone will profit.

7) *MOST IMPORTANT, DEVELOP AND PROMOTE A SPIRIT OF TOGETHERNESS.* Our nation has been crippled by the lack of leadership, as well as members forming uncooperative or hostile cliques. There is always hope! Even one person, by fair mindness and objectivity can bridge the gap between opposing sides. The "Chairman" will truly bless you if you have any hand in bringing this nation back together again and upholding the laws of the *"BLACK GANGSTER DISCIPLE NATION".*

8) *SEEK THE BEST INTEREST OF EVERYONE.* This is a double barreled point.
    a. It means ensuring that all members and not just a few share the benefits of the nation; and
    b. It involves taking into account the interest of the nation at large, and not just a few of the folks.

9) *ACT WISE AT ALL TIMES.* When misunderstandings arise, as well as disputes and clashes. You can help by trying to reach a peaceful accord. You may not completely succeed simply because talking about it isn't always the solution to the problem.

10) *GIVE CREDIT WHERE CREDIT IS DUE.* Many "Brothers of the Struggle" are annoying "Credit Grabbers", who are the first in line when it comes to taking a bow. On the otherhand, nowhere to be found when responsibility must be shared. If you are truly concerned with the continued success of the nation. Regardless of who gets the praise, you will be giving no small service to the nation.

Don't hesitate to praise a fellow member for a job well done. Your continuing effort to give praise will make this organization that much stronger and work that much smoother.

11) PREVENT SENSELESS MEETINGS. Whenever a meeting is to take place. Help keep things moving by making a clear distinction between essentials and nonessentials because of time limitations. Only matters of importance; practical and relevant should be proposed. Persuade capable people to seek positions. Point out to individuals with the capacity and motivation what great good they could do the nation by serving in positions of leadership. Find out before hand their qualifications and act on the basis of such qualifications; not personal loyalty or selfish advantages.

12) GIVE YOUR LEADERS RESPECT AND COOPERATION. Even if someone is calling shots whom you don't personally like. They represent you, as well as the "BLACK GANGSTER DISCIPLE NATION". They should receive the support you would expect if you were in that position.

13) OFFER CONSTRUCTIVE SUGGESTIONS. Don't tell them only what you think they want to hear. On the other hand, don't keep bringing up senseless complaints. Speak well of your leaders to outsiders. If you don't have nothing good to say about your leaders. Either shut up or refrain from needlessly publicizing any defects.

14) DON'T DODGE ISSUES THAT "MUST" BE DEALT WITH. The success of the Black Gangster Disciple Nation depends largely on the "Behind The Scene" plays of folks who never or seldom get recognition or acclaim. Your rights as a member of the Black Gangster Disciple Nation imply many responsibilities. Instead of seeking missions/responsibilities you like. You will accept those however distasteful, which are essential for the good running of the Black Gangster Disciple Nation. Small jobs well done will prepare you for bigger ones! The folks who are chosen for a mission/responsibility whose response is "why me"? Seldom or never get chosen for positions of responsibilities of greater opportunity. "HE WHO IS VERY FAITHFUL IN A VERY LITTLE, IS FAITHFUL ALSO IN MUCH"!!!

15) ENCOURAGE, DON'T DISCOURAGE. A "Wet Blanket" is defined as, a person or thing that quenches or dampens enthusiasm, pleasure or the likes. Wet blankets are quick to complain about a situation but are slow to do anything about it. They are more interested in fault finding, than fact finding. They are accustomed to speaking of the nation as "THEY" (i.e., Them people), instead of "WE". Anyone in that frame of mind is not needed in or around the Black Gangster Disciple Nation. Be more anxious to improve this powerful nation. Also, con-cerned with winning cooperation, than winning arguments.

16) BACK UP WORDS WITH ACTION. It has become the complete delusion of this nation to jump to the conclusion that because we have talked about a problem, we have rarely solved it. Discussions are needed to reach mature decisions but resolutions should be translated into performance.

17) KEEP EXPENSES UNDER CONTROL. Many organizations have had to close shop or severely curtail it's activities because of mismanagement of funds. Those who pay dues have a right to a strict accounting of the use of monies. If you take care of finances. The finances will take care of you.

18) WE MUST KEEP LONG RANGE GOALS IN MIND. Many organizations die because they let themselves get caught up in a mass of details and fail to lay long range plans for the future. The "Chairman" intuitively foresaw this and set goals for the Black Gangster Disciple Nation to reach. Unfortunately, our beloved "Chairman" is engaged in a battle for his life. A battle we must all help him win. For against the oppressor alone; you cannot win! In spite of this battle, we are still strong. But lately, in the midst of our crisis. Folks are beginning to ask, "Where are we headed"? "Is the nation fulfilling it's purpose"? "Do new conditions require a new change of directions"? "Do present methods meet current and future needs"? The answer to those questions are yes, and no! Just because the "Chairman" isn't physically present doesn't mean we can't move forward!

19) PERSEVERE AMIDST SHORTCOMINGS AND DIFFICULTIES. If we are working for high goals. Then, they are worth suffering for. Stay in the thick of things until the very end. Expect frustrations and difficulties. You won't be disappointed! Be ready to start and start again. The "Chairman" will bless you if you keep striving to strengthen the nation. Despite, misunderstanding or ingratitudes; Your willingness to keep going will strengthen both you and the "ALMIGHTY BLACK GANGSTER DISCIPLE NATION".

LOVE TO YOU ALL!

In October-November, 1992 the Chicago official "gang truce" button began appearing and was worn by many of the gang members whose gangs were signed parties to this truce. It was produced by the GDs through their "United in Peace" front group.

The "gang truce" button has the slogan "UNITED IN PEACE" with two hands (a left hand and a right hand) clasping, along with ten gang "logos" or symbols --- all in black on a white round background.

The logo symbols for the following gangs appear on this "gang truce" button: Vice Lords, New

El Rukns (seven in circle), Black P Stone Nation, Cobras, El Rukns, Four Corner Hustlers (+ sign, 440), Black Disciples, Black Gangster Disciples, and Black Gangsters.

This alliance of Black gangs arose in the aftermath of the sniper killing of a child in Cabrini-Green and the public uproar it caused. The pressure was put on the gangs. Political activists took advantage of the situation to "bring the gangs together". In this fashion, a tentative alliance was formed between rival gangs; giving them greater legitimacy and recognition in the mass media.

In 1992, the B.O.S. was clearly operating as effectively in Cook County Jail as it operated inside Illinois prisons. Thus, the modern gang member inmate has several codes of conduct to obey: that of the jail system itself and the "official rules and regulations", and the rules imposed by the gang --- the latter probably being the rules that get obeyed more often. Consider the following handwritten memo from the Brothers of the Struggle (BOS), an actual example, from Cook County Jail:

"DATE: 9-01-92
SUBJ: Violations
FROM: 4ou C.O.S.
TO: Decks C.O.S.

Greetings my 7/4 brothers, this memo is to inform you that <u>there will be no head</u> to toe violations given out unless you are given word from 2ft C.O.S. or BLD. C.O.S.. Anyone who goes against this will be bogus and violated on spot. Also all C.O.S. are to attend church on Sundays if not they are subject to disciplinary Actions. Pass word to your decks that all B.O.S. are to lace their right shoe by missing the bottom 2 holes. Example (‖:) This is so that we can identify each other. Brother security is to be on the entire yard; rec. when ever called. I leave as I came with plenty much love.

Important - all reports are to be in code, all minor and major incidents must be in report.

In the vision of our great leader and through his vision, we can become a more reckoning power of people beyond boundaries without measures.
2-15-19
(19-3-15-14-5-25) (7-4)".

As seen in the above B.O.S. memo, an elementary code is used: 1=a,2=b,3=c, etc. Thus the expression 7/4 means "G.D.". The expression "2-15-19" means "B.O.S.". The B.O.S. includes G.D.'s (Gangster Disciples), and B.D.'s (Black Disciples), and naturally, Black Gangster Disciples. It's Honorable Chairman of the Board is "King" Larry Hoover. "C.O.S." means chief of security. For additional information on GD's in the jail setting see: <u>American Jails</u> magazine (January/February, 1993, "Gang Or-

ganization in a Large Urban Jail", by George W. Knox).

In 1993 the first major efforts to win a parole release for Larry Hoover began. Larry's strategy would be infantile and would ultimately mean his complete downfall (i.e., a federal life sentence and transfer to the most secure prison in America). The strategy conceived by Larry Hoover was to make it appear he had the power to "turn his gang into something good" (i.e., Growth and Development). Thus, he initiate a political-action campaign at the same time: the plan - to make Larry look like he would be an asset to the community, he would reduce gang crime and gang violence if only the Illinois prison system would grant him a parole.

The official records for Larry Hoover's 1993 parole hearing were FOI'd through this journal, allowing access to the letters that became a part of a historical public record. It is useful to summarize some of these and provide examples.

First, there was a large scale "petition" drive as part of the 1993 parole bid for Larry Hoover. Printed on the front of each petition was an endorsement and a statement about Larry Hoover. Figure 40 provides a copy of this important historical document. Approximately 5,000 signatures were on the petition to free Larry Hoover.

Figure 40
A Copy of the Cover Sheet for the 1995 Petition Drive to Get Larry Hoover a Parole.

PETITION TO PAROLE LARRY HOOVER

We the undersigned do hereby acknowledge, agree and thereby join with Prince Asiel Ben Isreal, Co-Chairman, Target Hope--Crime and Violence Committee; Wallace "Gator" Bradley, International Spokesman, United in Peace Organization; Earl King, CEO and Founder, No Dope Express Foundation; Pat Hogan, Director, Community Affairs, 21st Century V.O.T.E.; Howard Saffold of PACT; Rev. Harold Bailey, Director and Founder, Probation Challenge; Diana L. Arnold, Proprietor, Absolute Secretarial Services and Graphics Design Layout, Inc; Rev. Helen Sinclair, Ma Houston Prison Outpost; Janette Wilson, Executive Director, Operation PUSH; Margaret Burrells, DuSable Museum; Sid Finley, Executive Director, NAACP (Chicago); Former Mayor Eugene Sawyer; Gary Gardner, President, Soft Sheen Products; Joe Gardner, Commissioner, Metropolitan Water Reclamation District; Alderman Allan Streeter, 17th Ward; Alderman Shirley Coleman, 16th Ward; Alderman Virgil Jones, 15th Ward; Pastor T.L. Barrett, Jr., Founder, Life Center Church of Universal Awareness; Hal Baskin, Executive Director, P.E.A.C.E. Organization; and Virgil

Martin, Honor Student, Fenger High School.

We hereby, individually and collectively, do believe, as evidence of his present actions, Larry Hoover, to be rehabilitated and of sound mind and judgement, and as such, an asset to the communities-at-large in the capacity of a prime component in the institution, maintenance and subsequent longevity of the existing United in Peace Coalition Nations' Truce that currently attributes to the continuous, dramatic drop in the percentage of violent crimes and homicides in the African-American communities from Chicago to Peoria and throughout the State of Illinois.

We hereby, individually and collectively, do ask Governor Jim Edgar and the Illinois Prisoner Review Board and its Chairman to grant Larry Hoover parole.

Some of the letters written to the Illinois Prisoner Review Board were on official government stationary. Some of these contain language of significance to this historical sketch. One of these was written by Alderman Allan Streeter who would a few years later be convicted in Operation Silver Shovel, a probe of corruption among Chicago alderman. Now former alderman Streeter's letter is provided in Figure 41.

Figure 41
Letter on City of Chicago Stationary From Alderman Allan Streeter on Behalf of Paroling Larry Hoover.

June 15, 1993

Mr. James Williams, Chairman
Illinois Prisoner Review Board
319 East Madison
Springfield, IL 62701

Re: Larry Hoover, C01829, Vienna Correctional Center

Dear Mr. Williams:

I am writing to you as a concerned citizen to support the release of Mr. Larry Hoover who has demonstrated a sincere desire and effort in working for the improvement of the African American Community.

For example, Mr. Hoover was one of the first to sign the Peace Treaty to stop the killings in the African American Community, which has been very successful. Also Mr. Hoover has been very instrumental in working for the capture of the Chatham Community

Rapist and working to assist in the apprehension of a serial killer in the Chatham area.

I strongly urge you as Chairman of the Illinois Prisoner Review Board to use your legal and executive powers to work for the release of this servant of the community.

Thank you in advance for your consideration and prompt attention to this matter.

Sincerely,

(signed)
Allan Streeter
Alderman, 17th Ward

Another alderman would write a letter on behalf of Larry's parole, and also face the same fate from the Operation Silver Shovel investigation: Alderman Virgil E. Jones. Alderman Jones was later convicted of taking $7,000 in bribes. Virgil Jones had been quoted in the Chicago Tribune "I'm not ready to say that Larry Hoover is such a bad man, I'm not sure Al Capone was such a bad person either" (See: Neal Pollack, "The Gang That Could Go Straight", Reader: Chicago's Free Weekly, Jan. 27, 1995, p. 16). Alderman Jones' letter is transcribed in Figure 42.

Figure 42
Transcription of the Letter on Official Chicago City Hall Stationary from Alderman Virgil Jones in Support of Larry Hoover's Parole.

June 17, 1993

Mr. James Williams, Chairman
Illinois Prisoner Review Board
319 East Madison
Springfield, IL 62701

Re: Larry Hoover C01829
Vienna Correctional Center

Dear Mr. William:

I am writing this letter to support the release of Larry Hoover who is an inmate in the Illinois Penal System. I feel that after two decades in the Illinois Penal System Larry Hoover has shown that he understands what it means to be a productive member of society.

Larry Hoover has shown that he can be a positive role model for youngmen and women in the African

American Community.

I recall recently in my ward 250 young men and women used brooms, rakes and shovels and cleaned up a whole mile square area because Larry Hoover said they must not destroyers (sic). This kind of resolve shows that rehabilitation has taken place.

A youngster named Delenna Williams was a gun shot victim and his outcry against such an act brought the alleged perpetrators forward. As a result of his calling for an end to killing, the city of Chiago (sic) has had a twenty percent murder rate reduction.

I believe that when an individual improves his educational background and tries to use his influence for constructive things to benefit the community the status quo owes that individual a chance.

I urge you to give Lary (sic) Hoover a chance to became (sic) a living example that an individual can change and become a productive member of society.

Mr. Chairman, everyone deserves a chance.

Sincerely,

(signed)
Virgil E. Jones
Alderman, 15th Ward

A number of other letters, such as from assistant principals at two different Chicago Public High Schools, offered to use Larry Hoover as a consultant to reduce their gang problems if only the parole board would release him. There were letters from churches, community groups, and one from a business that looked interesting. It was printed on business stationary, from a company called Benefit Planning, Inc, it is provided in Figure 43.

Figure 43
A Businessman Supports the Release of Larry Hoover.

Benefit Planning, Inc
150 South Wacker Drive
Suite 800
Chicago, IL 60606
(312) 781-2739
New York   (212) 557-6500
Fax   (312) 346-4825

July 2, 1993

Mr. James Williams, Chairman
Illinois Prisoner Review Board
319 East Madison - Suite A
Springfield, IL 62701

Dear Mr. Williams:

Greetings. This letter serves to confirm employment for Mr. Larry Hoover (C01829) upon his release from Viana (sic) in August. Mr. Hoover will be employed as an associate agent of Benefit Planning, Inc.

My personal visits to Viana (sic) and phone conversations with Mr. Hoover, along with community work by his family leave us extremely optimistic.

We have enjoyed a very positive relationship through our employment of Mr. Sam Dillon, former long time inmate. Mr. Dillon lived with us and was employed in Chicago for his first year. Currently, he runs our summer camp program for Cabrini Green's Near North Little League residing at the 4 Mounds Foundation in Dubuque, Iowa.

I personally attended the first week of camp last week and was extremely moved by Mr. Dillon's teaching re: negative gang activity, drugs, violence, and the benefits of hard work and truth.

We are confident that Mr. Hoover will prosper and be a strong force both in our company and for the youth of Chicago.

Please feel free to contact me if you have any questions.

At your service,

(signed)
Robert E. Muzikowski
President

Another letter on behalf of paroling Larry Hoover was written on state government stationary by State Representative Coy Pugh. A copy of the text of this letter is provided in Figure 44.

Figure 44
Copy of the Text of the Letter From State Representative Coy Pugh on Behalf of Paroling Larry Hoover.

July 15, 1993

Mr. James Williams, Chairman
Illinois Prisoner Review Board
319 East Madison-Suite A

Springfield, IL 62701

RE: LARRY HOOVER, C-01829

Dear Chairman Williams:

Please accept this communique as letter of support on behalf of Mr. Larry Hoover, who will be appearing before the parole board in August.

I am personally endorsing his release at this time. From all indication concerning his personal reform and evident rehabilitation I strongly urge that the Board consider this case with due diligence and in a positive frame of reference.

Mr. Hoover has more than demonstrated his willingness to take a responsible place in society. His work and efforts to bring about badly needed changes are quite known to myself as well as others in the community. With everything considered, he should be given a chance to re-enter society now.

I earnestly hope and trust that you and the Board will grant a favorable outcome.

Sincerely,

(signed)

Coy Pugh
State Representative

Thus, on August 10, 1993, when Larry Hoover actually appeared before the "parole board", he had amassed a wealth of political and community activists in support of his bid for parole. We had heard from a reliable source that some of those who did testify for Larry Hoover were handsomely paid, as much as $50,000; however, this has never been confirmed. The parole board voted 8-0 against giving Larry Hoover a parole.

Astute newspaper reporters like the Chicago Tribune's George Papajohn were skeptical of how rehabilitated Hoover was and how sincere he was about ordering his gang to "go straight". Reporters like Papajohn dug deeper, and they published their stories: they reported that it was a "hoax", it was a "scam", it was preposterous to assume that this notorious gang leader would be an asset to any community.

In the summer of 1993 summer Larry Hoover engineered a major gang organization accomplishment: a big GD picnic in rural Kankakee County, Illinois at a private farm. The official GD name for the event was the "Gala Illinois Family Day Voters Pic-

nic". Think of it as a "Woodstock" for GDs; because about ten thousand (10,000) of them showed up. They partied, ate, listened to music, got high, milled with the throngs of GDs, took pictures of each other in their finest gang clothing, and made quite a picture as a massive gang gathering, perhaps the largest ever recorded in U.S. history. They were bused in: the hundreds of buses were rented or paid for by the gang itself. Larry Hoover would make a call from his relative comfort in the Vienna minimum security facility, and speak to the thousands of GDs present at the picnic over a loud speaker system that was set-up for the event.

A major "coup" for the GD gang occurred in the fall of 1993. In October the GDs organized a "peace treaty summit meeting" in Chicago, bringing in Crips from all over the continental USA, as well as a lot of GD's and sympathizers to the GD "cause". The year 1993 would therefore signal the year in which "Crips" would align themselves into a national gang alliance system with the "Folks" (particularly GDs). Today, "Crips" and "Folks" are aligned in the national gang alliance system. It was not a hard allegiance to make: both Crips and GDs wear "blue" colors. As this initial alliance system developed and spread nationally, in local communities big and small, and inside correctional institutions everywhere, it basically forced the "Bloods" to align themselves with the "People" or "Brother" gang alliance system, by default in terms of what the power struggle had left them with: a choice of necessity, not convenience.

Obviously, the ability of the GD gang to hold this conference and stage other ludicrous events in Chicago during the Fall of 1993 made them formidable. Citizens were shocked and dumbfounded how the GDs had control over the Englewood High School in Chicago; where an "awards ceremony" was held for the Gang Peace Treaty Summit Meeting: it involved giving out awards for Community Leadership to the likes of persons like Larry Hoover and other notorious gang leaders. Some how the GDs had coopted and controlled an important government facility: a public high school, using the schools auditorium for an official gang event.

To our knowledge, no parent in Chicago who had a child attending Englewood High School at the time has ever filed a federal law suit against the Chicago Public School system for a civil RICO cause of action involving the criminal corruption of their children. But this author taught a gang class to the teachers at that school at that location during the same time frame: the teachers were obviously demanding gang information, because they sensed something was "amiss", the school was being turned over to a gang (the GDs). The teachers demanded an after school hours college course be taught about gangs at the Englewood High School, and they wanted me: I volunteered through my university to do this. I gained much valuable insight into the power of the GD gang at that time.

About time of the Fall of 1993, the federal government had its Operation HEADACHE, the official codename for the federal investigation of the GDs in full swing. It meant a unique way of gathering intelligence. The visitors who would come to see Larry Hoover in the Vienna Correctional Facility were given special visitor badges, inserted in between the thick lamination of the visitor's badges were subminiature radio frequency transmitter devices, designed to provide a listening station to the content of the "visiting" that went on with Larry Hoover. As one of the investigators on the case related to me, well into the investigation, one of the visitors with such a "wired" visiting badge simply walked out of the institution and kept the badge as a souvenir of visiting Larry Hoover. On their way home, they were still able to be monitored. But at some point the individual was so proud of getting this "trophy" of his visit to "King Larry" he kept playing with it, and noticed a small bulge in the middle, and his curiosity got the better of him, and he began to unravel the package to actually discover the transmitter device contained in it. Certainly Larry Hoover was soon notified of this development, but by then it was really far too late. Too much incriminating information had already been gathered in the preceding months of the court authorized intercept.

During the month of June, 1994 I.D.O.C. correctional officers complained through their union at the Pontiac prison that prison administrators were making deals with gang leaders; the CO's demanded a zero-tolerance policy towards gangs to improve CO safety. They would not get their zero-tolerance policy until after the infamous "Speck tape" hits the national news and makes the entire Illinois prison system appear to be corrupted. The Speck tape would shake up the prison system, and continue to have reverberations well up until the time of this writing in late 1999.

In the fall of 1994 Larry Hoover was transferred out of the Minimum Security Facility in Vienna and into a tighter facility at Dixon, Illinois. Obviously, IDOC knew at this point that the federal investigation, code-named "Operation HEADACHE" was underway and that they had scored evidence incriminating Larry Hoover, such that he was about to be indicted. From an investigator who was involved with that operation, we were told that over 8,000 conversations were recorded, amassing a wealth of intelligence on the GD gang. It would not look so bad if Larry was taken into federal custody if this were done at a more secure facility. But even at the Dixon prison, Larry Hoover's "job" was that of the visiting room: he had visitors every day; he ate steak

sandwiches, milk shakes, and chicken from the "grill" at the visiting room. He never ate off the "main line" in the inmate chow hall. He did not do any work, he had no assignment, he was busy EVERYDAY meeting with the endless number of visitors who would come to the prison to meet with him. He obviously had his own "section" of the visiting room staked out, it was "Larry Hoover's" area.

By the year 1994 "Bloods" were forced to ally with "People" and "Brothers" gangs in national gang alliance system started in 1993 where crips and folks joined.

Incredible, but true, in early 1994 Wallace "Gator" Bradley, spokesperson for GD front group "21st Century VOTE" meets with President Bill Clinton in the White House. He had the audacity to tell the president he represented a group called "Better Growth and Development". This issue never surfaced in any of the subsequent debate and campaign coverage when President Clinton began his run for a second term in office. But it truly was the first gang to get a representative into the inner sanctum of the White House. Some gang experts mistakenly refer to the case of Jeff Fort, the leader of the El Rukns, known more commonly as the Black P. Stone Nation, as the first person to pull this off, but that is factually untrue: Jeff Fort had an invitation to an inaugural event for President Nixon, but never actually got there. The photographic evidence of this is documented in the <u>Chicago Tribune</u>, February 18, 1994, section 2, p. 2.

During the time frame of 1994-95 the GDs fronted two candidates for election to Chicago City Council; both were defeated.

In March of 1995 Larry Hoover makes his last effort to gain a parole. This becomes one of the most sophisticated efforts to secure his release. It includes using the testimony of two Ph.D. university professors testifying for Larry Hoover (Dwight Conquergood from Northwestern University, Chicago, IL; and Clemens Bartollas, from the University of Northern Iowa). Obviously, his parole bid fails. The parole board voted 10-0 against giving Larry Hoover a parole.

On March 15, 1995 Larry Hoover issues a letter to all GDs in prison and out on the streets. It is a well-crafted letter, and thus probably actually written by one of his aides or attorneys. A copy of this letter is provided in Figure 45.

Figure 45
The March 15, 1995 Letter From Larry Hoover.

Larry Hoover
DIXON CORRECTIONAL CENTER
2600 North Brinton
P.O. Box 1200
Dixon, Illinois 61021

My Brothers and Sisters in the Struggle:

I learned this week, for the 13th time, that I have once again been denied parole. My thoughts, as they have been for years now, are of my family and of you. My sons, who have grown from infants to men during my imprisonment, and their mother, whose commitment has been unwavering: they all continue to pay, with me, the price for the terrible crime I committed, for which I am solely and fully responsible. They have been strong, as the families of tens of thousands of other black prisoners have been and must be strong every day of their lives.

But, Brothers and Sisters, we must have more than strength. We must have vision, too. We must see that we, ourselves, are the victims of the crimes that ignorance, poverty, hopelessness and drugs lead us to commit. We must see that, just as no man is an island, we all wear the shackles of the ghetto. We are all Ghetto Prisoners.

Our only hope for release is to use our strength and vision in the cause of change. Ignorance is our enemy; we must honor learning and those who learn. Poverty is our enemy; we must gather our pennies and dollars and use them in our own communities. Hopelessness is our enemy; we must organize and vote by the hundreds of thousands, to give voice to the voiceless. Drugs are our enemy, destroying many of us with the lure of profit, more of us with addiction, and still more with the crime that results; we must join our voices with those across the land, of whites and blacks, churchgoers and convicts, gays and straights - all who share the purpose of taking the profit out of drugs and ending the slaughter made easy by guns.

Whether and when I will be released is beyond my control. Whatever my personal destiny may be, I will fight to strike the shackles that imprison us all.

(signed)

Larry Hoover
Ghetto Prisoner #1829

The "Ghetto Prisoner" gimmick became the basis for Larry Hoover to gain recognition through a "rap music" group as well as through a new line of designer-gang clothing --- called the "Ghetto Prisoner" jerseys, which sold for about $45 each and were marketed through a company called Ghetto Prisoners, Inc, owned and operated in early 1995 by Larry Hoover's common-law wife Winndye Jenkins. These were hot items in the market of "gang apparel".

The feds, involving IRS criminal division, raided the Ghetto Prisoner company on April 10th, 1995. The IRS raided the company location and the home of Jenkins, seizing records and $67,000 in cash (see: Phillip J. O'Connor, "Cops Raid Businesses, Seek Gang Ties", Chicago Sun-Times, April 11, 1995, p. 12; Andrew Martin and George Papajohn, "Police Raid Firm Tied to Gang Chief Hoover", Chicago Tribune, April 11, 1995, Section 2, p. 9).

One of the professors who testified for Larry Hoover's release would in 1995 come to the aid of the GDs in another way: lending credibility to their school-based program at Englewood High School.

Dr. Clemens Bartollas, professor of sociology at Northern Iowa University, not only testified for Hoover, but also came to the benefit of the GDs in another way: by writing a OP-ED piece as a guest editorial in the Chicago Tribune (July 13, 1995) to defend the "gang deactivation program" at Englewood High School (formally now referred to as the Englewood Technical Preparatory Academy, a Chicago public school). The GD's are the single largest gang in the student population at Englewood High School. Recall, that during the 1993 Gang Peace Summit Meeting held in Chicago, that Englewood High School was also the scene for the infamous award ceremony that gave awards to gang leaders like Larry Hoover. Bartollas presented his credentials as a gang expert this way:

"for the last 35 years, I have been involved with gang and hard-core youth. I have worked with gangs in the community in two states, have interacted with them in correctional settings in three other states and have written a number of books about youth and adult crime in which gangs were d i s - cussed" (see Chicago Tribune, 7-13-95, p. 22, section 1).

Bartollas went on to defend the school's gang questionable gang program that involved gang members acting as hall monitors where they would physically punish students who violated discipline codes or did not attend school. The defense was his impression the school environment was delightfully innovative and effective. Earlier (Chicago Tribune, June 15, 1995) Bartollas was quoted as follows: "you have the deviant and quite radical suggestion that the gangs can, in fact, monitor themselves to promote a learning experience that is constructive to everyone" and on the basis of two visits to the school also said "it is working remarkably well".   August 31, 1995 becomes a landmark date in the developmental lifespan of the GD gang: this is the date that the U.S. Attorney for the Northern District of Illinois announces the indictment of Larry Hoover and 38 of his top associates, charging them with a 25-year conspiracy to distribute cocaine, crack, heroin and marijuana and to extort protection money from street dealers in Chicago and its suburbs, as well as operating a continuing criminal enterprise.

In September of 1996 the GDs release their book "From Gangster Disciple to Growth & Development: The Blueprint", shortly before Larry Hoover goes to trial.

In 1997 Larry Hoover is convicted, he is then immediately transferred to Terre Haute FBOP to await sentencing. While there he conducts a one hour videotaped interview with ESPN.

THE ORIGINAL PREDICTIONS ABOUT THE IMPACT OF THE GD PROSECUTION

The original predictions about the impact of the GD prosecution included short-term and long-term impact areas. Some of these predictions seem to have been accurate. Let us review the original predictions about the effect of the federal prosecution.

Projected Short-term Impact of the Federal Prosecution

Most of the media attention to the 39 indicted GDs during September 1995 looked at a short-term negative scenario in terms of the projected impact of Operation Headache. Gang-wise journalists were able to point to the succession effect: by prosecuting one gang, another gang would be able to step forward in the aftermath, that is other gangs would fill the void left by the GDs. Clearly, the dismantling of Jeff Fort's El Rukn gang empire in the 1980's --- also through federal prosecution ---was a context that allowed the GD's to take control of the turf previously held by the El Rukns.

Thus, the first major reaction to the 39 indicted GD leaders was a focus on how other gangs might now be able to become more effective. No programs of prevention and intervention were basically put into place in areas or buildings controlled by GDs at the time of the indictments. So, one cannot conclude that a "Weed and Seed" operation had been achieved. Only some weed whacking had been done on the largest criminal gang in the USA. It seems a reasonable fear, therefore, that in the cracks and crevices of social disorganization that we can expect other weeds to arise as an immediate short-term effect.

Two gangs stand to benefit directly from the effects of putting the GD leadership into disarray: (1) the Black P. Stone Nation (BPSN), and (2) The New Breed (or B.G.'s). Two factions exist in the BPSN, one being headed up by Jeff Fort's son. Both factions of the BPSN have been historical enemies of the "Folks" and GDs. Thus, the BPSN gang could see a strong revitalization. Even more likely, however, is that another faction of the Disciples will grow stronger. Two other Disciple factions most likely to benefit from the GD prosecution are: the BD's and the BG's. The BG's are today known as the New Breed, and are a very violent aggressive growing enterprise. Both the BD's and the BG's have their own separate and different written constitutions and by-laws and leadership structures. So in the short-term, the gangs most likely to benefit from the displacement of GD influence are opposition gangs like the BPSN and other Disciple factions like the BG's and BD's.

Projected Long Term Impact of the GD Prosecution Efforts

The projected long-term impact of Operation Headache consists of significant membership demoralization, significant organizational destabilization, substantial collateral impact, a strong deterrent effect, and a healthy dose of restoring public confidence in law enforcement's ability to counteract the gang threat. Each of these will be discussed briefly.

1. Significant Membership Demoralization Within the GDs.

We cannot lose sight of the fact that the GDs are the single largest centralized authoritarian formal organizational gang structure in the United States today, having 30,000 members in the Chicago area alone. One projected long-term impact of Operation Headache (and we are willing to assume that Hoover will be convicted and he will receive a life sentence to federal custody) is therefore the significant demoralization within the GD membership apparatus. The message sent to the other GD's after nearly a quarter of a century of a reign of terror is that their leaders are not invincible. Their gang leaders will no longer be able to call by phone to provide long speeches broadcast over a P.A. system to annual gang picnics, as Hoover was able to do in the past. For example, at the 1993 picnic on a private farm in Kankakee, Illinois with nearly 10,000 GD's and sympathizers listening, Hoover was able to provide an inspirational speech to the crowd from behind bars, calling over the phone to a public address system.

Any leadership succession in the GD's is likely to be a violent struggle over coveted positions of power. Thus, significant demoralization will occur over the next three years would be a prediction for the GD's here.

2. Significant Organizational Destabilization.

We must recognize that the GDs have grown over the last twenty years into a formidable crime threat. This is a threat not just to Chicago, not just to the State of Illinois, but to many midwestern cities, indeed GD activity is now known to exist in about 35 states. Over the years, with millions in illegal income, with attorneys, with training seminars for the gang's middle management, with forays into political life --- this gang has proven its ability to undermine and corrupt existing democratic structures. So one long-term impact of Operation Headache is that it will basically dismantle that leadership infrastructure of the GDs.

Hoover will now be effectively neutralized as a hands-on micro-manager of his gang empire. He will not be able to continue to run his gang from behind bars. Once he receives a life sentence he will be serving time in federal prison. The Federal Bureau of Prisons, unlike many state correctional systems, does not tolerate such machinations. While in state prison Hoover lived a life of luxury, he could have access to the phone anytime, and call a number on the outside that basically amounted to a "bulletin board" conference, where he could have a phone teleconference with gang leaders on the outside and in all other prison environments. While in state custody, he was able to sponsor "parties" in his correctional center to impress other inmates and staff. Hoover's power will no longer be so freely exercised from federal custody. Thus, Hoover will regret having such a centralized authoritarian structure, and without his ongoing control it can be expected that significant organizational destabilization will occur in the GD organization. It could fractionate into smaller units, it could become more decentralized, its "sets" could become more autonomous, and thus the GD organization will be significantly disrupted over time is the prediction here.

3. Substantial Collateral Impact.

That the GD's did exercise enormous power and influence seems unquestioned at this point in time. That Hoover was able to continue to orchestrate his gang activities even while serving a murder sentence in a state correctional system is also a matter of historical record. Thus, with the effective federal prosecution of Hoover and many other GD leaders, the astute gang analyst will also realize that the greater the gang threat, the greater the positive collateral impact from a law enforcement point of view. What this means is that with Hoover effectively neutralized, GD members who may have wanted to defect, who may have wanted to "flip" or snitch, will now feel more comfortable in cooperating with investigators.

Secondary positive impact could therefore in-volve other informants coming forward, as GD members may face the risk/benefit situation of facing greater costs of staying in the gang than trying to get out. Those GD members who had hero-worshipped Hoover, who may have wanted to erect a statue of Hoover, will now realize he is gone from public life and he will experience the civil death that the penal sanction in America is supposed to induce. In state custody, Hoover was able to create the myth that he was a legendary leader: he was not out on the gang line everyday, they are the ones making mistakes, not Hoover, so if something went wrong it was never Hoover's fault, it was someone else's.

Current research on gangs throughout the United States (see Project GANGECON, 1995, National Gang Crime Research Center) indicates that about one-third of all gang members, regardless of the nature of their gang, would "flip" or "snitch" given the right conditions. Such conditions are now ripe for the GDs.

It is important to understand that many types of crimes for which no statute of limitation exists (murder, homicide, arson, etc), can be traced to gangs like the GDs. It seems reasonable to expect substantial collateral impact in this regard in the future. Other GD crimes such as homicides will now be able to be solved and effectively prosecuted, as potential informants will feel safer to provide testimony, knowing that Hoover is locked up in supermaximum "no human contact" status in the new federal Alcatraz in Colorado.

4. Strong Deterrent Effect.

From a long-term impact perspective, we should expect a strong deterrent effect from Operation Headache. Again, the logic is as historical as the presumed negative short-term effect discussed earlier. Recall the federal prosecution of the top leadership of the El Rukn gang, where the straw that broke the camels back of public outcry was the fact that here was a gang that had sought to commit acts of terrorism "for hire" for hostile foreign terrorist organizations. What message got sent to other American gangs by the rapid dismantling of the El Rukns? The deterrent effect seems to have been effective in preventing hostile foreign and domestic terrorist organizations from manipulating ideal groups for such operations: gangs. We have not seen subsequent examples of major gangs becoming involved in political terrorism since the effective prosecution of Jeff Fort and his El Rukn gang back in the 1980's.

So the message sent to other gangs in the United States today is also very clear from Operation Headache: it can be risky business to try to achieve the status of being a supergang, for the moment one becomes the largest gang in the USA, the leaders are the first to be targeted for federal prosecution. It may therefore achieve the deterrent effect of forcing gangs into a more localized, less formalized style of organizational apparatus. Some shift from the vertical and formally organized style of gang organization to the more horizontal and loose knit style of organization could occur. This effectively reduces the gang threat as well. Why? Because the greater the organizational sophistication of a gang, the greater its objective crime threat.

Therefore it seems reasonable to expect a kind of lasting deterrent effect in the case of the GDs. Gang leaders throughout the United States who may have lusted for Hoover's status may now modify their lofty aims. For gang leaders will realize that the moment they "profile" in this way, they could be facing the same fate as Jeff Fort, John Gotti, and now hopefully Larry Hoover --- a life behind bars in no human contact status.

5. Restored Public Confidence in Law Enforcement.

Whether it was Al Capone, John Gotti, Jeff Fort, or now Larry Hoover, when a criminal organization is able to effectively operate over time in any community that same community experiences a decay in respect for the law. The fact that successful federal prosecution neutralizes such powerful crime figures is therefore also a factor that over time can be expected to restore public confidence in law enforcement. This is also a long-term prediction for Operation Headache.

Community support for anti-gang initiatives could be expected to rise with the effective neutralization of the largest gang in the United States. Community fear could be transformed into community mobilization against gangs. In Chicago neighborhoods where the GDs had operated for nearly a quarter of a century, the news of the 39 GD leaders being indicted by the federal government was equivalent to a kind of quiet individualized "D-day" celebration. Many prayers had been answered by victims of gang crime and gang violence. Those who celebrated the most with the news of the federal indictments in Operation Headache were those in communities who felt the daily devastation of GD influence. In many gang-infested communities today gangs like the GDs have successfully prevented millions of citizens from stepping forward to provide the eyes and ears necessary for law enforcement to successfully target the gang menace today. It is a matter of pervasive fear itself. So by alleviating that fear, we can extrapolate a long term positive benefit. This is true because gang tenure varies directly with the amount of fear the same gang can induce in a community. By reducing that fear, we believe the stranglehold of gangs on some communities can be broken.

DID OTHER GANGS BENEFIT FROM A SHORT-TERM IMPACT OF THE FEDERAL PROSECUTION OF THE GDs?

Yes, we believe that did occur, it is similar to the "displacement effect" in community policing. In community policing, where one geographical area "tightens up" and begins "zero-tolerance" campaigns to arrest for certain offenses, neighboring communities without this level of "target hardening" become the primary choice for offenders to move their business to, they set up shop in neighboring territories where there are similar opportunities but without the risks of arrest. Thus, when the GDs where prosecuted, we anticipated correctly that gangs like the BPSN and the BGs (New Breed, AKA "Braids") would benefit, and they have by some reports increased their operations in some regards. But another gang, we did not originally predict would benefit, actually did: the Latin Kings. In some jurisdictions, the Latin Kings have come to be the dominant threat group.

DID THE FEDERAL PROSECUTION ACHIEVE SIGNIFICANT MEMBERSHIP DEMORALIZATION WITHIN THE GD MEMBERSHIP?

We believe the follow-up evidence supports the conclusion that significant demoralization did pervade the GD membership. The evidence for this consists of (1) reluctance of GD members to take positions of authority any longer for fear of becoming a target of federal prosecution, (2) GD members defecting from their gang, joining other gangs, in both adult and juvenile correctional institutions in states that are geographical contiguous with Illinois, and (3) the actual defection of some high-level leaders inside the Illinois GD gang operation who have basically "dropped their flag" (or become informants).

Perhaps the most demoralizing effect of the federal prosecution of the GDs was the fact that numerous witnesses stepped forward to testify against the GD leadership. The federal government had an abundance of informants and GD members willing to testify. Snitches? Sure, but there is no honor in gangs today. The best estimate is that one out of three gang members in America would rat on their homies in a New York minute, if they had the proper motivation to do so (i.e., un-indicted co-conspirator, charges dropped, plea agreement, etc).

One of the professors who testified for Larry Hoover's release came to an NGCRC party ("wine and cheese reception" for gang researchers) at a national criminology meeting shortly before Hoover's trial. The professor was spotted immediately and I approached him, in order to have him photographed. He told me he was certain there would be only one or two informants at best and no one would be able to link Larry Hoover to any drug dealing. How wrong he was! And the GD gang realized, afterwards, the same cruel fact of life: it is hard being a Gangster Disciple when there are so many snitches in the organization.

DID THE FEDERAL PROSECUTION ACHIEVE SIGNIFICANT ORGANIZATIONAL DESTABILIZATION OF THE GDs?

We think yes. Certainly, one of the predictions was that the GD gang would become more decentralized without the "hands-on" micro-management of Larry Hoover, and that prediction seems to have been borne out since his conviction. The fact that in some areas within driving distance of Chicago we have seen the GDs "fractionate" into competing cliques is also evidence of this organizational destabilization. As well, we can point to the oral interview information from active and former GDs who tell the story same story that many GD "sets" today are "out for themselves". To the extent that there are relatively autonomous GD "sets" operating today is evidence of what would be unthinkable prior to Hoover's conviction: these "sets" would have been targeted by the central GD leadership for ruthless treatment, for being "renegade" GD factions. Leaders of such renegade factions would be ruthlessly executed. Today, almost anyone anywhere can claim they have a GD faction up and going as a gang operation and there really is no stable or verifiable central organization anymore to "check them out". For this reason astute gang specialists are aware of the fact that there exist in areas far away from Chicago, the epicenter of the GD gang, gangs that call themselves "GDs" but their symbols and their written materials they use bear little to no resemblance to the authentic gang materials from the original Chicago-based GD gang operation. In otherwords, one by-product of the GD prosecution has been that it enabled such "emulator" versions of the GDs to arise and function outside of the Chicago area. These persons running these autonomous GD operations know there is little likelihood of facing an "inspector" from Chicago headquarters.

One clear-cut piece of evidence of significant organizational destabilization is that we have searched and searched for new and recent "memo's" from Larry Hoover, or the Chairman, to their troops in recent years. The GD members themselves are probably as relieved as we are that these memo's have virtually disappeared since the federal prosecution.

Let us quote from one GD who gave us this statement:

"Because the feds stepped in, you have more people reluctant to step up and take leadership positions in the GD organization. The feds have these new laws and so people are reluctant to take on leadership roles."

Similarly the following GD quotation is compatible with this assessment:

"You still have some people who don't care, and those people would be leaders if they could work it out. You have people still associated with the organization who like me have been involved for a long long time, but they are not operating under one focus anymore".

THE PREDICTED EFFECT OF SUBSTANTIAL COLLATERAL IMPACT

The original prediction assumed that there would be secondary benefits to the GD prosecution. One clear-cut type of evidence in support of this premise is the "get tough" policy that was implemented after Larry Hoover's conviction inside Illinois prisons. Things have changed quite dramatically inside Illinois prisons with regard to gang activities. The evidence for this seems overwhelming, and is a major credit to the administration of the IDOC. Certainly, the GDs were the single most formidable gang organization that IDOC had to deal with, and the federal prosecution made it easier to "crack down" on gang activities. Add to this the one "wild card" of the infamous "Speck tapes" that produced national negative publicity for IDOC, and combined, we see that the impetus was there for IDOC to initiate major policy changes making it harder for gangs to operate they way they did in the past.

It may very well be that a lot of the GDs who witnessed the rise and fall of their esteemed leader, Larry Hoover, realize today that his preference for the "limelight" was his ultimate downfall. We may therefore see a more subdued GD organization in the future, one that does not intentionally "bring on heat" to the same organization in the same way that the ineffective leadership of Larry Hoover did for his gang: bringing it into the national spotlight, and thus also into the "sights" of federal prosecutors.

THE EVIDENCE OF A STRONG DETERRENT EFFECT

It is safe to say that a strong deterrent effect has been achieved with the federal prosecution of the GDs. This would not have been possible alone, but after the GD prosecution, the U.S. Attorney for the Northern District of Illinois also went after the north and south side factions of the Latin Kings, scoring huge take downs. The U.S. Attorney also effectively targeted the Black Disciples. Thus, subsequent gang prosecutions along with the original GD prosecution, have tended to substantially increase the cost faced by gang leaders in Chicago today.

Gangs will always operate in Chicago. Gangs have probably always operated, to some extent, in Chicago. But the evidence suggests a major curtailment of conspicuous gang operations since the GD prosecution. Obviously, the Chicago Police Department must take some of the credit for this, being able to strategically target various gang operations on a citywide basis.

But missing today are the large-scale gang picnics of the GDs and their massive protests in Chicago's loop. These just seem to have disappeared after the federal conviction of Larry Hoover. Disappearing from the Chicago media circuit, as well, have been some of the notorious "spokespersons" for the GDs that had previously become regular items in the print and electronic media. Their story is "gone now". And most importantly, their credibility is gone now. We still see some of them craning their heads and necks toward the cameras at police brutality or excessive force social protests, but their ability to draw a "news conference" is gone today.

THE EVIDENCE OF RESTORED PUBLIC CONFIDENCE IN LAW ENFORCEMENT

This seems the easiest, but may be the hardest to ever prove. The reason is the fact that no one tracks attitudinal measures of "respect for the law" as an ongoing, cyclical, or periodical measurement of the effectiveness of law enforcement, or simply put a measure of confidence in law enforcement. It is reasonable to assume that the fear of gangs has not subsided in places like Chicago. The best we can do on this type of prediction is say that Chicago appears to be headed in the right direction.

ADDITIONAL SPECIFIC FINDINGS ABOUT THE IMPACT OF THE GD PROSECUTION

Some definite areas of prosecutorial impact appeared from the interviews conducted for this assessment. Some remarkable effects appear to have been generated from this federal gang prosecution. These effects include: (1) the reluctance of some GDs today to want to fill leadership positions, (2) defection from leadership positions in the GD gang, (3) the movement towards decentralization and competition within the GD gang for the drug sale operations, (4) the GDs are losing their foothold in traditional areas of domination even though a lot of them still exist and still control other areas of Chicago, (5) some rival gangs think the GDs are getting weaker, (6) impact outside of the Chicago area appears positive as well, including inside juvenile and adult correctional institutions, (7) one jurisdiction near Chicago is reporting a "splintering" effect among the local GDs, where they now compete with each other on a more localized level, (8) Larry Hoover's power base has certainly eroded and an incapacitation effect is evident now that he is in federal custody and no longer able to spend all day visiting and communicating to his troops on the phone, (9) the political activism of

the GD gang has all but lost its steam and their front groups are no longer able to hold routine "press conferences" as they did in the past, and (10) it would appear that even inside the Illinois adult correctional system (I.D.O.C.) that the "zero-tolerance" approach to gangs has finally been implemented, making it hard for any gang to carry on business as usual, or at least compared to the past.

These effects are described below in greater detail.

RELUCTANCE OF SOME GANGSTER DISCIPLES TODAY TO WANT TO FILL LEADERSHIP POSITIONS

Several sources indicated the tendency today, among members of the Gangster Disciples, where members of this gang are very reluctant to fill leadership positions. In its heyday, it could be assumed that the opportunity to rise in the gang organization was more attractive. Today, several sources suggest quite the obverse: that some members do not want to step into the shoes of a leader and the reason is readily apparent.

The reason why some members of the Gangster Disciples are reluctant to accept a leadership position has to do with their perception that they would then be a target of prosecutors. This can be illustrated in the following quotation from a GD interviewed for this article:

"A lot of people don't want no functions no more, they are afraid of being snatched up".
Let us try to translate what this GD member is saying. By reference to "functions", he is saying that people in his gang do not want leadership positions (i.e., functions). The specific reason for this reluctance to assume vacant leadership positions is that they might be "snatched up" (i.e., investigated, targeted, and prosecuted).

DEFECTION FROM LEADERSHIP POSITIONS INSIDE THE GD's

This is a clear-cut example of the demoralization of middle management leadership within the GDs, clearly attributable to the federal prosecution, and resulting in a very high ranking member going "inactive". The subject is a 33-year-old African-American male, currently confined in an Illinois Department of Corrections facility in Centralia, Illinois. During the period from 1992 until 1995 he held the rank of "Institutional Coordinator" for the GDs at the Pontiac prison facility in Illinois. He is a good example of high level defection from the GDs attributable to the federal prosecution initiative. We thank him for sharing his extension collection of the GD memo's quoted earlier in this article.

Even after the federal prosecution, he reports that the GD operations in Illinois prisons still operated the same as before. Basically this meant that on a weekly basis written reports flowed up the chain of command from lower level leaders to persons like himself, and then directly to Larry Hoover in some condensed or verbal format on major topics of concern. Such weekly reports include who the members are in the gang, which members got violations, etc. In otherwords, the assessment from this subject is very consistent with that from others in the gang and from rival gang members in custody in Illinois. It seems that the GDs are still functioning, behind bars at least, like they have always functioned in the past.

There appear to have been a combination of factors that account for the defection of this subject from a top leadership position in the GDs. Most important was his increased alienation from the gang due to the sense he had been developing that it really was "all about money" and that in spite of his efforts and service to the gang, he was not getting what he felt was his "fair share". We can add to the factors leading to defection is age, at 33 perhaps he was ready to "mature out" or "age out" or "burn out" of the gang. We can add to the factors his fear of getting another "beef" while in custody. And it seems we can add the factor, in his case, that he did experience some cognition that the federal prosecution was sending a message to GD leaders like himself: he might be a target himself of federal prosecution.

So in 1997 he dropped his flag and now he just wants to get out of prison. He went "inactive" in the gang. He did not have to take a "violation" to do this. He explained that he just wanted to "step down" from his position in the gang, he needed to "chill out" to be able to get released from prison.

ARE GANGSTER DISCIPLES STILL INVOLVED IN DRUGS?

Yes, of course. Simply removing the top leadership did nothing to dismantle a large organization that has existed for years with its role in the underground economy being primarily that of drug sales. It seems fundamentally clear, from the interviews conducted for this assessment, that not much has changed in regard to the membership of the Gangster Disciple gang and their involvement in illegal drug sales. The issue that cannot be addressed here is a more quantifiable issue that does not have any know evaluation data source: to what extent has the market share, previously dominated by members of the Gangster Disciple gang, increased or decreased since the federal prosecution? This issue cannot be addressed here for the aforementioned reason.

One thing that has apparently happened, however, is that in some cases a previously cohesive and centralized gang organization called the "GD's", now may function as a network of independent players, still using their GD clothing and "props", but func-

tioning in relative autonomy from a centralized gang organization. In some jurisdictions the GD's have split into separate factions, to maximize the local profit from drug selling.

TURF CONTROLLED BY THE G.D.'s: NOT MUCH CHANGE

The GDs are still associated with Chicago's southside, even though there are chapters or factions that exist in other neighborhoods (i.e., Northside, etc). Basically, rival gang members still fear going into GD controlled neighborhoods on Chicago's southside. The evidence that GDs have lost much "territory" does not emerge from interviews with current and former GDs and other rival gang members.

One rival gang member did describe how the GDs had lost some territory or turf. The specific location of the turf that was formerly controlled by the GDs which is now controlled by another rival gang was described by one informant as being located at Roosevelt and Racine. This area is now controlled by BGs (i.e., Black Gangsters, AKA "New Breed", AKA "Braids").

The GDs are still "up and down" State Street and they are still "deep" as they would say, that is "very strong" in numbers, in their mother-chapter area of Englewood. Regarding their foothold along State Street, in the Robert Taylor homes, however, some of these buildings where the GDs were strong are now scheduled for demolition.

VIEWS FROM RIVAL GANGS ABOUT HOW THE GDs ARE DOING TODAY

Vice Lords ride under the five-pointed star, they are classified as a "People" gang, and often themselves use the term "Brothers" interchangeably with the designation "People" to describe their gang alliance system. Vice Lords have always been a rival gang for the Gangster Disciples. The one advantage in talking to rival gangs is that they are less reluctant to "give up information" when the information solicited is about their opposition. Here is what one Conservative Vice Lord said about the GDs:

"I'm a Vice Lord...a former 5-Star Malik...but I've got some family members who are Gangster Disciples. The Gangster Disciples are still strong in the prison system, they have the numbers in the prison system. On the street, I believe the Gangster Disciples are getting a little weaker, because so many of them are getting locked up for their gang-banging, killing each other."

There are several factions of the Vice Lords: Conservative Vice Lords, Travelling Vice Lords, Mafia Insane Vice Lords, Unknown Vice Lords, etc. The following view about the Gangster Disciples comes from a member of the Travelling Vice Lords:

"Ain't nothing changed with the GDs, their

still the same to me. I am always running into them. They are always flagging. Larry Hoover may be in federal prison, but he is still talking to people."

HAS LARRY HOOVER LOST POWER IN THE GANGSTER DISCIPLES?

Larry Hoover is still "honored" in his gang, the Gangster Disciples. Obviously, being in federal custody has curtailed his ability to micromanage gang operations. The best way to describe the GDs today is that they are kind of a "new society", somewhat on their own, facing the situation where they will in all likelihood never be able to communicate directly with their top leader. New leaders could emerge, and some say are emerging, from a crippled gang organization like the GDs.

There are mixed results in terms of whether Larry Hoover is still calling the shots for the GDs. Some say that in spite of being in a high security federal prison, that information still gets to him, and that he still makes decisions for the gang. Some say that his power has faded given the certain fact that he can no longer micro-manage the gang in a "hands-on" free-wheeling fashion. In as much as Larry Hoover has always been able to "appoint" his henchmen in the gang to positions of leadership, it is reasonable to expect that more than some duties and assignments had to be delegated given his federal conviction. But even here, the issue is the extent to which such appointees would truly be loyal to Larry Hoover or would they, like others in similar circumstances, simply pilfer from the proverbial gang till and amass their own private power structure in the gang?

Simply inducing such disorganization and disarray into a highly centralized gang like the GDs is a prosecutorial accomplishment and a measure of the effectiveness of the prosecution itself.

IMPACT OUTSIDE OF THE CHICAGO-AREA

The impact of the federal prosecution outside of the Chicago area, which is the epicenter for the Gangster Disciples gang, appears to support the original prediction (see Journal of Gang Research, Volume 3, Number 1). Confidential information from a neighboring adult state corrections agency revealed that the single largest number of gang inmates "defecting" from their gang are in fact inmates who had previously been members of the Gangster Disciples. Data at a local law enforcement level in the same neighboring state suggests, similarly, some "fractionation" is occurring in the GD gang: some type of decentralization and autonomy now characterizes "chapters" or "factions" of the GD gang. They may improvise on the traditional codes and constitutional by-laws, etc, of the GD gang, and basically "do their own thing". This development is similar to how easy it is for a "Crip" or "Blood" gang to form: no one

questions their right to use the name in a localized branch of the gang. Previously, it might have been possible for members of the GD gang to enforce local edicts and require "tribute" from local chapters of the GD gang.

So there does appear to be one very positive result of the federal prosecution of the GDs that was not anticipated in the original prediction made in this journal: in the neighboring state, the successful federal prosecution provided a "face shaving mechanism" for GDs who were prison inmates to "renounce" their gang and give up "gangbanging". The present author is therefore grateful to an adult corrections gang specialist in the neighboring state for this incredible insight. It would strongly suggest that a formal impact assessment consider this unique aspect of gang suppression in future studies.

SIMILAR DEFECTIONS OCCURRED IN A SECOND NEIGHBORING STATE IN THE JUVENILE CORRECTIONAL POPULATION

In a second neighboring state outside of Illinois, a gang specialist who works in that state's largest juvenile correctional institution provided a story that was nearly identical to what had happened in a state adult facility previously discussed above. Immediately following the successful prosecution of the GDs, in this particular juvenile institution, large numbers of GD members "flipped" or "switched" their allegiances, and joined other gangs. Some joined the Vice Lords, their historical rival and enemy gang! Remember the Vice Lords are a People or Brother gang alliance system, riding under the "five pointed star"; while the GDs were a "Folks" gang alliance system, riding under the six pointed star. Some GDs joined gangs other than the Vice Lords, but the important thing to note here is that many dropped the GD flag in order to affiliate with a gang other than the GDs.

Asked how this process worked, the gang specialist in the juvenile institution reported that "these kids are very impressionable to begin with", thus, when other gang members in the facility became aware of Larry Hoover's downfall, these other gangs would verbally harass and castigate the existing GD members to the effect "your king is gone now". This had a major effect on GD members in the juvenile correctional population. Many simply thought their enterprise was now defunct, and they "jumped ship", joining other gangs almost immediately.

SPLINTERING EFFECT OF GD's IN AURORA

Aurora, Illinois is located about an hour's drive southwest of Chicago, and is therefore in the immediate vicinity in terms of a "ripple effect" for gang impact. The report from one Gang Crime Specialist in Aurora tends to suggest that immediately following the federal prosecution of the GDs, a "splintering effect" occurred within the GD gang in Aurora. Basically, after the prosecution the GDs in Aurora split into five separate factions. That is, the GD population in Aurora decentralized itself to the neighborhood level. They still sell drugs. But now the five separate factions of the GDs are "out for themselves", they will fight each other if necessary in order to continue their focus on selling drugs. The loyalty to a centralized organizational GD structure has all but disappeared, leaving behind several fragmented and much less cohesive units of what was formerly a highly structured and centralized gang organization.

SPECIFIC DETERRENCE FUNCTION: DISINCENTIVE FOR BEING A G.D. LEADER

The federal prosecution of the GDs appears to have achieved a specific deterrence function by communicating a clear disincentive for being a gang leader in this particular gang. Offenders know that when Larry Hoover received a federal life-sentence, a life-sentence in the federal system really means "life", unlike many state systems of sentencing where persons can be eligible for parole after so many years even with a life sentence. The highly effective federal prosecution of the GDs sent a message to society that it does not pay to be involved in gangs, thus deterring others from such criminal gang involvement. But additionally it also sent a message to the larger membership base of the GD organization itself. And that message appears to be: if you want to be a GD leader, then the government will go after you.

HOW ABOUT THE POLITICAL ACTIVISM OF THE GD's IN CHICAGO?

As a necessary clarification, let it be made clear here that in no way can the GD involvement in politics be construed as legitimate political participation in their society. They were out to achieve one thing: obscure the criminal activities of their gang by conspicuously cloaking some of their activities in so-called political events. This included protests, voter registration, and slating their own candidates for local political office.

Recall that it was Larry Hoover's "defense strategy" to claim he was being prosecuted because he had his gang turned into a political machine which the status quo was threatened by. We must obviously reject such lunacy. Larry Hoover is no more a political prisoner than a common burglar or typical rapist is a political prisoner. For Larry Hoover and the GDs, political involvement was a public relations gimmick for the gang. Other gangs today fit this same profile: it is a way for them to operate in some communities by claiming they are a political group

or that they are in some strange ways a "liberation" group, or like the Neta's they may claim to have the aim to "free" the "country" of Puerto Rico from American imperialist domination.

On the political front, there are mixed results from the evidence of the impact of the federal prosecution. But let us review the good news first. There appear to be four areas in which some clear impact may have been achieved.

First, it appears that the GDs are no longer able to generate as large of a mass of juvenile and young adult GD members for their protests and activities.

Secondly, the GDs through their political front groups, including "21st Century V.O.T.E." have not been able to maintain the momentum they had during the time frame shortly before and during the federal prosecution of the GDs.

Thirdly, few today would be able to be "conned" or "snowed" into thinking that the GDs are genuinely concerned about "Growth" and "Development" for their communities. Most people today know that was a scam operation, and it is unlikely that some of the abuses of the past could be easily repeated (i.e., using a Chicago Public High school for a gang leader awards ceremony such as occurred during October, 1993).

Fourth, the GDs are not able to pull together large-scale massive picnics as they did in the past; one at a park in Starved Rock, Illinois drawing 5,000 in 1992; the one on a private farm in Kankakee County, Illinois drawing about 10,000 in 1993. Thus, a dampening effect on large scale public or semi-public operations seems to have been achieved.

Having mentioned four different examples suggestive of some deflation of the political activism of the GD gang, it must also be mentioned that there is evidence of continuing GD political involvement. One of the latest developments concerns how GDs have been trying to keep the City of Chicago from demolishing certain highrises in the "projects", the Chicago Housing Authority, particularly in geographical areas where they have historically been very strong: i.e., the Robert Taylor Homes on Chicago's southside, just east of the Dan Ryan Expressway. One Chicago Gang Specialist recently reported that the GDs were trying to force CHA into turning the buildings over to them to run their "school" or community enterprises. This has not been verified, but what is a matter of public record is that some families in these same public housing complexes have refused to move out in spite of concessions made by CHA for relocation (i.e., paid moving expenses, etc).

In summation, it would appear that there is still a lingering political capability within the Chicago-based GD gang; but most of the wind has been taken out of its sail would also be the assessment of this author.

THE SPECK TAPE

The infamous "Speck Tape" is a homemade VHS video program featuring Richard Speck doing drugs and having sex with another inmate while in an Illinois prison. There is much significance to the "Speck Tape" for this assessment of the GD prosecution. First, the release of the Speck tape came during the time period of the GD prosecution. Secondly, Speck himself was under the protection of the GDs while in prison. And, now thirdly, as has been speculated for some time in gang specialist circles, the GDs appear to have played a role in the production of that very same tape.

Here is what a former institutional coordinator for the GDs told us in late 1999, when we interviewed him for purposes of this follow-up study:

"Speck paid his way through prison life...by the GDs being the largest and most serious gang in the prison system at that time, he paid for protection, he kind of stood out, he would pay by cash and sex, moving drugs for the GDs and things of that nature."

Additionally, this former leader of the GDs inside the Illinois prison system remarked that:

"I heard the theory that Larry Hoover had the tape made, but I think some people under him actually had the tape made. For some reason or another they made it for their own personal gain and it was used against them in the long run. I think the tape was being used against the IDOC and in turn it eventually backfired, not only against the GDs but all gangs operating inside IDOC."

As he explained, the Speck tape led to a "crackdown" on gangs in the Illinois Department of Corrections:

"When the tapes came out of Richard Speck, that made a big difference, then the system changed fast. The IDOC officials have changed things dramatically, no more walking in groups, things are much more restricted now, and the prison officials will use more disciplinary procedures against gang members today than they did before the tapes."

Could the Speck tape have been made by one of the "programs" of the GD organization as a way to shake-down or extort IDOC officials into giving Larry Hoover special treatment? Could it be behind the transfer of Larry Hoover to a minimum security facility? We do not know. These are speculative issues without any substantiation.

HAS LARRY HOOVER'S POWER AND AUTHORITY OVER THE GANG BEEN DIMINISHED?

Yes, and no, again a kind of mixed set of findings on this aspect of the follow-up story regarding the prosecution of the GDs. Some say it has had a substantial effect in terms of eroding the power of the "Chairman" of the GD organization. Some say that his authority is still unquestioned, and that to a limited extent, he still sets policy for the gang.

Here is what an informant with over 20 years of experience as a Gangster Disciple told us:

"He (Larry Hoover) has left people behind to follow-up on what he is doing. From my standpoint it is not worth it at all, they are going against each other, laws are not being followed that are supposed to be followed, everyone is out for themselves now."

"He (Larry Hoover) had steps in place, chairman and cochairman, and cochair had people under him; now whether people are listening to him, I don't know, but from what I have seen, I doubt it."

The best answer we have is that incapacitation has been achieved for the GD leader Larry Hoover: he is no longer able to remotely control his gang from behind bars now that he is in supermaximum federal prison custody. With a federal life sentence, Larry Hoover has nothing to lose, but he has limited ability to carry out the attention to detailed organizational administration he once had while in the Illinois prison system. His phone privileges have been dramatically curtailed, his visiting and other contacts have been substantially reduced, and he is under the watchful eyes of the Federal Bureau of Prisons which has the ability to detect any attempts at continuing illegal gang operations under his direction. Thus, he and any of his colleagues who want to risk it, do so at great peril.

HOW HAVE THINGS CHANGED INSIDE THE ILLINOIS DEPARTMENT OF CORRECTIONS SINCE THE PROSECUTION OF THE GDs?

The evidence suggests, quite impressively, that a true zero-tolerance policy is now in effect regarding gang activities in the adult state correctional institutions in Illinois. This author was very skeptical when he first heard the reports. But the evidence seems overwhelming, from all possible sources, and most importantly the gang members themselves.

Here is how one GD described the I.D.O.C. in late 1999:

"Things have changed a lot in prison....I've been in 15 years.....the gangs ran the prisons then....now the DOC runs the prisons....back then we all stuck together....things we could do back then we cannot do now.....we could have big meetings on the yard and things of that nature, now you better not get caught with two in a crowd. Back then nobody cared, the prison was like the streets you had drugs money and sex, now you don't have any of that."

Someone recently released from Stateville remarked:

"Back in the old days, you could throw up gang signs, cock your hat to the right, and no problem. Today you can get another year added on to the time you are caught in any kind of gang activity. Back then they did not care if you was throwing up gang signs and stuff like that."

Another inmate told us: "the IDOC has full control of the prison system now...you may have isolated fights now and then, but gangs are not being tolerated in the prison system anymore."

Another similar remark was this: "You had a battle field back in the old days, prior to Speck's tape, all the correctional officers wanted was to get paid for their 8 hours, they didn't care as long as it didn't hurt them; but the Speck tape raised eyebrows, the prison system now is 200 percent different. The gang rivalry is still there, it is always going to be there, but the conflict in the prison system has slowed down."

One GD reported some degree of demoralization among the GDs when Larry was convicted, but qualified it to the following effect: "it's like everybody kind of got over it, ain't nothing they can do about it, but now they are reluctant to step up to leadership because the federal government is involved in it."

Similarly, a GD made the following analogy about the effect of the federal prosecution: "The size of GDs they will always be there, but the way things are going, there are going to be fewer and fewer. Like in the Al Capone days, you will always have some type of organized crime. You will always have different groups. Like the KKK, their organization was strong at one time, but they are in deep cover today, because they know the feds are always going to be after them."

Possible Successor to Larry Hoover:

The issue of gang leadership succession arises if Larry Hoover receives a federal life sentence arising from currently pending federal charges. Who would "take over" the top position in the gang as "Chairman of the Board" in actual continued functions of the gang as an organizational entity? As the current chairman would be functionally "ex-officio" should a harsh federal penal sanction. A high ranking informant in the BGs ("Smitty", AS) was the "celly" or cellmate of Melvin Haywood AKA "Head" or "Fatty". The informant stated that Melvin Haywood may take over the GDs, as he is "next in line".

At the Cabrini Green Public Housing complex in Chicago, after the federal indictment of Larry Hoover, the GD governor for Cabrini was made a board member when he got out of p prison; when he was in the Dixon Correctional Institution, he reported right to Melvin Haywood. Leon Holton "Milkman" is said to be Melvin Haywood's main man.

As one GD told us: "No attempt has ever been made to take over Larry's function. You had a lot of bickering at the time of the Speck tape, people did things in larry's name for their own personal benefit. They never had any loyalty in the first place, it is all about personal gain now, if they can get more by turning to another organization, better money, more drugs, bigger position, they will flip to another organization, people are a scared of the federal government."

SUMMARY OF THE DOWNFALL OF THE GANGSTER DISCIPLE GANG

To a very large extent the rise and fall of the Gangster Disciple gang is a case study in organizational dynamics for a criminal enterprise. First, the gang benefited from the formalization of the gang structure, including detailed memoranda, written rules and regulations, a lengthy "code" and "creed" or constitution, and even the use of a "suggestion box" for its incarcerated members. The increase in the formality of the gang, in terms of its organizational sophistication, certainly helped position it to grow steadily over the years and expand its influence. But this organizational formality and the information that it exposed would also be the ultimate basis for the effective federal prosecution of the gang as a continuing criminal enterprise as well. So while the efforts to make the gang a more complex social organization worked to help build it to be the largest centralized criminal gang in American history, these same efforts would expose the gang and make it vulnerable to prosecution at a later time.

So one lesson to be learned from the GD gang is that the increase in organizational sophistication carries with it the possibility of increased membership and ease of membership management, but this also means a major risk in terms of the vulnerability the gang has when the same information becomes available to investigators. Thus, a criminal organization, to be effective, must be secretive in nature; so a gang that systematically releases information about itself is a gang that opens itself up to investigative scrutiny. The GD gang's feeble attempt to make itself look like something other than a criminal enterprise was obviously ineffective, i.e., hiding behind a cloak of "do-gooderism".

A second major lesson in gang etiology learned from the GD gang has to do with involvement in politics and interaction with the news media. This was a gang that wanted the "limelight" anywhere it could get it. This was a gang that was effective in manipulating politicians and undertaking their own political initiatives. This was a gang that relished the opportunity to talk with news reporters, for they thought they had the ability to manipulate the mass media, and to some extent they did, but more often than not, every time the gang made itself available to reporters, some more damaging insight would appear in a growing scandal of how a gang leader can operate his gang with impunity from behind the walls of a prison and extend the gang influence into the outside communities. This was a gang that wanted to be a form of organized crime, but still functioned as a bunch of streetwise thugs wearing white hats when they tried to "con" the mass media.

The GD's, once they started dealing with the media, made the fatal mistake of trying to "spin" their image as being something other than a gang, laying claim to being about "Growth and Development" for their community. The persons who spoke for the GDs, including Larry Hoover himself, were simply not very gifted "spinmasters". They tried to live two lives in the same shadow: being a criminal gang enterprise, and claiming to be a bunch of "do-gooders". It was inevitable that the gang would attract some hard-hitting journalists who would dig deeper for the real story about the GD gang.

So certain was Larry Hoover that he could pull-off this social construction of portraying his gang as somehow having been transformed into a "do-gooder group", that to a large extent it became his basis for a defense strategy when he went to trial on federal charges. He bargained that if he was portrayed as a political prisoner, that he could sway the hearts and minds of a jury to acquit him. It backfired in a very big way, and in retrospect was exactly the kind of thinly disguised and deceitful posturing and megalomaniacal grandstanding that a prosecutor could benefit from.

The idea that Larry Hoover was being prosecuted because he had transformed his gang into a lawful and politically active community organization was the kind of "sham" and "scam" that any person of normal intelligence could quickly see through. Members of the jury simply did not buy the scam that Larry Hoover was being persecuted by the federal government because he was a major political figure in the African-American community. It was a bizarre and counter-productive defense to the kind of criminal charges he was facing.
Some legal scholars may eventually conclude that it was equivalent to having ineffective legal representation during trial.

POST SCRIPT: WHEN WILL THE MOVIE VERSION BE OUT?

We don't know, but we have heard the rumors to this effect. The NGCRC has not be privy to such developments, but obviously the story of the GD prosecution, the "rise and fall" of the gang, its uncertain, perhaps unpredictable future, make for interesting material for a movie script. We suspect it is a matter of time, and all we can hope for is that the real story gets out. Towards that end, we have gone on record here in presenting the facts about the effect of the federal gang prosecution against the GDs.

The author welcomes comments or observations from all concerned about this issue. Because, obviously as well, we have not yet written the obituary on the GDs. When there is money to be made in the underground economy of Chicago, and elsewhere, no matter how illegal it is, you can probably count on some GDs or someone just like them being involved. And that will always be the case. Gangs cannot be prosecuted out of business completely.

DISCUSSION QUESTIONS:

1. The government knew about Larry Hoover's various "memo's" for a decade before he was finally prosecuted, why do you think it took so long to finally convict him?

2. Describe how a gang that communicates to its members by written memo's has an organizational advantage in some respects, but also faces an incredible disadvantage in terms of prosecutorial vulnerability.

3. Describe how a gang that claims to be a "do-gooder" group has an advantage in terms of public relations, but may also face a disadvantage in terms of drawing investigative attention to itself.

FINDINGS FROM THE 1995 NATIONAL PROSECUTOR'S SURVEY
A Study by the National Gang Crime Research Center

ABSTRACT

There are approximately 4,000 state prosecution offices typically at the county level of government who make up the sampling universe for the present study. Approximately one-fourth of these were randomly selected for a mail questionnaire study. In March, 1995 about 1,000 were therefore sent the survey package and by May, 1995 only ten percent of these agencies (N = 101) had responded to the survey. This was absolutely the lowest response rate the NGCRC has ever achieved from any segment of the American criminal justice system.

The data analyzed here therefore consists of a sample of N = 100 prosecutors from 37 states. Thus, the typical respondent is the State's Attorney for the county.

As with all NGCRC projects, the survey focused on a host of relevant issues in addition to many gang issues.

The size of the agencies varied from the very small to the larger size with over 150 full-time attorneys on staff.

Attorney staff get little gang training, nationwide. Most believe tougher juvenile laws would help combat the gang problem.

Specialized gang prosecution units are very rare (5%), even though two-thirds report some level of a gang problem in their jurisdiction. Violence and drug sales were the most frequent gang crime patterns. Most (70.5%) report gang activity has become more violent in recent years. Few prosecutors (14%) have a strategic plan for dealing with youth gangs.

Many have state-level RICO statutes, but few have undertaken RICO prosecutions against gang members. Even fewer (5.3%) have used forfeiture statutes against gang assets, even though 62.2 percent believe this is an effective prosecution strategy.

Two-thirds believe curfew laws are effective against gang crimes.

Plea bargaining was seen to be somewhat less likely for gang members, and that gang members are less remorseful for their offenses. About half of the prosecutors want more laws that deal with youth gangs. There was not strong support for the idea that gun controls could reduce gang-related crime. There was strong support for trying juveniles as adults as a deterrent to gang crime.

Many believe some gangs like the Crips and Bloods can be considered forms of organized crime.

Two-thirds perceive the gang problem as having increased over the last five year period. Half are optimistic about the ability of their jurisdiction to combat the gang crime problem.

Most of the respondents (81.8%) are elected to office, which we believe was a factor suppressing the response rate to our survey.

Nearly all (90.6%) feel that parents should be held more accountable for the criminal behavior of their children.

Photo: Group of Latin Kings in the prison yard at Stateville
Penitentiary. From the back, and from the left, the second person
standing is Adolpho Matos, an FALN member. Fourth from the left
(in yellow shorts) is Rudy Rangel. Inside the prison system of
Illinois FALN members trained members of the Latin Kings in making
bombs and booby traps.

Chapter 25

GANGS AND ADULT
CORRECTIONAL INSTITUTIONS

INTRODUCTION

The correctional institutions of any society are open systems. As crime patterns change and as criminal prosecution patterns change, such societal output is the new input to corrections. That is, as their incoming prisoner population changes, the jails and prisons also change. As society changes, so does the prison. But maybe not as fast as it needs to. Here we examine a major problem facing all aspects of adult correctional institutions today: the gang problem.[1]

The gang problem, as will be seen, is tied into a number of other larger issues and problems associated with adult correctional institutions. Ultimately it is not the prison walls, the barbed wire, the machine gun turrets and rifle towers, and the threat of legitimate force that keep prisoners from escaping. It is the sense of control by legitimate authority. It is not an easy task. In fact, it is considerably more complex given the magnitude of the gang problem in American corrections as implied by the organizational nature of gangs in the correctional setting. As will be seen, the changing nature of the threat represented by gangs behind bars has meant that the correctional system itself has had to adapt as well: one response has been to seek to develop more secure "super maximum security" facilities for violent gang members who continued to be violent behind bars, such as that at Pelican Bay State Prison in California. Other states like Illinois are also seeking to implement such initia-

tives, with a super maximum prison in Tamms, Illinois scheduled to open in 1996.[2]

This chapter therefore examines a number of issues about gangs behind bars. Recent research on the problem in adult prisons and jails is also summarized.

WHAT GANGS ARE IN PRISON?

All gangs in prison are not simply "prison gangs". The fact is, most gangs are imported into the prison when their members and leaders are successfully prosecuted for major crimes. Most of the gangs that exist in prisons are also gangs that exist outside of the prison, what some simply call "street gangs". There are, however, some unique variations here; particularly where a threat group exists and may function as a gang inside the prison but is not known to exist as such an entity outside of prison. For a long time, many thought the Aryan Brotherhood were simply "prison gang" chapters. In fact, the Aryan Brotherhood does function as a criminal gang outside of the prison context.

In Illinois there are two such examples of gangs that originated in prison and appear only to function in the correctional setting: the Southern Illinois Association (SIA), and the "Northsiders". Both formed as a white extremist reaction against conspicuously organized minority inmates who had their gangs. The SIA was less successful in recruitment

431

and is not considered a major threat today. The "Northsiders", on the other hand, still continues to function by that name in Illinois prisons, but not on the northside streets of Chicago. The "Northsiders" are white extremist inmates, said to be first organized by an inmate named Joseph Ganci in Menard. The "Northsiders" gang appears, then, to fit the profile of the "self-protection" group formation process: it arises in reaction to the perceived threat or fear of other inmates who are organized into such a gang. The correctional setting is an ideal breeding ground for such gang formations.

The answer to the question "what gangs are in prison" is therefore all gangs that commit crimes in the free world whose members are sent to prison; in addition to those that form inside prison as a threat group to counter-act what the members may perceive as a threat from other gangs or gang members that exist inside prison society. That is, gangs can be "imported" into a prison; and they can naturally arise, typically in reaction to the existence of other threat groups or gangs.

IMPORTATION VERSUS INDIGENOUS FORMATION: GANGS BEHIND BARS.

The magnitude of the gang problem was not as bad as it is today, apparently, in the same institutions when Jacobs conducted his famous study of Stateville in the 1970s (Jacobs, 1974; 1977). Did society change, thereby reflecting the same problem in our prison system? Or were gangs targeted for prosecution above the priority of lone "non-gang affiliated" offenders? Importation theory sees subcultures such as gangs arising in the prison system because they have essentially been "imported" into the prison system via their targeted prosecution on the streets. Jacobs (1974, 1977) observed the empirical trend correctly in Illinois: most of the gangs that functioned behind bars were imported into the prison system.

Indigenous formation theory sees the gang arising naturally in response to threat, conflict, or victimization from an existing gang. Most gangs operating in adult correctional institutions would seem to fit the explanation offered by importation theory. Still there are examples known where gangs form in reaction to the obviously organized presence of other threat groups in the prison environment.[3]

The strongest evidence for the indigenous formation theory is that from Fong and his colleagues in research on gangs inside the Texas Department of Corrections (Buentello, Fong, and Vogel, 1991). Eight such gangs which represent most of the problem in the Texas correctional system are said to have basically grown and developed inside the prison. Fong and his colleagues see prison gangs arising in the following indigenous sequence: fearful inmates

enter into a "clique", which can become a "protection group", which can become a "predator group", which ultimately can become a "prison gang".

One gang begets another gang in opposition is the way some gangs form, both inside correctional settings and at the community level outside of the context of confinement. The clique or friendship patterns of group association found in prison life are comparable to those found in any institutional culture, such as the military, where the most common bond is the proximity of ones geographical origin (e.g., "where do you come from?", "where did you live?"). The social factor superceding this "homie factor" is that of racial differentiation in patterns of human interaction, which is of racism and patterns of racial enmity.

There is one major unique situation that must be taken into account in any theory that addresses the etiology of Texas prison gangs: the fact that until the federal courts said to stop it, Texas prisons were basically run by inmates called "Building Tenders" also known unaffectionately as "B.T.'s" by the inmates who they would often beat, and kill if necessary, to maintain order. The B.T.'s were trustees with the authority to administer discipline; and as inmates themselves, the amount of cotton picked by Texas prisoners was directly proportional to the amount of fear that the B.T.'s could induce among the prisoners. Another way of looking at the existence of "BT's" is that they were a state-sponsored "prison gang": the BT's "gang banged" on other inmates at the direction of state prison officials as a method for the control of the inmate population. The relationship between the Texas state government and the inmate "BT's" was basically that of the patron/client relationship often used to describe how corrupt foreign governments become involved with gangs and organized crime groups.

Texas correctional officials using "B.T.'s" was not an isolated instance in American corrections as institutions were being administered similarly in other states. Was it cruel and unusual punishment because it denied due process to inmates? It depends on your perspective. The Texas public probably wanted it that way, the BT system was in effect from the late 1800s to 1982.[4] So the Texas Department of Corrections was not doing anything that was not pretty much an accepted practice in its own state and existed in similar forms elsewhere in the United States. The "B.T. system" is known by other names in other states: the barn boss system, the trustee system, etc, its just that Texas did it in a big way. Did the Texas Department of Corrections stop using B.T.'s when the legislature ordered it to? Yes, of course.

But therein lies the problem. Prison culture --- the prison environment, the prison ethos, the prison organization, the inmate value system --- is hard to change over night. In the Texas prison inmate society the "B.T. system" had existed for a very long time. The essential feature of the B.T. system was cooptation; coopting some of the biggest and meanest inmates to control the other inmates. This process of informally granting disciplinary power to inmates was clearly violating the United Nations standards (1955) on the treatment of prisoners[5], it had just not been brought to the attention in a formal complaint until inmate law suits began to be filed and prison reform activists became involved. The Texas legislature in 1973 revised prison law to the effect of prohibiting the use of B.T.'s[6]. But apparently BT's continued well up until 1982. In 1983 many new correctional officers were hired to take the place of BT's. In 1984 the intelligence unit started to create gang files. In fact, the first few years after the actual end of the BT system is when a gang analysis begins. Before 1983 inmates controlled inmates officially, in roles as building tenders (BT's).

The problem then is that the Texas Department of Corrections was uniquely predisposed to the formation of such power groups, threat groups, or gangs forming indigenously once the B.T. system was abolished. The prisonization process Texas inmates went through was getting used to another inmate called a B.T. who would always get his way, and could have many amenities through the use of force or the threat of force. And what did the B.T.'s do when they were told "sorry guys, thanks for the help, but the feds say we can't use you any more". It is unlikely that all B.T.'s were suddenly paroled or released. The real research question then for any theory of the etiology of gangs in Texas was what role the B.T.'s played in such indigenous gang formation.

Prior to being abolished, the B.T.'s clearly functioned as a "goon squad" for the Texas Department of Corrections. The B.T.'s were, in a real sense, a gang with government approval. The B.T.'s functioned like vigilantes for correctional management; they made things run real smooth, very similar to the way Nazi concentration camps used prisoners to control other prisoners. As Fong and his colleagues report, no official records of "non-fatal stabbings" were kept in the Texas Department of Corrections before 1984 (1991: p. 4). So what we have here is a failure to communicate the scope and extent of violence in everyday life in the Texas correctional environment including such routine stabbings and other life-threatening injuries sustained from assaults. The modern correctional manager knows these kinds of injuries received by inmates are sources of legal liability to the correctional system itself.

**Indigenous Formation:
The C.O.N.S. Group in the 1970's**

The C.O.N.S. formally known as Church of the New Song became a nationwide force in the turbulent period of the early 1970's. They disappeared in the later 1970's. But in their heyday, they had their own outside published newspaper, they routinely filed enormous amounts of law suits against prison administrators, and were generally a pain in the neck for prison personnel. Their declared aim was prison reform within the "prisoners rights movement" which in that historical period was a popular issue.

Once it began in prison, with the help of outside activists willing to publish the newspaper and send copies to inmates everywhere in America, the group spread rapidly.

By the late 1970's, however, the group had disbanded. In later decades the group was thought to be completely defunct. Then in late 1999, a prison in Iowa reported that it had a "white extremist gang" called the C.O.N.S., which used the same name, "Church of the New Song". Basically, this new version of C.O.N.S. is said to be a self-protective type of gang, composed of white inmates. The "white racism" theme is something that could not be said to characterize the original 1970's C.O.N.S. group which was left of center politically. The new 1999 Iowa version of C.O.N.S. appears to be a genuine version of an indigenous formation gang: it started in the prison system. The new 1999 version of C.O.N.S. would qualify as a security threat group and perhaps even as a white racist gang if the reports are true that it is functioning in that capacity. What this new 1999 version of C.O.N.S. did was take a defunct or pre-existing identity and "transform" it to get a new gang/STG up and running inside the prison environment.

THE SCOPE OF THE PROBLEM

Shortly before the Director of the Illinois Department of Corrections transferred to another state agency outside of the field of corrections, he published an interesting account of gangs in the Illinois prison system (Lane, 1989). This article in <u>Corrections Today</u> estimated that "between 80-90 percent of the inmates in the Illinois system have some affiliation with street gangs" (Lane, 1989: p. 99). Implied in this article is that if prison administration is lax or incompetent, then the prison will be de facto "gang administered".[7] That is, the gangs will literally exert such power and influence that they will control the prison, not the warden. Recent reports tend to suggest this is close to being the reality now inside IDOC:

"According to one highly placed source, the gangs control the Stateville tiers and the correctional officers are cowed and intimidated by them. "If the officers refuse to allow friends and relatives to bring contraband into the prison for the inmates the correctional officers are shown that the prisoners possess photographs of their homes, their wives, and children".[8]

Multiple sources same to say the same thing adding greater validity to this story. Correctional officer Lawrence Kush was one of 30 on a gang's hit list at Stateville, these were prison employees who did their job, not taking any crap from the gangs, and not being compromised.[9] Kush was assassinated by the same gang on July 1, 1989. The same gang had warned in a letter this would happen unless the employees "eased up" on gang operations.[10] A level three gang operates as a formidable terrorist group behind bars is what the evidence suggests. The official record indicates correctional officers are being undermined in their work when administrators negotiate with gang leaders under the pretext of avoiding prison riots.

In early June 1994 correctional officers at Pontiac prison in Illinois complained through their union that the prison administrators were making deals with the gangs and demanded more of a zero tolerance approach to gangs. The authority of line correctional officers is systematically undermined when wardens grant special privileges and "discretion" to gang leaders. This 1994 problem is possibly a holdover from a previous administration, as once the gang has been "negotiated with" it is difficult to go back to a zero tolerance approach without inducing much change and population restructuring and staff reassignment. Gang violence is not limited to the maximum security units, but has also spread to the medium and minimum security facilities in Illinois.[11]

The single national survey of corrections regarding gangs reported in our literature is that by Camp and Camp (1985) conducted in 1983[12]. It focused on prison systems (i.e., one prison system per state), the adult component of corrections.[13] It found prison gangs existed in 33 states. State leaders in prison gang membership were Pennsylvania, Illinois and California. Some 29 states reported a combined gang membership of 12,624.[14] There has been no reported update of these statistics since then.[15] And from the prior literature we have no knowledge about the state of juvenile correctional populations.[16] What we do know is that nearly 96 percent of all prison inmates eventually return to society.

The Camp and Camp (1985) study was basically replicated by the American Correctional Association (ACA) with a federal grant from the National Institute of Corrections to conduct a national assessment of gangs in corrections. The ACA report (1993) estimated that only six percent of the American prison inmate population were gang members. This definition of gang members included security threat groups (STG's) like Muslims, or groups of two or more with a bad attitude. This gang density estimate is believed to be notoriously unreliable and more fictional than factual. Simple math helps us here: if only 6 percent of the one million inmates in America are gang members, that means we have a small problem nationwide, only 60,000 gang members behind bars to worry about. California is said to have more than that number alone in its adult system. The California gang density rate is estimated to be comparable to that in its juvenile division (CYA), about 75 percent.

What we also lack is an analysis of the differences, if any, in post-release behavior of such gang-affiliated prison releasees. Do they have higher rates of recidivism? In Illinois, current statistics tend to suggest that two out of every three such released state prisoners will be arrested and/or convicted of a new crime within a two year period. Even conservative criminological doctrines have been less than productive in this area of research, for we do not know if the "burnout hypothesis"[17] is applicable to such gang-affiliated felons.

One of the few quantitative researchers adding to our understanding of the prison gang problem is Fong (1990) who provides a very a detailed analysis of the gangs in the Texas prison system. Fong shows that the largest Texas prison gangs are organized in a military style hierarchy (1990, p. 39). Equally important Fong documents the existence of written gang constitutions in the Texas prison situation (p. 40). Finally, Fong shows that prison gangs do not simply disband when their gang members are released. In fact, quite the contrary there is much continued communication and involvement with the gang in a way that allows the gang to expand its criminal activities (p. 42). In this way, Fong[18] establishes that the gang problem is in fact "exported" to our communities outside of the prison.[19]

Understanding "Gang Density" Behind Bars

This book addresses the matter of the scope and extent of the prison gang problem in much greater detail. The next chapter, for example, provides a wealth of statistical information about gangs in adult corrections. At the heart of this is the issue of "gang density". Gang density refers to the percentage of all inmates who are gang members.

If an institution (jail, prison, halfway house, etc) has 100 inmates, and six of them are gang members, then the gang density for that institution is six percent.

The real issue is what is the best estimate for gang density at the national level. Much rides on the answer to this issue. If the estimate is artificially low, then it could offset efforts to address the gang problem behind bars, by means of diverting serious attention and minimizing the threat potential gangs represent behind bars.

One way this national gang density estimate gets obscured is through politics: the need to deny the gang problem. Gang denial exists in all phases of society, including correctional institutions, communities, schools, etc.

Another way this national gang density estimate gets artificially biased downwards is the use of clever "correctional semantics". That is, some states like California have used the phrase "validated gang members" as opposed to simply "gang members". Let us illustrate the critical importance of this subtle nuance. If such an institution were surveyed, they might reply "3 of our 100 inmates are validated gang members", but all they are really saying here is this (the translation): "there may be many, perhaps as many as 70 of the 100 inmates who were gang members before they came to prison, and still have their gang tattoos, still wear their gang colors, etc, but only 3 of them have been officially identified as leaders involved in ongoing violence in this particular facility" (i.e., they have been "validated").

The failure of some previous researchers to know the difference in reporting mechanisms in states like California has led them to grossly underestimate the scope and extent of the prison gang problem to the point of officially disseminating totally inaccurate information in their government funded research reports.

THE ROLE OF STANDARDS GOVERNING CORRECTIONAL SETTINGS

The existence of policy standards guiding the function and operation of correctional institutions is the essence of the role that the American Correctional Association (ACA) plays in accrediting correctional facilities of all types. Such standards are good. They provide for uniformity, fairness, continuity, and better structure. Standards promulgated by ACA cover virtually every aspect of correctional facilities from the physical plant and security to medical care and inmate grievances.

While gangs are such a critical aspect of correctional life, representing tremendous potential for violence, disruption, and security problems, the American Correctional Association at this point in time requires no standards for dealing with prison gangs. Particularly when it is shown that racial conflict among inmates tends to be a significant co-variate or surrogate measure of the inmate gang problem[20]. Perhaps some topics are taboo. Or perhaps here we see the "community denial" syndrome affecting American corrections as well. Recall that correctional institutions must be "safe and secure" facilities. Definitions of what constitutes cruel and un-

usual punishment evolve constitutionally as does society. So perhaps litigation could induce some change in corrections.[21]

In the 1992 Prison Warden Survey by the National Gang Crime Research Center, it was found that nearly half (52.8%) of the sample felt that the American Correctional Association should in fact establish such standards for controlling prison gangs.

In the absence of policy standards, correctional administrators are essentially in the awkward managerial position of "flying by the seat of their pants" regarding gangs. One might ask, logically, is it okay to group all gang members of one particular gang in one particular section of the institution; or reserve an entire correctional facility for one gang if its membership is large enough? Certainly, that would be the simple way to manage inter-gang violence. But is it really a good idea to segregate gangs? Or should gang members be mainstreamed, mixed in with the rest of the correctional population strictly on the basis of their security level classification?

Should correctional administrators officially recognize their inmate gang leaders and meet with them regularly, even hold "multi-gang conferences", allow them to have "group picnics" in the prison for their own gang members,[22] to work out more amicable relationships between the various gangs in the facility? Or does this official recognition[23] translate as legitimizing the gang as an organization? Could it even be tantamount to a condition of de facto gang administration of the correctional facility?[24]

It is a violation of the United Nations guidelines on the treatment of prisoners to place any inmate in a position of having "disciplinary power" over other inmates[25]. Therefore a correctional administrator cannot in good conscience urge a gang leader to do anything to control other prisoners. It is equal in force to a delegation of power.

Our prison systems have changed with the advent of extensive litigation dating from the 1960s which has created much case law establishing, in effect, prisoner rights. Inmate trustees can no longer be handed a 12 gauge shotgun, a whip, or a billyclub and be told to "restore order" or "keep them convicts in line".[26]

Effective management today means well designed policies and procedures, ongoing staff training, and effective security, all balanced by inmate rights. Therefore, in light of the management problem posed by inmate gangs, there appears only one logical choice. This involves using the law and disciplinary codes to suppress gang crime, gang violence, and gang disturbances within the correctional setting. It should mean no delegation of informal authority to gang leaders and it should mean no official recognition or deference to such influential gang figures.

For to officially recognize the gang leader is equivalent in function to recognizing all other gang members as "prisoners of war", feeding whatever existential notion they may have as being "political prisoners" because of racism, oppression, what have you. This is not to deny that such political prisoners exist, or prisoners of conscience as Amnesty International considers them. But our typical prison gang member is anything other than a educated intellectual or leader who came to the attention of law enforcement through political protest. Perhaps we should distinguish between prisoners with a developed political consciousness and political prisoners. In any case, recognition of gangs can only mean, ultimately, a larger problem of correctional management. And further problems, for society as a whole, when they return to our communities more organized than they were when they entered prison.

Prison should not be an opportunity to expand gang membership and to solidify gang operations outside of the prison context. Poor management is at the heart of any such condition of "de facto" gang control of the correctional facility. As a general rule of thumb, all correctional officers develop a reservoir of "good will" with their inmate charges, but this is done most effectively on an individual basis. Not in a group fashion.

The prison administrator who fosters such a "participatory management" alliance with gang leaders creates only a more difficult problem for correctional line staff. And remember, it is the line staff, the correctional officers, who do most of the most difficult work in corrections. The development of policy, procedures, an overall strategy, and effective staff training is an absolutely first step in even "getting a grip" on the gang problem in corrections today.[27]

"Race Riot At Pelican Bay Prison"

In February of 2000, a race riot erupted between black and Hispanic inmates at Pelican Bay Prison. Pelican Bay Prison, in California, is the place where serious gang members are sent to in the State of California. When the race riot erupted, correctional officers were forced to fire guns at the inmate rioters. One inmate was killed and 13 others were wounded.

This is the kind of racial disturbance that often is also a gang disturbance as well.

Source: Jeff Barnard, "California Inmate Killed in Riot", Feb. 24, 2000, Associated Press.

HOW VARIOUS LEVELS OF A ZERO-TOLERANCE POLICY MIGHT BE USED BEHIND BARS

Based on surveys of adult state correctional institutions, it has been possible to construct a bare minimum model, a medium "tough" model, and a "maximum strength" model for zero tolerance policies regarding gangs/STGs behind bars. These are "ideal types", not necessarily existing in pure form. In practice, institutions combine various elements of these models where practical and feasible.

THE MINIMUM STRENGTH ZERO-TOLERANCE POLICY FOR GANGS BEHIND BARS

The first rule is to be organizationally proactive with regard to gangs and Security Threat Groups (STGs) by having a full-time STG coordinator at every institution for every shift to monitor all gang and STG activity. Too often, the correctional officer assigned to this position is "part-time". Gang activity does not cease at a shift-change, it is an around the clock activity.

The correctional system must be able to identify, monitor, separate, isolate, transfer to maximum security institution, and prosecute where necessary any gang/STG activities using staff trained in gang issues. That means monitoring the mail and phone calls of all suspected or validated or renounced gang/STG members. If necessary displace gang members to different facilities to break up the leadership infrastructure.

It also means having a number of staff trained in gang issues.

THE MEDIUM STRENGTH ZERO-TOLERANCE POLICY FOR GANGS BEHIND BARS

In addition to the capabilities in the minimum policy stated above, the there should be a central state gang unit that all local STG coordinators report to. It should be practiced policy that all gang/STG members are placed in segregation or close-custody if found to be involved in gang/STG activity behind bars. Thereafter have a point system of graduated steps to allow cooperative gang inmates to return to the general population if they "debrief" and renounce their gang affiliation and show no sign of being of threat.

To increase the strength of the zero-tolerance policy requires, foremost, that the institution ensure that all correctional officers have some training in gang identification.

There is something that might be called "gang recidivism" behind bars. It operates when an inmate says he is denouncing his gang, gets released into the general population, and then renews his gang affiliation and a threatening pattern of behavior. In this type of situation, the inmate has "relapsed" back into gang/STG activity behind bars. Thus, most experts advocate that the inmate should be able to "renounce his gang" only once. After that, if subsequent gang involvement becomes detected, the person becomes permanently locked down for the duration of their sentence.

In this formulation, inmates would not be allowed to wear any individualized clothing. They would wear prison uniforms of a neutral color. This system of dress-uniformity would eliminate belts and shoestrings to prevent gang members from using colors to represent their gang affiliation. Remove any trappings of individuality or affiliation; make inmates all look and dress the same. This includes hair cuts.

Photograph all tattoos at the time the inmate first enters the correctional system; and thereafter as needed (when facing disciplinary sanction, investigation, etc).

"New Years 2000: Illinois Gang Leader Inmates Get Big Surprise"

Going into effect about the time of the New Year 2000, in Illinois gang leaders imprisoned at the Tamms Correctional Center were told: become "approvers" (see Sleeman, 18??) or spend the rest of their sentence in harsh super-maximum security conditions. IDOC did not use the term "approvers", IDOC asked the gang leaders to denounce their gang and give up information about their gang's activities. But any reader of Sleeman (18??) would know that is exactly what the "approvers" were in the British model of dealing with the Budhuk gangs of India. One new twist: IDOC would videotape the "denunciation" of their gang. That could come in useful.

Source: Gary Marx, "State Tries to Turn Its Top Gang Inmates: Leaders Offered A Way Out of Harshest Prison - If They Cooperate", Chicago Tribune, Jan. 10, 2000, pp. 1, 14.

THE MAXIMUM STRENGTH ZERO-TOLERANCE POLICY FOR GANGS BEHIND BARS

In addition to the capabilities of both the minimum and medium range models of zero tolerance discussed above, the maximum strength model would add a number of enhancements.

The first rule of this model is to clean house by removing those in administration as well as line-staff correctional officers who refuse to recognize that the gang problem exists and replace them with people who mean business. It also means more training for not just the line staff correctional officers, but all staff: teachers, healthcare, clergy, etc. The STG coordinators or investigators should be funded to attend as many gang training conferences as possible.

They should be developed into gang experts, including taking college/university courses on gang issues.

The second rule is that all active and verified gang members be removed from the general population at the earliest possible opportunity. They should be placed in a Special Housing Unit (isolation). They must be prevented from contaminating other inmates. This also prevents them from recruiting other inmates into the gang.

Third if the gang/STG inmate files a lawsuit, use the Interstate Compact agreement to transfer the inmate to a federal facility.

Fourth, the institution must have developed a new system of rules and regulations for inmates that reflect the reality of the modern gang threat behind bars. There must be disciplinary conduct hearings for even the smallest infraction of rules seeking to suppress gang/STG activity. The idea is to have severe and strict penalties for gang/STG behavior behind bars. This "disciplinary code of conduct" would impose mandatory sanctions against inmates who violate rules of conduct that pertain to gang activity. The "loss of good time" would be one of the possible sanctions that could be imposed against inmates who continue to be gang-involved behind bars.

Isolate even the suspected gang members in administrative segregation or close custody security units.

Ideally, remove by laser methods all inmate tattoos at time of intake into the correctional system. No tattoos would be allowed on any inmate. All communications entering and leaving the facility would be strictly monitored.

All inmates confined in no human contact status as suspected or verified gang members would have military style haircuts to accompany their standard uniform inmate dress modes. No personal clothing of any kind, no religious medallions, no allowances for rolling up a sleeve on the right or left, etc, would be allowed.

They cannot be released from 23-hour lockdown until: they debrief (giving up intelligence information on the gang), sign a form denouncing their gang, and have a videotape made of their gang denunciation for possible use at a later date, including release to the public and the mass media.

FIRST AMENDMENT RIGHTS AND PRISON GANGS

Does the first amendment's clause about "freedom of association" guarantee an inmate's right to hold gang meetings?[28] Or to congregate en masse in what could be viewed as an intimidating crowd? Or when a particular gang virtually "takes over" what was established as a legitimate inmate organization (e.g., Toastmasters, Jaycees, etc, etc,), and begins to operate in such a fashion as to use this, or even a religious occasion, for its gang meetings, is the correctional administrator at risk of violating first amendment rights by shutting down such groups from further activity? These are but some of the issues that need to be examined here. Generally, the need for security and to maintain order tend to override such concerns when there is the genuine threat to correctional discipline and good order.

"What Lengths Will Inmates Go To, In Order To Kill Rival Gang Members Behind Bars?"

No one is sure how long it took, but at the Coffield Unit of the Texas prison system in mid-March of 2000, inmate Antonio Lara was able to kill a rival gang member by sawing the bars off his cell. How did he saw the steel bars off his cell, so he could slip out at night to kill a rival? He used dental floss. He coated it with toothpaste and whatever abrasives he could find (sand, cleaning agents, etc) and took his time painstakingly cutting through the steel bars of his cell.

Once out of his cell he stabbed 41-year-old Roland Rios to death.

That is, running a "safe" correctional institution will tend to justify a number of restrictions. The difference between jails from one county to the next, both contiguous, may be enormous regarding visitation procedures. One may allow contact visits, the other (citing security grounds) may not. In the latter case, if the government agency can show a compelling interest in preserving order and security, it can clearly prohibit such contact visits. The same principle seems to apply to the gang organization situation.

Remember, the Constitution is a living document. Even notions of what constitutes "cruel and unusual" punishment may change as society and its moral standards change. As society changes, so does the prison. Or, more appropriately, so should the prison. But the fundamental policy question facing American corrections today is: what is the best policy for dealing with inmate gangs?

Also, this must be balanced with another constitutional right of prisoners: their right not to live in fear of physical harm. Gangs clearly represent a pervasive threat of physical harm. And those states that have the death penalty routinely have inmates sitting on death row for homicides committed against other inmates in gang conflicts within the prison setting.

This right to live free from fear of physical harm also has implications for the implemented policies in many of our nation's prisons and jails which is called among other things, the "off set" approach to

managing the gang problem. It means screening inmates as they come into the facility for their gang membership. Then inmates are assigned to units where a "balance of power" is established numerically in terms of inmates in the cell-house, unit, etc. Such an approach must be constantly monitored for frequent gang conflict flare ups, and therefore always needs daily "fine tuning" as a gang management method. But essentially, it means keeping two often warring groups in the same living unit.

The major problem with this approach is that it generates new gang members. Someone entering such a unit will have to join one side or the other. Neutrals or "neutrons" as they are called do not fare well. But again, this illustrates the kind of problems that can arise when local administrators are able to make their own decisions on how to handle the gang problem. In a situation where there are no written guidelines or standards promulgated by groups like the American Correctional Association, what happens is the informal process takes over. Then we get such policies as the "off set" method. An enormous variety of such methods that clearly recognize the gang and allow it to claim authority as a group exist.

OUTSIDE GANG RESOURCES SUPPLIED TO INMATE GANG MEMBERS

If Chicago's Latin Kings are representative of how gangs are capable of providing resources for their fellow gang members who are incarcerated, then we must recognize that gangs provide something unique to prison life generally. Gangs provide outside desirable resources, particularly cash, or commissary money. Historically, inmates have been in the situation of having nothing other than their family members to periodically send them "commissary" money to supplement the meager legitimate income they can make in prison. The same applies, in a stronger sense, to those locked up in our local jails; where there is no legitimate source of income that can be earned in the jail, you either have someone on the outside who can provide you with "cigarette" money, or you don't smoke.

Because the information here comes from what should be considered privileged sources, that is a well placed gang member holding office, who was able to provide the weekly minutes from each gang meeting, the specific identity of this particular Latin King gang chapter cannot be revealed.[29] The minutes, however, are hand written, often punctuated with gang insignia, and are considered authentic. They detail dues collection, gang unit accumulation of funds, expenditure of funds for the purchase of handguns, the specific instances of "violation" or giving disciplinary attention to other gang members, and also in some instances reveal a pattern of the local gang unit sending money to some of its members who are in custody. It also details minor expenditures such as "$6.00 was spent on spray paint to fix the hood". Mostly, it detailed a pattern of using dues money in amounts such as $30 to $40 to send to fellow gang inmates who are incarcerated.[30] By the way, after firearms being the major source of gang expenditures, gang apparel (shirts, etc) and gang totems (e.g, emblems for the meeting place, etc) constituted the next highest single item area for expenditures from gang income.

More organized gangs such as the Yakuza also use their dues to pay for basically "gate money" (i.e., post-release spending money) for their members who are released from prison (Kaplan and Dubro, 1986: p. 132).

CORRECTIONAL PROGRAMING FOR THE SOCIAL PSYCHOLOGY OF GANGS

If it is the gang that provides so many inmates under confinement with a sense of identity and a social role, then perhaps correctional programing should focus on inducing role distance. That is, role distance means having a sense of "self" apart from that of one's functional role. To manage a correctional facility with high levels of gang affiliation must necessarily mean struggling against the enormous power of the gang to reinforce individual identity. To provide identity alternatives to the gang is to provide an additional source of social control.

Role distance is not estrangement or alienation in the typical sense. Clearly, at the heart of gang affiliation is the deeper cluster of motives and experiences generally spelling out alienation. Alienation, anger and conflict tend to feed and reinforce gang membership. Therefore, to reduce alienation, anger, and conflict is potentially a logical method of countering the hegemony of the gang in a correctional setting. Conflict resolution is becoming increasingly popular in early childhood education as a primary prevention method for reducing violence.

The problem with the use of inmate organizations such as the Jaycees, Toastmasters, Dale Carnegie courses, and especially ethnic identity and religious "clubs", etc, inside correctional institutions, is that these are typically structured in a voluntaristic fashion. That is, anyone can join. Recognizing that the inmate population represents various gangs that may seek to control or influence these legitimate organizations, often correctional administrators have had no choice, once these officially sponsored meetings turned out to be dominated by specific groups, other than to eliminate them entirely or allow them to continue to operate knowing they are little more than "fronts" for specific gangs, and that realistically such inmate organizations "serve" only members of a specific gang rather than the entire inmate population.

The prison inmate culture portrayed in the 1950s as having the primary orientation of "do you own time" can be expected to disappear with the increased density of gang members in the same inmate population. Looking at this problem by interviewing released prisoners one study (Hunt, Riegel, Morales, and Waldorf, 1993) highlights this problem. It noted that the older "cons" view with some apprehension the arrival of a new "Pepsi generation" of aggressive younger inmate gang members who are basically out to make a reputation for themselves[31]. As the prison system is an open system this changing ethos of the inmate culture should come as no surprise. What it signals is a clear and major problem for correctional management: we are no longer dealing with the "lone offender" who believes in "doing you own time", what we are dealing with when we are facing a critical density of gang members in the inmate population is an entirely different management problem: such gangs represent sub rosa organizations.

THE QUEST FOR DOMINATION AND GANGS

Prison violence provides a unique look at race relations in America. The prison gangs tend to be clearly differentiated along racial and ethnic lines. The conflict pattern is both inter-gang and gang versus non-gang inmates. Regarding racism, prisons are more like steaming cauldrons than peaceful melting pots; it is an enmity that is deep-seated and rests along with a less than pro-social urge for the conquest and domination of others. And here lies one of the biggest challenges to correctional management today: how to reduce or control this enormous potential for violence.

For the social scientist, interested in race relations, this challenge is a natural for a field experiment in changing values and improving race relations.[32] But that has not been a pattern of much correctional research in America. If it is true that in all adversities there is a seed of equal or greater benefit, then the benefit of such controlled racial conflict environments is that they present an enormous opportunity for scholarly research and experimentation on improving the nature of race relations. If it can be effective in a prison, then it can replicated anywhere.

Unfortunately this is not a "hot research area" receiving much in the way of knowledge development reinforcement via government or foundation funding. The critical reader may ask "why"? For example, the American Correctional Association does not require programs regarding the encouragement of better race and ethnic relations within the correctional atmosphere. The Camp and Camp (1985, p. viii) report was quite direct in stating "the phenomenon of racism is fierce inside prisons and gangs usually organize along racial lines".[33] ACA mandates a variety of services and functions for inmates, such as education programs, hygiene, counseling, legal protections, and a host of factors making for a "safer correctional climate", but ACA requires nothing in the area of improving race relations among inmates. In spite of the historical evidence suggesting this pattern of conflict is one of recurring significance for all correctional institutions in America. It is a stunning and most curious situation. Let us hope it changes in the direction of becoming a more rational approach.

The Brotherwoods: An Indigenous Kansas Prison White Racist Gang

Published in the Journal of Gang Research (Vol. 6, No. 3, Spring, 1999), by Kansas DOC gang specialist Roger H. Bonner, was a profile of the rise and fall of the "Brotherwoods" gang. This was a strange gang. Unlike some gangs such as the Aryan Brotherhood that intentionally recruit only the most ruthless and hardcore inmates, who can fight and fight well, this gang called the "Brotherwoods" intentionally sought to organize all the weaker white inmates in the Lansing Correctional Institution in Kansas.

The typical member who would join the "Brotherwoods" was a weaker inmate who himself was subject to be "extorted" for protection from other gangs in the facility. One "leader" adapted some bizarre literature from Odinism to make the group sound like it was a quasi-religion and helped organize the gang. It did quickly get new members. This was a gang that, to show its power, began beating up homosexual inmates.

When the gang began to plan a hostage situation to gain publicity for their new identity, the snitches came forward, and the leaders were quickly rounded up. The gang had a lifespan of only about 2 years. It fizzled out and went defunct in a short period of time.

LAW ENFORCEMENT/CORRECTIONS INTERFACE

With so much in common, dealing with the same offenders, we would expect a higher level of cooperation and interface than currently exists between corrections and law enforcement. In addition to having an "institutional parole officer" what current gang problems suggest is also having an "institutional law enforcement officer". This more systematic interface is justified for several reasons.

First, much crime does occur inside the correctional institution, some of it very serious. Illinois criminal law is no friend here to prosecuting crimes that occur inside the prison. In Illinois, the State's Attorney Office in the county in which the prison is located may be used for criminal prosecution --- but the cost of prosecution must be paid for by the prison system itself.[34] Which is no incentive for criminal prosecution and may mean, ultimately, prosecuting only those more serious offenses such as homicide. Here again is an area of needed federal aid.

Secondly, from a social intelligence point of view correctional institutions are in a unique position to add to our knowledge about gang networks nationwide. As Daniels (1987) recommended, simply sharing information about known gang members could be used in a national computer-based analysis to more effectively manage the problem. Most such gang members do return to our communities. Therefore, is the only legal responsibility of state correctional institutions to notify the local law enforcement agency that a prisoner has been recently released, or should corrections also be required to alert local law enforcement to whether or not this person is still active in the gang?

Thirdly, the Camp and Camp (1985: pp. xiii-xiv) report indicated that about half of the correctional institutions reporting a gang problem had some basis for believing (e.g., informants, law enforcement contacts, etc) that the prison was the site for gang crime planning of major or serious crimes occurring in the outside community. Including, obviously, first degree murder. The prison as a base for criminal activity should be a major concern to law enforcement and a clear justification for providing a more systematic and effective interface with corrections. It is also bi-directional[35], gangs outside of the prison can apparently order "hits" on inmates or institutional staff inside a prison.[36]

Finally, the law enforcement needs cited above are for state and local purposes. As a fourth reason, more developed gangs now have a significant interstate web of influence. States like Iowa have not only gangs hailing from Chicago, Illinois (Vice Lords, Disciples, etc), but also members of the Crips, Bloods, Mexican Mafia, and Aryan Brotherhood.[37] Therefore, there should also be federal law enforcement representation in this interface.

CORRECTIONAL STAFF TRAINING

Not enough is being done to adequately train correctional staff in a competent manner to understand the vital role they play in dealing with the gang problem. Considering the magnitude of the problem there is embarrassingly little being done in terms of training academies for correctional officers. There are, however, some such gang materials that are being used by correctional institutions to train staff. Much of it is locally produced and reflects a clear lack of comprehension of the literature and often has a definite political bias.

THE LIMITS OF BUS THERAPY

Bus therapy, also known as "diesel treatment", is essentially the punitive transfer of a prison inmate from one facility to another.[38] Either in the same correctional system, or to another jurisdiction or state.[39] It was effective in the 1970s with the breakup of a protest/religious group of federal inmates, who under the impetus of a national prisoner's rights movement sought radical prison reform under the guise of a "religious" front. But "bus therapy" may not be as effective with some gangs.

One reason is that more than one source suggests, even in official correctional staff training materials, that for such gangs as the Aryan Brotherhood, giving them "bus therapy" meant not the dissolution of its gang influence, indeed it spread and inflamed the problem: "due to transfers of gang members to federal institutions, the Aryan Brotherhood has spread throughout the country" (Illinois Department of Corrections Training Academy, Gang Activity, July, 1985: p. 11). It could, then, contribute to the so-called contagion effect.

Unless we are prepared to send them to a truly remote region (upper Alaska, Yukan, Guam, etc), apparently many of these gangs will still be able to operate and flourish. No matter where they go they will still have communications rights (mail, telephone, visitors, etc) that cannot be lawfully taken away. And there exists no such central federal correctional unit to send hardcore gang leaders and members to.

"Prisons: Just Another Kind of Hood?"

The study by Zaitzow and Houston (1999) involved surveying N = 1,706 inmates in 29 facilities inside the State of North Carolina adult corrections system. Their gang density estimate for North Carolina was 27 percent based on self-report survey methods using the inmate as the unit of analysis.

Among other findings the study suggested (p. 23): (1) "prisons have become extensions of "the hood", (2) "prisons serve to solidify gang structure and criminal processes".

Among other things, their study recommended creating "programs and activities for inmates to avail themselves of to decrease the benefits gleaned from prison gang activity" (p. 30).

TRADITIONAL STRATEGIES FOR DEALING WITH PRISON GANGS

In the absence of standards and written policies for dealing with gangs in the correctional environment, gang administration amounts to little more than a local judgement call. That is, taking the best shot on an ad hoc basis. The research by Camp and Camp (1985) showed a variety of techniques were being practiced by those thirty three states reporting

a gang problem in correctional institutions. These techniques, included, in the rank order of their frequency used: (1) move or transfer (bus therapy) (N=27), (2) use of informers[40] and prevent events (N=21), (3) segregation of gang members (N=20), (4) lock up leaders (N=20), (5) lockdown (N=18), (6) prosecute (N=16), (7) intercept communications (N=16), (8) ID and track (N=14), (9) deal with situations case by case (N=13), (10) refuse to acknowledge (N=9), (11) put different gangs in particular institutions (N=5), (12) infiltration (N=5), (13) co-opt inmates to control (N=3).

The next chapter in this book provides more recent and longitudinal information on strategies used to control prison gangs.

It is also important to note that there has been absolutely no evaluation research whatsoever reported on the efficacy of any of these techniques or strategies for dealing with gangs in the correctional environment. This is doubly unfortunate. Because not only are we therefore in the situation of not knowing "what works" in controlling gangs in corrections, but as correctional institutions are highly controlled environments ideal for social experimentation we also are not generating any useful information for gang abatement, control, or dismemberment generally that could be applied outside of the correctional environment. We are wasting an enormous research potential here. A potential to develop knowledge on "what works" with gangs that could conceivably be applied for gang prevention and intervention methods throughout American society.

"Another Study of Prison Gangs in North Carolina"

In 1997 Mary S. Jackson and Elizabeth Gail Sharpe, in their article "Prison Gang Research: Preliminary Findings in Eastern North Carolina" (Journal of Gang Research, Vol. 5, No. 1, Fall, 1997: pp. 1-7), began research gangs in North Carolina. They noted that the 1993 gang study by the American Correctional Association reported that there were no gangs in North Carolina prisons. The authors found Crips, Bloods, Aryan Nations, Folks, Surenos, and other gangs (KKK, skinheads, bikers, white pride, etc) in their surveys of prison inmates.

TARGETING GANG RESOURCES

If it is true that one of the primary dynamics of gang organization is the accumulation of money and power, then some states like Illinois have unique statutory options for targeting gang resources. Under Illinois state law it is possible to enact such an economic emasculation policy:

Illinois Criminal Code and Procedure. Reimbursement for expenses. The Director may require convicted persons committed to Department correctional institutions or facilities to reimburse the Department for the expenses incurred by their incarceration to the extent of their ability to pay for such expenses. The Attorney General, upon authorization of the Director, may institute actions in the name of the people of the State of Illinois to recover from convicted persons committed to Department correctional institutions or facilities the expenses incurred by their confinement.

To the author's knowledge this statute has never been used in Illinois[41].

But the question remains: are there really such economic assets controlled or owned by gang members that can be readily discovered by means other than self-report? Real estate, bank accounts, motor vehicles, etc, in their name? If it takes a higher level of security to care for an inmate gang member, then would it not be possible to employ such a strategy? Remember, a prison term for adults is going to amount to a figure of around $20,000 per year; and can go well over $40,000 a year for juveniles.

It might be expected that certain prison inmates would regard this suggestion as cruel and unusual punishment to expect them to pay for their own incarceration. But as stated early in this text, we must be willing to consider all possibilities. This is a legal possibility. In fact, the situation is so severe in American corrections today that all legal recourses to the solution of crisis should be explored.

ANOTHER POSSIBILITY IS CONJUGAL VISITING (Have Something to "Take Away")

The value of Columbus B. Hopper's (1969) classic study of conjugal visits in the Mississippi prison system is that it demonstrated a powerful mechanism of social control.[42] Prisons today need all the social control they can get. If gang activities and gang conflicts were disciplinary infractions that a prison considered so severe that such behavior would mean forfeiting conjugal visitation privileges, then would there be a theoretical basis for expecting a safer correctional climate? It is certainly worth trying.

Recognizing, from discussion earlier in this text, that few prison inmates are legally married might mean a strong incentive for inmats to get legally married; as, presumably, it would be for married inmates. Objections relating to sexually transmitted diseases could easily be overcome by required testing. If there were child born as a result of conjugal visiting, then that would seem to have an additional potential positive effect instead of the arch-conservative objection that this would mean the systematic reproduction of criminals. It could mean, rather, strengthening family ties and instilling hope and perhaps even a higher level of responsibility. All of which translate into potential societal forces that could be enlisted in the war on gangs.

Generally, as was found in the 1992 Prison Warden Survey (N = 316 institutions in 50 states) by the National Gang Crime Research Center, few in the criminal justice system are actually supportive of allowing conjugal visiting. In fact, that study showed that only 8.7% of the respondents believed that conjugal visiting could be used as a reward to control gang problems in prison. There is some evidence, however, that "informal conjugal visiting" occurs in many different contexts of the adult correctional system. But no one talks about it, except in those rare cases such as happened in Chicago, where the El Rukn gang members who became informants and helped in the federal prosecution of other El Rukn leaders were allowed such "informal conjugal visiting", and other inmates heard about it and it became reported in that fashion --- in an effort to overturn the federal criminal convictions of El Rukn gang leaders.

Apparently, however, the gangs themselves (if we can believe what one El Rukn informant has recently claimed) have recognized the economic income potential of sponsoring such sexual favors from females for inmates. According to a story in the Chicago Tribune (May 25, 1993: section 2, p. 7) entitled "Prostitution Ring in Prison Detailed" a gang informant claims that before "flipping" as a mid-level leader of the El Rukn gang, he operated a prostitution ring from 1983 to 1987 inside the Stateville penitentiary. This informant claims to have been able to hire at least four female correctional officers in addition to six other women who provided, for a fee, sexual favors to Stateville inmates who could afford it. At this writing, none of these allegations have been proven. The same inmate turned informant also claimed that correctional staff were bribed to bring in illegal drugs and allowed the El Rukn gang to operate underground "restaurants" inside the prison as another income source.

GANG RECOGNITION AS OFFICIAL LEGITIMATION

Should a correctional administrator hold periodic chats with designated gang leaders? Or allow the gangs to meet regularly in the hope that this will appease them or reduce existing levels of intergang conflict in the correctional institution? Such a policy "experiment" in Illinois in the early 1970s, to essentially the above effect, backfired dramatically.

What appears to have happened is that in 1971 at the Pontiac prison in Illinois "special times were scheduled by the administrator for meetings of the respective gangs. This special class developed the power to create violence, pressure inmates and staff, and usurp authority from institutional officials. Gang jealousies and intra-gang strife were also by-products of gang recognition" (Illinois Training Academy,

July 1988: pp. 6-7). Recognition became equivalent in function to legitimating the gangs and giving them de jure justification to operate within and without of the correctional institution. It clearly exacerbated the problem.

"Who Gets High More? Guards or Inmates?"

It is commonly known that most drug activity, importation and sales at least, is typically gang-dominated inside correctional institutions. This story puts the issue of drug abuse in a different light.

This naturally occurring research comes from Illinois when in 1999 N=3,506 correctional staff were drug tested, compared with N =2,144 inmates tested for drugs in their system.

Results: 2.5 percent of the N = 3,506 correctional staff tested positive. At the Dwight Correctional Center, a facility for female state corrections inmates, some 4.1 percent of the N=97 staff tested positive for drugs. Less than one percent of the inmates (0.7%) tested positive for drugs.

Remember that correctional officers are also in the open-population where they can buy the "detoxifying" materials that many drug abusers use to "pass" drug tests. While inmates are not likely to have access to these kind of trick chemicals, pills, etc that are widely available in the open population (e.g., as commonly advertised to drug abusers in High Times).

Source: Dave McKinney, "Prison Guards Fail Drug Tests: Positive Results Top Inmates'", Chicago Sun-Times, Mar. 4, 2000, p. 1, 2.

It is a situation that is truly comparable to the matter of negotiating with terrorists. To negotiate is to recognize such a force as legitimate actors. Simple recognition provides political legitimation, which can be a larger gain than a military victory. In political science, similarly, an incumbent who enjoys name recognition or is widely known to the public is always advised to never debate with an opponent who is not so well known. What happens in such debates is the opponent automatically gains greater recognition and legitimacy, and the cognitive hegemony of the incumbent is systematically eroded. It is an attention/authority transfer phenomenon.

The same thing appears to happen in our dealings with the gang organization. In both law enforcement and in corrections, we can sometimes inadvertently reinforce gang strength. Recall that many authors in the gang literature assert that gangs emerge from, grow, or are reinforced in terms of identity and cohesiveness out of a pattern of conflict. Historically, this means the community labels them, other social institutions come to regard them as a gang,

the police respond to them as a gang, and they become a gang. Almost in a self-fulfilling prophecy.

Recall from the study of Jacobs (1977, pp. 82-83) that Warden Twomey ceased the practice of physically dragging a recalcitrant inmate gang member to the isolation unit. Rather, the policy became "cell lock in" until the inmate was ready to go peacefully. For otherwise, the witnessing gang members themselves had an opportunity to "rally" around such "brutality". They had a visible "enemy" (e.g., correctional officers using physical force) to protest. It meant higher solidarity for gang inmates. So taking away this opportunity to protest was a wise policy. The same implication also holds for local law enforcement. That is, perhaps it is much better to effect an arrest outside of the purview of other gang member witnesses.[43]

A HIDDEN PRISON INDUSTRY: THE MAKING OF "SUPERGANG" NATIONS

The prison or correctional setting as an arena of conflict provides, unfortunately, the organizational enhancement opportunity for establishing inter-gang alliances. Bobrowski (1988) posits that in the 1970s such an alliance was formed between the Black Disciple gang and the predominantly white Simon City Royals gang; where the latter agreed to be a connection for narcotics, and the former agreed to provide protection. In response to this alliance, the rival gangs (Latin Kings, Vice Lords, El Rukns) also established a pact. Thus was born the "Folks" and the "Peoples" and two large nations of gangs separated geographically (Bobrowski, 1988: pp. 30-31).[44]

Today in Illinois, to be in the Folks nation is to ride under the six-pointed star; to be "People" is to be about the five-pointed star. The "cause" of supergangs, then, is a finger pointed at the door of correctional agencies and their mishandling of the gang problem situation. Can prisons provide the setting in which we systematically provide a true training ground for new gang leaders? Yes is the general answer. For example, the Camp and Camp (1985: p. 152) report showed that a recurrent prison strategy for dealing with gangs was to "as a last resort, select leaders from the second layer of the organization and ship them out". Does that mean, afterwards, that within the shipping organization new middle-management are inducted into the gang hierarchy with an even higher level of commitment to the gang now that they have gained leadership or position status? And, similarly, does it mean that for the institutions receiving the shipped gang members these middle management gang leaders now have the charter to head up gang branches of their own at the new institutions? Again, the answer in both instances is probably yes.

The question then should be clear for the many other correctional systems outside of Illinois: could the conflict in the prison be such that gangs must establish such general alliances of almost equal proportion and in this manner facilitate the natural growth of groups of gangs? Whether intentional or not, this is the strongest argument yet that correctional institutions may in fact be "adding fuel to the fire" of the gang problem.[45] As society comes to understand the potential developments in this area we might expect more in the way of standards and guidelines for the handling of gang conflict in the correctional setting. It is no small problem.

LATINO GANGS AND THE TEEN ANGEL MAGAZINE: A FREEDOM OF THE PRESS ISSUE?

Organized deviant groups, extremists, and ideological fanatics can be expected to test the limits of constitutional protections. The Teen Angel magazine is a gang rights activist news organization. Its first magazine was published in 1980. Virtually every issue has photos of inmate gang members (always Hispanic/Latino/Chicano only) or their drawings, where they are seeking pen pals (e.g., females). Rapists and drug dealers are not allowed such pen pals according to magazine policy (Issue #107)[46].

While most such gang member inmates are in California prisons, other states are also represented. Sometimes a list of inmates and their numbers and addresses are provided where anyone interested can write directly to the inmate. More recently, such persons interested in being "pen pals" are instructed to simply write to the person "in care of" the magazine (enclosing $3.00 and stamps for the fee), where the letter is forwarded directly to the inmate.

This magazine is more than an outlet for Latino gang art. It is a self-described gang rights activist news organization. It does publish articles by jailhouse lawyers (pp. 12-13, Issue # 117) giving advice to gang members on the street on how to neutralize police interrogation and investigation techniques. It does reprint articles previously published by the ACLU. It also publishes agit-prop "information" handouts on prison reform/activist groups in California, such as the Pelican Bay Information Project[47].

It is useful to summarize some of the viewpoints from the Pelican Bay Information Project (PBIP)[48]. What the PBIP is all about is "prisoners rights", more specifically those confined in the Security Housing Unit (SHU) within the Pelican Bay State Prison which is a maxi-maximum facility for gang leaders and others who have committed violent crimes within the correctional system (e.g., assaulting correctional officers).

The SHU at Pelican Bay holds about one thousand inmates in lockdown status equivalent to that in the Marion Federal Penitentiary. What makes SHU unique and a security improvement on Marion is the architecture: inmates cannot successfully talk to each other through bars, there are no bars. The inmates are in solid rooms that are all monitored with audio-video equipment. It is similar to the "no human contact" status described in The Hot House (Earley, 1992). The inmates eat in their cells and do not get together in groups (e.g., for church, etc).

The SHU inmates are reported in the PBIP literature to experience a psychological pressure to "snitch": their choices are "debrief, parole, or die". To "debrief" is to explain the nature of ones gang affiliation, how one fits into the hierarchy, who else is involved, etc, and most gangs would regard such behavior as high treason and punishable accordingly. The PBIP report goes on to say that predominantly white correctional officers have made racist remarks to inmates, and that Pelican Bay may be increasing violence rather than reducing it, and that such treatment constitutes "torture". What the public does not know is that there is a very good reason for such super maximum security facilities. The reason has to do with the enormous amount of serious crime and violence that occurs inside prisons, or that is directed from behind prison walls by imprisoned gang leaders, and which never gets included in our national crime statistics!

D&D: DEBRIEFING AND DENOUNCING

A number of states have developed "D&D" initiatives in recent years to deal with the gang/STG problem behind bars. This hinges on the existence of whether the same prisons have the capability of "gang intelligence" in their security force. In recent years a new job category has been added to the prison security force, it is the "institutional gang investigator". This position has a number of equivalent job titles, including: "STG Coordinator", "Gang/STG Intelligence officer"', STG/SSU Supervisor, Intelligence Coordinator, STG manager, STG Investigator, Security Risk Group (SRG) coordinator, Intelligence & Investigations Unit, Gang Information Officer, etc. The job titles differ but the work remains the same across jurisdictions: identify, monitor, and coordinate gang/STG information and respond as necessary to the threats they represent to institutional safety and security.

One of the first things that an "institutional gang investigator" does when a new inmate arrives at the facility is to interview the inmate to ascertain current gang/STG status. Obviously, the investigator has access to a wealth of criminal justice information about the inmate which may or may not indicate the gang/STG involvement and affiliation. In the debriefing phase, the goal is to develop information about the gang/STG if possible by getting information from the inmates. Other methods also exist for developing this gang/STG information that are effective: (1) monitoring their telephone conversations with anyone they call from the institution, (2) monitoring their mail and correspondence, and (3) frequent inspections of the personal effects the inmate may have stored in his cell.

"The 'Set-Off' Policy: Mixing Rival Gang Members in Correctional Settings"

The "set-off" policy is an old one, used informally and formally in many different types of correctional facilities. It is easy to understand: according to the theory if you have a cell house that holds 25 inmates, put in 10 "Bloods", 10 "Crips", and maybe 5 "neutrons". The idea: let one gang counter-balance the other rival gang so that no single gang becomes dominant.

The "set-off" policy has one major theoretical problem: the potential for structurally inciting gang conflicts between rival gang members.

At the Corcoran Prison in California, the "Set-Off" policy was known as the "integrated yard policy": when inmates went to the yard for recreation, they were integrated or mixed in terms of their gang alliances. Some now say that this policy was equivalent to staging gladiator fights.

In April of 2000, eight correctional officers at Corcoran Prison went on federal trial after being indicted for their various roles in facilitating inmate violence; four of the officers face life prison sentences.

When the inmates would start fighting in the prison yard, obviously the correctional officers in the guard towers had the right to fire weapons. One of the fights in 1994 resulted in such an inmate being shot, where one of the officers was said to remark "It's going to be duck hunting season". The idea being inmates were easy to shoot.

According to the FBI the State of California obstructed an investigation and the fights were intentionally provoked between inmates to amuse the correctional officers. The family of one inmate killed by gunfire, Preston Tate, has already received a settlement of $825,000 for wrongful death.

Source: Kiley Russell, "Prison Guards Head to Trial", Associated Press, 4-11-00.

Sometimes it is the case that gang/STG members, once identified as such, are placed in more secure housing units. They can get released back into the general inmate population only if they debrief and denounce. This also goes into effect when a gang/

STG member continues to pose a threat to institutional security by "gang banging" behind bars, and gets sent to say "administrative segregation" where they will lose many of the privileges that other inmates in the general population have.

The idea is to get the inmate to "denounce" his gang. Sometimes this is done by means of signing a document, and sometimes it is even videotaped. If the inmate cooperates, gives up information, then he has been "debriefed"; and if he says "I quit this gang", then he has denounced the gang. After "D&D" the inmate may be released from a "Special Housing Unit" or "Security Housing Unit" (i.e., segregation), and allowed to gradually return to the general inmate population.

THE SNITCH FARM: PROSECUTING GANGS THAT ASSAULT AND KILL CORRECTIONAL OFFICERS

Someone who is willing to become an informant by providing testimony in court that can help convict gang members may in fact be a gang member, so what does a correctional system do with such persons who may automatically face a sentence of execution (e.g., a "hit") from their own gang? A recent idea that appears to be an effective solution and is consistent with the earlier work of Sleeman (1849). This recent idea is to create a separate and secure facility for such persons willing to cooperate with law enforcement agencies.

The snitch farm visited by the author was created in 1991 with a capacity of 60 inmates. It had 27 inmates on my visit. All of the inmates are known only by their initials (e.g., "G.D.C."), not their full and correct names. Correctional officers are not supposed to know their real names and also refer to them in routine interaction by their initials (usually a two letter combination, e.g. "D.C."). Obviously, though, that is to prevent casual use of the names in ordinary business. It is a security precaution taken to protect the identity and location of said inmates.

The units typically have their own separate budget. They are isolated physically and visually. No strangers can visit: one of the security precautions is that all visitors into the actual snitch farm complex itself are required to have a polaroid photograph taken of them, which is then shown to the inmate; the inmate then checks this photograph to make sure it is not an assassin sent by the gang that is trying to visit him.

Providing certain amenities and privileges that inmates outside of the snitch farm may not receive is not in any sense "pampering". For after all, without these inmates violent crimes including the assassination of correctional officers may have never been solved, nor the gang culprits convicted. By putting their life on the line for legitimate authority, we must come to recognize that such informants have earned some increased favorable treatment.

RECENT RESEARCH FINDINGS ON GANGS IN ADULT CORRECTIONS

The author as the director of the National Gang Crime Research Center initiated an ongoing series of national surveys dealing with literally all aspects of the criminal justice system and gangs. Here it is useful to summarize the findings from some of these various research projects that involve the adult corrections component of the criminal justice system.

Two different aspects of the adult correctional system are examined here. The first is a close look at gang problems in adult state prisons in America. The second is a close look at gang problems in adult local and county jails in America.

LOOKING AT THE QUANTITATIVE PICTURE IN ADULT STATE PRISONS

The gang problem has proliferated so much in recent years that almost all American cities, regardless of size, are now reporting some level of a gang presence or involvement in criminal code violation. The penal system is, as everyone knows, a filtering process that generally takes in as its "input" those individuals who have been found to be, after conviction for a felony crime, a genuine threat to public safety. All states report some level of a gang or security threat group (STG) problem in their correctional system today is the current situation the United States faces. It is not a matter of whether there is or is not a gang problem, the issue is just how serious is the gang problem in American corrections today? Answering that question is the substance of this report.

Both a qualitative and quantitative type of social change has taken place in the basic crime pattern of American society as well. This has to do with the extent to which gang members account for an increased amount of all crime in society. Correctional environments are the social contexts having the highest gang density rates today. Researchers from the NGCRC in their regular and ongoing on-site interviews of thousands of individual gang members throughout the United States have yet to find any correctional environment that does not have any gang member incarcerated therein. It is not uncommon to find correctional environments that contain gang members that were not known as gang members to the officials administering these same facilities or even to the gang intelligence officers working in these same facilities.

Knowledge about gangs in corrections is very limited. In fact, the only federally funded research recently conducted on gangs in corrections is itself very suspect, the reasons for which will be made abundantly clear. The most recent federally funded research report on gangs in corrections missed the boat entirely on the single most important issue (i.e., gang density) and was not able to obtain the cooperation of all states in its particular research strategy which used an over-aggregated unit of analysis. That research funded by the National Institute of Justice (NIJ) concluded that only 6 percent of our Nation's adult inmate population were gang members. That study was research carried out by the American Correctional Association and reported in 1993. The same year, the NGCRC 1993 Adult Corrections Survey showed the estimate to actually be twice as high!

The National Gang Crime Research Center (NGCRC) is the only organization in the world today that has researched and analyzed the gang problem in American adult state correctional institutions on a continuing basis since 1991. The annual gang assessments conducted by the NGCRC since 1991 is not only research, because the service component was built in from the very start: educating correctional administrators in a timely fashion about the "state-of-the-art" regarding gangs and corrections. Unlike most federal research projects that often take two years to be able to disseminate findings, at which point their usefulness may have been completely lost in terms of practical application due to an escalation in the nature of the problem being studied itself, the NGCRC has been able over the years to rapidly provide full non-technical feedback to all of its respondents requesting a complete copy of the research results. Thus, the respondents are not sent an executive summary only, they are provided with the full report. This kind of research is not a major analytical effort because it represents a very fixed and easily identified universe.

Previous Adult State Corrections Surveys by the NGCRC tended to show that the way in which researchers have tried to explain and analyze the "gang problem" in American corrections is substantially removed from reality. In otherwords, it is not sufficient to simply ask a summative evaluation question such as "DO YOU HAVE A GANG PROBLEM IN YOUR FACILITY". The reason is that a researcher must be able to measure the definitional components of what makes up a gang problem. As shown in the 1994 adult state corrections survey, if we examine the "components" of what makes up a gang problem in adult corrections, then almost everyone has some aspect of the problem. The only issue is the variation: some clearly have a greater problem than others.

The 1999 report extended our knowledge of the gang problem further and suggested some directions of change for policy makers.

RESEARCH METHODOLOGY

The research strategy for this study was to mail out questionnaires to every known state adult correctional institution. It is the individual state adult facility that is therefore the unit of analysis in this study. This study therefore does not deal with juvenile correctional institutions or federal correctional institutions.

The sampling strategy yielded the following samples for the various surveys summarized here:

1991: N = 184 (40 states)
1992: N = 316 (50 states)
1993: N = 174 (41 states)
1994: N = 290 (47 states)
1995: N = 323 (50 states)
1999: N = 133 (47 states)

FINDINGS

In presenting the descriptive statistical findings from the latest 1999 survey, the procedure is straight-forward by discussing the results in terms of the same item order as that found in the survey instrument itself. It should be noted that as in all survey research the total number of responses for any given item may in some cases be less than that of the total survey sample (N = 133). Overall, missing data was not a major problem, it is simply common for some respondents to not answer all of the many questions in the questionnaire. This will account for the fact that not all of the variables always have a total of N = 133 respondents which was our sample size.

Where appropriate, comparative results from the same surveys carried out in previous years are also summarized. Not all items were continuously used in all surveys. Sometimes new items were added, to focus on new issues. But by and large the most critical and more important issues do have this longitudinal data to allow comparisons over time.

Today About Two-Thirds of All Adult Correctional Facilities Have Specific Disciplinary Rules That Prohibit Gang Recruitment

The survey asked "does your facility have specific disciplinary rules that prohibit gang recruitment".

In 1995, some 59 percent (N = 187) indicated that their adult correctional facilities do in fact have such disciplinary rules that prohibit gang recruitment. Thus, 41 percent (N = 130) of the institutions responding to the 1995 Adult Corrections Survey reported that their facility did not have specific disciplinary rules that prohibit gang recruitment.

By 1999, this had increased to 66.7%.

	1995	1999
	%	%
YES	59%	66.7%
NO	41%	33.3%

Over Three-Fourths Believe the Supreme Court has Gone Too Far on Ruling in Favor of Inmate Rights

The survey asked "do you believe the Supreme Court has gone too far on ruling in favor of inmate rights".

In 1992 77.7 percent of the respondents agreed with the idea that the Supreme Court has been too favorably disposed towards inmate rights issues. By 1993 this increased to 83.5 percent.

In 1995, some 85.1 percent (N = 263) of the respondents did believe that the Supreme Court has gone too far on ruling in favor of inmate rights. Only 14.9 percent (N = 46) of the responding correctional administrators did not believe that the Supreme Court has gone too far on ruling in favor of inmate rights.

By 1999, though, we see that this dips somewhat to 79.1 percent of the respondents feeling that the Supreme Court has gone too far on ruling in favor of inmate rights.

	1992	1993	1995	1999
YES	77.7%	83.5%	85.1%	79.1%
NO	22.3%	16.5%	14.9%	20.9%

Only A Fourth of the Responding Correctional Facilities Indicated Their State Agency is Based on Decentralized Management

The survey asked "which best describes your state agency: __Centralized management __Decentralized management".

In 1995, some 71.9 percent (N = 215) of the responding agencies indicated that the state agency or parent organization is based on centralized management. About a fourth (28.1%, N = 84) did, however, report that their state agency is oriented towards decentralized management. This is a measure of correctional organizational style. The results suggest most adult state correctional institutions are still based on centralized management systems, as by 1999 72.1 percent were still centralized.

	1995	1999
	%	%
Centralized	71.9%	72.1%
Decentralized	28.1%	27.9%

About Half Believe That "No Human Contact" Status Is Not Effective For the Control of Gang Members

The survey asked "do you believe no human contact status is effective for the control of gang members".

In 1995, some 40.2 percent (N = 125) of the respondents indicated that they do in fact believe no human contact status is effective for the control of gang members. Still, there is not complete consensus, and perhaps this could vary by other factors (i.e., institutional security level, institutional type, gang density, etc). Because over half (59.8%, N = 186) did not believe that no human contact status is effective for the control of gang members. This had not changed significantly by 1999, it rose slightly to 49.2% believing that <u>no human contact status</u> is effective for the control of gang members.

	1995	1999
YES	40.2%	49.2%
NO	59.8%	50.8%

Two-Fifths Believe Gangs Could Be More Effectively Controlled if Gang Members Could Be Transferred to a Central-National Federal Unit

The survey asked "do you believe gangs could be more effectively controlled if gang members could be transferred to a central-national federal unit".

In 1993, about a third of the respondents believed in this idea, and it rose slightly, to level off at 41 percent for the 1993, 1995, and 1999 surveys.

In 1995, two-fifths (41.3%, N = 123) of the respondents indicated that they did believe that gang could be more effectively controlled if gang members could be sent to a central-national federal unit of correctional supervision. Some 58.7 percent (N = 175) did not believe that gang members could be more effectively controlled by transferring them to a central national style of correctional control. This rose to only 41.5 percent in the 1999 survey.

	1992	1993	1995	1999
YES	33.6%	41.8%	41.3%	41.5%
NO	69.4%	58.2%	58.7%	58.5%

Thus, as of 1999 there had been no change at all in this factor of beliefs about the effectiveness of "no human contact status" for controlling gang members behind bars, since the 1993 survey.

Gang Density: Percentage of Inmates Who Are Gang Members

Gang density refers to the percentage of inmates in any given facility who are gang members. One of the most important findings from the present research is that it is very rare for any of the adult state correctional institutions holding male inmates to report that they have no gang members at all confined in their facility.

In 1995, only 7.4 percent of the male institutions reported a gang density of zero percent. The gang density variable was measured by the question "among staff who know about gang members, what is the current estimate of what percentage gang members are of the total inmate population". Separate estimates were obtained for male and female inmate populations.

In 1995, the gang density for male institutions ranged from a low of zero percent (7.4%, N = 20) to a high of 100 percent. The mean, or average,

was 20.5 percent for the male inmates at a national level.

While the gang problem is felt more prominently in male correctional institutions, it is also clear that the gang problem has now converged on female correctional institutions. In 1995, the gang density estimates for female correctional institutions ranged from a low of zero percent to a high of 50 percent. The mean, or arithmetic average, for gang density was 3.1 percent for female inmates at a national level.

In 1995, the survey data reflects about a third of all adult correctional institutions in the United States today from all states. It is useful to look at the estimated gang population computed arithmetically by multiplying gang density by the more exact inmate populations for each responding institution. This analysis showed a total of N = 47,220 male gang members in just a third of the correctional institutions in the United States! We do not need to add the known female gang members to make the point here. The ACA report (1993) based its national estimate of a six percent gang density parameter on the fact that only N = 43,756 gang members were found in the way it conducted its survey.

Recall that the 1995 sample includes a third of the total overall universe of adult state correctional institutions in the United States. Thus, our sample of just a third of the American adult correctional institutions yielded a greater number of estimated gang members than the ACA estimated to exist in the entire adult correctional system!

When we look at gang density over time, we see a steady increase for males from 1991 up through 1999. The best estimate today is that one fourth of all male inmates confined in adult state correctional institutions are gang members.

	1991	1992	1993	1994	1995	1999
Males:	9.4%	10.2%	12.2%	15.6	20.5%	24.7%
Females:	3.5%	2.7%	2.3%	4.7	3.1%	7.5%

The gang density estimates for female inmates in adult state correctional institutions have, admittedly, been low and have fluctuated somewhat comparing results from 1991 to 1999.

There is a reason why it is necessary to measure separate gang density rates for male and female inmates: the males generally constitute the overwhelming vast majority of the inmate population. Since statistical records began to be kept and reported on gender in adult state correctional institutions, generally females have constituted about 5 percent of the overall prison population.

GANG DENSITY BY SECURITY LEVEL

Obviously, it would be expected that gang density levels would vary by the level of security of the institutions reporting this data. Thus, from the

1999 Survey, we find the following results. What this suggests is that overall in American corrections, gang members are in fact dispersed throughout the system regardless of security level of the institutions. But certainly it is true, as well, that the higher the security level of an institution, the higher the gang density it also faces.

Gang Density Means for Male and Female Inmates by Level of Institutional Security

The Three Levels of Institutional Security

	Minimum	Medium	Maximum
Male	16.1	23.6	32.7
Female	5.6	8.0	8.6

What this means, therefore, is that in a typical maximum security adult state correctional institution, in the year 1999, about 32.7 percent of the inmates could be expected to be gang/STG members. This reduces, by half, when we look at minimum security institutions in the same year. Generally, we would expect gang/STG members to probably be placed in the higher level security facilities.

Growing Trend: Providing Gang Training to Correctional Staff

The survey asked "do your staff receive formalized training in dealing with the gang problem". This factor has shown a progressively steady increase in the last decade is what the data shows. Gang training is becoming more necessary as the gang problem becomes more of a security threat to the adult correctional system.

In 1995, some 58.0 percent (N = 184) indicated that their correctional staff do in fact now receive such gang training. Still, two-fifths (42.0%, N = 133) of the correctional facilities survey indicated that their staff do not receive gang training. Obviously, there is a lag in staff training here that begs for more correctional resources. In otherwords, more institutions report a gang problem than do those do provide their staff with training in how to deal with gang members behind bars.

	1991	1992	1993	1994	1995	1999
YES	40.8%	45.4%	46.8%	49.5%	58%	67.4%
NO	59.2%	54.6%	53.2%	50.5%	42%	32.6%

What the trend indicates is that in 1991 about two-fifths of American adult correctional institutions provided gang training to their correctional officers. This rose to about half by the year 1994. And by 1999 two-thirds of all adult state correctional institutions are providing gang training to their correctional officers. It is fair to say that this longitudinal data suggests that gang training is now part and parcel of being able to do an effective job as a correctional officer today.

A separate follow-up question measuring the intensity of the gang training available to correctional staff asked "if yes, how many hours is the gang training session". In 1995, the results ranged from a low of 1 hour to a high of (in one instance) 132 hours. We suspect the one case of an institution providing 132 hours of gang training was a true exception to the rule, and may account for one gang coordinator's account of the amount of training he has received. Most of the respondents who provided gang training (88.8%) reported that the gang training amounts to ten hours or less or such training. Some 24.1 percent provided 2 hours of training. Some 22.4 percent provided 4 hours of training. And some 22.9 percent provided 8 hours of training. So viewed in this way, some 87.1 percent of the correctional staff receiving gang training in the United States actually get 8 hours or less of formalized gang training. That is, in most cases, it is one day or less of gang training. The mean amount of gang training nationally was 7.5 hours from the 1995 survey. Seven and one-half hours is enough to give someone training in gang awareness, but it would not make anyone a "gang expert" or "gang specialist".

A Growing Problem: Gang Members Assaulting Correctional Staff

The survey asked "have gang members been a problem in terms of assaults on your staff". In the 1992 survey only one out of ten institutions reported gang members being a problem in terms of assaults on the staff.

In the 1995 survey, about a sixth of all adult state correctional institutions in this large national sample (18.7%, N = 59) reported that gang members have been a problem in terms of assaults on correctional staff. Still, in 1995, most (81.3%, N = 256) of the respondents indicated that gang members have not been a problem in terms of assaults on their staff.

But by 1999, about one-third of all adult state correctional institutions would report gang members as a problem in terms of assaults on staff. If this data was controlled by type of institution, obviously we would see more dramatic increases perhaps in the maximum security facilities. Recall that the data includes all facilities: minimum, medium, and maximum security facilities.

The trend would suggest that this is a growing problem for corrections: assaults upon staff members from gang members.

	1992	1993	1995	1999
YES	10.4%	18%	18.7%	33.6%
NO	89.6%	82%	81.3%	66.4%

A Growing Problem: Gang Members Threatening Correctional Staff

A follow-up question on gang members assaulting correctional staff asked whether gang members had been a problem in terms of threats on correctional staff.

In the 1992 survey only about a fourth of the institutions reported gang members as a problem in terms of threats against staff members.

In 1995, over a third of all adult state correctional institutions in the sample (37.2%, N = 113) reported that gang members have been a problem in terms of threats against correctional staff. About two-thirds (62.8%, N = 191) indicated that gang members have not been a problem in terms of threats against correctional staff.

By 1999 we see that this problem escalates to about half of all correctional institutions in the United States today reporting that gang members have been a problem in terms of threats against staff members.

	1992	1993	1995	1999
YES	24.0%	32.5%	37.2%	53.5%
NO	76.0%	67.5	62.8%	46.5%

About Half of the Correctional Institutions Report Racial Conflicts Are A Problem Among the Offenders in Their Facilities

This question, like some others, is a replication of the same measure from previous yearly surveys. This problem has existed for quite some time and remains relatively stable. The specific question in the survey asked "are racial conflicts a problem among the offenders in your facility". In 1995, some 55.1 percent (N = 173) of the respondents indicated that racial conflicts are a problem among the inmate population. Similarly, the other half (44.9%, N = 141) indicated that racial conflicts are not a problem among the inmates. This was about the same as was found in the 1993 survey, and increased just slightly in the 1999 survey. It seems relatively stable over time as a very serious problem that is simply not disappearing.

	1993	1995	1999
YES	55.9%	55.1%	57%
NO	44.1%	44.9%	43%

Growing Trend: Institutions Reporting That White Inmates Have A Separate Gang in Their Facilities

The survey asked "do white inmates have a separate gang". Since 1991 this problem has steadily increased in a significant way. In 1991 about a fourth of the institutions were reporting white gangs.

In 1995, some 57.9 percent (N = 176) of the respondents indicated that the white inmates in their facility do in fact have a separate gang. Still some 42.1 percent (N = 128) did not report that white inmates have a separate gang.

By 1999, over two-thirds of the institutions were reporting the existence of separate white gangs among their inmates. What this is really measuring is the widespread nature of white inmate gangs in adult American correctional institutions today.

	1991	1992[49]	1993	1995	1999
YES	27.3%	41.1%	56.7%	57.9%	70.3%
NO	72.7%	59.6%	43.3%	42.1%	29.7%

The White Gangs In American Prisons Today

A follow-up question was designed for those adult state correctional institutions that did report their white inmates to having a separate gang. It simply asked the respondent to write-in the name of the gang in an open-ended format. While a wide assortment of white gangs exist behind bars today, it is clearly the Aryan Brotherhood that is the most frequently cited white gang. Other groups include: Aryan Nation, Aryan Warriors, Aryan Society, White Aryan Resistance, Ku Klux Klan, Neo-Nazis, Bikers (several factions: Prison Motorcycle Brotherhood, Outlaws, etc), Peckerwoods, Brothers of the White Struggle (B.O.W.S.), Northsiders (Illinois prison system), Simon City Royals (midwest gang), Texas Mafia, White Gangster Disciples, White Supremacists, Young and Wasted, other local gangs and STGs, as well as various religious-identity extremist groups (Church of Jesus Christ Christian, etc). From other sources (National Gangs Resource Handbook, 1995, Wyndham Hall Press, 52857 County Road 21, Bristol, Indiana 46507) we now know that white gangs like the Aryan Brotherhood are to be found in almost all states today, and they are not a gang that is limited to the adult correctional context.

In 1999, it was also discovered that a group from the 1970's thought to have been totally defunct, the Church of the New Song (CONS) was again up and running in the Iowa state adult corrections system. Today this CONS group is an all-white security threat group.

Inmate Racial Breakdown

The survey asked the respondents to estimate what percentage of the inmates in their facility were white, Black, Hispanic, and Other. For the white inmate population the estimated density ranged from a low of one percent to a high of 98 percent, with a mean or average of 43.5 percent. Black inmates were the single largest racial group represented in the adult state correctional institutions in this sample. The results for all racial groups are provided in Table 64.

Table 64

Inmate Racial Density Estimates in a Large National Sample of Adult State Correctional Institutions

	1995 Mean	1999 Mean
White Inmates	43.5	43.0%
Black Inmates	45.3	43.2%
Hispanic Inmates	9.7	12.2%
Other Races	5.0	6.4%

As an external check against the validity of the present findings, in terms of the degree to which this national sample corresponds to existing external population parameters, it is well known that Black or African-American inmates are in fact now highly represented inside the confined population. This is also the matter of DPM, or the concept of disproportionate minority confinement, which means that minorities are represented in the confined population at a higher rate than their overall proportion society-wide.

Today More Than Three-Fourths of Prison Wardens Believe That An Administrator Who Tries To Bargain With An Inmate Gang Leader is Similar To Trying To Negotiate With A Terrorist

We have seen this factor become more salient over the years, because some of the early work about gangs and corrections made the mistake of viewing gang leaders as a potential source of stabilization that could be coopted. A criminal gang cannot be coopted without enormous additional risk, and any benefits are likely to be short term for said administrator, and such a policy is bound to backfire in the long run.

So this is another replication item, a factor we have measured over the years. The survey asked the administrators "in your opinion, would an administrator who tries to bargain with an inmate gang leader be similar to negotiating with terrorists". In 1995, some 75.4 percent (N = 236) of the prison wardens agreed that an administrator who tries to bargain with an inmate gang leader is basically equivalent to trying to negotiate with a terrorist: it is a bad idea. This factor of staff recognition for gangs has varied and is now closing in on a more zero tolerance policy in adult state correctional institutions. In 1994's survey some 72.4 percent felt this analogy was true. In 1993 it was 59.3 percent. In 1992 it was 54 percent. Obviously, there is growing recognition that gangs cannot be easily coopted when a correctional administrator tries to bargain with a gang leader for prison safety.

Below, we can see how this factor has changed over the years in the minds of prison administrators.

	1992	1993	1994	1995	1999
YES	54.0%	59.3%	72.4%	75.4%	78.3%
NO	46.0%	40.7%	27.6%	24.6%	21.7%

The Growing Political Influence of Gangs: Nearly A Fourth of Prison Wardens Feel That Gangs or Gang Leaders Are Able to Influence Politicians in Their State

This is really an issue of political corruption or at the least a high level of naivete on the part of some elected officials prone to be gang apologists or easily manipulated by a gang. However, as demonstrated recently in the Journal of Gang Research ("Gang Profile: The Gangster Disciples", 1995, Fall Issue, Volume 3, Number 1, pp. 58-76), some midwest gangs like the Gangster Disciples have not only been able to slate their own candidates for local office, but have been able to have state elected officials try to change legislation for them, and have even shown up at large scale gang picnics. This is not a problem that affects only corrections, obviously. In fact, two recent large scale law enforcement studies, one examining gangs in Georgia (Project GEORGIA95) and one examining gangs in Wisconsin (Project WISCONSIN95), also showed that the problem of political corruption is linked in some municipalities to adverse gang influence, and it appears to be a growing problem.

The survey asked "do you feel that gangs or gang leaders are able to influence politicians in your state".

In 1995, the results showed that 23.6 percent (N = 74) of the respondents felt that gangs or gang leaders are able to influence the politicians in their state. Three-fourths (76.4%, N = 239) did not feel that gangs or gang leaders have political influence in their state.

We examined this variable more closely by selecting the subsample from 1995 who did feel that gangs do exert political influence in their state. Examining the distribution of actual geographical locations showed that 32 of the 50 states have one or more respondents who now report that gangs or gang leaders are able to influence politicians in their state. It is truly a nationwide problem and not a problem limited to areas like Illinois.

	1994	1995	1999
YES	20.3%	23.6%	25.4%
NO	79.7%	76.4%	74.6%

Which is More Dangerous: Street Gangs or Prison Gangs?

Most of the more organized gangs that are found behind bars have their equivalent outside of corrections, thus they are simply street gangs behind bars. The term prison gang is sometimes used in the restrictive sense of referring to those gangs that arose in prison and exist for the most part only behind bars. The term prison gang in its more restrictive meaning therefore seems to refer to gangs that has their origin in prison, and which may in fact have their counterparts outside of corrections (i.e., on the streets, in communities in a wide number of geographical areas).

One issue that has arisen in discussions about a national assessment of gangs in corrections is the matter of whether prison gangs are therefore more dangerous than street gangs represented as security threat groups among inmates. Any street gang represented among prison inmates is logically going to be considered a security threat group.

The 1994 survey asked "in general, which type of gang group poses more danger to your facility: a street gang (has its origins outside of prison), or a prison gang (has its origins inside of prison)". Over half of the facilities responding to the survey who provided information for this factor (N = 156, 62.2%) felt that street gangs posed greater danger. Still, over a third (N = 95, 37.8%) of the respondents felt that prison gangs were more dangerous.

Among those respondents not represented in the distribution above were "missing data" cases where the response could not be given, such as the situation where the respondent wrote in the margin "they are the same", or that they were "equally dangerous". We would recommend adding the response mode "No difference" to future uses of this item. But this item was not replicated in the 1999 survey.

The Largest Gangs Represented Among Inmates in American Corrections Today

The survey asked "what are the names of the top three largest gangs that are represented among inmates in your facility". Three blank lines were provided for this open-ended question series. By creating a name index file that would include up to three observations for each respondent, the names of the largest gangs were then possible to analyze. The way to interpret these results, therefore, is that any gang that shows up in this list is being cited as among the top three largest gangs in any given adult state correctional institution in the United States.

A very long list of gang names emerged in this manner. We can summarize these by looking at a few of the largest gangs represented among inmates in American corrections today. Table 65 presents these summary results about the largest gangs in adult corrections from the 1995 survey.

TABLE 65

Gangs Most Frequently Cited as Being Among the Top Three Gangs in American Correctional Institutions Rank Ordered (Percentage)

Name of the Gang	%
Crips (various factions)	15.4
Black Gangster Disciples	13.9
Bloods/Piru factions	1.7
Vice Lord factions	7.1
Aryan Brotherhood	6.8
Latin King factions[50]	4.5

As seen in Table 65, in 1995, Crips appear to have the edge, being cited by 15.4 percent of the adult state correctional institutions in this sample. They are closely followed by Black Gangster Disciples (13.9%), Blood/Piru sets (11.7%), Vice Lords (7.1%), Aryan Brotherhood (6.8%), and the Latin Kings (4.5%). The significance of this finding relates to the scope and extent of the same gang being represented throughout the American correctional system.

In What Year Gangs Were First Recognized As Being A Problem In American Adult Correctional Institutions

The survey asked "in what year did gangs first become recognized as a problem in your facility? 19___".

In 1995, the results showed a range from as early as 1965 to as recently as this year (e.g., 1995). Overall, the mean or average year for pinpointing the gang problem in this sample was 1988.6, meaning the later half of 1988. It is helpful to examine how this gang problem manifested itself over time by referring to Table 66.

The findings in Table 66 are therefore limited to those institutions that do in fact report a gang problem. There are some facilities that do not report a gang problem as having been "recognized" as such. Thus, the year of the emergence of the gang problem behind bars takes on significance only in reference to those facilities that are reporting a gang problem in the first place.

TABLE 66

**The Year Gangs Were First Recognized
As a Problem
In a Large National Sample of Adult State
Correctional Institutions (N = 232)
From the 1995 NGCRC Survey**

Year Gangs First Recognized As A Problem:	N	%
1965 - 1980	26	11.2
1981	4	1.7
1982	1	.4
1983	2	.9
1984	6	2.6
1985	11	4.7
1986	6	2.6
1987	5	2.2
1988	12	5.2
1989	21	9.1
1990	33	14.2
1991	16	6.9
1992	19	8.2
1993	35	15.1
1994	24	10.3
1995	11	4.7
	******	******
TOTALS	232	100.0%

As seen in Table 66, prior to 1981 the gang problem existed in only 11.2 percent of the correctional institutions. This began picking up in the 1980's, and in 1989-90 a sharp peak occurred. Only 31.5 percent of the facilities indicated their gang problem was first recognized on or before 1988. Nearly a fourth of American correctional institutions (23.3%) reporting a gang problem therefore indicate that they first recognized this gang problem in their facility during the 1989-1990 period. Another fourth (25.4%) first saw their gang problem in the period 1993-1994. The most important finding from Table 66 is that 59.5 percent of all of the American adult correctional institutions with a gang problem first recognized gangs as a problem in their facility on or after the year 1990! Thus, over half of the institutions first saw their gang problem arise in the 1990's.

One of the most important factors affecting the criminal justice system today is simply not monitored by any national group that has legal responsibility for it: the changing (i.e., increasing) gang density in these same institutions. The principal co-investigators for this study are not aware of any state that does not have a problem with gangs or gang members in its correctional system. The only issue is the matter of gang density, and the scope and extent

of the problem per se. Research suggests this is a growing problem, not a problem that is decreasing or disappearing nationally.

The 1993 survey showed mean date of 1987.

The 1999 survey showed that the mean date for when gangs were first recognized as a problem in their facility was about the time frame of June, 1990.

Nine Out of Ten Do Not Believe The Government Should Pay The Costs for Adult Inmates Enrolled in College Courses

The survey asked "do you believe that the government should pay the costs for adult inmates enrolled in college courses". In 1995, only 10.6 percent (N = 32) of the respondents indicated that they do in fact believe that public monies should be used to subsidize college courses for adult inmates. The vast majority (89.4%, N = 271) did not believe that the government should pay the costs for adult inmates enrolled in college courses.

	1995	1999
YES	10.6%	13.1%
NO	89.4%	86.9%

Four Out of Five Believe Federal Agencies Should Play A Greater Role in the Investigation and Prosecution of Gang Crimes

The survey asked "do you believe federal agencies should play a greater role in the investigation and prosecution of gang crimes".

In the 1995 survey, some 82.5 percent (N = 249) of the responding correctional administrators expressed the belief that federal agencies should in fact play a greater role in the investigation and prosecution of gang crimes. Just under a fifth (17.5%, N = 53) did not feel that federal agencies needed to play a greater role in the investigation and prosecution of gang crimes.

	1993	1994	1995	1999
YES	69.3%	69.6%	82.5%	84.0%
YO	30.7%	30.4%	17.5%	16.0%

Two-Thirds of the Correctional Institutions Responding to the Survey Thought That Chain Gangs Should Be Reinstated in Their Own State Correctional System

The survey asked "do you think chain gangs (i.e., hard labor crews) should be reinstated in your adult state correctional system". In the 1995 survey, some 64.8 percent (N = 199) of the respondents felt that chain gangs should in fact be reinstated in their own state correctional system. Among those favoring "bringing back chain gangs" were respondents from 43 different states! Only a third of the respondents (35.2%, N = 108) did not like the idea of bringing back chain gangs in their state correctional system.

This item was dropped from the 1999 survey to add a new variable on mentally retarded inmates.

Estimates of the Scope and Extent of Mental Retardation Among American Prison Inmates

The 1999 survey included the new question "please estimate what percentage of your total inmate population are mentally retarded (i.e., have IQ's less than 70)". The results indicated a mean value of 12.8% nationwide from the 1999 survey.

The Types of Economic "Rackets" Gangs Operate or Control in Adult State Correctional Institutions

The survey asked "what kind of economic rackets do gangs try to operate or control in your facility". A further instruction asked the respondent to check-off, among the options listed, those that are examples of economic "rackets" that gangs operate or control in their facility. A total of eight different economic "rackets" were separately listed in this check-off procedure. These rackets included: drugs, sex, food, clothing, loan sharking, gambling, extortion, and protection.

Table 67 presents the results of the descriptive statistical analysis for these eight different inmate rackets from the 1995 survey.

TABLE 67

Frequency and Percentage Distribution of the Types of Economic Rackets Reporting As Being Operated or Controlled By Gangs in a Large National Sample of Adult Correctional Institutions (1995 Results Compared to 1999 "Yes" Percentage)

Do Gangs Control/Operate These Rackets in Your Institution?

| Type of Racket | NO | | YES | | |
	N	%	N	%	1999%
Drugs	85	27.9	220	72.1	83.2%
Sex	198	66.7	99	33.3	30.5%
Food	171	57.2	128	42.8	46.6%
Clothing	211	71.8	83	28.2	29.0%
Loan Sharking	158	52.7	142	47.3	46.6%
Gambling	125	41.4	177	58.6	64.9%
Extortion	142	47.3	158	52.7	61.1%
Protection	128	42.1	176	57.9	56.5%

Table 67 shows that drugs, gambling, protection, and extortion are economic rackets that gangs attempt to operate or control in half or more of all of the adult state correctional facilities in this large na-

tional sample. The fact that many gangs engage in such behavior outside of the correctional setting simply means that they have been able to continue, to some unknown extent, this activity behind bars. The penal sanction does not mean we can expect a cessation of such criminal behavior that emanates from the gang as a group or organization is another way of interpreting the findings in Table 67. Where the gang was accustomed to victimizing the neighborhood in which it was located, the gang members behind bars appear to simply continue their behavior with new types of drug customers and new types of victims (i.e., other prison inmates).

What Table 67 also shows is the increased tendency for gangs to be involved in these prison rackets when we compare results from the 1995 and 1999 surveys. What is really on the rise: gang involvement in drugs and extortion behind bars would be the answer. The top three rackets for gangs behind bars would be drugs, gambling and extortion; in that order, according to the 1999 survey results.

Table 68
Comparison of Gang Involvement in Various Prison Rackets
Over Time from the NGCRC Prison Warden Surveys

Do Gangs Control/Operate These Rackets in Your Institution?

| | % YES | | |
Type of Racket	1994%	1995%	1999%
Drugs	67.8	72.1	83.2%
Sex	33.6	33.3	30.5%
Food	28.7	42.8	46.6%
Clothing	20.1	28.2	29.0%
Loan Sharking	45.5	47.3	46.6%
Gambling	50.9	58.6	64.9%
Extortion	50.5	52.7	61.1%
Protection	52.2	57.9	56.5%

What type of racket has shown a progressive increase in gang involvement behind bars? Table 68 above answers this question. Drugs, food, clothing, gambling, and extortion are inmate rackets that are showing increased gang involvement over time comparing the 1994, 1995 and 1999 survey results.

INMATE RACKETS: SIGNIFICANTLY MORE GANG INVOLVEMENT THE HIGHER THE SECURITY LEVEL OF THE INSTITUTION

When we examine the relationship between the security level of the institution and whether the same institution reports gang involvement in various inmate rackets, we see a significant and rather consistent trend. The trend is this: the higher the level of security for an institution, the larger the gang involvement in various inmate rackets. These findings are depicted below in Table 69.

Table 69

**Percentage Distribution of Institutions
Reporting Gang Involvement
in Selected Inmate Rackets
by the Level of Security
for the Same Institutions
From the 1999 Adult State Corrections Survey**

	Security Levels of the Institutions		
	Minimum	Medium	Maximum
Drugs	54.8%	89.7%	94.2%
	Chi-square = 24.0, p < .001		
Food	25.8%	51.0%	55.7%
	Chi-square = 7.51, p = .02		
Loan Sharking	22.5%	46.9%	61.5%
	Chi-square = 11.8, p = .003		
Gambling	45.1%	65.3%	76.9%
	Chi-square = 8.63, p = .01		
Extortion	29.0%	69.3%	73.0%
	Chi-square = 18.0, p < .001		
Protection	32.2%	57.1%	71.1%
	Chi-square = 11.9, p = .003		

Clearly, where the gang involvement in the inmate rackets becomes interesting is when we look at the variation within these adult state correctional institutions in terms of the security level of the facility. The minimum security level facilities consistently show the lowest degree of gang involvement in the various inmate rackets. The maximum security facilities consistently show the highest level of gang involvement in the inmate rackets (drugs, extortion, protection, etc).

Gang involvement in drug distribution is reported in only about half (54.8%) of the minimum security facilities; but this rises to 89.7 percent for medium security, and up again to 94.2 percent for maximum security facilities. The "protection" racket is one of the oldest rackets in the world: it means finding a weaker inmate, telling the inmate to 'pay up or face the consequences'. We see that only about a third (32.2%) of the minimum security facilities report gang involvement in this kind of activity, compared to 57.1 percent for medium level facilities, and 71.1 percent for maximum security facilities.

United States Currency Seized From Gang Inmates During the Last One Year Period
The survey asked "what was the largest amount of cash seized from gang member inmates during the last one year period". A blank line

($_____dollars) was used for this variable. In 1995, the results showed a range between a low of $5.00 dollars in cash to a high of $9,500.00 in cash being the largest amount of cash seized from gang inmates during the last one year time period. This included cash seizures from 88 different correctional institutions nationwide totalling $40,744 overall. Obviously, much more than this was probably actually seized, as the variable measured not the total amount seized, but rather the single largest amount seized from an inmate gang member during the last one year time period.   In the 1995 survey, the mean or average value of the largest amount of cash seized from a gang member in the last one year time period was $463.00 for this sample. We feel that it would be worthwhile to get a better handle on the scope and extent to which gangs dominate the correctional inmate underground economy, at least in terms of the amounts of money involved nationwide. It does suggest this may be a neglected area in terms of gang investigation and prosecution nationally.

In the 1999 survey, a total of $14,373 was seized by N = 45 institutions reporting this phenomenon, with a mean value of $319.40 nationwide.

About Four Fifths Report The Hardening Effect: Penal Sanctions Increasing Gang Ties
The survey asked "do you believe that gang members generally have a stronger affiliation with their gang after serving time". The hypothesis tested here is what we call the "hardening effect". It is similar, but different from, the hypothesized "conversion reaction" or solidifying effect. Nevertheless, it is a hypothesis consistent with that viewpoint which would argue that some suppression efforts can potentially increase gang solidarity, not decrease it. The variable measured here is simply a different and more focused factor about gang members in the correctional environment.

In 1995 the results of the survey showed that 80.5 percent (N = 235) of the responding adult state correctional administrators did feel that gang members generally have a stronger affiliation with their gang after serving time. This is consistent with the previous research) in that once a gang member is sent to a correctional institution, like being violated by his/her own gang, it may actually increase commitment to the gang in one sense: a greater opportunity for achieving gang "rank" exists behind bars, and a greater chance to meet up with the gang leaders occurs in that situation as well.

Thus, only a fifth (19.5%, N = 57) of the respondents did not feel that the penal sanction increases gang ties in 1995. This did not change much by 1999.

	1995	1999
YES	80.5%	78%
NO	19.5%	22%

Universal Support Among Prison Wardens In America: Public Notice Should Be Given Upon the Release of a Sex Offender

This question produced little variation is what our findings show. The survey asked "do you believe that public notice should be given upon the release of a sex offender". In 1995, the overwhelming majority (93.8%, N = 289) did in fact agree that such public notification should be given upon the release of sex offenders. In fact, only 6.2 percent (N = 19) of the responding correctional administrators did not support this idea.

It could be argued as well that correctional administrators are in a good position to know about the validity of the threat represented by sex offenders. We are aware of a growing trend in terms of victims rights and the prevention of sex crimes generally, where this process of public notification is coming to be adopted with varying degrees of strength in terms of public notice for the release of sex offenders.

	1995	1999
YES	93.8%	99.2%
NO	6.2%	0.8%

Less Than A Third Report Their Facilities Have Programs Designed to Improve Race Relations Among Inmates

The survey asked "does your facility have any programs for inmates which seek to improve race relations among inmates". In the 1995 survey, a third of the responding adult state correctional institutions (31.9%, N = 96) did report that their facilities to have programs that seek to improve inmate race relations. Thus, two-thirds (68.1%, N = 205) of the responding correctional institutions did not have such programs designed to improve race relations among the inmates in their facility.

It is important to point out that significant differences do exist in regard to facilities that do or do not have such programs designed to improve race relations among inmates. Table 70, for example, shows that a correctional facility that also reports there are racial conflicts among the inmates is almost twice as likely (40%) to also report having such programs designed to improve race relations among inmates, than when compared to correctional institutions that do not report that racial conflicts are a problem among their inmates (21.6%). Thus, Table 70 shows that having racial conflict problems among inmates is a factor that significantly differentiates whether the same facilities do or do not have such programs designed to foster better race relations among the inmates. In other words, institutions experiencing such problems are those more likely to adopt programs that focus on improving race relations among the inmates.

Not much changed in this regard comparing results for 1995 and 1999.

	1995	1999
YES	31.9%	29.8%
NO	68.1%	70.2%

What The Chi-Square Significance Test Means

This is an appropriate point to briefly explain to the reader how to interpret the meaning of the Chi-square test statistic used in this report. As seen in Table 70, the probability level for this Chi-square result is p = .001. What that means is that in only one time out of 1,000 could this result have occurred by chance alone, thus it is very significant. "Significant" in social research such as this basically means any probability level of .05 or less. Also, the higher the value of the Chi-square test statistic, the stronger the relationship between the two variables. A significant Chi-square test statistic means the two variables are not independent.

In the Chi-square statistic, the expected frequencies in a table are compared to the observed frequencies. The Chi-square test is therefore a test of independence. When the Chi-square test is not significant, that is the probability level if greater than .05, it is assumed the two variables are independent. When two variables are independent of each other, it basically means one has no major effect on the other. When the Chi-square test is in fact significant, that is the probability level is less than or equal to .05, then one can conclude that one variable does have a significant effect in differentiating the other variable (i.e., a relationship exists between the two variables).

TABLE 70

THE EFFECTS OF WHETHER RACIAL CONFLICTS ARE A PROBLEM IN THE INMATE POPULATION BY WHETHER PROGRAMS EXIST TO IMPROVE RACE RELATIONS AMONG THE INMATES (RESULTS FROM THE 1995 SURVEY)

		Does your facility have any programs for inmates which seek to improve race relations among inmates?		
		NO (N)	YES (N)	% Yes
Are racial conflicts a problem among the offenders in your facility?	NO	105	29	21.6
	YES	96	64	40.0

Chi-square = 11.3, p = .001

Few States Have Separate Facilities For Confidential Informants

Our research reveals that most state adult correctional systems do not have separate physical plants or facilities for confidential informants. Sometimes called "snitch farms", or Security Management Units, states with large gang problems find it inevitable to create these when seeking to prosecute gang members behind bars.

The survey asked "does your state have a separate correctional facility for confidential informants".

In the 1995 survey, only 11.4 percent (N = 35) of the respondents indicated their state has such separate facilities for confidential informants. Most (88.6%, N = 271) of the respondents indicated their state does not have separate facilities for confidential informants who are inmates.

From comparing data on this factor, over time, we do see a slight upward trend from the 1993, 1994, 1995 and 1999 surveys. However, it is a not a very remarkable upward trend.

	1993	1994	1995	1999
YES	10.5%	10.9%	11.4%	14.5%
NO	89.5%	89.1%	88.6%	85.5%

Recidivism Rates

Any study of adult corrections would not be complete without some focus on recidivism. There is no national standardized reporting format for recidivism that is lived up to. Although everyone understands its basic meaning. The basic meaning is "does the inmate return into the correctional system". So the survey asked "please estimate what percentage of your inmates have previously served time in your facility".

In the 1995 survey, the results ranged from a low of zero percent to a high of 98 percent. Suffice it to say, that great variation exists in this factor. The mean or national average was 39.1 percent.

	1995	1999
Mean	39.1%	42.3%

Vast Majority Support "Truth in Sentencing" Legislation

The 1995 survey asked "do you believe in the idea of truth in sentencing (i.e., a five year sentence really means serving 85 percent or more of that actual sentence)". Some 87.6 percent (N = 268) of the respondents indicated that they do in fact believe in the idea of "truth in sentencing". Only 12.4 percent (N = 38) indicated that they do not believe in the idea of "truth in sentencing". This item was dropped from the 1999 survey to include another factor about mentally retarded inmates.

The 1999 Factor on Mentally Retarded Inmates In Relation to Disciplinary Reports

The 1999 survey included the question "In your opinion, do the mentally retarded inmates (I.Q.'s less than 70) generally have a lower or higher number of disciplinary reports than other inmates?". Some 16.4 percent indicated "lower", some 52.3% indicated "about the same", and 31.3 percent indicated "higher".

Percentage of Inmates Who Are Mentally Ill

The survey asked "please estimate what percentage of the inmates in your facility are mentally ill". The 1995 survey results ranged from a low of zero percent to a high of 100 percent. The mean, or overall average, was that 7.6 percent of the inmates were mentally ill. The vast majority (83.4%) of the N = 283 respondents providing data for this variable gave estimates of ten percent or under.

	1995	1999
Mean	7.6%	12.8%

Increased Trend Towards State Political Pressure to "Play Down" Gang Activity

This is variable deals with the denial syndrome often associated with states having large adult correctional systems that also have high gang density rates. The survey therefore asked "do you receive any pressure from state officials to play down gang activity".

Results from the 1995 survey indicated that only 7.8 percent (N = 25) of the responding correctional administrators reported that they do in fact receive such pressure to engage in gang denial. The vast majority (92.2%, N = 294) of the correctional administrators responding to the survey indicated that they do not receive any such pressure to downplay the gang problem. This was certainly up from the 1993 and 1994 surveys, and increased somewhat again in the 1999 survey.

This would suggest an increased trend over time: the pressure to "play down" the gang problem behind bars may perhaps be more politicized today than in preceding years. In one sense, therefore, this aspect of "gang denial" is on the increase.

	1993	1994	1995	1999
Yes	2.3%	3.8%	7.8%	10.8%
No	97.7%	96.2%	92.2%	89.2%

Rising Factor: Correctional Facilities Report Disturbances Related to Gang Members in their Facilities During the Last Year

The survey asked "during the last twelve month period, have there been any disturbances related to gang members in your facility". In the 1995 survey, some 38 percent (N = 120) of the responding facilities did in fact report such gang disturbances during the last one year time period. Thus, about two-thirds (62%, N = 196) of the facilities surveyed reported not having any such gang disturbances during the last one year time period.

The trend indicates a significant rise over time comparing the 1993, 1995 and 1999 surveys for this factor. From the 1999 survey, about one-half of all adult state correctional institutions regardless of security level or where they are located are now reporting disturbances related to gang members in their facilities.

	1993	1995	1999
Yes	31.6%	38.0%	50.0%
No	68.4%	62.0%	50.0%

GANG DISTURBANCES: SIGNIFICANTLY MORE LIKELY IN HIGHER SECURITY LEVEL INSTITUTIONS

An interesting trend emerges when we look at gang disturbances in relationship to the level of security for the institutions that do or do not report this kind of security problem. Gang disturbances are like "mini-riots"; typically focusing on fights in a large area, a yard, a dining hall, a gym area, etc. The fighting is typically between rival gangs. The gangs carry their gang rivalry from the streets and into the prison with the same level of ferocity and animosity.

On the streets, the gangs may have their own "turf". In prison, they have to improvise. So the larger gangs in prison will take over a "function" in the prison: a weight-lifting area, a basketball court, a handball court, a section of bleachers, a specific area within the dining room, a section of grass or the ground, etc. These will be places they always congregate together.

The most serious type of injury from gang disturbances is a knife wound. The knife in prison is known as the "shank" or "shiv", it is typically homemade (i.e., an improvised weapon). The most typical injury is a "beating" of some kind, from the use of a blunt instrument or from kicking and punching of numerous attackers. Homicides that occur in prison are probably, in large part, "gang homicides"; however, these type of statistics are hard to come by.

Table 71 shows the relationship between security level of the facility and whether the facility reported gang disturbances during 1999. As seen here, a consistent and significant trend is evident. About one out of ten minimum security facilities (12.9%) reported such a gang disturbance. This rises quite dramatically to over half (59.1%) of the medium security level facilities. And increases further to 64.7 percent of the maximum security facilities reporting gang disturbances from the 1999 survey.

In minimum security facilities, inmates are often given only a "token" level of security: don't go past point X. Many of the inmates in minimum security may have outside work, education, and training opportunities. In otherwords, the inmates in a minimum facility have much more contact with the outside world. Still, even in these type of facilities, about one out of ten are in fact reporting such gang disturbances. What happens is the "offenders" get shipped back to a higher level of institutional security. Thus, the "hard core" predators are massed in the higher level facilities, where, not surprisingly, we also find the highest level of such gang disturbances as well.

Table 71

Distribution of Institutions Reporting a Gang Disturbance Among Inmates in the Last Year By Level of Institutional Security for the Facilities Represented in the 1999 Adult State Corrections Survey

	Levels of Security for the Institutions		
	Minimum	Medium	Maximum
Any Gang Disturbances During 1999?			
NO	27	20	18
YES	4	29	33
% Yes	12.9%	59.1%	64.7%

Chi-square = 23.1, p < .001

Two-fifths of All Correctional Facilities Report Disturbances Related to Racial Conflict in their Facilities During the Last Year

The survey asked "during the last twelve month period, have there been any disturbances related to racial conflict in your facility". In the 1995 survey, some 40.3 percent (N = 128) of the correctional institutions responding to the survey indicated that they have in fact experienced such racial disturbances during the last one year time period. Thus, 59.7 percent (N = 190) of the respondents reported no such racial disturbances during the last one year.

	1993	1995	1999
Yes	35.1%	40.3%	40.3%
No	64.9%	59.7%	59.7%

Comparing the 1995 and 1999 results, shows that there was absolutely no change in this factor during the 1995 to 1999 interval.

The Strong Relationship Between Racial Disturbances and Gang Disturbances in Correctional Institutions

Previous research by the NGCRC has shown that in adult and juvenile correctional contexts that racial disturbances are not independent of gang disturbances. The present research enables another very direct large scale test of this hypothesis. Table 72 provides the results of this test using the 1995 data.

As seen in Table 72 a strong significant relationship emerges here (p < .001) between racial disturbances and gang disturbances in adult state correctional institutions. Among those facilities that had no racial disturbances in the last year, only 13.7 percent also had gang disturbances. However, among those facilities that did in fact have racial disturbances in the last year, some 74.6 percent of these facilities also had gang disturbances in the same last one year time period.

These findings are very consistent with earlier research dating back to 1990 on the relationship between racial conflict and gang conflict (see Knox, 1994). In other words, having one of these problems tends to very substantially increase the likelihood of having the other problem as well. Thus, the problems are both closely related in a significant way.

Table 73 replicates this test using the recent 1999 data. Again, the same effect occurs, and it is again very significant. Any facility with a racial conflict problem stands a far greater probability of also facing a gang disturbance problem is what this data is showing.

TABLE 72

The Effects of Racial Conflicts on Gang Conflicts in a Large National Sample of Adult State Correctional Institutions (Results from the 1995 Survey)

	During the last 12 month period, have there been any disturbances related to gang members in your correctional institution?		
During the last 12 month period, any disturbances related to racial conflict in your facility?	NO (N)	YES (N)	% Yes
NO	163	26	13.7%
YES	32	94	74.6%

Chi-square = 118.6, p < .001

TABLE 73

The Effects of Racial Conflicts on Gang Conflicts in a Large National Sample of Adult State Correctional Institutions (Results from the 1999 Survey)

	During the last 12 month period, have there been any disturbances related to gang members in your correctional institution?		
During the last 12 month period, any disturbances related to racial conflict?	NO (N)	YES (N)	% Yes
NO	57	20	25.9%
YES	8	46	86.7%

Chi-square = 46.4, p < .001

Few Report That Their Staff Sometimes Find it Necessary to Negotiate With Gang Members in Order to Keep the Peace

The survey asked "do staff in your facility sometimes find it necessary to negotiate with gang members in order to keep the peace".

In the 1995 survey, only 12.2 percent (N = 37) reported that staff in their facility do sometimes find it necessary to negotiate with gang members in order to keep the peace. Most of the respondents (87.8%, N = 266) indicated that their staff do not engage in wheeling and dealing with gang members as an order maintenance device.

It is risky indeed to negotiate with any offender in custody, particularly gang members. Thus, not surprisingly, we find only 15.4 percent of the institutions engaging in this practice in the 1999 survey.

	1995	1999
Yes	12.2%	15.4%
No	87.8%	84.6%

An Empirical Test: Does Negotiating With Gang Members Lower the Risk of Gang Disturbances?

Can the casual process of negotiating with gang members to keep the peace among prison inmates help to also reduce the probability of gang disturbances? The present research allows us to directly test this hypothesis. We will use two variables already discussed in this report: (1) the issue of negotiating with gang members in order to keep the peace, and (2) whether there have been gang disturbances during the last year. The variable about negotiating with gang members is shown to have a significant effect in terms of differentiating whether institutions do or do not have gang disturbances. The results of this test are provided in Table 74.

TABLE 74

The Relationship Between Prison Staff Sometimes Negotiating With Gang Members to Keep the Peace And Whether The Same Facilities Actually Report A Gang Disturbance in the Last Twelve Months
(Results from the 1995 Survey)

	During the last 12 month period, have there been any disturbances related to gang members in your facility?		
	NO (N)	YES (N)	% Yes
Do staff in your facility sometimes find it necessary to negotiate with gang members in order to keep the peace? NO	183	81	30.6
YES	8	28	77.7

Chi-square = 30.3, p < .001

As seen in Table 74, there is a strong relationship between the two variables: one significantly differentiates the other, that is very clear. However, it is not consistent with the expectation that having staff who sometimes negotiate with gang members means having an institution with a reduced likelihood of also having gang disturbances. In fact, the relationship is very strong in the direction of suggesting something else entirely.

Survey research cannot prove causation, because survey research like the present research is cross-sectional in nature. However, one this is very clear: institutions that have staff who sometimes find it necessary to negotiate with gang members in order to keep the peace are also institutions that have a very high rate of gang disturbances in the last one year time period (77.7%). Only 30.6 percent of the facilities that did not have staff who periodically negotiate with gang members to keep the peace reported being institutions that also had gang disturbances in the last year.

While the causal nexus remains uncertain[51], the findings in Table 74 still bear great attention. For if the condition of having staff who negotiate with gang members is occurring to prevent gang disturbances from occurring in the first place, rather than

in dealing with gang disturbances ex post facto in a "cool down" mode, then what Table 74 might be saying is that negotiating with one security threat group or gang is enough to ensure a statistically significant increase, not a decrease, in the probability of an eventual gang disturbance in the same facility. The present researcher would highly recommend that this matter be subjected to further additional research. For the possibility exists that confused policies at an administrative level could adversely impact on the safety of correctional staff and inmates alike.

This research would recommend no negotiation with inmate leaders or members of gangs or STGs for anything other than for gang intelligence purposes. The reason is Table 74 suggests that it may be possible that the following scenario occurs: a pattern of concessions are made to gang leaders or gang members in the goals of conflict management, however the intense competition between rival gangs being as deadly as it is may also generate ongoing enmity by the symbolic consequences of "favoritism" towards one or another of the gangs. No special favors resulting from "negotiation" should therefore accrue to inmates who will interpret this action from legitimate authority to mean a delegation of power or control.

Gangs and STGs will always take the offer that confers upon them any unique power, authority, or control that they can further exploit against the mission statement of the correctional facility. Written policy statements for correctional mid-management and line staff should be prohibit disturbing the equilibrium of gang conflict among inmates in this fashion <u>as independent individual relationships</u> with gang or STG members; the reason is that where it occurs legitimately is in the intelligence area (strategic: for an overall management plan; and tactical: i.e., for purposes of immediate criminal prosecution), and this means the information must be codified, centralized, and analyzed in a feed-back loop to all others in this unique "social system" called the adult state correctional institution.

Hostage Situations Involving Inmates and Staff

The survey asked "when was the last time your facility had a hostage situation involving inmates and staff? 19____ or ____Never". In the 1995 survey, some N = 76 institutions provided dates for the last time their facility had a hostage situation involving inmates and staff. Some N = 240 of the respondents indicated "never". Thus, 24.1 percent of the respondents did report a hostage situation since 1969 with a mean value of 1985.2, meaning the early part of 1985.

The trend is easy to summarize for hostage situations. In the 1995 survey, the dates for the last hostage situation ranged from 1969 to present (1995).

A fourth (25%) of those reporting such hostage situations, last had a hostage situation on or before 1980. About half (52.6%) last had a hostage situation on or before 1986. However, some 28.9 percent of those reporting having ever had a hostage situation indicated their last hostage situation as occurring on or after 1992.

Three Fourths of Adult State Correctional Institutions Report That Most of Their Staff and Employees Have Received Training in Cultural Diversity

The survey asked the yes or no question: "have most of your staff and employees received training in cultural diversity". In the 1995 survey, some 74.1 percent (N = 237) indicated "yes", that in fact most of their staff and employees have received training in cultural diversity. Thus, only a fourth (25.9%, N = 83) of the responding adult state correctional institutions indicated that they had not yet met this condition.

From the 1995 data, there was no significant difference regarding gang disturbances or racial disturbances during the last year with respect to this training factor. Nor did this factor significantly differentiate beliefs about whether anything could be done to reduce racial conflicts among inmates.

Comparing the 1995 and 1999 surveys shows little change over time in regard to this factor.

	1995	1999
Yes	74.1%	77.3%
No	25.9%	22.7%

Date of Last Major Inmate Riot In Their State System

The survey asked "for your entire state correctional system, when was the last major inmate riot". For the 1995 survey, the results ranged from as long ago as 1954 to as recently as the present year (1995). About a fourth (26.7%, N = 73) reported their last major inmate riot in their state system on or before the year 1983. In fact, half (48.7%, N = 133) reported the last major inmate riot in their state system on or before 1988. Yet some 21.2 percent (N = 58) reported a riot during 1995.

From the 1999 survey the mean date was May, 1991 for the last major inmate riot.

Two-Fifths Report Staff Members In Their Facility Testing Positive for the PPD (Tuberculosis) Test in the Last Year

The survey asked "have any staff members in your facility tested positive for the PPD (tuberculosis) test in the last twelve months".

For the 1995 survey, data was available on N = 296 institutions. The results showed that 43.2 percent (N = 128) did in fact report staff testing positive for the PPD test during the last year. Some 56.8 percent (N = 168) reported no staff testing positive for the PPD test during the last year.

For the 1995 survey, there was no significant relationship observed between staff testing positive for the PPD test during the last year and the variable for whether the same institutions isolate inmates who also test positive for the PPD test. Where the significance comes in for the variable of staff testing positive for the PPD test is in relationship to inmates who have been diagnosed with TB during the last one year time period. Among institutions reporting that no inmates had been diagnosed with TB during the last year, only 22.5 percent also reported staff who tested positive for the PPD test. Yet among institutions reporting that they have had any inmates who have been diagnosed with TB during the last year, some 63.3 percent of the same institutions report that staff have in fact tested positive for the PPD test during the last year as well (Chi-square = 47.5, p < .001). The link between the two factors is very strong and significant enough to command the attention of policy makers.

In the 1993 survey, the item format was somewhat different, it asked HOW MANY staff members had tested positive for the PPD test in the last year. This yielded a mean of 4.57 staff members testing positive during the last year. Still, 49.6% reported one or more such staff members testing positive for the PPD test.

This is a politically sensitive survey item: some respondents were readily able to talk about gang problems among the inmates, but marked on their surveys "confidential information" when it came to this factor. We would want to assume, therefore, that these figures are very conservative estimates given the possible tendency to under-report on this factor.

Staff Test Positive for PPD

	1993[52]	1995	1999
Yes	49.6%	43.2%	43.5%
No	50.4%	56.8%	56.5%

Over Half of the Institutions Isolate Inmates Testing Positive for the PPD Test

The survey asked "are inmates who test positive for the PPD (tuberculosis) test isolated from other inmates".

In the 1995 survey, some 56 percent (N = 172) of the facilities in the sample indicated that inmates testing positive for the PPD test are in fact isolated from other inmates. Still, some 44 percent (N = 135) indicated that inmates testing positive for the PPD test are not isolated from other inmates.

This jumped to 65.6% in the 1999 survey. We might expect it to continue to rise in that a recent Supreme Court ruling rejected an inmate lawsuit challenging a correctional system's right to segregate HIV positive inmates, under the assumption that it was a safety issue that the institution had a right to enforce.

	1995	1999
Yes	56.0%	65.6%
No	44.0%	34.4%

Half of Correctional Administrators Would Regard A Gang Density Rate of Six Percent as A Moderate Problem

The most recent federally funded research on gangs in corrections concluded that only six percent of the American prison inmate population are gang members. The earlier Camp and Camp (1985) report had concluded that only three percent of the American prison inmate population were gang members at the time of their study. The survey asked "if you state prison system had six percent of its inmates involved in gangs or security threat groups how would you regard this as a problem for corrections? ___Minor problem ___Moderate problem ___Severe problem". From the 1995 survey, some 19.7 (N = 60) percent regarded it as a minor problem. About half (54.6%, N = 166) regarded a six percent density rate as a moderate problem. And 25.7 percent (N = 78) regarded a six percent density rate as a severe problem.

Not much changed in the 1999 survey: 24.4 percent regarded it as a minor problem, 55.0 percent regarded it as a moderate problem, and 20.6 percent regarded it as a severe problem.

The Gang Density Threshold for Having a Severe Gang Problem

The survey asked "at what percentage of the inmate population (% who are members of gangs or STGs) would you feel that a severe gang problem exists? ____Percent".

From the 1995 survey, the results ranged from a low of one percent to a high of 90 percent. The mode, or most frequently cited threshold level, was ten percent. The mean, or arithmetic average, threshold level was 16.3 percent. Only a fourth (27.2%) gave ratings of six percent or under. Some 48.4 percent gave thresholds of 11 percent or higher. A third (36.7%) gave thresholds of 20 percent or higher, while two-thirds (63.3%) gave thresholds of 15 percent or lower. In fact, 89 percent gave thresholds of 30 percent or under.

What we need to point out here is how this variable compares with the actual conditions estimated for the same institutions. This national sample indicated its gang threshold would be 16.3 percent, i.e., at the point of having 16.3 percent of the inmate population as gang or STG members a "severe problem" would exist in their evaluation. Recall from the earlier analysis of actual gang density rates that nationally our current estimate is that 20.5 percent of

all male inmates are in fact gang or STG members. Thus, the current estimate of gang density exceeds the threshold at which point a "severe problem" exists.

Gang Threshold

	1995	1999
Mean	16.3%	18.8%

Most Security Threat Groups or Gangs Behind Bars Also Exist By the Same Name Outside of Prison

The survey asked "do the more dangerous security threat groups that exist in your facility also exist by the same name in communities outside of the correctional environment".

From the 1995 survey, over three-fourths (83.9%, N = 230) of the respondents indicated that the more serious STG's in their facility also exist by the same name in communities outside of the prison environment. Thus, most of the more dangerous STG's in the American prison system are basically what some call street gangs, at least gangs that exist as well outside of confinement. Only 16.1 percent (N = 44) of the respondents answered the question "no".

From the 1999 survey, we are able to say that in about 9 out of ten cases, the gangs behind bars also exist by the same name outside of the prison situation. Thus, according to the 1999 survey, 89.6 percent of the gangs that exist in prison are also gangs that operate by the same name outside of prison.

	1995	1999
Yes	83.9%	89.6%
No	16.1%	10.4%

Growing Trend: Prison Gangs Have Tended To Result in More Improvised Weapons Production Among Inmates

The survey asked "in your opinion, have prison gangs tended to result in more improvised weapons production (e.g., shanks, etc) among inmates in your facility".

As early as the 1992 survey, 37.2 percent of adult state correctional institutions were reporting that prison gangs have tended to result in more improvised weapons production in their facilities. This then increased to 40.5 percent in the 1993 survey.

From the 1995 survey, about half of the correctional administrators in the sample (47.6%, N = 141) expressed the opinion that prison gangs have resulted in greater improvised weapons production. Similarly, about half (52.4%, N = 155) did not feel that prison gangs have resulted in greater improvised weapons production in their facility.

The most recent survey in 1999 showed that 55.6 percent of adult state correctional institutions were reporting that prison gangs have tended to result in more improvised weapons production in their facilities. This aspect of gang life behind bars is, therefore, clearly on the rise.

	1992	1993	1995	1999
Yes	37.2%	40.5%	47.6%	55.6%
No	62.8%	59.5%	52.4%	44.4%

Four-Fifths Agree: We Need Tougher Laws to Control the Gang Problem in Prison

The survey asked "do you feel we need tougher laws to control the gang problem in prison".

From the 1995 survey, some 81.2 percent (N = 254) of the correctional administrators responding to the survey expressed the opinion that tougher laws are in fact needed to control the gang problem in American corrections today. Only a fifth (18.8%, N = 59) did not feel that tougher laws are needed to control the gang problem behind bars.

There is no consistent pattern comparing the 1992, 1993, 1995 and 1999 survey results on this factor. There was an increase over time in the 1992, 1993, and 1995 surveys; and then this factor dipped back to 78.6 percent in the 1999 survey.

	1992	1993	1995	1999
Yes	73.4%	76.2%	81.2%	78.6%
No	26.6%	23.8%	18.8%	21.4%

Half Believe A Program to Improve Race Relations Could Reduce the Gang Violence or STG Problem as Well

The survey asked "do you believe a program that sought to improve race relations among inmates could reduce the gang violence or Security Threat Group (STG) problem in your facility". The correctional administrators were evenly mixed on this issue.

From the 1995 survey, about half (48.1%, N = 140) did believe that such a program to foster better race relations could reduce the gang or STG problem in their facility. Still, half (51.9%, N = 151) did not believe that such a program could reduce the threat posed by the gang problem in their facility. This extent to which someone might believe in this strategy for handling gang problems in correctional institutions may depend, we hypothesize, on whether or not the same administrators believe that anything at all can or cannot be done about race relations. We will come to this issue shortly in another section of this report.

This believe in reducing gang violence through improved race relations increases only slightly to 52.8 percent in the 1999 survey.

	1995	1999
Yes	48.1%	52.8%
No	51.9%	47.2%

Growing Trend: The Percentage of All Institutional Management Problems Caused By Gangs or STGs

The survey asked "in your estimate, what percentage of all institutional management problems in your facility are caused by gangs/STGs or gang/STG members? ____ Percent".

From the 1995 survey, the results for this variable ranged from a low of zero percent (23.3% indicated zero percent of their institutional management problems could be traced to gangs or STGs) to a high of 100 percent. The mean, or average, was that 17.2 percent of all institutional management problems in the facilities surveyed here were caused by gangs or STGs or their members.

This was up slightly from the mean of 16.4 percent in the 1993 survey. It jumps up again in the 1999 survey where the best estimate today is that about a fourth (25.7%) of all institutional management problems in adult state correctional institutions are causes by gangs or Security Threat Groups.

	1993	1995	1999
Mean	16.4%	17.2%	25.7%

Growing Trend: The Percentage of All Inmate Violence Caused by Gangs or Gang Members

The survey asked "in your estimate, what percentage of all violence among inmates in your facility is caused by gangs or gang members". From the 1995 survey, the results ranged from a low of zero percent (22.8% indicated zero percent) to a high of 100 percent. The mean, or average, was that 22.1 percent of all inmate violence in American adult correctional institutions was caused by gangs or gang members. This was up only slightly from the mean of 20.4 percent in the 1993 survey. Yet by 1999 we see this mean value rise to 29.2 percent.

	1993	1995	1999
Mean	20.4%	22.1%	29.2%

The Debate About Weight Lifting For Inmates: Two-fifths Say Eliminate It

The survey asked "do you feel it would be a good policy to eliminate weight lifting for inmates". From the 1995 survey, some 42.6 percent (N = 135) of the correctional administrators responding to the survey agreed that it would be a good policy to eliminate weight lifting for inmates. But 57.4 percent (N = 182) of the respondents did not feel it would be a good policy to eliminate weight lifting for inmates. Obviously, a debate exists about this issue even among corrections professionals.

We did examine this variable in relationship to several other factors. First, it did not vary by objective risk conditions such as whether gang members have been a problem in terms of assaults or threats on staff, nor did it vary significantly by institutional security level of the responding facility. Second, it did vary by what are essentially variables measuring beliefs: those who felt the government should not pay the costs for inmates enrolled in college courses and those who felt stronger laws are needed to control the gang problem were those who were more significantly likely to want to eliminate weight lifting for inmates.

In the 1999 survey, there appears to be even stronger support for the idea of eliminating weight lifting for prison inmates. Some 53.9 percent of the respondents in the 1999 survey were in favor of eliminating weight lifting.

	1995	1999
Yes	42.6%	53.9%
No	57.4%	46.1%

Most Now Agree: Telephone Monitoring Is Effective in Disabling Gang Leaders From Maintaining Ties to Outside Gang Members

The survey asked "in your opinion is telephone monitoring an effective technique to prevent gang leaders from maintaining their ties to outside gang members". From the 1995 survey, four-fifths (80.4%, N = 242) of the correctional administrators responding to the survey agreed that telephone monitoring is an effective technique in this regard. Only a fifth (19.6%, N = 59) did not believe telephone monitoring could be effective in this way.

	1995	1999
Yes	80.4%	91.4%
No	19.6%	8.6%

Most Also Now Agree: Mail Monitoring Prevents Gang Leaders From Maintaining Ties to Outside Gang Members

The survey asked "in your opinion is mail monitoring an effective technique to prevent gang leaders from maintaining their ties to outside gang members". In the 1995 survey, four-fifths (82.2%, N = 250) of the respondents did in fact feel that mail monitoring is an effective technique to prevent gang leaders from maintaining their ties to outside gang members. Only a fifth (17.8%, N = 54) did not believe in the effectiveness of this technique.

There was an increase in the perceived value of mail monitoring, as the 1999 survey showed that 91.5 percent of the respondents believed mail monitoring was an effective technique to prevent gang leaders from maintaining their ties to outside gang members.

	1995	1999
Yes	82.2%	91.5%
No	17.8%	8.5%

A Statistical Rarity: the Prison Warden Who Thinks that Prisons are Feared and a Deterrent to Gang Members

The survey asked "do you think prisons are feared and a deterrent to gang members". In the 1995 survey, some 95.4 percent of the respondents (N = 292) expressed the viewpoint that prisons are not feared by or a deterrent to gang members. Only 4.6 percent (N = 14) felt that prisons are feared and a deterrent to gang members. This is, after all, not very surprising to those in the field of criminal justice as it would be to most civilians unfamiliar with the gang problem.

In fact, by 1999, less than one percent of the respondents believed that prisons are feared and a deterrent to gang members. So it is a statistical rarity to find someone who works in adult corrections to express the belief that prisons are feared and a deterrent to gang members.

	1995	1999
Yes	4.6%	0.8%
No	95.4%	99.2%

Two-Thirds Believe It Is Possible to Reduce Racial Conflicts Among Inmates

The survey asked "do you think anything can be done to reduce racial conflicts among inmates". In the 1995 survey, some 69.4 percent (N = 211) did express the viewpoint that something can in fact be done to reduce racial conflicts among inmates. About a third (30.6%, N = 93) of the respondents were more fatalistic in taking the belief that nothing can be done to reduce racial conflicts among inmates.

In the 1999 survey some 71.3 percent of the respondents did feel that something can be done to reduce racial conflicts among inmates.

	1995	1999
Yes	69.4%	71.3%
No	30.6%	28.7%

The Greater The Belief That Racial Conflicts Can Be Reduced Among Inmates, The More That Race Relations Improvement Is Believed To Be A Way To Reduce The Gang Problem

This may be an issue of skepticism and disbelief generally, that is one of attitude alone. We had hypothesized, however, that the extent to which correctional administrators thought that a program seeking to improve race relations could have a positive effect on reducing the gang problem is itself a factor that would vary by beliefs about the extent to which race relations among inmates can be experimentally manipulated. It seems clear that to the extent that race relations can be deteriorated by ugly isolated incidents receiving much adverse publicity that one must admit that race relations among virtually all human beings is subject to experimental manipulation. The only question is the direction of the impact.

This is, we feel, still a vital and neglected issue that still remains somewhat of a taboo topic in nearly all correctional publications today. Few correctional textbooks, and fewer still publications targeting a correctional practitioner audience, address the issue of race relations among inmates. We are thankful that the correctional administrators in America continue to provide us with this meaningful information to analyze in light of this need for more useful knowledge on the issue. The NGCRC has, and continues to be, one of the few groups to address this issue directly, systematically, and objectively.

Table 75 shows, then, an important finding in this regard. Using the 1995 survey data, among those who do not believe much can be done about race relations among inmates, only 20.4 percent felt a program designed to improve race relations could possibly reduce the gang problem behind bars. Among those believing race relations can be shaped in a positive direction, the percentage triples to 60.4 percent for those believing that a program designed to improve race relations could also reduce the gang or STG problem as well.

TABLE 75

The Effects of Believing Whether Anything Can Be Done To Reduce Racial Conflicts Among Inmates by Whether the Same Prison Wardens Believe that a Program Designed to Improve Race Relations Among Inmates Could Also Reduce the Gang and STG Problem in Their Facility As Well
(Findings from the 1995 Survey Data)

	Do you believe a program that sought to improve race relations among inmates could reduce the gang violence or Security Threat Group (STG) Problem in your facility?		
Do you think anything can be done to reduce racial conflicts among inmates?	NO (N)	YES (N)	% Yes
NO	70	18	20.4%
YES	78	119	60.4%

Chi-square = 38.8, p < .001

Half of the Correctional Facilities Report Having Had Inmates Diagnosed With Tuberculosis During The Last Year

The survey asked "during the last year, have any inmates in your facility been diagnosed with tu-

berculosis". In the 1995 survey, some 53.8 percent (N = 157) of the responding adult state correctional facilities did in fact report such recent cases of TB being diagnosed among their inmates. Similarly, half (46.2%, N = 135) did not report such cases of TB being diagnosed among their inmates during the last one year period.

The 1993 data suggested a higher level of the TB problem, 62.9 percent reporting inmates being diagnosed with TB in the last year. But in 1999, this is still at about the 1995 level (54.1% for 1999, 53.8% for 1995).

	1993	1995	1999
Yes	62.9%	53.8%	54.1%
No	37.1%	46.2%	45.9%

Special Programs in Adult Corrections for Mentally Retarded Inmates

The 1999 survey included the question "does your facility have a special program (i.e., habilitation services) for mentally retarded inmates (inmates with I.Q.'s less than 70)?". Some 42.3 percent of the responding facilities indicated "yes", that they did in fact have such programs for the mentally retarded inmates. Still, about half (57.7%) indicated they did not have such programs.

Inmate Population Count

The survey asked "what is the total inmate population (count) for your institution as of today". The count for each respondent was used to generate a larger total sum. Thus, among the institutions in the 1995 sample, there were a total of N = 240,724 inmates incarcerated in their collective facilities. Female inmates made up 4.5 percent of the total sample which is very close to the national average. Historically, in the American adult state correctional inmate population females have constituted about five percent of the overall confined population.

In the 1999 survey a total of N = 155,663 inmates were incarcerated in the institutions surveyed; of which N = 151,840 were males, and N = 3,066 were females.

Security Levels of the Institutions

The survey asked "what level of security is your institution".   In the 1993 survey the results were as follows: 23.5% minimum, 42.4% medium, and 34.1% maximum security.

In the 1995 survey, just under half (45.2%, N = 127) were minimum security facilities. About a fourth (28.1%, N = 79) were medium security. And about a fourth (26.7%, N = 75) were maximum security institutions.

In the 1999 survey, 24.2% were minimum security, 37.1% were medium security, and 38.6% were maximum security facilities.

Nearly Half Believe Providing Tuition Support for Staff Could Help Deal With The Gang Problem

The survey asked "do you believe that providing tuition support for staff could help control the prison gang problem". The issue here is continuing education for correctional officers. Those with greater training, perhaps in social sciences and particularly in criminal justice where today many universities offer courses about the understanding/control/prevention of gang problems, would be better equipped to confront the intense personal dynamics of gang life behind bars.

In the 1995 survey, some 45.1 percent (N = 138) of the respondents did believe that providing tuition support for staff could help control the prison gang problem. Just over half (54.9%, N = 168), however, did not believe this tuition help to staff could help deal with the prison gang problem.

The trend in this data is up somewhat, but is just not consistent as a pattern over time. Both the 1993 and 1995 levels were at about 45 percent, this did jump to 56.9 percent for the 1999 survey.

	1993	1995	1999
Yes	45.3%	45.1%	56.9%
No	54.7%	54.9%	43.1%

The Year The Facility's Physical Plant Was Constructed

The survey asked "in what year was your physical plant constructed".

In the 1995 survey, the results for this variable were available on N = 289 institutions. The results showed a range from as old as 1836 to as recently constructed as the current year (1995). Only ten percent were built on or before 1900. Some 35.3 percent were built on or before 1950. Half (50.5%) were built on or before 1969, thus the other half (49.5%) were built on or after 1970. A fourth (26.3%) had been built on or after 1985. The average age of these physical plants was that they were constructed in the year 1957.

A Growing Trend: Having Full-Time Staff Employed as Ombudsmen for Inmates

The survey asked "does your institution have any full-time staff employed as ombudsmen for inmates".

In the 1995 survey, the results showed that only 16.1 percent (N = 48) of the respondents indicated that their facility had any full-time staff employed in the role of being ombudsmen for the inmates. Most of the respondents (83.9%, N = 250) reported having no such full-time staff employed in this capacity.

The use of staff employed as ombudsmen for inmates increased over ten points comparing the 1995 and 1999 surveys. By 1999 some 28.2 percent of the institutions reported using staff employed as ombudsmen for inmates.

	1995	1999
Yes	16.1%	28.2%
No	83.9%	71.8%

Most Believe Gang Members Gang Members Have a Higher Recidivism Rate

The survey asked "in your opinion, do gang members tend to have a higher recidivism rate".

In the 1995 survey, some 79.4 percent (N = 227) expressed the opinion that they do believe gang members tend to have a higher recidivism rate. A fifth (20.6%, N = 59) did not believe gang members have a higher recidivism rate.

In the 1999 survey we see this increased, where 87.3 percent of the responding facilities are reporting that gang members tend to have higher recidivism rates.

	1995	1999
Yes	79.4%	87.3%
No	20.6%	12.7%

Growing Trend: Institutions Taking Gang Membership Into Account in Their Classification System for Inmates

The survey asked "does your institutional classification system take gang membership into account".

In the 1991 survey, about half (51.9%) of the institutions reported that their classification took gang membership into account. That means that about half used the fact that the inmate was a gang member in the way they classified inmates; for purposes of security ratings, job and housing assignments, etc.

In the 1995 survey, some 60.3 percent (N = 178) of the respondents indicated that their inmate classification system does take gang membership into account. Thus, 39.7 percent (N = 117) indicated that their inmate classification system does not take gang membership into account.

Comparing the 1992, 1995 and 1999 surveys we do see a steady upward progression in the use of gang membership as a factor to be taken into account in the inmate classification systems in adult correctional institutions. By 1999, this had increased to 68.3 percent of the institutions taking gang membership into account in their inmate classification systems.

	1992	1995	1999
Yes	51.9%	60.3%	68.3%
No	48.1%	39.7%	31.7%

Strategies Currently Used to Control Gang Members Behind Bars

The survey asked "what strategies does your facility use to control gangs (check all those that apply)". The check off list was used, and included every previous known technique, plus new options known to exist. The results from the 1995 survey are presented in Table 76.

As seen in Table 76 the most frequently used techniques to control the gang problem in adult state correctional institutions today include: transfers (79.7%), case by case dealings (72.3%), monitor and track gang members (64.4%), monitor mail (61.2%), segregation (59.6%), and displacing members to different facilities (59.7%).

As seen in Table 76, few fortunately are using questionable techniques that are controversial in their own right such as: joint meetings between various gang leaders (3.5%), coopting of prisoners to control gangs (3.8%), and ignoring their existence (4.9%).

Sadly, while a great deal of gang research on a variety of topics has been funded by the federal government in recent years, absolutely no gang research has been funded that examines the more practical issue of the effectiveness of any of these gang control techniques listed in Table 76. It simply has been a neglected issue by federal funding sources.

So while we know a lot about the gang problem behind bars in terms of what control strategies are actually being used to deal with the gang problem, we still know very little about the comparative effectiveness of these different approaches, or whether some approaches in combination have the best overall impact on reducing the violence threat represented by gangs and STGs.

One option in the list in Table 76 is very new: involvement in the National Major Gang Task Force established through the American Correctional Association members. This is a relatively new initiative. But Table 76 does show a growing involvement in this effort to collaborate and share information across jurisdictions, as 13.8 percent indicated this was a part of their overall strategy. Still, the vast majority (86.2%) of the responding correctional institutions in this sample indicated that the National Major Gang Task Force is not included in their strategies used to deal with gang problems in corrections today.

Table 77 compares the use of these strategies to control gangs/STGs behind bars over time from the NGCRC surveys.

TABLE 76

Frequency and Percentage Distribution of Strategies Used to Control Gangs in a Large National Sample of Adult State Correctional Institutions (Results from the 1995 Survey)

| Gang Control Strategies Used: | Does Your Facility Use This Strategy to Control Gangs? | | | |
| | NO | | YES | |
	N	%	N	%
Transfers	61	20.3	239	79.7
Use of Informers	137	46.3	159	53.7
Segregation	118	40.4	174	59.6
Isolating Leaders	161	54.4	135	45.6
Lockdown	191	65.6	100	34.4
Prosecution	206	71.0	84	29.0
Interrupting communications	187	64.3	104	35.7
Case by case	83	27.7	217	72.3
Ignoring their existence	273	95.1	14	4.9
Infiltration	270	93.8	18	6.3
Displacing members to different facilities	119	40.3	176	59.7
Coopting of prisoners to control gangs	278	96.2	11	3.8
Meeting with gang leaders on an as needed basis	254	88.2	34	11.8
Joint meetings between various gang leaders	277	96.5	10	3.5
Balance the number of rival gang members living in the same unit	210	72.9	78	27.1
National Major Gang Task Force	250	86.2	40	13.8
Monitor and track gang members	106	35.6	192	64.4
Locking up gang leaders in high security facilities	201	68.4	93	31.6
Monitor mail	116	38.8	183	61.2
Monitor telephone calls	147	49.3	151	50.7
Other	277	96.2	11	3.8

TABLE 77

**Percentage Distribution of
Strategies Used to Control Gangs
in a Large National Sample of Adult State
Correctional Institutions
(Results Comparing the 1992, 1993, 1995
and 1999 Surveys)**

Does Your Facility Use This
<u>Strategy to Control Gangs?</u>
(percent by year)

Gang Control Strategies Used:	1992	1993	1995	1999
Transfers	65.5	73.0	79.7	80.8
Use of Informers	46.8	53.4	53.7	61.5
Segregation	48.1	57.5	59.6	69.2
Isolating Leaders	42.3	50.0	45.6	48.5
Lockdown	24.5	35.1	34.4	38.5
Prosecution	26.1	29.9	29.0	29.2
Interrupting communications	28.7	39.1	35.7	46.2
Case by case dealings	45.5	50.0	72.3	73.8
Ignoring their existence	5.5	4.6	4.9	4.6
Infiltration	1.6	4.0	6.3	6.2
Displacing members to different facilities	54.2	52.3	59.7	58.5
Coopting of prisoners to control gangs	2.6	5.7	3.8	3.8
Meeting with gang leaders on an as needed basis	5.8	13.2	11.8	10.0
Joint meetings between various gang leaders	1.3	5.2	3.5	3.1
Balance the number of rival gang members living in the same unit	16.5	19.5	27.1	25.4
National Major Gang Task Force	n/a	n/a	13.8	19.2
Monitor and track gang members	n/a	n/a	64.4	70.8
Locking up gang leaders in high security facilities	n/a	42.5	31.6	39.2
Monitor mail	n/a	n/a	61.2	83.1
Monitor telephone calls	n/a	n/a	50.7	74.6
Other	n/a	n/a	3.8	13.1

Obviously, some of the interesting findings comparing the 1992, 1993, 1995 and the 1999 survey results have to do with what has not changed. Things that probably would never work continue to show low usage: ignoring their existence, infiltration, coopting inmates, joint meetings with gang leaders.

Comparing the 1992, 1993, 1995, and 1999 surveys is useful to examine those strategies that show a slow, but steady increased usage to control gangs behind bars. These include: (1) transfers, (2) use of informers, (3) segregation, and (4) dealing with gang members on a case by case basis.

Comparing the 1995 and 1999 surveys, dramatic increased usage is shown in monitoring mail and telephone calls.

USING INFORMERS TO DEAL WITH THE PRISON GANG PROBLEM

The use of informers among prison inmates is clearly on the rise as a strategy to deal with the gang problem. However, an important controversy needs to be pointed out in regard to this issue.

Here is the problem: the use of informers, "rats", "stool pigeons", etc, has had its critics in correctional circles. It is the matter of long-term effectiveness, and the potential trade-offs. One of the potential trade-offs is that, in some circumstances, it creates a weakness in the correctional organization itself if a dependency develops from the use of informants. Some have also claimed that excessive use of this technique is conducive to prison rioting among inmates, as happened in the New Mexico Penitentiary case (Gettinger, 1980: p. 19). Certainly, prison officials using informers are inducing some degree of tension and suspicion among inmates. This was argued, for example, in the analysis by Serrill and Katel (1980) who noted that in the New Mexico Penitentiary riot, informers were systematically sought after for torture and execution by the rioting inmates.

Growing Trend: Gangs Significantly Affecting The Correctional Environment

The survey asked "do you believe that gang members have significantly affected your correctional environment".

In the 1992 survey about a fourth (27.7%) of the institutions reported that gang members had significantly affected their correctional environments. This rose to 41.4 percent in the 1993 survey.

In the 1995 survey, some 54.1 percent (N = 170) of the respondents indicated that they did in fact believe that gang members have significantly affected their correctional environment. Similarly, 45.9 percent (N = 144) did not feel that gangs have significantly affected their correctional environment.

In the 1999 survey, this factor of gang members significantly affecting the correctional climate, rose to 63.4 percent. Thus, a consistent steady progression over time suggests gangs may have significantly altered the correctional climates in adult American correctional institutions, and the "inmate cultures" found there.

	1992	1993	1995	1999
Yes	27.7%	41.4%	54.1%	63.4%
No	72.3%	58.6%	45.9%	36.6%

Number of Full-Time Personnel Employed By Their Facilities

The survey asked "how many full-time personnel are employed by your facility". In the 1995 survey, a total of N = 71,270 full-time personnel were employed in the sample of institutions surveyed here. A total of N = 45,495 full-time personnel were employed in 1999 survey sample.

Growing Favorable Ratings for The Federal Department of Justice: Providing Effective Leadership in Suppressing the Gang Problem in American Cities

The survey asked "do you feel the federal Department of Justice has provided effective leadership in suppressing the gang problem in American cities".

As early as 1993 only 7.3 percent of the responding correctional institutions expressed the belief that the federal Department of Justice has provided effective leadership in suppressing the gang problem in American cities. This "confidence vote" factor would rise in the subsequent 1995 and 1999 surveys.

In the 1995 survey, some 87.8 percent (N = 258) felt that the federal Department of Justice has not provided effective leadership in suppressing the gang problem in American cities. Only 12.2 percent (N = 36) of the respondents felt that the federal Department of Justice has in fact provided effective leadership in suppressing the gang problem in American cities.

In the 1999 survey this factor of the "confidence vote" for the federal Department of Justice rose to 21.3 percent. One might say that a goodly amount of additional progress is still warranted, given the fact that 78.7 percent of the 1999 respondents did not feel that the federal Department of Justice has provided such effective leadership.

Overall, however, these findings over time would suggest that a growing level of confidence exists, however small it remains.

	1993	1995	1999
Yes	7.3	12.2%	21.3%
No	92.7	87.8%	78.7%

Gang Involvement in Smuggling Drugs Into Correctional Facilities

The survey asked "in your opinion, what percent of all illicit drugs are brought into your facility by prison gang members".

In 1993 about a fourth (27.2%) of all drugs smuggled into correctional facilities were believed to be brought in by gang members.

In the 1995 survey, the results ranged from a low of zero percent to a high of 100 percent. The 1995 mean, or average, was that 32.6 percent of the illegal drugs were being smuggled into correctional institutions by gang members.

In the 1999 survey this increased, only slightly, suggesting that again about a third (34.1%) of all drugs are smuggled into prisons by gang members. While the trend is upwards in nature, it is not a very strong trend.

	1993	1995	1999
Mean	27.2%	32.6%	34.1%

Gang Involvement in Drug Sales Within The Inmate Underground Economy

The survey asked "in your opinion, what percentage of the illicit drug trade in your facility is dominated by gang/STG members".

In the 1993 survey, it was reported that 31.4 percent of the illegal drug trade behind bars was dominated by gang or STG members.

The 1995 survey results ranged from a low of zero percent to a high of 100 percent. The mean or average was that 35.0 percent of the overall illicit drug trade in these correctional facilities was dominated by gang or STG members.

In the 1999 survey, we see a progressive increase, but not a very substantial increase. In 1999, we find that 37.2 percent of the prison drug trade is controlled by gang members. Obviously, gang members have some work to do to continue to be a dominating force in this type of underground economy. Perhaps the fact that by inference, most of the illegal drug trade is not controlled by gang members will be the basis for conflicts and tension and/or gang violence in the years ahead behind bars. It is the issue of competition for this lucrative business of illegal drugs behind bars.

	1993	1995	1999
Mean	31.4%	35.0%	37.2%

Half Report That Overcrowding is a Problem in their Facility

The survey asked the yes/no question "Generally, is overcrowding a problem in your facility".

In the 1995 survey, half (52%, N = 166) of the institutions reported that generally overcrowding is a problem in their facility. Half (48%, N = 153) reported that generally overcrowding is not a problem in their facility.

In the 1995 survey, this factor was significant in relationship to the variable measuring whether any inmates had been diagnosed with TB during the last one year period (Chi-square = 5.95, p = .01). Among those facilities that reported overcrowding was a problem in their facility some 60.4 percent had also reported inmates being diagnosed with TB during the last year, this compares with 46 percent for those institutions that reported overcrowding was not a problem in their facility.

Comparing the 1993, 1995, and 1999 survey results on prison overcrowding, we see that there is a small overall steady increased in reported overcrowding.

	1993	1995	1999
Yes	47.7%	52.0%	53.0%
No	52.3%	48.0%	47.0%

Life-Threatening Violence Among Inmates in the Last Year

The survey asked "please estimate how many violent assaults among inmates that resulted in life-threatening injuries during the last twelve month period".

In the 1995 survey, the results ranged from a low of zero to a high of 178. In fact, half (49.1%, N = 139) of the respondents indicated zero such incidents in the last year of life-threatening violence among inmates in their facility. The mean, or average, was 3.8 such life-threatening cases of inmate violence during the last year.

In the 1999 survey the results ranged from a low of zero to a high of 300; for a total of N = 1,036 such assaults in the sample overall.

	1995	1999
Mean	3.8	8.5

Most Correctional Administrators Feel A Zero Tolerance Approach to Gangs is Best

The survey asked for a range of responses for their views about the statement "a zero-tolerance policy is the best approach for dealing with gangs and gang members".

In the 1995 survey, some 65.4% (N = 208) strongly agreed. Another 21.7% (N = 69) agreed. Thus, the vast majority (87.1%, N = 277) of the respondents agreed or strongly agreed with the zero-tolerance policy on gangs and gang members. Only 8.8 percent (N = 28) indicated they neither agree or disagree. Only 3.8 percent indicated they disagreed. And one lone respondent (.3%) indicated "strongly disagree".

Not much had changed as reflected in the 1999 survey, there is an increase in the "strongly agree" category however, in 1999 it shot up to 74.8% in strongly in favor of "zero tolerance".

	1995	1999
Strongly Agree	65.4%	74.8%
Agree	21.7%	16.8%
Neither A or D	8.8%	4.6%
Disagree	3.8%	3.8%
Strongly disagree	0.3%	0.0%

Inmate-Against-Inmate Assaults: Degree of Gang Involvement

The survey asked the respondents to estimate the percent of inmate-against-inmate assaults that in-volved gang members.

In 1995, the results ranged from a low of zero percent to a high of 100 percent. The mean, or average, was that 23.8 percent of all inmate-against-inmate assaults involved gang members.

By 1999 this had risen to 32.7 percent nationwide.

	1995	1999
Mean	23.8%	32.7%

Major Change: Having Staff Who Belong to State or Regional Gang Investigator Associations

The survey asked "do any of your staff belong to the state or regional Gang Investigators Association".

In 1993 only about a fifth (19%) of the institutions reported they had staff who belonged to state or regional gang investigator associations. This would rise dramatically over the years.

In 1995, some 28.9 percent (N = 88) indicated that they did have staff who were active in their local gang investigator associations. Most (71.1%, N = 217) of the correctional institutions did not have staff who belonged to these gang investigator associations.

As of 1999, about half (51.1%) of the institutions are reporting that they have staff members who are now involved with state or regional gang investigator associations. This represents a very significant increase over time comparing the 1993, 1995 and 1999 survey results.

	1993	1995	1999
Yes	19.0%	28.9%	51.1%
No	81.0%	71.1%	48.9%

No Change: Gang Members Do Not File More Law Suits Than Do Non-Gang Member Inmates

The survey asked "do gang members generally tend to file more law suits against your institution than non-gang member inmates". In the 1995 survey, some 92.7 percent (N = 254) of the responding correctional facilities indicated that gang members generally do not tend to file more law suits against them than non-gang member inmates. Only 7.3 percent (N = 20) indicated that gang members are more prone to this activity than non-gang member inmates.

In the 1999 survey we see that only 5.6 percent of the respondents are reporting that gang members tend to file more law suits. Thus, generally, gang members are not more litigious than other inmates would seem the fair conclusion.

	1995	1999
Yes	7.3%	5.6%
No	92.7%	94.4%

The Institutions That are Community-Based

The survey asked "is your facility community-based".

In the 1995 survey, some 45.5 percent (N = 137) indicated that their facility is in fact community-based. Some 54.5 percent (N = 164) indicated that their facility is not community-based.

In the 1999 survey some 39.1 percent of the responding institutions regarded their facility as being community-based.

	1995	1999
Yes	45.5%	39.1%
No	54.5%	60.9%

Types of Correctional Institutions Represented in the Study

The survey asked "which category best describes your facility" and the check-off options corresponded to currently used categories of correctional institutions.

In the 1995 survey, some 59.2 percent (N = 173) were adult correctional institutions. Only one (.3%) was a correctional medical facility. Some 9.9 percent (N = 29) indicated their facility was a prison or penitentiary. Some 4.8 percent (N = 14) indicated their facility was a reception and diagnostic institution. Some 8.2 percent (N = 24) indicated their facility was a work camp/farm/forestry/conservation center. Some 17.1 percent (N = 50) indicated their facility was a community correctional center. And one respondent (.3%) indicated the facility was a boot camp/shock incarceration facility.

In the 1999 survey, again 59.1 percent were adult correctional institutions, 23.5 percent were prisons/penitentiaries, 2.3% reception/diagnostic center, 2.3% work camp/farm/forestry/conservation, 10.6% community correctional centers, and 2.3% boot camp/shock incarceration.

Most Institutions Expect The Gang Problem in Corrections to Increase in the Next Few Years

The survey asked "in your opinion, do you expect the gang problem in corrections to increase or decrease in the next few years, or do you think the problem will remain at the same level it is at now".

In the 1995 survey, some 89.1 percent (N = 285) expected the gang problem in corrections to increase in the next few years. Some 2.2 percent (N = 7) actually felt the gang problem would decrease in the next few years, and these optimistic souls are clearly the minority in our sample. Finally, 8.8 percent (N = 28) felt the gang problem in the next few years would remain about the same level it is at now.

In the 1999 survey, we see a small decrease in the percentage who expect the gang problem to increase (80.3% in 1999). Another change comparing the 1995 and 1999 results is increase since 1995 in the percentage who expect this problem to "remain the same".

	1995	1999
Increase	89.1%	80.3%
Decrease	2.2%	1.5%
Remain same	8.8%	18.2%

Most Institutions Expect Inmate Gang Violence To Increase in the Next Few Years

The survey asked "in your opinion, do you expect the problem of inmate violence from gang/STG members to increase or decrease in the next few years, or do you think the problem will remain at the same level it is now". The results are very consistent with the previous finding.

In the 1995 survey, some 86.1 percent (N = 273) expect the problem of inmate violence from gang/STG members to increase in the next few years. Some 2.5 percent (N = 8) felt the problem would decrease in the next few years. And 11.4 percent (N = 36) felt the problem would remain at the same level it is at now.

In the 1999 survey a substantial shift was seen: lower expectation of increased gang violence, higher expectation for gang violence to remain at the current level. In 1999, 72.7 percent felt there would be an increase in gang violence among inmates in the next few years. A fourth (25.8%), in 1999, expected the level of gang violence to remain constant.

	1995	1999
Increase	86.1%	72.7%
Decrease	2.5%	1.5%
Remain same	11.4%	25.8%

SUMMARY: FINDINGS OF GANGS IN ADULT STATE PRISONS

This study has some clear messages for a national correctional policy on gangs. Several things are very clear from this study. Among the major warning signs that emerged from this study is that the vast majority of prison wardens in adult state correctional institutions do in fact believe that in the next few years the gang problem will dramatically increase behind bars. In the mean time, we still have no national knowledge other than that by the NGCRC that systematically tracks this problem. Most importantly, no evaluation research has been undertaken to assess the kinds of gang control strategies that work best.

It would appear that a crisis is facing adult corrections in America today and that the policy response is comparable only to what is called the ostrich phenomenon in law enforcement gang research: sticking one's head in the sand and hoping the problem will just go away. In the mean time as well, staff and correctional officers will continue to face the real and genuine threat of an increasingly dangerous situation from gang members and security threat groups (STGs).

The most recent federally funded research on gangs blamed prison administrators on the east coast for being in a denial mode (American Correctional Association, 1993). That same research was not able to obtain the level of cooperation we obtained here. Our findings suggests it is really a problem of knowing how to do good research. The same administrators said to be in a denial mode somehow cooperated with this survey. Only one state did not "cooperate", but we viewed this not as a reason to stop the research, but an opportunity to get even closer to the real "data". When New York state continued to instruct its wardens not to respond to our questionnaires, we simply contacted line staff in key positions who were obviously closer to the day-to-day problems that gangs and STG's represent behind bars. California, Illinois, and Virginia have historically had high resistance to our annual surveys, but in spite of their bureaucratized central office policies on answering questionnaires[53], some of the wardens there still complete our surveys.

The ACA study based on half a million dollars in funding by the National Institute of Justice appears to have been a major failure given the extent of misinformation it contains. The ACA report indicated no gangs in the adult state correctional systems of the following states: Georgia, Kentucky, Louisiana, Maine, Montana, New York, North Carolina, North Dakota, Vermont, and Wyoming. The problem may have been the way ACA conducted the study[54], using only one informant for each entire state it is possible that this over-aggregated unit of analysis was not able to reach to the individual institutional level of analysis, and was therefore more prone to basically be in the naive research situation of asking someone something the single respondent in each state did not really know. All we can say is that many of these same states over the years have indicated a gang presence to the NGCRC when we go to the individual correctional institutions and use the superintendent or warden as the unit of analysis.

The ACA report was overly simplistic in its research methodology by assuming a single person statewide would be knowledgeable and up-to-date about all gang or STG activities in all facilities in the same state. It was a "top down" research style, while the annual surveys conducted by the NGCRC are "bottom up". Here is what we do know: all fifty states and the District of Columbia today do in fact have some gangs or STGs in their inmate populations as of 1995. It is further possible that the ACA, being an agency that is also the accreditation body for correctional institutions, was not appropriate ethically as an awardee for the federally funded research on the same institutions; thus, while the ACA report

blamed many correctional state systems for being in the "denial mode", what may have actually been occurring is a natural and normal level of cautiousness in responding to gang surveys from the same agency that bestows or removes accreditation. The proof of this is the fact that the yearly adult corrections gang assessment surveys conducted by the NGCRC since 1991 have been able to obtain much more evidence of gang and STG activity than the ACA study. While the ACA report cost over half a million dollars in federal funding, the NGCRC yearly surveys barely cost $1,000 each year because no one was being paid and no profit was sought for this important service. It is an important issue because we are talking not only about the safety of inmates but of correctional staff!

Fortunately, the ACA was not effective at disseminating its research, thereby perhaps minimizing the damage of misinformation. We know, because we researched this too. The 1994 Annual Survey of Adult Correctional Institutions by the NGCRC had survey responses from N = 290 wardens or superintendents and asked them the following question: "Did you read the report entitled <u>Gangs in Correctional Facilities: A National Assessment</u> (ACA, April 12, 1993)". The data was collected in the fall of 1994. The majority (71.8%) of the respondents indicated they had not read the ACA report on gangs.

The NGCRC mission statement is based on the service model of research: provide a useful service while conducting research. Thus, most of our research over the years has been probono research. Good research is not research that generates lots of income to the researchers from federal agencies like OJJDP and NIJ. Unfortunately, many scholars today feel obligated to do research only when they have such funding. Good research is work that has both scholarly and practical applications, extending our knowledge of the problem and helping to clarify the national picture in a way that leads us towards consensus. We know what bad research is: studies that use poor methodologies, with low response rates, and with results that are meaningless. But when we are dealing with the gang problem some moral obligation exists for researchers when dealing with agencies to educate those same agencies. The researchers must be responsible for this because we cannot assume that agencies like NIJ and OJJDP are effective in dissemination based on recent research findings to that effect.

Now we come to the proof of a crisis about gangs in American adult state corrections. One of the questions in this 1995 survey asked the prison administrators what they thought would be the "threshold" for the point at which a severe gang problem would exist. Our research findings in this report showed that at the point where 16.3 percent of the inmate population are gang members, American corrections can at this point in time be said to be at the level of having a severe gang problem. That density rate of 16.3 was the national average for the threshold of determining when a facility would have a severe gang problem. The current national estimated gang density from this research is that at least 20.5 percent of all male adult state correctional inmates are gang members. Thus, we have already surpassed the point of a "severe gang problem" by this reasoning. It is further worthwhile to point out to the reader that our current estimate of 20.5 percent as the national estimate for male inmate gang density is over three times that estimated in the recent federally funded research on gangs in corrections.

This research has helped to answer the larger social policy question of "how serious is the gang problem in American state adult correctional institutions today?". The answer indicated in a state-by-state analysis of all fifty states is this: the gang problem in adult state corrections is very serious and it is expected to get a lot worse in the upcoming years.

• Some 15 states have one or more institutions reporting that they receive pressure from state officials to "play down" gang activity.

• About half the 50 states have one or more institutions reporting that gangs have been a problem in terms of assaults upon staff or correctional officers.

• Some 31 states have one or more institutions reporting that they feel that gangs or gang leaders are able to influence politicians in their state.

• Some 36 states have one or more institutions reporting that gangs have been a problem in terms of threats against staff or correctional officers.

• Some 37 states have one or more institutions reporting that white inmates have a separate gang.

• Some 37 states have one or more institutions reporting that during the last year there have been disturbances related to gang members in their facility.

• Some 40 states have one or more institutions reporting that prison gangs have tended to result in more improvised weapons production (e.g., shanks, etc) among inmates in their facility.

• Some 41 states have one or more institutions reporting that gang members have significantly affected their correctional environment.

• Some 42 states have one or more institutions that have now introduced disciplinary rules to prohibit gang recruitment in their facility.

• Some 49 states have one or more institutions reporting that they expect the problem of inmate violence from gang/STG members to increase in the next few years.

• Some 49 states have one more institutional

administrators who believe that tougher laws are needed to control the gang problem in prison.

• All fifty states have one or more institutions reporting that they expect the gang problem in corrections to increase in the next few years.

One disturbing overall finding compels attention from this report: the fact that while our findings from this national assessment of prison gangs and security threat groups (STGs) provide a conservative research estimate of the current national gang density, this rate is three times higher than that of the latest federally funded research! The ACA study estimated 6 percent of the American adult state corrections population were gang/STG members. Our data shows it was at least 20 percent in 1995! National law enforcement estimates of the "at large" gang member population, also Department of Justice funded studies, are also about one third of the size of the problem in research carried out and reported by the NGCRC. Sadly, it seems as if we can take the federally funded gang research estimates and triple them to arrive at what is closer to the truth about the scope and extent of the gang problem in the United States today.

GANG PROBLEMS IN LOCAL AND COUNTY JAILS

The first U.S. national gang research survey of local and county jails was carried out by the National Gang Crime Research Center and reported in the spring of 1993 representing a national sample of N = 140 jails[55]. Again, to our knowledge, this is the first effort to assess the scope and extent of the gang problem nationally in local and county jails[56].

The jail administrators were asked what percentage gang members constitute of the overall inmate population. For male inmates, the estimates ranged from a low of zero for 36.2 percent of all jails responding to the survey, to a high of 60 percent. For female inmates, again the estimates ranged from a low of zero for over two thirds (72.7%) of the jails, to a high of 85 percent. The mean or average estimate for all jails for male inmates was 5.05 percent, and 2.18 percent for female inmates.

Only about a fourth (26.6%) of the jails indicated that their staff receive formalized training in dealing with gang problems. Among those jails that did provide such gang training to its officers, in over four-fifths (83.8%) of these jails providing such training, the amount of training was eight hours or less. In fact, the average or mean hours of gang training was 6.6 hours. Two-thirds (67.9%) of the jail administrators responding to the survey expressed the opinion that their staff could benefit from professional outside training dealing with gangs.

Only 2.9 percent of the jails report that gang

members have been a problem in terms of assaults on their staff. Yet a fourth (26%) of the jails in the survey reported that gang members have been a problem in terms of threats against jail staff.

Very comparable to their adult state prison and juvenile correctional counterparts, some 43.2 percent of the jails in the survey reported that racial conflicts are a problem among the inmates in their facilities. In fact, some 19.8 percent of the jails report that whites have a separate gang.

About half of the jail administrators (52.9%) agreed that giving staff recognition to inmate gang leaders is similar to negotiating with terrorists.

Supporting the validity of the claim that gangs have vastly proliferated in a relatively recent period of American history, the jail administrators report almost identically to the views of law enforcement administrators reviewed in the previous chapter, that when asked in what year did gang problems among inmates first become recognized in your facility ---- 91.5 percent of the jails report that the gang problem first arose on or after 1981! The breakdown over yearly periods was as follows:

In what year did gang problems among inmates first become recognized?

	% of Jails
On or before 1980	8.5%
1981 - 1984	6.8
1985 - 1988	22.0
1989 - 1992	57.6
1993	5.1

Only ten percent of the jail administrators believed that conjugal visiting could be used as a reward to control gang problems in jails. When asked if providing college tuition support for staff could help control the inmate gang problem, some 38.5 percent of the jail administrators agreed. Some 18.6 percent of the jails expressed the opinion that inmate gangs have tended to result in more improvised weapons production among their inmates. Three fourths (76.9%) of the jail administrators felt we need tougher laws to control the gang problem among inmates.

Only about half (51.8%) of the jail administrators felt that their facility had enough resources and programs to control the gang problem. Stronger support exists among in jails than in prisons for establishing national and professional standards to deal with the gang problem. When asked if the American Correctional Association should establish standards for controlling inmate gangs, some 72.3 percent agreed. When asked if the American Jail Association should establish such standards, some 74.6 percent agreed.

Using the checklist approach, the respondents were asked to report what strategies were used in their jail facilities to control gangs. The following reflect the rank-ordered results from the most used

to the least used of the gang control techniques among the jails in this sample: segregation (39.6%), case by case dealings (33.1%), transfers (30.9%), isolating leaders (30.2%), lockdown (26.6%), use of informers (19.4%), interrupting communications (18%), prosecution (17.3%), displacing members to different facilities (15.1%), balance the number of rival gang members living in the same unit (14.4%), ignoring their existence (3.6%), meeting with gang leaders on "as needed" basis (3.6%), coopting of prisoners to control gangs (2.9%), infiltration (2.2%), joint meetings between various gang leaders (1.4%).

Still, only 11.6 percent of the jail administrators report that inmate gangs have significantly affected their correctional environment. The jail administrators were also asked a couple technical questions that yielded interesting results. When asked if they were familiar with the Camp and Camp (1985) report, only 5.9 percent indicated they were familiar with it. When asked if their jail facility has been able to make use of any of the research reports available from the National Institute of Justice, 55 percent said "no".

Gangs inside major urban jails operate very similarly to their counterparts in state adult correctional institutions. The larger gangs issue memos to their members, these gangs even maintain their own "disciplinary system" to control their members. So the modern gang member inmate has several codes of conduct to obey: that of the prison system itself and the "official rules and regulations", and the rules imposed by the gang --- the latter probably being the rules that get obeyed more often. of people beyond boundaries without measures.

SUMMARY AND CONCLUSION

The gang problem for corrections is growing, not declining, and is expanding throughout the United States. As a problem that may be responsible for assaults and threats on correctional officers the problem appears to be significant enough to establish written standards governing gang control strategies and techniques. These are necessary in order to cope with the changing character of prison populations. Programing for the social psychology of gangs should involve a closer examination of group capability to dominate legitimate prison organizations (Jaycees, etc).

Certainly, a stronger interface between law enforcement and corrections is essential for any effective strategy of gang control. Some prisons and state systems simply are not routinely interacting with law enforcement agencies in the sharing of gang intelligence. This may change now, however, as a recent issue of Corrections Today indicated that an intelligence clearinghouse is being created, allowing correctional officials in various states to share reports and information that might be helpful in gang control policies and procedures. Providing more effective gang training for correctional staff is equally important.[57] There are simply limits to the age-old technique of "bus therapy". No one wants gangs bussed in. Traditional strategies and techniques for dealing with prison gangs appear to represent a "shoot from the hip" approach to ad hoc correctional management and decision making rather than enjoying the benefits of a decision support system or any evaluation research on their efficacy. Some such techniques still in use are believed to be counterproductive and detrimental in the long term.

Targeting gang resources in some state statutes is permitted. Perhaps, as well, it is time to develop more "carrots" of social control and the time may be ripe for allowing conjugal visiting programs in more of our prisons. Not as an appeasement, but for the value of compliance and social control that such a program implies when offered as a "honor" for good behavior.

Gang recognition in the correctional setting is a common technique, but is a stop gap measure and an unsound gambit in the long run. It is equivalent to affording the gang organizational legitimation. In Illinois, a Chicago Police officer in a paper prepared for the American Society of Criminology argues that "super gangs" were made in prison (Bobrowski, 1988). Gangs can be expected to expand in the combat and racial strife that is endemic to some of our larger institutions. This suggests the merits of programing and services centered around the goal of improving race and ethnic relations among inmates. Alternatively, the absence of such policies and procedures to reinforce better race relations in a context of racial violence and racial enmity can only mean when trouble does erupt, and it can be anticipated, here we go again with another potential area of legal liability --- from both correctional staff and inmates.

DISCUSSION QUESTIONS:

(1) Do you think that prison holds as much fear as a deterrent today for gang offenders as it is assumed to have had historically for lone criminal offenders, when going to prison is like a "homecoming" for gang members, indeed a chance to earn higher rank and get to know their gang leaders better?

(2) If being a "neutral" or "neutron" (non-gang affiliated inmate) is next to impossible inside a correctional facility, do you feel that this poses some liability for correctional officials under the "cruel and unusual punishment" doctrine where inmates are assumed to have the right to live free from harm or violence?

(3) What policies, procedures, and initiatives would you develop to deal with gangs and STGs behind bars if you were the Director of the adult corrections department in your state? How would you ensure that these strategies to deal with gangs and gang members are actually effective?

Boot Camp Given the Boot: It Didn't Work!
        A fad that began in the 1980's is dying in the 1990's. Boot camps or shock incarceration. Sounds good. The public likes the idea of "getting tough" by using military-style discipline. But eventually someone had to ask "does it really work?".
        In 1997 Arizona shut down its boot camp, the Arizona Shock Incarceration Unit[59]. Like most boot camps, if someone from 18 to 25 years of age can make it through the 120 day sentence, they could get out. Sounded good. It was looked on as a way to relieve prison overcrowding as well. And judges like the idea of an alternative to incarceration.
        But a study of the N = 1,253 inmates sentenced to the Arizona boot camp during its first three years of operation showed that 70 percent were recidivists: they were back in the system doing time on a new charge typically within a 4 to 7 year period. Other states are following the same pattern: like other "fads" that have come and gone in American corrections.

WHO HOLDS THE WORLD RECORD FOR MOST INTENSIVE JAIL AND PRISON GANG VIOLENCE IN ONE DAY? ANSWER, VENEZUALA.
        On August 28th of 1997 it really got hot in the El Dorado jail in Venezuela, where 29 inmates were hacked and stabbed to death by rival gang members. Most of those killed were recently transferred into the jail from the La Sanbaneta jail. The issue was who would control the jail. Shortly before dawn, the local gang caught a lot of the transferred gang members sleeping: broke the locks on the cells, went in and hacked them up. When they could not get inside the cell, they set it on fire with incendiary devices. Some 29 gang inmates died and another 13 were injured.
        On Friday, April 28, 2000, the "El Modelo" federal prison in Bogata, Columbia became a second runner up; when 26 inmates were killed in a gang disturbance.
        So, South American prisons hold the record, that is clear.

END NOTES:

[1] Gangs in the correctional setting date back to the 19th century as illustrated by Hobsbawm (1965: p. 34) involving Mafia gangs in the Milazzo jail.

[2] See: "Prisons Boss Seeks Funds Hike", Chicago Sun-Times, March 30, 1994, p.22. Tamms is in southern Illinois. The same article indicates IDOC has 35,049 inmates in a system designed to hold 22,007.

[3] Here for those who are skeptical of the racism-oppression thesis we actually find motivation relating to racism playing a very large part in decisions to join a gang. Recall that Jackson and Mc Bride (1990) report the early formation of the Aryan Brotherhood (as the Bluebirds), not unlike Chinese gangs in New York, forming to protect against perceived threats. But also like the New York Chinese gangs, once established the Aryan Brotherhood and its equivalent youth gang counterparts, often take on a life of their own.

[4] For an excellent history of the BT system see: Aric Press, "Inside America's Brutal and Overcrowded, The Texas Prison System Was Told to Reform or Else", Newsweek, October 6, 1986.

[5] The United Nations Standard Minimum Rules for the Treatment of Prisoners and Related Recommendations, is U.N. resolution adopted 30 August 1955. Its provision # 28 says "No prisoner shall be employed, in the service of the institution, in any disciplinary capacity". (See John W. Palmer, 1977, Constitutional Rights of Prisoners, Anderson Publishing Company, p. 953).

[6] Steve J. Martin and Sheldon Ekland-Olson, 1987, Texas Prisons: The Walls Came Tumbling Down, Austin, TX: Texas Monthly Press, Inc; Ben M. Crouch and James W. Marquart, 1989, An Appeal to Justice: Litigated Reform of Texas Prisons, Austin, TX: University of Texas Press.

[7] Says Lane "if prison administrators are not in control of their facilities, the gangs will attempt to exert their influences" (Lane, 1989: p. 99). Another author (Bartollas, 1990) also explicitly asserts that some prisons are really "run" by gangs.

[8] See: p. 13, "High Noon at the D.O.C.: How Dick English Made It Work", Illinois Police and Sheriffs News, Spring, 1994.

[9] The killer in this instance, David Starks, 32, was sentenced to natural life; avoiding the death penalty by claiming he was ordered by his gang to commit the "hit". See: Jerry Shnay, "Inmate is Spared Death Penalty", Chicago Tribune, Section 2, March 15, 1994, p. 2. This law needs to be changed immediately, making it an automatic death penalty case for murdering a correctional officer, police officer, or public official.

[10] See: Jerry Thomas, "Gangs A Rising Threat to Prison Guards", Chicago Tribune, Nov. 28, 1993.

[11] See: Gary Marx, "Medium-Security Prisons No Longer Medium Secure", Chicago Tribune, Section 2, pp. 1, 4.

[12] Hunt, Riegel, Morales and Waldorf (1993) note that the first national study of prison gangs was that by Caltabiano (1981) involving 45 state prisons. Caltabiano's (1981) findings were not made known to the public as it is an unpublished report for the Federal Bureau of Prisons.

[13] The Camp and Camp data was collected in 1983 and reported in 1985. Just a few years would lapse until Lane (1989) would report that 80 to 90 percent of Illinois prison inmates are gang affiliated. What that means is either two things: (1) either there was an enormous rapid reproduction of gang membership in American prisons during this period, or (2) the Camp and Camp data seriously underestimated gang force strength. Camp and Camp (1985) estimated 12,624 prison gang members, nationwide. But Lane (1989) reports much more than that in Illinois alone!

[14] In the next chapter results will be shown for juvenile correctional institutions and the gang problem. As a comparison to Camp and Camp (1985), these juvenile institutions in the Fall of 1990 reported a combined total of 4561 male gang members and another 212 female gang members. Recall, however, that juveniles have always constituted but a fraction of the overall adult prison system population. But has always been a feeder or filtering mechanism to the adult system. This and other research suggests that today's prison gang force strength is many times the figure of 12,624 suggested by Camp and Camp (1985). A test of this is now in progress. Obviously, the Illinois prison system alone has more gang members than the total figure reported by Camp and Camp (1985).

[15] Such research is now underway by the author and is expected to be reported shortly. All that could be reported from this survey of all prison wardens in the United States were the preliminary results of gang listings. See the NGCRC for updated details.

[16] In the next chapter, such information will be provided based on results from 155 juvenile institutions in 49 states. This is the juvenile correctional institutions survey.

[17] The "burnout" hypothesis asserts, basically, that rehabilitation does nothing; what changes a felon to live a law-abiding life is a simple process of maturation and a sudden realization, around the age of the late thirties, that "this is a crumby life"; or some variation of "I fought the law, and the law won". This is not dissimilar from the point of view in Vigil (1988) "Gang members who secure a good job often refocus and redirect their lives into more conventional

routes; such a change in orientation is referred to as "maturing out" (Matza, 1964: 22-26)" (Vigil, 1988: p. 31).

[18] See also, Robert S. Fong, 1987, A Comparative Study of the Organizational Aspects of Two Texas Prison Gangs: Texas Syndicate and Mexican Mafia. Ph.D. Dissertation, Sam Houston State University, Huntsville, Texas.

[19] See also the recent and emerging work of Fong and his colleagues: Fong and Buentello (1991), Fong, Vogel and Little (1991).

[20] This was demonstrated earlier for juvenile institutions and re-emerged in the present analysis. For space limitations we shall summarize this finding here. Any report of racial conflict in the prison significantly differentiated whether these same prisons reported having five percent or higher of their inmates as gang members (Chi square = 7.54, p = .006). Racial conflict is more likely to be found where a higher density of gang members exist in the inmate population is what this finding suggests.

[21] This is cryptic comment is particularly directed against county jails in larger gang-oriented cities where the incoming inmate is asked at intake "WHO DO YOU RIDE WITH?", meaning what gang are you a member of? And no one can answer "I don't belong". They go in one or another designated categories, such as "neutrons", or neutrals. But they are rarely functionally neutral in such a facility that uses an "off-set" gang management policy of filling cell-houses with roughly "half and half" of the rival gangs. Once inside, anyone not a gang member (e.g., a "neutron") may find themselves having to affiliate just to eat.

[22] Livingston County Circuit Court Judge Charles Glennon is quoted to the effect that Illinois gang members in Joliet were allowed such picnics and that prison officials tried to work with the gang leaders up until the time of the 1978 riot, but that this "philosophy" still persists among prison administrators in Illinois. See Wes Smith, "Pontiac Prison Gangs' Ultimate Weapon is Fear", Chicago (Illinois) Tribune, September 20, 1987.

[23] Jacobs (1974) describes, almost like a scene out of Hogan's Heroes, how prison administrators would routinely call in a gang leader when they had problems with one of "their" members: "in numerous cases the chief guard has called the leaders to his office to discuss problems with one of their soldiers (Jacobs, 1974: p. 407)". It became status enhancing for the gang leader to then "cool out" the situation.

[24] Remember that the United Nations code for dealing with prisoners says it is forbidden to delegate any kind of disciplinary function to prisoners. It is a human rights violation. It is unconstitutional, as in the Texas prison system where "Building Tenders" were used, and the equivalent role functions in a variety of

other state prison system.

[25] John W. Palmer, 1985, Constitutional Rights of Prisoners, Anderson Publishing Company, p. 953.

[26] Some authors like Moore (1978) have, however, gone on record as stating something almost equivalent in contemporary corrections: "custodial staff often manipulates racial and ethnic differences, both for public relations purposes (to distract public attention from institutional malfunctioning), and for inmate control (the divide and conquer principle) (Moore, 1978: p. 136)". Which, if anything, is another reason to have ACA standards and policies enacted to promote better race and ethnic relations among inmates and staff and for handling the more specific problem of gangs in corrections.

[27] Camp and Camp (1985, p. xix) recommend, similarly, that "agencies should develop a general position (policy) and strategy concerning gangs".

[28] Regarding the freedom of religion, similarly, the question arises: given the tendency of prison gangs to self-segregate by race, is such a "religious front" group that really functions as a gang organization constitutional when it excludes persons of other races? No one has yet sued on this matter.

[29] Obviously, in no sense has the author felt confident about sharing all his information known about gangs in this text. There are risks of public disclosure.

[30] Incarcerated was spelled "incarserated" in the chapter notes, again showing a continued pattern of organizational sophistication without the highest level of literacy attainment.

[31] This "generation gap" problem simply says that gangs are subject to the same type of internal conflicts that other groups, organizations, and voluntary associations experience. For an example of how the "generation gap" also affects higher level gangs, like the Yakuza, see Kaplan and Kubro (1986: p. 128).

[32] And, of course, the obverse is also true: if little can be done to reduce gang violence in prison, where gangs are the surrogate force of ethnic and racial strife, by mode of attitudinal and value change; then a leap beyond social-psychology and into the arena of the political-economy is warranted.

[33] For an account of institutional racism and how inmate racism can fuel gang formations perhaps even in the other direction see Al Salvato, "Prison 'Ready to Blow' Racial Hatred Plagues Lucasville", Cincinnati (Ohio) Post February 19, 1990.

[34] Illinois Criminal Code and Procedure, Chapter 38, Section 1003-6-5, covers crimes committed by persons confined by the state department of corrections reads as follows: "When any person is charged with committing an offense while confined by the Department, cognizance thereof shall be taken by the circuit court of the county wherein such crime was committed. Such court shall adjudicate and sentence the person charged with such crime in the same manner

and subject to the same rules and limitations as are now established by law in relation to other persons charged with crime. The expense of prosecution shall be paid by the Department".

[35] Similarly, as Jacobs (1974: p. 398) observed at Stateville "gang fights on the streets are immediately felt behind the walls".

[36] See Wes Smith, "Gangs' Power Tied to Pontiac Policies", Chicago (Illinois) Tribune, September 6, 1987. This describes how the assassination style killing of an Illinois correctional officer was apparently "ordered" by gang members outside of the prison.

[37] See William Petroski, "Prisons See Surge in Gang Membership", Des Moines (Iowa) Register, February 14, 1990.

[38] Related approaches involve rotating gang leaders from one institution to the next.

[39] The idea for much of this policy option is to segregate gang leaders and hard core members from the general inmate population.

[40] Professor Carol Davis, Department of Corrections and Criminal Justice, Chicago State University, who has worked in a number of adult correctional institutions suggests that there are additional hidden problems associated with the cultivation of informants (1991, personal interview). That is, most informants want quid pro quo and it is a liability issue: if the informer is discovered and has to be placed in protective custody or faces danger, then the institution has essentially entrapped them. One solution, to be discussed shortly, is to create a special physically separate correctional unit for informants: a snitch farm.

[41] Apparently, then, those who say that members join gangs out of chiefly economic motivation must be saying as well that this is more "lure" than "reality". Because little such forfeitures on gang members have been reported in the literature through this statute or through RICO criminal and civil statutes. Shortly before going to press, in early October, 1993, the statute was used by the Illinois State Attorney General to sue John Wayne Gacey.

[42] See Columbus B. Hopper, 1969, Sex in Prison, Baton Rouge, Louisiana: Louisiana State University Press.

[43] This could be a formidable law enforcement strategy. Police officers can defer an arrest until a time that is more convenient in routine seizures of small amounts of drugs or other criminal code violations. Arresting in the presence of other gang members can, we hypothesize, therefore heighten gang cohesiveness and solidarity. It would be better to issue a warrant and randomly arrest the gang members in their homes when they least expect it and when there are no other gang members present to witness the event. Then arrests could be demoralizing, instead of a "cause celebre".

[44] But as early as 1967 the Vice Lords were a "level three" gang organization with its own not-for-profit corporation. Bobrowski is not saying that prisons trained gang members in higher levels of organizational training, management, strategic planning, etc, to convert level two gangs to level three gang formations. In fact, another view is that by Short (1974) that macro external processes (civil rights consciousness of the 1960s etc) created "supergangs". See also Sherman's (1970) account of the rise of "supergangs" as existing before Bobrowski's claim. Note, also, the lack of definitional clarity here: "supergang" can mean anything, and perhaps something different to, respectively, Sherman (1970), Short (1974) and Bobrowski.

[45] Daniels (1987: p. 66) agreed that prisons currently seem to function as an incubator for gangs --- that is, gangs "recruit, expand, and solidify in a prison setting". Similarly, Moore (1978: p. 191) indicates that Mexican super gangs exist in California prisons (Mafia and La Familia) and "were being used by correctional authorities as the rationalization for a newly repressive policy toward Chicano convicts". As in other discussions of "supergangs", this is little more than a colorful adjective; with little definitive power beyond implying these are "bigger and badder" kinds of gangs. I hope some authors that use this "supergang" concept can see the merits of perhaps instead considering these "level three" gang formations in the organizational development classification system advanced in the present work.

[46] "PEN PALS IN PRISON. Inmates in federal or state institutions may submit their art or photos and pen pal ads only if they first order Teen Angels. No more free-loaders! Also, we want no drug dealers or rapists. Do not send in anything! We don't want you! Also, no inmates in city or county jails, or people with less than one year to serve. Because pen pals get the letters because you are no longer at that address" (Teen Angels, Issue 107, p. 44).

[47] PBIP, 2489 Mission Street, #28, San Francisco, CA 94110; Tel. (415) 821-6545.

[48] The material printed in Teen Angels was the exact script from the Pelican Bay Information Project, but carried the by-line "White Guards Gang Up on Chicano Prisoners and Beat Them!"

[49] Slight difference in this statistic from the original 1992 report: due to more incoming data (i.e., late surveys were received that were added to the analysis).

[50] As explained elsewhere (Knox, 1995) there are two factions of the Latin Kings, the midwest original version and the east coast version. The midwest original version is most widely known, and the east coast version is therefore regarded as a renegade version because it operates under a totally different written constitution. The east coast version was developed by a former member of the midwest original Latin

King gang who had moved to New York.

[51] As cross-sectional research, normally "causality" cannot be addressed. The exception is where the variables are "time specific" or "time dated" (i.e., "in what year did X occur", "in what year did Y occur", etc). Only one of the variables here (a disturbance related to gang members in the facility) was specific about the time period, by referring to the last one year period.

[52] Means "one or more" staff members tested positive.

[53] Virginia is a case in point: a "director of research" at the state central corrections administrative office has asked us for years to seek his permission for our research. This went to the point in one recent year where the NGCRC did complete a full research proposal. Their research proposals were standard protocols for the protection of inmates as human subjects. We told Virginia we will not be talking to inmates, we would be talking to public officials: the wardens and superintendents. Virginia's research office every year has sent back our surveys it spends much time collecting from individual wardens in a panic. We did not need to use our back-up contingency plans for Virginia, California, or Illinois because of the fact that many wardens are knowledgeable about our research: it is responsible research and we deliver what we promise to a net positive effect for corrections nationwide.

[54] The research methodology in the ACA (1993) report basically copied and tried to update the Camp and Camp (1985) approach.

[55] The monograph "Findings From the 1993 Jail Survey: A Preliminary Report" was released on May 5, 1993 by the National Gang Crime Research Center. The author was the principal investigator. Research Associates included: Kenneth G. Brown, B.A., M.S.; Bettie Durrani, B.S., M.S.; Robert J. Edwards, B.A.; Janice Y. Evans, B.S.; Joseph F. Garrett, B.A.; Paul F. Hoffman, M.S.W.; Carlton Jackson, Jr., B.S.; William M. Misczak, B.A.; John E. Morris; Michael Walton, M.S.; and Steven E. Wright, B.S.

[56] A random sample of N = 613 jails were asked to participate in the study; mail questionnaires were completed by 140.

[57] According to Professor Carol Davis (personal interview, 1991) gang awareness and gang recognition training should be more, not less, refined than training outside of the institutional gang context: because it is more subtle in prison. Gang leaders do fear separation. Gang members will deny they are gang members. The gang problem may be less visible in terms of graffiti and territoriality in the community context. Who inmates hang around with may provide a better clue to whether or not they embrace gang membership.

[58] Published semi-annually by The Pennsylvania Prison Society, Three North Second Street, Philadelphia, PA 19106-2208 (215 352-2300).

[59] See: Misty Allen, "Arizona Gives Youth Prison Camp the Boot", Chicago Sun-Times, Nov. 24, 1997, p. 22.

New Breed
(AKA: "Black Gangsters", "B.G.N.")

They are a renegade gang defying classification along the folks/peoples gang alliance system. They are an all Black gang in mortal combat with the single largest "folks" gang, the Gangster Disciples (GDs). But they are not "Peoples", as they do not "ride under the five pointed star". Their symbol has four sides: a square. Who are they? They are the Black Gangsters (BGs), also called the "New Breed". While considered a "Folks" gang, they do not use the six pointed star, they use the "New Breed" symbol: a box, with a circle in it, with three corners marked "L", "L", "L", the meanings taken from the original disciple literature (Life, Loyalty, Love).

The single greatest enemy that the BGs have are the GDs. The history of this enmity stems from the fact that the BGs are a splinter group that originated within the BGDs. What is also unique about the BGs is that they transcend the classification system historically used by researchers studying midwest gangs (i.e., the "people" versus "folks" dimensions of gang nation alliances). It is a group on the rise. As is so typical of "genuine" gang symbols used by gangs, this example also illustrates another commonality about most gangs in Illinois: we know of none which have any literacy requirements for admission to membership, thus it is not uncommon to find such members who are willing to die for their gang, but really cannot correctly spell their own gang name!

Chapter 26

Gangs and Juvenile
Correctional Institutions

INTRODUCTION

Juvenile correctional institutions represent one of the most crucial components of the American criminal justice system. If they fail, much else fails. This assertion is true because these are institutions that are intended to re-direct the lives of serious law-violating youths into a more pro-social pattern. There has never been a war on youthful recidivism. But recidivism from such juvenile correctional facilities is very high and it is definitely a social problem about which something can and should be done.

Unfortunately, until rather recently, there has been little known about the youth gang problem nationally as it impacts on juvenile institutions. More has been known about gangs and adult state prisons. A series of research projects undertaken by the National Gang Crime Research Center focusing on the gang problem are described in this chapter.

PROSECUTING JUVENILES AS ADULTS

WIth an upsurge in violent crime committed by juveniles, in the late 1970s and in the early 1980s, many states began to pass new aggressive laws that allowed for juveniles to be prosecuted as adults under special circumstances. This is sometimes called "being bound over", or the "binding over" process (also called a "Transfer hearing" or proceeding, mean-

ing to transfer the minor from the juvenile into the adult criminal justice system), because a special hearing is held in juvenile court where the prosecutor must convince the juvenile court judge that the case is serious enough that the juvenile should be tried as an adult. In the late 1980s and the early 1990s, gang crime involvement by juveniles was added in some states as a new reason for trying juveniles as adults.

This is a "get tough" law for juveniles, the idea behind it is that will give such juveniles much stiffer adult sentences. Illinois is typical of such "get tough" states in terms of its laws in this respect. Any youth who is at least 15 years of age can be tried as an adult if the crime involves a forcible felony, and the youth had previously been adjudicated for an offense that if tried as an adult would have constituted an adult felony, and with regard to the instant offense "the act that constitutes the offense was committed in furtherance of criminal activity by an organized gang" [Illinois Criminal Code and Procedure, 1993, p. 98: 705, 405/5-4.(3.1)]. For purposes of that law, an "organized gang" was defined as "an association of 5 or more persons, with an established hierarchy, that encourages members of the association to perpetrate crimes or provides support to members of the association who do commit crimes" [Illinois Criminal Code and Procedure, 1993, p. 98: 705,

481

405/5-4.(3.2)].

Needless to say, prosecutors have been using such laws. Gang membership is a factor that prosecutors often use to convince a judge that a juvenile cannot be rehabilitated, and thus suitable for transfer to the adult system. The youths tried as adults often must continue to serve their time in juvenile correctional facilities until they become "of age"; at which time, if they can be transferred to an adult prison. Often the juvenile correctional system has the discretion as to when exactly, typically after the age of 17, the youth is transferred to an adult correctional facility. Such cases, however, are becoming more common to longterm juvenile correctional institutions.

THE 1990 SURVEY OF STATE JUVENILE INSTITUTIONS

On October 1, 1990 the questionnaire was mailed to approximately 300 state juvenile institutions[1]. These were sent to the superintendents or wardens identified through the 1990 American Correctional Association (ACA) Directory. Some 155 responded representing 49 states which constitutes the sample size used here[2].

Several check-off questions about service programs were similarly included in the questionnaire. The responding juvenile institutions were to indicate whether their facility did or did not have these types of service programs. The results indicate some 88.6 percent (N=132) indicated that they provided sex education. Some 94.1 percent (N=144) indicated that they provided drug rehabilitation/counseling. Some 85.7 percent (N=126) indicated that they provided job readiness skills training. Some 75.7 percent (N=109) indicated that they provided treatment for depression. And some 16.6 percent (N=24) indicated that they provided "gang deprogramming" even though we intentionally designed this item as a validity check, believing as we did from a review of the literature that no such program service actually existed anywhere other than "cult deprogramming" services in the private sector.[3]

A report from adult prisons in Illinois suggested that between 80 and 90 percent of all inmates were gang members (Lane, 1989). No comparable statistics have ever yet been reported nationally on juvenile institutions.[4] We sought to fill this gap in our knowledge by asking the reporting institutions to indicate "among staff who know about gang members, what is the current estimate of what percentage gang members are of the total population of your facility?" The percentages for males and females were sought.

Among male juveniles, our findings show this ranges from a low of zero percent for about one fifth of American juvenile institutions (21.7%)[5], to a high

of 97 percent. About half (52.2%) of these juvenile institutions report a rate of ten percent or higher of such male juvenile inmates as gang members. In fact, 30.4 percent of the institutions report a rate of one out of every four juveniles as gang members. In more than one of every ten American juvenile institutions (12.3%) this rate is fifty percent or higher.

Reported gang membership among females in juveniles institutions is substantially lower than for their male counterparts. Among female juveniles confined, the estimates of percentage of gang members of the total population ranges from a low of zero for over half of the institutions (60%), to a high of 40 percent. But in nearly one out of every five such female juvenile institutions we find a rate of 10 percent or higher for those who are gang members.

From our total sample, at least one of every five juvenile institutions (21.7%) reported that whites have a separate gang. These are called a variety of names, often simply "skin heads". Other names included, however, the following: Bootboys, Honky Love, Simon City Royals, White Knights, Supreme White Power, Supreme White Pride, Suicide White Power, White Gangster Disciples, Folkz, and others including skinheads and neo-nazis.

Clearly some gangs are more organizationally sophisticated, with written constitutions, and have definite political leanings that can be roughly characterized as an "oppressed peoples" ideology. Further, white gangs have traditionally shown a clear propensity towards white racism. Our findings here are in response to the question "to what extent are gang members involved in extremist political beliefs"? Recall that Camp and Camp (1985: pp. 59-61) reported 17 states with African-American activist prison gangs and 16 with white supremacist prison gangs.

What our findings show is that on a scale between zero (for not at all) to a high of 10 (for a great deal) most juvenile institutions (61 percent) indicated their gang members were not involved in political extremism. Over a third (39%) indicated at some level that this factor was evident in their juvenile institutions among gang members. Again, however, this is an under researched area about political ideology and gangs.

Several questions dealt with the matter of gang-related violence inside of the juvenile correctional institutions. This focused on both the correctional staff member as victim and on assaults generally. Thus, the findings have only indirect significance for estimating the potential impact of gang violence inside juvenile correctional institutions against other juvenile inmates.

When asked "have gang members been a problem in terms of assaults on the correctional staff", some 14 percent of the juvenile institutions reported yes.

When asked to "estimate the number within the last one year period, how many assaults or attacks on correctional personnel by gang members", more than one fourth of these juvenile institutions reported one or more such incidents (N = 39, 28.3%). Further, when asked "did any of these assaults by gang members on correction staff require hospitalization?", some eleven institutions indicated yes. Which suggests that in about a third of these institutions reporting gang assaults on correctional officers it was serious enough of an attack to require hospitalization.

For comparison purposes, Camp and Camp (1985: p. 50) reported eighteen such confrontations with staff in six adult correctional systems during 1983; of which only four states reported staff injuries. Here we find, among juvenile institutions during 1989-1990, that 150 different assaults or attacks by gang members on correctional staff were reported, which were serious enough to require hospitalization in eleven such institutions.

At a more global level, with no specification of victim status as either staff or inmate, when asked to estimate "within the last one year period, how many serious injuries occurred from attacks/fights/assaults involving gang members", some 33.1 percent indicated one or more such incidents. A total of 209 such incidents were reported in the sample. Clearly, this rate of violence is higher than all reported cases involving attacks or assaults on correctional staff, suggesting at least that some of the other victims had to be fellow juveniles confined in these institutions.

When asked "does the fear of violence represented by gangs, in your view, contribute to staff turnover in your facility?" thirteen (9.3%) of the juvenile institutions, nationwide, indicated this was true. Recall that four killings of correctional staff were attributed to gang members during 1983 by the Camp and Camp (1985) study.

Apparently, juvenile gang members inside the correctional institutions are also responsible for a considerable amount of damage to government property.[6] A question directed towards this line of inquiry asked "to what extent are gang members responsible for damage to government property in your facility?". The response modes included a low of zero for "none" to a high of 10 for "chiefly responsible". Our findings show that about half of the juvenile institutions (53.2%) report some level of gang member responsibility for such damage to government property while in juvenile correctional custody.

The gang problem in America has no panacea. And correctional institutions can do little about the conditions that give rise to gangs in our nations' communities. In fact, correctional institutions are the true "last resort" of our continuum of legal sanctions against gang offending. But no required standards currently exist from the American Correctional Association on the appropriate techniques for handling gang problems. At least one source has recommended such "strict standards to prevent gang activity or membership in custodial institutions where gang members are detained" (Stephens, 1988: p. 33). As Camp and Camp (1985: p. xix) recommended that correctional agencies should develop policy positions and strategies for the gang problem.

Our survey replicated previous research conducted on adult institutions and what techniques were used by corrections staff to deal with gangs (Camp and Camp, 1985: p. xvi). We also added some new dimensions to our investigation.

One question asked "would your facility function better if gang members could be transferred to a central/national federal unit?" Some 31.9 percent indicated yes.

A question about gang awareness training asked "do your staff receive formalized training in dealing with the gang problem?" About one third (33.1%) indicated this training was now in effect. But if training should be required to help "maintain order and prevent trouble" (Shannon, 1987: p. 173), then clearly the emerging gang problem will require more standardized and specialized training in dealing with gangs.

Finally, we sought to ascertain the extent to which previously documented techniques for dealing with gangs inside correctional institutions were also being used in juvenile corrections. Our findings show that, nationwide, the following techniques were used: transfers (33.6%), use of informers (17.8%), segregation (27.1%), isolating leaders (38.3%), lockdown (22.4%), prosecution (17.8%), interrupting communications (32.7%), case by case dealings (72%), ignoring their (gangs) existence (6.5%)[7], infiltration (0.9%), displacing members to different institutions (29%), coopting of prisoners to control gangs (2.8%), meeting with gang leaders on "as needed" basis (15.9%)[8], joint meetings between various gang leaders (9.3%), and other (19.8%).

Figure 46 below summarizes the differences between the rank ordering of techniques for dealing with gangs from the Camp and Camp (1985) study of adult prisons with this study of juvenile institutions. As seen in Figure 46, the present study has a larger sample but shows clear differences between the way adult prisons handle gangs in comparison with the way juvenile institutions handle gangs.

FIGURE 46

**RANK ORDERING OF MOST FRE-
QUENTLY USED METHODS IN DEALING
WITH GANGS COMPARING THE CAMP
AND CAMP (1985)
ADULT FINDINGS WITH THE 1990 STUDY
OF JUVENILE INSTITUTIONS**

ADULT PRISONS	JUVENILE INSTITUTIONS
Camp and Camp (1985) Study	The 1990 Survey
***************	****************
Move or transfer (N=27)	Case by case basis (N=77)
Use Informers (N = 21)	Isolate leaders (N=41)
Segregation (N = 20)	Intercept communications (N=35)
Lock up leaders (N = 20)	Move or transfer (N=36)
Lockdown (N = 18)	Segregate (N=29)
Prosecute (N = 16)	Lockdown (N=24)
Intercept Communi-	
cations (N=16)	Use informers (N=19)
Case by Case (N = 13)	Prosecute (N=19)
Refuse to Acknowledge	
(N=9)	Meet with leaders (N=17)
Infiltration (N=5)	Ignore (N=7)
Co-opt Inmates to	
control (N=3)[9]	Coopt (N=3) Infiltrate (N=1)

Another question to juvenile correctional administrators was "are racial conflicts a problem among juveniles in your facility?". Our findings show that nearly half (48.3%) indicated this was true. That some environments can foster a destructive demeanor appears to have some empirical support at least when examining this factor of racial conflict in relationship to reports of property damage, overcrowding, and even recidivism.[10] Recall from Chapter 4 in presenting some of these same juvenile institution findings in the context of the racism oppression thesis that the problem of racial conflict significantly differentiates those same juvenile institutions reporting a problem of gang damage to government property and high recidivism rates (e.g., over 20 percent). Also, overcrowding is significantly associated with reports of racial conflict.

Some 70 juvenile institutions provided written responses to an open-ended question about "what to do". Here is what juvenile correctional administrators recommend doing about the gang problem to make their facilities a safer place. It is clearly a staffing and training problem. Only a third of the institutions indicated that their staff receive formalized training in dealing with the gang problem. Many administrators see the need to hire more staff. This is justified because as one respondent indicated "the gang problem is 95% African-American, so hire an African-American with good group skills who can work directly with these youth". Having more staff would mean more people to deal with youth problems, with

social issues, and increasing the staffing ratios to reflect more counselors, not security guards.

Many also saw the need for increased training of staff. This would mean training staff in gang awareness and recognition of gang members, or generally to deal more effectively with gang problems. It can also mean setting up an educational curriculum along with intensive staff training. And the need to define gang behavior, to identify gang members and to increase staff understanding of the gang problem.

Providing more counseling is another major recommendation of the institutions surveyed here. This would mean increasing self-esteem because it varies inversely with gang affiliation. Or developing a speakers bureau using ex-gang members with reformed outlooks who are willing to discourage offenders from future gang activity. Providing an alternative to the gang life style. Perhaps even a program for parents of gang members. Or combined with an isolation policy, using staff with appropriate gang counseling skills.

Separation of the gang members in the institution was a policy recommended by some. It would mean designing facilities that separated youths into smaller, more manageable groups to decrease the contamination and contagion factor.[11] It can also mean a separate area of detention just for gang members. Or isolating gang members until they are ready to return to the general population and display appropriate behavior. Or transporting gang members to separate facilities, keeping them as separate as possible. Perhaps through new construction to provide a section to segregate disruptive residents, or placing them in a "special" program away from the facility. The idea being to divide and keep the gangs separate within the institution; secondly to isolate gang leaders from other youths.

But a few indicated this policy "does not work". They recommended keeping them together and providing therapeutic counseling. One simply indicated that isolation and separation do not work, perhaps joining some adult correctional agencies in the alternative method of "set-off" approaches, or balancing the gang problem by controlled gang affiliation assignments.

The largest single recommendation was a "get tough" policy. This view would make it a statutory offense to engage in gang activity in the institution, and prosecuting them for criminal activity inside the institution. Providing stiffer penalties. Increasing the use of restraints and tougher punishment to fit the crime. Such that those who refuse to dissociate from gangs would understand there are serious consequences. Or providing greater security measures (TV monitors, etc). Or transferring documented gang members to adult systems, prosecuting or "certifying" the violent or disruptive youths as unamenable to the juvenile system. Overall, this approach meant a "zero tolerance" for gang behavior. Prosecuting and extending their time in confinement if necessary, placing the gang members in a more secure setting (e.g., maximum security), providing more severe consequences for inappropriate behavior.

THE 1991 JUVENILE CORRECTIONS SURVEY

The findings reported here are from a national random sample of N = 274 state juvenile correctional facilities. This represents a 42.7 percent return rate for the sample frame of N = 641 facilities and includes responses from 44 states and the District of Columbia. Conducted in October, 1991 this survey sought to replicate some of the variables analyzed a year earlier (Knox, 1990). The findings relevant to gangs in juvenile corrections are summarized here from a much larger and more in-depth report on juvenile corrections generally[12]. The unit of analysis here is therefore the individual juvenile correctional facility or the views of its administrator.

Using a checklist approach, these juvenile correctional facility administrators were also asked to indicate if their facility had any of a list of specific service programs. Unfortunately, the term "program" can often be construed as any informal effort, as is likely here. That is, ideally we need to know if these are formalized, funded programs with full-time staff and resources allocated to these types of service programs. Such an analysis will have to wait for the 1992 survey. What we can present here is a comparison of the 1990 and the present 1991 surveys as shown in Table 78 below.

TABLE 78

DISTRIBUTION OF SERVICE PROGRAMS

| Type of Program: | "yes" have the Program | | | |
| | 1990 Survey | | 1991 survey | |
	N	%	N	%
Sex education	132	88.6	237	89.8
Drug rehab./counseling	144	94.1	237	90.5
Job readiness skills training	126	85.7	221	86.3
Treatment for depression	109	75.7	169	68.7
To enhance self-esteem	135	91.2	249	94.7
To increase life coping skills	143	94.1	249	94.0
To decrease propensity to commit self-destructive acts	109	74.7	204	80.3
Gang deprogramming	24	16.6	57	23.8

In the 1990 survey the "gang deprogramming" service program was included, initially, as a validity factor. That is, as the principal investigator had recently published the first full text book on gangs

(Knox, 1991) the research associates felt that one way to determine whether the survey was properly completed or not was to include a type of program that was not indicated anywhere in the literature (e.g., "gang deprogramming"). Thus, when the 1990 survey revealed some 16.6 percent reported having such a "gang deprogramming" service program in their juvenile correctional institution calls were made to these facilities to inquire about these unique initiatives. Generally, what this revealed was the belief that is empirically consistent with the drug-gang research literature, that secondary and tertiary prevention/intervention initiatives can be undertaken to erode "gang ties", to "dismember" gangs, to "coopt" those who are not hard core gang members, and to basically "siphon off" gang members whose commitment level is not very high. But these are informal, not formal, initiatives.

Another set of variables measured in both the 1990 and the 1991 juvenile corrections surveys dealt with the matter of gang force strength. The reader is simply cautioned that these are estimates of what percentage of the juveniles in their correctional facilities are gang members which were provided by agency administrators. We might reasonably expect some differences, for example, in comparing the estimates of administrators with line staff regarding what percentage of their juvenile charges are gang members. One dramatic research finding that cannot be reported here[13] (Knox and Tromanhauser, 1991) in specific detail is this: there is a much higher rate of gang membership when we directly ask the confined juveniles themselves through survey research than appears through agency administrator surveys.

The 1991 survey shows that for male juveniles the estimate of gang affiliation ranges between a low of zero percent (15.9%) to a high of 100 percent. And, similarly, the estimate for confined females ranges from a low of zero percent (58.3%) to a high of 100 percent. The 1991 means for the current estimate of what percentage gang members are of the total population of these juvenile facilities was 20.8 percent for males and 4.9 percent for females[14]. This compares with 17.7 percent for males and 4.4 percent for females from the 1990 survey. Obviously, from this kind of survey research methodology we cannot speak to whether there are objective increases in gang membership, per se, within American juvenile correctional institutions; because the increase in the 1991 survey may simply reflect a more open admission of the problem, overcoming agency denial, or a host of plausible rival hypotheses.

A similar gang finding trend is found in comparing the 1990 and the 1991 surveys with regard to the question "do whites have a separate gang in your facility?". From the present 1991 survey, about a fourth (25.4%, N = 57) indicated yes, that among whites who are confined in juvenile correctional facilities, there exist separate basically "white gangs". In the 1990 survey some 21.7 percent of the institutions reported the existence of such separate white gangs.

As in the 1990 survey, the 1991 survey included the question "to what extent are gang members involved in extremist political beliefs?". The response mode included the range between zero (not at all) and 10 (a great deal). Findings from the 1991 survey show that 44.5 percent indicated zero; or no such gang involvement with political extremism. But some 14.4 percent rated this factor at "five" or higher.

Another series of questions on the 1991 Survey dealt with gang violence inside juvenile facilities, again replicating the 1990 research[15]. When asked to "estimate the number, within the last one year period, how many serious injuries occurred in your facility from attacks/fights/assaults involving gang members", nearly three-fourths (74.6%, N = 194) indicated none. But the range was between zero such gang violence incidents and a high of 22.

When asked, "have gang members been a problem in terms of assaults on your staff?", some 92 percent (N = 242) indicated no for the current 1991 survey. And only 8 percent (N = 21) of these responding juvenile facilities indicated "yes" for such problems of gang assaults upon staff.

While 83.7 percent of the responding facilities indicated that no such assaults or attacks had been made on staff by gang members during the last one year period, some 16.3 percent indicated such attacks had in fact taken place. Among fourteen of the responding institutions these attacks on staff by gang members were serious enough to require hospitalization of the staff members involved. Further, some 8.2 percent of the responding juvenile facilities indicated that the fear of violence represented by gangs, in their view, contributes to staff turnover.

When asked "to what extent are gang members responsible for damage to property in your facility", using a response mode that ranged from zero (none) to 10 (chiefly responsible), the present 1991 findings are similar to the previous year (see Knox, 1991). Some 53.9 percent indicated zero, that is, gang members are not at all responsible for damage to such government property. Clearly, then, somewhat less than half indicated that this was to some extent true.

Another question was designed regarding the gang problem and corrections, and it was this "Would your facility function better if gang members could be transferred to a central-national federal unit?". Obviously, no such "gang Alcatraz" exists, nor has anyone proposed such a measure. What this really tends to measure, then, is the frustration with the gang problem and the tendency to want to "dump the problem" on someone else in the same way that gave rise to the gang presence within juvenile correctional institutions generally. Nearly a fifth, some 19.9 percent indicated "yes" they would like to transfer their youthful gang members to a central national unit.

As in law enforcement and adult corrections the term "gang training" can mean a lot of things. Some consider this equivalent to "group disturbance" training. As if all the gang problem implied was some factor of "potential disruptiveness" during correctional confinement. Like racial conflict, it is a problem found in many adult and juvenile correctional institutions, but it is not a factor that carries any guidelines from national groups like the American Correctional Association.

The 1991 survey showed that nearly a third (33.8%, N = 88) indicated their staff do receive such formalized training in dealing with the gang problem. Which means, of course, that about two-thirds of these same juvenile correctional facilities do not provide such staff training. One recent report (Knox, Mc Currie, and Tromanhauser, 1991) shows how juvenile institutions from the 1990 survey would prefer to deal with the gang problem.

Analysis of this gang training factor for the present 1991 survey reveals that several factors account for significant differences. Table 79 shows that long term facilities are much more likely to report such formal gang training. Similarly, those that are community-based are the least likely to provide such formal gang training as seen in Table 80.

TABLE 79

FREQUENCY DISTRIBUTION FOR TYPE OF JUVENILE CORRECTIONAL FACILITY (SHORT TERM, LONG TERM, OTHER) BY FORMAL GANG TRAINING

	Do Their Staff Receive Formal Gang Training?	
	NO	YES
Type of Facility:		
Short Term	95	28
Long Term	68	53
Other	7	5

Chi square = 12.4, p = .002

TABLE 80

FREQUENCY DISTRIBUTION OF WHETHER THE JUVENILE FACILITY IS COMMUNITY BASED BY FORMAL GANG TRAINING

Do Their Staff Receive
Formal Gang Training?
****

	NO	YES
Whether Community-Based:	*******	********
Not Community-based	71	54
Community-based	98	34

Chi square = 8.67, p = .003

As in the 1990 Survey, the 1991 Survey again examined the techniques that correctional administrators used to control gangs in their juvenile facilities. As shown below in Table 81, the "case by case" method is the most frequently cited strategy for dealing with gangs in juvenile correctional facilities. Genuinely, this "case by case" method simply means a catch all category of something approximating deal with it "as it arises", or on an individual basis.

As seen in Table 81 below, transferring gang members is the second most frequently cited method for dealing with the gang problem. Intercepting communications presumably relates to a variety of internal and external informational processes affecting the facility. It was interesting to see that "balancing the number of rival gang members living in the same unit" enjoyed such a prominent position in the rank ordering of methods for dealing with gangs in juvenile correctional facilities.

What this "balancing" option is often called is the "set off" principle, meaning in a particular ward, cell house, or living unit, provide a "balance of power" by basically putting in just as many "crips" as "bloods", essentially a "balance the opposition" under some conception of the famous divide and conquer thinking. As a way of dealing with the gang problem, however, this may not be very well thought out at all. In fact, such a strategy could conceivably increase the gang problem and induce conflict, including violence, within a juvenile correctional setting.

Let the record reflect the social scientific truth here: there has been absolutely no evaluation research reported anywhere regarding which, if any, of these gang control methods is effective, counter-productive, or having "null effect".

TABLE 81

FREQUENCY DISTRIBUTION OF METHODS FOR DEALING WITH THE GANG PROBLEM IN JUVENILE CORRECTIONAL AGENCIES

Method of Gang Control:	N
Case by case	130
Transfer	59
Intercept Communications	54
Balance the number of rival gang members living in the same unit	37
Isolate Leaders	34
Lockdown	25
Displacing members to different facilities	28
Ignoring their existence	16
Segregation	19
Use of informers	19
Meeting with gang leaders on "as needed" basis	23
Prosecution	19
Joint meetings between various gang leaders	13
Coopting others to control gangs	9
Infiltration	3

Those working in juvenile corrections, as elsewhere, who have to face the gang problem, are simply advised to "get the best facts". And the best facts are not necessarily from other practitioner points of view. The best facts are those that are based on hard research and an appraisal of the social science literature. Unfortunately for juvenile and adult correctional administrators today, the current federal gang research funding initiative gives no attention to evaluating these problems.

But the literature is suggestive to correctional administrators. The study by Brobrowski (1988) concluded that the rise of "gang nations" (confederations of previously oppositional gangs, e.g., "folks" versus "peoples" in Illinois prisons) was due entirely to a misdirected and misguided prison policy of allowing gang members to meet as groups, recognizing them as groups, and official negotiation with their gang leaders. It is fair to alert the reader that there is more than some level of legal liability implied by the use of some of these methods of gang control from a prisoners rights viewpoint. Mostly, if taken to its extreme logical conclusion the tendency to want to "do what others are doing about the problem" runs the serious risk that if the others truly are doing the wrong thing there is more than some social policy jeopardy represented by simply imitating or adopting procedures with unknown possible long term effects. They are unknown effects because none of these strategies have been evaluated.

The cost factor of juvenile corrections was also measured here in terms of the daily cost for one youth. This ranged from a low of $16 to a high of $300 in terms of daily costs[16]. The mean was $102.24 for the N = 238 respondents who provided this information. It is fair to assume that some significant variation exists with regard to the cost of care factor when controlling for type of facility. For example, an analysis of variance test showed a significant difference (F = 6.04, p = .01) in comparing the costs in terms of whether these were community-based facilities. The average cost for community based facilities was $94 compared to $110 for those facilities that were not community based. Community based juvenile facilities therefore reported significantly lower daily costs. No significance emerged in contrasting short term and long term facilities or whether the facility was located in rural or urban areas.

THE 1992 JUVENILE DETENTION SURVEY

Reported here are the findings of a survey of local juvenile detention centers with special attention on the gang problem[17]. A saturation sampling technique of all 576 juvenile detention facilities was used for this survey. The facility directors were asked to participate in a mail survey in February 1992. Some N = 228 facilities responded to the survey providing the sample used here, representing a 39.5 percent response rate. Stated alternatively, the data reported here represents 39.5 percent of all juvenile detention facilities (other than holdovers and group homes) as listed in the first edition of the National Juvenile Detention Directory (ACA, 1992).

Using a check list of nine different program services, the facility administrators were asked to indicate yes or no regarding whether their facility had any of these types of service programs. Often, in answering yes, the respondent would write in the margin of the survey a remark typically to the effect "not a formal program per se...but accomplished informally". Table 82 presents these results.

Estimates of Gang Membership Among Confined Juveniles. This question to facility administrators asked "Among staff who know about gang members, what is the current estimate of what percentage gang members are of the total population of your facility?" and separate estimates were sought for both males and females. Among males the estimate of gang membership ranged from a low of zero to a high of 100 percent. Among females the estimate ranged from a low of zero to a high of 90 percent. The mean or average for males was 14.6 percent.

The mean or average for females was 4.17 percent.

Table 82

The Availability of Various Service Programs Reported as Existing in Juvenile Detention Centers

Type of Service Program:	Does It Exist?			
	No		Yes	
	N	%	N	%
Sex Education	57	26.1	161	73.9
Drug Rehab./Counseling	54	24.4	167	75.6
Job Readiness Skills	111	51.6	104	48.4
Treatment for Depression	106	49.1	110	50.9
To enhance self-esteem	63	28.4	159	71.6
Increase life-coping skills	63	28.8	156	71.2
To decrease propensity to commit self-destructive acts	89	41.0	128	59.0
Gang Deprogramming	193	90.2	21	9.8
AIDS/HIV awareness	45	20.3	177	79.7

Another way of looking at this problem is in relationship to the actual population counts for males and females. Because both of these variables are on computer, it was possible to use simple arithmetic to multiply the "percentage" gang member by the respective gender population of confined juveniles. This yields 2062 male gang members and 62 female gang members represented in the facilities included in this study.

White Gangs. As illustrated elsewhere (Knox, 1991; Knox, Tromanhauser, and Laske, 1992) the correctional climate regarding gangs is very consistent: where minority gangs exist, separate white gangs are also commonly found. The reason for this has to do with the role that racial and ethnic conflict holds as a factor that fuels the gang problem. The data shows that 41 percent of the juvenile detention centers in the present study report that in fact whites do have a separate gang.

Gang Member Assaults on Staff. The data show that 10.3 percent of the juvenile detention centers report that gang members have, in fact, been a problem in terms of assaults on their staff. The estimate of the number of such assaults on staff by gang members ranged from a low of zero to a high of ten during the last one year period. However, only 5.3 percent of the administrators reported that the fear of violence represented by gangs has contributed to staff turnover in their facilities.

Gang Members Responsible for Damage to Property. The administrators were asked to rate the extent to which gang members have been responsible for damage to property in their facility along a scale of zero to ten, where zero represented "not responsible" and ten represented "chiefly responsible". Just over half of the facilities (52.4%) indicated the very lowest possible estimate in this range of estimates, suggesting that gangs or gang members were therefore not responsible to any extent for damage to property within these facilities. Yet some 13.7% indicated a rating of five or higher on this zero to ten point scale. The mean value was 1.57.

Formalized Gang Training for Staff. The data show that in 35 percent of the facilities the staff receive formalized training in dealing with the gang problem. The majority of these juvenile detention facilities (65%) report that their staff do not receive formal training in dealing with gangs.

Racial Conflicts Among Confined Juveniles. Racial conflicts are a problem among the confined juveniles in nearly half of the facilities studied here (49.6%).

Strategies Used to Control/Manage Gangs in Juvenile Detention Centers. The juvenile detention center administrators were asked about what strategies their facility uses to deal with gangs. A check list of known techniques was provided and the respondent was able to simply check off all those that apply. Presented in Table 83 are the results of the analysis that first controls for the density of the gang problem itself in these same facilities. That is to say, what strategies a facility uses to deal with gangs becomes important only to the extent of their gang problem. The extent of their gang problem was measured here by the percentage of the male youths who are gang members.

As seen in Table 83 the techniques used to control or manage gangs and disruptive groups do in fact vary with the density of the actual problem (e.g., percentage of males who are gang members). Three different density levels are used for analysis here. This basically partials out of the analysis any facility that claims none of its confined juvenile males are gang members. This shows that the higher the density of the gang problem, the more likely these juvenile correctional facilities are to use certain control strategies (use of informers, segregation, isolating leaders, lockdown, prosecution, interrupting communications, coopting of inmates to control gangs, joint meetings between various gang leaders, balancing the number of rival gang members in the same living unit --- also known as the "set off" technique).

Table 83 also shows that with increases in the density of the problem certain techniques do not show a consistent upward rate of utilization. Ignoring their existence, for example, is shown to be a

decreased option when 25 percent or more of the youths in the facility are gang members. Similarly, the lower the density of the problem the more likely these facilities are to report using the option of infiltration. Displacing gang members to different facilities (also known as "bus therapy" or "diesel treatment") is also shown to not be an option that varies directly with the density of the gang problem. Meeting with gang leaders on an "as needed" basis is also shown to not be an option that consistently increases with the density of the problem.

Table 83

Percentage Distribution for Strategies Used in Juvenile Detention Centers To Deal With Gangs By Three Levels of Gang Density

	Density Level of the Gang Problem (percentage of males: gang members)		
Gang Control Methods:	>= .02%	>= 5%	>= 25%
Transfers	20.9	22.3	22.7
Use of informers	11.1	12.5	15.9
Segregation	37.3	42.0	52.3
Isolating leaders	41.8	47.3	54.5
Lockdown	32.0	39.3	59.1
Prosecution	23.5	25.9	27.3
Interrupting Communications	35.9	41.1	56.8
Case by case dealings	56.9	59.8	59.1
Ignoring their existence	5.2	5.4	4.5
Infiltration	2.6	1.8	0.0
Displacing members to different facilities	11.1	9.8	11.4
Coopting of inmates to control gangs	2.6	3.6	4.5
Meeting with gang leaders on "as needed" basis	8.5	9.8	9.1
Joint meetings between various gang leaders	3.3	3.6	6.8
Balance the number of rival gang members in the same living unit	22.9	29.5	43.2
Other	8.5	10.7	18.2

Average Daily Costs for One Confined Youth. Overall, the average daily cost for one youth ranged from a low of $11.50 for a non-residential day detention facility to a high of $307 dollars for a secure detention setting. The overall mean was $100.40 per day for all such facilities represented in the sample. It is more meaningful, however, to look at costs in relationship to the security levels of the facilities and whether they are residential or non-residential facilities.

In short, the local juvenile detention centers which are designed to securely hold the juvenile awaiting trial or for very short term periods have much in common with the state juvenile correctional facilities that are designed to hold youths who have been sentenced and adjudicated for acts of juvenile delinquency.

"Profile of the Convicted Juvenile Gang Member"

The research by Santman, et a (1997) used data from one county in California to be able to profile and develop a prediction system for gang membership. Here are some of the aspects that emerged in the profile of the gang member: (1) Family: low socio-economic status where at least one parent had a criminal record, (2) Social: poor school attendance and diagnosis for conduct disorders, (3) Drugs and Alcohol: abuse of both at an early age, (4) Police record: early pattern of delinquency, conviction at early age (about age 13), followed by an average of seven other offenses in later juvenile years. Their prediction analysis showed that the drug/alcohol abuse and early delinquency were significant predictors of their gang involvement.

THE 1991 SURVEY OF CONFINED JUVENILES ON HEALTH RISKS

The study described here was a first large scale effort that examined gang membership at the level of the individual juvenile delinquent locked up in short and long term juvenile correctional institutions. Only a small section of the larger report dealt with gang membership[18].

This national survey data was collected during the period May-June, 1991. The survey itself contains forty five forced choice questions designed to be completed by respondents inside short and long term juvenile correctional institutions. In March-April, 1991 this survey instrument was pre-tested using juvenile correctional facilities in two states with over N = 100 respondents. The pretest indicated very little item difficulty for the lowest range of reading ability.

The sample of forty four (N = 44) juvenile correctional facilities was provided by NCCHC and these facilities represented a potential sample frame of N = 2533 respondents[19]. The superintendents of these facilities and their governing agencies were contacted by mail in April, 1991. The purpose of the NCCHC Health Risk Survey was explained, a copy of the survey instrument was provided, and their participation in the national research project was sought.

By July 10, 1991 a total of N = 1,801 completed surveys had been returned and processed for data analysis. This represents a slightly higher than 70 percent return rate of questionnaires for the complete sample frame of 44 institutions[20]. Summarized here are the findings about how gang membership among confined juveniles is significantly related to a number of other factors.

Outside of the Camp and Camp (1985) study where the unit of analysis was adult state prison systems (not individual correctional institutions) and which had much missing data on states reluctant to report on this problem, the only other research on gangs in corrections is that by Robert Fong and his associates (Fong, 1987, 1990; Fong and Buentello, 1991; Fong, Vogel and Little, 1991; Fong, Vogel and Buentello, 1991) focusing exclusively on gangs in adult Texas prisons and that by Knox (1991) focusing on juvenile and adult correctional institutions nationwide.[21] There has been little prior research reported in the literature involving a survey of actual juveniles detained in correctional facilities nationwide regarding the gang problem. The present effort, therefore, has much knowledge to offer regarding this most important social policy issue.

The most significant finding, not from a statistical viewpoint but from a knowledge development viewpoint, from the present analysis is that such a large proportion of these confined juveniles report ever having joined a gang. Recall that 46.1 percent of the juveniles from the present national survey reported such gang membership. The Camp and Camp (1985) research estimated that only three percent of our nation's adult prison population was gang affiliated; and while the national assessment of gangs in corrections by ACA (1993) estimated six percent, using a similarly flawed methodology to generate results that border on fantasy, it neglected entirely the field of juvenile corrections. The recent research by Knox (1991) using a more rigorous unit of analysis[22] showed that this figure was over ten percent for adult institutions, and even higher for juvenile correctional institutions[23].

The methodological improvement of the present study is that its unit of analysis is the individual confined juvenile and represents data from short and long term facilities in five different states. The findings below suggest that gang membership is associated with other health risk behaviors as well.

While age[24] and sex are independent of gang membership, race of these confined juveniles significantly differentiates gang membership. While our sample included few Native Americans or Alaskan Natives (N=31), 11 of them reported gang membership. Similarly, there were few Asian or Pacific Islander respondents (N = 32), but 21 of them reported gang membership. Overall, the largest proportion of gang membership was found among Hispanics (59.4%), followed by Blacks (46.3%) and whites (34.8%).

Time served showed that gang members had been incarcerated longer than their non-gang member counterparts (p = .03). Some 70.5 percent of the gang members had gone to the nurse or doctor for health problems since being incarcerated compared to 64.2 percent of non-gang member juveniles (p = .004). As might be expected from the hypothesis that gang members would be more aggressive or prone to conflict, the number of physical fights during the twelve month period before incarceration also significantly differentiated gang membership. Some 63.1 percent of the gang members reported two or more such physical fights compared to 50.5 percent of their non-gang counterparts (p < .001). Similarly, gang members were significantly more likely to report one or more injuries sustained from these fights (p < .001). The potential deadly nature of some of these conflicts shows gang members face a significantly higher likelihood of being injured as well when comparing the number of fights in which deadly weapons were used (p < .001). As an illustration, some 67.9 percent of the gang members had 4 or more such fights involving deadly weapons during their lifetime compared to 35.3 percent of youths who were not gang members.

Gang members are significantly more likely to report cigarette smoking when compared to non-gang members (p < .001). While 23.1 percent of the gang members reported suicide ideation compared to 20.7 percent of their non-gang counterparts this was not a significant difference. Where the significant difference emerges is in making a plan for suicide within the last twelve months. Gang members showed a significantly higher tendency to make a suicide plan (22.2%) than did non-gang members (17.2%) (p = .008). Also, gang members reported making more such actual suicide attempts than did their non-gang counterparts (p = .001). Also, gang members were more likely to have to be treated by a doctor or nurse for such attempts (p = .001). For example, 10.3 percent of the gang members reported requiring such medical treatment for suicide attempt injuries compared to 6.3 percent of their non-gang counterparts.

With the longstanding linkage between drugs and street gangs it comes as no surprise to find strong consistent relationships between drug and substance abuse variables and gang membership among these confined juveniles. Gang membership significantly differentiates all measures of drug and substance abuse as seen here.

DRUG AND SUBSTANCE ABUSE VARIABLES SIGNIFICANTLY DIFFERENTIATING GANG MEMBERSHIP AMONG CONFINED JUVENILES

Variable	Effect on Gangs	Probability
Item 17 (age 1st drink)	Gang drink earlier	< .001
Item 18 (days drinking)	Gang members drink more	< .001
Item 19 (heavy drinking)	Gang members drink more	< .001
Item 20 (age pot use)	Gang members use pot earlier	.02
Item 21 (# pot uses)	Gang members use more pot	< .001
Item 22 (cocaine use)	Cocaine use higher for gangs	< .001
Item 23 (# cocaine uses)	Gangs use more cocaine	< .001
Item 24 (crack use)	Crack use higher for gangs	< .001
Item 25 (other drugs)	Gangs use more other drugs	.03
Item 26 (IV drug use)	Gang members shoot up more	.006

In a recent survey providing a partial replication of the famous Chicago Safe School study (Tromanhauser, 1981) data collected in June, 1991 among over 500 Chicago high school students showed 32.5 percent of the gang members had permanent tattoos compared to only 9 percent of non-gang affiliated Chicago public high school students. In some of the more organized gangs in America, children at a very early age whose parents are gang members have their offspring tattooed with their gang sign, and for gang members the permanent tattoo is another form of gang expression and representation.

Among these confined juveniles having permanent tattoos significantly differentiated gang membership (p < .001). Some 45.7 percent of the gang members had permanent tattoos compared to 29.6 percent of non-gang juveniles. Gang members also reported getting these tattoos at an earlier age than their non-gang counterparts (p < .001).

While there was little variation among these confined juveniles in reporting whether or not they have ever willingly had sex, gang members showed a higher rate of reporting that they had willingly had sex (p = .02). Gang members were significantly more likely to report willingly having sex at age twelve or earlier than non-gang juveniles (p < .001) and to report having sex with more persons (p = .008). Consistent with the earlier tendency for gang members to have a higher drug and substance abuse history, they were also more likely to report using drugs and alcohol during the last time they had sex before their incarceration (p < .001).

During the last time these confined youths had sex before being incarcerated, gang membership also differentiated those who did not use any method to prevent pregnancy (p = .02). Gang members were more likely not to use birth control options. Of course, gang members were significantly more likely to report being pregnant or getting someone pregnant (p < .001). Finally, consistent with the findings just discussed, gang membership significantly differentiates reports of being diagnosed with an STD among these confined juveniles. Gang members are more likely to report an STD (19.3% for gang members, 14.1% for non-gang members) (p = .004).

SUMMARY AND CONCLUSION

The research projects on gangs and juvenile corrections reviewed in this chapter show that these facilities, like their adult prison and jail counterparts, face a large and apparently growing problem with gangs. There is a need for national standards to govern the handling of gangs within correctional settings and to address the matter of racial conflict. Racial conflict among confined juveniles significantly differentiates gang damage to government property; those with racial conflict were more likely to report a problem with damage to property. Juvenile correctional institutions could clearly benefit from more mediation programs (Smith, 1990).

There is a very large need for professional training for the correctional personnel who work in these institutions that specifically helps them to better understand gangs: not simply gang awareness, but more in-depth and advanced training. The reason this is true is the growing incidence of gang assaults upon these correctional officers and the violence that the institutionalized younger gang member is capable of. The study of the 1,801 confined juveniles, where the actual confined youth was the unit of analysis, not the superintendent of the correctional facilities, provides dramatic reason enough for this urgent training need. Beginning with the 1990 survey of juvenile correctional institutions where the respondent was the administrator of the facility, the estimates of the percentage of the confined juveniles that were gang members has been and continues to be very low. Their estimates differ greatly from the self-reported gang membership of the juveniles themselves. From the 1991 survey where the juveniles themselves where the unit of analysis, the estimate would be more likely that about half of all of these youths in short and long term juvenile correctional facilities in America are gang members.

These findings also have enormous implications for adult corrections as well; for after all, it is the juvenile institutions of America that feed our adult institutions through the recidivism process. Further, the research funded by the National Institute of Corrections in their award of the national assessment of gangs in corrections to the American Correctional Association, we find an inappropriate agency responsible for this kind of knowledge development and we should not be surprised that their results are far from reality. The present author did bid on that same research, but our proposal was rejected for being too scientific. Part of the problem is that federal agencies like the National Institute of Justice are politically-minded, and are not required to have true competitive bidding as they should be required when expending public monies. We still lack any valid national assessment of the gang problem in corrections generally, after two NIJ funded projects (1985, 1993), and we still have no information whatsoever about the scope and extent of gang problems in juvenile corrections nationally --- at least from federal agencies like NIJ. It is possible to contact a Washington consulting firm that would be used as a reviewer for NIJ, have them write your proposal and review it too, and it is still not a violation of the law under current procurement regulations --- something that would be called bid rigging and a felony crime in many other state and local government agencies.

DISCUSSION QUESTIONS:

(1) From the research reported here, does it seem like much has changed since the Shaw and Mc Kay (1949) study showing how our juvenile correctional institutions appear to be in the inadvertent business of producing adult criminals?

(2) Along with the gang problem for juvenile corrections, comes other problems: overcrowding, illiteracy, and more. Do you think those incarcerated in state training schools are probably already too far down the road of criminality and gang affiliation, or do you believe that secondary and tertiary prevention efforts can still work with them?

(3) This research is the first to demonstrate a strong link between racial conflict and the problem of gang damage to government property inside correctional institutions. Do you think anything can be done to reduce racial conflict through programs, services, education, training, etc?

(4) At a cost of about $50,000 per year to incarcerate one juvenile in a juvenile correctional facility, and knowing that these same facilities have notoriously high recidivism rates, can you envision a better solution; particularly knowing that the same system of juvenile corrections now faces a very large gang problem as well?

(5) The Illinois Youth Correctional Center at Joliet provides an olympic size swimming pool and premium cable television channels for the youths serving time there. Most of these youths are gang members. Should privileges and scarce resources be allo-

cated on the basis of the degree to which the confined juvenile does not continue to present a gang problem for the facility? Or do such convicted persons in your view automatically deserve the same type of services they would be entitled to if they were not locked up?

The "Set-Off" Method of Dealing With Gangs in Juvenile Institutions

One of the oldest juvenile correctional institutions in the world is that located in St. Charles, Illinois. Built at the turn of the century it is the "state reform school" for juveniles. It is formally known as the St. Charles Youth Center.

St. Charles uses the "set-off" method to deal with gangs[25]. There are enough rooms in the cottages for about 300 kids. But there are about 600 kids in St. Charles. So that means two kids to a room. St. Charles makes sure that when assigning kids to a room, that two kids from the same gang never get in the same room, but rather that the two kids must be from a different gang.

The "set-off" method, then, prevents increasing ties within the same gang by this "roommate selection/assignment process". But could it also inadvertently increase tension and conflict along gang lines? What do you think?

END NOTES:

[1] No federal facilities were included in this sample.

[2] Graduate students that assisted with this research undertaken by the National Gang Crime Research Center were as follows: Mary Castaneda, Dorenda K. Dixon, Glenn Evans, Sonya Hines, Bruce Jackson, Gloria W. Jones, Monice Lillie, Jordanette Matthews, Walter Mc Cullough, and Jamere Price. All helped in the instrumentation and mailing in a much larger study of juvenile institutions per se.

[3] This is one of the problems of researching the "gang frontier". In consulting with a noted Chicago gang expert about this finding, he indicated this was not unusual; there are such "gang deprogramming programs", perhaps patterned after "cult deprogramming", etc. I remarked that "cult deprogramming generally doesn't work", and he said "that doesn't matter". Which is to say, anyone with a Ph.D. in psychology can take a government report on gangs and summarize it, adding their own comments here and there, and put their name on the front and begin offering themselves as experts in "gang training" for criminal justice personnel.

[4] Our sample of juvenile institutions, nationwide,

reflecting 49 states, suggests that about 17 percent of the males in these institutions are identified as gang members, and about five percent of the female juveniles confined.

[5] Respondents were promised that their particular institution and their state as well would not be identified. Therefore the gang listing provided in Appendix A is "regional" for juvenile institutions in as much as the author was not permitted to identify these by state.

[6] This was a revised item focusing on what Camp and Camp (1985: pp. 46-47) reported about administrative problems reported by confined gang members. The Camp and Camp (1985) item measured "what percent of the problems are attributable to gangs?" The item as analyzed here reports any level of reported problems.

[7] Camp and Camp (1985: p. 14) showed that from adult prisons, submitting and ignoring are the two worst approaches administrators report taking towards gangs.

[8] Such a participatory management approach that essentially seeks out the gangs advice has also been recommended for dealing with gangs in our school system. For example, Stephens (1988: p. 28) recommends that to prevent conflict school officials should "discuss the solution strategy with student gang leaders and solicit their support". Obviously, these would not be recommended from the author's analysis presented in this book.

[9] Coopting inmates, juvenile or adult, as even through such "peer pressure" implied in required group counseling/confrontation sessions, might be interpreted as simply a more subtle but systematic version of Feld's (1977) finding, contra United Nations guidelines, of using inmates for the repression of other inmates in a disciplinary role. Obviously, some case law is now developing to suggest de facto gang control amounts to the same thing in some of our correctional institutions.

[10] In Juveniles and Jail (National Coalition for Jail Reform, 1985, pp. 1-15) overcrowding is argued to be a condition that will contribute to violence and conflict.

[11] The "subtle process of contamination" was mentioned in the foreign gang literature (see Robert and Lascoumes, 1974: p. 436). But presumably, here, as used by a warden, means essentially the same thing: one gang member "contaminates" another inmate. Therefore the policy should be to segregate gang members from non-gang members. Which is workable when there are only small proportions of gang members. Not when 97 percent of the entire institutional residents are gang members as in some states.

[12] The monograph provided to respondents to the survey was released in December, 1991 and is entitled "Findings from the 1991 National Survey of Juvenile

Corrections". The present author was the principal investigator. Research associates included: Bridgette Adams; Michael Adekale, B.S.; Bernard Akpan, B.S., M.S.; Robert Bonner; Raimondo Brown, B.S.; Ne'Cole Bryson; Nora Bush, B.S.; Rochelle Carey; Lashoney Carter; Cecelia Crenshaw, A.A., B.S.; Willie D. Cross, B.S., M.S.; Rolando Currington, B.S., M.S.; Harold Dade; Renee Delvecchio, B.S.; Mike Dooley; Linda Dozier; Yvette Gilmore-Hayes; Trenton Fedrick; Keith Griffin, B.S., M.S.; Abubakr Hamad, LL.B., LL.M., M.S.; Denise M. Hardin, B.S.; Paul Hoffman, M.S.W.; Carlton Jackson; Levelle Kimble, A.A., B.A.; Sam Lacey; David Laske, Ph.D.; Clara Massey, B.S.; Arturo Mota; Fitzgerald Mullins, B.S.; Willie Nance; Benita Parker, B.S.; Odessa Randle; Romelio Rogel, B.S.; Elvis Slaughter; Emile Spearman; Barbara Vasquez; David R. Williams, B.S., B.A.; Yolande Williams, B.S.; Deborach Y. Yackery, A.A.; and Carolyn Zook, A.A..

[13] This research was undertaken using the juveniles themselves as the unit of analysis in an anonymous "self-report" survey for 45 short and long term juvenile facilities in five states. The research agreement does not allow dissemination of the research report until the final version has been approved by the funding source. Thus, we can only relate a general trend here, rather than specific data.

[14] By multiplying the population count by these percentages of gang affiliation, a total of N = 4,736 male gang members and N = 514 female gang members would be facility administrator estimate for total gang force strength in this sample.

[15] Earlier work used the phrase "socialized delinquent" as being ideal candidates for long-term secure care facilities and made specific reference to gang members: "the ideal candidate is the older socialized delinquent: an extroverted gang member who is at least 16 years of age" (Grissom and Dubnov, 1989: p. 60). To speak of the over 16 year old gang member as a preferred correctional client is an anomaly in the literature.

[16] Mardon (1991: p. 33) reports a correctional program, a "marine/outward bound" type of program, that averaged $36 per day per client. Clearly, some of those at the lower end of the cost spectrum were of this type of correctional program variety: e.g., day centers, etc.

[17] The full report is 46 pages long and is entitled "Gangs in Corrections: Findings from the 1992 Juvenile Detention Survey", available through the National Gang Crime Research Center.

[18] The formal title of the monograph is "The 1991 NCCHC Health Risk Survey: An Analysis of N = 1,801 Respondents from Juvenile Correctional Institutions", by George W. Knox and Edward D. Tromanhauser, December, 1991.

[19] The original NCCHC list included 46 such institutions; however, one had been changed to a non-correctional facility and the other (a private program) had closed down. Thus, only 44 actual juvenile correctional institutions were able to be contacted.

[20] Partialing out those five institutions that refused to participate in the survey obviously increases the response rate to a somewhat higher level.

[21] See also the correctional training policy analysis on dealing with gangs inside juvenile institutions by Knox, Tromanhauser and Mc Currie (1991).

[22] Surveys of the wardens and superintendents of the individual correctional institutions, nationwide.

[23] The advantage to the anonymous survey approach such as that used in the present NCCHC Health Risk Survey is that self-reporting in this instance is likely to produce less of a reporting bias. Most correctional estimates of gang affiliation are based on self-reporting as well, but at time of intake, a time when detained persons are more likely to underreport their deviance.

[24] Age as an independent variable nears significance (p = .06).

[25] See: Lorraine Forte, "Teens Jammed Into Prisons: St. Charles Center Far Beyond Capacity", Chicago Sun-Times, Dec. 26, 1997.

A CONVERSATION IN GANG ARGOT

MAC: What's up G?
TRIGGER: Whatch you be about? Are you straight?
MAC: No. I'm a baller.
TRIGGER: I'm down with that.
MAC: Who'd you ride with? Are you a blob or a smelly?
TRIGGER: What set do you play? Are you a boofer? I got boo. I am working. I've got some boulders for your shoulders. I've got a bone for yo' stone. I got bud and bullion too. Maybe you want a dove?
MAC: Are you a bunny head? Or is you a buster? I know you ain't no crab.
TRIGGER: You look like a claimer to me. Are you looking for a demonstration? I bet you're with the slick boys, and you just want to cheese out on me.
MAC: Chill, man, no diss. I'm just dog city. I got my double duece here to prove it, and its got a rap on it.
TRIGGER: Yeah, I'm strapped with my my ooze so if you gonna dress down I can dress you up.
MAC: Chill, man. I just want my ends with my homies. We be eye to eye, we never die, we just multiply.
TRIGGER: Well you culprit, five high and six die. You'ze a donut.
MAC: I know you'ze eoples, probably vicky loose.
TRIGGER: You better stop that fussin. You gangstered me. You want to get off the gate lets go. Get out of my video. I drop a dime to your governor and you'll get a head to toe, you should stop stimulating what you're stressin' out your mouth. You could end up with a money bag on you.
MAC: Chill out my moe, you rushed me, I aint no frenemy, like I said hooks, I'm just getting my thirties on. No need to gun up, I'm into structure. You're talking like your head is pumped off. You might get yourself a Nelson if you're perpetrating.
TRIGGER: You sound like a hype. I'm just holdin' it down home boy. My ice cream truck is real close by. And if you ain't solid, don't howler it. As I said, I got my itchy. You looking for Cheese Cake or what?
MAC: You is jive. You ain't got no juice either. You probably aint got nothing but kibbles and bits. I would guess you got gank. But I could kick you down real good. Got a loaf right now. But I bet you is on the pipe. All is not well get their head swell.
TRIGGER: You gotta be packman. Maybe you want a Ph.D.?
MAC: You be getting the pumpkin head for punking out or for being a tweaker.
TRIGGER: Look man, be righteous, I'm raking grass and shoveling snow, what do you wanna do? I ain't no rock baby. Come on man, I got to go call my road dog. So stop the roo rah.
MAC: Are you serving?
TRIGGER: I said yes.
MAC: What kind of work you got? You got a sherman stick?
TRIGGER: No.
MAC: You slanging skonk weed? I bet you you just got wickets.
TRIGGER: No.
MAC: Do you sling space base or any time bomb?
TRIGGER: You doing some serious videoing. But the answer is no. And matter of fact, get them soup collars to spit me some literature Mr. Donut, before I tell you where my spot is.
    Unless you wanna do some talco and go swabbing some surfers.
MAC: Look I got to go to a service, G's up, hoes down.
TRIGGER: Okay glazed donut, I'll get up with you.

TRANSLATION

MAC: How are you, are you folks?
TRIGGER: What gang are you in, do you need any drugs? (straight = sober, thus: "no" = "yes, I need some drugs").
MAC: No, I am interested in making money.
TRIGGER: I am too.
MAC: What gang are you in? Are you a Blood?(a put down).
TRIGGER: What gang are you in? Do you use crack? I've got reefer. I'm selling drugs. I've got crack (rocks), and $50 bags of cocaine. (aka: Halfers). I got marijuana and rock cocaine too.   Maybe you want a $35 portion of cocaine.
MAC: Are you a member of a gang using the bunny symbol; with straight ears symbolizes people, with one right ear bent means folks? Or are you a fake? I bet you are in a People gang (a put down when used by Folks). I know you aint no Crip gang member.
TRIGGER: You look like a pretender to me. Are you looking for a

fight? I bet you're an informant and you want to snitch on me.
MAC: Calm down, no disrespect intended. I work for the money. I've got a .22 pistol here to prove it, and it is dirty (used in a shooting).
TRIGGER: Yeah, I am carrying my Uzi, so if you are going to flaunt your gang colors or symbols I can put you in a coffin.
MAC: Cool out, man. I just want to make money with my gang associates. (Then: solidarity expression of the BOS, a put down to peoples or brothers?)
TRIGGER: Well you (culprit=putdown used by Brothers/peoples to insult folks). (Then: solidarity expression used by people gang members). You are a Disciple (a putdown term used by Peoples).
MAC: I know you are a member of a Peoples gang.(eoples=putdown), probably a Vice Lord (put down name version used).
TRIGGER: Stop insulting me as a rival gang member. You slighted me. If you want to get on with it, let's start the fighting. Get out of my face, don't mess with my business. I rat you to your gang leader and you will be beaten (a violation) from head to toe. You should be silent because you are unaware of what you are saying. You could end up with a murder contract on you.
MAC: Relax (moe=term used by Brothers gang members to refer to each other) friend, you attacked me. I am not a person who pretends to be your friend but is really your main enemy. Like I said (hooks = putdown for peoples), I am just interested in making money. No need to fight, I show love for all gangs. You are talking like you are under the influence of drugs or alcohol. You might get a hit put out on you by your own gang (expression used by Folks), if you're pretending to be something you are not.
TRIGGER: You sound like someone sho smokes crack or ready rock. I am just gang banging my friend. My spot (typically apartment) used to sell drugs is real close by. (Then: Peoples solidarity gang expression, a put down to Mac). As I said, but I am ready, I've got my gun. Do you want crack or trouble?
MAC: You are jive (a major put down used by Folks against rival Peoples gang members who ride under the Five point star). You aint got no power in your gang either. You probably aint got nothing but crumbs of cocaine. I would guess you got imitation rock cocaine made out of Ivory soap or white cheese. But I could set you up with a good drug business. I've got a large quantity of cocaine (aka: bird, kilo) right now. But I bet you are someone addicted to freebasing cocaine. People gang members (All is not well = derogatory phrase against people gang members) will get their heads beaten.
TRIGGER: You gotta be a cop. Maybe you want a pumpkin head deluxe (Ph.D.), a brutal beating to the head?
MAC: You'll get the head beating for backing down from an opposition gang member or for being a crack user.
TRIGGER: Look, be nice, I'm selling marijuana and cocaine, what you wanna do? I aint no member of the Black P. Stone or El Rukn gang. Make up your mind, I have to call my close friend and partner. So stop the loud language game.
MAC: Are you selling drugs?
TRIGGER: I said yes.
MAC: What kind of drugs do you have? You got any PCP laced cigarettes or joints?
TRIGGER: No.
MAC: Are you selling marijuana that smells bad? I bet you just have cigarettes laced with formaldahyde.
TRIGGER: No.
MAC: Do you sell any PCP mixed with rock cocaine or any heroin?
TRIGGER: You are doing some intensive snooping into my business. But the answer is no. And matter of fact, get them big lips to tell me some of your gang's prayers and official codes (Mr. Donut = a put down), before I tell you where my drug house is. Unless you wanna get high by using some powder cocaine and go assaulting (without warning, sniper attack) some white kids who periodically "run with" or hang out with gangs (wannabes).
MAC: Look I have to go to a weekly gang meeting, my gang is great, your gang is nothing.
TRIGGER; Okay enemy, (extreme put down: glazed donut refers to "gangster disciple"), I'll see you again.

Latin Disciples

(AKA: "Maniac Latin Disciples")
(See Also: Maniac Latin Disciples)

Q. Why Does A Minority Group Gang Use the Nazi Swastica Symbol?
A. Most members of this gang could be classified as members of a racial or ethnic minority group. It is somewhat unusual, at first glance, to find that this gang (the LD's or MLD's) often uses a nazi swastica when they represent their gang symbols. The explanation for a gang composed mostly of Hispanics and Blacks using the swastica sign is that they are not showing any affininity to neo-nazis or white extremist groups when they use the swastica, which is sometimes put in a backwards or counter-clockwise position as well, what the gang is really doing by using the swastica in any fashion is typical of many gangs: it "honors a fallen comrade". One of their original gang leaders, long since deceased, used the gang name of "Hitler". Hitler was killed by the Latin Kings (the arch enemy of the LDs and MLDs) in 1970.

Chapter 27

GANG PREVENTION
AND INTERVENTION

INTRODUCTION

Can gangs be prevented?[1] Can we effectively socialize our children so as to "insulate" them from joining a gang? Can anything be done after they do join a gang? These are but some of the complex, but interesting, issues examined here. From an organizational viewpoint to prevent gang crime or violence at the primary level means to stop the flow of new members into the ranks of gangs. Here again, the open systems approach is helpful. Because a gang cannot continue indefinitely, especially when it is prone to lose it members through violent death or to the correctional system, without replenishing its membership through the induction of new members.

The issue from a primary level of prevention is therefore: how to prevent new gang recruits? And, from an organizational perspective, how to effectively compete with the social-psychological rewards afforded by the typical gang. This is the focus of the present discussion. A subsequent chapter will also critically examine some recent and specific "gang programs".

THE SOCIAL-PSYCHOLOGICAL BENEFIT STRUCTURE OF GANGS

In a nutshell, what psychic rewards can the gang offer? Is it just a matter of identity/recognition, protection/intimidation, and fellowship/brotherhood? To answer this question is to provide the agenda for counter-gang programs designed for American youths. Here, again, we shall review our gang literature to ascertain what these psychic benefits of gang affiliation entail. In so doing, we will also codify important aspects of the gang infrastructure and its function in the community.

According to Vigil (1988) what the gang does, social-psychologically, is fill the vacuum left by traditional sources. The gang provides, by the peer group's sense of belonging and group protection, a facility for the cultivation of self-identity. What is unique about the gang is that its emphasis, for males, is that on hypermasculine behavior. It is not easy to create a counter-hegemonic organization that can compete with the gang in this sense. Traditional youth groups (Scouts, 4-H, Junior Achievement and its re-

497

ligious variations such as National Foundation for Teaching Entrepreneurship, etc) cannot, easily, under law as not-for-profit organizations function with a sexist bias. Some volunteer groups, such as the Guardian Angels, may provide the kind of equivalent "macho" roles; as would Junior ROTC programs. The need, organizationally, however is for a "full time" group counterpart as a viable alternative for the gang. Here, perhaps, we as a social service society have been less than creative in responding to the needs of modern urban youths.

What gangs emphasize, in the prison context at least, in terms of social-psychological rewards for gang affiliation or membership is the dual combination of power and prestige (Camp and Camp, 1985).

One must ask, hypothetically, what would Saul Alinsky do in trying to organize an economically depressed urban neighborhood that was dominated by gangs? Would he mimic their own organizational styles, seek alliances with the gangs (e.g., if you can't beat em', join em'), declare a holy war against these traitor "quislings" in the community, or any combination of these? Some authors recommend more programs and assistance for community development. That is, a kind of "trickle down" approach, where with sufficient resources provided, presumably with federal aid comparable to CETA programs with a twist of being designed to attract the underclass, gangs would simply cease to be a problem.

The problem here is that the gang exists and functions over time not simply as a problem of economic determinism.[2] It clearly provides social and psychic rewards in the way of roles, status, recognition, and identity. It provides social relationships. Those needs will not necessarily go away simply through the provision of programs for education, training, and employment. One can read Kornblum's Blue Collar Community to realize that even with union scale jobs, some employees continue their gang allegiance and in fact it carries over into the work place.

It is the same problem with providing job placement and employment opportunities for ex-offenders generally. The skeptic tends to take the position that simply affording such legitimate opportunities is no guarantee of the offender's instant conversion to a legitimate life style. Indeed, the skeptic worries about how the employed offender will continue crime, slightly altered, combining a pattern of crime and legitimate employment.

From Klein (1967), youthful gang members are the "fallout" from the social-identity and emotional turmoil found in the transition from youth to adulthood. That is, we need to provide more suitable, more responsible, more attractive roles for youths to play in society. Bloch and Neiderhoffer

add the element of a gangs ability to confer status to youths under a powerful social structure that makes them, as many of us, motivated by the "search for status".

PREVENTION AT ALL LEVELS

As in the medical "prevention" analogy, someone who has not yet caught the "disease" is at the primary level of prevention, someone who has been exposed to the "disease" is at the secondary level of prevention, and someone who is suffering from the disease is at the tertiary level of prevention. Here we examine what choices our society faces in dealing with all levels of prevention. This necessarily means those persons who have been exposed to gangs or who are already members of gangs, who have been gang members, who are associated with gangs, and whom we want to prevent from returning to the gang, or whom we want to dissociate from the gang.

GRAFFITI REMOVAL: COMMUNITY SERVICE SENTENCING

Sending gang youths to our already overcrowded detention centers is itself becoming less of an option regardless of the severity of their offense. But community service sentences have proven effective for adults and are now a routine part of the adult criminal adjudication process. What is needed in many jurisdictions is the same sentencing sanction for use with juvenile offenders. At least one study has shown it to work (Agopian, 1989). Obviously, this kind of program needs to be supervised either by juvenile probation officers or a private-based program capable of such projects and working with communities that want their gang graffiti removed. In some cities, just keeping the gang graffiti off street signs and public places in the downtown business center is a recurring problem.

CONFRONTING THE GANG IDEOLOGY

While there are a number of commonalities in gang ideology, there are also likely to be some important differences. It is not as simple as Campbell and Muncer (1989) would have us believe. Their study compared American gangs with British subcultures. American gang members, from Campbell's earlier work, are not apparently interested in overthrowing capitalistic society as serious rebels; while British subcultures are more clearly antagonistic to the status quo. American gang members according to Campbell and Muncer (1989) simply use distorted versions of more main stream American values such as consumerism, patriotism, elitism, and competitive success.

More simply put, there exist two different strategies for dealing with gangs in terms of anticipating and using their ideology: (1) at the group or gang level, and (2) at the individual level. Recall, however, that no one has ever claimed to have "rehabilitated" an organization of offenders. At the best, individuals have been "reformed" or "rehabilitated" when the existential choice of the individual takes over and they basically want to "change their life".

GANG DISINTEGRATION SCENARIOS

According to Arnold (1965, p. 61) the gang disintegration process should proceed in this fashion: (1) first there is an erosion of normative consensus and solidarity, (2) secondly gang leadership becomes ineffective or lost, (3) thirdly, the gang ceases to meet, and (4) finally, the gang loses the value of its group name. The problem with this linear model of gang disintegration is that gangs are open systems. They can recruit new members and terminate old members.

Step one in Arnold's conception, if this disintegration scenario were to be taken as a blueprint for intervention at the secondary and tertiary levels, would be through a combination of community-based social services (education[3], training, subsidized work, or job placement, etc) to provide viable lifestyles for allowing gang members to enter into a productive role in their society.[4] Simultaneously, using the power of community-organizations at the neighborhood level, including religious institutions, to blanket current gang members with direct outreach including detached workers --- with the goal of preventing the escalation of gang attachment for marginal members and to sway their belief systems away from gang allegiance, and failing that counter with the natural threat to any organization: the internal competition for power and rank. Younger members of any organization are always eager to seize the power of older members. The question is can this internal competition be induced? Add a communications component that portrays local gangs as "anti-American", "racist", "latent homosexual" (ala Yablonsky), "quisling" (ala Taylor), etc, in a clear propaganda strategy to attack directly the primary social psychological values of gang membership (prestige, etc).

Gang leadership would then have to be targeted on multiple levels.[5] One is obviously prosecution and confinement; another is focused and calculated individual programing, which will require higher levels of resources. It could include intensive family services, housing/relocation assistance, special desired educational placements, etc. The idea being to fill up the leader's time as much as possible away from the gang formation by whatever means. Technically, it would be cheaper to send a gang leader on a long ocean cruise than to send them to prison. But the leadership vacuum from any such initiative must be calculated and dealt with strategically.

We must join Arnold in assuming that theoretically gangs can be disintegrated through social engineering. Indeed, it is a logical extension of the assumption that gangs can be artificially created. The informed reader will recall the infamous COINTELPRO counter-intelligence operations in the 1960s and early 1970s, the record reflects clearly that our government was able to establish "sham organizations for disruptive purposes" (see The Iron Fist and the Velvet Glove, 1975: p. 128). However, it would represent a most fascinating challenge involving a powerful mixture of social service administration and criminological sophistication. And, again, there are political trade-offs here; that is gang disintegration at what cost to the invasion of privacy and freedom.[6]

The hope for such a scenario is to be found in the very nature of gang organization and gang behavior: they have a natural tendency to exploit resources.[7] Therefore the "trojan horse" method could conceivably involve a planned strategy to intentionally allow a local gang to "take over" a resource designed in advance to be attractive to gang members. This could be a drop-in center with free video-games, pinball machines, pool tables, etc. It would be a strategy of cooptation and planned disintegration conditioned on advance knowledge of the structure and function of such a local gang organization.

The model suggested here is not too dissimilar from sting operations designed to prosecute large numbers of offenders in one large net. Some very successful efforts in law enforcement have been made in this fashion. A typical variation being that of the "phony fence set-up" where active offenders bring in their stolen goods for sale, and meanwhile they are on camera, and fully identified. They wake up one morning and find themselves, along with many others, indicted on criminal charges. Even bringing in fugitives en masse, such stings involving the "double con" clearly work: a hard to arrest offender is notified by mail that he has recently won a "grand prize" (superbowl tickets, etc) and can claim it by coming to the local hotel for the awards ceremony on a given date. The offenders show up eager to get their "free" booty, and much to their surprise find themselves under arrest.

History shows that gangs can be organizationally disintegrated and even experimentally manipulated. The implication this has for policy intervention is that within lawful means some measures should be used in the direction of gang abatement. This implies, of course, that a strategic plan for gang suppression exists in any geographical area considering this type of objective.

JOB PLACEMENT SERVICES

Everyone seems to point to the value of integrating potential gang members or gang members who want to "go straight" into the legitimate world of work. The biggest problem with this strategy is that in today's work place few employers want an illiterate, and unfortunately illiteracy, and other social handicaps, go hand in hand with the rank and file of today's gangs.[8]

There is one large segment of society, however, that is not thrilled at the idea of job placement services as a mechanism of solving the "gang problem": some very sophisticated employee "screening" firms, a kind of security service for employers, are very concerned about this issue. They are worried that gangs are trying to infiltrate employers for purposes of continued criminality. And when it comes to the issue of "violence": well, gang members are good for that, and no one wants an employee to go "postal", and if anyone can go "postal", a gang member probably qualifies.

Yet the hope of job placement services for ex-offenders and gang members, at the secondary and tertiary level of intervention, rests with the large amount of theory and research pointing to an inverse relationship between employment and crime generally.[9] What is somewhat unique about most of these job placement services, nationwide, is that when operated in the private sector it is a kind of service that can truly have an important positive impact. But a few observations are necessary here regarding the special case of the gang affiliated ex-offender.

Few of these job placement service programs ever have their ex-offender clients sign a "vow of good citizenship". That is, we simply hope they will straighten out after giving them a job. Contract programming could be useful here. Particularly regarding the gang affiliated ex-offender. Contract programming means give and take, between the service provider and the ex-offender client. What if, theoretically, such a job placement agency had the policy of obtaining such signed behavioral contracts where the offender declared, among other things, "I am not a gang member, and I will support no gang, nor will I affiliate with any gang, nor will I come to the assistance of any gang"?

If a moral wedge can be placed between the gang-affiliated ex-offender and the gang leadership, and such declarations as above might have that effect, as most gangs require a pervasive kind of allegiance, then perhaps there is at least the possibility of taking the offender outside the web of gang influence.

In some states, like Illinois, those persons released from state prisons have the statutory right to employment counseling and job placement services.[10] Job placement agencies become popular among offenders and are not as likely as correctional institutions to face offender-initiated court suits. The question, then, is can a private program establish administrative guidelines to protect the employers it works with by demanding, as a necessary condition for providing job placements, that the offender make such a declaration of non-gang allegiance? Where these kinds of private programs do end up in court is by being sued via "third party" law suits, typically, an offender is placed in a job, another employee at the work place is not aware of the offender status of the fellow employee, and the offender commits a serious crime (e.g., rape, etc), and the employee victim sues both the employer and the job placement agency for recklessness.

THE DECLINING DETERRENT VALUE OF IMPRISONMENT

The organizational and group aspects of gang life translate into a very unique situation for gang members and the threat of sending them to prison. It is not, in all instances, a very powerful threat. Because for the highly integrated gang member, that is one with a fervent and high level of commitment to the gang enterprise, and whose identity is shaped and molded around gang life, then the threat of sending such an individual to prison carries little of the traditional value of deterrence. The reason for this is simple: a prison term will not necessarily interrupt their gang career and status seeking behavior within the gang. Indeed, imprisonment for gang members can be a "homecoming".[11]

If imprisoned, they might be lucky enough to finally meet one of their esteemed gang leaders; and in this process, gain title and prestige that later transfer back to the outside community. From a social-psychological perspective, gangs also emphasize a "macho-man" value orientation. Prisons are some of the few "male-only" organizations that exist today. If Yablonsky was right, and there is an important latent homosexual component to gang affiliation --- speaking here only in terms of its theoretical value --- then, clearly, there is little "threat value" in sending such a person to an all-male prison where they get the chance to "hook up" with buddies.[12] Our prisons today are little more than gladiator training schools.

ACTORS IN THE GANG RESPONSE STRATEGY

A lot of finger pointing goes on today in regard to the gang problem. What we must realize is that the problem is here, and here to stay unless some major initiatives are undertaken. Who should be involved in any strategy for dealing with America's gang problem? A number of different sets of actors need to be involved.[13] They are described here not necessarily in order of their importance[14].

(1) The government. At the federal, state and local levels. Some of the problems that give rise to gang membership need to be confronted directly through new national policies. These include the problems of illiteracy and drug abuse. Drug rehabilitation services, programs, and shelters are urgently needed. Much more in the way of training and educational resources are also needed before it becomes realistic to assist these same youths to enter the into legitimate employment. For the higher level gang formations, perhaps new laws will be required for effective prosecution. But mostly, our government must be willing to invest in our nation's social infrastructure to combat gangs where they arise.

(2) Businesses and Employers. One need only talk to sales persons who have sold large ticket items (cars, furniture, jewelry, etc) to gang members or other offenders to find out that these businesses do not feel it is a moral problem to accept large amounts of cash, having a very reasonable suspicion that the money may be tainted in terms of its source. Transactions over $10,000 now require an IRS notification. Drug dealers and other "high roller" offenders obviously know about this and readily circumvent it by making installments under that level.

It is ultimately a choice for society. Should successful drug dealers and other offenders be able to readily enjoy the fruits of their crimes or should the IRS, state and local revenue agencies have greater latitude in being able to track such large scale cash expenditures according to the social security number of the purchaser? A sixteen year old illiterate youth buying a new Mercedes in three cash installments (each under $10,000) can now easily escape IRS detection. The question is should that escape be easy. A voluntary notification program with businesses would at least begin to provide some moral and ethical guidance to this problem. It is an another issue to tackle this problem with more regulatory structure.

Also, if government in cooperation with the social service industry and local community organizations begins to take seriously the problem of integrating our nation's youths into the legitimate opportunity system, then employers will also need to do their share. That will mean higher levels of involvement in such programs like JETPA.

Finally, employers will probably have to develop new and creative approaches to really providing a drug free work place. Perhaps it should rely less on coercive methods such as drug testing, and should provide incentives for those who are "drug free". Businesses need to be more concerned about the gang problem than simply trying to exploit it commercially by offering inner-city dwellers bullet-proof aluminum siding for their homes.[15]

The Special Matter of Advertising and Gang Symbols.

Professional business and commercial advertising has come to realize the importance of gang awareness, especially when mass media is involved with the unintentional use of gang symbols in targeting minority demographic markets. In the rush to develop hip advertising copy for the hip hop generation in particular, a softdrink (cola) bottling company advertising poster in the spring of 1994 showed the importance of using certain types of symbols. The poster featured about five different dress styles of minority youths around the boarder of the poster, one looking like a preppie, one looking collegiate, etc, and the one at the bottom of the poster was clearly decked out in hip-hop clothing and had his hand down with the pinky and index fingers extended, with thumb out. This poster was routinely put up one day as part of regular commercial advertising in the cafeteria at a Chicago Public High School where a substantial density of Latin Kings happened to attend school.[16]

The hand sign in the poster was basically "throwing down the crown", that is the upside down version of what the Latin Kings use as a hand sign. Any sign that a gang uses, the insult to them is to do the same sign upside down. It is a gesture that a truly suicidal person would find quite effective in a variety of communities throughout the United States. Anyhow, when the students entered the school cafeteria at lunch time, they immediately saw the posters showing what appeared to them as someone throwing down their sign. This caused a substantial school riot with violence and damage to property. The poster was immediately pulled off the market, but we kept one for our Gang Cultural Artifact Exhibit used in providing training by the National Gang Crime Research Center.

Another example of an exploitational approach to advertising in Chicago happened when a major beer company put up billboards with a picture of the beer product with a message to the consumer to the effect that Al Capone would prefer them to drink this type of beer while in Chicago. Mayor Daley protested the billboards, the media attacked them as tasteless, and the billboards about Al Capone were immediately removed.[17]

Language in advertising is also unfortunately subject to the same "double meaning" or "hidden meaning" trouble. Much more cultural awareness is needed on this particular issue. Language and symbols communicate social values, and sometimes even the best of intentions can generate controversy.

(3) Educational institutions. Both private, and public; both secondary schools, as well as colleges and universities --- all have an important role to play in addressing the gang problem. Unfortu-

nately, as recent research indicates (Knox, Laske, and Tromanhauser, 1992), many schools today are experiencing the gang problem. It is a problem that can reach well into higher education as well, as the recent policy discussion about allowing students to wear gang colors in college (Martin, 1993). Because gang behavior in the school setting tends to be regarded as threatening, if not an outright guarantee of violence and other disturbances among the student body, some schools have worked with the local police departments to implement a "zero tolerance" policy regarding gangs[18].

Rather than "giving up" our schools should accept gang members unless the federal and other governmental units along with the private sector programs are sufficiently capable of absorbing these youths.[19] Because otherwise, expulsion means the right to roam the streets; expulsion means no social control, expulsion means they have the right to be illiterate. Our nation's school buildings have many useful resources that can be put to effective use for after school programs in serving youths and in serving the community which subsidizes these physical plants. A school that is open only from the hours of 9:00 am till 3:00 pm is not one that is adequately serving its community.

Our colleges and universities need to become more directly involved in all communities having a gang problem. They can do this in the name of community service, but ultimately they will probably find it is in the name of self-help: they really need to get out into the community and into our secondary schools and mentor and attract minority students if they want to be effective institutions themselves. Also, there is a more fundamentally practical reason: colleges and universities are increasingly coming to experience the gang problem as a vulnerable target for gang crime.[20] They can also help by assisting with more GED programs and providing more college level instructional programs in our nations correctional institutions. Education works. There is very strong evidence that educational attainment level varies inversely with crime and recidivism. We also urge that this be done responsibly. An irresponsible version of this outreach would be where a college asks the permission of the gang to work in the community and tries to hire the gang or work with the gang in some financial relationship.[21]

(4) Community groups and associations. Addressing the gang problem means addressing a host of related problems and it is ultimately a question of democracy itself, a question of getting involved, a question of community empowerment. This should be the first step: get organized, get incorporated as a not-for-profit group. Many of the gangs are in places like Chicago. A community that is less organized than its own gangs is a community that needs to wake up. Should such community organizations suddenly arise throughout our Nation's neighborhoods, then perhaps that would bring greater resources than are currently available to fight the gang problem where it is most deadly and most visible: at the community and neighborhood level.

(5) Religious institutions. We should continue to pray for a solution, but in the mean time we should get off our duffs and really try to do something tangible about the gang problem. There are many possibilities for greater involvement of our nation's religious institutions. In Chicago's First Unitarian church an alternative to street gangs called the "Chicago Childrens Choir" brings about a "win/win" situation. It includes every racial and ethnic group and has successfully operated for decades. If nothing more, then even the buildings themselves should be open to greater participation in the community: making the space available for meetings, programs, etc, on a non-denominational and non-proselytizing basis. A large number of examples exist of cases like Rev. Greg Boyle --- persons who can "connect" with those at risk of gang violence, and this type outreach is about as genuine as we can get, and in this regard must be argued as equal to or superior to any "detached worker" style of gang intervention.[22] Some churches have taken to marching, to show a unity against gang violence. Some have established "anti-gang oaths" that kids can take with their parents in a pledge against the temptations of gang life. Some religious groups have simply created their business extension-training-employment programs, like in Chicago, and established their unarmed security guard firms that receive funding to regularly patrol public housing projects.[23]

(6) Healthcare institutions. Like businesses, our healthcare institutions that profit from the community also have some ethical obligation to put something back into the community which they benefit from. Most certainly there are many mental health and other services that can and should be provided on a true sliding scale basis: if they cannot pay, they should not have to pay. Some of our nation's neighborhoods have infant mortality rates that are not higher in many places of the less developed world. More drug detox centers are needed. Laser technology can now be more effectively used for tattoo removal than previous abrasion and surgical methods. Youths and young adults should be able to benefit from this kind of tattoo removal service when they want to get out of the gang life.[24] There are also many health related issues surrounding both juvenile and adult correctional institutions holding gang members.[25]

One this is for sure, the gang problem is now well known to the medical field and to health service agencies. In a youth mental health facility in Chicago, for example, a psychiatrist basically had to negotiate his own "gang truce" inside the facility between warring rival gang members who were patients.[26]

(7) The family. Everyone blames the family, everyone seems to want to say it is the family's responsibility to tackle our nation's gang problem and drug problem. Unfortunately, this has become a kind of national past time of kicking the dog. The family structure, its functions and roles, today is not the image that many have from 1950s Hollywood television shows. We should not expect more out of the family unless we put more resources into the family.

Perhaps the family itself, however, should at least receive its own "report card". What kind of grade does it earn for extra involvement at the school? What kind of grade does it earn for involvement in community and neighborhood organizations and affairs? What kind of grade does it earn for volunteer functions? What kind of grade does it earn for impressing neighbors that they are truly capable of adequately supervising their own children?

Those with good report cards might be enlisted in the war on gangs. The rest have many troubles of their own and might better be envisioned as being the recipients of strategic services.

(8) Social service industry. Social service programs have historically "followed the buck". When government funding dries out for one service, they drop that service. When new government funding for a new service is available, they suddenly provide that service. Like the Marine Corps, they improvise and survive. So, that is good news. It means some flexibility exists, and that if federal government resources were available for targeting our nation's gang problem, that there would be many bidders.

What we know about gangs is that they do respond to programs and services, as criminal offenders do generally. Social service providers have gotten a "bad rap" from incidents like Jeff Fort's involvement with Rev. Fry (which still today, in the minds of many, is interpreted falsely to the effect that it was the University of Chicago that was at fault, when in fact the University of Chicago had nothing to do with it --- Fry was simply operating in the ecological fringe of the university community, in Hyde Park) or like that scathing review of wasted federal money provided by Poston (1971).

The research reported in this book on social workers in juvenile corrections shows they do make a positive difference. We need more professional social service providers to have any positive impact on our nation's gang problem.

(9) Unions and voluntary associations. A significant problem that must be overcome is the view from many existing groups capable of doing something about it, but who take essentially the policy position "it is not our problem". These groups, particularly trade unions, professional and voluntary associations, need to be more directly involved. Crime is everyone's problem. A nation that lives in fear cannot itself survive as a democracy very long. Every such group should adopt a "neighborhood in need" and work with it in a coordinated strategy for doing something about the gang crime problem in America today.

(10) The military. Only exploratory research has been conducted to the present authors knowledge about how gang members actually represent a problem within the American military. There are some problems apparently, enough to justify a policy position. This is not the analogy of the war on drugs, to get the military more involved[27]. But historically this book has shown that when the gang problem does get out of hand and beyond local control, that the military is viewed as the choice of last resort[28]. With our nation's gang membership at this point in history outnumbering our nation's sworn police officers, it is a matter of some concern to prevent an escalation of violence. Our nation's gangs often have better firearms than their local police.

But this is not to advocate direct military action or involvement, although obviously as our American history demonstrates, the military has had a record of being called in when local police cannot handle the situation. Let us hope and pray it does not come to that stage of societal deterioration. The kind of low intensity conflict that an armed organization is capable of may be a real problem: it could be more violent than local law enforcement can control, and less violent than to justify a traditional military response.

Rather, this is to advocate the military in an outreach and training role as a primary level prevention alternative to gang life. The same youth who obediently follows a gang leader in neighborhood warfare, could equally serve his country to better effect. Military socialization is a good thing. The military is an option for many. Perhaps, as well, more Junior ROTC programs should be operated in areas that might otherwise feed youths into a gang organization.

Some programs have been established on a voluntary basis involving military personnel. These include mentoring programs that outreach to inner-city kids at risk of gang membership.

(11) The Mass Media and Hollywood Gang Movies.

The mass media and movie producers are often criticized over the gang issue. It is true that there are some gang movies that truly glorify gang life, and that their very existence as videos that can be rented at any local store are types of socialization and education that can in the hands of alienated youths generate a "copycat" phenomenon, where youths will try to emulate such behavior. It is equally true that artists have purposes that are not always our own. It is also true that simple gang exploitation movies are produced aimed at the gang-viewing audience. Just as it is also true that given the predictable nature of a bigot, that skinheads are easy to get on a television talk show, but should we still give them air time when the net effect is the vulgarization of the air waves?[29] Gangster movies romanticize criminal exploits. There is no hard evidence that watching gangster movies produces gangsters, but it is easy to show that criminals love gangster movies. We need to be concerned about this, then, in a wider sense of responsibility of how such products are consumed: as idols or as simply fictional messages.

There are those who want to take the mass media to task on the gang issue, no doubt. There is also the positive side of the effects of mass media: good investigative journalism, whether it be in print or electronic media form. Objectively educating the public without sensationalizing an issue is something that can only help in the long run. What most media critics object to is the amount of attention that gang apologists and gang members or gang spokespersons get, but again this is a very predictable behavior for some types of gangs. Some types of gang members love media coverage. It increases their "rep" much better than graffiti.

WHAT WORKS TO PREVENT CRIME, DELINQUENCY AND RECIDIVISM MAY WORK TO REDUCE THE GANG PROBLEM

The logic here is that of pragmatism. If evidence exists that it works, use it. That is, if any theoretical or research basis exists for expecting positive impact on the gang crime problem, then it deserves our expeditious, positive, consideration. Forget ideology and purist points of view. We need to apply the knowledge we have accumulated. We recognize, as well, the legitimate criticism that "general delinquency literature" is not the same as "gang literature". Gang members are a special subset of the wider field dealing with delinquents and criminal offenders. But to the extent that such theories offer constructive advice, it is worth pursuing how perhaps such theories could be extended to apply to gangs, or at least test these hypotheses in the spirit of scientific discovery where they are merited and hold promise.

The informed reader in the social sciences knows that a lot of things work in preventing crime, delinquency and recidivism. The astute reader in criminology knows that the dogma of "nothing works" is a political hoax created in part by Martinson, and revealed as such by Martinson before he took his own life. The truth is that some conditions are more easily manipulated than others, and some solutions may cost more than others.

But America is rapidly reaching a crisis point with regard to the gang crime problem.[30] It means examining all alternatives to the solution of the crisis. The evolving definition of citizenship may therefore mean doing what we can in terms of what is humanely possible to address this national problem. It may not be easy, it may not be cheap, but it is a social problem about which something can and should be done. Perhaps, further, about which something will have to be done if we want to insure any minimal level of the quality of life in America.

Clearly, there exist many current programs throughout America that have a direct involvement in addressing the gang crime problem. It is also a volatile period. Clearly not all of these programs have been described in this book. New programs and services can be expected to arise in response to this growing problem. And to the extent that they are informed about gang problems and cooperate with other criminal justice agencies we should welcome these services as new vehicles to provide a better way of life for many Americans.

The message here is obvious: we may best be advised not necessarily by surveys of what programs exist and what they are doing now, but rather we should be alerted in advance as to what SHOULD be done based on our social science knowledge of the problem.

TARGETING GANG RECRUITS: A PRIORITY POLICY ISSUE

To put any group or organization "out of business", whether we call it "gang busting" or just plain good social defense, will mean strangling it by preventing further growth in membership. That is, stopping new recruits. Historically local law enforcement has targeted gang leaders for prosecution under the common expectation that a leader's removal will mean maximum organizational disruption. As we have seen in the case of Chicago's Vice Lords, or in higher level gang formations, that strategy will not be as successful as it hopes to be. Such "shoot from the hip" gang-busting can, in fact, via conflict and induced opportunity for gang leadership training, be counterproductive.

Perhaps "gang busting" must also target new recruits.[31] But arrests, labels, and the shame brought upon the family unit will probably not be enough. Indeed it could be counterproductive. And sending such persons to correctional institutions will only guarantee they "make rank" in the gang organization. As a society, we need more options to effectively prevent new members from joining the ranks of our nation's gang organizations.

DIFFERENTIAL RESPONSES TO DIFFERENT GANG FORMATIONS

A prevalent error of policy is in assuming all gangs are equal and that one policy will work for all. That is a big mistake. Many authors believe that level zero gangs, and perhaps even level one gangs, can be coopted (Shaw and Sorrentino, 1956). That is, they can be redirected, channelled into potentially prosocial functions and activities that would be a blessing rather than a curse for the neighborhood or community in which they exist. The research on this matter is lacking, but we cannot equally reject such a hypothesis.

One thing is certain here: there exist differences in sophistication and capability between gangs today, and this must necessarily mean a differential response to them. We cannot treat a level zero gang in the same fashion that we respond to a level three gang. They cannot be treated alike, because they are not alike. A level zero gang is not really a true criminal gang at all, it is a pre-gang if anything. They are not gangs of equal public threat.

The gang classification system advanced in this book would therefore require differences in responding to gangs from all perspectives including law enforcement and corrections, not just community-based services. A level zero gang should be directly coopted and channeled into community organization functions. A level one gang should have its members coopted and its leaders dislocated. A level two gang and above should be prevented from expansion to dry up new recruits. And a level three gang should be treated as an emerging organized crime problem.

WHAT THE LITERATURE SAYS TO DO ABOUT GANG CRIME

This is for the skeptics, for those with nothing more than the "lock em up" mentality, and this is to show we are not as ignorant as we think we are. We are not in the situation of knowing nothing about what can work. We are not in the situation of having no guidelines or ideas useful towards a solution of the gang crime problem. We have many promising ways, from social science and specifically from the field of criminology, to tackle the gang crime problem in America today.

Following, we will show twenty-five ways to combat the gang crime problem in America today. These prescriptions are based on the existing literature showing theories with empirical support for these potential ways to crime, delinquency, and recidivism generally and as such can be equally effective in addressing the gang crime problem. These are factors that gang intervention programs should probably have incorporated as part of their stated goals.

(1) Social control theory has several variations, and is also choice theory, and social development theory. It tells us we would increase informal social controls and make formal social controls more effective.

(2) Differential social organization theory characterizes much of the Shaw and Mc Kay tradition and it tells us that we should increase local community organizational capability and improve our neighborhood social infrastructure.

(3) Differential opportunity theory (Cloward and Ohlin, 1960) advises us to increase legitimate opportunities in education, training, and employment, and decrease perceived closure or the view from potential gang members that "they will not fit in American society in a productive capacity".

(4) Differential opportunity theory also says we should decrease the attractiveness, the profitability, the viability as a career, of criminal opportunity systems. An affluent, conspicuously high spending, protected criminal offender sends the message to American youths that they too can be predators. It also says we should increase the feasibility of youths internalizing legitimate career goals, helping them to find a place in America's legitimate world of work.

(5) Differential association theory (ala Sutherland) says we should increase social ties with our youths to persons in their social network who have a more law-abiding and pro-social orientation. In doing so, their definition of reality is more likely to become one that says "conform". There is little that competes with the gang. We need to be creative in this regard.

(6) Differential association theory also says we should decrease the probability that our youths have as their primary group those who are criminal offenders and define the world as a "dog eat dog world", a Silver Rule world of "do unto others before they do unto you". It is not going to be easy to convince some of the potential for making it in America through education. But it is worth doing.

(7) Differential identity theory (ala Daniel Glaser) suggests we should increase more viable role models and in so doing communicate less from our culture that the way to make it in America is through the barrel of a gun. Hard work is the answer.

(8) Differential identity theory also suggests we should communicate less from the social structure that our culture accepts as legitimate heroes those who were nothing more than menaces (Al Capone, etc). That is, we must decrease the attractiveness of role models such as gang leaders and successful criminal offenders. Cultural awareness programs can help here to instill ethnic and racial pride.

(9) Differential integration theory (Knox, 1978) suggests we need to increase involvement with legitimate groups and mainstream society for our youths. And (10) decrease their participation and involvement with criminal or illicit subcultures.

(11) Self-concept theory says loud and clear, with support from the research reported in this book, that we should increase the self-esteem of our youths. Those with low self-esteem are most at risk of joining a gang. And (12) that among youths who have already affiliated with gangs, we need to re-mold their self-concept as being an offender, as being irresponsible, as being a predator. And show an alternative "pro-social", "productive" self-identity.

(13) Containment theory has several variations, but basically says we should seek to increase the internal locus of control among youths; their ability to "say no". And (14) we should decrease the external locus of control, or the tendency to follow gang leaders for whatever reason.

(15) Multiple marginality theory (Vigil, 1988) says we should increase the ability of those with multiple "marks" against them (e.g., minority status plus run in with the law) to still function in wider society in a positive, productive way. And (16) that we should as a society practice more of what we preach, e.g., forgiveness, salvation, equal opportunity, etc., and therefore decrease the impact of prior stigmas our society seems so highly capable of manufacturing. Or (17) as Dr. Martin Luther King said, we should judge persons on the nature of their character rather than on the color of their skin, or to update it slightly, by the size of their juvenile record. That is, (18) we should never throw away the welcome mat, anyone, any offender, hopefully at least our nation's youth, should be "welcome back to society", or else we create our own permanent class of enemies.

(19) Identity crisis theory (Erik Erickson) for youths generally tells us we should increase the ease of transition from youth to adulthood, it should not be as turbulent and as uncertain as to what the future holds. And (20) age-role integration (Suttles, etc) suggests we should have stronger, closer, more effective channels of interaction between youths and adults, our youths should not see their world as one of required rebellion. And (21) as Bloch and Niederhoffer showed, we should increase the role space for responsible, rewarded, desired, and prestige-filled positions available to youths, when they express a willingness to accept responsibility citizenship should mean to them the right to participate fully.

(22) Some psychological approaches (e.g., Yablonsky) have suggested that gang members are by their nature sociopaths, so perhaps we as a society should be doing more to increase prosocial beliefs and values, and the cultivation of citizenship, human and social capital generally.

(23) Labelling theory, in its many varieties, means we should increase personal achievement and human capital development among those at risk of joining gangs, and for those who have already found themselves involved in gangs, and in so doing opening up the possibility at least of another direction in life, that is, the development of attributional "off sets". (24) As a society we need to "cool out" on the need to have "someone at the bottom", we need to decrease the sticking power of prior stigmatizable labels if a person can show through good graces their value to society. It is well to remember that our history includes the granting of a presidential pardon for all crimes to a person that was technically never even convicted of a crime --- former President Nixon.

(25) And from surplus population and underclass theory, we need to give the poor and minority groups of our country a path to full participation in society --- we need to open up our social structure for allowing their productive involvement, and that will probably take major national initiatives to first focus on developing their human capital.

FOUNDATION FUNDING PATTERNS AND THE GANG PROBLEM

Figure 47 shows the distribution of all private foundation grants that involved the keyword "gang" for the past several years.[32] The first edition of this book pointed out what appeared to be a neglect by foundations in supporting gang programs. In pointing out the discrepancy the first edition noted

"Clearly, foundation funding patterns do not match up equitably with known reported national trends in gang crime severity. Some cities have clearly been ignored. This is an important social policy problem that will have to change. And foundation giving patterns will also have to change to reflect a more equitable commitment to the obvious problem of gang crime in America."

Someone got the message. Gangs are hot again for foundation grants. If that is the good news, then the bad news what the foundations have been funding. The best money spent is in pure prevention, not secondary prevention, not tertiary prevention. Once involved with a gang, the road back is very difficult. Most of the money is being spent on high risk populations, and they need help, no doubt about it. The thousands of gang members behind bars need help too. But to best spend foundation and public monies to most effectively do something about the gang problem requires a closer and more logical focus. The reason is that some Foundations have clearly been hustled again, reminiscent of the Jeff Fort and Rev. Fry period.

If the money is spent on a direct service program, the Foundation should require an independent evaluation research component: for otherwise we have no idea of any positive impact. If the money is spent on policy or programs, the theory behind the initiative should be clearly laid out, and special attention must be focused on "prove to the best of your ability that this initiative will not have a reverse-intended impact on the gang problem". Some of the best investment of public and foundation funds would be in the evaluation of such gang service programs at all levels of intervention/prevention. The same program should not be "evaluating itself"! The funding for a service program should be matched with a grant to an independent researcher, who holds credentials in the field of criminology (i.e., the field of study that deals with gangs directly), to carry out basic and evaluation research on the program. In this way we may be able to generate some useful information on "what works" and "what is needed" to put a dent in the gang problem.

Government funding, foundation funding, and private fund raising initiatives will all be required to seriously come to grips with the gang crime problem in American cities today. The worthy recipient of funding are those programs and initiatives based on a good theory of human behavior explaining why what is done will can be expected to have a positive impact on the "gang problem" rather than exacerbating the problem. Programs that the gangs directly benefit are the least worthy of funding, because we should not be in a position of advancing the organizational strength of any gang. We should not be assisting a gang in its public relations campaign, or the cloak of legitimacy the gang may masquerade behind. We should not be increasing the "influence" that any gang leader may have. We should not be rewarding the threat of violence against society, and unless someone has "dropped their flag", we should not be paying active gang leaders or active gang members to be the public liaison for the gang; as such a policy only helps the gang to persist over time, and gives the gang more legitimacy than it should have.

FIGURE 47

FOUNDATION GRANTS
RELATED TO GANGS 1985-1993

Foundation and Amount $	Recipient Agency/Year
The Boston Foundation 35,000	Gang Peace, Boston/1993
Weingart Foundation 30,000	Cal. Sch. of Prof'l..Psych./1993
Meyer Memorial Trust 154,000	Min. Youth Concerns Action, Portland/1993
Meyer Memorial Trust 184,000	Boys & Girls Club of Salem/1993
Chicago Community Trust 16,000	Network for Youth Svcs.,Chgo/1993
Greater Santa Cruz CCF 10,000	Barrios Unidos, Santa Cruz/1992
Chicago Community T. 1,000,000	United Way of Chgo./1992
Vira I. Heinz Endow. 750,000	YMCA, Metro Pittsburgh/1992
The McKnight Foundation 54,943	The City, Inc, Mpls,MN/1992
Cal. Community Found. 44,000	Soledad Enrich.Action, L.A./1992
Cal. Community Found. 25,000	Inland Co. Interfaith, San Bern./1992
James Irvine Foundation 40,000	Family Service Agency,Sacramento/1992
The McKnight Found. 30,000	Lao Youth Assn. of MN,Mpls/1992
The Boston Foundation 20,000	Gang Peace, Boston, MA/1992
The Frost Foundation 15,000	Open Door Youth Gang Alt., Denver/1991
Woods Charitable Trust 15,000	Northwest Neigh. Fed./1991
The Denver Foundation 15,000	Open Door Youth Gang Alts,Denver/1991
Anne Burnette/Tandy Fnd. 10,000	Citizens Crime Comm.,Fort Worth/1991
The Bodman Foundation 25,000	United Neigh. Houses of NY/1991
The Minneapolis Found. 10,000	The City, Inc, Mpls,MN/1991
Stuart Foundations 25,000	Sheriffs Youth Found., L.A./1991
M. & G. Cafritz Found. 25,000	Ctr.for Child Protect., DC/1991
W.K. Kellogg Foundation 100,000	F.I.R.S.T., Dorchester, MA/1991
The Hearst Foundation 20,000	Sisters of St. Joseph, L.A./1991
Woods Charitable Trust 15,000	N.W. Neighborhood Fed., Chicago/1991
Mc Inerny Foundation 10,000	Adult Friends for Youth, Honolulu/1990
The Freedom Forum 10,000	Adult Friends for Youth, Honolulu/1990
James Irvine Foundation 25,000	Sisters of St. Joseph, L.A./1990
The Freedom Forum 10,000	United Univ. Church, L.A./1990
New York Foundation 25,000	Hot Spots Program, Sunnyside,NY/1990
Calif. Community Foun. 12,480	Boys & Girls Club, Santa Clarita/1990
Greater Santa Cruz CCF 30,000	Pajaro Valley Gang Vio.Pre.Proj./1990
Island Foundation, Inc 20,000	Dorchester Youth Collaborative/1990
The San Francisco Foun. 25,000	Ella Hill Hutch Com.Ctr./1990
Dr. Scholl Foundation 13,000	BUILD, Inc, Chicago/1990
General Mills Found. 25,000	The City, Inc, Mpls., MN/1990
J.M. Kaplan Fund, Inc 25,000	Found. for Study of I.S.I, NYC/1990
The McKnight Foundation 60,000	St. Paul Amer. Indian Center/1990
Woods Charitable Trust 15,000	Lincoln Interfaith Council, Nebraska/1990
Adolph Coors Foundation 10,000	Open Door Youth Gang Alts, Denver/1990
Peter Kiewit Foundation 100,000	Chamber Foun. of Greater Omaha/1989
Ralph M. Parsons Foun. 51,200	Sisters of St. Joseph, L.A./1989
James Irvine Foundation 25,000	Sisters of St. Joseph, L.A./1989
Denver Foundation 10,000	Doctors of the World/1989
McBeath Foundation 25,000	Milwaukee Police Dept./1989
Woods Charitable Trust 14,000	Malone Com. Ctr., Lincoln/1989
Atlanta Community Found. 14,000	Urban Trng. Org. of Atlanta/1989
Cooper Foundation 7,332	Malone Com. Ctr., Lincoln/1989
The Bodman Foundation 20,000	United Neigh. Houses of NY/1989
California Community F. 50,000	Boys & Girls Clubs,Los Angeles/1989
Faye McBeath Foundation 30,000	N.W. Side Comm.Dev. Corp.,Milwaukee/1989
Gannett Foundation 10,000	Adult Friends for Youth, Honolulu/1989
San Francisco Foundation 25,000	Ella Hill Hutch Com. Ctr., San Fran./1989
Gannett Foundation 10,000	Urban League of San Diego, MAGIC/1989
Clark Foundation (NY) 25,000	Boys/Girls Club,Madison Sq.,NYC/1989
George Gund Foundation 35,000	Luth. Metro.Min. Assn. of Gtr. Cleveland/1988
Public Welfare Found. 21,000	Youth Service Project, Chicago/1989
Public Welfare Found. 74,900	Com. Youth Gang Srvs.Project,Los Angeles/1989
The Freedom Forum 5,000	M.A.G.I.C., Urban League, San Diego/1989
The Freedom Forum 10,000	Adult Friends for Youth, Honolulu/1989
Gannett Foundation 10,000	Com. Youth Sports&Arts Found.,Los Angeles/1988
Minneapolis Foundation 15,000	The City, Inc., Mpls, MN/1988
Mc Knight Foundation 150,000	Migizi Communications, MPLS/1988
The Freedom Forum 10,000	Commun. Youth Sports&Arts Found, L.A./1988
Columbus Foundation 55,000	United Way/Youth Outreach Project/1988
Public Welfare Found. 21,000	Youth Service Project, Chicago/1988
Gannett Foundation 6,000	City of Rochester, NY/1988

Figure 47: Continued

Foundation and Amount $	Recipient Agency/Year
Mc Knight Foundation 112,922	The City, Inc, Mpls, MN/1988
The George Gund Found. 35,000	Luth. Metro. Ministry Assn,Cleveland/1988
Johnson's Wax Fund, Inc 20,000	U. of Wisc-Racine/1987
JD+CT MacArthur Found. 15,000	United Block Club Council, Chgo/1987
Clark Foundation 20,000	Boys&Girls Club,Madison SQ,NYC/1987
Woods Charitable Trust 20,000	Logan SQ. Neighborhood Assn.,Chicago/1987
Public Welfare Found. 21,000	Youth Service Project, Chicago/1987
Milwaukee Foundation 50,000	Family Service of Milwaukee/1987
Com. Trust.Metro Texas 5,000	Fort Worth Boys Club/1986
Field Found. of Illinois 40,000	United Way/Marcy-Newberry Assn[33]/1986
Primerica Foundation 10,000	United Stoner Youth Found.,Santa Monica/1986
Arco Foundation 10,000	Los Angeles "Say Yes" Program/1986
Clark Foundation 20,000	Boys&Girls Club,Madison SQ,NYC/1986
Milwaukee Foundation 5,000	North Cott Neighborhood House, Milwaukee/1986
Gannett Foundation 15,000	Com. Youth Sports&Arts Foundation, L.A./1986
Ford Foundation 60,099	Boston-Fenway Project, Boston/1986
Chicago Comm. Trust 20,000	Youth Service Project, Chicago/1986
Bodman Foundation 40,000	United Neighborhood Assn of NY,NYC/1985
Achelis Foundation 15,000	United Neighborhood Assn of NY,NYC/1985
Primerica Foundation 10,000	United Stoner Youth Found.,Santa Monica/1985
Weingart Foundation 32,035	Com. Youth Gang Services Project, L.A./1985
Milwaukee Foundation 15,000	U. of Wisc.Milwaukee/1985
Mc Knight Foundation 26,000	Park Ave.United Meth. Church, Minneapolis/1985

SUMMARY AND CONCLUSION

As the gang crime problem in America is increasing, the programs, services, and intervention strategies are also currently changing to meet this challenge. A number of prior works have summarized the existing programs.[34] These include those in New York (Dunston, 1990), which were mostly delinquency prevention programs or prosocial groups such as Boy and Girl Scouts. No single program has been tested in multiple jurisdictions nationwide.

Stephens (1988) listed 22 school and community programs, giving a short profile and contact information. Eight were operated by police or correctional agencies, such as the "program" of the Gang Crime Section of the Chicago Police Department --- that is not a program, it is a police unit, it is not a social service program seeking to prevent gang crime at the primary, secondary, or tertiary level through services. Many of the others listed by Stephens were city agencies.

For a problem as large as the gang crime problem in America we are doing remarkably little about it. It has been an interstate problem for some time now. But the federal government as of this date has not responded to this problem with any major initiative other than fund "same old stuff" projects and research, which even when published and reported are never really known by those who need the information.

Something will have to be done. The major actors in the solution have been identified here. Some of the things that can and should be done have also be discussed. It is possible, in other words, to seek creative solutions, even solutions for funding the solution. In DuPage County, Illinois one such creative solution for funding not-for-profit groups like Moth-

ers Against Drunk Driving comes in the form of a state law permitting fines to drunk drivers as "contributions" to such not-for-profit service groups.[35] Just as those going to traffic school know about "traffic school", getting off the ticket by a short educational/video/lecture type of service, a "gang school" existed in Chicago for sometime until recently, where adults arrested for mob action and other gang crimes being referred to one court room were able to attend "Gang Free" sessions (similar to traffic school) and have their charges dropped.

The gang crime problem is a complex one. There will be no easy or simple solutions. The problem will not go away over night. And may never go away completely. There have always been gangs in America, and there may always be gangs in America. But they do not need to be as deadly and as destructive as they are today, or as much worse as they promise to be without the implementation of prevention and intervention services and strategies. Something will have to be done.

DISCUSSION QUESTIONS:

(1) Do you think a community organization can, by the provision of services and opportunities and adult prosocial supervision, redirect a local neighborhood gang out of the path of delinquency and crime and into the path of better citizenship?

(2) If you controlled a budget to spend on gang crime prevention and intervention, what percentage would you allocate to primary, secondary, and tertiary efforts? And why?

(3) Is it realistic to expect the major actors who should become involved in the solution to actually "get together" and work together towards a common goal of reducing the destructive impact of the gang crime problem? How could it work?

If You Are A Gang Member: This is The Kind of Program Counselor You Want To Have.

This can also be called the case of the "family counselor" who was also an "arms dealer" selling guns to gangs. David R. Goodman, age 38, from Gary, Indiana, worked as a "family educator" at the Aunt Martha's Youth Service Center in southeast Chicago. That is, until he was arrested in late 1997 for illegally buying 16 handguns with the intent to sell them to gang members[36].

But, hey, if you are a gang member, this is your kind of counselor.

END NOTES:

[1] "Yes", says your author: in any community, in any situation --- it is, however, a matter of how much effort we are willing to put into it. And how much in terms of resources.

[2] The astute reader will sense at this point that there is actually more in common between conservative police points of view and Hagedorn's analysis than might at glance be obvious. That is, some police may in a rejection of the "racism/oppression" thesis, point to a stronger role of economic incentives for joining gangs. Similarly, Hagedorn assumes this economic incentive as the primordial role for reducing the deleterious impact of gangs on a community.

[3] In one case study (LK29), this shows a perfect example of how gang members can be dismembered from their gang, even those like LK29 who were known as "loonies" who shoot rival gang members. LK29 was in a special program that involved relocation and college: it worked. He now is very much opposed to all gangs. And, thus, a great source of information on the Latin Kings; but equally, he was never arrested, and the statute of limitations has passed on his crimes, and he is currently working in a very responsible court role in Cook County.

[4] Apparently placement in the military for those who might qualify, while shown by Hans Mattick in his Master's thesis "Parole to the U.S. Army" to be likely to reduce recidivism, is not necessarily consistent with gang dismemberment. That is, Horowitz (1982, p. 7) states that gang members "in the Army were still considered gang members and likely to rejoin the group upon release".

[5] Examine Keiser (1979) on this point. Gangs like the Vice Lords simply "adapted" to the expectation that their gang leaders would be arrested. Therefore they "institutionalized" leadership positions in the gang-role structure. It provides for continuity of function even after an arrest and conviction (see Keiser, 1979: p. 6). It is not enough, therefore, in any gang dismemberment plan to simply assume that arresting an individual leader of any significance will actually in itself be sufficient to undermine the effectiveness of the gang organization. Indeed, as discussed elsewhere in this text, it can mean the inducement of "leadership training" for other gang members eager to "make rank".

[6] In a frustrated reply to a citizen demanding greater police surveillance of gangs in Chicago, a gang crimes police commander testifying at the Illinois Gang Crimes Study Commission stated "The city has gone into a consent decree with certain organizations, the Alliance to End Repression and the American Civil Liberties Union. Under that we are very, very limited to what we can do on their First Amendment rights" (see Nash, 1984: p. 75). He is referring to the law suits brought against the Chicago Police Department over its "red squad" spying on leftist groups, which was successfully battled in federal court, resulting now in restrictions even on gangs. Apparently, such surveillance and infiltration on groups also included Alinsky-style community anti-crime groups (see Candice M. Kane, 1976, Factors Related to Teacher Openmindedness as Measured by the Rokeach Dogmatism Scale and the Modified Kelly Exploration Questionnaire in a Neighborhood Undergoing Racial Change, Ph.D. dissertation, Northwestern University, pp. 23,25).

[7] From the case of LK29, apparently gang leaders are equally capable of this in the sense of taking off the "cream" of home invasions, burglaries, etc, and holding out on equitable income distribution to subordinate gang members involved in such crimes. It is a source of much potential friction between leaders and core members.

[8] One other problem has recently surfaced in the research reported by Taylor (1990: p. 131) whose findings showed that most gang members don't want a job, and are not looking for one; also, none would take a job paying the minimum wage.

[9] Vigil (1988: p. 31) joins this support for job placement services as a method of luring offenders away from the gang, in stating "gang members who secure a good job often refocus and redirect their lives into more conventional routes; such a change in orientation is referred to as "maturing out" (Matza, 1964: 22-26)".

[10] Illinois Criminal Code and Procedure, Chapter 38, Section 1003-14-3 Parole Services, "To assist parolees or releasees, the Department shall provide employment counseling and job placement services, and may in addition to other services provide the following: (1) assistance in residential placement, (2) family and individual counseling and treatment placement, (3) financial counseling, (4) vocational and educational counseling and placement, and (5) referral services to any other State or local agencies. The Department may purchase necessary services for a parolee or releasee if they are otherwise unavailable and the parolee or releasee is unable to pay for them. It may assess all or part of the costs of such services to a parolee or releasee in accordance with his ability to pay for them".

[11] In the case study of LK29, he remarked "just to get back in the gang, a loonie member or former member will to go excessive lengths in violence, to get back in the gang", like a conversion reaction, a compulsive kind of compliance to show affinity where "killing someone means automatic rank". Often, as well, means automatic prison terms. But not really a prison term as it means for most Americans, it means for these gang members a chance for status elevation.

[12] All we find on the topic of homosexuality from most of our so-called in-depth, richly detailed qualitative analyses are periodic reports of young gang members "jackrolling" gays. One of the few reports, actually, of gang interviews where the gang member admitted their homosexuality was that by Murphy (1978) in the case of Sandra --- a female member.

[13] Dr. Irving Spergel of the University of Chicago, has developed prototype/models for gang intervention on the following topical areas: general community design, community mobilization, police, prosecution, judges, probation, corrections, parole, schools, youth employment, community based youth agency, and grassroots organization.

[14] These are actors other than law enforcement. Obviously law enforcement has its hands full, or should have. Law enforcement policy should not be one that passively allows juveniles to roam the streets during the day when they are under law expected to be in school, or after curfew at night. Unfortunately, in some jurisdictions police have other more serious problems to contend with such that this aspect of youth welfare is often neglected.

[15] Such a product to protect from routine drive-bys has been developed and is being marketed by a firm in San Antonio, Texas. It is not so much exploiting the gang problem as it is a sign of the times that ordinary citizens do in fact have to consider this added level of physical protection to even feel safe in their own homes. See: Kelley Shannon, "Drive-By Protection: New Siding Also Shields", Chicago Sun-Times, May 30, 1994, p. 9.

[16] This was "Brite and Lymon registered trademark" ad entitled "Keys To The Future", with bubbles on the top. On March 22, 1994 these posters were put up at Farragut High School in Chicago and the Latin Kings demonstrated, a couple Latin Queens were arrested subsequently, and students and gang members alike ended up marching on the police station in a disturbance.

[17] See: Editorial "Don't Include Gangs In Youth Programs", Chicago Sun-Times, June 12, 1994, p. 47. At the time, a gang activist organization in Chicago was trying to pressure Mayor Daley into granting funding for "youth programs" that would be able to be administered by gangs. Mayor Daley fervently rejected such requests that then became protest demands, the gangs demanding a part of the pot of money allocated. Marion Stamps and Wallace "Gator" Bradley were on hand at a press event to protest against Mayor Daley's decision not to fund gang-run programs. See: "Fran Spielman and Mary A. Johnson, "Youth Jobs Event Turns Into Fiasco: Daley Avoids Clash With Gang Group", Chicago Sun-Times, June 10, 1994, pp. 1, 20. Marion Nzinga-Stamps was featured in the story "Run, Mural Help Promote Peace in Gang-Plagued Neighborhoods",

by Sonya C. Vann, Chicago Tribune, Sept. 13, 1993, section 2, p. 3. Stamps had been involved in a "peace walk" and media event for a mural on the organization she is an officer in, "Tranquility-Marksman Memorial Organization", 440 West Division Street, Chicago, Illinois, they claim the gang peace treaty they helped organize was responsible for the relative calm at Cabrini-Green after the sniper killing of 7-year-old Dantrell Davis there in 1992, not the sudden infusion of law enforcement and security improvements.

[18] Gang Specialist Thomas Fleming from the Park Forest, Illinois Police Department has pioneered a pragmatic approach by developing partnerships with the schools and the community --- called the School Liaison Program which has been operating since 1985.

[19] In some jurisdictions, like Elgin, Illinois, recent moves have been made to expel students who commit gang crimes regardless if this had anything to do with their school. The thinking in that regard is to prevent contagion: stop gang members from recruiting others into the gang. There is some merit to this idea, however legally we must presume that the school district would have to establish an "alternative school" program for such members.

[20] Numerous examples of shootings and drive-bys near the "ivory towers" can be found. See: "Police Seeking 2 Men in Shootings at ISU", Chicago Tribune, Section 2, p. 3, Jan. 23, 1994.

[21] Unfortunately, here again, we can find in Chicago how some gangs have been negotiated with. In the late 1960s one of the Chicago city colleges rented property from the Conservative Vice Lords and had gang members supervising functions of a college outpost program (see: Roger Flaherty, "College Name Outlives Controversy", Chicago Sun-Times, Apr. 26, 1994, p. 14). This is equivalent to the kind of foolishness that Rev. Fry engaged in: and ultimately gives the gang more power. One can easily develop a kind of personality profile from this literature, though, on who is the kind of person most likely to try and "buy" the good graces of the gang.

[22] Rev. Boyle worked in the Dolores Mission in Los Angeles and saw 26 gang members buried during a six year period. He did have their respect, enough so to earn him the street name of "G-dog". See: Hugh Dellios, "Barrio Misses Priest Who Tried To Stop Gang Wars", Chicago Tribune, Section 1, p. 21, March 21, 1993.

[23] See: "Maudlyne Ihejirika, "Muslims on Patrol at Rockwell", Chicago Sun-Times, May 5, 1994, p. 5.

[24] FCH17, a member of Chicago's "four corner hustlers" gang, who joined when he was 12 "because the money got good to me", felt that dropping out of the gang was not an option for him "because I have too many tattoos". Obviously, something that could be corrected with new modern methods of tattoo

removal.
[25] One group, the National Commission on Correctional Health Care (NCCHC), has been most active in providing quality training and technical assistance in areas dealing with known areas of risk to health (fighting, gang confrontations, drug/substance abuse, AIDS/HIV/STD infection, etc). Clearly, gang membership in a correctional institution can be considered a factor contributing to morbidity and mortality.
[26]See: Rob Karwath, "Youth Mental Facility Sought Gang Truce", Chicago Tribune, Section 2, P. 1.
[27] As in the politically popular "war on drugs", the traditional federal response is to simply put someone in charge (give them responsibility, with no authority), as "drug czars". One might predict, therefore, that "gang czars" could emerge in a conservative political climate favoring a "war on gangs". We lost the war on poverty, poverty won. We lost the war on drugs, drugs won. Any war on gangs, without taking into consideration some of the issues discussed by Miller (1990) will almost insure that gangs will win that war too.
[28]After the October 1992 sniper killing of a child in Cabrini Green, the Director of the Chicago Housing Authority was frequently cited in the local media to the effect that the Illinois National Guard was needed to restore peace to the area.
[29]Five skinheads appeared on a "Jerry Springer Show" in Chicago and left the set "ready for action, pumped up". They made the mistake of picking a target for their bias crimes after the show when they came over by Chicago State University (CSU). They tried to take over a fried chicken store across from CSU, had assaulted an employee, put up some racist graffiti, and as they tried to leave they were all captured and arrested by CSU police. See: Phillip J. O'Connor and Art Golab, "5 Skinheads Charged in Post-Show Vandalism", Chicago Sun-Times, April 29, 1994, p. 5.
[30] Case study LK29 stated that the gang problem, like AIDS, is an epidemic and getting worse; nothing can be done to eliminate it entirely, all we can do at this juncture is cope, adapt, prevent, etc, essentially "damage control".
[31] Targeting leaders means much work, and law enforcement are more prone to let "small fish" off the hook. Which can mean overlooking a significant portion of the problem. Especially in the case of female gang members, who as case studies indicated, may be those most likely to have the function to store weapons, firearms, and even money for other gang members. These are typically naive teenage girl gang members.
[32] This is based on an analysis of Foundation Grants Index information nationwide.
[33]The Marcy-Newberry Association in Chicago also received $25,000 in 1982 from the Chicago Community Trust in support of its youth gang outreach community service program.
[34] Spergel and Chance (1990) provided case studies in six cities that show the need for more pro-active gang program initiatives.
[35]See: Art Golab, "Price of Crime Rises in DuPage County", Chicago Sun-Times, May 20, 1994. This "fine" or "contribution" is simply enabled by state law, and could be easily modified to include the gang crime situation, and the gang prevention/intervention funding opportunity.
[36]See: Jerry Thornton, "Youth Counselor is Charged With Selling Firearms", Chicago Tribune, Dec. 18, 1997, section 2, p. 9.

Photos and "Business Card"
of the Simon City Royals,
a mostly white folks gang
from Chicago, Illinois.

C𝔐   **𝔍-𝔠**

Campbell-Lunt

Lil Capone
The Professor
Sandman
Sultan
Gilligan
Paz
Tyrant

Simon-City-Royals

Lil Satan - Jungle Jim
Sneaky - Lil Joker

Lil Dagger
Weasel
Beast
Pyro
Pest
Casper
Lil Rebel

Chapter 28

GANG PROGRAMS: AN OVERVIEW, ANALYSIS AND CRITIQUE

INTRODUCTION

Many persons want to do something about the gang problem, and more often than not the response involves establishing some type of gang program. There are many, many different gang programs; some are simply better known than others. Most knowledgeable citizens want gang prevention programs, they are just confused at what level of prevention should be targeted with strategic policy intervention or planning resources. Prevention can mean: (1) primary prevention, (2) secondary prevention, and (3) tertiary prevention. Primary prevention means getting to the person before they have been exposed to gangs, attempting with a good theory of human behavior to prevent the person from ever having any involvement with gangs. Secondary prevention means getting to the person who has already been exposed to gangs, and with a good theory of human behavior and based on what we know from criminology and delinquency prevention, and attempting to extract them from gang influence and prevent them from further gang involvement. Tertiary prevention means basically an intent to "rehabilitate", and means getting to the person who is a self-reported gang member and attempting with professional guidance based on theory, research, and sound policy to reduce the future crime impact of such persons.

Prevention carries a somewhat different meaning than intervention. Intervention implies working with gang youths. Tertiary prevention therefore comes closest to the full meaning of intervention in that it implies that some type or combination of services need to be provided to "those in the gang". Given a limited number of resources, the preference assumed by the social polity here is that of primary prevention rather than intervention. Intervention implies some ability to "rehabilitate" and the literature on the success of such efforts is truly mixed. A somewhat less ambitious goal in terms of impacting on human behavior is implied in primary prevention where the emphasis is on "insulating" someone from becoming involved in the problem behavior. Tertiary intervention with gang members is basically gang member rehabilitation programming, and enjoys little evidence of blanket effectiveness.[1]

As explained elsewhere in this book, there are different levels of gang involvement. This is not simply the difference between "hard core" and "fringe" members. There are leaders. There exists in most formal organizational gangs a middle management as well. There exist those who are "honorary" members or "ancianos" (i.e., older less active, almost retired, or honorary members) from whom less is expected. There always exists the regular "foot soldiers". But there also exists those who are simply "associates", or wannabes. Knowing what level of social integration the person has into any gang will vary proportionately to the difficulty of prevention efforts. The higher the gang integration, the higher the difficulty of inducing individual behavior change.[2]

The purpose of this chapter is to take a much closer look at gang programs; their ingredients (what they do), their structure (how they do it), their goals (what they hope to accomplish), their target groups (who they provide services to), and their assumptions if any (when and under what conditions do they logically expect to achieve a positive result based on the social sciences about human behavior).

GANGS RUNNING GANG PROGRAMS

A good deal of our psychological literature and common sense would tell us that professional help is needed when it comes to restoring someone to good mental health. That is to say, an active criminal cannot rehabilitate another criminal nor rehabilitate himself. The idea behind professional trained expertise is that it is unrealistic to lock someone up and basically say "go rehabilitate yourself or someone else". On the other hand, the indigenous approach works well in some contexts, for some persons, at some times, for some specific purposes. Alcoholics Anonymous (AA) and its many related forms (NA, etc) is viewed as an important and positive part of an overall solution throughout most of the literature and in common beliefs.

There are many examples of gang leaders and gangs being the primary administrators of "gang prevention/intervention" programs. These gang programs fit a definite profile. Once the government or foundation funding disappears, they disappear. Once the government or foundations discover they have misappropriated the funds, they disappear. They will resist to the bitter end any efforts to hold them "accountable" by the means of formal program evaluation research that involves a complete statistical accounting. They see "program evaluators" as the "G-men", the "funding five-oh". They want to be able to spend their money any way they want to. They do not want to have someone tell them they need a good theory of human behavior before attempting to intervene in the life of an individual regarding the protection of human subjects (e.g., what could happen afterwards if it really was not a good theoretically sound idea to do what they did to an individual in their field-service experiment).

How do gangs whose main goal is illegal income from criminal activity end up running gang programs? The fieldwork of Kotlowitz describes this process as it worked for Jeff Fort on Chicago's southside:

"By the late 1960s, the gangs had won some standing among the establishment, particularly with liberals who felt that these young hoodlums, given proper guidance, might turn their energies and enviable organizing and leadership abilities to bettering their neighborhoods" (Kotlowitz, 1992: p. 37).

Thus, Jeff Fort in 1964 got his real start and it was not from the from the University of Chicago as some are prone to believe in Chicago. Jeff got his help from Rev. John Fry in 1964, when Rev. Fry as the minister of First Presbyterian Church of Chicago at 64th and Kimbark, felt he could use his church to create a peace treaty between warring gangs, and it was Rev. Fry who helped Jeff get his Blackstone Rangers funding from Kettering Foundation, the Community Renewal Society, and the W. Clement Stone Foundation. It was in 1967 that Jeff had the opportunity to run a complete government job training program for gang members at The Woodlawn Organization (TWO), some $927,341 that was quickly misspent.[3] Similarly, for the Vice Lords on Chicago's westside:

"At Henry Horner, the Vice Lords gained a similar standing when a local hospital bequeathed a former Catholic boys' school it owned, coupled with a grant of over $20,000, to local gang leaders in the hope that they would open a neighborhood center" (Kotlowitz, 1992: p. 37).
Just like Jeff Fort, the Vice Lords used those assets for something other than community improvement.

The Federal government has not been a leader in clarifying "what works" in terms of gang prevention/intervention. It has been a leader in funding a wide number of 1960s style programs that were specifically targeting gang members or potential gang members. The Federal government has, over the last three decades, supported a wide number of gang experiments seeking to intervene in the gang crime problem. Some have clearly and most certainly achieved dramatic results, but in the opposite direction! That is, some programs have inadvertently increased the wealth and power, and thereby the persistence, continuity and expansion, of certain specific gangs. It seems reasonable to conclude that this has also meant, in its limited context, increasing rather than decreasing the gang crime problem.

The well-intended work of a member of the clergy known as Reverend Fry is one such example. Whether he said it or not in his applications for federal funding, Rev. Fry assumed the theory that gang members could be easily "coopted" into leading a law abiding existence. Rev. Fry hired Jeff Fort, the leader of the Black P. Stones and the Main 21, to help "solve the gang problem". Jeff Fort quickly manipulated the situation, ciphering off funds, hiring "ghost workers", demanding "kickbacks" from fellow gang members whom he hired under the authority of the program, and outright misappropriation (e.g., program fraud).

This sudden influx of hard money into the treasury of Jeff Fort's gang, meant it accumulated more weapons and more capital with which to eventually enter large scale narcotic trafficking. Overall, it meant never asking Jeff Fort, nor any other gang member, to ever sign a "pledge" that they had dropped their gang allegiance, that they would "give up on crime". Rev. Fry was concerned about gang violence and convinced the Federal government he could "do something about it". Rev. Fry assumed that offering a context for a "peace treaty" and a helping hand to these troubled youths would have a positive result. The result was not positive, the result was the El Rukns: a formidable, highly organized, tight knit, highly selective, extremely violent, criminal gang that still operates today in spite of the incarceration of its top leadership.

Jeff Fort wrote the book on how to run an outside gang from behind prison walls. He used his "prisoner rights", the right to use the telephone. Today in prisons such as those in Illinois, gang leaders continue to "issue marching orders" to their gang members on the streets. A common technique used to maintain communications even while incarcerated amounts to the use of a "safe house" telephone that the inmate gang leader calls collect. The "safe house" contains a sophisticated "call forwarding" fast dialing machine where all he needs to do is enter another digit from the keypad of the telephone he is using and he gets automatically connected to one of his henchmen who may have a cellular phone anywhere in the world. Conference calls are also routinely handled in this fashion.

While the Federal government has cracked down on the telephone activities of gang leaders like Jeff Fort (who is incarcerated presently at the Marion Penitentiary), gang leaders incarcerated in state and local correctional systems clearly have an edge. Many still continue, as in the case of gang leaders in Illinois prisons and elsewhere today, basically "running" their gang from the inside.

A genuine "bad idea" is to basically turn over assets to a hostile group like a highly organized criminal gang. Such an example is detailed in the case of the program started in 1976 known as "GET GOING, INC" (Madden, 1993: 7). It was an aftercare program for "Pintos" (released prisoners) located in East Los Angeles. It was run by the Mexican Mafia (EME). It was clearly, then, aimed at "tertiary prevention": the hardest to accomplish[4]. According to the report this program was "actually a front for the Mexican Mafia" (ibid). Thus, "Federal grants were used to purchase heroin in Mexico" and they used their access to the prisons to increase the gang presence throughout California. When someone was about to "spill the beans" in 1977 about this federal

fraud, she was killed by an EME member (ibid).

The cases of Jeff Fort and the Get Going Inc program illustrate what not to do. Providing assets that can be readily converted to the use of the gang (a criminal enterprise) is not the best idea if the goal is to reduce the gang crime threat problem. Similarly, a Boot Camp or "Leadership Training" program for some gangs might fit right into the agenda of a gang leader. A physically stronger and better disciplined gang member is the ideal soldier of any gang leader. Thus, program intervention cannot be predicated on the "terms" of the gang, but must rather be based on the "terms" and expectations of the community that must eventually face the gang problem if it gets much worse. The goals of the law-abiding community and the goals of the gang may be antithetical outside of the generalized context of "we all want a better world". In the context of specific issues, community members do not want armed gangs shooting up the neighborhood. No gang truce or "peace treaty" has yet to surface where gang members truly turned in their weapons. Someone who thinks the "gang truces" in Los Angeles, Chicago, Minneapolis[5], and elsewhere have resulted in a sudden permanent decrease in gang violence should get a police scanner and start listening to their local police calls like the organized gang-controlled drug-distribution rings do themselves to avoid serious arrests.

Gangs do aspire to control government funding for gang programs and sometimes appear to be able to reach to the very top of the local politicians for such support. More often than not, however, it backfires. Such was the case in October, 1985 when the mayor of St. Paul, Minnesota met with John Scruggs, the local leader of the Disciples gang who was seeking $58,000 in seed money to start a youth center. The very next day, this same gang leader executed a 16-year-old female member --- Christine Kreitz --- because he feared she could link him to a crime that if discovered would jeopardize the government grant. Scruggs was convicted of first-degree murder and received a life sentence in prison[6].

PROGRAMS WITHOUT THEORIES ARE RISKS NOT WORTH TAKING

As used here a theory means a model of etiological logic that is consistent with prior research support and/or common sense application of validated explanations of human behavior; in this instance, human behavior involving deviance, more specifically, crime and delinquency, as well as substance abuse and violence. Intervention or prevention implies an effort to "interrupt" a sequence of human behavior, at an appropriate point in time, to motivate behavioral change. This also presumes we are talking about individual behavior; not the treatment of group behavior. It is not assumed here that an entire group (i.e., gang in this case) is subject to such change[7].

The idea that no theory is used to guide program intervention efforts means it is an atheoretical model. In an atheoretical model, basically anything could happen as a result of the intervention because there is no logical sequence or justification for "what might happen". It is a "flip of the coin" situation. It could just as easily go "wrong" as go "right". If it goes wrong we produce criminals rather than preventing crime. The idea of having a theoretically justified model of intervention is that the program can logically expect positive impact at a higher level of probability than a flip of the coin (50/50 chance). A good theory of human behavior increases the odds of having a positive impact, which is why it is needed.

That any program of intervention or prevention dealing with crime or delinquency --- in this instance gang crime --- needs a theory justifying what it proposes to do is now one of the areas of consensus not just among gang researchers, but among almost all criminologists and social scientists[8].

It is important to have rigorous evaluation research conducted on all gang intervention/prevention programs. This should include both process (what happens during the program) and product evaluations (what happens afterwards, the "outcomes"). An atheoretical evaluation is also not a good idea. The "measures" used in the evaluation (reduction in recidivism, increased self-esteem, reduced interaction with gang members, etc) need to be as closely as possible related to the specific theory of intervention being used by the program.

PRIMARY PREVENTION IN THE SCHOOL SETTING

A number of program approaches have been described in the gang literature that are useful in the school setting (Knox, Laske, and Tromanhauser, 1992). The idea is to combine anti-gang education with anti-drug education, because so often in the school setting these two problems go hand in hand. Actually, a third problem --- conflict and violence --- can also be highly correlated with gang and drug problems. Thus, in the Cleveland Public Schools a special Youth Gang Unit was created in its Division of Safety & Security[9]. The concept behind this type of added expertise is that by training teachers on gang recognition issues, on conflict resolution, etc, and working with parents and community groups, that the school has a fighting chance to curb these interrelated problems[10]. Most teachers do not get training about gangs in college, however they need it to effectively carry out their mission.

PRIMARY PREVENTION IN THE NEIGHBORHOOD CONTEXT

Recreational activities structured and supervised in such a fashion as to provide a viable alternative to what the gangs offer in terms of fellowship and "excitement" are a common ingredient for the primary prevention of gang problems. Boys and Girls Clubs offer such activities in their drop-in centers as do many others (e.g., the YMCA/YWCA). Special initiatives such as the "Take Our Daughters to Work Club" work with large corporate sponsors such as Ameritech and in addition to providing a daily safe haven for kids also provide some social skills upgrading[11]. The goal is to prevent such "good kids" from ever joining a gang, and to keep them "off the streets" where the gangs are ever present.

A program that specifically incorporated such recreational activities as well as arts and crafts for youths, and which operated continuously for 52 years and is therefore regarded by some as the oldest anti-gang program in Chicago, is that started by the late Daniel "Moose" Brindisi who was the executive director of the Near Northwest Civic Committee[12]. This neighborhood based program also acquired its own summer camp, Camp Pompeii, which is located in Park Forest, Illinois. This program also used the recommendation of Thrasher (1918) that Boy Scout and Cub Scout groups could provide valuable socialization experiences as a way of gang prevention at the primary level. Groups like Boys Nation and Girls Nation also provide such general positive socialization experiences in an adult supervised context of legitimate social control.

There is a potentially endless list of positive, pro-social, skill-building, adult-supervised projects, programs and experiences that can be provided to children in an overall strategy to prevent gang affiliation at the primary level of prevention. At an elementary school near Chicago's Cabrini-Green, a drum and bugle corp was formed; while the staff volunteers could handle 80 children ages 5 through 9, some 300 actually applied to use the 36 drums available[13]. There are basically some very worthwhile programs that need to be funded that are not being funded. If we really want to do something for youths, then clearly there are a lot of ways to steer them away from gang involvement.

SECONDARY PREVENTION: WORKING WITH "AT RISK" YOUTHS

A common theme in secondary prevention is to target geographical areas that represent a "high risk". This has often meant targeting youths from 8 to 16 in public housing complexes. In such settings, the gang/drug/violence/crime problem is an ever present problem. Project FLOW (Future Leaders Of the World) in Philadelphia, for example, with

$875,602 in funding for the first 17 months seeks to serve 490 such at-risk youths. As described in its literature, this program includes a number of traditional and unique service components:

"The program activities developed to benefit these youth will include an education component involving tutoring, homework assistance, study groups, etc; comprehensive drug related services such as drug and alcohol education, prevention education, refusal skills building (Drugs/Violence/Alcohol) and counseling. The comprehensive gang prevention services will provide mentoring, individual and family counseling, conflict resolution and anger control workshops. Other activities will include summer programs, sports and recreation and other related cultural activities including trips to museums, parks etc. Parent support groups will also be formed to support and stabilize the family structures.

All Project FLOW youth will receive basic Health Care through the Philadelphia Department of Public Health. Another major component...will be the 'Rites of Passage' module which is designed to increase awareness and develop skills associated with positive culture and ethnic identities of the youth served"[14].

As should be expected, the FLOW program is evaluated by a University in its area. All programs with direct contact with youths should be subject to such thorough independent evaluation.

Some consulting firms have arisen rapidly to the potential market for such services to local government. It is not unusual for such consultants to be paid $100 an hour for their services in helping establish such programs[15].

THE COMMUNITY-BASED CONSORTIA APPROACH

In recent years, the federal funding for gang programs has emphasized a community-based consortia approach. What it means is bringing together a number of different programs and services under a larger umbrella-style program; all of the actors targeting a specific population for intensive prevention services. An example of such a program that bases its expectations for impact on the prior research and on sound theory is that of the "Mujeres Y Hombres Nobles" (Noble Men and Women) program of the Los Angeles County Office of Education. Funded with a $3 million grant that will last five years the consortium will serve 30,000 residents and 350 school age children in East Los Angeles. Its program components include: "gang risk reduction, drug prevention and treatment, HIV/AIDS prevention, vocational training, cultural pride and esteem, spiritual and moral rencounterment, mentoring by Madrinas and Padrinos, intergenerational gang family systems intervention, conflict resolution and mediation, educa-tion and community awareness, and linkages to services".

This program is unique in being capable of dealing with the intergenerational gang family situation. Unfortunately, it is a not infrequent problem apparently, and one of the least researched aspects of the gang/family area. The Mujeres y Hombres Nobles program summary gives an example:

Teen Angel Magazine, referred to elsewhere in this book, regularly publishes pictures submitted by teen mothers of their children and babies dressed in gang clothing and giving gang hand signs; these teen mothers are nurturing a new generation of gang members.

CONFUSED GANG PREVENTION: AN EXAMPLE OF A PROGRAM WITHOUT A THEORY

The Gang Project described here was funded by the Administration on Children, Youth and Families of the U.S. Department of Health and Human Services (DHHS). It had as its first broad purpose to "develop an action plan in the city which identified the community's vision for a gang-free city, the obstacles blocking that vision, new directions to take to overcome the obstacles, and implementation plans for each new direction". The strange idea here was that the gang problem could be solved with an administrative solution: some master plan that would take a couple years to develop. As the program "unfolded", it changed its goal away from "gang-free" to that of having gangs be less violent in their city. To quote their final report to DHHS:

"A shift occurred in the original language of the goals from 'gang free' to one that focussed on creating a climate in which gangs did not act in violent ways. It was felt that some hypocrisy would be in place if our goal was gang free but we said nothing about 'gangs' such as Rotary or Kiwanis or Lions." The project offered "training" of an unspecified nature to community groups and nonprofit staff, which along with "community meetings" were not well attended[16]. At some point, the project engaged in direct service to youths in schools and juvenile corrections; using former addicts and ex-gang members to speak to them on --- presumably --- the evil of gangs and drugs.

So what happened at the end of the project funding period? No such coherent strategic plan was ever actually written. The final report included a lot of vague generalities about the need for community empowerment. It evaluated itself, and felt it did a good job.

That is the danger of an atheoretical program: it can literally change its goals, which must be viewed with some criticism. The Project was probably not the best use of public monies. It probably sounded good to Washington (holding community forums, interfacing various agencies, etc), but the Project lacked any coherent theory and then changed its goals and began doing direct service work. This same program not only changed its goals and language after receiving federal money, it may have used the money to help sponsor a "Gang Summit Meeting".

A GANG OUTREACH PROGRAM THAT DOES NOT GET ALONG VERY WELL WITH GANG COPS

This is another federally funded program, but which as an "advocacy organization", receives funding from a variety of other sources especially foundations. A highly educated police officer who is also a gang researcher first told me about this program in his city. The word among police was that the program served as a site for gangs to hold their meetings and conduct their gang business. This program bills itself as a "gang outreach program". There is no theory of just how, exactly, it would prevent anything.

The idea itself was peculiar: not a traditional "detached worker outreach program" to individual gang members, for which there are a lot of materials that can be used for training such detached workers; but rather it sought outreach to the "gang" itself. Such on-line program service personnel would clearly have to be organizational and group psychology experts; which of course they were not, they were indigenous staff, paraprofessionals at best. What is the single most important criteria of program success in such detached worker programs is the ability to increase a more law abiding and prosocial lifestyle, and to reduce a delinquency and criminality lifestyle. Most prior evaluation research on such detached worker programs has not shown the ability to actually accomplish this goal (Mattick and Caplan, 1962; Klein, 1968; Miller, 1974; Quicker, 1983).

In the program being described here, what it did do is basically turn the program over to the gang. To quote from its final report: "Access to Gang Leadership: staff know the gang leadership in the city; some of the program staff have been recruited from this leadership". The program provides its staff with beepers and car radios, and thus claims it is a "round the clock" operation. The program employs active gang members, and "has hired most of its junior staff from the ranks of gangs in" the city. Without any indication of training for such staff, the report goes on to claim how it provides gang outreach, case management, crisis intervention, family services, school services, some type of "ministry to gang members"[17], security work at public events, and prison work. Hiring gang leaders and active gang members under the guise of working with the local gang scene somehow gets translated into establishing a Gang Council

and sponsoring a gang conference.

Here we see the real danger of an atheoretical program evaluating itself: of course, it claims to literally have walked on water. It provides a number of statistics which on their face would appear to be "doing something": during 1991, 235 meetings with gangs or gang leaders to prevent conflicts (does that include meetings the gang members themselves who work in the program have between each other, we don't know), 156 mediations of gang-related conflicts at schools (does that include the conflicts in its own school program that it runs, we don't know), 195 mediations between gangs in conflicts on the streets.

What we have here are paraprofessionals at best who while indigenous to the city, are employed in a social service and a crime prevention and public safety function, who might potentially be part of the problem itself. The media coverage gained by some of the gang leaders has certainly helped them to promote their gang as an organization "about Growth and Development" --- a code word for Gangster Disciple --- so it provides a public relations function for the local gangs. There is nothing in the program report documentation about success in reducing drug use or drug sales, of actual reductions in gang violence, or actual reductions in gang membership involvement. In fact, one would have to postulate from the declarations in this report back to the federal government that gang membership probably increased --- at least for those gangs whose leaders were put on the payroll. It is comparable to the early Jeff Fort and Rev. Fry phenomenon[18].

Needless to say this program did not have, as is apparently required of many programs receiving federal funding, any external quantitative process and product program evaluation. But it continues today. Is it possible that the beepers and car phones given to these gang members were used in anything other than "making peace"? Is it really a good idea to have gang members provide "security work" for concerts as this program does, is that not similar to hiring the Hell's Angels at Woodstock? What is the theory here for such a program that it is going to reduce the gang problem? It is certainly not well articulated.

WORKING WITH WOUNDED GANG MEMBERS

This is an example of what appears to be an unconditional style of tertiary prevention. In Chicago in early 1998, Mount Sinai Hospital announced it is teaming up with the Boys and Girls Clubs of Chicago in a $400,000 program to provide caseworkers for youths 10 to 24 years of age who have been treated in the hospital for being a victim of violence[19]. The idea is that a gang member may be more open to giving up the gang life while in the hospital recuperating from a gunshot or stab wound. Once released from the hospital the idea is to reach about 250 of these youths and offer service referrals by trying to get them involved with the Boys and Girls Club, perhaps teach them coping skills, at least the hope being that those treated in this fashion will be less likely to engage in "retaliatory violence" or "revenge" or "vendetta" style violence with rival gangs.

At a cost of $1,600.00 per client in this style of program, it would be equally effective to just send all 250 of the gang members on a six-month sea cruise.

ALTERNATIVE SCHOOLS: Tertiary Prevention With an Immediate Payoff.

When "zero tolerance" for gang mischief was introduced into the Chicago Public School system, obviously a lot of gang members had to be rightfully kicked out of schools: to keep the schools safe for the vast majority of good kids[20]. One by-product though is the matter of a lot of young gang kids on the street. Alternative schools are typically privately run programs and represent a way of reaching out to these gang-involved kids who still want a "school education". The alternative school provides necessary education and an important social control function: keeping the same gang kids off the streets at least a portion of the day that they are at the alternative school. A lot of the CETA programs in the 1970's provided a similar function by actually "paying" a small salary (i.e., minimum wage) to the program participants: they would be paid only if they showed up for the program, and would be "docked" by having to use a "time clock punch" just like they were working in a factory.

THE FEDERAL GOVERNMENT FUNDING FOR GANG PROGRAMS

The federal Youth Gang Drug Prevention Program was authorized by legislation in 1988 (section 3501 of the Anti-Drug Abuse Act of 1988). The federal Youth Gang Drug Prevention Program awards funding to actual gang programs "to prevent and to reduce the participation of youth in the activities of gangs that engage in illicit drug-relate activities and to promote the involvement of youth in lawful activities". The federal agency having the responsibility to administer this funding is the Administration on Children, Youth and Families (ACYF) and is managed by the Family and Youth Services Bureau, both within the Department of Health and Human Services. Since it first began in 1989, this federal initiative has provided over $50 million dollars in funding to over 100 different gang prevention programs.

The FYSB Youth Gang Prevention Program has issued a number of printed newsletters. The Connections newsletter provides updates on various programs funded by FYSB and other features such as its

National Conferences. At any particular time there are a sufficient number of such federally funded programs to hold a National Youth Gang Conference. The First National Conference was held June 5-7, 1991 in Alexandria, Virginia; the Third such conference was held in 1993. A number of other conferences have been funded by the FYSB as well.

Many of the programs funded by this federal initiative publish short guidelines in the Connections newsletter. Much very useful and important information is published in the newsletters[21]. It promotes practitioner/researcher interaction; gives advice on hiring gang outreach workers, provides highlights of gang programs in the news; and contact information.

PROGRAMS TO ESTABLISH "GANG TRUCES"

A number of efforts have been made historically to establish "gang truces". Typically these are ad hoc arrangements and do not reflect a formal program per se. Some programs seek "mini-truces" on an individual level, for example in the context of a single school, where this kind of gang program service is sometimes called "gang mediation". The Youth For Christ evangelical group in Chicago has been holding its "United Nations" meetings for a decade: bringing rival gang members together in groups representing over twenty different gangs over time (Mc Lean, 1991) - the goal being to allow the individuals to appreciate the Christian faith[22]. Such counseling and prosocial advice where the unit of service delivery being targeted is the individual does not seek to work with the gang as a collective enterprise, but rather simply seeks to apply conflict resolution skills at the level of the individual. Such work at the level of the individual is certainly worthwhile.

But what "gang truces" involve typically are not services, nor are they formal programs accountable for their actions, and the unit of service delivery target is the entire gang as a collective identity. A common theme of such truce efforts is to bring together warring or rival gangs and unite them under a larger umbrella organization. The position taken in the present book is that such endeavors are rarely successful and are indeed risky. Supporting the present position that negotiating with gang leaders basically means that through such official recognition the gang becomes stronger are a number of other analyses (Haskel and Yablonsky, 1982) and more recently Kodluboy and Evenrud:

"It is probable that mediation with gang members or gang leaders may sometimes be necessary to forestall immediate violence or prevent loss of life. It is also probable that such mediation increases the risk of validating the gang as a legitimate social entity, thus buying short-term peace at the price of long-term persistence of the gang (Goldstein and Huff,

1993: p. 285)."

Still, it is not hard at all to find those who felt the "truce" between the Crips and the Bloods in Los Angeles was a major positive development[23]; just as it is not hard to find the skeptics either. And there have been cases were one God-fearing man alone has achieved, it is claimed in media coverage anyhow, remarkable progress.[24]

It is helpful, however, to briefly outline some of the recent "gang truce" efforts. Four such efforts are critically examined here: (1) the Chicago Cabrini-Green case, (2) the Minneapolis case, (3) the Kansas City summit, and (4) the Chicago Gang Summit Meeting.

1. The Chicago Gang Truce.

In October-November, 1992 the Chicago official "gang truce" button began appearing and was worn by many of the gang members whose gangs were signed parties to this truce. The "gang truce" button has the slogan "UNITED IN PEACE" with two hands (a left hand and a right hand) clasping, along with ten gang "logos" or symbols --- all in black on a white round background. The logo symbols for the following gangs appear on this "gang truce" button: Vice Lords, New El Rukns (seven in circle), Black P Stone Nation, Cobras, El Rukns, Four Corner Hustlers (+ sign, 440), Black Disciples, Black Gangster Disciples, and Black Gangsters.

White gangs, Arab gangs, and Hispanic gangs were not a party to this "truce". Recall that such racial enmity is a part of the fuel that fires the engine of the gang problem. Any such genuine "truce" would have to include all ethnic gangs across the board. This alliance of Black gangs arose in the aftermath of the sniper killing of a child in Cabrini-Green and the public uproar it caused. The pressure was put on the gangs. Political activists took advantage of the situation to "bring the gangs together". In this fashion, a tentative alliance was formed between rival gangs; giving them greater legitimacy and recognition in the mass media. Gang leaders and gang activists claimed credit for the "calm" at Cabrini Green after the sniper killing of the 7-year-old child there, killed by a gang member shooting at someone else with an AR-15 assault rifle. No one should seriously believe any gang involvement caused any peace at Cabrini Green, rather this Chicago Housing Authority complex was flooded with international attention and was swarmed with new services and resources, including a vast number of intensive and proactive law enforcement initiatives by such agencies as the Secret Service.[25]

Gang killings, gang shootings, and gang violence continue in Chicago today in spite of any 1992 "gang truce". While the violence committed by gangs has not stopped in Chicago, this did give certain gang leaders who were a party to the "truce" a great deal of positive attention in the mass media. Some elected local Chicago politicians almost a year later believed the truce was successful enough to support a bid for parole by a major gang leader. The fact that the Chicago Police Department decentralized its gang unit during the same time frame has led others to believe that this simply unfounded much gang violence.

But the facts suggest the Chicago truce was little more than a public relations gimmick by the gangs. In July 1993, during the "truce", Chicago had the deadliest month in its entire history in terms of homicides. According to the "truce", anyone who engaged in such gang killings was supposed to be treated as a "renegade"; a term for a very errant gang member --- thus, they would be turned in by their peers to the police for prosecution. According to the Cook County State's Attorney, no gang ever turned in anyone during the time period up to and including August of 1993.

2. One gang truce in Minneapolis was paid for with federal funding, but just like the Chicago and Los Angeles version there is little evidence to show it was effective. The Minneapolis gang truce came out of a "gang intervention" program called The City, Inc which received grants from the U.S. Department of Health and Human Services --- through the FYSB federal initiative described above --- and additional funding from foundations and corporate donors.

"United For Peace" was the Minneapolis gang truce slogan and began in the spring of 1992. Did gang violence drop in Minneapolis? No is the answer, in fact gang-related violence may have increased according to one report[26]. In fact, a gang-war between two factions of the Vice Lords arose during the so-called gang truce[27]. So the factual evidence is that at a minimum, the gang shootings and killings continued.

For some time, the program that sponsored the gang truce also claimed as part of its success the fact that it had strong positive ties with the local police. Police had been meeting with the United For Peace leaders, but that ceased when on September 25, 1992 a Minneapolis police officer --- Jerome Haaf --- was slain execution style by gang members. One of the four members of the Vice Lords arrested for the murder was a relative of Sharif Willis[28] --- the Minneapolis leader of the Conservative Vice Lords and the president of United for Peace[29]. With federal funding The City, Inc --- the not-for-profit program that provided the financing for the Minneapolis gang truce --- was supposed to hold a Gang Conference to show social workers from around the country how effective it was in working with police. The conference was supposed to square off Spike Moss, the gang leader founder of the truce, and Minneapolis Police chief John Laux. The police chief did not attend the conference[30].

The facts of this "gang truce" are quite fascinating. Did the leader of the "gang truce" turn fellow Vice Lords who were charged with the murder of police officer Haaf? No! But the suspects were in fact arrested in the home of the leader of the "gang truce". Police learned that the plot to kill Officer Haaf to send a message about "police brutality" was in fact hatched in the same dwelling. In fact, A.C. Ford one of the persons charged with the assassination of Officer Haaf was a major Vice Lord leader and also a member of the United for Peace coalition[31]. In November, 1992, Jerome Copeland the Gangster Disciples gang leader who was the Vice President or second in command in the leadership of the United for Peace "gang truce" was himself arrested for firearms and narcotics charges![32] Copeland was a "gang outreach worker" employed by The City, Inc in Minneapolis. Some media attention to The City, Inc has likened it to the funding fiasco with Jeff Fort and his misuse of federal funding in Chicago[33]. It certainly seems to have the same elements in such a profile.

3. The Kansas City "Gang Summit"

During the period April 28 through May 2, 1993 at the St. Stephen Baptist Church in Kansas City, Missouri, the first National Urban Peace and Justice Summit was held. It was informally known as the "national gang truce summit". The Kansas City gang summit was truly historically unique. The Mayor, a minister, welcomed those attending at a special breakfast for them. The concept for this summit was originated by the political activist Carl Upchurch in Granville, Ohio. Although many others were obviously involved, including all those from the Chicago "truce" movement, the Minneapolis version, and those in Los Angeles. The single "inside story" indicated "one hundred and sixty four current and former gang leaders and members from 26 cities, and 53 observers" attended the event[34]. The organizer was Carl Upchurch whose group is called Council for Urban Peace and Justice in Columbus, Ohio.[35]

In the press release, gangs were given a Chicago-based public relations title "grassroot street youth organizations and nations". Calling it a "peace movement", the intent in the future is to hold such "summits" in every city and to have a yearly summit.

Much of the material reads similar to gang constitutions: it gives a "positive" side of gang life, it does not talk about how much death, destruction, and violence the gangs themselves have created. If we were to believe it at face value, some of it would lead us to believe these were a group of young republicans. Consider this excerpt[36]:

"Women's Issues: Sisters of the Summit.

We the mothers, the sisters, the girlfriends, women in organizations and the street gangs stand in unity to stop the violence!

As women we have always known violence. This violence is beyond street violence and police brutality; it includes domestic violence, rape, child abuse, and poverty. We insist that women be justly represented on any advisory group or board of directors at any future events.

Honoring our ancestors and elders is important to teach respect, family values, and cultural traditions to our youth.

We are committed to work with our brothers in teaching our children how to replace self-destruction with a commitment to life, family, education, and community empowerment."

It sounds good, but how many guns were turned in? How many signed pledges not to distribute illegal drugs? How many agreed to compensate innocent bystander victims of gang violence or the families of those who died from gang violence? A peace movement led by highly organized gangs for whom violence is a way of life is comparable only to a group of pyromaniacs who have been convicted of arson seeking to replace Smokey Bear as the spokespersons for a National Forest Fire Prevention Campaign.

Anyone who can get gangs to turn in their guns, give up on crime, violence, and drug distribution does however truly deserve not only a Nobel Peace Prize, but something much higher in recognition --- for they would have discovered the "magic bullet" of rehabilitation on a massive scale. Unfortunately, it is not realistic. Waiting for such a large scale of genuine change in deviant behavior is comparable only to someone leaving the porch light on in the hope that Jimmy Hoffa will return.

The Summit had a number of recommendations: reducing police brutality gained much discussion. Another recommendation was to repeal all laws against gangs: "Repeal of all anti-gang legislation, and ordinances, both state and federal, around the country, including existing statutes in California, Minnesota, and the City of Chicago, Oregon, and the federal program Weed and Seed." There were no recommendations in the Summit literature denouncing the use of automatic firearms, MAC's, AK-47's etc. There were no recommendations in the Summit literature demanding that drug trafficking cease and desist.

According to an ex-gang member from a Chicago program who attended, this Summit was a motivational seminar. "I heard a lot of feel good stuff", he reported. But he came back to Chicago believing that the program he works in must cooperate with this new peace movement. He also described a power-brokering incident that apparently resulted in the cessation of a rift between two factions of "Folks"; and in the process gave new meaning to the potential powers that could be held by an "ex-gang". The ex-gang member from the Chicago program was a Latino who was a former member of a Disciples gang faction that consisted primarily of Latinos. Another ex-gang leader from the Disciples, an African-American, also from Chicago, was also attending the summit. The Latino ex-gang member mentioned to the African-American ex-gang member how a rift now existed in a west side neighborhood in Chicago. Very quickly the African-American ex-gang member made a call to an Illinois prison[37]; almost immediately the African-American faction of the Disciples received a call from prison and were basically ordered to "chill out". The "rift" (a kind of discernible tension that could get out of hand) between the two different ethnic factions of the Disciples was immediately eliminated.

Is that an example of peace making or just good gang nation maintenance and management? These were two factions of the same gang nation. They were not traditional rival gangs, they were as ethnic gang factions gradually developing apart however.

What is most interesting here is just how "ex" the ex-gang member was who called the prison where the Disciples chief was serving time. Apparently this is some kind of social drift. The person has a marginal integration: highly integrated into gang life (enough to be able to call the gang leader), and simultaneously highly integrated into conventional society (representing himself as an "ex" gang member who wants peace and goodwill for humanity). Such a person moves in and out of both legitimate society and the deviant subcultures; gravitating to one or the other sectors of society as the need arises, drifting in and out at ease. It would seem reasonable to hypothesize that in the presentation of self to the imprisoned gang leader in the above instance would not be that of an "ex-member" of the gang. This is the kind of issue that needs to benefit from close-up research such as that of ethnomethodoly (i.e., hanging out with the gang). Does someone ever become an "ex-member" of a level three gang (e.g., the Aryan Brotherhood, the Latin Kings, etc) other than entering a witness protection program? Or can some persons, depending on personality and skills, actually penetrate the confidence and have influence over a gang?

4. The October, 1993 Chicago Gang Summit Meeting.

The Chicago Gang Summit Meeting drew enormous media attention and while it had its main events in a downtown hotel also held "field events" at various locations, including the Englewood Public High School for an awards ceremony honoring "community service for peace" leaders like Larry Hoover and Willie Lloyd and other gang leaders. When those attending the summit meeting went to hear Louis Farrakhan, what they heard was the message others also had for the gang members: "Peace cannot be a slogan...you have got to make it real...Put down the guns...You mean peace? You don't need a weapon".[38] Others also demanded that the gangs show a sign of good faith in making their rhetoric reality by turning in guns, but no guns were ever turned in. Actually the gang leaders attending the event got a mixed message in that regard, as one of their main speakers at the downtown main event challenged them "so you think you are bad and you can go and bum rush somebody huh, well if you think you're so tough you just go on up into the C.I.A. headquarters and you bust them up". The audience had heard of how the C.I.A. in Los Angeles was spying on gang members following them around and who also were said to use guns with tracer bullets[39].

Such gang truces appear to have some common etiological sequences. First, such gang truces are not limited to the United States, and have been reported among Asian gang crime groups in Hong Kong (Kaplan and Dubro, 1986: p. 219). What precedes such gang truces are periods of intermittent conflict with relatively equal losses and casualties or the onset of a sudden major surge in public opinion. The greater the intensity of police repression in response to such a public outcry, the greater the incentive for the combatant gangs to establish an alliance. The "heat" is on in otherwords, and public opinion may be developing rapidly as supporting even more intensive police repression. The more disruption in the income-producing functions of a gang from such developments, the more it is likely to agree to enter into an alliance with a rival gang. No one knows the long term effect of working with the gang as an organization and giving it a public platform, it is possible to at least hypothesize that the increased mass media role legitimating gang leaders as "keepers of the peace" may in fact further erode the willingness of potential crime witnesses to ever cooperate with law enforcement or testify if they had to --- as the fear of the gang will increase, it will make the gang appear to be "ever present".

Activist style leaders emerge in the context of such "gang truces" and "gang summit meetings" who represent themselves as being part of both worlds: the gang world, and the "straight" world. Others tend to act as spokespersons for the gang itself. None of these persons has ever really agreed to sign a statement accepting responsibility for the crime and violence of the gang it represents. They want the authority, esteemed status, and public recognition of a kind of Henry Kissinger to the gangs without the responsibility for their behavior and actions. They should not be taken serious until they are willing to accept civil legal responsibility --- and that means the many court suits that could potentially be brought against a gang, for its graffiti, for its theft crimes, for its robbery crimes, for its violence particularly, and such financial damages would be very enormous indeed in any city of 100,000 or more in the United States --- for the gang(s) they claim to represent in "peace" or "truce" negotiations.

Negotiating with gang leaders truly does set a bad precedent however. The logical extreme of such a criminal justice policy is that who knows, perhaps next burglars and rapists will want to negotiate --- "give us what we want....or else". Terrorists always want to negotiate, but anyone who knows anything about terrorism will advise that it is the worst of all decisions in practice and in policy to actually do so. Why? Because negotiating with terrorists provides the behavioral incentive for other terrorists to use extreme violence to achieve their ends as well. That is, negotiating with terrorists encourages more terrorism in the long run. Much gang violence can be considered "street" or "urban" terrorism.

SUMMARY AND CONCLUSION

The full and complete book the history of gang programs has yet to be written. It cannot be accomplished in the limited space here. Some of the programs that had the best theoretical basis for prevention were those making use of the social control that comes from involving the family of the youth in the process[40]. Such programs like the FOCUS Project in Washington, D.C. provided support group activities, family counseling, home visits, working with other social service agencies and police, and sought to prevent gang involvement and drug-abuse and with some promising results. It enlisted the parent in the effort to impact on the children in a systems approach. The good news is that there are a number of such positive impact programs throughout the United States. The bad news is that after the federal funding runs out after one or two years, the program services stop, and the problem returns. We cannot rely on band-aid approaches, the best strategy is the one that prevents new gang recruits from joining the gangs. The federal approach has been piecemeal and segmented. It may not even involve true competitive bidding, that is: politics still seems a factor in who gets funding. We never hear of how knowledge development is improved by these programs. We already know some such program models and services can truly have a positive impact. And yet, still today, such specific services are not standardized nor does the funding agency provide an overall summary of "what works". And it certainly does not do a very good job at disseminating this needed information to the communities that could benefit from it: just in case they wanted to do something without federal funding.

Examining a number of such current federally funded gang prevention programs the typical pro-

gram that operates at the primary level of prevention has the service components shown in Figure 48. By and large, the vast majority of these service components are indeed traditional social service approaches and can be found in many correctional aftercare programs with similar program goals (e.g., to reduce recidivism). Thus, they can be assumed to be useful as well in secondary and tertiary prevention programs.

A couple of the services in Figure 48 stand out as being uniquely related to the gang-drug problem. The "court advocacy" is not a new service, it was tried throughout the 1960s and 1970s and before. It simply motivates the client to participate in the program. But on a large scale, it basically means supplementing the resources of the juvenile public defenders office. Logically, it works against "Weed and Seed" and the strict accountability concept. Because through this service component, some juvenile offenders will get off the hook via the advocate from the program. It is a cheap way to generate clients: they may have to participate in the program as part of their probation agreement. But clearly, if the youth is at the level of being involved in the juvenile court system for delinquency, the program is operating for that youth at a secondary or tertiary level of prevention --- not a primary level of prevention. We cannot design our social structure to send mixed messages to the gang and expect the gang problem to cease operations. We need a logically consistent national strategy.

In none of the programs reviewed as funded by the recent federal initiative was there any breakdown by goals in terms of numbers of youths to be served at these various levels of prevention/intervention. This is truly remarkable in light of the vast accumulation of program knowledge and information in federal agencies. What this may imply is that the federal initiative should be dramatically changed. It should provide a model service intervention/prevention program and in its Requests For Proposals solicit who wants to run this specific type of Model Program (with no deviation, no changing of goals, etc). The evaluation research component would then be meaningful from a comparison and regional point of view. The federal initiative might then take on more structure and consistency. Currently, the initiative could be summarized as Requests for Proposals that solicit "do what you want to do....and if it sounds interesting we'll give you the federal money for it".

There are, however, important conceptual and policy issues in gang programs, especially the current federal initiative that need to be resolved. The foremost is comparable to the credo that physicians use: above all, do no harm. That is, whatever is done, make sure the program does not in fact increase the gang problem or the drug problem or the violence problem. The fact that very rigorous outcome evaluation research is sorely lacking in the current federal initiative unfortunately does not allow us to rule out such a hypothesis. Where that "reverse intended effect" hypothesis needs to be tested first are in those controversial programs that are substantially more than gang outreach, they may be subsidies for the gang (e.g., giving beepers and cellular phones to active gang members and leaders hired by the program).

Thus, any program that hires gang members as the staff who are involved in the prevention/intervention service delivery should probably have an intense process evaluation as well. It is not just Chicago or Minneapolis who have some history about hiring gang members, recently Fort Worth took six gang leaders on the payroll to provide dispute mediation for schools and agencies in Forth Worth.[41] History shows, however, such accommodationist efforts are more likely to backfire than to have positive results.[42] Evaluators familiar with offender programs know some of the dangers here. And clearly, some specific guidelines are needed at the secondary and tertiary levels of prevention. While it is rarely used as a sanction, probation and parole guidelines for adults and juveniles often allow for revocation because of associating with a gang.

In summation, to the extent that some government and private sources tend to reinforce the gang identity and its "public relations" function, allowing the gang to persist over time, allowing it to grow and expand and attract more youths, then to the same extent our intended policies and programs that seek to reduce the gang problem are actually designed for perpetuating the gang problem.

FIGURE 48
TYPICAL PROGRAM SERVICE COMPONENTS IN GANG PROGRAMS

Program Service Component	What it hopes to accomplish.
Referrals	Send the youth to a traditional service agency for specific type of assistance (e.g., health, addiction, housing, etc.).
Individual counseling	Motivate youth to change beliefs and behavior.
Group counseling	Apply positive peer culture to facilitate individual change in beliefs and behavior.
Family counseling	Apply the social control of family members to facilitate individual change in beliefs and behavior.
Peer/adult mentoring	Through one-on-one volunteers or staff, match with youth to motivate or reinforce change in beliefs/behavior.
Educational Upgrading	Increase the academic skills of the youth.
TECHNIQUES:	tutoring, independent study, homework assistance, computer instruction, etc.
Cultural enrichment	Increase youth awareness of the larger social order to motivate respect for conformity.
TECHNIQUES:	visits to museums, higher culture events, outings, etc.
Job placement	Motivate youth to seek legitimate opportunities for achievement.
TECHNIQUES:	subsidized employment, guaranteed summer job, meaningful work experience, etc.
Court Liaison Advocacy	Seek leniency in juvenile court for clients in return for their program involvement.
Parenting skills	Increase the knowledge and skills to nurture children.
AIDS/HIV prevention	Increase the knowledge of health risk behavior and motivate youth to avoid such risks.
Rites of passage awareness	Increase the awareness of youth about human development, the increased responsibilities over the lifespan, and to celebrate their own manhood and womanhood development.
Adult supervised recreation	Drop-in centers, day camp, etc. AKA: Social Recreation. Many such examples: Health & Physical education.
Parent Empowerment	Motivate parents affected by gangs and drugs to take back control of their homes, children, and neighborhoods. (E.G., Operation Parent Sweep).

DISCUSSION QUESTIONS:

(1) Would hiring active gang leaders to help administer a gang prevention program be similar to having the fox guard the hens? What guidelines should be used in hiring persons known to be previously involved as gang members if they are to be used in a gang prevention program? What ideal role should such ex-gang members have in a prevention program?

(2) Do you believe that an overall strategy is needed first before implementing programs at the secondary and tertiary levels? What should be the focus of such an overall national strategy?

(3) Should public funds for gang programs be allocated on the basis of the level of prevention impact and their probability of positive results? If you were in charge of the federal initiative what percentages of the overall program funding budget would you allocate for primary prevention, secondary prevention, and tertiary prevention?

EXERCISE: The Gang as A Modern Substitute for the Rites of Passage?

In his paper "The Death of Telemachus: Street Gangs and the Decline of Modern Rights of Passage", 1998, Andrew V. Papachristos hypothesizes one possible cause for gang membership which has direct implications for prevention: the disappearance or nonexistence of "rites of passage" for some youths. Some youths who have "rites of passage" built into their culture (Bar Mitzvah, Catechism, etc) may therefore be insulated from a social control perspective against gang influence. Some youths who go through the "turbulent times" of adolescence and experience no "rites of passage" may be those who are "ripe for gang membership".

In a small study of law enforcement agencies in South Carolina (National Gang Crime Research Center, 1998), some 88.6 percent of the police agencies surveyed indicated that they do believe that for some children the gang has become a kind of substitute for the rites of passage ceremony. Further, 86.8 percent of the same respondents agreed that a rites of passage or mentoring program for juveniles would be useful in their own jurisdictions for the purpose of gang prevention.

How would you design a gang prevention program at the primary level, that was based on good theory, which has a focus on socially enhancing "rites of passage" and mentoring activities for youths?

END NOTES:

[1] The most effective strategy is gang debriefing, converting the active gang member and even gang leader into a cooperative source of information for government prosecution (i.e., flipping). The gang member who becomes a government witness can be considered at the point of providing effective prosecution testimony to be a true "ex-gang member", a meaningful measure of program effectiveness from the point of view articulated in this book.

[2] The one exception to this general rule of thumb is when a gang member, including the very top gang leaders, basically "defect" (e.g., "flip") and agree to testify against other fellow gang members.

[3] For an excellent factual history of the rise of Jeff Fort in his experience up to 1988, see: Tom Brune and James Ylisela, Jr., "The Making of Jeff Fort", Chicago, November, 1988.

[4] It is the hardest to accomplish because in the extensive literature on "criminal rehabilitation", no one has yet been acknowledged as having discovered the "silver bullet", the true "cure". Some times, in some ways (typically job placements), their recidivism or relapse or return to prison seems to be reduced. It is a sufficient probability of potential impact to work on, however it is a voluntary process that leads someone to want to accept a job in the first place.

[5] Actually, it was a "Twin Cities" gang summit, scheduled for July 14-18, 1993 at the Mount Olivet Baptist Church in St. Paul, Minnesota. Louis Farrakhan who commands a speaking fee $25,000 (a rate quoted by a New York agency in 1991 for a speech fee to a Chicago university --- which could not afford the fee) is listed as one of the speakers at the gang summit entitled "All Nations Under God". The Vice Lords who are heavily involved in the Minneapolis gang summit swear allegiance to Islam in their gang constitution. The Twin Cities gang summit founders (e.g., of the United For and In Peace gang alliance) make no claims of being "ex-" gang members...they readily admit their gang membership. (See "Sharif Willis Shocked By Testimonies in A.C. Ford Trial", by Jae Bryson, Insight: The Journal for Business & The Arts, (20)(23): Monday, June 7, 1993, p. 1).

[6] See: Mark Brunswick, 1992, "A Tale of Two Cities and the Gangs that Couldn't Stay Straight", Star Tribune, Metro Edition, Nov. 19, 1992.

[7] Think about it, coopting a gang leader would not even work: how could a gang leader "order" his underlings to go straight in the same fashion any similar order comes down to violate the law? It is illogical and incomprehensible that any such genuine change could be affected in a level three gang. Certainly, much earlier work shows that non-gangs or 'pregangs', the level zero type of Alfalfa and Spanky groups, are certainly subject to redirection --- they

are easily provided with positive direction, because overall they do not have a criminal direction as of yet.

[8]Most recently Ribisl and Davidson (1993) also argue the need for such a theory at the base of any program; they also cite the work of Lipsey (1988). Well before this Daniel Glaser also showed that one of the biggest mistakes in program evaluation was not having a theoretical approach to work with.

[9]For additional information about this program contact: Kenneth S. Trump, Unit Coordinator, Youth Gang Unit, Division of Safety and Security, Cleveland Public Schools, 1380 East Sixth Street, Rm. 106-A, Cleveland, OH 44114.

[10]One of the most interesting spinoffs of the American gang problem is the emergence of corporate consulting firms that specialize in "gang intervention" and training. The city of Joliet, Illinois hired Urban Dynamics, Incorporated for such consulting services to the Joliet Gang Task Force; but then terminated the contract by a vote of 7-1 from the City Council --- apparently because gang violence did not subside, and rather increased. (See, Jerry Shnay, 1993, "Joliet Cuts Ties With 3rd Firm Hired to Help Fight Gangs", Chicago Tribune (Southwest), section 2, p. 1, Aug. 5, 1993).

[11]Founded by LueElla Edwards after her 15-year-old daughter was killed by stray gang gunfire at Chicago's Cabrini Green housing complex, the "Take Our Daughters To Work Club" works on identity and self-esteem issues for young females at a critical age when they may gravitate towards the gang or towards early motherhood. See K.T. Le, 1993, "After Child's Death, Mom Puts Grief to Good Work", Chicago Sun-Times, July 13, 1993, p. 17.

[12]Located at 1329 W. Grand in Chicago. Mr. Brandisi passed away in the summer of 1993.

[13]See "Cabrini Drummers Are Hard To Beat", Raymond R. Coffey, Chicago Sun-Times, Friday, June 25, 1993, p. 3.

[14]Project FLOW, Mayor's Office of Community Services, 101 N. Broad Street, 3rd Floor, Philadelphia, PA 19107.

[15]See "Jim Brown Joins Anti-Gang Team", Chicago Sun-Times, July 21, 1993, p. 20. The Chicago Housing Authority agreed to pay Jim Brown, from the Amer-I-Can Foundation, $100 an hour plus expenses up to $25,000 for establishing a program for kids at risk.

[16]This may have been due to a program lacking a "needs assessment".

[17]This should have been a "red flag" to the federal agency providing funding in the first place: the government has no business subsidizing "street versions" of religious prosyletizing. What religious doctrine was being "pushed" to these gangs?

[18]In fact, David Dawley was also involved indirectly

with this program and was quoted in the newspapers about the program. Dawley acts today as a consultant on gangs. Dawley was the one who helped the Vice Lords get federal and foundation funding in earlier Chicago gang history. Recall that Dawley claims to be the "only white member of the Vice Lords". See also: Mark Brunswick, 1992, "A Tale of Two Cities and the Gangs That Couldn't Stay Straight", Star Tribune, 1A, Nov. 19.

[19]See: Jim Ritter, "Breaking the Cycle of Violence: Program Targets Young Victims", Chicago-Sun Times, March 2, 1998, p. 12.

[20]See: Susy Schultz, "Alternative to Gangs: Back of Yards Community Plans a New School", Chicago Sun-Times, March 2, 1998, p. 16.

[21]The Connections newsletter is published and distributed by the Cosmos Corporation, 1735 Eye Street, NW, Suite 613, Washington, DC 20006.

[22]The program is privately, not government, funded and the director prefers it that way (private communication). Of course, like many of the government funded programs too, no evaluation research is ever reported on program success (e.g., number of sinners reached, number of souls converted, followup: commitment to a Christian lifestyle Lord one year later, etc).

[23]Fred Williams, an ex-member of the Harlem Crips "who works at the Cross Colours Common Ground Foundation, which helps to rehabilitate gang members", was quoted as one L.A. source who felt the gang truce was for real and the gangs need to be congratulated ("Probers Hint Gangs Used L.A. Riots To Get Guns, But Not All Agree", Chicago Tribune, June 18, 1992: section 1A, p. 41.).

[24]See: Jane Ammeson, "Peace on Turf", pp. 50-54,78-79, World Traveler, December, 1997.

[25]See: Ray Long, "Secret Service Plan Targets Cabrini-Green Gangs, Crime", Chicago Sun-Times, Oct. 4, 1993, p. 5.

[26]See quote of gang unit police officer in Randy Furst, 1992, "Can Gang Members Turn the Tide Toward Peace?: Praise and Skepticism Follow Effort to Cut Violence, Create Opportunity", Star Tribune, August 31, 1992, p. 1A.

[27]This reflects the tie between Chicago gang leader Willie Lloyd who has strong ties to Minneapolis, the leader of the Unknown Vice Lords. According to one report, "members of United for Peace acknowledge they have few answers to account for the increase in gang shootings, but say there is no war". See: Mark Brunswick, 1992, "As Deadly Vice Lords Feud Continues, Officials Point to Imprisoned Leader", Star Tribune, Metro Edition, p. 1A, Oct. 22, 1992.

[28]Four persons were arrested in the home of Willis after the assassination of police officer Haaf. See: Mark Brunswick, 1992, "As Deadly Vice Lords Feud

Continues, Officials Point to Imprisoned Gang Leader", Star Tribune, Metro Edition, Oct. 22, 1992.
[29] See: Laura Baenen, 1992, "Officer's Slaying Ends Anti-Crime Alliance Between Police, Gangs", Associated Press, Oct. 1, 1992. (I am grateful for these and other Lexis-Nexis articles on the Minneapolis gang truce to Doug Longhini, Producer, Prime Time Live, ABC News.)
[30] See: Patrick Howe, 1992, "Gang-crisis Success in Minneapolis Forum Indicates Otherwise", Star Tribune, Metro Edition, Oct. 8, 1992. However, the Police Chief for Minneapolis did write a letter of support and endorsement for The City, Inc in its initial application for federal funding (DHHS) which probably led enormous credibility to the proposal as the letter was included in an appendix. The present author made a Freedom of Information Act request to examine the full records of this and other programs in 1993. Anthony V. Bouza, Chief of Police, on August 2, 1988 wrote the letter addressed to The City, Inc in which he said "I am pleased to be able to enthusiastically support your impressive At Risk Youth Services proposal...I am a tough law and order advocate and practitioner....Yes there are risks, and there will be failures, but you'll be hard-put to match the existing system's impressive capacity for disaster. We've go (sic) to understand that even a 90% success rate connotes ten failures".
[31] See: Patricia Lopez Baden, 1992, "Councilman Cramer Says Backing Gang Coalition Was Naive: Mayoral Candidate Calls for End to Support for United for Peace", Star Tribune, Metro Edition, p. 1B, Nov. 24, 1992.
[32] See: Kevin Diaz and Mark Brunswick, 1992, "No. 2 Man at United for Peace charged: Firearms, Drug Crimes Alleged", Star Tribune, Metro Edition, p. 1A, Nov. 21, 1992.
[33] See Rogers Worthington, "Plan To Rehab Vice Lords Remake of 1970s Chicago: Gang Leader Claims to Bridge Both Worlds", (pp.1,4), Chicago Tribune, August 28, 1993.
[34] See Jim Wallis, "Special Report on the Gang Summit", Sojourner, August, 1993, p. 12.
[35] See: James Harney, "Gang Leaders Holding Peace Summit in K.C.", Chicago Sun-Times, April 30, 1993, p. 34.
[36] Marion Stamps from Chicago was active in "The Sister's Statement". According to Jim Wallis the females were virtually ignored the first day of the conference (p. 15), 1993, August, Sojourner's, "Special Report on the Gang Summit".
[37] I had been familiar with how gang members inside the Illinois Department of Corrections were able to effectively "run" their gangs using their access to the telephone, but it meant the inmate had to call collect to someone on the outside. I had not heard, prior to this account, of ex-gang members calling the gang

chief inside the prison.
[38] Scott Fornek and Frank Burgos, "Peace Means No Guns, Farrakhan Tells Leaders", Chicago Sun-Times, October 25, 1993, p. 3.
[39] The National Gang Crime Research Center did cover this event and have prepared a short instructional video suitable for law enforcement use and qualified criminal justice professionals. Instructors should contact the Center for use of this video in connection with a course using this book.
[40] For a "kit" by the Mc Gruff people (National Crime Prevention Council), see their Tools to Involve Parents in Gang Prevention that came out in 1993, created in consultation with the Boys and Girls Clubs and the Police Executive Research Forum. NCPC, 1700 K Street, NW, 2nd Fl., Washington, DC 20006-3817.
[41] The gang leaders were paid $204 a week, but without government benefits being temporary workers. See: "Town Battles Youth Gangs By Putting Them on Payroll", Daily Southtown, May 12, 1994, A13.
[42] See: Raymond R. Coffey, "City Shouldn't Be Fooled By Gangs Again", Chicago Sun-Times, June 12, 1994, p. 5.

CHAPTER 29

GANG THEORY

INTRODUCTION

A theory of gangs must be a theory that distinguishes between simple "errant" behavior, perhaps even deviance, and that of actual criminal behavior by the gang as a group, or by the gang as an organization, or by the individual members of the gang. A useful theory of gangs must be able to logically account for the many variations in gang formations. To be comprehensive, a theory of gangs must explain how gangs "arise", why gangs behave the way they do, how gangs have developed, and what future scenarios may unfold with regard to gangs. Mostly, a good theory must be able to be put to use: particularly in suppressing the gang-crime/violence problem, and in preventing an escalation of the gang problem.

This is a tall order for a theory. And it does not stop there. To be useful to the social sciences it must be a theory that can be tested. That is, it must be capable of generating hypotheses that can be evaluated empirically in actual research.

In the language of social theory, it must be falsifiable. A theory that says Great Scott created the Heaven and Earth is not falsifiable: because we cannot interview Mr. or Ms. G. Scott. Such non-falsifiable theories are subject to great abuse. One need only recall the "theory" of deviance held during the early American colonial period, the so-called "witch trials". In that rendition of "the devil made me do it" theory, women whose worst crime may have been that of some suspicion of deviant conduct, were brought to trial and accused of basically "being possessed". How can you prove that you are not possessed?

There are many complex and peculiar aspects about gangs that beg for a theoretical explanation. Why, for example, would five teenage girls in San Antonio, Texas agree to have sex with an AIDS infected gang member as a part of their initiation ceremony into the gang[1]? Unfortunately, a full and complete theory is not provided here. What is provided is a classification system and a set of propositions that begin to account for a portion of the analytical problem.

GANG THEORY PARAMETERS

Gang theory is needed to explain a variety of aspects about the origin, function, and persistence of gangs and aspects of their form of social organization. Figure 49 summarizes the five most important and essential theoretical specifications. The acronym FESPO therefore symbolizes that an integrated and complete gang theory must address itself to Function, Etiology, Structure, Process, and Outcome issues.

Many research interests today have to do with the functions of gangs. Obviously, a myriad of such possible functions exist. Another way to conceive of this is in terms of the capabilities and effects of gangs. In short, what do they do? What are gangs responsible for? One of the most controversial such current research areas concerns whether gangs "migrate" (i.e., set up shop in another non-contiguous geographical area, in another city, state, etc). Another has to do with the type of crime specialization, for example illegal drug distribution. These are issues of the function of the gang. The myopic focus on function alone leads some analysts to conceive of gangs as "drug gangs", "violent gangs", "entrepreneurial/corporate gangs", etc in a potentially endless list of such over-simplistic labels. In reality, any given gang has a variety of functions.

As in most "social problems", a theory should be able to explain the etiology of gangs: that is, how do gangs arise? Etiology implies a causal nexus, a series of conditions or experiences that may show a common pattern in explaining why, how, and when gangs form. Etiology accounts for the rise and fall of gangs, over time.

Another most important theoretical issue has to do with what variation exists in gang structure. Our literature now recognizes that such differences in organizational structure and sophistication do in fact exist. It may seem like a simple issue to assume that all gangs are not equal, either in sheer membership size, or in terms of how these social organizations are managed. But some gang researchers still do not specify these most important variables with the net effect of making comparisons problematic: for example, someone who studies a "Spanky and Alfalfa" gang cannot generalize their findings to gangs like the Gangster Disciples. Gangs do vary in the nature of their type of social organizational structures. A gang theory must account for such variations.

The process by which gangs achieve their objectives occupies a large and interdisciplinary theoretical area. How gangs function as they do is also a process issue. The logical basis for such process concerns is that gangs are open systems. Some gangs are more restrictive than others (i.e., a Black person would not be expected to join the Aryan Brotherhood, just as a caucasian would not be expected to easily join the Black Guerilla Family, but they are still "open" for the right candidates). The idea of open-systems theoretical issues has to do with the fact that to be successful gangs must have members, and some members leave the system (killed, jailed, flipped, etc), thus new members are needed to perpetuate the gang as an entity. What happens to the individual gang member is a major concern of the process question about gang theory. This is also the issue of being socialized into the gang, its values, its way or life.

The outcomes of initiatives undertaken by gangs or against gangs are of substantial theoretical interest. Programs to abate or prevent the gang problem have as their justification such an assumption that "something can be done about the gang problem". The theoretical issue is how successful such initiatives are. The debate about "gang truces" and "gang peace summits" similarly hinge around outcome assessments. For both the gang and society the issue of outcome assessment is that of effectiveness (i.e.,

the question "what works?").

FIGURE 49
F.E.S.P.O:
ISSUES TO BE EXPLAINED BY
GANG THEORY

The Larger Theoretical Concerns	Specific Issues About Gangs That Can Be Empirically Tested
Function	Why do some gangs migrate?
Etiology	How do gangs arise?
Structure	What variation exists in gang structure?
Process	Why do persons join gangs?
Outcome	What is effective in gang prevention or suppression?

Collectively these more generalized concerns about etiology, structure, function, process, and outcome regarding gangs, if they are integrated logically, provide the elements necessary for a genuine theory of gangs. This is not to deny that other major theoretical issues exist regarding gangs. There is no logical limit to such esoterica. But these five areas specified here provide the essence of what is needed to provide a beginning criminological explanation for the gang problem. Thus, a theory that deals with only one such global area is a mini-theory: it attempts to answer part of the overall puzzle. A full theory would have to address itself to all five of these theoretical concerns.

WHY DO WE NEED A VALID THEORY?

A theory helps us "make sense" of what may appear to be a complex situation. For example a detective, in order to solve a crime, seeks out a theory for a crime, and then systematically "tests hypotheses": ruling out suspects (rejecting null hypotheses). A theory helps to account for differences, variations, and what some may regard as contradictions in the social reality.

There is no single theory that has been professionally adopted, approved of as such, and therefore completely validated with regard to gangs. Not historically, and not today. Not in America, and not anywhere else. There exists no official "government version" of gangs that works. There exists no genuine comprehensive theory of gangs today. What we have in our gang literature are a number of fragmented perspectives on various facets of the gang problem.

There are, however, a number of what might be regarded as "single-factor" theories which look at specific aspects of the gang problem. Some of the good ones will be integrated into the framework generated in this chapter.

A major reason why we need to have a good theory about gangs is that --- as explained elsewhere in this book --- at some point we are responsible for "doing something about the problem". For example, to devise and implement an effective gang prevention program, a good theory will be needed or the results of the program in terms of actual impact on human behavior could be contrary to our good intentions.

Another major reason to have a good theory about gangs is that a valid theory can more effectively guide social policy. This is best illustrated in the negation. Let us assume someone wanted to adopt a biological theory of gangs which rooted its explanation of Los Angeles gang behavior in the work of Darwin:

"Although humans are much more complex, ethological research often suggests important similarities between the behavior of humans and that of animals lower in the phylogenetic system of classification. Understanding Darwin also helps in understanding certain aspects of the gang's behavior, especially male dominance and deference rituals and the predatory victimization of 'the weak' on the streets" (Goldstein and Huff, 1993: p. 18).

Such a theoretical explanation viewing the gang member as the "wolf" of the community would naturally bring the policy recommendation to citizens to "act like lions": get bigger teeth, or a louder bark, perhaps some Wild West solution: arm everyone, let kids carry their rifles to school, check them in at the gate as in the gang movie The Class of 1999. That is preposterous!

There is no better source for preposterous social policies and actions to "do something about the problem" than are found in the profoundly untenable theories of the problem itself (e.g., Darwinian genetics). Darwin's theory was good for what it was intended to explain: physiological facts. It does not explain social facts like gangs in America. Even if you accepted the notion that Darwin's theory applied to social problems, you could not implement such a theoretically-based prescription in America: and you would be forced to recall when such a Master Plan was attempted --- during Nazi Germany when six million Jews were viewed by Hitler to be "lower in the genetic system" and were therefore killed in concentration camps!

WHAT IS A THEORY?

The good news is that across the social sciences, there is a good deal of agreement on what we mean by "theory". And, after all, the study of the gang problem is one isolated primarily in the social sciences because of its human behavior and social context. Thus, it is useful here to provide a brief "primer" on what a theory is.

A "grand theory" covers everything about a problem. In terms of the gang problem, there are so many aspects of the problem where we truly do not know enough to be able to knowledgeably generalize about, that a "grand theory" covering all aspects of the gang problem is historically premature at this point. The theory advanced here certainly lays no claim to such a grandiose level of generalization; rather it seeks to capture the most important contemporary and salient issues about the gang problem. The theory advanced here is therefore more of what might be called a "middle-range" theory.

A theory is basically an abstract set of generalizations about a given problem (e.g., gangs). It explains the causality, the etiology, or the functioning of a given problem --- in this case, the gang and its behavior, its impact, its origin and persistence. Theories, typically because of the specialized nature of the training and disciplinary orientation (i.e., sociologists, psychologists, social workers, etc) of the theorists themselves, are often based solely on one social science discipline; and the remaining are bi-disciplinary theories (e.g., sociology and psychology = social psychology). Few theories are intentionally interdisciplinary theories, typically because few intellectuals are truly interdisciplinary in their training or their focus.   If there is one specialty field in the social sciences that is most specifically linked to the gang problem, it is not psychology, it is not general sociology; it is criminology. Criminology is a longstanding area of specialization within the field of sociology; and obviously many other disciplines have contributed to criminology as well. There is no discipline called "criminal justice", as it is an applied, eclectic, operations concept.

ASSUMPTIONS BASED ON THE LITERATURE AND PRIOR RESEARCH

A number of assumptions from reviewing the literature and the prior research on gangs appear to be justified generalizations.

(1) The greater the fear a gang can induce in a community, the higher the tenure will be for that same gang in the same community.

This assumption has to do with the impact of the gang on the community of which it is a part. Programs that have sought to organize citizens, to galvanize them into action against the proliferation of gang crime and violence at the community and neighborhood level, often report that success in such organizing depends on the level of fear that the gangs have successfully engendered in the populace. The ideal point in time to organize, of course, is when the gang problem is not a monumental one. For when the gang problem has existed over a long period of time, what happens is the flight of law-abiding citizens --- at least those who have the economic means to leave. Obviously, many of the urban trapped are just as law-abiding, but they cannot lift up their roots and move out. Who gets left behind are those who may be least able to resist the continuing influence of the gang.

Anyone who has tried to organize a "Crime Watch" program knows of the problem where because of the intense fear that some residents have, when they are asked to help out in such a crime watch program they are the hardest to get any cooperation from. The reasons are usually clearly articulated: they fear reprisals from the gang members, they just don't want to "get involved". They become "free riders". At the point in any community where the gangs have existed for such a long period that the gang members and the "free riders" outnumber the law-abiding citizens, that community is going to have a very hard time recovering.

In testing this proposition it would be necessary to look at the power of the gang. The gang persists because of fear that is not confronted. Incidents such as that of the Dantrell Davis killing in the Cabrini Green housing complex sparked an enormous public hue and cry to confront the fear that the gang induces in the community. Thus, it is possible that at some point a critical reaction can set in as a response to such ever present fears about safety. In such situations, sudden increased police and other attention can reduce the level of the gang problem the same way that community policing can effectively reduce the problem via the crime displacement effect.

A logical hypothesis to be tested from this assumption is that gangs in "new hot spots" (i.e., rural areas, suburban areas, smaller cities, etc) will be easier to suppress than those in major urban areas where the social recognition afforded the gang is comparable only to that of a social institution itself --- a group or organization that persists over time, after the businesses leave, after the housing deteriorates, after the social class flight occurs (i.e., those who can afford to leave do in fact leave), and can be found on the same battlefield many years later.

(2) The greater the economic competition in illicit commodities and services as income sources for local gangs, the more violent the rivalry between such gangs.

Illegal drug profits are at the heart of some significant share of the gang violence in America today. Some gangs at the lower level of the organizational sophistication spectrum may certainly be less involved in drug trafficking, but for many of the larger and more organized gangs what to other gangs is

viewed as "turf" is viewed instead as an illicit drug distribution market share or retail territory. Some areas within large cities may therefore be "contested areas" and subject to bitter competition including routine drive-by shootings. In other instances, market share takeover attempts are initiated at the neighborhood level; that is, a gang may intentionally initiate a series of violent attacks against a gang that competes for drug income in a contiguous area, the goal being to displace said gang and assume their share of the market. Such a common scenario is described in the Henry Horner public housing complex by Kotlowitz (1992).

A logical hypothesis to test from this assumption would be that economic parity between gangs would stabilize not just market share, but also the intensity of the conflict between opposition forces.

(3) The higher the sense of ethnic and racial provincialism in an area claimed as gang turf, the greater the likelihood of inter-ethnic and inter-racial gang conflicts; the higher the racial and ethnic tensions, the greater the ability of a gang to form and/or recruit members. There exists a wealth of anecdotal or qualitative evidence and much empirical data showing a strong relationship between "racial conflict" and various aspects of the gang problem. New immigrant youths are particularly subject to form their own gangs in response to gang threats from outside their own ethnic/racial group. In the prison, jail, and juvenile correctional contexts --- similarly --- the importation of gangs that are homogeneous with respect to race and ethnicity via effective prosecution, often provides the impetus for inmates of other racial and ethnic groups to form their own such threat groups. In schools, a similar phenomenon appears: when racial tension increases, we can expect an increase in the intensity of violence between rival gangs. In riot and civil disturbance contexts, from the 1919 Chicago race riot to the 1992 riot in Los Angeles, gangs are predisposed to exploit such social tensions and it is in their best interest (materially and objectively) to have such tensions continue: because in the absence of legitimate authority, they often become the most powerful functional group being an armed group, experienced in the use of violence, and benefiting from the financial gains (looting) and the opportunistic political leverage (they are looked upon as a "force" to be reckoned with) such disorders provide. Certain recurrent patterns of "hate crimes" that occur in the context of a group or organized effort also fit a similar pattern, where the law violating behavior of the offenders can be regarded in many instances as a functional gang.

(4) The higher the organizational capability of a gang, the higher its potential crime threat.

This assumption enjoys construct validity in the most obvious sense that the greater the resources and capabilities of any group or organization, the greater its potential threat, if it is an organization that finds itself at odds with wider society. Cults fit the same pattern. Terrorist groups fit the same pattern. A threat assessment for gangs, similarly, takes into account the objective and mobilizable resources at their disposal. In fact, there exists a multiplicative effect here when the gang organizational resources are assessed in relationship to its arsenal and mobilizable forces.

(5) The lower the organizational sophistication of a gang, the more likely it and its members are capable of being "redirected" into prosocial activities.

The issue here is commitment to the group or organization. Gang members frequently express the fear that they cannot simply quit the gang because their particular gang may be represented in one "faction" or another throughout the United States. Obviously, such a gang with a national penetration is able to instill higher fear among its members that "we can get you anywhere".

(6) The greater the communications network ability that an incarcerated gang leader has, the more likely it is that the same gang will continue unabated, essentially being managed in an absentee fashion from behind prison walls.

The leadership ability of a gang leader depends on communications. Unfortunately, today major gang leaders of very large gangs are still able to effectively administer their gangs remotely from behind bars. In Illinois, one major gang leader took out a full page ad in a Chicago newspaper describing how his gang was not about gangbanging and destruction, but was rather about "growth" and "development" for the community. Individuals involved in the Chicago gang truce were able to basically call the same imprisoned gang leader and quickly relay his orders to allied gangs on the streets. Such gang leaders could probably still carry out their administrative duties even if they did not enjoy the "prisoners rights" benefit of having daily access to a telephone. They could still maintain communications by interpersonal methods of visits and letters; or of using other inmates or corrupting criminal justice personnel to "smuggle out" such important messages and communiques.

(7) The higher the cooperation with agencies of social control (e.g., law enforcement), the more it can be assumed that an individual gang member has truly disavowed his/her gang identity.

The issue here is measuring when someone is truly an "ex" gang member. Those who are willing to testify against their former gang leaders must be recognized as having made a more fervent commitment to disavowing gang influence than someone who simply says in courtroom testimony "Oh, I was a gang member, but I am not involved in that kind of thing any more". It is a measurement of behavior actually. And, thus, judging someone by their deeds more than by their words.

(8) The lower the value of human life communicated to individuals by their perception of the social structure of their orientation[2], the higher the individual propensity for gang violence.

Here we are dealing with a very basic issue of human rights and the treatment of our citizens. Obviously some very serious discrepancies exist in the ideal notion of the chances of every American having a "piece of the American pie" and their likelihood of having to eat the crumbs of the pie intergenerationally. This is an issue of human capital, the surplus population, and the whole concept of the "underclass" in America. With such diminished objective and material chances of having a "good life" in America comes the many concomitant values of living in poverty and experiencing persisting conditions of economic deprivation.

Unfortunately, with the intensity of violence associated with such same conditions comes the message communicated from the larger social structure that: "human life is not precious....it is cheap". The messages we send our citizens who live at or below the poverty level are not messages that communicate the importance of human life. For a democracy to survive, this must change.

THE SOCIAL SPACE CONCEPT: EXPLAINING GANG EMULATION/REPRODUCTION

How do gangs form and originate? Is it possible that in the exposure to deviance during early and formative socialization that the social trajectory becomes, for many whose integration into deviant sectors develops over time in excess of their integration into legitimate sectors of society, a criminal career trajectory as well? This is the notion of the social production of gangs.

Gang suppression taken to its logical extreme means giving no harbor to gang values which perpetuate gang organizations and sustain the gang membership base. It can be seen that law enforcement alone is totally incapable of such complete suppression; police officers can enforce laws, but not values, not mores, not norms, not even folkways. Police can use their powers only to enforce laws, statutes passed by legislative bodies at various levels of government.

Gangs use all forms of power to perpetuate their values and the continuity of their social formation. Coercive power, the threat or actual use of force and violence, is at the base of gang values. Coercive power is used to generate income or resources for use by the gang leadership; and it is also used to sustain membership compliance. Once a gang has income or resources it has rewardive power: the power to pay, the power to buy, the power to impress; it confers titles, and status, rank and recognition to its members. With either coercive power or rewardive power a gang in the youth or deviant subcultures exerts social power: they are a force to be reckoned with, they have a "reputation", on the street corners they "run it", they gain prestige and come to be recognized as a "power", and deference patterns emerge. Ultimately, if the gang is able to acquire property or a business, or gain use or control of an established exploitable social-economic resource (e.g., a program site, a housing complex, etc), or simply gain tolerance by authority, it may gain legitimate power as well: the power to represent through public relations that they are not a "gang" per se, but rather are a civic organization, a religious group, a political group, etc.

GANG ADAPTATION TO THE SUPER STRUCTURE

The term "social structure" is inadequate to encompass the totality of all forms of power and social organization. The term super structure is used instead to encompass the historical and existing forms of power and social organization in any society. It therefore includes political parties, economic organizations, government agencies, organized subcultures, religious institutions --- in short, the aggregate of previous and existing forms of social organization. The universal phenomenon at work in explaining the emergence, the function, and the continuity/growth of gangs is that gangs adapt predictably to the types of organizational structures that exist in their society to which they have been exposed in their socialization.

In many respects criminal gangs emerge and develop as an infrastructure that is functional for the superstructure of any society. This does not mean, as some have misinterpreted Durkheim in terms of crime being functional for society, that "gangs are good for society". The functions of gangs certainly deserve more hard analysis, but certainly include a variety of effects and perceptions at all levels of the super structure. Some critics of federal law enforcement, for example, point to gangs as serving a "bogeyman" function that justifies their continued existence and expansion. Some community residents look upon their local turf oriented gangs as serving a kind of "junkyard dog" function[3]: they bark a lot when rival outside gang members come into the neighborhood, and in this sense provide a kind of local order enforcement function[4]. In the underground economy, gangs serve a most important function by processing large amounts of capital, little of which income is actually taxed.

Gangs therefore serve both latent and manifest functions. Gangs involved in illegal drug production and/or distribution in cities where tourism is a large part of the local economy are never going to be "eliminated", because like the prostitution trade this vice may be desired by the tourists themselves, thus the gang provides a latent function that is supportive of the tourist economy. Gangs that help politicians --- in providing protection, in carrying out "dirty tricks" in heated electoral campaigns, etc, provide a manifest function that both the gang members and the politicians recognize as valuable and deserving of the norm of reciprocity (i.e., the gang will want and get something in exchange for such services rendered).

Understanding how gangs adapt to the superstructure helps to explain some peculiarities and differences between gangs. Certain Asian gangs, for example the Vietnamese, engage in continuing patterns of crime that reflect a unique modus operandi: they case out the local Asian community they have travelled to from perhaps another city they may use as their home base, they gather intelligence and profile a target - typically a small businessman doing well - they then carry out a home invasion that may involve the use of torture and extreme violence to force the victim to reveal and turn over their "stash" of liquid assets (gold, cash, etc) knowing that such persons may have been themselves adapting to the superstructure by not trusting banks to hold their life earnings. The socialization pattern, then, impacts on gang organization and function. Youths who grew up around military violence and who at an early age were desensitized to the use of violence such as occurs in combat zones, are therefore predisposed toward similar solutions to their life problems. The continuity in the intensity of violence reflects not just socialization, but the organizational adaptation to the superstructure.

An understanding of how gangs adapt to the superstructure helps to predict the direction of future conflicts and developments. In a third world society that has a history of warlords and gunmen and rival tribes, the dimensions of the cleavage in terms of what the conflicts are really all about will constitute comparable structures that gangs can emerge as. In the United States, shortly after World War I the largest gang in terms of its membership was the Ku Klux Klan. In the period 1921-1922 there were literally several million KKK members in the USA[5]. The KKK was not the first hate group of its type in America; many others preceded it. The KKK peaked in its membership at a time of strained race relations. The Chicago riot of 1919 was one such example of how strained the relationship between whites and Black Americans was. The crime severity level of the KKK was no small issue: as many "lynchings" occurred during the first forty years of the 20th century as did legal executions in the subsequent forty year period! There was no Civil Rights Division of the United States Attorney's office in the heyday of the KKK: they got away with literally thousands of killings, and made lots of money from dues of KKK members. Like contemporary gangs, the KKK in the 1920s had its assortment of gang totems, symbols, clothing, and artifacts that were commercially produced for use by members[6].

Gangs therefore emerge, continue, and expand in the cracks and crevices of societal conflict. As some of the most intensive dimensions of such social conflict in America have centered around racial enmity and racial discrimination (e.g., racism, individual and institutional forms), some of the most predictable rises in gang patterns have followed similar superstructural forms. The intractable nature of racism in America is reflected in the proliferation of groups like the Aryan Brotherhood and skinheads. As much writing as the topic of race relations in America has generated, even in the academic circles on gang issues there appear to be some ongoing taboos. One of these taboos is equating the intensity of the accumulated experience of racial discrimination felt by African-Americans as a kind of American "caste" or "untouchable" social class --- and it has many academic names, the urban underclass, the permanent underclass, the dangerous underclass, the surplus population, etc[7], all of which mean pretty much the same thing: the systematic pattern of certain minority groups being held in a state of institutionalized poverty over several generations. As in legal issues regarding civil damages, it is not a matter of whether it is intentional or unintentional, in social policy as in civil law if the damage was done then compensation is owed. It is perhaps this aspect of the underclass concept that has the most dramatic implications for social policy[8]. The fact is, however, these are very legitimate issues and continue to be tied to unresolved conflicts in the American superstructure. Farthinking and truly patriotic American citizens who take serious their pledge to democracy will recognize that this issue cannot be put off very much longer. The strength of America is its racial and cultural diversity. Some small minded persons[9] would have us believe that such heterogeneity is a weakness, their preferred social policy does not include equity, they prefer the status quo. In short, an understanding of the history and contemporary forms of social organization in a given society helps to identify the pattern that gangs may seek to fill. Thus, it is possible to induce such conflict experimentally given sufficient knowledge of a given society using gangs as surrogate forces to disrupt a target society[10].

A GANG CLASSIFICATION SYSTEM

That gangs can vary in terms of the sophistication of their organization should now be widely known. A primary fact seems to be that "gangs" in our gang literature have varied in terms of their organizational development and sophistication.[11] The classification system advanced here is used to examine some of the many dimensions along which gangs vary.

Recall that a gang is a gang if and only if it engages in law violation behavior, either individually or collectively, and that deviance itself is not grounds for classifying a group as a gang. There is an enormous variety of deviance and deviant behaviors in any society, but many of these deviant behaviors are just that: they violate norms, customs, even mores, but they do not break the law. In America our law enforcement community has no right to investigate a group just because it is deviant. If it goes beyond deviance and into the realm of crime, then we are in a different situation and one where investigation is warranted.[12]

To believe otherwise is to be analytically in the situation of believing that if even a civil rights group that seeks a reduction in racism or seeks greater equality, in a situation where minority status and a change-oriented purpose implies deviance, therefore justifies law enforcement initiatives (spying, etc) such as Nixon's COINTELPRO operation. We cannot legally spy on, infiltrate, and monitor groups just because their beliefs are different than ours.[13] We cannot maintain "street files" just because a group is regarded as different or deviant from the mainstream of society.

What we need most in gang analysis is a classification system devoid of such bias. The one offered here is a step in that direction.

Figure 50 suggests from a social organizational perspective that gangs can be classified in terms of their level of formality, development, and sophistication.[14] Level "zero" is not a gang at all.[15] It could be become a gang. This encompasses much of "street-corner society" and loose knit groups with little such actual ongoing criminal code violation. It also includes much of Puffer's assumed tendency for all young males to "form groups".[16] Level "zero", therefore, is pre-gang or what some have called social gangs. It is comparable, certainly, to the so-called middle-class "gang" described by Meyerhoff and Meyerhoff (1964)[17], or that of Greeley and Casey (1963). It commits little, if any, real crime. It is a "Spanky and Alfalfa" kind of group (level zero) that can be assumed to be easy to study using field research, because they have little to hide, they are not involved in "drive-by" shootings.

Level "one" represents an emerging gang formation; it differs from the "pre-gang" level zero by having made a transition from an informal group to an informal organization. Horowitz (1982) description of the Lions gang in Chicago's lower west side seems to fit this description.[18] It functions as a primary group, with small size, no large arsenal, it does become recognized at early levels of "labelling" as a gang and regards itself as a unique entity. But they are typically "squatters", they do not rent or own their own "gang headquarters". They do represent a crime problem, but it is not the highest level threat in terms of crime and violence.[19] Often this kind of gang has a horizontal structure, such as the MOVE group in Philadelphia[20]. A typical burglary ring operates in much the same fashion as a level one gang.[21]

Level "two" represents a crystallized gang; one that functions as slightly more than a primary group. It has a stronger level of group commitment, it is also a reference group. Most importantly it represents two or more independent units of gang operation. It becomes a formal group because of the differentiation of roles and status positions within the gang members and it has a clear hierarchy. It may also function in two or more jurisdictions.

Level "three" represents the highest level of gang formation, aside from organized international crime cartels, and takes on the characteristics of a formal organization.[22] It is the formalized gang.[23] It typically owns its own real estate and therefore does not have to "meet on the street corner" or in a "shack". It is the highest level of threat for crime and violence as well. The threat comes from its larger size, its multi-jurisdictional boundaries, its age integration, pooled resources and higher levels of group commitment. When a gang author from the past talks about how it is "easy" to quit the gang, they were not talking about some of the gangs that exist today or, for that matter, that have truly existed throughout history.[24] In gangs like the Aryan Brotherhood (whites), El Rukns (Blacks), and Eme (Hispanics), one cannot simply say "I quit". Rather, membership becomes irreversible.[25] This kind of gang always has a vertical structure, reflecting different layers of authority inside the organization.

The need for such a system of classification is still great. At a minimum we must recognize there is certainly both a qualitative difference between a gang where one's parents are gang members[26], where the moment one was out of the hospital from child birth, one was "tattooed" with a gang sign.[27] Being born into the gang. And reinforcing gang identity through successive generations, such as in the famous early robber gangs of India. This IS going on in America.[28]

To take the position that gangs are not "Wall Street, Robert's Rules of Order, rational/calculating/goal achieving" organizations may be popular in some of our gang literature, but only as a political contrast to the portrayed assumptions from a law enforcement point of view or from "horror stories" created by the mass media. The careful reader will note that the previous discussions have not quoted much from "newspaper accounts". But they should not be denounced as a source of information. The true social scientific point of view should be open to all sources of information. Even though, obviously, in the university context some professors may encourage students to "steer clear" of journalistic impressionism, and encourage students rather to seek out "the best evidence", which is typically from our social science sources.

The classification system suggested in Figure 50 generalizes beyond the specific case of any one particular gang. Yet most gangs must necessarily follow a developmental sequence and have a particular level of maturation and function that will allow them to fall into one or the other of these categories. The advantage of this social organizational approach is that it allows for the conceptual continuity with prior gang authors, including everything from the work of Puffer to Thrasher (1927) to the present day. And perhaps the future. It allows for the integration of much prior knowledge about gangs. It looks at the gang as a unit of social organization rather than focusing solely on the social-psychological state of the individual gang member.

Most of Puffer's (1912), Furfey's (1926), and Thrasher's (1927) gangs were therefore, in all probability, level zero and level one gang formations. Level three corresponds to much of what is regarded as the "super gang" structure: Chicago's Disciples, Latin Kings, El Rukns, Vice Lords.[29] It is also possible for any specific gang to calculate its "severity of history or potential" ratings. By having this "severity of risk" assessment it is therefore possible to classify gangs by the scope and extent of the crime and violence problem they pose to society. Briefly, this corresponds to a typology of both organizational capability and level of threat as seen in Figure 50.

Obviously, much remains to be done to establish the rules of correspondence and the objective methods of comparative assessment prior to assigning such a "level of threat" rating for any particular gang. This must be left to a later analysis. For now it is sufficient simply alert the reader to this potential practical usage. Figure 51 suggests some of these features that might be included in helping to distinguish between various gangs by the nature of their organizational development features in terms of the typology advanced here.

Figure 50

A Gang Classification Typology By Organizational Capability and Level of Crime Threat

Level of
Organizational   Level of Crime/Violence Threat
Development: Low   Medium   High
                  0 1 2 3 4 5 6 7 8 9

****

Informal Group
  (level 0)

****

Informal Organization
  (Level 1)

****

Formal Group
  (Level 2)

****

Formal Organization
  (Level 3)

****

Figure 51 helps to quickly distinguish between a non-gang (level zero) group and the three types of criminal gangs. To apply a complete threat analysis system to any specific jurisdiction, however, would require looking at all of the classification variables. Figure 51 simply covers a few of the larger number of such classification variables that can be used. No effort is made here to apply this application to all gangs known America for the obvious reason that such data is not available for analysis here.

Figure 51
Level of Organizational Development in Gangs

INCIPIENT ===> higher formality, sophistication ===> COMPLEX
****

Level 0	Level 1	Level 2	Level 3
PRE-GANG	EMERGENT GANG	CRYSTALLIZED GANG	FORMALIZED GANG
GROUP FUNCTION			
Playgroup and recreation; a malleable near-group; the gang functions as an amorphous, at times solidary secondary group	A primary group emerging as a membership group; has a developing oral code or tradition.	Gang functions as a pseudo-family; usually with some adult participation. May not know all other members.	Gang functions as a total control institution; the level of group commitment is in many respects irreversible.
GROUP SIZE			
Very small size. (local only)	Size is "pack".	Multiple Groups.	Large Size. (interstate)
WEAPONS USE			
Fists, Clubs, Rocks, etc.	Knifes, and improvised weapons.	Stolen small arms; typically handguns, used.	Military arms, shoulder and fully automatic weapons.

CRIMINAL JUSTICE IMPACT			
Not yet labelled as a gang; and virtually unknown as an entity.	Recognized as a gang or group by police or their community.	Various social institutions and the mass media label as a gang threat.	Members are often found in the correctional system and on probation/parole.
MEETING RESOURCES			
Typically can meet only as a group on a public place or a street corner.	Typically meets as a group as gang site "squatters", or in host site.	Group may have pooled its resources to rent a gang meet site.	The gang or a member may own the real estate property for meetings.
LEADERSHIP FORMS			
Leadership is unstable. (Shifting)	Leadership is developing or controlled. (Charismatic)	Leadership is tiered and shared to some degree. (Authoritarian)	Leadership is highly stable; usually an older experienced adult (Royalty)
CODE OF CONDUCT			
Norms are those of situational loyalty.	Norms develop by an oral tradition.	Norms usually enforced by disciplinarian.	May have a written constitution and by-laws.
INCOME SOURCES			
Personal only.	Limited.	Specialized.	Diversified.
CRIME INVOLVEMENT			
None.	Passive.	Proactive.	Organized.
LEADERSHIP INSULATION			
Does not apply.	Leader is usually visible.	Leaders are somewhat shielded.	Leaders are very insulated. Buffered.
INTERNAL ORGANIZATION			
Ad hoc, no role structure. Loose knit.	Usually a two-level hierarchy: leader and followers.	Usually has multiple levels including a mid-management structure.	Very centralized hierarchy which may extend across jurisdictions.
MEMBERSHIP COMMITMENT			
Adjustable	Low (can still "quit" the gang easily)	Medium (cannot simply say "I QUIT" the gang)	High

WHAT CAN BE DONE WITH A "THREAT ANALYSIS" APPROACH TO GANGS?

The most useful thing a "threat analysis" approach to gangs offers, such as that advanced here, is that it can be used as the basis for a systems approach to dealing with the gang problem at all levels: primary, secondary, and tertiary prevention.

The most powerful thing that can be done with a systems approach is to achieve greater effectiveness in pure primary prevention. This comes from the ability to predict who is and who is not a current gang member in any school age population. Currently, about 4 out of 5 gang members can be identified with five simple survey questions. Knowing what predicts gang membership, we can focus on reducing those factors in a larger systems approach to gang prevention.

We have enough knowledge at present to detect who is really "at risk" of gang membership and possibly "steer away" those who are a collision course that is about to lead them into gang life.

And we can also predict who, inside the gang, will defect and who would cooperate with being a "snitch".

So there is a strong research basis to attack the gang problem at all three levels of prevention using a systems approach. Remember from a systems approach the gang is an "open system": it is therefore very predictable. We know how people get in (about half volunteer and seek out the gang to join it, about half are recruited into the gang). We know how people get out (by testifying, by taking a violation, sometimes by death). We can make it harder for a gang to get new members: and when a gang or any organization cannot get new members, guess what happens to it? It dies.

SUMMARY AND CONCLUSION

On closer examination some of the mysteries of gangs and the theoretical issues that gang life may pose are not as complex as they may originally appear. Some of what may appear to be "random" and "senseless" and "irrational" violence, may not be as lacking in motive and purpose as it may appear to be by the many stray bullets that hit and kill innocent non-gang member victims throughout the United States. Some of the ways that gangs continue to be able to operate even after their leaders have been imprisoned may not be any more complex than the theatrics of the Wizard of Oz who is finally revealed to be using little more than common technology to embellish his "presence".

No grandiose theory of gangs has been advanced here. Rather some of the common problems of gangs have been addressed and some of the best common sense has been applied to these gang problems. Throughout this book there is substantial evidence that something can and should be done about the gang problem in America. However, there is equally great evidence that we should approach this problem informed by the best evidence on the problem itself. That means having some conception of the origin and persistence of gangs as groups and as organizations.

The only caveat here is that the gang problem is so dramatically avoided as a priority in federally funded national policy making that the problem is most likely to expand and increase in its severity in the near future. Thus, the gang problem is a dynamic

one: it changes everyday. And literally a number of very frightening future scenarios are possible given the absence of any such coordinated and sensible national policy on the gang problem. Thus, the observations made here are relevant for the time frame of the present only; if the gang problem increases, then we are in a different and more severe stage of the gang crime problem and the present analysis would have to be substantially revised.

DISCUSSION QUESTIONS:

(1) What do you believe are the three primary and least disputed causal factors in explaining the existence and/or persistence of gangs?

(2) What do you believe are the three primary and most important factors about a community that may make it vulnerable to the onset and persistence of gangs?

(3) What do you believe are the three most important changes our society must make to address the gang problem today?

"Mama": First and Last Word Ever Learned or Spoken By One Gang Victim

Sarah Young wanted to go to the nearby store and buy some snacks. She took along her 18-month-old boy, Maurice. Maurice was in a stroller. Maurice had just learned his first word: "Mama". But when Sarah approached the intersection of Lawndale and Chicago Avenue in Chicago on the evening of Sept. 18, 1997, a local gang member decided it was time to start firing his gun at a car in the distance, a rival gang car that began shooting as well[30].

During the gunfire, Maurice was killed, and the mother was shot in the leg.

END NOTES:

[1]This story was given national coverage; for a summary see Law Enforcement News, a publication of John Jay College of Criminal Justice/CUNY, April 30, 1993: p. 3.

[2]I am grateful to James Sutton for this concept that is rooted in a socialization explanation for gang violence. The idea helps to explain how some Asian gangs (e.g., Vietnamese, Cambodian, etc), may be more prone to vicious torture in the kind of violence they use as a gang. The notion is that if someone

grew up in a country that was "war torn", where death by violence was an everyday event; that one becomes "de-sensitized" to such violence. One comes to accept, as legitimate options, similarly high levels of violence to achieve goals related to seeking income, power, etc.

[3]This is why, for example, many citizens who live around gangs have mixed feelings about gang members. They do not necessarily approve of their crimes and drug pushing for example, but on occasions do see the gang as a kind of local militia. Gangs make their most favorable impressions on local citizens when rival gangs establish gang truces and suddenly the shooting and open violence ends abruptly --- for a time at least --- in what was formerly a hot war zone (e.g., Cabrini Green in Chicago).

[4]This sense of ambivalence in the attitudes towards gangs and gang members are the neighborhood level --- combined with genuine fear of retribution and retaliation --- also accounts for why many citizens are less than cooperative about helping law enforcement to prosecute and suppress gang members. They might call anonymously to a police 911 number if the gang members get really excessive, but they will not sign a complaint.

[5]See Max Madden, 1993, "Hate Groups in America: Part I - White Supremacists", P.B.S.P.

[6]See Max Madden, op cit, p. 16. Madden (1993: p. 16) notes how the Gate City Manufacturing Company in Atlanta, Georgia sold a large variety of KKK items from the KKK mail order catalog including "a variety of robes, hoods, horse robes, carrying cases, pocket knives, and miscellaneous Klan related trinkets".

[7]Cummings and Monti (1993: p. 307) assert that "Despite its popularity, however, many social scientists are not enthused about the policy applications of underclass theory, and question its theoretical utility in the study of gangs". There is nothing wrong with the theory, what some may find objectionable is actually changing such a continuing pattern of social injustice. Such change would require major changes in the superstructure, particularly economic resources. Read "policy applications" (i.e., social policy) in Cummings and Monti (1993) as "American politics".

[8]The existence of the underclass is an ever present reality. The existence of the underclass is therefore not a "theory". What is theoretical about the underclass is how this situation came to be as it is. Members of the underclass are not theoretical entities, they exist in large numbers.

[9]Bigots and those who score high on dogmatism never get the "big picture"; they read books like the present one, and as soon as they see a chapter on the underclass or see "racism" presented as a legitimate issue involved in the gang problem, immediately label the author as a "gang apologist". They suffer from a factual deficit disorder in as much as they learn only what they are predisposed ideologically to want to learn.

[10]There has been some discussion about the possible role of the Central Intelligence Agency, for example, in fomenting conflict in Haiti using this type of controlled low-intensity conflict strategy. This is not to imply that the USA has been the only nation state to be involved in this type of gang social engineering.

[11] Jansyn (1966: p. 600) showed well before the appearance of "super gangs" that some gangs "have a relatively high degree of organization". Jansyn distinguished between "core" and "fringe" gang members.

[12] A gang is what a gang does. A gang is supportive of some forms of individual deviance (see Moore and Vigil, 1987). But deviance alone does not make a gang. Crime is the behavior or function that matters here. Still examples exist in our literature of "playful deviant" groups being analyzed as gangs (Sato, 1982) and it is not unusual that some of these reports therefore conclude "gangs lack formal organization" (see Lowney, 1984), because obviously these are probably level zero (pre-gang) formations.

[13] The Chicago Police Department's gang crimes unit, for example, is itself limited in what intelligence gathering techniques its can use because the Chicago Police Department has entered into a consent decree with the Alliance to End Repression and the American Civil Liberties Union. Here gang organizations benefit from protection of their First Amendment rights in an outgrowth of challenges to police spying that involved "red squads", that is surveillance of left groups (see Nash, 1984: p. 75).

[14] Your author simply believes that other contributors to the gang literature, while having good intentions, when they for whatever reason deny that "organizational sophistication" (see Best and Luckenbill, 1982: 25), they are taking the posture of a static rather than a dynamic analysis. And perhaps even an element of close-mindedness or dogmatism. Clearly, there exists much variation in organizational sophistication and in group capability functions.

[15] Arnold (1965: p. 67) takes essentially the same position regarding youth social clubs; they may have names, they may be integrated, but if they do not engage in conflict (typically with the police), then according to Arnold they are not gangs, per se. Here I would reserve level zero to encompass deviance, but no crime or delinquency.

[16] Perhaps as easy as some gang authors assert (who espouse a non-structured, non-organizationally sophisticated view of gangs only based on their own local data) "like forming a pick-up basketball game", they meet randomly, they start, and they are off and running as a functional gang. Or as Rahm and We-

ber (1958) said it is a very casual process (see Rahm and Weber, 1958, Office in the Alley). The truth is, joining a gang can be informal and it can be formal. It simply depends on what type of gang we are talking about. For lower level gang formations (level zero and level one) it probably is informal or casual; but initiation rites can also be very formal and can even include the prerequisite of carrying out a homicide among higher level gang formations. "Drafting", or coercive varieties of "compelling membership in a gang organization" does occur (Salisbury, 1958) and is today routine in our nation's correctional institutions.

[17] As indicated by Meyerhoff and Meyerhoff (1964) this "gang" was not exactly a professional crime group, it simply engaged in deviance. Indeed, its most serious "gang" offense history involved status offenses such as curfew violations, underage drinking, drag racing, and "much sexual activity". On this basis, such an analysis could be readily extended throughout the American middle class today to include, obviously, a large number of middle-class adult such "gangs". These are not true gangs in the classification system proposed here.

[18] Horowitz was unique in gang research traditions by returning to the study area and in this way obtaining "time series" data on the gang's status. The last time observation, however, was 1977. It would be interesting to know if this gang called the Lions was swallowed up by the Latin Kings or the Two-Sixers.

[19] This would include many of the so-called "Fagin" varieties of gangs which are very active in crime and do have a substantial local impact (burglaries, car thefts, etc) and perhaps even many of the local "skinhead" groups who venture out on criminal escapades only on an occasional basis (e.g., weekend gang members).

[20] Before the MOVE group became a crime problem (very similar to the Waco, Texas group led by David Koresh, MOVE stockpiled weapons), it was a "disruptive group" problem in the prison system of Pennsylvania. In Africa v. Commonwealth of Pennsylvania (662 F.2d 1025, 1981), Frank Africa the "leader", a minister who took on the title "coordinator", described MOVE as a revolutionary organization where the organization was described as a "family" that has "only one member, one family, one body". Regardless of stated gibberish by the MOVE group, it DID have a leader in its founder Frank Africa.

[21] A group called the "Yugo" gang, got their name from police, they were simply all members of a well organized burglary ring that also specialized in opening safes. See "Tempo Update", Chicago Tribune, April 3, 1994, Tempo Section, p. 1.

[22] This formalization process is supported by the key observations within correctional facilities with major gang problems. An Illinois Correctional Training

Academy document (1985, July) states "gangs are becoming more and more sophisticated, often moving toward a political power base. As was mentioned above, a number of larger gangs have applied and obtained charters, most for non-profit organization. By claiming to be religious organizations, voters leagues, etc., they are obtaining federal grands and influencing the political arena by getting out the vote" (p. 12).

[23] And highly structured, organizationally. It does not have to function as effectively as a military machine; please recall many of our own highly complex governmental organizations, as bureaucracies, do not necessarily function as effectively as we would like. Recall, too, Bernstein (1964) took the view that these "large highly structured" gangs had essentially faded away, but not altogether and are more common to the urban underclass.

[24] The national survey by Camp and Camp (1985) indicated that two-thirds of the gangs in our nation's prison system regard gang membership as a lifetime commitment. This is most certainly the case for all members of the Aryan Brotherhood; for as an Illinois Corrections Training Academy document expressed this "there is no known constitution for the Aryan Brotherhood. It has been learned through experience that it is for life. If you try to voluntarily drop out, they will kill you...The Aryan Brotherhood opted for the terms "hooked up" or "connected" in place of the term "member". They do not use the word "member" in order to avoid future conspiracy charges that may arise (Gang Activity, Illinois Dept. of Corrections Training Academy, July, 1985: p. 12)".

[25] In Chapter 15 we will review some of the actual, genuine, written constitutions and by-laws of level 3 gangs. In the Latin Kings for example we will find "the first and most Law of the Almighty Latin King Nation is "Once a King, always a King", unless he is expelled from the Nation for violation of its Laws". Here presumably "expelled" is equivalent to termination with prejudice. As will be seen from the three stage "theory" in their constitution, as well, this gang leader/writer was apparently aware of the maturation hypothesis (see Tice, 1967, p. 48).

[26] Moore and Devitt (1989) describe the context where females who were gang members during their adolescence go into adulthood to be mothers, but with a high rate of heroin addiction, and drug use during pregnancy.

[27] Lane (1989) states similarly "sadly, gang allegiance is often passed from one generation to another. Entire families become gang members in some cases" (p. 99).

[28] In dramatic terms, a photograph seized via search warrant of the Spanish Cobras shows a young child holding an automatic pistol, it is entitled "indoctrination of gang being a 'family affair'" (see Nash, 1984:

p. 56).

[29] A new phrase for the "supergang" is the "corporate gang" which is contrasted with the less developed scavenger gang (see Taylor, 1988). The corporate gang being, I believe, equivalent to a level three gang; and the scavenger gang a less developed organizational pattern, typical of the level one gang.

[30] See: Michelle Roberts, "Police Hunt Gang Members in Toddler's Fatal Shooting", Chicago Sun-Times, Sept. 20, 1997, p. 17.

The Gang Funeral: The Final Ceremony.   Members are often buried with their gang artifacts.   They do not often cooperate with police to help prosecute the murder of "one of their own".   Rather the gang continues the process of murder: by means of revenge and retaliation.

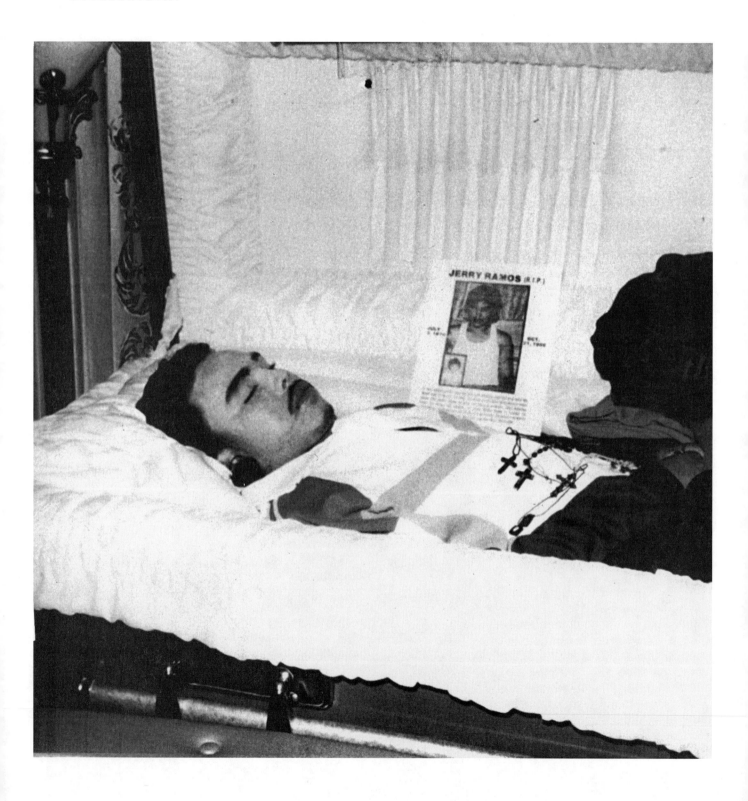

Chapter 30

GANGS AND THE FUTURE:
Towards Theoretical Integration and Policy Options for Reducing the Gang Problem.

INTRODUCTION

This book has reviewed a large number of concepts and ideas from a variety of authors who have contributed to the gang literature. Gangs have been examined historically, in terms of their organizational development patterns, in terms of their "threat" to the public, in terms of "what can be done" from the family, education, the community, law enforcement, correctional institution, and prevention perspectives. Now we must face the harsh reality of ill-informed and misguided efforts, segmented and partisan-politically shaped, disjointed and often having reverse-intended effects as we examine the hope of the future.

The author's hope is that the gang problem, like any social problem, is one about which something can and should be done. The question is always: at what cost, and who is going to pay for it? It can currently cost $50 to $100 thousand per youth to incarcerate that youth for a year in a juvenile detention facility. As Americans we are already spending large amounts of public monies to administer public facilities that have no track record of effectiveness whatsoever! All Americans know that the poor exist, but rich and wealthy Americans and the corporations owned by Americans and by foreigners are not all willing enough to extend assistance to help the American poor to "pull themselves up by the bootstraps". It is also a fundamental question of racial justice; another issue that many Americans simply pray that it will "go away". It will not go away. And like any primordial matter in the psyche of the collective thinking of Americans today, it is the most healthy response to finally face this issue and make some genuine changes.

And what of the future of America and other countries in our ever-increasing sense of living in a "world community"? Will effective American gangs become transnational gangs?[1] In what sense do gangs represent a threat to freedom itself? Will some larger more organized gangs develop such effective "public relations" images as do-gooders that they can run their own candidates in local elections? These are but some of the issues that remain on the agenda described as "gangs and the future".

WHAT NOT TO DO

What has always amazed this author is that so much of our gang literature seems to be so radically estranged from our social sciences dealing with the core related problem of what we know about social groups, patterns of group affiliation, and organization development. If there can be no other single contribution to our gang literature that will have a generally positive historical impact, then it is in knowing "what not to do" in terms of gang intervention/interdiction/prosecution/etc policy. As mentioned early in this book the problem of gang studies is really one of finding solutions.

Something as admittedly complex as gang formations and being as rampant throughout our society as gangs are, is not likely to have any easy quick-fix solution. We have previously addressed the policy recommendation of Moore (1978) regarding the legalization of heroin for gang dismemberment via choked drug income. Not everyone is fully convinced of such a positive "gang fading" scenario from hard drug legalization. And there is the "slippery slope" ethical problem here as well: by providing legal heroin, do we simply find a more oppressive method of containing and controlling the surplus population? And after such a systematic devaluation of human potential itself, is there any return from this moral decline? How much moral difference is there between America in the 21st Century having a huge population of official addicts and Nazi Germany's en masse extirpation policies or the Nazi T-4 program? It seems only a difference between de facto and de jure racism, when those who may be expected to gravitate towards this "life option" are predominantly from the ranks of minority groups.

What not to do is to repeat some of the mistakes of the past. A primary consideration should be not to facilitate further organizational development, wittingly or unwittingly, through public and private sector initiatives. Inducing an organizational succession in goals in a gang, getting it to lay down its arms and give up lucrative areas of income-producing crime (e.g., narcotics trafficking), is not realistic. Making it hard for such organizations to function and preventing further new recruits is at least one way to organizationally choke some American gangs. Unfortunately, in some public and privately funded initiatives under the banner of being "anti-gang" have actually encouraged youths to join the gang by giving the gang leaders status, power, and resources --- the examples of this are legion, and stretch from New York to California, from Minnesota to Texas; and these lessons from gang history stretch back far in time, and include contemporary examples as well.

"If you can't beat em, join em" in the sense of vigilantism is another non-option. Organized vigilante groups would give gangs what they thrive on: conflict[2]. A gang or "street organization" as some may prefer to be called is weakened only by the loss of useful resources. Thus providing any exploitable resources to gangs, under whatever well-intended pretext, may very well exacerbate the very same problem --- a problem that truly does require intervention services, and prevention services, and public funding. But not necessarily in the tradition of trying to "coopt" gang leaders. Such intervention programs should be strictly monitored and evaluated in both process and outcome, much in the manner shown by the Agopian (1991) research on such a program in the Los Angeles probation department, and Spergel's (1990) evaluation of a Chicago program.

It is an issue of accountability. Recall from Taylor (1990), the "quisling effect". And some of the early warnings about the advisability of using former gang leaders to convince non-gang aligned youths not to join a gang, not dissimilar from the issues about using well dressed articulate ex-heroin addicts lecturing children on the evils of drug or substance abuse. What message really gets communicated: don't do drugs, or you can in fact do them, get addicted to them, but still be prosperous, well-dressed, and get a job with the government? Some examples discussed in this book, like the case where a public high school in Chicago was used for a gang awards ceremony, would appear to illustrate an important concept: some Americans are really confused about gangs, or use this naivete effectively as an excuse. Should the parent of a child that joins the gang after such an event rightfully sue the school system?

This is not an exclusionary viewpoint or one that says close down all such programs that use gang members. We need to balance the dominant reintegration philosophy in the case of gang services with what the research literature shows. And gang programs more than any program, because we are talking also about the rights of human subjects, should probably live up to a much higher level of program accountability in terms of quantitative program evaluation research. We don't need any "black boxes" in gang intervention services. We truly need to know exactly what is being done and if it really works.

What should also not be done is to send mixed messages to our children which imply that gangs active in crime are in any sense "legitimate groups". Inviting a gang member or leader to speak to teachers and students at a local school is a bad idea unless the speaker is prepared --- as such "ex-gang member" street-outreach workers should do to qualify for the job --- to denounce the gang, or testify against it in court. Such events and conditions may really communicate a tacit approval of gangs, particularly when the message communicated is an apology for the existence of the gang.

What not to do is to fall victim to the psychological warfare that some larger and more sophisticated gangs are capable of today. A gang leader that portrays himself as a leader of poor kids, who claims to be doing "good" for society, who claims to be the new political messiah for the underclass --- this is the contemporary rhetoric that is being replayed on television, in the newspapers, at parole boards, etc --- because gang leaders are successful in manipulating the media on occasions. It is, of course, little more than twisted rhetoric; and all too often, beneath the thin veneer of pro-social intent is a deep pattern of crime and violence.

What not to do is to negotiate with gang leaders. What not to do is to tacitly allow gang leaders to continue to effectively administer their organizations from behind bars. What not to do is to continue to deny the problem when everyone knows it exists. Some states like California, Illinois, and Virginia --- to name a few --- will not allow their prison wardens to fill out surveys about their correctional institutions for fear of the political repercussions of "gang news". The political image maintenance strategy seems to assume that if the public realizes it happened on "their shift", they will get the blame. This is counterproductive to everyone, especially those who must work in corrections, because the public will never know the resources they deserve and need to deal with the problem.

What not to do is to continue to have the U.S. Department of Justice agencies like the National Institute of Justice to continue their historical pattern of granting research contracts to the bidder with the highest political clout, not the most capable bidder. True competitive bidding has not yet become the norm among our federal agencies for crime research. The public should not be paying for misinformation passing as criminological research.

What not to do is to allow gangs to freely attract and recruit juveniles into the gang without sanctions and without penalties. Gang membership translates into objective material health risks: the morbidity and mortality that comes from gang violence. Children must be legally protected. Children are not legally protected in America today from the gang that like a hungry vampire feeds constantly on the unending supply of young blood. Adult gang leaders must be held accountable. Our laws should discourage, not encourage, children from joining a gang.

TOWARDS THEORETICAL INTEGRATION

The foregoing discussion has urged the value of a social organizational approach to gang analysis. We must recognize, logically, the limited variation in a crosstabulation of "unit of analysis" and "frame of reference" in gang analysis. As discussed earlier, our units of analysis have typically been the individual,

the community, organizations or institutions, major political jurisdictions (cities, states, etc) and entire societies.

Obviously, at the individual unit of analysis we may also want to include an examination of non-gang affiliated youths with the same eagerness that some contemporary authors fervently advocate focusing on the individual gang member via field studies or ethnographic accounts. Our logic here is that to understand criminality or deviance, generally we should want to understand what makes someone conform first. Similarly, in areas with gang problems the analysis of non-gang affiliated youths may present some stronger basis for programming and services.

A legitimate criticism of prior research was given by Jackson and Mc Bride (1990: p. 5) to the effect that "for every sociologist who has studied gangs there seems to be a different theory". Such is the nature of much of the social sciences, as social scientists seek to position themselves, not necessarily integrating theory or testing multiple theories, but advancing their own unique perspective. As if what drives knowledge development is the need to be different.

The time has come for a more interdisciplinary and empirical approach. A period of theory testing. Hopefully this book has demonstrated that many of these views are not necessarily inconsistent ideas. These competing theoretical concepts should rather be viewed as rival hypotheses to be tested. What explains the onset and persistence of gangs may, obviously, be some combination of several such theoretical orientations.

The value of an organizational approach to the study of gangs is that we begin by recognizing that natural variation is to be expected in the complexity and sophistication of styles of gang organization. The value of an organizational approach is that we can therefore subsume much undeveloped psychological approaches, by looking at the type of personality profiles and behavioral profiles that emerge from empirical gang research, and use this research in policy. We can systematically identify the type of gang that needs to be the focus of law enforcement investigation, by applying threat analysis to these gangs. We can systematically identify persons who are gang members without asking them what gang they belong to, gang membership can be predicted. We can systematically identify those in the gang who are most likely to defect or provide testimony against gang leaders, all we have to do is apply good criminological research to the problem. This has not been the agenda of most federal and foundation knowledge development research agendas.

WHAT KIND OF GANGS ARE THERE?

The truth that we have tried to impart here is that there exist many variations in the organizational complexity and sophistication of gangs today. Some are obviously more of a threat than others. The truth also is that even within a gang there exists a continuum of risk in terms of violence and crime among individual gang members --- that is, their level of commitment to the gang.

Throughout this book we have seen that a variety of concepts have been used to account for the diverse nature of gang behavior and gang organizations. In the prior gang literature we have seen a variety of such "gangs" each having a salient caption:[3] social gangs, conflict gangs, fighting gangs, violent gangs, defensive gangs, delinquent gangs, criminal gangs, retreatist gangs, hedonistic gangs, instrumental gangs, predatory gangs, scavenger gangs, corporate gangs, party gangs, etc. In the interests of trying to "tie together" much of this previous work, an organizational continuum approach has been advanced as a more objective basis for gang classification.

What this analysis has shown is that unpopular or potentially stigmatizable groups of youths or otherwise should probably not enjoy the definition of being a gang. A "gang" should probably be reserved for various forms of group crime pursuits. And the answer to "what kind of gangs are there?" is simply different levels of organizational capability and sophistication. From the informal group to the formal organization. Ultimately, if they succeed where we fail, then organized crime.

The approach recommended here does not use such salient caption labels (e.g., conflict gang, party gang, etc), nor does it reduce a social group problem to a simple dichotomy of motivational choices (e.g., instrumental vs. integrative/expressive). It is a social organizational approach that examines the varying levels of organizational complexity and sophistication in terms of group behavior. As seen in Figure 52 below, historically gangs have been classified by impressionistic attributions and salient captions. Obviously, these do not meet the rigorous requirements of a true typology.[4]

Similarly, in Figure 53, it is shown that types of gang membership also vary enormously, by author(s). Using these various categories of gang membership may help establish here a continuum reflecting level of integration into or involvement with a gang. It is, therefore, possible to conceive of gang membership as reflecting varying levels or stages of attachment and involvement.

FIGURE 52

TYPES OF GANGS BY AUTHOR(s)

Author(s)	Gang Classification System
Taylor 1990	Scavenger, Territorial, Organized/Corporate
Huff, 1989	Hedonistic, instrumental, predatory
Rosenbaum 1983	Fighting, moneymaking
Yablonsky 1962	Delinquent, violent, social
Cloward and Ohlin 1960	Criminal, conflict, retreatist
Stephens, 1988	Hispanic, Black, Asian, Punk Rockers, etc,
Fagan 1989	Social, Party, Serious Delinquents, Incipient Organizations

FIGURE 53

TYPES OF GANG MEMBERSHIP BY

Author(s)	Gang Membership Categories
Vigil, 1988	regular, peripheral, temporary, situational
Camp and Camp, 1985	Full-fledged, associates, affiliates
Quicker 1974	Auxiliary (females)
Jacobs 1974	Chiefs, Indians (prison inmates)
Davis 1982	Hardcore, affiliates, peripheral, cliques
Short and Strodtbeck 1974	Core, fringe.
Klein 1965	Core, fringe
Leissner 1969	Core, regulars, fringe
Patrick 1973	Core, Marginal
Hagedorn 1988	Topdogs, maingroup, wanna bes.
Taylor 1990	Corporate, scavenger, emulator, auxiliary, adjunct member
Fong 1990	Leaders, soldiers (members) vs. associates, sympathizers (non-members).

We can add to Figure 53 gang membership categories a number of others that have surfaced in the literature. These include: leaders, regulars, sleepers, emeritus, veteran members, defacto members, neutrals or neutrons, and of course if we have "core" (Gerrard, 1964) then we have "hardcore". Hardman (1969) notes the category of "peripheral adults", as "hangers-on" or as dabblers, who were not members but who did benefit in some way from the gang activities. Similarly, from the gang members themselves we find additional "salient caption" categories: loonies, druggies, hangarounds, renegades, and dropouts.

There is no easy solution to what constitutes membership. But we can try to integrate this literature. We can try to "pull together" much of what is implied by these very different types of terminology.

This would suggest a gang membership classification system in terms of five ascending stages of gang integration as follows:

1. Top Leadership
2. Mid-Management or Second Level of Leadership
3. Core/Regular members/soldiers
4. Auxiliary/Associate/Adjunct/Emeritus members
5. Fringe/Peripheral members/sympathizers/marginal

From this codification, categories one through three are essentially the "full time" gang members who can be readily mobilized. Categories four and five provide a more supportive function and are less mobilizable. Ideally, gang prevention must be aimed at preventing entry to, and advancement in, membership integration. Clearly gang intervention must seek to move members down the ladder of gang integration, and ultimately out of it. Theoretically, it can be done.

Therefore, the gang typology developed in this text uses four categories. This can be used in a tabular form for purposes of eventually determining the actual level of severity of the gang crime problem in America today. Figure 54 shows such a needed "blank table" that represents the primary knowledge development need for future research. We clearly need to know how serious the problem is nationwide.

GUESSTIMATES OF THE IMPACT OF GANG CRIME

At least a hundred reporters have asked me "how many gang members and gangs exist in America?" Even more have asked "how much crime do they commit?". I always tell them the truth as I know it: no one is in charge of that. No one has the legal responsibility for that public issue. Yes, we have some guestimates, a lot of ongoing research on the issue, but we are a small group of unfunded criminological researchers. It is time for federal law to change: to mandate that the Uniform Crime Reports and other crime statistical surveys now include gang members in the unit of analysis, and gang crime in the national reporting system. The citizens have a right to know, and the government has the obligation to inform us of the scope and extent of this problem. The time is long overdue for this change in federal policy.

FIGURE 54

TYPE OF GANGS BY TYPE OF GANG MEMBERS: Needed National Data

Stages of Gang Membership Integration

Stage 1	Stage 2	Stage 3	Stage 4	Stage 5
*******	********	*******	*******	*******

Levels of
Gang Formations:

Level 0 (We have no idea, no clue, no guesstimate, no suggestion whatsoever, of what the

Level 1 figures would be for these various levels of gangs in terms of the numbers of actual

Level 2 members by their member level of gang integration; indeed, law enforcement agencies

Level 3 do not themselves know what these figures are.)

A sure sign of the brutal neglect by the federal government in protecting its citizens from criminal gangs is the inability of any federal agency to say with any level confidence how much crime in America is explained by the gang problem. Crude estimates are all that can be currently made of the scope and extent of the impact of gangs on crime in America. By most accounts, this is a very large problem.

One of the most curious features of this issue is the undocumented crime that is committed everyday in America. The assertion here is that the Uniform Crime Reports compiled by the Federal Bureau of Investigation are substantially in error in underestimating the scope and severity of the American crime problem. The most dramatic proof of this assertion is that the crimes that prison inmates commit on each other every day are virtually never reported unless these incidents hit the front pages of our newspapers in a riot or similar disturbance.

Vetter and Territo (1984: p. 517) asserted a decade ago that "today, urban gangs are responsible for roughly one quarter of all juvenile crimes committed each year". And along with the changes in society and our urban communities has also come the changes in technology used by gangs. They no longer use "zip guns", they are more likely to use "sophisticated weaponry --- AR-15s, M-16s, grenades, and plastic explosives --- that would do credit to a military assault troop" (Vetter and Territo, 1984: p. 517).

Police estimates are somewhat different. Huff (1989) reports that police chiefs tend to minimize the scope and extent of the problem. In fact, minimized to a level of either fantasy or intentional misrepresentation. That is, several police chiefs in Ohio felt gang crime constituted less than one percent of all total crime, and less than 2 percent of all juvenile crime (Huff, 1989). Perhaps the real issue is this: to what extent is gang crime reporting also a political issue? Does reporting seriously high levels of gang crime tend to convey the impression that a police department is ineffectual in controlling crime in the community?   One problem here is the reporting bias. Generally, we must assume that at the community level the fear of gang retaliation, or the perception by the citizen complainant that "nothing will be done", or that the knowledge that prison and jail overcrowding means at the most a few hours or days off the street for a serious offense, must have some deflationary effect on gang crime reporting. The bias is likely to underreport gang crime. We would probably feel more comfortable, as a victim, reporting on crimes involving lone offenders than a group or gang of offenders.

Recall Short and Strodtbeck's estimate on the probability of arrest for gang violence. It is a low risk. A probability of .04 or .02 for the very skillful (Short and Strodtbeck, 1974: p. 258). Our police view this probability of an arrest as obviously being much higher.

In Illinois, the Director of the state prison system estimated that between 80 to 90 percent of all inmates were gang affiliated. Campbell (1984, p. 20) quotes findings from the Los Angeles juvenile hall to the effect that 40 percent of the youths detained there are gang members. The research reported on juvenile institutions by the present author revealed a total of 212 female gang members and a total of 4,457 male gang members in the sample of juvenile correctional institutions. Overall, this meant an average of 17.7 percent of the males confined were gang members compared to 4.4 percent of the females. Adult state prisons appear to have a national average of at least ten percent of their inmates being gang members. Again, recall that these figures come from administrators of social control facilities. When we actually ask those who are confined in the facilities, as occurred in the survey of youths in correctional institutions, a much more dramatic and higher figure emerges: nearly half of both males and females readily admit to having ever joined a gang. And as these juvenile institutions effectively do one thing --- they feed the steady stream of adult criminals to adult correctional institutions --- we might realistically assume that the actual percentage of prison inmates in America who are gang members is substantially higher than their principal keepers are prone to admit.

Tannenbaum (1938, p. 21) cited the previous research by Shaw and Myers (1929) in the specific crime offense category of theft, and of 6,000 such cases, some 90.4 percent were committed in a group context of two or more boys.

Astute criminologists know that official crime data is always problematic. But homicide data is always the most reliable; simply because a dead body must be processed, and it involves not just the police, it involves the coroner's office. While we can assume some such homicides are never detected, and may perhaps even be passed into our statistics as simply "drug overdose" deaths, etc, if the corpus delicti has a bullet hole in it, then it is more likely to be reported as a homicide, but not always. The point is this: perhaps in the absence of required and standardized reporting systems which are obviously not in place in our communities today, one reason being the lack of standardized definitions of what constitutes a gang, then perhaps our best estimate of the parameter of "gang related crime" comes from homicide data.[5]

In a nutshell, nationwide we simply lack accurate data from the law enforcement end of the problem (Bensinger, 1984: p. 1). In fact, the survey on law enforcement agencies by Needle and Stapleton (1983) had to conclude it lacked adequate information:

"Unfortunately, this preliminary survey's attempts to use these measures were inhibited by responding police agencies' inability to supply the requisite statistical data. With the exception of a few departments, reliable gang-related statistics are not compiled, and while many estimates were provided, these could not be cross-checked for reliability" (Needle and Stapleton, 1983: p. 13).
Additional research to replicate and extend the Needle and Stapleton study is now underway by the present author as part of a larger study to ascertain the scope and extent of the gang crime problem nationally.[6]

Correctional institutions seem to have information relevant to this analysis. Many correctional institutions, adult and juvenile, have a fairly good idea of the extent of gang membership among inmates. In many of the states indicated by the Camp and Camp (1985) study to not have a gang problem in adult institutions, more current research shows their juvenile and adult institutions to now report a definite gang presence.

In summary, outside of a capture/recapture analysis supplementing official statistics with self-report information, which is a research project likely to pose some difficulty, we really have no idea factually how much crime in America gangs are responsible for. It can be assumed to be quite significant. Nor does anyone know exactly how many gangs and gang members exist in the United States. We have some rough ideas, but little systematic and comprehensive data exists. Without information, no new knowledge will be developed that can tackle this problem. So in this sense America still has its blinders on regarding gang crime. While many continue to die daily in gang violence, no one is taking responsibility for tracking and monitoring and most importantly reporting on the scope and extent of this problem. A problem that is escalating, not fading away.

One hopeful sign is that the Los Angeles definition of what constitutes a "gang related crime" is being adopted more readily than Chicago's overly restrictive definition (see Klein and Maxson in Huff, 1990). Much of this has to do with the dedication of one police professional: Sgt. Wesley D. Mc Bride and his career long work in developing an appraisal of the scope of the gang crime problem (see Jackson and Mc Bride, 1990). Cities that want to honestly confront the gang crime problem will use the Los Angeles definition, those that want to politicize the problem and obscure it, hoping it will "just go away," will use the Chicago definition.

Finally, some data is emerging here. Again, however, these are estimates provided by a national survey of police chiefs. What this data shows is that among those police chiefs who report a gang problem existing under five years (N=130) when asked to estimate the percentage of gang-related crime within all crimes a mean of 11.9% emerges, and a mean of 16.3 percent for all youth crime. Among those police chiefs who report a gang problem existing for over five years (N = 30) these estimates rise to 20.6 percent for all crime, and 32.0 percent for all youth crime. Until we have a change in the FBI's Uniform Crime Reporting system, to include a new data element on all arrestees in the United States (is the person a gang member?), we are probably never going to have the type of basic information needed to plan an effective solution to the gang problem.

Clearly, from this less than herculean effort of trying to assess the problem, the problem still appears to be a very large one.[7] Some recent federal estimates suggest there are about half a million gang members in America, but again these are estimates. We need to stop guessing and get serious about this issue. We need new federal legislation to require the tracking and monitoring of offense patterns by gang members arrested in the United States and have this information published routinely in the FBI's Uniform Crime Reports.

WHY DO GANGS ARISE?

Our literature and research suggests that several factors are important in explaining the onset and persistence of gangs. Obviously, a great many such hypotheses have been reviewed in this book. But summarized here are those that appear to have some theoretical and empirical support.

The theoretical factors are these: (1) being economically disadvantaged, (2) racism/oppression, and (3) political corruption. These are contexts of recurring inequality that engender a sense of hopelessness for the individual. These are not problems existing only in the minds of individuals, these are real problems: objective, material conditions. They

are social structural problems that require our serious attention. These are, furthermore, theoretical explanations. We are not at a stage in the development and accumulation of gang research that we can extrapolate much in terms of generalizations to the entire American society. When you ask gang members why they join, we find a wide variety of explanations: to make money, to be with friends, a family member was involved, etc. We can take no pride in the lack of systematic national research assessing the scope and extent of this problem. We have a very long way to go in terms of developing useful knowledge about the gang problem in America.

Obviously, these theoretical factors for why gangs arise can operate just as easily in rural as in urban areas, and can be assumed to figure prominently in the emergence of small-town gangs as well as in large cities. And they know no jurisdictional or national boundaries. Any community, any society can have gangs if it has these political-economic factors operating to its overall detriment. Although, obviously, our history shows gangs have been traditionally urban problems; today rural areas also have gang problems.

Differences in the motivation for joining a gang can help to explain the level of commitment to the gang, and may therefore be useful in gang intervention. The more serious hard core gang member in some recent research has simply joined the gang for income purposes "to make money".[8] The reasons for joining do vary significantly by attempts to quit the gang. Those who join for "protection" or because they were "pushed into it" are more likely to later try to quit the gang, while those who joined for income purposes apparently adjust to the gang life as if it were an alternative career and are much less likely to later attempt to quit the gang.

WHAT IS BEING DONE ABOUT GANGS IN AMERICA TODAY?

Not enough. Clearly, much more is claiming to being done about gangs than is actually being done about the gang problem. Further, it cannot be assumed from the literature reviewed in this book that all such efforts are going to be productive. Our history shows that a number of "experiments" have clearly gone awry and have generated reverse-intended effects. They have added fuel to the fire in some instances. These reverse-intended effects did not stop in the 1960s. They continue today, with government funding, by confused policy makers, whose federal files contain numerous examples of such federally funded programs that actually helped to strengthen the gang, not destabilize it.

In a nutshell, not much is being done about gangs other than improving intelligence gathering capabilities and locking up the gang members. A number of programs exist in the United States that I believe do have the necessary theoretical grounding from which we can expect positive impact and have some evidence of positive impact. Many of these programs have never been replicated in areas outside of their own jurisdiction. Most certainly much more must be done about this problem.

But programs must change too. We must adopt a more scientific and a more responsible attitude about program evaluation. Any applicant for federal or state funding should agree in writing to make all agency files and provide cooperation with a totally independent evaluation researcher who is trained in criminology. The program should not be able to pick its local friend to write a fluffy report that has no grounding in criminology, and where legally the evaluation requirement becomes satisfied, but no real knowledge ever results from the public investment. A national pool of qualified and certified evaluation research professionals should be established from which to draw upon for mandatory independent evaluations of any program dealing with gang members or persons at risk of joining a gang. Using groups like the Academy of Criminal Justice Sciences and the American Society of Criminology as a recruiting pool for this initiative would be a good first step in the right direction. There is too much riding on this issue to make mistakes. This is not a problem that can simply be used for traditional pork barrel politics and 1960s style programs. True accountability must be established for programs dealing with gang issues.

CAN GANGS BE "PUT OUT OF BUSINESS?"

Not easily in the United States is the answer. Using penal sanctions could be very expensive and would only transfer the problem from our communities to our correctional institutions. Seizing assets, effective use of immunity and pardons/amnesty, etc, could be useful in demoralizing gangs. But as social organizational forms of group affiliation something will have to take its place. Our communities will have to have something to offer the future gang members of America unless we want to reproduce the problem again and again in a cyclical historical fashion.

National Service could be an answer.[9] If it targeted economic disadvantage, if it was systematic in overcoming problems of intergenerational poverty, if it could significantly enhance human and social capital, and if it could reduce our society's overall problem with regard to race relations and social stigmatization. To be a truly "homogenizing" influence, it might have to be mandatory for all youthful citizens: a common requirement of service to their country. No one gets excluded. No one. It would be a viable way to attack the drug problem which is also

so closely tied into the gang problem as well.

But it could be done. Either way it is going to cost America a great deal. But at least there is some hope attacking it frontally, with substantial preventative and intervention efforts.

CAN WE TAKE THE FUEL OUT OF THE GANG ENGINE?

The fuel of the gang engine in America is the constant supply of new children who become the new input and the new recruits into gang life. Yes, this may be the most effective strategy from a systems point of view. Because once the gang is unable to replenish its members, all that will exist are the hardcore, those at the top who with long prison sentences, and no one to do their bidding, and it is theoretically possible that nationally we could do much to rapidly suppress the gang problem in this fashion.

However, it would require legislation that defines allowing an underage child in a gang to be a sanctionable offense. It would require holding adult gang members accountable for the prima facie evidence that any child is a member of the gang. Allowing a child to freely join a gang is to allow the child to be morally corrupted systematically. We must creatively explore how gang membership translates into a new form of child abuse. We must have laws that will make it harder for adult gang leaders to take advantage of our many alienated youths. We cannot allow such criminal organizations to continue to systematically recruit and indoctrinate children and turn our children into young killers.

CAN "DETACHED WORKERS" HAVE A POSITIVE EFFECT?

Yes. But they could also have a negative effect. It depends on how the program is organized and administered. Such workers should obviously be subject to drug testing because illicit drug abuse is one of the primary corrupting influences of gangs today. It may matter less if the detached worker is a professional social worker than it matters what exactly the overall program impact is on the gang organization. Simply providing the gang another resource to exploit is not going to result in aborting new recruits to the gang organization. Ex-offenders and former gang members, with some record of successful reintegration, can be just as effective, perhaps more so, than degreed social workers in making outreach to gang members. The question for theory and program development is not what to do when that outreach has been made,[10] rather the question is what can we as a society offer them?

No simple small local project is going to solve the problem, because the gang problem extends across all jurisdictions. The gang problem is not a local problem, it is a national problem, and it requires a national solution. Some recent federally funded studies that would like to pass as professional research would have us believe no such national problem exists. I claim differently.

I claim the gang problem not only exists in virtually all states, but also that there is interaction among and between gangs nationally. We can thank the federal government for that too: for knowingly or unknowingly funding some gang summit meetings in the guise of "anti-gang programs"[11], thus solidifying the relationships between gang leaders nationally.

So it is not totally incorrect to be able to conclude that we what we have in current federal policy regarding gangs is some agencies (i.e., DHHS) helping gangs to become stronger, others denying the problem exists (i.e., NIJ), and others (FBI, ATF, DEA, etc) who take the heat and have to clean up the mess. We need a nationally coordinated strategy, not one that both facilitates gang development and gang prosecution simultaneously.

The reader with a good ear will recall the current presidential incumbent in his 1992 nominating speech did promise to do something about the gang problem, making specific reference to gangs. The American voter must decide in 1996 whether this promise was fulfilled, forgotten, or flipped. Some gang analysts point to the case of El Rukn gang leader Jeff Fort at one point earlier in his career benefitting from a visit to the White House for the inauguration of President Nixon; this actually did not happen that way specifically, Jeff Fort was invited, but he sent two underlings in his place, and it did not mean they met with the president. However, during the last year a well-known gang activist in Chicago did in fact meet with the President.

GANGS AND AMERICA'S FUTURE

We all live in a world community, we are inseparable by a large number of factors. Whether or not a society that imprisons significant proportions of its members can continue as a democratic society very long may be the question. Clearly many prisons could probably be abolished (adult and juvenile) and replaced with more effective forms of community-based correctional services --- especially community-service --- and programs without any risk of increase in recidivism and at a significantly lower cost.

Gang crime in America is an issue of citizenship. It is an issue of "who really belongs?", of who is really accepted and capable of being integrated into wider society. It is an issue of the apparently enduring need that many Americans have for stigmatizing and labelling; to derogate and subjugate with status degradation, as if manufacturing such a social substrata actually meant any elevation for anyone else. It doesn't.

Gangs today clearly constitute a major national problem. Gangs hold much power locally in their communities, in their purchasing power, in their capability for extortion and violence, in outnumbering municipal police officers, and in their continuing domination of our correctional institutions --- and even more recently in their political influence. What most Americans seem to forget is that even among adult prison inmates, 96 percent of them are eventually released. And guess where they are coming? You've got it. Back to your community.

The Archie Bunkers among us will advise: "well, don't let them out of prison then". But as any informed reader of criminal justice knows, that is not a viable solution. Long term prisoners represent long term fiscal commitments of the government. The new national debt would be that of projected imprisonment costs if we took the advice of those reacting without thinking.

The ethical contradiction of our time is that we as a society are willing to spend so much for non-investment options such as prisons and jails and so little for the actual quality of life (education, healthcare, etc) and human capital development to make our nation stronger and more competitive. We have gotten into the habit of relying on formal social control for handling our concerns about order and security. The absurdity of it all is very apparent in some instances, such as the two year prison sentence given in June 1993 to a 21-year-old Illinois man for stealing a cheese snack valued at three dollars from a grocery store. The judge wanted to send this thief a "wake up call". A pretty expensive wake-up call. About fifty thousand dollars worth of criminal justice resources over a three dollar piece of cheese![12]

This is not to say we do not have serious violent criminals for which no other appropriate option exists other than secure modern prisons. The emphasis is on modern. Traditional ways of dealing with prison inmates will have to be replaced by styles of management that focus on dealing with groups of affiliated inmates. Affiliated by gang membership that is.

WILL WE ALWAYS HAVE GANGS?

Yes, in one form or another. But we do have choices here. One choice is whether we want to facilitate the organizational development of our nation's gangs or do we want to "bring their members back into the fold"? Gangs today have an enormous capacity for violence, much more than they have actually used. Gangs, as organizational forms of criminal endeavors, have for the most part always existed in America and in other countries[13] in one way or another, and probably always will. Another choice is whether we want to continue to allow gangs to freely grow and expand using American children as their new members, their shooters, and their killers, knowing juveniles will receive less severe penal sanctions. We should not allow American gangs to continue to systematically recruit our young children. We must rise to the defense of our children. We must by legislation enable the enhancement of the rights of children to include the right to not be freely captured by adult gang leaders whose overall corrupting influence is no less than that of a total control institution-style "cult". We get upset when religious cults try to attract our young, but not when the gangs attract our young is the apparent conclusion here. The other choice we have for the future of our society is that gangs need not be so large, so growing, so powerful, so potentially violent and destructive. There are some things we can do about this problem. The first step is to get educated about the problem. That is why I wrote the first full text book on gangs and have continually updated and expanded it over a ten year period.

Gangs are normal and expected in any society with problems of racial enmity, institutionalized poverty, and the mathematical jeopardy of social stigma (e.g., multiple marginality, ala Vigil). There is nothing abnormal about wanting to join a gang when you are a child, particularly an alienated unloved child: look what the gang offers --- adults who do care for you, they care how much money you can make for them, but they care; guns, drugs, sex, violence, togetherness, an entire gamut of cultural, economic, and psychic benefits. Remember, gangs are a national problem. Most states now report gangs as a problem in either adult or juvenile correctional institutions. One urgent and present research need is to track the status of these other "non-gang problem" communities and truly assess them. Because of their dwindling numbers, they represent the last chance to ascertain, as it happens, whether gangs are franchised interstate from higher level gang formations; or whether they grow indigenously, ala social imitation, perhaps emulating mass media or Hollywood "social space" or the "psychology of enmity" imaging given to gang roles; or if it is some kind of "seed spreading" contagion; etc.

IT IS NOT JUST A LAW ENFORCEMENT ISSUE

The gang problem is a crime problem that is a part of a national social problem.[14] It is inconceivable that law enforcement alone could solve the gang crime problem in America. So federal resources should go to the communities first before going to direct law enforcement aid. Such policy initiatives as LEAA were good for police. But federal policy should not be to systematically encourage use of the criminal sanction, it should encourage peace. Domestic peace. And a reduction of conflict levels. This

is best accomplished by systematically enhancing the human capital of our Nation. We do know how to identify potential "informants" or gang defectors from their social, psychological, and behavioral profile; we can siphon off a lot of core gang members into legitimate pursuits; we can certainly prevent new gang recruits (our own children) from entering the fray; and we can isolate and <u>effectively</u> sanction those hard core persisting gang members who want to continue to disrupt and threaten our society. We have always had the choice. We have not always been educated enough to make the right choice. And we have not had the political leaders with sufficient law enforcement experience to be able to guide us along a safer path.   No doubt about it, the private security field of the future will continue to burgeon and expand, as a market phenomenon in response to our nation's perceived fear of crime. Much of it will be related to the gang problem. Some businesses will get their protection either way[15]. What needs protecting are the communities and civil rights. Because, after all is said and done, the gang crime problem in America is a problem of social justice[16]. And the solution must start with realizing that children have the right not to be targeted for gang membership. Foreign journalists seemed amazed when I would tell them that absolutely no criminal sanction existed whatsoever for adult gang leaders who systematically corrupted young children --- having them as loyal young soldiers of their gang, without the parents permission, without any American governmental or private group whatsoever even objecting to this chain of human circumstances. It is totally legal to corrupt and guide young children into being killers is the message our society is now sending to adult criminal gang leaders. We arrest a child killer who is a gang member and we never hold the adult gang leaders involved responsible, how long will we be suckered by this device? We need to change the message our society sends to adult gang leaders, and it is my personal prayer that the reader acts on this problem.

PRISONS ALONE ARE NO GENUINE ANSWER EITHER

Those who advocate building more prisons, perhaps even centralized federal "gang security centers" to warehouse gang members only, are not advocating genuine solutions to the problem. They are advocating their self-interest in expanding the penal apparatus. They are advocating expanding and exacerbating the gang crime problem when our focus should be on prevention, but I am saying nothing different here than what has been said for a terribly long time, it is simply my moral duty to repeat it. Our conceptions of prisons and correctional institutions have historically been predicated on the notion that who goes there are lone, individual offenders. That has changed.

Today's correctional systems may have less deterrent value for gang members.[17] Going to prison may not seem like the punishment many "hang em' high" citizens might think it to be.[18] For many gang members, a short prison stint is much like a home-coming affair; and, indeed, a chance to improve leadership skills and to develop and advance organizationally.[19] For seven years the leader of the Gangster Disciples was able to run his gang on a day to day basis from within the prison system in Illinois --- and from the relative comfort of a minimum security facility, even though he was serving time for murder. We must cease allowing our politicians to make concessions to gang leaders. The coopted gang leader may not bite the hand that feeds from correctional administrators, but the gang leader will go for the neck of the society that allows it to freely administer gangs on the streets from behind bars. No one should question this finding other than the gang member or those who would apologize for the gang member. What correctional institutions need to do is to divert large numbers of their inmates to community-based corrections; including the heavy use of supervised community-service in a fashion as to increase the informal social controls in our nation's communities. Use this enormous manpower potential to rebuild our nation's burned out, dilapidated inner-city areas or for repairing the infrastructure of our cities. What correctional institutions need to consider is contract programming: giving up the gang in favor of valued training, education, and treatment. What correctional institutions need to consider is isolating the gang leaders who continue to manipulate and control other inmates in an overall course of action designed to increase the threat or use of violence in any fashion. For it is by violence that the gang survives and persists. We must take that power away from the gang. Yes, even if it means having no-human contact status for such persons.

COMMUNITIES RESTORED WITH HOPE VERSUS THE PRODUCTION OF MONSTERS[20]

At what cost to freedom can anyone take the position that nothing can be done about gang crime in America? Such a distrustful and negativistic psychological orientation is that which is most often projected onto our most hardened criminals. If hate breeds crime, then hope can slow it down. If cynicism breeds low expectations of performance, then a more fervent commitment to accountability can increase it. If racism fuels gang crime, then equity and social justice can put that fire out. But something will have to be done, unless we want to manufacture our gang problem into something more serious than it already is.

The hope is that what can grow is a sense of local power to address and solve problems; what can grow is a tolerance of other points of view and plurality generally; what can grow is a true and genuine defense of the meaning of liberty and freedom for all and an elimination of racial enmity and hatred; and in so doing all Americans will be allowed to grow morally and spiritually as human beings. That our nation's communities need more resources should be apparent to all. Perhaps this change can come from freeing up scarce resources: particularly those spent most unproductively in the area of imprisonment, and unnecessary expenditures in military defense.

The default option ---- that is, what will happen in the wake of not seeing a rebirth and revitalization of local community spirit and citizenship which encompasses local responsibility for social control ---- is "business as usual" in corrections: the production of zombies who return to our communities angry at the way society has treated them, becoming ever-committed enemies of society, fulfilling the labels thrust upon them. Monsters[21], stamped and numbered "MADE IN AMERICA". Dependably effective monsters. Truly reliable monsters. Because we made them.

American society made little monsters like Robert "Yummy" Sandifer and many other young, underage killers. What we may have that is unique in American history is the first generation of adults that pays tribute by symbolization alone to the rights of children, but by deeds avoids the fulfillment of the rights of American children today. This kind of benign neglect correlates highly with conservative ideology that resists government spending for youth services to produce better human beings, but encourages spending to put them in gladiator training schools where they can learn to become adult criminals. We are a very confused society. More than some Americans learn most of what they know about the gang problem from those who are least capable of educating us about anything: television talks shows and Hollywood images of the gang.

LONGTERM VERSUS SHORTTERM GOALS FOR GANG CRIME ABATEMENT

In the absence of a miracle we must assume it is not going to be easy to eliminate racism and racial enmity in America overnight. America is a cultural melting pot, but one that often steams with antagonism and intolerance. Both short and long term goals should include addressing this enduring issue shown to be so historically associated with gang crime in America. Gangs thrive on conflict of any kind, especially racial and ethnic conflict, even cultural conflict in dress styles. We must not allow gangs to exploit conflicts, but establish instead environments that defuse conflict and increase recognition for the value of diversity.

The highest level of demonstrating moral superiority as a nation state in the years to come shall certainly rest not with military power, but with domestic peace; and the ability to function in the world community not from a position of shame, but from a position of strength on the home front. Prisons filled to the walls are not a source of strength, they are a weakness. Criminal gangs dominating our neighborhoods are not a source of strength: if foreign invaders with superior firepower arrived, then gang members as quislings ala Taylor (1990) might be the first to collaborate with them, not fight them.

A sure fire formula for the debasement of the very essence of democracy and the progressive deterioration of America as a leading world nation is to continue current policies in the spirit of "business as usual". It will guarantee for every child from every home an equal opportunity to be a gang member. Why? Because we looked the other way as the adult gang leaders continue to produce future examples of young children like Robert "Yummy" Sandifer. In fact, we encouraged adult criminal gang leaders to exploit our children by providing no specific sanctions for this kind of organizational crime.

Gang members are not foreigners or aliens with no right to be here operating as they do, they are our neighbors and more often than not persons we have failed to responsibly integrate into a productive capacity in our society. They are our brothers and sisters in the larger sense of the meaning of citizenship. They are our fellow citizens and we cannot ship them abroad as "unwanted offenders" in the same manner that gave rise to our own country. It is possible to get out of the gang. It is possible to become inactive in a gang. There is no limit on the dimension of human possibilities.

It is well to recall America rising as a colony of offenders and miscreants escaping from oppression and persecution. It is well to imagine, at least, the possibility that we have reproduced a comparable form of oppression and persecution in our own society; of our own making. The shame is in not admitting it will be a costly and expensive proposition to be committed to a policy of such enormous and forceful debasement. As Houston (1994) has shown there appears to be more symbolism than substance to recent National legislation about the gang problem. It is truly a time for taking a collective moral inventory. And, after sermonizing, putting our money where our mouth is.

ON INTELLECTUALIZING THE GANG CRIME PROBLEM

Obviously, criminologists are those in the most advantageous position to be able to speak to the gang crime problem in America. But they are not the only educational or intellectual discipline with a vested interest in the outcome of solving this problem. In fact, criminologists are best served objectively and materially by allowing the gang crime problem to escalate, and in so doing increasing the legitimacy of their "focal concerns".

And what are the "focal concerns" of criminologists? Teaching and reproducing other criminologists to serve them; getting funding grants to advice policy makers that they are on the right track, "just keep the research funding coming in"; and there are no structural defects of any significance, only minor adjustments, fine tuning, and alterations from a change perspective that need be considered. No dramatic changes are required. Such are the focal concerns of not only criminologists, but many who are a part of the status quo in a society bent on a pattern of institutional non-productivity and counter-productivity. A business of managing problems that reproduces at an alarmingly efficient rate its own problems that the rest of us must pay for. Unfortunately these are the problems affecting all citizens. It would be fortunate indeed for Ph.D.'s to finally stop arguing about "what is a gang" and recognize the facts. The facts are some gangs are greater threats than others. If some scholars want to consider Spanky and Alfalfa a gang, fine, let them do so. Their research will certainly help us better understand adolescents generally. But we need to focus our criminological expertise on what are genuinely formal gangs, gangs that some would want to call organized crime, but which are not really classical versions of organized crime; we cannot define criminal gangs out of our vocabulary of scholarly research by simply declaring them by policy or definition to be organized crime.

With the rapidly growing interest in "gang" issues, the public demands more gang books. We have seen a virtual explosion of gang books in recent years. Gang courses at the university level are now being offered across the United States, in many disciplines. Why? Because it is practical and useful for survival? Not primarily. Rather because the gang problem overlaps with so many other human functions: social services, education, the family, the community, and obviously all of course criminal justice. Some books are better than others is the advice offered here.

WHO IS REALLY "FREE"?

In a national atmosphere of intense fear and loathing, when ordinary citizens "lock themselves up" in their impregnable homes at sundown, or in their condos with armed guards, and would not hazard to walk the streets of their city or community any more than they would walk through a poison gas mine field, who is really free? Who is free is the person who has nothing to lose.

The typical American gang member is such a person. The gang member does not fear prison. Prison means friends. The gang member does not fear violence, violence was probably always a part of everyday solutions to their life problems in America. The gang member does not fear loss, for there is little to lose materially that cannot be regained through cunning or stealth; the clothes on ones back, immediate possessions, a car, money in the pocket. Yours could be theirs. The gang member has a good reason not to place much value on human life, for little has been invested in his own human capital. The typical gang member takes on a combative personality and adapts to this situation quite nicely, surviving one day at a time.

To rebuild America is to rethink our assumptions about what can or cannot work regarding problems that face us daily. The gang problem will not go away even if we send every gang member to prison. For they will come back, perhaps stronger; and if they vote, perhaps citizens who are not gang members may be the ones in custody ultimately, in one way or another; because only half of our citizens vote anyway. If they cannot vote, then we can look to more violent scenarios. Because as official "outcasts", gang members are probably more prone than the rest of us to political extremism.

THE NARROWING OF SOCIAL CHOICES IN THE 21st CENTURY

Predictability is a weakness, organizationally and militarily. America is currently committed to a narrow set of choices for dealing with the gang problem. Unless of course it is willing to take perhaps a brand new perspective, a "no holds barred", a "let the chips fall where they may" kind of analysis. The author has endeavored to provide such an analysis of the gang crime problem in America here.

While this book has sought to be comprehensive, there are certainly many contributions that may have deserved closer scrutiny. The author has endeavored to maintain ongoing consistent research in the area of gangs: as they affect our community, our schools, our police departments, our jails, our prisons, our juvenile institutions, and other aspects of modern society. The author currently serves as the editor-in-chief of the Journal of Gang Research which disseminates the best gang research our world has to offer. The author is not a simple "dabbler" in gang issues, but is committed enough to the issue to have established a think tank that continues to produce ongoing useful gang research. The gang problem is a dynamic problem, not a static problem. The direction of change, however, is very predictable in light of the lack of any coherent national federal policy regarding the gang problem. It will get worse. The

rising evidence of gang members shooting police officers is consistent with this prediction. The recent case in Chicago where the Four Corner Hustlers felt so much in control of their community that they could conceive of simply blowing up the police station as a way to stop the police from interfering with their drug sales operations is another case in point.

The true power of a democracy is in the last analysis probably a power of offering choices to the solution of a crisis. The gang crime problem in America is, if not now, then soon reaching such a "crisis" point. We shall certainly need more choices than are currently available. Hopefully a scholar of crime contributes, what we mean in our more positive moments of what a criminologist should have as a job description, to more choices rather than restricting them.

Unfortunately America as a nation seems under the gun of an ideological imperative, of a progressively decreasing number of choices for dealing with its problems such as gang crime. As if it were neurotically compulsive in having only the option of imprisonment in responding to American gang members. It is truly not a solution, it is simply an expensive option. We will most certainly need more choices in the 21st century.

Because without choices we shall not be free. We will be as imprisoned by our lack of creative imaginations as we would be if we were locked up with the gang members themselves. Recall, that gang members have successfully adapted to limited choices. We shall also have to adapt. By generating new choices. Choices of responsible social justice. Choices that can work.

WHAT WILL IT TAKE TO DO ANYTHING ABOUT THE GANG CRIME PROBLEM?

Resources. Plenty of them. More sophisticated training and education for our nation's police officers and criminal justice personnel. Recall that gang members in America outnumber the ranks of all our Nation's municipal sworn police officers. Social defense is a quality of life issue. If a city cannot aggressively confront its crime problem, then fear intensifies and the tax base flees the city leaving behind those least able to solve the problem --- almost in the fashion of Gresham's law of conflict.

Gang crime is a national, even international problem. It will require that scope of attention as well. Which clearly means much more from the federal budget earmarked for the suppression of gang crime, along with more logically allocated funding for prevention service initiatives. Which is to imply, yes --- some federal funded initiatives from the 1970s to the present have been substantially less than logical. Many such recently funded programs lacked any theoretically consistent basis for having a positive impact. It comes as no surprise then that we find examples of federally funded programs providing "beepers" and cellular phones to active gang members, under the guise of "staying in touch with the program"[22].

WHAT IS THE LIKELY FUTURE DIRECTION OF GANG POLICY?

We think we have a good idea of what the future may hold in terms of gang policy. First, it depends on whether the FBI's Uniform Crime Report is ever changed to include crimes committed by gang members, if this does happen, shortly after the first new FBI report, there will be a lot of intensive concern throughout the USA about gang crime, because Americans will discover that gang members do more than "sell drugs", "do drive-bys", and "put up graffiti". If, repeating, if this change does occur in the next few years, then we predict a logical sequence in gang policy will follow as well.

To predict the future, we need to critically understand the past. In the 1960's and 1970's, American gang policy could be characterized as one of "positive tolerance" for gangs: the idea was we could "coopt" them, or "treat them with social services", and redirect their energies into positive or prosocial functions. We were wrong. We sent a message of basically "saying yes" to gangs. The guiding philosophy was to "give the gangs a bone", and it included providing government and foundation grants directly to gangs and to gang leaders, who predictably abused these funds.

In the 1980's and 1990's, America discovered what it thought was the true "get tough" message: "Say no to gangs", the guiding philosophy became that of "taking the bone away from gangs", if they were living in federally subsidized public housing, they were threatened with eviction if they committed crimes in the housing complex, etc. But still the overall funding focus, continuing up to the present, has seemed to have a goal of seeking to "moderate", mitigate, and control the gang problem. It has not worked in checking the spread of gangs or the objective material threat represented by gang crime nationally.

That is our prediction for the future of gang policy in the United States. What could "short circuit" the process would be gang involvement with terrorist groups from hostile foreign nations seeking to disrupt American life. History has shown that it really take a "major event" to get American's off their collective butts and do something about a social problem like gangs.

Our prediction, then, for the future of gang policy is that: (1) if we do get smart on "gangs" and get "hard data" about gang crime by changing the FBI's Uniform Crime Report to track crimes committed by gang members arrested in the USA, or (2) if American gangs become used by hostile nations in terrorist attempts on U.S. soil, then the "sleeping giant will wake up": and look out when it does if you are an adult gang leader previously enjoying an "open season" or "a historically laissez faire policy" in the criminal exploitation of underage American youths. For you will be in big trouble if the sleeping giant of American ingenuity wakes up.

SUMMARY AND CONCLUSION

The development and accumulation of useful knowledge in the social sciences is different from that in the physical sciences (e.g., biology, chemistry, physics, etc). In the latter, "major moves forward" can occur with experimental discovery. There is much less opportunity to experiment on human beings, social groups, communities, or societies. So, in the field of criminology we can categorically say that we really do not have all the answers yet in terms of addressing the gang crime problem in America. Some profoundly simple questions have no answers from our federal leaders, such as "What proportion of the crime in America is committed by gang members?", or even "How many gangs and gang members are there in America?".

Further, no single contribution is likely to change national thinking. What this book has endeavored to provide, therefore, is an eclectic and comprehensive view of the gang crime problem. What it has also sought is to provide a discussion of the major issues today. And some of those we may face in the years to come.

Our best bet is not on intuition, our best approach is not a "belly button" method, our best solution is not a "let's vote on either punishment or rehabilitation" method; in fact, our best friend in finding solutions is that of the social sciences and what we know about human behavior and social groups generally. This has been the view articulated here. It is the view of what social science can offer in terms of understanding and solving the gang problem today.

Ideology is less important than proof of effectiveness when it comes to the gang crime problem. We need, at least, to aspire to a social scientific solution. That means leaving our prejudices and stereotypes out of the analysis. Unfortunately, politics has always been a factor in what gets researched and what knowledge gets produced and who gets funded and who does not. The fact that the gang problem in America quietly spread like a virulent plague during the second term of the Reagan administration and the term of office held by President Bush implies that some government agencies are would rather simply ignore this problem and let it fester like a local sore. Sadly, the new Clinton administration has also not done much of anything as of this date to address or even recognize this problem. The current "business as usual" policy of the federal government on gangs is that law enforcement agencies will continue to stay busy and attract media attention in arresting gang members, but that little will actually be done about the underlying causes of the problem. We are literally headed for a criminal justice disaster until some officials recognize that administering the penal sanction is not a guaranteed solution to this problem.

The gang classification system advanced here is a preliminary effort towards getting a handle on what really is going on in American gangs today. We obviously, as a society, lack the information we really need to evaluate how serious this problem truly is. But advances are occurring rapidly in the area of gang research because more and more criminologists are entering this area of study.

Many authors have had an enduring impact on our knowledge of what kind of gangs exist in American society, and how they came to exist. Not all of these can be considered true criminologists. Gang studies for some was just a "passing fancy". For others, it was their life focus. The most important point here is that all of the social sciences have something to offer to the gang crime problem when it comes to "solutions".

Some truths have emerged here. They are commonalities and historical continuities found in many different contributions to the gang literature. One of these is the racism/oppression thesis. It appears to have considerable support from a number of different authors. It means, basically, that in American society race relations is such that gangs act out the violent conflict that is often just below the surface in daily life.

Another continuity in thinking about gangs is the problem of politics and crime. That is still a problem today. Not all politicians will refuse a cash donation or "volunteer muscle". And clearly, in some urban areas, gangs are making a political statement if not in fact organizing full-scale political action committees. The PAC for the Gangster Disciples in Chicago quickly had over $100,000 in its coffers to run their own candidates for election to local offices and to support others.

Another continuity is the method of researching gangs. While many research methods have been used in the present book to describe the problem and address the issues of gangs in America, an enduring form of research has been the "conversation analysis" form of qualitative analysis. Call it oral history, case study, field study, whatever, it means getting the story from the mouths of gang members. We need only remind our fellow criminologists that we need the same attention provided to gang crime victims and neighbors of gang members. And those who work with gang members in correctional settings and in community service agencies.

But there are some quirks in our history of studying gangs as well. One of these is the apparent misrepresentation of what if anything Shaw and Mc Kay had to offer about the understanding of gangs. Hopefully this book has clarified their important historical role in the study of American gangs.

There have been a lot of "mistakes" in the study of American gangs. Some of these would be hard to commit again with currently existing standards for professional ethics and the need for the protection of human subjects. This is another justification for truly understanding gangs in a historical context. We are not in a situation of truly having "zero knowledge" on gangs. We know some things. We know absolutely nothing about other aspects of American gangs --- particularly, how much variation they explain in the overall American crime problem and how much potential mobilization they represent in terms of gang organization levels and stages of gang membership.

By the historical patterns of neglect and the decay of our neighborhood social infrastructures, gangs have become an urban way of life. The challenge of the coming decade is whether they also become a rural and suburban way of life. And whether the quality of life, in terms of security, can be preserved sufficiently to prevent en masse migration from our central cities, thereby further eroding the income base and escalating the problem.

What this book has demonstrated is that what knowledge we want to develop in the years to come regarding the gang crime problem in America is often dependent on the frame of "user" reference. Our society is organized like any other society. Each segment has a different function and need. Many, unfortunately, would like to pass on the gang problem (like the federal deficit) to someone else. We are rapidly approaching the point where we can pass on the gang crime problem to no one. It comes back to haunt us nightly. We must begin to take responsibility for this problem, recognize for what it is, take proper measures, and be prepared to pay for the costs of a massive national effort.

Violence, hate, and destruction are part and parcel of the gang crime problem. It shows no sign of anything but escalation. Historically, gangs have but a small jump to make to become urban guerrilla organizations. If ever there was a time to take seriously the prospect of intervention and prevention it is now. For to wait much longer may mean it could be too late. Conflict should be mediated and diffused. It should not be systematically manufactured as seems to be the current de facto national policy.

Gangs are groups of human beings. They speak our language, albeit, often, somewhat differently. The gang members are our neighbors, our students, our employees, and our constituents. They do have the right to vote. It is a mistake to treat them as anything other than as a human social group. They are not simply a bunch of haphazardly associating sociopaths as some gang authors would have use believe.[23]

Drugs and gang crime, today, are intertwined. They exploit the contradiction in American society that drugs are illegal, but large numbers of people want these drugs. Legalizing heroin may not be the complete answer. But we should approach such decriminalization and legalization issues from a social science point of view. We clearly need more research on this. The scenarios presented in this book, regarding heroin, include not just a "sunny tomorrow", they include a "turbulent tomorrow". We need to keep an open mind about everything.

This book has examined gang crime and organized crime. It suggests that most criminal gangs do in fact aspire to become a new type of organized crime. Gangs can and have displaced the rackets in a number of ways. It has been shown that a level three gang has but to make some prosocial adjustments to "front" a social legitimacy to impact on society as has traditional organized crime groups (Mafia, etc). Some federal wiretap conversations between gang leaders like King Larry Hoover (leader of the Gangster Disciples) and Willie Lloyd (leader of the Insane Vice Lords) show how such gang leaders talk about using politics to carve up a large city like Chicago, in the same vein that traditional organized crime groups divide up territories.

Everyone blames the family. Beware of those who do little more than blame. They often have few answers. Clearly, the family and other social correlates of gang affiliation need further analysis. We need to understand what causes someone to join and sustain their membership in a gang, just as we need to know why similar persons avoid and never join gangs. The only blame the author has been willing to engage in is the blame that must be placed at the door of our elected officials for systematically ignoring this ever increasing problem.

The community, like the family, has a much larger role to play than it is apparently willing or able to play. Like the family, it cannot do it alone, without resources, on a "boot strap" total-volunteer basis. Our families, like our communities, are going to need some national help to deal with the American gang crime problem.

What the police should do and what they actually do are two separate analytical entities. In the best of all worlds, politics would not enter into law enforcement agencies. Rather law enforcement would be driven by career professionalism alone. But that is not necessarily the situation today nationwide, and is not likely to change anytime soon. Politicians always want to control their police forces. Hopefully the present analysis has suggested some proscriptive and prescriptive issues.

If any basis for rampant fear existed about the American gang crime problem today, then it is in the statistics compiled on gangs within our adult and juvenile correctional institutions. We seem, as a society, to have dumped this problem into the field of corrections. What few citizens seem informed about is that correctional officials are mandated to ultimately dump the problem back into our communities. Few prisoners in America are really "in for their natural life". What is also clear is that the gang density problem in American corrections today is not as low as some recent federally funded research would suggest.

Prevention and intervention in the gang crime problem are both feasible, and indeed desirable. We have not tried everything. We have in fact only begun to understand the scope and extent of the problem itself. We have focused, as a society, on repression. Repression has turned out to be the sticking of the harsh finger into the Chinese finger trap. It has a reverse-intended effect. Gangs can thrive on conflict. We need new answers. We need genuine solutions. We need non-ideological advice. We don't need extreme leftists giving their views about how good gangs really are for the community and we don't need extreme right wingers giving us their views about how gangs are part of some national conspiracy to socially engineer the gang problem and increase the intensity of its impact in an effort to invoke martial law.

What we really need is simply to begin using our social sciences in a straight-forward, common sense, non-political way. The fields of sociology, criminology, corrections and criminal justice, psychology, anthropology, political science, economics, and more. Social groups are not new. Gangs are not new. Gangs are social groups we fear. Conflict, violence, and crime are not new. We have accumulated some knowledge on these issues.

The primary lesson of this book then is abundantly clear: we simply need to begin using this knowledge.

DISCUSSION QUESTIONS:

(1) Do you think gangs could have an important latent function for American society in spite of their manifest function? Or, lacking any appreciation for Durkheim, do you think that gangs and gang members should command our highest priority in terms of investigation and prosecution?

(2) Why do some societies like America have a more pronounced problem with gangs than other societies? What might distinguish high gang-problem societies from low-gang problem societies?

(3) What is your solution to the gang crime problem in America today?

END NOTES:

[1] Obviously, some of our outlaw motorcycle gangs already meet this criteria.

[2] There have been numerous incidents throughout the USA, such as in the recent case in Joliet, Illinois (Chicago Tribune, 1993, Section 2, p. 7) where a family "fought back" a gang that was pressuring a child into joining a gang by assaulting the youth. The family members fired their guns back at the gang and hit their target: two gang members were wounded. Guess who was arrested? You got it, the family members trying to fight the gang.

[3] The predatory and social forms seem to have been first described by Henry D. Sheldon in "The Institutional Activity of American Children", American Journal of Psychology (1898): pp. 425-428.

[4] In fact, most of the gang types listed in Figure 1 appear to be based on the attribution of goal orientations or motives to these gangs. Gangs, simply, do more than get high (hedonists) and drink wine. They do more than fighting and violence. They adapt to their environment and the opportunities it provides. Thus, the categories in Figure 1 are, in essence, little more than what Schwendinger and Schwendinger call social type names: greasers, skinheads, jocks, etc.

[5] With the obvious qualification: because of the political nature of defining what is or is not crime, particularly gang crime (see Klein and Maxson, in Huff, 1990), a jurisdiction like Chicago can use "very conservative" definitions of what constitutes gang crime, while another (e.g., Los Angeles) may use a rather straight-forward method. Chicago's Police Department reported, for example, only 74 homicides, 31 armed robbery victims, 26 strong arm robbery victims, 979 aggravated battery victims, 269 aggravated assault victims, 4 burglary victims, 2 theft victims, and 2 arson victims as constituting all of what is "of-

ficial gang victimization" from the period January 1, 1990 through September 30, 1990 for an overall of 1,347 such gang related crime victims. Obviously, that barely touches the surface of the larger impact that gangs have when their members commit such offenses alone, in small groups, or where they do not leave their calling card to the effect "Hey, Chicago Police: We the _____ gang did this job".

[6] This is an agency/systems study examining police chiefs, probation/parole agencies, correctional institutions, community organizations, etc, in an effort to gauge the actual force strength of gangs in America. It also includes an analysis of $N = 3,000$ youths held in confinement nationwide in terms of the actual extent of prior gang membership, age at joining, and the relationship of these two factors to other problems: fighting, drug/substance abuse, etc. Unfortunately this information could not be included in this here. We shall have to wait.

[7] How many gang members are there in America? Assume ten percent of the prison population, ADD 100,000. Assume 15 percent of the juvenile confined population, ADD ANOTHER 15,000. Assume 5 percent of the local and county jail population, ADD ANOTHER 15,000. Assume 5 percent of the population on probation ADD ANOTHER 75,000. Here our most conservative estimate would show at least 200,000 gang members who are under some form of criminal justice control. And, if we can assume there are at least as many gang members in the community who escape the penal sanction, we are probably looking at about half a million gang members as a bare minimum.

[8] See: Gangs and Guns: A Task Force Report, National Gang Crime Research Center, Nov. 11, 1994. George Knox, Tom McCurrie, Ed Tromanhauser, Jim Houston, and John Laskey.

[9] Muehlbauer and Dodder (1983: pp. 127-129) recommend this very thing --- "a compulsory, two-year program of service for the common good" (p. 128). They also provide some other programmatic aspects, such as a flexible enlistment option (e.g., right to enter at age 16).

[10] Fossett (1974) described service results for one such program called the North Central Youth Academy, operated by the Philadelphia Committee for Services to Youth. All we learn is that the NCYA staff had made contacts on 15 different gang corners, enrolled 149 applicants, 58 of which were counseled on education, and 42 were provided with job referrals; 71 were enrolled in vocational training, and 21 were enrolled in a GED program. Such programs can therefore clearly establish ability to "reach out", and often attract some youths "at risk" of gang affiliation.

[11] Clearly, the Gang Summit meeting held in Minneapolis, Minnesota enjoyed the benefits of federal fund-

ing, because it was a federal grantee in a DHHS anti-gang program that sponsored the gang summit meeting. Other examples also exist.

[12]The man actually received a four-year sentence for violating a previous probation involving retail theft; plus the two years for the cheese crime. <u>Chicago Sun-Times</u>, Friday, June 25, 1999, p. 4, "Metro Briefings: Cheese Thief Get Prison".

[13]   Clearly, the literature shows gangs existing in France (Faz, 1962; Legree and Fai, 1989), Canada (Rogers, 1945), London (Scott, 1956), Israel (Leissner, 1969), and as reviewed by Tompkins (1966) in Japan, Australia, Ceylon, Taiwan, and others. Gangs are not unique to America. Much new evidence is emerging on gangs in many other countries, as well as gangs with international movement and/or international connections.

[14] See Dolan and Finney, 1984 for a similar position that it is a national problem.

[15]Some private security and loss prevention companies now provide gang training, gang awareness, and gang identification, to staff. The National Gang Crime Research Center has conducted a number of such contractual training seminars, but mostly for the more elite and expensive security companies.

[16]   As Davis (1988) indicates, context is everything, and the context that must be addressed involves such policy issues as unemployment and racial inequality.

[17] Gang members are simply more predisposed to get a prison sentence for a variety of reasons, including the fact that as law offenders gang members are more likely to commit homicide than are non-gang members (see Klein, Gordon and Maxson, 1985).

[18] The case study of LK29 showed he felt "some loonies kill just to get back in the gang, they don't care if they go to prison, prison don't worry them, they just want back in, back in the gang".

[19] Arnold (1969, p. 177) showed that for gang members a prison record is status enhancing.

[20] I am indebted to the paper by Harris, Abdullah and Rowe (1990) presented in the scheduled session of student papers at the American Society of Criminology (held at the Maryland State Penitentiary), for the concept of "zombies." See Guy Harris, Tarif Abdullah, and Joe Rowe, 1990, "Penal Philosophy and Public Policy: Cohesion Requires Some Fundamental Change", pp. 26-37, in Raymond L. Ellis, Ph.D., <u>Student Panel Papers, Theme: Behind Bars: Perspectives on the Administration of Justice On Location at Maryland State Penitentiary.</u>, Baltimore, Maryland: Coppin State College.

[21]The reader must note for the historical record that my 1991 book used this same language. I did not try to emulate anything in the gang authored book <u>Monster</u>, in fact my use of the term appears before that of the Crip gang member who tells his heroic tale of being a new type of urban freedom fighter. This is

standard inmate language I gained from my visit with prison inmates. The book bearing the same title of this expression appears to be an orchestrated and stylized account from do-gooders working with such a gang member in a predictable direction of logic: the gang member is never responsible for the violence and mayhem he or she creates. It is a commercial exploitation of the gang problem. It is not social science.

[22]Actually, such an initiative would be a great idea if the person using the equipment acknowledged in writing by their signature that they forfeited any expectation of privacy: to wit, monitoring these communications to see what they were actually doing for the "program".

[23] We cannot oversimplify the problem by labelling gangs as psychotic (Bolitho, 1930), or assume they all have such mental health problems just because some authors have taken a psychiatric approach (Baittle, 1961) or like Schwitzgebel, have sought to use experimental therapy on gang members (Brotman, 1949; Beier, 1951).

Selected Bibliography on Gangs

Abel, Ernest; and Barbara Buckley
  1974 The Handwriting on the Wall: Toward a Sociology and Psychology of Graffiti. Westport, CT: Greenwood Press.
Ackley, Ethel and Beverly Fliegel
  1960 "A Social Work Approach to Street Corner Girls", Social Work, (5): 29-31.
Ackley, N.
  1984 Gangs in Schools: Breaking Up Is Hard To Do, U.S. Dept. of Justice, Office of Juvenile Justice and Delinquency Prevention, Washington, D.C.
Ackerley, Ethel G. and Beverly R. Fliegel
  1960 "A Social Work Approach to Street-Corner Girls", Social Work (5)(4): 27-36.
Adams, Stuart
  1967 "A Cost Approach to the Assessment of Gang Rehabilitation Techniques", Journal of Research in Crime and Delinquency (Jan.).
Adler, P.A.
  1985 Wheeling and Dealing: An Ethnography of an Upper-Level Drug Dealing and Smuggling Community. New York: Columbia University Press.
Allegro, Donald B.
  1989 "Police Tactics, Drug Trafficking, and Gang Violence: Why the No-Knock Warrant is an Idea Whose Time Has Come", Notre Dame Law Review (64)(4): 552-570.
Alonso, Alejandro A.
  1999 Territoriality Among African-American Street Gangs in Los Angeles, M.A. Thesis, Geography, University of Southern California.
Anslinger, Harry J.; and Will Ousler
  1961 The Murderers: The Story of Narcotics Gangs. American Book-Stratford Press: New York.
Anyah, Morris Azuma
  n.d. Urban Street Gangs (1974 to August 1991): An Annotated Bibliography, Office of International Criminal Justice, University of Illinois at Chicago.
Agopian, Michael
  1991 "Evaluation of G.A.P.P. - Gang Alternative Prevention Project in the Los Angeles Probation Department", paper presented at the Annual Meeting of the Academy of Criminal Justice Sciences, Nashville, Tennessee.
Aiken, Carol; Jeffrey P. Rush; and Jerry Wycoff
  1993 "A Preliminary Inquiry Into Alabama Youth Gang Membership", The Gang Journal: An Interdisciplinary Research Quarterly (1)(2): 37-47.
Amandes, Richard B.
  1979 "Hire a Gang Leader: A Delinquency Prevention Program", Juvenile and Family Court Journal (30)(1)(Feb): 37-40.
Anderson, Elijah
  1978 A Place on the Corner. Chicago: University of Chicago Press.
Anderson, James F.
  1993 "Review Essay: A Methodological Critique of Islands in the Streets", The Gang Journal: An Interdisciplinary Research Quarterly (1)(2): 49-57.
Anderson, James F.; and Laronistine Dyson
  1996 "Community Strategies to Neutralize Gang Proliferation", Journal of Gang Research, Volume 3, Number 2, Winter.
Armor, Jerry C.; and Vincent Keith Jackson
  1995 "Juvenile Gang Activity in Alabama", Journal of Gang Research, Volume 2, Number 3, Spring.
Armstrong, Richard M.
  1997 "Identification of Gangs Within Indian Country", unpublished paper.
Arnold, William R.
  1965 "The Concept of Gang", The Sociological Quarterly (7)(1): 59-75.

Arthur, Richard F.
    1989 "How to Help Gangs Win the Self-Esteem Battle", School Administrator (46)(5)(May): 18-20.
Asbury, Herbert
    1927 Gangs of New York. New York: Garden City Publishing Co.
    1939 The Gangs of New York. New York: Alfred A. Knopf.
    1971 The Gangs of New York. New York: Capricorn.
Austin, David M.
    1957 "Goals for Gang Workers", Social Work (2)(4): 43-50
Axelson, Roland G.
    1984 "The Psychological Influence of Street Gangs on School-Aged Youth: A Case Study in Hartford, CT". The I.N. Thut World Education Center, Hartford, CT.
Bailey, William C.
    1969 "Educational and Occupational Experience, Perception, and Future Expectations of Lower Class Negro Gang Delinquents", Master's thesis, Washington State University.
Baird, L.H.
    1986 "Prison Gangs: Texas", Corrections Today (18)(July):   22.
Baittle, Brahm
    1961 "Psychiatric Aspects of the Development of a Street Corner Group: An Exploratory Study", American Journal of Orthopsychiatry (31)(Oct): 703-712.
Barker, George C.
    1950 Pachuco: An American-Spanish Argot and Its Social Function in Tucson, Arizona. Social Science Bulletin No. 18 (Vol. XXI)(No. 1)(Jan), Tucson, Arizona: University of Arizona Press.
    1979 -----
Batsis, Tom
    1997 "Helping Schools to Respond to Gang Violence", Journal of Gang Research, Volume 4, Number 3, Spring.
Barrett, Leonard E.
    1988 The Rastafarians. Boston: Beacon Press.
Bartollas, Clemens
    1990 "The Prison: Disorder Personified", chapter 1 (pp. 11-22) in John W. Murphy and Jack E. Dison (Eds.) Are Prisons Any Better? Twenty Years of Correctional Reform, Sage Criminal Justice System Annuals, Newbury Park, CA: Sage Publications.
Beck, L.M.
    1962 Three Groups of Delinquents of the Family Court of East Baton Rouge Parish, Ph.D. dissertation, Louisiana State University.
Becker, Harold K.; George T. Felkenes; Lisa Magana; and Jill Huntley
    1997 "A Socioeconomic Comparison of Drug Sales by Mexican-American and Mexican Immigrant Gang Members", Journal of Gang Research, Volume 4, Number 4, Summer.
Beier, Ernest G.
    1951 "Experimental Therapy With a Gang", Focus (30) (July): 97-102.
Bell, J. and D. Sullivan
    1987 Jackson, Mississippi Mayor's Task Force on Gangs: Final Report, Jackson, MS.
Bennett, James
    1981 Oral History and Delinquency: The Rhetoric of Criminology. Chicago: University of Chicago Press.
Bensinger, Gad J.
    1984 "Chicago Youth Gangs: A New Old Problem", Journal of Crime & Justice (VII): 1-16.
Bernstein, Saul
    1964 Youth on the Streets -- Work with Alienated Youth Groups. New York: Associated Press.
Bessant, Judith and Rob Watts
    1992 "Being Bad is Good: Explorations of the Bodgie Gang Culture in South East Australia, 1948-1956", The Gang Journal: An Interdisciplinary Research Quarterly (1)(1): 31-55.
    1994 "The American Juvenile Underclass and the Cultural Colonisation of Young Australians Under Conditions of Modernity", Journal of Gang Research (2)(1)(Fall): 15-33.

Bing, Leon
    1991 <u>Do or Die</u>. New York: Harper-Collins.
Bjerregaard, Beth; and Carolyn Smith
    1993 "Gender Differences in Gang Participation, Delinquency and Substance Use", <u>Journal of Quantitative Criminology</u>, (4): 329-355.
Blanchard, W.H.
    1959 "The Group Process in Gang Rape", <u>Journal of Social Psychology</u>: 259-266.
Bloch, Herbert
    1963 "The Juvenile Gang: A Cultural Reflex", <u>Annals of the American Academy of Political and Social Science</u> (347)(May): 20-29.
Bloch, Herbert and Arthur Niederhoffer
    1957 "Adolescent Behavior and the Gang: A Cross-Cultural Analysis", <u>Journal of Social Therapy</u> (3): 174-179.
    1958 <u>The Gang: A Study in Adolescent Behavior</u>. New York: Philosophical Press.
Block, Carolyn Rebecca and Richard Block
    1993 <u>Street Gang Crime In Chicago</u>. National Institute of Justice, Research in Brief. December.
Blumberg, Leonard
    1964 "A Possible Application of the Epidemiological-Public Health Model to Civic Action-Research", <u>Social Problems</u> (12)(Fall): 178-185.
Bobrowski, Lawrence J.
    1988 "Collecting, Organizing and Reporting Street Gang Crime", 82 pp., Chicago Police Department, Prepared for the 40th Annual Meeting of the American Society of Criminology, CPD: Special Functions Group.
Bochenek, Brian M.
    1996 "Views from the Field: Not Just Removing Tattoos", <u>Journal of Gang Research</u>, Volume 4, Number 1, Fall.
Bogardus, Emory
    1943 "Gangs of Mexican-American Youth", <u>Sociology and Social Research</u> (28): 55-66.
Bolitho, W.
    1930 "The Psychosis of the Gang", <u>Survey</u>: 501-506.
Bonner, Roger H.
    1999 "Gang Profile: The Brotherwoods - The Rise and Fall of a White-Supremacist Gang Inside a Kansas Prison", <u>Journal of Gang Research</u>, Volume 6, Number 3, Spring.
Bookin, H.
    1980 "The Gangs That Didn't Go Straight", paper presented at the Society for the Study of Social Problems, New York.
Bookin-Weiner, Hedy and Ruth Horowitz
    1983 "The End of the Youth Gang: Fad or Fact?", <u>Criminology</u> (21)(4)(Nov): 585-601.
Bordua, David J.
    1961 "Delinquent Subcultures: Sociological Interpretations of Gang Delinquency", <u>Annals of the American Academy of Social Science</u> (338): 119-36.
Born, Peter
    1971 <u>Street Gangs and Youth Unrest</u>. Chicago: Chicago Tribune Educational Service Department.
Bowker, Lee H.; H.W. Gross; and Malcolm W. Klein
    1980 "Female Participation in Delinquent Gang Activities", <u>Adolescence</u>, (14): 509-519.
Bowker, L.H. and Malcolm W. Klein
    1983 "The Etiology of Female Juvenile Delinquency and Gang Membership: A Test of Psychological and Social Structural Explanations", <u>Adolescence</u> (18)(72)(Win): 739-751.
Boyle, J. and A. Gonzales
    1989 "Using Proactive Programs to Impact Gangs and Drugs", <u>Law and Order</u> (37)(8)(Aug.): 62-64.
Breen, Lawrence; and Martin M. Allen
    1983 "Gang Behavior: Psychological and Law Enforcement Implications", <u>FBI Law Enforcement Bulletin</u> (52)(Feb): 19-24.
Brooks, William Allan
    1952 <u>Girl Gangs</u>. A Survey of Teen-Age Drug Addicts, Sex Crimes, Rape, Kleptomania, Prosti

tution, Truancy, and Other Deviations. New York: Padell Book Company.

Brotherton, David C.
    1997 "From Gangs to Street Organizations: The Changing Characteristics of Street Subcultures in New York City", paper presented at the Annual Meeting of the American Society of Criminology.

Brotman, Richard
    1949 A Group Approach to the Treatment of the Aggressive Gang, Master's Thesis, City College of New York.

Brown, Waln K.
    1977 "Black Female Gangs in Philadelphia", International Journal of Offender Therapy and Comparative Criminology (21): 221-228.
    1978 "Black Gangs as Family Extensions" & "Graffiti, Identity, and the Delinquent Gang", International Journal of Offender Therapy and Comparative Criminology (22)(1): 39-48.

Brownfield, David; Kevin M. Thompson; and Ann Marie Sorenson
    1997 "Correlates of Gang Membership: A Test of Strain, Social Learning, an Social Control Theories", Journal of Gang Research, Volume 4, Number 4, Summer.

Brueckner, William H.
    1960 "Corner Group Work with Teen-Age Gangs", Federal Probation (24)(Dec): 84.

Bryant, D.
    1989 Community Responses Crucial for Dealing With Youth Gangs, U.S. Dept. of Justice, Office of Juvenile Justice and Delinquency Prevention, Washington, D.C.

Brymmer, R.A.
    1967 "Toward a Definition and Theory of Conflict Gangs", (mimeo) paper presented at the annual meeting of the Society for the Study of Social Problems (August 26).

Buentello, S.
    1986 Texas Syndicate: A Review of Its Inception, Growth in Violence and Continued Threat to the TDC, Texas Department of Corrections, unpublished.

Burns, E. and T.J. Deakin
    1989 "New Investigative Approach to Youth Gangs", FBI Law Enforcement Bulletin (58)(10)(Oct): 20-24.

Burris-Kitchen, Deborah
    1997 Female Gang Participation: The Role of African-American Women in the Informal Drug Economy and Gang Activities. The Edwin Mellen Press: Lewiston, NY.

California Attorney General's Youth Gang Task Force
    1981 Report on Youth Gang Violence in California. California: Department of Justice.

California Council on Criminal Justice
    1986 Final Report: State Task Force on Youth Gang Violence. Sacramento, CA.
    1989 State Task Force on Gangs and Drugs. Sacramento, CA: 95823.

Camp, George and Camille Graham Camp
    1985 Prison Gangs: Their Extent, Nature, and Impact on Prisons. Washington, D.C.: U.S. Dept. of Justice.

Campbell, Anne
    1984 The Girls in the Gang: A Report from New York City. New York: Basil Blackwell Ltd.
    1984 "Girls' Talk: The Social Representation of Aggression by Female Gang Members", Criminal Justice Behavior (11): 139-156.
    1987 "Self Definitions by Rejection: The Case of Gang Girls", Social Problems (34)(5)(Dec): 451-466.

Campbell, Anne and Steven Muncer
    1989 "Them and Us: A Comparison of the Cultural Context of American Gangs and British Subcultures", DeviantBehavior (10)(3): 271-288.

Candamil, Maria T.
    1992 Female Gangs: The Forgotten Ones. U.S. Department of Health and Human Services (DHHS), Administration for Children, Youth and Families, Washington, DC.

Caplan, Nathan S.; Dennis J. Deshaies, Gerald D. Suttles, and Hans W. Mattick
    1963 "The Nature, Variety, and Patterning of Street Club Work in an Urban Setting", pp. 135-169 in Malcolm W. Klein and Barbara G. Meyerhoff (eds), Juvenile Gangs in Context: Theory,Research, and Action, Conference Report, August 25-26, 1963, Youth Studies

Center, Los Angeles: University of Southern California.

1964 "Factors Affecting the Process and Outcome of Street Club Work", <u>Sociology and Social Research</u> (48)(Jan): 207-219.

Carey, Sean

1985 "I just Hate 'em, That's All", <u>New Society</u> (73) (1178)(July): 123-125.

Cartwright, Desmond S. and Kenneth I. Howard

1966 "Multivariate Analysis of Gang Delinquency: I. Ecologic Influences", <u>Multivariate Behavioral Research</u> (1)(July): 321-71.

Cartwright, Desmond S.; Kenneth I. Howard; and Nicholas A. Reuterman

1970 "Multivariate Analysis of Gang Delinquency: II. Structural and Dynamic Properties of Gangs", <u>Multivariate Behavioral Research</u> (5)(July): 303-24.

----- 1971 "Multivariate Analysis of Gang Delinquency: III. Age and Physique of Gangs and Clubs", <u>Multivariate Behavioral Research</u> (6)(Jan): 75-90.

----- 1980 "Multivariate Analysis of Gang Delinquency: IV. Personality Factors in Gangs and Clubs", <u>Multivariate Behavioral Research</u> (15): 3-22.

Cartwright, Desmond S.; B. Tomson; and H. Schwartz

1975 <u>Gang Delinquency</u>. Monterey, CA: Brooks/Cole.

Cavanagh, Suzanne and David Teasley

1992 <u>Youth Gangs: An Overview</u>. Washington, DC: Congressional Research Service.

Cellini, Henry D.

1991 <u>Youth Gang Prevention and Intervention Strategies</u>. Albuquerque, NM: Training and Research Institute, Inc.

Center for Child Protection and Family Support, Inc

1989 <u>Final Report: Youth Gang Drug Revenues: A Possible Hidden Source of Family Financial Support, An Exploratory Investigation</u>. Washington, D.C.

Chang, Jean

1996 "A Comparative Analysis of Female Gang and Non-Gang Members in Chicago", <u>Journal of Gang Research</u>, Volume 4, Number 1, Fall.

Chazal, J.

1964 "A Current Criminological Problem: Juvenile Delinquency in Gangs", <u>Quebec Society of Criminology Bulletin</u> (3)(2): 5-11.

Chesney-Lind, Meda

1993 "Girls, Gangs, and Violence: Reinventing the Liberated Female Crook", <u>Humanity and Society</u> (17): 321-344.

Chesney-Lind, Meda; and John M. Hagedorn (eds)

1999 <u>Female Gangs in America: Essays on Girls, Gangs and Gender</u>. Lake View Press: Chicago, IL.

Chicago Area Project

n.d. "Shaw's Thoughts".

1939 "Chicago Area Project", March, 1939.

n.d. <u>Chicago Area Project: The Nation's First Community-Based Delinquency Prevention Program.</u>

Chicago Police Department

1989 <u>Murder Analysis</u>. Richard M. Daley, Mayor. Leroy Martin, Superindendent of Police. Chicago, IL.

Chin, Ko-Lin

1986 <u>Chinese Triad Societies, Tongs, Organized Crime, and Street Gangs in Asia and the United States</u>. Ph.D. dissertation, University of Pennsylvania.

1988 <u>Chinese Gangs in New York City: 1965-1988</u>. Baltimore, MD and Taipeh, Taiwan: Loyola College and National Taiwan University.

1990 <u>Chinese Subculture and Criminality: Non-traditional Crime Groups in America</u>. Westport, Conn: Greenwood Press.

1993 "Methodological Issues in Studying Chinese Gang Extortion", <u>The Gang Journal: An Interdisciplinary Research Quarterly</u> (1)(2): 25-36.

Christensen, Loren W.

1999 <u>Gangbangers: Understanding the Deadly Minds of America's Street Gangs</u>. Boulder, CO: Paladin Press.

Cintron, Ralph
    2000 "Listening to What the Streets Say: Thoughts on Gangs and the Logic of Violence", The Annals of the American Academy of Political and Social Science, Vol. 567, January.
Clark, J.H.
    1981 A Report of the Gang Activities Task Force. Chicago Board of Education, Chicago, Illinois.
Cloward, R.A. and L.E. Ohlin
    1960 Delinquency and Opportunity. New York: Free Press.
Coghlan, Michael P.
    1997 How to Prevent Gangs and Drugs in Your Home, School and Community!!.
    1998 "The Rural Gang Problem: A Case Study for the Midwest", Journal of Gang Research, Volume 5, Number 2, Winter.
Cohen, Albert K.
    1955 Delinquent Boys: The Culture of the Gang. Glencoe, IL: The Free Press.
Cohen, Bernard
    1970 "The Delinquency of Gangs and Spontaneous Groups", Chapter 4 in Delinquency: Selected Studies, Thorsten Sellin and Marvin E. Wolfgang (eds.), New York: John Wiley and Sons.
Cole, Juan R.I. and Moojan Momen
    1986 "Mafia, Mob and Shiism in Iraq: The Rebellion of Ottoman Karbala 1824-1843", Past and Present (112)(Aug): 112-143.
Collins, H. Craig
    1977 "Street Gangs of New York: A Prototype of Organized Youth Crime", Law and Order (25)(1)(Jan): 6-16.
Collins, Jessie
    1993 "Joe: The Story of an Ex-Gang Member", Gang Journal: An Interdisciplinary Research Quarterly (1)(3): 45-50.
Conrad, J.P.
    1979 "Who's in Charge? The Control of Gang Violence in California Prisons", in Correctional Facility Planning edited by Robert Montilla and Nora Marlow, pp. 135-147, Lexington, Mass: D.C. Heath.
Cook, James I.
    1993 "Targeting Gang Violence in the City of Westminister", Westminister Police Department, Westminister, CA.
Corbiscello, George V.
    1997 "Gang Profile: The Almighty Latin King and Queen Nation of New York", Journal of Gang Research, Volume 4, Number 2, Winter.
    1998 "Gang Profile: A Nation of Gods - The Five Percent Nation of Islam", Journal of Gang Research, Volume 5, Number 2, Winter.
Covey, Herbert C.; Scott Menard; and Robert J. Franzese
    1992 Juvenile Gangs. Charles C. Thomas Publisher: Springfield, IL.
Cox, V.
    1986 "Prison Gangs - Inmates Battle for Control", Corrections Compendium (10)(9)(Apr): 1,6-9.
Cozic, Charles P.
    1996 Gangs: Opposing Viewpoints. David Bender & Bruno Leone (series editors), San Diego, CA: Greenhaven Press.
Crane, A.R.
    1951 "A Note on Pre-Adolescent Gangs", Australian Psychology (3): 43-45.
    1958 "The Development of Moral Values in Children: IV; Pre-Adolescent Gangs and the Moral Development of Children", British Journal of Educational Psychology (28)(Nov): 201-208.
Crawford, Paul I.; Daniel I. Malamud; and James R. Dumpson
    1950 Working With Teenage Gangs. A Report on the Central Harlem Street Clubs Project. New York: Welfare Council of New York City.
Crime Control Digest
    1976 "Detroit Mayor Against City's Growing Youth Gangs: Citizen Involvement in Crime

Prevention", Aug. 30, 1976,   p. 5, (10)(35).

1980 "Gangs - Police, Community Relations", Mar. 30, 1980, pp. 7-8, (14)(9).

1984 "Police Community Relations: Gangs - Chicago Police Department: Citizen Involvement in Crime Prevention", Mar. 26, 1984, pp. 5-6, (18)(12).

1987 "Detroit Mayor Unveils Plan to Fight Youth Crime: Gangs and Crime Prevention", Jan 26, 1987, p. 6, (21)(4).

1987 "California's Vietnam Refugees Work on Their Own to Divert Teens from Street Gangs", June 8, 1987, pp. 9-10,(21)(23).

Crowner, James M.

1963 "Utilizing Certain Positive Aspects of Gang Phenomena in Training School Group Work", American Journal of Correction (25)(July-August): 24-27.

Cummings, Scott and Daniel Monti (eds.)

1993 Gangs: The Origins and Impact of Contemporary Youth Gangs in the United States. Albany, NY: State University New York Press.

Cureton, Steven R.

1999 "Gang Membership: Gang Formations and Gang Joining", Journal of Gang Research, Volume 7, Number 1, Fall: 13-21.

Curry, G. David; and Scott H. Decker

1998 Confronting Gangs: Crime and Community, Roxbury Publishing Company: Los Angeles, CA.

Curry, G. David and Irving A. Spergel

1988 "Gang Homicide, Delinquency, and Community", Criminology (26)(Aug): 381-405.

Curtis, Richard

1997 "The Improbable Transformation of Inner-City Neighborhoods: Crime, Violence, Drugs and Youth in the1990s", unpublished paper.

Cusson, Maurice

1989 "Disputes over Honor and Gregarious Aggressions", Revue Internationale de Criminologie et de Police Technique (Geneva, SWITZ) (42)(3): 290-297.

Dahmann, J.

1981 "Operation Hardcore: A Prosecutorial Response to Violent Gang Criminality", interim report, MITRE Corporation, McLean, VA.

Daniels, S.

1987 "Prison Gangs: Confronting the Threat", Corrections Today (29)(2)(Apr): 66,126,162.

Dart, Robert W.

1992 "The Future is Here Today: Street Gang Trends", The Gang Journal: An Interdisciplinary Research Quarterly (1)(1): 87-90.

David, J.J. and M.H. Shaffer

1988 Intelligence Gathering in the Investigation of Motorcycle Gangs, National Institute of Justice, NCJRS, Rockville, MD.

David, J.J.

1988 "Outlaw Motorcycle Gangs: A Transnational Problem", paper presented at the Conference on International Terrorism and Transnational Crime, University of Illinois at Chicago, August, 1988.

Davis, James R.

1978 The Terrorists: Youth, Biker and Prison Violence. San Diego, CA: Grossmont Press.

1982 Street Gangs: Youth, Biker and Prison Groups. Dubuque, Iowa: Kendall/Hunt Publishing.

Davis, Mike

1988 "War in the Streets", New Statesman & Society (1)(23)(Nov): 27-30.

Davis, R.H.

1982 Selected Bibliography on Publications Related to Outlaw Motorcycle Gangs, U.S. Dept. of Justice, FBI Academy, Quantico, VA 22134.

1995 "Cruising for Trouble: Gang-Related Drive-by Shootings", FBI Law Enforcement Bulletin, 64: 16-22.

Dawley, David

1973 A Nation of Lords: The Autobiography of the Vice Lords. Garden City, NY: Anchor Press.

1992 A Nation of Lords. Prospect Heights, IL: Waveland Press.

Day, D.
      1987 "Outlaw Motorcycle Gangs", <u>Royal Canadian Mounted Police Gazette</u> (49)(5): 1-42.
Decker, Scott
      1996 "Gangs and Violence: The Expressive Character of Collective Involvement", <u>Justice Quar-terly</u> (11): 231-250.
Decker, Scott; and Janet L. Lauritsen
      1996 "Collective and Normative Features of Gang Violence", <u>Justice Quarterly</u> (13): 243-264.
      1996 "Breaking the Bonds of Membership: Leaving the Gang", in <u>Gangs in America</u> (C. Ronald Huff, Ed), Sage Publications: Newbury Park, CA.
Decker, Scott; ;and K. Kempf-Leonard
      1991 "Constructing Gangs: The Social Definition of Youth Activities", <u>Criminal Justice Policy Review</u> (5): 271-291.
Decker, Scott; and Barrik Van Winkle
      1996 <u>Life in the Gang: Family, Friends, and Violence</u>. New York: Cambidge University Press.
Dees, M.
      1996 <u>Gathering Storm: America's Militia Threat</u>. Harper-Collins: New York.
Delaney, J.L. and Walter B. Miller
      1977 <u>Intercity Variation in the Seriousness of Crime by Youth Gangs and Youth Groups</u>, Report to the Office of Juvenile Justice and Delinquency Prevention.
Delaney, Lloyd T.
      1954 "Establishing Relationships with Antisocial Groups and an Analysis of Their Structure", <u>British Journal of Delinquency</u> (5)(1): 34-42.
De Leon, Aleister
      1977 "Averting Violence in the Gang Community", <u>The Police Chief</u> (44)(7)(July): 52-53.
Denisoff, R. Serge and Charles H. McCaghy
      1973 <u>Deviance, Conflict, and Criminality</u>. Chicago: Rand McNally & Company.
Destro, Robert A.
      1993 "Gangs and Civil Rights", pp. 227-304 in Scott Cummings and Daniel J. Monti (Eds.), <u>Gangs: The Origin and Impact of Contemporary Youth Gangs in the United States</u>. Albany, NY: State University of New York Press.
Deukmajian, G.
      1981 <u>Report on Youth Gang Violence in California</u>. State of California: Department of Justice.
DeZolt, Ernest M.; Linda M. Schmidt; and Donna C. Gilcher
      1996 "The 'Tabula Rasa' Intervention Project for Delinquent Gang-Involved Females", <u>Journal of Gang Research</u>, Volume 3, Number 3, Spring.
      1997 "We Ain't No Gang, We A Family!: Gangs as Projects", paper presented at the Annual Meeting of the American Society of Criminology, San Diego, CA.
Dolan, Edward F. and Shan Finney
      1984 <u>Youth Gangs</u>. New York: Simon & Schuster, Julian Messner.
Donohue, John K.
      1966 <u>My Brother's Boy: A Treatise on Criminology.</u> St. Paul, MN: Bruce Publishing Co.
Douglas, Jack D.
      1970 <u>Youth in Turmoil: America's Changing Youth Cultures and Student Protest Movements</u>. Center for Studies of Crime and Delinquency, National Institute of Mental Health, Washington, DC: Government Printing Office.
Dumpson, J.R.
      1949 "An Approach to Antisocial Street Gangs", <u>Federal Probation</u>: 22-29.
Dumpson, James R., et al
      1952 "Gang and Narcotic Problems of Teen-Age Youth", <u>American Journal of Psychotherapy</u> (6)(Apr): 312-46.
Dunbar, Ellen A.
      1963 "How to Help the Gang Member Through His Family", Special Service for Groups, Los Angeles: unpublished.
Dunston, Leonard G.
      1990 <u>Report of the Task Force on Juvenile Gangs</u>. New York State Division for Youth. Albany, New York.

Dunston, Mark S.
  1992 Street Signs - An Identification Guide of Symbols of Crime and Violence. Powers Lake,
        WI: Performance Dimensions Publishing.
Duran, M.
  1975 "What Makes a Difference in Working with Youth Gangs?", Crime Prevention Review (2):
        25-30.
Earley, Pete
  1992 The Hot House: Life Inside Leavenworth Prison. New York: Bantam.
Eisenstadt, S. N.
  1951 "Delinquency Group Formation Among Immigrant Youth", British Journal of Delinquency
        (2)(1).
Elder, Alice P. Franklin
  1996 "Inside Gang Society: How Gang Members Imitate Legitimate Social Forms", Journal of
        Gang Research, Volume 3, Number 4, Summer.
  1999 "Goal Displacement at Leadership and Operational Levels of the Gang Organization",
        Journal of Gang Research, Volume 6, Number 3, Spring.
Elliott, D.S.
  1962 "Delinquency and Perceived Opportunity", Sociological Inquiry (32)(Spr): 216-27.
English, T.J.
  1990 The Westies: The Irish Mob. New York: St. Martins Press.
  1995 Born to Kill. New York: William Morrow and Company.
Erlanger, Howard S.
  1979 "Estrangement, Machismo and Gang Violence", Social Science Quarterly (60)(2): 235-49.
Esbensen, Finn-Aage
  1995 "Overview of the National Evaluation of GREAT", paper presented at the Annual Meeting
        of the Academy of Criminal Justice Sciences, Boston, MA.
Esbensen, Finn-Aage; and David Huizinga
  1993 "Gangs, Drugs, and Delinquency in a Survey of Urban Youth", Criminology, (31)(4)(Nov.):
        565-587.
Etter, Gregg W.
  1995 "Tattoos and the New Urban Tribes", Journal of Gang Research, Volume 3, Number 1, Fall.
  1998 "Common Characteristics of Gangs: Examining the Cultures of the New Urban Tribes",
        Journal of Gang Research, Volume 5, Number 2, Winter.
  1999 "Skinheads: Manifestations of the Warrior Culture of the New Urban Tribes", Journal of
        Gang Research, Volume 6, Number 3, Spring.
Evans, William; and Alex Mason
  1996 "Factors Associated With Gang Involvement Among Incarcerated Youths", Journal of
        Gang Research, Volume 3, Number 4, Summer.
Eyres, John
  1997 "On the Rise of Vietnamese Gangs in Southern California: An Analysis of Los Angeles
        Times News Reports", paper presented at the Annual Meeting of the American Society of
        Criminology.
Fagan, Jeffrey
  1989 "The Social Organization of Drug Use and Drug Dealing Among Urban Gangs", Criminol-
        ogy (27)(4): 633-664.
Fagan, Jeffrey and Ko-lin Chin
  1989 "Violence as Regulation and Social Control in the Distribution of Crack", in M. De la Rosa;
        B. Gropper; and E. Lambert (eds.), Drugs and Violence, National Institute of Drug Abuse
        Research Monograph, Rockville, MD: U.S. Dept. of Health and Human Services.
Fanscali, James
  1999 "Views from the Field: Gang Homicide Investigation", Journal of Gang Research, Volume
        6, Number 2, Winter.
Feinstein, M.D.
  1976 "Youth Gangs: The Problem and the Approach", Crime Prevention Review (4): 21-25.
Felkenes, George T.; and Harold K. Becker
  1995 "Female Gang Members: A Growing Issue for Policy Makers", Journal of Gang Research,
        Volume 2, Number 4, Fall: 1-10.

Ferrell, Jeff
    1992 Crimes of Style: Urban Graffiti and the Politics of Urban Criminality. New York: Garland.
Fishman, L.
    1988 "The Vice Queens: An Ethnographic Study of Black Female Gang Behavior", paper
          presented at the Annual Meeting of the American Society of Criminology.
Florida House of Representatives
    1987 Issue Paper: Youth Gangs in Florida. Committee on Youth. Tallahassee, FL.
Foner, Philip S.
    1995 The Black Panthers Speak. Da Capo Presss: New York.
Fong, Robert S.
    1987 A Comparative Study of the Organizational Aspects of Two Texas Prison Gangs: Texas
          Syndicate and Mexican Mafia. Ph.D. dissertation, Sam Houston State University,
          Huntsville, Texas.
    1990 "The Organizational Structure of Prison Gangs: A Texas Case Study", Federal Probation
          (54)(1)(Mar): 36-43.
Fong, Robert S. and Salvador Buentello
    1991 "The Management of Prison Gangs: An Empirical Assessment", paper presented at the
          Annual Meeting of the Academy of Criminal Justice Sciences, Nashville, Tennessee.
Fong, Robert S.; Ron Vogel; and Robert Little
    1991 "Behind Prison Walls: Racially Based Gangs and Their Level of Violence", paper presented
          at the Annual Meeting of the Academy of Criminal Justice Sciences, Nashville, TN.
Fong, Robert S.; and Ronald E. Vogel
    1995 "A Comparative Analysis of Prison Gang Members, Security Threat Group Inmates and
          General Population Prisoners in the Texas Department of Corrections", Journal of Gang
          Research, Volume 2, Number 2, Winter.
Fong, Robert S;; Ronald E. Vogel; and Salvador Buentello
    1995 "Blood-in, Blood-out: The Rationale Behind Defecting from Prison Gangs", Journal of
          Gang Research, Volume 2, Number 4, Fall.
Fossett, Christine A.
    1974 Evaluation Report: North Central Youth Academy. Educational Management Associates,
          Consultants, Facilitators, Applied Behavioral and Management Sciences, Design,
          Development and Audit of Urban Programs, Philadelphia, PA (NCJRS#
          09900.00.027469).
Fox, Jerry R.
    1985 "Mission Impossible? Social Work Practice with Black Urban Youth Gangs", Social Work
          (30)(Jan/Feb): 25-31.
Fox, Robert W. and Mark E. Amador
    1993 Gangs on the Move: A Descriptive Cataloging of Over 1500 Most Active Gangs in
          America. Placerville, CA: Copperhouse Publishing Company.
Freed, D.
    1971 Agony in New Haven: The Trial of Bobby Seale, Ericka Huggins, and the Black Panther
          Party. Simon & Schuster: New York.
Frias, Gus
    1982 Barrio Warriors: Homeboys of Peace. Los Angeles: Diaz Publishing.
Friedman, C.J.; F. Mann; and A.S. Friedman
    1975 "A Profile of Juvenile Street Gang Members", Adolescence (10): 563-607.
    1976 "Juvenile Street Group: The Victimization of Youth", Adolescence, (44)(Winter): 527-533.
Fry, John
    1969 Fire and Blackstone. Philadelphia: J.B. Lippincott.
    1973 Locked Out Americans. New York: Harper and Row.
Furfey, Paul Hanley
    1926 The Gang Age: A Study of the Pre-Adolescent Boy and His Recreational Needs. New
          York: The Macmillan Company.
Furman, Sylvan S. (ed).
    1952 Reaching the Unreached. "Working with a Street Gang" (pp. 112-121) New York: New
          York City Youth Board.

Gandy, John M.
    1959 "Preventive Work with Street-Corner Groups: Hyde Park Project, Chicago", <u>Annals of American Academy of Political and Social Science</u> (323)(Mar): 107-116.
Gannon, Thomas M.
    1967 "Dimension of Current Gang Delinquency", <u>Journal of Research in Crime and Delinquency</u> (Jan)(4)(2): 119-131.
    1970 -----. Chapter 34 in Marvin E. Wolfgang, Leonard Savitz, and Norman Johnston (eds.), <u>The Sociology of Crime and Delinquency</u>, New York: John Wiley & Sons, Inc.
Garner, Stephanie
    1983 <u>Street Gangs</u>. New York: Franklin Watts.
Geis, Gilbert
    1965 "Juvenile Gangs", <u>President's Committee on Juvenile Delinquency and Youth Crime</u>, Washington, D.C.
Gerrard, Nathan L.
    1964 "The Core Member of the Gang", <u>British Journal of Criminology</u> (4)(Apr): 361-371.
Gertz, Marc; Laura Bedard; and Will Persons
    1995 "Hispanic Perceptions of Youth Gangs: A Descriptive Exploration", <u>Journal of Gang Research</u>, Volume 2, Number 3, Spring.
Giles, H. Harry
    1957 "Case Analysis of Social Conflict", <u>Journal of Educational Sociology</u> (30)(Mar): 289-333.
Giordano, P.C.
    1978 "Girls, Guys and Gangs: The Changing Social Context of Female Delinquency", <u>Journal of Criminal Law and Criminology</u> (69): 126-132.
Glane, Sam
    1950 "Juvenile Gangs in East Side Los Angeles", <u>Focus</u> (29)(Sept): 136-141.
Glazier, Mary H. and Rikardo Hull
    1997 "Getting Props: Gangs, Graffiti and Identity", paper presented at the Annual Meeting of the American Society of Criminology.
Goldstein, Arnold P.
    1991 <u>Delinquent Gangs: A Psychological Perspective.</u> Champaign, IL: Research Press.
Goldstein, Arnold P. and Barry Glick, et al
    1994 <u>The Prosocial Gang: Implementing Aggression Replacement Training</u>. Thousand Oaks, CA: Sage Publications.
Goldstein, Arnold P. and C. Ronald Huff
    1995 <u>Gang Intervention Handbook</u>. Research Press: Urbana, IL.
Gonzalez, Alfredo
    1981 <u>Mexican/Chicano Gangs in Los Angeles</u>. D.S.W. dissertation, University of California at Berkeley, School of Social Welfare.
Goodman, Mark
    1996 <u>Perceptions of Gang Territories in Fresno, California</u>. M.A. Thesis, California State University, Fresno.
Gordon, Robert A.
    1963 <u>Values and Gang Delinquency</u>, Ph.D. dissertation, University of Chicago.
    1967 "Social Level, Disability, and Gang Interaction", <u>American Journal of Sociology</u> (73)(July): 42-62.
Gordon, Robert A.; James Short, Jr.; Desmond S. Cartwright; and Fred L. Strodtbeck
    1963 "Values and Gang Delinquency: A Study of Street-Corner Groups", <u>American Journal of Sociology</u> (69)(2): 109-128.
    1970 "Values and Gang Delinquency: A Study of Street-Corner Groups", Chapter 33 in Wolfgang, et al (eds.), <u>The Sociology of Crime and Delinquency</u>, New York: John Wiley & Sons, Inc, pp. 319-339.
Gorn, Elliott J.
    1987 "Good-Bye Boys, I Die a True American": Homicide, Nativism, and Working-Class Culture in Antebellum New York City", <u>Journal of American History</u> (74)(2) (Sept): 388-410.
Gott, Raymond
    1991 (Audio Training Tape) "Juvenile Gangs and Drug Trafficking", available through the Na

tional Juvenile Detention Association, 217 Perkins Bldg, Richmond, KY 40475-3127.

Greeley, Andrew and James Casey
  1963 "An Upper Middle Class Deviant Gang", <u>American Catholic Sociological Review</u> (24)(Spr): 33-41.

Grennan, Sean; Marjie T. Britz; Jeffrey Rush; and Thomas Barker
  2000 <u>Gangs: An International Approach</u>, Prentice Hall: Upper Saddle River, NJ.

Guagliardo, James G.; and Michael Langston
  1997 "Introducing Gang Evidence Against a Criminal Defendant at Trial", <u>Journal of Gang Research</u>, Volume 4, Number 4, Summer.

Hagedorn, John M.
  1987 <u>Final Report: Milwaukee Gang Research Project</u>, Milwaukee: University of Wisconsin-Milwaukee.

Hagedorn, John M. and Perry Macon
  1988 <u>People and Folks: Gangs, Crime and the Underclass in a Rustbelt City</u>, Chicago: Lakeview Press.

Hagedorn, John M. and Joan W. Moore
  1987 "Milwaukee and Los Angeles Gangs Compared", paper presented at the Annual Meeting of the American Anthropological Association, Oaxaca, Mexico.

Hailer, Julie A.; and Cynthia Baroody Hart
  1999 "A New Breed of Warrior: The Emergence of American Indian Youth Gangs", <u>Journal of Gang Research</u>, Volume 7, Number 1, Fall: 23-33.

Haire, Thomas D.
  1979 "Street Gangs: Some Suggested Remedies for Violence and Vandalism", <u>The Police Chief</u> (46)(7)(July): 54-55.

Hamm, Mark S.
  1990 "Dealing with Skinheads, the Ku Klux Klan and other Idiots with Ideology: Toward a Correctional Education to Reduce Racial Hatred in Prison", paper presented at the International Conference of the Correctional Educational Education Association, July 8-11, 1990, Burnaby, British Columbia.
  1993 <u>American Skinheads: The Criminology and Control of Hate Crime</u>. Westport, Conn.: Praeger Series in Criminology and Crime Control Policy.

Hanson, Kitty
  1964 <u>Rebels in the Streets: The Story of New York's Gang Girls</u>. Englewood Cliffs, NJ: Prentice-Hall.

Harding, J.
  1952 "A Street Corner Gang and its Implications for Sociological and Psychological Theory", In J.E. Hulett and K.R. Stagner (eds.), <u>Problems in Social Psychology</u>, Urbana: University of Illinois Press.

Hardman, Dale G.
  1963 <u>Small Town Gangs</u>, Ph.D. dissertation, University of Illinois, College of Education.
  1967 "Historical Perspectives of Gang Research", <u>Journal of Research in Crime and Delinquency</u> (4)(1): 5-27.
  1969 "Small Town Gangs", <u>Journal of Criminal Law, Criminology and Police Studies</u> (60)(2): 173-81.

Harris, Mary G.
  1988 <u>Cholas: Latino Girls and Gangs</u>. New York: AMS Press.

Harrison, F.V.
  1988 "The Politics of Outlawry in Urban Jamaica", <u>Urban Anthropology</u> (17)(2,3)(Sum/Fall): 259-277.

Haskins, James
  1974 <u>Street Gangs: Yesterday and Today</u>. New York: Hastings House.

Hehnly, Raymond E.
  1998 "Gang Profile: Association Neta", <u>Journal of Gang Research</u>, Volume 6, Number 1, Fall.

Helfgot, Joseph H.
  1981 <u>Professional Reforming: Mobilization for Youth and the Failure of Social Science</u>, Lexington Press, Lexington: MA.

Helmreich, W.B.
  1973 "Black Crusaders: The Rise and Fall of Political Gangs", Society (11)(1)(Nov/Dec): 44-50.
Hendry, Charles E., et al
  1947 "Gangs", John Dewey Society, Ninth Yearbook: 151-175, New York: Harper.
Hobsbawm, Eric J.
  1965 Primitive Rebels. New York: W.W. Norton & Co., Inc.
  1969 Bandits. Delacorte Press.
Hodge, Patricia
  1964 Self-Descriptions of Gang and Nongang Teen-Aged Boys, Master's thesis, Department of
        Sociology, University of Chicago.
Hoenig, Gary
  1975 Reaper: The Story of a Gang Leader. Indianapolis: The Bobbs-Merrill Company, Inc.
Hoffman, Paul
  1993 "A Nation of Lords: Book Review", The Gang Journal: An Interdisciplinary Research
        Quarterly (1)(2): 71-72.
Hogrefe, Russell and John Harding
  1947 "Research Considerations in the Study of Street Gangs", Applied Anthropology (6)(Fall):
        21-24.
Holmes, Shirley R.
  1995 "Potential Research Areas for Addressing Gang Violence", Journal of Gang Research,
        Volume 2, Number 4, Summer.
Holmes, Shirley R.; and Susan J. Brandenburg-Ayres
  1998 "Bullying Behavior in School: A Predictor of Later Gang Involvement", Journal of Gang
        Research, Volume 5, Number 2, Winter.
Horowitz, Ruth
  1982 "Masked Intimacy and Marginality: Adult Delinquent Gangs in a Chicano COmmunity",
        Urban Life (11): 3-26.
  1983 "The End of the Youth Gang", Criminology (21)(4): 585-600.
  1983 Honor and the American Dream. New Brunswick, NJ: Rutgers University Press.
  1986 "Remaining an Outsider: Membership as a Threat to Research Rapport", Urban Life
        (14)(4)(Jan): 409-430.
  1987 "Community Tolerance of Gang Violence", Social Problems (34)(Dec): 449.
Horowitz, Ruth and Gary Schwartz
  1974 "Honor, Normative Ambiguity and Gang Violence", American Sociological Review (39):
        238-51.
Houston, James G.
  1993 "An Interview with Lewis Yablonsky: The Violent Gang and Beyond", The Gang Journal:
        An Interdisciplinary Research Quarterly (1)(2): 59-67.
  1994 "National Policy Neglect and Its Impact on Gang Suppression", Journal of Gang Research
        (2)(1)(Fall): 35-62.
  1996 "What Works: The Search for Excellence in Gang Intervention Programs", Journal of Gang
        Research, Volume 3, Number 3, Spring.
  1998 "Prison Gangs in South Africa: A Comparative Analysis", Journal of Gang Research,
        (5)(3)(Spring, 1998).
Houston, James G.; and Johan Prinsloo
  1998 "Prison Gangs in South Africa: A Comparative Analysis", Journal of Gang Research,
        Volume 5, Number 3, Spring.
Howson, Gerald
  1970 Thief-Taker General: Jonathan Wild and the Emergence of Crime and Corruption as a Way
        of Life in Eighteenth Century England. New Brunswick: Transaction Books.
Huang, Hua-lun
  1996 "Chinese Secret Societies\Gangs and Transnational Organized Crime: The Triads and
        Chinese Gangs in the Global Enterprise of Human Smuggling", paper presented at the
        Annual Meeting of the American Society of Criminology, Chicago, IL.
Huff, C. Ronald
  1988 "Youth Gangs and Public Policy in Ohio: Findings and Recommendations", paper
        presented at the Ohio Conference on Youth Gangs and the Urban Underclass, Columbus:

Ohio State University.

---- "Youth Gangs and Police Organizations: Rethinking Structure and Functions", paper presented at the Annual Meeting of the Academy of Criminal Justice Sciences, San Francisco.

1989 "Youth Gangs and Public Policy", Crime & Delinquency (35)(4)(Oct.): 524-37.

---- "Gangs, Organized Crime, and Drug-Related Violence in Ohio", In Understanding the Enemy: An Informational Overview of Substance Abuse in Ohio, Columbus, OH: Governor's Office of Criminal Justice Services.

1990 Gangs in America: Diffusion, Diversity, and Public Policy. Newbury Park, CA: Sage Publications.

Hunsaker, A.
1981 "The Behavioral-Ecological Model of Intervention With Chicano Gang Delinquents", Hispanic Journal of Behavioral Sciences (3): 225-239.

Hunt, G.; S. Riegel; T. Morales; and D. Waldorf
1992 "Keep The Peace Out of Prisons: Prison Gangs, an Alternative Perspective". San Francisco, CA: Institute for Scientific Analysis, Home Boy Study.
1993 "Changes in Prison Culture: Prison Gangs and the Case of the Pepsi Generation". San Francisco, CA: Institute for Scientific Analysis, Home Boy Study.

Hunt, Matthew B.
1996 The Sociolinguistics of Tagging and Chicano Gang Graffiti, Ph.D. dissertation, University of Southern California.

Hutchison, Ray
1993 "Blazon Nouveau: Gang Graffiti in the Barrios of Los Angeles and Chicago", in Gangs: The Origins and Impact of Contemporary Youth Gangs in the United States (Scott Cummings and Daniel Monti, Eds.), State University Press of New York: Albany.

Hutson, H. Range; Deidre Anglin; D.N. Kyriancou; Joel Hart; and Kelvin Spears
1995 "The Epidemic of Gang-Related Homicides in Los Angeles County from 1979-1994", Journal of the American Medical Association, 274: 1031-36.

Ianni, Francis A.J.
1974 Black Mafia: Ethnic Succession in Organized Crime. New York: Simon and Schuster.

Illinois Department of Corrections
1984 Gangs and Gang Awareness. Training Academy.
1988 Gangs and Gang Awareness. Training Academy.

Inciardi, James A.
1984 Criminal Justice. Orlando: Academic Press, Inc.

Intl. Assoc. of Chiefs of Police
1986 Organized Motorcycle Gangs, Gaithersburg, MO 20878.

Jackson, George
1970 Soledad Brother: The Prison Letters of George Jackson. New York: Bantam Books.

Jackson, Mary; and Elizabeth Gail Sharpe
1997 "Prison Gang Research: Preliminary Findings in Eastern North Carolina", Journal of Gang Research, Volume 5, Number 1, Fall.

Jackson, Pamela Irving
1991 "Crime, Youth Gangs, and Urban Transition: The Social Dislocations of Postindustrial Economic Development", Justice Quarterly (8)(3): 379-397.

Jackson, Patrick G.
1989 "Theories and Findings About Youth Gangs", Criminal Justice Abstracts (21)(2)(June): 313-329.

Jackson, R.K. and W.D. McBride
1985 Understanding Street Gangs. Sacramento, CA: Custom Publishing.

Jacobs, James
1974 "Street Gangs Behind Bars", Social Problems (21)(3): 395-408.
1977 Stateville. Chicago: University of Chicago Press.

Jah, Yusuf; and Sister Shah'Keyah
1995 Uprising: Crips and Bloods Tell the Story of America's Youth in the Crossfire. New York: Scribner.

James, Don
  1963 <u>Girls and Gangs</u>. Derby, Conn: Monarch.
Jameson, S.H.
  1956 "Policeman's Non-Official Role in Combatting Gangs and Vandalism", <u>Association for Professional Law</u> Enforcement, Quartly Journal (3)(June): 1-3.
Jankowski, Martin Sanchez
  1991 <u>Islands in the Street: Gangs American Urban Society</u>. Berkeley: University of California Press.
Janowitz, Morris
  1970 <u>Political Conflict</u>. Chicago: Quadrangle Books.
Jansyn, Leon
  1960 <u>Solidarity and Delinquency in a Street Corner Group: A Study of the Relationship between Changes in Specified Aspects of Group Structure and Variations in the Frequency of Delinquent Activity</u>, Master's thesis, University of Chicago.
  1967 "Solidarity and Delinquency in a Street Corner Group", <u>American Sociological Review</u> (31): 600-14.
Jayasuriya, J.E. and Sundari Kariyawasam
  1958 "Juvenile Delinquency as a Gang Activity in the City of Colombo", <u>Ceylon Journal of Historical and Social</u> Studies (1)(2)(July): 202-215.
Jensen, Eric L.
  1995 "An Interview with James F. Short, Jr.", <u>Journal of Gang Research</u>, Volume 2, Number 2, Winter.
Jensen, Gary F.
  1996 "Defiance and Gang Identity: Quantitative Tests of Qualitative Hypotheses", <u>Journal of Gang Research</u>, Volume 3, Number 4, Summer.
Jenson, Jeffrey M.; and Matthew O. Howard
  1998 "Correlates of Gang Involvement Among Juvenile Probationers", <u>Journal of Gang Research</u>, Volume 5, Number 2, Winter.
Jereczek, Gordon E.
  1962 "Gangs Need Not Be Delinquent", <u>Federal Probation</u> (26)(Mar): 49-52.
Joe, D. and N. Robinson
  1980 "Chinatown's Immigrant Gangs: The New Young Warrior Class", <u>Criminology</u> (18)(3)(Nov): 337-345.
Joe, Karen
  1980 "Kai-Doi's: Gang Violence in Chinatown". Paper presented at the Annual Conference of the Rho Chapter of the California Alpha Kappa Delta association. Los Angeles, CA: University of California at Los Angeles.
  1993 "Issues in Accessing and Studying Ethnic Youth Gangs", <u>The Gang Journal: An Interdisciplinary Research</u> Quarterly (1)(2): 9-23.
  1995 "Delinquency in Chicago During the Roaring Twenties: Assembling Reality in Ethnography", <u>Journal of Gang Research</u>, Volume 3, Number 1, Fall.
Johnson, Clair; Barbara A. Webster; Edward F. Connors; and Diane J. Saenz
  1995 "Gang Enforcement Problems and Strategies: National Survey Findings", <u>Journal of Gang Research</u>, Volume 3, Number 1, Fall.
Johnson, Gwendolyn
  1949 <u>The Transformation of Juvenile Gangs into Accommodated Groups: A Study of Eight Boys' Gangs in Washington.</u> Master's Thesis, Howard University.
Johnson, Patrick
  1989 "Theories and Findings about Youth Gangs", <u>Criminal Justice Abstracts</u> (June): 313-327.
Johnson, W.C.
  1981 "Motorcycle Gangs and White Collar Crime", <u>The Police Chief</u> (47)(6)(June): 32-33.
Johnstone, John W.C.
  1981 "Youth Gangs and Black Suburbs", <u>Pacific Sociological Review</u> (24)(3)(July): 355-375.
  1983 "Recruitment to a Youth Gang", <u>Pacific Sociological Review</u> (24): 355-375.
Joselit, Jenna Weissman
  1983 <u>Our Gang: Jewish Crime and the New York Jewish Community 1900-1940</u>. Bloomington: Indiana University Press.

Joseph, Janice
      1997 "Black Youth Gangs", <u>Journal of Gang Research,</u> Volume 4, Number 2, Winter.
      1999 "Jamaican Posses and Transnational Crimes", <u>Journal of Gang Research,</u> Volume 6,
            Number 4, Summer.
Juvenile Justice Digest
      1980 "Police Community Relations: Crime Prevention of Gangs", Feb. 22, 1980, pp. 7-8 (8)(4).
Kantor, David and William Ira Bennett
      1968 "Orientation of Street-Corner Workers and Their Effect on Gangs", In Stanton Wheeler
            (ed.), <u>Controlling Delinquents,</u> New York: Wiley.
Kaplan, David E.; and Alec Dubro
      1986 <u>Yakuza: The Explosive Account of Japan's Criminal Underworld.</u> Reading, MA: Addison-
            Wesley.
Karacki, Larry and Jackson Toby
      1962 "The Uncommitted Adolescent: Candidate for Gang Socialization", <u>Sociological Quarterly</u>
            (32)(Spr): 203-215.
Karp, Hal
      1999 "Teen Gangs Invade the Suburbs", <u>Family Circle,</u> 4-20-99: pp. 51-55.
Kasimar, Yale
      1971 "When the Cops Were Not 'Handcuffed'", pp. 46-57 in Donald R. Cressey (ed.), <u>Crime &</u>
            <u>Criminal Justice,</u> Chicago: Quadrangle Books.
Keiser, R. Lincoln
      1969 <u>The Vice Lords: Warriors of the Streets</u>. New York: Holt, Rinehart and Winston.
Kelly, Robert J.; Ko-lin Chin; and Jeffrey Fagan
      1992 "The Structure, Activity, and Control of Chinese Gangs: Law Enforcement Perspectives",
            <u>Journal of Contemporary Criminal Justice</u> (8)(3)(Sept): 256-278.
Kennedy, David M.; Anthony A. Braga; and Anne M. Piehl
      1996 "The (Un)Known Universe: Mapping Gangs and Gang Violence in Boston", forthcoming in
            <u>Crime Mapping and Crime Prevention,</u> (Eds), D. Wisburd and J. Thomas McEwen, New
            York: Criminal Justice Press.
Kinnard, Albert; and Marlon Wilson
      1993 <u>Shorty-Four,</u> Chicago, IL: Self-published 100pp, stapled softcover book.
Kirk-Duggan, Cheryl A.
      1997 "Kindred Spirits: Sister Mimetic Societies and Social Responsibilities", <u>Journal of Gang</u>
            <u>Research,</u> Volume 4, Number 2, Winter.
Kleeck, Mary van; Emma A. Winslow; and Ira De A. Reid
      1931 <u>Work and Law Observance</u>. An Experimental Inquiry into the Influence of Unemployment
            and Occupational Conditions Upon Crime for the National Commission on Law
            Observance and Enforcement, No. 13, June 26, 1931, pp. 163-333.
Klein, Lloyd
      1990 "Running on the 'Wild Side': The Central Park Jogger Case and Adolescent Criminal
            Activity", paper presented at the Annual Meeting of the American Society of
            Criminology, Baltimore, MD.
Klein, Malcolm W.
      1964 "Internal Structures and Age Distribution in Four Delinquent Negro Gangs", Youth
            Studies Center (Dec.), Los Angeles: University of Southern California.
      1965 "Juvenile Gangs, Police, and Detached Workers: Controversies About Intervention",
            <u>Social Service Review</u> (39): 183-190.
      1966 "Factors Related to Juvenile Gang Membership Patterns", <u>Sociology and Social Research</u>
            (51): 49-62.
      1967 <u>Juvenile Gangs in Context</u>. New Jersey: Prentice-Hall.
      1968a "Impressions of Juvenile Gang Members", <u>Adolescence</u> (3)(59): 53-78.
      1968b From Association to Guilt: The Group Guidance Project in Juvenile Gang Intervention.
            Los Angeles: Youth Studies Center.
      1968c The Ladino Hill Project. Los Angeles: Youth Studies Center.
      1969a "Violence in American Juvenile Gangs", in D. Mulvihill and M. Tumin (eds.), <u>Crimes of</u>
            <u>Violence,</u> National Commission on the Causes and Prevention of Violence, Vol. 13: 1427-
            1460.

1969b "On the Group Context of Delinquency", <u>Sociology and Social Research</u> (54): 63-71.
1969c "Gang Cohesiveness, Delinquency, and a Street-Work Program", <u>Journal of Research in Crime and Delinquency</u> (July).
1971 <u>Street Gangs and Street Workers</u>. Englewood Cliffs, NJ: Prentice-Hall.
1990 "Having an Investment in Violence: Some Thoughts About the American Street Gang", The Edwin H. Sutherland Award Address to the American Society of Criminology, Annual Meeting, November 9, 1990.
Klein, Malcolm W. and Lois Y. Crawford
1967 "Groups, Gangs, and Cohesiveness", <u>Journal of Research in Crime and Delinquency</u> (4): 63-75.
Klein, Malcolm W.; Cheryl Maxson, and Margaret A. Gordon
1985 "Differences Between Gang and Non-Gang Homicides", <u>Criminology</u> (23)(2): 209-20.
1986 "The Impact of Police Investigations on Police-Reported Rates of Gang and Nongang Homicides", <u>Criminology</u> (24): 489-512.
Klein, Malcolm W.; and Cheryl L. Maxson
1985 "Rock' Sales in South L.A.", <u>Social Science Research</u> (69): 561-565.
1989 "Street Gang Violence", In Marvin E. Wolfgang and Neil A. Weiner (eds.), <u>Violent Crime, Violent Criminals</u>, Newbury Park, CA: Sage Publications.
Klein, Malcolm W.; Cheryl Maxson; and Lea Cunningham
1990 "'Crack,' Street Gangs, and Violence", Center For Research on Crime and Social Control, University of Southern California.
Klein, Malcolm W.; Cheryl Maxson; and Jody Miller
1995 <u>The Modern Gang Reader</u>. Los Angeles, CA: Roxbury Publishing Company.
Klein, Malcolm W. and Barbara G. Meyerhoff (eds)
1964 <u>Juvenile Gangs in Context: Theory, Research, and Action</u>, Conference Report, August 25-26, 1963, Youth Studies Center, Los Angeles: University of Southern California.
Klein, Malcolm W. and Neal Snyder
1965 "The Detached Worker: Uniformities and Variances in Style", <u>Social Work</u> (10)(Oct): 60-68.
Klofas, John; Stan Stojkovic and David Kalinich
1990 <u>Criminal Justice Organizations: Administration and Management</u>. Belmont, CA: Brooks/ Cole Publishing Company.
Knox, George W.
1976 <u>The Urban Crisis in Southwest Chicago: A Research-Based Discussion of Racial Conflict</u>, (Dec., 1976), unpublished monograph.
1978 "Perceived Closure and Respect for the Law Among Delinquent and Non-Delinquent Youths", <u>Youth and Society</u> (9)(4)(June): 385-406.
1978 "Determinants of Employment Success Among Exoffenders", <u>Offender Rehabiliation</u> (2)(3)(Spr): 204-214.
1980 "Educational Upgrading for Youthful Offenders", <u>Chidren and Youth Services Review</u> (2)(3): 291-313.
1981 "Differential Integration and Job Retention Among Exoffenders", <u>Criminology</u> (18)(4)(Feb): 481-499.
1981 "A Comparative Cost-Benefit Analysis of Offender Placement Programs", <u>LAE Journal of the American Criminal Justice Association</u> (43)(1,2): 39-49.
1984 "How Criminologists View Rehabilitation", <u>Indian Journal of Criminology</u> (12)(1)(Jan): 26-32.
1989 "Family Services in Corrections", <u>The State of Corrections</u>, Proceedings of the Annual Conferences of The American Correctional Association, pp. 179-182.
1991 <u>An Introduction to Gangs</u>. Berrien Springs, MI: Vande Vere Publishing, Ltd., First Edition.
1991 "Gangs and Social Justice Issues", chapter 1 (pp. 1-19), in Sloan T. Letman (Ed.), <u>Prison Conditions and Prison Overcrowding</u>, Dubuque, IA: Kendall/Hunt Publishing Company.
1992 "Gang Organization in a Large Urban Jail", <u>AmericanJails</u>.
1994 <u>An Introduction to Gangs</u>, 2nd edition, Vande Vere Pubishing, Berrien Springs, MI.
1995 "Findings on African-American Female Gang Members Using a Matched Pair Design", <u>Journal of Gang Research</u>, Volume 2, Number 3, Spring.
1995 <u>An Introduction to Gangs</u>, 3rd Edition, Wyndham Hall Press, Bristol, Indiana.

1996 "Gang Profile: The Black Gangsters, AKA 'New Breed'", Journal of Gang Research, Volume 3, Number 2, Winter.

1996 "Gang Profile: The Black Disciples", Journal of Gang Research, Volume 3, Number 3, Spring.

1996 "Gang Profile: The Black P. Stone Nation", Journal of Gang Research, Volume 3, Number 4, Summer.

1996 "Gang Profile: The Latin Kings", Journal of Gang Research, Volume 4, Number 1, Fall.

1997 "Crips: A Gang Profile Analysis", Journal of Gang Research, Volume 4, Number 3, Spring.

1997 "Special Report: The Gang Problem in Chicago's Public Housing", Journal of Gang Research, Volume 4, Number 4, Summer.

1997 "The 'Get Out of the Gang Thermometer': An Application to a Large National Sample of African-American Male Youths", Journal of Gang Research, Volume 5, Number 1, Fall.

1997 "An Update on the Chicago Latin Kings", Journal of Gang Research, Volume 5, Number 1, Fall.

1998 An Introduction to Gangs, 4th Edition, New Chicago School Press, Inc, Peotone, IL.

1998 "Research Note: A Comparison of Two Gangs - The Gangster Disciples and the Vice Lords", Journal of Gang Research, Volume 5, Number 2, Winter.

1998 "Special Report: How to Gang Proof Your Child", Journal of Gang Research, Volume 5, Number 4, Summer.

1999 "The Promulgation of Gang-Banging Through the Mass Media", Journal of Gang Research, Volume 6, Number 2, Winter.

1999 "A Comparison of Cults and Gangs: Dimensions of Coercive Power nd Malevolent Authority", Journal of Gang Research, Volume 6, Number 4, Summer.

Knox, George W.; Benito Garcia; and Pat Mc Clendon
1983 "Social and Behavioral Correlates of Gang Affiliation", paper presented at the Annual Meeting of the American Society of Criminology, Nov. 10, 1983, Denver, CO.

Knox, George W.; and Curtis J. Robinson
1999 "Trying to Live Gang-Free in Cicero, Illinois", Journal of Gang Research, Volume 6, Number 4, Summer.

Knox, George W.; Edward D. Tromanhauser; and David Laske
1992 Schools Under Siege. Dubuque, IA: Kendall/Hunt Publishing Company.

Knox, George W.; Edward Tromanhauser; and Thomas F. Mc Currie
1991 "Gangs in Juvenile Corrections: Training Issues", Journal of Correctional Training .

Knox, George W.; and Edward Tromanhauser
1991 "Gangs and Their Control in Adult Correctional Institutions", The Prison Journal (LXXI)(2)(Fall-Winter): 15-22.

1991 "Gang Members as a Distinct Health Risk Group in Juvenile Correctional Facilities", The Prison Journal (LXXI)(2)(Fall-Winter): 61-66.

1992 "Comparing Juvenile Correctional Facilities: A Brief Overview", Journal of Juvenile Justice and Detention Services (7)(1)(Spr): 7-13.

1993 "Gang Training in Adult Correctional Institutions: A Function of Intensity, Duration and Impact of the Gang Problem", Journal of Correctional Training.

1999 "Research Note: Juvenile Gang Members - A Public Health Perspective", Journal of Gang Research, Volume 6, Number 3, Spring.

Knox, George W.; Edward D. Tromanhauser; Pamela Irving Jackson; Darek Niklas; James G. Houston; Paul Koch; and James R. Sutton
1993 "Preliminary Findings from the 1992 Law Enforcement Mail Questionnaire Project", Gang Journal: An Interdisciplinary Research Quarterly (1)(3): 11-27.

Knox, Mike
1995 Gangsta in the House: Understanding Gang Culture, Troy, MI: Momentum Books, Ltd.

Kobrin, Solomon
1959 "The Chicago Area Project - a Twenty-five Year Assessment", Annals of the American Academy of Political and Social Science (322): 19-29.

1961 "Sociological Aspects of the Development of a Street Corner Group: An Exploratory Study", Amerian Journal of Orthopsychiatry (31)(4): 685-702.

1964 "Legal and Ethical Problems of Street Gang Work", Crime and Delinquency (10)(2): 152-156.

Kobrin, Solomon and Malcolm W. Klein
    1983 Community Treatment of Juvenile Offenders: The DSO Experiments. Beverly Hills, CA:
        Sage Publications.
Kobrin, S.; J. Puntil; and E. Peluso
    1967 "Criteria of Status Among Street Groups", Journal of Research in Crime and Delinquency
        (4)(Jan): 98-119.
Kolender, W.B.
    1982 Street Gangs (Revised). In-service Training. San Diego Police Department, Training
        Section.
Kornblum, William
    1974 Blue Collar Community. Chicago: University of Chicago Press.
    1987 "Ganging Together: Helping Gangs Go Straight", Social Issues and Health Review (2): 99-
        104.
Kornhauser, Ruth R.
    1978 Social Sources of Delinquency. Chicago: University of Chicago Press.
Kotlowitz, Alex
    1991 There Are No Children Here. New York: Doubleday.
    1992 There Are No Children Here. New York: Anchor Books.
Krajick, K.
    1990 "The Menace of Supergangs", Corrections Magazine (June): 11-14.
Kramer, Dale and Madeline Karr
    1953 Teenage Gangs. Henry Holt and Co., Inc.

Krech, David; Richard S. Crutchfield; and Egerton L. Ballachey
    1962 Individual in Society: A Textbook of Social Psychology New York: McGraw-Hill Book
        Company, Inc.
Krisberg, Barry
    1971 Urban Leadership Training: An Ethnographic Study of 22 Gang Leaders. Ph.D. disserta-
        tion, University of Pennsylvania, Philadelphia.
    1974 "Gang Youth and Hustling: The Psychology of Survival", Issues in Criminology
        (9)(1)(Spr): 115-131.
    1975 The Gang and the Community. School of Criminology, University of California, Berkeley.
        San Franciso, CA: R and E Research Associates.
Lagree, J. and P.L. Fai
    1989 "Girls in Street Gangs in the Suburbs of Paris" (from Growing up Good: Policing the
        Behavior of Girls in Europe, pp. 80-95, Maureen Cain, editor), Newbury Park, CA: Sage
        Publications.
Laidler, Karen A. Joe and Geoffrey Hunt
    1997 "Violence and Social Organization in Female Gangs", unpublished paper.
Landesco, John
    1929 Organized Crime in Chicago. Part III of the Illinois Crime Survey. Illinois Association for
        Criminal Justice, 300 West Adams Street, Chicago, IL. In Cooperation with the Chicago
        Crime Commission.
Lane, Michael
    1989 "Inmate Gangs", Corrections Today (51)(4)(July): 98-99, 126-128.
Langston, Michael
    1998 "Views from the Field: Guidelines for Operating an Effective Gang Unit", Journal of Gang
        Research, Volume 5, Number 4, Summer.
Laskey, John A.
    1996 "Gang Migration: The Familial Gang Transplant Phenomenon", Journal of Gang Research,
        Volume 5, Number 2, Winter.
    1997 "The Gang Snitch Profile", Journal of Gang Research, Volume 4, Number 3, Spring.
Lauderback, David; Joy Hansen; and Dan Waldorf
    1992 "Sisters are Doin' It For Themselves: A Black Female Gang in San Francisco",
        The Gang Journal: An Interdisciplinary Research Quarterly (1)(1): 57-72.
Lavgine, Yves
    1987 Hell's Angels: Taking Care of Business. Toronto: Deneaua and Wayne.

1996 Hell's Angels, Toronto: Deneaua and Wayne.
Law and Order
1977 "Gangs: Police Community Relations", (25)(12): 20-23.
Le Blanc, Marc; and Nadine Lanctot
1998 "Social and Psychological Characteristics of Gang Members", Journal of Gang Research, Volume 5, Number 3, Spring.
Leissner, Aryeh
1969 Street Club Work in Tel Aviv and New York. London: Longmans, Green and Co., Ltd.
Lerman, P.
1967 "Gangs, Networks, and Subcultural Delinquency", American Journal of Sociology (73): 63-72.
Liang, Bin
1997 Chinese Tongs and Gangs in America, Master's thesis, Arizona State University.
Liebow, Elliot
1967 Tally's Corner: Study of Negro Street Corner Men. Boston: Little, Brown and Co.
Little, Bertis B.; Jose Gonzalez; Laura Snell; and Christian Molidor
1999 "Risk Behaviors for Sexually Transmitted Diseases Among Gangs in Dallas, Texas", Journal of Gang Research, Volume 6, Number 3, Spring.
Loo, C.K.
1976 The Emergence of San Francisco Chinese Juvenile Gangs from the 1950s to the Present, unpublished Master's thesis, San Jose State University.
Los Angeles County Probation Department and Youth Studies Center
1962 Progress Report, Study of Delinquent Gangs, July 1, 1961 - June 30, 1962. Los Angles and University of Southern California.
1963 Second Annual Progress Report: Study of Delinquent Gangs, July 1, 1962 - June 30, 1963. Los Angeles and University of Southern California.
1964 Third Annual Progress Report: Study of Delinquent Gangs, July 1, 1963 - June 30, 1964. Los Angeles and University of Southern California.
Lotter, J.M.
1988 "Prison Gangs in South Africa: A Description", The South African Journal of Sociology (19)(2)(May): 67-75.
Lowney, Jeremiah
1984 "The Wall Gang: A Study of Interpersonal Process and Deviance Among Twenty-Three Middle-Class Youths", Adolescence (19)(75)(Fall): 527-538.
Lyman, Michael D.
1989 Gangland: Drug Trafficking by Organized Criminals, Springfield, IL: Charles C. Thomas.
Madden, Max
1993 The NACGI Journal. Various Copyrighted Materials.
Majors, Richard and Janet Mancini Billson
1992 Cool Pose: The Dilemmas of Black Manhood in America. New York: Lexington Books.
Malcolm, Dino.
1981 "D To the Knee! Stone To the Bone!", Best of Hair Trigger: A Story Workshop Anthology, pp. 81-91, Chicago: Columbia College Writing Department.
Martin, Richard H.
1993 "Gang Colors: Should Students Be Allowed to Wear Them in College?", The Gang Journal: An Interdisciplinary Research Quarterly (1)(2): 69. 69.
Matthews, Mark
1997 "Train Tramps Ride Rails of Crime Across United States", Police magazine, November, 1997, pp. 14-18.
Mattick, Hans W. and Nathan S. Caplan
1962 Chicago Youth Development Project: Street Work, Community Organization and Research, April, University of Michigan Institute for Social Research, Ann Arbor, Michigan.
1964 The Chicago Youth Development Project, February, University of Michigan Institute for Social Research, Ann Arbor, Michigan.
Maxson, C.L.; M.A. Gordon; and Malcolm W. Klein
1985 "Differences Between Gang and Nongang Homicides", Criminology (23): 209-222.

Maxson, Cheryl L. and Malcolm W. Klein
   1983 "Agency versus Agency: Disputes in the Gang Deterence Model", in James R. Kluegel
      (ed.), Evaluating Contemporary Juvenile Justice, Beverly Hills: Sage.
   1986 "Street Gangs Selling Cocaine "rock": The Confluence of Two Social Problems", Social
      Science Research Center, University of Southern California.
   1989 "Street Gang Violence: Twice as Great, or Half as Great?", paper presented at the annual
      meeting of the American Society of Criminology, Reno, Nevada, November.
   1995 "Investigating Gang Structures", Journal of Gang Research, Volume 3, Number 1, Fall.
Maxson, Cheryl L.
   1983 "Gangs: Why We Couldn't Stay Away", in James R. Kluegel (ed.), Evaluating Contempo-
      rary Juvenile Justice, Beverly Hills: Sage.
   1993 "Investigating Gang Migration: Contextual Issues for Intervention", The Gang Journal: An
      Interdisciplinary Research Quarterly (1)(2): 1-8.
Maxson, Cheryl L.; Monica L. Whitlock; and Malcolm W. Klein
   1998 "Vulnerability to Street Gang Membership: Implications for Practice", Social Service
      Review (March) pp. 70-91.
May, Melvyn
   1999 "Views from the Field: The Impact of Gangs on Private Security in the Workplace", Journal
      of Gang Research, Volume 6, Number 4, Summer.
Mazon, M.
   1985 The Zoot-suit Riots: The Psychology of Symbolic Annihilation, Austin: University of
      Texas Press.
McCaddon, Jeff
   1993 "Jakes: Jamaican Posses, The Most Violent Crime Groups Operating in North America!",
      P.B.S.P, February.
Mc Carthy, J.E. and J.S. Barbaro
   1952 "Redirecting Teenage Gangs", in S.S. Furman (ed.), New York City Youth Board.
Mc Connell, Elizabeth H.
   1990 "Assessing Youth Gangs in an Urban High School", paper presented at the Annual Meeting
      of the American Society of Criminology, Baltimore, MD.
   1994 "Youth Gang Intervention and Prevention in Texas: Evaluating Community Mobilization
      Training", Journal of Gang Research (2)(1)(Fall): 63-71.
Mc Currie, Thomas F.
   1998 "Special Report: White Racist Extremist Gang Members - A Behavioral Profile", Journal of
      Gang Research, Volume 5, Number 2, Winter.
   1999 "Research Note: Asian Gangs", Journal of Gang Research, Volume 6, Number 2, Winter.
Mc Guire, P.
   1986 "Outlaw Motorcycle Gangs - Organized Crime on Wheels", National Sheriff (37)(2)(Apr-
      May): 68-75.
   1988 "Jamaican Posses: A Call for Cooperation Among Law Enforcement Agencies", The Police
      Chief (55)(1): 20-25.
Mc Kay, Henry D.
   1949 "The Neighborhood and Child Conduct", Annals of the American Academy of Political and
      Social Science (Jan): 32-41.
Mc Kinney, K.C.
   1988 Juvenile Gangs: Crime and Drug Trafficking, U.S. Dept. of Justice, Office of Juvenile
      Justice and Delinquency Prevention, Washington, D.C.
   1988 "Juvenile Gangs: Crime and Drug Trafficking", Juvenile Justice Bulletin, 2-7.
Mc Lean, Gordon
   1991 Cities of Lonesome Fear: God Among the Gangs. Chicago: Moody Press.
   1998 Too Young to Die: Bringing Hope to Gangs in the Hood, with Dave and Neta Jackson,
Wheaton, IL: Tyndale House Publishers.
   1999 "Views from the Field", Journal of Gang Research, Volume 7, Number 1, Fall: 72-75.
Mc Pherson, James Alan
   1966 "The Blackstone Rangers", The Atlantic (223)(5)(May).
Mendenhall, Barbara; and Troy Armstrong
   1997 "Finding and Knowing the Gang Nayee: Navajo Nation Youth Gangs and Public Housing",

paper presented at the Annual Meeting of the American Society of Criminology, San Diego, CA.

Meyerhoff, Howard L. and Barbara G. Meyerhoff
1964 "Field Observations of Middle Class Gangs", Social Forces (42): 328-336.

Mieczkowski, Thomas
1986 "Geeking Up and Throwing Down: Heroin Street Life in Detroit", Criminology (24): 645-666.

Miethe, Terance D. and Richard C. McCorkle
1997 "Gang Membership and Criminal Processing: A Test of the 'Master Status' Concept", Justice Quarterly (14)(3): 407-427.

Miller, J. Mitchell; William J. Ruefle; and Richard A. Wright
1997 "Ideology and Gang Policy: Beyond the False Dichotomy", Journal of Gang Research, Volume 5, Number 1, Fall.

Miller, J. Mitchell; and Jeffrey P. Rush (Eds)
1996 Gangs: A Criminal Justice Approach, ACJS Monograph Series, Anderson Publishing Company.

Miller, Jody
1996 "Gender and Victimization Risk among Young Women in Gangs", presentation at the Annual Meeting of the American Society of Criminology, Chicago.

Miller, Walter B.
1957 "The Impact of a Community Group Work Program on Delinquent Corner Groups", Social Service Review (31): 396-406.
1958 "Lower Class Culture as a Generating Milieu of Gang Delinquency", Journal of Social Issues (14)(3): 9.
1962 "The Impact of a 'Total Community' Delinquency Control Project", Social Problems (10)(Fall): 168-91.
1963 "The Corner Gang Boys Get Married", Transaction (1): 10-12.
1966 "Violent Crimes by City Gangs", Annals of the American Academy of Political and Social Sciences (364): 219-230.
1969 "White Gangs", Transaction (6)(1).
1976 Violence by Youth Gangs and Youth Groups as a Crime Problem in Major American Cities. Washington, D.C.: U.S. Government Printing Office.
1980 "Gangs, Groups and Serious Youth Crime", In D. Schichor and D. Kelly (eds.), Critical Issues in Juvenile Delinquency, Lexington, MA: Lexington.
1981 "American Youth Gangs: Past and Present", Current Perspectives on Criminal Behavior: Original Essays on Criminology, 2nd edition, edited by Abraham S. Blumberg, New York: Knopf (also 1974).
1982 Crime by Youth Gangs and Youth Groups in the United States, report prepared for the National Youth Gang Survey, Washington, DC: Office of Juvenile Justice and Delinquency Prevention.
1983 "Youth Gangs and Groups", In Sanford H. Kadish (ed.), Encyclopedia of Crime and Justice. New York: Free Press.
1985 "Historical Review of Programs and Theories of Work With Youth Gangs: 1920-1985", in D. Ingemunsen and G. Johnson, Report on the Illinois Symposium on Gangs, Springfield, IL: Illinois Department of Children and Family Services.
1989 "Recommendations for Terms to Be Used for Designating Law Violating Youth Groups", paper presented at the Conference of the National Youth Gang Suppression and Intervention Project, Chicago.

Miller, Walter B.; Hildred Geertz; and Henry S.G. Cutter
1961 "Aggression in a Boys' Street-Corner Group", Psychiatry (24)(4): 283-298.

Milner, John G.
1959 "Working With Juvenile Gang Members", California Youth Authority, Quarterly (12)(Spr): 3-7.

Mitchell, R.
1951 "Capturing Boys Gangs", Human Organization (Summer).

Molland, John, Jr.
1967 Cross Pressures: A Study of the Reconciliation by the Gang Boys of Perceived

Expectations of Others, Ph.D. dissertation, University of Chicago.
Moore, Jack B.
1993 Skinheads Shaved For Battle: A Cultural History of American Skinheads. Bowling Green, OH: Bowling Green State University Popular Press.
Moore, Joan W.
1977 "The Chicano Pinto Research Project: A Case Study in Collaboration", Journal of Social Issues (33)(4): 144-158.
1978 Homeboys: Gangs, Drugs, and Prison in the Barrios of Los Angeles, Philadelphia: Temple University Press.
1983 "Residence and Territoriality in Chicano Gangs", Social Problems (31): 182-194.
1985 "Isolation and Stigmatization in the Development of the Underclass: The Case of the Chicano Gangs in East Los Angeles", Social Problems (33)(1)(Oct): 1-12.
1988 "Changing Chicano Gangs: Acculturation, Generational Change, Evolution of Deviance or Emerging Underclass?", In J.H. Johnson, Jr. and M.L. Oliver (eds.), Proceedings of the Conference on Comparative Ethnicity, Los Angeles: Institute for Social Science Research, UCLA.
1989 "Is There a Hispanic Underclass?", Social Science Quarterly (70)(2): 265-285.
1989 "Gangs, Drugs, and Violence", in M. de la Rosea, B. Gropper, and E. Lambert (eds.), Drugs and Violence National Institute of Drug Abuse Research Monograph, Rockville, MD: U.S. Department of Health and Human Services.
1989 "Gangs and Gang Violence: What We Know and What We Don't Know", paper presented at the California State University, Los Angeles, CA.
1991 Going Down to the Barrio: Homeboys and Homegirls in Change. Philadelpha, PA: Temple University Press.
Moore, Joan and Mary Devitt
1989 "The Paradox of Deviance in Addicted Mexican American Mothers", Gender & Society (3)(1)(Mar): 53-70.
Moore, Joan; J. Diego Vigil; and Robert Garcia
1983 "Residence and Territoriality in Chicano Gangs", Social Problems (31): 182-194.
Moore, Joan W. and J.D. Vigil
1987 "Chicano Gangs: Group Norms and Individual Factors Related to Adult Criminality", Aztlan (18)(2)(Fall): 27-44.
Moore, Mark and Mark A. R. Kleiman
1989 The Police and Drugs. Washington, D.C.: National Institute of Justice.
Moore, Winston; Charles P. Livermore, and George F. Galland, Jr.
1973 "Woodlawn: The Zone of Destruction", The Public Interest (30)(Winter): 41-59.
Morales, Armando
1963 "A Study of Recidivism of Mexican-American Junior Forestry Camp Graduates", Master's Thesis, Social Work, University of Southern California.
1982 "The Mexican American Gang Member: Evaluation and Treatment", in Mental Health and Hispanic Americans by Rosina M. Becerra, Marvin Karno, and Javier I. Escobar (eds.), New York: Grune and Stratton.
1989 "A Clinical Model for the Prevention of Gang Violence and Homicide", In A. Morales and B.W. Sheafor, Social Work: A Profession of Many Faces, Boston: Allyn and Bacon.
Morash, Merry
1983 "Gangs, Groups and Delinquency", British Journal of Criminology (23): 309-331.
1990 "Gangs and Violence", in A.J. Reiss, Jr..; N. Weiner; and J. Roth (eds.), Violent Criminal Behavior, Report of the Panel on the Understanding and Control of Violent Behavior, National Academy of Sciences, Washington, DC: National Academy Press.
Morici, J. and D. Flanders
1979 "Chinatown Youth Gangs - Past, Present and Future." California Youth Authority Quarterly (32): 19-24.
Mottel, Syeus
1973 CHARAS: The Improbable Dome Builders. New York: Drake Publlishers, Inc.
Muehlbauer, Gene and Laura Dodder
1983 The Losers: Gang Delinquency in an American Suburb. New York: Praeger Publishers.

Mundel, Jerome J.
    1962 <u>Differential Perception of Gangs.</u> Master's Thesis, Social Work, University of Southern
        California.
Murphy, Suzanne
    1978 "A Year with the gangs of East Los Angeles", <u>Ms.</u> (July): 55-64.
Nash, Steven G.
    1984 <u>Gang Crimes Study Commission.</u> State of Illinois. Legislative Council Service Unit Order
        841246 (May).
National Council of Juvenile and Family Court Judges
    1988 "Youth Gangs - A Special Problem", <u>Juvenile &</u> <u>Family Court Journal</u> (39)(4): 47-51.
National School Safety Center
    1988 <u>Gangs in Schools: Breaking Up is Hard to Do.</u> Malibu,CA: Pepperdine University Press.
National Youth Gang Suppression and Intervention Program
    1989 <u>Report of the Law Enforcement Youth Symposium.</u>
    1990 <u>Literature Review: Youth Gangs: Problem and Response.</u> University of Chicago, School of
        Social Service Administration, Chicago, IL.
    1990 <u>Survey of Youth Gang Problems and Programs in 45 Cities and 6 Sites.</u>
    1990 <u>Community and Institutional Reponses to the Youth Gang Problem.</u>
    1990 <u>Law Enforcement Definitional Conference - Transcript.</u>
    1990 <u>The Youth Gang Problem: Perceptions of Former Youth Gang Influentials. Transcripts of</u>
        <u>Two Symposia.</u>
    n.d. <u>Preventing Involvement in Youth Gang Crime.</u>
Needle, Jerome A. and William Vaughan Stapleton
    1983 <u>Police Handling of Youth Gangs.</u> Washington, D.C.: American Justice Institute.
Neely, David E.
    1997 "The Social Reality of Street Gangs", <u>Journal of Gang Research,</u> Volume 4, Number 2,
        Winter.
Negola, Todd D.
    1998 "Development of an Instrument for Predicting At-Risk Potential for Adolescent Street
        Gang Membership", <u>Journal of Gang Research,</u> Volume 5, Number 4, Summer.
Neisser, Edith G. and Nina Ridenour
    1960 <u>Your Children and Their Gangs.</u> U.S. Children's Bureau. Publication No. 384. Washington,
        D.C.
New York City Youth Board
    1960 <u>Reaching the Fighting Gang.</u> New York.
Nieburg, H.L.
    1970 <u>Political Violence: The Behavioral Process.</u> New York: St. Martin's Press.
North, Paul
    1997 "Gang Behavior Within The Community", unpublished paper.
Oehme, Chester G. III
    1997 <u>Gangs, Groups and Crime: Perceptions and Responses of Community Organizations.</u>
        Durham, NC: Carolina Academic Press.
Oetting, E.R. and Fred Beauvais
    1987 "Common Elements in Youth Drug Abuse: Peer Clusters and Other Psychosocial Factors",
        <u>Journal of Drug Issues</u> (17)(1-2)(Win-Spr): 133-151.
O'Hagan, F.J.
    1976 "Gang Characteristics: An Empirical Survey", <u>Journal of Child Psychology and Psychiatry</u>
        (17): 305-314.
Oleson, Jim
    1988 <u>Treating Street Youth: Some Observations.</u> Community Research Associates, 115 N. Neil
        Street, Suite 302, Champaign, IL 61820.
Olivero, J. Michael
    1991 <u>Honor, Gangs, Violence, Religion and Upward Mobility: A Case Study of Chicago Street</u>
        <u>Gangs During the 1970s and 1980s.</u> Edinburg, TX: The UT-Pan American Presss.
Ontario Police Department
    1989 "Gangs, Move 'Em Out of Your Life", (video). Ontario, CA 91761.

Oppenheimer, Martin
  1969 The Urban Guerrilla. Chicago: Quadrangle Books.
Orlandella, Angelo Ralph
  1995 "A More Effective Strategy for Dealing With Inner City Street Corner Gangs", Journal of
        Gang Research, Volume 2, Number 2, WInter.
Padilla, Felix
  1992 The Gang as an American Enterprise. New Brunswick, NJ: Rutgers University Press.
Padilla, Felix and Lourdes Santiago
  1993 Outside the Wall: A Puerto Rican Woman's Struggle. New Brunswick, NJ: Rutgers
        University Press.
Palacios, Wilson R.
  1996 "Side by Side: An Ethnographic Study of a Miami Gang", Journal of Gang Research,
        Volume 4, Number 1, Fall.
Palumbo, Dennis; Robert Eskay; and Michael Hallett
  1994 "Do Gang Prevention Strategies Actually Reduce Crime?", Journal of Gang Research,
        Volume 1, Number 4.
Papachristos, Andrew V.
  1998 "The Death of Telemachus: Street Gangs and the Decline of Modern Rites of Passage",
        Journal of Gang Research, Volume 5, Number 4, Summer.
Paramount Plan
  1988 The Paramount Plan: Alternatives to Gang Membership. City of Paramount, California.
Parra, Fernando
  1997 "Views from the Field: A Street Gang in Fact", Journal of Gang Research, Volume 4,
        Number 3, Spring.
Parrot, Philippe and Monique Gueneau
  1961 "Gangs of Adolescents: The History of Such a Gang", Excerpta Criminologica (1): 397-
        399.
Patrick, James
  1973 A Glasgow Gang Observed. Trowbridge, Wiltshire: Redwood Press Ltd., Great Britain.
Pennell, Susan and Christine Curtis
  1982 Juvenile Violence and Gang-Related Crime. San Diego: San Diego Association of
        Governments.
Perkins, Useni Eugene
  1987 Explosion of Chicago's Black Street Gangs. Chicago: Third World Press.
Perry, Anthony
  1995 Original Gang Truce. Beverly Hills: Ant Valley Book Productions.
Pfautz, Harold W.
  1961 "Near-Group Theory and Collective Behavior: A Critical Reformulation", Social Problems
        (9)(2): 167-174.
Phelps, Roy David
  1988 The History of the Eastside Dudes, a Black Social Club in Central Harlem, New York City,
        1933-1985: An Exploration of Background Factors Related to Adult Criminality. Ph.D.
        dissertation, Fordham University, Bronx, New York.
Philobosian, R.H.
  1986 State Task Force on Youth Gang Violence. Sacramento, CA: California Council in Criminal
        Justice.
Pleister, Margaret A.
  1963 An Exploratory Study of Factors Influencing Nine Adolescent Girls in their Movement To
        and From Both School and the Gang, Master's thesis, Social Work, University of
        Southern California.
Poirier, Mike
  1982 Street Gangs of Los Angeles County. Los Angeles: Self-published, P.O. Box 60481, Los
        Angeles, CA 90060.
Police Chief, The
  1979 "Gangs, Violence, Vandalism: Citizen Involvement in Crime Prevention", (46)(7): 54-55.
Pope, Whitney
  1962 Detached Workers, Delinquent Boys and the Theory of Exchange, Master's Thesis,

University of Chicago.

Porter, Bruce
    1982 "California Prison Gangs: The Price of Control", <u>Corrections Magazine</u> (8)(6)(Dec): 6, 19.

Poston, Richard W.
    1971 <u>The Gang and the Establishment</u>. New York: Harper & Row Publishers.

President's Commission on Organized Crime
    1986 <u>The Impact: Organized Crime Today.</u>

Propper, Leonard M.
    1957 "Juvenile Delinquency and the Gang Problem", <u>Juvenile Court Judges Journal</u> (8)(Mar): 24-28.

Puffer, J. Adams
    1912 <u>The Boy and His Gang</u>. Boston: Houghton, Mifflin Co.

Quicker, John C.
    1974 "The Chicana Gang: A Preliminary Description", paper presented at the Pacific Sociological Association meeting.
    1983 <u>Homegirls: Characterizing Chicana Gangs.</u> San Pedro, California: International Universities Press.
    1983 <u>Seven Decades of Gangs: What has been done, and what should be done</u>. Sacramento, CA: State of California Commission on Crime Control and Violence Prevention.

Quicker, John C.; and Akil Batani-Khalfani
    1998 "From Boozies to Bloods: Early Gangs in Los Angeles", <u>Journal of Gang Research</u>, Volume 5, Number 4, Summer.

Quinn, James F. and Bill Downs
    1993 "Predictors of the Severity of the Gang Problem at the Local Level: An Analysis of Police Perceptions", <u>Gang Journal: An Interdisciplinary Research Quarterly</u>, (1)(3): 1-10.
    1993 "Non-Criminal Predictors of Gang Violence: An Analysis of Police Perceptions", <u>Gang Journal: An Interdisciplinary Research Quarterly</u> (1)(3): 29-38.
    1995 "Predictors of Gang Violence: The Impact of Drugs and Guns on Police Perceptions in Nine States", <u>Journal of Gang Research</u>, Volume 2, Number 3, Spring.

Quinn, James F.; Peggy M. Tobolowsky; and William T. Downs
    1995 "The Gang Problem in Large and Small Cities: An Analysis of Police Perceptions in Nine States", <u>Journal of Gang Research</u>, Volume 2, Number 2, Winter.

Rafferty, Frank T. and Harvey Bertcher
    1962 "Gang Formation in Vitro", <u>American Journal of Orthopsychiatry</u> (32)(Mar): 329-330.

Ralph, Paige H; James W. Marquart; and Ben M. Crouch
    1990 "Prisoner Gangs in Texas", paper presented at the 1990 Annual Meeting of the American Society of Criminology, Baltimore, MD.

Ranker, Jess E., Jr.
    1958 <u>A Study of Juvenile Gangs in the Hollenbeck Area of Los Angeles</u>, Master's thesis, University of Southern California, Dept. of Sociology.

Reckless, Walter
    1969 <u>Vice in Chicago</u>. New Jersey: Patterson-Smith.

Redl, Fritz
    1954 "The Psychology of Gang Formation and the Treatment of Juvenile Delinquency", pp. 367-377 in <u>The Psycho-Analytic Study of the Child</u>, Vol. 1, New York: International Universities Press.

Rees, Thomas A.
    1996 "Joining the Gang: A Look at Youth Gang Recruitment", <u>Journal of Gang Research</u>, Volume 4, Number 1, Fall.

Regulus, Thomas A.
    1994 "The Effects of Gangs on Student Performance and Delinquency in Public Schools", <u>Journal of Gang Research</u> (2)(1)(Fall): 1-13.

Reuter, P.
    1989 <u>Youth Gangs and Drug Distribution: A Preliminary Enquiry</u>. RAND Corporation, Paper prepared for the U.S. Office of Juvenile Justice and Delinquency Prevention, Washington, DC.

Ribisl, Kurt M. and William S. Davidson, II
 1993 "Community Change Interventions", Chapter 11 (pp. 333-355) in Arnold P. Goldstein and
  C. Ronald Huff (Eds.), The Gang Intervention Handbook, Champaign, IL: Research Press.

Riccio, Vincent and Bill Slocum
 1962 All The Way Down: The Violent Underworld of Street Gangs. New York: Simon and
  Schuster.

Richards, C.
 1958 "Can We Get a Focus For Our Working With Hostile or Hard To Reach Youth Gangs,"
  Welfare Council of Metropolitan Chicago.

Ridgeway, James
 1990 Blood in the Face: The Ku Klux Klan, Aryan Nations, Nazi Skinheads, and the Rise of a
  New White Culture. New York: Thunder's Mouth Press.

Riley, William E.
 1988 "Prison Gangs: An Introduction, Crips and Bloods", Washington State Penitentiary.

Rivera, Ramon J.
 1964 Occupational Goals: A Comparative Analysis, Master'sThesis, University of Chicago.

Rivera, Raymond
 1998 "Views from the Field of Corrections: A Speech to Inmates by Major Raymond Rivera",
  Journal of Gang Research, Volume 6, Number 1, Fall.

Rizzardini, Laura
 1997 "Vigilantes, Gangs, and Terrorists: The Marginalization of Social Control", paper presented
  at the Annual Meeting of the American Society of Criminology.

Robert, Phillipe and Pierre Lascoumes
 1974 Les Bands D'Adolescents: Une Theorie de la Segregation. Paris, France: Les Editions
  Ouvieres.

Robins, Gerald
 1964 "Gang Membership Delinquency: Its Extent, Sequence, and Pattern", Journal of Criminal
  Law, Criminology, and Police Science (55): 59-69.

Robinson, Curtis J.
 1997 "Views from the Field: GD Peace Treaty Fails in Gary", Journal of Gang Research, Volume
  4, Number 3, Spring.
 1999 "Profiling the Satanic/Occult Dabblers in the Correctional Offender Population", Journal of
  Gang Research, Volume 7, Number 1, Fall: 35-66.

Robinson, N. and D. Joe
 1980 "Gangs in Chinatown", McGill Journal of Education (15): 149-162.

Rodeheffer, I.A.
 1949 "Gangdom: Fists to Reasoning", Journal of Educational Sociology (22)(Feb): 406-15.

Rodriguez, Luis J.
 1994 Always Running: La Vida Loca, Gang Days in L.A.. Curbstone Press.

Rogers, Kenneth H.
 1945 Street Gangs in Toronto. Toronto: The Ryerson Press.

Rosenbaum, Dennis P. and Jane A. Grant
 1983 "Gangs and Youth Problems in Evanston: Research Findings and Policy Options", Center
  for Urban Affairs and Policy Research, Northwestern University, July 22, 1983.

Rosenbaum, Jill Leslie
 1996 "A Violent Few: Gang Girls in the California Youth Authority", Journal of Gang Research,
  Volume 3, Number 3, Spring.

Rothman, Edwin, et al
 1974 The Gang Problem in Philadelphia: Proposals for Improving the Programs of Gang-Control
  Agencies. Pennsylvania Economy League (Eastern Division) in association with the
  Bureau of Municipal Research Liberty Trust Building, Philadelphia, Pa. 19107, Report
  No. 375; supported by a grant from the William Penn Foundation.

Rush, Jeffrey Paul
 1993 "An Interview With Richard Cloward", The Gang Journal: An Interdisciplinary Research
  Quarterly (1)(3): 51-53.

Sale, Richard T.
 1971 The Blackstone Rangers. A Reporter's Account of Time Spent with the Street Gang on

Chicago's South Side. New York: Random House.

Salisbury, Harrison E.
    1958 The Shook-up Generation. New York: Harper.

Sanchez-Jankowski, Martin
    1991 Islands in the Street: Gangs in American Urban Society. Berkeley: University of California
        Press.

Sanders, Willliam B.
    1994 Gangbangs and Drivebys: Grounded Culture and Juvenile Gang Violence. New York:
        Aldline De Gruyter.

Sanders, William B.; and S. Fernando Rodriguez
    1995 "Patterns of Gang Activity in A Border Community", Journal of Gang Research, Volume 2,
        Number 4, Fall.

Santamaria, C; et al
    1989 "Study of a Juvenile Gang in a High Risk Community", Salud Mental (12)(3)(Sept): 26-36.

Santman, Jennifer; Julye Myner; Gordon G. Cappeletty; and Barry F. Perimutter
    1997 "California Juvenile Gang Members: An Analysis of Case Records", Journal of Gang
        Research, Volume 5, Number 1, Fall.

Sarnecki, J.
    1986 Delinquent Networks. National Swedish Council for Crime Prevention, Research Division:
        Stockholm.

Sato, Ikuya
    1982 "Crime as Play and Excitement: A Conceptual Analysis of Japanese Bosozoku
        (Motorcycle Gangs)", Tohoku Psychologica Folia (41): 1-4,64-84.

Savitz, Leonard D.; Michael Lalli; and Lawrence Rosen
    1977 City Life and Delinquency --- Victimization, Fear of Crime and Gang Membership. National
        Institute for Juvenile Justice and Delinquency Prevention. U.S. Department of Justice,
        Government Printing Office, Washington, D.C.
    1980 "Delinquency and Gang Membership as Related to Victimization", Victimology (5): 152-
        160.

Scallan, J.H.
    1987 Prison Gang Codes and Communications. Texas Department of Corrections, unpublished.

Scharr, John H.
    1963 "Violence in Juvenile Gangs: Some Notes and a Few Analogies", American Journal of
        Orthopsychiatry (33)(1)(Jan): 29-37.

Schrag, C.
    1962 "Delinquency and Opportunity: Analysis of a Theory", Sociology and Social Research
        (46)(Jan): 167-75.

Schwendinger, Herman and Julia
    1967 "Delinquent Stereotypes of Probable Victims", in Malcolm W. Klein (ed.), Juvenile Gangs
        in Context, New Jersey: Prentice-Hall, pp. 91-105.
    1985 Adolescent Subcultures and Delinquency. New York: Praeger.

Schwitzgebel, Ralph
    1965 Street-Corner Research: An Experimental Approach to the Juvenile Delinquent.
        Cambridge, MA: Harvard University Press.

Schlossman, Steven and Michael Sedlak
    1983 The Chicago Area Project Revisited. A Rand Note. Prepared for the National Institute of
        Justice. Santa Monica, CA: The Rand Corporation.

Scott, Peter
    1956 "Gangs and Delinquent Groups in London", British Journal of Delinquency (7)(1): 4-26.

Shakur, Sanyika (aka Monster Kody Scott)
    1993 Monster: The Autobiography of an L.A. Gang Member, New York, NY: Penguin Books.

Shaw, Clifford R.
    1929 Delinquency Areas. Chicago: University of Chicago Press.
    1931 The Natural History of a Delinquent Career. Chicago: University of Chicago Press.
    1939 "Group Factors in Delinquency Among Boys", Society for Research in Child Development,
        Proceedings of the Third Biennial Meeting: 14-26.
    1951 The Natural History of a Delinquent Career. Philadelphia: Albert Saifer.

Shaw, Clifford R. and Jesse A. Jacobs
    1939 <u>Chicago Area Project</u>, March, 1939. Chicago Area Project, Chicago, Illinois.
Shaw, Clifford R. and Henry D. McKay
    1931 <u>Social Factors in Juvenile Delinquency: A Study of Community, the Family, and the Gang in Relation to Delinquent Behavior</u>. Volume II in the National Commission on Law Observance and Enforcement. U.S. Government Printing Office.
    1942 <u>Juvenile Delinquency and Urban Areas.</u> Chicago: University of Chicago Press.
    1956 <u>Juvenile Delinquency and Urban Areas.</u> Chicago: University of Chicago Press.
Shaw, Clifford R. and Earl D. Meyer
    1920 "The Juvenile Delinquent", Chicago: The Illinois Crime Survey.
Shaw, Clifford R. and Maurice E. Morre
    1931 <u>The Natural History of a Delinquent Career</u>. Chicago: University of Chicago Press.
Shaw, Clifford R. and Anthony Sorrentino
    1956 "Is 'Gang-Busting' Wise?", <u>National Parent-Teacher Magazine</u> (50)(Jan): 18-20+.
Shelden, Randall G.; Ted Snodgrass; and Pam Snodgrass
    1992 "Comparing Gang and Non-Gang Offenders: Some Tentative Findings", <u>The Gang Journal: An Interdisciplinary Research Quarterly</u> (1)(1): 73-85.
Sherif, Muzafer; O.J. Harvey; Jack White; William R. Hood; and Carolyn W. Sherif
    1961 <u>Intergroup Conflict and Cooperation: The Robbers Cave Experiment</u>, Norman, OK: University of Oklahoma Institute of Group Relations.
Sherman, Lawrence W.
    1970 <u>Youth Workers, Police and the Gangs: Chicago 1956- 1970</u>, Master's thesis, University of Chicago.
    1973 "Street Work History Includes Three Stages", <u>The Forum</u> (May): 17-24.
Sheu, Chuen-Jim
    1990 "Nonsyndicated Organized Crime in Taipei, Taiwan", paper presented at the 1990 Annual Meeting of the American Society of Criminology, Baltimore, Maryland: Nov. 7-10, 1990.
Shimota, Helen E.
    1964 "Delinquent Acts as Perceived by Gang and Nongang Negro Adolescents", Youth Studies Center, presented Dec. 12, 1964 before the California State Psychological Association; Los Angeles: University of Southern California.
Shireman, Charles H., et al
    1957 <u>An Examination and Analysis of Technique Used by a Street Worker</u>. Chicago: Hyde Park Youth Project.
    1958 <u>An Analysis of the Dynamics of the Interrelationship of Agency, Group and Community in Providing Staff ServiceTo A "Street Club"</u>. Hyde Park Youth Project. Welfare Council of Metropolitan Chicago.
Short, James F.
    1963 "Street Corner Groups and Patterns of Delinquency: A Progress Report", <u>American Catholic Sociological Review</u> (28): 13-32.
    1964 "Gang Delinquency and Anomie", pp. 98-127 in Marshall B. Clinard (ed.), <u>Anomie and Deviant Behavior</u>, New York: Free Press of Glencoe.
    1964 "Aleatory Risks Versus Short-run Hedonism in Explanation of Gang Action", <u>Social Problems</u> (12): 127-140.
    1965 "Social Structure and Group Processes in Explanations of Gang Delinquency", in M. and C. Sherif (eds.), <u>Problems of Youth</u>. Chicago: Aldine.
    1968 <u>Gang Delinquency and Delinquent Subcultures</u>. New York: Harper and Row.
    1968 "Comment on Lerman's 'Gangs, Networks, and Subcultural Delinquency'", <u>American Journal of Sociology</u> (73)(4)(Jan): 513-515.
    1974 "Youth, Gangs and Society: Micro and Macrosociological Processes", <u>Sociological Quarterly</u> (15): 3-19.
    1975 "Gangs, Violence and Politics", In Duncan Chappell and John Monahan (eds.), <u>Violence and Criminal Justice</u> Lexington, Mass: Lexington Books.
    1976 "Gangs, Politics, and the Social Order", in J.F. Short (ed.), <u>Delinquency, Crime and Society</u>, Chicago: University of Chicago Press.
    1989 "Exploring Integration of Theoretical Levels of Explanation: Notes on Gang Delinquency", in S.F. Messner, M.D. Krohn, and A.E. Liska (eds.), <u>Theoretical Integration in the Study</u>

of Deviance and Crime: Problems and Prospects (pp. 243-259), Albany: State University of New York Press.

Short, James F., and John Molland
    1976 "Politics and Youth Gangs: A Follow-up Study", Sociological Quarterly (17): 162-179.

Short, J.F.; R. Rivera; and R.A. Tennyson
    1965 "Perceived Opportunities, Gang Membership and Delinquency", American Sociological Review (30)(Feb).

Short, James F., Jr. and Fred L. Strodtbeck
    1965 Group Process and Gang Delinquency. Chicago: The University of Chicago Press.
    1974. _____.

Shukla, K.S.
    1981 "Adolescent Criminal Gangs: Structure and Functions", The International Journal of Critical Sociology (5): 35-49.

Sibley, James Blake
    1989 "Gang Violence: Response of the Criminal Justice System to the Growing Threat", Criminal Justice Journal (11)(2)(Spr): 403-422.

Sifakis, Carl
    1987 The Mafia Encyclopedia. New York: Facts on File Publications, Inc.

Sipchen, Bob
    1993 Baby Insane and the Buddha. New York: Doubleday.

Sirpal, Suman K.
    1997 "Causes of Gang Participation and Strategies for Prevention in Gang Members' Own Words", Journal of Gang Research, Volume 4, Number 2, Winter.

Skalitzky, William G.
    1990 "Aider and Abettor Liability, The Continuing Criminal Enterprise, and Street Gangs: A New Twist in an Old War on Drugs", Journal of Criminal Law & Criminology (81)(2): 348-397.

Skolnick, J.H.
    1990 "Gangs and Crime Old as Time: But Drugs Change Gang Culture", Commentary, Crime and Delinquency.

Skolnick, Jerome H.; Blumenthal, Ricky and Theodore Correl
    1990 "Gang Organization and Migration", Berkeley, CA: University of California at Berkeley, Center for the Study of Law and Society (2-18-90).
    1993 "Gang Organization and Migration", pp. 193-217 in Scott Cummings and Daniel J. Monti (Eds.), Gangs: The Orgins and Impact of Contempoary Youth Gangs in the United States, Albany, NY: State University of New York.

Skolnick, J.H. Correl, T.; Navarro, E.; and R. Rabb
    1989 "The Social Structure of Street Drug Dealing". Sacramento, CA: Office of the Attorney General, State of California.

Slack, Charles W.
    1963 "SCORE -- A Description", in Experiment in Culture Expansion, Report of Proceedings, U.S. National Institute of Mental Health, Bethesda, MD.

Sleeman, Lieut.-Col. W.H.
    1849 Report on Budhuk alia Bagree Decoits and other Gang Robbers by Hereditary Profession and on the measures adopted by the Government of India for their Suppression. Calcutta: J.C.Sherriff, Bengal Military Orphan Press.

Snyder, P.Z.
    1977 "An Anthropological Description of Street Gangs in the Los Angeles Area", prepared for the Department of Justice, Santa Monica, CA: Rand Corporation.

Song, John
    1991 "Lost in the Melting Pot? The Causes of Asian Gangs in the United States", paper presented at the Annual Meeting of the Academy of Criminal Justice Sciences, Nashville, Tennessee.

Song, John Huey-Long and John Dombrink
    1990 "Gangs, Groups and Organized Crime: Defining Asian Racketeering", paper presented at the Annual Meeting of the American Society of Criminology, Baltimore, MD.

Song, John Huey-Long; John Dombrink; and Gilbert Geis
  1992 "Lost in the Melting Pot: Asian Youth Gangs in the United States", The Gang Journal: An Interdisciplinary Research Quarterly (1)(1): 1-12.
Song, John Huey-Long; and Lynn M. Hurysz
  1995 "Victimization Patterns of Asian Gangs in the United States", Journal of Gang Research, Volume 3, Number 1, Fall.
Sorrentino, Anthony
  1995 "Implications of the Shaw-McKay Studies and the Problems of Intervention in Gang Work", Journal of Gang Research, Volume 2, Number 3, Spring.
Spaulding, Charles B.
  1948 "Cliques, Gangs and Networks", Sociology and Social Research (32)(July-August): 928-937.
Spergel, Irving
  1960 Types of Delinquent Groups, D.S.W. dissertation, Columbia University. Dissertation Abstracts (21)(Jan): 2034-35 (1961).
  1964 Racketville, Slumtown, Haulburg: An Exploratory Study of Delinquent Subcultures, Chicago: University of Chicago Press.
  1966 Street Gang Work: Theory and Practice. Reading, MA: Addison-Wesley Publishing Company, Inc.
  1984 "Violent Gangs in Chicago: In Search of Social Policy", Social Service Review (58): 199-226.
  1985 The Violent Gang Problem in Chicago. Chicago: Social Services Administration, University of Chicago.
  1985 Youth Gang Activity and the Chicago Public Schools. Chicago: Social Services Administration, University of Chicago.
  1986 "The Violent Gang Problem in Chicago: A Local Community Approach", Social Service Review (60)(1)(Mar): 94-131.
  1988 "The Youth Gang Problem: A Preliminary Policy Pespective", draft, Prepared for the Juvenile Gang Suppression and Intervention Research and Development Program, Office of Juvenile Justice and Delinquency Prevention, U.S. Dept. of Justice.
  1989 Youth Gangs: Problem and Response: A Review of the Literature, Executive Summary. U.S. Dept. of Justice, Office of Juvenile Justice and Delinquency Prevention, Washington, D.C.
  1989 Survey of Youth Gang Problems and Programs in 45 Cities and 6 States. Washington, DC: Office of Juvenile Justice and Delinquency Prevention.
  1989 "Youth Gangs: Continuity and Change", In N. Morris and M. Tonry (eds.), Crime and Justice: An Annual Review of Research (12): Chicago, University of Chicago Press.
  1990 "Youth Gangs: Continuity and Change", in Norval Morris (ed), Crime and Justice: Annual Review of Research, 267-371.
  1990 "The Violent Gang Problem in Chicago: A Local Community Approach", Social Service Review (60)(1)(Mar): 94-131.
  1995 The Youth Gang Problem, A Community Approach. New York: Oxford University Press.
Spergel, Irving A. and Ron L. Chance
  1990 Community and Institutional Responses to the Youth Gang Problem: Case Studies Based on Field Visits and Other Materials. National Youth Gang Suppression and Intervention Project, School of Social Service Administration, University of Chicago (Jan.).
Spergel, Irving A.; Glen David Curry; R.A. Ross; and R. Chance
  1989 Survey of Youth Gang Problems and Programs in 45 Cities and 6 Sites (Technical Report, No. 2, National Youth Gang Suppression and Intervention Project), Chicago: School of Social Service Administration, University of Chicago.
Srivastava, S.S.
  1981 "Problem of Dacoity in India - A Sociological Perspective" The International Journal of Critical Sociology (5): 23-34.
Stallworth, Ron
  1998 "Views from the Field of Law Enforcement: A Speech by Sgt. Ron Stallworth", Journal of Gang Research, Volume 6, Number 1, Fall.

Stapleton, W. Vaughn and Jerome Needle
    1982 Police Handling of Youth Gangs. Washington, D.C. Office of Juvenile Justice and
        Delinquency Prevention.
Stevens, Dennis J.
    1997 "Origins and Effects of Prison Drug Gangs in North Carolina", Journal of Gang Research,
        Volume 4, Number 4, Summer.
Steward, Samuel M.
    1990 Bad Boys and Tough Tattoos. New York: Harrington Park.
Stinchcombe, Arthur L.
    1964 Rebellion in a High School. Chicago: Quadrangle Books.
Stone, Sandra S.
    1999 "Risk Factors Associated with Gang Joining Among Youth", Journal of Gang Research,
        Volume 6, Number 2, Winter.
Stone, Sandra S.; and Jerry Wycoff
    1996 "The Extent and Dynamics of Gang Activity in Juvenile Correctional Facilities", Journal of
        Gang Research, Volume 4, Number 1, Fall.
Strodtbeck, Fred L.; James F. Short, Jr.; and Ellen Kolegar
    1962 "The Analysis of Self-Descriptions by Members of Different Gangs", Sociological
        Quarterly (24): 331-356.
Stover, Del
    1986 "A New Breed of Youth Gang is on the Prowl and a Bigger Threat Than Ever", American
        School Board Journal (173)(8)(Aug): 19-24,35.
Stum, Karen; and Mayling Maria Chu
    1999 "Gang Prevention and Intervention in a Rural Town in California", Journal of Gang
        Research, Volume 7, Number 1, Fall: 1-12.
Stumphauzer, Jerome S; Esteban V. Veloz; and Thomas W. Aiken
    1981 "Violence by Street Gangs: East Side Story?", in Robert B. Stuart (ed.), Violent Behavior.
        New York: Brunner-Mazel.
Suall, Irwin and David Lowe
    1988 "Shaved for Battle - Skinheads Target America's Youth", Political Communication and
        Persuasion (5)(2): 139-144.
Sullivan, John P. and Martin E. Silverstein
    1995 "The Disaster Within Us: Urban Conflict and Street Gang Violence in Los Angeles",
        Journal of Gang Research, Volume 2, Number 4, Fall.
Sun, Key
    1993 "The Implications of Social Psychological Theories of Group Dynamics for Gang
        Research", Gang Journal: An Interdisciplinary Research Quarterly (1)(3): 39-44.
Sung, B.L.
    1977 Gangs in New York's Chinatown (Monograph No. 6), New York: City College of New
        York, Department of Asian Studies.
Suttles, Gerald D.
    1959 Territoriality, Identity, and Conduct: A Study of an Inner-City Slum with Special Reference
        to Street Corner Groups, Ph.D. dissertation, University of Illinois at Champaign.
    1968 The Social Order of the Slum Chicago: University of Chicago Press.
Swans, Bennie J., Jr.
    1985 "Gangbusters! Crisis Intervention Network.", School Safety, Winter, 1985, pp. 12-15,
        National School Safety Center.
Sweeney, T.
    1980 Streets of Anger, Streets of Hope: Youth Gangs in East Los Angeles. Glendale, CA: Great
        Western Publishing.
Takata, Susan R.; and Charles Tyler
    1995 "A Community-University Based Approach to Gang Intervention and Delinquency
        Prevention: Racine's Innovative Model for Small Cities", Journal of Gang Research,
        Volume 2, Number 2, Winter.
Takata, Susan and Richard Zevitz
    1987 "Youth Gangs in Racine: An Examination of Community Perceptions", Wisconsin
        Sociologist (24)(4)(Fall): 132-141.

1990 "Divergent Perceptions of Group Delinquency in a Midwestern Community: Racine's Gang Problem", Youth and Society (21)(3)(Mar): 282-305.

Taylor, Carl S.
1988 "Youth Gangs Organize Quest for Power, Money", School Safety (Spr): 26-27.
1990 Dangerous Society. East Lansing, Michigan: Michigan State University Press.

Tennyson, Ray A.
1966 Family Structure and Gang Delinquency. Ph.D. dissertation, Washington State University.

Thompkins, Douglas E.
2000 "Gangs in Schools and a Culture of Fear", The Annals of the American Academy of Political and Social Science, Volume 567, January.

Thompson, Craig and Allen Raymond
1940 Gang Rule in New York. New York: Dial Press.

Thompson, D.W.
1986 Preventing Youth Membership in Urban Street Gangs: The Evaluation of a Behavioral Community Intervention. Dissertation Abstracts International, 47, 3987B.

Thompson, David W. and Leonard A. Jason
1988 "Street Gangs and Preventive Interventions", Criminal Justice and Behavior (15)(3)(Sept): 323-333.

Thompson, Kevin M.; David Brownfield; and Ann Marie Sorenson
1996 "Specialization Patterns of Gang and Nongang Offending: A Latent Structure Analysis", Journal of Gang Research, Volume 3, Number 3, Spring.
1998 "At-Risk Behavior and Group Fighting: A Latent Structure Analysis", Journal of Gang Research, Volume 5, Number 3, Spring.

Thornberry, Terrance;; Marvid D. Krohn; Alan J. Lizotte; and Deborah Chard-Wierschem
1993 "The Role of Juvenile Gangs in Facilitating Delinquent Behavior", Journal of Research in Crime and Delinquency, (30): 55-87.

Thrasher, Frederic M.
1927 The Gang. A Study of 1,313 Gangs in Chicago. Chicago: University of Chicago Press.
1936 _____. 2nd revised eidition. Chicago: University of Chicago Press.
1936 "The Boys Club and Juvenile Delinquency", American Journal of Sociology (41): 66-80.
1968 _____. Third Impression, Abridged and with a Introduction by James F. Short, Jr. Chicago: University of Chicago Press.
2000 The Gang: The Full Original Edition. New Chicago School Press: Peotone, IL.

Tice, Lawrence Clinton
1967 "The National Avenue 'Rebels': A Study of a Puerto Rican Gang in Milwaukee", M.A. thesis, Department of Social Welfare, University of Wisconsin-Milwaukee.

Toby, Jackson
1957 "Social Disorganization and Stake in Conformity", Journal of Criminal Law and Criminology (48)(May- June): 12-17.

Todorovic, Aleksander
1978 "Special Conditions and Causes That Influence the Forming of Juvenile Gangs", Socioloski Pregled (7): 27-38.

Toll, Joseph F.
1944 "Converting the Gang into a Club", Probation (23)(Dec): 49-55.

Tompkins, Dorothy Campbell
1966 Juvenile Gangs and Street Groups - A Bibliography. Institute of Governmental Studies, University of California, Berkeley.

Torres, Dorothy M.
1979 "Chicano Gangs in the East Los Angeles Barrio", California Youth Authority Quarterly (32)(3): 5-13.
1980 Gang Violence Reduction Project 3rd Evaluation Report. Sacramento, CA: California Department of the Youth Authority.
1981 Gang Violence Reduction Project: Fourth Evaluation Report, July 1979-June 1980. Department of the Youth Authority, Sacramento, CA.

Toy, Calvin
1992 "Coming Out to Play: Reasons to Join and Participate in Asian Gangs", The Gang Journal: An Interdisciplinary Research Quarterly (1)(1): 13-29.

Tracy, Paul E.
    1984 "Subcultural Delinquency: A Comparison of the Incidence and Seriousness of Gang and
        Nongang Offensivity", University of Pennsylvania: Center for Studies in Criminology and
        Criminal Law.
Tracy, Paul E. and E.S. Piper
    1984 "Gang Membership and Violent Offending: Preliminary Results from the 1958 Cohort
        Study". Paper presented at the Annual Meeting of the American Society of Criminology,
        Cincinnati, OH.
Tracy, Paul E. and M. Epstein
    1979 Subcultural Delinquency: A Comparision of the Incidence and Seriousness of Gang and
        Nongang Member Offensivity. Center for Studies in Criminology and Criminal Law,
        Philadelphia: University of Pennsylvania.
Tracy, Paul E. and Elizabeth S. Piper
    1982 "Gang Membership and Violent Offending: Preliminary Results from the 1958 Cohort
        Study", paper presented at the annual meeting of the American Society of Criminology,
        Cincinnati.
Tripp, Dean
    1997 "Jungian Thought and the Etiology of Gangs", unpublished paper.
Tromanhauser, Edward
    1981 "The Problem of Street Gangs", chapter IV in Chicago Safe School Study, Board of
        Education, City of Chicago.
Trostle, Lawrence Charles
    1987 The Stoners: Drugs, Demons and Delinquency: A Descriptive and Empirical Analysis of
        Delinquent Behavior, Ph.D. dissertation, Claremont Graduate School, California.
Turner, Ralph H and Samuel J. Surace
    1956 "Zoot-Suiters and Mexicans: Symbols in Crowd Behavior", American Journal of
        Sociology (62)(July): 14-20.
Tursman, Cindy
    1989 "Safeguarding Schools Against Gang Violence", School Administrator (46)(5)(May):
        8,9,11-15.
Useem, Bert and Peter Kimball
    1989 "A Gang in Rebellion - Joliet (1975)", Chapter 4 (pp. 59-77) in States of Siege: U.S. Prison
        Riots, 1971-1986 New York: Oxford University Press.
Vaz, Edmund W.
    1962 "Juvenile Gang Delinquency in Paris", Social Problems (10)(Sum): 23-31.
Van De Kamp, John K.
    1988 Report on Youth Gang Violence in California. Sacramento, CA: Office of the Attorney
        General.
Venkatesh, Sudhir Alladi
    1997 "The Social Organization of Street Gang Activity in an Urban Ghetto", American Journal
        of Sociology, 101: 82-111.
Vercaigne, Conny
    1997 "Views from the Field: Gangs in Sight", Journal of Gang Research, Volume 5, Number 1,
        Fall.
Vetter, Harold J. and Leonard Territo
    1984 Crime & Justice In America: A Human Perspective. St. Paul, MN: West Publishing Co.
Vigil, James Diego
    1983 "Chicano Gangs: One Response to Mexican Urban Adaptation in the Los Angeles Area",
        Urban Anthropology (12)(1)(Spr): 45-75.
    1987 "Street Socialization, Locura Behavior and Violence Among Chicano Gang Members", in J.
        Kraus et al (eds.), Violence and Homicide in Hispanic Communities, Washington, DC:
        National Institute of Mental Health, Office of Minority Health.
    1988 "Group Processes and Street Identity: Adolescent Chicano Gang Members", Ethos
        (16)(4)(Dec): 421-445.
    1988 Barrio Gangs: Street Life and Identity in Southern California. Austin, TX: University of
        Texas Press.

Vila, Bryan; and James W. Meeker
    1997 "A Regional Gang Incident Tracking System", <u>Journal of Gang Research</u>, Volume 4, Number 3, Spring.

Vold, George B.
    1958. <u>Theoretical Criminology.</u> Oxford University Press.
    1981. <u>Theoretical Criminology.</u> New York: Oxford University Press.
    1986. With Thomas J. Bernard. Third edition.

Waldorf, Dan
    1993 "When the Crips Invaded San Francisco - Gang Migration", <u>Journal of Gang Research</u>, Volume 2, Number 1.

Walker, Jeffery T.; Judge Bill White; and E. Ashley White
    1995 "The Evolution of Gang Formation: Potentially Delinquent Activity and Gang Involvement", <u>Journal of Gang Research</u>, Volume 2, Number 2, Winter.

Wang, Zheng
    1995 "Gang Affiliation Among Asian-American High School Studenets: A Path Analysis of Social Development Model 1", <u>Journal of Gang Research</u>, Volume 2, Number 3, Spring.
    1998 "Special Report: An Update on Asian Gang Affiliation", <u>Journal of Gang Research</u>, Volume 5, Number 3, Spring.

Wattenberg, William M. and James Balistrieri
    1950 "Gang Membership and Juvenile Misconduct", <u>American</u> <u>Sociological Review</u> (15)(Dec): 744-752.
    1959 "Gang Membership and Juvenile Misconduct", pp. 169-177 in Sheldon Glueck (ed), <u>The Problem of Delinquency</u> Boston: Houghton.

Watts, T.J.
    1988 New Gangs: Young, Armed and Dangerous. Monticello, IL: Vance Bibliographies (P.O. Box 229, Monticello, IL 61856).

Webb, Margot
    1991 <u>Coping With Street Gangs.</u> New York: Free Press.

Weiner, Arthur K.
    1965 "C-r-a-c-k-i-n-g The Hard Core Area", <u>Police Chief</u> (32)(Jan): 27-31.

Weisfeld, Glenn and Roger Feldman
    1982 "A Former Street Gang Leader Re-Interviewed EightYears Later", <u>Crime and Delinquency</u> (28): 567-581.

Weissman, Harold (ed.)
    1969 <u>Community Development in the Mobilization for Youth.</u> New York: Association Press.

Werdmolder, Hans
    1997 <u>A Generation Adrift: An Ethnography of a Criminal Moroccan Gang in the Netherlands.</u> Kluwer Law International: The Hague.

Werthman, Carl
    1964 <u>Delinquency and Authority,</u> Master's Thesis, University of California, Berkeley.
    1966 "Police Action and Gang Delinquency", in D. Bordua (ed.), <u>The Police,</u> New York: Wiley.

Werthman, Carl and Irving Piliavin
    1967 "Gang Members and the Police", in David Bordua (ed), <u>The Police: Six Sociological Essays,</u> New York: Wiley.

West, Pat and Tony Ostos
    1988 Pilot Study: City of Paramount Alternatives to Gang Membership Program. City of Paramount, 16400 Colorado Ave., Paramount, CA 90723.

Whyte, William Foote
    1943 <u>Street Corner Society: The Social Structure of an Italian Slum.</u> Ph.D. dissertation, University of Chicago.
    1943 <u>Street Corner Society.</u> Chicago: University of Chicago Press.
    1981 <u>Street Corner Society.</u> Chicago: University of Chicago Press, third edition.

Williams, Hampton; Rex Leonard; and Phillip Terrell
    1991 "Students' Perceptions of Some Selected Conditions that Might Lead to Gang Membership: An Exploratory Investigation", paper presented at the Annual Meeting of the Academy of Criminal Justice Sciences, Nashville, Tennessee.

Wilner, Daniel M.; Eva Rosenfeld; Robert S. Lee; Donald L. Gerard; and Isidor Chein
    1957 "Heroin Use and Street Gangs", Journal of Criminal Law, Criminology, and Police Science (48)(4): 399-409.
Wilson, Everett
    1971 Sociology: Rules, Roles, and Relationships. The Dorsey Press.
Wilson, James Q. and George L. Kelling
    1989 "Making Neighborhoods Safe", The Atlantic Monthly (Feb): 46-52.
Wilson, William J.
    1987 The Truly Disadvantaged. Chicago: University of Chicago Press.
Wise, John M.
    1962 A Comparison of Sources of Data as Indices of Delinquent Behavior, Master's thesis, Department of Sociology, University of Chicago.
Wolfe, Tom
    1968 The Pump House Gang. New York: Farrar, Straus and Giroux.
Wooden, Wayne
    1989 "Profile of Stoner Gang Members in the California Youth Authority", paper presented at the American Society of Criminology, Annual Meeting, Reno, Nevada, November.
    1990 "Contemporary Youth Identities: Problems and Issues", paper presented at the Western Society of Criminology, Annual Meeting, Las Vegas, Nevada (February).
Xu, J.
    1986 "Brief Discussion of New Trends in the Development of Juvenile Delinquent Gangs", Chinese Education (19)(2)(Sum): 92-102.
Yablonsky, Lewis
    1958 A Field Study of Delinquent Gang Organization and Behavior With Special Emphasis on Gang Warfare. Ph.D. dissertation, New York University.
    1959 "The Delinquent Gang as a Near-Group", Social Problems (7): 108-117.
    1962 The Violent Gang. New York: MacMillan.
    1999 "The Affirmation of Hanging Out: The U.S. Supreme Court Ruling on Gang Busting Laws and Their Consequences", Journal of Gang Research, Volume 6, Number 4, Summer.
Youth Gang Task Force (California)
    1981 Report on Youth Gang Violence in California. State of California Department of Justice. Sacramento.
Zaitzow, Barbara H.
    1998 "Nickname Usage by Gang Members", Journal of Gang Research, Volume 5, Number 3, Spring.
Zaitzow, Barbara H.; and James G. Houston
    1999 "Prison Gangs: The North Carolina Experience", Journal of Gang Research, Volume 6, Number 3, Spring.
Zatz, Marjorie S.
    1985 "Los Cholos: Legal Processing of Chicano Gang Members", Social Problems (33): 13-30.
    1987 "Chicano Youth Gangs and Crime: The Creation of a Moral Panic", Contemporary Crises (11)(2): 129-158.
Zhang, Lening and John W. Welte
    1997 "Youth Gangs, Drug Use, and Delinquency", unpublished paper.
Zhang, Lening; Steven F. Messner; Zhou Lu; and Ziaogang Deng
    1997 "Gang Crime and Its Punishment in China", Journal of Criminal Justice (25)(4): 289-302.
Zinn, Elizabeth
    1959 "He Begged that Gang Violence End With His Life", Federal Probation (23)(Sept): 24-30.

APPENDIX A:

WRITTEN CONSTITUTION AND BY-LAWS OF THE ALMIGHTY LATIN KING NATION

CHAPTER CONSTITUTION OF THE ALMIGHTY LATIN KING NATION

IN THE SIXTH DECADE OF THE TWENTIETH CENTURY THE A.L.K.N. WAS FORMED. GENERATION AFTER GENERATION OF KINGS HAVE LIVED BY A CONSTITUTION OF PRINCIPLES BASED UPON THE IDEAS OF KINGISM. THOSE IDEAS, OUR LAWS AND PRINCIPLES WE NOW IMPACT TO ALL KINGS WITH THIS CONSTITUTION.

FROM THIS DAY FORWARD WE SHALL ORGANIZE OURSELVES UNDER CONSTITUTIONAL LAW TO INSURE THAT WE AS A NATION SHALL LEAD THE WAY TO PROGRESS AND NO LONGER STAND IN THE SHADOW OF IT: WE AS A NATION SHALL LEAD THE WAY FOR TRUE KINGISM.

DEVOTING YOUR LIFE TO THESE PRINCIPLES IMPLIES A LIFE OF SERVICE TO EACH OTHER AND TO THE ALMIGHTY LATIN KING NATION.

LOVE - HONOR - OBEDIENCE
SACRIFICE - RIGHTEOUSNESS

INCA

The Inca is the highest ranking officer in every chapter of the Nation. The Inca is elected by majority vote of his Chapter's membership. His term of office is indefinite. However, he must run in an election for a "vote of confidence" every two years in order to retain as position as Commander-In-Chief.

The Inca is responsible for the actions of his Chapter, its security, the treasury and the general well-fare of the membership. He is responsible for promoting academic and vocational skills and for providing the aid and way in our search for peace, unity and freedom.

The Inca must file a State of the Nation report every three months with Los Coronas concerning the affairs of his Chapter. Any action taken by the Inca shall be enforced through the Cacique.

CACIQUE

The Cacique shall be second in command of his chapter. He, like the Inca, is elected by majority vote of the membership of his Chapter and his term of office is indefinite. However, he too must run in a vote of confi-

dence election every two years.

The Cacique is to work hand-in-hand with the Inca and assume the responsibilities of the Inca in case of the Inca's absence.

The Cacique is responsible for keeping the Inca informed on all actions taken by the Officers of his Chapter.

Any action taken by the Cacique shall be enforced through Chapter Enforzador.

ELECTIONS

The elections will be conducted by the Chairman of the Chapter Crown Council for both Inca and Cacique. Elections for these officer must be held within thirty days of their departure from office. However, if the Council Chairman has prior knowledge of an immediate or forthcoming departure of either the Inca or Cacique then he has the option of proceeding with an election thirty days prior to such departure.

The Crown Council members will each select five members as candidates of whom in their opinion are the most qualified to run for Office. The two candidates that receive the highest number of votes from the Chapter Crown Council members will automatically run for Office. The candidate that receives the highest number of votes from that Chapter's membership will be elected as Inca and the other candidate as Cacique.

In order to run for office a Brother must be a member of the Nation for a minimum of three years. This is the basic requirement. Other requirements include but are not limited to the following:

1.   He must be a member in good standing and have some type of prior experiences an Officer of the Nation with the rank of Chairman of the Crown Council, Chapter Enforzador and/or previous Inca and Cacique.

2.   He must also have been in the chapter for a period of six months so that he has gained e x p e r i ence and knowledge in understanding the policies and principles of the Almighty Latin King Nation.

Every two years the Inca and Cacique must run for re-election. This is called a Vote of Confidence and is to assure that the membership is satisfied with the leadership. A vote of confidence is not an election of new officers but a vote by the Chapter's membership to determine if the Inca and Cacique have fulfilled the responsibilities of their Office.

If the majority of the Chapter's membership is dissatisfied with their elected Officers, the People's will shall be manifested by a vote of NAY - one who votes no. If the majority of the Chapter's membership is satisfied with the rule of their Inca and Cacique they shall cast a vote of YEA - one who votes yes.

LAS CORONAS

Las Coronas are the highest ranking Officers of the Nation. Their term of office is indefinite. Las Coronas are responsible for seeing that all Officers of the

Nation abide by the Constitution and respect the rights of our membership.

Las Coronas have the power to bring justice where the abuse of power or corruption has occurs by the Inca and Cacique in any Chapter. In the event the Inca and Cacique violate the Laws of this Constitution, Las Coronas have the power to place all rank on hold pending investigation and appoint temporary positions of rank until a new Inca and Cacique have been elected.

Las Coronas have the power to give Crowns to new members of the nation without them being required to be voted in by the Chapters' Crown Councils.

Any member seeking re-entry into the Nation must be approved by Las Coronas.

Once a proposal has been put to a vote and approved by the Chapter and Council, the Inca and Cacique, final approval must be given by las Coronas before it is added to the Constitution and Law.

EL CONSEJADOR

The Inca's advisor shall serve as an consejador and Cacique. This position is usually reserved for members who have served as past Inca and have been in the nation for a long period of time with a record of having served wisely.

All members reaching the age of fifty (50) years, who are members in good standing and have during their years in the Nation held the rank of Inca, Cacique, Chapter Crown Council Chairman and Chapter Enforzador shall, with the approval of Las Coronas, hold the title of National Consejador and are to be treated with the respect of an Officer.

The name of this association shall be the ALMIGHTY LATIN KING NATION.

An organization of international brotherhood with exists for the purpose of:

　　1.　　Promoting prosperity and freedom through love and understanding to all oppressed people of the world.

　　2.　　To train our People to become aware of our social and political problems and of the conditions we are subjected to live under as a Third World People.

　　3.　　To provide the aid and way in our search for peace and unity.

　　4.　　To promote and encourage education and vocational learning in order to train our People in the art of survival.

MEMBERSHIP

Membership shall be available to anyone who is willing to change their life-style for the doctrine of Kingism.

Membership shall be denied to anyone who has willfully taken the life of a Latin King or a relative of a member of the Nation.

Membership is forbidden to anyone addicted to heroin and denied to rapists.

Membership is forbidden to anyone who is expelled from Nation unless his re-entry is approved by Las Coronas. Anyone seeking re-entry into the Nation must find an Officer with the rank of Chapter Enforcer, Chapter Crown Council Chairman, Inca or Cacique, to sponsor him before las Coronas will even consider him for re-entry.

CHAPTER ENFORZADOR

The Enforzador will be in charge and responsible for the security of every member Chapter. He shall be appointed by the Inca and Cacique and report to them directly. The Enforzador shall see that the Laws are enforced and the orders of the Inca and Cacique are obeyed.

CHAPTER TESORERO

The Tesorero will be appointed by the Inca and Cacique. It shall be his responsibility to collect and invest Chapter funds. However, members of each Chapter shall determine by majority vote, the amount of dues they pay monthly and how their Chapter funds are to be spent.

The Tesorero shall file a report with the Inca and Cacique at the first of every month on his Chapter's financial status. Brothers who are delinquent in payment of dues are not members in good standing and are not allowed to vote in how Chapter funds are to be spent.

CHAPTER SECRETARIO

The Secretario will be appointed by the Inca and Cacique. His duties shall consist of the following:

　　1.　　Collection and distribution of Nation literature.

　　2.　　Keeping records of all business conducted by the Chapter Crown Council. Although the Secretario sits in all matters of business conducted by the Crown Council, he may not interfere with the proceedings and must abide by the Rules of the Council.

　　3.　　Keep Communications open to all Chapters through the Secretario of every Chapter.

CHAPTER INVESTIGATOR

The Chapter Investigator shall be appointed by the Inca and Cacique. He shall conduct an investigation of all new members. All prospective new members shall be placed on hold until the investigation is completed.

The Investigator shall also conduct all investigations requested by the Inca, Cacique, Chapter Crown Council, Enforzador, Tesorero and Secretario. A report of all investigations, no matter what Officer makes the request, must be filed at the completion with the Inca and Cacique.

CHAPTER CROWN COUNCIL

The Chapter Crown Council shall have its powers delegated to it under this Constitution. Council members do not maintain any power outside the Council. However, Council members shall be recognized as Officers of the Nation. Council members shall be responsible to the Council Chairman, the Inca and Cacique.

The Chapter Crown Council shall be the Law making body of the Chapter and guardian of the Constitution. The Council shall the authority to make their own Rules and Regulations concerning the procedures they are to follow in order to function effectively as a Council.

The Council shall be composed of not more or less than seven of most qualified members of the Chapter.

The Chapter Crown Council shall have the absolute power of holding trials for everyone in the ALMIGHTY LATIN KING NATION regardless of who they are or their position of rank, this includes the Inca and Cacique.

Thee Chapter Crown Council has the prerogative of asking for the resignation of the Inca and Cacique but only a majority of the entire Chapter can remove either of them from Office.

The Council, under the leadership of the Chairman, shall automatically take control of the Chapter in the absence of the Inca and Cacique.

The Council shall have the power, by majority vote, to dismiss a member of the nation under the recommendation of the Inca and Cacique or Las Coronas.

Once the seven members of the Council have been selected and approved it will then become the Council's responsibility; to choose any new members whenever a seat has been vacated. A new member of the Council can be selected by majority vote from the remaining members of the Council.

Whenever the Chairman's seat is vacant, the Inca, Cacique and remaining Council members shall, by majority vote, select a new Chairman.

A council member can be removed from office by the Inca or Cacique's vote along with the majority vote of the remaining Council members.

ALTERNATE COUNCIL MEMBERS

Members of the Chapter Crown Council, by majority vote and with the approval of the Inca or Cacique, shall select members of the Chapter to serve as alternate Council members. Alternate Council members may be selected for the following purposes:

1.   In order to form a full quorum.
2.   In the event a member appearing before the Council requests that a Crown Council member be excused for possible prejudice.
3.   In order to train new members as prospective permanent Council members.

The Chapter Crown Council shall have the power, by majority vote, to accept an individual as an Almighty Latin King or reject him from membership. All individuals seeking membership shall be screened by the Council. The Council shall also interview any member that wishes to make any comments in support of or against any person seeking membership.

The Chapter Crown Council shall try all cases that involve Constitutional violations. The Council may also try cases where an infraction has been committed outside the Constitution but only under the recommendation of the Inca, Cacique or Las Coronas.

Council members are not allowed to discuss any issues or business before it with any members outside the Council until the procedures are completed. This or course does not include their investigative work.

The Chapter Crown Council Chairman shall have no vote in the proceedings but may vote in case of a tie vote among Council members. It is the Chairman's duty to conduct the proceedings and make recommendations on all actions taken by the Council. The Chairman must also keep records of all proceedings conducted by the Council.

If the Inca and Cacique issue an order or implement a Rule that the Chapter Crown Council feels is detrimental to the Chapter, the Council by majority vote, has the authority to null and void such rule or order. However, Las Coronas must be informed in the event of such action is taken by the Council.

CHAPTER CROWN COUNCIL MEMBERS

The first Council member will be appointed by the Inca and Cacique and he shall be the Chapter Crown Council Chairman. The Chairman will then select six other members to complete the quorum of the Council. The members chosen by the Chairman must be approved by the Inca and Cacique.

Council members will be referred to ass Council members and never as "Crown" member. Only Nation Crowns of this rank will be recognized by this title.

Every member of the nation shall honor, respect and protect with his life the lives and reputations of all members of the Almighty Latin King Nation.

When a member gives another member the Nation Salute it should always be returned.

There shall be no stealing inside the Nation and proliferation of the community by acts of vandalism, destruction of property and graffiti is strongly discouraged.

No member shall use his membership or position in the Nation to exploit anyone inside or outside the Nation.

No member shall incur debts with other members that he cannot afford to repay.

Nation affairs are to be kept within the Nation and are not be discussed in the presence of anyone outside the Nation.

No King shall strike or disrespect another King unless it is in self-defense. And any Officer that strikes another member (with the exception of the Inca and Cacique) will automatically lose his rank and may be subjected to further disciplinary action pending an investigation and hearing before the Chapter Crown Council.

Any member found guilty of being a traitor or police collaborator shall automatically lose his position (if he has one) and be expelled from the Nation.

No member shall take the Law into their own hands especially when he knows that what he does will reflect upon the Nation and jeopardize the health and well-being of every member of the Chapter.

No member shall take a lie detector test without the approval of the Inca and Cacique.

No member shall conduct an interview with any person from the news media concerning Nation affairs without the approval of the Las Coronas.

Any member accused of rape shall be put on hold pending investigation by the Chapter Crown Council and subject to approval by the Inca and Cacique.

No member shall bring false charges or statements against another member of the Nation.

Any member or group of members caught disrespecting the Inca and Cacique in public, or conspiring against them or any other member of the Nation shall be brought before the Council on a charge of conspiracy and treason.

No King shall stand idle while another King is in need of assistance.

The use of what is commonly known as angel dust (tick, tack or animal tranquilizer), glue, L.S.D. (acid), heroin, downers and free-basing is unlawful, and cannot be sold in our communities.

Those who are known to have previously used heroin for the purpose of addiction cannot obtain a position of rank without the approval of Las Coronas.

Nothing which can be construed as an emblem of another organization can be worn by a member of the Almighty Latin King Nation.

In recognition of our culture, each January the 6th will be recognized as Kings Holy Day - a day dedicated to the memory of our departed Brothers and Sisters; a day of sacrifice in which each and every member of the nation will observe by fasting.

The first week in the month of March of each and every year is a Nation holiday. This holiday is known as King's Week or Week of the Sun. This holiday is the nation's anniversary and is week of celebration.

TRIAL PROCEDURES

Any member that violates a Law shall be brought before the Chapter Crown Council within a reasonable time to stand trial for his offense. If he is unable to appear he may present a written defense.

Any member that violates a Law must be presented with a copy of the charges as soon as possible so that he may be allowed adequate opportunity to prepare his defense.

Every member of the Nation has the right to have another member of the Nation represent and assist him at his trial. They shall also be allowed the privilege of one continuance for the purpose of presenting witnesses on their behalf and to give them an opportunity to gather information to prove their innocence. If the Chapter Crown Council feels that further investigation is necessary in order to assist them in their work, then they may

order a continuation for such purpose. The Chapter Crown Council also maintains the right to call witnesses.

When an Officer of the Nation must stand trial, the Inca or the Cacique must be present. However, the Inca nor the Cacique has the right to vote in such matters as their responsibility is to review the decision of the Chapter Crown Council.

If a member if found guilty of an offense by the Council, the Council will determine the punishment, subject to the approval of the Inca or Cacique. If the member is an officer, the Inca and Cacique, with the recommendation of the Chapter Crown Council, will determine the punishment.

In order to try the Inca or Cacique, any charges brought against either one of them must be brought before the Chapter Crown Council. Any member has the right to bring charges.

If the Council feels the charges are valid, the Council must immediately inform Las Coronas before proceeding with a hearing. If the charges are serious enough to warrant a public trial, the Inca and/or Cacique has the option of abdicating their throne or submitting to the trial.

If the Inca and Cacique do not receive approval of their performance by a majority of their Chapter's membership, a new election of Officers shall be held according to Constitutional law.

HOW LAWS ARE MADE

Any member of the Almighty Latin King Nation has the right to make a proposal, requesting that said proposal be made a part of our Law. A proposal is introduced first to the Chapter Crown Council by any member of the Chapter.

Once the proposal has been submitted, reviewed and debated by the Council, the majority vote will then decide whether or not the submitted proposal has been approved or denied. Once the proposal has been approved by the Chapter Crown Council it will be presented to the Inca and Cacique for their approval.

If the proposal is approved by the Inca and Cacique it will be submitted to Las Coronas. The proposal cannot be Chapter Law without the approval of Las Coronas.

LAWS

Rules and regulations may vary from Chapter to Chapter but the laws of all Chapters are the same. Rules and regulations implemented by the Inca and Cacique falls under their jurisdiction and they will handle all such infractions. The violation of a Law falls under the jurisdiction of the Chapter Crown Council and they will handle all such violations.

The first and most Law of the Almighty Latin King Nation is "Once a King, always a King", unless he is expelled from the Nation for violation of its Laws.

AMENDMENTS

As of this date

,_____,
passage of the following proposal has been enacted into the Constitutional Law as the First Amendment to the Constitution of the Almighty Latin King Nation.

AMENDMENT I.

AMENDMENTS

An amendment is an amelioration of the Constitution without involving the idea of any change in substance or essence.

For the purposes of continued growth, the modification or alteration proposed under an amendment is, as of this date, given its force and effect in the following manner:

Once the passage of a proposal to amend is given by a Chapter Inca and Cacique and approved by Las Coronas it shall be added hereunder as Constitutional Law. Amor!

APPROVED:

ALMIGHTY LATIN KING NATION

He who knows, and knows that he knows, is a wise man,
Listen to him!
He who knows, and does not know that he knows, is asleep,
Wake him up!
He who does not know, and knows that he does not know,
Wants to learn... Teach him!
He who does not know, and does not know that he does
Not know, is a fool... Avoid him!

Confucian

A LOVE MEASURED IN GREAT HARMONY TOWARDS YAHVE
LATIN AMERICAN TRIBE ILLUMINATING NATURAL
KNOWLEDGE, INDESTRUCTIBLE NOBILITY and GLOWING STRENGTH
NATURAL ALLIES TOGETHER IN ONE NUCLEUS

HOLY PRAYER

Almighty Father, King of Kings, Maker of the Universe and Foundation of Life, bring peace to our souls, to the here present, to those not present, to the young and to the old.

As an Almighty Nation under one Sun protected by thine love and guidance we bring our right fist upon our heart for sincerity, love, wisdom, strength, knowledge and understanding. Three hundred-sixty degrees of Strong King Wisdom.

Illuminate our minds and our hearts. Guide our thoughts with thine righteousness. Guide and protect the thoughts of our Coronas and all those holy and righteous lovers and followers of our beloved family and tribe - the Almighty Latin King Nation.

Let the manifestation of our departed Brothers be the path to thee and let it be as it was in the beginning - Strong King Wisdom on both continents, Peace in Black and Gold.

King love! Yesterday, Today, Tomorrow, Always and Forever.

KINGS AND QUEENS PRAYER

Oh King of the Universe, Supreme maker of all things, We the Almighty Latin King and Queen Nation ask you, Almighty King, to bring peace our cause. As an Almighty Nation under the Sun, protected by your love and guidance, we bring our right fist upon our hearts for love, honor, obedience, sacrifice and righteousness.

We ask you Almighty King to bless our departed Brothers and sisters, members of our beloved and mighty Nation, who on this very day rest in the bosom of your sanctuary. May they rest in your care and may they have found the peace and freedom they sought. In our critical moments bring us comfort and guide us through those days of confusion and oppression. May the blessings of the ancients and the wisdom of the ages guide us and keep our Nation strong as we battle the forces that seek to deny us.

We, the Almighty Latin King and Queen Nation, are entrusted with a divine mission, one that transcends personal gains and recognition. As Kings and Queens we pledge ourselves ever faithful to that mission. Make us all aware that others look to us for guidance, and let us always prove ourselves worthy of providing it. For, though we are of different Nationalities, we all share the same cultures of our ancient ancestors whose every word is law throughout the world. It is our destiny to lead rather than to be led.

We, the Almighty Latin King and Queen Nation, have the blood of royalty in our veins. We are the guiding light of our People. Place wisdom in our minds love in our hearts, and fortitude to withstand the trials of time. Guide and protect our Coronas so that they may lead us to our ultimate goal - the awakening of our People to their oppressed state that they may lift our heritage to its rightful place among the thrones of Kings and Queens,

LET THE MANIFESTATION OF OUR SAC-
RIFICED BROTHERS AND SISTERS
BE THE PATH SO THEE, AND LET IT BE AS
IT WAS IN THE BEGINNING:
STRONG KING AND QUEEN WISDOM -
PEACE IN BLACK AND GOLD....

ALMIGHTY LATIN KING NATION

The Almighty Latin King Nation is a religion which gives us faith in ourselves, a national self-respect, power to educate the poor and relieve the misery around us.

It is the Brotherhood of man, blending like the waves of one ocean, shinning as the Sun, one soul in many bodies bearing fruit of the same tree.

It creates in us a thirst like the heat of earth on fire, a thirst for knowledge, wisdom, strength, unity and freedom.

It is the Sun glowing in the essence of our being, the brightness in our eyes that cast reflections of its rays spitting fire in all directions.

It is the unshakable spirit and the nobleness of our hearts, the limitless power of the mind, the unrelentless will to be free.

It is pride, ambition, love, sacrifice, honor, obedience and righteousness, all our powers and all our desires thrown into the mission of human service and united into one Single Gold Sun.

If you want to find Yahve serve the Almighty Latin King Nation. Put on the Gold Sun - Black and Gold colors, place your right fist upon your heart and pledge devotion to the Almighty Latin King Nation, to Yahve and all oppressed people. This is the Nation of Kingism....

BEHOLD KING LOVE!

ICONA

The history of all hitherto existing gang feuds is the History of label struggles for the sake of "click" recognition. It is thin egotistical force for recognition which leads to rivalry and senseless disputes which often cost the high price of human life. The life of our People, the oppressed Third World People.

With the intentions of changing this social and oppressive phenomena the King Manifesto is written; to serve as a guide and enlighten our deplorable conditions under the existing order of things. With this thought in mind we proceed to create the New King, the Moral King, the King of Others, the lover of men and the Turning Wheel of Change.

Devoting your life to the principles of Kingism implies a life of service to your fellow man. We can be of service in no other way. If you turn your back on your Brother simply because of a label you are turning your back on the Almighty Latin King Nation.

One who does not know the Almighty Latin King Nation and its Laws is like a plant growing in the shade. Although it knows not the Sun, it is nevertheless abso-

lutely dependent upon it.

The Nation is in your hands. If you turn your back on the Nation you are denying yourself the sole purpose of your existence - the right to be free!

BEHOLD LATIN KING

KINGISM

Kingism is the doctrine of the Almighty Latin King Nation. There are three stages or cycles of Nation life that constitutes Kingism. They are:
PRIMITIVE STAGE
CONSERVATIVE STAGE
THE NEW KING STAGE

In order for one to grasp a good understanding of each stage and its development, one must understand and consider the social factors surrounding each stage.

THE PRIMITIVE STAGE is that stage in life where the King Warrior acts on impulse, executing his actions without giving them the serious thought that they demand. A stage of immaturity where the King Warrior's time is spent "gang-banging", getting high and being recognized as big and bad.

This can also be classified as the wasteful stage to a certain extent; to the extent that what is being done is being done unconsciously. Yet it is not wasteful in the sense that the environment conditions this type of behavior in order for one to survive the hardships of ghetto life - that undesirable level at the lowest plane of social existence. It is wasteful in that energy is being misused. There are no objectives for one's actions except for the factual phenomena that the entire affair is centered around recognition, label recognition and personal recognition. This egotistical tendency often leads to a blind alley.

Regardless of how senseless one's nations may seem at this level, this is the original stage of Kingism and from the roots of the Primitive Stage emerges the second stage. It is at this level where one either breaks or becomes strong. True lovers of the Nation develop at this stage.

THE CONSERVATIVE STAGE (also known as the Mummy Stage) is the stage of so-called maturity. At this level the King Warrior becomes tired of the Primitive Stage. He no longer wishes to participate in the senseless routine of gang fighting, hanging on the corner or being recognized as big and bad. Most often at this level the King Warrior gets married and retires, alienating himself from the boys and the Nation, concentrating his energies and devotion to his Queen, his children and his responsibility to them; ignoring the fact that he has unconsciously been neglecting his main responsibility to them and himself i.e., to make himself and his loved ones free!

It is inappropriate to call this stage the maturity Stage due to the fact that the King Warrior at this time does not really become mature in the true sense of maturity. Instead he becomes mummified or reaches a level of mummified maturity. He, in his conservative role, lives with no future, accepting life as it has been taught to him by the existing system that exploits all People of color - dehumanizes them and maintains them under the economic and social yoke of slavery.

True members of the Nation do not quit at this level, they do not cease to identify themselves with the Kings, instead they alienate themselves from them. They do not cease to be who they are, they conserve what they are; they become conservative. There are more Kings at this level than at any other level. And, although this stage has all the characteristics of a regressive stage, it is really the stepping stone into the third stage of Kingism - the New King Stage.

THE NEW KING is the stage of awareness and decision. The Primitive and Conservative stages are a compliment to the third. They go hand-in-hand with this stage of maturity, it does not keep the King Warrior in the limbo state of being i.e., the mummy like stage. At this level there is a stage of awareness, an awareness of one's self as a subject of decision.

Under the New King stage the world takes a completely new form. One no longer continues to visualize the street corner as his turf or being tough as a man of survival as in the Primitive stage nor does he remain in the mummy stage. Instead he learns to appreciate the values of organizational work, the values of life and Brotherhood. One no longer views the rival warrior as the cause of one's ills, instead his vision broadens to the extent of recognizing himself as a subject of decision. He learns that his ills lie at the roots of a system completely alien to his train of thought and his natural development due to the components of dehumanization that exist therein.

This stage is what determines righteousness, for it is at this stage where awareness leads to the point of decision, that point where one must decide one's future. This is where he either becomes an accomplice to that anti-King system or a subject of decision - A New King!

The New King recognizes that the time for revolution is at hand. Yes, revolution - a revolution of the mind! The revolution of knowledge! A revolution that will bring freedom to the enslaved, to all Third World People as we together sing and praise with joy what time it is - it's Nation time! Time for all oppressed People of the world to unite. The young warriors and future leaders look at the New King with the hope of someday being free. We shall not destroy the faith they have in us, for in doing so we destroy ourselves.

The New King is the end product of complete awareness, presieving three hundred-sixty degrees of enlightment. He strives for world unity. For him there are no horizons between races, sexes and senseless labels. For him everything has meaning, human life is placed above materialistic values. He throws himself completely into the battlefield ready to sacrifice his life for the ones he loves, for the sake of humanization.

The New King is endowed with the supreme natural powers that surpass the human scope of comprehension. This highly complexed energical entities separate him from the abstract world and all those who surrender themselves to vanity and idleness and place materialistic values above and beyond human principle.

The New King sees himself as a subject of decision, a Sun that must glow forever to enlighten those not so fortunate as he. He feels the rays of the Sun glowing in the essence of his being, giving him life, energy and strength - the strength of his unshakable spirit and the nobleness of his heart. The hypnotizing profundity of his gaze reflects the limitless power of his mind and the unshakable will to be FREE.

THE CODE OF KINGISM

Every member of the Nation shall honor, respect and protect with his life the lives and reputation of all members of the Almighty Latin King Nation.

Stand up for those who stand up for themselves in their quest for peace, justice, freedom, progress and prosperity.

Never exploit or bring harm to any member of the most righteous Tribe - The Lion Tribe - the Almighty Latin King Nation or any other oppressed person or nation.

Respect and protect with your life Brown Women for they are the mothers of our beautiful color the life of the future Suns of the Universe.

Love and respect children of all races, sexes, cults and religions. Protect them with your life for they are the leaders of tomorrow's Nations.

Honor and respect the Nation Salute for it means. "I DIE FOR YOU; the Sacred Colors for they represent the People we love and live for - the memory of those who rest in peace in the sanctuary of the Almighty Father, King of Kings.

Educate yourself, for an illiterate King is a weak King and a weak King has no place in a Strong Nation.

Learn your King Manifesto and live by it for it shall lead to Peace - Freedom - and Justice.

BEHOLD LATIN KING

NATIONAL EMBLEM

The Crown is the National Emblem of the Almighty Latin King Nation. It displays our royalty among men; our sovereignty and our Kingdom among Nations. The Crown is a symbol that is recognized all over the world and although there are many different types, the two that the Almighty Latin King Nation identify with the most are the Imperial and the Coronet.

The Imperial is the one most generally used to represent our beloved Nation because of its very meaning and magnificence.

Each of the Coronet's five points has a special meaning. They represent Love, Honor, Obedience, Sacrifice and Righteousness. The Crown enthrones our idealism, our belief and attitudes towards a better way of life in the universe....

SACRED COLORS

BLACK represents the solid dominant color of the universe, the brave and the bold, the darkness of the immense night. It represents People of one idea, one body, mind and soul, the Alpha and the Omega.

GOLD represents the fabulous brilliant Sun at its highest peak; the splendoring glow of hope in oppressed People, the brilliance of the mind and the solid unity in strength, love and sacrifice.

Two colors of natural creations existing since the beginning of time and enduring forever.

NATIONAL SALUTE

A fist upon our heart.... it means, "I DIE FOR YOU" for you are flesh of my flesh, blood of my blood, son of my mother who is the Universal Nature and follower of Yahve who is the Almighty King of Kings; it also means Love - Strength - Sacrifice.

BEHOLD LATIN KING

Glory to the Queens and Power to the Kings
Almighty Latin King Love, Yesterday, Today, Tomorrow, Always and Forever!

FEARLESSNESS

To the Almighty Latin King Nation, fearlessness implies absence of all kinds of fears. It is the freedom from such fears as hunger, humiliation, wrath and criticism of others. It is also the freedom from the fear of resistance, the freedom from the fear of loss of courage and the freedom from the fear of physical death. It is a necessity for a true Latin King because cowards can never be moral. Fearlessness is indispensable for the growth of other noble qualities.

How can one seek liberation, truth, or cherish love without fearlessness? Moral Bravery is, for the Nation, the highest heroism. And it consists in the readiness to sacrifice patiently and fearlessly, everything, including life for the good of other members of the Tribe of Righteousness out of love for them....

BEHOLD LATIN KING

NATION FLAG

The Flag shall consist of either two stripes - one Black and one Gold - running horizontally with a circle in the upper left corner of the top color with a Crown in the center of the circle or the Flag may consist of three stripes running vertically with a circle in the center stripe and a Crown in the circle.

The Flag shall never touch the floor or be placed where dishonor may fall upon it.

BEHOLD LATIN KING

The New King is the turning wheel of change, he recognizes what time it is - It's Nation time! He sees the rulers of our present system lavishing their treasures freely on the means of destruction, then towards that which would promote the happiness of mankind. These strifes and this bloodshed and this discord must cease and all oppressed People unite as one Nation, as one kindred, as one family.

The New King is aware of the fact that in the Almighty Latin King Nation all are servants, Brothers and Sisters - natural allies together in one nucleus. As soon as one feels a little better than the other, a little superior to the rest, he is in a dangerous position and unless he casts away the seed of such evil thought, he is not an instrument for the service of the Nation. Just as calamity is due for disobedience, so deliverance form calamity can be obtained by obedience. Turning from the Nation brings inevitable disaster and turning to the Nation brings blessings.

In order to establish the Kingdom of freedom in the world, it must first be established in the hearts of men. The King that lives the life according to the teachings of this Nation is the True King. A King who loves his Nation, his People and freedom; one who works for universal peace, universal freedom and universal Brotherhood. A man may call himself a King just as an ugly man may call himself handsome, yet if he does not live the life of a True King, he is not a King, and a ugly man deceives no one.

He who would be a New King needs to be a fearless seeker and lover of freedom. If his heart is pure and his mind is free from prejudice he shall not fail to recognize freedom from slavery. The call of the New King to mankind is that men should open their eyes and use their reason, not suppress it. It is seeing and free thinking, no servile credulity that will enable the True King to penetrate the clouds of prejudice, to shake the fetters of blind imitation and attain from the realization of truth a new revelation.

The New King will not only believe in the teachings of his Nation but will find in them the guide and inspiration for his life and joyfully impart to others the knowledge that is the well-spring of his own being. Only then will he receive the full measure of power of the Almighty Latin King Nation.

When a man becomes a New King the will of the nation becomes his will, for to be at variance with the Nation is one thing that cannot endure. The Almighty latin King Nation requires while-hearted and compete devotion.

How can divine King Love be demonstrated to an unbelieving world its capacity to endure to the utmost blows of calamity and the treachery of seeming friends; to rise above all t his undismayed and unembittered, still to forgive, bless and unite? The light of King Love irradiates his foggiest days, transmutes his suffering into hope and martyrdom itself into an ecstatical bliss. The New King longs to see believers of freedom shouldering the responsibilities of the cause. Now is the time to proclaim the Kingdom that is rightfully ours. Now is the time for union and concord. Now is the day of unity because it's Nation time!

The New King recognizes that the day of resurrection is here. A time for the appearance of a new manifestation of truth. The rising of the dead means the spiritual awakening of those who have been sleeping in the graveyard of ignorance. The day of the oppressor must now be judged by the oppressed.

BEHOLD LATIN KING

THE ALMIGHTY EYE

When a King Warrior accepts Kingism as described in the King Manifesto, his life takes a complete turn. For him everything changes. His vision is no longer limited to narrow horizons, instead he is gifted with the power of the Almighty Eye - a Sun that glows to enlighten, through the sense of sight, the New King and the Nation.

The eyes of the Nation are everywhere there is a Nation man, a True King. His perceptions, viewed in the concept of universal human progress, is the reflections of his soul, his ideology, his quest for freedom and his desire for unity among his People. His observations are free and independent; his thoughts are not clouded by any form of prejudice and his actions are based on common sense and knowledge.

Seeing, perceiving and observation by all Kings is the network of the Nation - the eyes of the Almighty Latin King Nation are everywhere.

BEHOLD LATIN KING

KING AM I

> Whether in front or profile I stand
> On that finished form let glory bestow
> Black its midnight shadow, Gold its morning glow
> In precision clear, a vision ever so bright
> That over the rest the domineering light
> Spreads the extensive vigor of its rays
> Any yields to me the power they praise
> That majesty, that grace, rarely given
> To remove the restraints with which they confine
> To pass before the turning wheel of change
> With supreme perfection my aim
> Love, truth and knowledge my claim.
> Below the thunderous lofty arch of light
> The whole in loveliest harmony unites
> For a True King the brightest glories soar
> The King of Kings applauds him and the

> world adores
> Let then each be firm allied
> And let no one separate or divide
> United in strict decorum, time and place
> An emulous love and genuine faith
> Be Grace, Be Majesty thy constant strive
> That majesty, that grace - King Am I.

Be it always remembered that the original Manifesto was written and dedicated to all oppressed people of the world, to the People and the Nation and to all our beautiful Sisters by the Brown Prince of Darkness. Amor!

BEHOLD LATIN KING

BROWN FORCE

The Latino can draw additional strength from another force too if he has the will and the faith.

Anonymous millions of Brown Men and Women have given their life in the fight for liberation. They have fought against colonialism, hunger and ignorance and for the human dignity of our People. They have drawn from one another, through unity, a force of fortitude - Brown Force - the force which provides the splendoring glow of hope in oppressed people. The seed they cast into the founding of a Nation - the Almighty Latin King Nation - has withstood the trials of time.

Drawing upon the endurance and fortitude of Brown Force, we continue our quest to unify and insure free political and culture expression among the Third World People and among the commonwealth of individuals. We are the People's liberating force - Brown Force - the foundation of the Nation.

BEHOLD LATIN KING

NATION MEN

Who is a Nation man and who is not? The difference lies in what they do, how they carry themselves and how they talk. But in order for one to really understand the contrast one must know and understand the principles of the King Manifesto and Modern Kingism.

One of the clearest contrastive examples is when the so-called Nation Man claims to be a Latin King, a member of the Almighty Latin King Nation, and by the same token says, "I am a Little; A Coulter King; A Pee Wee; I'm from such and such a branch or chapter, etc." He might be a Latin King, that is true, but he definitely is not a Nation Man.

This clearly testifies that this so-called Nation Man is really a demagogue, a preacher of a false philosophy, an agent of confusion and disunity. His mind is broad only to the scope of where his particular "click" is concerned. Outside of that click mentality his mind meets with the brick-wall of prejudice and individualism.

Nation Men on the other hand are devoted followers and believers of unity, supporters of the harmonious whole. For Nation Men there are no horizons between clicks and branches for they identify only with the Nation, not with a particular click, branch or section - natural allies together in one nucleus, one Nation, the Almighty Latin King Nation.

Your position of leadership requires that you become totally knowledgeble in planning projects and conducting our nations business, we can make being members of the S.G.D.N. a beneficial and meaningful experience. Remember that our objective is to give our family members tools through which they can personally benifit and apply to their lives.

I urge you brothers to put in all your heart and mind, and participate in helping our nation have years of pride and accomplishments. I bid you peace love an loyalty and deep respect for our fallen comrades.

> Our deeds will travel
> with us from afar, and
> what we have been,
> makes us what we are'"
>   VICTOR

(2) INSIGNIA

The Spanish Cross derives from our heretic ways, the first word in our Nations name, in which we find our race, our creed, our essential belifs and our faith.

These guiding principals unite us closer together and bound us as one. The circular disc behind the cross represents the highest degree of unity, unity being the reason for which we have constructed the S.G.D.N.

To unionize and coordinate the structure of all our branches under one foundation of S.G.D.N.

The disc behind the cross is to be carved on edge with "WREATH" type circles, for our loving memories of our dead.

Each stone on the cross will represent the color of our branches, the middle stone is to be the color of your original branch, all colors on the insignia are there to show respect and tribute to each of our affiliate organizations, which secure peace, praise, and credit to the foundation of our Nation.

This "Insignia" is to be worn proud, with a constant loyalty shown to the people of thee:
S.G.D.N.

(4) PREAMBLE

We, of thee: S.G.D.N. grateful to all our brothers for thier participation in our years of struggle, for our brothers with thier years of loyalty to our nations life. Through our nations decades we've enjoyed providing security, a sure safety and domestic tranquillity amoung the lives of our people.

We, brother's of the S.G.D.N. must ordain and abide by the nations constitution, to eliminate poverty and inequality amoung our people, to provide a structure of potential developments for the individual of our nation, to maintain a liberty for our children and a more gratifying style of social living. We bless all our people along with our families and we will constantly obtain a future for the descendants of our nation.

(5) CODE OF S.G.D.N.

"All code word's must be in a set of quotation's."
Stateville
    "Vic's Crib"
Pontiac
    "Imoky's Crib:
Manard
"Slim's Crib"
Administration
    "Neek's"

APPENDIX B:

WRITTEN CONSTITUTION AND BY-LAWS OF THE SPANISH GANGSTER DISCIPLE NATION

CONCEPT'S OF THEE 20th CENTURY

TABLE OF CONTENTS
(1)   GREETING'S
(2)   INSIGNIA
(3)   CROSS
(4)   PREAMBLE
(5)   CODE OF S.G.D.N.
(6)   A BROTHER'S OATH TO THE NATION
(7)   ADMINISTRATORS OF OUR NATION
(8)   ORGANIZATIONAL STRUCTURE
(9)   COMMUNICATION AND MEETING'S
(10)   AMENDMENTS OF S.G.D.N.
(11)   AMENDMENTS OF THEE INCATCERATED
(12)   EDUCATION AND EMPLOYMENT
(13)   SECURITY
(14)   DISCIPLE'S HISTORY
(15)   GANGSTER'S HISTORY
(16)   MOTTO - IDEALOGY - GOALS
(17)   LOVING MEMORIES OF OUR BROTHER'S & SISTER'S
(18)   GLOSSARY

(1) GREETING'S TO OUR COMRADES

Greeting's Comrades

Before I proceed any futher into this letter, I would like to extend our nation's love to all our family members who in their time of incarceration have served our distinguished organization faithfully and effectively.

My sole purpose is to speak to our comrades in arms through these unspoken words, in order that I may convey the basic information that you may need to function effectively in our dignified organization. It also gives me great pleasure to acquaint you with our new ideology and some of the needed changes that have taken place within our nation. To begin with, changes in our nsential for the "total S.G.D.N." to be a reality.

We must all be aware that in the history of anyone of our organizations, we have shown failure in many ways, and we have also accomplished some achievements, as for instance, the 60's for us was not a decade of many accomplishments, and the same applies for the 70's, but the 80's will be a new day for us, and not to mention a more successful decade. "No other success can compensate for failure in our Nation".

Here is something we must all acknowledge! The S.G.D.N. makeup is a composite of all the organizations that came together to form it. If we all play active roles, the S.G.D.N. will become a strong nation. And if we don't all agree to participate, our nation will become weak. "It's that simple". We can all make a difference.

Police
> "Pig"

S.G.D.N.
> "Folk's"

Familia Disciple's
> "Gente"

Cobra's
> "c"s"

Gangster's
> "Division"

Disciple's
> "Rockwell"

Satan Disciple's
> "Taylor's"

B.G.D.N.
> "Allies"

B.D.N.
> "Discipulo Negro's"

King's
> "Corona"

S.C.R.
> "Peaches"

Joliet
> "Angel's Crib"

Mail
> "Carta"

Nation
> "Nasióa"

Segragation
> "Pit"

Parole Board
> "Tabla de Violar"

Law's
> "Leyes"

Constitution
> "foundation"

Literature
> "Fact's"

Organization
> "La Unión"

Incarcerated
> "Pared"

Penal Institution's
> "Chßteau"

Figa
> "Old Spice"

Add words as needed -

(6) A BROTHER'S OATH TO THE NATION

A sworn oath to the nación in sound form from each of our hearts, a oath to the people, for the people and accepted by the people. As a brother of the Spanish Gangster Disciple nación, I, in belief of the nación's ideology and teachings of the constitution, swear to uphold the honor and protect the nación, to show love and endure 100% loyalty toward the people of our nación.

To maintain silence in our nación, in respect to abiding by the law's of our constitution, giving my life to my brother's; never to betray a brother in code of *Death*Before*Dishonor*, securing our rights to love, to carry life, and to pursue the loyalty we share.

As this statement to be truth I, swear to our beloved insignia to carry the name Spanish-Gangster-Disciple-Nación-, and to serve as a prophet to the faith of our Nación until my death...

(7) ADMINISTRATOR'S OF OUR NACIÓN

Governor:

Our Governor is the chief executive of our Nación. Our Governor's responsibility is to maintain and oversee his administrator's functions toward the people of the Nación.

Lt. Governor:

There is one Lt. Governor in our Nación while incarcerated, his function is to exercise and perform duties handed down to him by the Governor.

Ambassador's:

Ambassador's are officials appointed by the Lt. Gov.- an ambassador's functions are to carry out duties handed down to them by the Lt. Gov.; an appointed ambassador must carry himself in form as follows:

1. A)   Our ambassador's must carry a positive and firm attitude, this be mentally as well as physically. He has to maintain a strick discipline upon himself in which those of our Nación can see and recognize: "A Explicit Character".

1. B)   Our ambassador is an official appointed in position of commands, but the ambassador is not to constantly impose his position upon our brother's of the Nación.

2. A)   Ambassador must have a wide understanding along with patience to relate to any situation that may arise. To be able to comprehend all information before making the decision to make a move, the ambassador must consult with the Lt. Governor before he makes the move in question.

2. B)   An ambassador has to approach and speak to all brother's of our Nación in a manner in which all the brother's understand what has been said, and to make sure all brother's comprehend the idea at hand.

3. A)   A ambassadors mental attitude must be to maintain peace at all times, this is amoungst our Nación; we are to bare arms after all avenues have been exhausted.

3. B) A ambassador must realize for faulty decisions he is to expect the same penalty as any brother in transgression.

VICEROY- Appointed by the ambassador to maintain a cell-house!

(8) ORGANIZATIONAL STRUCTURE

There is no ideal organizational structure that fit's the needs of every single S.G.D.-member, but there is one that is right for your's, which is, "The Board Of Directors", the board of directors merely figures out all the job functions and activities that are needed. The board sensibly and fairly distributes them to certain officers on the board.

Fortunately we have been in existence long enough to assist you with the assignment. As you design your structure there are a few guidelines that will assist you, they are:

1.)   No one person should be required to manage more than six (6) to ten (10) member's.

2.)   The workload should be balanced between the Board Member's.

3.)   The system must be flexible so that additional people and programs can be added during the coming years. It must also be flexible enough to handle a reduction in the number of people and programs.

4.)   Each Ambassador must know what is expected of him, the importance of his role in achieving the overall objectives, and the standards by which his performance will be judged.

These are examples of how you can shift workloads to a new officer when it is necessary. Whatever structure you finally choose, let it be flexible enough to accommodate the growth of your section. As you grow, al the management functions of your section increase. It's far better to add new positions to alleviatae some of the new burdens than to let the present Board members become overworked. Don't be afraid to change your structure when it is necessary.

(9)   COMMUNICATION AND MEETING'S

If you don't communicate effectively, you won't lead effectively. Leadership involves getting things done through people. How well you do this, this will be determined by your ability to communicate. You have to look upon communication as your most valuable asset, other than your own personal communication methods there is one primary way that a section can comunicate with it's member's. Thee primary way is through: Meeting's!

MEETING'S

Board meetings are the single most important time where all aspects of the management of your section should be reviewed and discussed. Items that should be discussed are such items as follows:

1.)   The status of all projects.
2.)   Attitude of older and younger member's.
3.)   Whose dues are due next month.
4.)   Budget review and your sections plan of
        action.
5.)   Review of last membership meeting's, the
        good point's and the bad point's.
6.)   Plan for next Board meeting!

You should be an active participant at all Board meeting's, it is your elected responsibility. Regular membership meeting's are equally important. It is during these meeting's that several things are accomplished. Direction for your section is decided, the member's are informed, motivated, and the opportunities available in your section are on display.

Even though it is the direct responsibility of your Governor, Lt. Governor, or Ambassador to insure that you have effective and productive meeting's, it is your responsibility to assist them in several areas. Areas such as:

1.)   You should actively participate in the planning of the next membership meeting at each   B o a r d meeting.

2.)   You should insure that your reports, and reports of your Directors and committee chairman are always short, clear, and concise. (To the Point)- Nothing turns off members more than long and unprepared committee reports.

3.)   If the meeting or an individual becomes unruly you should assist the Governor in getting the meeting back to order as soon ass possible. Or Chairman -

NOTE:

Always arrive at Board meetings one half hour before starting time of the meeting. You can help with any last minute set ups. Be sure that you also review the basics with all members so that they can more effectively participate in meeting's.

Speaking of Board meeting procedures, you should have a basic idea of how it works and it's importance in conducting the affairs of our organization. You don't have to be a lawyer to understand the Board's procedure. All you must do is realize that it is merely a tool to shorten meeting's, conduct business and ensure fairness to all our member's.

(10)   AMENDMENTS OF S.G.D.N.

1.)   All members must respect and participate in maintaining a code of silence within our family, and at all times conduct themselves in accordance with our family's laws. All members must display faithful allegience to the family's organization and to thier appointed superiors.

2.)   Discourtesy, rude, or impolite remarks will not be tolerated, absolutley no fighting amoung family members.

3.)   No family members shall at anytime consume any addictive drugs, or encourage the use of drugs to any family member.

4.)   All family members will acknowledge authorative commands handed down to them by thier appointed superiours. Insubordination, will not be tolerated from any member towards thier superiours.

5.)   "At No Time" - will any member put up with, or tolerate any offensive critisizm towards this organization - by those non-affiliated with our family, nor shall we see any members outrage the moral feelings of any righteous family member.

6.)   All members of this family are expected to sacrifice and devote thier lives for this family's cause.

7.)   All members will be at any aid to the members of thee B.G.D.N. - and to this family, in any difficulty or problem that they may have, be it mentally or physically.

8.)   Misrepresentation of this family, or of any appraisales, flags, embloms, or colors will not be tolerated.

9.)   All members- regardless of rank or position must strive to assist each other, not to compete with one another.

10.)   All members must make a solemn declaration to uphold all commands handed down to them, and to make a oath from thier heart and soul to this family- that all members will be a part, even if there are times of depression.

11.)   All members will experience and undergo the same penalties imposed on any member of this organization who breaks or goes beyond the limits of our set laws. "No exceptions will be made!" Regardless of rank or position.

12.)   The penalty for any transgression made against this organizations laws- will be left up to the discretion of your superiors, considering the nature of the law that was broken, then the member in the wrong will be dealt with according to the law broken.

13.)   Ignorance of our laws are of no excuse, all members shall make it thier initiative to come and know each and every law, and percieve to understand the full meaning to our laws, and also apply yourselfs to them.

(11)   AMENDMENTS OF THEE INCARCERATED

1.)   In each place of where you are confined, there is a box... All family members who are able must contribute to help others in the family who are not as fortunate as other members. (This includes for the people of orientation).

2.)   At no time shall we disrespect any member of another nation - all grudges from the street are to be held until you return to the streets. We as a nación, are in no position to participate in meaningless struggles which will only prolong our stay in these confinements. If any problems occur, a decision will be made by high authority.

3.) We shall not play with any officer of the jail, they have a job to do. It is to keep us here. Unless you can gain off the situation, leave it alone. Our struggle is to show love to each other, and one day be set free. The administration holds us. So consider them off limits, unless it benifits you, or any other member of this family.

4.) We are allies of the B.G.D.N., but we are an independant nación, we are our own ruler, we take orders from our own organization only... Give the members of the B.G.D.N., all due respect at all times.

5.) Attend to your personal needs, ask one another for what you lack, we shall not hold back on anything that will make one of our people be without...

6.) All members shall take orders from thier appointed superiours of any cellhouse. Disrespect in any form is an immediate violation of King Vic's laws.

7.) We shall represent with (2) fists across the chest. We all have an original way of representing. Either way will be proper. We all understand the love and meaning behind representing.

8.) We all know who we are, and what we stand for. If in any place or situation you cannot represent, well, we know one doesn't have to hit his chest to be 100% loyal to this almighty family.

9.) We are Gangsters, Disciples, Cobras, Eagles, all united into one familia de amor, We are Disciples of each other-we are King Vic's Disciples. We be about the latino organization, so spread out the laws and the teachings of our supreme Nación.

(12) EDUCATION + EMPLOYMENT

This section is specifically for all our fellow familia members to gain as much knowledge in these two areas as possible. Education and Employment are two essential needs throughout your confinement and also in todays society.

During ones confinement, if an individual has not yet obtained his diploma, he should take advantage of the educational system. We find in our confinement areas that there are two types of educational programs. 1.) One is the school for individuals to obtain a G.E.D. The other educational program is the vocational school, a place where a individual can learn a trade. Actual learning experiences in trades such as: welding skills, electrical training, small engines, computer programing, and a print shop trade. Of these mentioned vocational skills an individual can obtain a verified certificate of his achievement. An individual can further the achievement into becoming a "Journey Man" in one of these specific field's.

Members of our organization with these achievements are important assets to our daily progress, but also as an individual with these skills you can become financially stable. Employment is most important to our people's needs, whether it is employment while incarceration, or in society. But a structure of development must be set to raise our peoples standards and classification.

While in confinement there are jobs where a individual can learn a specific skill, such as; tailoring, cooking, barbering, electrician skill, plumbing or even legal aid's. Our ideas toward our people are; not letting thim sit around to let time pass by, each of our people must take a day in life to make the decision of what he or she wants out of life, and to set the structure of obtaining the set goal, whether it be through Education or Employment.

(13) SECURITY

In maintaining security of the lifestyle we live, one must have eyes that memorize and see at the same time. The importance of memory can be vital to you and any brother around you. Communication amoung our brothers is our greatest virtue, for what one brother misses in his sight, another brother can carry the blind to see the light of a situation; as in understanding, teach our brothers understanding until they are capable of being the prophet.

In maintaining security of a organization; all information that is kept within one brothers mind can be vital to other brothers who are left in the dark of a situation. Our guard is to be up at all times and we are to strike first if need be, because for our people to be struck at first is a sure sign of being lax.

It is always best to be in the pressance of another brother at all times, if not, for best results let another bother know of your whereabouts, in case of any occurrance that may come about. When the question is asked about a brothers whereabouts, someone should know at all times. In case of any unusual happening it is a brothers first obligation to notify others, a brother is always to handle the situation at hand, any revengious act of a brother is not tolerated, especially a act alone- consult other brothers in the surrounding's to make the wisest decision as a whole, never leaving any brother in the dark.

As a individual in a organization, to maintain personal security it is wise to be properly clothed at all times, and also to have showes on instead of "Thongs", or slippers. When returning from a shower it is best to put on shoes, never lounge around - especially in jail where a incident may occur at any given time.

In maintaining personal security it is wise to sleep with the door locked, never sleep with the door open. Then again in parable form, "Never Sleep"...

(14) WORDS OF HISTORY

The history and concepts of thee: Maniac Latin Disciples. The current slogan "You've come a long way baby" certainly applies to the "Maniac Latin Disciples".

We have evolved from the dream of a small group of youths in the late part of the sixties into a vital, effective organization.

When the scope of the Spanish Gangster Disciple Nation, of today is considered, it is difficult to concieve it's beginning as the Latin Scorpions of Rockwell and Hirsch.

The Maniac Latin Disciples, are not of recent vintage, of course. The organization had been built exactly a decade and a half ago, and it's purpose, the social elevation of it's members, a goal the organization rapidly attained. By the mid-seventies it was the most outstanding organization in the vicinity and it prepared to merge with several other similar groups to form the federation of the Maniac Latin Disciples.

During the early years of our emergence, followed a series of clashes with our rivals, a wawr that to this day is still in existence. Where upon we lost a great number of our comrades, our members pride themselves on dealing with the enemy in thier terms, I could describe hundreds of episodes that relate to the wars we've had, but it would take me forever. Also, during the early years of our existence the Maniac Latin Disciples gained support from many of it's members, but none was greater and more valuable than the support gained from our allies.

This history culminates today into what we now term "The Spanish Gangster Disciple Nation Concept". It, then, can be understood as a convenient label pinned to a whole way of life, a living system that develops and changes in the course of time.

(15) WORDS OF HISTORY

The life of a common street gang, a historical document manufested for future purposes of: Our descendants having questions of how we as a people came about, and how we as a people still progress in todays era, as well as the yesterdays.

Speaking vividly as a original member of the Imperial Spanish Gangster's, I can only try to put over 15 years of events on paper in a brief menner, many events here with will remain known only to those of the Imperial Spanish Gangsters who lived through the history of the Nation.

To bring out the reason why we as a people became a Nation; our first lable was not Gangsters, we were just a bunch of young kids attending school, but being that the school was dominated by the white, as Latino's, we fought against the white almost every day- never having intentions of being any specific group, so as time went by more Latino's attended the school, thus giving the Latino's more power and making survival easier.

In the year 1969 a section of Imperial Gangsters had became known in the area of Armitage and Drake, by people like; Pito a said leader as well as Jabar, Lil Mexico, Lil Bug's, Goyo, and Killer, not having any real goal in mind but to be as a defense to the white street gangs.

At the end of the same year another section of people came about which added another name to the already - Imperial Gangsters, being that most members were of latin origin the second section became — Imperial Spanish Gangster's, the section was labled the division and grand people, or Cameron Gangster's. In that same year a sweater was brought about by one- Jesse Rodreguez, or known as "Lil Bug's" R.I.P., the sweater being black with baby pink cuts and trim. The first sweater thought of by the people of Cameron was to be black and white, but this unballanced the two sections so to unite the two sections Cameron people accepted the pink and black, for a emblom which was a Imperial crown- it is always to be a rounded crown at the top, with 5 head band diamonds to distinguish the crown from the three point crown of the latin kings, a later enemy to the Nation.

As Imperial Spanish Gangsters, the two sections decided to have thier leader's, which was a president, a vice president and a war chief. The first leaders started to live thier personal lives with wives and from that the people of armitage and drake had to take a step of advancement, the section of armitage and drake had to move the section to a different place and vote on we leadership.

The Imperial Gangsters of armitage and drake had the business on armitage tied up in thier favor, resturants, a theater, a cleaners, and parshally a liquor lounge. These businesses were important because of the donated money handed to the people of armitage and drake. As a street gang many shootings took place, shootings against the white gangs who just didn't like the latino, and the shootings against a street gang of latinos who wanted all latins to became latin kings. But the two sections of Imperial.

Gangsters held thier ground and kept what was thier's.

A meeting took place in 1972 for the section of Armitage people to move because they were to open for target and to open for the enemy of the law. The meeting was held in the Armitage theator which was a known place of the Gangster people. During the meeting it was known that the leaders of the new section was to be Lil Mexico as president, Goyo as vice president, and the move was to be on Palmer and Drake.

Lil Bug's was considered for position, but because of his military involvment, he "Lil Bug's" didn't want position.

For positions of the Cameron people, the first leader was Spanky as president, Tito as vice president-the people of Cameron had a change in leadership after a year or two, and the leadership was in one man known as; Godfather, he was the president and instead of a vice president, or war chief, the people of Cameron had thier "main" people. People like; Tiny, Casanova, Jauquin, Mr. Doc, M.D.Ron, Cisco, "secret squarral James", Caveman R.I.P., Lil man, Alberto, Tomo, Modesto, Fingers, Lil Joe, and Miguel "Chulito", White Boy.

The Cameron people had a section of future's who were; Sinbad, Cat, Milton Juni, Speedy, Armondo "Chico", and moreno, Moreno with his aggressive style and attitude became one of the main people and participated in the Gangster Nation with his life. A credit to the future's for being young and having the heart of survival.

With Cameron being the back bone to the Nation of Gangster's and with Armitage people having thier money businesses, more sections were formed, as Palmer and Drake became larger, a section of people came about, being the Sawyer and Armitage people, stemming from the help of people like- Lil Bug's and Lil Mexico, as for other factions of Gangster's, there were- Continental Gangsters- originated by the minister, Ghetto Gangsters originated by Mijo and the newest section of Imperial Spanish Gangster's on North & Hamlin.

Two brother's by the name of Smokey and Ellio are the ones who came up with the name Gangster's. The Supreme Gangster's, turned into the Imperial Gangster's.

There were always the lady Gangster's to each section, ladies being mostly latin and dedicated in our ways; ladies like; Morena R.I.P., Miss Lee R.I.P., Flac, Goofie, Bozo, Jeanie, Liz, Luz, Anita, Chiqueta, Happy, Smiley, Troubles, Peanut, Tita Maria, Elsa, Patty, Cateyes, Mary, GiGi, Herliena and Gym shoes. These ladies being a important part in our life, being mother to our peoples children and mostly by getting bonds together for thos who found themselves in jail.

As jail became part of the Nations life it brang about different ideas and made the members of the Nation smarter with sophisticated acts instead of openly-where jail was the next step.

Jumping to the year of 1976, this was the year the Imperial Spanish Gangsters had thier share of dealing with the law, until 1976 members were going in jail and finding it hard to get out, so the next thing to do was deal with the jail system because there were more Gangster's coming in jail then leaving the jail. In the jails the people of the Imperial Spanish Gangster's found other allies that they've dealt with on the street, by allies I speak of; Maniac Latin Disciple's, Satans Disciple's, Latin Eagle's, Spanish Cobra's, O-A;S, Milwalkee Kings and the Y.L.O. DISCIPLE'S.

In the jail wa've found the enemy still existed so a merge was constructed and these Nations became silently united in the struggles of the jail, we found ourselves fighting just to go to court in peace, to be able to get the proper share of food, or because of what you belonged too and to survive in jail as a whole was a duty you had to plan, there were only a hand full of people; Vic, M.D.R., Sach-Mo, Pito, Moreno, Bad-Boy, Aggie, Slim-D, Beaver, Mustang, Killer and Lucky plus Chino. We were never able to put our guard down against the whole system and the only people who could be trusted was these members of the silently put together Nation.

After years of seperation from these people because of convictions and seperated joints the silent Nation was at a stand still, but during the past year steps have been taken to unite and foundate all the Nations under one main title, neverto forget your originating people, and instead of all the different titles and beliefs, a structure was set up by leaders of these Nations for all the people to understand one way in one belief as a whole. In this one way we all have to follow a pattern to survive, to prosper in our growth, and to set forth a accomplishing goal.

We as a Nation have to have morals, to teach our young in every subject, to abide by our set of laws, to carry our Nations oath in our heart, to accept our prayer for our desceased and accept our constitution to keep our "Families" and "Nation" in a state of peace and well being.

— Constantly in Thought —

Always a special tribute to our ladies,
and to our families for putting up with
our chaotic ways, to all the people who
have suffered in making our Nation possible, all the goods and bads we've dealt
with and we still live. My special love
too two aggressive brothers of the Nation.
Moreno— and TopCat.

(16) MOTTO OF S.G.D.N.

Motto being a structure of words to express ones beliefs, ones conduct; a phrase suitable to it's character;

"Our deeds will travel with us from afar, and what we have been, makes us what we are".

IDEOLOGY OF S.G.D.N.

INGREDIENTS

1. LOYALTY

2. SECURITY

3. PROGRESS

GOALS

1. Freedom for our confined brother's

2. Enbetterment of our people, and our children.

3. Unity-North and South - Harmony within the Latino Barrios.

(17)   LOVING MEMORIES OF OUR BROTHER'S & SISTER'S

:   Please, with a powerful unseen faith, with a meaning-ful trust and for the sake of loving memory, let us combine our hearts in a true moment of silence for our Brother's & Sister's who have lost thier lives in being part of our Nation's struggle...

:   A mere moment is vaguely enough to show tribute for the feelings we have. With this dedicated thought to you of our desceased, we will carry you in our hearts for the peace we have had in our daily lives...

:   We feel you through music we hear, we feel you through things we see, we feel you through our conversations, and most of all we have a hold on each other's heart...

:   At times we have a picture in our hand, at times we have a vision in our mind, and at this time we praise what you be rested in your peace...

:   In Loving Memory
of our's who —:
REST IN PEACE

MESSAGE:

Our Nation will continue, and it's through these changes that our nation will grow to it's height. Changes come through the new ideas proposed by any family member. Each individual who is an active member of this supreme nation, is given the opportunity to grow and develop along with it.

To further the growth of our nation, I have proposed an idea that will advance the unification of all our allies. My presentation to our allies is for us to go under one name, not only in these penal institutions, but also in the free world.

I discussed my proposal over with Mad-Dog, in re-spect that he is looked upon as a leader among his peoples organization, and with some of our other allies, and they all endorsed my proposal. So our strength of minds were mutual.

We will assume the name of - Spanish Gangster Dis-ciple nation, those of you who oppose our proposal will just have to step to the side and let our nation lunge forward and gain ground.

Mad-Dog and I, have dispatched word to the free world informing our comrades of the S.G.D.N. movement. All of us as a whole are obligated to spread the word to our com-rades who are in different penal institutions, and to those who are in the free world.

Through full and total participation we shall achieve the development and growth of our nation, and thereby stimu-late the personal development of each of our members. Those members who show leadership potentials should be prepared to assume leadership roles in our organization.

Asymbol had to be thought up, one which would char-acterize and represent our newly founded nation, and we came up with the idea to devise a cross that will symbolize the Span-ish Gangster Disciple Nation. So Sach-Mo and I designed it. The cross bares five(5) stones, with the colors of each of the original organizations that came together to form the S.G.D.N., the cross is a process by which the "whole nation" can offer it's member's, a total experience, personal development, and not to forget, effective service to the S.G.D.N.

APPENDIX C:

INTERNAL DOCUMENTS AND
OFFICIAL MEMORANDA
OF THE BROTHERS OF THE STRUGGLE (B.O.S.)

(typed Memo dated July 14, 1982: From an Illinois Prison; reproduced here "as is" in the original style, spelling, and syntax)

Date: July 14, 1982

From: The Chairman and Board of Directors

To: All Brothers of the Struggle

Subj: Awareness Session

The Movement

It is a fact, without contradiction that the success of any movement depends largely upon the participation of the mass of people involved in that particular struggle. Leadership without active support, is as useless as spitting in the winds to aid in putting out a major fire. (The fire in this case is the burning effects of povery, lost direction, and progressive states of self-destruction.) The same is true with the lack of Leadership for the people. The two must combine to coordinate the movement, and each part must do it's share in reaching the goals of the group. What is more important is that the directions of the Organization be set forth, and that each concerned member adher to those directions, making the necessary sacrifices required to accomplish the objectives.

The Objectives

A group of people organized around the idea of reaching common objectives is called an Organization. Without that Unity that comes from having a common purpose, the same group of people qualifies as a Mob, Gang, etc., Therefore it is essential that each member realize the objectives of the group. Know what it is that inspire the need for Unity, and what it is that binds them One to the Other. Otherwise, their membership becomes questionable.

One of the basic objectives of the Black Gangster Disciple Nation is: "To obtain the means to Self-Determination for our People." We can not possibly determine anything without being AWARE of our situation, as well as our alternatives.

This AWARENESS does not come from acting foolish, nor from beng lax in your efforts to learn. Therefore the Leadership has opened up avenues for you to gain a perspective on life, our situation, and all aspects of progressive AWARENESS. One such avenue is the AWARENESS SESSIONS, conducted by the Legal Arm of the Organization.

Awareness Session

The interest of our members are many, therefore the subjects of the Awareness Sessions are many. Listed below are the objectives of the Awareness Session.

1. Bring a vast range of Intelligence to the availability of the people.

2. Promote an environment of creativity among the people.

3. Practice the art of debate.

4. Inspire dignity in our people, by introducing them to a Black History, as well as a Black Heritage.

5. To in general, uplift the mental, emotional, and spiritual growth of our people.

All sessions shall be in accordance with the six points of the Star of David, signifying the six principles upon which our Organization is founded. These principles are: Love, Life, Loyality, Knowledge, Wisdom & Understanding.

The goals we have set to reach in these AWARENESS SESSIONS are valid goals. We expect to range from Politics to Stock Markets. We shall speak of wars and cultures, as well as the law.

Rules of the BGDN

1. Silence and Secrecy. No member shall give any information or discuss any matters that concerns any member or the function of the organization to any individual that is not a standing member.

2. Drugs. No member shall consume or inject any drug that is addictive.

3. Stealing. No member shall steal from any convict, inmate, or resident.

4. Respect. No member shall be disrespectful to any member or non member. Being disrespectful to others only entices others to become hostile and disrespectful to you which leads to unnecessary and stilly confrontations. Always be respectful, dignified, honorable, loyal and thoughtful.

5. Breaking and Entering. No member shall break in or enter any building that will cause unde heat and pressure to others making moves that cause institutional lock-ups and shake-downs is prohibited.

6. Gambling. No member shall gamble in any games unles all parties have their money up front.

7. Guards. No member shall engage in any unnecessary confrontations with any officer's or administrative personnel.

8. Sportmanship. No member shall engage in any heated arguments or fights while participating in any sport or games. Use good sportsmanship at all times.

9. Personal Hygiene. All members must look presentable at all times and all living quarters should be kept clean.

13. Exercising. All members are required to jog three times around the yard and do fifty jumping jacks together at the beginning of each yard period except on Saturday, Sunday and night yard.

14. Exploiting. No member shall use his membership, staff or office to exploit funds or favors from any member.

15. A.R. 804. All members are required to read and become familiar with the D.O.C. A.R. 804 administration discipline.

16. Rape. No member shall use threat or force to make any one engage in homosexual acts.

July 23, 1983

TO : ALL BROTHERS OF THE STRUGGLE

FROM : THE CHAIRMAN AND THE BOARD OF DIRECTORS

RE : MIRANDA WARNINGS

FELLOW BROTHERS OF THE STRUGGLE

"Nothing hurts a duck, but its Bill (MOUTH)." The leadership is sure that you all are familiar with this old and truthful saying, because if any one of you have ever had the opportunity to go on a hunting trip (in the free world) before being locked up, then you know full well that if the duck had kept his mouth shut, instead of quacking, he wouldn't have given his position away, and naturally, would'nt have been our dinner.

This comparison with the duck, our Brothers, is used to stress home to everyone the value and importance of keeping your mouths shut, especially when you are confronted by investigators of the D.O.C., police, Counselors, med techs, even the ministers and others.

As you are all aware, situations occur where it may be necessary to take care of organizational business. Naturally it should be understood that there will be steps taken by D.O.C. messengers to find out who, and how the business was taken care of.

Not all business can be taken care of in a smooth way without a large mass of people actually seeing what has taken place, but they are in the immediate area., naturally, you should know that there will be a general round up of everyone in the vicinity.
Lets recount these steps very briefly, because they are very important. First some business is taken care of., Second, some one saw what occurred, but due to the amount of people in the vicinity at the time of discovery, everyone is detained and checked out.

Third, Whether your name was given by a notorious messenger, or you are being checked out by a group of investigators, state police, state's attorney, etc., due to the fact that the group you're in at the time (recreation period etc)., is being questioned, etc. The main question is "How do you handle yourslef at this time? What will be your reaction while you and maybe two, three, four, or more (B.O.S.) are being singled out as the persons to allegedly took care of the business, what would you say to these investigators who you know are tying to pin something on you with hopes of getting you the electric chair?

If, for whatever reason, you said you would talk to them in any way, (regardless of the exchange of words) you have just made the biggest mistake of your life, why? because, you are not, or were not to say anything at all to them. Let us explain further, here is the situation, the police, investigators etc, don't have enough information to go on that would give them a better than average chance to obtain a conviction., The only hoe they have is that they can make you convict yourself by breaking, thus implicating others, and making confessions etc. Say for instance that those of you being charged or investigated, were separated from one another and placed in different rooms, or different joints so you could'nt communicate with each other to find out what the other is saying or has said so far.

While you are in separate rooms, by yourselves for awhile, in comes two, three, or more investigators with a pen, pad or tape recorder. One of them offers a cigarette, coffee, food, or whatever, you accept it, or you Don't, its up to you. If, however, you take their offerings, then, you have implicated by your acceptance that the possibility of you breaking is very great, because, not everyone has the strong will to accept their offerings and turn around and say, "Go to hell", or "I have nothing to say".

Before any questions have been asked, you were supposed to have been given or read your rights, formerly known as the Miranda Warnings.

These warnings come from a 1966 case, (Miranda vs. Arizona), Under these wardings yu must be informed of the following:

1. You have the right to remain silent under the due process of law, 5th and 14th amendments, and that anything you say can and will be held against you in a Court of law.

2. You have the right to have a lawyer present and to consult with a lawyer during questioning., If you cannot afford one, a lawyer will be supplied by the government.

3. You are entitled to make one free telephone call so don't waste it, contact a lawyer or somebody who can obtain one for you.

While this is going on and afterwards, it is extremely important that you don't sign anything, papers, etc., without the advice of your lawyer.

Our Brothers, all of the above must be remembered, as well as, all that you say, if you made a statement or statements to the investigators in the presence of others, but did not sign it, it may still be used against you, so it is best to just remain silent, its as simple as that.

The investigators, police, state's attorney, etc., use a number of techniques to get a person to tell on himself and implicate others.

That which seems natural our brothers, is often times unatural, let us explain. Say for instance you were on your way to take care of some business and the cop stopped you, asking you for your pass but you don't have one and he tell you to return to your cellhouse, then somebody, member, non-member, etc, came passing by you and the cop, but the cop said nothing to them as he had you, and you blurt out to the cop "you let them go by why did you stop kme, and he call them back and ask for a pass, but they don't have one, this may appear to be a natural quesiton, but, what yu have done is told on someone and kept them from taking care of their business because of your big MOUTH.

This is called dry snitching and will not be tolerated from anyone, what one do reflects on the whole which you all know., To say that you let so and so do this or that, or they are doing this why can't we do it seems a natural question to ask the authorities but it clearly is not and cannot be justified, and most certainly will not be tolerated.

SINCERELY

YOUR CHAIRMAN AND BOARD OF DIRECTORS

(undated typed document)

Preface

Our governing body has decided to take on a New Concept of Organization. A concept that will bring us into the 80's and prepare us for the political and economical realities of Black America. Our Leadership feels that we must take advantage of our imprisonment; we must learn what's necessary to be a productive and disciplined organization while we're confined. If we are successful here in this inferior situation, there's no limitations on our potential in the outside world.

The Leadership doesn't expect miracles from the people in our new undertakings. We are aware of the fact that it took us eighteen (18) years to get into this shape. The Leadership also realizes without the full support of the people, it will take another (18) years or more to make this New Concept of Organization a reality. Unfortunately we don't have that kind of time to waste. Therefore, the Leadership is requesting that all qualified members help us make this transition in to the New Concept. We have wasted enough time dwelling on insignificant matters. Let's prepare ourselves for the World.

In the process of going from the Old to the New, we will have a few complications. It must be understood from the outset that we are not forgetting our past, (as some of you know, we have had good moments as well as bad moments in the past) we're putting our past where it belongs, behind us. Our past will serve as a motivating force that will enable us to have a glorious future. It's a necessity that we go through changes. You're either growing or dieing. To stand still is to Die, our Leadership has decided that we will live and flourish into something great.

All Organizations have Discipline. Discipline is a necessity in all things pertaining to development. Our organization is in transtion. Discipline is essential and must be enforced. All members will adhere to all laws governing the organization. The governing body has updated the laws. We want our laws to reflect our intelligence as well as our strength. These will be absolutely No!!!! exception or exemption from the laws.

Our governing body will be invested with the power to make policies and laws. Our Chairman will have final say on all policies and laws. Our governing body will be called board of directors. All board members will be appointed by the Chairman.

Organizational Structure
1. When it comes to the organization; the individual is subordinate to the organization.
2. The minority is subordinate to the majority.
3. The entire membership is subordinate to the Chairman and the governing body. Whoever violates these articles of organizational structure will be charged with disrupting organizational unity and dealt with in that fashion as an enemy of the people.

We have witnessed what comes from a lack of Unity and Discipline. Now, observe what comes from Unity and Discipline.

If we are to become a power to reckon with, We must take on the concept of organization. Everyone must do their share. Everybody has a responsibility. For we make up the organization as individuals who have come together as a collective.

THE COMMON SENSE APPROACH

Notations: To be rememberd at all atimes:

Because of inadequate prevention against organization, organiz-

ing exist, a new engineering solution must be introduced for the present and future goals of this nation. In composing these solutions to the problems that deeply stagnates the body of this organization, the solutions to eradicate these problems will be given in a self-explanatory and compehensive dialogue, so that everyone may better understand the goals and concepts of our nation:

(Dialogue)

There seems to be a syndrome orientation of negativism, meaning an attitude or system or thoughts characterized by doubt and question, rather than approval and acceptance. An attitude characterized by ignorning, resisting, or opposing suggestions and orders coming from people that are in a position of authority......

(Findings)

A majority of our people are guility of this negativism, reasons are, "most people are unaware of the definition of organization, "therefore it will be spelled out as followed: (Organization is a unified & consolidated group of people, with an executive structure that deals with the well-being of all it's people. It's an executive structure of business & enterprise for individual growth and collective excelleration of the body as a whole. It does not mean a bunch of disorganized, wild radicals who have trouble in distinguishing the 80's from the 60's. Or feel they must hate and fight other organizations because their concepts are different from their own.

There is also this attitude that some members think they have to be around the executive staff that governs the nation to be recognized. "All members will be judged on their character, loyality and ability to think; and above all, your ability to function as part of the organizations structure we have built, and is continuing to build." If we are to ascertain our success, security and endurance in this world, or the free world:

It has been noted that quite a few of our members have this attitude that they will rebel against decisions or judgement that has been made by the executive staff of this nation:

(Understanding)

It will be written here, and it will be UNDERSTOOD, "That the actions above will in no-way be tolderated by anyone, nor will we accept any group of people to disrupt the laws, the goals, and concept of progress of thils Nation:"

(Dialogue)

For effective functioning of this and other solutions, all persons with governing authority must be sincere about his responsibility, and sincere to the people the executive staff gave him authority to govern. Sincere means being sincere enough to step down from a spot if you feel that you are not capable of fulfilling it to its full capacity. Don't forsake the nation for your own personal faults, because only you can correct you, and as your people we are behind you in all that's positive and for the betterment of all. One must radiate a vibe that will let the people know that you are for the whole of our nation. With this attitude, you will generate a vibe that will let the young people of this nation know that we are for each other and about helping each other excell. Our cause is to have a successful "COSMOLOGY", which means - "the world for which we will make and live in, will be organized".

(Ignorant Outburst)

It has long been recognized that some of our people seem to have a problem in controlling the things they say out of their mouths. It should be first stipulated that the word "IGNORANT" does not mean that a person is stupid, it means a person having little knowledge, or education and experience in a particular area, subject, or matter. When a person makes a statement without first weighing it's value or logic, his out-burst in most cases become harmful to the management of this nation. When someone does this, he is being ignorant without having knowledge of it. THis kind of attitude should be eradicated to ensure that there will be no stupid rumors formulating out of our organization. This stupidity has in the past, and will in the future get people hurt unnecessarily. It also causes confusion and sometimes spookism among people that are not involved. This should be acknowledged by all the people. It is extremely necessary and important to check and evaluate all information before you spread something you only got a part of, or heard somebody else say;. If a person in authority is not around during a period in which some vital information has been passed to you, then you must begin to think about the best decision or judgement to render the situation. THis is done by simply weighing the value of the information, and the credibility of the source from which it came. 8 out of 10 times, a person in authority will be around.

(Hand written, printed, document)

We the Brothers of the Stuggle pledging whole heartedly our live, life, loyalty have embraced the teaching of our "Chairman", are covenet until fully chance, teaching laws and policy set forth by our Chairman, and Executive staff. The Doctrine of New Concept, will be a guiding light that will for ever burn in our heart and mind. This light will serve as a constant reminder and motivating force with each of us. Also it will instill in us dedication and discipline. We standing firmly in our six point stance. Concepts of Organization, Politic, Economics, Serenity, Eduction, Unity.
1) Head - life
2) Right shoulder - love
3) Left shoulder - loyalty
4) Right elbow - knowledge
5) Left elbow - understanding
6) heel of feet - wisdom

I agree to as long as I stand proudly under the blue sky to serve this glorious organization and its every cause aid and assist my fellow Brothers of the Struggle in our righteous endeavors. I will do that I can can to help us both to reach our fullest potential as the organization grows. I know that I will for our goals are inter-related. Positive organization produces poxitive productive people. That which we are, my every action and behavior, and attitude will vividly reflect the positive, dignified principle that the organization is built upon I will never do anything that would cause embarrassment or disrespect to the integrity of our organization. Standing strongly upon our six point stand I shall utilize knowledge wisdom & understanding as I strive in our Struggle for education, economical, political, social development, I will learn, look, and listen to anything that may be conductive towards the excelleration and never abandon our struggle, as in all struggles I realize that sacrifices must be made. I will not be selfish but for the sake of the preservation of our organization; I am willing to endure my share, I believe in the goal of the organization and its honor, to aid and assist in our struggle for success. We are with a great leader. Together we shall see the vision. May His visions become our vision. For his visions are for us to grow into a productive successful people with the consolidation and diligent efforts of everyone, our visions will be manifested into a reality.

(Undated typewritten document)

KEEP-UP NOT CATCH-UP

The affairs of these modern times are designed for the thinking man, the rational logical man, the man that contemplates beyond a 24 hour span of time. We as a organization are not thinkers that only realize their existence of today, but we are men of vision with foresight with future objectives of growth and development. My brothers this is a fast-pace competitive world where the pace isn't won by those that are just trying to catch-up, but is wond by those that keep up. The term (catch-up) signifies not up to a general or expected level of development. The key word is behind and behind is a place or time and here again I state, this is a different era of time now, the modern age of existence, an age in which races arent won by the behinders, and we all know what a behind is dont we? And we dont want to be a continuous ass, a Beast of Burden. My brothers, the Preface of our Organization is a clear sign of the timesk our Preface is a Beckoning Light of Knowledge, Wisdom, and Understanding of the Concept of Unity.

This concept has....anization can win this race, its not an easy race, the strenght to endure the trials and tribulations of this world. Whats to be gained by winning this race? The realization of the Growth and Development of a nation.
Remember a wise man changes his mind often, but a fool never does...
Keep Up With The Times My Brother

BOS PRAYER

Looking out the window as far as I can see,
All my BOS brothers standing around me,
GD's and BD's has combined,
As we both unite our star will shine,
King David he recuted gave the (G)
Strength on the street,
He recuted the (D) on the history of our G
will last forever,
As the Brothers of the Struggle
Struggle together.

GD PRAYER

All GDs must use the knowledge on the six point star, 360 base on the life we belive and the love we have for one another. Wisdom is what we use to grow knowledge on the six point star in our nation flag in order to be real you must be willing to appear in front of Larry Hoover.

G.D. Creed

We believe in the teaching of our Honorable Chairman; in all laws and polices set forth by our Chairman and Executive Staff.

In the concept of ideology of the organization in aid and assisting our fellow brother of the struggle in all righteous Endeavors.

And standing strongly upon our six points utilizing Knowledge, Wisdom, and Understanding as we strive in our struggle for Education, Economical, and Political and Social Development that we are a special group of people with Integraty and Dignity.

In the vision of our great leader and throuh his vision we can be come a reckoning power of people beyond Boundaries without measures.

INTERNAL RULES OF THE B.O.S.

1. SILENCE AND SECRECY. No member should give any Information or discuss any matter that concerns any member or function of the organization to any individual that is not an outstanding member.

2. DRUGS. No member shall consume or inject any drugs that are addictive.

3. STEALING. No member shall steal from any convict inmate or resident.

4. RESPECT. No member shall be disrespectful to any member or non-member being disrespectful only intices other to become hot-stely and be disrespectful to you which leads to unnecersery silly confrontation. always be respectful, dignified, honorable; loyal and thoughtful.

5. BRAKEING AND ENTERING: No member shall breake in or enter any building that cause un-due heat and presure to other. Making institutional move that leads to lock-up and shake down is prohibited.

6. GAMBLING. No member shall gamble in any game unless all parties have there money up front.

7. GUARD. No member shell engage in any unnissery confrontation with any officers or administrative personnel.

8. SPORTMANSHIP. No member shell engage in heated arguments or fights while participating in any sports or games. Use good sportmenship at all time.

9. PERSONAL-HYGENE. All member must look presenable at all times and livin quarters should be kept clean.

10. INCIDENTS. All incidents minor or major concerning the health and well being of any member or members should be reported to the coordinatorors.

11. AID AND ASSISTING. All member shell Aid and assisting one another in all righteous endeavors.

12. DUES. All member are required to give 2 pack a month if able.

13. EXERCISING. All member are required to job three times around the yard and do fifty jumping jacks together at the beginning of each yard period except Saturday, Sunday and night yard.

14. EXPLOITING. No member shall use his membership, staff, or office to exploit or favor for any member.

15. A.R. 504. All member shall read and become familiar with the D.O.C. A.R. 504 Administrative disaplene.

16. RAPE. No one should use threat or force to make anyone engage in any homosexual act.

Disciplinary Report Form Used by The B.O.S.

MINOR:_____

MAJOR:_____

TIME:_____
DATE:_____
INCIDENT:_____

WE BELIEVE IN THE TEACHING OF OUR HONORABLE CHAIRMAN; IN ALL LAWS AND POLICIES SET FORTH BY OUR CHAIRMAN AND EXECUTIVE STAFF.

INCIDENT
:_____

_____

_____

_____

_____

IN THE CONCEPT OF IDEOLOGY OF THE ORGANIZATION IN AID AND ASSISTING OUR FELLOW BROTHERS OF THE STRUGGLE IN ALL RIGHTEOUS ENDEAVORS. IN THE VISION OF OUR GREAT LEADER AND THROUGH HIS VISION WE CAN BECOME A RECKONING POWER OF PEOPLE BEYOND BOUNDARIES WITHOUT MEASURE.

WITNESS:

_____

_____

_____

NOTE: WHEN THE DOCUMENTS IN THIS APPENDIX REFER TO THE "CHAIRMAN OF THE BOARD", THIS IS REALLY REFERRING TO "KING LARRY HOOVER", THE LEADER OF THE GANGSTER DISCIPLES.

Appendix D:

Constitution Of The Vice Lords

CONSTITUTION OF THE VICE LORDS

Amalgamated Order Of Lordism
Lah Via Va Va Illilaha Halaliil, Allah Akbun
Supreme Chief, Al-Ugdah

Salutations my brothers I greet you in the name of V/L, With dedications to V/L, And sincerity of V/L. My brothers I greet you under the master sign.

This literature is a revelation of the nature of V/L, It's principals and its superiority.

It is manifested at this time to steer this nation to its proper course and to unify V/L the world over into and Amalgamated Order Of V/L dedicated to V/L's and Lordism.

There also is another reason for the manifestation of this revelation. there is a demonstration in our midst that has confused, misled and divided V/L's. This demonstration is called the (L.O.I. Lords Of Islam Nation. V/L's have been led to believe that this is the literature and or law of the V/L's. IT IS NOT! The Supreme Chief Of V/L's is Al-Ugdag, And he has not order or give consent to V/L's being govern by the dictate of L.O.I. Every true V/L is a V/L by choice. The V/L Nation is comprised of various branches of V/L's, This has always been and will be. Every V/L has personalize roots in any particular branch and those will not be uprooted. So awaken brothers and remember from whence you came that loi is not V/L. It is a chartered motorcycle club with bylaws and laws of already set stipulations. Law governs all events. Justice is Supreme.

We leave you as we came, In Peace, In Love, and in Lordism. As the wind shall blow the whole world shall know we come as we are, We are as we come, In the name of Almighty most glorious V/L.

Behold the truth and the Law Nov, 17, 1989 Chief Al-Ugdah.....

Why we chose the name Amalgamated Order Of Lordism because we as V/L's are a diverse people, Meaning we are people with a choice, And are autonomous in our same representations of Lordism. We have different precinct preference, And yet the same principals, And Concept. These precincts, And autonomous in nature, And in essence for us the core of versatility, Such fundamentals sameness, And different are the ingredients necessary for the continuity, development, And prosperity of the Amalgamated Order Of Lordism. Question; Is that a contradiction?

Answer;NO!

Explanation; That sameness that we experience together that we are all expressing and practicing, And living Lordism as true V/L'.

The difference is that we all belong to different precincts, Our

Unifying, Common Denominator is summed up in one word, Amalgamated; Draw Brothers, Amag means that we are a conglomeration of people, A family. For clarification. (And elaboration see key 14 of keys to the throne of power).

Lah Via Va Va Illilaha Halaiil, Allah Akur.....

Amalgamated Order Of Lordism.....
Supreme Chief, Al Ugdah.....
Chair of Command.....

Supreme Chief King Of Kings.....

The Supreme Chief holds the reigns of the nation in his hands. He has the power, And the authority to delegate responsibility and make law to and for all representatives of V/L. His decree shall keep the nation moving in an organize and constructive manor down the golden path of Lordism. He was, Is, And will be the choice of the consensus of the kings of V/L's, And in effect is the king of kings of V/L's, And the precepts, Of V/L's, And in effect is the king of kings is V/L. The precepts, Policies, And laws set down by his administration are absolute. The Supreme Chief does not indulge in precinct policies, He allows all precinct to be autonomous, Thus self govern. (Note: The price to appeasing certain people is total subjugation). I'm determine not to setup to any level that will compromise my manhood, Or principals in any shape fashion Or form. I will never become subservient to the wills, And expectations of others especially when such projections conflict with my own.

Prince Of The Nation.....

This brother is second only to Supreme Chief, He is to be held in high regards. In the event of Unforeseen absence of the Supreme Chief, The Prince is responsible for keeping the nation on the golden path, And is to keep a line of communications open with the Supreme Chief, And other Kings. In the event of death of this Supreme Chief (may Allah forbid) the Kings of V/L will convene to reestablish a King of Kings, And a Prince from the Amalgamated Order from their own ranks, The selections of the Nation Prince is manifested in the same fashion as the Supreme Chief (King Of Kings), Is selected, By the panel of Kings.

Minister Of Justice.....

He is to be both respected, And honored by all representatives of V/L. His functions is to make sure orders and laws directed by Supreme Chief are put into manifestation in an orderly, Prompt, Effectively fashion, He is also to advise the Supreme Chief as to the need of modification, Amending of any existence of oppose laws. He is also responsible for balancing justice within our nation, And making sure that the law and principal are adhered to.

Kings Of Nation.....

These individuals are few. They are the distinct leaders of precinct. Kings of each precincts have universal appeal, And influences, And are to be respected and honored by all precincts, And all V/L's period. In the history of V/L every branch (Precinct) head has been traditionally recognized and respected as kings. This tradition will continue to be in effect.

Universal Elites.....

In the not to distant pass, Without the express consent or authorization of the Supreme Chief, Universal Elite were appointed. That practice as is of now terminated! The Supreme Chief alone has this authority. Recommendation for brothers to be appointed will be accepted from any king, Universal status, And some circumstances from representative. All existing Universal Elites will continue to be honored, And carried in highest regard by the Supreme Chief, And all representatives of the Amalgamated Order Of Lordism, That status, Contributions, And sincerity to V/L is reviewed by the Supreme Chief, And or whomever he may appoint to an elite review committee, Which such committee will be establish in the near future, And will consist of representatives from each precinct.

Ambassador.....

The brothers, Or sisters that are blessed with the position of Ambassador have a great responsibility to undertake. They act as missionary. They are to propagate, And promote Lordism in any area designed which lack organizational structure. They will spread. And correctly expound on the way of life as V/L. And Ambassador is appointed by the Supreme Chief, And is to inform him weekly of the progress, Problem, Needs, Ect., Of the designated area which he/she has been sent. And Ambassador has Universal appeal, And require a Universal star upon his/her appointment. (Note: Kings of precincts can appoint precinct ambassadors at there own discretion., However, They will not be a Universal nature but are to be respected by all representatives.

Minister Of Command.....

These brothers will be chosen by the kings of there respected branches. There function are to insure that Laws, Orders, And directed issue by the Supreme Chief, By way of the minister Of Justice, Or issued by there respected Kings, Are being adhere to in there respected precincts. It is there responsibility to communicate with the Minister Of Justice to insure that they have the proper understanding of the letter spirit of any Laws, Orders, or directives of the Supreme Chief. They also serve as sounding post for there administration as to any difficulty do to circumstances, Or environment surrounding any particular precincts regarding effective manifestation of Laws, Orders, Or directives. (Note: In the past there has been manifestation, And demonstration of abusiveness).

(Due to display of ignorance from one Lordself to another who apparently lacks the knowledge that one branch part, Or precinct constitute in nature one nation whole. The continuity, And self reliance dictate that we adopt this new measure of identity once referred to as branches, And now precincts. This has a two fold affect. One, being the inextricable ties of precinct, And to All precincts inherently, An intrinsic relationship with the Amalgamated Order Of Lordism, So in this literature from here out branches are referred to, And indeed are precincts.

Precincts Elite.....

These brothers are to be respected, Honored, And carried high by all representatives, As it there due, And our nature. A

Precinct Elite authority is to be restricted to his particular precinct, And his appointment is left to the discretion of the king of his precinct. Precinct Elite may require stars based on having a particular number of representatives in his following, And or, Meritoriously. His functions include assuring the overall effectiveness of his particular precinct, And can be viewed as a trouble shooter for his precinct.

Lieutenant.....

Appointment of Lieutenant is left to the discretion of the respective administration of each precinct. Its function is also left to the same discretion.

minister of Literature.....

This position is a very essential position in our nation. The brother holding this position in any precinct must be respectful as well as respected at all times. His functions include teaching of the Amalgamated Order Of Lordism literature As well as any precinct literature, To his brothers, And making sure that they know the meaning behind the words. He would also help representatives to acknowledge and understand there spiritual selves.

(Note: In the past their has been disrespect from one precinct to another under the Amalgamated Order Of Lordism, Such display, Reflection, Or infractions will no longer be intolerated justice is the call today, And in this event justice will be swift).

(Note: All Universals appointed will move under the sign of the Amalgamated Order Of Lordism. Although they still have there precinct roots in there heart, As they should be, But there promotions of Lordism will encompass the totality Of Lordism. Such expression must be express thru the Amalgamated Order Of Lordism to insure proper adherence, Unity, And Respect.)

Summation.....

This Chair Of Command is a structure that is in the tradition of V/L. Time, As circumstances as time dictate change. As we move into the 90's we have the opportunity to realize past mistakes, That we now put them behind us as we travel on the golden path. Gone are the days of many chief, And few indians, Gone are the days of fractured Unity, Gone of the days of selfish motives. With the strength of lions and wills of ants we will move forward for a better tomorrow for every V/L present, And future. Every V/L has a moral, And Lordly obligations to work both within, And outside of this nation to bring about a nation of V/L truth. Every position of leadership whether of a Universal Nature, Or a precinct Nature is to be honored, And Respected. We must, And will work together for the common good of all, For only together are we a nation, Lord to Lord, Precinct, And all into the Amalgamated Order Of Lordism.

Lah Via Va Va Illilaha.....
Amalgamated Order Of Lordism.......

Code Of Conduct.....

(A) Respect: This is a very essential ingredient of a V/L character. Every V/L will at all times give proper respect to every representative in our organization, And to representatives of other organizations. We will demand by conduct, Character, Demeanor, Actions, Deeds, Respect in return. We will always give respect to persons who are not representatives of any organization also. Disrespect is a very serious violation of the principals of law of our Amalgamated Order, And will be judge according. Therefore it will not be tolerated.

(B) Discipline: Discipline has a multiple faceted character. It must, And will be maintain in all it aspects for the successful function of the nation. Discipline does not only entail efficiency in following orders. Representatives must also be discipline mentally as well as spiritually. Lack of discipline in any area could very easily be detrimentally to a representative, "Other Representatives" Or the whole nation as a whole. For those reasons one understands discipline is of the utmost importance. Every order you receive pertaining to nation business has a specific reason, And will not question unless a representative does not understand the specific order being given, failure to be a discipline representative will result in discipline actions that will be taken.

(C) Meetings: General meetings of the Amalgamated Order Of Lordism are held for the purpose of the nation business, And will be conducted accordingly. During all meetings the highest ranking representative will be first to start business of the meeting, (Unless someone else has been designed for that purpose). That representative will be followed by administration representative if they have input at that time. Then each representative will be given the opportunity to speak about matters in relation to those being discussed at that time. When any representative is speaking at meetings all other representatives will be quite, And Attentive, Failure to do so constitute disrespect and will result in immediate disciplinary action. Any problem relating to any particular precinct will be discussed once the business of the nation as a whole is resolved every one will uphold the character, And demeanor of V/L while meetings are in progress.

(D) Fighting: While it is the unspoken obligation of every V/L to defend himself and every other V/L to the extent of giving his life if necessary, No representative of the Amalgamated Order Of Lordism will place his or herself or other representative in any situation where he is needlessly involve in fights over trivia matters. If any V/L is attacked it is the sworn duty of every V/L to overcome his or her attacker by whatever means is necessary. If any representative regardless to his or her authority within the nation, take it upon themselves to fight with another representative it is a violation of all our laws of the Amalgamated Order of Lordism, And will be addressed immediately. Therefore no representative of the Amalgamated order Of Lordism will ever fight with another representative unless authorized by someone with the authority to do so.

Amalgamated Order Of Lordism
Lah Via Va Va Illilaha Halaliil, Allah Akbun
Supreme Chief, Al-Ugdah

Dues.....

It is understood that every organization in existence needs a financial foundation in order to sustain itself, Our organization is no exception. There is an economic program establish for the Amalgamated Order Of Lordism, However it will not be manifested at this time. Interim representation of the or-

der are to continue with the existing program relating to dues that are establish in there respected precinct.

Lah Via Va Va Illilaha Halaliil.....
Amalgamated Order of Lordism.....

Rules and Laws.....

(1) Each and every representative of the Amalgamated Order Of Lordism will be aware of, An Knowledge of these precise Chain Of Command. (Supreme Chief, Prince Of The Nation, Minister Justice, Kings, Universal Elites, Ambassador, Minister Of Command, Precinct Elite, Lieutenant, And Minister of Literature.)

(2) Every member of the Amalgamated Order Of Lordism will at all times maintain him or herself within the Code Of Conduct Chain Of Command, And the Principals of law in the highest manor. In the past representatives have failed to honor parts of the code, The change, And the laws due both to ignorance, And lack of enforcement. These laws and bylaws of the Amalgamated Order Of Lordism Will be enforce, And adhered to.

(3) It is the responsibility of the kings of each precinct to revise a plan within there precinct to keep and accurate account, And are census of the representatives and elites in his precinct.

(4)(5) The king of each precinct must have a way of communication with each other, As well as with the Supreme Chief and the Minister Of Justice. This is to assure readiness, And the alertness in the event that assistance is needed in another precinct. If not directed by the Supreme Chief, Prince, Or the Minister Justice, The Kings of the Precinct involve are the only ones that have the authority to call on another precinct and its representatives for assistance. No representatives can take it upon him or herself to deal with a problem that arises. He or she shall always use the proper chain with in his of her precinct. Taking things in your hands is taking the chance of making a bigger problem, And is out of accord with the chain.

(6) All precinct problems and altercations will stay within the precinct. No representative will ever take a from one precinct to another. Pertaining to the Amalgamated Order Of Lordism, Unless the problem in that particular precinct cannot be handle in that precinct due to extenuating circumstances.

(7) Representatives of the Amalgamated Order of Lordism will be nobly respected because as V/L's we demand respect by our actions, And deeds and give respect in the same matter as we demand it. Representatives disrespecting each other will not be tolerated.

(8) Every representative upon given the laws, And Principals of the Amalgamated Order Of Lordism will never stray from this principals that we stand by, And die for. The guidelines established thru out our Laws, Principals will be strictly adhered to by all representatives.

(9) All representatives are expected, And encouraged to strive for self development this include but it is not limited to acquiring high school diploma or its equivalence, College Course, Vocational training, And especially the study of Laws, And Principals of Lordism.

(10) Upon attending Religious services or nation meetings all drugs, And alcoholic beverages will be left outside the par-

ticular place. Everyone will carry themselves respectfully, And orderly at these function. Because we need not promote anything but the higherself, And to be in the right frame of mind.

(11) No V/L should ever overlook our main purpose, Which is to be a organization thru out these times, Our objective is to be sincere about what we believe in, And what we will die for. We aim to show the world what we stand on, And that is Lordism.

(12) If a representative fail to realize to meet the high standard of V/L by continuing expression of the lowerself thru continuing misuse of our divine principals, And concept, It will be incumbent on the kings of the particular precinct (Or his representative) to make the decisions as to whether that representative should be placed on hold, Or worse. We have no time for individuals who threatening to stunt our growth.

(13) As a representative of the Amalgamated Order Of Lordism we will continually seek solutions for the betterment of all our people.

(14) As a representative of the Amalgamated Order Of Lordism we must learn to live with and respect other representatives, Including those before us who paved the way for us to walk the golden path of righteous. We must also learn to with, And respect other representatives life principals, And Religious denomination, Even if they defer from our own.

(15) We the representatives of the Amalgamated Order Of Lordism should not worry about possing threat to each other person prestige, But should concentrate our united effort, And thoughts upon solving the hurt, And injustice done daily to our representatives, And our Nation as a whole.

(16) We as representatives must understand, And highly respect that instead of arrogance that will be humility among each other, As oppose to being drunk with power, There will be stronger realization to serve our nation in the spirit of Lordism.

(17) Representatives of the Amalgamated Order Of Lordism will be guided by tenants of morality, And the divine principals of love that governs Lordism, And will show the world that we are Lords of the world.

(18) All representatives of the Amalgamated Order Of Lordism will be fair, Straight Forward, And Honest in his dealings. He or she at all times uphold the truth, And justice, Even at the cost of his or her life.

(19) We of the Amalgamated Order Of Lordism will accent our youth. The young seeds essential. They can, And should provide New Ideas, New Methods, And New approaches. Your representative following the truthful teaching of Lordism that have potentials to be in any position to benefit the nation will not be overlook because of there youth.

(20) Every representative of the order will be conscious of there appearance at all times, And will always appear neat and clean.

(21) Every representative should make it his her sworn duty to uphold the Laws, And Principals of Lordism wherever they may be where other representatives are present.

(22) If at anytime a representative of the Amalgamated Order Of Lordism wishes to remove his or herself from the nation it will be upon the king of that particular precinct or (His Representatives) to grant the request of the representatives.

Note: We are not making anyone by force be a part of the Amalgamated Order Of Lordism. We became V/L's by choice, And the choice is ours.

Principals Of Laws.....

(1) I as a representative of the A/V/L/N swear with my life never to dishonor our most high Chief, All appointed of the A/V/L/N.

(2) I as a representative of the A/V/L/N will teach our people, Protect our people, Love our people, And if is the will of Allah die for our people, So that one day they will walk the golden path of V/L as free people, As productive people progressing in the love of V/L, The knowledge of V/L, Wisdom of V/L, Understanding of V/L, And the future of V/L.

(3) I as a representative of the A/V/L/N will never go astray from the truthful teachings of our most wise, And beloved high Chief.

(4) I as a representative of the A/V/L/N will help my people with any problem that they may have, Be it mentally, Or Physically, For there problems are my problems and my problems are there problems.

(5) I as a representative of the A/V/L/N will never take word of another before that of any representative of the V/L Nation without placing the burden of proof on there accusers.

(6) I as a representative of the A/V/L/N swear with my life never to put anything or anyone before most high and beloved Chief, Any appointed Chief, Or any representative of the V/L nation.

(7) I as a representative of the A/V/L/N swear that I will never deny any V/L Materially, Apiritualy, Mentally, Financially or Physically, My help under any circumstances at all or be denied.

(8) I as a representative of the A/V/L/N swear with my life that I will never lie on any representative of the A/V/L/N or V/L from another precinct or take anything from any representative of the A/V/L/N. I swear by my life to live by these laws under any circumstances.

Flag: The flag is the national identification for any nation of people. It is what the people represent and live for. This flag is a symbol of the entire order of the Amalgamated Order Of Lordism and consist of the following:

(1) Circle: The circle means 360 degrees of knowledge and what was will always will be, That Black people once ruled the world and will once again rule.

(2) Fire: The circle is surrounded by fire. The fire means and represent our nation true knowledge of themselves as being suppressed. The flame prevent our reaching 360 degree of knowledge because of the heat (Rome or Europeans).

(3) Darkness: Inside the circle is darkness (Jet Black) and represents that universaly Black people are a majority of people, Not a minority.

Note: If we were not brainwashed into thinking that we are different from other Blacks around the world, We would have a population of over 700 Million! There are 400 Million Blacks in mother land (Africa) alone, The darkness that we have been kept in so long.

(4) Moons: Inside the darkness are (Two) crescent moons. They represents the splitting of one nation into two. One in the east (Asia And Africa) and the other in west our nation. They also represents entity of the male and female factor.

The Flag: When these two moons come together they represent the marriage between the Lord and his Lady a union which is mandatory if we are to acquire 360 degrees of pure Knowledge, Wisdom, And Understanding.

(5) Star: Also in this darkness is a golden star. This is the eye of Allah keeping watch over his people, A just and justice seeking people.

(6) Pyramid and Triangle; The darkness also engulfed the Pyramid Triangle which is our strength. It is the phenomena that puzzle the white world today. There is still no knowledge of Pyramids building today, Even with all this technology of the white man's world, This society cannot even begin to build or understand how to build the Pyramid., Yet the pyramid was build by Black people many centuries ago. We V/L's are sheltered by this pyramid of strength, Until we are able to cleanse our minds. There are three aspects to the formation of the might puzzling pyramid. The are Physical, Mental, And Spirit. He must decide now how we want to live. Are we going to let our physical cravings take control of our minds? Or are we going to control our bodies as it is suppose to be? As V/L's, We have one choice.

(7) Sun: Inside the pyramid is the sun. This represents the raising truth in our nation. Once our minds have gained control over our physical body, We will then think as men and be able to understand and to respect one another life position. Then we can move men (One in a righteousness direction_ We, Like all Black people who are living within the shelter of the pyramid and under the watchful eye of Allah, Are guided down the proper path.

(8) Hat: The Hat represents the shelter of our heads until we can get them together.

(9) Cane: The Cane is our staff of strength. As we need the cane to help us walk when we are old, The cane represents the need for us to support one another in these trying times.

(10) Glove: The glove represent purity., That we keep our hands clean of any acts that cause division among our people. This is also the reason for representing the way we do now. Our palms out and upward, showing each other that our hand are clean and that we mean no harm.

Lah Via Va Va Illilaha Halaliil

Supreme Chief, Al-Ugdah

A message To My Muslim Brother.....

To my brother in Islam, I greet thy with the high sign of Love, In **Peace I come**, In tune I am. For what is Islam but Lordism, And Lordism but Islam? Each when served properly will give the people a different flavor of the same thing. "Almighty" is Allah, "Allah is Almighty."

Chocolate, Strawberry, and Vanilla is purposely design to meet the critera of the people taste, Yet the flavor doesn't subtract from the substance, Or change the ingredients that make up the ice cream. That which is righteous under any other name will turn out right.

I am as you are a true believer of Allah traveling the same pass you are own, But in a different vehicle adhering to the same law of caution.

I am the true V/L self and you are the true Muslim, But by virtue of our seeded part we are brother's under Allah's influence. We represent two establishments, Yet stand upon one stone, Our house built on the same foundations, "Brother," Islam, Or Lordism is just the umbrella we walk under, That Allah is the rainmaker, And sense we both acknowledge him we can walk in warmth, And confidence without the fear of getting drench, For our intentions are good, And our steps are righteous inclined.

Lah Via Va Va Illilaha Halaliil

The Keys Of V/L.....

(Key1) What is Lordism?

It is a Philosophy. Ideology, And Guidelines of a chosen way of life. A lodestone made manifest through the primitive teaching of it first teacher, The Honorable "Pep Pillow," And chiseled by devoted believers from various schools of thought into a structure of today.

(Key2) What is the philosophy of Lordism?

We believe in its authenticity in the sight of God, But we don't believe that any one person can have a monopoly on God, Or any one religion can claim Him exclusively. We believe all men are equal in the sight of God and that righteous V/L will be recipients of God's grace, The same as any other religious person regardless of their religion persuasion. The Quran says that man was put here as Vicegerents. We take that as man was put here to be V/L's in this physical world.

(Key3) The meaning behind the name:

Vice means one having faults. (The Human Being) and being of second importance, Second only to God, God being the ruler of all the worlds and the universe and man was elected by him to his "Vice Lord" Or Vice Ruler, We see ourselves as God's highest creation, His custodians of the physical world. So whether you address yourself as a Baptist, Christian, ect., By the definition of that which just been defined, You are still "Vice Lord" the only difference is interpretation and acceptance.

(Key4) What is the religion of V/L?

Lordism is the religion, Yet we are not religious fanatics. The Quran and all religion books tell men to "Take the bounties of the earth" We interpret this as a sign that man should always strive to improve his life's condition. The A/V/L should strive to balance himself Physical, Mentally, Spiritual, and materially. Man seeks to promote himself in the sight of God, But also has concerns and needs here in the physical world.

(Key5) About Religion:

A Lord is a seeker of truth and Lordism encompasses every facet of life. It acknowledge the existence of God in people and it acknowledge every person's right to communicate with him. It is a complete way of life, A life of involvement with both God and state and the belief in one true God whose proper name is (Allah) and associate no partners with him.

(Key6) What is the Religion book of V/L?

A Lord will study any Religious book and use them selectively as reference points and guidelines as long as it will contribute to his development, But always in the frame of mind that man and not God is the author of such books. Everything in print deals with relative truth and not absolute. Absolute truth are the things that only the mind of God knows, While the relative truth are the things that the highest reason man understands them to be, But still, Of all the religious people tend to favor the Quran.

(Key7) Why does the Lord tend to favor the Quran?

We believe that there is knowledge to be gained even from the Bible, But only after tedious process of shifting through its maze. On the other hand, Regardless of the fixation of relative truth that we automatically apply, We still find The Holy Quran the best book for our people, It corresponds with our way of thinking and supportive to our way of life, But still, we are Vice Lords and not Muslims, There exist that degree and that difference.

(Key8) What's the difference between a Vice Lord and a Muslim since both acknowledge the Quran?

The difference is our guidelines, names, application and interpretation of faith.

(Key9) Explain the difference a Lord and a Muslim:

Our names and Prayers, And the belief that all religious books deal with the relative and not the absolute truth. And that the righteous "Lord" will be made manifest in this physical realm of creation and we see ourselves as Allah's temple and that God exists in that temple.

(Key10) A Lord do not pray in the conventional style of a Muslim. A Lord making prayer bring his fingers to fingers, Making a pyramid over his head (A symbolic Gesture) and says, "O Allah, I seek shelter from the forces of evil and schemes and threatening plans of my enemies," And then brings his hands down to the palms up position and recites the "Al-Fatiha" The Universal Prayer.

(Key11) Greetings!

It would not subtract any degree from you if you would greet your Muslim brother as he would greet you, But when greeting one of our brothers, Greet him under the master sign of Lah Via Va Va, Illilaha Halaliil With your palms up and he should return that greeting with "Via Va Va Lah, Halaliil Illilaha.

(Key12) The meaning behind the greeting:

Lah (Love), Via (vice), Va Va (Lord), Illilaha (My Sword), Halaliil (My Shield).

(Key13) What are the master signs?

Palms up and all greets of V/L's, The flag Of V/L, The Emblem Of V/L, The Meaning of V/L, And the righteous representation, These are the master signs of V/L.

(Key14) Why the various schools of thought?

Because the A/V/L/N is symbolic to the real blood line family, It represents the highest principals of the real blood line family: Love, Truth, Peace, Freedom, Justice, Harmony, and Understanding. As every family the Lord (Father) and the Queen (Mother) upon producing life have bestow a name of their favor upon that life, For every life they produce they honor that life with a first name for distinguishing proposes, And the child automatically inherit the last which will affirm his identity. Such is the composition of the various precincts or fractions that make up the A/V/L/N that have been granted autonomy and have form the various schools of thought according to their father, The brother of our father who share the family name. No matter what the first name the child or parents call that child, As long as that adheres to the dictated of his parents ads accept the family name, One must remember the root of its existence is in the family.

The teachings as administered by Chief Al-Ugdah, From the unknown school of thought.

Statement Of Love...

To you my Brother, Sister, My love for you began at birth, has manifested through out our Heritage. Because of my Black skin, which is yours, My Blood and Flesh, Which is us I am you, And you are me. Our minds are for the same goal, Our effort is for the same cause, Our souls are bound by the same determination. To this nation I give my unity, And all my vitality. To you my Brother, And Sister, I give my love.

Oath.....

In the name of the almighty, I do solemnly swear, That I as a representative of the Amalgamated Order Of Lordism will not dishonor my most sacred weapon meaning Lord unity, Nor under the threat of death will I deny those that stand beside me. I as a representative of the Amalgamated Order Of Lordism will listen well to the truthful teachings of our king, And Elites. I will use my time constructively, I will become, And remain useful to my Nation, My community, And Myself as a whole. Let the Almighty God (Allah) bear witness to this oath by birth in the Spirit, And to, And thru the heart core. I come as I am, I am as I come, Almighty Vice Lord. Lord love means I have a undying love for this Nation, And I'll die for it. Lah Via Va Va, Illilaha Halaliil.

The Warning On Treason.....

Treason is a act by no less than a life of misery. The nature of such punishment constitute by its very nature one of two extremes. The above prescription is in order when circumstances, And events dictates (So as not to jeopardize the life, Or freedom of the righteous) That we spare the most serious extreme out of consideration. And preservation for our most truest, And righteous representative. Under no circumstances will treason Or disrespect be tolerated against the crown. The crown represents the embodies of V/L world wide. This is true regardless to which king sit on the crown. The crown is the glorious representation of the V/L. Speak on it with unrighteous intent, And you speak against the nation whole. Pain will come to you as a consequence of speaking on the crown with indignation. Scheme clandestinely against it, And such scheme will be made manifest at your own expense.

The crown has the resiliency of the people support. Those who will be in grievous error head this warning. There is a boomerang around the crown. Test it at your own risk. Lah Via Va Va Illilaha Halaliil.

Knowledge Of V/L Existence.....

Let our enemies take heed to these words, we shall pay any price for V/L, Bear any burden for V/L, Meet any hardship for V/L, And support and friend for V/L, Condemn any person that tries to upset the tranquility of V/L, To assure the survival, And success of this Nation.

Faith Of V/L.....

I am a V/L, In my possession I take pride, But without vain glory. To it I owe solemn obligations that I am eager to fulfill. As a V/L I will participate in none but honest enterprise. To him that has engage my service as soldier or warrior, I will give the utter most of perfection and fidelity. When needed my skills and knowledge they will be given without reservations for the (Nation) good. From special capacity springs obligations to use it well in the service of humanity, And I accept the challenge that this implies jealousy of the high repute of my callings, I will strive to protect the entrance and good name of any V/L that I know to be deserving, But I will not shrink should duty dictate from disclosing the truth regardless anyone that unscrupulous act has shown himself unworthy of the profession. Since the age of stone human progress has never been condition by the genius of my professional forebearers by them have been rendered usable to mankind nature resources of the material and energy. By them have been vitalize, And turn to practical account of principals, Science, And Revelations of technology. Accept this heritage of accumulate experience, My Efforts will feeble, I dedicate myself to dissemination of Lordism knowledge, And especially to the instructions of younger members of my profession in all is art and tradition. To my Lord brother I pledge in the same full measure I acts of them, And interpreted, Dignify of our profession. With the consciousness always that our special expertise carries with it the obligation to serve humanity with Lords. I am proud to live, This place, And love V/L with the highest Devotion, Loyalty, And Honor.

Lordism In Focus.....

The Amalgamated Order Of Lordism is built on the laws and principals that govern everyday activities, And life of V/L. If followed properly these laws, And principals will guide our people on a path which is straight, And progressive. These codes of law is based on external principals of righteousness, And Fair Dealings, Sobriety, Cleanliness, Helpfulness, And Honesty to one another, Yet shaped into concrete form suites, And circumstances. Our goals are to abolish blood feuds, Help the weak, And the need, And harness wrong doing. Lordism is design to appeal our intellect so that we'll be able to make the best of our lives. We must not waste, Nor misuse our life for individually and indeed together we have a lot to

offer. Lordism is more than just a religion of faith. It is the sewing together of knowledge, And logic, This a cooperative expression, A fraternal order which allows men as Lords of various religions the nominations to come together and the common denomination of Lordism, Thus enjoy true meaning of Lords.

Putting It In Perspective.....

We the members of the Amalgamated Order Of Lordism will continue to represent our beloved nation with Sincerity, Love, Commitment. Those who are pure in heart will no doubt be overcome by the common enemy which is rome. We as members of the Amalgamated Order Of Lordism will devote our time, Energy, And resources to advance, And uplift not only our nation, But all poor, And oppressed people with in our reach. We of the Amalgamated Order Of Lordism will greet, And honor each representative with greetings of the master sign, Not with the sign of our precinct. This is to identify with the fraternity of which we belong, And the cause that we all share. This greeting signify the meaning of poor nature, And is automatically a sign of our love, One together will cause nor show division among the m embers of the Amalgamated Order Of Lordism. We take not our oath to practice deceptions among ourselves, Nor should we attempt to promote discord. Time thru the ages bear's witness that nothing remains but faith, Good Deeds, And the teachings of Truth, Patience, And continuity. Do not slip off the golden path of Lordism my beloved brother, And for sure do not cause another brother foot to slip, You surely will experience the consequences of having rendered men from the path of God, And a mighty wraith will descend on you.

The Movement Mandates.....

We are under obligation to our nation, Our Supreme Chief, Our Elites and all the righteous representative, Of the master sign. We encourage our Elites, For its through their support for our Supreme Chief that our Supreme Chief is able to reach out, And grow it into us, And we into him, And together into the movement. But most of all we encourage ourselves, For we are the soldiers of growing nation, We are the architect for a better tommorrow. For we through our dedication, And total commitment shall build out of nothing, Something of great apprizal. We shall take an old nation and make a new movement dedicated to upliftment of our people. We shall take the name of the Amalgamated Order Of Lordism and like the world take seasons, And nature leaves her mark on man, We shall leave ours on the world.

Steps To Live By.....

In the name of the Almighty. I greet thy, All of you with the honorable thump of the thumping V across my chest. And with palms.

Greetings Righteous Seed.....

I want to spend some time on a paramount importance "What do we, You and I do as members of A/V/L/N? First, Or more directly, You must at one time or another ask yourself this question. What do I do now that I am V/L? As Ruler, Protector, And Teacher of the people, We have a really profound test ahead of us. One that cannot be viewed as being easy. How do you let other people know the beauty of your dreams of a new nation? How do you teach people, Reeducate the people to the philosophy of Lordism? Simple "By your example, By your reflective character. You my brothers and sisters are manifestations of V/L. If you profess to be about all its sublime beauties and grace, Then live it," There should never be any defamation of the V/L character. There will be acceptance and forgiveness for your fault and error. These can be corrected and improved upon. However willful Injury. Insults, Stealth, Deception, and Defamation of the V/L character shall not be condoned or tolerated. It will result in Fines, Restrictions, Or Expulsion. Your image should always be one of Love, Dedication, And Sincerity. The golden beam of Lordism should always Radiate, And Reflect from the glow of your presence. That will be the true indication of your sincere and pronounce devotion and dedications to the reconstruction of t his V/L Nation. Your conduct should be one that is full of confidence but yet not arrogance, "Respectful and yet not ostracizing. We should be on top of our knowledge, Sounding our knowledge, But not to the point that we talk to people. We are rulers, Protectors and Teachers of the people. Thus, We must be able to reach those that we need to tach and raise up to a level of awareness. We can b certain that we will have a very difficult time if we take on the air of better that thou. How many people at all times and among all nations close there heart to any distinction of knowledge or spiritual influence because of some little fragment which they have got and which they think is the whole of God's truth? Such an attitude shows really want of faith and a blasphemous limitations of Gods unlimited spiritual gift to his creatures. (Commentary 92 H.Q.).j

The times are over where we don't have to prove anything to anyone. The great fact that the longevity of our existence is a sign that we are here to stay. We have survived the necessary physical aspect of our formation. We have involve into the mental stages. This development dictated the focus on Revising, And Reconstruction from point one. We have to be professional. We are talking about a securing a future for our children. About a place in the future where the proper recognition will be giving to V/L. This will never come into existence without expertise and know how. It will never materialize without mind, And the proper effort motoring it. Obviously the present system is not *at all concerned about realistic educating our children. They are still systematically destroying them. "Force Busing". That is a illusion, Why are we so short on qualified teachers? Black Teachers? Why not upgrade the school facilities? We as a people are responsible for the teaching of our children. That and itself is the answer to this illusion.

If we qualify ourselves there will be no need to bus our children anywhere. We can teach them ourselves. But first we must feel our own heads with the necessary knowledge. Or groom and cultivate our own people so that they may fill the void. Yet that they shall never reach the thresh hole of reality unless we qualify ourselves first. We're gonna have to make a few adjustments in order to qualify ourselves from a mental perspective. We must cease being old fashioned, And modernize our ideas, And way of thinking to better serve us, All of us older Lords have or are down for game. We can do that very good. Let us put as much emphasis into seriously tightening up our knowledge and applying that knowledge to our everyday life. Lets do this so that our mere presence can demand it's respect. Its time we raise from the dark and ignorance, Into the light and knowledge of who we truly are. Its time we exhaust our energy and exploit our ability by building, Not to do so will surely reflect a cripple image of V/L's?

May Allah bless and protect us in our infancy, And grant us the Strength, Desire, Dedication, And Preseverance that is needed in order to build our character and thus our nation.

Trichinosis.....

All products made of pork are forbidded to representatives of the Amalgamated Order Of Lordism. The pig was put here for medicinal, And is unfit for human consumption. There is a worm know to medical science, As the trichinosis worm. Its a parasite that attacks, And infests the organ structure of pigs. Our bodies became contaminated by these poisonous parasites whenever we eat pork. Ironically, The deterioring effect it has on us is intricately masked by the staking of times, In essence creating genetics disease. People tend to under estimate the actual danger that exist in our health. Pork is synonymous to dope. Its a gun pointed in the direction of the Black community. Every time we eat pork, The trichinosis worm penetrate our intestine and muscle tissue. Once this process begin our health slowly begin to deteriorate. The affect of pork on our health is devastating. It will inedibility induce a cycle of illness, And forgetfulness. No not immediately, Nevertheless no one really escape this parasite. Hypertension is the number one killer amongst Blacks. Why? Trichinosis! Its a killer that takes its dwelling in pork. No matter what you read about curing pork, The only solution to trichinosis is abstinence. You can smoke it, Burn tar baby black, Freeze it, Ect., But trichinosis will remain in its poignant, And deadly state. The pig have no veins, If bitten by a poison snake it will just turn around, And gobble the snake up. The pig is the world filthiest animal. Its a combination of the Cat, Rat, and Dog. Examine it microscopically if you like. It has the tail of a rat, The eyes of a cat, And the snout of a dog.

Yet most people love it. Biblical scripture has Jesus casting demons into pigs, And then driving them over a cliff.

The same scripture tells us not to eat the meat of the hoofed animal. Most religious leaders fail to mention this. Jews, Muslems, Buddist, ect., All obey Gods law when it comes to abstinence from swine, That is all about the Christian World. Most Black people state out of ignorance that their Mother, Father, Grandparents, Ect., Ate swine, and lived to be Sixty, Seventy, Or even 100, But none ever ask themselves how much older they have been if they had not consumed swine. Think about that. How can you love someone on one hand, And then turn around, And feed them that metamorphic swine?

Destiny From The V/L Point Of View.....

Being V/L mean we are in control of own destiny. If we who represent the true Lordism because victims at all or conquers, We have done it in our minds and wills, Or without faulty judgement and or illusion. If a Lord permit others to exploit him in private life, Or government he chooses it, Or he has made the fatal error of acquiescence and he should be condemned. The world forgives everything except weakness and submission. Universally men have been known to take advantage of these two traits. A V/L have no fear of battle, Even if it means a Lords death. In any event death come's to all men. How you die is your own choice. The Lord know that life is full of battles, On various levels and stages, In various forms, Which by law dictate battles that take shape by various means. Fighting or Submitting out of options, There is no halfway station in between offering supplementary premium,

Lordism demands that we chose the warrior choice. Some men are born free even under the adversity of unfavorable times. Even under persecution. Even in slavery. It is strictly a matter of man's spirit on whether not man is free. V/L's are free at birth, In the spirit, And thru the heart core. If not at the birth of his mother, So at the birth of his chosen nation, For is not the master teachings of Love, Truth, Peace, Freedom, And Justice? The choice is ours that we wish to be.... No one impels us or compel us.... We may delude ourselves that is so but it is not! (Quote) "The same wind which blow a ship on the rock can blow it into a safe harbor just as well.... In short it is not the wind it is the set of the sail. (Unquote) A man who denies, That is a weakling who wishes to blame others for his life. V/L you are what you are by choice, And you have given some deliberation to the parts you have played and play in life. Move with the conscious that you can affect the outcome of many things, And cause many things to happen, Realize the two degrees of involvement, The direct and the indirect shoot of it, And set yourself up to take charge of every situation possible, For you posses the keys to do so. There are consequences involve with actions, Be man enough to accept the consequences of yours. Never say you are completely blameless without chewing on the two degrees of involvement. A V/L should strive to master total control over his life. A Lord knows he must pass away from this world some day and you have no control over this. In this sense his destiny is set. But in his dealings with the world what becomes of him will depend on his own efforts and state of mind. Allah gifted man with ability.

Thus place his destiny on earth outside of pasting away from this plan of being into his own lap.

A/V/L/N "Misrepresentation".....

In advocating the principals of this organization we find that we have been very much misunderstood, And very much misrepresented by men from within our organization, As well as others from without. Any reform movement that we seeks to bring about changes for the benefit of humanity is bound to be misrepresented by those who always taking it upon themselves to administer to and lead the unfortunate, And to direct those who may be place under temporary disadvantages. It has been so in all other movements whether social or political. Hence those of us in the "A/V/L/N" who lead, Do not feel embarrassed about this MISREPRESENTATION. About this misunderstanding as far as the aims and objectives of the "A/V/L/N" is concerned. But those who has taken timely notice of this great movement seeks not to develop the good nation within the nation, But to give expression to that which is most destructive and most harmful to society and the government. We desire to remove the misunderstanding that has been created in the minds of millions of people thru out the world in there relationship to the organization. The A/V/L/N stands for the bigger brotherhood. The A/V/L/N stands for human rights, Not only for the nation of V/L's, But all Black people world wide. We ask for nothing but the rights of all V/L's. We are not seeking to destroy or disrupt the society or the government. We of the "A/V/L/N" are determined to unite all V/L's for there own Industrial. Political, Social, And Religious Emancipation. Some have said that this organization seeks to create discord and discontent among the races. Some say we are organize for the purpose of hating other people. The A/V/L/N has no such intentions. We are organize for the absolute purpose for bettering our conditions, Industrially, Economically, Religiously, And Politically.

What Are The Master Teaching?.....

The master teachings are the master teachings of Lordism. The teachings of man as V/L second only to Allah in his relationship with the world. They are the teaching that places man in charge of his/selves and the world he live in.

"On The Selves Of (Mind) Man".....

Truth and falsehood are two absolutes, Personified they represents the develop man (Minds) and the deform man (Mind) which signify the virtuous and unvirtuous state of man (Mind). Or the higher self in coexistence with the pigmy self. The self that control will depend on the feed of the man. There entire composition of the human being rotates from the axis of these two absolute. The selves of man are inextricable. Man can only subdue his lower self not separate himself from it entirely. Destractions or temptation can open the valves and allow the lower self to seep thru. The Lord Man, Lord Father, The V/L every action, Every Reflection, Every deed spring from the balcony of the mind (His Virtuous Self) Or the basement of it. (His Virtuous Self). All the selves of man (Mind) are tied to these absolutes. This axiom is universal, Each of the three dimension of V/L spin from this fundamental truth.

The Spin Off From The Selves Of Man (Mind).....

Lord Man: The Lord man is V/L in his infancy not yet developed into the maturity of the true Lord self. His is the physical manifestation of the character of keys. He have been impress by the physical aspects of the nation, But is not yet cemented in the faith do to his lack of spiritual and mental reinforcements. He is either a new representative that the teachings have not had a chance to take firm of, Or a old unrighteous deceptor that will never graduate from the caterpillar state and in fact whole appearance and representation is false. The Lord Man is in his most vulnerable stage, He will either fall to external influences and pressures and forfeit his V/L self, Allow himself to be suspended in the stagnant caterpillar state, Or open his mind and heart to the teachings and love of V/L Thus growing into a true crowning glory.

Lord Father: The Lord Father signifies a harmonious balance of the physical and mental aspect of V/L, And a growing awareness and acceptance of the spiritual nature of it. He is one mindful of his responsibilities to his family and nation, And goes about interrupted, He knows the nation is not here to infringe upon the privacy or disrupt the order of the family but enhance the quality of the family life thru its teachings. His is the image of a righteous supporter and provider. Of love, And undying determination. He is not a stranger to trials and tribulations of life, Or the external and internal pressure and influences, Still his strength and constancy is unfaltering. His strong Lord father self bears witness to the splendor of V/L.

The V/L Developed: The fully formed V/L is in the ethereal state of the selves of man. Here the character keys are all balance and being a V/L is a state of euphoria. Lordism is a unconflicting way of life for him. A natural expression and thought form. He is V/L in his weakest moment as well as his strongest, And will die a pure state of Lordism. He have elected out of faith to carry the nation high and not to let the golden light be extinguish by the dark deeds and deception clock work by those of the caterpillar persuasion, Or the other debilitating and evenly subversive forces of men. He is loyal to his brothers and sisters and will cut his own heart out before he would betray a righteous believer. He upholds and enforces the principals of laws and articles of faith. None of the selves of man can pass hie righteous manifestation of his true Lord self because he superiorly demonstrate all the selves of man. He is the true crown and glory.....He forever V/L...., Shining!!!!!

Who Are The True Believers.....

The true Lord self is the true believers. The Lord that is not self servant or pertinacious in his representation so as to gain advantages. A true believer is one that do not falsify our love. One who has unshakable Faith, Confidence, And Trust in the nation. A true Crown And Glory.

Crown And Glory.....

A believer that exemplifies good Personal Hygiene, Good Habits, Self Discipline, Strength Of Character, Pursues Knowledge, Upholds The Principals Of Laws, And the Articles Of Faith, And truly has committed the nation to heart, Is indeed a Crown And Glory to V/L.

The Glory Of The Sisterhood And Brotherhood Of V/L.....

The sisterhood to V/L's are our biggest inspiration. Every dedicated and righteous sister is available and precious gem to us. As a jewel throws forth a light that is magnified by the light of the sun, So does the V/Lady throw forth life, And sustain life, Thus light up the sole and life of V/L. The Lord is a sun unto her, Magnifying the spirit of her soul, And given warmth to her as the sun give warmth to everything under its scope. Like the sun aid the vegetation in its growth, The Lord and Lady aid the vegetation in its growth, The Lord and Lady aid each other in there needs development. For whatever struggle or endeavor they undertake, Its done with each other in mind. Thus is the glory of the sisterhood and brotherhood of V/L.

What do A/V/Lady Represents.....

She represent the diversified transition of queen woman, to queen mother, To V/Lady. A cherish his woman and think of her and refer to her as his queen, To him every V/Lady is majestic and occupy a seat on his heart throne. This three dimensional view of our vision of beautiful also symbolizes the three character keys in the human being that every believer should be striving to develop. They are Spiritual, Physical, And Mental composition of the believer. (Referral to what a righteous represent).

Different Selves Of The Vision Beautiful.....

Queer Woman..... And The First Level of Development.....

Queen Woman is V/Lady unpredictable. Her primary entrance is in a specific V/L and not necessary the master teachings. Its the first level of development that is really responsible for her coming under the master sign, Her physical attractions to a particular Lord. If by chance things don't work out for her Lord Man she may decide to fall out of tune with the master teachings. She may develop a certain amount of spiritual and

mental strength but not nearly enough to maintain fer faith. However (All praise to Allah) there are those that due come into the nation under the physical and enticement of a Lord Man and gained the spiritual and mental prowess necessary to embrace the master teachings and if there relationship with there Lord Man fail they will still exalt the master teachings, For they to are the vision beautiful.

Queen Mother..... And The Second Level Of Development.....

Queen Mother symbolizes the mental aspect of the Lord Child and also there responsibilities of being a good homemaker. Although she is dutiful in the her contributions to the life and the nation transcend beyond. Queen Mother is V/L as exemplifying the highest qualities of motherhood. Her image is Love, Concern, And Devotion to the family. Here is a true portrait of strength and a good balance of the three character keys that enhance the beauty of the human being. No mistakenly her for anyone else when you see her for she to is the vision beautify.

Different Selves Of The Vision Beautiful Cont.....

Queen Lady.....And The Third Level Of Development.....

Queen Lady is V/Lady in her highest manifestation of the teaching of Lordism. Because of the high esteem V/L holds for V/Lady the noble title of queen is granted, However whether the principal is called queen or V/Lady the substance remain, Either one is still the highest tribute a Lord can pay to the vision beautiful. The spiritual level of development is attached to her because as a true V/Lady her faith is unshakable, Given her a deeper spiritual sense of God in relationship to the master teachings and how it realistically comes together. She is dedicated to the principals of laws and the articles of faith. She honestly believes in V/L and will never forsake the faith. She respects all V/L's and is jealous of none for she know they are truly her brothers. She is well adjusted Spiritual, Physical, And Mentally. She is one concerned with the development of the nation and will sacrifice the best of her efforts for it. She is the true vision beautiful!!!!!

Oh Righteous Believers Never Forget.....

The V/Lady is a confinement and good manors. She is a pillar of strength to V/L. She is most ardent advocate and supporter, A buffer making him shine. She is second only to Allah in importance but most important after Allah to V/L. She is always the lady of the house, Always second in command to V/L. She is the vision beautiful!!!!!

The Collected Forces Of The Character Keys Made Manifest.

The V/L and Lady should always strive to enhance their Spiritual, Physical, And Mental state of being to draw the maximum benefits such conditioning has to offer. The proper collective force of these once balanced can open up the doors and secrets of life and help shape the believer into that righteous and harmonious self. These keys are essential to our development for they will allow for a smooth transition into this beautiful way of life. These are the keys that offer Security, Truth, Prosperity, And True Love.

The Queen Power.....

Article 1: Queenship is the highest status a V/Lady can achieve. A number of factors must determine this course of action. Sometimes emotions dictate under the guise of rational, Often times group appeal without the full season, In Essence, Dedication, Preseverance, Cultivation, Refinement, Commitment, And a Diligent application of Faith, And efforts towards the way of V/L. Because the autonomous set of order (Precinct) there can be several queens. However only one Supreme Queen. Know one can grant such a royal title, Or suspend, revoke or rescind, Other than the crown king. It is not only a expectation of the crown, But law! And law governs all events. Alternatives or Altercations: If due to circumstances beyond the crown king control dictates so, Appointment of queenship can be decreed by his prince, Or special elected committee consisting of all his elites. Under the existence circumstances the decree will be at most temporary, And subject to the capriciousness, Whims, And judgement of the crown king. Only he can pronounce with certainty, and surety (Which translate into law) the true crowning of his queen.

Article 2: The queen may appoint who ever she pleases to office, Including, But not limited it to princess. Her system of ranking, And organization take own the same structure of her kingship. Only the crown can dictate measure of law to her. She must always be studious and loyal to the (His kingship) crown. The queen can call meetings of the sisterhood at random, Or schedule fashion. All V/Ladies are to honor, And protect there queen. They must adhere to all the Precepts, Principals, And Articles of law in the same fashion, and fortitude exhibited by there brothers. V/Ladies, You have a obligation to yourself, And your nation to be morally conscious of your Hygiene, Appearance, Grooming, Conduct, Living Conducts, And Food Consumption, As well as your vocal output. ; You should always strive to exhibit these traits, And attributes that are distinguished by Refinery, Cleanliness, Sobriety, And Dedication

Article 3: The queen power is such in scope that it encompass the whole, Or part of the Amalgamated Order. Influence: If a precinct queen, Her influence will be categorize by, And limited to her precinct. On the other hand the supreme queen influence will be pervasive, Acknowledge and respected thru out our entire order. She will be carried highly and honored always, Whether precinct, Or not, by the entire order of V/L. Conduct in her presence must be one of Protectiveness, Sobriety, And Discipline. To dishonor or disrespect her image is a descration of our faith, Its a insult, And fragment disrespect to both crowns. Honor, Respect, And Protect her always! For such is law and law governs all events!

The V/L Manifesto.....

In The Name of Allah, We the righteous people of the Amalgamated Order give honor to our king Al-Ugdah, And all pioneers, Lords Of The Amalgamated Order Of Lordism. There has been tears, Bloodshed, Trials, Tribulations, And Trauma, By the pioneers of our most beloved order, We have witness the continue surfacing, And resurgence of a dedicated Ideology, And pedigree that refuses to die. We honor Prince Dank, And all the other countless Lord pioneers. For the dedicated pioneers with there Love, Knowledge, Wisdom, And Understanding, Have given Strength, Beauty, And a sense of direction, And purpose to our people. We honor our pioneers, And may Allah blessing forever be upon them for there sacrifices have been our gain. There dedication, Understanding And Tenacity has given birth to a new breed of V/Ladies, And Lords, The engineer. The engineers who strive to make a past ideology a present reality. The engineers who strive to be righteous, And productive in accordance to the vision that the pioneer held dearly. The pioneer have given the engineers a seed to nourish. And with a Love knowledge, Wisdom, And understanding even comparable to that of the pioneers, These engineers will design and perpetuate a flourishing nation second to none!!! May Allah forever bless, And Strengthen the sisterhood, And brotherhood, And inspire them to uphold the laws, And principals of the master sign, For we realize the difficult task ahead for all.

Foremost, We give the highest praise to Allah for blessing the Amalgamated Order Of Lordism with our most beloved, And dedicated pioneers, For it is thru perseveration that we are here today representing V/L..... We give the highest to Allah from blessing the Amalgamated Order Of Lordism with support, And love of our beautiful sisterhood, For they are the Delight, Love, And glory of the V/L nation.... They, And the lord child are our most precious treasures. We give high praise to Allah for blessing the V/L nation with you. The people of the most persecuted of faith, For it is thru dedication that we prevail Vice Omnipotent, For you are the engineers! Some of the pioneers are gone, Maybe some of the engineers will stray, But we rest assured with the knowledge That V/L is here to stay!!!!!

A/V/L/N "Righteous Sons".....

Almighty Righteous Sons, Of the most High, Reflecting true Lordism is not easy, Nor is it a righteous reflection displaying unrighteous acts. V/L is not sometimes, But always. Every moment, Every hour, Every week, Every month, Every year, Every breathe we take is V/L, Every step we take is V/L, Every thought we have is V/L, And know, V/L is not easy!!!!!

But each moment of our lives we righteous lords strive toward a deeper conscience of ourselves and what we are about. Knowing who and what we are give courage to stand temptation and reflect who and what we are in our weakest moment! The righteous for those who die fighting for the cause of V/L and every fallen lord spirit in the heart of us all!

We the righteous sons of the "Almighty" will never retrogress from our righteous principals and concepts. We the righteous sons of the most highest, Will defend these "Principals and Concepts" With our lives and discipline anyone found in violation of them!

In The Name of Allah, In The Name of our most High Chief, In the name of all appointed Chiefs, In The Name of all the righteous representatives of V.L's, We vow to uphold these truth's!

Lah Via Va Va Illilaha

Creed of the V/L.....

We the younger generation especially must feel a scared call to that which is before us. I go out to do my little part in helping my untutored brother. We of this less favorite race realize that our future lies chiefly in our hands, And we are struggling on attempting to show knowledge can be obtain under difficulties, That neither the old time slavery, Nor continued prejudice need extinguish self respect, Crush manly ambitions, Or paralyze effort. We know that neither institution, Nor friends can make a race stand unless it has strength in its own foundation, And that racist like individuals must stand, Or fall by there own merit, And for that to fully exceed they must practice the virtues of self reliance, Self respect, Industry, Perseverance, And Economy.

The Classifying of the young seeds.....

A young seed is a new member, Or young V/L. They are referred to as young seeds because the message (seed) of faith is being planted with in the rich soil of there fertile mind.

(A) The Way.....

Young seeds you are caterpillars not yet transformed into a butterfly (The True Believer). The possibility for such a transformation, But You must put your heart, And honest efforts into this nation.

(B) The Warning.....

There are older seeds around older seeds around that have been confined to being caterpillars, They are cripples missing the righteous attributes that are necessary in order to reach the butterfly state. They will l never become a CROWN AND GLORY, They are simply Teaches just hanging on to bleed us But one day they will be examine.

(C) Treachery of the old caterpillar seed.....

The old seed that have been confined to the caterpillar stage are like stagnant water, They collect bacteria, And its unfit to drink. They will poison your mind. If you wade in there water, Weak in your faith in the first place.

(D) The personification of V/L's at its. beset.....

Study, Be for real when you fly the love. Learn to discipline yourself, Learn patience, And Understanding. Fight against the negative influences of the unrighteous pretender, They will inevitably let there own action trip them up. They stand before a mirror, And lack the sense to know it. Don't just settle for being a caterpillar, Be a butterfly. There are degrees to everything in life even to being a V/L.....

In The Search Of The Golden Path Or Righteous.....

In the silent of the night bountiful spoke to hunger, His voice was very vibrant, And his message touched his spirit, His soul, His heart core, There was no introduction necessary for bountiful, For the golden light of knowledge was a trademark to his degree of pureness. As hunger stared intently into the eye's of bountiful, The golden rays of compassion betook bountiful. Bountiful said I am here as a sign of what can be. I have witness your affliction. Behold hunger, For I can be of great comfort to you. I bring with me a mirror of your inner most desire's, Look into me, Now what do you perceive? Hunger answered said, "I see all the things I ever wanted out of life, I

see an altruistic concern for your brother man, The flying of two great flags in the iris of your eye's. I see the coming of a new nation, A new way of life. I see a strong masculinity tide and a similar femininity one, They symbolizes the coming together of a King and Queen, They also symbolizes one purpose in life. I see little children who take pride in what they are as they adjust their golden sun's upon their heads. I see a multitude of happiness, A lack of poverty. I see a very proud people, A real display of unity, Vitality, And love, Oh bountiful, How can I be as you are? Surely all of this is merely a state of mind? Bountiful Replied.

Hunger I came you in the form of inspiration you had little hope, Little direction in life, And as you are now, Little meaning, Now I'll represent myself as truly am, So open your minds eye, Look around you, For I am a Vice Lord, A new way of life, And hunger replied "You deceived me, For I knew of you," And bountiful replied "No hunger, You only deceive yourself, As in the beginning, So shall it be in the ending, Vice Lord."

Introspection.....

Yesterday I was alone in the world, A flower growing in the shadows whos existence, Life was not aware of, And who was not aware of life. But today my soul has awakened, And I beheld V/L. I rose to my feet, And rejoice in the love of V/L, The knowledge of V/L, The wisdom of V/L And the understanding of V/L. All praise unto Allah, Today I am A V/L, And may Allah the Lord And master continue to lead me in the righteous path of V/L. Yesterday the touch of the frolicsome breeze seen breeze harsh, And the sunbeams seem weak. A mist hid the face of the earth, And the waves of the ocean roared like a tempest. All praise unto Allah, I am V/L. Yesterday I look all about me, But saw nothing but my own suffering self standing by myself, Wild pandoms of darkness rose, And fail around like ravenous vultures. All praise unto AL-LAH, The Lord, And master, Today I am V/L. Whenever I look I see life's secrets lying open before me. Yesterday I was soundless word in the heart of the night. Today I am a song on the lips of time. All praise unto ALLAH, The Lord, And Master, I am V/L.....

All Praise.....

All praise to the kings and Elites, Sons of the Almighty and righteous warriors and prophet of the Amalgamated Order Of Lordism. All praise to the kings and Elites, Lord of Lords, Lord the World. All praise to the kings and Elites who have died in the name of V/L. All praise to the kings and Elites who suffered thru all the enemy had and will now lead there people to victory thru the truthful teaching of Lordism. All praise to the kings and Elites, The Way, The truth, The light. And thru them comes knowledge, Wisdom, and understanding of Lordism. All praise to the kings and Elites, who teach us to love one another, To become strong in one another, And to become one in Body, And Souls, In the true meaning of V/L. All praise to the kings And Elites, Nation builders, Builders of Nation, Mighty Nations under the golden banor that lets all righteous people walk in he golden light of 360 degrees of Lordism.....All praise to the Kings and Elites of V/L.....

Allah Akbur!!!!!

Deeper Revelations.....

Allah is the ominpotent, The Almighty, Second to none first to all. He is the face of sublimity in the appearance of the creation that exhales the holy breath of life, And hale that life by recall at the point of his readiness. He is uninfluence by the plans men have for he knows the rotation of everything that move from square to circumference, That is seen, And Unseen, of jiins, And of men for all that moves does so by his consent. His body extends, And overlaps all in creations, for his is the realm of all worlds, And nothing exist beyond him in any state, The ethereal, or material, For all that exist is thru him. He is the circle engulfing all spheres, The key that unlock all doors. His thought is beyond minds compactsity For the mind itself only coputes by his decree. He is the mind in man and far beyond the portion he receives as a result of his grace. Even if we could unite all our minds into one it would still retain its shadowness in comparison to Allah, For his depth unmeasureable. Almighty is Allah, Master of the world both seen, And unseen Thought, And behold Thought did manifest. Man he did create in his own image, And made him subservient to his will. Allah did give to ability, And capability, And it is unmatched. For by Allah design man as V/L, second to him, Lord of all fears of matter. Yet do they know? No! Indeed a sad affair. It was not Allah that reduce men to negro, Or caucasian, A Chinaman, A Mexican, Or A Romanian, Or Hulgarian, A Jew, Or even Native American. All never reduce man into a slave, Or referred to him by color simply because of the geographical conditioning of his skin. No he created men, And made him his servant, His custodian, His Vicegerent, His V/L, Second only to himself. Man took being in Allah's favor for granted and was punished, And made to scatter. Because of their shame they cloaked themselves in the garment of funny names, And cloaked every people in every direction with a differentiate between themselves in hope of vanishing blame for there Holy infractions committed in the garden of eve.

Allah did create man, And made him V/L. Man distort it, And disfigured himself. It was man that gave names to the multitude of religion, Each claiming there's to be the one true religion. But Allah put his presence in every man unchristian, And all man has to do to communicate with him is to mediate. And call within himself. Allah created man, And gave him the rank of V/L. Man created confusion, And his subself, And every atrocious act against his bother, And they tell a notorious lie by saying Allah sanction such extremities ALLAH is the ALMIGHTY, ALMIGHTY IS ALLAH, And we that are subservient to him hurl his honorable attributes before us his people A/V/L/N. Vice which signifies that we are a people weak in the flesh who submit themselves only to a higher authority of ALLAH, And lord to affirm our position as his Vicegerent, And rulers of the physical world. ALLAH sign is the master sign, Although not exclusively, For no people have monopoly on ALLAH, And wherever truth, And righteous dwells so does he.

LAH VIA VA VA ILLILAHA HALALIIL, ALLAH AKBUR

Almighty Vice Lord Prayer.....

In the name of Allah, The Beneficient, The Merciful..... We the righteous people of the Vice Lord Nation seek thy understanding and thy blessing, As we commit ourselves to our chosen way of life.

We pray that you strengthen us Allah, And bestow upon us your favor. And that you help us in our strive to turn from wrong into right. We seek thy guidance and assistance in every phase of our development. And thy patience with us as a striving people.

We pray here in convenient form. YOUR SERVANTS AND VICE AGENTS, VICE LORDS OF THIS PHYSICAL WORLD. We pray for the good of our nation, And our people. And that you help us overcome our faults. We ask that you grant us the strength to carry this burden, For being V/L is not easy!

We thank you for the gift of life, And the glory of your love. And offer our gratitude for the potential and ability you have granted us as a people.

We pray that you will help us better utilize these keys, So that we may unlock the secrets and doors of both this life and the mystery after. We ask that you bless those who have died and lived in the name of V/L. And that you help us make this work if for none, Than for the Believers.............................Amen.............................Amen

Almighty Vice Lord Prayer.....

In The Name of Allah, We the righteous of the Almighty Vice Lord Nation give praise to our Supreme Chief, righteous son of the Almighty and a divine prophet of V/L.

Behold, Here our prayers O'Lord of lords, And give us your people of the A/V/L/N the continuous courage to represent our nation, So that the world will know that we are V/L, And as such will never stray from our divine principals and concepts, The laws by which we the most righteous of your people live by.

By your divine grace and generosity, You have instilled with us thy divine seed of love, Knowledge, Wisdom, And Understanding. And as a representative of this Almighty Vice Lord Nation, It is our responsibility to apply these precious gifts to the interest of our beloved nation And all poor and oppressed people of color world wide.

It is known that if we retrogress from our divine principals and laws the wrath of this A/V/L/N will surely fall upon us. For we pledge our life, Love And Loyalty to this Nation.

..........This Almighty Vice Lord Nation..........

Let our conduct O'Lord of Lords be judged by you according to our deeds.....By Birth .....In The Spirit.....And Through the heart core.....Behold, Behold, We come as we are..... V/L.....Ar

Quranic Justice.....

The man of faith holds fast to his faith, Because he knows it is true! The man of the world rejecting faith, Clings hard to worldly interests, But let him not force his interest on men/women, Sincere, And true by Favor, Force, Or fraud. Let not men/women be intoxicated with power, Or material resources. To each is a goal to which Allah turns him/her, Then strives together as in a race towards all that is good where ever ye are. Allah will bring you together, For Allah has power over all things. Mankind was one single nation, And God sent messages with Glad Tidings, And with them he sent the book and the truth to judge between people where they differed, But the people of the book, After the clear signs came to them they did not differ among themselves, Except through selfish contumely. God by his grace guided the believer to the truth concerning that where in they differed, For God guides whom he will to a path that is straight Draw Brothers!

Ingredient of 360% Of Lordism.....

In order to obtain 360 degree's of Lordism, We as striving Lords must give fully of ourselves from ourselves.....We must apply the supreme degree of determination in all our endeavors, For through this all shall be accomplished..... Our level of conscience must be most high or life will pass..... We must incorporate all the essentials of a blood line family and from the hardcore give our support, And our Love, And if a situation dictates so. Our life..Thurst, Respect, Discipline, And Loyalty must be our appetizer, As for the main course, We through in our commitment, Our Queen should be taught of the Lords, For it is through them that our growth is finalized. With proper guidance and understanding a sister can reach 120% of pure Lordism...When a person lives it, Love it, Dream it, Eat it, Speak it, And Die in it, Then and only Then can they be called a righteous Lord to and through Hard Core. This and only this is the essence 360% of pure Lordism.

A/V/L/N Economic Program.....

1.   It will be incumbent on every representative of the A/V/L/N to pay membership dues on a regular and basis.

2.   The initial dues shall be fifty dollars per year each year there after shall be thirty dollars.

3.   A workable timetable shall be set up to accommodate each individual to alleviate and eliminate the crush of a financial strain.

4.   All monies will be placed in the subnations account in the following manner fifty percent goes to general account, forty percent subnation account.

5.   All monies will be under the authority of treasure(s): National Headquarters treasure in Chicago will be the paramount treasure and must be afforded a monthly treasure report from all Subofficers. These reports shall be submitted to the Chief or his appointed representative.

6.   No monies will be drawn from accounts without approval of Chief and representing office of SubNation. (1) NOTE, Other necessary funds for upkeeping and daily functioning of nation, In essence Rent, Salaries, Expenses.

7.   Each SubNation acting in accordance with this economic program shall be recipients of all the benefits and advantages that this entails.

One of our economic goals: Set a work program based on commitment and a work pledge. With a two hundred minimum given for the building and buying of a Lords center. Our goal will be to raise a million settling for no less than five hundred thousand dollars. Each Elite must donate five hundred dollars. Our Center/House of Lords, will be constructed from the ground once we gain the necessary funds for such a project, But initially we will settle for a building of comfort and conviency.

The National Athem.....

Throw your palms to the sky, Fly your Love most high, Be forever proud, forever real, And dedicated to the cause. Whether you be man, woman, Or Child it make no difference which one are thou. All that believe are the same. A fruit from (a) tree from which the nation sprang. Be V/L, And forever real. Oh precious people always strive to excell, Build upon your dreams, our faith, But don't let that stand in your way. We too are a living people of life with every right to be. Oh fruit from the tree which the Nation sprang, Beautiful, sweet bearing the V/L name, Throw your palms to the sky, Fly your love most high, be forever proud..........

(Note): THE CONSTITUTION OF THE UNITED STATES OF AMERICA GRANTS US THE RIGHTS TO ASSERT OUR RIGHT TO AN IDEALIZED WAY OF LIFE. LORDISM IS OUR CHOICE, AND ANY BELIEVER HAVE A RIGHT TO GIVE EXPRESSION TO IT..........

Conclusion.....

This Code Of Conduct, Chain Of Command, Principals Of Law, And all the other material containing this revelation has been designed, And arranged with great care, And consideration of every representative of the Amalgamated Order Of Lordism. It is the Law, Philosophy, And Structure of a great nation. It is established so that every V/L will know who he/she is, And who his/her Brother and Sisters are. This literature also serves to maintain a Security, Discipline, Safety, And Integrity of the order. This literature contains some of the truthful teaching of Lordism, But as Lordism literature a way of life, And the righteous truth seeking V/L cannot help but learn more truth as he/she travels the golden path of Lordism. You as V/L & V/Lady are expected to know, Respect, And Honor the Code, The Chain, And the principals of laws of this Almighty Amalgamated Order Of Lordism, And also know what Lordism is about, For in no other way can we sincerely represent V/L. Behold V/L, The Truth has now been revealed, Hold fast to it, And you will surely walk the golden path of Lordism as a true V/L.

Via Va Va Lah Halaliil Illilaha

APPENDIX E:

The Illinois Streetgang Terrorism Prevention Act
ACT 147. STREETGANG TERRORISM OMNIBUS
PREVENTION ACT

Section
147/1.   Short title.
147/5.   Legislative findings.
147/10.   Definitions.
147/15.   Creation of civil cause of action.
147/20   Commencement of action.
147/25.   Venue.
147/30.   Service of process.
147/35.   Injunctive relief, damages, costs, and   fees.

147/1. Short title
        1. Short title. This Article may be cited as the Illinois
Streetgang Terrorism Omnibus Prevention Act.
P.A. 87-932, Art. II, 1, eff. Jan. 1, 1993.
Formerly Ill.Rev.Stat., ch. 38, 1751.

Title of Act:
        An Act to create the Statewide Organized Gang
Database Act and the Illinois Streetgang Terrorism Omnibus
Prevention Act. P.A. 87-932, Art. II, approved Aug. 27, 1992,
eff. Jan. 1, 1993.

147/5. Legislative findings.
        5. Legislative findings.
        (a) The General Assembly hereby finds and declares
that it is the right of every person, regardless of race, color,
creed, religion, national origin, sex, age, or disability, to be
secure and protected from fear, intimidation, and physical harm
caused by the activities of violent groups and individuals. It is
not the intent of this Act to interfere with the exercise of the
constitutionally protected rights of freedom of expression and
association. The General Assembly hereby recognizes the
constitutional right of every citizen to harbor and express beliefs
on any lawful subject whatsoever, to lawfully associate with
others who share similar beliefs, to petition lawfully constituted
authority for a redress of perceived grievances, and to participate
in the electoral process.
        (b) The General Assembly finds, however, that urban,
suburban, and rural communities, neighborhoods and schools
throughout the State are being terrorized and plundered by
streetgangs. The General Assembly dins that there are now
several hundred streetgangs operating in Illinois, and that while
their terrorism is most widespread in urban areas, streetgangs
are spreading into suburban and rural areas of Illinois.
        (c) The General Assembly further finds that streetgangs
are often controlled by criminally sophisticated adults who take
advantage of our youth by intimidating and coercing them into
membership by employing them as drug couriers and runners,
and by using them to commit brutal crimes against persons and
property to further the financial benefit to and dominance of the
streetgang.
        (d) These streetgangs' activities present a clear and
present danger to public order and safety and are not constitutionally protected. No society is or should be required to endure
such activities without redress. Accordingly, it is the intent of
the General Assembly in enacting this Act to create a civil
remedy against streetgangs and their members that focuses upon
patterns of criminal gang activity and upon the organized nature
of streetgangs, which together have been the chief source of their
success.
P.A. 87-932, Art. II, ° 5, eff. Jan. 1, 1993.
Formerly Ill.Rev.Stat., ch. 38, 1755.

147/10. Definitions
        10. Definitions.
        Course or pattern of criminal activityö means 2 or more
gang-related criminal offenses committed in whole or in part
within this State when:
        (1) at least one such offense was committed after the
effective date of this Act;
        (2) both offenses were committed within 5 years of each
other; and
        (3) at least one offense involved the solicitation to
commit, conspiracy to commit, attempt to commit, or commission of any offense defined as a felony or forcible felony under
the Criminal Code of 1961.1
        Designee of State's Attorney or designee means any
attorney for a public authority who has received written permission from the State's Attorney to file or join in a civil action
authorized by this Act.
        Public authority means any unit of local government or
school district created or established under the Constitution or
laws of this State.
        State's Attorney means the State's Attorney of any
county where an offense constituting a part of a course or pattern
of gang-related criminal activity has occurred or has been
committed.
        Streetgang or gang means any combination, confedera-
tion, alliance, network, conspiracy, understanding, or other
similar conjoining, in law or in fact, or 3 or more persons:
        (1)(I) that, through its membership or through the
agency of any member and at the direction, order, solicitation, or
request of any conspirator who is a leader, officer, director,
organizer, or other governing or policy making person or
authority in the conspiracy, or by any agent, representative, or
deputy of any such person or authority engages in a course or
pattern of criminal activity; or (ii) that, through its membership
or through the agency of any member engages in a course or
pattern of criminal activity.
        (2) For purposes of this Act, it shall not be necessary to
show that a particular conspiracy, combination, or conjoining of
persons possesses, acknowledges, or is known by any common
name, insignias, flag, means of recognition, secret signal or
code, creed, belief, structure, leadership or command structure,
method of operation, or criminal enterprise, concentration or
specialty, membership, age, or other qualifications, initiation
rites, geographical or territorial situs or boundary or location, or
other unifying mark, manner, protocol or method of expressing
or indicating membership when the conspiracy's existence, in
law or in fact, can be demonstrated by a preponderance of other
competent evidence. However, any evidence reasonably tending
to show or demonstrate, in law or in fact, the existence of or
membership in any conspiracy, confederation, or other association described herein, or probative of the existence of or membership in any such association, shall be admissible in any action
or proceeding brought under this Act.
        'Streetgang member' or 'gang member' means any
person who actually and in fact belongs to a gang, and any
person who knowingly acts in the capacity of an agent for or
accessory to, or is legally accountable for, or voluntarily associates himself with a course or pattern o f gang-related criminal
activity, whether in a preparatory, executory, or cover-up phase
of any activity, or who knowingly performs, aids, or abets any
such activity.

'Streetgang related' or 'gang-related' means any criminal activity, enterprise, pursuit, or undertaking directed by, ordered by, authorized by, consented to, agreed to, requested by, acquiesced in, or ratified by any gang leader, officer, or governing or policy-making person or authority, or by any agent, representative, or deputy of any such officer, person, or authority:

(1) with the intent to increase the gang's size, membership, prestige, dominance, or control in any geographical area; or

(2) with the intent to provide the gang with any advantage in, or any control or dominance over any criminal market sector, including but not limited to, the manufacture, delivery, or sale of controlled substances or cannabis; arson or arson-for-hire; traffic in stolen property or stolen credit cards; traffic in prostitution, obscenity, or pornography; or that involves robbery, burglary, or theft; or

(3) with the intent to exact revenge or retribution for the gang or any member of the gang; or

(4) with the intent to obstruct justice, or intimidate or eliminate any witness against the gang or any member of the gang; or

(5) with the intent to otherwise directly or indirectly cause any benefit, aggrandizement, gain, profit or other advantage whatsoever to or for the gang, its reputation, influence, or membership.
P.A. 87-932, Art. II ° 10, eff. Jan. 1, 1993.
Formerly Ill.Rev.Stat., ch. 38, 1760.
1 720 ILCS 5/1-1 et seq.

147/15. Creation of civil cause of action
15. Creation of civil cause of action.
(a) A civil cause of action is hereby created in favor of any public authority expending money, allocating or reallocating police, firefighting, emergency or other personnel or resources, or otherwise incurring any loss, deprivation, or injury, or sustaining any damage, impairment, or harm whatsoever, proximately caused by any course or pattern of criminal activity.
(b) The cause of action created by this Act shall lie against:
(1) any streetgang in whose name, for whose benefit, on whose behalf, or under whose direction the act was committed; and
(2) any gang officer or director who causes, orders, suggests, authorizes, consents to, agrees to, requests, acquiesces in, or ratifies any such act; and
(3) any gang member who, in the furtherance of or in connection with, any gang-related activity, commits any such act; and
(4) any gang officer, director, leader, or member.
(c) The cause of action authorized by this Act shall be brought by the State's Attorney or attorneys, or by his or their designees. This cause of action shall be in addition to any other civil or criminal proceeding authorized by the laws of this State or by federal law, and shall not be construed as requiring the State's Attorney or his designee to elect a civil, rather than criminal remedy, or as its officers, directors, leaders, and members shall be joint and severable subject only to the apportionment and allocation of punitive damage authorized under Section 35 of this Act.1
P.A. 87-932, Art. II, ° 15, eff. Jan. 1, 1993.
Formerly Ill.Rev.Stat., ch. 38, °1765.
1 740 ILCS 147/35.

147/20. Commencement of action.
20. Commencement of action.
(a) An action may be commenced under this Act by the filing of a verified complaint as in civil cases.
(b) A complaint filed under this Act, and all other ancillary or collateral matters arising therefrom, including matter relating to discovery, motions, trial, and the perfection or execution of judgments shall be subject to the Code of Civil

Procedure,1 except as may be otherwise provided in this Act, or except as the court may otherwise order upon motion of the State's Attorney or his designee in matters relating to immunity or the physical safety of witnesses.
(c) The complaint shall name each complaining State's Attorney or his designee, and the public authority represented by him or by them.
(d) The complaint shall also name as defendants the gang, all known gang officers, and any gang members specifically identified or alleged in the complaint as having participated in a course or pattern of gang-related criminal activity. The complaint may also name, as a class of defendants, all unknown gang members.
(e) When, at any point prior to trial, other specific gang officers or members become known, the complaint may be amended to include any such person as a named defendant.
P.A. 87-932, Art. II, ° 20, eff. Jan. 1, 1993.
Formerly Ill.Rev.Stat., ch. 38, 1770
1 735 ILCS 5/1-101 et seq.

147/25. Venue
25. Venue.
(a) In an action brought under this Act, venue shall lie in any county where an act charged in the complaint as part of a course or pattern of gang-related criminal activity was committed.
(b) It shall not be necessary for all offenses necessary to establishing a course or pattern of criminal activity to have occurred in any one county where the State's Attorneys of several counties, or their designees, each complaining of any offense, elected to join in a complaint. In such instance, it shall be sufficient that the complaint, taken as a whole, alleges a course or pattern of gang-related criminal activity, and each count of any such joint complaint shall be considered as cumulative to other counts for purposes of alleging or demonstrating such a course or pattern of activity.
(c) Where a course or pattern of activity is alleged to have been committed or to have occurred in more than one county, the State's Attorney of each such county, or their designees, may join their several causes of action in a single complaint, which may be filed in any such county agreed to by or among them, but no such joinder shall be had without the consent of the State's Attorney having jurisdiction over each offense alleged as part of the course or pattern of activity.
P.A. 87-932, Art. II, ° 25, eff. Jan. 1, 1993.
Formerly Ill.Rev.Stat., ch. 38, 1775.

147/30. Service of process
30. service of process.
(a) All streetgangs and streetgang members engaged in a course or pattern of gang-related criminal activity within this State impliedly consent to service of process upon them as set forth in this Section, or as may be otherwise authorized by the Code of Civil Procedure.1
(b) Service of process upon a streetgang may be had by leaving a copy of the complaint and summons directed to any officer of such gang, commanding the gang to appear and answer the complaint or otherwise plead at a time and place certain:
(1) with any gang officer; or
(2) with any individual member of the gang simultaneously named therein; or
(3) in the manner provided for service upon a voluntary unincorporated association in a civil action; or
(4) in the manner provided for service by publication in a civil action; or
(5) with any parent, legal guardian, or legal custodian of any persons charged with a gang-related offense when any person sued civilly under this Act is under 18 years of age and is

also charged criminally or as a delinquent minor; or

(6) with the director of any agency or department of this State who is the legal guardian, guardianship administrator, or custodian of any person sued under this Act; or

(7) with the probation or parole officer of any person sued under this Act; or

(8) with such other person or agent as the court may, upon petition of the State's Attorney or his designee authorize as appropriate and reasonable under all of the circumstances.

(c) If after being summoned a streetgang does not appear, the court shall enter an answer for the streetgang neither affirming nor denying the allegations of the complaint but demanding strict proof thereof, and proceed to trial and judgment without further process.

(d) When any person is named as a defendant streetgang member in any complaint, or subsequently becomes known and is added or joined as a named defendant, service of process may be had as authorized or provided for in the Code of Civil Procedure for service of process in a civil case.

(e) Unknown gang members may be sued as a class and designated as such in the caption of any complaint filed under this Act. Service of process upon unknown members may be made in the manner prescribed for provision of notice to members of a class in a class action, or as the court may direct for providing the best service and notice practicable under the circumstances which shall include individual, personal, or other service upon all members who can be identified and located through reasonable effort.

P.A. 87-932, Art. II, ° 30, eff. Jan. 1, 1993.
Formerly Ill.Rev.Stat., ch. 38, 1780.
1 735 ILCS 5/1-101 et seq.

147/35. Injunctive relief, damages, costs, and fees

° 35. Injunctive relief, damages, costs, and fees.

(a) In any action brought under this Act, and upon the verified application of the State's Attorney or his designee, the circuit court may at any time enter such restraining orders, injunctions, or other prohibitions, or order such other relief as it deems proper, including but not limited to ordering any person to divest himself of any involvement or interest, direct or indirect, in any illegal streetgang activity and imposing other reasonable restrictions on the future illegal activities of any defendant.

(b) A final judgement in favor of a public authority under this Act shall entitle it to recover compensatory damages for all damages, losses, impairments, or other harm proximately caused, together with the costs of the suit and reasonable attorney's fees. Punitive damages may be assessed against any streetgang, against any streetgang officer or member found guilty of actual participation in or to be legally accountable for a course or pattern of criminal activity under this Act.

P.A. 87-932, Art. II, 35, eff. Jan. 1, 1993.
Formerly Ill.Rev.Stat., ch. 38, 1785.

Appendix F:
The GANGSTER DISCIPLES:
A Gang Profile

Introduction

The Gangster Disciples, formed in 1974 as a 60-man operation, today has matured into a centralized criminal organization with nearly 30,000 members in Chicago alone, spreading its tentacles out to at least 35 other states and several thousand more members.

With an estimated annual revenues in excess of $100 million from Chicagoland narcotics sales and street tax (its total income from various front organizations, social service scams and other illegal income sources is difficult to assess), the gang is one of Chicago's most successful, albeit illegal, home-grown corporations in the modern American underground economy.

The Gangster Disciples' entrenched presence in city life, from West Side drug sales to political protests at City Hall, is a painful reminder that Chicago has a long and well-earned reputation as a gangster town.

It is also a testament to the gang's reach.

Like an aggressive, mutating virus, the Gangster Disciples gang has penetrated and exploited legitimate authority structures and democratic processes that could have endangered its existence: media, government, social service agencies, academia, church, even the penal system.

Reminiscent of the U.S. Army's recruitment promise to "be all you can be" the gang has lured members with opportunities far overreaching illicit financial gain from narcotics sales, from merchandising "prison fashion" to meeting with the President of the United States.

As they climb within the gang hierarchy, GD members have increased access to political internships, media exposure, preaching engagements, contracts and jobs with social service agencies and high schools and the prestige of associating with national leaders.

Chicago's Gangster Disciples have benefited from a societal vulnerability created in part by the naivete, ignorance— and often apathy— of journalists, politicians, religious leaders and government officials.

In this article, we will provide an overview of this powerful and dangerous gang, including information on: recent federal indictments and ongoing investigation; thumbnail sketches of gang leaders; organizational chart; historical overview with gang constitution; political and social service fronts;

use of religion; and media strategies.

This article will conclude with an assessment of the gang's current power in light of recent federal indictments. Also included: excerpts from a yet-to-be released study by the National Gang Crime Research Center, prepared from a survey of Atlanta law-enforcement officials, including data on their beliefs of the gang's intent and ability to menace the upcoming Atlanta Olympic Games.

Federal Indictments: United States of America v. the Gangster Disciples

On Aug. 31, 1995, U.S. Atty Jim Burns boasted in a Chicago news conference that a five-year federal investigation had "torn the head off the snake" by indicting 39 GD members and associates, including leader Larry "The Chairman" Hoover. Hoover and 38 other GD middle management gang leaders now face long federal prison sentences for among other things using juveniles in their large scale drug sales operations. Hoover himself faces a federal life sentence if convicted.

Officers and officials from the U.S. Bureau of Alcohol, Tobacco & Firearms, U.S. Drug Enforcement Agency, the U.S. Marshal's office, Internal Revenue Service, U.S. Customs, Illinois State Police, Chicago Police and Chicago Housing Authority Police were also to savor that day. "Operation Headache" culminated in 21 arrests without injury to either officers or arrestees.

Hoover himself was flown from prison in Dixon, Ill. into Meigs Field, and subsequently taken to the Dirksen Federal Building.

But did "Operation Headache" cut off the head of the gang? Was it a beheading— or merely a migraine?

By the middle of September, a community activist with acknowledged ties to the gang led a serpentine chain of self-identified GDs into City Council chambers, where they claimed every public seat for a hearing on how the State's Atty. had handled a political hot potato homicide investigation.

And on Sept. 22, Chicago Police officers who had enjoyed the televised August spectacle of handcuffed GDs got a CPD Special Bulletin advising them that 10 men named in the indictment were still free.

The bulletin read:

"Published herein is Federal Arrest warrant information on individuals wanted in connection with 'Operation Headache'... this bulletin concerns those 10 subjects who are still wanted on outstanding Federal arrest warrants. All are members of the Gangster Disciples street gang and should be approached with caution. Though all the wanted subjects have southside addresses, investigation revealed a strong Gangster Disciple presence in westside and northside districts."

The bulletin featured 10 booking photos of the wanted men, along with their addresses, ages and descriptions.

As this issue went to press, Darryl "Pee Wee" Branch, William "Too Short" Edwards, Russell "Poncho" Ellis, Johnny "Crusher" Jackson, Dion "Knuckles" Lewis, Sherman Moore, Timothy "Willa" Nettles, Quan "Q" Ray, Kevin "K-Dog" Williams and Tirenzy "Bible" Wilson remained at large.

Jackson (IR# 899836) is reputedly a member of the gang's Finance and Communication Division, while Edwards (IR# 887190) was listed among the GD Governors/Area Coordinators, as was Darryl "Pee Wee" Branch, also known as Darryl Brent (IR# 350360). (See An Introduction to Gangs, 1995).

Brief Historical Sketch: Evolution of the GDs

The gang's genesis dates to 1960, with a South Side gang called the Devil's Disciples had become sufficiently large to warrant being given an outreach worker by the Welfare Council of Metropolitan Chicago Youth Services (source: Chicago Historical Society). The Devil's Disciples were mostly male African-Americans, 15-18 years of age, frequenting the intersection of 53rd St. and Kimbark Ave., and operated from 53rd and Woodlawn to 49th St. and Dorchester Ave. In the early 1960s this gang known as the Devils Disciples became the "Black Disciples" (see Explosion of Chicago's Black Street Gangs: 1900 to Present, 1990, by Useni Perkins). The three major players in the Devils Disciples were David Barksdale, Shorty Freeman, and Don Derky.

Most accounts date the founding of the Black Disciples to the year 1966 as a southside gang. The founding leader of the Black Disciples was David Barksdale, referred to in gang materials as "King David." As a boy, Barksdale trained as a boxer at the Better Boys Foundation, later making an unsuccessful attempt to turn pro in New York City before returning to Chicago.

Even in the 1960's, the Black Disciples were enemies or rivals of the Black P. Stone Rangers led by Jeff Fort.

The gang's center of influence in the 1960's appeared to be he Englewood community of Chicago, where "to raise money to fund their illegal enterprises Disciple leaders staged fundraising parties at the Maryland Theatre, located at 63rd and Maryland" (See Illinois Police and Sheriffs News, "Paying the Price of Our Neglect: Street Gangs are the New Organized Crime", Spring, 1994).

Barksdale, seriously wounded by gunfire from a rival gang member in 1969, died in 1974 of kidney failure related to those injuries.

Barksdale's arrests consisted mostly of disorderly conduct, weapons and drug possession (i.e., marijuana), with no actual convictions of drug pushing, according to one relative interviewed in July 1995.

Regardless of Barksdale's own arrest record, by the early 70's it was clear that his gang was involved in narcotics trafficking. And when he died, the narcotics territory and leadership of the Black Disciples was up for grabs.

Two men attempted to fill the power void: Jerome "Shorty" Freeman rose to become the leader of the existing Black Disciples; and Larry "King" Hoover created his own thing — the Black Gangster Disciples.

Freeman tried to secure Barksdale's territory for the benefit of his gang, the Black Disciples or BD's (which continues today as a separate organization with its own unique by-laws and constitution.)

From prison, Hoover fused remnants of Barksdale's organization with that of his own gang, "The Family." Hoover had founded "The Family" at age 23, about a year before Barksdale's death. (See Chicago Tribune, Dec.11, 1973). Members of the Supreme Gangsters, a transition gang identity, became the Gangster Disciples.

Mississippi-born Hoover lived at 121 E. 104th St., in what today is called the "hundreds" area of Chicago's southside.

His gang's territory stretched from Chicago to Gary, Ind.   On Nov. 5, 1973 Hoover was found guilty of the kidnap murder of reputed addict William Young. Joshua Shaw was prepared to testify against Hoover, but he too was murdered Sept. 27, 1974.

But Shaw had already given his deposition at a preliminary hearing, detailing how he saw Hoover and his lieutenant, Andrew Howard, kidnap Young from 69th Street and Wentworth Avenue on Feb. 26, 1973. Young, whom Hoover suspected of stealing from The Family's narcotics supply, was found shot to death in an alley at 6814 S. Lowe St. later that day.

Both Howard and Hoover received sentences of 150 to 200 years in the Illinois Department of Corrections. When Barksdale died in 1974, Hoover was ideally positioned to begin organizing his own gang following.

Howard, later known as "Dee Dee" was to continue his association with Hoover, and would himself be included in the Aug. 31 indictments.

Hoover flourished in his quarters at the Illinois Department of Corrections (IDOC), growing in influence and power. How powerful? Hoover was indicted for ordering the inmate uprising in Pontiac Correctional Center in 1978 in which three officers died. But charges against Hoover were dropped because GD's would not testify against their leader.

Did Hoover mastermind the riot? Here are the colorful opinions of a high ranking gang informant, excerpted from a July 1995 interview:

"Hoover practically masterminded the riot in 1978. He ordered his members to burn the commissary down. Three guards got killed; he looted it first, then burned it. He also had one of our guys killed back in Pontiac in 1982, a kid named Smiley. Which started a big thing. One of his guys, a GD named Shannon, has a statewide hit out on him from our gang becase of it; Shannon is still alive though, he is inside, he was one of the GD hitmen."

"Hoover was hit only once, after Barksdale died, there was a guy named Nissan. Nissan was a BG. Nissan had a homosexual hit Hoover because he wanted to humiliate Hoover. The homo stabbed Hoover two or three times before Hoover's security got a hold of him. This guy Nissan is in Danville now, he made a training tape for the corrections academy on how to disarm an inmate with a weapon."

In 1993, when Hoover began serious efforts to win parole through political and public pressure, he would appear at the parole board hearing "dressed as though on a European vacation: black loafers, black pleated slacks and a white, short-sleeve shirt" (George Papajohn, "Killer Hoover Pleads to Go Free: Broker, Even Ex-Prosecutor Stand Up For Convict", Chicago Tribune, 8-11-93).

And Hoover was until the Fall of 1994 held in the Vienna Correctional Center in Vienna, Illinois — a very comfortable, minimum security, college campus style facility with no fences. The historical issue is what major type of power brokerage was Hoover able to use to gain a transfer to this Vienna facility.

Why could a gang leader serving a life sentence for murder wield such clout? One explanation is that prison officials and gang members alike believed that Hoover held the power of life and death in his hands. They believed that Hoover was able to order all GD's incarcerated in the IDOC to not assault a correctional officer or employee without his direct authorization — thus, any assaults against prison staff anywhere in Illinois would be considered a major "violation" in the gang laws that GD's live by behind bars.

Gang Leader's Prison Status: Ability to Lead From Behind Bars

This ability of a gang leader to operate from behind state prison walls amazes most people who do not understand modern gangs. The public is equally unaware of how in the Federal Bureau of Prisons such gang leaders would face a no human contact status facility like that of California's Pelican Bay Correctional Center. Illinois state facilities have a long history of trying to manage gangs by providing special concessions to gang leaders such as Hoover.

If the story of the Gangster Disciples and Hoover has any lesson, it is that negotiating with gangs is a futile strategy. The gang will not be coopted, it will be strengthened by the recognition and implied delegation of authority that such recognition brings.

There have been several major efforts over the years by the collective bargaining units for line staff correctional officers to stop correctional administrators from the practice of granting special favors, concessions, and privileges to gang leaders in Illinois state correctional facilities.

The Illinois Department of Corrections has a very confused and therefore politically vulnerable policy on gang issues. First, it denies it has much of a gang problem. Some background history is useful here. Secondly, the historical record is quite clear: a national pattern of serious mistakes about handling gangs behind bars was detected early in Illinois. Prison administrators did negotiate with gang leaders. Gang leaders were able to hold banquets and picnics on their "Nation days", thereby undermining the authority of the line correctional officers who dealt with these gang members on a daily basis.

The official central office administration in the Illinois Department of Corrections forbids its wardens and administrative staff from revealing information to the public, particularly researchers, about gangs. Other states having a strong gang denial syndrome at the state correctional level include: California, New York, and Virginia.

Alliances

The Gangster Disciples are the leading national group in the "Folks" alliance system for gangs, which flourishes within correctional settings, but somewhat less strong when gang members operate in the larger community.

Inside a jail, juvenile or adult correctional setting, Folks gang members, including the Gangster Disciples, are mixed in with their rivals (i.e., People or Brothers), and thus find a powerful motive to create a mutual assistance pact.

The Gangster Disciples are also aligned with the Los Angeles-founded Crips, and both brandish the colors blue and black.

The GD ties with the Crips were evident during the series of national Gang Summit meetings held in various U.S. cities during 1993, when the gangs claimed they held the key to create "peace."

The GD-Crip alliance is also apparent in smaller cities that lie between Los Angeles and Chicago. In cities located in the "heartland", where comparatively small numbers of the two gangs exist, they will often "ride together".

The 1993 Maneuvers to Get Hoover A Parole

The Aug. 10, 1993 parole board hearing showed the ability of Hoover to orchestrate a large public relations campaign for his release. First, a petition for his release with 5,000 signatures was submitted to the Illinois Prisoner Review Board. He was able to promote the impression that the entire community eagerly awaited his return. But according to one witness interviewed for this article, some signatures were coerced. The witness, who requested anonymity for obvious reasons, asserted that the GD's showed up at her home one night and told, rather than asked, her to sign the petition. She admits to past ties with the gang, but claims she had not given them her new address, and did not know how they got it. (The National Gang Crime Research Center did attempt to secure a copy of the complete list from the Illinois Prisoner Review Board by a FOIA request for purposes of gang research; but this effort was not successful. The Board chairman reported that the list had been destroyed.)

It was at this 1993 summer parole hearing that Hoover had felt comfortable enough that the GD public relations campaign had been successful, that he himself claimed at the hearing that he had now converted the Gangster Disciples into a new pro-social group called "Growth and Development". Thus, he was basically claiming that the group that he led was no longer involved in blood, guns, and drugs — rather his new organization was that seeking better growth and development.

While a number of important community leaders, business leaders, and politicians (including former Chicago mayor Eugene Sawyer) had come to testify in favor of his release, Hoover was denied a parole.

The 1995 Parole Gambit Enlists the Help of Two University Professors

The modus operandi used by Larry Hoover to obtain expert testimony on behalf of his bid for a parole involved having his attorneys basically contact the university-based professors in the midwest who had previously been quoted in the newspapers on gang issues. Two professors did in fact testify on behalf of Larry Hoover at his parole hearing in early 1995. As a side note, Hoover's attorney did contact the NGCRC, and we said we might be able to determine if Hoover was in fact rehabilitated because we use facts: we would have to give Larry a series of tests and do some serious interviews on him before we could be certain he was "rehabilitated", needless to say the attorney quickly gave up on the NGCRC in Chicago as a source of manipulating gang apologists to benefit the gang itself.

One of these was Clemens Bartollas, a professor of sociology at the University of Northern Iowa. The other was Dwight Conquergood, a professor at Northwestern University in Evanston, Illinois.

Dr. Bartollas not only testified for Hoover, but also came to the benefit of the GDs in another way: by writing a OP-ED piece as a guest editorial in the Chicago Tribune (July 13, 1995) to defend the "gang deactivation program" at Englewood High School (formally now referred to as the Englewood Technical Preparatory Academy, a Chicago public school). The GD's are the single largest gang in the student population at Englewood High School. Recall, that during the 1993 Gang Peace Summit Meeting held in Chicago, that Englewood High School was also the scene for the infamous award ceremony that gave awards to gang leaders like Larry Hoover. Bartollas presented his credentials as a gang expert thusly:

"for the last 35 years, I have been involved with gang and hard-core youth. I have worked with gangs in the community in two states, have interacted   with them in correctional settings in three other states and have written a number of   books about youth and adult crime in which gangs were discussed" (see Chicago   Tribune, 7-13-95, p. 22, section 1).

Bartollas went on to defend the school's gang questionable gang program that involved gang members acting as hall monitors where they would physically punish students who violated discipline codes or did not attend school. The defense was his impression the school environment was delightfully innovative and effective. Earlier (Chicago Tribune, June 15, 1995) Bartollas was quoted as follows: "you have the deviant and quite radical suggestion that the gangs can, in fact, monitor themselves to promote a learning experience that is constructive to everyone" and on the basis of two visits to the school also said "it is working remarkably well".

Efforts to Get Hoover Released by Legislative Change: The Effort to Convert "C-Numbers"

NGCRC members realized years ago that Larry Hoover had several plans to get out of state prison, one of which included changing state law to convert "C-numbers" to the current determinate sentencing system (i.e., thus allowing for the immediate release of most C-number inmates like Hoover). It is a simple issue: among the inmates in the I.D.O.C. today are the older cons having "C-Numbers", these are inmates sentenced to prison before 1978. The "C-Number" inmates basically were sentenced under the indeterminate system of prison sentences (i.e., zero to five years, 10 to 20 years, etc). If legislation were passed to convert C-numbers to the fixed or determinate system of prison sentencing that affected all inmates sentenced in the 1980's and 1990's, then basically most of the C-number inmates would have to be immediately released on an issue of parity or equivalence in sentencing standards. Today in Illinois, while such a bill for converting C-numbers to fixed sentences was previously introduced in the Illinois legislature by a politician whose name appeared on the petition for getting Hoover released and who also showed up in a photograph at the huge GD picnic in Kankakee in 1993, it was a legislative effort that was quickly killed: and today, C-number inmates are still going up for parole every year, because they are eligible for parole under the old sentencing guidelines.

GD's Take Leadership in Gang Peace Media Manipulation

Although Wallace "Gator" Bradley, who admits being a past enforcer for the Gangster Disciples, the GD's have also been able to manipulate the mass media and gain press for their gang. Bradley was the primary mover and shaker for the Chicago branch of "United In/For Peace" nationwide gang truce movement: an effort to gain press supporting the notion that gang leaders from the GDs, Crips and Vice Lords were "peacemakers" divinely appointed to serve and protect American communities today.

It is important, perhaps, to note the problem Bradley has had over time with the issue of gang identity. During the peace treaty meeting held in Chicago in 1993, Bradley represented himself as a "gang member" but "not a gang banger", implying of course that gang allegiance is no bar to good citizenship. During the 1995 City Council elections, he sought office under the banner of being an "ex-gang member." Finally, on Feb. 28, 1995, during Bradley's intoxicating night of victory in which he forced incumbent Ald. Dorothy Tillman (3rd)into a run-off election, he was asked again if he was a gang member. His response, on-camera, was: "I am a Gangster Disciple!"

Bradley's counterpart in Minneapolis, Minnesota was Samuel Sharif Willis, a Vice Lord leader turned political activist.

The Gang Peace Summit Meeting held in Chicago in October, 1993 was headed up by Bradley. It was a media circus, with marches, protests, symbolic gestures in church and mosque settings, and formal meetings on a variety of topics of organizing for the future held at the Congress Hotel in Chicago's loop.

Gang Written Codes, Memos, Constitution and By-laws

The Gangster Disciple gang operates as a centralized authoritarian formal organization, with written codes, regularly-appearing memos, a lengthy written constitution and membership rules and regu-

lations. The gang uses a membership application form, which is used in conjunction with a background check in the same way an legal corporation such as United Parcel Service or IBM cautiously investigates potential employees. (For a list of gang prayers, statutes of the constitution, by-laws and a recent chain of command see An Introduction to Gangs, 1995).

Female Involvement

Women and teenaged girls are allowed gang membership, but rarely exercise command or even symbolic authority. In this aspect, the Gangster Disciples is typical of a centralized authoritarian gang headed by male convicted offenders.

School-aged girls are organized in a subsystem called the "Sisters of the Struggle" or "Intellectual Sisters," while male members of the Gangster Disciples are regarded as "Brothers of the Struggle."

The chivalry hypothesis operates for the most part in the Gangster Disciple gang with regard to the treatment of women. But the underlying misogyny is sometimes revealed. During the 1995 aldermanic runoff, 21st Century V.O.T.E. candidate Hal "Mad Maniac Maine" Baskin said his opponent, incumbent Ald. Shirley Coleman (16th) was responsible for the horrendous crimes of her ex-husband. Baskin, who believed Coleman had distributed a campaign flier featuring his old booking photo and arrest record, told reporters for the City News Bureau and Chicago Sun-Times that Coleman's sexual shortcomings had led to her ex-husband Hernando Williams' 1978 abduction, rape and murder of Lamaze instructor Linda Goldstone. Coleman, who denied introducing Baskin's arrest record as a campaign issue, subsequently defeated Baskin by a two-to-one margin on April 4, 1995.

Further information on female members of this gang is available elsewhere (see Journal of Gang Research, Volume 2, Number 3, Spring, 1995, pp. 61-71; An Introduction to Gangs, 1995).

Gang Identifiers and Symbols

While many different gangs are allied under the umbrella of "Folks" or the "Folks Nation", they use two common methods of identifying themselves: display of the six-pointed Star of David and "signing to the right."

A gang member may thus cock his hat to the right, roll up his right pants leg, cross his arms to the right, or modify the shoelaces on the right shoe.

The Gangster Disciples also code messages using the "7 4" alpha-numeric code system; where 7 stands for the seventh letter of the alphabet (i.e., G), and 4 stands for the fourth letter of the alphabet (i.e., D).

The six points of the Star of David symbol used by the Gangster Disciple gang have symbolic significance, which is recorded in the written constitution of the gang.

From clockwise, beginning at the one o'clock position on the star, the points correlate with the six "King David" principles: Love, Life, Loyalty, Knowledge, Wisdom, and Understanding. The principles are also called the universal laws of existence and/or the six principles of "Growth & Development".

A common coded ritual of greeting for Disciples is "All is One", just as "All is Well" is the greeting of Peoples or Brothers gang members. More common to the GD's is the greeting ritual of "What's Up G?", just as "What it Be?" is common among Brothers/Peoples gang members. "What's up moe?", being a common greeting ritual of Black P. Stone Nation gang members.

Special codes and a complex linguistic system tend to characterize the subcultural argot of gangs like the GDs today. Rival gangs (i.e., Peoples/Brothers) have special "put downs" or insults for Disciples, they call the Disciples "Donuts", they call GD's "Glazed Donuts". Similarly, GD's call Vice Lords "hooks" because of their use of the waling cane symbol. These type of "put-downs" are commonly used as status threats and constitute serious insults to the rival or opposition gang.

Folks use the term "eeples" as a term of derision against all Peoples gang members. Folks use the phrase "Eye to eye, we never die, we just multiply" as a group solidarity expression. Similarly, rival or opposition groups (i.e., peoples/brothers) use the phrase "Five to the sky, the six gotta die". Folks use the phrase "G's up, hoes down" as a put-down on Four Corner Hustlers and "Moes" (i.e., people gang members).

Influence and Control in Chicago Public Housing Buildings

The GD's have been particularly effective in controlling public housing buildings for their use in highly organized drug retail distribution systems. In the Robert Taylor and Stateway Gardens public housing buildings on Chicago's southside, GDs as recently as this spring of 1995 controlled the following buildings: 4444 S. State, 4429 S. Federal, 4410 S. State, 4352 S. State, 4331 S. Federal, 4101 S. Federal, 4037 S. Federal, 4022. S. State, 3919 S. Federal, 3737 S. Federal, 3739 S. Federal, 3651 S. Federal, 3653 S. Federal, 3542 S. State, 3544 S. State, 3717 S. Federal, and 3719 S. Federal. All other buildings in the two complexes were controlled primarily by the Black Disciples.

Drug distribution systems using public housing buildings are often very complex. It involves the use of gang members "on security" in the lobby, who literally search persons entering the building, as well as the extensive use of "look outs". Once a drug customer enters the building he/she is directed to the "spots". There may be separate apartments being used as "spots" for separate types of drugs: heroin, cocaine, marijuana, etc.

Influence and Control: High Schools, Govt Grants, and Police

1. A Chicago public high school: Englewood awards ceremony for gang leaders. This happened in the fall of 1993 at the time of the "gang peace/ truce summit meeting" held in Chicago. Students at the Englewood High School were told to go to the auditorium with teachers where they were joined by others coming to attend this "awards ceremony". The awards ceremony involved giving out awards for "Community Service" and "leadership excellence" to Willie Lloyd and Hoover. Despite sweeping changes implmented by the new Chicago School Board, the school administrators responsible remain in place today.

2. Government grant: $1/2 million for Poverty Program. The Illinois Department of Public aid awarded three contracts in excess of $500,000 to the "Save the Children" group said to be a front group for the GDs (see Chicago Sun-Times, 9-3-95). Also known as the "D & D Save the Children Community Organization", the group received the funding to providing training and provide job placements for the "Earnfare" program: an anti-poverty program that is designed to get people off of welfare and into mainstream employment opportunities.

3. Police officers assisting gang members. There have long been rumors about gang members becoming police officers, even more rumors about police officers corrupted by gangs. Sadly, some of these rumors have proved true. One of those 39 indicted in Operation Headache was Chicago Special Detail Ptl. Sonia Irwin (Star 08700), who lived with Gangster Disciple chieftan Gregory "Shorty G" Shell (IR#704666). Even before the federal indictments, this issue had been raised. Following the killing of rookie police officer who was killed responding to a call near a known drug house yards from the Austin District Police Station, Mayor Richard M. Daley fund himself besieged by press questions as to how a drug house could operate next door to the Chicago Police Department. The Chicago press corp received no answer on this issue from politicians or police but the questions remain about why the drug house was able to continue its operations at all.

4. Ability to corrupt correctional officers. There have been reports over the years in Illinois, of continued ability of large gangs to corrupt correctional officers. This includes the ability of gangs to operate prostitute rings involving female correctional

officers to provide service to other inmates. This includes, obviously, a long list of contraband smuggling operations.

Threats to Disrupt the 1996 Democratic National Convention

It is a matter of public record, that some political activists linked to the Gangster Disciples threatened to make the 1996 Democratic National Convention to be held in Chicago "look like a slumber party" compared to the 1968 event.

Law enforcement beliefs about the seriousness of the threat could be based on fear and speculation, but appear to exist is our finding regardless of the cause. As discussed in the next section of this profile, the GD's have spread throughout the United States and are well known to many law enforcement agencies in the State of Georgia. The Georgia study was undertaken as a follow-up on an inquiry about the potential for GD's to disrupt the 1996 International Olympics event to be held in Atlanta. The findings, discussed in the next section in this profile, suggest much support for the belief that such a threat exists. Additional research data is now being processed for the entire State of Wisconsin, the preliminary results do suggest that similar trends will appear supportive of the conclusion that the GD's are perceived outside of Chicago as a genuine threat to both major public events (see Project GANGWISC, A Service-Research Task Force Model of Useful Knowledge Development Collaboration Between Law Enforcement Agencies and Academic Research Agencies: A Study of Local Gang Problems in the State of Wisconsin, 1995, NGCRC, not yet released).

The GD's Go Down to Georgia

A report about to be released, a joint research undertaking of both the National Gang Crime Research Center and the Chicago Crime Commission, examined among other issues the GD connection in Georgia using a sample of N = 107 law enforcement agencies in Georgia (see Gangs in Georgia: An Assessment of Law Enforcement Agencies, NGCRC, 1995). Among the other findings were these pertaining to the GD's:

•Among Georgia law enforcement agencies experiencing gang migration, a fourth (24.4%) report the Chicago-based Gangster Disciple gang as having had contact in their Georgia communities.

•Half (51%) of the law enforcement agencies surveyed in Georgia felt the GDs could be considered a form of organized crime.

•A small number of Georgia law enforcement agencies (15.2%) reported the spread of the Chicago-based public relations gang gimmick (i.e., Gangster Disciples masquerading under the title of being a group dedicated to "Better Growth and Develop-

ment" for their community).

• Only two of the Georgia respondents indicated the GD front group known as "21st Century V.O.T.E." had been active in their jurisdictions. Gangs involved in politics in Georgia is still a small problem there at this time.

•Most of the Georgia respondents (84.3%) did believe that some of the more organized gangs like the Gangster Disciples could pose a crime threat to major events like the 1996 Olympics to be hosted in Atlanta next year; just as most (80%) believed the GD's could be a crime threat to the 1996 Democratic National Convention to be held in Chicago.

• Statewide, the GD's are among the top gangs represented in the State of Georgia according to this study about to be released.

Twists on the Gang Identity

The Gangster Disciple (GD) (also known as the Black Gangster Disciple (BGD) or by its original name, the Black Gangster Disciple Nation (BGDN). It is also referred to as the "Brothers of the Struggle", and thus females are also called "Sisters of the Struggle". As indicated below, the GD's have also effectively used modern "public relations" gimmicks, including efforts to convince some politicians they have made a transition from "Gangster Disciples" or gangbanging to a new prosocial gang called "Growth and Development". Similarly, rather than BGD's (Black Gangster Disciples) spokespersons for the BGD's will portray themselves as representing a group dedicated to "Better Growth and Development". That was how Wallace "Gator" Bradley presented himself when he had a personal meeting with President Clinton in the White House in 1994.

Proliferation of the GD's Outside of Chicago

In recent years the GDs have spread to at least 35 states throughout the continental United States (see National Gang Resource Handbook: An Encyclopedic Reference, 1995). This is considered a conservative estimate.

Rivalry With Other Gangs

The rule of thumb is this: while in a correctional setting (prison, jail, juvenile facility, etc), GDs will "ride with" other Folks in a pact of alignment necessary to deal with the present threat of Peoples/Brothers gangs, however outside of the correctional setting the GDs can have conflict with any gang, including Folks gangs. Some factions of the GDs often fight with each other, leading to the prediction that the removal of top leadership from the gang could contribute to decentralization or some type of successive fractionation of the gang into smaller, more autonomous, less centralized factions, units, or "sets".

How Hoover Was Able to Operate His Gang From Behind Bars

Shortly before the Director of the Illinois Department of Corrections transferred to another state agency outside of the field of corrections, he published an interesting account of gangs in the Illinois prison system (Lane, 1989). This article in <u>Corrections Today</u> estimated that "between 80-90 percent of the inmates in the Illinois system have some affiliation with street gangs" (Lane, 1989: p. 99). Implied in this article is that if prison administration is lax or incompetent, then the prison will be de facto "gang administered".[1] That is, the gangs will literally exert such power and influence that they will control the prison, not the warden. Recent reports tend to suggest this is close to being the reality now inside IDOC:

"According to one highly placed source, the gangs control the Stateville tiers and the correctional officers are cowed and intimidated by them. "If the officers refuse to allow friends and relatives to bring contraband into the prison for the inmates the correctional officers are shown that the prisoners possess photographs of their homes, their wives, and children".[2]

Multiple sources same to say the same thing adding greater validity to this story. Correctional officer Lawrence Kush was one of 30 on a gang's hit list at Stateville, these were prison employees who did their job, not taking any crap from the gangs, and not being compromised.[3] Kush was assassinated by the same gang on July 1, 1989, by the same gang that warned in a letter this would happen unless the employees "eased up" on gang operations.[4] A level three gang operates as a formidable terrorist group behind bars is what the evidence suggests. The official record indicates correctional officers are being undermined in their work when administrators negotiate with gang leaders under the pretext of avoiding prison riots.

In early June 1994 correctional officers at Pontiac prison in Illinois complained through their union that the prison administrators were making deals with the gangs and demanded more of a zero tolerance approach to gangs. The authority of line correctional officers is systematically undermined when wardens grant special privileges and "discretion" to gang leaders. This 1994 problem is possibly a holdover from a previous administration, as once the gang has been "negotiated with" it is difficult to go back to a zero tolerance approach without inducing much change and population restructuring and staff reassignment. Gang violence is not limited to the maximum security units, but has also spread to the medium and minimum security facilities in Illinois.[5]

One of the early, less than rigorous studies, a survey of corrections regarding gangs, was that by Camp & Camp (1985) conducted in 1983[6]. It focused on prison systems (i.e., one prison system per state), the adult component of corrections.[7] It found prison gangs existed in 33 states. State leaders in prison gang membership were Pennsylvania, Illinois and California. Some 29 states reported a combined gang membership of 12,624.[8] Basically, Camp & Camp (1985) concluded that only 3 percent of the American adult prison inmate population were gang members.

That study was basically replicated in 1993 by the American Correctional Association (ACA) with a federal grant from the National Institute of Corrections to conduct a national assessment of gangs in corrections. The ACA report estimated that a mere six percent of the American prison inmate population belonged to gangs. Furthermore, the definition of gang members included security threat groups (STG's) like fringe Muslim groups, or groups of two or more with a bad attitude.

If only 6 percent of the one million inmates in America are gang members, that means we have a minute problem nationwide, only 60,000 imprisoned gang members to worry about! Untrue. California is believed to possess more than that in its adult system alone. The California gang density rate is estimated to be comparable to that in its juvenile division (CYA), about 75 percent.

Needless to say, other research such as the yearly survey of prison wardens by the National Gang Crime Research Center (1990 to present), suggest that gang density is significantly higher than government claims. But research including that conducted by Camp & Camp (1985) and the ACA study has permitted a systemwide denial of gang density rates current in American correctional institutions.

Gangs inside major urban jails operate similarly to their counterparts in state adult correctional institutions. Larger gangs issue memos to their members, maintain a "disciplinary system" and enforce several codes of conduct: the "official rules and regulations" of the prison system itself, and gang rules — the latter probably being the rules that get obeyed more often. Consider the following handwritten memo from the Brothers of the Struggle (BOS), an actual example:

"DATE: 9-01-92
SUBJ: Violations
FROM: 4ou C.O.S.
TO: Decks C.O.S.

Greetings my 7/4 brothers, this memo is to inform you that <u>there will be no head</u> to toe violations given out unless you are given word from 2ft C.O.S. or BLD. C.O.S.. Anyone who goes against this will be bogus and violated on spot. Also all

C.O.S. are to attend church on Sundays if not they are subject to disciplinary Actions. Pass word to your decks that all B.O.S. are to lace their right shoe by missing the bottom 2 holes. Example|: This is so that we can identify each other. Brother security is to be on the entire yard; rec. when ever called. I leave as I came with plenty much love.

Important - all reports are to be in code, all minor and major incidents must be in report.

In the vision of our great leader and through his vision, we can become a more reckoning power of people beyond boundaries without measures.
2-15-19
(19-3-15-14-5-25) (7-4)".

As seen in the above B.O.S. memo, an elementary code is used: 1=a,2=b,3=c, etc. Thus the expression 7/4 means "G.D.". The expression "2-15-19" means "B.O.S.". The B.O.S. includes G.D.'s (Gangster Disciples), and B.D.'s (Black Disciples), and naturally, Black Gangster Disciples. Its Honorable Chairman of the Board is "King" Larry Hoover. "C.O.S." means chief of security. For additional information on GD's in the jail setting see: American Jails magazine (January/February, 1993, "Gang Organization in a Large Urban Jail", by George W. Knox).

Projected Short-term Impact of the Federal Prosecution

Most of the media attention to the 39 indicted GDs during September 1995 looked at a short-term negative scenario in terms of the projected impact of Operation Headache. Some gang-savvy journalists pointed out the succession effect: other gangs may exploit the void left by the GDs, just as the GDs themselves expanded in the 1980s when Jeff Fort's El Rukn gang empire was unraveled through federal prosecution.

One likely beneficiary: the Black P. Stone Nation (BPSN). There are two BPSN factions, one headed by Jeff Fort's son, both historical enemies of the "Folks" and GDs. But some law-enforcement officials believe it is much more likely that a Disciples splinter group will grow stronger. The two Disciple factions most likely to benefit from the GD prosecution are: the BD's and the BG's. Today's BG's are known as the New Breed, and are already credited with numerous robberies, gang-related shootings and some homicides. Both the BD's and the BG's have their own separate and different written constitutions and by-laws and leadership structures.

Projected Long Term Impact of the GD Prosecution Efforts

The projected long-term impact of Operation Headache consists of significant membership demoralization, significant organizational destabilization,

substantial collateral impact, a strong deterrent effect, and some restoration of public confidence in law enforcement's ability to counteract the gang threat. Each of these will be discussed below

1. Significant Membership Demoralization Within the GDs.

The GDs are the single largest centralized authoritarian formal organizational gang structure in the United States today. One projected long-term impact of Operation Headache (assuming Hoover is convicted and receives a life sentence) is demoralization within the GD membership. The message sent to the other GD's after nearly a quarter of a century is that their leaders are not invincible. And gang leaders' ability to communicate with, inspire and influence gang membership will be severely restricted. For example, no longer will jailed GD leaders be able to broadcast via a telephone-P.A. link to annual gang picnics, as Hoover did. (In the summer of 1993, in what was undoubtedly one of the more surreal moments in Chicago's gang history, Hoover gave a rousing speech to the crowd of nearly 10,000 GD picnickers gathered to munch hamburgers and hot dogs on a private farm in Kankakee.)

Additionally, gang unity will be fractured, as members vie for leadership positions. Thus, significant demoralization will occur over the next three years would be a prediction for the GD's here.

2. Significant Organizational Destabilization.

In two decades, the GDs have grown into a threat not only to Chicago or the State of Illinois, but to midwestern cities, from Indianapolis to Milwaukee, Detroit to Des Moines.

In the recent years, much has been written about the importance of "institutional memory" and the impact upon corporations whose leaders retire prematurely. In effect, the Gangster Disciples have just lost part of its memory and decision-making ability. In a federal prison, Hoover will be effectively neutralized as a hands-on micro-manager of his gang empire. In the past he has enjoyed round-the-clock access to the phone, and could could call teleconferences with gang leaders on the outside and in other prison environments.
While in state custody, he was able to sponsor "parties" in his correctional center to impress other inmates and staff. Hoover's ability to call such corporate functions is over.

3. Substantial Collateral Impact.

With the effective federal prosecution of Hoover and many other GD leaders, the astute gang analyst will also realize that the greater the gang threat, the greater the positive collateral impact from a law enforcement point of view. With top GD leadership effectively neutralized, GD members who may have wanted to defect, who may have wanted to "flip" or snitch, will now feel more comfortable in cooperating with investigators.

Secondary positive impact could therefore involve other informants coming forward, as GD members may face the risk/benefit situation of facing greater costs of staying in the gang than trying to get out. Those GD members who had worshipped Hoover as a hero face the disillusioning realization that he is gone from public life and is suffering the severe civil restrictions that the penal sanction in America is supposed to induce.

An organization founded upon the cult of personality may compel allegiance unto death, but rarely provides a structure that can be replicated. Most corporate historians would agree that McDonald's has sold millions of hamburgers not because founder Ray Kroc possessed unusual charisma, but because he created a business plan for hamburger restaurants which could be reliably replicated again and again.

This is key to predicting the future of the Gangster Disciples. To what degree is the GD organizational structure that different from those of other gangs? To what degree has the gang been run as a cult of personality, with Hoover held up to thousands of young men and women as a legendary leader, an untouchable icon, a symbol of black pride?

In state custody, Hoover could craft the myth of his own perfection, a man to powerful to be constrained even by a prison sentence. And paradoxically, prison life shielded and nourished him, protecting him not only from assassination attempts, but from having to answer for his own leadership mistakes. He was not out on the frontline every day. If something went wrong it was attributed to others, rarely himself.

Current research on gangs throughout the United States (see Project GANGECON, 1995, National Gang Crime Research Center) indicates that about one-third of all gang members, regardless of the nature of their gang, would "flip" or "snitch" given the right conditions. Such conditions are now ripe for the GDs.

It is important to understand that many crimes for which no statute of limitation exists (murder, homicide, arson, etc), can be traced to gangs like the GDs. It seems reasonable to expect substantial collateral impact in this regard in the future. Other GD crimes such as homicides will in all likelihood now be solved and effectively prosecuted. Potential informants will feel safer to give their testimony, knowing that Hoover is locked up in supermaximum "no human contact" status in the new federal Alcatraz in Colorado.

4. Strong Deterrent Effect.

From a long-term impact perspective, we should expect a strong deterrent effect from Operation Headache. Again, the logic is as historical as the presumed negative short-term effect discussed earlier. Recall the federal prosecution of the top leadership of the El Rukn gang, where the straw that broke the camels back of public outcry was the fact that here was a gang that had sought to commit acts of terrorism "for hire" for hostile foreign terrorist organizations. What message got sent to other American gangs by the rapid dismantling of the El Rukns? The deterrent effect seems to have been effective in preventing hostile foreign and domestic terrorist organizations from manipulating ideal groups for such operations: gangs. We have not seen subsequent examples of major gangs becoming involved in political terrorism since the effective prosecution of Jeff Fort and his El Rukn gang back in the 1980's.

So the message sent to other gangs in the United States today is also very clear from Operation Headache: being a supergang, claiming the spotlight as the largest gang in the USA, means you are first to be targeted for federal prosecution. It may therefore achieve the deterrent effect of forcing gangs into a more localized, less formal style of organization. This effectively reduces the gang threat as well. Why? Because the greater the organizational sophistication of a gang, the greater its objective crime threat.

Therefore it seems reasonable to expect a kind of lasting deterrent effect in the case of the GDs. Gang leaders throughout the United States who may have lusted for Hoover's status may note his fate and modify their ambitions, just as gang leaders did when Al Capone was finally jailed. They will realize that the moment they "profile" in this way, they will become federal targets, like Jeff Fort, John Gotti, and Larry Hoover.

5. Restored Public Confidence in Law Enforcement.

Whether it is run by Capone, John Gotti, Jeff Fort, or Hoover, when a criminal organization operates unchecked in any community that same community experiences a decay in respect for the law. The fact that successful federal prosecution neutralizes such powerful crime figures is therefore also a factor that over time can be expected to restore public confidence in law enforcement. And this restoration of confidence is another long-term prediction for Operation Headache.

In Chicago communities where the GDs had operated for nearly a quarter of a century, the news of the 39 GD leaders and associates being indicted by the federal government was equivalent to a kind of quiet individualized "D-day" celebration.

Many victims of gang crime and violence greeted the news with the thanksgiving given to answered prayers. Significantly, those who celebrated most were in the communities facing the daily devastation of GD influence: the Chicago communities of Englewood, Avalon Park, Chatham, Woodlawn and others. In the past, the false perception that gangs such as the GDs were invincible has filled citizens with paralyzing fear and apathy.

During this period of gang destabilization, in the wake of federal charges, many pastors, community leaders and residents may now seize the opportunity to act as witnessing "eyes and ears" to law enforcement.

Endnotes:

[1] Says Lane "if prison administrators are not in control of their facilities, the gangs will attempt to exert their influences" (Lane, 1989: p. 99). Another author whose name appeared in this gang profile (Bartollas, 1990) also previously explicitly asserted that some prisons are really "run" by gangs.

[2] See: p. 13, "High Noon at the D.O.C.: How Dick English Made It Work", Illinois Police and Sheriffs News, Spring, 1994.

[3] The killer in this instance, David Starks, 32, was sentenced to natural life; avoiding the death penalty by claiming he was ordered by his gang to commit the "hit". See: Jerry Shnay, "Inmate is Spared Death Penalty", Chicago Tribune, Section 2, March 15, 1994, p. 2. This law needs to be changed immediately, making it an automatic death penalty case for murdering a correctional officer, police officer, or public official.

[4] See: Jerry Thomas, "Gangs A Rising Threat to Prison Guards", Chicago Tribune, Nov. 28, 1993.

[5] See: Gary Marx, "Medium-Security Prisons No Longer Medium Secure", Chicago Tribune, Section 2, pp. 1, 4.

[6] Hunt, Riegel, Morales and Waldorf (1993) note that the first national study of prison gangs was that by Caltabiano (1981) involving 45 state prisons. Caltabiano's (1981) findings were not made known to the public as it is an unpublished report for the Federal Bureau of Prisons. Many research projects over the years have been conducted by the National Gang Crime Research Center.

[7] The Camp and Camp data was collected in 1983 and reported in 1985. Just a few years would lapse until Lane (1989) would report that 80 to 90 percent of Illinois prison inmates are gang affiliated. What that means is either two things: (1) either there was an enormous rapid reproduction of gang membership in American prisons during this period, or (2) the Camp and Camp data seriously underestimated gang force strength. Camp and Camp (1985) estimated 12,624 prison gang members, nationwide. But Lane (1989) reports much more than that in Illinois alone! Obviously somebody does not know the truth or is not telling the truth in the issue of "gang density" in American corrections today.

[8] Research for juvenile corrections on the gang problem is an area not covered by the Camp and Camp or the ACA reports. As a comparison to Camp and Camp (1985), juvenile institutions in the Fall of 1990 surveyed by the NGCRC reported a combined total of 4561 male gang members and another 212 female gang members. In a 1991 analysis using the juveniles as the unit of analysis, nationwide the estimate then was that half of both females and males in juvenile facilities nationwide were self-reported gang members — i.e., a gang density of 50 percent. Recall, however, that juveniles have always constituted but a fraction of the overall adult prison system population. But has always been a feeder or filtering mechanism to the adult system. This and other research suggests that today's prison gang density level is many times the density rate (3%) suggested by Camp and Camp (1985) and even the recent ACA federally funded (NIJ) research (6%). Both estimates amount to misinformation, but are convenient for a national denial policy on the gang problem in America.

[9] Published semi-annually by The Pennsylvania Prison Society, Three North Second Street, Philadelphia, PA 19106-2208 (215 352-2300).

Appendix G:

GANG PROFILE:
The Black Gangsters, AKA "NEW BREED"

INTRODUCTION

They are a renegade gang defying classification along the folks/peoples gang alliance system. They are an all Black gang in mortal combat with the single largest "folks" gang, the Gangster Disciples (GDs). But they are not "Peoples", as they do not "ride under the five pointed star". Their symbol has four sides: a square. Who are they? They are the Black Gangsters (BGs), also called the "New Breed".

The single greatest enemy that the BGs have are the GDs. The history of this enmity stems from the fact that the BGs are a splinter group that originated within the BGDs. What is also unique about the BGs is that they transcend the classification system historically used by researchers studying midwest gangs (i.e., the "people" versus "folks" dimensions of gang nation alliances). It is a group on the rise and therefore the gang profile of the BGs will help gang researchers and analysts to better understand the complexity of gang life in America today.

LITTLE PRIOR DOCUMENTATION ABOUT THE ROLE OF THE BGs

Most privately published gang identification manuals do not provide any clue to even the existence of the BGs or the New Breed. The recent privately published gang manual by Beckom (1993) does not mention the BG's or New Breed, although it does differentiate between BGDs and GDs. However, the BGs are not the BGDs.

The gang identification guide by Fox and Amador (1993, p. 13) does mention the "Black Gangsters", but provides false information by indicating that the Black Gangsters is an AKA for Black Gangster Disciples. Reports like that by Fox and Amador (1993) are part of the problem of confusion in the gang arena, because it also incorrectly indicates that Black Disciples (BDs), Black Gangsters (BGs), and Black Gangster Disciples (BGDs) are aliases for the BGDs. We have labored to point out that there are some important differences between the three separate gangs known today as the GDs, BDs, and BGs. To briefly illustrate the importance of this difference, let us assume that gang identification guide or some variation of it was used for training correctional officers in a local jail or juvenile lock-up. Upon arrival at intake a BG might be placed in the same unit with a group of GDs, where the gang coordinator may have concluded from gang

training materials they were "all folks". The BG might die as a result of such a mistake of being placed in a unit containing GDs.

One report that correctly describes the colors and identity of the BGs is the report on gangs from the Chicago Crime Commission (1995, p. 27). The gang identification manual by Gang Prevention Inc (1993) also correctly identifies the BGs.

The gang identity of "New Breed" has been specifically identified in the print media of Chicago (see "Man Guilty of Murder", Chicago Sun-Times, Dec. 2, 1995, p. 10 for a story of one BG member convicted of killing another BG member).

GDs, BDs, and BGs: What's The Difference?

Many researchers and gang analysts fail to realize that at least in their area of origin (i.e., Chicago), the GD's, BD's, and BG's today are basically three completely different gangs. These three gangs have completely different types of written constitutions. And the gangs have different leaders, and as shall be seen in the case of the BG's, somewhat different organizational styles. The GDs are the Gangster Disciples (AKA: GDN, Gangster Disciple Nation). The BD's are the Black Disciples (AKA: BDN, Black Disciple Nation). The BG's are the Black Gangsters (AKA: Black Gangster Nation), but today they prefer to be called the "New Breed".

OUR INFORMANT BOB

Bob was interviewed while he was still in confinement and again after his release from prison. Bob held a very high level rank in the BG gang (i.e., General) and had extensive direct contact over the years with Boony Black and other BG gang leaders. Bob's credentials as an informant were vigorously tested for validity. There was nothing inconsistent in the information provided by Bob. Bob became an informant, as is often typically the case, because of unfair treatment by his fellow gang leaders.

Bob confirmed much of our story in this gang profile, including all names of the current gang leadership. He also provided detailed information on businesses owned by some of the gang leaders, such as a large night club owned by one of the gang leaders that is still in operation on Chicago's west side.

Our access to Bob was through another informant. A small honorarium was paid to Bob and the other informant for the use of their time. They were paid after their information was checked-out.

A SHORT HISTORY OF THE GDs, BDs, and BGs

The GD (Gangster Disciple) history was explained in Volume 3, Number 1 of this journal (Gang Profile: The Gangster Disciples). The GD's basically emerged out of the gang known as the Devils Disciples. At about the same time that David Barksdale was leading the Devil's Disciples in the Englewood area of Chicago, a group that was coming into conflict with Jeff Fort's Black Stone Rangers aligned themselves with Barksdale. This group was known as the Eastside Disciples and were located closer to Lake Michigan and would later become the Black Disciples. Some readers may recall the sad story of Robert "Yummy" Sandifer, the 11-year-old shooter who was killed by his own gang. Yummy was a BD.

So while the GDs and the BDs arose about the same time and were both "Folks" gangs, the Black Gangster Disciples prior to 1980 included not only Larry Hoover but other powerful leaders such as Boony Black - the founder and leader of the Black Gangsters. This is important to understand, because the BG's are basically a splinter group of the BGDs. Many GDs are simply BGDs, the BGDN being another descriptor of the GDs; as all acknowledge Hoover as their leader. However, about 1979 Boony Black split off from the BGDs. If there was a single culminating event that signaled the birth of this nation it was the fact that Nissan made an attempt on the life of Larry Hoover.

In splitting off from the BGDs, Boony Black's group simply "dropped the D, took half the star, and the three Ls" as their gangs developmental history is commonly explained by BG members. Apparently much more was dropped than simply the letter "D" for disciple. That is the nature of the significance of this gang profile.

EARLY ANTAGONISM BETWEEN THE BGs and GDs

As described in the gang profile of the Gangster Disciples (Knox and Fuller, 1995: pp. 60-61), the only known attempt to assassinate Larry Hoover, the leader of the Gangster Disciples, while Larry was in prison, was orchestrated by a BG named Nissan (also spelled Nisan in BG internal documents). This attempted hit occurred after the death of David Barksdale, who was the undisputed leader of all the Black Gangster Disciples, who died without anointing a successor thereby leaving behind a number of leaders beneath him who sought power as well. Nissan (AKA "Nee") is acknowledged in the BG internal literature as having been a major player, holding various leadership positions, but that he also resigned from the gang. There is actually a long history of violent antagonism between the BGs and the GDs. Today they remain mortal enemies, in and out of jail. What the BG's signal is a third column in gang alliances: there is not only a "six" pointed symbol for folks, a "five" pointed symbol for peoples or brothers, there is also a new alternative: the four pointed symbol. In fact, BG members were observed defending their turn in a small section of Englewood in Chicago's southside against the ever present and surrounding GDs, and the three BGs were in the accompany of a Four Corner Hustler who "rode with" the BGs against the GDs. The strong bond between the Four Corner Hustlers (a Vice Lord faction) and the BGs continues today. It is truly a unique and hybrid gang in this respect.

WHEN IS SOMEONE CONSIDERED A "BG"?

A BG is someone who also uses the term "New Breed" to describe their gang and/or acknowledges the leader of their gang is Boony Black. Someone who calls

him "Boony" is often someone who really does not personally know this gang leader. Those in the gang that really know Boony do not call him Boony, but rather call him the "old man" or "skull". Other indications of membership or affiliation with this gang include the use of the very specific symbols and logos used by the BGs. Another indicator is the use of the written material of the BGs, as the BGs have their own separate written constitution and bylaws which are completely different than those of the BDs or the GDs. They are required to study and recite from memory a number of these rules and codes of the gang. They are not required to adorn themselves with tattoos that "prove" their dedication to the gang.

COLORS AND DRESS PATTERNS OF THE BGs

Black and grey are the official colors of the BGs. A black t-shirt or sportswear with grey lettering is the battle dress uniform of this gang. A black Georgetown sportswear jersey with grey lettering (i.e. Georgetown) is a popular casual wear clothing preference for this group because it communicates the two color combination of the BGs and "Georgetown" is often interpreted as "G-Town". The grey and black Nike sports line is also in wide use by BG's to "represent" their colors and their gang identity.

LOGOS AND SYMBOLS OF THE BGs

The logo of the BGs is not very complicated or fancy. It is simply a box with a circle in it. Inside the box, but outside of the circle area, are three L letters: one in the upper left inside corner, one in the lower left inside corner, and one in the lower right inside corner. The three L's of course mean: Life, Loyalty, and Love. Some of the prayers, the laws, and other written materials of the BGs, discussed elsewhere in this profile, provide information about this gang as well.

THE RECENT SPREAD OF THE BGs THROUGHOUT THE CHICAGO AREA

It is clear that the BGs are now to be found in almost all areas of Chicago. Some "sets" or groups of BGs are to be found in public housing projects as far south as Altgeld Gardens. Their graffiti is also an indication of their presence and is also found in a number of other public housing projects throughout the City of Chicago. This includes Cabrini Green.

Several BGs from a set that is geographically isolated and located in Englewood help to clarify something that is unique about the BGs. They can exist even within a GD stronghold. In the four block section of 67 to about 66th street near Winchester in Englewood on Chicago's south side, the BGs are very conspicuous. They guard their neighborhood with great pride and fanfare. They are guarding it from GDs. They are literally surrounded by GDs. They do indeed have a need to be on guard from the GDs as will shortly be explained. It is only in the recent couple years that the BGs have been able to "hold down" a complete section of turf within the GD stronghold of Englewood. Similarly, it is only in recent years that BG's have been able to control an entire building as their own in the Cabrini Green housing project. In the last few years, the BGs have made their presence known through their distinctive graffiti along south 95th Street just east of the Dan Ryan as well.

But one of the single largest concentrations of BGs in Chicago is to be found in the Abla Homes public housing project. This Chicago Housing Authority property is located just south of the University of Illinois at Chicago campus on Chicago's near southwest side. Unquestionably the single most dominant gang in the Abla Homes are BGs. The BGs have a long history in this location from the boundaries of Roosevelt Road on the north to Grenshaw Avenue on the south, and from Throop on the west to Loomis on the east. Prince Larry Burton lives in the same area and this is generally regarded as BG headquarters. Prince Gam, on the other hand, hangs out on the westside with Vice Lords and the Four Corner Hustlers.

BOONY BLACK: LEADER OF THE BGs

George Davis holds the title of "Don", the top leader of the BGs, and may be receiving up to a half of all the proceeds from the BG drug sales operations according to our high ranking source from the same gang. The "don" is most widely known by his gang name of "Boony Black". Boony Black was himself the target of a "hit" while serving time in the Illinois Department of Corrections (IDOC). When Boony Black was in Stateville, according to several informants, he was stabbed by members of the Black Souls gang. This happened on January 7, 1987. In fact, according to this source, Boony Black and two of his generals were hit at the same time in E-house of the Stateville Penitentiary. One of the BG lieutenants was killed (Luke). However, Boony Black is alive and well today, but still serving a sentence in IDOC. Yet this early conflict with the Black Souls would prove to be of continuing historical significance.

For the record, the Black Souls are a folks gang that are closely tied to the GDs, but operate independently of the GDs. The violence between the two gangs arose out of the organizational alienation from one of the members of the BGs. Shortly before the hit from the Black Souls a BG named Gabby held the position of Field Marshall in the BGs. However, Boony put a violation on Gabby. "Gabby was whupped" said the informant. Then Gabby flip-flopped into the Black Souls. When Gabby joined the Black Souls, the Black Souls retaliated and hit Boony and the other BGs in Stateville.

This earlier violence between the Black Souls and the BGs continues today inside and outside of prison. Both the Black Souls and the BGs operate lucrative drug distribution systems in. The BGs and the Black Souls are at war with each other today in Chicago over drug sale territories. BGs are not above informing on the Black Souls allowing for the recovery of illegal guns and filing UUW charges against the Black Souls during times of intense conflict.

Boony is serving a long prison sentence consisting of consecutive terms on multiple felony convictions. Boony is described by his colleagues in the BGs as someone who "wants to have a crowd with him every where he goes", similar to the behavior engaged in by the El Rukn

gang leader Jeff Fort who would take a large entourage of loyal soldiers along with him everywhere and anywhere he went.

Another area where Boony Black parallels other gang leaders like Larry Hoover is how they are able to effectively operate their gang from behind bars. The Gangster Disciple leader Larry Hoover was said to have a fax machine in his cell that enabled communication with the gang troops. When we asked the informants about Boony's communication system, the informant who held a very high rank reported "Boony has the whole works....access to cell phones, you name it he can get it, the BGs have a telephone line that only the Don uses, and one guy is assigned to monitor the phone 24 hours a day."

So, even if Boony were "on the circuit", he would still be able to stay in touch with his gang if he had access to a telephone.

To his trusted associates in the gang, Boony is known by two other names: "the old man", or "skull". Boony is called "the old man" because of his age. While young gullible teens, and other manipulable offenders constitute the bulk of the membership, their leader is no juvenile: he is over 50 years of age!

One of Boony's trusted associates became a law enforcement informant that we had access to for this profile research. When asked to describe the one thing that Boony was most effective at, this is what our high ranking informant said: "Boony played the extortion game, that's what he did best. He taught us: extort, extort. He never really owned an automobile, someone else would always get used to drive him around for his errands. To extort is to pressure other people, intimidate them. He had the businesses on Roosevelt Avenue terrified, they feared him enough so they could not really say NO to him."

DISAFFECTED LEADERS IN THE BGs

A number of major leaders in the BGs have become disaffected and/or killed by their own gang. These cases have all involved conflicts and disagreements with the top leader of the BGs (i.e., the Don). Gabby was a field marshall who was basically squeezed out of the gang along these lines. Nissan did not see eye to eye with the Don either, and while still alive today was a king or founder of the BGs, but was similarly forced to leave the gang. Moto was the first prince, he was the Don's "rap partner", but Moto too was squeezed out of the gang owing to his inaction when an attempt was made on the life of the Don. The rumor was that Moto knew the hit was coming down on the Don and did not get involved to help the Don, and further that Moto had been developing ties with the GDs. Baldy was another major leader in the BGs, but he was killed around 1991 by a member named Joe; Baldy had been extorting Joe and pressuring younger members of the BGs for homosexual favors. Apparently before being executed by his same gang, Baldy had been using his power in the gang to "give young kids lieutenant spots or rank to have sex with them". Prince Gam did initiate a non-lethal assault on Baldy before Baldy was actually killed. And, of course, there is one of our key informants for this profile — Bob — who was a general in this gang.

ORGANIZATIONAL SIMILARITY TO THE GDs: ISSUING MEMOS TO THE SOLDIERS

Clearly, the GDs are the most organizationally sophisticated with respect to regularly issued memorandums from the gang leader in prison. However, the BGs also do this. When we asked the top ranking informant in the BGs about this process of writing memos, our source replied "its a money thing, he is telling them {the gang members} they must be productive, selling drugs or whatever, they have to be about something, they cannot be about nothing". Here is an example of a recent memo to the troops:

Project Up-Lift: It has come to my attention that the majority of our people have incurred "DEBTS" which by some strange twist of fate they are unable to repay. There are some who simply, out of negligence on their own who cannot pay. Therefore, giving the impression "we are a worthless bunch of nothings".
NOTICE!!!
"DEBTS"
If after this date, **"one of us"** incurs a debt which he cannot repay by time of agreement, then he will have gone beyond the scope of his word, thereby causing confusion and possible dissention. So I am telling **each of you**, "if you   have to deprive yourself of the habits of luxuries you have acquired, be strong enough to do so." Don't borrow without having the means to repay!!!!!

ORGANIZATIONAL SIMILARITY TO OTHER GANGS: INVOLVEMENT IN POLITICS

In the early 1980's Prince Gam (at one time also called Prince Corn) was setting up a political wing of the gang, billing this as a voter registration drive. The idea was to sell their services to the political figures in Chicago. According to one high ranking informant interviewed for this profile, who held the position of general in the gang, the plan was "to set up a political move with Mayor Byrne". The identity of the group established by one of the BG princes was the Concerned Youth Association (CYA). The CYA did exist for a time, but faded away from lack of recognition.

AN ORGANIZATIONAL FEATURE VERY DIFFERENT FROM GANGS LIKE THE GDs OR LATIN KINGS

Some gangs like the Gangster Disciples and Latin Kings, when they hold their weekly meetings, spend an inordinate amount of their time "trying cases" of rule violations of their own members. Much ceremony in the Latin Kings, for example, centers around the administration of "violations" (i.e., physical punishment to fellow but errant gang members). The BGs do not physically punish their members to join, nor do they engage in the administration of "violations" to members involving the kind of physical punishment often found in groups like the GDs and Latin Kings. Such physical punishment or violations in the GDs and Latin Kings would typically involve a

time period of 30 or 60 seconds during which other members of the group physically punch the errant member, and the errant member must "accept" the punishment. The BGs are not like that.

The BGs have a somewhat different organizational philosophy on the issue of maintaining internal discipline in their gang. This feature of the BGs was confirmed by interviewing members in the field, as well as the high ranking member who flipped. The high ranking informant explained it this way: "if you violate a BG you kill him. No beatings, just kill him. How are you gonna beat a man and ask him to watch your back. So if two members are in a dispute of a personal nature they either let it pass, or let the two talk it out or work it out, or maybe even fight and make up so they can get on with their life. But if someone really has done something to the gang, and deserves a violation, they get eliminated entirely. They are executed."

So the BG's are similar to most other criminal gangs profiled in this journal by being highly authoritarian structures that maintain membership compliance by the threat of violence and fear, but it is not a regular diet of ritualized torture: it happens swiftly and with finality. As such an extreme measure, it is a less frequently used type of violation, as it is a "death V". It clearly does happen in the BGs however.

In the internal documents of the BGs there is a reference to "K-Baldy" this means "King Baldy". Baldy was an example of the death V. He was hit by his own gang according to one informant: "Baldy was hit for having sex with the young kids in IDOC. Baldy was one of the Kings of the BGs".

Fights between members of the BGs are therefore not uncommon because the violation process is reserved for those who deserve the "death V". Sometimes this internal fighting between members has deadly consequences. This happened on April 5, 1995 when a BG member with known rank and influence (i.e., Marcellus Ward) confronted fellow member BG gang member Corey Tolliver, both aged 27, regarding Tolliver's sexual assault on a female friend:

"In a statement to police, Ward said he confronted fellow New Breed member Tolliver in the 1200 block of West Roosevelt on April 5, telling him "I ought to shoot you right now." Tolliver responded, "Go ahead." Ward did, with a .32-caliber handgun, Assistant State's Attorney Timothy Tomasik said. ("Man Guilty of Murder", Chicago Sun-Times, Dec. 2, 1995, p. 10).

INTERNAL WRITTEN DOCUMENTS FROM THE BG GANG

According to our informant Bob, who held the rank of general in the BGs, with a long tenure in the gang, a very old African-American man named "Jeepers" known for his ability to file law suits while an inmate in the Illinois Department of Corrections "helped write the BG concepts, he was the brains behind Boony, he also helped Boony do his law work". Jeepers is well known to the NGCRC and was interviewed several years ago on an unrelated event. Jeepers is known affectionately to a great many gang members in Chicago neighborhoods as "Godfather". As Jeepers explained it in a luncheon interview set up by the NGCRC for a <u>Time Magazine</u> writer several years ago, "I can go in any neighborhood anywhere no matter what gang exists there, because I am an advisor to the four, the five, and the six". Jeepers is said to live on Chicago's westside and is a historical figure with much oral history knowledge of Chicago gangs. Apparently, according to Bob our informant, he also had a written contribution as well. Bob indicated that some of the written documents reviewed in this profile could have been written by Jeepers. Jeepers could not be reached for comment.

According to another informant, Jeepers (who has been out of prison for some time) still engages in legal work acting as his own attorney and was last known to be involved in filing a class action law suit over the discrimination of "C-Number" inmates in IDOC (see Knox and Fuller, 1995).[1]

THE BG BY-LAWS

We have reproduced the BG by-laws exactly as they are available in print to their members in Figure 1. Here we see another similarity to the GDs: the BGs are similar in being a centralized authoritarian violent structure. However, a close analysis of the By-laws in Figure 1 also reveals some stranger features of the BGs. Not dissimilar from other gangs, these internal written documents of the BG gang are blasphemous in equating "Men/Leadership" of the gang with "GOD". Some of the authoritarian elements commonly found in cults appear here as well: whatever the leader says, that is the law. The BG leader is clearly the "DON".

The self-selected title of "don" for the top banana of the gang hierarchy appears in other internal documents of the BGs to be traced to some fascination with the Sicilian "Black Hand" mafia group. Not dissimilar from the psychological profile of other gang leaders, this would imply he wants more than anything to be an organized crime figure leading a vast and powerful criminal empire. Currently the BG criminal empire is still in a state of applying its better guidance, because it still engages in strong arm robbery (mugging), robbing other kids of their jewelry at knife point, and robbing rival gang drug dealers on the street of their drugs and money.

HOMOGENEOUS MEMBERSHIP

The membership is composed exclusively of African-Americans. Persons of other races may be found with the gang in a capacity of aiding and assisting, but they are not eligible to join the gang. The gang fits the traditional pattern of being homogeneous with respect to race.

Figure 1

By-Laws of the BGs

BETTER GUIDANCE CONCEPT OF THE NEW BREED B.G.N.

<u>GOD</u>	<u>COUNTRY</u>	<u>FAMILY</u>
Men/Leadership	Nation B.G.N.	Bloodline Relative

As of this date, the order to everyman is to first <u>obey the laws</u> of L.L.L., maintain the principles of **Love, Life,** and **Loyalty**, as every committed man must prove his worthiness by deeds, progress and accomplishments.

1. We will abolish all nonsense and direct ourselves in the fashion of **MEN** of respect.

2. We look forward to peace, prosperity and the education of **Love, Life,** and **Loyalty**.

3. We must and will think positive. In this modern era, it is necessary in order to obtain our goals.

4. We will achieve success regardless of the efforts and sacrifices it takes and with dignity and respect, **L.L.L.**

5. We will discard the <u>envy</u>, <u>jealousy</u> and <u>negativism</u> from our vocabulary, and replace them with <u>steadfastness,</u> <u>initiative</u> and <u>positiveness</u>.

6. We must swear to uphold all secret laws decreed by the **"DON"**.

7. We honor the **"DON"**. He is the father of our Nation. His law is unquestionable.

8. We take the oath never to betray our flag, or the brother's of our nation. It is against the law to participate or contrive any form of conspiracy or treason....wrath is **SWIFT**.

9. We honor the nation by following the laws and concepts set down by our leadership.

10. **We don't lie, steal or cheat among us**. Our word is our bond. We **die** for that...

11. We must place aside the old tradition **"don't trust no one"**. We must trust those brothers that are beneficial and who treasure life as we do....

Forever I swear to that....L.L.L.

With honor I sign_____

THE B.G. PRAYER

Similar to other gangs, the BGs have their own unique prayer. This is an internal written document of the BGs. It is reproduced in Figure 2. It too betrays a centralized authoritarian organizational structure similar to that of a violent cult. Because here again "THE DON" is the top gang leader, and joining this gang is basically a new form of slavery: a lifetime of servitude to basically anything the "don" wants. It is intermixed with the typical mumble-jumble statements of do-gooderism and concern for member welfare, but overall it is one of the most unique such gang prayers in being so overtly and patently authoritarian. It is not unique in calling for members to be able to sacrifice their lives if necessary for the gang, the GDs have this clause and the BDs have this clause as well. So there is more than some imitation going on in Figure 2. There is a very strong element of the threat of violence or death to members who do not want to go along with the program. So, the "prayer" here is again not atypical of gang prayers in being more of a declaration of allegiance and service to the gang and especially the spiritual leader or gang leader.

FIGURE 2

The "B.G. PRAYER"

We are **NEW BREED B.G.'s** pride of the nation. Dwelling in the house of wisdom, knowledge and understanding, under the sworn oath of **LOVE, LIFE,** and **LOYALTY**. We honor **"THE DON"** and pledge ourselves to the nation. I am as I am **Black Gangster always and forever**.

1. I support the nation with my life.

2. I walk in the righteous way and will adhere to the laws according to the concepts handed down from **"THE DON"** and his worthy appointees.

3. I will never disgrace the nation in any acts of cowardliness or treason. To betray either will naturally spell doom.

4. I will answer every call to service and respect the honor bestowed upon me by my superiors and commanding officers without question.

5. I have faith in being selected to share in the burden of responsibility.

6. I believe in progress, peace and prosperity.

7. I stay alert and prepared, for at any given moment I might be called upon to carry out an act.

8. I am **"NEW BREED"**. Intelligent, Expressive, Ambitious and Righteous. I stand willing to make any contribution to the success of our nation.

I am devoted for **LIFE**. In our struggle I honor **"THE DON"**.

OTHER INTERNAL DOCUMENTS OF THE BGs

Figure 3 shows an internal communique apparently from up high in the command structure of the BGs, perhaps the Don himself, that was sent to the troops of the BGs. All soldiers of the BGN are required to study this and other types of written messages designed to motivate the BG members. The clear message is that the top gang leader is a very authoritarian leader.

Figure 4 shows an example of an internal written notice regarding new promotions in the gang

chain of command.

Similarly, Figure 5 provides more of the cult-like gobbledygook "literature" in this gang. Perhaps a naive researcher could hear some of this from a gang member and then conclude this must be what some are now calling by the phrase "a pro-social gang" (actually the phrase is non-sensical as a contradiction in terms).

Overall these internal documents of the BGs are similar in regards to many other such midwestern gangs. The language allows for moral neutralization among the gang members. The language basically excuses them for the criminal responsibility of their behavior.

OVERALL THREAT ASSESSMENT

The threat level is rated medium for the BGs. The membership base in Illinois is still small, with only about 3,000 members (includes leadership, regular members, and associates). The aggressiveness level of this gang is very high, again owing to the nature of the gang itself: it recognizes itself as a renegade gang, and it is regarded as a renegade gang. It is this "grey area" of gang classification that brings the gang threat level up to medium, because of its potential to offer a new model for the gang merger and gang consolidation scenario (gangs uniting under a larger umbrella organization). Given the current leadership, the likelihood of such a scenario of attracting lots of new members from other gangs is considered low. There has been a great deal of defection from the leadership over the years owing to conflicts with the top leader (i.e., "The Don", Boony Black).

FIGURE 3

Example of B.G.N. Internal Communique

*I come out of the house of B.G.N. I am **DON** of my castle. Every time I utter a word or make an impression, it is law, unless in the face of jest.*

*I greet you, **"my people"**, in the ancient principles of **Love, Life,** and **Loyalty**, always and forever B.G.N.*

It comes a time and point in every mans life, a critical decision must be made. So for the overall development of our nation, I have decided to expel bad blood and grant the people a privilege of the better-guidance concept of the new breed.

*In order for our nation to be fruitful and multiply, **"law"** must be established...**our business is our business**. The code of silence teaches us this faith...trust in the father of our nation, **"the DON'S word is law"**.*

I have the qualifications, but I limit myself to one concept. I took the oath and swore never to betray what I stand for...B.G.N. I believe in the three L's, which is the foundation of our way of life. If I go against these principles, , the law teaches me only death will heal the wrong...

Our concept comes through the teachings of Hannibal, "whose first born son, by a Sicilian woman was entrusted with the laws of omerta", code of silence and therefore according to the law, was the first Don, ruler of, and law giver of those closely-knit Black-hand.

B.G. was established by a common bond between four different leaderships, united for one cause, unity of our brothers; equal rank applied to all four with the exception of the Don. His was the first and last say-so because of his age, his wisdom, and his leadership abilities, the Don's word was law...

K-Ram[2] was the first elected King, only through the Don's support was he afforded the throne. His duties were to enforce the law, educate the people, and represent the first "L", LOVE is his honor...retired[3].

K-Baldy[4] was one of two (2) princes. He wore a resigned crown through aggression, but to be accepted by the people as a whole he had to have the support of the Don. He represented the second "L", his honor was LIFE.

The foundation of any unit organization family is the "L", which is last and first. "The Don represented loyalty, the basis of our being...B.G.N.

Nisan...a number of titles...resigned. Cochise[5]...one of the original heads, N-active as of the present.

Any time a brother has passed the test, he deserves the honor. Only the righteous shall reside in the house of the Don, those living according to the concept of B.G.N., and the principles of Love, Life and Loyalty.

We will give our all for the betterment of the "New Generation". Our future survival depends on every brother contributing his share. We will exercise our rights to Life, Liberty, and the pursuit of Happiness.

In order to succeed, we must stand together. Without unity there is no hope. The law is for the benefit of the Nation as a whole; it governs our daily lives...up-holding the laws are the first step we take in our...sworn oath to the nation...L.L.L.

FIGURE 4

Example of B.G. Hierarchy Appointments: Giving Notice of New Promotions to the Troops

Laws of "THE DON" B.G.N. L.L.L.

Prince M. Representative, Advocator
Commander PM. Chief Dog Treasurer & Developer of Businessmen.
Fieldmarshall Chief Dog Entrusted with the safety and security of all.

B.G.N. Chief of Security of the nations as a whole, run the joint.

General B. Commander of all the troops here and abroad.

General BL. "Special Forces".

Until further notice, these aforementioned names will carry the responsibility of enforcing the law; their word is unquestionable. Also, each is held accountable for their actions and in turn must account to their man in rank.

The first right everyman has as a member of this nation is to be represented properly. Simply by learning and complying with the law, no man will dare harm you. If you have been following the laws and the law has said you are right, only the law can condemn or redeem a brother...

The duty of the ranking officers is to carry the responsibilities of Justice...The real influence of man convictions for his nation, comes through those who share in Love, Life, and Loyalty.

Soldiers who will lay down their life for the betterment of the Nation and Honor themselves as true B.G.'s.

FIGURE 5

Example of the Internal Written Documents of the B.G.N. Designed for Motivating Members

Laws of "THE DON" B.G.N. L.L.L.

Each man, our concepts teaches us has a different approach. He's a man, nature to react in response to his environment and the actions of others, know thyself.

We Rally "this our cause"
Better Guidance New Breed B.G.N. L.L.L.

SEVEN DEADLY VIRTUES
1. Traitor. 2. Greed. 3. Envy. 4. Cheating. 5. Lying. 6. Stealing. 7. Adultery. Equal Violations = unforgivable, penalty is FINAL.

SEVEN VIRTUOUS PRINCIPLES
1. Intelligence. 2. Shrewdness. 3. Kindness. 4. Wisdom. 5. Knowledge. 6. Understanding. 7. Loyalty. Love = Honorable Heart traits. Progress, success and future.

A man reaches his destination either by the will of God, or the course of action he takes, courage and strength...

Honor more than any moral principle on earth your "avowed word" L.L.L. expresses this characterization...or Dishonor!

All young brothers need support coming up; they inherit strong traits and rebel against authority; other than those they choose to listen to. The ghetto produces strength and once that is put into relations with intelligence, adult manhood is developed.

The brothers that reach this plateau gains what's commonly called Respect.

A Firm Step

We defend our territories and protect our families, L.L.L. Honor thy family bloodline, mother and father, brother and sister as well as relatives. Respect our elders and children and friendships. As they are so deserving. Carry the image of dignity always and forever...

Each day we spend studying and concentrating on our

Laws puts us closer to the precious gifts of freedom, success and happiness.

We must be able to do for self and property as well as effectively represent ourselves and our intent in all things productive and progressive; Growth and Security; Plan, Prepare, and Preserve.

*As a **B.G.** you shall serve a special Interest and learn through the law how to specialize in **B.G.** profession...*

*I leave you in the folds of **New Breed Concepts** and the hands of **Love, Life and Loyalty**!*

I appreciate your cooperation, my people!

L.L.L.

THE BG CHAIN OF COMMAND

At the top of the BG organizational ladder is the "don", George "Boony Black" Davis. Directly under the don are two "princes": (1) Larry Burton, and (2) Prince Gambrell, aka's "Gam", "Dre", "Andre Crawford". Burton is out of prison, but Gambrell just received another prison sentence. Under the two princes of the BGs are the field marshalls: (1) Marco Brown, (2) Young[6], (3) Shawn "Chief Dog" Bally[7], and (4) Lucky.

Under the field marshalls are the generals: (1) Calvin Kuyhendal, (2) Carbindine, (3) Kenny Allen, (4) Alvin "Country" Mazie, (5) Kemp, (6) Maurice, (7) Artrel "Dean" Jackson, (8) Gilbert "Mu-Mu" Kuykendal (brother of Calvin). All of this top leadership are middle-aged men, in their thirties. Among the rising stars in the generals is "Kemp", who according to our informant is expected to rise up in the organization in the next year or so. Our informant was a general who was eager to work with law enforcement personnel, for a price.

Under the generals are a host of lieutenants, some of the more active including: (1) "Twin" Wilberton, (2) Lawrence, (3) Lance "Boo-Bye" Baggett, (4) Orlando, (5) Kent Dickens, (6) Fred Curtis, and (7) Little Reese.

Under the lieutenants are the soldiers, the lowest rank in the BG organization. Some of the more active soldiers jockeying for position in the BGs include: Mandy, Ricky Battles, Allen Young, Little Allen, Louis "Lo Down" Harris", "Monchie", "Shenell", "Coal Shawn", "Clarence Dabney", Johnnie "Black Boy" Galloway, Ronald Hayes, and Darnell Wilberton. There are an estimated 3,000 members of the BGs active in Illinois (some participate in the gang's Chicago activities even though they live in suburbs like Skokie). It is, however, a gang on the move. It is aggressive, violent, and imperialistic.

STRATEGIC SUPPRESSION OPPORTUNITIES

It might be useful to target this group for prosecution because of the high level of violence their members have in recent years become known for. The high level of dissatisfaction among midmanagement and older members could yield cooperative information

sources for prosecution. The fact that the gang is led by an older adult leader means the gang profiles as one that should be targeted for suppression to send the message that the manipulation of juveniles for the criminal benefit of older adult offenders will not be tolerated by society.

The fact that the gang maintains its main base in a federally funded housing complex (Abla Homes), again presents a strong case for targeted prosecution efforts. A number of homicides the gang has been responsible for involve victims who were members of the same gang: these cases would be the easiest to prosecute.

There are a number of business enterprises that are owned or operated by key figures in this gang. The centralized flow of income to key leaders in this highly authoritarian gang whose leaders regard themselves as godlike figures and royalty would also justify a criminal tax evasion investigation.

BIBLIOGRAPHY

Beckom, Jesse Jr.
  1993 Gangs, Drugs and Violence: Chicago Style.
Published by Gangs, Drugs and Violence Prevention Consultants, P.O.Box 288833, Chicago, IL 60628-8833.

Chicago Crime Commission
  1995 Gangs: Public Enemy Number One. Chicago Crime Commission, 79 West Monroe, Suite 605, Chicago, IL 60603.

Fox, Robert W. and Mark E. Amador
  1993 Gangs on the Move: A Descriptive Cataloging of Over 1500 Most Active Gangs in America. Copperhouse Publishing Company, 1590 Lotus Road, Pacerville, CA 95667.

ENDNOTES:

[1] The "C-Number" issue involves inmates sentenced before the Illinois fixed sentencing guidelines. C-number inmates (some are still in IDOC) still have indeterminate sentences. Larry Hoover had such a C-number.

[2] About 1992 or 1993 King Ram had a falling out with Prince Larry; King Ram was a supplier for Baldy; King Ram is still alive and about the same age as Boony.

[3] According to Bob, our highest ranking informant in the BGs, "you can get out of the gang according to your age, you can retire at the age of 35, other than that there is no way out other than death".

[4] King Baldy was killed around 1990 or 1991 by a BG member named Joe (age 36 or 37) who was being extorted by Baldy.

[5] Cochise is said to be as old as Boony, one of the original founders of the BGs, but now out of the gang.

[6] According to our informant Bob, Young was released from IDOC custody about a year ago.

[7] Chief Dog, as he is known, is said by our informant Bob to be low key in the gang but very active.

INTRODUCTION

The Black Disciples (BDs) are the Chicago "folks" gang that gained international notoriety in 1994 by executing its eleven-year-old member "Yummy". It is also unique in its comparison with another African-American gang, the Gangster Disciples (GDs). While the GDs are structured like a corporate enterprise, the BDs are structured more like a religion where gang leaders are called "ministers". The BDs trace their historical roots directly to "King David Barksdale". In other respects, the BDs are like many other American gangs in that this type of gang is able to exist over time only by the criminal exploitation of children.

THE BDs ARISING FROM A SPLINTERING EFFECT IN A LARGER GANG

The GDs, BGs, and BDs all became separate gang entities through splintering from the Black Gangster Disciples. It all began with "King David", chief of the Devils Disciples. When King David died in 1974, the new umbrella organization was the Black Gangster Disciples (BGDs). However, in 1978 three groups splintered off from the BGDs all having their origins from the original Devils Disciples (BGs, GDs, and BDs). The splintering was due to the individual leaders. This profile of the BD's shows that even within the BD's a splintering has occurred. This gang phenomenon has also been seen in "people" or "brothers" gangs, like the Latin Kings, where the East Coast version of the Latin Kings has a completely different written constitution than that found in the original Chicago version of the gang. Given the natural way in which this splintering phenomenon occurs in gangs, it is theoretically possible to induce the same effect by the separation and promotion of leadership skills. We are not implying this should be done in the form of social engineering, but rather that conflict among gang leaders in the same gang also occurs naturally and predictably. However, rather than allowing the gang to "settle" its internal disputes, in a correctional setting it may be worthwhile to transfer out one of the members along with some of his most earnest supporters. This could potentially create a "schism", unresolved conflict in the leadership structure of the gang, and therefore provide the basis for a splintering effect. The theory that a smaller decentralized gang would be more "manageable" would be the basis for viewing the splintering effect as a positive development from a gang control strategy viewpoint.

ORGANIZATIONAL STRUCTURE

As of this writing, there may be as many as 300 "sets" of the BDs throughout the Chicagoland area. Each "set" typically has 30 to 40 members, and is identical in the format of its organizational structure. Each "set" is actually called a "dynasty" in the language of the BDs, and refers to a specific section of the BD organization.

In each set or dynasty of the BDs, the lowest ranking members are soldiers or representatives. The permanent leadership ranks include: Minister, Assistant Co-Minister, and the Demetrius. One rank above the ordinary members is the "First Demetrius". One rank above the First Demetrius is the "Assistant Co-Minister". Above this in each set is the "Minister". All sets revere "King David" at the head of their organization, even though "King David" is dead. The living top boss of this mob is "King Shorty", also known as the "crowned king" (Jerome Freeman).

Each set or dynasty also has the following temporary positions of rank that exist underneath the First Demetrius: (1) Chief of Violations, (2) Chief of Security, and (3) Assistant Chief of Security. These positions may rotate periodically, because the labor is basically unrewarded (the responsibility outweighs the authority and economic benefits).

Overall each set, chapter, or "dynasty" as the BDs call it is a middle management leadership structure that is comparable to the BG's gang. There are several generals or "dons", each of which may have "deputies". It is through this middle management leadership that money passes up the ladder from the set, chapter, or "dynasty" to the higher echelon in the BD gang hierarchy.

THIS IS A GANG WHERE DRUG SELLING IS A GANG SPONSORED BUSINESS ENTERPRISE

This gang does not exist solely and exclusively to sell drugs and do nothing else. It has meetings, parties, and reaches into many non-contiguous geographical areas. It has unique hand signs, gang logos, and written codes. However, it is like other adult dominated centralized authoritarian gang structures in that the vast majority of the "members" are youths, more specifically underage juveniles, and there is one long recurring activity that this gang can at any time day or night be found to be engaging in: selling illegal drugs.

The term "putting in Nation work" means selling drugs for the gang set. The phrase "getting new work" from the gang means collecting a new batch of drugs for sale. This may mean picking up ten bags of marijuana, the proceeds from seven of the bags must be returned to the local gang leader, the proceeds from the other three are "profit" for the individual member.

The vast majority of the illegal drug income goes directly up the ladder of this adult-driven enterprise. Every BD member we talked to indicated illegal drug sales was the primary activity of the BDs and this was in fact a gang sponsored activity. Much of the "internal rules" for gang members in the BDs are designed to shield the gang and especially the leaders from criminal prosecution regarding this activity.

SOMETHING UNIQUE: SYNDICATED GAMBLING BY THE BDs

Several informants mentioned the gambling enterprises of the BD's were intermixed with the drug sales operations. An apartment in a public housing complex, a house use for selling drugs, an open deserted area: all qualify for settings for running large scale crap games. Clearly, the same kind of gambling goes on at the BD annual gang picnics (24th or 25th of May). But we began to take more notes on the gambling operations when they were a repeated them for this gang. As one informant detailed it: "the BDs are into gambling everywhere and gamble on everything, the fights, superbowl, you name it, they do all types of betting, but dice and large crap games are their specialty...like they will have a big ole crap game, 30 or 40 people there betting all at once, they have so much security that nothing else is moving....because you have some guys....Derky started it....sticking up the BDs trying to take their work money....they have lots of security always at the craps....and there are a lot of weapons present...because there is so much money involved in crap games that big."

The BD's also make use of what they call "safe houses". These safe houses are commonly used for business: meetings, drug packaging, and gambling.

DUTIES OF THE BD LEADERS

The "Minister" is the head position of a BD set. The Minister is typically about 25 years of age and supervises the Assistant Co-Minister and the First Demetrius in the BD set. The assistant co-minister facilitates drug sales or "putting in work" for the "Nation" (i.e., their BD gang), and also collects dues from the BD members. It is the First Demetrius who has hands-on supervision of the BD members. The First Demetrius calls the meetings, distributes gang literature, and makes sure members do "work" for the gang ("work" means selling marijuana, cocaine, and heroin). All of these positions of rank (First Demetrius, Assistant Co-Minister, and Minister) are positions that are only available to members who are 18 years of age and older.

RITUALIZED VIOLENCE: MAINTAINING INTERNAL DISCIPLINE

The BD's are typical in this respect: the members face "violations" for conduct or behavior that is a threat to the social solidarity of the gang organization. The "rules" of this gang are clear, and in writing. These are shown in some of the internal written documents of the BDs to be discussed later in this gang profile.

Members who violate internal rules face a type of ritualized, violent, punishment in front of other members of the same gang. This punishment occurs at the meetings of the gang. Smaller violations can be met with a "thirty second violation", meaning thirty seconds of punishment meted out by several members of the gang while the member being punished is held, with his arms behind his back, as other members punch the victim in the chest for the time duration of the "violation" being administered. A small violation might be not paying dues or not showing up at meetings. A larger violation may entail a five minute beating. And, of course, BDs have been known to kill their own (i.e., Yummy).

The typical smaller violations are for conduct that plagues any organization: failure to attend meetings or pay dues. The most serious violations have to do with "nation work". When a member returns an insufficient amount of money (comes up "short" on his "ends") this calls for a major violation. The same occurs when a member "loses" the drug stash that is supposed to be sold in "nation work". Another major violation would be insulting or disrespecting any BD leader, including chapter or set leaders (Minister, Assistant Co-Minister, First Demetrius, etc).

HOUSE PARTIES: A SOLIDARITY BUILDING MECHANISM FOR THE BDs

The BDs regularly organize "house parties" in their neighborhoods. Members and non-members alike will pay a small amount such as $3 for admittance. Age is not a concern, anyone may come to the house parties if they have the admittance fee. In the house parties, the BDs present establish the social status pecking order. Members with rank in the gang clearly stand out. Non-members take second seat to the BD members. It is therefore an opportunity to recruit new members to the BDs. As it affords a time for social interaction, drinking and smoking marijuana, with local BD leaders it is also a solidarity building mechanism for the gang. They are able to have their "good time" on a social basis where their membership counts for something. It is in this context of the "house parties" that the rules of the gang really come into play, particularly about disrespecting leaders or other members. Members are careful about the jokes and the expressions they use in their conversations and interactions with other members. They learn to be "on guard" socially. For example, they may want to express how they detest another member, but they really cannot do so, as it would call for a "violation".

House parties are also occasions to honor the birthdays of area BD leaders. A cake will be decorated with the BD gang symbols, honoring the birthday of the BD leader, which is also an occasion for taking polaroid photographs. The NGCRC has obtained quite a collection of these over the years. The main gang symbols decorated on the birthday cake will be the six pointed star of david, inside the star will be the "III" symbol. The "III" symbol is a key logo to the BDs. At the top of the Star of David will be "King" and at the bottom of the star "David". To the left and right will be names of other important gang members, perhaps including some deceased and some active members who are honoring the gang leader with the cake.

HAND SIGNS: BEWARE THESE ARE NOT BOY SCOUTS

The BD hand sign looks similar to that used by the Boy Scouts. The hand sign for the BD's is to depress the thumb tip to cover the depressed little finger, leaving three extended fingers pointing upwards. Most use the right hand, but depending on the occasion or context the left hand will also do. This is signifying the "trey", the "III" sign. Another sign is the fists clenched, knuckles out, with right hand on top of the left hand in front of the body.

In the BD hand sign the three extended fingers are slightly separated giving the "I I I" effect, also known as the "trey" sign to the BDs. A naive adult might mistake this sign for that used by Boy Scouts.

TATTOOS

Tattoos are common among the older BDs and among more hardcore younger members. The most common tattoo is a Star of David six pointed star with the "III" (trey) symbol, or simply "B.D.N." or "B.D.". Most of the juvenile members do not have the permanent tattoos. It would not be in the best interests of the BD gang to have its very young members with the tattoos, that way being easy to identify by the parents of the same children. Without the gang tattoo, the parent still has plausible deniability as well: some just do not want to know for certain their child is in fact in a gang. It is common for parents to bury their children who have been members and claim "I never knew he was in a gang or I would have done something about it".

MEETINGS AND MEETING PLACES

There is great variation in the scheduling of meetings and places where BD meetings occur. In good or warmer weather, a large back porch may be used as a meeting site for the BDs. Sometimes an enclosed garage large enough to accommodate the meeting may be used. Homes and abandoned buildings are also used.

The two most common items on the agenda of any BD meeting are: violations and paying dues. The violations to members are dispensed at these meetings. Dues are also collected at meetings. Dues are typically $5.00 for a member payable every time there is a meeting. It seems there is no fixed date for BD meetings, they are called by the set leaders on an as needed basis. This averages about two meetings a month for a typical BD set.

Going to meetings for the BD gang, perhaps as in other gangs, can be a time for fear for the gang members. One of the things they fear most is that they will be singled out by their own gang. Here is how one informant described the situation: "when they have meetings they call on someone to recite the prayer at random...whoever they call upon better know the prayer from front to back by memory, because if they do not they will be dealt with harshly....they will get a violation....the members have to know their gang literature....they regard it as sacred material...at the meetings they put a religious meaning on it".

GANG FRANCHISING: THE BDs IN MILWAUKEE

We have run across numerous examples of Chicago gangs making intentional forays into Milwaukee, Wisconsin over the years. If we were to believe the qualitative data from the book People and Folks we would believe no such real Chicago connection exists. The El Rukn's were the first to discover the value of selling Chicago drugs in laid-back comfortable Milwaukee. Louis Hoover (an El Rukn) "was one of two generals who ran El Rukn's Milwaukee drug operation in the late 1970's and 1980's" (see: Chicago Tribune, May 27, 1992, section 2, p. 9, Matt O'Connor). We have heard from several informants interviewed specifically for this BD profile that a BD chapter was intentionally formed in Milwaukee as well in the mid 1980's.

As one BD informant described it: "We had plenty of BDs in Milwaukee....I stayed there half a summer in 1992...the way they got started is guys from Chicago went up there to sell drugs, it is a better environment for the drug scenery....you get your own strip....your own spot....that's your strip...you run that....its like a McDonalds....how do you get a strip in Chicago, its almost impossible, everything is being used. The BD leaders have got it scouted out everywhere, so to open up your own operation in a place like Milwaukee, what you got to do is talk to the man in Stateville, he will give you the okay to open up this place, but without the word you cannot make a move.....BDs are nationwide.....its a nationwide thing".

THE YUMMY STORY

The 4'6", 86 pound eleven year old Robert "Yummy" Sandifer brought unwanted international attention to the BD gang in late August, and early September, 1994. Yummy belonged to the BD set called the "8 balls", because this particular set of BDs was geographically located at 108th Street. Yummy was not a peewee, nor simply an associate, he was a BD member. Yummy got his name "Yummy" because he liked cookies so much. By the time Yummy reached the ripe old age of 11, when he would be executed by his own gang, he had already accumulated a record that included 12 felony arrests. His set of the gang sent Yummy out to shoot at some GDs. His gang chief gave Yummy a 9mm semi-automatic pistol. The result was predictably tragic: Yummy did fire the weapon and was able to wound two members of the GDs, however, a stray round from the gun fired by Yummy ended up killing a non-gang member, a 14-year-old girl named Shavon Dean, who was simply an innocent bystander. Chicago was outraged and horrified at this event. Yummy hid and went back to the 8-Balls. Then members from an adjoining BD set (Edbrook) executed Yummy, shooting him in the back of the head with a .25-caliber semiautomatic handgun.

The geographical grid of Chicago is used to give each set of the BDs its distinct name. Yummy belonged to the "8-Ball" set of the BDs, this set is still based at 108th Street and Perry in Chicago. The set whose members actually killed Yummy is located at 107th and Edbrook, called the Edbrook set. Another nearby set includes "Dirty Perry", the BD set at 107th and Perry.

Two youths, both BD's, were arrested for killing "Yummy": Derrick Hardaway (14) and his brother Cragg Hardaway (16).

Both told police their gang leader directed them to get rid of Yummy. Their gang leader had provided them with a car to transport Yummy in, the ruse being that they would take Yummy away from Chicago.

FEMALE INVOLVEMENT

Female involvement in the BDs fits the pattern of the chivalry hypothesis: "sisters" can be full fledged members, but are unlikely to rise to prominence in the male dominated authoritarian cult-like organization. In some sets, up to 30 percent of the members are females. Generally, females are not "sexed in" as an initiation ceremony, which may be due to the fact that most of the sets are very provincial in nature: sometimes covering only a one block area of "turf". Leadership positions are, in theory, open to women. However, no women are known to have had major positions in the BDs over a long period of time.

Similar to other gangs, the BD's have a separate "wing" in their membership for older or hardcore female members. It is called the "Daughters of the Universal Star". It is basically a female branch. As one informant described it: "they have their own sessions; they have their little meetings; they have to appoint a chief over them; you respect them and their rank; they make decisions, and if you are asked to do something and get it cleared, you have to use your judgement, they will mislead you....they sell drugs, they kill, they give violations, just the same as the men do". Still, there is limited realistic opportunity for "rank advancement" for females in the BDs.

MAIN ENEMIES OF THE BDs

The main enemies of the BDs, for all practical purposes, are the Black P. Stone Nation, Mickey Cobras, and Vice Lords (i.e., brothers or peoples, gangs riding under the 5 pointed star). However, on the streets BDs have been known to battle it out with GDs on a regular basis as well. One informant described how a BD had drugs stolen from him by a GD. The BDs subsequently administered a brutal beating to the GD. Not surprisingly the GDs then came to the BD set and "blasted away", shooting up the neighborhood.

Recall that the primary activity of "work" for BD members is selling illegal drugs. So this risky activity can place them in conflict with virtually any other gang that is also involved in drug trafficking.

Inside the correctional population, the BD's are most closely aligned with the BG's. Both the BD's and the BG's fight regularly with the GD's.

SIMILARITY TO OTHER CHICAGO GANGS: HOLDING LARGE PICNICS

King David's birthday is a time for one of the most important yearly rituals of the BDs: their gang picnic. The BD's celebrate his birthday with a large gang picnic, usually on May 24th or May 25th. It is the equivalent of a kind of Mardi Gras for the BD's. At Ogden Park at 63rd and Racine, a public park on Chicago's southside, every May 24th there is a picnic in honor of the memory of "King David". One will also find an assortment of other parties and celebrations occurring in individual residences at this important date in Chicago.

The "King David" commemorative t-shirt is often worn at these events. It is a professionally made full size picture of King David. The cheapest version sells for around $50.

The BDs are similar to other gangs in Chicago like the GDs in that the BDs hold large scale "picnics" for their members at least once a year. The GD picnics were very well organized and involved many restrictions on the members: no drugs, no guns, no fighting, because to a large extent it was also a publicity gimmick --- there were elected officials (i.e., politicians) who were attending the GD picnic. The BD picnics sound like a lot more fun from a gang member point of view.

A 1995 BD picnic was similar to the GD style in that members were transported on commercially leased busses. What is different is that one of the BD picnics in 1995 was actually held in the State of Minnesota, thus members were transported across state lines. We interviewed one of the BD members who attended the 1995 picnic in Minnesota.

The BD picnic had bountiful amounts of food just like the GD picnic. But it also had drugs. Members were given as much marijuana as they could smoke for free. There was also a large amount of gambling going on. So the BD picnic is more expressive (i.e., have a good time), while the GD picnic is more instrumental (i.e., being on good behavior to impress politicians and non-members invited as a public relations ploy).

SHORTY FREEMAN: Leader of the BDs

Jerome Freeman, known as "King Shorty", has been described similarly by different informants: prefers late model Cadillacs, wears a lot of gold and a rolex watch and a lot of blue jogging suits. However, currently he has only the "props" available to him in a correctional context, as he is serving time in Stateville. He is described as: "quiet, but a very very smooth character, just like Willie Lloyd", "flamboyant in a way, but like an educated banker on the street level", "quite an operator, a real manipulator", "a real shrewd guy, always competing with Don Derky", "Shorty has more class than most gang members, Shorty is a family man with several kids from the same wife". So he is described as being rather calm and collected, but with another side that can sometimes manifest itself. We can illustrate this below.

One incident where Shorty Freeman "lost his cool" was described to us. This happened when Shorty Freeman was still in Cook County Jail during his trial, before he went to IDOC (Illinois Department of Corrections) where he is currently incarcerated. Here is how an informant who was present at the incident described it:

"One of our members was in the day room with his boxer shorts on, and it was the time for the day visits in this unit of Cook County Jail. Shorty Freeman was getting a visit from a female at the time and saw our member walking around in his boxer shorts and got offended. Shorty Freeman told the guy to put his clothes on because it was disrespectful to walk around like that in the jail dayroom when his lady could see him. Our member said basically fuck off. The next day the BDs started a confrontation with our mob, so we tore it up with the BDs."

King Shorty is today serving out his sentence in Stateville Penitentiary.

INSIGHTS INTO KING SHORTY: FROM ONE OF HIS DRUG SUPPLIERS

A major narcotics trafficker who "flipped" was interviewed sometime ago by the NGCRC. The information about dealing with gang leaders was useful to the present profile. This narcotics trafficker has been and continues to be a confidential reliable informant for various agencies including the DEA. This particular informant was in a different gang but he dealt directly with Shorty Freeman on the streets of Chicago over a long period of time. Here is his story:

"I know Shorty Freeman....drugs is his livelihood...I dealt with him on the street....he used to cop anywhere from 10 to 50 keys of cocaine a month....he got a lot of drugs on consignment....he was always good for it".

"Shorty had four guys who were in his inner circle, they stuck with him like glue, they were with him at all times, one actually lived with Shorty. Shorty had a house on 51st and

Morgan....as I recall Don Derky's house was not too far away from there, they kept a watch on each other's operations, Shorty had more followers, but Don Derky did everything short of having Shorty killed to mess with him".

"The BDs pretty much look up to Shorty the same way the GDs look up to Larry Hoover, except with the BD's its more like a close knit family, they are not as organized as Hoover's mob. But as far as business is concerned, Shorty does not take any prisoners, I dealt with him hand to hand for about five years I should know. He was real careful."

INSIGHTS INTO KING SHORTY FROM ONE OF HIS FORMER HENCHMEN

We interviewed a BD who was no longer active who was in prison with King Shorty and who had rank in the BD's. This informant described his impressions of Shorty Freeman and they are largely consistent with the previous information:

"Shorty treated me with respect, he is a real quiet guy, he does not front himself a lot, but you do not know what his moves are, he is very secretive."

The informant continued that what he like about the BD's was they were "about business", but he also liked the parties, and the money making opportunities in the gang. He also described that King Shorty basically runs his gang remotely from behind bars almost the same way that Larry Hoover administered the GDs: "in Stateville he sits back and lives like a king, inside he is treated like he is on the outside, he dresses like he is on the outside wearing clothes most inmates cannot have, he wears a lot of jewelry inmates cannot have, and he has cash money on him that no inmate is supposed to have, and he has it with him on his possession at all times, like he is on the street...he has guys on security with him where ever he walks, he is never alone.. in prison the way he runs it, its just like Hoover runs it...they have their gatherings.....most of the time they go to church...they use church as a shield....protestant church....you can't be in no big crowd because of prison rules....except in church....they spread the word among themselves in small groups when they meet in church."

Several informants described how King Shorty seems to have a full time job as a inmate with constant time in the visiting room of Stateville. This is how he sends his "orders" to the streets, through his emissaries. Said one informant "he is just like Hoover....Shorty has steady stream of visitors every day, like Hoover they send out the orders for the streets".

DON DERKY: The Splinter Group Phenomenon in the BDs

Don Derky is a BD and according to one informant "he's got his own crew, Don Derky used to be a real character, he started an ugly riot in Division 1 at Cook County Jail, Don is a lot older than Shorty, Don Derky started a chapter in Milwaukee, Wisconsin in the early 1980's." Thus, the Don Derky faction of the BDs appears to be a renegade faction within the BDs. However, there is no doubt about the fact that Shorty Freeman is the acknowledged leader of most factions of the BDs. It is obvious as well from different sources that there is a strained relationship between Shorty Freeman and Don Derky. The best way to describe the renegade gang leader Don Derky is that while the BDs have a kind of religious structure to their gang, Don Derky's faction splintered off like a separate sect using the same type of gang gospel, just on a smaller scale.

THE INITIATION CEREMONY: TREYS ON THE HEAD OF CHILDREN

The initiation ceremony for new members who are becoming BD's is a relatively simple procedure. The members are not required to engage in a violent crime to show their commitment to the gang. The members are not beaten to test their physical ability to withstand pain. The members simply recite the gang prayer and afterwards the other members present at the meeting put the "treys" on the head of the inductee. "Treys on the head" is the expression describing when the BD member places the three fingers of the right hand, the BD gang hand sign, on the head of the initiate. During the initiation ceremony several members present will place their three finger gang hand sign to touch the head of the new member as a "blessing". Once that is done, the child is a member of the BDs and can begin paying dues and doing their "Nation work". As with other gangs, most new members are children, with an average age of 12. They have about six years of "Nation work" (i.e., selling drugs for the gang) before they are eligible to hold any official position of rank in the gang organization of the BDs. If they are fortunate to live that long, then they typically have accumulated a juvenile arrest record that hardens and prepares them for an adult criminal career.

LEAVING THE BD's: NOT HARD UNLESS CAUGHT DISRESPECTING OTHER BD's

A member of the BD's can leave the BD gang with relative ease, that is compared to other gangs where it is "blood in, blood out". Leaving simply involves an agreement not to join any other gang in the future. Leaving should have a justification: "taking a job", "going back to school", "family problems", etc, that is any legitimate "face saving" excuse to sever ties to the gang. Under these optimal conditions, the gang member attends the last meeting, the member invokes the prayer and becomes instantly "inactive" in membership status. However, sometimes when it is known a member is trying to get out other members will provoke a conflict.

If the member trying to get out of the gang, and through either provocation or natural inclination makes a verbal insult to any other member of the same gang, then the exit ceremony comes with a "violation". The member must endure a ritual physical beating in addition to the other requirements.

The grip the gang has on its members is very strong and cult-like. The same members reside in the same small geographical area, typically a one block area. They are in constant daily contact with each other in this environment. It is therefore very hard not to associate with the same gang members even after leaving the gang. Such inactive members cannot use any gang signs or associate with any gang members and are expected not to reveal the "nation secrets" of the BDs. A child literally needs to go on "house lock down" status to avoid daily contact with these other gang members. And even this is of limited value when contact arises at school or in routine activities (i.e., meeting at the neighborhood store, fast food place, etc).

Similar to some other gangs, at age 35 one can "retire" from active status in the BD's to inactive status.

WHAT BENEFIT DOES THE BD TYPE OF GANG PROVIDE THE NEIGHBORHOOD IN WHICH IT RESIDES?

Mostly, it provides a subcultural economic benefit: a reliable ongoing continual source of illicit drugs for casual drug users who may also reside in the same neighborhood, work there, or routinely visit there. The BD gang provides the drugs of choice: marijuana and cocaine on the southside, add heroin to the list on the westside.

For the casual drug abusing customers of the gang, they may feel "protected" in this community setting. The nature of their contact to the drug supply is friendly and courteous. They never worry about being "ripped off" or sold "bad drugs". They are satisfied customers. If they live in the same area, the reciprocal ties that develop help to ensure that the gang does not steal their car parts, or harass them, in fact, quite the obverse, they may in the spirit of modern drug pushing "protect their customers".

The gang resides in the same area where it does its drug business. The community sees these children on the street and knows they are "local boys". The community rarely sees the concealed weapons. When the community hears the routine gun shots the same community wants to believe this was from "outsiders". News flash: no community anywhere in the world wants to believe its own members are responsible for any of its own problems. Thus, the local rumor mill always helps the local gang: the gunshots were "outsiders", but fortunately the local gang was there to "protect the hood" from invading outsiders. Thus, the myth persists that gangs have a prosocial function to protect the neighborhood. The gang protects its business only. The gang's business is drug sales.

THE INSIDE STORY ON THE "KING OF KINGS": KING DAVID

A strong ongoing interest of the National Gang Crime Research Center focuses on historical details about gangs and gang members, particularly the impact of gangs. We maintain a long list of these issues that are yet to be resolved, including the need for interviewers to interview historical figures in the field. We have still not been able, for example, to interview the famous Rev. Fry regarding some issues of the long term impact of assisting Jeff Fort's early gang career.

We are pleased, in this gang profile, to be able to disclose a good number of previously unknown, very factual details about what may be one of the most famous gang leaders in the United States (i.e., the famous King David). We are not able to disclose the sources of the data, as a book is now in progress about this same issue.

King David was really DONISE DAVID BARKSDALE, born May 24, 1947, the seventh child of Charlie and Virginia Barksdale. David Barksdale died on September 2, 1974 at the age of 27, from kidney failure as a result of a rival gang gunshot injury sustained four years earlier. He was buried in Restvale Cemetery.

David Barksdale was born in Sallis, Mississippi. He came to Chicago when his parents (Charlie and Virginia) moved to Chicago in 1957. He did visit his grandfather (John Roby) in Mississippi, but is not known to have done much other travel over his short life span.

The funeral for David Barksdale was at the Golden Gate Funeral Home, 2036 West 79th Street, Chicago. Officiating at the funeral and delivering the eulogy was an Elder J. Jackson. The funeral director was Bro. E. Edwards. The M.C. was Glorie Watson. The obituary was by John Taylor. There were two solos: one by Charline Dawson and one by Bob Hudson.

At the time of his death, David Barksdale was survived by his wife (Yvonne "Cookie" Barksdale), three children: David Junior (then age 4), and twins Melinda and Ronald (then aged 17 months); thirteen brothers and sisters and a great many relatives and friends.

The wife of David Barksdale died on Saturday, June 24, 1978. Yvonne Barksdale was born on December 17, 1948 in Chicago, Illinois. Her parents were James and Rose Yarber. Yvonne attended Kershaw Elementary School and Englewood High School. She married David Barksdale and they had three children: David Jr., Melinda, and Ronnie. At the time of her death she was engaged to be married to Lee Faulker and they were parents of a son, Derrick (three months old). Yvonne was survived by her mother, fiancee, four children, four brothers, and many friends and relatives. She is buried at the Archerwood Cemetery. The funeral was held at the Stonecrest Funeral Home, 2122 West 79th Street, Chicago.

THE "RAP SHEET" OF KING DAVID

If someone were to read the "rap sheet" of David Barksdale they would have no idea this was someone as powerful as he was, or as "notorious" as he is made out to be, as a historical figure in the world of Chicago gangs. We are reviewing the Chicago Police Department rap sheet here.

The rap sheet of King David never once lists his full and correct name (i.e., Donise David Barksdale). This is not uncommon. Arrestees often may give names other than their own is the reason. So the official rap sheet maintained by the Chicago Police Department (I.R. #101573) is for "David Jones". But it is really David Barksdale.

There are no felony convictions in this rap sheet. There are a number of what might be considered "minor offenses", and typical gang member offenses (disorderly conduct, mob action, etc). It does help, however, to provide a glimpse into the developmental lifespan of this legendary gang figure.

The rap sheet begins with the arrest of David Jones, 5 May 65, for Criminal Trespass to Vehicle (dismissed by Judge Comerford). On 13 July 65 the arrest is for "resisting", and again 28 July 65 "Resist. & Disorderly G.B.". The case also went to Judge Comerford.

* The first twist on the real name begins on 2 December 65, "David L. Barksdale" with investigation for aggravated battery.

* The next alias (Davis Jones) comes on 31 Dec 66 for Strong Arm robbery. His gives a home address of 8407 S. Morgan.
Arrested as Davis L. Barksdale 14 Feb 67 for investigation of Burglary, released without charge, and listed as living at 522 W. 64th St.

* Arrested then again on 26 April 67 as Donise Barksdale for assault and resisting, it was non-suited. Address given: 6452 S. Union.

* An entry on 10 Aug 67 for David L. Barksdale (6452 S. Union) indicates "Appl. Chicago Urban Oppt.", which presumably means an anti-gang program or gang-treatment program.

* David Barksdale was arrested on 13 Sept 67 for possession of marijuana, but it was a case dismissed by Judge Wendt.

* George Walker was an alias used in the arrest on 13 Oct 67 for disorderly conduct; but again the charge was non-suited (Judge Wendt again).

* David L. Barksdale on 1 Feb 68 was arrested for resisting and disorderly conduct (Xparte $25, Judge Cerda).

* On 7 April 68 David Barksdale was arrested for curfew, but again the case was dismissed (Judge Lee).

* On 28 May 68 David L. Barksdale was arrested for aggravated assault, battery and criminal damage to property, but also dismissed (Judge Cerda).

* On 8 June 68 David Barksdale was arrested for disorderly conduct (Xparte $25 & NC, Judge Zelezinski).

* David D. Barksdale arrested 27 June 68 for mob action. Again on 3 July 68 for Agg. battery.

* Arrested 24 July 68 for warrants on the two prior arrests, receives 6 months in the "House of Corrections" (i.e., today known as Cook County Jail) by Judge Zelezinski.

* On 3 August 68 charged with criminal damage to property, but on 3 Nov 68 it is dismissed (Judge Zelezinski). Similarly, 4 August 68 charged with resisting arrest and disorderly, again dismissed (Judge Zelezinski).

* Arrested 7 Mar 69 for a battery warrant, dismissed (Judge Zelezinski). On 4 Sept 69 again for "mob action", again dismissed (S.O.L., Judge Genesen). Arrested 14 August 69 for unlawful use of weapon, and defacing I.D.; dismissed (Judge Mooney).

* Arrested 15 January 70 for intimidation, dismissed (S.O.L., Judge Hechinger).

* David Lee Barksdale arrested for resisting arrest on 7 May 70, discharged on 10 Mar 71 (Judge Genesen). Arrested 4 Sept 70 for mob action, held to the grand jury (Judge Dunne). He is indicted for Mob Action by the Grand Jury. Verdict: not guilty (Judge Aspen).

* On 9 Jan 71 arrested for defacing firearms and discharging a weapon, gets 6 months in the county jail (Judge Dunne).

* Next record entry is 12 Jan 71, for traffic court. Arrested 26 January 71 for armed robbery conspiracy, dismissed by Judge Murphy. A 21 June 71 entry for traffic court. A blank entry for 11 July 1972 in the 6th district (CB No. 3586047).

* On 18 Jan 74 John David Barksdale arrested for gambling (dice), dismissed by Judge Neal.

* Last entry, 13 Feb 74 for possession of marijuana and fictitious license plates (3 days in jail, and $100 fine, Judge Murphy).

That is the full rap sheet of King David. It shows he met a lot of Cook County judges. It shows he got to see Cook County Jail a couple times. It shows he may not have given his full and correct name when repeatedly arrested. But it does not show convictions for murder, drug pushing, or literally any felony crime.

Three major African-American gangs today pay some tribute to this gang leader: the BD's first and foremost still regard him as their true king; the GD's who acknowledge his historical influence; and the BGs who arose out of his death, splintering away as a separate faction from the BGDs.

HOW DO THE BD's RECRUIT NEW MEMBERS?

Answer: the BD gang has simply twisted the elements of enhancing salesmanship skills of youthful members not too dissimilar from the way a Junior Achievement group would also raise money collectively. The BD gang offers young members a chance to have some "pocket money" from selling drugs for the gang. It offers kids a way to have a "good time" with adults in their community: the adult gang leaders. It has parties, out of state picnics, and provides an assortment of "thrill seeking" opportunities.

A casual review of the internal written documents of the BDs suggests much of this "gang literature" is aimed at children. The gang becomes their "religion". The local gang leader who hands out the drugs to be sold becomes their "minister". The top banana of the gang leaders becomes the equivalent of a God-like figure that members are expected to be willing to kill or die for. The young members of the gang regularly engage in "prayer" with fellow members: but the kind of prayer we are talking about here is an abomination. Clearly, these materials show the kind of cult-like "hold" that this gang is capable of having on its young members, once they do join. The fact is the BD's like other gangs often do not have to spend an ounce of effort in "recruitment" per se. Kids will come to them.

LIKE A UNION GUILD, THE BD'S WILL HELP THEIR OWN MEMBERS

The BD's are similar to other gangs in being an organization that provides some "benefits" to those who are arrested or end up in jail. This is common for most gangs like the BD's that qualify as being a formal organization. Explained one informant "they will send members money for cosmetics, books, cigarettes in jail; but if you are not true to the gang, don't hold your hand out because you've got nothing coming".

THREAT RATING OF THE BDs

Given the nature of the organization and that it is unable to keep many older members, and therefore operates much like a business franchise: where any leader in good standing can have his own "plantation", the level of threat here is not as high as a more centralized corporate structure. The BDs profile more for migration-franchising: opening up new operations in new geographical areas (i.e., Milwaukee). They do not control sections where they do not live. The top gang leadership is able to make a good living off of this type of youth slavery and except in the case of Yummy, has been able to avoid "heat" from the media or community. It minimizes its risks, and maximizes its gains to the older adult leadership structure. It could persist for decades, being careful not to draw much attention, not engaging in politics, and sticking to its criminal mission: drug profits for the adult leaders from the "nation work" of its underage juvenile members who are lured into this kind of oppression.

So, the threat level is medium from a crime perspective, because all a community needs to do to challenge and undermine this kind of gang is directly confront it and its leaders and its "teachings". The threat level is not high because this kind of gang does not profile as one capable of acts of domestic terrorism, unless a hostile foreign national group were to approach the adult leaders. Something as simple as a civil RICO action, or a wrongful death 3rd party law suit against adult leaders of the BDs would be sufficient to put a good dent in this kind of gang. On the other hand it may take a new type of "radio free inner city" to get the message across that this type of gang is more than a gang: it is a new kind of slavery cult run by adult criminals. The slaves are the children of the community who get sucked into the gang and its weird belief system.

However, since the GD prosecution we have noted a number of "flippers": GD's joining the BD's. So if the BD's are able to capture a lot of GD members, it is possible the BD threat rating could increase in the coming years. The BD's and the BG's are the most likely to benefit from alienated members of the GD's trying to find a better gang.

Still, for the present the threat rating for the BDs must be regarded as medium for a variety of reasons explored in this profile. One "ex" BD expressed it best: "the BDs are not that deep, they are real shallow, their king is not an entrepreneur, he is more or less a dictator".

INTERNAL WRITTEN DOCUMENTS OF THE BDs

Figures 1 through 9 provide examples of the internal written documents of the Black Disciples (BDs). Each of these will be briefly explained here.

Figure 1 is the basic prayer of the BDs. Here Donise David Barksdale is truly in direct competition with every local church in Chicago for known spiritual leaders. Note that "God" does appear in this prayer. But King David Barksdale is the one regarded as the true prophet for these believers.

Another prayer, provided in Figure 2, is interesting as a historical reference, for it acknowledges the original BGD six point star meanings currently still used by the GDs: Love, Life, Loyalty, Knowledge, Wisdom, and Understanding. In a later document we will see that "unity" becomes a new organizing principle.

Figure 3 provides the first set of "rules" or "laws" that BD members must abide by. Rule #6 becomes definitive: "I will accept no other teachings than that of our KING or that which refers to the Nation". Clearly, this rule establishes an ideological press upon members that whatever type of religious training or socialization they may have had, what they now must believe and act upon are the "creeds" of their gang. Rule # 8 continues in this theme, to the effect of almost inoculating

BD members against any outside religious influence.

They truly are "devil's disciples": a cult-like group with blasphemous dogma at the heart of its belief system that is enforced by violence and the threat of violence against its believers. Note the "top down" vertical authoritarian structure implied by rule # 10: "I will abide by all commands given to me by the KING and all appointed chiefs". Clearly, there is little room for individual thinking or even an ability to resist this coercive compliance structure when the older adult leaders ask a younger member of the gang like "Yummy" to perform an act or behavior that pleases the central leadership. Note also the rule #16 about the clenched fist "salute", the warrior sign for ritually greeting other BD members.

Figure 4 is the second part of the rules or laws of the BD gang. In some versions of this internal written document of the gang, the word "soldier" has been translated to "member". "Soldier" was the original version. This is interesting as a psychological mechanism, for the first part of the rules (Figure 3) may not seem too bad for a potential new recruit to the BD gang being "courted" or lured into the gang. However, once initiated the member will find out there is another set of rules: those in Figure 4. The rules in Figure 4 are centered around protecting the gang leaders from criminal prosecution. This second set of rules requires "silence" on the criminal drug operations of the gang or any other nation business, and specifically lays out rules about exposing the gang leaders to unnecessary risk.

We interviewed a retired member of the BD's who knew King Shorty personally. He was now in a drug program, in his late 30's, and had spent about 15 years in the BD's. The highest rank he achieved was that of a chief of violations, a kind of temporary rank that is more service than power. This informant indicated these rules are taken literally by the members. Even the rule about prostitution: "if you get caught with a sister of the gang ho'ing, that is going to bring you some punishment, you cannot use your sisters like that in the BD's".

The same informant described the importance of rule # 7 on protecting or shielding the "Crowned King", King Shorty: "if we pull up on the set, and the King was in a building up stairs, you cannot tell anyone the King is there in an apartment. When we go to a funeral, there will be a lot of guys just surrounding the King, so many that you will not see him". He went on to describe a funeral in 1984 where 6 or 7 hundred members attended.

Figure 5 is internal propaganda designed to enhance the social solidarity of members and give them their unique gang identity and belief system. Thus, Figure 5 gives literal meaning to the gang symbols used by the BDs. A photograph of the actual layout of a BD "banner" using all of these symbols is provided (Photograph #1) for reference purposes. This banner and a host of other artifacts used by the gang are a part of the National Gang Cultural Artifact Exhibit which includes such materials from a large number of major gangs in the USA that is maintained by the NGCRC for training purposes.

Figure 6 is an introductory lesson for BD members: basic essential items of indoctrination they must commit to memory.

Figure 7 is another brainwashing component in the BD curriculum of youth socialization. Note that here we see "unity" added as one of the principles of the six pointed star, while the original BGD item of "wisdom" disappears from the map. No one in this organization in their right mind would challenge the fact that earlier documents include "wisdom" but apparently this item is lost in more updated documents: to question this obvious inconsistency would be tantamount to treason against the BD leaders. Clearly, a typical BD member with any ability to discern such factors would obviously also have to develop a strong sense of being able to survive in a situation of ambiguity and dissonance.

Figure 8 begins to show us how in the pseudo-biblical language used by the gang leaders to make demands on BD gang members, that this is truly a criminal cult organization, where the continuity of the gang is predicated on its ability to underage juvenile manipulate members along a spiritual dimension that allows the members to engage in moral neutralization (i.e., an adult sponsored justification for their criminal behavior). Note the language of "thou shall" in these "commandments". Here young children with unknown levels of religious training are getting new "homework": things they really must study or they will be physically punished by their own gang and they will not dare report it to anyone outside of the gang.

This new "homework" makes the gang leader the new GOD, and some gang henchman who wrote the material the real "Moses" imparting the 10 commandments.

This is more than a "put on", young children like "Yummy" are routinely being killed over this kind of new modern gang-criminal-cult style organization. It should be patently obvious to us all that the last person to probably ever see this kind of material is the local church or religious institution and its legitimate spiritual leaders in the same community!

Religious leaders in America who have worked with gangs to sponsor their events, activities, and public relations functions are going to have to come to grips with this kind of evidence. This kind of gang is not going to be coopted.

Finally, Figure 9 provides the equivalent of a daily scripture or a daily prayer to reinforce the identity and commitment to the adult driven criminal gang leader. Whatever the gang leader "says" is what "goes". We see in none of these internal documents anything that spells out in great detail what the "teachings" are of the "crowned" King Shorty. Apparently his will is the gospel.

Churches in inner city areas like those affected by the presence of gang organizations like the BDs need no longer speculate about why they are having difficulty attracting younger persons to worship in their religious institutions. The message should be very clear from this gang profile that gangs like the BDs have been competing for years with churches for the control of the "minds, bodies, and souls" of inner city children.

U.S. FEDERAL PROSECUTION EFFORTS AGAINST THE BD's

In 1998 a number of BD leaders were arrested for federal charges. Some of them, like Robert Allen Jr. and Charles Jackson, agreed to cooperate with federal authorities. This is a standard "trade-off": those who snitch usually get lighter sentences.

Thus, in 1999, some 21 members of the BD gang were indicted for federal drug charges in Chicago. The federal authorities were able to get a large number of indictments due to the prominent help from informants within the leadership of the BD gang.

BD leader Robert Allen made statements against 16 of the 21 BDs indicted in 1999. Allen did get a 20 year sentence, but he was facing life in federal prison, like many of his colleagues he testified against (See: Cam Simpson, "21 in Black Disciples Named in Drug Charges", Chicago Sun-Times, Dec. 9, 1999, p. 18).

HOW TO SUPPRESS THE BDs AND SIMILAR GANGS

There are two known historical truths about the persistence and continuity of criminal gangs that have so much support they can be likened to social laws. The first is based on systems theory, the idea that a gang without new members to do its "work" is a gang that will die off and fade away, a gang

needs a steady supply of new young recruits to stay in business. The second is based on risk/benefit analysis: a gang cannot exist in a community without providing some benefit to the same community, so once the reciprocal benefits are terminated, and there is no benefit to the gang, the gang will disappear. Both help to clarify "what should be done" about gangs like the BDs.

First, our society needs additional laws protecting the rights of juveniles, both civil and criminal penalties need to be attached to the conduct of adult gang leaders who use children to do their dirty work. Increasing the penalties for using juveniles in adult-run gangs, and doing everything else possible to cut off the flow of new recruits into a gang, will do much to destabilize any gang anywhere in systems theory.

Secondly, the risk-benefit equation currently favors adult gang leaders: they face little risk and almost no sanctions for using juveniles to do their dirty work (selling drugs, committing acts of violence against opposing gangs, etc). We as a society need to increase the "costs" to the adult gang leaders in this known national pattern of the criminal exploitation of children. We need to also eliminate any social benefits the gang claims to provide a community: involvement in voter registration, involvement in publicly funded services, anything that appears to give the gang "legitimacy" erodes the power of the community to fight back against the gangs. Some leaders in Chicago and elsewhere still have not figured this out.

Third, educating clergy, civic leaders, and parents about gang profiles like the BDs may help them recognize that the gang is not a benefit to the community, nor is it a benign social force that can be "turned into good": it is, plain and simple, a criminal organization. What we have in America today is a legal lag: gangs have continued over time, outpacing the ability of American policy makers to pass legislation to control their operations. In otherwords, due to the inaction of policy makers, modern American gangs like the BDs continue with "business as usual" and are able to flagrantly manipulate the system to their own benefit.

Figure 1

BLACK DISCIPLES PRAYER

Let us open up this prayer with a lot of love to KING of all Kings, KING DAVID, our crowned KING, KING SHORTY, and all righteous Black Disciples of the world. . .

We are stronger together, we are stronger together, my love and yours forever. We are as ONE.

King David said that is must be done! God put the stars in the sky, and with the reflection they shine.

Yes said King David, we must combine, Body, Souls, and Minds, with the D's Love for now and all times.

-

Figure 2

(LOVE)

ALMIGHTY BLACK DISCIPLE NATION * * * * * *
Once the D's thang was just an idea until KING DAVID said it's time to bring it here. Just like everything else it had to begin, but the BLACK DISCIPLE NATION will never end.

Love, Life, and Loyalty will get it all started but without WISDOM, KNOWLEDGE, and UNDERSTANDING it will soon be departed.

The SIX POINTED STAR will connect them all together, since it is the STAR OF KING DAVID that will make it all last forever.

Being able to use 360 degrees of pure knowledge in any situation means nothing is impossible for the BLACK DISCIPLE NATION.

*By using the knowledge of the SIX POINTED STAR means we can better our situation no matter where we are, whether behind these walls, out there on the streets doing our own thang the BLACK DISCIPLE NATION shall remain the same. Let us give thanks. I AM WHAT I AM, A BLACK DISCIPLE, AND THAT I AIN'T I WILL NEVER BE * * * * * ***

We are going to close this prayer with a lot of love to KING of all Kings, KING DAVID, our CROWNED KING, KING SHORTY, AND ALL RIGHTEOUS BLACK DISCIPLES OF THE WORLD.

Figure 3

ALMIGHTY BLACK DISCIPLE NATION
UNIVERSAL CODE OF LAWS
PART I

1. I solemnly swear to never disrespect the KING or "any" member of the Black Disciple Nation.

2. I will not tolerate anyone scandalizing the name of the Black Disciple Nation.

3. I will sacrifice my life for the Nation's causes.

4. I will Love, Respect, and Honor every member of the nation as I so love, respect, and honor myself.

5. I will be of any assistance to any member of the Nation in any problems or difficulties that he have, be it physically or mentally.

6. I will accept no other teachings than that of our KING or that which refers to the Nation.

7. I will not tolerate anyone, even a Black Disciple to misrepresent or disrespect our appraisal emblem or flag.

8. I pledge my soul, heart, love and spirit to the Black Disciple nation and will be a part of it even in death.

9. I will not affiliate myself with our opposition.

10. I will abide by all commands given to me by the KING and all appointed chiefs.

11. I will not tolerate the criticizing or abusive sayings of those who are not Black Disciple.

12. I will not tolerate anyone criticizing the KING or any righteous member of the Black Disciple Nation.

13. I will ask and accept the same penalty that any Black Disciple is given for my transgression against the Nation's Laws.

14. I will not fight or mistreat any Nation member unless told

to do so otherwise.

15. I will not fight against any member of the Black Disciple Nation and will not stand to see any member of the Black Disciple Nation fight among themselves.

16. I will greet and salute any member of the Black Disciple Nation with the crossing of the CLENCHED FIST, the warriors sign whenever and where ever I see any Black Disciple.

Figure 4

ALMIGHTY BLACK DISCIPLE NATION
UNIVERSAL CODE OF LAWS PART II

1. All soldiers must share and respect a code of silence, loyalty to friends inside the nation, also becomes a part of that code and the two (silence and loyalty) join to establish the soldiers as insiders and everyone else as outsiders.

2. Family disrespect cannot and will not be tolerated either toward each other or family members of his fellow soldiers.

3. No soldier shall encourage the use of drugs to any soldier or family members of his fellow soldiers.

4. No soldier shall consume any addictive drugs.

5. No soldier shall encourage prostitution from the women in their families or families of fellow soldiers.

6. No soldier shall point out, refer or introduce any fellow member to an outsider without first screening and checking into the background of that outside person.

7. At no time shall a soldier shall point out, refer, or introduce any outsider to the "King", or any of the places the "King" might be without permission from the proper chain of Command.

8. No soldier shall bring inside the nation new members without a screening and a observation period and the approval of an evaluation report by the top of the chain of command.

9. All soldiers regardless of rank or position must strive to help each other and not to compete with each other.

Figure 5

MAY THE STAR OF DAVID WATCH OVER US ALL AS DISCIPLES
BLACK DISCIPLES NATION THIS EMBLEM STAND AS FLAG
FOR THE BLACK DISCIPLE NATION

1. The HEART represents the LOVE we have for our Nation.

2. The CROWN represents our Nation's Crowned King, KING SHORTY.

3. The SIX POINTED STAR of KING DAVID represents what our Nation is based on.

4. The SWORD represents Life and Death in our Nation, Life and the survival of the Nation at all cost. But Death before Dishonor.

5. The DEVIL'S PITCHFORKS represents our Nation's powers and our struggle to overcome the oppression we are under.

6. The HORNS represents our Nation's determination to overcome all obstacles.

7. The DEVIL'S TAIL represents the oppression that Blacks, Latinos, and Third World people live under and is not a white issue.

8. The FLAME represents our Nation's eternal philosophy of Self-Help.

9. The Insignia "78" represents the year of our Nation's New Day of Teachings and Inspiration.

Figure 6

THE SIX POINTED STAR AND OUR COLORS

The STAR OF KING DAVID is our Nation's symbol. It has six points, and each point of the star stands for: LOVE, LIVE, LOYALTY, UNITY, KNOWLEDGE, and UNDERSTANDING.

The Disciple's colors are: RED, BLACK, and BLUE. Red is for the bloodshed of our Nation. Black stands for all black people. Blue is for the heavenly sky which blesses all Disciples. True blue also represents the love we share, which is as deep as the deep blue sea.

Figure 7

THE SIX POINTS AND THEIR MEANINGS

1. LOVE: Love of the Nation is greater than mere love alone, because we have a brotherhood in which love is as deep as the deep blue sea. TRUE BLUE LOVE.

2. LIFE: Life commitment to the Nation for the betterment of ourselves as well as the Nation and each committed brother within the Nation, and our Nation's teachings, laws, creeds, symbols, philosophy and defense.

3. LOYALTY: To yourself, and each committed brother of our Nation.

4. UNITY: Collectively embraces all concepts, ideas, and actions that apply to our Nation. Togetherness is essential in order for us to continue our survival.

5. KNOWLEDGE: Is insight, therefore it is priceless, it gives one the ability to apply rational judgement. Knowledge is the ability to have a conscious awareness, and knowledge gained and not passed along is wasted knowledge.

6. UNDERSTANDING: Shows that we are able to communicate effectively, bringing about agreements, and a positive state of mind.

"Repeat these six points (PRINCIPLES) until they are fully understood, because they apply to you (ALL) as BLACK DISCIPLES. KING SHORTY IS KING! AND LONG LIVE THE KING.

B.D. LOYALTY

Figure 8

ALMIGHTY BLACK DISCIPLE NATION'S TEN COMMANDMENTS

1. Thou shall love the nation with all thy heart, soul and spirit.
2. Thou shall teach the warriors of thy nation diligently and shall talk with, advise them, and in the event that some go astray, thou shall be there to understand and restore in them the determination of a true Disciple.
3. Thou shall bind them together in UNITY and LOVE, and they shall be as true as one that will never be divided.
4. Thou shall make it known in the streets, jails and penitentiaries that this Black Disciple Nation is indestructible.
5. It shall be that when we have fully accepted the teachings of our deceased KING DAVID and our CROWNED KING, KING SHORTY, then and only then shall we acquire the riches that is rightfully ours as Disciples in the armor of blue.
6. For the nation is full of good things that thou has brought us into, therefore, we can never fail but shall prosper at all cost.
7. Beware lest we forget the teachings of the King that brought us into awareness of this Black Disciple Nation.
8. Thou shall feel the warmth of this Black Disciple Nation and serve the King and swear by the power of his name which he has invested in the Nation.
9. You shall not seek the safety of other nations around you, but hold steadfast to the teachings of the Black Disciple Nation.
10. For the King is a jealous King, he loves his people, and unless we return this love as it is freely given, we shall anger the King, and thus bring forth upon ourselves the wrath of the Black Disciple Nation.

Figure 9

A DAILY REMINDER

WHAT IT MEAN TO TRULY BE A DISCIPLE

*I AM WHAT I AM, A BLACK DISCIPLE, AND THAT I AIN'T WILL NEVER BE * * * * * **

1. As a true Disciple I am a follower of thy Crowned King, KING SHORTY, and a student in the teachings of our nation's Founder and King of all Kings, KING DAVID.
2. I shall strive and succeed in showing myself to be disciplined in my actions, and thoughts, reflecting to the fullest of my ability and potential the SIX PRINCIPLES WITHIN THE STAR OF DAVID.
3. I shall seek to be mindful of the TEN COMMANDMENTS of our nation and the UNIVERSAL CODES OF LAW.
4. I shall do whatever is possible, or whatever is asked, and required of me to support the leadership of our organization.
5. I shall especially be conscious of my environment, its elements and dangers therein, and shall secure myself and each righteous member of our organization from the dangers and pitfalls before us.
*6. I shall remind myself and my brothers that * * * * * * WE ARE STRONGER TOGETHER, WE ARE STRONGER TOGETHER, MY LOVE AND YOURS FOREVER. WE ARE AS ONE. KING DAVID SAID THAT IT MUST BE DONE! GOD PUT THE STARS IN THE SKY, AND WITH THE REFLECTION THEY SHINE. YES SAID KING DAVID WE MUST COMBINE, BODY, SOULS, AND MINDS, WITH THE D'S LOVE FOR NOW AND ALL TIMES.*

I vow this day to shine . . .

Appendix: I

GANG PROFILE: The Latin Kings

INTRODUCTION

The Latin King gang is one of the most violent gangs in the United States today, with leaders unafraid to order "hits" on correctional officers and followers unashamed to obey their orders. The history of this gang is written in blood, with episodes so bizarre that they read like chapters from a pulp fiction novel. Members of the Chicago branch of the Latin Kings cherish a history that includes the theft of military ordnance; the murder and subsequent cannabilization of one disobedient inmate member; consorting with a notorious terrorist group; and a high school riot over a Coca-Cola poster.

Nor is their strange history complete: as we go to press in late September, 1996, the search continues for three guns believed to be hidden somewhere in Pontiac Prison. Law enforcement officials continue an urgent search for these weapons, in the belief they are intended for use in the assassination of correctional officers.

OVERVIEW

The Latin Kings began in Chicago over three decades ago and today its influence stretches into 34 states (AL, AK, AZ, AR, CA, CO, CT, FL, GA, IL, IN, IA, KS, LA, MA, MI, MN, MO, NE, NV, NH, NJ, NM, NY, NC, ND, OH, OR, PA, TX, UT, VT, WA, and WI). In Chicago today the Latin Kings (LKs) are the second largest gang (the GDs have held 1st place for some time, but are now waning somewhat). The Latin Kings have an estimated 18,000 members in Chicago alone.

There are actually two versions of this gang: (1) the Chicago original, and (2) the east coast splinter version. Both operate as violent formal organizations with lengthy written constitutions and by-laws and elaborate ceremonies. The Chicago version is the largest and has a very stable infrastructure where the loyalty of members is maintained by fear. The east coast version is newer and is off-shoot of the Chicago original, and it takes on more of a political tone. These are basically two different gangs today.

This profile focuses mostly on the original Chicago version. Thus, unless otherwise stated, any information provided here applies to the largest and oldest of the Latin King gangs: the Chicago original.

There are some unique aspects of the Latin King gang that are noteworthy and which will be detailed in the profile that follows. One of these is that this is a gang that has a connection to the F.A.L.N. terrorist group. Some evidence to this effect will be provided in this gang profile. Another trait of the Latin Kings is their ruthlessness, they are a particularly violent gang: to other gang rivals, and even to their own members. This gang profile will detail the case of how the Illinois Department of Corrections for years listed Carlos Robles as an escapee, escaping a couple days before his parole the official story went, but who was really "chopped up" in a meat grinder and served to the inmates in the "meat loaf" for dinner at Stateville Prison: the skull of the inmate would be found years later buried in Stateville's yard.

Our direct sources, quoted in this profile, included many "regular" members of the gang, in Chicago and in many other areas outside of Chicago, as well as high-ranking leaders of the gang (two who attained the status of being a "Prince" in the gang).

The NGCRC has scheduled a number of gangs for profiling in future issues of the Journal of Gang Research. The Latin Kings were not scheduled originally for this issue. What prompted us to give priority to the Latin King profile was the fact that this gang has a history of assassinating correctional officers and in early 1996 threatened to kill three more. We have every reason to believe the threats are genuine. To perhaps provide the basis for better prospects of prosecution against this gang, we accelerated the schedule to give attention to the Latin Kings at the earliest possible opportunity.

METHODOLOGY

There were several sources of information and strategies used for this gang profile. A large body of knowledge was accumulated on this gang, enough for an entire book. The primary source of information was that obtained directly from cooperative members of the gang, through intensive multiple interviews over time. Good informants and those with rank were therefore often interviewed repeatedly over a time span of four years.

Many "secret" internal documents of the LKs, both the Chicago original and the east cost version, were obtained for this gang profile. If published in their entirety, a minimum of 600 pages would be required for the length of this profile.

We have spent a great amount of time in prisons, jails, and juvenile detention centers in a number of states routinely getting information directly from LK members, but we do not have any delusions of grandeur that would motivate us to call this "ethnomethodological research of prison gangs". What we got are good informants, and plenty of them. Some of the best resources for information were those who were not in custody, but still wanted to "make a deal" or share their story.

Finally, quantitative research that is nationwide in scope allowed for capturing LK members in the general gang population. We have this information as well from a number of studies that allowed "picking out" or identifying LK members for special analysis. The NGCRC currently works in over 20 states with a large number of other investigators allowing for the collection of information on gangs like the Latin Kings, and it is not uncommon for such members to simply volunteer further information, that is information above that which we sought using a standard national gang assessment survey instrument.

In summary, both qualitative and quantitative research methods were used. The methodology also had access to important historical information: the secret writings and files of the gang, and we were able to acquire a large number of the cultural artifacts of this gang to add to the National Gang Cultural Artifact and Weapons Exhibit maintained by the NGCRC[1].

One final comment is useful here and it is addressed to gang apologists. Gang apologists are typically very liberal persons in a confused state who come to the defense of gangs, the extreme version specializes in testifying for gang members in court or at parole hearings for gang leaders. Gang apologists claim that the media and others "demonize" gangs by giving them "bad labels". Here is what we have to say about this: if a gang like the Gangster Disciples or many of its other "Disciple" affiliates uses the symbols of the "Devil" (i.e., devil's head, devil's tail, devil's pitchfork, devil's horns, etc), then it is a gang that labels itself, the media did not do it; if a gang over time develops an earned reputation for "killing", it was not a criminologist or a criminal justice practitioner who gave them the label, they sought that label themselves. The NGCRC does not develop gang profiles on fraternities, sororities, or informal play groups like "Alfalfa and Spanky": the NGCRC develops profiles on known criminal gangs.

VALIDITY ISSUES: QUESTIONS WE WOULD ASK CHICAGO-BASED LATIN KING MEMBERS TO SCREEN THEM AS BEING RELIABLE SOURCES OF INFORMATION

Anyone can "claim" to be a gang member. Gangs call these persons "claimers". We had to develop certain questions, as we do with all gang profiles, to make sure we would not be wasting our time. We do not normally share this type of information as it is the kind of material more usefully shared in training provided by NGCRC staff. However, we will share a couple of these "lie tests" here. These would be useful questions to prosecutors trying Latin King cases where a gang apologist testifying for the defense acts as an "expert witness" and presents himself as a "scholar and research expert" on the Latin Kings.

When we would interview a cooperative person who reported his or her membership affiliation with the LKs, one of the first questions we asked was a cognitive item. This question measured the extent of knowledge about the gang itself, so an older member or someone who claimed to be in the gang for a considerable period of time should know the right answer. The question was "Who is Papa King and where is he today and how did he get there?". Papa King is a legend in the Latin Kings, also known as Papa Santos, he help found the Latin Kings. Papa King is dead today, killed by his own gang in 1988. This was one of the few "organizational shakeups" in the Latin Kings. Countless members repeated the same oral history: "Lord Gino wanted the organization to go in one direction and Papa King wanted the organization to go in another direction and in the summer of 1988 Papa King was killed". Papa King was in his 40's when he died. There still remains, among some older members of the LKs, an enormous resentment over the killing of Papa King. It is a "sore" in the organization today that is still not fully resolved. Papa King was one of the five original "King of Kings", the other four were: Jose Rivera (now out of prison, AKA "Cadillac Joe"), Eddie Rodriguez (AKA "Tiger"), Joe Gunn, and Fast Eddy. They were the first original Latin Kings.

If we had someone who considered himself an "OG", or original part of the organization, then we had another question based on the physical and cultural anthropology of the LKs. We asked the question, "what hair style did the Latin Kings use to identify themselves in the 1960s?". During their early stages as a gang, the LK's had one distinguishing physical trait: they would wear their hair in "Afro's". We knew this from early photographs of the LKs in our files and numerous interviews with older members who later became useful for purposes of prosecuting LK members. As one founder told us: "The LKs in the 60's had Afro's, huge Afro's, to identify themselves. Crow was the last LK to have a huge Afro. Crow (Rivera) was an Inca from Armitage and Kedzie. He died in Menard from an overdose. He swallowed a balloon filled with heroin and cocaine trying to smuggle it in during a visit, the balloon busted inside him".

One question each and every LK member must know the answer to regardless of how much time they have spent in the gang relates to a "sign" the LKs make in ritual greetings to each other. We would therefore ask: "What does this gesture represent: placing the clenched right fist on my heart?". To LKs it means one thing only: "I will die for you". In the

Latin King constitution it is regarded as the "National Salute": "A fist upon our heart....it means, "I DIE FOR YOU " for you are flesh of my flesh, blood of my blood, son of my mother who is the Universal Nature and follower of Yahve who is the Almighty King of Kings; it also means Love - Strength - Sacrifice".

Another question all current members should know the answer to if they have been exposed to any of the LK internal written "literature" is this: "What does Yahve mean?". In the LKs, "Yahve" stands for "God". "Yahweh" is how it is normally spelled. The LKs intentionally spell it differently as "Yahve". The Latin King constitution identifies "Yahve" as the "Almighty King of Kings", implying sacrilegiously that God himself is a Latin King, or not uncommonly as such gangs are prone to do: that their gang leader is a God.

Another question any member should be able to answer is this: "What are the holy days for Latin King's?". Many gangs have such "high holy days" where they celebrate various things of importance to their gang, such as their gang leaders birthday, or whatever. The answers to this question for validity purposes in assessing members of the LKs is in the LK written constitution and by-laws. We can share some of this LK constitution here: "In recognition of our culture, each January the 6th will be recognized as Kings Holy Day - a day dedicated to the memory of our departed Brothers and Sisters; a day of sacrifice in which each and every member of the Nation will observe by fasting". In the Christian religion, of course, January 6th is the Ephihany or "Three Kings day". The LK constitution also specifies when the LK's "party": "The first week in the month of March of each and every year is a Nation holiday. This holiday is known as King's Week or Week of the Sun. This holiday is the Nation's anniversary and is a week of celebration".

What the LK's use themselves to "test" another member for validity is also a question the answer to which can be found only in the written constitution and by-laws of the LKs. It is the question: "What are the three stages of Kingism?". We do not need to share the answers here, the point should be clear: we had elaborate controls on the validity of our "data". We would routinely cut short interviews with persons who could not answer basic questions about the LKs. We would listen to, reward, and record information from those we judged by our assessment center approach to be knowledgeable members of the LK gang.

The NGCRC has for years functioned as a resource for state and federal prosecutors in gang cases by providing such insights on a large number of gangs. The NGCRC has a policy of not assisting the defense in gang cases, with one exception: cases where a member "flips" and provides testimony against his or her own gang, we have helped such persons who flipped against their gang, saving them from imprisonment and/or reducing their sentences and/or getting them out early.

THE GENESIS OF THE LATIN KINGS

The NGCRC accumulates a lot of historical material on gangs, official records from social service programs serving gangs, archived official records, etc. Prior to 1961 we have no record whatsoever of the Latin Kings. Up until about 1960 there were a great many active gangs in Chicago that had "gang outreach workers" assigned to them by social service agencies: Imperials, Egyptian Cobras (and Cobrettes), Braves, Vice Lords (Senior, Junior, Midget, Pee Wee, Vice Ladies; various chapters like the Maypole Vice Lords), Burpies, Aces, Flames, Iron Dukes, Tomahawks, Clovers, Vampires, Noble Lords, Vikings, Simon City Royals, Autocrats, Mumchecks, Lancers, Spanish Cobras, Latin Counts, etc. Similarly, there were many other gangs that had no such workers assigned to them as of 1959: Angels, Apaches, Bandit Counts, Barrons, Blue Notes, Chaplains, Cherokees, Clicks, Comos, Condors, Conquerors, Cool Click, Corvettes, Del Vikings, Diggers, Dolphins, El Commandos, Emeralds, Jr. Blue Flames, Jr. Romans, Jr. Saints, Jr. Vikings, Gladiators, Kansas City Gang, Latin Lovers, Little Loafers, Monarchs, Muscatels, Navahoes, Night Owls, Ohio Dukes, Old Angels, Pacers, Pharoahs, Primo Raiders, Ravens, Rebels, Red Devils, Red Lions, Regents, Romans, Royal Kings, Saints, Satan's Angels, Scorpians, Shady Oaks, Shy Lads, Skulls, Sex Club, Shamrocks, Sharks, Sixteenth Street Rats, Sons of Satan, Spanish Gents, Tarantulas, Taylor Bishops, Tigers, Texans, Tornados, Trotters, Valley Boys, Warriors, White Ghosts, and others.

The gang "Ambrose" did exist as early as 1960 according to these same historical records, and it fought with a Mexican/Puerto Rican gang at that time called the "Royal Kings". The Royal Kings operated in a number of areas and "hung out" for example at a snack shop located at Loomis and Filmore, they operated from Madison to 26th street, from Halsted to Western. The members were in the age range of 16 to 22. Another hangout for the Royal Kings was at Polk and Laflin, and operated in the geographical turf defined by Harrison to Roosevelt, and from Loomis to Ashland. The "Gaylords" existed back in 1960 as well, as did the Latin Counts[4].

By 1963 some additional gangs got detached social workers to work with them: Spanish Kings, Junior Sinners, the Jokers, and others, but still no record of the Latin Kings as an entity by the name "Latin Kings".

But by 1966 the "Latin Kings" were up and going strong throughout the City of Chicago. So our best estimate for the genesis of the Latin Kings is in the time frame of 1964-65. From our view of Chicago gang history, the YMCA "detached gang worker" program basically invented what today is known as a "shout out". The YMCA gang program used a newsletter distributed to gang members throughout the city called The Turning Point. Gangs like the Latin Kings and the Simon City Royals in 1966 could publish their "shout outs" in the YMCA newsletter. Here are some examples:

"BOOM: LATIN QUEENS REPORTING

This is Chiqrita reporting for those hip Jr. Queens. Everyone in the territory is keeping things tight and right. We all took a trip to Leaning Tower, it turned out to be big thrill. The trip was sponsored by Carlos Castro and Rory Guerra and it made a big hit with all the juniors. We're planning to cut out of the neighborhood on other trips, so soon as Carlos says the word. Nina has been getting raps from all the guys but she already knows who her man is. Olga is ready to get married as soon as G.I. Joe (RICCO) finishes his term in the Army. Theresa the Polock has been given the guys looks with green eyes. This is one of the Latin Queens reporting. We have seen lots of workers operating from the Y.M.C.A. We have seen Mr. Rivera and Mr. Bach and the rest of the workers. We respect them all."

"LATIN KINGS REPORTING

This is Robert reporting from the mightiest of the mighty Latin Kings. We had a boss time on our trip to Paw Paw, Michigan. We went swimming, boating and to town. We are planning to go horse back riding in a few days. A lot of the boys are splitting up. Gruk and Lora broke up. Apache is back from California with his strong raps. You know his rap. Whats happening, thats his rap. He keeps all his women up tight."

What basically went on in early Chicago gang history, if anyone is looking for advice on WHAT NOT TO DO in gang prevention, is that in the late 50's and early 60's kids who joined gangs or formed gangs got services, the badder the gang, the more "fun resources" they got, the incentive was there to continue as an organizational entity. This early "gang work" was done with good intentions by probably sincere social workers, but basically was not very well thought out on a more abstract level in as much as basically boiled down to "gang management" by means of providing attractive benefits to gang members. Clearly, the Latin Kings was one of these gangs our society inadvertently nourished as an organizational entity. Like a simple principle from what we know about "crowd control", gang members should be dealt with as individuals, not as a group or organizational entity is one fundamental lesson from the history of gangs.

It is possible, then, reviewing the above material that the southside faction of what is today known as the "Latin Kings" may have evolved from what clearly existed as the "Royal Kings". Secondly, the "Royal Kings" fought with the "Ambrose", and the "Latin Kings" (People) continued a pattern of enmity with the Ambrose (Folks) up to the present day. Early in its genesis, the Latin Kings on the northside at least, learned that the badder you act, the more benefits you get from government funded programs. We should not be surprised, then, that today as this gang profile is being written the Illinois Department of Corrections is in a crisis because of what amounts to the same thing.

Finally, we must report that there is no "perfect" historical chain of evidence here about the genesis of the Latin Kings. The truth is probably somewhere in-between the official records and the oral history of the gang. According to the oral history of the gang the very first chapter of the LKs was founded at 18th Street and Wabash, and it was founded by Papa King, AKA "Papa Santos". Before that Papa Santos was in the Young Lords from NYC. After Papa Santos left the southside, he moved to Levitt and Schiller on Chicago's northside, this became the original chapter of the LKs on the northwest side (this is different from the Northside chapter of the LKs). The first chapter of the LKs on the Northside is said have grown out of the Noble Knights. All of this is from the "oral history" recollections of old-timers in the LKs.

SYMBOLS

A "people" gang, the Latin Kings use the colors black and gold/yellow to represent their gang, and the most common symbol they use is a "crown" for "King". The "crown" may have three or five points. They also make exclusive use of the trademark symbol known as the "master", often with a tear drop. Some of these Latin King symbols are provided here in Figure 1. Figure 1 illustrates examples of the symbols for this gang obtained directly from members of the Latin Kings. Thus, each "drawing" was done by a different member. Like most gangs, where about a third of the members will "flip" and cooperate with authorities to the point of providing testimony given the right circumstances, it was not hard to get information on the Latin Kings.

We have an interesting story we use in our gang training program about the symbols of the Latin Kings that is valuable to include here. The Latin King hand sign is made by all fingers and thumb extended, but with the two middle fingers down; and of course the extended fingers or hand pointing up: this "puts up the crown". Rival gangs that want to "throw down the crown" or insult the Latin Kings use the same hand sign but upside down.

In the spring of 1994 (on 3-22-94) the Cocacola company had an advertising campaign that reached into public schools, posters displaying the words at the top called "Keys to the Future". The poster included minority youths in different dress styles, bubbles from the Cocacola, a number of different youthful "dress styles", including one youth in hip hop dress style who is definitely "signing" in gang language. The "gang representation" here was, we must believe, accidental; but included a youth in the advertising poster who was basically throwing down the crown by the upside down Latin King hand sign.

At Farragut High School that day (3-22-94) the posters were displayed throughout the lunch room. This just happened to be a school where a lot of Latin Kings are represented in the student population. When the students had their lunch period, and the Latin Kings saw the poster, a riot broke out. The Latin Kings were infuriated, ripping down posters, breaking up the cafeteria and the school, the police swarmed in, arrests were made, that inflamed the gang riot even more, and the students marched towards the police station to confront the police again.

It became a major disturbance. Needless to say the "Keys to the Future" posters rapidly disappeared from the market place. We still have one we use in gang training however, but we must remark that we have never had anyone from the advertising industry attend any of our sessions yet.

WHO's WHO IN THE LATIN KINGS

The original Chicago-based Latin King gang is a formal organization. We are grateful for the information provided here from a high ranking defector who is currently working with federal investigators to bring down this organization. The authors of this profile have been working with this intelligence asset for several years. Thus, it is fair to say that a strong positive relationship existed with this very reliable source who held a position near the very top of the organization, just under the Sun-King and the Corona positions.

At the very top of the Latin King gang is the Sun-King: Raul Gonzalez, AKA "Baby King". He was from Chicago's southside faction of the Latin Kings, but is now out of prison, and therefore as a Corona, has control of all Latin King operations outside of that in the correctional system. The "La Corona" controls the gang's activities now behind bars: Gustavo Colon, AKA "Lord Gino". These are the two top leaders of the Latin Kings and have held their positions unchallenged for many years. Underneath these two leaders are an assortment of positions and middle-management slots. We will only identify those positions of substantial "rank" in the gang as a whole. These are positions of authority and leadership that transcend individual chapters of the gang.

The "Crown Prince" is such a position that exists as an administrative assistant to the top leaders. The current Crown Prince is Pedro Rey, AKA "Forehead". His job is basically that of the chief overseer of the gang.

Both the Sun King and the Corona have their appointed "Advisors" as well. These are the personal executive assistants to the top leaders of the gang. Current such advisors to Lord Gino include: Charlie Padilla, AKA "Big C"; "Kike"; "Havao"; and "Compa". Current advisors to Baby King include: "Sex Machine", "Beretta", "Dino", and Rudy Rangel (AKA "Kato").

There is also the "Council of Princes". This group consists of leaders from various chapters of the gang who function as administrators of the operations of the organization and implement the policies and goals set by the Sun-King and the Corona. The current chairman of the Council of Princes is Pedro Rey, hailing from the Northwest side chapter of the LKs. Other members include: Caspar Rosario, AKA "Casper"; Felix Jusino[5], AKA "Lil Kato"; Rudy Martinez, AKA "El Cubano"[6]; Juan Perea, AKA "Mustang"; Arturo Zambrano, AKA "Tino"; and Michael Contreras[7], AKA "Country".

Another important council in the LK organization that is also organization-wide is the "Crown Council". This body is led by the "Crown Chairman", currently Eddie Rodriquez, AKA "Tiger". The purpose of this group is that it is capable of making new laws for their gang or modifying old ones, and it also functions as a "court" or "trial procedure" for the gang. Current members of the "Crown Council" include: Paul Diaz, AKA "Popeye"; Willie Cabrera, AKA "The Beast"; Juan Padilla, AKA "Meme"; Radame Velasquez, AKA "Kato"; Edward Ranconi, AKA "Scar"; and Chris Novak, AKA "Novak".

Chiefs of Security for the LKs provide the "enforcer" function for the gang and work together across the geographical territory controlled by the LKs. Current members include: William Gonzalez, AKA "Kong" representing the Northwest side; William Chacon, AKA "Spade" representing the Northside; and Moe Garcia, AKA "Moe", representing the Southside.

Treasurers for the overall organization are an important position, obviously, as they handle financial transactions. Current treasurers include: Jose Rivera, AKA "Cadillac Joe", who handles the Northwest side and suburbs; Sam Madhi, AKA "Arabian Joe", who handles the Southside; and Paul Diaz, AKA "Popeye", who handles the Northside.

The position of "Investigators" is a powerful position in the LK organization. The duty of the Investigator is to check into the background of all new LK members during their 30-day probationary period and report their findings to the Crown Council. They are the "eyes and ears" of the LK organization by gathering intelligence on rivals as well. Current "investigators" for the LKs include the following members: Freddy Quinones, AKA "Lil Freddy", who represents the Northwest side; Frank Periche, AKA "Flaco", who represents the Northside; and Juan Mendiola, AKA "Ricco", who represents the Southside.

There are also the "Finance Committees" and the "Business Committees". These parallel the controlling geographical influences of the gang, where the differentiation is between the Southside as one influence, and the North and Northwest sides as the other influence. It is important to note that "B.K." the Sun-King hails from the Southside; while "Lord Gino" hails from the North and Northwest side. This is an important differentiation that has affected the gang in its historical development and evolution over the years. It is equivalent to "what barrio are you from?".

The work of the "Finance Committees" and the "Business Committees" explains why it is so difficult to put a gang like the Latin Kings out of business in their drug trade operations. Those who sell the drugs might, in a lucky case, be able to trace the chain of accountability for drug conspiracy charges back to one of the operatives of the Business Committee, but would never be able to put a dent in the "Finance Committee". And it is the "Finance Committee" that purchases the drugs at wholesale. It is the "Business Committee" that distributes the drugs by selling them at retail prices. The "Finance Committee" would have the funds from the gang to make substantial purchases of the "pure product" directly from Colombian drug cartel sources in the case of cocaine products. While it is the "Business Committee" that would mix or "cut" the drug, package it and arrange for its sale and distribution.

Current members of the "Finance Committee" for the Northside and Northwest side include: Gustavo Colon (the Chairman); Rudy Martinez; Jose Rivera; Frank Periche; William Gonzalez; Sophia Matarazzo; and Oscar Burgos. Current members of the "Finance Committee" for the Southside include: Raul Gonzalez (Chairman); Michael Contreras; Rudy Rangel; Arturo Zambrano; Edward Ranconi; Juan Perea; Juan

Mendiola; and Linda Guzman.

Current members of the "Business Committee" for the Northside and Northwest side include: Kike Rivera, AKA "Kike"; Edwin Rivera, AKA "Shorty"; Ramon Rivera, AKA "Baby"; Edward Mendez, AKA "Spanky"; Felix Jusino; Paul Diaz; and "Buff". Current members of the Southside "Business Committee" include: "Beretta"; "Sex Machine"; "Mando"; Linda Guzman, AKA "Queen Linda"; Juan Mendiola; Rudy Rangel; Juan Perea; and Edward Ranconi. Obviously, there is some overlap between these organizational functions that allows for interfacing between the two different geographical operations.

Finally, there is the "Secretary" of the Latin King Nation: Sophia Matarazzo, AKA "Sunshine". She takes the minutes of all inner circle meetings, keeps records of membership, and distributes the Latin King literature.

CHAPTER INFRASTRUCTURE OF THE CHICAGO-BASED LATIN KINGS

The organizational infrastructure of the Chicago-based Latin Kings is a command structure that is specified in writing in their constitution and by-laws. This infrastructure provides for a variety of leadership positions at the "chapter level". These are not equivalent in rank and status to the "gang nation" positions outlined in the section "Who's Who in the Latin Kings". Persons who hold the "ranks" described here have no authority outside of their street chapter or prison chapter of their respective gang.

The typical street chapter of the Latin Kings has the following organizational arrangement from top down: Inca, Cacique, Enforcers, Treasurer, Investigator, Secretary, Cleaners, Throwers, and the basic rank and file member. There may be a female associated group, called the Latin Queens, but must be attached to a male driven chapter, they do not exist on their own as independent operators. There may also be "pee wee" members, but they are not privy to the secret operations of the chapter of the gang and are not normally allowed to attend its weekly meetings. This has very important implications for those who consider themselves "experts on the Latin Kings". This warrants separate commentary below.

One of the two university professors conned by the GDs into testifying at the Illinois Prisoner Review Board hearing in February of 1995, <u>for</u> the release of Larry Hoover[8], Dwight Conquergood of Northwestern University, can be found in the print media presenting himself as a scholar and research expert on the Latin Kings. Conquergood's research methodology or way of getting information is called "ethnography", or getting close up to the culture by living in it or with it. Did he do that? Well, he did get funding to rent an apartment in Chicago, where he claims he was able to observe the goings-on of gangs including the Latin Kings. Naturally, he suggests that society should not place such harsh "labels" on gang members and that if they just had jobs that gangs like the Latin Kings would be less attractive lifestyles (see: "Trust Enables Professor to Study Gang Culture", by Scott Fornek, <u>Chicago Sun-Times</u>, June 12, 1994, p. 12). We seriously doubt someone who pays the bail money for gang members or acts in the capacity as a exploitable resource for them is going to get access to the "secrets" of a gang. Mostly, simply dealing with "pee wees" is not going to be a valid source of information about the gang.

We will shortly be detailing what really goes on inside a typical Latin King meeting. The "pee wees" are not allowed inside these meetings. Thus, only regular members are allowed inside the gang meetings. The "pee wees" and "associates" are, however, systematically "courted": they are given every possible positive impression the gang can give

them, some of the associates, but not all, are invited to the meetings as a way of "courting" new members. Yet the truth remains: only when they become regular members will they discover the truth about the gang - it is a gang based on crime and violence as a way of life.

CHAPTER INFRASTRUCTURE OF THE LATIN KINGS INSIDE CORRECTIONAL FACILITIES

The Latin King chapters inside correctional facilities operate much like those on the streets and share the bulk of the rules and regulations and the "literature" of their outside counterparts. The structure looks like this from the top down: at the very top is the Inca. Each facility may have an "Inca". This is a spot that does not necessarily "transfer" to other facilities or the outside. Underneath the "Inca" are the following positions: Cacique, Enforcer, Crown Chairman, Investigator, Treasurer, and Secretary. Where the gang in one facility is dispersed into different "cellhouses" or buildings, there will also be separate roles for: cellhouse chief, cellhouse enforcer, cellhouse treasurer, and cellhouse security.

STATISTICAL PROFILE OF THE TYPICAL LATIN KING MEMBER

Project GANGPINT in 1995 carried out by the NGCRC was able to survey about 2,000 gang members in several states. Some N = 82 members of the Latin Kings were able to be pulled out of this sample for the statistical profile provided here. Here are the major lifespan developmental milestones of the LK member:

Mean Age	Developmental Factor in the Lifespan of the LK Member
8.8	Age first heard anything about "gangs".
8.9	Age first met someone who was in a gang.
9.0	Age first "bullied" by someone in school.
9.9	Age first "bullied" someone else in school.
11.0	Age first fired a pistol or revolver.
11.5	Age first saw some killed or seriously injured by gang violence.
11.6	Age first arrested for any crime.
12.3	Age they first joined the gang.
12.6	Age first got their own real gun.
12.8	Age first got a permanent tattoo.
15.6	Age at time we surveyed them for this profile.
23.0	Age they expect to get legally married to someone.
25.1	Age they expect to quit the gang.
57.8	Age they expect to die.

Other important trends found among members of the LK gang are as follows:

• Typical member has an average of 16.8 prior arrests.

• 95.1 percent worry about the safety of their family members.

• 89 percent think their parents/family worry about the LK member of the family being killed.

• 78.5 percent believed that "fear is the only effective means that you can use to control children".

• 72.8 percent felt "there is hardly anything lower than a person who does not feel a great deal of love, gratitude, and respect for his/her mother", while only 57.5 percent felt the same way about father.

• 55.1 percent have been in court-mandated psychological counseling or therapy.

• 33.8 percent have been in a drug/substance abuse counseling program.

• 91.0 percent indicated "I believe in God", and 28.2 percent expected to go to hell in the afterlife.

• 91.0 percent do not want their own children in the

gang.

• 94.9 percent have been suspended from school, 65.4 percent have been expelled from school.

• 44.7 percent have tried to quit the gang.

• 64.8 percent have been "violated" by their own gang.

• 69.3 percent had other family members who are in a gang.

• 74.7 percent have fired a gun at someone to defend their gang turf.

• 57.3 percent have been a shooter in a drive-by shooting.

• 66.7 percent are willing to die for their gang friends.

• 73.3 percent have recruited other persons into the gang.

• Most confirmed that their gang has written rules and that their gang has adult leaders who have been in the gang for a very long time, and that their gang holds regular meetings, that their gang has a treasury, and that their gang has existed for about 20 years.

THE MEAT LOAF STORY

We first learned of this true story in 1992. We did not find out who the two guys that did the killing were until shortly before going to press with this profile: a hard core Cuban member of the LKs who came on the boat lift, described as "a cold blooded Cuban who killed without regard" and the other guy was a small white guy that Gino and BK took under his wing.

As of the fall of 1996 no one has ever been prosecuted for the murder. And to our knowledge the Illinois Department of Corrections still lists the victim as an "escapee".

This is a story of how ruthlessness one gang, the Latin Kings, can be in disciplining its own members. Our information comes from the 2nd in command (a Prince) of the gang at that time who is now a federal informant in the witness protection program. We have spent much time with this particular ex-member of the LKs over a three year period: including about 40 hours of face-to-face interviewing, and about 80 hours of telephone interviewing.

In 1981, the leader of Chicago's southside chapter, one Raul Gonzalez (AKA "Baby King") of the Latin Kings had a "run in" with a member of the northside chapter of the Latin Kings. What happened was that the leader "Baby King" was basically "disrespected" by an inmate known as Carlos Robles. Because Rolez was basically in the same gang, just in a different geographical unit, Baby King approach the leader of the northside chapter of the LKN, Gino Colon, and got his "blessing" to change Carlos Robles permanently before he is released.

About two years later, when he was in the Illinois State Penitentiary, inmate Rolez would get his "violation" for disrespecting the southside leader of the ALKN. Two of the most whacked out members of the southside LKN chapter were chosen for the "hit". Rolez was to be murdered. These were two gang members who were heavy PCP users.

The way the "hit" was carried out was quite clever. The two Whacko's intending to kill Carlos, basically told him they were throwing him a "going away party". Carlos was scheduled to be paroled in two days when the hit took place in July, 1983. As is common in corrupting correctional staff, the two hitmen got permission from the cellhouse guard to use the basement for the going away party. The basement of the cellhouse unit has the showers the inmates use.

Carlos entered the basement of the cellhouse with the two whackos for his "parole party". They proceeded to use their homemade weapons. Not little "shanks" as homemade knifes are called, but rather the much larger Machetes, usually about two feet long and made out of heavy gauge steel.

First they cut off Carlos' head. Then one arm, then the other arm. With a little hacking, off went one leg, then the other. They chopped at the torso, cutting it into smaller pieces. The head was the only body part that could not be sliced up into smaller pieces. The arms and legs were then chopped into smaller pieces. Blood was everywhere. But all the two whackos did was turn on the showers and let the blood run down the drain. Basically washing off the body parts.

Members of their own gang, cooperating upstairs in the cell house, helped next. As the two whackos placed the body parts into plastic bags, a "diversion" fight was staged. This allowed the two whackos to go through the tunnel which led to what was then the butcher shop area of the prisons kitchen.

The Black inmate working in the butcher shop that day was a Gangster Disciple, and as a "Folks" gang, is always opposed to Latin Kings (a "Peoples" gang). The two whackos asked him for a favor, for which they would reward him with some drugs and cash money. They asked him to "grind" up the body parts in the older meat grinder that was there, a very large commercial grade meat grinder. On the menu for the evening meal that night at Stateville Penitentiary was "meat loaf".

The GD in charge of the butcher shop, once offered the drugs and money to grind up the body parts, simply asked "who is in the bag". The two whacko's replied "he is one of our own", not one of yours.

The GD agreed, and ground up the body parts with the pork and beef that was also going into the meat loaf for the evening meal.

Shortly before the bells rung for the inmates to go to evening chow in the inmate dining room, two gangs already had much advance warning about what not to eat that night. The GD's and the Latin Kings spread the word amongst themselves: don't eat on the main line tonight.

In the dining hall that night, only the gangs that did not know the real recipe for the meatloaf ate their food. Some inmate chow hounds were pleasantly surprised to find so many friendly Latin Kings and GD's offering their entre for the evening meal to other hungry inmates.

No traces of the skin, bones, teeth, or blood of Carlos Robles were ever found. That is for years. The skull bone apparently simply "rolled around" in the meat grinder like a basketball spinning on a net rim, and thus it had to be buried. The skull was dug up in 1995 in the yard at Stateville (see: "Skull Dug up in Stateville Prison", Chicago Tribune, April 16, 1995, p. 2).

To this day, the official position of the Illinois Department of Corrections is that "Rolez escaped a day before his parole when a tour of church visitors was in the facility". Did Carlos really escape one day before his parole?

Or do we believe the gang that killed him?

Why do you think some people call meatloaf "mystery meat"?

I guess our message to the other prison gangs is that you really are what you eat, in this case at least.

This has been a true story. One of the two whackos is still serving his life sentence in Stateville. The other whacko has since been released and is now happily married and could be working as a chef at a government center employee cafeteria somewhere.

ONE BOOK WAS BASED ON THE LATIN KINGS

Another commonality between gang types (People, Folks, Crips, Bloods, Other) is an issue that has previously appeared in the at least one contribution to the literature in Felix Padilla's The Gang as an American Enterprise (1992, Rutgers University Press, 109 Church Street, New Brunswick,

NJ 08901). In his ethnographic study of the Latin Kings in Chicago, he concluded that some gang members become alienated from their "gang work" (i.e., selling drugs). That is they feel just as exploited financially as they would feel if they worked at a local fastfood franchise, being paid the minimum wage: the real profits go to the top owners of the enterprise, not to the workers.

So Padilla (1992) asserts, we believe correctly, that the economic income activities of the gang become sometimes viewed as exploitive. Or as other authors in the Journal of Gang Research have argued: gangs imitate other social forms. This is the only way we can account for the fact that in September of 1996 the Gangster Disciples came out with their own book: claiming now that Larry Hoover is a kind of "God" who speaks with thunder and that he leads a group formerly known as "Gangster Disciples" but who are now all about "Growth and Development" for their community: it is a public relations gimmick, plain and simple, and gangs that have that kind of money can easily do what corporations do when they face "heat": they engage in a public relations function.[9]

This theme is easy to understand in analyzing the historical minutes of one chapter of the LKs that will be detailed later in this gang profile. The LKs are meticulous about keeping "minutes" of their meetings and accounting for money, who owes what, and how much is spent on what. Our analysis is certainly consistent with that of Padilla (1992). However, this "exploitive" aspect is not in anyway unique to the Latin Kings. It is an aspect that gang members find out about only when they join gangs and to our knowledge applies to most such centralized authoritarian formal gangs that exist in the United States today.

HOW THE LATIN KINGS TOOK DOWN A NATIONAL GUARD ARMORY

In the late 1970's the Latin Kings took down a national guard armory making away with a number of military weapons. This contributed to some of the Chicago gang folk lore in the 1980's about how the Latin Kings were a "heavily armed" gang and had powerful military weapons. We asked a leader who had spent 20 years in the gang, before being forced to basically testify against his own gang in a situation comparable to that in the movie American Me except this particularly member was not going to accept being killed and he flipped instead, to tell us how the Latin Kings took down the armory and here is his story:

"In 1977 or 1978 we hit the armory at North Avenue and Kedzie. We got an M-60, thousands of rounds of ammunition, two crates of M-16's, and a crate of hand grenades. The next day after the burglary, the cops went postal on us. They were all over the Humboldt Park area for a couple of days, it looked like martial law. We took the M-60 to hid it at Hector's house, so what does Hector do, he has it on its stand, the tripod, in his attic, and it is visible through the window to the outside street...two gang cops stop on Spaulding and Beach, they look up at Hector's attic window, and they see the M-60 in plain view. So the cops got the M-60 back, but not any of the hand grenades or the M16's. We tried one of the hand grenades in Humboldt Park, it left a crater. We sold one crate of the M16's to the Spanish Lords and the Unknowns who were allies at the time. And we kept one crate of the M16's for ourselves. A lot of the M16's are still out there. I know, my brother still has one of them."

THE LATIN KING CONNECTION TO THE F.A.L.N. TERRORIST GROUP

We had first heard of a possible linkage between some members of the FALN terrorist group and the Latin Kings back in 1990 when one cooperative member of the LKs claimed such a connection existed. We discounted it at the time, but information developed over the years and culminated in hard evidence. The typical report we would get from LK members was this: "When Luis Rosa was imprisoned at Stateville the SGD's (Satans Gangster Disciples) tried to pull him their way because he is a bomb expert, but we got him to ride under our flag instead, he taught us how to make some wicked shit down there, Rosa taught us how to make some shit with batteries and remote control with a cell phone, taught us stuff about wiring bombs, taught us how to make homemade napalm, it was toxic substance, like a gluey toxic substance, some killer shit to make Molotov cocktails out of". Luis Rosa was one of 11 FALN members arrested in 1980 in Evanston, Illinois and later convicted.

Luis Rosa is listed in the Libertad, an extreme leftist publication of the National Committee to Free Puerto Rican Political Prisoners of War (2048 W. Division, Chicago, IL 60622, email address: ncprpowpp@aol.com), as serving a 105 year sentence at Joliet presently (IDOC #N02743, DOB 8/6/60).

We continued to be skeptical of such accounts. Then they appeared over and over. Then we got lucky. In our historical approach to developing gang profile information we routinely collect old photographs of the gang, and gangs like the LKs are very predictable in this regard: they love to pose for pictures that members keep in their gang photo albums. We have collected dozens of these photo albums over the years, and literally thousands of such photos, usually paying a small fee to the LK member to acquire these artifacts. We got lucky in one of the photo albums when we found the photograph showing a group of Latin Kings posing in the yard of Stateville Penitentiary that included, guess who, Luis Rosa.

THE MOLOTOV COCKTAIL: A FAVORITE ARSON TECHNIQUE OF THE LATIN KINGS

In Illinois arson is one of the only six crimes for which there is no statute of limitation: prosecution may commence at any time. The Latin Kings seem to have had a particularly strong history of using the Molotov cocktail in arsons against: (1) rival gang member homes, (2) homes or businesses of citizens who testify against Latin Kings, and (3) buildings where the family of suspected informants in their own gang may reside in.

We can illustrate one particularly gruesome case from Joliet, Illinois involving this MO of the LKs.

On November 21st, in 1993, in what used to be a quiet neighborhood on Joliet's east, but poorer, side of town, 91-year-old, Nicolasa Esquibel was confined to a bed for health reasons. Living in the same house was a young gang member that the Latin Kings wanted to send a message to. The message was gunfire and a Molotov cocktail. The young "folks" gang member residing there was not even home at the time. But Nicolasa Esquibel was. Because she was bed-ridden, she was burned alive when the Joliet chapter of the Latin Kings decided to "light up" her house. Nine members of the Latin Kings were brought to trial, four were convicted of arson-murder, two were convicted of theft charges (one of whom had his case overturned completely as was set free: Eddie Olender), and three others were acquitted. Two of the local LK leaders brought to trial were Anthony Montoya and Fidel Nino. Nino got a 75-year sentence, Montaya got a 80-year sentence, Freddie Gonzalez got a 40-year sentence, and Mario Gonzalez got a 35 year sentence for the arson-murder. Just as we were going to press with this gang profile, Anthony Montoya won a new trial because of prosecutorial errors in the Will County, Illinois trial (see: Jerry Shnay, "2nd Case Overturned in Fatal Fire: Will County's Errors May Free 2 Others", Chicago Tribune, 1996, September 17, 1996). Earlier in 1996, Fidel Nino had his case overturned for prosecutorial misconduct as well.

For this reason, arson investigators need to know about the gang profile of the LKs. Also, as gang members are prone over time to "give up the story", it is also useful that prosecutors in states where arson has no statute of limitations to consider prosecuting such older cases that can be linked to the LKs.

LATIN KINGS ON THE CHICAGO POLICE FORCE

The controversy that unfolded in Chicago in the fall of 1995 was not limited to the Latin Kings, but basically boiled down to the fact that there were active gang members who were also Chicago police officers. The information seemed overwhelming, from 1992 to 1995 "at least 15 cops have been charged with crimes, forced to resign" who were from "some of Chicago's most notorious street gangs, including the Gangster Disciples, the Latin Kings, and the Latin Lovers" (see: Jorge Oclander, "Gangs Move Into Police Ranks", Chicago Sun-Times, October 6, 1995, pp. 1, 22-23. For example, two officers charged with robbing a store in the summer of 1995 of $700 to $1000 worth of fireworks were identified by the CPD's Internal Affairs Division as being Latin King members (see: Jorge Oclander, "Something Fishy Going On: Neighborhood Wary of Gangs' Link to Cops", October 9, 1995, pp. 1, 8).

CHRISTIANITY: ONE WAY OUT OF THE GANG

We have not been able to get consistent agreement on this issue in debriefing LK members, but at least one high ranking leader of the LK gang told us that one way out of the gang is for a member to convert to Christianity. As he explained: "in the Latin Kings....unity is very strong in this gang....membership is very loyal to those in command, often borne out of fear, because the gang will kill its own members routinely, so the first and foremost law of the gang is once a King, always a King: the only exception is to go to the Corona and ask for permission to retire on the basis you are a Christian, but you better not backslide, or get caught faking, because the penalty is death..."

Another member reiterated this possibility of getting out of the gang through a religious conversion: "guys do it in the joint all the time, if you make a sincere conversion, they will not even violate you out, but if they find out you were faking it, then it's a death violation".

GOING UNDERGROUND: A MORE COMMON WAY OUT OF THE GANG

Simply "disappearing" and cutting off all ties to the gang and moving to a new city where there is no known LK activity is a more common way out of the gang. One LK member who "dropped his flag" in this fashion provided substantial information on the Latin Kings that is reported elsewhere (see: An Introduction to Gangs, 1994, by George Knox, Wyndham Hall Press). This LK member after shooting a rival gang member simply panicked, thinking he may have killed the victim, and moved out of state to attend college. This LK member returned a few years later and took a job in the Cook County Court system (having no arrest record, because he quit the gang shortly after doing the shooting which was a part of his initiation into the LKs). His nightmare, however, was that he would be walking the hallway of the court building someday and see his old homies from the LK gang.

FLIPPING: A SURE FIRE WAY OUT OF THE GANG

Flipping is a sure fire way out of the gang. Flipping can mean "dropping your flag" and joining another gang or providing testimony against the LKs. If a LK member joins

another gang, the member will always face an uncertain future. The Latin Kings are described by one ex-member of the gang as being "a ruthless organization where the main focus is economics, they've gone from being a one-chapter group to being a nationwide organization". The only way we have been able to verify that someone becomes a true "ex" member of the gang is to testify against other members of the same gang. As in the Aryan Brotherhood where the motto is "kill to get in, die to get out", the Latin Kings use the expression: "once a King, always a King". In other words, you can run, but you cannot hide, if they catch up with you, there will be a reckoning. It is routine for the LK gang to put a "money bag" on its members who flip and cooperate with investigators, that is a "hit". This is why in Illinois and elsewhere new improvements have been made in the state criminal code to provide for "witness protection and relocation assistance".

THE FEMALE AUXILIARY UNIT OF THE GANG: LATIN QUEENS

For the past twenty years in Chicago female students who attended Chicago public schools have had to live with the fear of the well-earned reputation of the female members of the Latin Kings. The female members are called "Latin Queens". They exist to aid and assist the male members. Not surprisingly, it is not exactly a feminist organization, the men run this gang. But as one high ranking source told us who had become a resource for federal investigators: "Latin Queens make our gang similar to an extended family...we treated our Queens like they were our true sisters...the penalty for disrespecting a Queen is death...you can disrespect a male member, and depending on the situation --- whether the guy had any rank, etc --- you can walk away alive...but you can get killed just for calling a Latin Queen a bitch especially if she is married to a Latin King...we trained them to be just as ruthless as we were....we trained them to never back down from business...you will have to do it.....they fight with any rival gang females and with guys....they will shot at them, the whole nine yards....".

ALLIES AND ENEMIES OF THE LATIN KINGS

The Latin Kings are a "people" gang, they use the "5 pointed star", or more appropriately the 5 pointed crown, but still maintain today an alliance structure with other people or brother gangs. Consequently, the Latin Kings have as their "enemy" all "folks" gangs.

The Spanish Cobras are perhaps one of the single largest enemies of the LKs, the Spanish Cobras are a folks gang, they are an enemy because the LK's gave the Unknowns the greenlight to kill the Spanish Cobra leader (King Cobra, "KC", about 1979).

The Latin Disciples would probably be the second main enemy of the LKs, because they still believe the LKs were behind the hit of their leader "Hitler", even though the LKs say it was the C-Notes who really killed "Hitler".

The Maniac Latin Disciples, or MLDs, are one such folks gang that are an enemy to the Latin Kings. As one LK member explained: "The MLDs are very violent....something they replicated from the Latin Kings.....they seek to be as ruthless as the latin kings, their primary enemy....their existence depends on ruthlessness because they are not as large an organization as the Latin Kings...they used to be called the Latin Scorpians from Rockwell and Hirsch in Chicago".

Another gang that basically emerged to a criminal gang almost overnight simply because of violence with the Latin Kings is seen in the case of the Orchestra Albany gang (i.e., the OA's). As detailed by a LK member: "Orchestra Albany started as a Puerto Rican salsa band until the Latin Kings from Arlington and Kedzie went over and attended one of their block parties...the OA's colors were brown and gold....the Latin Kings were there in their war sweaters....LKs mistook the brown and gold for black and gold and thought the OA's were perpetrating and misrepresenting Latin King Nation colors...a fight broke out and then shots rang out, one of the OAs got killed, and they turned from a street band to a street gang over night, and a few nights later the OA's killed "Queen Lefty", she was the first Latin Queen to ever get killed". There is no group more hostile to the Latin Kings today than the OA's. The OA's arose as a criminal gang because of violence from the Latin Kings.

The Maniac Latin Disciples is another fierce rival to the Latin Kings, a folks gang obviously.

A standard MO of the Latin Kings is to drive in a car, with about 4 Latin King occupants, and go out "hunting" for an opportunity for a drive-by. It is often an initiation ceremony as well.

The single largest or best ally of the LKs is the "Insane Unknowns". The gang originally called themselves Unknown Latin Kings, but changed their colors to Black and White, and became the Insane Unknowns.

The Spanish Lords, a people gang, are one of the LK allies; as a LK member told us: "the Spanish Lords are like a second cousin to us.....their chief was Corky...he OD'd in Stateville in 1989....but their gang has been around since the 60s.....they have never been too deep though".

The Cullerton Deuces were running with the LKs at one time and then the entire gang (the Cullerton Deuces are not a very large gang) "flip flopped" its alliance system: changing from a People gang to a "Folks" gang when a confrontation with LK's left one of the CD's dead.

The "Metros" is another Illinois gang, operating in East St. Louis, Illinois, and in the IDOC, that the Latin Kings have an alliance with. According to one of our sources in the Latin Kings: "Gino was the one who first hooked up with them, Gino had the job of driving a garbage truck in Menard where he is currently serving his sentence, that's how they move drugs from one cellhouse to the other in Menard, and it was there that we established a cooperative linkage with the Metros".

A LOOK AT THE ECONOMIC FUNCTION OF THE LATIN KINGS

Some of this information on the economic structure and function of the Latin Kings was previously made available in the book length report from the NGCRC "Project GANGECON" (**THE ECONOMICS OF GANG LIFE: A Task Force Report of the National Gang Crime Research Center**, Co-Principal Investigators: George W. Knox; Edward D. Tromanhauser; James G. Houston; Brad Martin; Robert E. Morris; Thomas F. McCurrie; John L. Laskey; and Dorothy Papachristos, 1995). The Latin Kings are known to own or control a number of what might appear on the outside to be "legitimate businesses", typically "cash" businesses, such as: Beeper communications, a dance hall, a pool hall, etc, which are cash businesses, perfect as well for laundering money from the gang's drug proceeds. Explained one high ranking member of the LKs: "we had a lot of businesses, we had a car wash right across the street from Humboldt Park, we had to shut it down when the feds found out we were selling drugs out of there, but we also had video stores, apartment buildings, restaurants, you name it, hell we are one of the biggest enterprises in Chicago today -- drugs -- and we have been holding it down for thirty years, so what do you think."

One reason, a high ranking member of the LKs told us, why little may be known about the financial aspects of gang life is that this is a sub rosa and secret activity. Many gangs, do however, have "dues" requirements:

"Every member has to pay a certain amount, say $5.00, and in the Latin Kings a treasurer will go around to the chapters to collect the dues. It is always kept balanced, so if somebody goes out and takes care of business, he is supposed to be provided with bond money and a lawyer (they keep lawyers on retainer), the guys at the top have certain crews in each chapter that sell drugs directly for them...the sellers they get a percentage of everything they sell...and then of course they are allowed to make their own money also...but whatever they sell for the organization the profits end up in the hands of the guys at the top...the council I sat on...a lot of this structure still remains the same....except we branched out to some new cities...and the money is coming in everyday seven days a week. It is always wise to....a lot of it is spent, it is a risky business, you might as well enjoy what you can make while you've got it. Its a big thing to have a nice ride. They spend $19K on the car and spend another $10k on toys: stereos, car phone, etc. We had a couple of those, with door panels secretly fitted, if the car was going to hold 5 keys of cocaine, if they got pulled over, five oh (the police) would not have a clue as to where to look. When we would go do drops or pickups we always had a chase car, 4 guys armed to the teeth just in case something happened they would be right there, a security measure so to speak."

"The only way a lot of these guys can hide their finances you can never put anything under your name, it has to be a third party....I had a relative who was heavily involved in real estate....we let him handle a lot of our finances....we always kept bank accounts under fictitious and false names...I don't know how they are doing it...but the bankers we dealt with, they never question it..."

"The people they are dealing with, they have their own way of getting around modern banking regulations..."

"The first very large sum of cash I saw at one time while in the Latin Kings was one I saw for about two bills....that's two million dollars...later I learned that was small. it was split up 8 different ways...the ones that had their investments in it...it was counted out...and split up...no big thing..." "Trying to pass laws against gangs that exist because there is money in it is like trying to outlaw ice cream....what people want they are going to get...whether its bud (reefer, marijuana, etc)...or harder drugs....Al Capone taught us that. There is always going to be somebody else to step in...you can't put the gang out of a business that has faces no regulations....the boys might be arrested....but the business will go on. Gang business is pure business...no regulations other than what it agrees to, just the opposition or competition to worry about."

Regarding drug sellers for the Latin Kings: "a lot of em were exploited...we treated a lot of ours good though...they made 20 cents on the dollar...the other 80 percent was split upstairs...we made sure they had the props...we set them up in apartments so they did not have to work on the streets...i was given the responsibility to oversee our operations in 5 states...all some of the outlying groups were lacking was product which we quickly provided them with....the territories in question were virgin territories, and were considered neutral turf, but other organizations did exist there and when they learned what we were doing...they wanted a piece of the action and they wanted a war if they did not get a piece....i went out there to start a business, i had a sit down with the heads of these other organizations, let them know the product being sold is being sold to you guys and not their customers, we are doing this on neutral ground, we started selling them products at lower prices and a higher quality than they could not get elsewhere...they eventually ended up becoming our allies...which had the effect of strengthening our own network..."

About gang economics behind bars: "When I flipped.... a guy in (the prison) was holding some of my money and would not give it to me because I was in seg waiting for transfer...it was $3800 bucks...he had it hid in his tv....I asked the warden if they could collect it for me...and they sort of agreed if I would tell them where the money was hidden...I told them, but they burned me....they gave me a bogus move...they gave me a hundred bucks as like a little reward for the tip....the warden said it was all dirty money....we cant prove it was yours...we'll give you a hundred bucks...we'll put the rest in the inmate fund...."

A LOOK INSIDE THE FINANCIAL RECORDS OF A LATIN KING CHAPTER

The present researchers had access to what must be regarded as very sensitive documents already in the hands of law enforcement agencies, because we obtained this information again from the gang member involved who had "flipped" and turned this same information over to law enforcement agencies investigating and prosecuting members of the same gang. Appendix A contains the exact transcripts of this information that were as accurate as we could transcribe them. These are hand-written documents, not typed original source documents that are laboriously transcribed in Appendix A. We have intentionally omitted certain specific information about addresses and full names and telephone or other numbers relating to the same internal record information. For reference purposes, Appendix I 1.1 is provided at the end of this gang profile.

The information being referred to in Appendix A is therefore very genuine and reflects the detailed membership, dues, internal structural change, and expenses associated with one Chicago chapter of the Latin Kings. There are many such chapters or sets, which exist non-contiguously not only within the City of Chicago, but the entire Chicago metropolitan area extending deep into the midwestern United States.

The "data" here therefore consists of actual genuine documents maintained by the gang as its official records. We have included only a transcription of a six month period of activity during 1990 for the purposes of illustrating some issues about the economic functions of gangs. We feel that a short analysis of these documents in Appendix A provide the basis for discussing the legitimacy of some hitherto unexplored aspects about gang economics.

About this "data", it was in handwritten form, transcribed literally in Appendix A for purposes of cross-reference here. Here are some of the trends in this data:

*** Associates of the gang, whose names appear in records, do later become full gang members.

*** A very democratic process operates in voting for sanctions and for promotions in rank.

*** A frequent activity of the gang is order maintenance: sanctioning its own members for infractions and not meeting financial obligations.

*** Such sanctions typically are "violations" or monetary fines. The violations are beatings from up to four members of the gang lasting specific time limits: 30 seconds, 60 seconds, etc. The fines sometimes involve situations where the individual gang member may lose a gun owned by the gang, that is a gun purchased from its treasury money (i.e., paying a $50.00 fine for losing a $150.00 pistol).

*** The gang does seem to benefit from the underground economy in having opportunities over time to purchase firearms at reasonable prices. This type of gang is a rational, calculating, and self-supporting enterprise is the image that emerges from the data in Appendix A. It has costs for maintaining its operations, it collects dues, and keeps accurate account of its gang treasury money, its income sources over time and its expenditures over time.

*** The gang does spend its treasury money on guns,

gang clothing, spray paint to "fix the hood", and in what appears to be a structured general welfare benefit program to its needy or incarcerated members.

*** The gang has this general welfare benefit character by being able to provide money to its needy members in or outside of jail/prison. The gang does in this sense function as an economic benevolent society for its members in a small but very symbolic way.

*** The gang becomes politically correct in voting to have "non-smoking" meetings, and then sanctions several members for subsequently smoking behavior. Violations are also given for being late to, or missing, required meetings. The required weekly meetings are held promptly and neatly organized as any formal or voluntary organization might behave. The notes and ledgers are also meticulously maintained by the gang secretary. Where this type of organizational meeting differs from others that might be held in the same neighborhood (religious or political meetings, community groups, advisory groups, etc), is that internal control can be achieved by the use of violence against detractors to organizational effectiveness.

*** The gang spends money on parties, and does maintain a relationship to the larger Nation (other chapters or sets, i.e., attending the yearly gang picnic, having other chapter gang members visit their own meetings, etc).

*** All of the gang income to the treasury is dues money. The gang is steadfast about requirements for paying regular dues. It even passes new laws to punish deadbeats.

*** The amount of cash in the treasury varies over this six month period from a low of $1.00 to a high of $437.00 at any one particular time during this period. And averaged about $200 during the six month period.

*** Typical expenses included in this gang's ledgers included: (1) the purchase of guns ($75.00/357 revolver; $70.00/22 revolver; $150.00/32 pistol; $250.00/9mm pistol), (2) payments to incarcerated members as direct payments of cash ($192.00) in small increments to several different members, and (3) misc. operating expenses (spray paint, gang t-shirts, etc $277.00).

*** The gang spends an inordinate amount of time with internal conflicts and with disciplining its members. Cohesion, compliance, and conformity are maintained through the use of violence by the gang against its own members.

*** These findings are based on the written minutes of weekly punctual gang meetings over a six month period, and suggest clearly the importance of understanding the gang in terms of its internal friction in relationship to its own fiscal solvency. This type of level three formal organization gang does have regular meetings, and does require dues to be paid regularly from its members.

Apparently, there is another side about gang life in America that has not emerged in anthropological studies of younger gang members who may not be at all knowledgeable of this larger picture. "Shorties" or "Peewees" as associates of a real gang might be easily approached by such anthropological techniques, but these type of data sources are the least likely to actually be knowledgeable about the larger financial and economic issues of gang life today. Someone who pays dues, is someone who might be privy to the kind of economic functions that gangs may have today. A peewee or very young wannabe or associate may not be required to pay dues because they are not considered genuine or official members of the gang, and therefore will never be attending gang meetings on a regular basis to overhear "Nation business".

THE 1989 ASSASSINATION OF OFFICER LAWRENCE KUSH

On July 1, 1989 a correctional officer at the Stateville Correctional Center, Lawrence Kush, Jr., was assassinated by the Latin Kings while on the job. Attacked from behind with pipes and other weapons, Kush would die a day later, but was one of 30 officers on a "hit list" prepared by the Latin Kings (see: Jerry Thomas, "Gangs a Rising Threat to Prison Guards", Chicago Tribune, November 28, 1993). Why did the Latin Kings target correctional officers? Clearly, all evidence points to one thing: the officers were doing their job, and that meant they were a threat to the inside drug business of the Latin Kings.

The key issue readers need to understand here is that any ordinary member of the Latin Kings, or even one with "rank" or power, cannot on his own order or undertake a "hit" against anyone, especially a correctional officer. This type of serious activity must be "approved" of by the top gang leaders. This is important to understand because of the fact that the top gang leaders of the LKs have never been held accountable as of this date. Let us share some information from middle-management leaders of the Latin Kings who were in fact in this same penitentiary and were directly knowledgeable of the Kush assassination:

"Kush was the type of officer who came to work to do his job, he was young. He was not like Officers ____ and ____ who were shake-down artists, who really started it, they started fucking with Lord Gino, Lord Gino told them I was doing time before you were born, so fuck off, they didn't back off, in fact they searched Lord Gino's cell, Lord Gino had a strainer in his cell used for mixing and preparing cocaine and it had cocaine residue on it, Kush wrote up Gino, then Gino told our mob: I want Kush hit today."

Said another high-ranking source in the LKs:

"Gino summoned me to the law library where carried out our executive meetings and he said I want Kush hit. I was not in agreement with him, you can deal with him on the outside is what I tried to argue, I suggested sending Kush pictures of his wife and children. Then Gino got kind of pissed that me and ____ may have been obstructing his authority, by not endorsing the hit on Kush, and he said If you two guys try to have this hit blocked I will have you both hit. In our gang you cannot order a murder of a correctional officer without it being approved and called by the top leader (Lord Gino)."

Three inmates were indicted for the murder of Officer Kush: William Cabrera, David Starks, and Salvatore Giancana. These Latin Kings were prosecuted in Will County, Illinois, and there was some thought among our informants that the prosecution was bungled. First it took about four years to bring the killers to trial. By then one, Sal Giancana, had already died. That left Starks and Cabrera. Starks was spared the death penalty (see: Jerry Shnay, "Inmate is spared death penalty: Prisoner convicted in guard's death awaits sentencing", Chicago Tribune, March 15, 1994). Secondly, the one ranking LK gang member that did flip in the case and provide the testimony for prosecution of the three killers was someone we interviewed for this gang profile, and this person clearly indicated that he had provided substantial information that could have been used to go after the top leaders of the LKs, but the evidence was not used[10].

PREVIOUS FAILURE TO PROSECUTE THE LATIN KING LEADERS IN THE KUSH ASSASSINATION BRINGS ABOUT ANOTHER CRISIS IN THE ILLINOIS PRISON SYSTEM IN 1996

On January 12th, 1996 a LK member named Florencio Pecina was an inmate in the Pontiac prison, who was holding a knife in his hand in a threatening manner and when a correctional officer demanded he surrender the weapon refused to do so, and a watchful armed officer backing up the unarmed officer fired a fatal shot at Pecina.[11] This is straightforward as any inmate knows, it was a justifiable homicide: the same thing would occur on the street if a police officer faced the same incident. But the Latin King leadership had become bolder having successfully insulated their leadership from prosecution in the Kush assassination. So soon the word came down from the LK top leadership: retaliate.

Latin Kings throughout Illinois, but especially in the Pontiac Prison, began chanting "Three for One". This echoed the LK leadership approval for retaliation against employees of the Illinois Department of Corrections and meant: if you killed one of ours (Pecina), we will kill three of you (IDOC staff or officers).

Throughout the spring and summer of 1996, the tension mounted and escalated, rioting ensued, institutions went on complete "lock down", and well up until the time of going to press with this gang profile, the threat to kill three IDOC employees continues, as does the search for handguns and ammunition believed to have been smuggled in by the Latin Kings to carry out this retaliation (see: Gary Marx, "Fearing that inmates have weapon, state squad scours Pontiac", Chicago Tribune, September 8, 1996, p. 4). Currently, the "three for one" threat has escalated to a crisis condition.

Have the LKs tried to carry out the "three for one" threat after the death of Pecina? Yes. In February of 1996, a LK member was ordered by Pedro Rey, a LK middle management leader, to kill an IDOC officer, but the member turned himself in and the assassination was prevented. About two weeks later, an officer in Pontiac was severely wounded in a knife attack but recovered from his wounds.

The "back drop" for this "three for one" threat was the political fall out from the infamous "Richard Speck tapes", these were videotapes of Richard Speck and another inmate known as "Hooks" having sex and snorting from a bowl of cocaine, tapes believed to have been made by GDs, that showed the inmates having run of the prison; other tapes emerged showing gang "parties", with open sex going on with female visitors in the family visiting room. The Illinois legislature investigated, the media attention spiraled upwards, and finally in the late summer of 1996, the IDOC itself implemented stiff reforms as the legislative investigation "cooled out" until after the election.

In late September, 1996 IDOC officials were still overturning every source they could to locate the guns believed to have been smuggled in by the Latin Kings.

We have been interviewing one high ranking member of the Latin Kings for over three years, spending over 40 hours with him as he is an enormous intelligence asset for federal investigators, and this is what he had to say about the "three for one" threat: "they are definitely going to carry it out, the man behind the three for one deal is no one other than Lord Gino. A Latin King member, no matter what his rank, in Pontiac cannot on his own have an officer hit. Only Lord Gino can order it. So if Lord Gino sent that order down it is not a matter of if the hits will take place, but when the hits will take place".

The logic here is that anyone in the LK organization who carries out the "3 for 1" threat will probably gain immediate elevation in their rank and status in the gang, and there are plenty of such individuals around eager to please their top gang leaders and get a "promotion" at the same time. Asked to examine some scenarios for timing, more than one source suggested the attack would be likely to occur on a commemorative date: a date when Latin Kings remember a "fallen comrade", or an anniversary for when a Latin King member was killed.[12]

The other historical factor of importance here is the individual history on Florencio Pecina. Pecina had himself developed a "reputation" for being able to literally get away with murder. Here is the background on this issue from one of his fellow LK members: "Pecina got away with a murder in Stateville....he only served 30 days in the hole for killing a guy they found out was actually serving time for being a child molester.....they cut off his penis and put it in his mouth; when we discovered one of our own had a rap sheet that included child molesting I had recommended that we send him to PC, but they hit the guy anyhow; if they say they are going to hit 3 officers they are going to do it, Gino does not care, he is not worried about being indicted, his soldiers are going to carry out his orders regardless of the consequences".

THE LATIN KINGS ARE A RACIALLY INTEGRATED GANG

We have routinely found white and Black members of the LKs, as well as members whose families recently moved to Chicago from Iraq, Palestine, Poland, Asian countries, etc. In regard to ethnic composition, the LKs are predominantly Latin (Mexican and Puerto Rican, and Cuban), but clearly their membership is a veritable "rainbow" when it comes to ethnicity and race.

THE EAST-COAST VERSION OF THE LATIN KINGS

Pedro Millan (AKA: "Chico"), a Chicago-based Latin King, moved to New York and Spanish Harlem in 1978 and is said to have spread the gang to the east coast at this time. He was soon joined by Luis Filipe (AKA "King Blood"). Pedro moved to Connecticut, and formed another chapter of the LKs out there. Pedro Millan did have Papa King's blessing to start a new chapter in New York, but Pedro did not have the blessing of Lord Gino to operate as an equal in status, i.e., a "Corona" or "Chief Crown". Pedro was supposed to go through Lord Gino being from the Northside LKs, but he went to Papa King instead for the blessing to be a "missionary" to spread the LKs to the east coast.

So theoretically there is more than some potential for friction between the east coast version of the LKs and the Chicago original. The primary reason is this: the east coast version has its own written lengthy constitution and by-laws, and as well as an assortment of "gang forms" such as "handling deaths and paying for the burial of LK members". Chicago has never tried to compete with Connecticut and New York for who is the supreme command of the LKs. The issue is who is the "national crown". If the east coast members and their leaders meet the Chicago members and Chicago leaders, there could be friction. A worse scenario, however, would be that an amalgamation or consolidation/merger scenario might unfold where a true national council would develop for an even stronger LK gang system.

The east coast version of the LKs has gained a great deal of media coverage in recent years and they seem to enjoy it. The Chicago original LKs are skilled at avoiding any media coverage and shy away from the media as if reporters and TV crews were the plague.[13]

A couple things can be said about the East Coast version of the Latin Kings. Their written constitution and by-laws and other internal documents reflect the highest level of organizational skill we have seen in any gang anywhere in the world. This east-coast version of the LKs is a gang that emulates a federal bureaucracy in its detail given to policies and procedures and illustrates a high level of sophistication in its micro-management of membership behavior (i.e., standards, guidelines, etc). In fact, when we first saw the East-Coast LK constitution around 1991 we thought it was an experiment gone bad: perhaps a federal project or something

where the "sting" got out of control or went awry, because the gang's internal documents and by-laws, forms, etc could not have been written much better if a federal attorney had done so. So in terms of displaying a sense of organizational sophistication, at least on paper, the East-Coast version is clearly superior to its Chicago original. Figure 2 illustrates this kind of exceptional "style". Figure 2 is an internal memo of the east coast Latin Kings restructuring the gang by means of appointing "regional commanders".

OVERALL THREAT RATING FOR THE LATIN KINGS

The Latin Kings are a Level Three gang organization: they exist as a centralized, authoritarian, violent formal organization complete with a written constitution and by-laws. As a gang they have often taken advantage of any political corruption they could, but do so on a "case by case" basis: where it helps, they do it for business, and in this sense fit the more classic pattern of organized crime. From a perspective of size of the gang, its penetration of communities outside of its epicenter (i.e., Chicago), and its propensity for violence, we would give this gang an 8 on a zero to ten point scale (the higher the number the higher the threat), making it one of the most threatening gangs in the United States today.

RECOMMENDATIONS FOR GANG SUPPRESSION

This gang is particularly vulnerable to the loss of leadership: the two main heads of the two main branches in Chicago --- (1) Lord Gino from the Northside, and (2) B.K. (Baby King) from the Southside. These two branches have always existed in a tenuous competition with each other. If these two leaders were in federal custody facing federal charges, then a succession crisis could ensue. As Lord Gino has control of state prison operations, it might be a more effective strategy to prosecute B.K. on state charges and Lord Gino on federal charges, if the State of Illinois prison system was able to open up its super-max facility for keeping B.K. and major "middle management" figures. There already exists a hierarchy of LK control in the federal prison system. So there are really not many guaranteed effective options for the suppression of the LK leaders by allowing them in the general inmate population.

Federal prosecution is urgently needed to remove Latin King leaders from the Illinois prisons where they are still free to administer their gang from behind bars. The Illinois state prison system currently lacks the capability to deal with such hard core gang leaders who know how to use their "inmate rights" to continue to administer their gang even while incarcerated. Currently the Illinois state prison system is in a crisis generated by the Latin King gang. It is a crisis that will not be solved without federal assistance.

APPENDIX I 1.1

Transcription of the Internal Records of
The Albany Park Chapter of the Latin Kings
For A Six Month Period in 1990

Member list: Flaco, Kasper, Hitman, Shy, SHort, Mousie, Joker, House, Gunner, Lotto, Angel, Sinbad, Killer, Al, Turtle, Wedo, Ponyboy, Sinister, Delfino, Whitey, Babyslick, Lover, Slick, Flaco.

January 13, 1990 6:30 P.M. Flaco's House

I Kato becomes A Latin King: he is on preliminary probation until March 13, 1990

II New counsel:

Since 2 members of the present counsel have been incarserated and I cannot attend the meting regularly, we picked 3 new counsel members. The new counsel is as follows: Chairman - Stony; members - Hitman, Wedo, Shy, and Shorty. Slick and Sir Lover have the chance to gain their rank back when they get out.

III (Marked in large letters OVERRULED FEB. 11, 1990)

It was decided today by a majority vote that Baby Slick will have to pay $50.00 for the .32 pistol because he told the police where to find the gun during the interrogation. Baby Slick will have a chance to defend himself as soon as possible.

IV Violations:

Today Flaco got a 15 second violation because he let his lady thrown down the crown to his face.

Stony got a 30 second violation for disrespecting Flaco by telling him "I wish you weren't a King so I could smash you".

signed by secretary: Angel

January 20, 1990 6:30 P.M. Flaco's House

I Today Kasper took his violation out of Albany: the violation was 3 minutes long and was given by 4 people.

II NEW RANK: Because Kasper left his rank of enforcer we chose to move Stony up to rank of enforcer. Wedo is the new chairman of the counsel and our newest counsel member is Joker.

III Spending ALBANY money:

Today it was decided that we will send $10.00 a piece to Slick, Sir Lover and Baby Slick. $31.00 was given to Kato so he can give it to Carol.

IV Violations: Wedo got a violation today because he left his post while standing security for a southside meeting.

February 11, 1990 6:30 P.M. Flaco's House

I. New Recruits:

Today Kasper took his violation back into the Latin Kings. The violation was 30 seconds long and there was no probation given.

II Violations: Joker got a 45 second violation for coming to the meeting intoxicated. Shy and sinister both got a 45 second violation for not going back to Loco when he got shot.

III On Tuesday February the 6th Loco got shot while taking a march to 60th. He is healthy and will be in perfect health.

IV New Laws: It was decided today that from now on at the end of every month, whoever is not paid up on their dues has a 30 second violation and if the person is overdue for 2 months then it's a 60 second violation.

V. We decided today that we will start up the Latin Kings of 53rd. As far as we know Claudia will be holding it down for them. We will meet with her next week.

VI We will soon be holding a party for the 1st anniversary of our chapter of the Latin Kings. All the boy's have until April 21st to pay the $20.00 fee for the party. Angel was put in charge of organizing the party.

VII $70.00 was collected in dues today which brings our current balance of $112.00

1-13-90 $26.00 was collected today and $25.00 was paid to Ghost of the LLKs. $5.00 is still owed to Ghost and we have $1.00 left.

1-20-90 $30.00 was collected today and was decided that we will send $10.00 a piece to Slick, Sir Lover and Baby Slick. $31.00 was given to Kato so he can give it to Carol.

1-27-90 $19.00 was collected today.

February 17, 1990 6:30 P.M. Flaco's House

I We talk about the party again.

II Collect $19.00 today. Balanced $131.00. Signed Prowler.

Feb. 24, 1990 6:30 Flaco's House

I Today we over ruled to pay the dues because all the boys were not here. We're going to do it next week.

II Today Stony got a violation for missing the meeting for getting a tattoo. Joker and Hitman gave him the violation.

III Today we collected $21.00 dollars for dues money. It balances out to $152.00 dollars.

IIII Today all the boys that were at the meeting talk about the party but it was canceled to next week.

Signed Joker

2-3-90 $19.00 was collected in dues today. That makes the balance currently $42.00

2-11-90 $70.00 was collected in dues today which brings our current balance to $112.00

2-17-90 $19.00 was collected in dues today. That makes the balance $130.00 in cash.

2-24-90 $21.00 was collected in dues today. That makes the balance $152.00 in cash.

March 3, 1990 6:30 P.M. Flaco's House

I. Sinbad became Latin Kings of 53st. He is on preliminary probation until May 5, 1990.

II. We cancel the meeting early because nobody came.

III Nobody had dues money, today so our balance is still $152.00

Signed Flaco

March 8, 1990
Member check list:
Flaco check
Kasper check
Prowler check
Stony check
Hitman check
Shy EX.
Shorty EX.
Mousie EX.

Joker check
Smoky
Mando check
Gunner
Kato
Sinister check
Loco check
Angel check
Sinbad check
Wedo EX.
Sir Lover EX.
Slick EX.
Baby Slick EX.
Paco EX.

March 10, 1990 6:30 P.M. Flaco's House

I. New Members: Today Insane Gus became the newest Latin King. He is on preliminary probation until May 12, 1990. Killer also took his violation into the ALKs and he also will be on probation until May 12, 1990.

II. New Rank: Kasper was Appointed by the Inca and the Cacique to be the chapter investigator. His term is indefinite.

III. Violations - today Gunner got a 30 second violation for missing an emergency meeting that was called last Thursday.

IV Chapter rules + regulations: It was decided today that members will no longer be able to smoke during indoor meetings due to the mess and the congestion. It was also decided that anyone coming more than 5 minutes late to a scheduled meeting will not be admitted in. The person will also be getting a violation for missing a meeting.

V $63 was collected in due's today. That brings our current balance to $215

Signed Angel

March 17, 1990 6:30 P.M. Flaco's House

I We collect $26.00. $241.00 together.

II Vote for new rule's. We talk about the heads. Talk about the due's. Kato get out probation. Kato lost the pistol owe's $50.00

signed Prowler

March 24, 1990 6:30 P.M. Flaco's House

I Today Delfino and Alex and WHitey became a Latin King. All are on two months probation until May 26th, 1990.

II Kato was put on 30 day probation for the fact that his girlfriend knew about our emergency meeting two weeks ago

III 27 dollars was collected in dues today which brings our balance to $268

IV $6.00 was spend on spray paint which is needed to fix the hood.

V It was decided unanimously today that Smokey be kicked out. He will be given a violation on sight.

signed Angel

March 31st, 1990 6:30 P.M. Flaco's House

I Alex has decided today that from here on he shall be known as Al - of the Latin Kings.

II Violations - Kasper, Stoney + Joker all have received violations for not keeping up with their dues during the month of March.

III $75.00 was spend on artillery this week which brings the balance down to $193.00

IV $95.00 was collected this week which brings our balance back up to $288.00

signed Angel

Whitey join pd.
Alex join pd.

3-3-90 Nobody had dues money today so our balance is still $152.00

3-10-90 $63.00 was collected in dues today that brings our balance to $215.00

3-17-90 $26.00 was collected which brings our balance to $241.00

3-24-90 $27.00 was collected in dues which brings our balance to $268.00 but $6.00 was spent on spray paint to fix the hood.

3-31-89 $95.00 was collected which brings our balance to $288.00 but $75.00 was spend on the "357".

April 7, 1990 6:30 P.M. Flaco's House

I No dues was collected today, but we collect dues from the past which is $35.00 an it bring the balance to $317.00

II Loco is now off probation

Signed Paco

April 14, 1990 6:30 P.M. Flaco's House

I. Violations, Gunner got a 30 second violation for not keeping up with his dues.

II. 30 dollars was taken out for Big Slick, who is incarserated.

III 47 dollars was collected in dues today which brings our balance to $334.00

signed Angel

April 21, 1990 6:30 P.M. Flaco's house

I Today $59.00 was collected which brings our balance up to $393.00

signed Flaco
-----
delinquent dues list:
Ponyboy 2.00
Kasper 9.00

Turtle gave 10 owes 2.75
Angel 17.75 + 250.00
Al 42.00
Hitman 6.00
Shorty 23.00
Joker 23.00
Wedo 9.00
Gus 13.00
Wicked 43.00
Kalo 63.00
Lover 24.00
Slick 101.00
Gunner 36.00
Smoky 24.00
Bush 100.00

Missing from dues: $746.50

April 28th, 1990 6:30 P.M. Flaco's House

I. Wicked becomes Albany with Turtle both are on preliminary probation until June 30, 1990

II Violations: Stony got 60, for no dues, 60 for no party money and 60 for fighting with Joker. Stony also lost his rank of enforcer because he fought with Joker. Shorty got 60 seconds for no party money. Joker got 60 second for no party money and 35 for fighting with Stony.

III $44.00 was collected for dues which brings our balance to $437.00. $164.00 was spent on shirts and 82.00 was spent on paint for the emblem which brings our balance to 191.00

signed Angel

May 5, 1990 12:00 P.M. Flaco's House

I Today was a quick meeting because we were late for the nation picnic. Nothing official was talked about. All matters were continued to next meeting.

signed Angel

May 12, 1990 6:30 P.M. Flaco's House

I. Violations: Wicked, Lil Al, Stony, Joker all got violations for owing more than $9.00 to the dues - 30 seconds.
    Stony got a violation for running from the Ambrose and leaving Angel hanging - 1 1/2 minutes.

II Joker lost his rank as a counsel member because he has been missing counsel meetings. Mousie is a new permanent member of the counsel and Loco + Killer are temporary members until Wedo + Shorty get out of jail.

III Insane Gus got another 1 month probation because he still hasn't proved himself.

IV $47.40 was collected today which brings our balance to $237.40

signed Angel

May 19, 1990 6:30 P.M. Flaco's house.

I. Violations: Joker got 30 seconds for missing the last meeting and 30 seconds for going over the $9.00 limit.
    Delfino got 30 seconds for not coming to the last meeting.

Stony got 15 seconds for smoking in the last meeting.
Sinbad took 15 seconds for smoking in the last meeting.

II. $64.00 was collected this week. $80.00 was spent on donations for brothers in need. $30.00 was sent to Gunner. That leaves $182.00 total for the dues.

Signed Angel

May 26, 1990 6:30 P.M. Flaco's House

I. Violations.
    Angel got a violation for taking the pistol out of the hood - 30 seconds.
    Mousie got a violation for missing the last meeting - 30 seconds.

II Delfino and Alex are off preliminary probation and are now official members.

III $164.00 was collected in dues today. $70.00 was used to buy a .22 caliber 6-shot and $150.00 was used to buy a 32 automatic. That makes the total $126.00 dollars in the dues.

Signed Angel

June 2, 1990 6:30 P.M. Flaco's House

I. Today we collected $26.00 in dues. That makes the total $152.00 in the dues.

II Short meeting

Signed Flaco

June 9, 1990 6:30 P.M. Flaco's House

I. Today we collected $83.00 for dues which is the total of $235.00 in balance.

II Today the boy's decided that Kasper and Shorty has to pay $20.00 each for the 357 pistol that we lost.

III And also we had a short meeting this week.

Signed Flaco

June 6, 1990 We had a get together meeting:
Flaco check
Prowler check
Kasper check
Stony check
Shy check
Shorty check
Mousie check
Lotto check
Turtle check
Killer
Delfino check
House check
Lil Angel check
Hitman check
Joker check
Sinbad check
Al check
Gus
Wicked check
Kato

June 11, 1990 we 7:00 pm had a get together meeting just for:
1) Hitman check
2) House check
3) Shy check
4) Shorty
5) Killer check
6) Mousie
7) Lotto check
8) Angel check
9) Prowler
10) Flaco check
11) Kasper check

June 11, 1990 7:00 Flaco's House

Today we had a meeting to talk about whether or not Cheryl was tricking to Nicole's mother. The next page was given to the boys by Nicole. Cheryl was found innocent and it came out that Nicole was with folks saying she is a Queen.

6-11-90

6/1 9:00 pm she left here in a Escort, 2 guys to pick up Joanne. I called Joanne and told her she can't go she said she would bring her back when they come to get her. She wasn't in the car. They dropped her off at 79 & Pulaski to beep Ramsey; Joanne called me back could find her anywhere.
6/2 I called Joanne- she said her ____ didn't come home-- also _____ was kicked out. Cheryl called, I ask where Nikki was she said in the hood by Flaco's partying, gang banging at _____ so we went by Flaco's they said they haven't seen her and ____ left 15 minutes ago.
6/3 Called police at 12:30 to report her missing.
6/4 Mike found her with ____ by accident. He brought her home.

June 16, 1990 6:30 P.M. Flaco's house.

I. Violations: Sinbad got 30 seconds for interrupting todays meeting and 60 seconds for interrupting last monday's meeting.
   Hitman got 30 seconds for interrupting todays meeting and 30 seconds for calling Sinbad an "Arab".
   Stony got 30 seconds for interrupting todays meeting.
   Kasper got 30 seconds for lieing on the crown.
   Turtle got 15 seconds for interrupting last Mondays meeting.
   Angel got 20 seconds for hitting Hitman in the arm.
   Mousie got 15 seconds for interrupting todays meeting.

II. Visitors: Oso and Neto sat in on our meeting representing Albany and 21st.

III. Dues: $29.00 was collected today in dues. $21.00 was sent to Whitey who is presently incarserated. Total balance $231.18

IV. Angel's trial has been continued for 2 weeks.

Signed Angel

June 23rd, 1990 6:30 P.M. Flaco's House.

I. New Rank: Shy is the new secretary as of next week.
   The vote for new cacique has been continued for 1 month.

The running contenders are Hitman, Kasper, Flaco, Wedo.

II $56.75 was collected today that brings our balance to $288.03

signed Angel

June 30, 1990

I. Mama's, Ann, Lisa became Queen's from Albany.

II. Wicked, Stoney, Joker got 1 minute for not having all the dues at the end of the month. Turtle got a 30 second for not having his dues in. Bob gets his next week.

III Mousie, Stony, Wicked, Turtle, and Sinbad got 30 seconds violation for getting out of hand during the meeting.

IV $250.00 dollars were taken from the dues to purchase a 9mm.

V $92.25 dollars ere collected for dues.

END NOTES:

[1] The NGCRC has collected gang cultural artifacts since 1990 and uses this enormous museum quality "display" in professional gang training seminars.
[2] The prison-based Latin King chapters may modify their constitution slightly to include new roles and positions needed in that environment. The best expert we know on this issue has shared these insights with gang intelligence agencies long ago (see: David Tibbetts, 1993, The Front Line, Drug Enforcement Administration, Chicago Field Division, Vol. 3, Issue 1, pp. 1,3,9).
[3] We get a lot of inquiries about how to get this book. It can be ordered through the American Correctional Association's publication division.
[4] Clearly, two Latin or Spanish gangs, the Ambrose and the Latin Counts existed before the Latin Kings. Some "gang awareness" pamphlets produced by Illinois police departments for purposes of training and public education therefore mistakenly identify the Latin Kings "as the oldest Hispanic street gang in Chicago". The Latin Kings might be the largest, but they are not the oldest continuing such ethnic enterprise.
[5] Rey and Rosario are from the Northwest side LKs, while Jusino is from the Northside LKs.
[6] Oversees the LK membership in the federal prison system.
[7] Perea, Zambrano, and Contreras are from the Southside LKs.
[8] See: George Papajohn, "Two Pictures of Hoover Emerge at Parole Hearing", Chicago Tribune, Feb. 8, 1996. Here Professor Dwight Conquergood admitted he had never talked to Hoover, but still felt he deserved a parole, because "racist attitudes and sensationalized media reports have demonized gangs" and that "a gang leader who had mended his ways could have a powerful impact".
[9] Sadly we must report a couple disturbing trends about this new book being distributed by the Gangster Disciples. First, the "book release" press conference was knowingly held on state property, a large auditorium at the southside campus of North Eastern Illinois University. And secondly, one of the volunteers helping with the distribution of the new GD book was an administrator of an alternative high school operated by DePaul University who promised the media she would use the book in her curriculum. And thirdly, that one of the 39

GDs indicted by the feds who got out on bail and was supposed to be on electronic home monitoring was at this same event carrying what looked like a walkie-talkie affecting a kind of "security role", as he told one reporter "I am a educational specialist now" working for a new GD front group that seeks to do research on African-American youth (the walkie-talkie may have been a converted RF-signal device because he was supposed to be on home electronic-monitoring). And fourthly, one of the figures in the at Englewood High School (where the GDs held their infamous "awards ceremony" several years ago) who until recently served as the assistant principal and who had joined in the efforts to gain Larry Hoover an early release, shows up as the main spokesman for the book release having written the foreward to the new GD book, while at the same time being on medical leave from the Chicago Public School system.

[10] As a "Prince" in the Latin Kings that had become a primary source of federal intelligence on the gang told us: "The Kush killing - that's where the evidence was for indicting Lord Gino, and it was never used".

[11] Our sources in the gang gave this account of what happened: "Pecina was doing security, that means protecting another Latin King leader above him, at the time. When you are doing security you are always armed. An officer wanted to shake him down, so Pecina pulled out the knife and told the guard "back up, I'm doing security on this guy". The guard in the cage saw what was going down, here is an inmate holding a knife in a life threatening way at a correctional officer and he shot the inmate, simple as that. But you see the Latin Kings thought it was a hit by the IDOC. IDOC investigators had said to the Latin Kings if you hit us, we will hit back, and what you see now is what you get out of a situation like that".

[12] Unfortunately, there are several possible such dates coming up in the near future: (1) October 29, 1994 represents the date for the slaying of Latin King member Antonio DeJesus, killed by basketball star and Maniac Latin Disciple member Dana Garrett, (2) October 28, 1995 represents the date for the slaying of Latin King member Marcelino Lopez, shotgunned at his home in the CHA Lathrop Homes projects at 2620 N. Hoyne Avenue in Chicago; and (3) October 18, 1990 three Latin Kings were killed at a gang party in Joliet by Michael Blackwell, who was convicted and sentenced to death but who recently won a new trial in Will County, Illinois because "prosecutors deliberately excluded too many women from the jury" (see: Jerry Shnay, "Jury Hears Dead Witness' Testimony : Man Being Retried in 3 Gang Kills", Chicago Tribune, Sept. 25, 1996). We advise any investigators dealing with the Latin Kings to keep track of such important "dates", because the Latin Kings profile as a group engaging in calculated symbolic retaliation. Explained one LK member serving time for murder: "my case was on an anniversary date, the poor guy who got shot, that was his unlucky day, December 31st was the date, at New Year's eve, that was the date Lord Gino ordered me to carry out the hit. I killed the chief of the Latin Stylers, they were an independent gang, not folks or people, their only chapter was North Avenue and Bell, the December 31st date was chosen because that's the day one of our guys was killed the year before, Lord Gino had wanted to kill this chief of the Latin Stylers for some time, but Lord Gino simply waited until December 31st, the anniversary date for when we lost one of our own."

[13] For example, during the October 1993 Chicago Gang Summit organized mostly by the GDs, there was little if any Latin gang involvement (people or folks) in any of the "affairs". However, at one southside church where one of the "affairs" for the 1993 Gang Summit was being held, a small contingent of the LKs did come in, they immediately took seats in the very rear of the church, when asked one of them said "we

are the Latin Kings", but they refused to answer any questions from any media representative at a time when any other gang (Crips, Vice Lords, GDs especially) were fighting each other to get in front of the TV camera.

AN UPDATE ON THE CHICAGO LATIN KINGS

INTRODUCTION
A year after the Journal of Gang Research featured the Chicago Latin Kings in a gang profile (Volume 4, Number 1, Fall, 1996: pp. 43-72) there were some significant developments with regard to the Chicago Latin Kings that are worthy of the update provided here.

LORD GINO: LATIN KING LEADER'S SCHEDULED RELEASE
On Friday morning, September 19th, 1997 the undisputed chief of the Chicago-based Latin Kings, Gustavo Colon, known among Latin Kings as "Lord Gino", was scheduled to be released from the Menard Correctional Center. At the time of his scheduled release from state custody, Lord Gino had been serving time at the Menard state prison in Illinois from a murder conviction in 1971. Clearly, this leader of the Latin Kings had served almost his entire sentence, and he was ready to be released back to the streets. News reports indicated that Lord Gino's gang had made preparations for the release of their leader by arranging for a limousine to pick him up from the prison.

SURPRISE: LORD GINO LEAVES STATE PRISON ONE DAY EARLY
However, Lord Gino was to leave the Menard prison one day early. Lord Gino was actually picked up at the Menard prison on Thursday morning, September 18th, 1997. It was not a limousine that Lord Gino would ride back to Chicago. It was not his gang that got him out of the prison a day early either. It was the fact that the United States Attorney for the Northern District of Illinois (Chicago) announced federal indictments against 14 members of the Latin Kings --- one of the indictments was against Lord Gino. So Lord Gino was picked up a day before his release and transferred by federal authorities to the Metropolitan Correctional Center (the federal detention center in Chicago).

THE NEW ROUND OF FEDERAL INDICTMENTS AGAINST THE LATIN KINGS
The new round of federal indictments against the Latin Kings were announced on 9-18-97. The indictments are similar in nature to those brought against the Gangster Disciples. In the Gangster Disciple prosecution, 39 GD leaders including Larry Hoover himself were convicted. The new round of federal indictments allege that the Latin King leader --- Gustavo "Lord Gino" Colon (age 43) --- was able to run his gang's business affairs from behind bars and that like the GD prosecution the "gang business" involved illegal drug sales.

Lord Gino and 13 others were indicted. Among the others indicted were Lord Gino's wife, Marisol Colon (age 31). The indictments allege that Lord Gino's wife was instrumental in the administration of the gang's business, including the drug business and being a conduit for the upward flow of money from the Latin King gang from activities such as protection payments involved in the drug business end of the gang.

Two of Lord Gino's top dogs were also indicted: (1) Jorge D. Martinez (age 32) from Chicago, and (2) Jose Souffront (age 28) from Springfield, Massachusetts.

Several ranking members of the Latin Kings in Chicago were also indicted: (1) Wilfredo Escobar (age 35), (2) Rene Herrera (age 23), (3) Ariel Ginjuama (age 43), (4) Christobal Ruffin (age 39), (5) Angel Nieves (age 47), (6) Caesar Diaz (age 24), (7) Luis Montalvo (age 48), and (8) Luis Valdez (age 39).

Others indicted included: (1) Charlie Alejandro (age 31), Puerto Rico, and Heriberto Sanchez (age 45).

Lord Gino would serve a life sentence in federal custody if he is convicted of the new federal charges.

The indictments describe how the Latin Kings require members to pay dues, how the gang amasses a treasury controlled by the elite leaders of the gang, how monies are set aside for retaining lawyers for the gang, how the gang buys firearms, etc. Much of this activity has been known for years by gang experts but not generally known to the public.

Appendix: J

GANG PROFILE: Black P. Stone Nation

INTRODUCTION

This gang, the Black P. Stone Nation (BPSN), has been shouting "Stones Run It" for over three decades. This gang is also unique in that several books have been written about it. However, as this gang profile will show, it has significantly changed over the years. For example, it now has a strong Islamic influence which pervades the various branches of this gang and its internal written codes. It is a gang which since its inception has been based on illegal drug income and violence.

Perhaps what is most interesting about this gang is the fact that Jeff Fort (who has been in federal prison for his role in seeking to do contract terrorism work for Moammar Gadhafi back in 1986, when Jeff Fort headed up the El Rukn gang) is actually the acknowledged top leader of the BPSN. Further, Jeff Fort continues to carry out significant gang management duties from the highest level of security in federal custody!

METHODOLOGY

The findings reported here come from a variety of sources and data presented are derived from several methodological approaches. The sources include: (1) historical sources, published and unpublished, as well as in-depth oral history interviews with persons having an intimate knowledge of the BPSN since its inception, (2) qualitative sources particularly detailed depth interviews with cooperative current and former members of the BPSN, (3) documents from the BPSN informants, and (4) quantitative data from survey research on BPSN members. Thus, both qualitative and quantitative methods were used in developing this gang profile.

The most important methodological issue that should be made here is what information was left out. A great many direct primary sources of data were used: interviews. Much of this information was not used here. Also, a wealth of other internal written materials on and about the BPSN gang were collected that have not been presented here. These internal gang documents tended to be historical matters and related to the creed and "constitution" of the gang. Given the length of this particular BPSN profile, these and other materials were not able to be presented here. Clearly, the information developed allowed for an entire book length report on the BPSN. What is presented here is therefore a synopsis of the major important issues about this gang.

WHEN AND WHERE DID THE BPSN BEGIN? LIKE VICE LORDS: IN A JUVENILE CORRECTIONAL CENTER (St. Charles Reform School)

Reverend John Fry, who became a close confidant and advisor to the BPSN through his tutelage of Jeff Fort and Eugene Hairston (the two founders of the BPSN), probably got very close to understanding the etiology of the BPSN. One caveat here, Rev. Fry was basically "duped" by the gang and substantial new historical information developed through interviews with other key figures during this time frame will reveal insights that are clearly not indicated in Rev. Fry's "gang apologist" account of the BPSN. Rev. Fry suggested that the

BPSN is more like a "prisoners organization", and that it in fact started in St. Charles. St. Charles is a state reform school in Illinois.

It is of historical interest that Rev. Fry places the birth of the BPSN in the time frame of 1957-1960. The Vice Lords began during that same time frame, also in St. Charles. The law of natural group opposition formation would hold that some other group had to exist besides the Vice Lords during that same time frame.

During the early 1960's the BPSN existed as a small ragtag group of misfits; juvenile delinquents of the classic type. It was not until the mid-1960's, in fact, until they came into contact with Rev. Fry that the BPSN became a formidable force. The BPSN would grow exponentially with the financial, social, political, and other support from Rev. Fry. This little known aspect of gang life in Chicago is explained elsewhere in this gang profile.

Another account of the origin of the BPSN comes from the book by R.T. Sale (1971, <u>The Blackstone Rangers: A Reporter's Account of Time Spent with the Street Gang on Chicago's South Side</u>, New York, Random House). Sale described the process by which consolidation, alliances, and mergers took place to allow the BPSN to grow to be a menacing force in Chicago:

"He told me then how, back in 1959, there had been a small street clique on 66th Street that had a modest ten members. Jeff Fort was the man at is head and controlled a turf known as Jackson Park. But there had been a rival gang, a small one as well...on 70th Street....the gangs clashed...They fought together many times. When they found that neither one could inflict a final, decisive defeat, they came together and talked. A short time later they combined" (Sale, 1971: pp. 63-64).

The federal indictments against the El Rukn leadership from an April, 1987 federal Grand Jury indicated that the gang really got off the ground and was up and running in the year 1966. This would be consistent with viewing it as a criminal gang at that point in time. The reasons will be made clear later in this gang profile, when we examine how the gang was able to rapidly increase its membership during the same time frame.

A gang training document for the Illinois Department of Corrections states that the origin of the name "Blackstone Rangers" began in 1959 because then Jeff Fort lived at 6536 South Blackstone and his clique gathered nearby at the corner of 64th and Blackstone.

WHO ARE THE BLACK STONES?

Members of the Black P. Stone Nation (BPSN) ride under the "five pointed" star, they are therefore "Brothers" or "People". The BPSN was first known as the Blackstone Rangers gang. In the Blackstone Rangers there were two gang leaders: Jeff Fort and Eugene "Bull" Hairston (AKA "King Bull", and "King Ball"). Only Jeff Fort survived. This helps to explain how Jeff Fort today is in fact the undisputed leader of the BPSN. Many gang experts thought Jeff Fort's group, the El Rukns, was "put out of business" and that his gang involvement ended when Jeff and many of his "generals" gained federal prison sentences in the late 1980's. Untrue. Jeff somehow took over control of the BPSN after the series of convictions against the El Rukn's.

The Black Stones today are the Black P. Stone Nation. It includes several branches all of which trace their history to the original Blackstone Rangers. These branches include: (1) Gangster Stones (led by "Moose") who control the southside, (2) Jet Black Stones, (3) Rubinites (AKA "Rubes"), (4) Future Stones, (5) P.R. Stones, (6) Corner Stones, and (7) the Almighty BPSN (led by Wakeeta, Jeff Fort's son). The Almighty BPSN is the largest branch. Another name the BPSN uses for "Jet Black Stones" is "Jack Black".

Prior to Jeff Fort's 1976 coup over the BPSN, there was also a separate group known as the "Titanic Stones" that had been considered BPSN. That is, until Jeff Fort ordered them killed. Also, the Mickey Cobra Stones were a founding branch of the BPSN, again until Jeff Fort had their leader killed, and the Mickey Cobras then splintered off from the BPSN.

COBRA STONES: SPLINTERED FROM THE BPSN, BECAME MICKEY COBRAS

The "Cobra Stones" were a part of the BPSN at one time. The Cobra Stones was from the beginning of the BPSN to 1977 an official branch of the BPSN, and this gang faction was led by Mickey Cogwell. In the early days of the BPSN, Mickey Cogwell as in fact a founding member of the "Main 21" and was therefore a leader within the BPSN. Cogwell was one of those convicted in 1972 for defrauding the federal government grant of $927,000 (U.S. Office of Economic Opportunity) that helped the BPSN get a jump start on gang organization in Chicago in connection with Rev. Fry's church sponsored "gang program". This gang experienced the "Splintering effect" when Jeff Fort had Mickey Cogwell killed on February 25, 1977. At this point the gang became a separate entity that is today known as the Mickey Cobras gang. The Mickey Cobras refused to join the "El Rukn" leadership of Jeff Fort.

In fact, in 1976 Jeff Fort declared his intent to kill Mickey Cogwell in a large BPSN gang meeting. Shortly thereafter (February 25, 1977), Cogwell was in fact killed. Cogwell had been working as an organizer for a southside union at the time of his death. In 1970 the commander of the Gang Intelligence Unit for the Chicago Police Department portrayed Cogwell as the link between gangs and organized crime. According to one high ranking BPSN informant (among the many interviewed for this profile): "they was at war with us in 1994", thus the early history of friendship is not a guarantee of civility in relationship with the BPSN. Today the Mickey Cobras are "People" or "Brothers" in gang nation alliances, just like the BPSN. However, the Mickey Cobras exist in areas of the southside that compete for membership with the BPSN. And no one could say that just because both the BPSN and the Mickey Cobras today are a "people" or "brothers" gang that they are in any sense cooperative or friendly towards each other.

This is a good example of how gang alliance systems involving competing criminal offenders are not likely to be readily manipulated for purposes of "gang truces": the enmity between these gangs that should theoretically be "together" in an alliance against rival gangs is a long standing problem that has festered over the years. Still, today few seem to recognize that gang apologists and representatives of the gangs themselves who attract mass media attention with their claim of being able to "create gang peace treaties" are basically hustlers exploiting public ignorance on these rather complex issues.

Today the Mickey Cobras are known formally as the "Kingdom of the Mickey Cobra New Movement", AKA "Almighty Cobra Nation", AKA "Almighty Mickey Cobras Nation". In their original identity, they were known as the Egyptian King Cobras. In their third generation, they now like the BPSN, have a strong Islamic influence. The Mickey Cobras now have their own unique written constitution and by-laws. These documents show a strong Islamic influence, just like those of the modern-day BPSN. So what we have here are basically two Black gangs operating under some variety of Islamic beliefs that are in an armed struggle with each other. The NGCRC does maintain a file on the Mickey Cobras, like almost all gangs that have been tracked since 1990, but it is not a gang whose force strength and threat analysis ratings currently justifies a separate "gang profile" in this journal.

THE BPSN, LIKE OTHER GANGS, EXPLOITED LIBERAL CONFUSION

The BPSN got a major boost from sympathetic liberals willing to help the gang. One keen observer described it this way:

"These white liberals were awed by the potential political power of the Mighty P. Stone Nation, and they attempted to translate this power into constructive activities. While this in itself was noteworthy, the romantic image many had of the street gang made it difficult for them to realize the magnitude and complexity of the problem." (Useni Eugene Perkins, 1987, Explosion of Chicago's Black Street Gangs: 1900 to Present, Chicago: Third World Press).

As discussed later in this gang profile, the largest help to the gang came from a member of the clergy. A Presbyterian pastor named Rev. John Fry was the culprit. Rev. Fry basically turned over his church and the churches resources to the gang. If that meant using the church's money for bailing out gang leaders, fine. If that meant allowing the gang to hold its citywide meetings in the church, fine. For a description of the significance of this error of large scale gang meetings, one of the most dramatic accounts is that provided from one of the youths who attended one of these events and who later attended Columbia College: "D to the Knee ! Stone to the Bone!" by Dino Malcolm (Best of Hair Trigger: A Story Workshop Anthology, pp. 81-91, Chicago: Columbia College Writing Department). It describes how the very appearance of gangs being able to use a large church to hold a large gang meeting adds an important resource to the benefit structure of the gang as an organization. Most gang analysts today recognize that a gang will predictably exploit any resource it can. Thus, in a true zero-tolerance policy no such resource should be made available to a gang that could make it stronger or more organizationally effective (i.e., increasing its ability to recruit youths, adding to its legitimacy, etc).

Unfortunately, many Americans have yet to realize this important lesson about the history of gangs. For example, when Wallace "Gator" Bradley (the chief political spokesperson for the Gangster Disciples and their political wing known as "21st Century V.O.T.E.") was able to go to the White House and personally meet with President Bill Clinton on January 24th, 1994, subsequent pictures published in newspapers of this "photo session" with the President of the United States (see Chicago Tribune, Friday, February 18, 1994; section 2, p. 6) expectedly added much new momentum to the GD's political movement in Chicago. Apparently, Gator had the audacity to introduce himself to President Clinton as representing a group called "Better Growth and Development": i.e., using the "put on" that they are not Black Gangster Disciples (BGDs), a criminal drug gang, but are something "pro-social". But, historically at least, many liberals have been sucked into the beguiling language used by gang leaders as will be evidenced by the important role of Rev. Fry in the historical development of the BPSN.

ESTABLISHING THE BPSN AS A STREET GANG GOVERNMENT

Rev. Fry selected as the director of the First Presbyterian Church's¹ "Ranger Staff" one Chuck Lapaglia. Rev. Fry's 1973 book explains how they helped the BPSN (Jeff Fort and Bull Hairston) deal with their sudden expanded membership base, particularly their fear of police informants. As described in the 1973 book, Fry and Lapaglia took Fort and Hairston to a luncheon to discuss organizational advice to the BPSN.

Lapaglia advised Jeff Fort and Bull Hairston to "age grade": create a two-tiered organization, one level for younger members, and one level for older "reliable" presumably more hardcore "Stones".

As described in Fry's 1973 book, the two gang leaders immediately took this advice to heart. Jeff Fort headed up the younger faction. Bull Hairston headed up the older faction (see Fry, 1973: pp. 16- 23).

Throughout both of Fry's self-aggrandizing books, he recognizes that gangs like the BPSN are dangerous and armed offenders. How then do we account for the fact that Fry and his assistants in the church and its programs helped the BPSN to become a "street gang government". Which would mean an armed criminal street gang government, capable of exercising the most formidable power in the African-American communities in which the BPSN existed. What kind of unique spiritual insight did Fry have to think that it would be a good idea for the African-American communities of Chicago to have "more organized street gangs"?

Our latest intelligence is that Rev. Fry has assiduously avoided any media interviews regarding these issues for a very long time. Further, our information is that he is currently working in a remote area of the USA that is virtually untouched by the aftermath of helping gangs to become more organizationally sophisticated. The need to debrief persons like Fry remains an important element of developing gang knowledge, so anyone who would be interested in this type of assignment, please contact the NGCRC.

THE GANG SYMBOLS OF THE BPSN

The crescent moon and the five pointed star are today important symbols used by the BPSN because of the strong Islamic influence in this gang. The pyramid with one side showing twenty-one small rectangles that could be "bricks" is another important symbol that also refers to the "Main 21": the founding fathers of this gang. Jeff Fort was one of these founding fathers. Most of the other original "main 21" are dead. The "main 21" was like a commission for organized crime and still functions today. When someone on the "main 21" makes a mistake or gets too close to competing with OG's like Jeff Fort, they just seem to die violently, and someone new takes their "seat" on the "main 21".

Other symbols associated with the BPSN include their code words: such as "C.S.A." which stands for "Cold Soldier Army". The name of their "set" or "hood" is also commonly used in their graffiti: an example would be "Terror Town", which refers to Chicago's southeast side. An expression of solidarity for this gang is also commonly used: "Stones Run It", meaning the BPSN are "in control" or are "very powerful".

The two word phrase "Chief Malik" will often appear in BPSN graffiti. This phrase ("Chief Malik") refers to one of the aliases of Jeff Fort. Jeff Fort is known to the BPSN as "Chief Malik" (pronounced "malique"). Jeff Fort's earlier AKA's included: "Black Prince" and "Angel".

Contemporary BPSN members can often be identified at a distance: they like to wear their hair in braids.

THE ORIGINAL MAIN 21 MEMBERS

At the top were Eugene "Bull" Hairston (#1) and Jeff Fort (#2). Other early "O.G.'s" in the Black Stones included the following members who are not listed in any order of hierarchical power (see: Chicagoland Monthly, June, 1979):

#a George Rose (AKA "Watusi", "Mad Dog")
#b Lee "Stone" Jackson (DECEASED)
#c William Troop (AKA: "Sweet Pea", "Sweet Jones") (DECEASED)
#d Melvin Bailey (AKA: "Lefty")
#e Herbert Stevens (AKA: "Thunder")

#f Lawrence White (AKA: "Tom Tucker")
#g Adam Battiste (AKA: "Leto")
#h Sylvester Hutchins (AKA: "Hutch")
#i Charles Franklin (AKA: "Bosco")
#j Theotis Clark (AKA: "Thee")
#k Henry Cogwell (AKA: "Mickey") (DECEASED)
#l George Martin (AKA: "Porgy") (DECEASED)
#m Andrew D. McChristian (AKA: "A.D."
#n Fletcher Puch (AKA: "Bo Peep", "Old Man")
#o Edwin Codwell (AKA: "Little Charlie", "Caboo")
#p Leroy Hairston (AKA: "Mr. Maniac", "Baby Bull")[2]
#q Charles Edward Bey (AKA: "Benbolaman", "Bear")
#r Herman Holmes (AKA: "Moose")
#s Moses Robert Jackson (AKA: "Dog")
#t Paul Martin (AKA: "Crazy Paul") (DECEASED)
#u Lamar Bell (AKA: "Bop Daddy")
#v Johnnie Jones (AKA: "Cool Johnnie")
#w Bernard Green (AKA: "Droop", "The Colonel")

SPORTSWEAR AND GANG CLOTHING

When the "Blackstone Rangers" first appeared, their distinguishing clothing was a red felt beret.

When Jeff Fort returned to Chicago from Milwaukee after his first federal sentence and started the "Moorish American" group (circa 1975-76) that would evolve into the El Rukns, their distinguishing clothing item was a red fez cap.

BPSN members wear an assortment of highly stylized, expensive air-brushed gang designs on t-shirts and sweat shirts and hats. There are numerous examples of these in the National Gang Cultural Artifact collection maintained by the National Gang Crime Research Center for its gang training services. Most typical is a BPSN gang argot expression such as "ALL IS WELL" or a logo symbol such as the use of the pyramid.

One of the most popular items of gang apparel for BPSN members today is their sportswear line. This particular style of clothing is clearly gang designed. It has the large words "Black Stone" on it, but between these two words is the crescent moon with a five pointed star. Underneath this rocker reads the words: "ATHLETIC WEAR, Chicago, New York, Los Angeles". These are three of the larger cities where the BPSN operates today. A casual observer would look at this t-shirt and never figure out the put-on.

THE HISTORY OF THE B.P.S.N.

The BPSN may have started in 1959, making it as old as the Vice Lords, but it did not really become a strong and institutionalized gang until the mid-1960's. It existed side by side with the Devil's Disciples. The BPSN first gained strength up and along Blackstone Avenue on Chicago's southside. Their main enemy was not the Vice Lords who had existed since 1959. Rather the main enemy of the BPSN was the Devil's Disciples, who existed in closer proximity and competed for gang loyalty among disaffected southside youths. The Devil's Disciples would later become three gangs: the Gangster Disciples (led by Larry Hoover), the Black Gangsters (AKA: New Breed, led by Booney Black), and the Black Disciples (led by Jerome "Shorty" Freeman).

SACRED CALENDAR DATES FOR THE BPSN

A sacred day for the BPSN is August 8th. Jeff Fort selected August 8th as the "anniversary celebration day" for the BPSN. August 8th is also called the "feast day" for BPSN members. The first annual "feast day" occurred on August 8th, 1976. It was held in Milwaukee, Wisconsin. The reason Jeff Fort selected August 8th as the "feast day" or time for the annual gang celebration is that it commemorated the anniversary of planning the murder of Chicago Police Officer James Alfono.

Officer Alfono was a Gang Intelligence Officer doing surveillance in a car around 67th and Stoney Island, when the BPSN shot out the street lights, and then shot through the trunk of the car with a high-powered rifle, killing Officer Alfono instantly.

ALLIES OF THE BPSN

The BPSN has always been a "people" or "brothers" gang. It therefore rides under the five pointed star if it uses any star. It is most closely aligned with the Vice Lords and Latin Kings, owing to the prison connection for gang alliances. It is clear, though, that some other "people" gangs like the Mickey Cobras are dedicated enemies of the BPSN even though both had the same background. As will be explained, the Mickey Cobra's are no longer "Cobra Stones", due to the gang splintering phenomenon. In fact, the Mickey Cobra's remain mortal enemies of the BPSN even though both gangs are "people". But for all practical purposes, the main day to day enemy or rival of the BPSN are members of the Gangster Disciples gang.

THE ROLE OF ISLAMIC RELIGIOUS BELIEFS IN THE BPSN

None of the previous books written about the BPSN describe the role that Islamic religious beliefs play in this gang. This is partially a problem of timing, the books are older and predated the development where Jeff Fort's influence over the BPSN brought about this religious influence. It is important to note, however, that this is not regarded as a legitimate religious influence. Rather the role of religious beliefs in the gang serves a two-fold purpose: (1) it gives a cloak of legitimacy and social acceptability for an organization that at its core is basically criminal in nature, and in correctional settings is often necessary for purposes of holding "gang meetings", thus having religious beliefs as the outward appearance of the gang gives it certain protective powers, and (2) the religious beliefs add to the level of social control that the gang exercises over its members, and it also provides an ideology useful for purposes of "moral neutralization" (i.e., the beliefs help members to justify their criminal activities).

Thus, like a cult, the stronger and more extreme the beliefs, often the more the members are pressed into submission to the centralized authoritarian organizational structure of the gang.

Thus, what Jeff Fort learned from his association with Rev. Fry was that having some association with or appearance of a religious operation was very functional for an effective gang organization. The other gangs that have come to have such a religious component to their internal belief system may have simply copied the tradition started by Jeff Fort. This is another way in which gangs exploit a free society: they know that religion is a "sacred" aspect of society that most do not want regulated, inspected, monitored, or investigated. So the ability to predict the future organizational styles of gangs comes from knowing that gangs will exploit the "rights" and "freedoms" that any society offers.

The BPSN have adopted a decidedly Islamic belief system. Elsewhere in this gang profile we will examine, in detail, some of these aspects of the Islamic influence. The one question we can answer here relates to WHY Jeff Fort began this tradition. It would appear that Jeff Fort was looking for a way to overcome the federal parole restrictions about "gang association" when he was first released from his first federal prison sentence after being put away for embezzling federal monies in the Rev. Fry "gang program".

A gang training document in use by the Illinois Department of Corrections states[3]:

"The El Rukn Moorish Science Temple of America's name appeared in March of 1976 coinciding with the release of Fort from the federal prison. Fort tried to join the Black Muslims and the Regional Church of the Moorish Science Temple of America. Both groups rejected him and his followers. Fort then started his own religious organization."

EARLY INVOLVEMENT IN POLITICS

During the "El Rukn" phase of the BPSN developmental history, the gang was similar to other Chicago gangs in trying to get involved in electoral politics. The El Rukns established an organization called the "Grassroots Independent Voters of Illinois". The involvement continues today, but as will be seen later in this gang profile, by a new name and a new organizational identity.

THE HISTORY OF JEFF FORT AND THE BPSN

Jeff Fort must be understood in terms of the different phases of his gang development: (1) his original years in relationship to getting liberal do-gooders to obtain foundation funding and government grants for him to abuse, (2) his stint in federal custody as a result of that early activity, (3) his return from living outside of Chicago and organizing the Moorish American "group" and his involvement in an anti-nazi protest group on Chicago's southwest side called the "Martin Luther King Movement", (4) his subsequent organizing of the "El Rukn" gang in 1976, (5) the federal prosecution of his "El Rukn" gang, and (6) the aftermath of the federal prosecution of El Rukns and his current ability to continue to reach out to gang troops in Chicago.

History of Black Stones and Jeff Fort: Their Help From Rev. John R. Fry (1965-1971)

A Presbyterian pastor named John R. Fry had an earthly mission but was beguiled by gangs into helping them grow stronger in Chicago. Reverend Fry was perhaps the first major American gang apologist. His two books describe this well: Fire and Blackstone[4] (1969, J.B. Lippincott Company, New York) and Locked-Out Americans: A Memoir (1973, Harper & Row, New York). Rev. Fry became the pastor at the First Presbyterian Church of Chicago in 1965. Under his spiritual leadership the congregation studied such books as Frantz Fanon's The Wretched of the Earth (a leftist classic) and thus this church took a decidedly political turn: where the City of Chicago was trying to suppress the gang problem, the church thought it could coopt and reform the gangs.

What happens in 1965-1971 under the influence of Rev. Fry later becomes an expensive historical lesson about gangs. Obviously, with federal funding and foundation funding and private donors, the money did come in that allowed Rev. Fry's church to start its gang program. The church had a close relationship with TWO (The Woodlawn Organization), indeed Fry's 1969 book claims the church was vital in getting TWO started. So the gang program was based at TWO. The gang program accomplished two things: (1) it gave existing gang leaders like Eugene "Bull" Hairston and Jeff Fort further legitimacy and influence in their community, and (2) it provided direct financial support to the gangs through the payroll system that would later be the basis for federal convictions. The community did not benefit, but the gangs did benefit. The community got weaker, the gangs got stronger.

The gangs were not coopted, nor reformed. What did happen is now a historical fact: the influx of money and the added benefit of being able to add the legitimacy of a mainstream religious institution (the First Presbyterian Church of Chicago) to the defense of the gang and its leaders did one thing --- it institutionalized the Black P. Stone Nation in Chicago and gave impetus to other gangs. Sadly, the historical record is clear here: this was tantamount to an insidious "experiment" on the African-American community that feels the most immediate effects of violence from gangs such as the BPSN and the Devil's Disciples (which would later become three separate gangs: Gangster Disciples, Black Gangsters, and the Black Disciples --- See respective gang profiles in Journal of Gang Research, Volume 3, Number 1 through Volume 3, Number 3).

The BPSN did not "fade away" into prosocial legitimacy under the tutelage of Rev. Fry. Fry indicated, in fact, that "between April, 1966, and the end of the year, the organization grew from 500 to 1,500 members. During the twelve months of 1967 the number doubled" (Fry, 1973: p. 15). So the BPSN did in fact rapidly flourish from such economic, political, and social nourishment is what Chicago history shows.

Both of Rev. Fry's books make him appear saintly and persecuted. Not surprisingly, he has some bitter words for law enforcement officers. The legacy of Rev. Fry's unconditional positive regard for the welfare of gang members can still be seen today in Chicago. It allowed a small gang group to become further organized and even more powerful. As this gang profile will also show, Rev. Fry totally failed in any proselytizing mission: this gang today is very Islamic. What gang leaders like Jeff Fort did learn in this early formative stage was that the cloak of religion gave legal and social benefits to the gang. So there was an enduring impact from Rev. Fry. Unfortunately, it was completely detrimental in the long run.

One other very important fact needs to be repeated here that is discussed elsewhere in Chicago gang history (see An Introduction to Gangs, Wyndham Hall Press, 1994). Many mistakenly recall this aspect of Chicago's gang history as having an important connection to the University of Chicago. That is not true. Rev. Fry existed on the geographical fringe of the University of Chicago but had nothing to do with the university per se, other than hiring some staff from its students. There was no official connection. Rev. Fry was an independent actor who basically turned his church over lock, stock and barrel to the Blackstone Rangers (i.e., BPSN).

History of BPSN and Jeff Fort: His First Federal Sentence for Defrauding the Chicago "Gang Program".

The foundation and government funding in the 1960's was as confused then is it is today regarding the role of active gang members. Rev. Fry's influence in the late 1960's allowed funding specifically to hire active gang members. The first "heat" came in 1968 when the United States Senate began an investigation into such a "Job Training Program". In March of 1972 three BPSN members were convicted of conspiring to defraud the federal government. Jeff Fort was one of these, and he got his first federal prison sentence. When Jeff Fort finished his federal sentence, he relocated temporarily to Milwaukee, Wisconsin. Jeff Fort continued to have a strong connection to Milwaukee even after this time period.[5]

To be able to understand the societal benefits of targeted prosecution against gang leaders, one must understand the pressure that was building due to the fear that gangs like the BPSN were able to generate on the streets of Chicago. Fortunately, there is a book available on this topic. It is the 1971 book by R.T. Sale: The Blackstone Rangers: A Reporter's Account of Time Spent with the Street Gang on Chicago's South Side (New York, Random House).

Sale's book about the BPSN is 186 pages of a "novel or narrative" informal writing style. It makes no effort to really understand the larger literature on gangs, therefore it is not a professional contribution. It does describe the flow of government money, particularly Rev. Fry 's involvement with the BPSN. It provides an accurate summary of how Senator

McClellan headed the committee to investigate allegations of wrongdoing with the federal money that did wind up in the hands of the BPSN (Sale, 1971: pp. 86-87). It also documents the angst of Chicago's civic leaders in response to the BPSN being able to benefit from federal funding.

The record is clear on a related point, however, that Jeff Fort and another gang leader (Mickey Cogwell) were in fact invited to the inauguration of Richard Nixon in 1968.[6] Some speculated this might have been due to the BPSN helping republicans. The record indicates that Jeff Fort did not attend, but sent one of his henchmen instead to the inauguration.

What is also an interesting part of the true history of the BPSN, as documented by Sale (1971: pp. 66-67) is how tension was induced between street gangs like the BPSN and the Black Panthers that were operating in the same areas of Chicago's southside. The evidence seems to be that Jeff Fort's gang were in fact paid by someone to engage in conflict with the Black Panthers, thus preventing the Black Panthers from effectively operating in certain areas (i.e., distributing/selling Black Panther newspapers, etc). No evidence has yet been reported on who exactly provided such funding to the BPSN to covertly suppress the Black Panther operations in Chicago (see: Knox, An Introduction to Gangs, 1994 for further background information).

However, it established a clear pattern of behavior for Jeff Fort's gang: a willingness to do "dirty tricks", for a price. Jeff Fort moved to Milwaukee, Wisconsin upon his release from federal custody. This is significant, because later evidence would show that the El Rukn gang that he would form after the "Moorish American" transition period (when he returned to Chicago), would in fact be involved in drug sales operations in Milwaukee. Coincidentally, Rev. Fry's "gang director", Charles LaPaglia, was working in an educational program in Milwaukee at the time Jeff Fort was released from Leavenworth on March 12, 1976 and had some role in Jeff's parole plan.

Jeff Fort's Return to Chicago: A Moorish American Fighting Nazis in Marquette Park

Jeff Fort returned to Chicago, Rev. Fry was long gone, but Jeff now had his own "religious" identity. Jeff Fort adopted the cloak of a religious front: the Moorish American (AKA: MSTA, Moorish Science Temple of America). Today, this religious group has been adapted as a "front" for other prison inmates throughout the USA and is regarded in many correctional facilities as an STG. The time frame here was middle 1970's. It was during this period (circa 1976) that Jeff Fort's mob adopted the use of the large red fez caps, similar in appearance to those worn by Shriners.

Jeff Fort had returned at a time when a Neo-nazi group led by Frank Collin (National Social Party of America, NSPA) had established its operations in the southwest side neighborhood of Marquette Park. Jeff Fort started the Martin Luther King Movement as an umbrella organization to fight the nazis: protesting the nazi presence, marching on Marquette Park, etc. Jeff Fort at the time had use of a small warehouse in Englewood that was used as a staging area for these protests.

Jeff Fort's El Rukn Stage of Gang Involvement

In the El Rukn stage, Jeff Fort focused almost exclusively on "gang business": selling illegal drugs. This allowed him to buy a building that became known as the "Fort", or his own personal "Mosque". Jeff Fort's gang members in the El Rukn's were a hardcore group of older felons. Once becoming an El Rukn, the gang member changed his name by adding the "-el" suffix. In this fashion, "Shay Bilker" became "Shay Bilker-el". The gang members used this name in everything they did: any paperwork, student loans, applying for government programs, welfare, etc. Thus it became easy to "pick off" the El Rukns on a computer in the late 1970's and throughout the 1980's, all one had to do was search the last name field in any file for the character string "-el".

Jeff Fort's El Rukn gang also had operations in Milwaukee, Wisconsin. This was simply an extension of the Chicago-based drug sales operation. The evidence for this is clear. As described in the gang profile of the Black Disciples (Journal of Gang Research, Volume 3, No. 3, Spring, 1996, p. 48): Louis Hoover (an El Rukn) "was one of two generals who ran El Rukn's Milwaukee drug operation in the late 1970's and 1980's (source: Chicago Tribune, May 27, 1992, section 2, p. 9, Matt O'Connor).

The best source of information places the birth of the El Rukn identity at an April, 1976 event. In April, 1976, according to federal indictment information, Jeff Fort held a large meeting for members of the BPSN at which he announced that the name of the organization was from then on to be known as the "El Rukn's" and that he, Jeff Fort, was the sole leader of the El Rukn Nation. The meeting has held at a site the gang called "The Camp" (located at 4233 South Indiana Avenue in Chicago). Also at this same large BPSN meeting involving all branches, Jeff Fort basically abolished the Main 21 as leaders and replaced them with his hand-picked generals and his top cronies. These new management staff for the gang included: Felix Mayes, Jake Crowder, Alan Knox, Derrick Porter, Floyd Davis, Walter Pollard, Edward Williams, Roger Bowman, Bernard Green, Thomas Bates, Fred Giles, Eddie Franklin, and Andrew Fort.

So in April, 1976 Jeff Fort basically achieved a complete coup over the BPSN. Jeff Fort at the meeting declared Mickey Cogwell, who had been a founding member of the "Main 21", to be an enemy. Jeff Fort made clear the need to murder Mickey Cogwell because of disloyalty to the "Main 21". Further, on February 25, 1977 Mickey Cogwell was in fact killed.

On April 14, 1978 the El Rukns formed their own corporation to purchase a number of apartment buildings and hotels in Chicago. The corporation was called the "El-Pyramid Maintenance and Management Corporation". One of the first buildings to be purchased was the property at 3945 - 3959 South Drexel in Chicago, previously it had been the "Oakland Square Theater" building but under Jeff Fort's ownership became known as the "El Rukn Grand Major Temple of America", AKA "The Fort". The "Fort" was demolished in June of 1990.

Many gang experts did not realize, then, that El Rukn empire was basically the top leadership of the BPSN. Thus, putting the El Rukn leadership out of business through federal prosecution would still leave intact a vast original organization known as the BPSN. In fact, today Jeff Fort still rules over the BPSN. Further, it will be shown in this profile that Jeff Fort continues to micro-manage the gang even from behind bars in the most secure federal correctional facility in America today!

The Prosecution of the El Rukn's

What appears to have brought an abrupt end to Jeff Fort's El Rukn drug-selling empire was the fact that he made overtures to a hostile foreign nation about contracting to carry out acts of political terrorism. This involved Libya's leader Moiamar Khadafy (see Bert Useem and Peter Kimball, 1989, p. 77, States of Siege: U.S. Prison Riots, 1971-1986, New York: Oxford University Press). The idea was Jeff Fort would be willing to blow up some planes in America for a large price.

To understand the complexity of the situation where a modern American street gang would be willing to perform terrorist acts for a hostile foreign government, we really need to return to the very first issue of this gang journal (Volume

One, Number One, 1992: Views From the Field, "The Future is Here Today: Street Gang Trends", pp. 87-90, by Robert W. Dart). As Dart explained (then commander of the gang unit for the Chicago Police Department, and now director of security for the Chicago Transit Authority):

"In the summer of 1986, Libyan operatives from Colonel Moammar Gadhafi met for the first of two clandestine meetings in Panama with Chicago street gang representatives. Speculation about the purpose of these meetings ranged from negotiations for asylum from prosecution in Chicago to seeking money to carry on terrorist activities. It was then that they (i.e., the El Rukns) purchased a LAW missile from FBI agents with the intent to create terrorism by targeting a law enforcement facility or specific gang officers, or both. Later it was reported that this gang sent members half way around the world to Libya and other middle east countries" (Dart, 1992: p. 89).

This was obviously the turning point for the El Rukns. And the beginning of their demise, that is in that form. Hence with clear gang involvement in terrorism, federal prosecution came swiftly and strongly. Jeff Fort received an 80 year federal prison sentence for plotting to engage in acts of terrorism in the U.S. on behalf of Libya. If he ever did serve all the federal sentence, he would still face a consecutive sentence of another 75 years in Illinois' prison system for a 1988 murder conviction. So thanks to effective federal and state prosecution, Jeff Fort is never going to see the streets again.

The El Rukn Prosecution Aftermath: The Federal Prosecutor is Fired

We probably should have mentioned that some problems from a defense point of view did emerge during the federal El Rukn prosecution. The issue was about allowing government witnesses certain "privileges" even though they too were in custody. The lax supervision accorded some of these witnesses resulted in allegations that the prosecution witnesses were able to consume drugs and engage in sex while in federal custody. The bottom line: the leading assistant U.S. Attorney who prosecuted and won convictions against over fifty El Rukns including their leader Jeff Fort, William R. Hogan, Jr. was fired on April 11th, 1996.

Fifteen El Rukns who had been convicted were able to win retrials and many others were able to plea bargain for lighter federal prison sentences, because their defense attorneys petitioned a federal judge that there was prosecutorial misconduct. It was never clearly established that the "misconduct", if any, was attributable to U.S. Attorney Hogan. The only factual issue made public, because of the secrecy being maintained by the U.S. Department of Justice on this issue, was the existence of a 1989 memorandum from another federal attorney that mentioned possible drug abuse among some of the governments witnesses that were in custody. The judicial issue here was that of suppressing evidence.

The untold story about the aftermath of the El Rukn prosecution is that Jeff Fort is still in the drivers seat and continues to have remarkable influence over street gang activities even from behind federal bars. The new evidence accumulated for this gang profile may force some serious effort to reconsider ways of dealing with gang leaders in custody.

JEFF FORT'S INFLUENCE OVER THE BPSN WHILE CURRENTLY IN FEDERAL PRISON

We don't know how he does it, all we know is what we see: Jeff Fort is still able to influence the BPSN even while currently in federal prison. One BPSN informant gave us a current photograph of Jeff Fort that shows Jeff in his cell: his cell is adorned with an Islamic picture, he has a entire "rack" of commissary goodies in his cell in the photo suggesting he is not wanting for much. And the photo shows Jeff holding his right hand up where the first index finger is pointed upwards. This is actually a fairly new gang hand sign for the BPSN that few gang experts seem to recognize: it means "we are one". Jeff Fort appears very muscular in this photo. This photo of Jeff in his federal prison cell has been copied and recopied many times by BPSN members who keep it as a memento of their leader.

JEFF FORT'S LETTERS TO THE BPSN TROOPS: NEW LITERATURE AND STARTING A NEW POLITICAL FRONT ORGANIZATION IN ILLINOIS

A letter bearing Jeff Fort's current BPSN gang name (Khalifa-Abdul Malik) and dated 3-13-95 demonstrates how the gang helped the GD front group "21st Century V.O.T.E." to stage protests in Chicago as well as how quickly the BPSN then were able to start their own political front group. Here is the full text of the letter:

"In the name of Allah, the Beneficient, the Merciful.

As-salaam Alaikum.

Wali! It is a good demonstration as far as the assistance you have been giving 21st VOTE. But, I feel we should have our own political base, that we can call our own. We should train our own brothers and sisters, even the ones that are not into organization's.

I want you to start training our brothers and sisters, but we must first get a political base and choose a name for our base before any training takes place. We should also reach out to our allies heads to get their support. I want Wai-keeta, Jack Black and Sandman, also Moose to support our movement. I want each one of the four to put up one hundred members each, which make a total of four hundred to be trained by you. I want Musambay to work with you. Get back with me about this! 3-13-95."

Why was Jeff Fort jealous of the GD political front group (21st Century V.O.T.E.)? Because one of the main operatives of 21st V.O.T.E. (Wallace "Gator" Bradley) was able to meet with President Bill Clinton in the White House's oval office in early 1994, and this legitimacy given to the GD gang provided a lot of political momentum that allowed the GD's to run several candidates for local elections in Chicago in 1995 as well. What happened to the BPSN after this letter from the Chief Malik? Well, things happened fast.

A typed memorandum addressed to "All Mahdi's" appeared quickly to provide new marching orders to the BPSN troops. Mahdi's are BPSN with any rank. The "Chairman" here is the outside BPSN leader who manages the BPSN members for the Malik. We are providing this memorandum in its entirety here:

"To: All Mahdi's
From: The Chairman
Re: Programs and Projects
Date: April 13, 1995

Before starting let us say 20 to the Honorable Body of Mahdi's.

As Chairman for the next 3 years I want to first outline a few Programs that will be Implemented throughout this City, throughout this State and throughout this Country, that will produce the Political, Economic and Social Growth of Our Nation.

As Responsible members of the Governing Body, it is your duty and responsibility to Plan, Organize and Implement Proclamation 1-A and Any and All Additions and/or Attachments to it.

Through unity, political action and community service, we can and shall reach our goals.
UNITY
We all bear witness to the indisputable fact that "In unity there is strength and in people (numbers) there is power". Therefore, when we pull all of our people together and we all aid and assist in the following programs and work towards the same goals, we will have the political power to influence the decisions that are made that affect our everyday lives. This will be done through voter education & voter registration.

We will have the economic power to open and operate legitimate businesses, real estate and provide jobs for our people.

We will also develope social power by instilling pride, self-respect, honor and love, truth, peace, freedom and justice in the hearts and minds of the membership.

Our Nation will be networking with organizations all over the City. Representatives must be selected, groomed and prepared so they can be dispatched to establish lines of communication and working relationships in the areas of politics, business, jobs, peace in the communities and any other area that contributes to the uplift of the Afro-American people and community.

Our first network and relationship has been established with an organization called C.R.E.S.T. (Citizens Responding to Emergency Situations Today). They are lawfully chartered and headquartered at 2440 E. 75th Street (75th & Phillips). They will be holding a membership drive seeking volunteers to aid and assist in implementing their programs through political action and community service.

The board of directors of C.R.E.S.T. has offered us an office in their headquarters through which we can operate out of to plan, organize and implement the programs and projects in Proclamation 1-A. We will have community meetings every 2 weeks with all community leaders.

Through and with the assistance of C.R.E.S.T., we can be about improving the image of our community and lead our community leaders into the light of legal, strong and clean image.

Leadership is responsible and accountable for the implementation, establishment and teaching of Proclamation 1-A. The outpost of C.R.E.S.T. is there to assist you in all affairs, and you must be available to assist C.R.E.S.T. in its legitimate aspirations. Your cooperation in making C.R.E.S.T. a success is and should be mandatory and one of your top priorities. The phones are not on as of yet, but are anticipated to be on soon. The number will be made available to you when service is on.

I want to thank you in advance for any and all aid and assistance you have given and will give in the future.

My brothers & sisters, it takes finance to uplift the Nation, therefore, we shall establish an account with the local banking industry, so any and all financial donations and/or contributions can be sent to the treasurer.

To our brothers and sisters who are incarcerated, letters can be sent to the same address, as C.R.E.S.T. has a program geared towards maintaining family ties between those incarcerated and their families.

I welcome and encourage any positive, legitimate ideas, plans and/or programs geared towards the uplift of our Nation, the Islamic community and the Afro-American community as a whole.

Peace,

The Chairman"

Obviously, C.R.E.S.T. was formed rather quickly. Other documents were also analyzed from BPSN informants about this development. These documents show that C.R.E.S.T. did in fact gain a legitimate official state charter as a not-for-profit corporation in the State of Illinois. Other documents show C.R.E.S.T. to be very similar in nature to the front group used by the Gangster Disciples (i.e., 21st Century V.O.T.E.): they are really concerned about street gang violence, school drop outs, unemployment, the rising number of people going to prison, teenage pregnancy, etc.

The internal written gang document cited above called "Proclamation 1-A" is actually signed by Chief Malik (i.e., Jeff Fort) and dated 4-23-93. We feel it is useful to provide all of this internal written code of the BPSN in its entirety here:

"Proclamation 1-A.

To all brothers of the B.P.S.N. who recognize me as their Chief Malik and who for whatever reason are not at this time inclined toward the true religion Al Islam, this is my request.

As of this day each leader of each branch of B.P.S.N. will be referred to (title) Al Akbar, which means servant of the Greatest and Allah (God) is the Greatest.

His function as the leader of his particular branch will be to keep in touch with the following.

1. All Al Akbar's (leaders) of each branch will be responsible and in charge of their own finances.

2. Each Al Akbar must seek to have more communication with the other Al Akbars to demonstrate unity of strength of purpose, and this love and understanding must be filtered down throughout the body.

3. Brothers who are in Aliens as well as in society are to be friends and aiders of the muslim community who follow the sunna of Prophet Muhammad (S.A.W.) and work hard to prevent any conflict between the two organizations.

4. The Chief Malik is the only one over each of the Al Akbars, however my Amirs are to be respected in terms of considering their (Amirs) suggestions and adhere to all instructions that comes to you, from me, through them.

5. I do not insist that you attend Jumah (Friday Prayer) at this juncture. I do ask you to recognize Allah as God Almighty and that you discontinue the consumption of the swine (Pork) because it is an abomination and hazzard to your health.

6. The flag of the Masjid Al Ka'bah and the B.P.S.N. will continue to be Red Black and Green, the only difference will be that the B.P.S.N. flag will have those initials on it written in gold and the Masjid Al Ka'bah will have that name and the name of Allah written on it. The Red represents the blood we have shed, the Black represents our people and the Green represents the land we must obtain and the growth we must produce. The B.P.S.N. symbol will still be the Pyramid with a five pointed green star in the center of the Pyramid with Almighty written over the top of the sun with Black P. Stone under the pyramid and the word Nation at the bottom of the circle.

7. In our efforts to bring the city together to promote peace, success and financial security for our people, we must reach out for our Allies and other groups that want to attach (Stone) to the end of their name and bring them into the Nation.

8. All leaders of Allies and groups who agree to embrace the Nation will still maintain their leadership status of their particular groups and their leaders will be called Al Akbar also.

9. The Lords and Latin Kings are independent Nations who have been our long standing Allies. This proclamation does not refer to them nor does it change the relationship that we have always held with them.

10. In all Aliens, only the Amirs will choose who will be Al Akbars regardless of what organization or group you are in as long as your particular leader has given allegence (sic) to the Chief Malik. This is necessary in order to maintain peace and the recognition of leadership inside the aliens.

11. All Al Akbars are free to appoint leadership positions under them.

The Chief Malik extends his love to all the Al Akbars and to all the members of B.P.S.N.

We love each other more as we grow.

(signed) Chief Malik, 4-23-93"

At this point in the BPSN profile the reader should realize, of course, that "Chief Malik" is and always has been Jeff Fort. In 1993 Jeff Fort was in the custody of the Federal Bureau of Prisons or "Aliens" as he refers to correctional institutions. Jeff Fort learned during his leadership of the El Rukn gang that requiring members to modify their name was a way to increase the solidarity of the gang members: i.e., requiring an El Rukn member named Jimmy Jones to become "Jimmy Jones-El" basically helped to increase the gang identity in a cult-like fashion. Of course, it meant these persons could be picked off easier on a computer name search of public records as well. Such persons would apply for jobs in the name of "Jimmy Jones-El", own property or obtain licenses and execute legal documents in the same vein. By modifying the persons name, the members become "married" to the gang identity. Any gang that does this is a sophisticated organization in this respect in that it exploits the psychology of human identity.

THE RISE OF GANGS AND THE INMATE RIGHTS MOVEMENT: WHY WE NEED TO MOVE FROM "ZERO TOLERANCE" ON GANGS TO "NEGATIVE TOLERANCE"

Gang leaders behind bars, or "Aliens", as Jeff Fort calls prisons, quickly learned that hiding behind a religious identity was a way to adapt, improvise, overcome and persevere in a correctional environment. This was due to the lifting of the "hands off doctrine" in courts regarding inmate rights. Beginning in the 1960's and well established in the 1970's, prison inmates obtained a large number of new "rights". Inmates tend to know their legal rights and how to exploit them. Gang leaders are most adept at exploiting a free and open society that extends rights to the individual.

We need to recall these are rights extended to the individual and not to the gang or any organization that represents a security threat. Gangs and gang leaders since the 1970's have systematically exploited these inmate rights to be able to more effectively operate behind bars. We also need to realize that in explaining the rise of gangs inside correctional institutions and their ability to operate behind bars in the last two decades must be understood in the context of the inmate rights movement. When the judicial branch of government decided it could micro-manage the executive branch of government the inmate rights movement probably did increase the well-being of individual inmates, but it did so at the expense of increasing the ability of the gang to operate as an organization and entity even though its leaders were behind bars. Many gang experts point to state prisons like those in Illinois where gang leaders like Larry Hoover have been able, in this context, to continue to manage their gang from behind bars; however, this gang profile shows that federal prisons also must face such criticism.

Some correctional institutions today, whether operated as a part of a state government or as private proprietary contractors, allow gang members to wear gang clothes behind bars. These conditions which can be said to have an atmosphere of "positive tolerance for gangs" that this author has seen over the years have one thing in common: the administrators are typically very ignorant about the threat of gangs or gang members and therefore the gangs typically operate right under the nose of such officials. Obviously, these gang members are therefore enjoying more rights than children in a lot of schools where such restrictions are now in place. The reason that many schools and some correctional facilities and court rooms have prohibitions against the wearing of gang clothing is that from a zero-tolerance perspective it is clear that wearing gang attire creates an atmosphere of fear and intimidation: and any administrator that tolerates this does potentially face some legal liabilities.

Zero tolerance means not allowing any gang activities and having policies in place that prohibit the ability of the gang or gang members from instilling fear and intimidation. Zero tolerance with regard to gangs is a concept going back to 1991. A more proactive approach is probably justified today: negative tolerance for gangs. A policy of negative tolerance for gangs would not simply prohibit such gang activities, it would attach sanctions and penalties to such behavior.

Correctional administrators have a long way to go towards dealing with the modern American gang threat. However, the smartest idea would be to move towards a "negative tolerance" policy on gangs. In the zero tolerance policy, laws or regulations are established to the effect that gangs are not tolerated, in other words it amounts to an admonition against gang activity. In the negative tolerance policy, some "muscle" is added to the zero tolerance policy to act as a deterrent to gang activity. The way to keep gangs out of a community, or from increasing in threat level, is to simply begin with a negative tolerance policy not a zero tolerance policy. The crime threat from individuals is different from the crime threat posed by a group or organization (i.e., a "gang"). To deter a gang, one needs to increase the "cost" side of the equation when gang members can benefit and gain in a situation of exploiting individual rights in a free and open society such as our own.

THE FUSION OF ISLAMIC RELIGION AND THE GANG IDENTITY IN THE B.P.S.N.

Jeff Fort learned from Rev. Fry that any time a gang can attach itself to a legitimate social institution such as a church, one can increase the power of the gang. The reason this is true is that it confers of legitimacy to the gang and therefore shields the gang in the same community.[7] Jeff Fort's career up to the present demonstrates this lesson and provides a blue print we can probably expect to be followed by other gangs. Jeff Fort first applied this when he was in his Moorish American stage and then had his empire of "El Rukns" where he had his own "temple" or "mosque" with an MSTA type of identity. On the fringe of religious sects, anyone is free to establish their own religious identity in America and to do so unchallenged.

Today, what also makes the B.P.S.N. unique is the fusion of an Islamic religious identity with regular gang operations. This is apparent in the internal written document of the BPSN entitled "Addition to Proclamation One & One A". This is provided in its entirety here.

Addition to Proclamation One & One A

(1.) Abdul, is our Nations family name, The B.P.S.N. is our Nation. There are two sides which make up the membership of this Nation. The "Masjid Al-Ka'Bah" makes up the religious side of our Nation, yet there is only one nation!

(2.) If a brothers name is stated as Abdul "Tye" Ka'bah this speaks of two things. It states his being a member of the B.P.S.N.. He attends the Masjid Al-Ka'bah for Fridays Jumah Prayer Service. Also this brother attends the Nations meeting as a B.P.S.N. member. He shall refer to me as, "Imam Abdul Malik Ka'bah".

(3.) If a brothers name is stated as Abdul "Pawnee", it states that this brother is a member of the B.P.S.N. and he has yet to decide on attending Jumah prayer services. He shall refer to me as "Chief Abdul Malik". I shall not and will not judge the Government Body nor members by whom attends Jumah or does not attend the services. But by those whom know only one God, that being "Father-God Allah", and those whom Pledge their allegiance to me and strive for the upliftment of our Nation. Should a brother desire to embrace the teaching of Islam, I look for him to attend the Masjid Al Ka'bah. Whenever one of our brothers passes to the heavenly plane and burial services are given, we want an Islamic minister present to speak in terms to our love for that divine brother. This can only be done with the permission of family & relatives. We have dealt with the way all B.P.S.N. members will carry their titles example: Abdul and their second name as they so choose.

This now concerns the Government body of the whole Nation. This is the correct way the Government body titles are to be stated. Should a brother state his title as being: Al Akbar Prince Abdul "Kimani". Then such is correct. All Generals titles must be: (1.) General (2.) Abdul (3.) the name they choose. All Officers (1.) Officer (2.) Abdul (3.) the name they choose. So these names without "Ka'bah" are our brothers who do not yet attend Jumah. And no one is to attempt to force any of these brothers to attend services. Important is the factor of our names being "Abdul". It states a Family being one. We are one!

Now all Amirs are to function as Amirs in their full confirmation within "Masjid Al Ka'bah", yet in the Nation they shall function as Al Akbars. All Mufti's shall function as Mufti's within the "Masjid Al Ka'bah", yet in the Nation they shall function as Generals. All Sharieff's will function as "Sharieffs's" within "Masjid Al Ka'bah", yet in the Nation they shall function as Officers.

No one is to get upset or angry with neither a Government member nor member of the Nation. We must display Love and Unity amongst our brothers. We must strive to building our Nation together.

Your Imam Abdul Malik Ka'bah

MIXING THE GANG ROLES WITH RELIGIOUS ROLES: HIDING BEHIND THE CONSTITUTIONAL RIGHT OF RELIGIOUS EXPRESSION TO PLAY OUT GANG ROLES

There is another internal written document of the B.P.S.N. called "Attachment to Proclamation's 1 & 1A". It basically shows how ludicrous these internal written gang documents can be today. For example, here is a centralized authoritarian organization that enforces compliance with the threat of violence or death to members and demands such members to change their name and then has the audacity in its written documents to imply a value of autonomy in a statement deriding "robots". This is a gang that has found a way to try to conceal its organization as being a "gang" by using a religious "front".

In the document entitled "Addition to Proclamation One & One A" we saw that religious meetings are held: but gang roles are clearly defined inside such religious meetings. In the document entitled "Attachment to Proclamation's 1 & 1A" we will see more of how the BPSN structures itself so as to conceal itself as a gang organization. We also see how its own version of Islamic "religion" is differentiated from the genuine version of Islam: BPSN members have been granted certain exemptions in terms of behavior from their "Chief Malik": their gang leader is the head of their religion.

Attachment to Proclamation's 1 & 1A

(1.) Within the A.B.P.S.N. within society each branch shall have an Al-Akbar. This Al-Akbar shall appoint three generals and three officers. The "Malik" is also putting together a group called the Main 21.
(2.) The Government body of the A.B.P.S.N. consists of Al-Akbars, Generals, Main 21, and Officers. The total body in general will be called "Mahdi"...just as the Government body of the Masjid Al-Ka'bah consists of Amirs, Muftis, and Sharieff's. This government body being called Iquaams.
(3.) Together the Iquamms and Mahdis represent the entire body of this Nation.
(4.) Within the Aliens, the Iquamms are responsible for placing the "Mahdis" in positions within the Aliens..Then in order to place more Mahdis in position. It shall be did through the sanctioning of Mahdis within both society and the Aliens. Yet within society it is strictly the decision of both the Iquaams and Mahdis in their positions.

I want both the Iquaams and Mahdis to seek out for righteous Brothers to be a part of this movement. If we see the Elders and our youth being taken advantage of, we must stop that.

We must never ask of our brothers and sisters to do anything that we would not do ourselves.

We must live in accordance to our principles: Love, Truth, Peace, Freedom, and Justice.

None of us are to give the impression that our Nation is a gang. We are in no way a gang...we are the Vanguard of our people.

In regards to our brothers within the Masjid Al-Ka'bah, we must be aware of those whom strive to lead our Muslim brothers down the path of trouble and disunity. We have some Muslims whom teach that rapping, singing, dancing, and etc.

are forbidden, yet we the members of the members of the Masjid Al-Ka'bah, are believers in the teachings of Allah, we are human beings, we sing, we rapp, and we dance. This is just so long as we dance where it is not in a profanatory and seducing manner. What the people of our Nation are not, are Robots.

We shall never use "Racist" slurs in regards to other nationalities, nor in speaking in terms to ourselves.

Imam Abdul "Malik" Ka'Bah...Chief Abdul "Malik".

HOW A GANG LEADER THAN CANNOT CORRECTLY SPELL "COLLEGE" WANTS TO OPERATE HIS GANG ON COLLEGE CAMPUSES

One of the newest areas of training services that the National Gang Crime Research Center has had to focus on is in the college and university arena. We have provided such gang awareness, identification, and policy development training to judicial officers: these are the persons in higher education who face the issue of dealing with discipline against errant college and university students. Today it is not uncommon that such incidents calling for the role of the judicial officer (theft, assault, intimidation, drugs, etc) on college campuses involve gang members. Gangs do operate and recruit on college and university campuses throughout the United States.

But it is rare to find hard direct evidence of serious gang involvement on college campuses as a matter of an overall design or plan by the gang to extend its influence from being a "street gang" to being also a "campus gang" as well. The internal written materials of the BPSN made available from a BPSN informant, however, demonstrate exactly that: an intent from the BPSN leader, Jeff Fort (while currently serving time in federal prison), to organize on college and university campuses. Apparently the gang leader does not have to be able to correctly spell "college" to accomplish this goal. We have verified such BPSN gang members on campus from the Chicago area to as far south as Mississippi.

The internal document we are referring to here is a letter from the Chief Malik himself. The letter is transcribed exactly as it appears in its hand-printed style.

In the name of Allah, Most gracious, Most merciful.

Amir-Abdul Rasheem Ka'bah.

As salaam Alaikum!

Amir, I want you and Prince-Abdul The Sheik Ka-bah, Imam-Abdul Saber Ka'Bah, Akbar Prince-Abdul Raheem, and Akbar Prince-Abdul Wali to go to Imam-Abdul Hasamadeem Ka'Bah house and Imam-Abdul Ka'bah house and see Imam-Abdul Raymoe also Imam-Abdul Ben. I want you to express to Hasamadeem, that I have resituated everything and put it in proper order. Let him know that he "is not" to present himself as the Prince of the ABPSN. We have Madhis over the ABPSN. The Iquaams are to put Madihs in place through out there particular collage. Make sure the Iquaams get copies of that 2nd letter. I don't want anyone to second guess what I say. It is six chairman over the meetings of the madihs. I want the appointed chairman who are Akbar Princes to establish close ties with the Madihs at all collages (sic) as the madihs put them together. I want one Akbar-Abdul in every major and junior collage. The madihs that seek counsel from the Iquaams are to be clear on how the Khalifa wants it to be carried. I want the Iquaams to push forward so that the Masjid Al-Ka'bah Nation can push forward for the ABPSN. But guard against Iquaams or Madihs who try to make brothers there (sic) own personal solieders (sic) as far as using brothers for there (sic) own personal gain. That won't be allowed. I want the Iquaams and Madihs to go to every major collage (sic) within a three month span. To make sure the Khalifa program is clear. Make sure copies be made of this letter and sent to all of the collages (sic) and all the collages (sic) where Imam-Abdul Omar Ka'bah and Sheik-Abdul Reeco Ka'bah attens (sic) collage.

Extend my salaams to all of the brothers and sisters of the Masjid Al-Ka'bah Nation also extend my stone love to the brothers and sisters of the ABPSN.

Khalifa-Abdul Malik Ka'bah,
3-26

THE SOCINT PROFILE OF BPSN MEMBERS

A sample of BPSN members was able to be identified from Project GANGPINT (see the Project GANGPINT report, 1995, NGCRC, the first national needs assessment for gang prevention and gang intervention that systematically analyzed nearly 2,000 gang members in many parts of the USA) for a quantitative look at BPSN members. Using this data provides a comprehensive social, behavioral, psychological, and developmental lifespan profile of gang members. A sample of N = 41 such BPSN members in the much larger Project GANGFACT national sample was available for the social intelligence profile here.

Most were interviewed in Chicago (Audy Home, Cook County Jail, an Alternative High School) but others came from sites in the following areas: Gary, IN; Los Angeles, CA; Ohio juvenile correctional system; and a private program in Rock Island, Illinois.

Here is the age developmental lifespan analysis:

Age   Gang/Risk Developmental Factor Over the Lifespan
9.1   First heard anything about gangs and met someone in a gang
10.7   First saw someone killed or injured by gang violence
10.8   First "bullied" by someone else in school
11.1   First joined the BPSN gang
11.6   First fired a pistol or revolver
11.8   First "bullied" someone else in school
12.0   First got their own real gun
12.2   First got a permanent tattoo
12.7   First arrested for any crime
15.7   Average age today at time survey for this profile
25.4   Age they expect to get legally married
26.6   Age they expect to quit the gang

The average or mean ages are shown above. Thus, the typical BPSN member profile is very predictable in terms of life events. It is clear the BPSN, like most gangs in America today, exploits young children in a systematic criminal fashion. It draws its new recruits from "pee wees", children still in elementary school. Further it does this "at will" facing no known criminal or civil penalties anywhere in the United States: as no state and no federal law exists prohibiting adult criminal gang leaders from corrupting children in this fashion.

Here are some other traits and characteristics of the typical BPSN member:

*** 48.6 percent have been in court-mandated psychological counseling or therapy.

*** 33.3 percent have been in a drub/substance abuse counseling program.

*** Average age of members surveyed for this profile is 15.7 years of age.

*** Typical member last completed the ninth grade in education.

*** Half have permanent tattoos.

*** Most (82.1%) indicate they do believe in God (of which 40 percent expect to go to hell, and 60 percent expect to go to heaven in the afterlife).

*** Half (55%) have been demoted in school.

*** Half believe that some parents benefit financially from having a child who is a gang member.

*** Most (78.9%) have seen friends or family members killed by gangs.

*** Most (82.1%) do not want their own children to grow up to be gang members.

*** Half (57.5%) report someone in their family has a substance abuse problem.

*** Typical member has an average of 10.2 prior arrests. The average age of first arrest for this BPSN sample is 12.7 years of age as indicated in the lifespan analysis above.

*** Most (84.6%) have been suspended from school before. About half (56.4%) have been expelled from school before.

*** Some 41 percent have tried to quit the gang.

*** Most (73.7%) report having held some rank in the gang.

*** Over half (59.5%) have been violated by their own gang.

*** Some 73 percent have fired a gun at someone in the defense of BPSN turf.

*** Half of these BPSN members (48.6%) have been a shooter in a drive-by shooting, typically defending the gang's drug business.

*** Three-fourths of these BPSN members (75.7%) have helped to recruit others into the gang. Thus, they are aggressive recruiters for the gang, perhaps owing to some extent to the religious zealotry aspect of this gang's version of Islamic ideology. Thus, it could pose a genuine threat to college campuses if this gang is indeed targeting college and university environments for its new activities.

*** Over half (55.6%) reported that "in my gang, the things the gang does are approved by a higher up leader".

*** Most (74.4%) report their gang has written rules; and (84.2%) adult leaders who have been in the gang for many years; and that their gang (86.8%) provides money to needy members in or out of jail/prison; and most members report (89.5%) that they have family members who are also in a gang; and that their gang holds regular meetings (73.7%); and that their gang keeps an account that pays for only legal defense (69.4%); that their gang keeps a treasury (67.6%).

Overall, the profile here is very consistent with that of the gang member who belongs to a centralized, organized, authoritarian gang structure. This person has the same profile of an hard core offender: an early start in delinquency, troubled home life, school failure, etc. The gang for them functions more like a trade union guild for hard core offenders.

GANG THREAT ANALYSIS

The BPSN gang is a level 3 gang: it is a formal organization, complete with written internal codes, by-laws, etc; it operates in numerous geographically non-contiguous areas; it is interstate in criminal function; and its tenure and history make it one of the oldest active gangs in the United States today.

On a scale of 0 to 10 this gang would rate a 7.5 or higher in terms of the gang crime severity threat level. This is a high crime threat group. The reason for this designation is twofold: (1) the top leader of the gang is currently in federal prison for acts of domestic terrorism and is still able to have substantial influence over his gang, (2) the gang dances on the border of being an authoritarian religious cult/criminal organization in its blending of Islamic beliefs and symbols with its crime patterns, and (3) this gang is expected to pose continuing problems for a number of communities throughout the United States.

It is a sophisticated adult-run gang that aggressively recruits young gullible children. This gang also operates on college and university campuses. This gang, therefore, unlike many law enforcement agencies in the United States does in fact have a strategic plan.

HOW TO EFFECTIVELY PREVENT THE RISE OF GANGS LIKE THE BPSN

Gang leaders want to have their own version of a "government", one that has the real control over the streets of any given community in which the gang exists. Anything any person does to aid or assist a gang or its members will strengthen that gang. This includes not only the obvious: the manifest function of supporting a gang --- by giving it direct financial aid in the form of grants (e.g., the Rev. Fry phenomenon). This also includes indirect activities, or the latent function of support, such as not reporting the activities of local gang members, such as the drug customers who rely on the gang as a source of illegal narcotics. This also includes any level of "negotiating" with the gang, its leaders, or its members, because in negotiating with the gang one is basically acknowledging their legitimate control or influence or status an equal bargaining agent. A gang has no legitimate control. A gang has only that control that is illegal (the power of armed conflict, threats, intimidation, violence, etc), or that control that is surrendered to the gang. It is a major mistake to surrender any control over any resource to any gang or gang member. It is a major mistake of any legitimate social institution to collaborate with a gang or a front group operated by a gang. These are lessons many American communities have yet to learn.

Gang members thrive under weak and naive government policies. In fact, to understand the gang viewpoint on government is similar to understanding the viewpoint of the typical gang member on gun control: there is a double entendre, or double meaning to the issue. One can ask a simple question of a gang member such as "do you believe in gun control" and ask them to write out their answer and invariably you will find someone write something to the effect: "yes...I believe in gun control, if there are any guns around I want to be in control of them". This is not dissimilar to how gang members view government. Gang organizations emulate government and other legitimate social forms. To a gang member "government" means control and authority. They want control, authority, and the power. To have a meaningful national gang abatement strategy we are going to have to systematically remove any control and authority that gangs and gang members illegally use or abuse. Minimally, we are going to have to develop consensus that at least there will be no continuation of the kind of informal "gang development support" that characterized the rise of the BPSN empire in Chicago and elsewhere.

Some gangs like the Gangster Disciples have been able to translate their ability to get close to elected government officials into their own political power. Like a tick sucking the blood of a dog, gangs cozy up to naive politicians and leaders in order gain direct and indirect parasitic benefits. This is not a new phenomenon, this is human history. When the leader of "21st Century V.O.T.E." (Wallace "Gator" Bradley), the political front group for the Gangster Disciples, was able to personally meet with President Bill Clinton in the Oval Office of the White House on January 24th, 1994, the GD's gained enormous political momentum in Chicago communities. The GDs gained so much from the positive attention bestowed on their front group's representative that they were able to slate several persons to run for office in the Chicago city council elections. Some gangs like the BPSN have been able to manipulate liberal or "do gooder" members of the clergy in a similar fashion. More responsibly enlightened public educa-

tion is urgently needed to effectively address this issue. Finally, we are going to have to rethink the idea that federal prison necessarily neutralizes a gang leader. This gang profile revealed that Jeff Fort has continued to have an active influence on the BPSN up to the current day. Our Nation's prison system was not designed for the kind of calculating criminal adult gang leader like Jeff Fort: there are far too many privileges and rights that can be abused in the name of the gang organization (i.e., the rights to telephone calls, mail, uncensored communication with the press and legal counsel, etc). It is time to rethink these rights in light of the imminent risk and jeopardy facing not only the security of the correctional institution itself (i.e., inmates and staff), but also the continuing threat to the wider outside community whose judges sent the offender to that very same correctional system! In other words, incapacitation is apparently not working for gang leaders in America today even when it involves a federal prison sentence.

End Notes:

[1] The church is located at 6400 South Kimbark, Chicago, Illinois.

[2] This is the younger brother of Eugene "Bull" Hairston. The son of Eugene "Bull" Hairston is BPSN member "Omar Bull" and heads up the Titanics branch of the BPSN.

[3] The same, almost identical writing can be found in Chicagoland Monthly (June), 1979: p. 12. The I.D.O.C. gang training materials are notorious for plagiarizing other gang authors. So it is often dangerous to quote from these materials.

[4] This book basically provides Rev. Fry's defense of his legacy to Chicago. A good portion of the book simply provides copies of some of his sermons. The sermons are worth reading to understand the psychological profile of this kind of person. For example, in the sermon "The Church and Blackstone" (p. 150) he states: "I am a fallible man who is prone to error. Quite possibly I am crazy. But at least as of now I am your pastor and as such am called to make theological statements". The statements were 99% 1960's style radical leftist critiques of the "Establishment" and about 1 percent biblical in nature.

[5] The indicted El Rukn's who were selling or supervised the selling of cocaine in Milwaukee, Wisconsin included: Louis Lomas, Roger Bowman, Lewis Hoover, Jake Crowder, Felix Mayes, and Henry Leon Harris. Also on October 9, 1987 the El Rukn's invaded Hank's Fun House Tap in Milwaukee, firing numerous shots, in order to prevent Henry Leon Harris from cooperating with law enforcement agencies regarding the interstate murder-for-hire of Leroy Barber.

[6] Apparently they were invited to the inauguration of Richard M. Nixon in 1969 by then Senator Charles H. Percy.

[7] A gang like the Gangster Disciples illustrates this same general historical principle. The GD front group, "21st Century V.O.T.E.", like an aggressive parasite was able to sneak its way into a highly publicized "voter registration" coalition with a major civil rights group in Chicago: the Chicago Urban League. In early 1996 when this became public knowledge, there was much criticism from law enforcement and other responsible public officials. Several months later the Urban League "backed off" and facing public criticism then fully severed its ties to "21st Century V.O.T.E.".

Appendix: K

CRIPS: A Gang Profile Analysis

INTRODUCTION

Crips are no longer a gang limited to Los Angeles, they can be found anywhere in the United States today. They outnumber their rival "Bloods" in and out of custody. They have aligned with "Folks" gangs.

This profile will show that in some regards, a Crip gang member may appear to be a less formidable threat than a member of a more centralized, authoritarian gang like the GD's, but that what we have here is simply a difference in the style of gang organization. Crips are more decentralized, GD's are more centralized. The violence propensity, the drug involvement, and their tenacious commitment to gang life make Crips a ongoing crime problem in America today.

IMITATIVE INFORMAL STRUCTURE

The Crips tend to be less formalized in their style of gang organization. This is certainly true in comparing them to more formalized gangs like the Gangster Disciples. As one police officer in a southern rural town explained his local "set" of Crips: "they seem to get their organizational inspiration out of Power Rangers or something they can imitate from a comic book or a television cartoon series...". This gang profile will provide more detailed information on the structure and function of the Crips, but suffice it to say here that this is a gang that is easier to get into and perhaps easier to get out of than a more centralized authoritarian gang like the Black P. Stone Nation (B.P.S.N.) or the Gangster Disciples (GDs), both of which have been previously profiled in this journal.

Because Crips have an imitative informal structure, it is a gang that is easily "transplanted". Using the "familial gang transplant phenomenon" (see Laskey, 1996[1]) as an explanation, a mother might upon discovering her son was a "Crip" decide to "move" to a new geographical area, thinking this move would remove her son from the evil clutches of gang influence, only to find that in the new location her son starts up a new chapter of the same gang!

A Crip gang is easily "imitated" as well and can therefore begin within in any new geographical area simply by means of "emulation". There are few rules, few "prayers", no lengthy written constitution to remember. Unlike the Gangster Disciples, there are no detailed typed "memos" from the top leader that are regularly distributed to the "troops" on the front line. The dress colors, the demeanor, the hand signs, the music forms, the cultural argot and linguistic expressions[2], the "values" — these are all spread through the mass media, and are therefore readily available to the "wannabe" gang member.

THE CRIPS/FOLKS NATIONAL ALLIANCE SYSTEM

This trend has now hit all areas of the United States: the Crips "ride with", or are "allied with", Folks gang members. Thus, a Crip gang member will be allied with a Gangster Disciple (i.e., the largest "Folks" gang in the USA). There have been several explanations for this development.

The most common explanation offered for the Crip/Folks alliance is their mutual color preference (i.e., Blue). In other words, the gangs have similar color patterns: Crips like "Blue", and Gangster Disciples also use "Blue" in their way of "representing" their gang affiliation.

Another explanation offered for the Crips/Folks alliance system that now definitely exists nationwide is the fact that as early as 1993 the two gangs were in close communication by means of the "peace treaty" "gang peace" talks and summit meetings held in various parts of the United States. We are not saying any "peace" came out of these efforts, we are saying only that an alliance was struck between groups like the Crips and groups like the Gangster Disciples. The now infamous "gang peace/treaty summit meeting" held in Chicago in October of 1993 brought together mostly Crips and GDs. Their "rivals" (Bloods and "peoples"/"brothers") were not attending this event to any large degree. It became a "Crips/Folks" convention! They "partied" together, they had a good time, they gave each other speeches, and they were all dressed alike: in BLUE.

NO SINGLE RECOGNIZED NATIONAL LEADER

In gangs like the Black P. Stone Nation (BPSN), or in gangs like the Aryan Brotherhood, or in gangs like the Gangster Disciples, one will find a leadership structure that has been crystallized over the years by the continuity of the gang and its members and its increased formalization. In a gang like the Gangster Disciples, everyone knows who the real "national" leader of the gang is: Larry Hoover. In a gang like the Black P. Stone Nation everyone knows who is the real "national" leader is: Jeff Fort. However, there is no single individual that has recognized leadership command authority over all "Crip" gangs in the United States.

Within some of the larger "sets" of the Crip gang (Rolling 20's, etc) the pattern of family involvement in the membership of the gang tends to establish a clear "lineage" of authority. This would apply, for example, in the areas of the epicenter[3] for the gang: Los Angeles in particular. In the "neighborhoods" where the gang has its identity embedded into the gang name, the leadership exists for particular chapters of the gang, such persons are called "OG's" or the "original gangsters" of the gang. But across the many chapters or "sets" of Crips, there really is no one spokesperson for the "Crips".

This lack of any single national leader is certainly not an impediment to the spread of the gang, indeed this decentralization may help in the process of gang proliferation. Over the years we have seen many examples of some local youths simply "emulating" the Crip identity and doing it successfully: at some point in time they are arrested, and while in a correctional facility they meet "the real thing", they gain momentum and learn more of the "walk and talk" of Crip life, and can be up and running as a Crip faction in a relatively short period of time.

This is not to say that there are not "Crip leaders". There are many to be found in and out of custody. In custody, the leader of the group with the most members tends to be the shot caller. But like the "Disciples", not all "Crips" are alike and they can and do fight with each other.

Most "Crip" gangs are more informal and fluid in nature. In fact, the further away from the epicenter of the Crips (i.e., Los Angeles), the more informal such Crip "sets" can be. The notable exception, however, is where in remote regions the "Crips" mix and match their symbols and argot with "Gangster Disciple" lingo, and become a kind of "hybrid" gang.

A better way of conceiving the relationship between various Crip "sets" is that they are competitive. While various Crip sets may be conceived of as being homogeneous and a kind of monolithic entity, there is actually much variation between the "sets". Each has its own unique variations in language, hand signs, etc. And when they come into contact with each other, the commonality of being a "Crip" has some value admittedly as an organizing principle, but there will be much competition and sometimes rivalry as well even among different factions of Crips. Crip gangs are best conceived of as a kind of "Union Guild" for criminal offenders, there are a lot of such "Union Halls" to report to, they are somewhat autonomous in nature, but are all affiliated under the umbrella identity of "Crips".

SOME FINDINGS ABOUT CRIPS FROM PROJECT GANGECON

Project GANGECON was a large scale national gang research project carried out by the National Gang Crime Research Center to examine the economic function, infrastructure, and activities of American gangs. One section of the Project GANGECON report provided a comparison of "Crips" with Bloods, People, and Folks. Here are some of the ways in which the "Crips" stood out or distinguished themselves in the Project GANGECON analysis:

• Crips were more likely (27.8%) to report having ever collected protection money on behalf of their gang than were People (19.9%), Folks (16.7%), or Bloods (20.5%).

• Crips were much more likely to have ever assaulted a school teacher (50%), than compared to People (30%), Folks (33.2%), or Bloods (28.3%).

• Crips were less likely to have ever attempted to quit the gang (32.7%) than compared to People (44.5%), Folks (49%), or Bloods (48.4%).

• Crips were much more likely (79.3%) to report that they have ever committed a crime for financial gain with their gang than compared to People (56.3%), Folks (52.6%), or Bloods (67.1%). Further, this trend gain validity when breaking down specific crime patterns for analysis as well.

• Crips were the most likely to report having committed a robbery crime for financial gain with their gang (65.9%), than compared to People (35.7%), Folks (33.3%), or Bloods (56.8%).

• Crips were the most likely to report having committed a burglary crime for financial gain with their gang (48.4%) than compared to People (23.5%), Folks (23%), or Bloods (45%).

• Crips were the most likely to report having committed a car theft crime for financial gain with their gang (54.7%) than compared to People (30%), Folks (32.7%), or Bloods (39.2%).

• Crips were the most likely to report having committed an arson crime for financial gain with their gang (23.1%) than compared to People (13.8%), Folks (9.6%), or Bloods (15.6%).

• Crips were the most likely to report having committed shoplifting crimes for financial gain with their gang (45.2%) than compared to People (17%), Folks (20.6%), or Bloods (23.5%).

• Crips were the most willing to dies for their fellow gang members (61.6%), than compared to People (42.4%), Folks (33.5%), or Bloods (45.3%).

The Profile of N = 873 CRIPS: Project GANGFACT Data

Project GANGFACT surveyed over 4,000 gang members in 17 states during 1996. Data on N = 873 Crips was available in the Project GANGFACT database. Crips were found in 68 of the 85 correctional facilities surveyed in Project GANGFACT. The profile information from Project GANGFACT on this large sample of Crip gang members is summarized below.

Types of Crip Sets

The types of "sets", units of, or chapters of the Crip gang included in this sample involves a long, seven page list. These include: Rolling 20's Crips, Rolling 30's Crips (an assortment: Rolling 40's, Rolling 60's, etc), Hoover Crips (a large assortment, i.e., 59th Street Hoover Crips, 74th Street Hoover Crips, East Side Hoover Crips, etc), Eight Tray Gangster Crips, Grape Street, West Side Crips, Shotgun Crips, Compton Crips. The rule of thumb seems to be: in an area that is high in gang density, the gang name may be localized to a specific geographical coordinate; or the gang name may refer to a section of the community (east, west, etc); or if it is a small community, the gang name may take the city name and use it in the full gang identifier (i.e., Venice Crips).

Demographic Factors

Their age ranged from 11 to 45 years of age.

Nine out of ten Crips (91.5%) are males, only 8.5 percent were female.

While African-Americans are the single largest ethnic group represented among this sample of Crips (60.6%), clearly all other groups are also represented in its ranks: 23.7% white, 6% Hispanic, 2.9% Asian/Chinese, 2.5% Native American Indian, and 4.3% "other".

Personality Factors

A fourth indicated they always or usually "get what I want even if I have to take it from someone".

About half feel "excluded from legitimate opportunities": 46.4 percent answered "true" to the statement "I feel that I am not a part of legitimate opportunities in my city or town and am cut out of good possibilities". Thus, the other half (53.6%) did not feel "excluded from legitimate opportunities".

Over half (62.8%) of these Crip members responded "no" to the question "if more juveniles who committed violent crimes were tried in court as adult offenders, would this stop you as a juvenile from committing a violent crime".

Over two-thirds (73.5%) similarly answered "no" to the question "if gangs were investigated and prosecuted as if they were organized crime groups, would this put some gangs out of business".

Nine out of ten (89.4%) indicated true to the statement "I believe that I will be able to find a good job and eventually support a family".

Early Childhood Experiences

A third (34.3%) report that they were "bullied" by someone while in school.

Two-thirds (66.4%) report that they were themselves a "bully" in school; and 72.6 percent did believe that bullying in school can lead to gangbanging.

Some 18.2 percent report that they have been forced to have sex that they did not want to have.

Religious Factors

About half (58.5%) indicated that they "rarely if ever attend church".

The vast majority (92%) claim they "believe in God", only 8 percent claim they "do not believe in God".

The vast majority (92.4%) claim they are on "God's side", only 7.6 percent claim they are on "Satan's side".

A fifth (20.6%) of all Crips report that their gang involvement has affected their religious beliefs.

Family Factors

The typical Crip member is from a mother-only family structure (60%); some 31.8 percent came from an intact family (mother, father and siblings); only 8.2 percent from a father-only family (family, self, and siblings).

Over a third of all Crips conceal their gang identity from their parents. Our survey included the question "do your parents know you are a member of a gang?". While 64.1 percent of the Crips indicated that their parents did in fact know they were gang members, some 35.9 percent of the Crips indicated that their parents did not know that they were a member of a gang.

Some 8.2 percent of Crips report that their father encouraged them to join a gang. Some 5.6 percent of Crips report that their mother encouraged them to join a gang.

About half (55.1%) of all Crips report that "my mother and father would be embarrassed if they knew I was in a gang".

Almost half (47.8%) of all Crips report that one of their parents has served time in prison.

Ethnic and Racial Diversity in Crip Gangs

While certainly the Crips began as a gang that was homogeneous with respect to race, originally consisting of African-American members exclusively, it is today diverse would be the best evidence we can present. There are Asian sets of Crips, there are Black sets of Crips, there are Native American Indian sets of Crips, etc, etc. The Project GANGFACT survey provides some evidence of this ethnic and racial diversity. The Project GANGFACT survey asked the Crip members to describe their gang with respect to the issue. A fourth (26.4%) described the Crip gang as consisting only of members who represent one racial or ethnic group. Some 29.6 percent described their gang as consisting mostly of one racial or ethnic group, with some members who are from other racial groups. But 44 percent described their gang as consisting of a variety of racial and ethnic groups on an equal basis.

Entering a Crip Gang

Illegal income as an explanation for getting into the Crip gang: about a fourth (25.8%) indicated that the chance to make money was "very important" in their decision to join the Crip gang. Some 31.5 percent indicated it was "important", and the rest (42.7%) indicated it was "not important".

Seeking "protection" as an explanation for getting into the Crip gang: only 17.8 percent indicated that seeking protection was "very important" in their decision to join the Crip gang; another 24.8 percent indicated it was "important", while most (57.4%) indicated it was "not important".

Crip members are more likely (63.3%) to report that they were "recruited" into the gang, than they were to report that they volunteered or asked to join the gang (36.7%).

Crips join their gang like most other gang members: at any point in the age span, but typically very young. Some 44.6 percent joined the gang on or before the age of 12. Some 86.6 percent joined the gang on or before the age of 15.

Female Involvement in Crip Gang Life

High female involvement characterizes Crip gang life. Most Crip gangs have female members. Nearly nine out of ten (88.8%) of Crip members report that there are female members of their gang. In fact, 44 percent report that there are female leaders in their gang.

Some 45.1 percent of all Crips report that they have known males in their gang who have forced females to have sex.

Crime Patterns Among Crip Gang Members

When asked "do you think most gang members get arrested for crimes they committed for their gang or for crimes they committed for themselves", 55.9 percent indicated for the "gang", and 44.1% indicated for "self". Two thirds (68.4%) of these Crip members report that they have sold crack cocaine. A third (35.4%) of these Crip members report that they have fired a gun at a police officer.

Crip gang crime: 1/4 for the gang, 3/4 for self interest. The Project GANGFACT survey asked the Crips "of the crimes that you committed, were these mostly for the benefit of the gang or were they for your own personal benefit?". Some 24.8 percent of the Crips indicated their crimes were for the benefit of the gang. Yet 75.2 percent indicated their crimes were for their own personal benefit.

About two-thirds (64.5%) report that they have committed a crime for financial gain with their gang.

A fourth (26.2%) of all Crips have made false "911" calls to the police emergency telephone number in connection with their gang activities.

Drug Sales Patterns Among Crip Gang Members

Crips sell crack cocaine. Repeat: Crips sell crack cocaine. A careful review of both the gang research literature, and the statements to the print and electronic media by some gang experts from southern California, will show the claim that "GANGS DO NOT INVOLVE THEMSELVES IN CRACK COCAINE SALES". Such outrageous over-generalizations about gang life are often cloaked in blanket political criticisms of agencies like the Drug Enforcement Administration (DEA). Our data is conclusive: Crips sell crack cocaine. We had N = 826 Crip members answer the question "has your gang ever sold crack cocaine?". Some 90.1 percent of the Crip members reported to us that they gang has in fact sold crack cocaine.

Three-fourths (77.9%) have been involved in organized drug dealing. When asked if they did it for themselves or if they did it for the gang, the image that emerges is that of a group of individual entrepreneurs: most (89%) indicated they engaged in the drug dealing "for myself", while only 11 percent indicated they did it "for my gang".

Violence Propensity Among Crip Gang Members

The effects of the Brady Bill on the Crips appear to be minimal: 10.8 percent of these Crip members indicated that it has been "harder" since March of 1994 to buy illegal guns. But 48.7 percent indicated it has been "easier", and 40.5% indicated no change in difficulty regarding the ease or difficulty or buying illegal guns.

A third (35.3%) of all Crips report that "shooting at a police officer would bring me more status and 'rep' in my gang".

Infrastructure of Crip Gangs

Crip gang infrastructure is in many cases poorly articulated. The classic local neighborhood Crip gang set may therefore appear to be "loosely organized" in comparison to gangs like the El Rukns or the Gangster Disciples. Yet the Crips have sprung up all over the United States, so how do we account for this "success" of the Crip gang when it is felt to be so "unorganized"? The answer seems to be that decentralized gangs can compete with centralized gangs in an illicit market place.

One of the questions in the Project GANGFACT survey instrument specifically asked (in a follow-up of "have you ever held rank or any leadership position in the gang") what the title of their rank or leadership position was in the Crip gang. The information here is based on the infrastructure data provided by a large sample of Crip members.

One trend is for a simple age differentiation: "Baby G" or "Baby Gangster", would be a "rank" for a "Young Gangster", a "Baby O.G.", a "Baby Loco", a "Tiny Mite", a "Young Hoodster", a "Pee Wee", a "Lil' Homie", a "young rider", all would designate a younger child member of the gang.

Another trend is towards egalitarianism where there is no discernible leadership by outward appearances, yet like a "pick up basketball team" the one with the ball is the leader. This person may be designated as an "O.G.", an "Original Gangster", the "shot caller", the "chairman", the "coordinator", the "general", the "set king", the "president", the "Chief", the "over lord", etc. There appears to be no uniformity in the chain of command among Crips as there would be by examining the same data from a gang like the GD's, the explanation would appear to be in the fact that the GDs are more centralized and have elaborate written rules, by-laws, and a constitution, while the Crips are more decentralized.

So while there is a top leader of each set of the Crips, when that person dies or disappears (i.e., goes to prison, etc), someone else in the gang will simply fill the position. The person to fill the position was typically the protege, the "vice president", the "2nd banana", the "2nd star", "co-captain", the "2nd seat", the "2nd lieutenant", the "right hand man", a kind of executive assistant who was the top confidant or "aide" to the top leader or "head".

Regular members take on typical gang status designations: trooper, foot soldier, etc. Female members take on gender status designations: "first girl", "set queen", "big sister", etc.

So it is not as if there is no organization at all in the Crips, the organizational sophistication may not be as formalized as that within some Chicago-based gangs (i.e., GD's, BPSN, etc), but it is there and it does exist. The infrastructure of Crips is simply, therefore, more informal in nature. In other words, it may not be dependent on a "written code or constitution", but may simply reflect a style of organization based on the oral history of the gang. Because of this, Crips may have a tendency to be more provincial in nature.

There are "positions" available in the Crip gang to perform certain "functions". These could include "treasurer" for financial functions, the "chief assassin" or "hitman" for violence functions, etc.

Missing from the list of "functions" in the Crips gang are those positions of authority we would normally find in more sophisticated gangs like the GDs for instilling "discipline" and "order": the "chief of violations". Few positions of rank or leadership in the Crips seemed to imply this ability to achieve gang goals by means of violence against their own members. However, we do know that Crips administer such "violations" to their members in ways that are very comparable to the People/Folks style of administering ritualized physical punishment to errant members

Crip Gang Structure Factors

About two-thirds (65.4%) of the Crip members claim to have held some type of rank or leadership position in their gang.

About two-thirds (69.5%) of the Crip members do claim that their gang has a special language code; and that their gangs has written rules for its members (66.2%).

Most Crip members (87.4%) report that their gang does have adult leaders who have been in the gang for many years.

Only about half (53.6%) report that their gang holds regular weekly meetings.

Less than a fifth (18.1%) report that their gang requires its members to pay regular weekly dues.

Crips members fit another clear profile: about a fourth (24.2%) "do whatever the gang expects of me", while about three-fourths (75.8%) "do what I want to do, regardless of what the gang expects me to do".

Half (50.3%) of all Crips claim their gang has established a relationship with real organized crime.

A fourth (28.3%) of all Crip members have never met the top leader of their gang.

Just under half (44.4%) of all Crip members believe they may someday be the top leader of their gang.

Only a fifth (21.5%) of all Crips believe that their gang is aiding their race or ethnic group to overcome society's prejudices.

Two-fifths (41.2%) of all Crips report that they have been told by someone in their gang (i.e., leaders, etc) to perform an act that they felt was wrong.

Regarding the source of their gang nicknames, 37.4 percent of Crips report that "I picked the nickname myself". While 62.6 percent report that "my gang friends picked the nickname for me.

Getting Out of A Crip Gang

Some 43.3 percent of the Crip members have tried to quit the gang.

Four-fifths (79.1%) of all Crips would quit the gang if they could get a more satisfying life. The Project GANGFACT survey presented the scenario to the Crip members as follows: "if you were offered a second chance in life, with a clean slate, and if you are given the opportunity to finish your education and/or receive job training while working with a person that truly cares about you and your needs, would you be willing to quit the gang and start your life over again?". Only a fifth (20.9%) of the Crip members indicated they would not quit the gang under these conditions. Our impression is that based on this, and related findings presented here, the Crip gang has a very weak "hold" on its members; there are fewer membership expectations, there is less cohesiveness and less solidarity, because of the decentralized nature of the gang. Three-fourths (75.6%) of all Crips do believe that their gang has kept the promises made to them when they first joined. Still, about a fourth of all Crips (24.4%) report that their gang has not kept the promises made to them when they first joined the gang.

CRIP GEOGRAPHICAL DISPERSION

The following is a partial list of known geographical dispersion of Crip gangs. Two categories of listings can exist for each state: (1) correctional facilities, and (2) cities and counties. Correctional facilities include jails, adult prisons, juvenile institutions and juvenile detention centers. The source of this information is the National Geographic Guide to Gangs, a computer file maintained by the National Gang Crime Research Center.[4]

ALABAMA:

Correctional facilities: Atmore, Birmingham, Childerburg, Elmore, Montgomery, Mt. Meigs, Phenix City, Springville, Troy, Union Spring.

Cities and counties: Baldwin Co., Birmingham, Barbour, Bay Minette, Bibb Co., Calhoun, Dothan, Gadsden, Huntsville, Jefferson Co., Montgomery, Moulton.

ALASKA:

Correctional facilities: Anchorage, Eagle River, Fairbanks, Juneau, Palmer, Seward.

City: Anchorage.

ARIZONA:

Correctional facilities: Douglas, Florence, Goodyear, Jonesboro, Phoenix, Pichaco, Safford, Tucson, Winslow.

Cities and counties: Cochise Co., Coconino Co., Graham Co., Maricopa Co., Mesa, Navajo Co., Phoenix, Scottsdale, South Tucson, Tucson, Winslow, Yuma.

ARKANSAS:

Correctional facilities: Grady, Little Rock, Pine Bluff, Tucker, Wrightsville.

Cities and counties: Fayetteville, Hope, Little Rock.

CALIFORNIA:

Correctional facilities: Blythe, Corcoran, Crescent City, El Centro, Eureka, Fresno, Frontera, Indio, Los Angeles, Merced, Nevada City, Norwalk, Ontario, Paso Robles, Placerville, Redding, San Diego, San Francisco, San Jose, San Louis Obispo, San Quentin, Santa Cruz, Stockton, Whittier, Yreka.

Cities and counties: Alameda Co., Anaheim, Bakersfield, Butte Co., Chula Vista, Claremont, Compton, Concord, Covina, Crescent City, Downey, Freemont, Fresno, Fullerton, Glendale, Jolo Co., Kings Co., La Mesa, Livermore, Lodi, Long Beach, Los Angeles, Modesto, Monrovia, Monterey Park, Nevada Co., Oakland, Oakton, Oceanside, Orange Co., Pismo Beach, Placer Co., Rancho Domiguez, Rialto, Riverside, Sacramento, San Benito Co., San Bernardino, San Diego, San Francisco, Santa Ana, Santa Monica, Shasta Co., Stockton, Torrance, Upland, Vallejo, Ventura Co., Ventura, Visalia, Walnut Creek, West Covina, Yuba City.

COLORADO:

Correctional facilities: Brighton, Burlington, Canon City, Colorado Springs, Crowley, Delta, Denver, Englewood, Golden, Grand Junction, Pueblo, Rifle.

Cities and counties: Adams Co., Arapahoe Co., Arvada, Aurora, Boulder Co., Boulder, Cherry Hills, Colorado Springs, Denver, Douglas Co., Englewood, Golden, Larimer Co., Littleton, Milliken, Pueblo, Silverthorne, Walsenburg, Wheat Ridge, Yuma.

CONNECTICUT:

Correctional facility: Windsor Locks.

DISTRICT OF COLUMBIA (WASHINGTON, D.C.):

Correctional facilities (juvenile).

FLORIDA:

Correctional facilities: Bushnell, Cross City, Jacksonville,

Cities and counties: Fort Lauderdale, Orange Co., Palm Beach Co., Panama City, Polk Co.

GEORGIA:

Correctional facilities: Columbus, Decatur, Lawrenceville, Milledgeville, Rock Springs, Savannah.

Cities and counties: Atlanta, Clayton Co., Forest Park, Marietta.

HAWAII:

Correctional facilities: Hilo, Kailua.

Cities: Hilo, Honolulu, Kailua.

IDAHO:

Correctional facilities: Boise, Cottonwood, Orofino.

Cities and counties: Ada Co., Boise, Kootenai Co., Madison Co., Pocatello.

ILLINOIS:

Correctional facilities: Dwight, Joliet.

Cities and counties: Alton, Arlington Hts., Aurora, Chicago, Colllinsville, Edwardsville, Kankakee, Knox Co., LaSalle Co., Madison Co., Maywood, Mounds, Rockford, St. Clair Co., Washington.

INDIANA:

Correctional facilities: Fort Wayne, La Porte, Michigan City, Pendleton, Plainfield, Rockville, Tell City.

Cities and counties: Anderson, Bloomington, Fort Wayne, Indianapolis, Marion, Marion Co., Monroe Co.

IOWA:

Correctional facilities: Anamosa, Council Bluffs, Eldora, Fort Madison, Indianola, Michellville, Oakdale, Rockwell City, Waterloo.

Cities and counties: Black Hawk Co., Cedar Falls, Davenport, Des Moines, Jessup, Ottumwa, Scott Co., Woodbury Co..

KANSAS:

Correctional facilities: Atchison, Beloit, El Dorado, Ellsworth, Hutchinson, Lansing, Larned, Norton, Osawatomie, Topeka, Wichita, Winfield.

Cities and counties: Ellsworth Co., Kansas City, Lawrence, Olathe, Sedgwick Co., Shawnee Co., Shawnee Mission, Topeka.

KENTUCKY:

Correctional facilities: Eddyville, Elizabethtown, LaGrange, Lexington, Louisville, Newport.

LOUISIANA:

Correctional facilities: Baton Rouge, Bridge City, DeQuincy, Homer, Monroe, New Orleans, Pineville, Shreveport, St. Gabriel, Winfield.

Cities and counties: Caddo Parish, Concordia Parish, Covington, Hammond, Port Allen, St. Martinville, W. Baton Rouge Parish.

MAINE:

City: Lewiston.

MARYLAND:

Correctional facility: Westover.

MASSACHUSETTS:

Correctional Facilities: Boston, Bridgewater, Carver.

MICHIGAN:

Correctional facility: Ionia.

Cities and counties: Flint, Ottawa Co., Saginaw, Southgate.

MINNESOTA:

Correctional facilities: Fairbault, Minneapolis, Jackson, Lino Lakes, Moose Lake, Oak Park Heights, Red Wing, Sauk Centre, St. Cloud, Stillwater, St. Paul, Willow River.

Cities and counties: Anoka Co., Arden Hills, Bloomington, Hennipenn Co., Maple Grove, Maplewood, Minneapolis, Rochester, Roseville, Stearns Co., St. Louis Park, Waite Park.

MISSISSIPPI:

Correctional facilities: Gulfport, Leakesville, Lucedale, Parchman.

Cities and counties: Hinds Co., Pascagoula, Waveland, Westpoint.

MISSOURI:

Correctional facilities: Boonville, Chillicothe, Farmington, Fordland, Fulton, Harrisonville, Jefferson City, Kansas City, Lawson, Liberty, Mexico, Mineral Point, Osage Beach, Poplar Bluff, Springfield, St. Louis, Union.

Cities and counties: Andrew Co., Jackson Co., Springfield, St. Charles Co., St. Louis.

MONTANA:

Correctional facilities: Helena, Swan Lake.

NEBRASKA:

Correctional facilities: Geneva, Lincoln, Omaha, York.

Cities and counties: Atkinson, Dakota Co., Lincoln, Lancaster, Omaha, Ralston.

NEVADA:

Correctional facilities: Carson City, Caliente, Elko,

Ely, Jean, Las Vegas, Reno.
        Cities and counties: Douglas Co., Henderson, Las Vegas, North Los Vegas, Reno, Sparks, Washoe Co.
NEW HAMPSHIRE:
        Correctional facilities: Concord, Manchester.
NEW JERSEY:
        Cities and counties: Mercer Co., Monmouth Co.
NEW MEXICO:
        Correctional facilities: Alamogordo, Albuquerque, Clovis, Farmington, Fort Stanto, Hagerman, Las Crueces, Springer.
        Cities and counties: Alamogordo, Albuquerque, Las Crueces, Los Lunas, Mesilla.
NEW YORK:
        Correctional facilities: Elmira, Flushing, Industry, Moravia, Rensselaerville.
NORTH CAROLINA
        Correctional facility: Washington.
        Cities and counties: Davidson Co., Greensboro.
NORTH DAKOTA:
        Correctional facility: Mandan.
        Cities: Bismarck, Minot.
OHIO:
        Correctional facilities: Chillicothe, Cincinnati, Columbus, Delaware, Grafton, Lebanon, Liberty Center, London, Mansfield, Marysville, Massillon, Orient, Painesville, Sandusky, Springfield.
        Cities and counties: Butler Co., Canton, Cincinnati, Cleveland, Columbus, Dayton, Franklin Co., Loraine Co., Mahoning Co., Maple Heights, Stark Co., Toledo, Wood Co., Xexia.
OKLAHOMA:
        Correctional facilities: Boley, Granite, Helena, Hodgen, Hominy, Lexington, McAlester, Sand Springs, Tecumseh, York.
        Cities and counties: Del City, Idabel, Lawton, Midwest City, Morris, Oklahoma City, Stillwater, Temple, Tulsa.
OREGON:
        Correctional facilities: Baker City, Eugene, Grants Pass, Hillsboro, Pendleton, Salem, Tillahook, Woodburn.
        Cities and Counties: Clackamas Co., Clatsop Co., Columbia Co., Corvallis, Lane Co., Marion Co., Morrow Co., Portland, Sheridan, Troutdale, Wasco Co., Yamhill Co.
PENNSYLVANIA:
        Correctional facilities: Camp Hill, Cresson, Pittsburgh.
        City: Weatherly.
SOUTH CAROLINA:
        Correctional facility: Fairfax.
        City: Greenville.
SOUTH DAKOTA:
        Correctional facilities: Plankinton, Springfield.
        City: North Sioux City.
TENNESSEE:
        Correctional facilities: Knoxville, Lebanon, Nashville.
        Cities and counties: Chattanooga, Davidson Co., Jackson, Memphis, Murfreesboro, Williamson Co.
TEXAS:
        Correctional facilities: Abilene, Austin, Beaumont, Brazoria, Brazos Co., Brownwood, Bryan, Corpus Christi, Dallas, Del Rio, El Paso, Fort Worth, Groveton, Huntsville, Longview, Lubbock, Lufkin, Pyote, Raymondville, Richmond, Rosharon, Rusk, San Antonio, Tarrant Co.
        Cities and counties: Abilene, Arlington, Austin, Baytown, Castroville, Collin Co., Grand Prairie, Itasca, Jefferson, Laredo, Longview, Midland, Randall Co., Richardson, San Antonio, Temple, Waco.

UTAH:
        Correctional facilities: Cedar City, Draper, Ogden, Provo, Roy, Salt Lake City.
        Cities and counties: Provo, Utah Co., Wasatch Co., Woods Cross.
VIRGINIA:
        City: Norfolk.
WASHINGTON:
        Correctional facilities: Belfair, Bellingham, Centralia, Clallam Bay, East Wenatchee, Ephrata, Gig Harbor, Littlerock, Monroe, Shelton, Snoqualmie, Spokane, Steilacoom, Tacoma, Woodinville, Yakima.
        Cities and counties: Clark Co., King, King Co., Klickitat Co., Pierce Co., Richland, Seattle, Skagit Co., Snohomish Co., Spokane, Walla Walla Co., Yakima.
WEST VIRGINIA:
        City: Huntington.
WISCONSIN:
        Correctional facilities: Chippewa Falls, Dodgeville, Milwaukee, Oshkosh, Sturtevant, Winnebago.
        City: Milwaukee.

WYOMING:
        Correctional facilities: Casper, Torrington.
        County: Laramie Co.

OVERALL THREAT RATING OF CRIPS
        Crips get an overall threat rating of 8 on a scale of 1 to 10 (where 10 is the highest threat rating). The reason for this high threat analysis rating is their consistently strong tendency towards extreme violence, their high commitment to gang life, and the track record of crime that occurs in the context of organized gang life for Crip members. For Crip members the gang functions like a kind of "Union Guild" for criminal offenders; to carry the analogy further, there are many "Union halls" for these offenders to report to, which are all affiliated under one organizing umbrella (i.e., Crip).

END NOTES:

[1] John A. Laskey, "Gang Migration: The Familial Gang Transplant Phenomenon", <u>Journal of Gang Research</u>, Volume 4, Number 2, Winter, 1996, pp. 1-15.

[2] A common Crip slogan is "Crippin' ain't easy, but it sure is fun.". Coded words that have special meaning also are used: "LOVE" means "let our vision educate". The term "Cuz" refers to any fellow Crip member. The term "Blob" is a putdown that refers to "Blood" gang members, similarly Crips are insulted by the word "Crab" as a putdown on Crips.

[3] We gratefully acknowledge the social-linguistic origin of the "epicenter" concept to NGCRC researcher Avery Puckett, of Nashville, Tennessee.

[4] The Geographical Guide includes the full gang names, which have not been used here, and it also includes the time frames for data collection sources.

AUTHOR INDEX

Ackley, N., 365
Agopian, Michael, 544
Alonso, Alejandro, 34
Armstrong, Richard M., 76
Arnold, William R., 121, 215, 224, 276, 499, 539
Asbury, Herbert, 64, 92, 185
Axelson, Roland G., 30, 36
Bales, Robert F., 214
Bartollas, Clemens, 391
Bastian, Lisa D., 299, 308
Beauvais, Fred, 224
Beier, Ernest G., 560
Bell, Daniel, 86, 361
Bennett, James, 110, 111, 114
Bensinger, Gad J., 104, 276, 548
Bergman, Brian, 81, 308
Berk, Richard A., 82, 88
Berland, David I., 308, 311
Bernard, Thomas, 64, 358
Berstein, Saul, 540
Blanchard, W.H., 145
Bloch, Herbert, 41
Blumenthal, Ricky, 263
Bobrowski, Lawrence J., 215, 224, 443, 487
Bonn, Robert L., 3
Bonner, Roger H., 224, 232
Bookin-Weiner, Hedy, 4, 166
Bowker, L.H., 86
Braga, Anthony A., 382
Breed, Ailen F., 74
Brooks, W.A., 57
Brotman, Richard, 560
Bryant, D., 361-362
Buentello, Salvador, 432, 490
Burgess, Ernest W., 125
Burns, E., 374, 380, 391
Burris-Kitchen, Deborah, 55
Caltabiano, Michael L.,
Camp, George, 10, 22, 70, 74, 276, 434, 440, 441, 476, 483, 498, 549
Camp, Camille Graham, 10, 22, 70, 74, 276, 434, 440, 441, 476, 483, 498, 549
Campbell, Anne, 46, 67, 92, 94, 103, 127, 230, 327, 332, 493, 448, 548
Capeci, Jerry, 298

Capote, Truman, 110
Carey, James T., 66, 139
Cartwright, Desmond S., 49, 64
Chin, Ko-lin, 76, 271, 299, 308
Christenson, Loren W., 379
Clark, J.H., 89
Cloward, Richard A., 41-42, 64, 79, 86, 94, 128, 299, 300, 305, 308, 324, 325, 505, 549
Cody, Monster, 336
Coghlan, Michael P., 54
Cohen, Albert K., 41, 47, 59, 76, 128, 300, 304, 308
Cole, Juan R.I., 209, 268
Cole, George F., 77
Coleman, James S., 89
Correl, Theodore, 263
Covey, Herbert C., 49, 188
Cozic, Charles P., 53
Crutchfield, Robert D., 71, 74
Cummings, Scott, 51, 539
Curry, G. David, 299
Cusson, Maurice, 209
Daniels, S., 390, 440, 478
Davis, James R., 145
Dawley, David, 59, 121, 285
Deakin, T.J., 374, 380, 391
Deng, Ziaogang, 310
Denisoff, R. Serge, 59, 131, 313
DiChiara, Albert, 105
DiRenzo, Gordon J., 224, 268, 276
Disch, Robert, 65, 69, 74
Dodder, Laurel, 188, 380, 559
Dolan, Edward F., 560
Dubro, Alec, 77, 105, 201, 260, 391, 439, 477, 522
Dunston, Leonard G., 49, 188, 215, 508
Earley, Pete, 117
Edelman, Marian Wright, 328
English, T.J., 308
Etter, Gregg. W., 138
Evenrud, Loren A., 519
Eyres, John, 308
Fagan, Jeffrey, 299, 308, 353, 546
Fishman, L., 55
Fletcher, Colin, 150
Fong, Robert S., 74, 188, 276, 433, 434, 477, 490, 546

Fossett, Christine A., 539
Fox, Robert W., 57
Fry, John, 5
Furfey, Paul H., 6, 536
Galland, George F., 80, 88
Gannon, Thomas M., 64, 66
Geis, Gilbert, 165, 173, 298
Gerrard, Nathan L., 546
Giordano, P.C., 55
Glaser, Daniel, 86, 145
Glasgow, Douglas G., 85, 88
Goffman, Irving, 51, 110, 111
Goldstein, Arnold P., 8, 48, 51, 52, 519, 531
Gonzalez, Alfredo, 66, 75-76, 145
Gordon, Robert A., 89
Gorn, Elliott J., 14
Gott, Raymond, 389
Graham, J., 308
Gramsci, Antonio, 88
Greeley, Andrew, 535
Green, J.H., 181, 185, 273
Grennan, Sean, 55-57
Gurele, Jim, 261
Guttentag, Marcia, 86
Hagan, Frank E., 4, 124
Hagedorn, John M., 11, 46-47, 55, 60, 64, 66, 67,
        76, 80, 81, 82, 88, 112, 124, 126, 187-188,
        209, 509, 546
Hamm, Mark S., 51-52, 70
Hansen, Joy, 51, 286
Hardman, Dale G., 19, 546
Harris, Mary G., 60
Haskins, James, 45, 75, 104, 391
Hasselbach, Ingo, 111
Helmreich, W.B., 200
Hess, Karen M., 215, 269, 313
Hicks, Robert, 230
Hindelang, Michael J., 328
Hirschi, Travis, 328
Hobsbawm, Eric J., 166, 230, 277
Hochhaus, Craig, 308
Hoenig, Gary, 276
Hoffman, Paul, 121
Hopper, Columbus B., 478
Horowitz, Ruth, 4, 59, 121, 166, 180, 215, 269,
        536
Houston, James G., 77, 559

Huang, Lua-lun, 308
Huff, C. Ronald, 8, 14, 48, 51, 59, 89, 130, 188,
        313, 364, 390, 391, 519, 531, 546, 547
Hunt, G., 294, 439
Ianni, Francis A.J., 269-270
Irwin, John, 89
Jackson, Robert K., 77, 215, 276, 333
Jacobs, James, 276, 432, 446, 477, 478
James, Don, 300, 309
Jan, Lee-jan, 309
Janowitz, Morris, 87, 198
Joe, Karen A., 173
Johnstone, John W.C., 332
Kalanich, David, 70
Kane, Candice M., 509
Kaplan, David, 77, 201, 260, 391, 439, 477, 518,
        522
Karr, Madeline, 120, 360
Kasimar, Yale, 4, 389
Keiser, R. Lincoln, 44-45, 75, 121, 191, 209, 277,
        509
Keen, Sam, 183
Kelling, George L., 377
Kennedy, David M., 382, 389
Kimball, Peter, 94, 192
Klein, Malcolm W., 43, 52, 57, 59, 215, 389, 498,
        518, 549
Klofas, John, 70
Knox, George W., 48, 49, 69, 77, 80, 86, 94, 148,
        219, 230, 232, 248, 263, 280, 299, 300,
        305, 306, 307, 309, 311, 315, 322, 324,
        331, 332, 485, 486, 488, 490, 494, 502,
        505, 516, 559
Kobrin, Solomon, 361, 389
Kolender, W.B., 376
Kotlowitz, Alex, 10, 48, 93, 514, 532
Kornblum, William, 68, 74, 498
Kovel, Joel, 65
Kramer, Dale, 120, 360
Krisberg, Barry, 19, 45, 75, 192
Lacey, Robert, 298, 309
Ladler, Karen A., 294
Landesco, John, 92, 165
Lane, Michael, 164, 433, 482
Laske, David, 49, 74, 77, 264, 280, 300, 307, 315,
        331, 332, 502, 516, 540
Laskey, John, 77, 322, 488, 559

Lattimore, Pamela K., 74
Lauderback, David, 51, 286
Leissner, Aryeh, 59, 546, 560
Lenihan, Kenneth J., 82, 88
Liang, Bin, 309
Lipsey, Richard G., 81
Little, Bertis B., 490
Livermore, Charles P., 88
Loeber, R., 309, 311
Long, Patrick Du Phuoc, 309
Lu, Zhou, 310
Lyman, M.D., 390
Majors, Richard, 66, 80
Marquart, James W.,
Mattick, Hans, 518
Mays, G. Larry, 307
McBride, Wesley D., 46, 59, 63, 77, 331, 368, 389
McCaddon, Jeff, 94
McCaghy, Charles H., 59, 131, 313
McCurrie, Thomas F., 7, 52, 494, 559
McKay, Henry D., 12, 113, 125-128, 130, 131,
        140, 167, 173, 299, 309, 361, 541
McLean, Gordon, 48, 55, 115, 135-137, 141-143,
        201, 221, 519
Merton, Robert K., 59
Miller, Walter B., 518
Mok, Bong Ho, 309, 311
Molland, John, 91
Momen, Moojan, 209
Monti, Daniel, 51, 539
Moore, Jack B., 52
Moore, Helen B., 329
Moore, Joan W., 11, 12, 45-46, 66, 80, 88, 127,
        163, 198, 258, 259, 260, 261, 477, 544
Morash, Merry, 131, 299, 309, 389
Morre, Maurice E., 125
Mottel, Syeus, 59
Muehlbauer, Gene, 188, 380, 559
Mustain, Gene, 298, 309
Nash, Steven G., 276, 277, 509, 539, 540
Needle, Jerome A., 380, 382, 548
Nieburg, H.L., 197-198
Niederhoffer, Arthur, 41
Oates, Joyce Carol, 58
O'Connor, James, 80
Oehme, Chester G. III, 54
Oetting, E.R., 224

Ohlin, Lloyd E., 41-42, 64, 79, 86, 94, 128, 299,
        300, 305, 308, 324, 325, 505, 549
Olivero, J. Michael, 57, 60
Oppenheimer, Martin, 198
Padilla, Felix, 49, 111
Palmer, John W., 477
Papachristos, Andrew V., 525
Parsons, Talcott, 187
Patrick, James, 145, 209, 360, 546
Peiar, J., 309
Pennell, Susan, 389
Perkins, Useni Eugene, 74, 75
Petersilia, Joan, 74
Peterson, Alan H., 230
Philobosian, R.H., 389
Piehl, Ann M., 382
Poston, Richard W., 45, 59, 503
Puffer, J. Adams, 6, 137-138, 536
Quicker, John C., 55, 518, 546
Quinney, Richard, 80, 81
Rader, Arthur F., 74
Raper, Arthur F., 69
Raymond, Allen, 64
Redl, Fritz, 145
Reid, Sue Titus, 86, 180, 313
Reuter, P., 389
Rice, Kent, 86
Ridgeway, James, 68, 74
Riegel, S., 439
Roemer, William F., Jr, 298, 309
Rosenberg, M., 300, 309
Rodriguez, Luis J., 49, 111
Rossi, Peter H., 82, 188
Rothman, Edwin, 198, 215
Rush, Jeffrey Paul, 53, 55
Sale, R.T., 104, 182, 270
Sanchez-Jankowski, Martin, 10, 48, 117, 299, 306,
        313, 320, 331
Sanders, William B., 52, 150
Santamaria, C., 166
Santiago, Lourdes, 111
Schwartz, Audrey J., 299, 309
Schwartz, Barry, 74
Schwartz, Gary, 65, 69
Schwitzgebel, Ralph, 60, 155, 216-217, 225
Shaw, Clifford R., 12, 113, 125-126, 128, 130,
        131, 135-137, 140, 141-143, 184, 221,

299, 309, 361, 505
Sheldon, Randall G., 116
Sherer, Moshe, 299, 309
Sherif, Muzafer, 215
Sheu, Chuen-Jim, 224
Shireman, Charles H., 14, 182
Short, James F., 44, 59, 64, 67, 70, 71, 88, 92, 131, 183, 197, 214, 299, 309, 324, 358, 383, 390, 547, 549
Shukla, K.S., 34
Sibley, James B., 198, 209, 276, 381
Sifakis, Carl, 276
Sipchen, Bob, 389
Skolnick, Jerome H., 263
Slack, Charles W., 60
Sleeman, W.H., 59, 183, 185, 194-197, 201, 272, 313
Smith, Robert E., 74, 151
Snyder, Howard N., 74
Song, John, 298, 309
Sorrentino, Anthony, 84, 505
Spergel, Irving, 18, 34, 43-44, 52, 59, 84, 86, 89, 127, 299, 309, 331, 389, 483, 508
Stapleton, William V., 209, 380, 382, 389, 548
Stephens, Ronald D., 33, 365, 368, 483, 493, 508
Stinchecombe, Arthur L., 207, 299, 300, 303, 309
Stojkovic, Stan, 70
Strodtbeck, Fred L., 44, 59, 64, 67, 70, 92, 131, 183, 191, 214, 299, 309, 358, 383, 549
Sullivan, D., 361
Sung, Betty Lee, 311
Sutherland, Edwin, 110, 131, 245
Suttles, Gerald D., 64, 67, 74, 75, 92, 127, 131, 351, 366
Takata, Susan, 224, 299, 309, 362
Tannenbaum, Frank, 191
Taylor, Carl S., 47, 145, 199, 209, 261, 270, 276, 299, 331, 509, 541, 546
Territo, Leonard, 215, 224, 268, 309, 547
Thio, Alex, 268, 372
Thompson, Craig, 64, 309, 358
Thrasher, Frederic M., 6, 19, 39-40, 55, 59, 64, 66, 69, 92-93, 100, 137, 148, 151, 185, 215, 231, 299, 309, 339-341
Tompkins, Dorothy C., 172, 560
Touhy, Roger, 298, 309
Toy, Calvin, 309

Tromanhauser, Edward D., 49, 74, 263, 280, 300, 305, 306, 307, 315
Truckenmiller, James L., 307
Tucker, Ruth, 248
Turner, Susan, 74
Tyler, Charles, 362
Useem, Bert, 94, 192
Vetter, Harold J., 215, 224, 268, 547
Victor, Jeffrey S., 230
Vigil, James Diego, 80, 120, 144, 145, 357, 390, 497, 509
Visher, Christy A., 74
Vold, George, 193-194, 358
Wadsworth, M., 86
Waldorf, Dan, 51, 182, 286, 439
Werdmolder, Hans, 117
White, Joseph L., 116, 174
Whyte, William F., 40, 59, 69, 93, 155, 165, 209, 215, 225
Wilson, James Q., 377
Wilson, William Julius, 74, 88
Winfree, L. Thomas, 307, 309
Woodside, Arch G., 116
Wrobleski, Henry M., 215, 269, 313
Yablonsky, Lewis, 42, 64, 66, 89, 127, 215, 224, 299, 304, 310, 519, 546
Young, T.R., 80, 81
Yun, Steve Chong, 14, 74, 299, 309
Zatz, Marjorie, 86, 183
Zevitz, Richard, 224, 299
Zhang, Lening, 310
Zimbardo, Phillip, 224

SUBJECT INDEX

Accentuation (or over-reaction) hypothesis, 285-286

Adult correctional institutions, 431-479

Adult involvement, 67, 229

Advancement opportunity, 25-26

Age of gang members, 366

Age-grading, 24-25, 42

Age-role integration, 59n

Aggressive personality profile of female gang members, 282

AIDS/HIV infection, 319-321

Aleatory risks, 44, 59n

Aliases, 30

Alienation, 166, 245

Alliances, 182, 443-444

Allowance, 283, 306, 315

American Correctional Association, 75n, 435-436

American Indian Movement, 154

Animal Liberation Front (ALF), 206, 263

Arsenal, 32

Articulation hypothesis, 207, 299, 300

Aryan brotherhood, 7, 14-15n, 21, 34n, 56, 69-70, 77n, 117, 154, 155, 452

Asian gangs, 297-311

Asian pragmatism, 299

Assassination, 99, 105n, 207, 364, 478n

Attempts to leave the gang, 241

Authoritarian leaders, 228

Background information, 112

Barrio gangs, 45-46, 163-164

Belief in God, 233

Belief in luck, 304-305

Benefit structure (of gangs), 26,

Bias crimes, 7, 65-66, 75n

Black Disciples gang profile, 653-662

Black Gangsters (gang profile of), 645-652

Black Guerilla Family, 191, 199-200, 277n

Black Muslims, 57

Black Panthers, 102, 104n, 107n, 154, 355-356

Black P. Stone Nation, 168, 681-692

Blood-in, Blood-out,

Bloods, 43, 72, 89n, 239, 452

Boot camps, 475

Brothers of the Struggle (BOS), 22, 612-616

Budhuk gangs of India, 194-197

Building tenders (BTs), 432-433, 476n

BUILD program, 358

Burnout hypothesis, 476n

Businesses and employers (role of), 145n, 353-354

Capone, Al, 3, 14n, 27, 91

Car theft, see also Chop shop, 36n,

Case analysis, 116-117

Case study, 109, 135-145

Central Intelligence Agency, 94, 345

Chain gangs, 453-454

Changing criminal laws, 377

Changing police patrol strategies, 377

Chicago Area Project, 356-357

Chicago School, 39, 110, 123-132, 135-145

Chicago's EDGE and SNAG initiatives, see chap. 23

Chicago's gang loitering law, 378

Children of war, 359-360

Chivalry hypothesis, 279-280

Chop-shops, 29

Churches, 354-355

Citizen patrols, 356

Citywide gang-free task force, 364

Civil remedies against gangs, 365

Clergy (role of), 55

Client-Patron relationship, 94-95

Clinton (President Bill Clinton), 99, 362-363

Cliques, 274

Cocktail criminologists, 173n

Colleges and universities, 356, 361-362

Communities Dare to Care program, 359

Community denial (of gang problem), 360-361

Community relations, 379-380

Community's role in dealing with gangs, 351-369

Community organizations, 178

Components of organized crime, 269

Compulsion, 242

Confidential informants, 457

Conjugal visits, 442

Consolidation, 182

Conspiracy, 7,

Contamination, 493n

Convergence hypothesis, 279-280

Cool pose, 66-67, 80

Copycat (see also Contagion effect), 387

Correctional institutions, 128-129, 287, 431-479,

481-494

Correctional service/treatment programs, 178-179

Correctional staff training, 440-441, 449, 486-487

Counterfeiting, 29

Courthouse criminologists, 173n

Crack cocaine, 263n

CRASH unit in LAPD, 374

Crips, 18, 31, 43, 71, 72, 89n, 239, 277n, 336, 452, 371-372, 693-698

Cults, 6, 20, 25, 34, 170, 218-219, 227-251

Cultural diversity training, 461

Cultural enrichment, 131n

Dangerous underclass, 79-89

Dating profile of female gang members, 282

Death V, 238

Debriefing and denouncing (D&D), 444-445

Defiant individualist character, 299

Definitions of organized crime, 268-269

Delinquent subcultures, 41

Demonizing, 88

Denial syndrome, 457

Dependency-Critical Thinking effect, 237-238

Deprogramming, 215-216, 247-248

Depth interview, 109

Detached workers, 93, 235, 357-358, 384

Differential access, 197-198

Differential association, 131n, 245

Differential identity, 131n

Differential integration, 131n

Differential opportunity, 41-42, 79, 299, 300, 324-325

Differential socialization, 127

Dismembering, 220-221

Disorderly conduct, 193

Disorganized neighborhoods, 135-137

Displacement effect, 355

Disruptive life event, 243

Dramatic narrative, 120n

Drive-by shootings, 52, 367n

Drug abuse by gang members, 253-256

Drugs and gangs, 253-264

Drug legalization debate, 257-261

Drug sales by gang members, 256-257, 469

Drug smuggling, 469, 253-264

Drug trafficking, 207, 253-26

Drug use by juvenile gang members, 491, 253-264

Dual labor market, 71

Dues, 407-408

Dyad, 215

Economic rackets controlled by inmate gangs, 454-455

Educational lag, 83-84

El Rukns, 27

El Salvador, 35n

Employment, 305

Ethnic antagonisms, 76n

Ethnic diversity, 298

Ethnic homogeneity, 64-65

Ethics (and gang research), 179

Ethnic homogeneity, 22

Ethnic succession hypothesis, 269-270

Ethnography, 109, 179-181

Ethnomethodology, 109

Etiology of gangs, 32-33, 40

Exclusion, 144n

Explosives, 208

External locus of control, 244

External organization, 20,

Extortion, 29, 348

FACE Act, 5

Fagin law, 225n

False Flagging, 59

Familial gang transplant phenomena, 322, 332n

Family and the gang, 53, 313-332

Family conditions, 183

Family life profile, 282

FBI, 5, 9, 157, 381

FBI's Uniform Crime Report, 119-120

Federal effectiveness in suppressing gangs, 469

Female involvement, 30

Female gang members, 30, 46, 51, 279-295

Feminism, 58, 284-285

Fertility of gang members, 317

Field work, 109

Fighting behavior of gang members, 306-307

First amendment rights and gangs, 437-438

Five Percenters, 57

Flakes, 177

Focal concerns of the lower class, 169-170

Folks gangs, 239, 443

Formalized or written code, 181-182 (see also gang constitutions)

Force strength, 32

Four Corner Hustlers, 50-51, 336

Frame of reference in analyzing gangs, 164-165
Franchising, 390n
Freedom fighters, 50
Free will, 245-247
Freight and warehouse theft, 30
Freight Train Riders of America (FTRA), 157
Fruits of Islam (FOI), 57
Fry, Rev. John, 4, 263n, 270
Function and behavior of the gang as a group, 215
Gambling, 28-29
Gang assaults on correctional staff, 449, 482
Gang classification, 8, 17-36, 271-272
Gang clothing, 36n,
Gang colors, 46
Gang constitutions, (see also appendices), 21,
Gang constitutions and by-laws, 21, 181-182
Gang defection, 422-423, 424
Gang density, 200, 434-435, 448-449, 462
Gang deprogramming, 3, 485, 488, 493n
Gang disturbances, 457-458
Gang emulation, 26-27
Gang evolution, 270
Gang forming instinct, 137
Gang "front groups", (see also Public Relations
Function) 18, 147
Gang funerals, 14n
Gang initiations, 42
Gang intelligence files, 375-376
Gang investigator associations, 388, 470,
Gang mapping, 151, 382
Gang moles, 390n
Gang mothers, 290
Gang myths, 10
Gangology, 1, 39,
Gang peace/truces, 170, 411-412
Gang picnics, 35n,
Gang population in America, 75
Gang recognition and official legitimation, 442-443
Gang recruiting, 447
Gang-related crime, 9-10, 13, 221-222, 256, 380,
383, 385
Gang rights activist movement, 95-96, 444
Gangs and social institutions, 167
Gangs as an urban way of life, 161-174
Gang spirit, 151
Gangster Disciples (see also B.O.S.), 20, 240, 288,
335-336, 393-428, 612-616, 634-644

Gang theory, 169, 193-194
Gang typology, 184
Gang violence, 275, 438, 470
Gangwear, 164
Geneva convention, 353
Gang summit meetings, 95
Gang symbols, 297-298
Gang theory, 173
Gang truces, 170
Gang violence, 290-291, 331, 475
Gang warfare, 209
Gender difference, 301-302
Gender grading, 25
Generation gap, 41
Government gangs, 100
Graffiti, 335
Grand jury (use of against gangs), 379, 384
GREAT program, 381
Group characteristics in defining the gang, 215
Group factors in understanding gangs, 213-225
Group identity, 229
Group size, 224n
Group think, 138, 236
Guerilla warfare, 191-211, 197
Guns, see arsenal, see firearms, 208
Habitual association, 40, 59n, 209
Hard core gang members, 242
Hate groups, 386
Health risks of juvenile gang members, 490-492,
254-255
Heterogeneity, 22
Homosexuality, 138, 145n
Hoover, King Larry, 20,
Hostage situations involving inmates, 460-461
Human capital, 79-89
Hybrid gang formations, 65
Hypermasculinity, 145n
Ideology, 4, 10, 166
Illinois Department of Corrections, 426-427, 433-
434, 437
Importation hypothesis, 69-70, 432-433
Indian reservations (and gangs), 67, 76n
Informants, (see also confidential informants), 112,
468
Informed consent, 113
Initiation rites, 31, 42
Intellectual Sisters (see also: Sisters of the

Struggle, SOS), 25, 281-284
Internal locus of control, 243-244, 299, 303
Internal organization, 19-20
Internet, 338
International involvement of gangs, 28
Interrogation, 114-116
Interviewing, 393-394
Jails, 473-474
Jamaican gangs, 199
Jeff Fort, 192, 198-199
Job placement services, 59n, 82
Juvenile correctional institutions, 481-494
Juvenile gang members, 366
Klika, 45
Ku Klux Klan, 6, 7, 14n, 15n, 45, 67, 223
Labelling, 43, 75-76n,
Latin Kings, 29, 56, 97-99, 232, 272-274 (see also
New York Latin Kings), 452, 597-605, 663-680
      (gang profile)
Law enforcement (see also: Police), 275, 294, 297,
      371-391
Law enforcement/corrections interface, 440
Leadership, 19, 24
Legalist definition of crime, 15n
Legitimate opportunity, 299
Level of cohesion, 23
Level of morale, 25
Level of stability, 24
Life-span approach to gang analysis, 142, 331n
Loan sharking, 29
Local media (role of), 360
Los Solidos, 105n
Macroanalytic approaches to gang analysis, 164-
      165
Mafia, (see also: organized crime), 267-277
Mail monitoring, 464
Malcolm X, 57
Management strategies for dealing with prison
      gangs, 441, 466-468, 483-484, 487, 489
Marginality, 302
Marriage, 314
Masculinity crisis, 145n
Mass media, 15n, 335-349
Mass suicide, 234
Maturation hypothesis, 276n, 287-290, 476n
Maxwell Street, 59n
Membership demoralization, 420-421

Membership expectations, 23-24
Mentally ill inmates, 457
Mentally retarded inmates, 457, 465
Mergers, 182, 260
Microanalytic approaches to gang analysis, 164-
      165
Midcity Project, 357-358
Migration (gang), 26-27, 322, 332n, 391n
Military, 201-206
Mind control, 227-228
Mob action, 5, 218
Moral development, 138
Moral neutralization, 236-237
Moral panic, 321-322
Morale, 23, 398-399, 406-407
Mothers against gangs, 359
Motorcycle gangs, 56, 386
Movies and motion pictures, 335-349
Multi-jurisdictional police investigation, 375
Multiple marginality, 60n, 144n
NAACP, 102, 206
Narcotics trafficking, see drug sales, 28
National Gang Crime Research Center, 27
National guard, 201-206
Near group, 224n
Negotiating with inmate gang leaders, 451, 459-
      460
Neighborhood watch programs, 352-353
Neo-nazis, 6, 15n, 68-69, 93-94, 105n, 219-220
New York Latin Kings, 103
"No human contact" status, 447-448
"Nothing works Martinson", 132n
Nuisance abatement statute, 365
Obedience, 244
Ombudsmen for inmates, 466
Opportunity structure, see Differential Opportunity
Offense patterns of gangs, 28
Oppressed peoples belief system, 273-274
Oral history, 109-121
Organizational approach to gang analysis, 177-188
Organizational continuum for gang analysis,
Organizational destabilization, 421
Organizational vulnerability to gang influence, 186
Organized crime, 40, 162-163, 267-277
Paranoia, 299, 304, 305
Parental help with homework, 314
Parents, 321, 386

Parents against gangs, 359
Participant observation, 109, 180
Penal sanction increasing gang ties, 455
People/brothers gang members, 239, 443-444
Perceived closure, 86, 324-325
Personality changes, 228-229
Pessimistic racial beliefs, 73
Pirates, 196
Police, 371-391
Police chiefs, 382-387
Police views on gangs, 143-144
Political extremism, 100, 200-201
Political ideology, 230-232
Politicians cultivating gangs, 92-95, 104
Politics (gangs involved in), 27, 91-107, 165-166, 231-232, 412-416, 425-426
Post traumatic stress disorder (PTSD) and gangs, 49
Predicting gang membership, 307
Prestige, 26
Prison, (see: Corrections), 164, 257, 431-479
Prison gangs, 431-432, 451-452, 462-463
Prison drug smuggling by gangs, 257
Prison riots, 461
Prosecution, 393-428, 381, 391n
Prosecuting juveniles as adults, 481-482
Pro-social, 27, 32
Pro-social intent, 272-273
Prostitution/vice, 29,
Provincialism, 367n
Public education, 390
Public relations function (in gangs), 27-28, 170, 229
Pumpkin head, 238
Qualitative research, 109-121
Race relations, 66-67, 456, 463
Race riots, 436, 458-459
Racial conflict, 72-73, 200, 450, 456, 458, 464-465
Racial and ethnic slurs, 66
Racism oppression thesis, 63-77
Rap music, 387-388
Rational choice model, 59n
Real Great Society, 45, 59n
Rebuilding community fabric, 361
Recapitulation theory, 137
Recidivism, 73, 128-129, 325-326, 457
Recurrent illegal acts, 24

Reliability, 114
Religious or political trappings (of gangs), 20-21, 168, 232-234, 273
Religious institutions (role of), 55
Renegade gangs, 27,
Respect for the law scale, 324-325
Retired gang members, 48, 179
RICO, 5, 272, 372
Rights of children, 291-292
Riots, 193, 287
Risky shift, 138, 235-236
Robbery, 29-30
Role definitions, 22-23
Rumors, 67-68
Runaways, 284
Safe zones, 366n
Satanism, 230, 233, 384
Satellite gang units, see also Franchising, 390n
School discipline profile, 282, 301-302
School system, 49, 293, 382
Screening for risk, 373-374
Screening tenants, 355
Security Risk Group, 9
Security Threat Group, 9, 234
Self-concept scale, 322-325
Self-esteem, 299, 303-304, 322-325
Set-off method (of dealing with gangs behind bars), 445, 493
Sex offenders, 172
Sexual abuse of gang members, 286, 289-290, 315-317
Sexual behavior of gang members, 318-319, 491
Shaw and McKay tradition, 123-132
Sheriff's, 384-387
Shifting membership, 22
Simon City Royals, 288
Sisters of the Struggle (SOS), 281-284
Skinheads, 6, 51-52
Smuggling illegal aliens,
Snitch farm, 445-446
Social athletic clubs, 2, 149, 158-159n
Social conflict, 191-211
Social Darwinism, 137-140
Social engineering, 15n, 217-220
Social estrangement, 245
Social gangs, 2, 14n,
Social psychology of gangs, 439

Social stigma, 182-183
Spanish Gangster Disciples, 606-611
Statewide gang assessments, 53-54
Status attainment, 145n
Status threat, 34, 44
STEP act, 381-382
Stoner gangs, 263n
Straight Edge, 263
Street gangs, 8
Street Gang Terrorism Act, 14n, 631-633
Subcultural argot, 276n
Subcultural diffusion, 31-32
Substance abuse profile, 282
Supergangs, 18, 267, 443-444
Supreme Court, 447
Surplus population, 79-89
SWORD gang computer files, 376
Symbionese Liberation Army, 7, 198, 234
Targeted Offender Program, 374
Targeting Gang Resources, 441-442
TARGET program, 381-382
Tattoos, 30
Telephone monitoring, 464
Television and news programs, 339
Territoriality, 19, 34n,
Territorial function of gangs, 351-352
Terrorism, 55-56, 94, 191-211, 263
Thrasher's approach to gangs, 147-159
Threat analysis, 390n
Threat assessment, 33
Threat group, 213
Tongs, 64
Total control institutions, 234
Totems, 31
Tracking and monitoring gang-related crime, 380
Trench Coat Mafia, 234
Tuberculosis in prison, 461-462, 465, 469
Turf, 19
Underclass, 79-89
Underground economy, 87
Unemployment, 85
Unfounding gang crime, 10
Urbanism and gangs, 161-174
Urban guerilla analogy, 198-199
Validity issues in gang research, 114
Vice Lords, 44-45, 56, 59n, 154, 240, 277n, 336, 452, 617-630

Victim assistance, 373
Vietnamese youth gangs, 14n
Vigilante justice, 342
Violations, 228, 235, 238-242
Violence socialization profile of female gang members, 282
Vulnerability factor, 299
Wannabe gang members, 2,
Weed and seed program, 261
Welfare, 284
White Aryan Resistance (WAR), 27-28
White racism, 126
White racist extremist gangs (WREGs), 234, 440, 450
Witness protection, 372
Written gang constitutions, 272-274
Written rules (internal gang literature), 228, 396-428
Yummy, 292
Zero tolerance policies, 436-437, 470
Zoot suit "military riot", 201